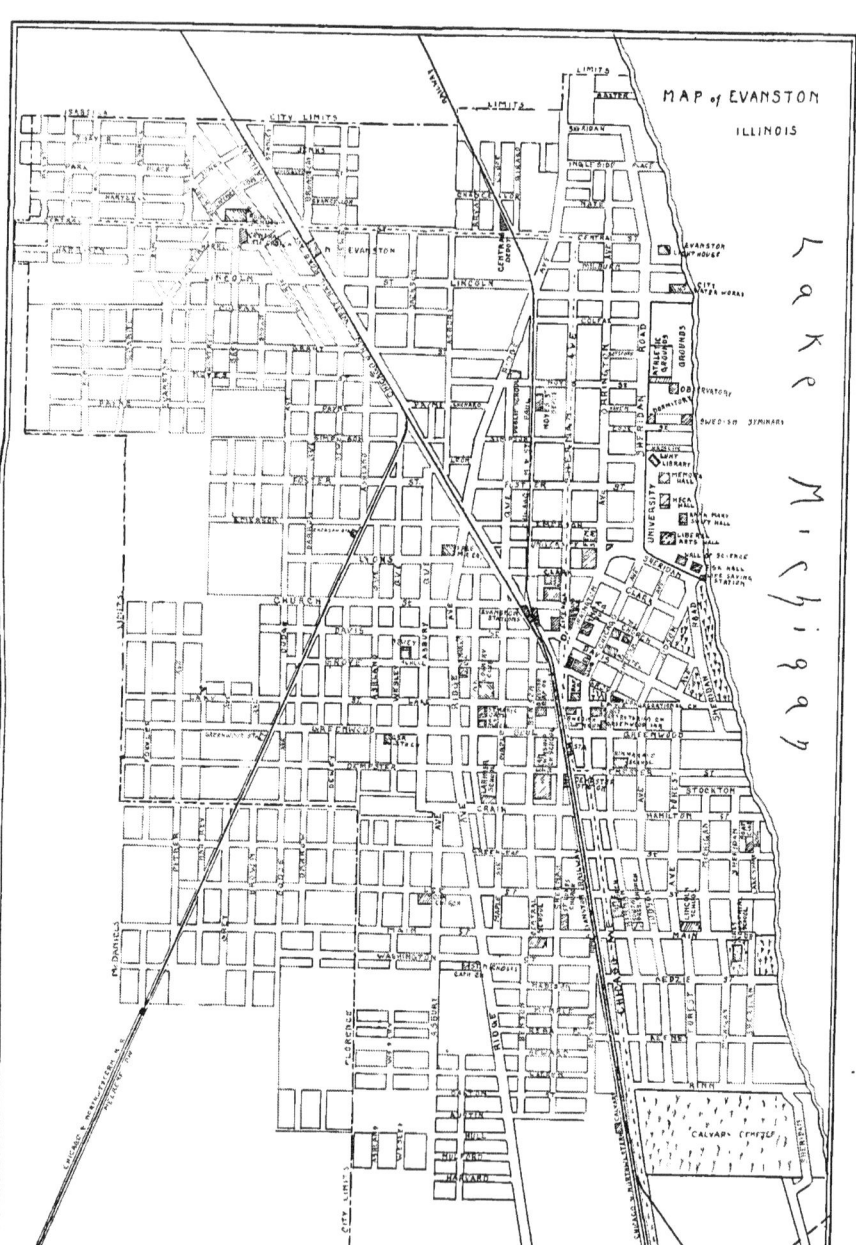

MAP of EVANSTON
ILLINOIS

HISTORY

OF

NORTHWESTERN
UNIVERSITY

AND

EVANSTON

EDITED BY

ROBERT D. SHEPPARD, D.D.   HARVEY B. HURD, LL.D.

CHICAGO:
MUNSELL PUBLISHING COMPANY,
PUBLISHERS
1906

PREFACE

An analysis of the motives which have induced Evanstonians to join in the furnishing of material for this record of local history would afford evidence, not only of a feeling of obligation to the past and present, but also to future generations; and this, it is but just to say, has been the impelling force in the conception and preparation of this volume.

Book-making is an expensive undertaking, and the limited sale which a work treating of a small community would obtain, would inevitably involve heavy financial responsibilities. The publishers of that excellent work, "The Historical Encyclopedia of Illinois," have deemed it practicable to produce a special Evanston edition of that work embracing, as a feature of added interest and value, a supplemental volume largely devoted to Evanston history, prepared and edited by Evanstonians. The business management of the enterprise rests with the publishers who have had a long and successful experience in the publication of works of this character, and to whom great credit is due for successfully financing the cost of production and carrying to a faithful completion this important work.

This history has been written in the belief that it is needed; that man's immortal instincts revolt at the thought of the good of the past being buried in oblivion—that the fruitage of lives which have accomplished results, epitomized in the word "history," should be forgotten—that lessons of faithful doing, accompanied by self-sacrifice, zealous faith and daring courage little short of the heroic, should fail of their highest accomplishment by inspiration and example, because no one has recorded them—that present and future generations should be deprived of these teachings, examples and educational forces, simply for the want of a proper and available published record of many facts now having an existence only in the memory of individuals who cannot long remain, and whose passing away will place the foundation facts of our history beyond the reach of those who come after them.

Hence this history, with the imperfections and shortcomings always incident to human authorship, yet the results of the best thought and intelligent efforts of many accomplished writers and contributors who have produced, in concise but comprehen-

1

sive form, a carefully prepared and faithful record of facts and events relating to the various topics assigned to them. Without attempting to enumerate all of them by name, I here wish to express my personal obligation to Robert D. Sheppard, D. D., as my Editorial Associate, and to each author for the faithful and intelligent service rendered in the preparation of this work, as well as the lasting debt of gratitude due to them from the home-loving and Evanston-loving people of to-day and the future.

The conception that our city's history, together with the memoirs of its founders and builders, was deserving of record, received its first practical suggestion in the organization, about seven years ago, of the Evanston Historical Society, which is doing such noble work in its chosen field of research and collection of historical material. To the influence and labors of this association is due, not only the conception of the need of an authoritative published History of Evanston, but, in a large degree through the labors and co-operation of its members, the success which has attended the preparation of such a work. Believing that it will have a permanent value, not only to citizens of Evanston and Cook County, but to many others interested in State history, I herewith bring my labors in connection with the volume to a close, with thanks to my associates and co-laborers and hope that it will meet the expectation of its patrons and have for them an interest corresponding with the labor required in its preparation.

Harvey B. Hurd

Editor

FOREWORD

. ———

The preface to this work, written by the late Hon. Harvey B. Hurd, after the various manuscripts furnished by the many contributors were well in hand, quite fully sets forth the inception of this undertaking and the potent influences leading thereto. It is self-evident that the preparation of so extended a history of Evanston was a more formidable task than originally contemplated, and unavoidable delays were experienced incident to receiving the completed manuscripts from some of our friends contributing the same, and still further delays were occasioned by the sending to each author a copy of the printer's proof of his or her portion of the work. To do this was thought important in order, first, that each writer might thus have a last opportunity to correct and make more complete his or her department; and, second, that each chapter might, by this means, receive any necessary additions extending its scope to a more recent period.

Credit is due to the publishers for the pecuniary outlay which they necessarily have borne, and for the great care evidently taken by them in the preparation of the whole work and in placing it in completed form before its readers.

I have every reason to believe that the various chapters, furnished by about forty special contributors to the city's history, have been prepared with great care; that the completed work will constitute a valued addition to the library of all Evanstonians, and will be accorded a prominent place in the historical collections of Illinois.

Robert D. Sheppard,
Associate Editor,

INDEX

CHAPTER VIII.
AN ERA OF PROGRESS.

CHAPTER IX.
SOME SIDE ISSUES.

CHAPTER X.
NORTHWESTERN UNIVERSITY MEDICAL SCHOOL.

BIOGRAPHICAL

ILLUSTRATIONS

CHAPTER I.

HISTORY OF EVANSTON

INTRODUCTORY.

*The Evanston of 1905—Gem Suburb of a
Great Metropolis and Seat of Learning—
Results Accomplished by Fifty Years
of Development—Contrast Between Past
and Present—First Township Organization Under Name of Ridgeville—Evanston Township Organized in 1857—The
Village Platted in 1854—Later Changes
in Township and Municipal Organization
—Old Name of Ridgeville Township Resumed in 1903, with Boundaries Identical
with City of Evanston—Garrett Biblical
Institute Precedes the University—City
Government Organized in 1892—Early
Evanston Homes and Their Occupants—
Advent of the First Railroad—The Career of Dr. John Evans.*

The Evanston of 1905 is justification of
an effort to unfold the story of its planting
and its development. Gem of suburbs as it
is, lying contiguous to the greatest of western cities and the home of many of its
most active men of affairs, it also occupies
a commanding position as a seat of intelligence and learning. It has crowded into
its short career so much of human interest,
it has been the source of so many wide
spreading and helpful influences, it is so
endeared to the people who have found in it
a home, that the narration of its fifty years
of progress must be told. Like many another American city closely associated with
a metropolis, it has attained its present
proud position within the memory of men
now living, among whom is included the
general editor of the present work. It possesses no ruins and no ivy-covered walls.
Its oldest buildings bear the marks of recent construction, and its well paved streets
have but lately passed from the hands of
the contractor. Unlike some of the historic towns of the United States, whose
history has been written covering two centuries or more, and which reflect the growth
and history of the American people, this
tidy suburban town has developed quickly
within itself all the forces that make up our
active, advanced American life, of schools
and churches, of clubs and cabals; in religion, society, politics, philanthropy and
pleasure it is an epitome of distinctly modern progress. Numerous helpful hands have
been employed to draw the composite picture that is meant to convey a lasting impression of the facts and forces that make
up the idea of Evanston, and placing them
side by side, or mingling them in one's

thought, we have the resultant of as wide-awake, up-to-date, eager, intelligent, interesting and hopeful a community of men, women and youth as the world can furnish.

Perhaps you have at some time paused to listen to the mingled din of a great city and, with a quick ear, analyzed the individual sounds that make up the hum of the city's life. That task has been ours. The hum is well nigh deafening to the ear, sensitized by attention even in a town which boasts few noises of factories or traffic. But its hum is not less real, of activities which employ the finer faculties of men and women. It will be told otherwheres how the particular region that now bears the name of Evanston came to be selected as the site of a college town. Delving into the political conditions that antedate the modern city, we find that Cook County, Ill., in which Evanston is located, was, previous to 1849, under what is known in this State as County Government; that is, the county affairs were managed by a Board of Commissioners, who supervised the community business of the neighborhoods that had not yet emerged into local government. Many of these were designated by a name which might later attach to a township, but there was no township government, though there were townships indicated in the United States Survey, and designated by numbers, which were used before 1849, and have been since used in connection with school purposes, as illustrating this condition.

It is interesting to note that the records of Township 41—in which Evanston is located—now in possession of the Evanston Historical Society, were begun in 1846, and that they record the election of Township Trustees for school purposes four years before the first election of officers of the town of Ridgeville, which included Evanston; and, as throwing a little light upon the onerous duties of these early

Trustees, we read from the minutes of their third meeting, held May 20, 1846, at the Ridge Road House: "It was ordered that we proceed to hire Miss Cornelia Wheadon to teach our school the present season, at one dollar and twenty-five cents a week. Also, it was ordered that the school house should be repaired as soon as possible, and furnished with a water-pail and dipper."

Evidently Township 41 had enjoyed the blessing of a school house long enough for it to get out of repair, probably under the regime of County Commissioners. In the Code of By-Laws of the School Trustees, it was provided that, in case a patron of the school refused, or was not in position at the appointed time, to receive the teacher the required number of days, the teacher should select his or her own boarding place, and the board bill should be taxed with such patron's tuition bill. From such germs has Evanston's splendid school system developed.

Township Organization.—By the Constitution of 1848 the Legislature was required to provide by general law for township organization, which it did by Act of February 12, 1849. By this act the people were permitted to divide their counties into towns or townships, which were to conform as nearly as might be with the congressional townships. Commissioners were appointed for the purpose of dividing the county, and the people were permitted to select the names of the townships. When they could not agree, the Commissioners were authorized to select the names for them. The people of fractional Town 41 North, Range 14 East, chose the name of Ridgeville. This continued to be the name of the town until by act of the Legislature of February 15, 1857, it was changed to Evanston, and the township was enlarged by the addition of a tier of sections taken from Niles Township on the west and the Archange Reservation and several sections in Township 42, taken from New Trier on the north. The language of the act reads: "The name of Ridgeville shall be changed to Evanston, and the Town of Evanston shall comprise all of fractional Township 41 North, Range 14 East, Sections 12, 13, 24, 25 and 36, Township 41 North, Range 13 East, the Archange Reservation and fractional Sections 22, 26 and 27, Township 42 North, Range 14 East, and the same shall form and constitute a township for school purposes and be known as Town 41 North, Range 14 East."

Dreary reading—perhaps, dry as dust—but thrilling none the less, because it is the record of a creative act of great importance. Under an enabling act, approved May 23, 1877, and amended May 15, 1903, the territory embraced within the present limits of the city of Evanston has been formed into a township under the old name of Ridgeville, which makes the boundaries of the city and the new township identical and in effect consolidates the township and city governments. The new township as now constituted embraces what previously formed the southern part of New Trier Township and a small section from the northeast corner of Niles Township. The remainder of the former Township of Evanston now constitutes the northern portion of the City of Chicago, with a small section south of the Chicago city limits and west of the southern portion of Evanston, these two sections remaining under the old name of Evanston Township, though not embracing any part of the city of that name.

Village and City Organization.—Such are Evanston's present geographical and political relations to the county and the State. Under the loose system of county and township government it subsisted till 1863. It had been platted as a town in 1854, and outstripping all other sections of the township, and taking on exclusiveness and individuality, it demanded a narrower and more intensive government of its platted territory. The agitation culminated in a meeting of voters on December 29, 1863, when it was decided, in accordance with the law on the subject, to organize an incorporated town, and the decision was consummated by the election of five Trustees, January 6, 1864. The new town was bounded by Lake Michigan on the east, Wesley Avenue on the west, Crain and Hamilton Streets on the south, and Foster Street on the north. In 1869 a special act of the Legislature permitted the incorporation of the City of Evanston, but content with their simple form of government, the citizens decided against its adoption by a vote of 197 to 82. Yet within three years they organized under the Act of 1872 for Cities and Villages, but continued their village form of government by Trustees selected from the village at large instead of by Aldermen from wards, with a Village President instead of Mayor.

In 1872 new territory was annexed to the town on petition of property owners of the district lying north of Foster Street and east of Wesley and Asbury Avenues, and extending to the present limits of the city. On October 19, 1872, village organization was adopted under the general City and Village Incorporation Act of April 10, 1872, and the first village election took place April 15, 1873. Further increase of territory was made January 7, 1873, by the annexation, on petition, of the region bounded on the north by Grant Street, on the south by Church and Foster Streets, on the east by Wesley and Asbury Avenues, and on the west by Dodge Street. Then followed, during the same month, the accession of the region bounded on the north by Grant and Simpson Streets,

on the south by Church Street, on the east
by Dodge Street, and on the west by Hartrey .and McDaniel Avenues. April 21,
1874, the Village of North Evanston succumbed to the acquisitive mood of its larger
neighbor, and, in September of the same
year, the territory lying between Hamilton
and Greenleaf Streets, with the lake on
the east and Chicago Avenue on the west,
was included by petition. In April, 1886,
the territory bounded by Church Street,
Wesley Avenue, Crain Street and McDaniel
Avenue, was likewise annexed on petition.
Finally, on February 20, 1892, the important
question of the annexation of South Evanston was submitted to the vote of both villages and approved by a small majority.

Thus the chapter of territorial expansion
for Evanston was closed for the time being. It had now outgrown the swaddling
clothes of village government and demanded the habiliments of a city. The
question of the adoption of city organization was submitted to the people on March
29, 1892, and was adopted by a vote of 784
to 26. The first city election took place
April 19, 1892, when Dr. Oscar H. Mann
became the first Mayor of the city.

Physical Characteristics.—The physical
characteristics of Evanston have changed
but little in the progress of the years. Its
main features, north and south, were the
Lake Shore on the east, more wooded than
now, with two ridges, one called the East
Ridge, comprising the land purchased by
the University, and the other the West
Ridge, comprising the lands of Brown and
Hurd, which were a part of the first town-
plat. The latter ridge was some forty-five
feet above the lake level. Between the
ridges was a level valley, receptacle of the
drainage of the ridges, often giving the
impression of a swamp, but easily susceptible of being drained to the north or by
ditches to the Lake. The trend of these

ridges constrained the surveyors in the
platting of the town, so that the streets
running north and south paralleled the
ridge roads, and the east and west bound
streets crossed the former at right angles.
The original plat comprised three hundred
and fifty acres, purchased by the Trustees
of the University from John H. Foster, in
1853, and nearly two hundred and fifty
acres, purchased about the same time, by
Andrew J. Brown and Harvey B. Hurd,
from James Carney. The tract was well
wooded, especially along the shore of the
Lake, chiefly with oaks, some few of which
remain to give a hint of the noble forest of
which they formed a part. The plat, which
perished in the Chicago fire, bore the names
of streets that kept fresh in memory some
of the active spirits who were associated
with the early days of the enterprise, such
as Dempster, Hinman, Judson, Benson,
Sherman, Davis, Orrington and Clark;
while to the west, such names of streets as
Oak, Maple Grove and Ridge were a
tribute to the conditions that then prevailed, and help the late-comers to picture
the leafy shade, overlooked by the old-time
thoroughfare that crowned the ridge; and
still farther west, Wesley and Asbury
Avenues flanked the town, testifying to
the loyal Methodism of the settlers who
dwelt within it.

The Town Platted.—The purchases of
the land were made in 1853, and, during
that year, the town was staked out and
streets thrown up, but the plat was not
acknowledged till 1854, in which year a
number of lots were sold, houses built and
families settled. The plat made by the
Northwestern University provided generously, in its portion of the town, for public
parks such as now beautify the town. The
streets were spacious, and a constituency
was appealed to such as might be attracted
to an educational center. This was the

chief magnet. The idea of the suburban residence had not yet emerged. The families who came were chiefly those that were attracted by the idea of residence in a college town. Garrett Biblical Institute preceded the University on university ground, and John Dempster, at Old Dempster Hall, realized to the early students of the Institute, as Mark Hopkins did to the students of Williams College, how a very few facilities in the hands of such a master will serve to develop the minds and hearts of men eager for an education. Obadiah Huse early ministered to the physical wants of students at Dempster Hall in such manner that their slender purses might provide for a not too luxurious existence. Philo Judson was the advance guard of the University, selling lots, vending scholarships, drumming up settlers and promoting the town. Hurd, Brown, Beveridge, Pearsons, Judson, Evans, Clifford and Ludlam were among the people who picked their way over the newly made thoroughfares of the new town to their new homes, with wet and muddy feet ofttimes, during the years 1854 and 1855. And, until the summer of 1855, if they went to Chicago, they must do so by their own private conveyance. They were sturdy people; practical, religious, neighborly, genuine pioneers who could curry a horse, build a house, lead a class-meeting and finance a town and two institutions of learning. On the West Ridge Road lived the Huntoons, the Crains and the McDaniels and Carneys, the Pratts and the Garfields, antedating the town. The home of John L. Beveridge was on Chicago Avenue, near Clark Street; of John A. Pearsons on Grove Street, near Chicago Avenue; of Philo Judson at Ridge Avenue and Davis Street; of Judge H. B. Hurd in the same vicinity; of G. W. Reynolds where the Avenue House now stands; and Dempster Hall and the home of Dr. John

Dempster on the Lake Shore north of Simpson Street. The Snyders home was on Chicago Avenue, near Dempster Street.

These were the scattered centers of life in the ambitious hamlet. They were soon reinforced by the families of the Professors of the University and Institute, and such families as the Willards, from which was destined to proceed that bright and shining light in philanthropy and temperance reform, Frances E. Willard, probably the best known product of Evanston life, its historian in "A Classic Town," an orator and writer of rare power. George F. Foster soon took up his home on Chicago Avenue near Church Street—a shouting Methodist and social to his finger tips, whose house was a seat of hospitality and elegance. George W. Reynolds was on Davis Street, near to the corner of Chicago Avenue, on which corner the Reynolds House, still a part of the Avenue House, was built. We take exception to him as a builder, for on one occasion at a caucus, or neighborhood meeting, the floor of his house suddenly collapsed, precipitating the company into the cellar, and the same performance was re-enacted at the house of George F. Foster, also built by Mr. Reynolds. There was no "Index" or "Press" in those days to note these happenings, but the survivors tell the tale with more laughter than they then experienced.

Church Street took its name from the donated site of what was to be the Cathedral Church of the town, the center of the religious and social life of this God-fearing community, chiefly of the Methodist persuasion, but broad-minded enough to welcome those of other communions in their worship, and disposed, when the time of separation should come, to give them a site on which to raise their own roof-tree, as the title deeds from the University to Trustees of the older churches of Evanston will testify—consid-

eration one dollar and other valuable benefits, such as good will and gladness at their
coming, their loyalty and their prosperity.

Advent of the First Railroad.—The
Chicago and Milwaukee Railroad was being located in 1853, and the Trustees of the
University, by resolution of October 26,
1853, requested the company to locate their
road through the land of the University so
as to strike the center, or within thirty-five
rods south of the center of Section 19 of
Township 41 North, Range 18, and offering to donate the right of way and one acre
of land for a depot, providing the railroad
company would make such location and
agree not to allow any establishment for
the sale of liquor or gambling houses, or
other nuisance, to be placed on such right
of way or depot ground. March 28, 1854,
the Trustees passed another resolution requesting the railroad company to locate its
station on a line west of Davis Street—
which terminated at Sherman Avenue—on
a small ridge on the Carney farm, or as
near as may be expedient in the judgment
of the agent, providing the owner of the
Carney farm lay off suitable streets for the
same. Mr. A. J. Brown, who held the title
of the Carney tract for himself and others,
conveyed the right of way and depot ground
to the railroad company about the date of
the resolution referred to, and it appears on
the plat of the town. It was not, however,
till the summer of 1855 that trains began
running through the town. Two through
trains and one accommodation train were
all the facilities that were offered. Evanston seldom filled the single passenger car
of the accommodation (or "Waukegan")
train, as it was most familiarly known,
and the grumbling railroad authorities
threatened to take off the train, declaring
that it did not pay and gave no promise

of ever paying. But they took it out in
grumbling. It did pay, and was destined to
be their best paying piece of road through
its suburban traffic, as a prosperous community grew around the cheerful, hospitable nucleus that had grouped itself near
to the Northwestern University and Garrett
Biblical Institute.

Such are some of Evanston's beginnings
with which we introduce the reader to the
more elaborate story, as told in detail by
those familiar with it. One word more we
cannot refrain from saying concerning Dr.
John Evans, the man whose chief monument
(though he has many others) is the
Classic Town; in whose brain was chiefly
conceived the thought of this educational
and home center, and by whose skill and
suggestions and influence the plans were
chiefly made to compass the acquisition of
the land that should be the Northwestern
University's chief source of endowment,
and by whom the enterprise was financed
for all the coming years. Close to him
wrought Orrington Lunt, imbibing his zeal
and supplementing his labors by his unselfish devotion and tireless energy. John
Evans was as far-seeing a man as ever
wrought in the formative days of cities or
States; a plain man who dreamed of large
things, and whose heart kept pace with
his swift moving intellect. The sphere of
his activity was changed all too soon from
the region that bears his name to a distant
State, where he built railroads, planned
Titanic enterprises, supervised the beginning
of a great commonwealth and helped to
found another University in the Far West.
Evanston is honored in her name, as she
honors the name of her founder.

Kind reader, if you have read thus far,
read on.

CHAPTER II[1].

OUR INDIAN PREDECESSORS.

(By FRANK R. GROVER, Vice-President Evanston Historical Society.)

*The First Evanstonians—Indian Relics—
Stone Implements and What They Indi-
cate — Early Explorers—Joliet, Mar-
quette, La Salle and Tonty—First White
Visitors—Indian Tribes—The Iroquois,
Illinois and Pottawatomies—Ouilmette
Reservation and Family—The Fort Dear-
born Massacre—Home of the Ouil-
mettes—Treaty of Prairie du Chien—In-
dian Trails and Trees on North Shore—
Aboriginal Camps and Villages—Indian
Mounds and Graves—Reminiscenses of
Early Settlers—Important Treaties—An
Englishman's Story of the Treaty of Chi-
cago in 1833.*

Since the discovery of this continent the
North American Indian has ever been the
subject of constant study, discussion and
contention. His origin, his traditions, his
character, his manners and customs, his
superstitions, his eloquence, the wars in
which he has engaged, his tribal relations,
his certain destiny, the wrongs he has done
and those that he has suffered have, for four
centuries, been favorite themes for the historian, the poet, the philanthropist, the eth-
nologist. And yet, with all the countless
books that have been written upon the subject, there is still room for inquiry, for
speculation, for historical research.

Every political division of this country,
from state to hamlet, has a mine of untold
facts, which must ever remain undisclosed.
Still, the diligent and the curious can, with
all due regard to the limitations to truth
put upon the honest historian, gather old
facts that will in the aggregate be of interest as local history. With that end in view
I wish to tell you what I have been able
to learn of our Indian predecessors—the
first Evanstonians.

**Stone Implements Found in This Vi-
cinity and What They Indicate.**—There
is no more interesting field for historical research than that of the implements and
weapons of the prehistoric Indian. There is,
too, a later time of which there is no written history, before the coming of the Jesuit
Missionary and his early successor, the Indian Trader, who was the first vendor of
steel hatchets and arrow points, that is of
no less interest.

Much of the Indian history of those times
must of necessity remain forever undisclosed. Some of it has been gathered from
credible traditions, some of it distorted by
the frailty of human recollection and by the
fragile partition that oft divides memory
from imagination, and truthfulness from
the inclination to boast of the prowess of
Indian ancestry. All of these factors, of

---

[1]Compiled from two papers: (1), "Our Indian
Predecessors—The First Evanstonians," read before the
Evanston Historical Society, November 2, 1901; and (2)
"Some Indian Land Marks of the North Shore," read be-
fore the Chicago Historical Society, February 21, 1905,
with some supplemental notations by the writer.

course, result in endless confusion, and what the exact truth is must be left, for the most part, to uncertainty and speculation. But a portion of that history, as applied to the North Shore, is told as simply and plainly by the stone implements and weapons as though written in words on monument or obelisk. The entrance to this field of inquiry opens, of course, more easily and widely to the man of science—the archæologist—but the merest novice, if he be curious and diligent, will there find a mine of historic facts that are both interesting and reliable.

One of the greatest orators of modern times has entertained thousands of his hearers and readers with the topic, "The man of imagination—what does he see?" And so the student, whether he has great learning or that next best substitute—industry—when he finds the chippings of flint, chert or cobble-stone left in the workshop of the ancient artisan of the North Shore, or when he sees the many finishing wares that have been worn and used and lost by the ancient customers of this ancient artisan, and then found again, can reproduce a reasonably accurate picture of the red man, who sat ages ago on the West Shore of old Lake Michigan, and, with untold labor and deftness, prepared the arrows and spear-heads that his red brothers, in due time, hurled at deer, or buffalo or dusky foe; and this student can, in fair and truthful speculation, follow these red brothers in all they saw and did through the forest and across the broad prairies, in the hunt and in the chase, to the wigwam and to the camp fire, on the war path and in their idle roamings from place to place.

These implements may, for convenience in this discussion, be divided into two classes: first, those found along the lake shore near the beach, which are often imperfect in form, consisting of "rejects" and chippings, and found in the aboriginal quarries and shops; and, second, the perfect forms found farther from the lake, where they were in use. I will refer to them in the order named.

It must be borne in mind that, from Wilmette to Waukegan, there are high bluffs, reaching to the beach, so that in that locality the remains of these shops or chipping stations have, to some extent at least, been obliterated by the waves. But, both north and south of these high bluffs, many of these shops have been located and clearly indicate that the Lake Shore, with its ready material among the gravel constantly thrown up by the waves, not only furnished an inexhaustible supply of material ready for use and easily accessible, but that it was resorted to in preference to the more laborious method of seeking and mining materials to the West. Indeed, it is quite probable, and a plausible theory, that the Indian population, for many miles to the west and for untold centuries, used the Lake Shore almost exclusively for the manufacture of stone implements and weapons. These shops, or chipping stations, have generally been found in the sand dunes or ridges immediately adjacent to the beach, where there was shelter from the wind and waves. Many, of course, have long since disappeared by the action of the lake; but at least four of them were located along the shore at Edgewater and Rogers Park, one immediately south of the Indian boundary line at the city limits. In the early days of Evanston and, to my personal knowledge, even as late as 1870, the chippings, rejects and broken arrow-heads, indicating one of the largest of these shops, could easily be found in Evanston extending from what is now Main Street to Greenleaf Street, and about on a line from the Industrial School to the present Evanston residences of Messrs. John C. Spry,

Charles E. Graves and Milton H. Wilson. This particular shop was not only the resort of the idle school boy in his quest for arrow points, but was, in the year 1884, the subject of scientific investigation by Dr. William A. Phillips, a member of the Evanston Historical Society (Science, Vol. 3, page 273, 1884), who made a collection at that time of the chert refuse, "illustrating the successive stages of the chipping or flaking work, beginning with the water-worn pebble from the beach and ending with the nearly completed, but broken, implement," which collection is now in the Museum of the Northwestern University at Evanston (Rep. Curator N. W. University Museum, 1884, Smithsonian Report, 1897 —1161, pp. 587-600).

At the present site of the Dearborn Observatory, on the campus of the Northwestern University, was another of these shops, although a smaller one, which was partially obliterated in the construction of that building, and several others have been located at different times along the lake front of Rogers Park and Evanston.

Indeed, the various collections of these implements, chippings and also of broken pottery would indicate not only an unusual Indian population, but that this industry was general along the lake shore, and much nearer the Chicago river than the sites just described. This situation can easily be demonstrated by the merest glance at the collection of the late Karl A. Dilg, in possession of the Chicago Historical Society.

Immediately north of Waukegan, east of the Northwestern Railway, and extending nearly to the Kenosha city limits, and between the bluff that was formerly the shore line and the present lake front, are some 1,200 to 1,300 acres of low sand dunes, all of which have, from time to time, constituted the shore of the receding lake. This district is replete with shops and stations of

this character, especially so at what was formerly Benton, and now Beach Station, and extending from there north, a distance of about five miles, through Doctor Dowie's "City of Zion" to the state line. As early as 1853 this locality was also the subject of scientific investigation on this subject. (Prof. I. A. Lapham, Antiquities of Wisconsin, Smithsonian Contributions to Knowledge, Vol. 7, page 6, 1885).

These investigations have been further pursued by Dr. Phillips, assisted by Messrs. W. C. Wyman and E. F. Wyman, of Evanston, and by Mr. F. H. Lyman, of Kenosha. In the district between Beach Station and the State line no less than thirty-two sites were located, and a new group or variety of implements found, viz.: weapons and utensils in endless variety, made of trap rock or cobble-stone, and which are now designated, "The Trap Flake Series." A very entertaining and instructive description of this locality and these implements, their uses and the method employed in flaking them, with plates and pictures, will be found in the Smithsonian Report for 1897, pages 587-600, in an able paper by Dr. Phillips, under the title, "A New Group of Stone Implements from the Southern Shores of Lake Michigan."

The implements and weapons, made in these localities along the shore from the Chicago River to Kenosha, represent almost unlimited varieties, from the ordinary arrowhead and the net weight or stone sinker used by the Pottawatomie fisherman, or his ancient predecessor, to the finest of polished hatchets, spear-heads and drills.

It is not within the scope of this discussion to go further into the details of this lost art, in showing how these implements were made and for what they were used— that inquiry should be left to more able hands; but the field for exploration is as boundless and unlimited as the enthusiasm of the archæologist, and is full of interest even to the layman.

The second class, in this subdivision of these implements, are the finished weapons and utensils that, in the long ago, left the work-shop of the artisan, on the beach and elsewhere, were placed in the hands of his warrior customer and have been scattered, used and lost on the land which we have designated the North Shore. Generally speaking, these implements are found in about the same variety and number as in any ordinary Indian country, with one or two remarkable exceptions that will receive special attention. The materials used in their manufacture indicate the presence of Indians from remote parts of the continent, or barter and exchange with remote tribes. They also indicate that the North Shore—especially for from three to six miles from the lake—was not only a great hunting ground, but that the western shore of the lake has been the scene of many a bloody battle between these red warriors of the olden time. They also further indicate, in one or two localities that will be mentioned, an extended Indian population during a long period of time. I am told by members of the Academy of Sciences and others, who have the best means of information, that it is hard to distinguish the particular peoples by these relics, as there is great similarity in manufacture among respective tribes—the distinguishing marks being more especially in the wooden handles or hafts, which, of course, cannot be found —and that some of these implements are of prehistoric origin.

The nearest locality where these implements are found in the greatest variety and number is what was formerly known as Bowmanville—being the vicinity of Rose Hill Cemetery and extending from there to the North Branch of the Chicago River and throughout the territory north of there, extending to Forest Glen, Niles Center and High Ridge, where they have been found in such abundance that a great ancient village—and probably several such villages in that district, is a certainty—all of which will receive later mention when we consider the sites of the Indian villages. The locality west of Evanston, in the town of Niles, which is now a gardening district, has supplied many excellent specimens ploughed up by the farm hands, and it has been an easy matter, with a little patience and attention, to secure a good collection in these localities; and there are many of them— notably the collection of William A. Peterson, of the Peterson Nursery Company, gathered largely from the lands of that company at Rose Hill, the collection of Dr. A. S. Alexander, formerly of Evanston, gathered very largely in Evanston and the township of Niles; also the interesting collection of Karl A. Dilg, already referred to, and that of Adolph Miller at Bowmanville. Still another locality is the neighborhood of the Indian Village at Waukegan, and from there north to the State line, in the locality investigated and described by Dr. Phillips in his paper.

These land marks—these bits of clay, and flint and cobble-stone—to which has been made but very scant and imperfect reference, tell, as they have ever told, a perfect, and yet an imperfect, story; perfect, because we know from that, in some far off day, the North Shore was, as it is now, a favorite abiding place; perfect, too, because the man of science can tell us in some measure of how these people lived and what they did; imperfect, because we must rely to some extent upon theory and speculation and cannot open wide the door with what is understood by the term written history.

The Early Explorers.—All the writers upon the early history of the Northwest, of necessity describe, in more or less detail, the expeditions, exploits and adventures of the explorers and Jesuit missionaries, who first saw the Indians, who were the first white men in Illinois, and who have been the greatest contributors to the history of the Indians of the Northern States. Among these the names of James Marquette, Louis Joliet, La Salle, Henry de Tonty, Hennepin and Claude Allouez are so prominent that the youngest student, who has read even the average school history of the day, can give, with reasonable accuracy, an outline of where they went, what they saw and what they did.

In most of their travels they were accompanied by friendly Indians as guides and assistants, to whose fidelity and attention we owe quite as much as to the explorers themselves. Reference to the extended travels of these daring and hardy men would be useless repetition, but it certainly is of interest to know that such famous voyagers as Father Marquette, Joliet, La Salle, Tonty, and Fathers Hennepin and Allouez, with their Indian friends, all in their day and in their turn, visited the site of Evanston or coasted its shores in their canoes. To the circumstances of some of these early visits to this locality, I briefly direct your attention.

It was the month of June, 1673, over two hundred years ago, when Louis Joliet —educated as a priest, but with more love for exploration and adventure—and James Marquette—who longed to see and trace the course of the great river that De Soto had discovered over one hundred years before, and who, godly man that he was, loved still more to carry the tidings of the Christ to the red man of the prairies—with five French companions in two canoes, started upon that long and toilsome journey through Green Bay, up the Fox River of Wisconsin, from thence into and down the Wisconsin and the Mississippi, and up the then nameless river to the Indian village of the Illinois, where they arrived late in the summer and tarried until September.

The first visit of a white man to Evanston, in September, 1673, is thus described by Francis Parkman in his life of La Salle and the "Discovery of the Great West": "An Illinois chief, with a band of young warriors, offered to guide them to the Lake of the Illinois, that is to say, Lake Michigan; thither they repaired," via the Illinois, Desplaines and Chicago rivers, "and, coasting the shores of the lake, reached Green Bay at the end of September."

The month of November the following year (1674) found Marquette again coasting the western shores of Lake Michigan, accompanied by two white men, "Pierre Porteret and Jacques ———" (Marquette's diary), a band of Pottawatomies and another band of Illinois—ten canoes in all—on his way from Green Bay to his beloved mission of the Illinois, to which he had promised the Indians surely to return. Frail and sick in body, but strong and rich in energy and religious fervor, he made this, his last voyage, from which there proved to be no return for him. Parkman (La Salle, pp. 67, 68) describes the journey: "November had come; the bright hues of the autumn foliage was changed to rusty brown. The shore was desolate and the lake was stormy. They were more than a month in coasting its western border."

Marquette's diary (brought to light nearly two centuries later) gives an interesting account of this journey, describing the land, the forest, the prairie, the buffalo, the deer and other game, the Indians they met, their camp fires at night on shore and their battles with the waves by day, and tells the story of their arrival at the Chicago

River on December 4, 1674, and finding it frozen over; but what is of special interest to us, his diary shows almost conclusively that, on December 3, the day before, the party landed somewhere near the light-house within our present city limits. His notation is as follows:

"December 3, having said holy mass and embarked, we were compelled to make a point and land on account of floating masses of ice."

The only point of land within the day's journey shown upon our present maps, and even the maps of those days, including that of Marquette, is what is known to-day by the sailors as "Gross Point," where the Evanston light-house stands.

Father Allouez made the same journey in the winter of 1676 and 1677, on his way with two companions to the Illinois coun-try, to take the place of Father Marquette in the Illinois mission. They encountered untold hardships, dragging their canoes for many weary miles over the ice-floes of the lake and the snow along its shores.

Two years later is the date when white men were next here (November, 1679), when La Salle, Father Hennepin (the his-torian of the expedition), a Mohegan In-dian (La Salle's faithful servant and hunt-er), and fourteen Frenchmen in four large canoes deeply laden with merchandise, tools and guns, made the same voyage from Green Bay and to St. Joseph, Mich., then called Miami, on their way to the Illi-nois country, to build a fort and to further establish the trade and colonies of New France. They skirted the entire western and southern shores of the lake, while Ton-ty proceeded by the eastern shore.

An interesting account of their adven-tures, hardships and meetings with both hostile and friendly Indians, can be found in Parkman's Life of La Salle (pp. 142-150). As the author says:

"This was no journey of pleasure. The lake was ruffled with almost ceaseless storms; clouds big with rain above, a tur-moil of gray and gloomy waves beneath. Every night the canoes must be shouldered through the breakers and dragged up the steep banks. . . .

"The men paddled all day with no other food than a handful of Indian corn. They were spent with toil and sick with the wild berries which they ravenously devoured and dejected at the prospects before them."

That they, too, may have camped at night or rested by noonday within the limits of our present city is entirely probable.

"As they approached the head of the lake game grew abundant." Marquette verifies this latter statement, for in his diary (entry of December 4, 1674), he says: "Deer hunting is pretty good as you get away from the Pottawatomies." And his next entry (December 12), made after arriving at Chicago, is further verification. He says:

"Pierre and Jacques killed three cattle (buffalo) and four deer, one of which ran quite a distance with his heart cut in two. They contented themselves with killing three or four turkeys of the many that were around our cabin. Jacques brought in a partridge he had killed, in every way re-sembling those of France."

It was winter time a year later—1680. La Salle had not returned from his memo-rable and heroic tramp from the Illinois back to Canada. His men had deserted; his goods had been destroyed by mutineers and In-dians; Hennepin was on the Mississippi. The Iroquois had dispersed and all but de-stroyed the Illinois, and all that remained of La Salle's party was his faithful lieutenant and friend, Henry de Tonty, and two fol-lowers—Membre and Boissondet. Tonty had failed to pacify the Iroquois, had been seriously wounded in battle by them, and he and his two surviving companions, without food or shelter, fled for their lives. Sick, wounded and maimed, he reached the shores of Lake Michigan at Chicago, and he and his companions began their long northward journey on foot, along the dreary and ice-bound shores of the lake to old Michilimackinac. Parkman ("Life of La Salle," p. 220) thus describes their journey: "The cold was intense and it was no easy task to grub up wild onions from the frozen ground, to save themselves from starving. Tonty fell ill of a fever and swelling of the limbs, which disabled him from traveling, and hence ensued a long delay. At length they reached Green Bay, where they would have starved had they not gleaned a few ears of corn and frozen squashes in the fields of an empty Indian town."

A volume could easily be written describing the exploits of the later but still early white and Indian visitors to these shores. The western shore of the lake was the great highway between the Chicago portage and Green Bay and Mackinac. We need not depend upon imagination to paint the picture of the white voyageur and his Indian companion plying the paddle with steady stroke, keeping time to the notes of his boat song, while their birch bark canoes skimmed the surface of the lake, for the "Jesuit Relations" of those early days will supply the facts.

[These travels along the shore of the lake call to mind the early maps, tracing the shore lines made by these explorers, and a fact of local interest is, that in all probability the shore line here at Evanston, in the seventeenth century, extended much farther into the lake—how much cannot be told from the maps, as they were not drawn to scale. This fact appears from a large bay shown on the maps immediately north of the site of our city, indicating that the shore to the south has since been washed away. The maps referred to are (1) one

called Marquette's map, Hist. of Ills., by Sidney Breese, p. 78; (2) map copied by Parkman found in the "Archives of the Marine" at Paris, dated 1683—"may, in fact, have been one drawn by Joliet from recollection"; (3) Joliet's earliest map (1673-74), "Windsor's Geographical Discoveries in the Interior of North America"; (4) Haines' "American Indian," p. 344.

On the map first mentioned Marquette locates a copper mine near Evanston. This was probably done from tales of the Indians describing such mines as being to the north, and Marquette misunderstanding the distance.]

Indian Tribes.—For two hundred years preceding the advent of the white man to Illinois—and for how much longer we do not know—the territory lying between the Mississippi and the Atlantic, and from the Carolinas to Hudson Bay, was occupied by two great families of Indian tribes, distinguished by their languages. All this vast wilderness, with the exception of New York, a part of Ohio and part of Canada, was the country of the tribes speaking the Algonquin language and dialects. "Like a great island in the midst of the Algonquins lay the country of the Iroquois." The true Iroquois, or Five Nations, often called the Six Nations, occupied Central and Western New York, and the remainder of this linguistic group contiguous territory to the west, in Ohio and Lower Canada. (The only exception to this general statement is the Winnebagoes of Dahcotah stock, who were at Green Bay and in Southern Wisconsin, and a few scattering bands of the Dahcotahs, who were at times on the eastern banks of the Mississippi.)

All the Indians who have held and occupied this part of Illinois as their homes, so far back as history tells us, or can be ascertained during the past four hundred years, were of the Algonquin family; and while scattering bands of the Sacs and Foxes (Outagamies), Miamis, Ottawas and other Algonquin tribes, and also the Kickapoos, Shawaneese, Sioux and Winnebagoes, have at times, roamed over and, perhaps, for very brief periods, in roving bands occupied the lands lying along the western shores of Lake Michigan in this locality, the Indian ownership, as indicated by extended occupancy, was confined almost, if not entirely, to the tribes of the Illinois and the Pottawatomies. Therefore, to those two tribes and their eastern enemies, the Iroquois, who at times paid unwelcome visits to their western neighbors, I direct your attention.

It must be borne in mind that Chicago was as important a point to the Indian as it has since been to the white man, partly on account of the portage leading to the Desplaines River, and, as the lake was the great water highway, so also was its western shore an important highway for these Indian tribes when they traveled by land.

[The early explorers and missionaries often mention a tribe called by them the "Mascoutins," and on some of the very early maps of this locality appears the name of such a tribe as occupying parts of northern Illinois. The better opinion is, there never was in fact such a tribe of Indians. This word—"Mascoutins"—in the Algonquin language means people of the prairie or meadow country, and it was applied, it seems, indiscriminately to indicate the locality from which the Indians it was applied to had emigrated or were located. Haines' "American Indian," p. 151.]

It is claimed by several reliable writers that, from 1700 or 1702 to 1770, the country about Chicago had no fixed Indian population, but that the only Indian residents were roving bands of Iroquois and "Northern Indians." (See Andreas' "Hist. of Chicago," Mason's "Illinois.")

The Iroquois.—The Iroquois have received the enthusiastic admiration of many writers: the best, and some of the worst, traits of Indian character found its highest development among them; they are designated by one enthusiast as "the Indians of Indians." And they are well worthy of mention in our local history, for, after exterminating and subduing their nearest neighbors, including the Hurons, the Eries and other tribes speaking the same language, their thirst for conquest led them westward from their far away eastern homes; their war parties penetrated the intervening wilderness of forest and plain, navigated the western rivers and great lakes, and destroyed or drove their enemies in terror before them across the prairies of Illinois and along the western shore of Lake Michigan. Distance, hardships, winter and time expended in travel, presented no obstacles to them, and they scattered, and all but destroyed, the great and powerful Algonquin tribes of the Illinois, from which our State takes its name; and, as early as 1660, they were known to have pursued their ancient enemies, the Hurons or Wyandots, across our State. (Mason's "Land of the Illinois," p. 4.)

The Iroquois are thus described by Parkman ("Conspiracy of Pontiac," p. 7): "Foremost in war, foremost in eloquence, foremost in their savage arts of policy, . . . they extended their conquests and their depredations from Quebec to the Carolinas, and from the western prairies to the forests of Maine. . . . On the west they exterminated the Eries, and Andastes, and spread havoc and dismay among the tribes of the Illinois. . . . The Indians of New England fled at the first peal of the Mohawk war cry. . . and all Canada shook with the fury of their onset. . . . The blood besmeared conquerors roamed like wolves among the burning settlements, and the colony trembled on the brink of ruin. . . Few tribes could match them in prowess, constancy, moral energy or intellectual vigor." They, in turn, and within a quarter of a century (1650-1672), exterminated four powerful tribes, the Wyandots, the Neutral Nation, the Andastes and the Eries, and reduced the ancient and powerful Hurons, from whom the great lake takes its name, to a small band of terror-stricken fugitives; their ferocity and torture of captives were revolting traits in their character; they were the worst of conquerors and their lust of blood and dominion is without parallel in Indian history.

Mr. Mason says of them ("Land of the Illinois," pp. 113,114): "Though numbering but 2,500 warriors, their superior weapons and experience in warfare had enabled them to defeat and finally exterminate all their neighbors. . . . They destroyed more than thirty nations; caused the death of more than 600,000 persons within eighty years, and rendered the country about the great lakes a desert"—and Mr. Mason's statement had ample corroboration.

Such were the Indians who were often transient residents of this locality before the coming of the white man, and their depredations furnish the basis for much of the historical references to the process of self-extermination of the Indian, by the wars among themselves in progress when the white man first saw the American Indian.

The French were never successful in gaining the friendship of the Iroquois tribes, as they were with almost all the other Indians of the North and Northwest; but the Iroquois were the friends of the English and Dutch.

In Colden's "History of the Five Nations," printed in the old English style of that day (1750), the author, in describing one of the campaigns between the French and English, in 1693, where Peter Schuyler, a Major of the New York Militia, was in charge of the English and their Indian allies, the Iroquois, says:

"It is true that the English were in great want of Provisions at that time. . . . The Indians eat the Bodies of the French that they found. Col. Schuyler (as he told me himself) going among the Indians at that Time was invited to eat broth with them, which some of them had ready boiled, which he did, till they, putting the Ladle deep into the Kettle to take out more, brought out a French Man's Hand, which put an end to his Appetite."

The quaint humor in this record of an Englishman eating such French broth in the seventeenth century, or at any subsequent time, for that matter, and losing his appetite, needs no comment; the author may unconsciously have offered a fair explanation of this circumstance, for he says in another connection, "Schuyler was brave, but he was no Soldier."

The Illinois.—In the year 1615, five years before the landing of the Mayflower, Champlain reached Lake Huron. Upon his crude map of New France appears indications that he then heard and knew of the far-away prairie land, in which dwelt the tribes of the Illinois—the land of the Buffalo. (Mason, supra.) Jean Nicolet saw or heard of the Illinois again in 1638 and two young French explorers again in 1655 (Mason, Id.) October 1, 1665, ten years later, the Illinois sent a delegation to attend an Indian Council at the Great Chippewa (Ojibway) Village, on Lake Superior, with reference to war with the Sioux, which Claude Allouez attended and there addressed the many Northern tribes assembled in council, assuring them of the friendship and protection of the French, who would "smooth the path between the Chippewas and Quebec, brush the pirate canoes from the intervening rivers and leave the Iroquois no alternative but death and destruction." (Brown's "History of Illinois," p. 115.) There is abundant evidence to show that, during the preceding years, the Illinois had suffered greatly by wars with the Sioux from the West and with the Iroquois from the East.

In 1673 Joliet and Marquette found the Illinois on the western bank of the Mississippi and on the Illinois River, where there were many villages; one village found by these explorers consisting of seventy-four cabins, each containing several families. In 1675 Marquette paid his second visit to the same locality and "summoned them to a grand council on the Great Meadow between the Illinois River and the modern village of Utica. Here five hundred chiefs and old men were seated in a ring; behind stood 1,500 youths and warriors and, behind them, all the women and children of the village. Marquette standing in the midst," told them the story of Christ and the Virgin (Parkman's "La Salle," 69); Allouez visited them again in 1677.

In 1680 Tonty and Hennepin found the lodges of the great Indian town, 460 in number, constructed of poles "in shape like the arched tops of a baggage wagon," covered with mats of rushes, closely interwoven; each contained three or four fires; the greater part served for two families. The population has been variously estimated at 2,400 families, 1,200 warriors and 6,000 souls. "The lodges were built along the river bank for the distance of a mile, sometimes far more." (Parkman's "La Salle," 156.)

Among the varying estimates as to population of the Illinois tribes (none of them very accurate), one early Jesuit writer (1658) describes their number at "about 100,000 souls, with sixty villages and quite 20,000 warriors." (Mason, Id., 4.) "Their

great Metropolis, near Utica, in La Salle County, was the largest city ever built by northern natives." (Caton, "The Last of the Illinois.") Mr. Mason locates the village four miles below the present city of Ottawa. ("Land of the Illinois," p. 44.)

These facts indicate not only a powerful and populous nation, but their cemeteries, traditions, implements and cultivated fields, a long residence in the same locality—how many the years or how many the centuries can never be known.

Their most permanent homes were along the Illinois River, but they seem to have had entire control of all the northeastern portion of Illinois, as far back as any record can be found and to the time of the occupation by the Pottawatomies. The Chicago portage seems to have been a frequent and popular rendezvous, and they were so identified with this locality that Lake Michigan was generally known to the early explorers as the "Lake of the Illinois."

The Illinois were a kindly people; hospitable, affable and humane; and it was said of them by one of the Jesuit missionaries, "When they meet a stranger they utter a cry of joy, caress him and give him every proof of friendship." They lived by hunting and tilling of the soil, raising great crops of Indian corn and storing away a surplus for future use; they were great travelers by land, but, unlike most northern Indian tribes, used canoes but little; they had permanent dwellings, as well as portable lodges; they roamed many months of the year among the prairies and forests of their great country, to return again and join in the feasts and merry-making, when their whole population gathered in the villages. These habits of travel indicate that they were frequently along the western shore of the lake.

In September, 1680, soon after La Salle and Tonty reached the Illinois country, and while Tonty was still there, the Iroquois from New York again attacked the Illinois. "With great slaughter they defeated this hitherto invincible people; laid waste their great city and scattered them in broken bands over their wide domain. From this terrible blow the Illinois never recovered." (Caton, "Last of the Illinois"; Mason, Id., pp. 99-103.)

During the succeeding century the Illinois—lovers of peace, who had welcomed the explorer and the missionary—broken in spirit, their courage gone, decimated by drink and disease and scattered by their enemies, struggled with waning fortunes, ending their existence in the historic tragedy of Starved Rock, about the year 1770, from which but eleven of their number escaped.

An Indian boy—a Pottawatomie—saw the last remnant of this once proud and powerful nation, brave warriors, their women and little children, huddled together upon the half acre of ground that crowns the summit of Starved Rock; saw the fierce and war-like Pottawatomies and Ottawas swarm for days around them, and perform by the torture of siege and starvation what they could not do by force of arms. When the little stock of food was gone, and despair drove the Illinois to make the last brave dash for liberty in the darkness of the stormy night, he heard the yells and clash of the fighting warriors and the dying shrieks of the helpless women and children. Years afterward, when this Indian lad (Meachelle) had grown to be the principal chief of the Pottawatomies, he related these incidents to Judge Caton. Let him who cares for tragedy read what the learned Judge says of this—the last of the Illinois.

The Pottawatomies.—The Pottawatomies were of the Algonquin tribes. Their power was severely felt by the British when at war with the French and in the later Indian war led by Pontiac. When Allouez and the other Jesuit Fathers first visited Green Bay, in 1670, the Pottawatomies were living along its shores, and these Jesuits are probably the first white men who saw them in their homes. Green Bay at that time was their permanent abode, though they roamed far away and extended their visits over much of the territory around Lake Superior, where delegations of them were seen as early as 1665, and in 1670, '71 and '72 by the Jesuit Fathers, whom they frequently visited and invited to their homes at Green Bay. In those days they were not known in this locality, for Joliet and Marquette, returning from the Mississippi and the Illinois country in 1674, met none of the Pottawatomies in this region.

The date when they left Green Bay is not certain, or whether they emigrated from there as a whole or in parties, but it is a matter of history that, early in the eighteenth century (authorities differ as to the date), they scattered to the south and east and, thereafter, occupied the Southern Peninsula of Michigan, Northeastern Illinois and the northern part of Indiana. Their advance into Illinois was sometimes accomplished with good-natured tolerance on the part of the Illinois tribes, and sometimes by actual violence. This emigration divided the tribe into two rather distinct classes, so that we often find, even in recent Government reports, the Pottawatomies of Michigan and Indiana designated as those of the Woods, and those of Illinois as those of the Prairie, or "The Prairie Band."

The exclusive possession of this territory by the Pottawatomies dates from the siege of Starved Rock and the extinction of the Illinois. The Pottawatomies and Ottawas supposed that the Illinois were accessory to the murder of Pontiac, who was killed in

1769 by an Illinois Indian, bribed for the deed with a barrel of whiskey. They loved and obeyed this great Indian chieftain of the Oattawas and wreaked dire vengeance for his death upon the luckless Illinois, and the date of the massacre at Starved Rock and their permanent occupation of this territory is generally fixed as soon after Pontiac's death. No record of their permanent residence at Green Bay succeeds this date.

The Pottawatomies were of commanding importance in this locality thereafter, and even before, for in 1763 they sent a delegation of 450 warriors to the Algonquin Conference at Niagara Falls, and, as we all know, they were the last Indians to yield their place in this State to the inevitable westward march of the white man, when the tomahawk gave way forever to the plowshare.

As already stated, the Pottawatomies of the Woods became, in time, a different people than their western brothers; they were susceptible to the influence of civilization and religion; took kindly to agriculture to supplement the fruits of the chase.

It was very different, however, with the Illinois Pottawatomies—the prairie Indians. Judge Caton says of them: "They despised the cultivation of the soil as too mean even for their women and children, and deemed the captures of the chase the only fit food for a valorous people." They paid little attention to the religion of the white man.

"If they understood something of the principles of the Christian religion which were told them, they listened to it as a sort of theory which might be well adapted to the white man's condition, but was not fitted for them, nor they for it. They enjoyed the wild, roving life of the prairie, and, in common with most all other native Americans, were vain of their prowess and manhood, both in war and in the chase.

They did not settle down for a great length of time in a given place, but roamed across the broad prairies, from one grove or belt of timber to another, either in single families or in small bands, packing their few effects, their children, and infirm on their little Indian ponies. They always traveled in Indian file upon well-beaten trails, connecting, by the most direct routes, prominent trading posts. These native highways served as guides to our early settlers, who followed them with as much confidence as we now do the roads laid out and worked by civilized man."

Schoolcraft says they were tall of stature, fierce and haughty.

The portable wigwams of the Pottawatomies were made of flags or rushes, woven and lapped ingeniously together. This material was wound around a framework of poles, meeting at the top. Through a hole in the apex of the roof, left for the purpose, the smoke escaped from the fire in the center; the floor was generally of mats of the same material spread around the fire. Their beds were of buffalo robes and deer skins thrown over the mats. The door consisted of a simple opening covered with a mat or robe.

Chicago was an important rendezvous for them, as it had previously been for the Illinois. There they signed an important treaty with the United States in 1821, ceding some 5,000,000 acres in Michigan and other treaties, which will receive later mention, and here they held, in 1835, immediately preceding their removal to the West, their last grand council and war dance in the presence of the early settlers of Chicago and 5,000 of their tribe.

The Ottawas were the firm allies of the Pottawatomies, as were also the Chippewas (Ojibways) and all three tribes were closely related, not only as friends and allies, but by ties of blood and kinship, and they generally joined in signing treaties; some writers assert that they were formerly one nation.

In the war of 1812 the Pottawatomies, at least in part, were against the United States, although they fought the British under Pontiac in 1763. In the Black Hawk War of 1832 they remained true to our Government, although it was with difficulty that some of their young warriors were restrained from joining the Sacs and Foxes. They participated in the Battle of Tippecanoe, and stamped their names forever upon the history of Chicago by the Fort Dearborn massacre. They were not only actively concerned in all the warlike transactions of their time, but among their numbers were some of the most noted orators of history.

Ouilmette Reservation and Family. —The Ouilmette reservation and its former occupants and owners have been the subject of much solicitude and investigation, not entirely for historical purposes, but more especially that the white man might know that he had a good, white man's title to the Indian's land. The southern boundary was Central Street, or a line due west from the light-house; the eastern boundary the lake; the northern boundary a little south of Kenilworth, and the western boundary a little west of the western terminus of the present street-car line on Central Street, from which it will be seen that some 300 acres of the Reservation falls within the city limits of Evanston, while the remainder includes almost the whole of our nearest neighbor to the north—the Village of Wilmette.

The reservation takes its name from its original owner, Archange Ouilmette, wife of Antoine Ouilmette, described in the original Treaty and Patent from the United States as a Pottawatomie woman. The name given the village—Wilmette—originates from the phonetic spelling of the French name "O-u-i-l-m-e-t-t-e."

There are many interesting facts regarding Ouilmette and his family, some of which I will mention: Antoine, the husband, was a Frenchman, who, like many of his countrymen, came to the West in early days and married an Indian wife. He was one of the first white residents of Chicago; some of the authorities say that, with the exception of Marquette, he was the very first. He was born at a place called Lahndrayh, near Montreal, Canada, in the year 1760. His first employment was with the American Fur Company, in Canada, and he came to Chicago in the employ of that company in the year 1790.

This striking figure in our local history is sadly neglected in most, if not all, the historical writings. Almost every one knows that the Village of Wilmette was named after its former owner; many misinformed persons speak of him as an Indian chief; a few of the writers merely mention his name as one of the early settlers of Chicago. And that has been the beginning and the end of his written history.

Ouilmette's occupation cannot be more definitely stated than to say that, at one time, he was an employe of John Kinzie, and in turn Indian trader, hunter and farmer. He was a type of the early French voyageurs, who lived and died among their Indian friends, loving more the hardships and excitement of the Western frontier than the easier life of Eastern civilization.

If a detailed account of all he saw and did could be written we would have a complete history of Chicago, Evanston and all the North Shore during the eventful fifty years intervening between 1790 and 1840.

It appears from a letter signed with "his mark," written and witnessed by one James Moore, dated at Racine, June 1, 1839, that he came to Chicago in July, 1790. A facsimile of this letter, which is addressed to Mr. John H. Kinzie, appears in Blanchard's History of Chicago (p. 574), and contains some interesting facts, both historical and personal. He says:

"I caim into Chicago in the year 1790 in July witness old Mr. Veaux . . . and Mr Griano . . . These men ware living in the country Before the war with the winnebagoes. Trading with them I saw the Indians Brake open the Door of my house and also the Door of Mr. Kinzie's House. At first there was only three indians come. They told me there was Forty more coming and they told me to run. i Did So. in nine days all I found left of my things was the feathers of my beds scattered about The floor, the amount Distroyed By them at that time was about Eight hundred Dollars. Besides your fathar and me Had about four hundred hogs Distroyed by the Saim indians and nearly at the Saim time. further particulars when I See you. I wish you to write me whether it is best for me to come thare or for you to come hear and how son it must be Done"

"Yours with Respect"

"Jas. Moore"
his
Antone X Ouilmette"
mark

Ouilmette owned and occupied one of the four cabins that constituted the settlement of Chicago in 1803. The other residents were Kinzie, Burns and Lee (Kirkland's "Story of Chicago," "Andreas' History of Chicago," Mrs. William Whistler's letter, written in 1875.)

Ouilmette had eight children, four sons and four daughters, viz.:—Joseph, Louis, Francis, Mitchell, Elizabeth, Archange, Josette and Sophia; also an adopted daughter, Archange Trombla, who, on August 3, 1830, married John Mann, who in early times ran a ferry at Calumet. (Authority John Wentworth and Sophia Martell, the only surviving daughter of Antoine Ouilmette.)

Ouilmette was in Chicago at the time of the massacre of the garrison of Old Fort Dearborn in 1812 by the Pottawatomies, and his family was instrumental, at that time, in saving the lives of at least two whites. Mrs. John H. Kinzie in her book, "Wau-bun" (the early day), describes the circumstances:

"The next day after Black Partridge, the Pottawatomie Chief, had saved the life of Mrs. Helm in the massacre on the lake shore (commemorated by the monument recently erected at the place), a band of "the most hostile and implacable of all the tribes of the Pottawatomies" arrived at Chicago and, disappointed at their failure to participate in the massacre and plunder, were ready to wreak vengeance on the survivors, including Mrs. Helm and other members of Mr. Kinzie's family. Mrs. Kinzie says ("Wau-bun" pages 235, 240):

"Black Partridge had watched their approach, and his fears were particularly awakened for the safety of Mrs. Helm (Mr. Kinzie's step-daughter). By his advice she was made to assume the ordinary dress of a French woman of the country. .

"In this disguise she was conducted by Black Partridge himself to the house of Ouilmette, a Frenchman with a half-breed wife, who formed a part of the establishment of Mr. Kinzie, and whose dwelling was close at hand. . . It so happened that the Indians came first to this house in their search for prisoners. As they approached, the inmates, fearful that the fair complexion and general appearance of Mrs. Helm might betray her for an American, raised a large feather bed and placed her under the edge of it, upon the bedstead, with her face to the wall. Mrs. Bison, the sister of Ouilmette's wife, then seated herself with her sewing upon the foot of the bed."

It was a hot day in August and Mrs. Helm suffered so much from her position and was so nearly suffocated that she entreated to be released and given up to the Indians. "I can but die," said she; "let them put an end to my misery at once." When they assured her that her discovery would be the death of all of them, she remained quiet.

"The Indians entered and she could occasionally see them from her hiding place, gliding about and stealthily inspecting every part of the room, though without making any ostensible search, until apparently satisfied that there was no one concealed, they left the house. . . All this time Mrs. Bison had kept her seat upon the side of the bed, calmly sorting and arranging the patch work of the quilt on which she was then engaged and preserving the appearance of the utmost tranquillity, although she knew not but the next moment she might receive a tomahawk in her brain. Her self command unquestionably saved the lives of all present. . . From Ouilmette's house the party proceeded to the dwelling of Mr. Kinzie."

The Indians had just left Ouilmette's house when one Griffin, a non-commissioned officer, who had escaped and had been concealed among the currant bushes of Ouilmette's garden, climbed into Ouilmette's house through a window to hide from the Indians. "The family stripped him of his uniform and arrayed him in a suit of deer skin, with belt, moccasins and pipe, like a French engage," in which disguise he also escaped.

After the massacre, when John Kinzie and all the other white settlers and their families fled from the place, Ouilmette and his family remained, and he was the only white resident of Chicago for the following four years, 1812 to 1816. (Kirkland's "Story of Chicago"; Hurlbut's "Chicago Antiquities.")

In 1814 Alexander Robinson (afterwards chief of the Pottawatomies) came to Chicago, and he and Ouilmette cultivated the field formerly used as the garden of old Fort Dearborn; they raised good crops of corn and sold the crop of 1816 to Captain Bradley, after his arrival at Chicago to rebuild the fort. (Andreas' "History of Chicago.")

He was still in Chicago in 1821. (Andreas', Id.; Kirkland, Id.)

He had horses and oxen and other stock in abundance. In early days he kept a small store in Chicago and used to tow boats into the Chicago River with his ox teams. He also furnished the Fort Dearborn garrison with meat and fuel and carried on trading operations with the Indians along the North Shore and in Canada, where he frequently went. (Authority, Sophia Martell.)

Mrs. Archibald Clybourne says that Ouilmette raised sheep when he lived in Chicago, and that her mother, Mrs. Galloway, used to purchase the wool of him with which she spun yarn and knit stockings for the Fort Dearborn soldiers.

Ouilmette was a thrifty Frenchman. In 1825 he was one of the principal taxpayers in Chicago and paid $4.00 taxes that year upon property valued at $400, as appears by an old tax roll, dated July 25th of that year (Blanchard's "History of Chicago," p.

517), from which rate of taxation it would seem that the burden of "taxing bodies," of which we hear so much in these days, began very early in Chicago's history. With one exception, none of the fourteen taxpayers of that year owned property in excess of $1,000. John Kinzie's holdings appear on the same roll as worth $500, while those of John B. Beaubien are set down at $1,000; the lowest man on the list is Joseph La Framboise, who paid fifty cents on property valued at $50, and Ouilmette's taxes appear considerably above the average in amount. He also appears as a voter upon the poll book of an election held at Chicago on August 7, 1826, at which election it is said he voted for John Quincy Adams for President (Blanchard, Id., p. 519), which is the last record I have been able to find of his residence in Chicago.

The Treaty of Prairie du Chien, in describing the boundaries of a part of the lands ceded by the Indians, and dated July 29, 1829, begins the description as follows:

"Beginning on the western shore of Lake Michigan, at the northeast corner of the field of Antoine Ouilmette, who lives near Gross Point, about twelve (12) miles north from Chicago, thence due west to the Rock River," which is the first evidence I have found of Ouilmette's residence in this vicinity, although he was married to Archange in 1796 or 1797 at "Gross Point," or what is now Wilmette Village, this being the first North Shore wedding of which there is any history. (Authority, Sophia Martell.)

Ouilmette was a Roman Catholic. In April, 1833, he joined with Alexander Robinson, Billy Caldwell, several of the Beaubiens and others, in a petition to the Bishop of the diocese of Missouri, at St. Louis, asking for the establishment of the first Catholic Church in Chicago. The petition (written in French) says: "A priest should be sent there before other sects obtain the upper hand, which very likely they will try to do." The early enterprise of the church is demonstrated by the fact that the petition was received on April 16th and granted the next day. (Andreas' "History of Chicago.")

From the foregoing facts it is evident that Ouilmette located in Chicago in 1790, and lived there for over thirty-six years, and that some time between 1826 and 1829 he located within the present limits of Evanston or Wilmette Village, and certainly within the Reservation.

Mrs. Kinzie took Ouilmette's daughter Josette with her to the Indian Agency, of which her husband was in charge at Old Fort Winnebago in Wisconsin, on her return from Chicago in 1831. She describes her ("Wau-bun," 300) as " a little bound girl, a bright, pretty child of ten years of age. She had been at the Saint Joseph's Mission School." Mrs. Kinzie, at the time of the Black Hawk war (1832) fled from Fort Winnebago to Green Bay in a canoe and took this same little Josette Ouilmette with her ("Wau-bun," 426).

That Josette was a protege of the Kinzie family, and that they took a lively interest in her welfare, further appears from the treaty of 1833 with the Pottawatomies at Chicago. She is personally provided for, probably at the demand of the Kinzies, in the following words: "To Josette Ouilmette (John H. Kinzie, Trustee), $200." The other children did not fare so well, for the Treaty further provides, "To Antoine Ouilmette's children, $300."

Archange Ouilmette, wife of Antoine, was a squaw of the Pottawatomie tribe, belonging to a band of that tribe located at the time she was married at what is now Wilmette Village, although the band were constant rovers over what is now Illinois, Michigan, Indiana and Wisconsin. While Archange was of the Pottawatomie tribe her father was a white man, a trader in the employ of the American Fur Company, a Frenchman, bearing the rather striking name of Francois Chevallier. Archange was born at Sugar Creek, Michigan, about 1764 and died at Council Bluffs, Iowa, in 1840. (Authority, Sophia Martell, daughter, and Israel Martell, grandson of Antoine.)

John Wentworth says in his reminiscences that Ouilmette's daughter, Elizabeth, married for her first husband on May 11, 1830, Michael Welch, "the first Irishman in Chicago."

This wedding, with the son of Erin groom and the Pottawatomie bride, was celebrated in an old log cabin that stood until some two years ago (1903) on the east side of Sheridan Road, at Kenilworth, and about two blocks north of the Kenilworth water tower. I secured a kodak picture of this log cabin shortly before it was removed, copy of which appears on an adjoining page. This cabin was built by one John Doyle, who, considering his name and date of residence, may be safely designated "the first Irishman of the North Shore," for I am sure there are few who can successfully dispute my statement, nor do I see any reason why the North Shore should not have its "first Irishman" as well as Chicago.

My authority as to this being the house where the wedding was celebrated is Mr. Charles S. Raddin, of Evanston, who secured the information some years ago from Mrs. Archibald Clybourne, who may have been present at the wedding, although Mr. Raddin neglected to ask her. Mr. Raddin was further neglectful in failing to get the name of the best man and the maid of honor, and whether they were Irish or Pottawatomie. The ceremony was performed by John B. Beaubien, a Justice of the Peace, as is shown beyond question by the records of Peoria County.

Ouilmette and his family lived in this cabin at the time of this wedding, and for some time thereafter (authority, Sophia Martell, who also corroborates Mr. Raddin regarding her sister's marriage), although their most permanent abode was about a mile south of there, as will be shown later.

The Treaty of Prairie du Chien with the Chippewas, Ottawas and Pottawatomies, by which the Reservation was ceded to Ouilmette's wife, was concluded July 29, 1829. Among other provisions of land for Indians and others, Article 4 of the Treaty provides as follows: "To Archange Ouilmette, a Pottawatomie woman, wife of Antoine, two sections for herself and her children on Lake Michigan, south of and adjoining the northern boundary of the cession herein made by the Indians aforesaid to the United States. . . . The tracts of land herein stipulated to be granted shall never be leased or conveyed by the grantees, or their heirs, to any person whatever, without the permission of the President of the United States."

The land was surveyed by the Government surveyors in 1842, and the patent therefor was issued October 29th of the same year.

Site of Evanston Lands Acquired From the Indians.—This treaty is of special historical interest. By it the United States acquired title from the Indians to all of the land within the city limits of Evanston and great tracts to the west, bounded as follows: Beginning at the north line of Ouilmette's reservation, or a little south of Kenilworth on the Lake Shore, due west to the Rock River, thence down the river and east of it to the Indian boundary line on Fox River, established by the treaty of 1816; thence northeasterly on that line to Lake Michi-

gan, thence north along the lake shore to the place of beginning. (The line mentioned as running "northeasterly to Lake Michigan" is the center of the street in Rogers Park, known for many years and in our records as the "Indian Boundary Road," now unfortunately changed by direction of the City Council of Chicago to "Rogers Avenue." It is about half way between Calvary Cemetery and the Rogers Park depot; crosses Clark Street or Chicago Avenue at the site of the old tollgate and Justice Murphy's birthplace on the opposite corner).

There should be active co-operation in restoring the name "Indian Boundary" to this highway. I am informed that the name was changed at the solicitation of Mr. Rogers' family. He was, no doubt, a worthy pioneer, but his name seems to have been sufficiently perpetuated by the name Rogers' Park, which was the former village now annexed to Chicago. There is, too, a railroad station there of that name, and many real estate subdivisions also bearing his name. This Indian Boundary line is not only a great land mark, but the treaty which fixed it had great historical significance in the development of Illinois. This line is referred to in many maps, surveys, deeds and conveyances, is in part the dividing line between the cities of Chicago and Evanston, runs in a southwesterly direction, intersecting other roads and streets in such manner as to make it an important and distinctive highway, the importance of which will grow more and more as the years go by. The disinclination of the City Council to disturb historical landmarks by changing the names of old highways should surely have been exercised in this instance, and one of the aldermen of that ward, Mr. W. P. Dunn, assures me that he agrees with this sentiment.

This treaty also included a vast territory lying between the Mississippi and Rock rivers in Illinois and Wisconsin, and was planned, it is said, with reference to the succeeding Treaty of Chicago in 1833, to finally clear Western Illinois and Southern Wisconsin of the Indians. "By its provisions the Indians became completely hemmed in or surrounded. To use a common saying in playing checkers, the Indians were driven into the 'single corner' before they were aware of it." Haines, p 554.)

This treaty was the entering wedge, designed, as above stated, to eventually oust the Pottawatomies and other tribes from Illinois and Wisconsin, and the manner in which its execution was secured reflects no credit upon our nation. If the writers who have investigated the subject can be relied upon, hardly any treaty with the Indians ever made is subject to more just criticism.

Story of the Ouilmette Reservation.— It is claimed by Elijah M. Haines, author of "The American Indian," that the two sections of land constituting the Ouilmette Reservation, were given to Ouilmette's wife and children as a bribe for the husband's influence in securing the execution of this treaty. Mr. Haines, late of Waukegan, was for some years Speaker of the Illinois House of Representatives, and spent a portion of each year, for many years, among the Indians. In his book he devotes some ten pages (550-560) to "the ingenious work in overreaching the Indians in procuring the execution of this treaty," from which it appears, if Mr. Haines is correct, that plans were laid in advance by the Government's agents to carry it through by electing chiefs to fill vacancies in the Pottawatomie tribe, who were not only friendly to the whites, but who were parties to a prior conspiracy to dupe the Indians. As the author says, "the

jury being thus successfully packed, the verdict was awaited as a matter of form." Mr. Haines seems to have reached this conclusion after careful investigation, including personal interviews with some of the principals, among whom was Alexander Robinson, one of the chiefs who was elected at the very time the treaty was signed. Mr. Haines sets out a personal interview between himself and Robinson on the subject, which is as follows: ·

"Mr. Robinson, when and how did you become a chief?"

"Me made chief at the treaty of Prairie du Chien."

"How did you happen to be made chief?"

"Old Wilmette, he come to me one day and he say: Dr. Wolcott" (then Indian agent at Chicago, who Mr. Haines says, planned the deal) "want me and Billy Caldwell to be chief. He ask me if I will. Me say yes, if Dr. Wolcott want me to be."

"After the Indians had met together at Prairie du Chien for the Treaty, what was the first thing done?"

"The first thing they do they make me and Billy Caldwell chiefs; then we be chiefs . . . then we all go and make the treaty."

Chiefs Robinson and Caldwell were handsomely taken care of, both in this treaty and subsequent ones, in the way of annuities, cash and lands, as were also their friends. Archange Ouilmette, Indian wife of the man designated by Chief Robinson as "Old Wilmette," and her children thus, according to Mr. Haines, secured the two sections of land constituting the Reservation under discussion, and which seems to show that Ouilmette was, indeed, as already stated, a thrifty Frenchman.

There is ample ground, however, for disagreement with Mr. Haines in his voluntary criticism of Ouilmette in this transaction. It must be borne in mind that Ouilmette and his family were not only friendly to the whites during the stirring and perilous times at Chicago in the War of 1812, but they themselves had suffered depredations at the hands of the Indians, as shown by Ouilmette's letter to John H.

Kinzie. Then, too, he was occupying this very land, then of little value, and considering his fidelity to the Government, notwithstanding his marriage to a Pottawatomie wife, it would seem that this cession of these two sections of land, under the circumstances, was entirely right and probably very small compensation for his friendly services. Then, too, it must be remembered that he did not get the land, but it went to his Pottawatomie wife and her children.

Mr. Haines says of this transaction and of Dr. Wolcott's and Ouilmette's connection with it (p. 557): "In aid of this purpose, it seems he secured the services of Antoine Wilmette, a Frenchman, who had married an Indian wife of the Pottawatomie tribe, one of the oldest residents of Chicago, and a man of much influence with the Indians and a particular friend of Robinson's."

It is fair to say that Mr. Haines excuses both Robinson and Caldwell for their action in the matter, on the ground that they had long been friendly to the whites and were misled into believing that the integrity of their white friends was as lasting as their own (p. 556). It is to be regretted that Mr. Haines did not express the same views as to Ouilmette, for history clearly demonstrates that he was richly entitled to it.

Ouilmette was also on hand when the Treaty of Chicago (1833) was negotiated, as he was at Prairie du Chien, for the treaty not only provides for the donations already mentioned to Chiefs Robinson and Caldwell, to Ouilmette's children and others, but he secured $800 for himself, as the treaty shows. Whether this was compensation for his hogs that had been "distroyed" some thirty years before by the Indians, or as further compensation for his prior services at Prairie du Chien or at Chicago in 1812, is not disclosed, but it certainly is evidence of his desire to see that his finances should not suffer in deals made with his wife's relations.

Joseph Fountain, late of Evanston, now deceased, father-in-law of ex-Alderman Carroll, says in an affidavit dated in 1871, "that when he first came here he lived with Antoine Ouilmette; that at that time he (Antoine) was an old man, about 70 years of age, and was living upon the Reservation with his nephew, Archange, his wife, being then absent. . . . That within a year or two thereafter the children returned and lived with their father upon the Reservation The children went away again and returned again in 1844. They were then all over lawful age, had usual and ordinary intelligence of white people and were competent to manage and sell their property. . . . That he was intimate with the children and their father and after their return assisted them in building a house to live in on the Reservation. That during the last twenty (20) years the Indian heirs have not been back there. . . . That in the years 1852 and 1853 the land was not worth over $3.00 per acre."

I find by inquiry of Mary Fountain, Joseph Fountain's widow, a very old lady, in Evanston, still living in 1901[1], and by like inquiry of Mr. Benjamin F. Hill[2] and others, that the house just mentioned was built of logs, situated on the high bluffs on the lake shore, opposite, or a little north of Lake Avenue, in the Village of Wilmette, and that the former site of the house has long since, and within the memory of old residents been washed into the lake, many acres of land having been thus washed away. Mr. Hill says that this house was at one time occupied by Joel Stebbins, who used it as a tavern.

[1] Mrs. Fountain died in Evanston February 17, 1905.
[2] Benjamin F. Hill died in Milwaukee, Wisconsin, October 7, 1905—his residence up to that time, however, having been in Evanston.

The affidavit of Mr. Fountain indicates that Ouilmette lived on the Reservation until 1838. His letter of 1839 indicates a residence at Racine, at which place he had a farm for several prior years, and while living in Chicago, or at least a tract of land where he frequently went. (Authority, Sophia Martell.)

Mr. Benjamin F. Hill says that he knew him about the year 1838; that he was then a very old man, rather small of stature, dark skinned and bowed with age; that about that year he went away. He died at Council Bluffs, December 1, 1841.

Mr. Hill says that Mr. Fountain omits in his affidavit one item concerning the acquaintance between Ouilmette and Fountain, viz.: a lawsuit, in which Ouilmette prosecuted Fountain and others for trespassing upon the Reservation by cutting timber, which resulted unfavorably to Ouilmette; that there was a large bill of court costs which Fountain's lawyer collected by having the Sheriff levy upon and sell a pair of fine Indian ponies belonging to Ouilmette, which were his special pride, and that it was immediately after this incident that Ouilmette left the Reservation never to return.

(The value of the timber probably accounts for the selection of this land by Ouilmette when the treaty was drawn.)

There are many other interesting reminiscences among old settlers of Evanston regarding Ouilmette. One from William Carney, former Chief of Police of Evanston and for many years a Cook County Deputy Sheriff, who was born in Evanston, is to the effect that Ouilmette often went through Evanston, along the old Ridge trail on which the Carneys lived, on foot and always carrying a bag over his shoulder; that the children were afraid of him, and that Carney's mother, when he was a small boy, used to threaten him with the

punishment for misconduct of giving him to "Old Ouilmette," who would put him in the bag and carry young Carney home to his squaw. Mr. Carney says, "Then I used to be good"; and it is local history that, in later years, my youthful associates used to say something to the same effect about being good after an interview with Mr. Carney himself, when he had grown to manhood and become the first Chief of Police of Evanston, his brother John constituting the remainder of the force. In those days, too, "*Carney* will get you if you don't look out!" was a common parental threat in Evanston.

As already shown, neither Archange Ouilmette nor her children could, under the treaty and patent, sell any of the land without the consent of the President of the United States. Consequently there is much data respecting the family, both in the Recorder's office of this county, in the form of affidavits and in the office of the Interior Department at Washington, especially in the General Land Office and the office of Indian Affairs. To some of these documents I refer:

By a petition dated February 22, 1844, to the President of the United States, signed by seven of the children of Ouilmette (all except Joseph), it appears that Archange Ouilmette, the mother, died at Council Bluffs on November 25, 1840; that six of the children signing the petition then resided at Council Bluffs, and one (probably the former little Josette) at Fort Winnebago, Wisconsin Territory; that in consequence of their living at a remote distance, the land is deteriorating in value "by having much of its timber, which constitutes its chief worth, cut off and stolen by various individuals living near by," which would seem to indicate that people were not so good in those days in Evanston as they have been reputed to be in some later days, if the Chicago newspapers can be believed in this respect. The petition further says:

"The home of your petitioners, with one exception, is at Council Bluffs, with the Pottawatomie tribe of Indians, with whom we are connected by blood, and that your petitioners cannot, with due regard to their feelings and interests, reside away from their tribe on said Reserve"; also that they have been put to expense in employing agents, whose employment has not been beneficial.

The petition then asks leave to sell or lease the land, and the prayer concludes in the following words:

"Or, that your Excellency will cause the Government of the United States to purchase back from us said Reserve of land, and pay us one dollar and twenty-five cents per acre therefor."

"And your petitioners further show that they are now at Chicago on expense, waiting for the termination of this petition, and anxious to return home as soon as possible," and request action "without delay."

As the result of this petition and subsequent ones, Henry W. Clarke was appointed a Special Indian Agent to make sale of the Reservation, or rather that part of it owned by the seven petitioners, so that a fair price could be obtained, and sale was made to real estate speculators during the years 1844 and 1845. In the correspondence between the various departments of the Government with reference to the sale, appear the signatures of John H. Kinzie, John Wentworth (then member of Congress), William Wilkins, Secretary of War, President John Tyler, W. L. Marcy, Secretary of War; also the signatures of Presidents James K. Polk and U. S. Grant.[1]

[1] For copies of these documents see "Historical Collections," Evanston Historical Society.

The south half of the Reservation, including all that is in Evanston (640 acres), sold for $1,000, or a little over $1.50 per acre. The north section was sold in separate parcels for a larger sum. The correspondence tends to show that the seven Ouilmette children carried their money home with them, but as the Special Indian Agent had no compensation from the Government and there were several lawyers engaged in the transaction, the amount that the Indians carried back to Council Bluffs can be better imagined than described.

Joseph Ouilmette in the year 1844 took his share of the Reservation in severalty, deeding the remainder of the Reservation to his brothers and sisters, and they in turn deeding his share to him. The share that he took was in the northeastern part of the Reservation; he secured the best price in making a sale and seemed inclined, not only to separate his property interests from his brothers and sisters, but to be more of a white man than an Indian, as he did not follow the family and the Pottawatomie tribe to the West for several years, but adopted the life of a Wisconsin farmer, removing later to the Pottawatomie Reservation in Kansas.

An affidavit made by Norman Clark, May 25, 1871, states that Joseph Ouilmette was in 1853 a farmer, residing on his farm in Marathon county, Wis., "about 300 miles from Racine," and that the $460 he received for his share of the Reservation "was used in and about the improvement of his farm," upon which he lived for about seven years, and that he was capable of managing his affairs "as ordinary, fullblooded white farmers are"; that from 1850 to 1853 he carried on a farm within two miles of Racine, presumably on the land formerly owned by his father, Antoine.

It appears from various recorded affi-

davits that all of the children of Ouilmette are now dead. Such affidavits must
have been made from hearsay and with a
view of extinguishing upon the face of the
records all possible adverse claims, for I
find by investigation that a daughter of
Ouilmette (Sophia Martell) is still (1905)
living on the Pottawatomie Reservation in
Kansas, at a very advanced age, but with a
good memory that has served a useful
purpose in supplying the writer with a few
of the facts here noted. With this exception, all of the children are dead, but many
of their descendants are still living on this
same Reservation, and several of them are
people of intelligence and education, priz-
ing highly the history of their ancestors.

Mitchell Ouilmette, on May 2, 1832, (as
John Wentworth says) enlisted in the first
"militia of the town of Chicago until all
apprehension of danger from the Indians
may have subsided"—probably referring to
the Black Hawk War. Mr. Wentworth's
authority is a copy of the enlistment roll,
where, in transacting the copy, his name
is stated as "Michael," an evident mistake
in transcribing from the original signature.

While it is true that Captain Heald, of
Fort Dearborn, was notified on August 7 or
9, 1812, of the declaration of war against
England by a message carried by the
Pottawatomie chief Win-a-mac, or Win-
nemeg (the Catfish), from General Hull at
Detroit, warning Captain Heald that the
Post and Island of Mackinac had fallen
into the hands of the British, of the consequent danger to the Chicago garrison, and
the probable necessity of retiring to Fort
Wayne, still it is stated upon good authority that Louis Ouilmette, son of Antoine,
learned the same facts from a band of Indians on the North Shore, who had come
either from Mackinac or from that vicinity, and at once carried the information to

the garrison several days before the arrival
of Win-a-mac. (Authority, data in hands
of C. S. Raddin.)

The only relic of Antoine Ouilmette in
the hands of the Evanston Historical Society is an old chisel, or tapping gouge,
used by him in tapping maple trees in making
maple sugar on the Reservation, at a point
a little west and some two blocks north of the
present Wilmette station of the Northwestern Railway, immediately west of Dr. B. C.
Stolp's residence. This chisel, or gouge,
was secured by Mr. Benjamin F. Hill in
this sugar bush soon after Ouilmette went
away, and there is not the slightest doubt
of its being the former property of Ouilmette; for Mr. Hill, who has been quoted
frequently in this paper, is not only the
John Wentworth of Evanston in the matter of being an early settler (1836), with a
great fund of authentic information, but
he is a man of force and intelligence, of excellent memory, unquestionable integrity,
and always interested in historical subjects, as his many valuable contributions
to the Evanston Historical Society abundantly show.

Convincing evidence of the shortness
of the span between the wigwam, the log
cabin and the modern home, is presented
when we consider that there are many liv-
in Evanstonians who knew the Ouilmette
family, and who saw their North Shore
Reservation in all the primeval beauty of
its ancient forest and towering elms.

Indian Trails of the North Shore.—
"Red Men's Roads" have of late been the
subject of much investigation. Passing
reference, therefore, to some of the Indian
Trails of the North Shore will not be
out of place here. My information is confined largely to Evanston and that immediate vicinity. For over a quarter of a
century the Northwestern Railway has
operated what the North Shore residents

call "The Green Bay Train." A quarter of a century before that the white pioneer went to "Little Fort" or Waukegan on the "Green Bay Road," and before that old settlers say it was the "Green Bay Indian Trail." Along this trail, in the year 1680, fled the wounded Henri de Tonty and his two or three followers, in their historic flight from the blood-thirsty Iroquois, who time and again had also chased their red enemies in terror before them along this same Indian trail, and, in the later days, the white pioneer saw, in the same trail, the tracks of many moccasined feet and of many Indian ponies wending their way to and from the treaty making councils at Fort Dearborn.

Evanston historians have long been at loggerheads as to the location of this Green Bay Road. They all agree that it followed the line of Clark Street north, to a point opposite the north line of Rose Hill Cemetery, and there the trouble begins. Some insist that it went due north, following Clark Street and its Evanston extension—called there Chicago Avenue—to a point a little north of the Evanston lighthouse, there reaching "the Ridge." Others claim that its divergence to 'the Ridge" was at the point of difference. Probably Both are right, each route being used, according to the wetness or dryness of the season. At all events, there is no doubt—for old settlers all agree, from Benjamin F. Hill, who came to Evanston in 1836, to Frances E. Willard, author of "The Classic Town" in 1892—that through Evanston there were at least two well-defined north and south Indian trails, one following "the Ridge" or the high ground that extends from the terminus of Lincoln Avenue at Bowmanville, or Rose Hill, on the south, to the high bluff on the lake front to the north of Evanston, and the other trail was right on the bank of the lake shore. This latter

trail, however, there is reason to believe, was a very ancient trail, leading to the chipping stations or shops already described; and, in the later days, when the settlers began to arrive, and when weapons were purchased of traders—and, therefore, no further use for the primitive article—this latter trail was used only in following the game that also used it. "The Ridge" trail ran to the south, along the high ground, through Rose Hill Cemetery, reaching both the ancient and the modern Indian Village somewhere in that vicinity—probably at or near the western limits of the cemetery or on the North Branch. There is abundant evidence to show that north of Evanston, this trail, which reaches the Lake Shore in the north part of Evanston, led to Milwaukee and even north of that, following generally the present line of Sheridan Road—with a branch around the south end of "The Skokie," reaching the North Branch of the Chicago River at or near its source, and in turn the Desplaines River and the Lake region to the northwest. One authority places the "Little Fort (Waukegan) Trail" six miles west of Evanston, on one of the sand ridges there. As these ridges (of which there are several) lie generally alongside low, marshy places between the ridges, and as these ridges extend north and south, it is no doubt true, considering the Indian population and the important points both north and south, that there were well defined Indian trails on all of them, with branches in varying directions, that would lead to Little Fort; but whatever may have been the name of this western trail, the most direct ones from Chicago to Little Fort were through Evanston.

The existence and location of these Evanston trails is not left in doubt, for there are several living witnesses, both in Chicago and Evanston, who have seen them and have traveled them. The Ridge Trail had been in such constant use that the path was worn more than a foot into the ground from constant travel. Major Mulford, one of Evanston's pioneers, had his home adjoining his trail, immediately west of the present site of Calvary Cemetery, and was frequently visited there by his Chicago friends, among them Fernando Jones. The site of this trail is known as Ridge Boulevard, in Evanston, and upon it live many of Chicago's leading citizens.

Mr. B. F. Hill, in describing the Ridge Trail, says: "On each side of the Ridge and close to it, were two Indian trails, where the Indians traveled north and south. One was about where Ridge Avenue now is, and the other in the neighborhood of Asbury Avenue, or perhaps a little west of that. These trails were so much used that the path was worn more than a foot into the ground from the constant travel, showing that these trails had been used for many years."

Indian Trees of the North Shore.— There are, at various places along the North Shore, and following closely the line of several of the old Indian trails, some curious trees that apparently have been broken, or rather bent and tied down while saplings by Indians to mark these trails; that custom has been followed in other localities, among which, it is said, is the Braddock trail, several localities near Fox Lake, Ill., also in the vicinity of Mackinac, and it is entirely probable here. The trees are invariably large and, if this convenient and plausible theory is correct, some of this work of so marking the trails must have been done a century and more ago, for many of the trees are white oaks of considerable size. These trees, and this theory, present also a most interesting field for inquiry and speculation. Photographs of some of these trees were taken by Mr. A. W. Watriss of Rogers Park, who, as well as Mr. C. S. Raddin of the Evanston Historical Society and Vice-President of the Chicago Academy of Sciences, have taken great interest in this subject. One of these trees is located on the county line, beside the railroad tracks of the Northwestern Railroad at the southwest corner of the Highland Park Cemetery, and can easily be seen from passing trains; and another at Calvary Cemetery, west of the railroad, can also be so seen; and one of them long stood in the dooryard, at Davis Street and Hinman Avenue, of the late Dr. Miner Raymond, of Evanston, father of Messrs. Samuel, James and Fred D. Raymond.

But some six years ago there were eleven of these trees in perfect alignment, leading from the site of the old Indian Village at Highland Park in a northwesterly direction for several miles. Most of them are still standing and can be easily identified; and what is particularly of interest is the fact that all of these trees are white oaks, while another old trail farther to the south, near Wilmette, are without exception white elms, indicating system in the selection. Those in the City of Evanston were oaks, and supposed by the supporters of this theory to lead to the chipping stations or shops on the lake shore. Two or three of these trees were also located on the North Branch of the Chicago River, near the Glen View Golf Club, probably marking the trail to one of the near-by villages. Another circumstance that gives color to this contention is, that where those trees are found was once a dense and heavy forest, where it is probable that an Indian trail would be marked, if marked at all.

There is still another theory to the effect that these trees were bent down when young saplings, and used in the construction of wigwams by covering them with mats—a common method among the Algonquins;

but as these trees generally stand alone, with no near-by duplicates, there seems to be little to warrant this contention.

Another North Shore tree that has become historic on account of the attention of the modern newspaper reporter, is what was known as "the Pottawatomie tree," located about three miles west of Wilmette, on the farm of M. A. Kloepfer, who secures quite a revenue from its exhibition. This was a remarkable tree, but is now dead, having been partially destroyed by fire and cut off some thirty feet from the ground. It was said to be the largest tree in Illinois, a cottonwood, 160 feet high and eighteen feet in diameter, with a hollow trunk that would hold thirty-one people. All sorts of Indian traditions, of the impromptu variety, have been related with reference to its Indian history, most of them being about as reliable as the average historical novel, or the relation of an old settler in his dotage, who sometimes has been found to know many things that were not so. Still, it may be true that such a tree, towering so high above the surrounding forest, may, on account of being such a conspicuous landmark, have been a place of Indian rendezvous.

Indian Camps and Villages.—A picture of an Indian country would be sadly disappointing and deficient without the Indian camps and villages, and, therefore, I direct your attention to the sites of such camps and villages as I have been able to locate in Evanston and vicinity.

The village near Bowmanville, already referred to, was designated by the late Karl Dilg, in an article published in "The Lake View Independent," as "Chicago's Greatest Indian Village," and it is quite certain that there is every reason for giving it that name. The vast number and variety of the weapons, utensils, chippings, bits of pottery and litter of many descriptions not only indicate an unusual population, but extended residence for a very long space of time. Some of these utensils are claimed to be pre-historic and very ancient, and the area covered by them, extending practically over the territory from Rose Hill Cemetery to the North Branch of the Chicago River, with like finds as far north as High Ridge, would indicate a very extensive village. Another populous village is said to have been at Niles Center, one at Forest Glen, or Edgebrook, and still another on the North Branch of the Chicago River, near the Glen View golf-grounds. One of these villages is, in all probability, the one referred to in Marquette's diary as being six leagues (or some 18 miles) to the north. These locations by Mr. Dilg are further corroborated by Mr. Albert F. Scharf, who has made extensive personal examination of the ground, and has shown many of the locations upon a map, which not only seems to have been prepared with great care, but which is, in many instances that I could name, entirely corroborated by other independent investigations. Mr. Dilg locates also another village on the Ridge Trail at Rogers Park, which he says is practically a continuation of this Bowmanville village, "as there are chips everywhere" in this vicinity indicating this fact and such inhabitants to the Evanston City Limits on "the Ridge"; and further claims that these villages are of great antiquity, reaching back to the time of the Mound Builders, and corroborated, he says, by the utensils found, some of copper, and by the further fact that there is no written history concerning any such population as must have lived for a long space of time in this locality.

Whether Mr. Dilg be right or wrong in these conclusions, it is certain that these were populous villages in times of which there is no written history of this vicinity, and these same localities were in later times favorite camping grounds and smaller village sites for the Pottawatomies, as is abundantly shown by the testimony of many early pioneers who saw them here along the North Branch of the Chicago River.

Mr. Budlong, proprietor of the present extensive truck farm, or garden, at Bowmanville, very recently (1904) in excavating a gravel-pit, unexpectedly opened and exposed to view an Indian grave of more than ordinary interest. The grave contained fourteen skeletons buried in a circle, the feet without exception pointing toward the center. Although apparently well preserved when uncovered, they soon crumbled to pieces after being exposed to the air. The site of this grave is about ten rods north of Foster Avenue, and of the center of Section 12; and, when California Avenue is opened, the site of these graves will be in that highway (authority, William A. Peterson, who pointed out the location to the writer.) It is reasonable to suppose that these fourteen mute tenants of Mr. Budlong's gravel-pit were Pottawatomies, who were some of the later residents of the Bowmanville Indian Village.

Two small villages are said to have been located at Rogers Park, on the Indian boundary line, and between Clark Street and the Lake, one of them within the present limits of Evanston (authority, Albert F. Scharf's map). The same authority locates a small village at the foot of Dempster Street, in Evanston, which must have been done by the litter of a temporary village or camp that was there about the year 1840, during the summer season, and occupied by a small roving band of Pottawatomie fishermen, described by an Evanston pioneer, James Carney, who visited them. Still another small village was on the north side of Hill Street, in Wilmette, about 300 feet east of Sheridan Road, on the north boundary of the Evanston golf-grounds, and one also at Gross Point, I am informed.

In 1835, when the Carney family first came to Evanston, there was, at about the southwest corner of Davis Street and Wesley Avenue, in Evanston, a log hut, with roof of straw, that is said to have been constructed by Indians, and that was, in fact, inhabited by them (one or two families), for quite a time while hunting in the vicinity.

Immediately north of Sheridan Road, where it turns to the west, some two or three blocks north of the Evanston lighthouse, fronting the lake shore and on the property belonging to Mr. Charles Deering, was another Indian Village consisting of from fifteen to twenty wigwams. It must have been quite a permanent place of abode, for they had a cornfield there, and the mounds showing where the corn grew in rows could be seen but a few years ago. Mr. James Carney, of Evanston, visited this village when a small boy, and has a vivid recollection of the wigwams built of rushes and mats, the Indians, their squaws, the children, the dogs, and especially of five or six of the Indians who followed him home after one of his visits to secure a certain black pup to which they took a fancy, which Mrs. Carney, his mother, gave them, much to his disappointment, for he, too, was fond of the dog. This was done while James was in hiding in a hay stack back of the house.

In 1852 Dr. Henry M. Bannister and a companion, while hunting on the Lake Shore discovered the site of an Indian village immediately south of what is now Greenleaf Street and east of the present Sheridan Road and lying east of the shop or chipping station before described. The site was well defined, not only by the fire places, but by the litter of many kinds, including broken utensils and pottery. This discovery of Dr. Bannister's has received ample corroboration by other investigations.

Still another village is thus described by Mr. B. F. Hill, of Evanston:

"The Indians had winter quarters at Wilmette and lived in wigwams made of poles and mats of rushes. The village was where the Westerfield place used to be, near the present intersection of Lake Avenue and Sheridan Road. It was their custom to come there late in the fall and stay for the winter." (This village was composed, not only of Indians, but French and half-breeds, the Ouilmettes and some of the Beaubiens are said to have lived with them part of the time).

A part of the same interview with Mr. Hill is also of interest in this connection. I quote from it as follows: "Evanston was quite a hunting ground for the Indians on account of the deer being plenty there. During the early years of my residence here Indians were coming and going all the time, traveling north and south from Chicago, Green Bay and other points, including the winter village at Wilmette, and to and from the lake on hunting expeditions. The last band that I remember of seeing was some time in the early forties; they were camping temporarily on the side of the road and at about what is now the intersection of Lake Avenue and Eighth Street in Wilmette.

"I remember seeing John Kinzie Clark, who had a ranch in Northfield, where he raised ponies, on one occasion, coming along through the Wilmette woods with three or four Indian ponies. He was a great hunter, and, on this occasion, had three or four deer tied onto the backs of the ponies. He was riding one pony and the pony to the rear had his bridle tied to the tail of the pony Clark was riding, and the whole string was thus tied together, Indian file or tandem fashion.

"The Indians I have described were all Pottawatomies. Roaming bands frequently camped near my father's house and would call and trade." ("Our Indian Predecessors," 23.)

The wigwams of all these North Shore camps and villages have, like their builders, disappeared forever from the earth, but it is a pleasing reverie to think of them and of the forests and the ridges and the North Shore, as in those olden days they used to be.

The Indian Mounds and Graves of the North Shore are also most interesting land marks. Indian graves have been found in Evanston in many localities along the lake front, one on the property of Dr. Robert D. Sheppard, by Mr. C. S. Raddin and Dr. William A. Phillips, two by my father, Aldin J. Grover, in the year 1866, in laying the foundation for "Heck Hall," the first building constructed on the Northwestern University campus; two more about a block north of Mr. Charles Deering's residence, on the bank of the lake; another in the excavation for the foundation of James Rood's building on Davis Street, some ten years ago.

The emblematic or totemic mound, in the form of a huge lizard that was under the present site of the Wellington Street Station of the Northwestern Elevated Railroad, may well be classed among the North Shore landmarks, and I was informed its existence has been fully authenticated. Another one used for burial purposes, and now also obliterated, was located near the Saint Paul Railway viaduct, at the intersection of Ridge Boulevard in Evanston. This mound was excavated some fifty years ago by Evanston pioneers, Joel Stebbins, Paul Pratt and James Colvin, who found a collection of "war instruments and skeletons." (Authority, James Carney, of Evanston.)

Another landmark that may well be classed under this heading is across the ravine from the residence and on the premises of the late McGregor Adams, at Highland Park, which is circular in form, and about thirty feet in diameter, with a round elevation in the center, and is said to have been the site of a huge wigwam used as a "council house," with trails leading to it from the west, marked by the trees elsewhere described.

But to return to Evanston: there was an Indian cemetery beside the Green Bay or Ridge Avenue trail, some four or five blocks northwest of the Evanston lighthouse, and extending from the Evanston Hospital north to the lake, terminating about at the property now owned by Mr. P. W. Gates, and extending across the eastern edge of the Evanston golf-grounds. The last burial there is fully described in Frances E. Willard's history of Evanston, "The Classic Town" (page 21). The last burial in this cemetery is well authenticated by old settlers.

"This Indian's coffin was made of poles or saplings, laid up like a log house and bound together at the corners with withes of bark, and the top was also of poles fastened in like manner. With him was buried his gun and tomahawk and his dog. He was buried in a sitting posture, above ground, and facing the east." (See Mr. Hill's account of this in Miss Willard's "Classic Town.")

Some old settlers (then boys) were kept awake many nights by visions of the grinning skeleton, which they saw by peeping through the cracks between the poles, which immediately preceded their flight in terror to their home. The tomahawk buried with this Indian was found on the site of the grave of this identical Indian in 1875, and is now the property of the Evanston Historical Society. The exact site of this burial is on the west side of Ridge Boulevard, a little north of the intersection

of Sheridan Road and thirty to forty feet south of Joseph Nellessen's house, and it may be of interest to Evanston golf enthusiasts, who pursue the game until the shadows of evening fall, to know that Hole or Green No. 9, of the Evanston Golf Club's course, is within less than fifty feet of this former sepulcher. (Authority, B. F. Hill, who saw, when a boy, the grave, procured the tomahawk and presented it to the Evanston Society, and who has described to the writer the exact location as determined by the modern landmarks just mentioned.)

The many burials, so wildly scattered over Evanston, have an important significance in the respect that they indicate more than the ordinary scattering Indian population.

Recollections of Later Settlers.—In later years and, even as late as 1870, single Indians and very small bands or families, came through Evanston, traveling to and from the north and Chicago, following the railroad and the lake. I have personal recollection of such visitors on two or three occasions between 1866 and 1870, when they would camp and spend the night under the oaks at the northeast corner of Sherman Avenue and Lake Street; but these were not the wild prairie Indians of the olden time, and their character may be illustrated by an anecdote. A year or two ago I was visiting the summer home of a Kentucky gentleman on Lake Huron. His family had a colored cook—"Aunt Caroline"—who had never before been in the North. My friend had in his employ, about his grounds, several half-breed Chippewas (Ojibways). The next morning, after "Aunt Caroline's" arrival, one of the children of the family tried to alarm her by saying that the Indians were apt to scalp her, to which she replied: "Law no, honey! them's pet Indians."

Five Great Treaties—Removal of the Pottawatomies.—Five important treaties preceded and were effective in divesting the Pottawatomies of their title to this part of the land of the Illinois. The first was the treaty of Greenville, effected by William H. Harrison, as aid-de-camp to Major-General Anthony Wayne, August 3, 1795, by which the Indians ceded "one piece of land six miles square at the mouth of the Chikago River, emptying into the southwest end of Lake Michigan, where a fort formerly stood."

The second was the treaty of Saint Louis, concluded August 24, 1816, and negotiated by Gov. Ninian Edwards, by which the Indians ceded twenty miles of lake front, directly south of Evanston, and a great adjacent territory lying to the west and south. The northern boundary of this cession (ten miles north of the Chicago River) is what has been known by Ridgeville and Evanston citizens, for some fifty years, as "the Indian Boundary line" and "Indian Boundary Road," above referred to. The southern boundary of the land ceded by this treaty began on the lake shore, ten miles south of the Chicago River. The Indians retained by the provisions of this treaty the right to hunt and fish, within the tract of land ceded, "so long as it may continue to be the property of the United States." The object of the Government in securing this land, was said to be "to construct a military road to facilitate the building of the proposed ship canal." (Blanchard, supra, 419.)

The third of the treaties referred to was the Treaty of Chicago, concluded August 29, 1821, by which the Pottawatomies ceded some 5,000,000 acres of land in Michigan, and thus began the most important cessions of their large domain. It was at Chicago at this time that the Pottawatomie Chief Me-te-a made his eloquent and historical speech, so often quoted by Indian historians. It is of interest to show the feeling of the Pottawatomies in regard to parting with their lands. The following quotations are from Samuel G. Drake's "Book of the Indians":

"You know that we first came to this country a long time ago, and when we sat ourselves down upon it, we met with a great many hardships and difficulties. Our country was then very large; but it has dwindled away to a small spot, and you wish to purchase that. . . . We have brought all the warriors and the young men and women of our tribe that one part may not do what the others object to. . . . Our country was given to us by the Great Spirit, who gave it to us to hunt upon, to make our cornfields upon, to live upon, and to make our beds upon when we die, and He would never forgive us should we bargain it away. When you first spoke to us of lands at St. Mary's we said we had a little and agreed to sell you a piece of it; but we told you we could spare no more. Now you ask us again. You are never satisfied. We have sold you a great tract of land already, but it is not enough. . . . You are gradually taking away our hunting grounds. Your children are driving us before them. We are growing uneasy. What lands you have you can retain forever, but we shall sell no more. You think, perhaps, that I speak in passion, but my heart is good towards you. I speak like one of your own children. I am an Indian, a red-skin, and live by hunting and fishing, but my country is already too small, and I do not know how to bring up my children if I give it all away. . . . We speak to you with a good heart and the feelings of a friend. You are acquainted with this piece of land—the country we live in. Shall we give it up? Take notice it is a small piece of land, and if we give it away what will become of us? . . . If we had more land, you should get more, but our land has been wasting away ever since the white people became our neighbors and we now have hardly enough left to cover the bones of our tribe. You are in the midst of your red children. We all shake hands with you. Behold our warriors, our women and children. Take pity on us and on our words."

The fourth of the treaties in question was that of Prairie du Chien, concluded July 29, 1829, ceding the lake front from Kenilworth to Rogers Park, including Wilmette and Evanston and lands to the west, fully mentioned in references to Ouilmette, his family and Reservation.

The fifth of the treaties mentioned was the final treaty of Chicago, concluded September 26, 1833, by which the Pottawatomies ceded to the United States all that remained of their lands in Illinois and Wisconsin ("supposed to contain," the treaty says, "about five million acres"), and which provided for and resulted in their removal from Illinois and west of the Mississippi.

There is a very numerous class of American writers who have little or no sympathy with the Indian or his supposed rights; they look upon him and the land he has occupied as not only the inevitable, but the just spoil of advancing civilization. It must, however, be a man with a heart of stone that could view, without some feeling of sentiment, this once proud and powerful nation, compelled by circumstance to which they had made no contribution, to desert the land of their fathers and terminate a residence of more than a century and a half, at the demand of more powerful masters.

Chicago in 1833 was an insignificant frontier village; but it was then the scene of a great and historic drama, both picturesque and pathetic. At the time the treaty was concluded an English writer, a gentleman of learning—Charles J. Latrobe—was making a tour of this country, and was in Chicago. In a book dedicated to Washington Irving, entitled "Rambler," printed in London in 1835, he describes the scene from which I quote:

"When within five miles of Chicago we came to the first Indian encampment; five thousand Indians were said to be collected around this little upstart village.

"We found the village on our arrival crowded to excess, and we procured with great difficulty a small apartment, comfortless and noisy from its close proximity to others, but quite as good as we could have hoped for. The Pottawatomies were encamped on all sides—on the wide level prairie beyond the scattered village, beneath the shelter of the low woods on the side of the small river, or to the leeward of the sand hills near the beach of the lake. They consisted of three principal tribes with certain adjuncts from smaller tribes. The main divisions are, the Pottawatomies of the prairie and those of the forest, and these are subdivided into distinct villages under their several chiefs. . . .

"A preliminary council had been held with the chiefs some days before our arrival. The principal commissioner had opened it, as we learned, by stating that, 'as their great father in Washington had heard that they wished to sell their land, he had sent Commissioners to treat with them.' The Indians promptly answered by their organ 'that their great father in Washington must have seen a bad bird which had told him a lie, for that, far from wishing to sell their land, they wished to keep it.' The commissioner, nothing daunted, replied: 'That nevertheless, as they had come together for a council, they must take the matter into consideration.' He then explained to them promptly the wishes and intentions of their great father, and asked their opinion thereon. Thus pressed, they looked at the sky, saw a few wandering clouds, and straightway adjourned sine die, as the weather is not clear enough for so solemn a council.

"However, as the treaty had been opened, provision was supplied to them by regular rations; and the same night they had great rejoicing—danced the war dance, and kept the eyes and ears of all open by running and howling about the village.

"Such was the state of affairs on our arrival. Companies of old warriors might be seen sitting smoking under every bush, arguing, palavering or 'pow-wowing' with great earnestness; but there seemed no possibility of bringing them to another council in a hurry. . . .

"Next in rank to the officers and commissioners, may be noticed certain store-keepers and merchants here; looking either to the influx of new settlers establishing themselves in the neighborhood, or those passing yet further to the westward, for custom and profit; not to forget the chance of extraordinary occasions like the present. Add to these a doctor or two, two or three lawyers, a land agent, and five or six hotel-keepers. These may be considered as stationary, and proprietors of the half a hundred clap-board houses around you.

"Then, for the birds of passage—exclusive of the Pottawatomies, of whom more anon—and emigrants and land speculators as numerous as the sands. You will find horse-dealers and horse-stealers; rogues of every description, white, black, brown, and red; half-breeds, quarter-breeds, and men of no breed at all; dealers in pigs, poultry and potatoes; men pursuing Indian claims, some for tracts of land, others, like our friend Snipe (one of his stage coach companions on the way), for pigs which wolves had eaten, creditors of the tribes or of particular Indians, who know that they have no chance of getting their money, if they do not get it from the government agents—sharpers of every degree; peddlers, grog-sellers, Indian agents and Indian traders of every description, and contractors to supply the Pottawatomies with food. The little village was in an uproar from morning to night, and from night to morning; for, during the hours of darkness, when the housed portion of the population of Chicago strove to obtain repose in the crowded plank edifices of the village, the Indians howled, sang, wept, yelled and whooped in their various encampments.

"I loved to stroll out toward sunset across the river, and gaze upon the level horizon, stretching to the northwest over the surface of the prairie, dotted with innumerable objects far and near. Not far from the river lay many groups of tents constructed of coarse canvas, blankets and mats, and surmounted by poles supporting meat, moccasins and rags. Their vicinity was always enlivened by various painted Indian figures, dressed in the most gaudy attire. The interior of the hovels generally displayed a confined area, perhaps covered with a few half-rotten mats or shavings, upon which men, women, children and baggage were heaped pell-mell.

"Far and wide the grassy prairie teemed with figures; warriors mounted or on foot, squaws and horses; here a race between three or four Indian ponies, each carrying a double rider, whooping and yelling like fiends; there a solitary horseman with a long spear, turbaned like an Arab, scouring along at full speed; groups of hobbled horses, Indian dogs and children, or a grave conclave of gray chiefs seated on the grass in consultation.

"It was amusing to wind silently from group to group—here noting the raised knife, the sudden drunken brawl, quashed by the good-natured and even playful interference of the neighbors; there a party breaking up their encampment, and falling with their little train of loaded ponies and wolfish dogs *into the deep, black narrow trail running to the north.* You peep into a wigwam and see a domestic feud; the chief sitting in dogged silence on the mat, while the women, of which there were commonly two or three in every dwelling, and who appeared every evening more elevated with the fumes of whisky than the males, read him a lecture. From another tent a constant voice of wrangling and weeping would proceed, when suddenly an offended fair one would draw the mat aside, and taking a youth standing without by the hand, lead him apart and sitting down on the grass, set up the most indescriable whine as she told her grief. Then forward comes an Indian, staggering with his chum from a debauch; he is met by his squaw, with her child dangling in a fold of her blanket behind, and the sobbing and weeping which accompanies her whining appeal to him, as she hangs to his hand, would melt your heart, if you did not see that she was quite as tipsy as himself. . . .

"It is a grievous thing that the government is not strong-handed enough to put a stop to the shameful and scandalous sale of whisky to those poor, miserable wretches. But here lie casks of it for sale under the very eyes of the Commissioners, met together for purposes which demand that sobriety should be maintained, were it only that no one should be able to lay at their door an accusation of unfair dealing, and of having taken advantage of the helpless Indian in a bargain, whereby the people of the United States were to be so greatly the gainers. . . .

"Day after day passed. It was in vain that the signal gun from the fort gave notice of an assemblage of chiefs at the council fire. Reasons were always found for its delay. One day an influential chief was not in the way; another, the sky looked cloudy, and the Indian never performs an important business except the sky be clear. At length, on September 21st, the Pottawatomies resolved to meet the Commissioners. We were politely invited to be present.

"The council fire was lighted under a spacious open shed on the green meadow, on the opposite side of the river from that on which the fort stood. It was late in the afternoon when they assembled. There might be twenty or thirty chiefs present, seated at the lower end of the enclosure, while the commissioners, interpreters, etc., were at the upper. The palaver was opened by the principal Commissioner. . . .

"The relative positions of the Commissioners and the whites before the council fire, and that of the red children of the forest and prairie, were to me strikingly impressive. The glorious light of the setting sun streaming in under the low roof of the council house, fell full on the countenances of the former as they faced the west—while the pale light of the east hardly lighted up the dark and painted lineaments of the poor Indians, whose souls evidently clave to their birthright in that quarter. Even though convinced of the necessity of their removal, my heart bled for them in their desolation and decline. Ignorant and degraded as they may have been in their original state, their degradation is now ten-fold, after years of intercourse with the whites; and their speedy disappearance from the earth appears as certain as though it were already sealed and accomplished.

"Your own reflections will lead you to form the conclusion—and it will be a just one—that even if he had the will, the power would be wanting for the Indian to keep his territory, and that the business of arranging the terms of an Indian treaty—whatever it might have been two hundred years ago, while the Indian tribes had not, as now, thrown aside the rude but vigorous intellectual character which distinguished many among them—now lies chiefly between the various traders, agents, creditors and half-breeds of the tribes, on whom custom and necessity have made the degraded chiefs dependent, and the Government agents. When the former have seen matters so far arranged their self-interests and various schemes and claims are likely to be fulfilled and allowed to their hearts' content, the silent acquiescence of the Indian follows of course; and till this is the case, the treaty can never be amicably effected. In fine, before we quitted Chicago on the 25th, three or four days later, the treaty with the Pottawatomies was concluded—the Commissioners putting their hands, and the assembled chief their paws, to the same."

Thus, as so ably described by the English writer, was consummated the transfer by which Illinois ceased to be the land of the Indian. The Indians received as compensation for this vast grant $100,000 "to satisfy sundry individuals in behalf of whom reservations were asked, which the Commissioners refused to grant"; $175,000 to "satisfy the claims made against" the Indians; $100,000 to be paid in goods and provisions; $280,000 to be paid in an annuity of $14,000 each year for twenty years; $150,000 "to be applied to the erection of mills, farm houses, Indian houses, blacksmith shops, agricultural improvements," etc., and $70,000 "for purposes of education and the encouragement of the domestic arts."

One remarkable feature of this treaty is the fact that, by its provisions, some five hundred to one thousand persons, most of them with no Indian blood in their veins, derived personal gain from the transaction; the allowance and payment of individual claims ranging in amount from a few dollars to many thousands, and, as already noted, about one-third of the cash consideration was thus disbursed. Among the individual beneficiaries also appear the following: Alexander Robinson, $10,000 cash and $300 annuity, "in addition to annuities already granted"; Billy Caldwell, $10,000 cash and $400 annuity, "in addition to annuities already granted"; John Kinzie Clark, $400; allowances to Ouilmette and his family, already noted; "John K. Clark's Indian children $400" (John Kinzie Clark —see B. F. Hill's interview supra), and various allowances to the Kinzie family.

The mere reading of the treaty demonstrates that the "birds of pasage," "land speculators," "men pursuing Indian claims," "creditors of the tribe," "sharpers of every degree," and "Indian traders of every description," so graphically described by the English tourist, constituted no small minority of the assembly at Chicago on this occasion, or of those who had to do with framing that part of the treaty that provided for the payment of individual claims.

Three years after the signing of this last treaty and in the years 1835 and 1836, the Pottawatomies—or at least the most of them—then some 5,000 in number, were removed west of the Mississippi, into Missouri, near Fort Leavenworth. They remained there but a year or two on account of the hostility of the frontier settlers, and were again removed to Council Bluffs, and in a few years again to a reservation in Kansas, where three or four hundred of their number still exist, while others are in the Indian Territory. Their history since leaving Illinois has been in the main that of all the Indian tribes—a steady dwindling, until less than what was one-fourth of their numbers in 1836 now remain.

These transactions are all within the memory of many living citizens. A little more than half a century has rolled by since these children of the prairie and of the forest took their farewell look at old Lake Michigan and crossed, for the last time, in their westward journey, the plains and woods and streams of the land of the Illinois. Their fathers entered here with strong and bloody hands; peaceably, yet by still stronger hands, have they gone the way of all their race. They have caused the white man to hear and to speak of the last of the Illinois; and soon—too soon—will the white man also hear of the last of the Pottawatomies.

CHAPTER III.

NORTHWESTERN UNIVERSITY

The Beginning—First Meeting of the Founders—Prime Movers in the Enterprise—Resolutions and Draft of Charter Adopted—The Legislature Acts—First Board of Trustees—Organization Effected—Search for a Site for the New Institution—The Present Location at Evanston Finally Selected—Acquisition of Lands—Valuable Real Estate in Chicago Retained as Part of the Endowment— Election of a President is Decided Upon.

Most American Universities that have attained to a position of strength and wide usefulness have had humble beginnings, and have gathered volume and momentum through a long period of years. They have acquired, too, in that time, a style and a spirit, all their own, which it is difficult to portray in words. It needs the experience and interest of an alumnus to give life to what would be the dreary details of its progress; yet these details are what we call history. They are the footprints of its forward march. What Northwestern University is now, is—to most of us—the thing that makes the story of interest. This will be hinted at in the progress of this narration, and will be told more fully by other writers. The period of the existence of Northwestern University has been under the close observation of men now living. One of its original founders—then a young man, now full of years—still tarries among us, and some of its earliest graduates are still in the vigor of life. Its records are all accessible, unfaded as if written only yesterday. Its growth coincides with that of the town in which it is located and the neighboring city. It is a perilous task to deal with names so familiar as the names of the men who have chiefly wrought out its fortunes, or with events so recent. We can deal more bravely, and perhaps more freely, with men and events of a few centuries gone.

First Meeting of the Founders.—It was on May 31, 1850, that a little company of men gathered by appointment in the dingy law office of Grant Goodrich, on Lake Street, between Clark and Dearborn, in the City of Chicago, over the hardware store of Jabez K. Botsford. That region was then the very heart of the business life of Chicago. These men were convened for the ambitious purpose of establishing a university at what they considered the Center of Influence in the Northwest, under the patronage and government of the Methodist Episcopal Church. Chicago then had three Methodist Churches: Clark Street, the munificent Mother of Chicago Methodism, on the South Side; Canal Street on the West Side; and Indiana Street Chapel on the North Side. The men present were representatives of those churches. The

53

most positive and aggressive among them were Grant Goodrich and John Evans. The latter was most likely the leader, for he was a man who dreamed great dreams, and then set to work to realize them. The roll of the founders who disposed themselves in the law office that day were: Rev. Richard Haney, then pastor of Clark Street Church; Rev. R. K. Blanchard, Pastor of Canal Street Church; Rev. Zadok Hall, Pastor of Indiana Street Church; Grant Goodrich, Andrew J. Brown, John Evans, Orrington Lunt, Jabez K. Botsford and Henry W. Clark; three ministers of the gospel, three attorneys, one physician and two merchants evidenced that the future would not neglect the departments of Theology, Medicine, Law and, possibly, Commerce. These were devoted men, men of zeal, enthusiastic Methodist Christians who had faith in the future and wished their church, in its educational work, to share in the opportunities they believed the future had in store. There was, at that time, no institution of college rank nearer than Galesburg, Illinois, where Knox College was situated. The only other colleges in the State at that time were Illinois College at Jacksonville, Shurtleff at Alton, and McKendree at Lebanon; and inasmuch as Chicago was to be the metropolis of the Northwest and a great center of population, it should also be a seat of learning.

The chair was taken by Grant Goodrich. The work of the meeting had been cut and dried. Brother Goodrich had a little paper in his pocket which he was prepared to read, explaining the purpose of their gathering. He was the Methodist attorney of Chicago. There were other Methodist lawyers in Chicago, but he over-topped them; he was earlier in the field; keen, combative, persistent, devoted to his clients and of stainless honor, a man who wanted his own way and fought for it. There were men in that company who would give Brother Goodrich good battle if he left any weak points exposed, notably Dr. Evans, who had a mind of his own and no hesitancy or lack of skill in expressing it. The scheme of Northwestern University bears the marks of his far-seeing mind, whose plans were uniformly bold and full of faith, and which, with the added element of time, have, in almost every scheme with which he was connected, achieved a splendid result.

Steps Taken for Founding the University.—The purpose of the meeting was briefly explained. Andrew J. Brown was made Secretary, and then the paper was produced—the first formal step in the establishment of the University. That paper read as follows:

"WHEREAS, The interests of sanctified learning require the immediate establishment of a university in the Northwest, under the patronage of the Methodist Episcopal Church:

"*Resolved*, That a committee of five be appointed to prepare a draft of a charter to incorporate a literary university, to be located at Chicago, to be under the control and patronage of the Methodist Episcopal Church, to be submitted to the next General Assembly of the State of Illinois.

"*Resolved*, That said committee memorialize the Rock River, Wisconsin, Michigan and North Indiana Conferences of the Methodist Episcopal Church, to mutually take part in the government and patronage of said university.

"*Resolved*, That a committee of three be appointed to ascertain what amount can be obtained for the erection and endowment of said institution."

These resolutions were spoken to by Rev. Richard Haney, the foremost preacher in Rock River Conference, at that early day pastor of its leading pulpit, a man of commanding presence and persuasive speech, and very loyal to his church and all her agencies, against whom posterity has no charge to make that he did not labor tirelessly or wisely, or plan broadly for the coming years, and a man who was destined

UNIVERSITY HALL

to be associated with Northwestern University, as a Trustee, till his death, and who, during that time, never missed an annual meeting of its Board of Trustees, save one, when sickness interfered.

Then Dr. Evans spoke, with kindling eye and with the fervid speech of a great promoter. He saw the future in the instant. He would associate the cause of education with the inevitable growth of Chicago and the increase of values of property. Let men sacrifice something now, and the coming peoples would pay tribute to their devotion and sagacity, was the burden of his speech.

The resolutions were unanimously adopted. The two committees suggested were appointed: First, On the Charter—John Evans, A. J. Brown, E. G. Meek, A. S. Sherman and Grant Goodrich; Second, On Co-operation of Northwest Conferences —Rev. R. Haney, Rev. R. H. Blanchard and Dr. John Evans. They were requested to report in two weeks from that date, at three o'clock p. m., at the Clark Street parsonage. They meant business, and the committees went immediately about their work. Promptly at three o'clock of the day appointed, the brethren gathered in the parlor of Brother Haney's parsonage on Clark Street, in the rear of the First Church. Dr. Evans reported for his committee the draft of a charter as follows:

Form of Charter Proposed.

Section 1.—Be it enacted by the people of the State of Illinois, represented in the General Assembly: That Richard Haney, Philo Judson, S. P. Keyes and A. E. Phelps, and such persons as shall be appointed by the Rock River Annual Conference of the Methodist Episcopal Church to succeed them in the said office; Henry Summers, Elihu Springer, David Brooks and Elmore Yocum, and such persons as shall be appointed by the Wisconsin Annual Conference of said Church to succeed them; four individuals, if chosen, and such persons as shall be appointed to succeed them by the Michigan Annual Conference of said Church; four individuals, if chosen, and such persons as shall be appointed to succeed them by the North Indiana Annual Conference of said Church; H. W. Reed, I. I. Stewart, D. N. Smith and George M. Teas, and such persons as shall be appointed to succeed them by the Iowa Annual Conference of said Church; four individuals, if chosen, and such persons as shall be appointed to succeed them by the Illinois Annual Conference of said Church; A. S. Sherman, Grant Goodrich, Andrew J. Brown, John Evans, Orrington Lunt, J. K. Botsford, Joseph Kettlestrings, George F. Foster, Eri Reynolds, John M. Arnold, Absalom Funk and E. B. Kingsley, and such persons, citizens of Chicago or its vicinity, as shall be appointed by the Board of Trustees hereby constituted to succeed them; be and they are hereby created and constituted a body politic and corporate, under the name and title of the Trustees of the Northwestern University, and henceforth shall be styled and known by that name, and by name and style to remain and have perpetual succession, with power to sue and to be sued, plead and be impleaded, to acquire, hold and convey property, real, personal or mixed, in all lawful ways; to have and to use a common seal and to alter the same at pleasure; to make and alter, from time to time, such by-laws as they may deem necessary for the government of said institution, its officers and servants, provided such by-laws are not inconsistent with the Constitution and laws of this State and of the United States, and to confer on such persons as may be considered worthy such academical or honorary degrees as are usually conveyed by similar institutions.

Section 2.—The term of office of said Trustees shall be four years, but that of one member of the Board for each Conference enjoying the appointing power by this act, and (the) term of three of the members whose successors are to be appointed by the Board hereby constituted, shall expire annually, the term of each member of the Board herein named to be fixed by lot at the first meeting of said Board, which Board shall, in manner above specified, have perpetual succession, and shall hold the property of said institution solely for the purposes of education, and not as a stock for the individual benefit of themselves or any contributor to the endowment of the same; and no particular religious faith shall be required of those who become students of the institution. Nine members shall constitute a quorum for the transaction of any business of the Board, except the appointment of President or Professor, or the establishment of chairs in said institution, and the enactment of by-laws for its government, for which the presence of a majority of the Board shall be necessary.

Section 3.—Said Annual Conference of the Methodist Episcopal Church, under whose control and patronage said University is placed, shall each also have the right to appoint annually two suitable persons, members of their own body, visitors to said University, who shall attend the examination of students, and be entitled to participate in the deliberations of the Board of Trustees and enjoy all the privileges of members of said Board, except the right to vote.

Section 4.—Said institution shall remain located in or near the City of Chicago, Cook County, and the corporators and their successors shall be competent in law or equity to take to themselves, in their said corporate name, real, personal or mixed estate, by gift, grant, bargain and sale, conveyance, will, devise or bequest of any person or persons whomsoever; and the same estate, whether real, personal or mixed, to grant, bargain, sell, convey, devise, let, place out at interest, or otherwise dispose of the same for the use of said institution in such manner as to them shall seem most beneficial to said institution. Said corporation shall faithfully apply all the funds collected, or the proceeds of the property belonging to the said institution, according to their best judgment, in erecting and completing suitable buildings, supporting necessary officers, instructors and servants, and procuring books, maps, charts, globes and philosophical, chemical and other apparatus necessary to the success of the institution, and do all other acts usually performed by similar institutions that may be deemed necessary or useful to the success of said institution, under the restrictions herein imposed: Provided, nevertheless, that in case any donation, devise or bequest shall be made for particular purposes, accordant with the design of the institution, and the corporation shall accept the same, every such donation, devise or bequest shall be applied in conformity with the express conditions of the donor or devisor; provided, further, that said corporation shall not be allowed to hold more than two thousand acres of land at any one time, unless the said corporation shall have received the same gift, grant or devise; and in such case they shall be required to sell or dispose of the same within ten years from the time they shall acquire such title; and, on failure to do so, such lands, over and above the before-named two thousand acres, shall revert to the original donor, grantor, devisor or their heirs.

Section 5.—The Treasurer of the institution, and all other agents when required, before entering upon the duties of their appointment, shall give bond for the security of the corporation in such penal sums, and with such securities as the corporation shall approve, and all process against the corporation shall be by summons, and the service of the same shall be by leaving an attested copy thereof with the Treasurer, at least sixty days before the return day thereof.

Section 6.—The corporation shall have power to employ and appoint a President or Principal for said institution, and all such professors or teachers and all such servants as shall be necessary, and shall have power to displace any or such of them as the interest of the institution shall require, to fill vacancies which may happen by death, resignation or otherwise, among said officers and servants, and to prescribe and direct the course of studies to be pursued in said institution.

Section 7.—The corporation shall have power to establish departments for the study of any and all the learned and liberal professions in the same, to confer the degree of doctor in the learned arts and sciences and belles-lettres, and to confer such other academical degrees as are usually conferred by the most learned institutions.

Section 8.—Said institution shall have the power to institute a board of competent persons, always including the faculty, who shall examine such individuals as shall apply, and if such applicants are found to possess such knowledge pursued in said institution as, in the judgment of said Board, renders them worthy, they may be considered graduates in course, and shall be entitled to diplomas accordingly on paying such fee as the corporation shall affix, which fee, however, shall in no case exceed the tuition bills of the full course of studies in said institution. Said Examination Board may not exceed the number of ten, three of whom may transact business, provided one be of the faculty.

Section 9.—Should the corporation at any time act contrary to the provisions of this charter, or fail to comply with the same, upon complaint being made to the Circuit Court of Cook County, a scire facias shall issue, and the Circuit Attorney shall prosecute, on behalf of the people of this State, for the forfeiture of this charter.

This act shall be a public act, and shall be construed liberally in all courts, for the purpose herein expressed.

The draft of the charter was approved as read, and it was agreed that the Legislature, at its ensuing session, should be asked to enact it into law. A memorial was framed at the same meeting to the different conferences in the region of the Northwest, asking their participation. Minnesota, Nebraska and the Dakotas were then unknown quantities in their conception of the Northwest, and were not included in the memorial.

Organization is Effected.—The charter became a law at the ensuing session of the Legislature, the act being signed by Sidney Breese, Speaker of the House, and Lieutenant-Governor William McMurtry, as President of the Senate, and received the approval of Gov. A. C. French, January 28, 1851. On the 14th of June, next ensuing, the first meeting of the corporation was held for purposes of organization, and their first formal action was the election of Dr. N. S. Davis as Trustee, to succeed Eri Reynolds, one of the charter members, who had died. They accepted the act of the Legislature, divided the members into classes by lot, and adopted a plan of operations for the establishment of the College of Liberal Arts, with a President who should be Professor of Moral and Intellectual Philosophy, a Professor of Mathematics, one of Natural Sciences, and another of Modern Languages. A Preparatory School was likewise contemplated in the City of Chicago, where there was not, at that time, even a high school, and steps were taken to raise money for these purposes. Beginning at the bottom, their thought was, first, to set the Preparatory School in operation. For this purpose twenty-five thousand dollars was needed. It was firmly resolved, "that no debts should be contracted or money expended, without the means be first provided," and Congress was to be memorialized for a grant of lands to the Northwest-

ern University. Nothing ever resulted from this memorial, but the Trustees were not idle in other directions. They organized by the election of Dr. John Evans, the master spirit among them, as President; A. S. Sherman as Vice-President; Andrew J. Brown as Secretary; and Jabez K. Botsford as Treasurer. These, with Grant Goodrich, George F. Foster and Dr. N. S. Davis, constituted the Executive Committee of the Board.

Seeking a Site.—The Committee on Site for the Preparatory School reported August 4, 1852, recommending the purchase of the property of the First Universalist Society in Chicago, which had a frontage of eighty feet on Washington Street, about the middle of the block east of the Clark Street Methodist Episcopal Church, at a cost of four thousand dollars, one-half cash and the balance in three years, at six per cent interest. On August 28th they raised their bid on this property to forty-eight hundred dollars, and started a subscription for the purpose of securing funds. Evidently there was a hitch in the negotiations, for the Board appointed Dr. Evans and Orrington Lunt to view other lots for the same purpose. That committee turned aside from the Universalist Church property, and recommended the purchase of a lot about two hundred feet square at the corner of LaSalle and Jackson Streets, from P. F. W. Peck. This situation was thought to be a little remote, but, the lot being larger, it was deemed more desirable for the proposed Preparatory School, and the purchase was consummated—a thousand dollars being paid down, contributed by a few of the brethren. The title was taken in the name of John Evans, to be later transferred to the Trustees of Northwestern University. The consideration was eight thousand dollars.

Erection of Building Authorized.—On September 22, 1852, the erection of a building upon this property was authorized, to accommodate three hundred students, and, on the same date a committee was appointed, consisting of S. P. Keyes, N. S. Davis and Orrington Lunt, to recommend a site for the Collegiate Department. The ambition and scope of these early founders is seen in a series of resolutions adopted at this meeting, appealing to the Methodist people of the Northwest not to multiply higher institutions of learning, but to concentrate their effort upon a single institution, viz., the Northwestern University, and to make it an institution of the highest order of excellence, complete in all its parts; and, further, they resolved to ask from the Legislature power to establish preparatory schools in different sections of the Northwest, and to affiliate preparatory institutions already in existence.

In the following October Rev. Philo Judson was appointed to solicit subscriptions for the new enterprise. He had been pastor of the Clark Street Church, was an accomplished and influential preacher and a man of affairs, with just the make-up to appeal to the constituency of the new institution. His first duty was to obtain funds for the Preparatory School on La-Salle Street.

Site for Collegiate Department Sought. —But the developments with reference to the site of the Collegiate Department were destined to turn the Trustees away from Chicago. The Committee on Site considered a location at Rose Hill, strongly commended by William B. Ogden; a farm near Jefferson was looked upon with favor; then the Lake Shore in the region of Winnetka and Lake Forest. The region contiguous to Chicago on the north, because it was swampy, was usually avoided in going north by taking what was known as the "Old Sand Road." This road veered to the northwest at a point half a mile west of the northern limit of Lincoln Park—at that time an old Chicago Cemetery—and struck the Ridge Road just north of what is now Rose Hill Cemetery, then known as Rose's Ridge. Thus, to the ordinary traveler, the region north of Lincoln Park, adjoining the lake, was a terra incognita. Orrington Lunt had casually visited that region and demanded, before a location was settled upon, that the Lake Shore be explored. He delayed a decision upon the Jefferson property and arranged a tour of inspection of the Lake Shore. Andrew J. Brown recalls it as of the Fourth of July, 1853. Disposed in various vehicles, the Trustees took the Sand Road, stopped for lunch at the Rose's Ridge Tavern, and pursued their way along the Ridge Road to what is the corner of Ridge Avenue and Clark Street; thence following an old cow path easterly, over the slough in the region of Davis Street and Sherman Avenue, they found themselves in a splendid oak forest skirting the Lake Shore, the remains of which will help us to recall that scene of exploration for a university site fifty years ago. To see it was to desire it. Three hundred and eighty acres lay in a single tract, owned by Dr. J. H. Foster. The price asked was twenty-five thousand dollars—far in excess of its value, as values were then estimated. The terms were easy; one thousand dollars down, the balance in ten years at six per cent interest. Releases might be given from time to time on payment of one hundred dollars per acre. The purchase was consummated, and the college site and college town, made up of forest and swamp, was permanently located.

It was decided that it was "inexpedient to erect a Preparatory School in the City of Chicago at the present time"; the chosen site for that building, however, was good enough to keep, and, in the years to come, as the site of the Grand Pacific Hotel, and later, of the Illinois Trust and Savings Bank, would furnish valuable endowment for the fledgling college.

The Trustees decided likewise to elect a President of the institution, whose first duty should be to procure subscriptions and plan for the establishment of an endowment for the University.

CHAPTER IV.

INSTITUTION IN DEVELOPMENT

At the meeting of June 23, 1853, Dr. Clark T. Hinman was unanimously elected the first President of the University. He was thirty-six years of age, a Trustee from Michigan Conference and principal of Albion Seminary. He was a graduate of Wesleyan University, Connecticut, and had been principal of Newbury Seminary, in Vermont. He was a man of zeal and method. He laid hands upon one and another of the Trustees, and took them out among their business acquaintances to give him an opportunity to present his cause. The scheme of raising money, which was adopted, and which Dr. Hinman was especially to present, was by the sale of scholarships. Perpetual scholarships were issued, which were to entitle to tuition the purchaser, his son or grandson and other descendants by will, and were sold for one hundred dollars; transferable scholarships were sold for one hundred dollars, entitling the holder to five hundred dollars in tuition; and scholarships were sold for fifty dollars, entitling the holder to two hundred dollars in tuition. A bond was issued on the first payment, and the scholarship was to be issued on the completion of payments within an allotted time. One-half of the funds from these sales was to be used for purposes of instruction, and the other half for the purchase of lands, not to exceed twelve hundred acres, as a site for the University and for the erection of buildings. The Trustees evidently thought that some tangible equivalent must be tendered for money spent for education in that early day. Scholarships certainly proved marketable; and, if the same zeal had been exercised in the careful collection of the amounts pledged for them as was shown in their sale, the growth of the institution would have been more rapid; for Dr. Hinman disposed of them with great success among all sorts and conditions of men—on Water Street, among commission men and grain dealers; on Canal Street, to the lumber men; in town, to the merchants; and in the country, to the farmers. In the short period of his service he sold scholarships to the amount of $64,600, while others, under the stimulus of his activity, sold $37,000 worth. He was dreaming, meanwhile, of the institution whose financial foundations he sought to lay, but death overtook him ere his dream had been realized. He died in 1854, one year before the formal opening of the institution in which he hoped to teach as Professor of Moral and Intellectual Philosophy.

Town Platted and Named—Public Parks. —In the meantime, the land purchased by the Trustees from Dr. Foster, and some two hundred and forty-eight acres adjoining it on the west, which had been purchased by Andrew J. Brown and Harvey B. Hurd, was laid out into lots and blocks, and platted and named Evanston, in honor of Dr. John Evans. The University's part was bounded on the west by Sherman Avenue. What lay west of Sherman Avenue was in the Brown and Hurd tract. Many of the avenues and streets bear the names of the favorite friends of the University—as Orrington Avenue, named for Orrington Lunt; Sherman Avenue, for A. S. Sherman; Hinman Avenue, for Dr. Hinman, the first President; Judson Avenue, for Rev. Philo Judson; Davis Street, in honor of Dr. N. S. Davis.

Six public parks were included in the plan to beautify the future Evanston, and the Lake Shore, from Davis Street to University Place, east of Michigan Avenue, was dedicated to the same purpose. The contemplated campus extended from the projection eastward of the south line of Foster Street to the north line of University Place—a beautiful and spacious campus, respected Founders, but hardly enough for a university of so ambitious a title as yours. But Block 1, to Simpson Street—so they thought—might be used as a campus in an emergency, and they still held lands to the north, unplatted, which might be used for the same purpose, but which, in their wildest dreams, they did not fancy would be needed for the campus of the institution they were founding.

Garrett Biblical Institute Founded. —The scheme of a Biblical Institute had been started in Chicago by the same founders, and Eliza Garrett, by her will, had arranged for the endowment of such an institution; but the beginnings of the institution were had in February, 1854. To them the Trustees of the University offered a site at a nominal rent. The offer was accepted and an institution established on the campus that was destined to make splendid history in theological education. Streets were graded in the growing town; transportation was furnished by the Chicago & Milwaukee Railroad—now the Milwaukee division of the Chicago Northwestern—the right of way for which was given by Brown & Hurd. It is notable that this gift was coupled with the agreement that all passenger trains should stop at Evanston—an agreement that it would be difficult for the road to fulfill.

Not content with their three hundred acres of ground, the Billings farm (contiguous to their first purchase) was bought, consisting of twenty-eight acres, for three thousand dollars. They chose to forget, for the time being, one of their earlier resolutions, viz.: "Resolved, That no debts shall be contracted or money expended without the means be first provided." It was a purchase on time, and time, they believed, was on their side. Values of their subdivided property were advancing. They could soon open their school, possibly in 1855. To this end they elected a small corps of professors in June, 1854: Henry S. Noyes, Professor of Mathematics; W. D. Godman, Professor of Greek; and Abel Stevens, Professor of Literature.

When the Treasurer made his report in 1854, the assets of the University, in land, notes and subscriptions, were estimated at $281,915, with liabilities of $32,255.04. The Foster purchase had increased in value from $25,000 to $102,000; the Billings farm from

SOUTH END OF THE CAMPUS

$3,000 to $4,200; and the Peck purchase, from $8,000 to $43,400. Subscriptions to scholarships made up the remainder of the estimated wealth.

Site of the University Described.— It was probably at the annual meeting in June, 1854, that the hopeful feeling and aggressive spirit of the Trustees of the institution were voiced in a report which was of the nature of a proclamation and formulation of their plans, as thus far developed. They offered devout praise to God and their sincere thanks to the founders for the present success and the future prospects of the University. They described the location at Evanston in glowing terms, stating that, "On the shore of Lake Michigan, eleven miles north of the City of Chicago and on the line of the Chicago & Milwaukee Railroad—the site being large, beautiful and healthful, including some four hundred and forty acres of land, sufficiently elevated above the lake and the surrounding country to afford an extensive view of each, extending nearly two miles along the shore and about one-half of it covered with a young and thrifty forest in its natural state, affording the lovers of good taste every facility desirable for the most lovely residence in the country—a town has been laid out and named Evanston. The University buildings will occupy the latitudinal center of the town and the highest point of land, covered with a beautiful grove, and inclining at an angle of some thirty degrees toward the lake shore." They add that, "In respect of the motive in selecting the site of the University and establishing the institution, neither local prejudice nor a spirit of opposition to kindred institutions has had any place in the hearts of its friends, but rather a desire to meet adequately the growing need in the Northwest of a university of the highest grade, adapted to the country, to its increasing prosperity and the advanced state of learning in the present age. Its location makes it central for the entire Northwest: and the magnitude of the enterprise, by developing the educational resources of the country on a large scale, and by stimulating a spirit of noble, generous rivalry, will benefit institutions of every grade. We very frankly, and we hope not ostentatiously, aver our design of making it an institution second to none, and worthy of the country in which it is located and its name, 'The Northwestern University.'"

Teaching Features of the University.— They then proceed to state its distinctive features: Undergraduate courses of instruction; Post-Graduate courses; a Medical Department in the near future; a Law School. But immediate attention was to be given to the College of Literature, Science and the Arts, with a classical course of four years, a scientific course and an elective course of the same duration. The conditions of admission were to be the same as those of other colleges of the country, not excepting Yale or Harvard. The scheme of contemplated professorships numbered fourteen, among which were some not yet realized; as a Professorship of the Fine Arts and Arts of Design, a Professorship of Didactics, of Physical Education and Hygiene. Young men were had in mind for these various chairs, some of whom were to increase their efficiency by devoting a year or more to travel in Europe and to study in the best Eastern Universities, comparing their own modes of instruction and profiting by the society of the ripest scholars of the age. Abel Stevens, William D. Godman and Henry S. Noyes had been selected for Literature, Greek and Mathematics. The merits of these men were set forth in a manner that showed their confidence, as, for instance: "To speak of their qualifications is superfluous"; and then, speaking of

Abel Stevens, they say: "As a rhetorician and finished scholar in English Literature, Abel Stevens stands beside the finest writers of the nation, and as a preacher, and particularly a platform speaker, is unsurpassed in America." The commendation was doubtless merited; but their expressions lead us to say, verily those founders knew how to blow the Northwestern trumpet.

They hoped to fill the remaining chairs, or such as were needed, at the subsequent session. They presented a tabulation of their net assets, showing the estimate of their resources in land and promises at $250,000, to which they proposed to add $150,000 by the sale of scholarships, and $100,000 by donations—the last for the purpose of erecting suitable buildings, including an observatory, and purchasing a library, cabinet, apparatus and other university fixtures. This report, or proclamation, was signed by Grant Goodrich, Chairman of the Committee, attorney and special pleader for the infant University, and bears date July 4, 1854 —the spirit of the day, no doubt, giving color to his rhetoric and a touch of extravagance to the document. But he was in earnest, and so were they all.

When the Board met in June, 1855, Dr. Hinman, was no longer with them. That eager spirit had succumbed to the burden of his labors. He had undertaken to increase the endowment from the sale of scholarships to $250,000, and to secure the needed $100,000 for the erection of buildings. There is every probability that, with his rare faculty for influencing men, he would have accomplished even more than he had undertaken had time permitted. Fitting resolutions were passed, recounting the service which this gifted young man had rendered and the hopes that were entertained of him. Those inadequate resolutions have perished; at least, they are not

of record. His monument is in the institution he helped to found; and, while it lives, his name and his service will not be forgotten. They sought two years later to perpetuate his memory by some monument on the college grounds. It is, perhaps, well that they failed in this, for he partakes, with others, in the monumental character of the entire University enterprise to the devotion and sacrifice of its founders.

At this session of the Board the liberal policy of the institution was signalized by the grant of a large lot for the Evanston public schools, and it was decided that the formal opening of the University should take place on November 1st of the same year. A building was in course of erection, at the southeast corner of Block 20, on Davis Street, near Hinman Avenue, in which to house the infant college. Subscriptions, running through three years had been taken for this purpose. That building is with us still: the "Old College" on the campus, a building about fifty feet in width and forty feet in depth, of three stories in height with an attic and a belfry. It contained six class-rooms, a chapel, a small museum and halls for two literary societies, with three rooms in the attic, where, with a little oat-meal for food, a few aspiring students might board themselves and compensate the University for their rent by ringing the college bell. The chapel furnished the meeting place of the Society of the First Methodist Church until they erected a church edifice of their own. Other meetings, political and social, were also held there.

The liberal spirit of the founders was further evidenced at this meeting by the adoption of the report of the Committee on Professorships, which declared that, "In the election of Professors of Northwestern University, the Board of Trustees will have reference to character and qualifications alone: that is to say, that a professor need not necessarily be a Methodist."

The Anti-Liquor Limit Established.— It was at this meeting that an amendment to their charter, enacted at the last session of the Legislature, was accepted, two sections of which were fraught with tremendous issues for the future institution. Section 11 provided that, "No spirituous, vinous or fermented liquors shall be sold, under license or otherwise, within four miles of the location of said University, except for medicinal, mechanical or sacramental purposes, under a penalty of twenty-five dollars for each offense, to be recovered before any Justice of the Peace in said County of Cook; provided, that so much of this act as relates to the sale of intoxicating drinks within four miles may be repealed by the General Assembly whenever they think proper." This created a prohibition district, ostensibly for the protection of the students against the temptations of the saloon, and incidentally protecting the city that should grow up about the University from the evils of the liquor traffic; and against this prohibition, the arts and persistence of the traffic in ardent spirits were to be continuously exerted. The third section of the amendment organized the University into a Trust Company, presumably for its own benefit, but its language was broader than that. It said, "The said corporation shall have power to take, hold, use and manage, lease and dispose of all such property, as may in any manner come to said corporation, charged with any trust or trusts, in conformity with such trusts and direction, and to execute all such trusts as may be confided to it." Section 4 conceded the public value of such an institution as the Northwestern University, and ordained, "That all property, of whatever kind or description, belonging to or owned by said corporation,

shall be forever free from taxation for any and all purposes. This act shall be public and take effect from and after its passage." It was signed by the Speaker of the House and President of the Senate, and approved by Joel A. Matteson, Governor, February 14, 1855.

On June 15th the chosen corps of teachers was sought to be increased by the addition of Dr. J. V. Z. Blaney, to the prospective faculty, as Professor of Chemistry, of whom similar high praise could be given, as to fitness for the work upon which he was expected to enter, as to his colleagues in the notable pronunciamento of July 4, 1854; but it was discovered that there was not a sufficient number of Trustees present to constitute a quorum for the election of professors, so the election was declared void, but, in 1857, he was duly elected to the chair of Natural Science.

It was now apparent that it would be difficult to hold the entire territory of the Northwest to the policy of a single institution, for the Trustees were requested to permit cancelling of notes taken in Iowa for the sale of scholarships, or to allow the notes and subscriptions to be transferred to the Iowa Wesleyan University. The request was not granted, but it gave evidence of a tendency which was sadly noted to localize interests in the matter of education in portions of the district, which had been chosen as the field for the University.

In July, 1855, a movement was started by Dr. Evans, and strongly advocated by him, seeking to fasten upon the Trustees the policy of withholding its property from sale and reserving it exclusively for purposes of lease. That far-sighted man saw clearly the value of the property for purpose of endowment, but overlooked the practical difficulty of successfully maintaining possession of a large body of land within the limits of a corporation such as

Evanston was destined to be, on such a basis. With their usual sagacity, the Trustees laid his resolution on the table, even though Dr. Evans urged it with his usual vigor and persistence.

University Opened—First Students.— The frame building on Davis Street was completed for occupancy by November, 1855, and circulars had been sent out inviting the Northwestern students to assemble. Professor Noyes was on hand to teach mathematics, and Professor Godman, likewise, to teach the classics. Professor Abel Stevens did not appear; nor was he greatly needed, for there were only ten students in all, and their requirements could be easily met by two instructors. Indeed, though Professor Stevens was announced for the following year, he did not even then appear; and the name of Abel Stevens, the gifted historian of Methodism, is connected with the fortunes of Northwestern only as a "Might have Been." The roll of pupils for that year will always be of interest, as the advance guard of that great company that, in time, should be permanently enrolled as students of the University. There were Thomas E. Annis, Winchester E. Clifford, Samuel L. Eastman, J. Marshall Godman, Horace A. Goodrich, C. F. Staf-

ford, Hart L. Stewart, Albert Lamb and Elhanon Q. Searle. There is one name lacking, but history has often to bewail that there are blanks that cannot easily be filled. These were, somehow, grouped in a Freshman Class—an awkward squad, I warrant, of unequal preparation; but the professors had time to spend on individual cases, so that the awkward squad were drilled into the uniformity of a Freshman Class. A literary society was organized and named in honor of the lamented Dr. Hinman. It inherited his library as a part of its equipment, and was assigned a room for its sessions in the northeast corner of the third story of the college building. Greek, Latin and Mathematics, with declamations on Saturday, formed the program of instruction. Permits must be secured for absence from town, and church services must be religiously attended on Sunday; such was the routine of that first college year. Tuition, when not covered by a scholarship, was forty-five dollars per annum, with other fees amounting to nine dollars. The price of board was from two dollars and a half to three dollars and a half per week, in homes of the early settlers. The college bell tolled out the hours of recitation and devotion, and the beginnings of college life in Evanston were laid.

CHAPTER V.

Trustees Meet in Their Own Building— Dr. R. S. Foster Elected the Second President—The Faculty Enlarged—Absorption of Rush Medical College Projected— Competitors Enter the Field—Professor Jones' "Fem. Sem."—President Foster Visits the University, but Obtains a Year's Leave of Absence—He Joins the Faculty in 1857—The Assets of the Institution Increased to Nearly $316,000— Reinforcement of the Faculty—First Graduated Class in 1859—Dr. Foster Resigns the Presidency and Dr. E. O. Haven Becomes His Successor.

In June of 1856 the Trustees met under their own roof in the little chapel of the University Building. They had made a beginning. Two professors had been at work at salaries of fifteen hundred dollars per annum. An agent had been busy in the sale of lots and scholarships. Their land was assuming the character of a settlement. The frogs were still croaking in the low places, but drainage had been started by "The Drainage Committee," and the frogs were given notice to quit or, at least, to go as far south as Dempster Street.

Dr. Foster Elected Second President.— The Board of Trustees thought they required a President soon, to give direction and leadership and help them in acquiring the resources needful for their work. Two

names were especially canvassed: Those of Randolph S. Foster and E. Otis Haven. both rising men of unusual talent. The election resulted in fifteen votes for Dr. R. S. Foster and nine for Dr. E. O. Haven. The election of Dr. Foster was made unanimous, with but one dissenting vote. He was thirty-six years of age and had already acquired a brilliant reputation as a pulpit orator, and was then serving a prominent church in New York. He was to fill the chair of Intellectual and Moral Philosophy in connection with the Presidency. His salary was to be two thousand dollars a year. A thousand dollars was appropriated for books. The chair of Latin Language and Literature was filled by the election of Daniel Bonbright, a young man of great promise, then a tutor in Yale College. His service was not to begin at once, but he was to be allowed a year's absence in Europe before taking up the work.

Tentative steps were taken at this meeting to carry out the university idea, to which the Trustees tenaciously held, by requesting Rush Medical College, which was now in its infancy, and Garrett Biblical Institute, to unite with them in a University organization for the purpose of conferring degrees; but the doctors and theologians preferred their single blessedness, at least for the present. They were willing to occupy a sisterly relation, but nothing more. There

67

was little use for a seal as yet on diplomas, but one was desirable in the execution of scholarships and real estate instruments of the corporation. For this purpose a design was chosen, consisting of an open book with radiating rays of light encircled by the words, "Northwestern University." This was to give place, later, to a somewhat more ornate design; but it was destined to do duty for many years in the authorization of titles to land and scholarships, and upon the parchments of the early graduates.

The minds of the brethren were deeply stirred over an incident that was brought to their notice at this time. They could not easily understand why Iowa Wesleyan University should spring up within their territory, but the matter was brought very close to them when Rev. W. P. Jones secured a charter for the Northwestern Female College and Male Preparatory School, and flung out his banners within easy hail of the building where they were assembled. He had appropriated their name and function; he was aggressive and purposeful. They appointed a committee, on which was the shrewd attorney, Grant Goodrich, and the saintly Hooper Crews, to dissuade him. But neither the law nor the gospel were effective to divert the professor from his chosen name or purpose. Threats of prosecution from the lawyer and persuasion from the preacher were alike futile. He even had the temerity to appear, later, before the Trustees and request the use of their building until such time as his quarters should be ready for occupancy. It does not require historical or other imagination to picture the promptness with which Professor Jones was shown the door. However, the establishment of what was known as the "Fem. Sem." was not similarly hailed by the students of the college. It was counted a boon, and often, I doubt not, when the assiduous attention of college students by day

and by night made life a burden to the said professor, he was led to wonder if, indeed, he had not committed an error in invading the territory of Northwestern University with his Northwestern Female College. However, it lived on, doing good work until it was merged in the institution whose Trustees it at first defied.

In July, 1856, the President-elect appeared to look over his heritage and exhort the Trustees to larger undertakings. New and appropriate buildings he evidently thought necessary, for the Board immediately resolved to prepare plans for permanent structures. He asked them to excuse him from entering upon his office for the period of one year, so that he might continue for that time in the service of Trinity Methodist Episcopal Church of New York. His request was granted and the funds that otherwise would have been devoted to his salary were appropriated to the enrichment of the library. Evidently Dr. Foster came again in September to the opening of the college year, for the first recorded minutes of the faculty bear date, September 16, 1856. It took place in the study of Professor Noyes. There were present: Randolph S. Foster, President; Henry S. Noyes, Professor of Mathematics; and William D. Godman, Professor of Greek. It was agreed that, in the absence of the President for the ensuing year, the duties of the faculty should be divided as follows: Professor Noyes should assume the administration of discipline and act as Treasurer; Professor Godman should be Secretary and Librarian. One other item of business is recorded: "Resolved, That a Bible class be formed and taught on the Sabbath day, Professor Noyes to teach it." The next meeting took place October 13, 1856, and its record is as follows:

"In Faculty assembled, Resolved, That a student whose credit in recitations falls

POOL ON THE CAMPUS

below the average for the term, shall fall out of his class to the next lower; if a Freshman, his recitations are postponed for the year. W. D. GODMAN, Sec'y."

Thus these two, in faculty assembled, carried on the interior legislation of the infant University during that year, collecting fees, attending to the library, doing all but the janitor work, which was discharged by some embryo statesmen who lived in the attic, at the munificent compensation of two dollars a week.

Dr. Foster appeared on the 5th of June, 1857, and then there were three. They were not so lonesome. They even held two faculty meetings in a month, and the records lengthen to a page and bristle with suggestions to the Trustees as to what should be done to push the fortunes of the little college. There had been twenty-two students in attendance during the year—a gain of over one hundred per cent. Among them I note the familiar names of Henry M. Kidder, W. A. Spencer, A. C. Linn, Homer A. Plympton, James W. Haney and I. McCaskey. There were two classes now. The library had grown to two thousand volumes. The museum had been begun under the enthusiastic labors of Robert Kennicott. They issued a circular in the summer of 1857, promising three classes for the ensuing year, and a fourth, if students with advanced standing should make application; also an academic school, which should be a private enterprise where preparatory branches of study would be taught, students, partially prepared for college, being permitted to spend a part of their time in college, the rest in the academy. They hesitated about the establishment of an academy under university auspices. They had not issued a catalogue as yet. Professor Bonbright was given permission to remain abroad another year, and the working force of the college was to be reinforced by the

arrival of Dr. J. V. Z. Blaney, Professor of Natural Science, and the sum of one thousand dollars was appropriated for the purchase of philosophical and chemical apparatus.

Financial Conditions During 1857.— The sessions of the Trustees for 1857 give out no sign of the embarrassment that was prevailing in the business world. They took careful account of their assets in various schedules, and reported them as $315,845.30 in excess of their liabilities. The jubilant Financial Agent, in his fourth annual report, says: "Seldom, if ever, has it been the good fortune of an institution, unless endowed by very liberal bequests, to present in its infancy such a pecuniary basis as is shown by the exhibit herewith submitted. Four years since this institution was an experiment, and, by many, thought to be a visionary one. The entire capital consisted in whatever of profit or advantage might accrue from the ownership of sixteen lots in Chicago, which were held by Dr. Evans, and upon which a few individuals had made advances of one thousand dollars, with the intention of placing the investment to the account of the University. During that and the ensuing year, subscriptions to the amount of $22,440, payable in four equal annual installments, were obtained. The site of the institution and that part of the now flourishing city of Evanston, constituting the original purchase—about three hundred and eighty acres—was bought of Dr. John H. Foster for $25,000, which sum, less one thousand dollars, was to remain for ten years at six per cent interest. This purchase, and the sixteen lots in Chicago which were subsequently conveyed to the Trustees at the original cost of $8,000 and expenses, together with two parcels of land since purchased and sold at an advance, constitute the principal sources from which the present capital of the University has been derived. To the amount thus obtained add the proceeds of scholarships sold, and you have the assets above indicated."

It is small wonder that Brother Judson was jubilant, and, with the rapid settlement of Evanston and sale of lots, could meet the hard times with a smile. The schedule of expenses shows to some extent the rough work that the University was called upon to do in order to provide for its educational plant. It is largely made up of items, such as surveying and platting, grading, clearing streets, ditching, chopping, fencing, bridging, draining, grubbing, building breakwaters—indeed, the whole vocabulary of the pioneer was taxed to describe their operations. Meantime, while the Trustees were grubbing and chopping their way to the material enrichment of their institution, students and teachers were grubbing and chopping their way, under disadvantages, to the accomplishment of their ideals. One of the reported schedules of this year gives the names of purchasers of homesteads in Evanston—some eighty-five in number, all well known Methodist names—who were to make up the members left of the delightful company of old settlers, whose neighborliness and hospitality, whose simple kindliness and approachability, made Evanston a good place for a homesick boy to happen into. Most of these people purchased in blocks contiguous to University Place, usually a hundred feet front, and at prices ranging from five to ten dollars a foot. The catalogue of 1859 announced that there were twelve hundred inhabitants in Evanston. The desert and the solitary place were being made glad by habitation. The hard times were somewhat reflected in the financial report of the following year, when a gain of only about three thousand dollars was reported; and, though the purchase money on Evanston lands was not due until 1863,

they passed a resolution setting aside fifty thousand dollars in securities, for the payment of that debt and for the erection of buildings, provided no other resources were received for those purposes.

Professor Bonbright was notified to appear in Evanston and take up his work in 1858. More students were expected that year, and arrangements were made to insure for them board with G. W. Reynolds, at $2.50 per week, including washing, light, fuel and room, and he was loaned five hundred dollars to assist in carrying out the difficult project. Surveying and leveling instruments were furnished Professor Noyes in connection with his work, which were to be procured "with the least possible outlay of funds." If the Trustees had known what good use he would make of them, and how much he would save them as a practical surveyor, they would not have been so niggardly in their grant.

The year 1857 passed uneventfully in the little college. The faculty was reinforced by the service of a tutor, S. L. Eastman, whose duty it was to assist in preparatory classes. The library was increased and the foundations of the museum were growing, in the Northwestern class-room, under the skillful hands of Robert Kennicott. Thus, another year rolled round with Dr. Foster as President. There were twenty-nine students in all, and they were on the eve of sending out the first graduating class. On recommendation of the faculty, the degree of Bachelor of Arts was conferred upon Thomas E. Annis, Winchester E. Clifford, Samuel L. Eastman and Elhanon Q. Searles, and the degree of Bachelor of Philosophy upon Henry M. Kidder. These were to be the advance guard of the army of Northwestern graduates. In June of 1859 the members of this class made their graduating orations and departed from the scenes of their scholastic training. These early graduating exercises were events in Evanston, when the men who had developed under the eye of the community took their leave of scenes that had become familiar. The people were interested in them, and thronged the little church to hear their orations. The farewell of the President was touching and personal, for he knew these men, had interested himself in them personally, and regarded their going away as a father regards the departure of his sons from the old home. The coming years might add the dignity of numbers to commencement occasions, but they would lack the sweet flavor of personal acquaintance and the inspiration of departure amid the regrets and tender farewells of a community who would watch the careers of the departing students with solicitude and hope.

The Financial Agent, Rev. Philo Judson, had now resigned and Prof. Henry S. Noyes, in addition to his duties as professor, was appointed Agent of the University. He had previously looked after the financial affairs incidental to college expenses, tuition, etc., and now, in the most painstaking way, he was to carry, for a time, the burden of property management and business detail that was so vital to the institution. Though an excellent scholar and thorough mathematician, he was a man of affairs. He knew men and things as well as books, and was not niggardly of service of any sort that might advance the work that was dear to him.

The Trustees were a little alarmed lest the expenses of the growing college should outstrip the receipts, and their alarm took the form of a resolution instructing the Executive Committee to bring the expenses of the institution within the available income. The budget showed expenses of five thousand dollars a year in excess of the income. It was truly alarming. They raised a subscription to lessen the deficit and arranged to pay teachers in land when other resources failed.

Dr. Haven Succeeds to the Presidency. —By June, 1860, Dr. Foster had resigned the presidency; his library was added to the University library, and he returned to what was, to him, the more attractive work of the pastorate in New York City, leaving behind him memories of his genial and helpful presence and his inspiring eloquence that graced any occasion when he was the orator. Dr. E. O. Haven was elected in his place. His name had been turned down at the previous election; this time the Trustees were turned down, and that all-round, indefatigable, and adaptable professor, Henry S. Noyes, was made Vice-President. Dr. Foster's departure was signalized by a resolution which voiced the deep regret over his going: "Resolved, That the intercourse of Dr. Foster with the Board has been that of the Christian minister and the Christian gentleman, and that his connection with the University has manifested his intelligence and earnest devotion to the cause of education, and that his influence of the members of the University was such as endears his memory to all the friends of the institution, and that the best wishes of the Board attend him to the avocation of the Christian ministry." They were still under the spell of his charming presence and engaging speech when they wrote that. And what opportunities those Trustees and students had in those days, to sit under the preaching of such men as Foster and Simpson and Dempster!—giants whom the moderns have hardly duplicated. But there were serviceable men to come. Professor Noyes, if not showy, was substantial and useful beyond many more brilliant men. In matters of discipline he was kind. Mischievous fellows used to hyphenate his name and called him Professor No-yes. But they found to their sorrow that, when occasion demanded it, in matters of discipline, his Yes was Yea, and his No, Nay—and there was no appeal. He met the in-coming student with a warm greeting that dissipated his homesickness, and his lovely wife supplemented his labors with such graceful kindness as made the new-comer feel that, Evanston was all right as long as these people were in town.

There were thirty students in 1859-60, and the ranks of the graduates were increased by the names of A. C. Linn, W. A. Lord, H. A. Plympton, E. Q. Searles, M. C. Spaulding, B. A. Springer and H. L. Stewart, who received the degree of A. B., and W. H. H. Raleigh who received the degree of Ph. B. The Academy was now duly organized, with a principal of its own. Warren Taplin being first called to that office.

CHAPTER VI.

PERIODS OF DEPRESSION AND GROWTH

Changes of Faculty—Charter Amendments Adopted—Effect of the Civil War on Number of Students—Accessions to the Faculty—University Land Debt is Liquidated—Orrington Lunt Land Donation for Benefit of Library—University Hall Projected—Accession of Students and Teaching Force Following the War Period—New Prizes Serve as a Stimulus to the Students—First Honorary Degrees Conferred—Corporate Name is Changed —Professors' Salaries Increased and Erection of University Hall Prosecuted —A "Gold Brick" Donation—Encouraging Financial Development—Death of Acting President Noyes.

In 1860-61 there had been forty-three students in College and forty-nine in the Academy, the library had been increased to over three thousand volumes, and the curriculum had remained the same, with its emphasis on Latin, Greek and Mathematics. Dr. Godman resigned his chair in Greek in 1860, thereby reducing the teaching force of the college. The presumption is, that the burden of his work fell on the broad shoulders of Professor Noyes, who was already carrying Mathematics and the Acting Presidency, besides acting as Secretary of the Board of Trustees and Financial Agent; and, in view of his responsibilities, six hundred dollars was added to his salary over that of the other professors. It was an efficient and economical arrangement; but how about the not too strong Professor? He is weaving his life into his work without stint.

A formal transfer of assets was now made to J. G. Hamilton, as Trustee, to the extent of $37,949, to meet approaching indebtedness, and, as a result, he was ready to meet Dr. Foster, the mortgagee of the Evanston lands, when he called for payment in 1863. Dr. Bonbright now takes his place as Secretary of the faculty, to keep its records almost continuously till 1873.

In 1861 amendments were added to the charter, regulating the number and work of Trustees appointed by the Annual Conferences, and providing that any chartered institution of learning may become a department of this University, by agreement between the Boards of Trustees of both institutions. They are still coquetting with Rush Medical College and Garrett Biblical Institute, and have serious intentions as to a Law School. They had made some investment in the property of Rock River Seminary at Mt. Morris, Illinois, probably in the neighborhood of five thousand dollars. A creditor had seized upon it and it was liable to be alienated. They were willing to relinquish their claim if it could be saved by local friends, but it passed from under Methodist control, and the first of their ventures in affiliated preparatory schools, as provided for by their charter, was a failure.

The Civil War—Financial Conditions. —The existence of the War of the Rebellion was reflected in college life in 1862, in the resignation by Dr. J. V. Z. Blaney, of the Chair of Natural Science. He was parted with sadly, and the best wishes of the little college followed him in the patriotic service in which he engaged. Many of the students followed him in the service, among them being Plympton, McCaskey, Spencer and Haney, H. A. Pearsons, O. C. Foster, Charles F. Smith and M. C. Springer, and many others whose names are lost to us; and, from time to time, the Recruiting Sergeant, with his fife and drum, found Evanston and its students a fruitful field for recruiting operations, seriously thinning the ranks and causing the faculty to invoke the authority of the distant parents as to whether or not their boys should be permitted to enlist.

In consequence of the depletion of the faculty, Drs. Dempster and Bannister were called to assist in the work of instruction. Clark Street Methodist Episcopal Church offered in 1862 to open its church doors in Chicago for the commencement exercises— a proposition which was declined on the ground of the smallness of the class; so that, on that occasion, the rafters of the Methodist Episcopal Church at Evanston resounded with the eloquence of Robert Bentley, Isaac McCaskey, William T. Rose, David Sterrit and Bennett B. Botsford The number of students, all told, that year, had dwindled to eighty-nine. The Senior class of 1862-63 was reduced by enlistments to two persons, and one of these had no sooner doffed his scholastic gown than he put on the soldier's uniform and marched away to his country's service. Still, there was a gain of preparatory students that

year, and the aggregate number on the college roll was slightly increased.

June 18, 1862, Oliver Marcy was elected to the Chair of Natural Science and Physics, to succeed Dr. Blaney, who was made Professor Emeritus. Professor Marcy had been teaching at Wilbraham, Mass. He was an enthusiast in his work and a most genial and painstaking teacher, who was destined to a long and honorable service in his new relations. Rev. N. H. Axtell, later an honored member of Rock River Conference, was likewise added to the teaching force during the year as Principal of the Academy, assisted by A. C. Linn, a graduate of the class of 1860, as Tutor in Mathematics and Latin—a sturdy, thorough-going teacher who was soon to enter the service of his country and lay down his life in her cause.

The income of the University was now estimated by a judicious committee, consisting of Bishop Simpson, J. G. Hamilton and Prof. H. S. Noyes, at $5,594, and its whole property was valued at $225,000. Evidently there had been a great shrinkage from former valuations, or a strong desire to stimulate donations by putting an exceedingly conservative estimate upon the property. At any rate, the pressure was upon the Trustees to provide better buildings and better boarding accommodations, in order to appeal to new students and to hold those already in attendance. From time to time the matter was earnestly discussed by the Trustees. A building known as the Club House, now located on Orrington Avenue, near Clark Street, capable of accommodating about twenty students, was the result of this agitation—the first experiment of the University in the matter of dormitories. Fifteen thousand dollars worth of scholarship notes was likewise set apart as a building fund, besides ten thousand

THE OLD OAK

dollars from prospective sales of University lands. The rest must wait upon donations.

In November, 1863, James G. Hamilton, the University Treasurer, announced the fulfilment of his trust in the matter of the payment of the University debt, for which $39,000 of assets had been put in his hands. It was a happy consummation. It realized the forethought of the fathers and nerved them to still larger undertakings. A definite plan for locating upon the campus the buildings that were sure to come with the progress of time was now devised; and the services of the eloquent Dr. Tiffany were secured, as Financial Agent, to see if his powers of persuasion could not unlock the pursestrings of numerous patrons to the extent of providing funds for the projected buildings. The cost of the main building was to be one hundred thousand dollars, and some were sanguine enough to believe that, in the space of a few months, that silver-tongued orator could coin his speech into the needed amount. But the task was too difficult; few contributions were secured by the gifted agent, and Rev. S. A. W. Jewett took up the task with little better success.

Accessions to the Teaching Force.— In 1865 the name of Rev. Louis Kistler appears as a temporary appointment to the Chair of Greek and Principal of the Preparatory Department. This appointment was made permanent the following year. He was an animated instructor, full of action, and knew his subject well. His eccentricities were such as to interest his students and give rise to those mischievous pranks that students are wont to play where there is opportunity. He had his favorite pupils: among them a young Scot, fresh from the farm in Lake County, appealed to his partiality by his conscientious devotion to his work and his uniform excellence in his classes—Robert Baird, who was destined to write after his name, "Professor of Greek Language and Literature." Those of us who sat under Prof. Kistler will readily concede to him that, in the class-room, he put a spirit and fire into Homer's heroic lines that we were unable to acquire in the ordinary use of our lexicons.

It was during the year 1865 that Orrington Lunt, upon whose heart rested heavily the educational work of the church, donated a tract of one hundred and fifty-seven acres of land in George Smith's Sub-division, adjoining Wilmette, which was to be applied to library endowment. The conditions of this donation involved a few financial obligations on the part of the University, which were gladly met in view of the prospective value of this library endowment, and, stimulated by the gift, the Trustees set themselves afresh to the task of college buildings. They employed an architect—G. P. Randall, of Chicago—who designed the building that is now known as University Hall. It was a fascinating thing, when drawn on paper as it would be when drawn in stone, dominating the campus and sounding out the hours from its watch-tower to the generations of coming students. But how to build it was the question which still remained unanswered.

In 1865 and 1866 we note the name of George Strobridge as Principal of the Academy. He had returned from the war to the peaceful pursuit of pedagogy, and John Poucher was his assistant.

In 1866 a new name was added to the corps of instructors—that of David H. Wheeler, Professor of History and English Literature—a genial and accomplished scholar and elegant writer, who had seen much of the world and was destined to make a marked impression while he remained in this corner of it.

The items of Trustee business of these years are somewhat dreary reading—made up, as they were, of transactions concerning the property of the University, of repairs and improvements of one sort or another, the discussion of the problem of shore protection, and of various ways and means for the enlargement of property interests and the raising of funds. But all this is of exceeding importance, in order that the professors may be supported in their work and the students kept at their tasks with the increasing facilities that they require. And the work goes on. Evans, Lunt, Botsford, Hamilton, Cook, Noyes and Hoag—as the Executive Committee—did the business that must be done, held things together and hoped for improvement and growth.

The increase of college students was not rapid, but the academy numbers had reached one hundred and five in 1866, with a roll of seven teachers, among them being the new names of John Ellis and Edmund W. Burke—the Judge Burke, that is to be, though, to be honest, we did not then suspect it. The catalogue of that year blossoms out unexpectedly with the announcement of the Lunt Prize in Philology, the Haskin Prize in Mathematics, the Hurd Prize in Physical Science, the Kedzie Prize in Declamation and the Hamilton Prize in Composition and Reading. These prizes gave a marvelous stimulus to things. It all came out of the effort of John A. Copeland to start a prize declamation contest, a few years before, when a petition was presented to the faculty, which was duly discussed and about which there was much hesitation, though the petition was granted that a prize declamation contest be permitted. Tom Strobridge won the first prize and Will Comstock the second. The occasion aroused an interest such as the University had rarely known. The contestants had raised the funds for their prizes, but thereafter, as it appeared, kind friends would furnish them.

One incident of 1866 shows how difficult

it was for the Trustees to anticipate the future requirements of the University. A deed was given to the heirs of John Dempster for what was known as Dempster's Sub-division, which cut the campus in twain in the region of the deep ditch which runs from Sheridan Road to the Lake, north of Cook Street. This was the result of a previous contract, executed at a time when the Trustees might have been forgiven for their lack of foresight. The Garrett Biblical Institute had been located on the campus just south of the property described; and, to imagine that the remainder of the campus would suffice for the needs of the growing institution, was a fallacy that it required but little time to prove. In the same year the Presbyterians were given a site for a church. The Baptists and Congregationalists were similarly treated, and when they had no house of worship, they were welcome to the College Chapel. During the same year the corporate name of the University was changed from "Trustees of the Northwestern University" to "Northwestern University." Other names were suggested, but the Trustees clung tenaciously to the idea with which they started, of a university for the Northwest. The Treasurer's report for that year showed assets to the amount of $419,751.50 and subscriptions to the University Hall amounting to $48,000.

The first honorary degrees given by the University were bestowed in 1866, when George W. Quereau, George M. Steele, and George S. Hare were given the degree of Doctor of Divinity, and, upon Randolph S. Foster and Joseph Cummings were conferred the degree of Doctor of Laws.

Professor Bonbright continued to act as Secretary of the Faculty till 1869, when Professor Marcy relieved him for a number of years. During this period the faculty remained unchanged.

Increase in Salaries and Assets.—
A strong desire was manifested in 1867
to see the erection of University Hall
pushed to completion. Matters were looking much more hopeful. The income from
endowment had been found sufficient to
warrant increasing the salaries of the professors from $1,500 to $2,000 per annum,
and within a year the assets had increased
over $40,000. The building was now under-
taken in a very cautious manner. It was to
be constructed of Athens stone, and, with
the discreetness that always characterized
them, the Trustees proposed to stop and
roof the building over when it reached a
point beyond which their available funds
would not enable them to proceed. H. B.
Hurd proposed in this emergency—and the
proposition carried—that the building be
completed to the roof and enclosed before
halting in the enterprise. Their hearts were
gladdened by the announcement made
by Prof. Louis Kistler, that one William
Walker, of Kankakee, proposed to give the
munificent sum of thirty thousand dollars
for the completion of the building. It was a
cruel disappointment when the discovery
was made that Lord Walker's specialty was
subscribing to various benevolent enterprises. His benefactions, however, were of
the "gold-brick" variety. The Trustees of
Garrett Biblical Institute were treated to a
similar experience at the dedication of Heck
Hall. But there were those who promised
and performed; and in an emergency, a
loan could be safely made, so the University
Hall was assured. The building went on,
giving marvelous stimulus to the work of
the college, as voiced in the last report of
Professor Noyes as Secretary and Financial
Agent, made in June, 1868, in which he
says: "The work of the new college building is progressing with gratifying rapidity.
Its erection has greatly inspired public confidence in the permanent growth of Evan-

ston, and had a marked influence in enhancing the prices of University property.
It can no longer be doubted that the resolution adopted at the last meeting of the
Board, to proceed at once with the building,
was a wise and prudent measure. The
early completion of the edifice will hasten
the day of its more complete and generous
endowment."

He reported the assets of the institution
at $703,706.08, with a net income of nearly
seventeen thousand dollars during 1866.
The Snyder farm had been purchased,
south of Dempster Street, running from
Chicago Avenue to the lake, at a cost of
$26,623.12, and, by June 10th, sales and
leases of that property, were made by Professor Noyes, amounting to $42,445, leav-
ing a profit above the original investment
of $15,821.88, to which should be added, as
a conservative estimate, lots unsold to the
value of $74,470, and all within the space
of two years. Verily, if subscriptions to
the new building were not forthcoming,
they could turn aside to their old procedure
of building up the University on the increase of land values. This transaction
Professor Noyes carried through; surveyed and sub-divided the grounds, mar-
keted the property up to 1868, and it has
since proved one of the choicest of the
University's holdings. His work was nearly
done. His strength, never great, was breaking under the load that he had carried and
he needed rest and change. The Trustees
complimented him for his fidelity as he laid
down his tasks—all but his teaching and
secretaryship of the Board. Miss Willard
has well said of him: "No one ever connected with the institution has placed upon
it a more skillful hand, or at a time when
it was more plastic to his touch. To the
last syllable of recorded time, his name
should be associated with the Northwestern

University, and doubtless it will some day be permanently connected with some building of the growing group upon the College campus." He relinquished his work in 1869 and his secretaryship in 1870, and was tenderly laid to rest, at Rosehill Cemetery, in 1872. Professor D. H. Wheeler succeeded him in the Acting Presidency of the institution. T. C. Hoag, the former Treasurer of the University, now succeeded to the duties of Agent, bringing to the task a large business experience and orderly habits in the conduct of affairs. For more than twenty-five years he was to continue in the discharge of that office or of the treasurership, giving good account of his stewardship.

CHAPTER VII.

A DECADE OF CHANGE

The Chicago Medical College had now become an integral part of Northwestern University, located on the corner of Prairie Avenue and Twenty-sixth Street, Chicago, in close conjunction with Mercy Hospital. The University aided in the erection of its building and felt great pride in the new connection, which was largely brought about through the agency of Dr. N. S. Davis, an early Trustee of the University and deeply interested in the cause of medical education. The income of the University had now been enhanced by returns from the La Salle Street lots, which had been leased to the Grand Pacific Hotel corporation, and the future looked brighter.

In the catalogue of 1868-69 there appears, for the first time, the name of Robert M. Cumnock, Instructor in Elocution, with the modest compensation of three dollars a week. His time as an instructor would command that much an hour a few years later. His services proved so acceptable that he was paid three hundred dollars the following year for such services as he rendered in connection with the College students. He was a rising man and has risen to be one of the fixed stars in the firmament of the University. The name of Robert Baird now appears, too, as Instructor in Greek in the Academy. He, too, was a rising man, on his way to become a fixed star, so to speak, in the University constellation, but died deeply regretted during the year 1905.

Town and Gown Contest—New Buildings.—Most colleges have had their town and gown experiences and, growing up, as the Town of Evanston has done, under the shadow of the University, it would almost seem that experiences of hostility would be avoided; but the student body was constantly discovering that they were regarded as an element that had few rights at the hands of the native-born, and more than once they had rough treatment at the hands of the town boys. Nor is it to be wondered at that the owners of melon patches, to the south and on the ridge, regarded the student community with some suspicion during the period when the juicy melon ripens on its vine. But the Trustees, too, had their troubles in 1869, when the Town vs. Gown spirit was manifested by a visitation of villagers to the Trustees' Board on the subject of taxation. They were respectfully heard and were told that the Trustees had troubles of their own in maintaining an institution that would be a credit to all concerned, even with the subsidy given by the State in the form of exemption from general taxation; and, then, Grant Goodrich took the floor and informed the visitors as to what the University had done for the town, was doing and would continue to do, and what were its rights under its charter, and how the scheme of mutual benefits ought at once and forever to quiet the incipient murmurings on the subject of tax-burdens because of University exemption. He did not fully lay the ghost. It has since walked abroad and, perhaps, will never down, for there never yet was a college town but had its war 'twixt "town and gown."

The lease of part of the campus to Garrett Biblical Institute was put in form, as it now exists, after long and tedious conferences—indeed, after Heck Hall had been erected—and the mutual relations were so adjusted that they might live ever after happily and helpfully, side by side.

University Hall was now well-nigh complete and the formal dedication and occupation was designed for 1870. It was considered desirable that a President should be elected to begin service simultaneously with the occupation of this Hall, and thought turned again to Dr. Erastus O. Haven. He was then President of the University of Michigan—a man whose coming would give new dignity and prominence to the University.

Dr. Haven Assumes the Presidency.— The Trustees fixed his salary—*mirabile dictu!*—at $4,500 per annum, and elected him without a dissenting vote. President Haven was then forty-nine years of age. He had graduated from Wesleyan University in 1842; had been Principal of Amenia Seminary; had been Professor of Latin in Michigan University, and later of English Language, Literature and History; had been editor of "Zion's Herald"; a member of the Massachusetts State Senate, and Overseer of Harvard University; then President of the University of Michigan for six years before accepting the Presidency of Northwestern. He was a clear, earnest and logical speaker, and his long experience and eminent qualifications strongly commended him in his new relations. His first year was signalized by the admission of women to the college classes—almost a new departure among colleges in the United States, but a movement that he had championed and concerning which he had assurances before coming to Evanston. The working union with the Chicago Medical College was consummated in his first year, and there were added to the roll of University instructors the conspicuous names of Davis, Andrews, Johnson, Byford, Isham, Hollister, Roler and Bevan, with N. S. Davis—then in his prime —Dean of the Medical School. The summary of names of University students counted three hundred and thirty-seven, of which two hundred and sixty-two were in Evanston. The curriculum had been greatly enriched. Julius F. Kellogg had entered the College Faculty as Professor of Civil Engineering—a splendid mathematician, an excellent teacher and well beloved.

The north end of the third story of University Hall had been set apart as a library, in which the accumulated treasures of twenty years were installed, and to which

NORTHWESTERN FEMALE COLLEGE

was added the Greenleaf Library of twenty thousand volumes, rich in classics, in philosophy, in art and education, the private library of Dr. John Schulze, Minister of Education in Prussia. The funds for this rich and timely purchase were the gift of Luther L. Greenleaf, one of Evanston's large-hearted and well-disposed citizens, a friend and a Trustee of the University.

The Advent of College Journalism.— College journalism began during the presidency of Dr. Haven, with the issue of "The Tripod"—a serious and well edited publication, whose columns represented the College and the Medical School. A rival entered the field in 1878, and, for three years, made matters interesting, as only rival papers with an inadequate constituency can. These papers were combined in 1881 in the "Northwestern," the present college paper, which has held the field alone, except during a single year, when the "Barbs," who concluded that they were discriminated against in the make-up of the editorial staff, entered the field of college journalism, in which Sidney P. Johnston won his newspaper spurs. The "Evanston Press," too, was an outgrowth of college journalism, bringing out the latent talent of Robert Vandercook and giving direction to the bent of Edwin L. Shuman, afterwards the accomplished literary editor of the "Chicago Tribune," and still later of the "Record-Herald." And what shall we say of the numerous reporters who have reported Evanston news for the Chicago press? Eager for news, they have sometimes created it, and very often magnified some trivial incident into a harmful sensation. Many of them have graduated into journalism, however, and given a good account of themselves. For many years James W. Scott, of the "Chicago Herald," maintained the Herald Scholarship and Mr. H. H. Kohlsaat has continued it. A publication

that has reflected much of the spirit of college life was the "Pandora," issued in 1884 and published by the senior class. In 1885 the name was changed to "Syllabus," and its publication was assumed by the fraternities. In 1893 the publication was undertaken by the junior class and so continues.

"Sketches in Purple" is a most creditable exhibit of literary work done in the classes of Prof. J. S. Clark, first published in 1901, with hope of an annual appearing.

The list of prizes as stimulants to all sorts of intellectual activity had been increased by the addition of prizes for excellence in literary composition, leading up to the Blanchard Prize of one hundred dollars for the best English oration, and sundry prizes for excellence in debate and elocution.

The Catalogue of 1869-70 is the most attractive issue of that periodical thus far published, and it impressed the founders that their hopes of Northwestern were reaching some fruitage. A cut of the new University Hall adorns its pages, giving the impression of amplitude of accommodation in which to do the college work. The joy of teachers and students in the spacious quarters, which contrasted so strongly with the stuffy quarters on Davis Street, amounted almost to intoxication. Then, too, the freedom of the splendid campus, with its oak-tree shade, its outlook on the open lake, were means of intellectual growth and culture that could not be overrated. The museum, that was growing to splendid proportions under the loving care of Professor Marcy, was given spacious quarters in the lofty upper story of the building. The Preparatory School was given the cast-off garment of the College on Davis Street; and it, too, took on new dignity and importance, with its little campus all its own, where Preps. would no longer be over awed by the lordly airs of college men. Amos W. Patten, and Charles W. Pearson and E. P. Shrader, names that will figure more prominently by and by, were added to the teaching force of the Academy. Through Dr. Haven's efforts, the hospitality of the College was extended to the Evanston College for Ladies, and an opening made for the co-operation of the Scandinavians in the work of the College. Prof. H. S. Carhart, fresh from Middletown, was added to the faculty in the Chair of Civil Engineering, while Professor Kellogg assumed the Chair of Mathematics. Professor Carhart likewise took up the duties of Secretary of the Faculty, which Professor Marcy and Professor Bonbright had carried. Few colleges were then better equipped with bright, earnest men, or had a better share of hope and the stimulus of manifest progression.

Another Change of Administration.— The administration of Dr. Haven was all too short. His ambitions were, no doubt, ecclesiastical. The General Conference called him away to the Secretaryship of the Board of Education, and he inclined to the summons. Gentle, loving persuasion was of no avail to divert him from this public call. In October, 1872, Dr. C. H. Fowler was elected President of the University for the second time, he having declined an earlier election. His career, since 1861, when he graduated from Garrett Biblical Institute, had been in the adjacent City of Chicago, where he had acquired the reputation of a pulpit orator of the highest rank. His brilliant parts and large influence promised well for a splendid career at Evanston. He magnified his work and made it honorable and, with the stimulus of youth, he planned for large things in connection with his charge. He planned a School of Technology. A School of Music was established. The Evanston College for Ladies was merged in the Uni-

versity, and a Law School was established in conjunction with the University of Chicago, which was destined to become exclusively the Northwestern University Law School. The catalogue, never larger than eighty pages in any previous issue, now became an imposing document of one hundred and eighty pages, with broadened curriculum, lists of professional schools and affiliated preparatory schools, and an enrollment of eight hundred and sixty-six students, together with a double-page engraving of the campus and its buildings and the adjacent lake—enough to fire the prospective student with an eager desire to be a part of such a school. The succeeding catalogue is less ambitious, composed of one hundred and twelve pages, of lighter paper and smaller type. The President had doubtless heard from the business office as to the cost of printing and the matter of postage; but the roll of students had increased to eight hundred ninety-one.

Organization of Teaching Force.— Frances E. Willard had become associated with the University, as Professor of Esthetics, on the merging of the Evanston College for Ladies in the University. Her students came with her and the roll of the graduates of the Northwestern Female College, to which the Evanston College for Ladies succeeded, was included among the alumni of Northwestern University. That brilliant woman did not tarry long in educational work. She was calculated for leadership rather than for service in the ranks. She chafed under the restraints of a conservative Board of Trustees. Her career was to be world-wide. As the President of the Woman's Christian Temperance Union she found her sphere; she wielded her pen with the most polished grace, and she spoke as one inspired, when her theme involved the welfare of men and women. The College was proud of her, of her genius and of the sacrifice and devotion with which she applied it. Her successor, as Dean of the Woman's College, was Miss Ellen Soule, who became Mrs. Professor Carhart, and gave place, in turn, to Miss Jane M. Bancroft. With the merging of the College for Ladies a new element was introduced in the Board of Government by the election of three lady Trustees, one of whom, for a time, served on the Executive Committee—Mrs. Emily Huntington Miller having the distinction to be the first woman to take her place in the "Seats of the Mighty."

A much needed improvement on the campus was made in 1876 by the building of the Gymnasium by a stock company of students, with a bowling alley in the basement and a large room for exercise above, in size about forty feet by eighty. It was not adequate to the needs of the institu-. tion, but it would do as a step towards better things,—a long step, perhaps, ere the new Gymnasium is to be erected—but the need was so great that students took hold of the enterprise, managing it by a Board of Directors.

New names appear in 1876 as donors of prizes to stimulate various sorts of effort: the Easter Prize displacing the Blanchard, the Gage Prizes, the Mann Prize, the Phillips Prize, and others given by the University.

Prof. Herbert F. Fisk came to the Preparatory School in 1875, with the rank of Professor, and later became Professor of Pedagogics in the College. He had graduated early from Wesleyan University, and since his graduation had taught continuously in academies in the East. He was destined now to find a field of continuous labor, and to make a record as teacher and disciplinarian. The Old College Building had been enlarged and moved to the campus, to serve, for a long series of years, as the scene of his labors where he should preside, a terror to evil-doers and a praise to them that do well. The discipline of that end of the campus was safe while Dr. Fisk was in town.

Financial Situation—New Burdens.— It has already been indicated that President Fowler had started things at a more rapid pace than they had previously been going. Such movements require money. The absorption of the Ladies' College increased the debt and a dangerous deficit was piling up. One large subscription of twenty-five thousand dollars proved to be of the Walker variety and the Trustees were greatly disturbed. Some advocated the rapid sale of property and its use to diminish the debt and to defray the expenses upon which they had entered, rather than take a backward step. The records of 1875 fairly reflect the earnestness of the controversy over the question of the policy to be pursued by the University with reference to unproductive property. In the communications of Governor Evans, of T. C. Hoag, of W. H. Lunt and of Rev. Philo Judson on this subject, almost the last word was spoken on behalf of the respective policies of holding for lease or selling out the residence property of the University, at going prices to actual settlers, and investing the resultant funds. When this discussion again arises—as arise it will from time to time—the minutes of 1875 will prove an armory of weapons to the contestants. Governor Evans wrote as one deeply interested in the institution, as having given to it with generous liberality and having put it under restraint to withhold from sale a certain portion of its property. Philo Judson wrote as one who met the actual situation in his work as Land Agent, and reached a height of eloquence and argument in his plea for generous and unrestricted sales that seems unanswerable. If he or Governor Evans had never written anything else than these two papers, these recorded documents of two of the founders of the institution would reveal to us of a later generation that they were men of keen intellectuality and good fighters.

So far as the policy with reference to the sale of property is concerned, this discussion was without practical result. The limitations which Governor Evans placed upon the sale of property, by conditional grants to the University of sundry pieces of Chicago property, were revoked by a later instrument. Indeed, the limitations agreed to by the Executive Committee in receiving gifts from Governor Evans were not approved by the Board of Trustees, and the whole question of the sale of property, with a view to limitations, was referred to a committee of three, in 1871, the report from whom has never been called up. Rev. Philo Judson's communication on this subject was his last word to the University, and it is indeed a heritage. He died a few months later and a feeling tribute graces the record, describing him as "one of the founders of the institution"; as "the first—and, for many years—Business Manager and Financial Agent, and later Trustee and Executive Officer, who has rendered long and efficient service to the University. To his intellectual force, sagacity, wisdom, integrity, unselfishness and fidelity, the cause of education is lastingly indebted." And much more to the same effect, which was inspired by a genuine appreciation of a man of most sterling and serviceable qualities.

The Board started out upon the year 1876 with a discouraging budget, showing a probable deficit of nearly sixteen thousand dollars; but the end of the year was reached with a somewhat better showing, though, on the whole, not entirely satisfactory. A judicious Committee on Ways and Means was appointed to look matters in the face, and see if some remedy could not be devised

to avoid a crisis. They could only figure out a probable deficit of $23,750 per annum. They reminded their brethren that, in their great desire for rapid development, they had forgotten the old adage, "Make haste slowly," and they recommended a return to the old ways of making no appropriations for salaries or other expenses in advance of current income. This policy, said they, must be adhered to rigidly, in the future, for we cannot afford to mortgage the future usefulness of the institution.

Dr. Fowler having been elected editor of the "Christian Advocate" in New York, in May of that year, resigned his position, to the great regret of the Board, who passed resolutions of warm commendation of his work and his influence. The Chairs of English Literature and Chemistry were likewise vacated and the work distributed. Thus the ship was lightened and proceeded on its voyage with a better prospect of reaching port. Dr. Oliver Marcy was made Acting President—a work which, although not at all to his taste, he took up and administered with the same fidelity and zeal that he gave to his own department, winning respect and confidence at every step and administering government and discipline with an even hand.

A new menace came in 1876 to try the patience of the Trustees who were heroically struggling with the problem of finance, in the listing of their property by the assessors for taxation. The expense of testing the legality of the claim was appalling, and the possibly unfavorable outcome of litigation was even more discouraging. But they stood firmly upon their chartered rights. The contest in the lower court of the State was adverse, as was expected. The decision in the State Supreme Court was similarly adverse, but not unanimous, there being two dissenting Justices. The case then went to Washington, with Grant

Goodrich, Wirt Dexter and Senator M. H. Carpenter as attorneys for the University, and their efforts were crowned with the happy result of a reversal of the decision of the State Courts. The contention of the tax-collector was that, though the property of the University was exempted from taxation by the amendment to the charter in 1855, a subsequent statute of 1872 limited this exemption to land and other property in immediate use by the school. The Supreme Court of the United States construed the charter in harmony with the powers granted to the Legislature under the Constitution of 1848, and, therefore, not limited by the new Constitution of 1870. We cannot say if any bonfires blazed on the campus when the decision was made known. It is quite certain that a new light gleamed from the faces of the surviving founders, and especially from the face of the surviving attorney, Grant Goodrich, who drew the charter amendment that had been controverted and which meant so much to the institution.

Life Saving Station is Established.— During 1876 the Life Saving Station of the United States was established on the campus, manned by students and presided over by Captain Larson, an "old salt" who is the soul of discipline and fidelity, as devout as he is brave, whose influence upon his boys has been the very best. The work of life-saving at the station has been a source of honest joy and pride to the friends of the University. The lease of University grounds for this purpose was for twenty years, and in 1896 was renewed for fifty years, so that it has a future in connection with the institution.

Without serious diminution in numbers, but on a more even keel, the University kept on its course under the wise administration of Dr. Marcy, till 1881. Prof. Kistler had retired and his old-time pupil was made instructor in Greek. Charles W. Pearson, too, had risen to an instructorship in English Literature in place of D. H. Wheeler. New names were appearing in instructorships which will afterwards figure in connection with professorships in the institution. The financial burden that had been much relieved was still oppressing, and the heroic method of reduction of salaries was applied, with the hope that it would not be for long.

George F. Foster, one of the charter members of the Board of Trustees, passed away in 1878 and was memorialized in the records of the Trustees. He was a man of zeal and generous liberality; a shouting Methodist, ardent in his temperament, earnest and persistent in the discharge of what he believed to be his duty. He was a warm and devoted friend, an open and honorable opponent. William Wheeler, too, had gone, and the ranks of the early Trustees were sadly thinning.

CHAPTER VIII.

AN ERA OF PROGRESS

Dr. Marcy was becoming weary of tasks that took him from his class-room and his beloved museum, and, in June, 1881, Joseph Cummings, the Nestor of educators in the Methodist Episcopal Church, long-time President of Wesleyan University, an old man but full of vigor, was chosen for the Presidency. He was coming to his own; for, had not the Northwestern, for years, paid tribute to Middletown in the filling of its chairs? There were Marcy, and Fisk, and Carhart, and Cumnock, and Morse, and there were others coming. Surely, the grand old man might take up his work with no sense of novelty in his new situation. He

was a man of noble parts, full of dignity but full of gentleness, as devoted to his work as is the sun to shining. He was an ideal College President of the old school; great in the recitation room, great as a disciplinarian, strong in administration, a financier, an economist, a mighty man in the pulpit or on the rostrum, able to do great things and small, considerate of his colleagues, no tyrant, but a believer in faculty government and, without coercion of their opinion, willing to abide by it. What a mighty man he seemed on commencement days, in his square Doctor's cap and silk gown, bidding candidates "ascendat," and conferring degrees in Latin without a slip, a task over which his successors stumbled. Before his work was done, two hundred thousand dollars of indebtedness from former years had been cleared off. Governor Evans helped nobly; William Deering bore the lion's share; and one and another lifted, under the persuasive power of Dr. Cummings or Dr. Hatfield, till the work of liquidation of indebtedness was wrought, and then, relieved of burden, the college work went on more hopefully. New professors were secured, development took place in the line of true, logical growth under the hand of a master. His annual reports were and are still the strongest and most helpful papers ever submitted to the Board of Trustees, full of stimulus and suggestions. The

Fayerweather Hall of Science was secured, the gift, for a long time, of an unknown donor into whose ear Dr. Hatfield, at a timely moment, had dropped a word concerning Northwestern, and it resulted in this anonymous gift—and would result in more when his will should be opened—that helped mightily in the development of the work in Chemistry and Physics. Professor Carhart was tempted away to Michigan University just as he was about to enter into his heritage of the new building, to carry on the brilliant career of a physicist, which he had so well begun at Northwestern.

Organization of New Departments.— Then, too, on the north campus arose the graceful pile of Dearborn Observatory, the gift of James B. Hobbs, equipped with the splendid instruments that were formerly in the old Dearborn Observatory at the rear of Chicago University. The gift was made without ostentation, after the manner of the princely giver that he is, and there was installed Prof. George W. Hough as astronomer, to keep up his vigil over Jupiter, with whom he is so well acquainted, and to increase the list of double stars whose hidings he has such facility in finding out.

Then, as a result of Dr. Hatfield's efforts, a dormitory was erected on Cook Street to house thirty young men, the second experiment of the University in that direction.

The death of Robert F. Queal was chronicled in 1883, one of the later most valuable Trustees of the institution, a man of grace and tact, and loyal to the core. In 1886 James S. Kirk, a stalwart, useful member of the Board was taken away; and, in 1887, Philip R. Shumway, who had given great promise of valuable aid in the counsels of the Executive Committee.

In 1884 the Illinois School of Pharmacy became the property of the University, thereafter to be known as the Northwestern School of Pharmacy—this through the labors of Dr. D. R. Dyche, one of the most self-forgetful, public-spirited Trustees that ever helped to carry the burdens of the institution. The School of Dentistry was likewise taken on, to become one of the most flourishing departments by and by.

The celebration of University Day was begun February 22, 1886, by the assembling of all departments in Evanston, who marched through the streets to the strains of martial music, and were addressed by representatives of the University culminating in a collation and a reception at Willard Hall. This happy custom was continued into the administration of President Rogers, and fell at last into innocuous desuetude.

The Passing away of Dr. Cummings. —For almost ten years, in the ripeness of his wisdom and powers, without dimness of vision or abatement of natural vigor, Dr. Cummings kept on his way as President of the University, with a broadening curriculum and increasing number of students, large graduating classes and a splendid faculty that were harmonious and enthusiastic and united in honoring their chief and following his leadership. Though disease was preying upon him, he gave out no sign of weakness. He called the regular meeting of the faculty to assemble in his room when the hand of death was upon him, and passed away as a soldier in battle, with his armor on. His name and character is a heritage to those of us who knew him well, stimulating to duty. Not less useful, on the social side of college life, in that eminently successful administration, was the influence of the queenly woman who presided in the home of the President. She was a woman of striking presence, of tact and sprightliness, with a keen eye to take in difficult situations and a skillful hand to relieve all embarrassments. These two were a marvelous combination in a college community. I do not wonder that Middletown students are ready to bow down at the mention of their names. Northwestern students, between 1880 and 1890, are ready to do likewise. Dr. Cummings' last appearance in chapel was a scene long to be remembered. He would not be relieved of his accustomed task of leading the devotions, though his breath came quick and his utterance was choked. He read the hymn,

"My Jesus, as thou wilt,
Tho' seen through many a tear,
Let not my star of hope
Grow dim or disappear."

A solemn stillness pervaded the little chapel. The broken voice that led the devotions was speaking for the last time among us, and it spoke out in prayer and Scripture and hymn, as if conscious that it was a farewell, the keynote of a life attuned to duty, "My Lord, thy will be done." Cheerful and serene, though feeble from acute disease, he left the chapel that day amid faces sad with fear and eager with sympathy, and went home to die as bravely as he went to work. We carried him to his final rest a few days later, and enshrined him in our hearts as one of the few great men that we had known. He was not a writer of dreary pamphlets or a seeker after notoriety. He felt called of God to do the work of a Christian educator by character, example, precept and wise and prayerful administration, and he did it well, and thereon rests his abiding fame.

Then Dr. Marcy was called once more to take up the task of administration till some new man could be found, with youth and strength and scope of vision, fit to take up the work that had developed somewhat after the hope of the founders.

A new appraisal had taken place of the property on La Salle Street that had been clung to tenaciously during the vicissitudes of forty years, which resulted in an increase of income of more than fifty thousand dollars per annum. It meant the accomplishment of much that had been dreamed of, and the long hoped for development.

Dr. Rogers Called to the Presidency. —In September, 1890, Dr. Henry Wade Rogers was called to the Presidency of the institution. He had been Dean of the Law School of the University of Michigan, and entered most auspiciously upon his work at the most fortunate moment in the career of the University.

In June, 1892, T. C. Hoag, having declined to serve longer as Treasurer and Business Agent, retired from the arduous duties of his office with an enviable record for fidelity and skill in the conduct of the affairs of the University, and Prof. R. D. Sheppard was invited to assume the business cares of the institution, in addition to his college work. The work of the decade was to be one of development on the material side, far in excess of any similar period in the history of the University, as the annual reports of receipts and expenditures will show. The spacious buildings on Dearborn Street, near Twenty-fourth, were erected for the proper housing of the Medical School and School of Pharmacy, on land that had been purchased largely by the gift for that purpose of William Deering, and an adjacent lot had been purchased for the prospective occupancy of Wesley Hospital. The Woman's Medical College on Lincoln Street, Chicago, was purchased at a cost of twenty-five thousand dollars, and it became an integral part of the University, with a goodly list of alumnæ and an eminent faculty.

In 1892 the American College of Dental Surgery was combined with the Northwestern Dental School, with a student attendance of over five hundred and an equipment unsurpassed, over which presided Theodore Menges, a phenomenon of energy and tact in the organization and management of such an institution, whose untimely death, a few years since, left that school sadly orphaned but still vigorous and a monument to his energy and devotion.

The Law School was reorganized and made one of the best of its kind, with better quarters and with an enriched curriculum.

Orrington Lunt Library Dedicated.— On the campus the new Orrington Lunt Library was erected and named in honor of its principal benefactor, the genial, saintly Orrington Lunt, who walked among us in the evening of his days as the spirit of peace and benediction. Justin Winsor came on the dedication and spoke a splendid message, but the charming address of the founder of the library who, for so long had believed in books as a prime requisite of a student community, and who had manifested his faith by his works, was the great event of that dedicatory occasion.

Then, too, the School of Music was housed in its own quarters, with a hall for recitals and rooms for instruction and practice, presided over by Prof. P. C. Lutkin, whose skill and devotion have made it one of the important features of the University work.

Then, too, in this favored time arose the Annie May Swift Hall, devoted to elocution and oratory, the gift chiefly of Gustavus F. Swift, in honor of his daughter, who died during her career in college. It was the graceful tribute of the bereaved parent to a beautiful girl. Others contributed to this building at the solicitation of Professor Cumnock, but Mr. Swift's gift made it possible, and there its enthusiastic Director has made a school unique in its character and unsurpassed anywhere.

At last the Fayerweather bequest of one hundred thousand dollars came to hand, the result of Dr. Hatfield's timely suggestion to the generous leather merchant whose benefactions to American colleges have been one of the phenomenal things in the history of those institutions.

Then Fisk Hall was constructed—the dream of Dr. Fisk for twenty years— crowning the labors of his devoted life. William Deering built it with a capacity to care for six or seven hundred students, with a chapel that is the best auditorium on the campus, and with all the appointments and equipment of an academy of the first rank.

Woman's Hall was enlarged by the same generous giver, so that its capacity was almost doubled.

Then the campus was fenced and the gateways were built, giving an air of individuality and dignity to the college enclosure. William Deering did that; and one quiet afternoon, on his way to town, he left at the business office a package of papers that the dazed Business Manager found, on inspection, to consist of over two hundred thousand dollars worth of securities; and, a little later, when Wesley Hospital was needed, not only for the charity work of the Methodist Episcopal Church, but also an adjunct to the work of the Medical School, he dazed the same easily dazable Business Manager by the offer of fifty thousand dollars for that purpose, and property worth one hundred thousand dollars for the future endowment. Yet this was not all; for, when Onarga Seminary was to be saved from loss and made an affiliated academy of Northwestern University, Mr. Deering gave five thousand dollars to help that enterprise to a consummation; and, again, when the Tremont House was under consideration, his gift of twenty-five thousand dollars helped to acquire that splendid property. The chapter of his gracious deeds on behalf of the University might be prolonged, but the historian is not permitted to dwell over-much on the deeds of living men. Of the records and events of the last ten years—its men and its transactions—he feels compelled to speak with cautious reserve. But these have been years of progress.

Early in Dr. Rogers' administration, on the suggestion of David Swing, the annual commencement exercises were taken to Chicago and held in the Auditorium, where an oration was delivered by some orator of note before a magnificent assembly. Men like Theodore Roosevelt, Ex-Governor Chamberlain, Bishops Warren and Galloway, Drs. Northrup, Canfield, Day and Buckley have been numbered among the orators, and thousands of Northwestern graduates have ascended the stage and received their diplomas at the hands of the President of the University. Formerly all honorary degrees had been given on the recommendation of the Faculty of the College of Liberal Arts, and now that service was rendered by a University Council, consisting of representatives of the different departments, who, in addition to this function, might recommend to the Trustees action upon such matters as were of general University interest.

On the La Salle Street property of the University was erected a building, unrivaled among the bank buildings of the world, for the use of one of the strongest institutions in the West, and leased for one hundred years at a rental that will be one of the principal supports of the University in beneficent work during that long period. It has improved the property on Kinzie Street, Chicago, donated by William Deering, and leased it for fifty years to a strong corporation at a very satisfactory rental. It has acquired the Tremont House at a cost of five hundred thousand dollars, as the future home of the Law School, the Dental School and the School of Pharmacy, devoting to these schools a space as great as that comprised by any three of the buildings on the college campus, and has still reserved the old parlor floor of the Tremont House for general University purposes, offices, parlors, alumni headquarters, and a small assembly hall, while still retaining the first floor as a source of revenue.

CHAPTER IX.

SOME SIDE ISSUES

Athletics and College Societies—Women's Educational Associations—"The Settlement" and the University Guild—Dr. Rogers Resigns the Presidency in 1899, and is Succeeded by Dr. Bonbright as Acting President—A Long List of Notable Friends of the University Who Have Passed Away—Tribute to Their Memory—Dr. E. J. James' Two Years' Administration—He is succeeded by Dr. Abram W. Harris.

And what shall we say of College Athletics that have flourished during these ten years, in spite of the fact that the expected donor of a great gymnasium has not come to view? The old "Gym." has done a noble work, but it is confessedly a back number. Still, the students have made good use of it and the Athletic Field on the north campus has been the scene of vigorous sport and rare athletic performances. It is largely within the last ten years that athletic sports have formed a prominent feature in the life of Western colleges, and during that period, Northwestern has often ranked with the best, and, even when defeated, has been undiscouraged; and, in the trials of forensic and dialectic skill with the great institutions of the West, she has proved herself a foeman not to be despised.

Y. M. and Y. W. C. A.—Other Societies. —In the religious work of the college, its general conduct in these later years has been in the hands of the Young Men's and the Young Woman's Christian Associations. The responsibility has been largely on the students, with the sympathetic aid of members of the faculty. A house has been occupied by the young men as an Association headquarters; secretaries have been employed, with University aid, by both Associations; and the evangelistic spirit with marked results has attended both these associations.

Greek Letter Societies have taken deep root in the University and detracted somewhat from the vigor of the old debating societies that were of such educational value in the early history of the University. "Phi Kappa Psi" was founded in 1864, and the "Alpha Phi" in 1881. Now there are numerous other organizations, with their cliques and politics, and other redeeming features of good fellowship, that are among the pleasant recollections of college life.

For a few years, beginning in 1893, the "University Record" was published, with a compendium of information of interest to the alumni and the public. Professor Caldwell and Professor Gray were editors, and performed their task well. The last issue was of June, 1895. The scheme will bear resurrection when some fit man with adequate support can give it attention.

Collateral with the work of the University, and springing out of it, has been the work of the Woman's Educational Aid Association, of which, for many years, Mrs. J. A. Pearsons has been President, and with whom have been associated such elect ladies as Mrs. Cummings, Mrs. Morse, Mrs. Gage, Mrs. Townsend, Mrs. Clifford and others, in an effort to furnish a home for young women during their college life, where they can board cheaply, assisting in the work, and yet be provided with the comforts and elegances that are so desirable from an educational point of view. With the aid of Dr. Pearsons they have sustained the College Cottage for many years, which has been once enlarged; and now, by the timely gift of thirty thousand dollars from the same philanthropic source, they have under their charge the new Chapin Hall, which was dedicated in the fall of 1901 by its generous donor, and where sixty young women are housed as a happy family in elegance and comfort.

Another collateral institution has been that of "The Settlement," started and presided over during her presence in Evanston by Mrs. Henry Wade Rogers, to minister, as such institutions do, to the life of the neglected poor in the Northwestern section of Chicago. There University graduates are in residence and University students help to carry on the various forms of life and service peculiar to the settlement. To carry on this work and erect their commodious building, Mr. Milton Wilson gave the munificent sum of twenty-five thousand dollars, and the finished structure—with its perfect appointments, the property of Northwestern University—stands as a monument of his interest in the welfare of his fellowmen.

Another collateral institution founded by Mrs. Rogers was the University Guild, an association of women whose pursuit has been culture, and who, in a few years, have

gathered together a beautiful collection of art treasures which are deposited in Lunt Library. These are now the property of the University, and may serve as the nucleus of an Art Museum, when these treasures, and those which Dr. Marcy gathered during his long career, are fitly housed.

Resignation of President Rogers.— In 1899 Dr. Rogers resigned the Presidency of the University and returned to a law professorship at Yale University, and Dr. Bonbright was persuaded to take up the Acting Presidency during a brief interregnum, while the quest for a new president went on. The period ended in January, 1902. It is not often in American life that a man is planted in a community to grow as a tree grows, from the sapling period to the period of advanced maturity, becoming a landmark and a source of benefit to all passers-by. But all this is true of the Professor of Latin, Acting President of Northwestern University. Seized upon as a stripling tutor, rounded out in culture and methods by foreign study and observation, he has spent an ordinary lifetime in his chair; devoted as a lover to a single love; doing his part with a wisdom, thoroughness and grace that has left nothing to be desired as a teacher, gentleman, friend and inspirer of youth.

From the very first date of graduations at Evanston he has seen the stream of students go by; has known them all and taken a place in their memories as an integral part of their culture, their character and ideals. He has noted every step of progress, every movement of whatever sort that has gone to make up the traditions of Northwestern University, so that his were safe hands in which to entrust for any length of time the discipline, the growth, the care of the institution, with the assurance that the administration would be without caprice or doubtful experiment. Eager to escape pub-

PRESIDENT ROOSEVELT'S VISIT IN 1903

licity and diffident under public gaze, he took up his public cares with the easy grace of one born to the purple; and, when public utterance was needed, he spoke with the charm of one accustomed to public address, with a play of fancy and with such aptness of illustration and vigorous marshalling of ideas, that we were made to wonder that these talents had been so long concealed. With all the honors that Northwestern could confer upon him, after the term of his Acting Presidency, he quietly returned to his class-room to preside with the same simple dignity as of old, as if nothing unusual had happened in his career.

Passing Away of University Founders. —The past ten years has been a time of harvesting of the ripened grain among the surviving toilers in the early years of University history. John Evans, the first President of the Board, at a ripe old age passed away in the distant State of Colorado, of which he had been Governor, and where he displayed the same enterprise and leadership in affairs that characterized him in Chicago and Evanston. He had been one of the University's chief benefactors, and at a time when gifts were most acceptable. Two principal professorships were named in his honor; and while he was in Evanston, the weight of his judgment was well-nigh preponderating in University counsels. He aided in founding another university in Denver, but the University at Evanston was the child of his youth and the pride of his old age.

J. K. Botsford, too, passed away in this decade—the quiet hardware merchant on Lake Street, over whose store the meeting was held that launched the infant University. An unobtrusive man who built up a good competence in honorable trade; who loved the Church and all her enterprises; who talked little and thought much; who sat quietly in Trustee meetings, made no

long speeches, and always voted right. He was the soul of honor, a good man for Treasurer and serviceable in any situation that required prompt action, integrity and discreetness.

J. G. Hamilton was another of the old-time Trustees whose name was added to the death roll: Treasurer, Agent, Secretary of the Board, a prosperous and useful man in his time—so useful that, when misfortune and feebleness seized upon him, and he was left alone in the world and without resources, his fellow Trustees pensioned him, and gave him the honorable consideration that was due to the valuable and unselfish service he had rendered to the cause of education.

Richard Haney was another who came to the councils of the Trustees with each recurring year, till he could come no longer. A giant in stature, with the heart of a child —under his eye the institution had grown for nearly fifty years. Children whom he had baptized in infancy were filling important chairs in the University and, like a fond father, he smiled with joyful benignity upon the large heritage that had come to him and his comrades, most of whom had gone before him to their reward. It was one of the features of the Trustee meetings of later years to listen to his opening prayer— for that was his assigned part—and, when the meeting closed, it was with his benediction and with a farewell word that spoke of the joy of his heart over what God had wrought at the hands of his servants, and the assurance to his brethren that he could not expect to meet with them often in the future, perhaps never. He was waiting daily for his summons to ascend. Such incidents pertain to a distinctly Christian institution. They lift the business side of education out of the region of ordinary business, and inspire those who toil therein with the thought that they are doing a God-like work in the world that will beget sweet memories, such as kindled in the heart of the old founder when he looked back on his own labors and saw the work still going on, larger in volume and with a far-reaching influence such as he had never dreamed it would attain.

Then, too, Orrington Lunt, who succeeded to John Evans as President of the Board, was another of the surviving group of founders that passed away, than whom no single man connected with the institution had given to the University more of his thought and attention, or sacrificed more for it. The library was his darling project, and to it, as already noted, he gave an endowment and a building. Without Orrington Lunt, we cannot say what would have been done; but true it is, that the Trustees took no step in which he did not actively participate. No important committee was complete without him. No difficult negotiation could be carried on without his help. Wise, forceful, gentle, devoted as he was, his colleagues caught his spirit and were braced by his example to a like fidelity and devotion. When disease prevented his meeting with them, they took their meetings to his home; and when the end came he summoned them, one by one, to a sunny farewell. He loved them in the bonds of a common labor of love. Verily, when we speak of the endowment of the University, though the things that might seem most important may be lands and buildings and securities, we must not overlook, among its chief assets, the undying investment of the prayers, and love and labor of such choice spirits as are reckoned among the men whose names adorn our history, among whom there was no whiter soul than Orrington Lunt.

Then there was another Trustee, who does not rank with the founders, but who took his place naturally among the later Trustees who efficiently labored in the up-building of the institution—Robert M. Hatfield. In his time, a peerless pulpit orator, with a diction unsurpassed, an intensity and fervor that enthralled and possessed men, and a mastery of scorn and invective that was a terror to all shams, injustice and deceit, his forceful speech and influence meant much for the University endowment.

And there was David R. Dyche, who could drop his business cares any time to talk and plan for the University's good; who carried the burden of the four-mile limit on his heart; who gave generously of his substance, as of his time and influence, and by his wisdom and his gentleness helped on the march of progress.

And in March, 1899, Oliver Marcy, the grand old man who had been connected with the University for nearly forty years, finished his work. He had been twice Acting President; had taught an immense range of subjects, and had become the most striking figure in connection with the institution. He did not grow old. His body failed, but his keen intellect retained its edge; his love for the things of nature never failed; he wrought to the last in his dear museum, fondling his specimens as of old. They spoke to him of the mighty universe of which they were a part. They disclosed chapters of flood and fire that ordinary vision could not see in them, and which he delighted to reveal to any interested listener. His daily walk made us love him and the things he loved. It spoke to us of duty and devotion and joy in learning. He was called of God to be an educator, and he fulfilled his calling. His career is a part of the University's richest endowment.

Julius F. Kellogg, too, long time Professor of Mathematics, faded away in this decade, and was borne to rest by the loving hands of his old comrades, who knew him as a thorough mathematician, an excellent teacher and a simple hearted Christian. But I have played the role of Old Mortality long enough. These, and others of similar spirit, have served the University well, have gone to their reward and others have taken up their work.

It would be difficult to reach an exact statement of the number of young men and women who have shared the educational opportunities furnished by the University since its organization. Like a stream rising in the mountains—a rivulet at first, then a river, with increasing tributaries and enlarging volume—so the stream of students has enlarged, from ten in number in 1855, to nearly three thousand in 1901. Very many, of course, have attended the institution for a longer or a shorter course without graduating. Of those who have graduated, fifteen hundred have been from the College of Liberal Arts; eighteen hundred and forty-four from the Medical School; five hundred and fifty-nine from the Woman's Medical School; eleven hundred and eighty-six from the School of Pharmacy; sixteen hundred and five from the Law School; and fifteen hundred and thirty-one from the Dental School—in all, eight thousand, two hundred and twenty-five men and women, who have given a good account of themselves in the varied walks in life, and some of whom have attained to conspicuous positions and shed luster on their Alma Mater.

College Administration of Today.— Little has been said of the labors of living men in connection with the history of the University, either in the faculty or the board of government. This much ought to be stated, however: that the body of teachers in the College of Liberal Arts are a devoted, harmonious body of men and women, devoted chiefly to under-graduate work, and are hence confined largely to the work of instruction, though they do find time, now and then, to publish a volume in connection with their various specialties.

In the large faculty of the College nearly every study that would be selected as a culture study is represented by a specialist who knows his work; and, when they meet "in faculty assembled," according to the phrase adopted from Professor Godman of an early date, they are a distinguished body of men and women, keen in debate, deferential to each other, and with a single eye to the interests of the youth committed to their care.

And it is with unusual restraint that I refrain from writing of the labors of the men who have cared for the material interests of the institution, and who still carry on that work; men as conspicuous, able and devoted as any who have toiled in former generations, and who have finished their work and gone to their reward. When Orrington Lunt ascended, William Deering took his place as primus inter pares, administering his office with a dignity and discreetness that commends him to the confidence and affection of his colleagues, and with such a knowledge of the situation, such solicitude for progress, and such generous liberality as to constitute him easily the chief patron in our history. Beside him are eminent men who take up his work when absence or illness interferes.

And the able Secretary and Auditor, Frank P. Crandon, who has carried forward the work of the secretaryship since J. G. Hamilton laid down his pen, has put the University under a debt of obligation for service which it can never adequately reward. The volume of University business has become so great and its transactions so important—all of which pass through a central office and must be scrutinized from week to week—that it makes demands upon this officer that few appreciate as do those nearest his work, but to which he addresses himself with a constancy and painstaking fidelity that are beyond praise. I have referred to endowments that are not expressed in lands and buildings or notes of hand; such labors as his enter into this list, and swell the wealth of the favored institution that has commanded such services as his without fee or reward.

The Executive Committee are busy men of large private interests, but they are always about the Trustees' table when called; and they are regularly and irregularly called, and, without haste and after full discussion, they give all the time that is needful, in committee and out of committee, to carrying on their trust, with generous gifts of valuable time and other resources as they are able.

Dr. James Two Years' Administration. —From small beginnings, by careful management and timely benefactions, the University has acquired a property conservatively valued at six million dollars, and has done its work for fifty years with increasing vigor and enlargement as the years have advanced. In the summer of 1902, Dr. Edmund J. James was selected to fill the vacant Presidency, and for two years carried on the work with great vigor and promise, infusing fresh life into all departments of the institution. But in 1904, the claims of the Illinois State University upon him were too strong for him to resist, and he resigned to be succeeded by Prof. Thomas F. Holgate, as Acting President.

The service of Professor Holgate as Dean of the College of Liberal Arts has fitted him well for the duties that have been thrust upon him, while his familiarity with the history and traditions of the University justify the belief that, under his guiding hand, the institution will maintain its steady and healthy progress, growing as the tree grows, nourished by the kindly care of the men and women who stand forth as its representatives—its Trustees, its Professors, its Alumni, and the great Church in whose name it was founded, and whose zeal for Christian culture it expresses.

The University Finds a New President —On February 1, 1906, the Trustees of Northwestern University closed their long quest for a successor to President James, by the election of Abram W. Harris, LL.D., of Tome Institute, Maryland, to the Presidency. Dr. Harris was born in Philadelphia, November 7, 1858, graduated from the Wesleyan University, at Middletown, Conn., in 1880, and has followed an educational career since that time, except for a few years when he was in government service. His experience in University work and the secondary schools gives promise of great usefulness in his new field. His term of service was designated to commence July 1, 1906, un-til which time the interests of the University are presided over by Acting President Holgate, who has borne well the burdens and responsibilities of his office for nearly two years past.

CHAPTER X.

NORTHWESTERN UNIVERSITY MEDICAL SCHOOL
(By N. S. DAVIS, JR., A. M., M. D.)

Object of its Organization—Early Conditions and Methods of Medical Education—Dr. N. S. Davis Begins the Agitation for Graded Instruction and Longer Courses—Lind University Established in 1859—Institution affiliated with Northwestern University in 1860—Changes of Name and Location—Growth, Present Conditions and Methods of Instruction—South Side Free Dispensary—Hospitals: Mercy, Wesley, St. Luke's and Provident—Clinical and other Advantages—Influence of the Founders of the School Shown in its Growth and Character of its Graduates—Positions Won by its Alumni.

Northwestern University Medical School was founded to demonstrate the practicability of what were admitted to be good methods of teaching the art and science of medicine. So long as this country was sparsely settled and means of rapid transit were wanting, it was difficult for physicians educated abroad to find communities of sufficient size or of such character as to tempt them to settle here. It was equally difficult for those of our own people inclined to study medicine to obtain suitable opportunities. For many years most practitioners of medicine received their training from others to whom they were apprenticed. For half a century after the Revolutionary War the medical colleges, which were established,

were regarded as not essential to the making of physicians and surgeons, but as useful places for the review of studies pursued under a preceptor and for the prosecution of practical studies in anatomy. The annual course in these schools was from four to five months in duration. During this time all the students attended all the lectures. These courses they repeated a second year, when they were granted a diploma. It is evident that such schools in no sense supplanted the work of preceptors or general practitioners who received apprentices, but supplemented it. The colleges contained no laboratories, and few were connected with hospitals or attempted clinical teaching. During the next twenty-five years a gradual evolution took place; clinics were established in most schools and a better quality of teaching was done. By both practitioners and laymen colleges were regarded as of more importance for the acquisition of the knowledge which medical men must have.

In the second decade of the last century Dr. N. S. Davis began to agitate the need of graded instruction in medical schools and of longer courses. This he did in medical societies and by writing a small treatise upon medical education. Later, in order to further this end, he induced the leading teachers and practitioners of various States to assemble to form a National Medical Society. He hoped that, by agitating the subject in such a body, reforms might be inaugurated simultaneously in all the States. Although medical societies by numerous resolutions urged such reforms upon the colleges, they were not made. In 1859 a group of men, most of whom had been teachers in Rush College, Chicago, established a new school in that city, which was to demonstrate the feasibility of some of these long-needed reforms. Minimum requirements for entrance to the school were made; three years of study, at least two of which must have been in a medical college, were demanded for graduation, and the studies were graded so that the most elementary were taught first and the others followed in logical order. Clinical teaching was made a prominent feature of the instruction from the beginning. Surprising as it seems, considering the evident need of these changes, it was nearly ten years before any other college in the country followed its example, and many more before it was followed by all.

Originally this college was not a department of Northwestern University. In 1859 Lind University was established and Doctors Hosmer A. Johnson, David Rutter, Edmund Andrews, and Ralph Isham organized a medical department of it. N. S. Davis, William H. Byford and numerous other leading physicians of this small city were invited to form its faculty. Lind University soon went out of existence for want of sufficient financial support, but the medical school was re-organized under a charter of its own and was called Chicago Medical College. Under this name it made a permanent reputation. In 1869 it was affiliated with Northwestern University, because it was thought that a university connection would enable it to stimulate students to prepare better for college and to maintain a higher grade of instruction itself. From

this time until 1890 the institution was known as "Chicago Medical College"—the Medical Department of Northwestern University. In the latter year a close union with the University was effected, and the name was again changed, this time to Northwestern University Medical School.

With each of these changes of title a change of location was made. Originally the college was housed in the Lind Block in the heart of the city; later it moved into a building of its own on State Street near Twenty-second. In 1870 it was compelled to move, as its home was destroyed in the process of widening State Street. It then built anew at the corner of Twenty-sixth and Prairie Avenue, immediately adjoining Mercy Hospital. Here it remained twenty years; but the growth of the hospital in time necessitated abandonment of this site. New and entirely modern buildings were constructed for its accommodation in 1890 on Dearborn Street, between Twenty-fourth and Twenty-fifth Streets; and, in 1901, Wesley Hospital was built beside it.

While in material possessions the institution has grown, it has also steadily advanced, and even led, in most of the reforms in teaching which have taken place. In 1868 it demanded attendance upon three annual courses of instruction in the college for graduation, and lengthened each course to six months. By 1870 the number of departments of instruction had been increased from eleven to thirteen, and, during the next twenty years, to eighteen. In 1890 the annual term was lengthened to seven months, and four years of study in college were required for graduation. For several years before these changes were made a fourth year was offered but not required. In 1894 the annual term was made eight months. In 1892 Latin and physics were added to the entrance requirements and, three years later, algebra, and in 1896 several other branches of a high school course. A year later the requirements for entrance to the medical school were made the same as those of the College of Liberal Arts.

Laboratory and clinical teaching were conspicuous elements of instruction from the inception of this college. When it was established, the only laboratory teaching done in medical schools was in chemistry and anatomy. Some years later a laboratory of histology was opened. In 1886 laboratory instruction was given to all students in pathology. Bacteriology was taught for several years as an optional study, but work was required of all students in the bacteriological laboratory in 1891. In 1894 laboratories of experimental physiology and pharmacology were opened, although for several years prior to this, instruction had been given in physiological chemistry; still more recently those of clinical pathology were established. This kind of practical teaching has so grown that it now constitutes the largest part of the work done by students in their first two years of medical study. The development of this kind of teaching, which is largely individual, has necessitated the employment of numerous teachers who devote their entire time to the school. In the earlier history of this institution, these branches were taught by practitioners of medicine who devoted only a few hours per week to the work, a practice which is still continued by many colleges.

Clinical teaching bears to the studies of the last two years the same relationship that laboratory teaching does to the first. It practically illustrates all instruction in the various departments of medicine, surgery and the specialties, and brings students in personal contact with patients and teacher. As laboratories have multiplied so have clinics, and in each the amount of teaching has been increased and improved. A few

clinics are introduced into the second year course to illustrate methods of examination, a subject taught at that time in order to prepare students for the study of disease which completely occupies their attention during the junior and senior years. The senior year is given up almost exclusively to clinical teaching. Northwestern University offers its students much more clinical instruction than most other schools do, and especially a large amount of bedside instruction to small groups of them. The clinical laboratory enables students to apply all kinds of scientific methods of research to the examination of patients. In it they make blood examinations, sputa examinations and analyze the other secretions and excretions of the body. The aim of this school is not simply to afford students an opportunity to learn what is known of disease, but to become intimately acquainted with it by contact with patients, to obtain experience by watching the course of disease and the effect of remedial procedures.

The unusual clinical facilities of this college are made possible by the South Side Free Dispensary—which is in Davis Hall, one of the University buildings—by Mercy Hospital, St. Luke's Hospital, and by Wesley and Provident Hospitals. These hospitals together accommodate from eight hundred to one thousand patients. In the South Side Free Dispensary twenty-five thousand patients are prescribed for annually, and are treated, in many cases, by the best physicians, surgeons and specialists of the city. Rooms are arranged for the proper examination and care of eye and ear, nose and throat, gynecological, skin, nervous, surgical and medical cases, as well as of children. Trained nurses assist in several of these departments. This dispensary is not only an important educational institution, but one of the best philanthropies in Chicago. Davis Hall, in which the dispensary is housed, was constructed for its accommodation. The building is a well planned and commodious out-patient hospital.

Mercy Hospital, which is the oldest and one of the largest public hospitals in the city, has been intimately associated with this school ever since its founding. The hospital consists of a series of buildings, with a total length of six hundred feet. It is located on the corner of Twenty-sixth Street and Calumet Avenue, and covers nearly half a block of land. It owns property adjoining its present buildings, which will enable it to grow and ultimately to cover nearly a square of land. A part of this vacant property is an attractive garden, which is much frequented by convalescent patients during the summer.

There has recently been completed an addition to the hospital devoted to a large operating and clinic hall, which will accommodate four hundred students. This is one of the most attractive and perfect operating rooms in the city. In connection with this are numerous small rooms for private operations, for the care of instruments and surgical supplies, for preparing patients and for preparing operators and their assistants. These rooms are of the most modern and approved construction and contain the best equipment known.

Mercy Hospital has also one of the best training schools for nurses in the city. Instruction and training is given them in the hospital by the staff, as well as by regular teachers devoting their time to the school.

The attending staff of physicians and surgeons is selected from the Faculty of Northwestern University Medical School. Eight resident physicians and surgeons are chosen annually from the graduating class of the college, and serve for eighteen months in the hospital. During the college year from one to four clinics are given daily in this institution.

The most notable recent addition to the equipment of the Medical School is Wesley Hospital. It is located beside the college building, and is connected with Davis Hall by an enclosed bridge. Neither expense nor time has been spared to make this one of the best equipped hospitals in the world. It is the last built in Chicago and contains all of the newest improvements in hospital construction.

With its laboratories for sterilizing and preparing dressings and instruments, its amphitheatre, its clinical and pathological laboratories, drug-room and morgue; with its sun-baths and suites of private rooms, and with its commodious, light and well ventilated wards, this institution would seem to have reached the highest mark in hospital construction and equipment. The staff of this hospital is also selected from the faculty of the college. Four resident physicians and surgeons are chosen annually from the graduating class. It also has an excellent training school for nurses.

The instruction given to the students in Wesley Hospital makes a very important portion of their clinical course. This is naturally consequent upon the close relation of the two institutions—the hospital standing beside the College Building and connected with it by corridors.

St. Luke's Hospital is situated on Indiana Avenue, near Fourteenth street. Owing to its central location, it receives a large number of accident cases, and its surgical clinic is, consequently, an extensive one. Clinics are given regularly in Medicine, Nervous Diseases, Surgery, Gynecology, and Diseases of the Eye and Ear. The clinics and autopsies of St. Luke's Hospital are attended principally by the third year students.

Provident Hospital, located at the corner of Thirty-sixth and Dearborn streets, has recently been much enlarged. Besides its 100 beds, which can accommodate 800 to

1,000 patients annually, there is a large dispensary in which about 6,000 ambulatory patients receive treatment each year.

The students of the Northwestern University Medical School have an opportunity to attend clinics by the Medical Staff and operations by the Surgical Staff, and are assigned, in small classes, to ward visits in Surgery and Gynecology.

The college possesses, in addition to the equipment of its laboratories and clinics, a fine collection of pathological and anatomical specimens. Its present museum is crowded and more space is needed. It also has an excellent reference library, which is in constant use by the students. This is in charge of a librarian who devotes her entire time to it.

The inspiration which its founders gave this school, to maintain in it the most thorough and complete instruction possible, has never been lost. Its success is shown by its growth and, best of all, by the character of its graduates. For a number of years past from one-third to one-half of each graduating class has received hospital appointments, in which they obtain from a year to eighteen months of practical post-graduate training. Many of its alumni are filling important professorships in colleges from the Atlantic to the Pacific coasts. They are found leaders in the communities in which they live and in the societies of their profession.

CHAPTER XI.

NORTHWESTERN UNIVERSITY LAW SCHOOL
(By F. B. CROSSLEY, LL. B.)

Historical Sketch—Law School Founded in 1859—Hon. Thomas Hoyne Leads in Endowment of First Chair—Only Three Law Schools then West of the Alleghenies—First Faculty—Notable Members of Faculty of Later Date—Union College of Law Result of Combination of Northwestern and University of Chicago—First Board of Managers and First Faculty Under New Arrangement—University of Chicago Suspended in 1866 and Northwestern Assumed Entire Control of Law School in 1891—Subsequent History—Changes in Requirements of Supreme Court as to Law Course—Present Home and Conditions—Acquisition of Gary Collection—Present Outlook.

The present Northwestern University Law School was founded in 1859 through the generosity of the Hon. Thomas Hoyne, who contributed five thousand dollars to the original University of Chicago to endow a "chair of International and Constitutional Law" which contribution enabled the University to establish a Law Department.

At that time there were but three other law schools west of the Allegheny Mountains, and the need of an institution that could offer a better legal training than could be obtained in a law office, was becoming

more and more apparent with the growth of the city.

The School was first opened for instruction in 1860, with Honorable Henry Booth and Judges John M. Wilson and Grant Goodrich as professors. Dr. Booth was the first to be called as a professor and to serve as Dean, and continued in that joint capacity for thirty-two years, retiring as Dean Emeritus in 1892. The inauguration ceremonies of the School took place in Metropolitan Hall, the chief address being made by the Hon. David Dudley Field, of New York; the Chief Justice of the Supreme Court of Illinois, Sidney Breese, and several other Judges of prominence being present and assisting.

The School was conducted continuously by the University of Chicago until 1873, becoming better known throughout the United States each year for the thorough character of its instruction and the high standard of scholarship set for its graduates; and though the dominating control of the School has changed several times from the date of its organization, the policy outlined by Dean Booth and his co-workers has been followed, and at no time has the School lost in influence or prestige through any attempt by the different interests to lower the quality of its instruction or the standard of its scholarship. The faith of these different interests in the policy of its first Dean and his fellow-laborers is illustrated by the long tenure of office and the service on the Faculty of one of Evanston's best known citizens, the Hon. Harvey B. Hurd, who became a Professor in the Law School in 1862, and remained in active service until May 23, 1902, when he retired as Emeritus Professor of Law.

In 1873, for the purpose of strengthening the School and adding a department of law, Northwestern University entered into an agreement with the University of Chicago whereby the Law School came under the joint control of the two Universities. By the terms of this agreement the School was placed under the direct management of a "Joint Board," "comprising an equal number of persons from the Board of Trustees of each University," the announcement of the change setting forth that "it should not be overlooked by any of the graduates of the Law School of the University of Chicago, that this School is a legitimate offspring and successor to its claims, and, as such, is entitled to receive all the honors and support of the large number of those, fast rising into professional eminence, who acquired the rudiments of their legal learning within the walls of this School." The joint agreement provided that the School should be known as the Law Department of both Universities, "with full right to each to publish the same in all catalogues and circulars, as its law department; that diplomas should be signed by the President and Secretary of both Universities, under the seal of each, and that, "as far as practicable, the graduating exercises of the law classes shall be held in the name of, and attended by, the Trustees, officers and Faculties of both Universities"; that, "for the purpose of placing said Law School upon a sure and

substantial financial basis," each University should pay annually towards its support not less than two thousand dollars and, in case of default for six months, the party in default should forfeit its interest and control in the School.

Northwestern University was represented on the first Board of Management, as above provided for, by Hon. Grant Goodrich, Wirt Dexter, Esq., Robert F. Queal, and Rev. Charles H. Fowler, President of the University.

The first Faculty under joint control of the two Universities was composed as follows: Hon. Henry Booth, Dean and Professor of the law of Property and of Pleading; Hon. Lyman Trumbull, Professor of Constitutional Law, Statute Law, and Practice in the United States Courts; Hon. James R. Doolittle, Professor of Equity Jurisprudence, Pleading and Evidence; Van Buren Denslow, Esq., Professor of Contracts and Civil and Criminal Practice; Philip Myers, Esq., Professor of Commercial Law; Hon. James B. Bradwell, Lecturer on Wills and Probate; Dr. Nathan S. Davis, Lecturer on Medical Jurisprudence.

The School was now known as the Union College of Law, and was located at this time (1873) in the Superior Block, fronting the Court-House. Sixty regular students were registered during the year 1872-73— and, after three years of joint management, one hundred and thirty students were enrolled in one year. The requirements for admission at this time were low in all law schools, this School requiring merely a common school education, but recommending a college training, and during the year 1876— or three years after Northwestern University assumed partial control—almost one-third of the students in the Law School possessed academic degrees. The course, as in nearly all the better schools, covered a period of two years and the diploma of the School admitted to the bar of Illinois.

The joint management was continued until 1886, when the original University of Chicago ceased to exist actively, and later surrendered its charter. For a period of about five years (1886 to 1891) the control of the Law School was still exercised by a "Joint Board," but in 1891 Northwestern University assumed entire control and the School received its present name. The agreement under which the Northwestern University assumed exclusive control of the Law School was made July 1, 1891, with the Union College of Law represented by Hon. Oliver H. Horton and William V. Farwell; Northwestern University being represented by Orrington Lunt, its Vice-President. This agreement, among other provisions, set forth that the School should thereafter be known as Northwestern University Law School, with the privilege to continue the name "Union College of Law" in brackets, and that "all persons who are alumni of Union College of Law are hereby made alumni of Northwestern University Law School."

Since Northwestern University obtained sole control of the Law School, its position among the foremost in the country has been maintained and the School has led in all attempts to raise the standard of legal education and of the legal profession in the West. An academic training equivalent to that of a graduate of a high school was soon made a requirement for admission, and, in 1897, the required period of study in the School of all candidates for a degree was extended to three years, although at that time the Supreme Court of Illinois required but two years' study for admission to practice within its jurisdiction. This change in the requirements for graduation was soon followed by a new rule of the Supreme Court of Illinois, governing admission to

the bar and requiring an academic training equivalent to that of a high school graduate, and three years' study of law of all applicants for admission to practice. A change was also made in the Law School in the method of instruction by the adoption of the case system instead of the text, the curriculum was greatly enlarged and the Faculty increased.

The policy of the University toward the Law School has been, at all times since its assumption of executive control, one of commendable liberality, and because of it the School has been able to keep up its progress and maintain its prestige. To do this, because of the large gifts of money contributed in recent years to Universities throughout the country other than Northwestern, and the consequent increase in efficiency and equipment of their various departments, the University found it necessary, in 1902, to increase very largely its annual financial contribution to the Law School, and this was done by adding thereto the income from a quarter of a million dollars and, in addition, an appropriation of ten thousand dollars for the immediate increase of the library; so that, when the School ceased its migratory career and moved into its present permanent home in Northwestern University Building, purchased and equipped at a cost of nearly one million dollars by the University, as a home for its professional Schools other than Medical, it possessed a Faculty of six professors giving the whole or the substance of their time to the School, besides an excellent staff of instructors and lecturers, and a library of over 12,000 volumes. The present home of the School, in what was widely known for more than half a century as the "Tremont House," is well adapted to its needs. It occupies the entire third floor of Northwestern University Building, in the heart of the business section of Chicago. The twenty-three thousand square feet of floor space is divided into well equipped library, lecture, study and court rooms, and offices. The library reading room will accommodate 450 students at its tables. The students' assembly room provides pleasant quarters for rest and conversation. The walls of the School are hung with an interesting collection of portraits of prominent Judges, and legal writers, teachers, and lawyers of all countries—a collection that is probably not equaled in the United States. The equipment throughout, aside from the library, was made possible by generous money contributions from alumni, Trustees and other friends of the School upon its removal to its permanent home.

Through the generosity of Hon. Elbert H. Gary, '67, the School in 1903 acquired the Gary Collection of Continental Jurisprudence. This Collection, the most complete of its kind this side the Atlantic, comprises an extensive collection of the laws and jurisprudence of all the countries of Continental Europe. It is of incalculable practical value to Chicago and the Northwest, and to students of the law in this country interested in the study of comparative laws. Judge Gary has also made it possible for the School to greatly increase its collection of English and American laws and treatises, and placed it (1905) in a position for the first time to compare favorably in this respect with the best law school libraries in the country.

After forty-six years of existence the Law School stands for the best in legal training. During the past it has occupied constantly a high place as one of the best law schools, although greatly handicapped by lack of proper equipment and insufficient financial support. Today, with its large body of alumni, many of whom are of State and National reputation, scattered over thirty-five States and Territories, with its excellent equipment and its increased financial support, the future of this department seems almost assured.

CHAPTER XII.

NORTHWESTERN UNIVERSITY DENTAL SCHOOL
(By G. V. BLACK, M. D., D. D. S., LL. D.)

Dental Education as a Distinct Branch of Professional Training — First Dental School Established in 1839—Development Due to State Legislation—Dental Schools in Eastern Cities—Chicago College of Dental Surgery Graduates its First Class in 1885—Dr. Thomas L. Gilmer Leads Movement for Establishment of North-western University Dental School—Consolidation with American College of Dental Surgery — Dr. Theodore Menges Chief Promoter — First Faculty of the Consolidated School — Present Condition — It Finds a Permanent Home in Historic Tremont House Building.

In order to understand the conditions influencing the growth of the Northwestern University Dental School, it seems necessary to intermingle with the more direct account of it, a brief explanation of some of the general conditions peculiar to dental education which have had so large an influence on its development.

Dental education, as a distinct branch of activity in the development of science and art, began in 1839, when Dr. Chapin Harris and his colleagues, who had been teaching oral surgery in a medical school in Baltimore, withdrew and founded an independent school of dentistry, establishing the degree of Doctor of Dental Surgery as earned by a definite course of study. The effort was so successful that since that time dental education in America has been on a separate basis from general medical education. Yet it has always been regarded as a branch of the healing art, having much in common with general medicine, and especially as requiring similar preparation in the fundamental branches, viz: anatomy, physiology, histology, pathology and chemistry. Dental schools made slow progress, however, in the earlier years of their existence. It had been the custom that one desiring to engage in the practice of dentistry became a student in the office of a practitioner, and, when considered sufficiently proficient, entered upon the practice independently without question. So firmly fixed was this practice that, for a time, few students entered the dental schools; though from year to year they increased in numbers and new schools were organized and operated successfully in several of the larger cities.

About 1870 there was a general movement for the better education of dentists. The need for the better education of physicians was being urged, and laws for the regulation of the practice of medicine, and incidentally requiring improvement in educational qualification, were being enacted by the different State Legislatures. Dentistry followed, and laws were also rapidly adopted regulating the practice of dentistry. These laws have been sustained by the sentiment of the people for whose benefit they were drawn, by the profession and by the courts of law. Those entering upon the practice of dentistry then found that the easier way to obtain an education that would satisfy the State Boards of Dental Examiners, was by attending the dental schools. This brought about a very rapid increase in the number of students, and also a similar increase in the number of dental schools. In 1870 there were eight dental schools in operation, from which were graduated 140 students. This, with the conditions of graduation then prevailing, would indicate a total attendance of but little over 200 students. In 1901 there were fifty-four dental schools and from these about 2,300 students were graduated. This would indicate a total attendance of about 7,000 students.

This seemingly extreme educational activity in dentistry was also accompanied by a similar activity in the development of dental science and practice. Many active men were coming forward with new facts and with new thought for the betterment of the treatment of dental diseases. The people were gaining confidence in dental operations and making larger demands on the dental profession, and increased numbers of dentists were required to satisfy these demands, thus giving substantial support to the educational impulse. Baltimore and Philadelphia were the earlier seats of dental educational work, though successful dental schools were being developed in other cities. In Chicago the first dental school in actual operation (some charters for dental schools were obtained earlier) was Chicago College of Dental Surgery, which graduated its first class in 1885. In the activity of the time many efforts failed, or were imperfectly organized and continued but a short time.   .

Dr. Thomas L. Gilmer inaugurated, and was principally instrumental in carrying through, the initial movement which resulted in the organization of the present Northwestern University Dental School. In 1890 there were a number of men in Chicago who had obtained some prominence as teachers in dentistry who were not then engaged in teaching. Having noted this, and having carefully studied the conditions, Dr. Gilmer gave a dinner at the Leland Hotel, to which Drs. George H. Cushing, Edgar D. Swain, Edmund Noyes and W. V-B. Ames were invited, and to whom he opened the subject of the organization of a new dental school. There were at the time several dental schools in the city that were not doing well, and the question of the reorganization of some one of these was discussed, with the result that Dr. Gilmer was authorized to investigate the advisability of the purchase of the American College of Dental Surgery, then under the control of Dr. Clendenen. At a subsequent meeting Dr. Gilmer reported adversely to the purchase of that school. Chicago University was then in process of organization, and an interview was had with President Harper with reference to the organization of a dental school as a department of that university, but at the time they were not ready for such an undertaking. The discussion of various schemes continued from time to time until the resignation of the faculty of the University Dental College seemed to create an opening in that direction.

The University Dental College was finally organized under a charter granted from the State of Illinois in 1887. The first session was held in the winter of 1887-88, with a class of six students, the dental faculty consisting of W. W. Allport (Emeritus), L. P. Haskell, R. F. Ludwig, John S. Marshall (Dean), A. E. Baldwin, Charles P. Pruyn, R. C. Baker and Arthur B. Freeman. An agreement was effected between President Cummings of Northwestern University, Nathan S. Davis, Dean of Chicago Medical College, and the faculty of the new Dental College, by which the students should take lectures in anatomy, physiology, histology, materia medica, pathology and surgery with the medical classes; but this agreement involved no further connection with the Medical College. Also the connection with Northwestern University was nominal and prospective only, the University assuming no responsibility for the Dental College.

The new college was located on Twenty-sixth Street, Chicago, near the Medical College. The students were required to take a course of three years, of seven months each, before graduation. This was the first dental college to make this requirement, and this fact operated very much against its success in obtaining students; so that its classes remained very small. There were only eleven students at the end of the second year. At the beginning of the third year the three-year course was made optional, and the students were allowed to elect to take a two years' course. At the end of the fourth year the class numbered nineteen. The college could not continue to meet its expenses on the income derived from this number of students and, at the end of the year, the Faculty resigned, as has been noted above.

At that time Dr. Henry Wade Rogers had recently become President of Northwestern University, and was actively engaged in bringing the professional schools, which had previously but a nominal connection with the University at Evanston, into a closer relationship. He was seen by Dr. Gilmer with regard to the reorganization of this college, and he actively favored it. After a number of conferences between the parties interested, which included especially Drs. Chas. P. Pruyn, I. A. Freeman, A. B.

Freeman and A. E. Matteson, of the old faculty, the officers of Chicago Medical College, and Drs. T. L. Gilmer, E. D. Swain, Geo. H. Cushing, Edmund Noyes, W. V-B. Ames and others, an organization was effected under the charter of Northwestern University, and the charter of the University Dental College from the State allowed to lapse. In making this change the word college was dropped and the word school substituted, in accord with a policy of the University, in which the teaching organizations under its jurisdiction are called "schools" rather than colleges. The new school took the name Northwestern University Dental School. The Chicago Medical College also came into closer relationship with the University and took the name Northwestern University Medical School.

The new dental faculty was composed of Edgar D. Swain, Dean; Edmund Noyes, Secretary; G. V. Black, George H. Cushing, J. S. Marshall, Charles P. Pruyn, Isaac A. Freeman, Thomas L. Gilmer, Arthur B. Freeman, B. S. Palmer, W. V-B. Ames, Arthur E. Matteson, E. L. Clifford, G. W. Haskins, D. M. Cattell and H. P. Smith. Arrangements were made with the medical school by which the dental students took lectures on the fundamental subjects with the medical classes. The school was removed to more commodious quarters on Twenty-second Street, but near enough to be convenient to the Medical School, which was also moved to new quarters on Dearborn Street, near Twenty-fourth. In the summer of 1891 the National Association of Dental Faculties passed an order which required all schools affiliated with it to extend the course of study to three terms of not less than six months each, in separate years before graduation. This order was complied with at once, and the new organization began its first session with a class of fifty-three students, only six of whom came from the old school.

The National Association of Dental Faculties was formed in 1884, having as its object the improvement of the methods of dental education and harmony of action among the separate schools. The National Association of Dental Examiners had been formed a year earlier, having for its object the promotion of harmony of action among the separate Examining Boards of the different States. These associations, while remaining distinct, have, for the most part, worked in unison, both having for their prime object the better education and professional qualification of young men for the practice of dentistry, and their influence has been too important to be passed without some consideration. It must be understood that, before this time, dental schools were without law or rule other than such as each might adopt at will, and there was little harmony of action among them. Some were graduating students on a single course of six months. There was no standard of educational requirement for matriculation, etc. The object of the Faculties Association was to bring about harmony and establish rules regarding all such matters.

Perhaps the best definition of the objects and purposes of this organization will be expressed in its first official acts. It was agreed by the association at its first meeting that, after the close of the sessions of 1884-85, each college belonging to the Association would refuse to allow a candidate to come up for final examination who had not attended two full courses of lectures, the last of which should have been spent in the college where the candidate for graduation proposed to take the degree. A preliminary examination of all students not possessing an academic or high school education was also ordered to go into effect at the same time. It was ordered that an examination of junior students should take place at the end of their first course, and that certificates should be issued showing their fitness to enter the senior class of any one of the chain of colleges, and that no college belonging to the Association would allow a student to enter the senior class who did not exhibit such a certificate of qualification, and this class of legislation has since been continued. This organization quickly gathered into its membership all of the dental schools regarded as reputable; and, although a purely voluntary organization, it has attained such power through the general support of the dental profession that its edicts have the force of law.

It was under these general conditions that the new school began its work. After two years in its location on Twenty-second Street, the school was moved into new buildings erected on Dearborn Street, between Twenty-fourth and Twenty-fifth Streets, and was housed with the Medical School; each, however, having its own rooms, clinical outfits and laboratories. In this location, and with these arrangements, the school was fairly prosperous and the number of students increased so that, in the fall of 1895, the whole number was one hundred and twenty-eight. With this number in the Dental School and the continued increase in the Medical School, the space was overcrowded, so that it became necessary to procure additional buildings outside for a portion of the laboratories of the Dental School. This arrangement proved very unsatisfactory, as it required much running to and fro, and it became clear that something else must be done in order to accommodate the increasing demands. The extension of the course to three years instead of two, as had been the former custom, had not served materially to diminish the number of applicants for matriculation.

In the meantime the American College of Dental Surgery, previously mentioned, had been purchased by Dr. Theodore Menges and others, its equipment had been improved, it was being put in better condition for giving instruction and its classes were rapidly increasing in numbers. Dr. Menges, who was showing much energy and tact, especially in gaining students, proposed in the winter of 1895-96 the consolidation of these two schools. After numerous conferences usual in such proceedings, this was effected during the following spring on terms which, for the time, left the principal management of the school in the hands of Dr. Menges, but provided for the ultimate complete ownership by the University. The faculty was again reorganized, a part of each of the old faculties being retained. The new faculty at the beginning of 1896-97 was composed of Edgar D. Swain (Dean), G. V. Black, George H. Cushing, Thomas L. Gilmer, J. S. Marshall (Emeritus), B. J. Cigrand, A. H. Peck, E. H. Angle, Edmund Noyes, I. B. Crissman, W. E. Harper, G. W. Haskins, James H. Prothero, G. W. Swartz, William Stearns, Charles B. Reed, F. B. Noyes, T. B. Wiggin, W. T. Eckley, L. B. Haymen, George Leininger, C. E. Sayre, V. J. Hall, with Theodore Menges as Secretary and Business Manager. The Dental School was removed to the building that had been occupied by the American College of Dental Surgery, on the corner of Franklin and Madison Streets, where it has since remained. In this building additional space could be had from time to time for indefinite expansion. In this arrangement the American College of Dental Surgery went out of existence, and, as its graduates would have no *alma mater*, it was agreed that those students who had graduated in 1891 and since should be made alumni of the Northwestern University Dental School.

Northwestern University Dental School now undertook to teach all of the departments, including the fundamental branches, by its own professors and instructors, thus separating it entirely from the Medical School. The work was now with much larger classes than had before been assembled in dental schools, and, as the year passed, it was seen that, while the general methods of instruction in vogue were well adapted, much improvement in the systematization of the work of the teaching force was desirable. At the end of the year the Dean, Dr. Edgar D. Swain, resigned. Dr. G. V. Black was then appointed Dean, and was charged especially with the systematization of the methods of instruction. Each of the departments of instruction was gradually brought under the control of a single responsible professor, who controlled the methods of presentation of the subjects in his field of work by those associated with him, and the courses of study were so graded that the classes of each year remained separate in the class room. Personal teaching was provided for by the separation of classes into sections and the arrangement of quiz-masters and demonstrators for special duties, so that the individual student could, at any time, obtain a personal answer to his question or the demonstration of a technical procedure.

In following out these arrangements, subjects that had been divided among different members of the faculty were grouped under one head and managed by a single professor with the aid of assistants, so that the faculty was reduced in number and the assistant teachers, demonstrators and quiz-masters increased. In 1899-1900 the faculty was composed of Greene V. Black (Dean), Thomas L. Gilmer, John S. Marshall (Emeritus), Adelbert H. Peck, Edmund Noyes, William E. Harper, James H. Prothero, Frederick B. Noyes, Twing B. Wiggin, William T. Eckley, Vernon J. Hall, George A. Dorsey, Theodore Menges (Secretary of the Faculty) and James N. McDowell.

This faculty was assisted by about thirty assistants, teachers, demonstrators and quizmasters.

Northwestern Dental College, a small school also located in Chicago, had given much annoyance on account of the similarity of name, especially in the confusion it caused in the delivery of mail. In 1898 this was purchased, the college closed, and its plant added to the Northwestern University Dental School. This arrangement included the recognition of the recent graduates of the Northwestern Dental College as alumni of Northwestern University Dental School.

The school as thus organized prospered, and the classes steadily increased until, in 1899-1900, they numbered six hundred students—the largest number ever collected in one dental school. Additional space in the building was obtained from time to time for new laboratories and class rooms. In 1899 an entire floor was added to gain additional space for necessary class rooms, lecture rooms and laboratories, and also to provide space for a library, museum and reading room. It has been found particularly desirable that students should be provided with well-arranged space in the school building, to which they could go during any leisure hour for the purpose of reading and study, or which they could occupy at regular hours and where they could find books upon any topic in dentistry. The work of assembling a library and museum of comparative dental anatomy and dental pathology was actively undertaken, and the material has been rapidly brought together, so that, at the present time, these may be justly regarded as excellent and as quite fully supplying the needs of a dental school. To these members of the profession have contributed books, journals and specimens liberally, and have in this way very materially aided in the gathering of the collection. This work is still in progress. Members of the profession are also permitted to make use of this library and museum.

On the first of June, 1900, Dr. Theodore Menges, Secretary and Business Manager of Northwestern University Dental School, died of appendicitis, after an illness of a little less than one week. He was thus cut off, seemingly before his time, in the midst of a robust manhood and mental vigor, while in the active prosecution of the work that seemed to have been allotted him to do. His sudden death threw a wave of grief over all connected with the school, upon its alumni, the dental profession and all who knew him and the work he was doing. He was an active, energetic and persistent worker, devoting his life to the upbuilding of the dental profession.

With the death of Dr. Menges the dental school became completely the property of Northwestern University. Dr. W. E. Harper was appointed Secretary and the school went regularly forward with its work without other change in its faculty. Its alumni now number about fourteen hundred.

In 1901 the University purchased a new building at a cost of half a million dollars, which two years since became the permanent home of the Dental School, as also of the schools of Law and Pharmacy. This building—formerly the "Tremont House," for more than fifty years one of the most widely known hostelries in the city of Chicago—is located at the corner of Lake and Dearborn Streets, within the downtown loop of the elevated roads, is convenient of access from all lines of travel, both general and suburban, and furnishes especially commodious quarters for the uses of the school. It has a frontage of 180 feet on Dearborn Street and 160 feet on Lake Street, and since it came into the possession of the University, has undergone thorough reconstruction, fitting it for the several departments there located.

The several schools in this building are entirely separate and distinct from each other in their respective rooms, equipment and special work—as much so as if in separate buildings—so situated as to have a much closer community of interest and of helpfulness with reference to each other than had previously existed. The annual sessions of the Dental School are held in this new building, and there is every reason to believe that in its new and permanent home the Dental department has entered upon a new period of increasing prosperity and usefulness.

ADDENDUM

Since the above was written Northwestern University Dental School has gone regularly forward with its educational work. Dr. Elgin MaWhinney has been appointed to fill the place made vacant by the resignation af Dr. A. H. Peck. A vacancy occuring through the resignation of Dr. E. H. Angle is filled by Dr. Ira B. Sellery. Secretary Dr. W. E. Harper resigned and his place was filled by the appointment of Dr. C. R. E. Koch. Also three of the younger men who had been serving the school as Demonstrators and Lecturers, have been appointed Asistant Professors to the chair of Operative Dentistry and Bacteriology. These are Dr. E. S. Willard, in charge of Bacteriology; Dr. F. W. Gethro, in charge of Dental Anatomy and Operative Technics; and Dr. A. D. Black, in charge of the Junior work in Operative Dentistry.

The annual session has been lengthened to include thirty-two weeks exclusive of holidays, teaching six days per week, making the actual work of instruction equal to the full nine-months' academic course. The educational requirements for registration have also been advanced to graduation from a recognized high school or an equivalent preliminary education.

The school continues in a prosperous condition.

CHAPTER XIII.

UNIVERSITY SCHOOL OF PHARMACY
(By PROF. OSCAR OLDBERG, Pharm. D., Dean)

Founding of the School of Pharmacy in Connection with Northwestern University—Promoters of the Movement—School Opened in 1886—Its Extensive Equipment—Instruction Rooms and Laboratories—Number of Students in Eighteen Years—They are Drawn from Practically All the States and Territories—Present Location of the Institution—Library and Value of Equipment—Annual Expenditures—Faculty of 1905.

The Executive Committee of the Board of Trustees of Northwestern University, upon the motion of Dr. David R. Dyche, at its regular meeting April 10, 1886, adopted a resolution favoring the establishment of a School of Pharmacy and invited the co-operation of friends of sound pharmaceutical education in the project. Associated with Dr. Dyche in this movement were Messrs. Ezekiel H. Sargent, Theodore H. Patterson, Wilhelm Bodemann, Henry S. Maynard, Oscar Oldberg and John H. Long. The organization of the school was completed and the addition of this department of the University was formally approved by vote of the Board of Trustees in June. The new school was opened to students on the first day of October, 1886, with a more extensive equipment than that of any other American pharmaceutical school existing at that time. In addition to its other instruction rooms

the School of Pharmacy of Northwestern University provided four laboratories. One of these—and the first of its kind in the history of pharmaceutical education—was a special laboratory for systematic practical training in the work of preparing and dispensing medicines in accordance with physicians' prescriptions. This "dispensing laboratory" proved to be one of the most important and useful features of the new institution. The other laboratories were a chemical, a microscopical, and a manufacturing laboratory.

During the first eighteen years of its career, from 1886 to 1904, the School of Pharmacy of Northwestern University has had an annual attendance averaging 215 students. These students have come from all the States and Territories of the United States except Nevada and Delaware. Degrees have been conferred by this school upon 1,516 graduates up to the end of the academic year 1903-1904. The number of students in attendance in 1903-1904 was 284.

The School of Pharmacy is now housed in Northwestern University Building, corner of Lake and Dearborn streets, Chicago, where it occupies all of the fourth and part of the fifth floor, the twenty-six rooms used exclusively by this school having a total floor space of about 27,000 square feet. It has now seven laboratories, with an aggregate floor space of 10,780 square feet and provided with over 300 individual work-tables, enabling that number of students to be concurrently at work. There are two lecture rooms, one capable of seating 184 pupils and the other 96.

The library of this school contains about 1,000 bound volumes, of an estimated value of not less than $3,400 (March, 1905). The museum contains over 2,000 selected specimens of drugs, pharmaceutical and chemical products, industrial materials, etc.

The value of the furniture, fixtures, apparatus, instruments, books, museum specimens and other educational equipment and materials is not less than $26,500 (March, 1905).

The annual expenditures, including salaries, furniture, apparatus, materials and other necessary current school expenses, amount to about $29,000. It should be remembered that this sum does not include any rent.

The teaching staff of the School of Pharmacy in 1905 embraced the following names:

Thomas Franklin Holgate, Ph. D., Acting President of the University.

Oscar Old'erg, Pharm. D., Dean. Professor of Pharmacy and Director of the Pharmaceutical Laboratories.

William Edward Quine, M. D., Emeritus Professor Physiology, Therapeutics and Toxicology.

Harry Mann Gordin, Ph. D., (University of Berne, Switzerland), Professor of Organic Chemistry and Director of the Organic Chemical Laboratory.

Theodore Whittelsey, Ph. D. (University of Goettingen, Germany), Professor of Inorganic and Analytical Chemistry, and Director of the Inorganic Chemical Laboratories.

Raymond H. Pond, Ph. D. (University of Michigan), Professor of Botany, Microscopy, Pharmacognosy and Bacteriology, and Director of the Microscopical and Bacteriological Laboratories.

Maurice Ashbel Miner, Pharm. M. (University of Michigan), Assistant Professor of Pharmacy, in charge of the Manufacturing Laboratory. Curator.

Charles Waggener Paterson, Sc. B., Ph. C. (Northwestern University), Assistant Professor of Organic Analytical Pharmaceutical Chemistry, in charge of the Organic Chemical Laboratory. Registrar.

Harry Kahn, Pharm. M. (University of Michigan), M. D. (Northwestern), Assistant Professor of Physiology and Materia Medica.

David Charles Eccles, Sc. B., A. M. (Columbia University), Instructor in Pharmacy, in Charge of the Dispensing Laboratory, Secretary of the Faculty.

Gustave E. F. Lundell, Sc. B. (Cornell University), Instructor in the Inorganic Chemical Laboratories.

Gerhard H. Jensen, Sc. B. (Cornell University), Instructor in Botany and Pharmacognosy.

John Ferd. Fischnar, Ph. C. (Northwestern), Assistant in the Pharmaceutical Laboratory.

William Henry Harrison, Ph. C. (Northwestern), Assistant in the Chemical Laboratories.

Ernest Woollett, College Clerk, Instructor in Bookkeeping and Business Methods.

Lee R. Girton, Ph. G., Lecture Assistant in Inorganic Chemistry.

All these teachers devote their time to the School of Pharmacy exclusively, with the exception of the Professor of Physiology and Materia Medica, who has no laboratory courses under his charge.

The professors are provided with private offices and laboratories for the effective performance of their duties under the most favorable conditions and for research work.

CHAPTER XIV.

THE WOMAN'S MEDICAL SCHOOL
(By ELIZA H. ROOT, M. D.)

Demand for Higher Education for Women —First Steps in Founding Woman's Medical College—Promoters of Movement in Chicago — "Woman's Hospital Medical College" Founded in 1870—First Faculty —Story of "The Little Barn"—Career of Dr. Mary H. Thompson, Drs. Byford, Dyas and Others—Some Notable Graduates—A Period of Struggle—Institution Reorganized in 1877 as Woman's Medical College—President Byford Dies in 1890 —Institution Affiliated with Northwestern University—Is Discontinued in 1902 —Graduates in Foreign Missionary and Other Fields—Alumnae Organization.

About the middle of the nineteenth century there was a great awakening along lines of intellectual freedom. It spread like a tidal wave over the country, and it traveled into the frontier West in "the prairie schooner." The slave question became a burning one, and one that required courage to attack openly. Women caught the spirit of the times and began to enter their own claims for greater freedom. Equal suffrage came to the front, enlisting men as its champions, and brought women before the public with a most unprecedented frequency and prominence. The question of a more liberal education for women became a question of fervent heat, permeating every walk of life. Women began to teach in our public schools and to plead for better preparation for their work.

No question, perhaps, has enlisted the championship of noble, free-minded men and women more than did the question of admitting women to our colleges and universities on the same terms as men. Among the innovations of that time was the urgent appeal made to the medical colleges by women seeking a medical training. There was no use in trying to evade the question; it was up and sides must be taken, and were taken. Men of noble stamp took the affirmative and advocated the right of women to a medical education. Men of equally noble stamp, but less liberal in their views, took the negative, and would lock all doors of learning against the importuning woman. In the eastern part of our country medical schools were approached, but no entrance was obtained until Dr. Elizabeth Blackwell succeeded in gaining entrance to the Geneva Medical School in New York, from which she graduated in 1849. In Philadelphia the movement met with an opposition that led to the founding, in 1850, of the Woman's Medical College of Pennsylvania, which is still a prosperous school of medicine. In the Middle West women were repeatedly asking for admission to the Medical Colleges of Chicago and elsewhere.

In 1852 Emily Blackwell attended a course of lectures in Rush Medical College.

She was denied admission the second year and went to Cleveland, Ohio.

There are very incomplete records of this case, but referring to this period of inquiry that led to the founding of the Medical College for Women in Chicago, the late Professor Charles Warrington Earle says: "This much, however, is known: the Illinois Medical Society, saturated with the then prevailing prejudices against female medical education, censured the college for admitting women to its institution."

Six or eight years after this Dr. Mary H. Thompson came to Chicago and entered upon practice. The city had poor hospital facilities at this time, and when the Civil War broke out between the North and the South, many women—soldiers' wives—were left with children helpless and nearly destitute. To meet the demands for medical care made by these women and their children and the poor generally, the Chicago Hospital for Women and Children was founded in 1865. This hospital, founded on the basis of a charitable institution, soon won a clientele among the poor, its dispensary and wards being well patronized. The clinical advantages afforded by the hospital consequently provided the nearest approach to an institution for medical instruction that was open to women in the West seeking a medical education. Applications were made to the hospital for clinical instruction; but while the hospital could furnish excellent clinical advantages, there was no place provided for giving didactic instruction, and no properly organized body to bestow a medical diploma when the course was finished.

Dr. Mary H. Thompson, who took an active part in founding the hospital, asked at two different times for the admission of women into Rush Medical College and was refused. In the meantime she became acquainted with Dr. William Heath Byford, of the Chicago Medical College, which was

then, as now, the Medical Department of the Northwestern University. Dr. Byford espoused the cause of the women who were asking for admission to medical lectures. He laid the matter before his Faculty, giving the measure his hearty support. This college consented to admit women, but only four entered. The remainder of the applicants, pending the discussion and aware of the uncertainty of what the decision might be, had gone East to the Woman's Medical College in Philadelphia, to New York, or had given up the idea of studying medicine. The four women who entered the Chicago Medical College—one of the number being Dr. Thompson herself—attended lectures in that institution for one year. Dr. Thompson, already a graduate in medicine, received the diploma of the institution, which was granted, after some hesitancy and warm discussion upon the propriety of granting the degree of Doctor of Medicine to a woman. Dr. Thompson was thus the first and only woman, for years, to hold a diploma of the Northwestern University Medical College of Chicago.

The following year "mixed classes" were found to be objectionable, and women were refused further admission. This refusal, together with the increasing number of applications, determined the founding of the Woman's Hospital Medical College in 1870.

Once decided upon, the despatch with which this college started, notwithstanding the lack of money for the enterprise, is remarkable, and is characteristic of the energy and push that existed among the citizens of a young and growing city.

Dr. Byford was the instigator, by suggestion and generous aid, of the establishment of the new college. He was, in fact, its founder.

"The first meeting," according to the records, "was held at Dr. Byford's office, at No. 60 State Street, Chicago, August 2,

1870." This meeting was held "for the purpose of considering the expediency of the organization of a Woman's Medical College in Chicago." There were eight physicians present at that first meeting: Drs. William H. Byford, Mary H. Thompson, Eugene Marguerat, R. G. Bogue, Norman Bridge, Charles Warrington Earle, Addison H. Foster and T. D. Fitch. A Faculty was formed, in part, that night, and was composed of those present at the meeting, with Dr. William Godfrey Dyas added to the list. Of this original number, only three are now living (March, 1905), Drs. Marguerat and Foster, both now weighted with years, and men who have followed an active pioneer practice that has been crowned with achievements that have contributed to the making of modern methods in medical education and practice possible, and Dr. Norman Bridge, now of Pasadena, Cal., who has won an honorable and honored place in the medical profession and who is widely known as an authority on tuberculosis and climatology.

At this same meeting—a most important one in its relation to the medical training of women in the West—committees were appointed for the purpose of procuring a place in which college work could be commenced.

A little band of nine physicians, without means and without professional sympathy or approval, was now a college without a home. But this difficulty was soon overcome. By October 1, 1870, the faculty was completed and a home secured.

The records are very meager in regard to this important event. But it is evident that some ceremony was observed, for Dr. Byford was chosen on September 12, 1870, "for the opening address to be given in a public hall." At this same meeting a "time table" was adopted, and a committee on announcement was appointed.

The college was founded under the name of "The Woman's Hospital Medical College of Chicago," with Dr. Byford as its President. Drs. Byford, Thompson and Dyas (with his noble and high-minded wife, Miranda B. Sherwood Dyas) were active promoters of the new college and the hospital; in fact, the hospital was more than once saved from ruin by the energy, influence and faith in the cause by Mrs. Dyas.

In an address delivered February 27, 1879, Dr. Dyas said of the school's origin: "Whatever merit attaches to the project— whether in its inception, in its furtherance, or in its subsequent progress—can be claimed by no one to the same extent as by Professor Byford." Just and true as this tribute is, to one who gave so much of his life to this institution, it must not be forgotten that Dr. Dyas himself, and his wife, took no small part in promoting the college, especially in its early history and its struggles against adversity, prejudice and fire.

The first regular course of lectures began with seventeen students, and was given in the building occupied by the hospital referred to above, then situated at 402 North Clark Street, Chicago. The session was a greater success than the most sanguine friends of the movement had dared to hope. The year closed with the first graduating exercises (1871). A class of three were given diplomas by the college. All three of these ladies had had a first year's course in some other college—two of the number— Mrs. Kent and Julia Cole-Blackman—having taken theirs in the Chicago Medical College the year before.

A spring course, from April 1 to July 1, 1871, was held, and was attended by fifteen students. The second session began October 3, 1871, in rooms fitted up at Nos. 1 and 3 North Clark Street, near the bridge, with the following named Faculty, which was practically the same as that for the first year: William H. Byford, M. D., President of the Faculty and Professor of Clinical Surgery of Women; William G. Dyas, M. D., F. R. C. S. I., Professor of Theory and Practice of Medicine; A. Fisher, M. D., Professor Emeritus of Surgery; R. G. Bogue, M. D., Treasurer of the Faculty and Professor of Surgery; T. D. Fitch, M. D., Secretary of the Faculty and Professor of Diseases of Women; Eugent Marguerat, M. D., Professor of Obstetrics; Charles G. Smith, M. D., Professor of Diseases of Children; Mary H. Thompson, M. D., Professor of Hygiene and Clinical Obstetrics and Diseases of Women; Samuel C. Blake, M. D., Professor of Diseases of the Mind and Nervous System; G. C. Paoli, M. D., Professor of Materia Medica and Therapeutics; S. A. McWilliams, M. D., Professor of Anatomy; Charles W. Earle, M. D., Professor of Physiology; Norman Bridge, M. D., Professor of Pathology; A. H. Foster, M. D., Professor of Surgical Anatomy and Operations in Surgery; M. Delafontaine, Ph. D., Professor of Chemistry; Samuel Cole, M. D., Professor of Ophthalmology and Otology; P. S. MacDonald, M. D., Demonstrator of Anatomy. Six of this Faculty were clinical instructors at the Chicago Hospital for Women and Children and at the Cook County Hospital. The Board of Trustees was chosen from the Faculty and from the Hospital Board (see second annual announcement 1871-72), which united the two institutions, ostensibly in oneness of purpose, if not in harmony.

The work of the young College was scarcely well begun when the Great Fire of October 9, 1871, swept away the college and hospital, with all their material belongings. The fire swept away the larger part of the city, including its entire business portion. Desolation and ruin were complete throughout the city. Although three-fourths of the Faculty had lost their homes, their offices and libraries, the members convened on the 10th of October, amid the smoking ruins of a destroyed city, and decided that the College should be continued. The scattered students were notified and lectures were resumed on the West Side—the only considerable portion of the city that had escaped the fire. A residence at 341 West Adams Street afforded shelter to the College, while the hospital was re-established at another residence, 600 West Adams Street, which is still standing. To this location the College was soon again moved. In 1872 the College was moved again, this time to a home of its own, the first in its hitherto checkered existence. This home is known in the history of the institution as "The Little Barn." This barn was of mean proportions, situated in the rear of the lot occupied by the hospital—and on which the hospital now stands—on the corner of Adams and Paulina Streets. The barn, as it stood, was offered gratuitously by the hospital authorities to the Faculty for a college building. Enough money was expended upon this shabby old barn, built of wood, to make a fairly comfortable and moderately convenient Woman's Medical College. On the first floor was a small lecture room, which served as a library, faculty room and museum. The second floor was used for practical anatomy.

There were five classes graduated from "the little barn," the members of which have attained to honor and able distinction in the medical profession. Among those most successful may be mentioned the following:

Dr. Julia Cole-Blackman, of Geneva, Ill., whose life has been devoted to matters pertaining to medicine, as the wife of one of the leading surgeons of Kane county, Ill., and the only surviving member of her class. She was the first woman to become a member of the Fox River Valley Medical Society, and has been an active and honored member for years.

Dr. Rosa Engert, of the class of 1873 (there was no class graduated in 1872), was of German birth and practiced medicine in Chicago for many years, when she retired to private life. She came to Chicago after receiving a training in a German school of midwifery. She was not satisfied with the limits to which this training confined her, so she entered the College and became one of its honored graduates. She was at one time attending surgeon at the Chicago Hospital for Women and Children, and connected with the College as instructor. She also established the Engert Prize for the best work with the microscope and maintained it for several years. Dr. Margaret E. Holland, of the same class, served the Chicago Hospital for Women and Children, as interne, for one year after graduation, and then went to Houston, Texas, where she still is in practice. She has done praiseworthy pioneer work for the medical woman, winning the respect and confidence of the medical profession of a conservative Southern city and a practice that has brought her a fitting competency. She has served in various positions in which her work has promoted the public health and welfare.

Of the class of 1874 Dr. Lucinda Corr, of Carlinville, Ill., has won distinction as a physician of skill and as an active philanthropist. She has always been an active member of the Illinois State Medical Society, taking active part in its proceedings, and has won an honorable place in the ranks of the profession in Illinois, where she stood shoulder to shoulder with her husband, a broad-minded man of ability and endowed with an enterprising public spirit. Dr. Lettie Mason Quine, of the same class, was the first medical missionary sent

to China from this College and the third medical woman sent to China by the Woman's Foreign Missionary Society of the Methodist Episcopal Church. After her return to America she became the wife of Dr. William E. Quine, of Chicago, and continued active in missionary society work and never lost her interest in the medical missionary. She died an honored and valuable member of the Northwest Branch of the M. E. Woman's Foreign Mission Board.

Last, but not least of this class, may be mentioned Dr. Sarah Hackett Stevenson, who is widely known and who has won place and position in college, hospital and society excelled by none and equaled by few. After graduation in medicine with honors, she was appointed to the chair of Physiology in her Alma Mater, which she filled until 1881, when she resigned this chair to take that of Obstetrics, which she filled until 1894, when she resigned from the Faculty. While a member of the Faculty she was, for a time, its Secretary. Her vote on questions of standards is found recorded in favor of the highest, even when expediency demanded a medium policy. She founded the Chicago Maternity Hospital, an unique institution, in that it has connected with it a training school for nursery maids. She was the first woman to secure membership in the American Medical Association.

Of the class of 1875 Dr. Edith A. Root, of Denver, Colo., may be mentioned as the most prominent figure. She has practiced in Denver, where she first located over thirty years ago, and has done her share of pioneer work in winning confidence for the medical woman. Of the class of 1876 Drs. Margaret Caldwell of Waukesha, Wis., and Harriet E. Garrison of Dixon, Ill., are both conspicuous examples of successful achievements attained by medical women.

Leaving the alumnæ of "the little barn"

and returning to the history of the College proper, we approach a new epoch in the history of the institution. As early as 1873 there began a growing dissatisfaction among students and Faculty regarding "the little barn" as a properly equipped college building. Many means of escape from the increasing dilemma were thought of, chief among which was a new building. Union with the Northwestern University was also discussed, and a committee was appointed as early as 1875 to confer with the University regarding the matter. Nothing more than a report "of progress" ever came of this committee's efforts. There was no money for University affiliation nor for the new building; still the idea of a new college building was not lost sight of by the more interested and progressive members of the Faculty who were anxious to put the College upon a more substantial footing. During this same year several resignations from the Faculty took place; the office of Corresponding Secretary was created and Dr. Mary H. Thompson was elected to fill the position; some amendments to the constitution and by-laws were enacted for the purpose of improving the existing standard for entrance upon the study of medicine and for graduation, and Dr. Sarah Hackett Stevenson was appointed to the chair of Physiology. The new building remained a matter of prime importance in the minds of those who strongly favored the movement, while others as strongly opposed it, believing it to be "an unwarranted venture." The prospects for further progress were certainly not very encouraging; finances were low, and some of the most desirable members of the Faculty were threatening to resign if the building was undertaken. As an indication of the financial standing we find these figures for the year 1874: "Receipts, $758; expenditures, $958, with but few assets and a debt on the present building."

Notwithstanding these gloomy and discouraging conditions, there were those on the Faculty who firmly believed that the means for a new building were within reach, if a proper plan could be agreed upon. While desirable progress must remain at a standstill, for awhile at least, the college course must be provided for. Vacancies, caused by resignations, were filled; the course (1874) was made to consist of twenty-one weeks; holiday vacations were provided for and the summer courses were continued.

During this period of the College history, Dr. William Godfrey Dyas was President of the Faculty; he was elected in April, 1873, and served until the year 1877, Dr. Byford meanwhile remaining President of the Board of Trustees and on the list of teachers. In 1876 finances were a little easier. The total receipts for that year were $1,105; expenditures, $893.93, with assets $533.57; liabilities, $555.50. This year the munificent sum of $25 was appropriated for the Department of Chemistry, to which Dr. Plymon S. Hayes had been appointed to succeed Dr. Delafontaine, resigned. The facilities for teaching were seriously affected by the financial stringency, and students naturally complained. "The little barn" was uncomfortably small and wholly inadequate for proper class work.

In May, 1876, a committee was appointed on a new building, progress was slow and conditions began to be desperate. At a meeting held early in 1877, we find it recorded that, "Professor Earle delivered the same old speech on a New College." This year proved a revolutionary year in the history of the College. In February and March of this year of 1877, it became imperative that something be done. The number of students was falling off; the restraining conservatism of a large number of the Faculty, together with the half-hearted interest they took in the work of "teaching women," blocked all progress. A committee was appointed, composed of Professors Byford, Dyas and Bartlett, to investigate the institution in all its bearings upon medical instruction. This committee reported that, for the future life and progress of the school, it was indispensable to secure a better building and apparatus for teaching purposes, and that the poor attendance and half-hearted interest on the part of the Faculty was working great harm to the institution. To build or rent a building was now the question. The latter would involve a large expenditure of money and add little or nothing to the property holdings of the College. This step was advocated by some and opposed by others. The new building idea was strongly held to by a few devoted and progressive members of the Faculty, and it was strongly opposed by those who held illiberal and pessimistic views on the cause they had practically espoused. It was impossible to arrive at any agreement. Affiliation with the Northwestern University was again considered, but there were financial reasons on both sides that made affiliation impracticable.

At a meeting held March 27, 1877, Dr. Byford spoke warmly of the lack of apparatus, and means of illustrating lectures, the tardiness and want of interest shown by the Faculty, and the extreme poverty of the College. Something must be *done* or close the College. At this meeting a committee of three was appointed with Dr. William H. Byford, Chairman, for the purpose of suggesting a name for a new College, to be reorganized "on some basis which would insure better facilities for teaching and a better place to teach in." A motion prevailed at this meeting that every member of the Faculty, except the committee on reorganization, resign. Resignations were handed in and Dr. Dyas

vacated the chair, which was now occupied by the Chairman of the Reorganization Committee.

The Faculty as reorganized consisted of William Heath Byford, A. M., M. D., President and Professor of Obstetrics; T. Davis Fitch, M. D., Secretary of the Faculty and Professor of Gynecology; Charles Warrington Earle, A. M., M. D., Treasurer and Professor of Diseases of Children; Isaac Newton Danforth, A. M., M. D., Professor of Pathology; John E. Owens, M. D., Professor of Surgery; Henry M. Lyman, A. M., M. D., Professor of Theory and Practice of Medicine; Daniel Roberts Brower, A. M., M. D., Professor of Materia Medica, Therapeutics and Nervous Diseases; Sarah Hackett Stevenson, M. D., Corresponding Secretary and Professor of Physiology; David Wilson Graham, A. M., M. D., Professor of Anatomy; Plymon S. Hays, M. D., Professor of Chemistry. Dr. Mary H. Thompson was invited to the chair of Clinical Medicine, but refused to accept. This was certainly a missed opportunity, for the doctor had absolute control of the clinical material at the Chicago Hospital for women and children, the one institution where women could or should have been able to receive bedside instruction—a privilege decidedly limited in the men's colleges at that time. The new Faculty organized, it now became necessary to form a plan that would secure the means needed for building.

This new organization began business with the sum of ten dollars in its treasury. Nothing daunted, it organized a stock company, in June, 1877, under the name of the Woman's Medical College of Chicago, severing all organized connection with the Chicago Hospital for Women and Children. A fair-sized modern residence, at 337 and 339 South Lincoln Street, was bought and remodeled into a very complete College building. This building contained two amphitheaters, a comfortable anatomical laboratory, and a fairly well equipped chemical laboratory. It was a vast improvement on the previous accommodations. Indeed, it placed the Woman's Medical College of Chicago among the recognized Colleges of Medicine. Classes doubled in size. The increase in requirements and demands for better opportunities soon made it necessary to erect a new and larger building, which was completed in 1890. The old building was remodeled for laboratory and dispensary purposes, and was connected directly with the new one.

The new building had two amphitheaters with a seating capacity each of one hundred and fifty, new laboratories and other additional conveniences. From a poor, penniless and despised institution, the Woman's Medical College had grown to a well equipped institution with valuable property holdings, and its earnings allowed all running expenses and a fair dividend rate on the money invested. The year that marked the completion of the second and entirely new building also marks the death of Dr. Byford, which was a great shock to the College and to the profession at large. He died on May 21, 1890, after his life-work and hope had been realized. A noble, strong and practical friend had been called home, but another who had been equally devoted, and who had worked hard for the accomplishment of these results, remained to us, namely, Charles Warrington Earle, who was elected President by the Faculty, to succeed his life-long friend and co-worker.

With the change that had taken place in public sentiment concerning the admission of women to higher educational institutions, and the high standing which the College itself had attained, it now seemed practicable, on the part of the Northwest-

ern University and on the part of the College, that the two institutions should become allied. This question of alliance had been considered before, but was never taken up with the same seriousness of purpose as now. In 1892, the College was made a department of the University, and assumed the name "Northwestern University Woman's Medical School." The former graduates of the College, "by the action of the Universities Authorities, were made Alumnæ of the University." The University made additions to the College building, at considerable expense, which were equipped as a chemical laboratory and commodious and convenient dispensary rooms.

The school continued prosperous for a few years, when the number of students began to fall off in consequence of co-education being adopted in many of the leading medical colleges of the country. As a financial investment it began to fall behind—there being a small deficit each year —and the University sold the property and closed the school in June, 1902.

Dr. Byford served the College, except for an interval of about four years, from its organization in 1870 until his death in 1890. He was succeeded by Dr. Charles Warrington Earle, first as President of the Faculty and later as Dean, serving until his death in November, 1894. Dr. I. N. Danforth was then appointed Dean by the University authorities, and continued in office until 1899, when he resigned and was succeeded by Dr. Marie J. Mergler, a graduate of the class of '79, who held the office until her death in May, 1901. Dr. Eliza H. Root, also a graduate of the school (class 1882), was appointed Dean by the University Trustees, and went out of office with the closing of the school. Dr. John Ridlon succeeded Dr. Mergler as Secretary of the Faculty and its Executive Committee, in

1899, and continued in office until the school was closed.

The school was built up, maintained and its welfare promoted at the expense of much energy, faithfulness and self-sacrifice on the part of its most interested friends. For many years it was necessary for the Faculty to assume large financial responsibility, which was, in fact, assumed chiefly by Drs. Byford and Earle. The work accomplished by the school has not been a small or an insignificant work.

Early in its history, missionary societies began to inquire for terms for the education of their students designed for the medical mission field in foreign countries. Fees were reduced one-half for these students when the institution needed money, and each member of the Faculty was doing the work assigned him or her without pay or price. The training which these students received made it a desirable and profitable measure for the missionary societies to establish scholarships for the education of their medical missionaries.

In 1884 a scholarship—*"The Grace Chandler Scholarship"*— was created by Mrs. Chandler, of Detroit, Michigan, for the Woman's Presbyterian Board of Missions of the Northwest. This scholarship was secured through the influence of Dr. Sarah Cummings-Porter, a graduate of the School and, for many years, medical missionary in Japan, and Dr. D. W. Graham, a loyal friend of the institution from the time that he came onto the Faculty in 1877. Other scholarships were founded from time to time as follows:

Nos. 2-3. *"The Emily W. N. Scofield Scholarship,"* by Mrs. Scofield, of Elgin, Ill., for the Northwest Branch of the Woman's Foreign Missionary Society of the M. E. Church.

No. 4. *"The Woman's Board of Missions of the Interior"* (of the Congregational church).

No. 5. *"The Woman's Presbyterian Board of Missions of the Southwest."*

No. 6. *"The Elizabeth Skelton-Danforth Memorial Scholarship."*

This scholarship was founded by Professor I. N. Danforth, in memory of his late wife, and in recognition of her long and active interest in all that related to the education of women.

The *"Lucy S. Ingals Prize Scholarship"* was founded by Professor E. Fletcher Ingals, long a member of the Faculty, and who served the institution as Treasurer for several years. This scholarship was founded for the purpose of encouraging original work in Medical Science and to promote higher medical education. It was conferred as a prize for excellent original work done in some branch pertaining to the Science of Medicine.

Five of these scholarships were purely missionary, while another was at the disposal of other students when a missionary student was not offered as a beneficiary. Consequently, the Alumnæ of this school have furnished some fifty women medical missionaries who are working, or who have worked, in India, China, Japan, Korea, Persia, Africa, Mexico and Alaska. China alone has been supplied with twenty-two women medical missionaries from this school. Dr. Lettie Mason-Quine, previously mentioned, was the first one sent out from this school; Dr. Anna D. Gloss, of Pekin, China, class of 1885, has been in the mission field since her graduation, and is still there doing heavy medical work. Dr. Gloss was sent out to aid Dr. Estelle Akers-Perkins, of the class of 1881, who is still in Pekin. Boxer uprisings, plague or famine have in no way deterred these women from the work in which they have engaged heart and soul. Of the number sent out, so far as we know to date, only two have died in the field: Dr. Anna Larson, in China, and Dr. Yasu Hishekawa, in Japan. The latter was a native Japanese woman who was sent to America by one of the school's alumnæ, a medical missionary to Japan, for the purpose of receiving a medical education in this school. Two have died since their return home. These medical missionaries are all in charge of hospitals where they practice general surgery and medicine and are training native women as "helpers" in their work, caring for the sick and afflicted natives.

Drs. Ellen M. Lyons, in Foochow, China, and Izilla Ernsberger, in India, are examples of the faithful and persevering work that is being carried on by medical missionaries sent our from the Woman's Medical School by Methodist, Presbyterian, Baptist and other Foreign Missionary Societies.

Turning from the foreign field to the home-workers, we find that a large percentage of the graduates have filled, or are filling, hospital and college positions. that involve responsibility and skill.

The graduates of this school have been the first and only women, so far (1905), to secure, by competitive examinations, the position of interne in Cook County Hospital. Dr. Mary E. Bates, now of Denver, Colo., was the first, receiving her appointment in 1881. She has been followed by seven others, all of whom filled their terms of service with credit.

Positions in State and other institutions and in other States of the Union, have been won by these earnest women. Colorado, Indiana, Iowa, Michigan, Texas, and Massachusetts are among the States, outside of Illinois, where they are filling responsible positions in State institutions. One has been a member of the Colorado Legislature and one was at one time Railroad Surgeon for a road in the West, and the first woman to fill such a position. Others have been and are members of Boards of

Health. The first woman to pass the examination for the position of interne in the public institutions at Dunning, Cook County, Illinois, was Marie J. Mergler, of the class of 1879. She passed with high credit, was recommended for appointment, but was never indorsed by the County Commissioners because she was a woman.

"We believe that nothing in the entire history of the College was so conducive to the high rank which it attained, as the persistent efforts on the part of the students to be given an opportunity to fairly test their ability by entering into the competitive examinations, and by insisting on equal privileges with the men in holding positions in their public institutions." (Dr. Mergler.)

A total of 575 women were graduated from the school. The large majority have been and are successful members of the medical profession. Death has claimed a considerable number. Chief among these, we find the name of our lamented friend, Dr. Marie Josepha Mergler, who by means of persistent, hard and faithful work, won a place among the foremost surgeons of the West, and who enjoyed the confidence of the medical profession. She stood high with her colleagues, and was an active member of local and State Medical Societies. She began teaching in her Alma Mater after she graduated, in the Spring Course. The following year she studied abroad, and further prepared herself to fill the chairs of Histology and Materia Medica. Later she succeeded Dr. William H. Byford, at the time of his death in 1890, to the chair of Gynecology, which she held at the time of her death. She was Secretary of the Faculty from 1885 to 1899, when she was appointed Dean of the Northwestern University Woman's Medical School (her Alma Mater) by the Trustees of the University, on the nomination to the position by the Faculty of the School. She won a lucrative practice and left at her death a competent estate. She was prompt and faithful to duty and never betrayed a trust or confidence. During her lifetime she held several important hospital positions, retaining them until her death.

The writer, Eliza H. Root, matriculated in 1879, graduated in 1882, doing her first teaching in the school in the Spring Course of the same year. From the day of matriculation to the closing of the school, her connection with it was never severed. She served her Alma Mater as Assistant, Professor (State Medicine and Medical Jurisprudence, later on Obstetrics and Clinical Obstetrics) and as Dean.

There is an organization of the Alumnæ known as the Alumnæ of the Woman's Medical School (nee College). This Association placed a portrait bust of Dr. Byford in the College building, founded a Charles W. Earle Memorial Library that had accumulated over 600 volumes at the time of the school's closing. In 1896 it issued a history of the "Alumnæ of the Woman's Medical College of Chicago—1870 to 1896." The organization still exists and is the only organized body representing what was once one of the leading and prosperous institutions of the City of Chicago and the Middle West.

CHAPTER XV.

UNIVERSITY SCHOOL OF MUSIC

(By PROF. P. C. LUTKIN, Mus. D.)

Sphere of Music in Higher Institutions— Its Influence on Character and as the Hand-Maid of Religion—Higher Aspects of the Art—Its Growth in the Universities—History of its Connection with Evanston Educational Institutions—Northwestern Female College Merged into Evanston College for Ladies in 1871— Two Years Later the Latter becomes a Part of the Northwestern University— Struggles, Changes and Growth of Later Years—Some Notable Teachers—Increase in Roll of Pupils—Need of Ampler Buildings—Music Festivals.

Universities and colleges have been rather tardy in recognizing the proper sphere and scope of music in the economy of intellectual and psychical development. It has been looked upon as a graceful accomplishment and a more or less fascinating and attractive art, but its far-reaching influence on character, its importance to many of the practical relations of life, its complexity as an art, its discipline as a study, its manifold demands upon the intellectual, physical and spiritual faculties, and its vital relation to the emotions, religious and otherwise, are all matters that have been but little appreciated or understood.

That music has a definite influence in molding and developing character there can be no doubt. Beginning with the cradle,

the mother's lullaby soothes the restless babe, and the songs of childhood have a direct bearing on the ethics of the young. In the school-room, music lessens the tedium of study and can be made the vehicle for inculcating good morals and awakening a love for the beautiful, both in verse and music. An appreciation of the emotional qualities of music tends to keep alive the gentler states of feeling, and the finer intuitions of youth, which are only too often blunted, if not entirely destroyed, by contact with the selfishness and sordidness of social and commercial amenities in later life. Song is the core and essence of college spirit, and the only concrete and adequate expression of that spirit. It is the only means by which unity of sentiment or feeling can be jointly and satisfactorily manifested. It heightens our joys and pleasures, lessens our griefs and sorrows, increases our affections and incites to worthy endeavor.

But it is principally as the hand-maid of religion that music has its greatest value. From the street-corner rally of the Salvation Army to an oratorio performance in cathedral walls, music voices and intensifies every shade of religious emotion. Here again it forms the one medium of expression in which rich and poor, saint and sinner, join in common utterance of praise or supplication. It is hard to conceive of the services of the church without the aid of music. It is equally indispensable at the revival meeting or the most elaborate ceremonial, at the wedding, or at the funeral service, for the joy of Christmas or Easter, or for the sorrow of penitential seasons. Sermons can be preached with mighty eloquence in the musical settings of the Crucifixion, the Nativity or the Resurrection, but no spoken sermon can replace the hymns of the church.

In its higher aspects as an art, music is a world of unceasing delight to the initiated, a world devoid of cares and anxieties and free from evil associations or suggestions. Far beyond the power of words it depicts the finest gradations of feeling and the subtlest shades of expression. It has logic, proportion, order and symmetry, in the highest degree. To infinitely more rhythmic possibilities than exist in poetry, it adds the warm color of painting, the beauty of outline and dignity of sculpture, and the structural principles of architecture. No other study combines, to the same degree, the esthetic and the mechanical, the spiritual and the physical. The science of music is an extremely complex and intricate matter. It has to do with elements that are inexhaustible in their rhythmic, melodic and harmonic combinations, even when confined to a single instrument, such as the piano or organ. When they are applied to works for chorus and full orchestra, the element of tone color is added with its infinite possibilities, and the command of all this material only comes after years of study involving harmony, counterpoint, form and instrumentation. Even if these are mastered, they count for little without the saving grace of artistic intuition and a keen sense of esthetic values.

In the study of music as an applied art, totally different factors come to light. Phys-ical dexterity is a prerequisite and, to this foundation, a long and arduous schooling is necessary before the demands of a modern technique are approximated. This rigid disciplining of brains and fingers in muscular and nerve control, often means the deliberate sacrifice of much that is attractive in the social or intellectual life, and gives rise to perplexing problems in the process of elimination. Be this as it may, the fact remains that the study of music alone, in any wide sense, is a liberal education in itself, calling upon a fine perception of mathematical niceties, logical development, artistic symmetry and emotional expression.

The study of music, theoretically, is rapidly finding its way into all of our leading universities. For a number of years, courses in harmony, counterpoint, fugue, musical form and musical history have existed at Harvard in charge of Professor John Knowles Paine. The result has been that Boston comes nearer giving us a distinctive school of American composition than any other city in the country. Yale followed the example of Harvard by installing Horatio W. Parker in a chair of music, a few years ago. Professor Parker is unquestionably the greatest American composer of large choral works with orchestral accompaniment. His oratorios are given at the prominent English musical festivals, where they are most highly esteemed and considered quite on a par with similar productions from any living composer. Not only is credit allowed at Yale for theoretical studies as at Harvard, but also for proficiency in performing ability as well. Another gifted American composer, Edward A. MacDowell, was appointed to the recently endowed chair of Music at Columbia College. Professor MacDowell has written some important orchestral compositions, but his fame lies principally in his works for the piano. In this regard he is a conspicuous figure among modern composers. His works possess a rare and distinct personality, and his workmanship is characterized by extreme finish and delicacy.

This tendency to make room for our most gifted tone-poets in our leading universities is most commendable and is full of promise for the future. It is only through freedom from the harassing cares of the ordinary professional connection that a man can give himself up to the creation of the larger and more pretentious works of art. A generously endowed chair, with a limited amount of routine duties, gives opportunity for the necessary abstraction and concentration, and the university environment will be an additional incentive to scholarly work.

Under its cultured Professor of Music, Hugh A. Clarke, the University of Pennsylvania has won an enviable reputation with its theoretical courses in the higher mathematics of music. Professor Clarke has perfected a system of instruction by mail that has largely extended his sphere of influence. Cornell and Princeton have not as yet made official recognition of music, but Syracuse University has a finely developed School of Fine Arts, which not only embraces music, but painting, sculpture and architecture as well. It ranks next to the College of Liberal Arts in numbers and importance, and each department has its own faculty.

The University of Michigan maintains a chair of theoretical music, ably filled by Professor Albert A. Stanley, who is also Director of an affiliated "University School of Music," which supplies excellent instruction in all branches of music. Professor Stanley has evolved and developed a series of May Festivals, which are the event of the college year at Ann Arbor, and which bring the masterpieces of musical art before large and enthusiastic audiences. His ex-

ample is followed on a smaller scale by a number of Western State Universities, where provision for the study of music is made, both theoretically and practically.

A school that has had a notable influence for good is the Conservatory of Music at Oberlin, Ohio. It is the largest and most widely known of the departments of Oberlin College. It is finely housed in a hundred-thousand-dollar building, the gift of an Oberlin graduate who has since come to fame and fortune. Its success and prosperity are almost entirely due to the foresight, good judgment and abiding faith of its late director, Professor Fenelon B. Rice.

These facts are very encouraging, and all this artistic activity must have a direct and important bearing on our national development. We sadly need the counterbalancing influence of art in these days of intellectual and commercial expansion. It is the best antidote for materialism, realism and anarchy. The appreciation of the beautiful is not a question of birth, of wealth, of social position or even of intellect or education. It is the common ground on which all innately refined and sensitive souls meet in a brotherhood of mutual love and kindly feeling.

The first definite record of musical instruction in connection with Evanston educational institutions is found in the catalogue of the Northwestern Female College in the year 1865. Instruction in music had doubtless been given previously to this date, and in all probability from the founding of the College in 1855; but printed information to that effect is missing. In 1865 Nicholas Cawthorne is mentioned in the annual catalogue as teacher of the piano, organ and voice. He was organist of the First Presbyterian church in Chicago. He had an assistant instructor, James A. Doane. The following quotation from the catalogue will give an idea of the advantages offered:

"The course of study in the Department is intended to furnish a solid musical education, both in practice and theory. Instruction will be given in the following branches: System of Notation, Harmony, Composition with reference to Musical Forms, and Instrumentation, Practice in Chorus singing, Pianoforte and Organ. A complete course of study will extend through four years, a new class opening each term. Diplomas certifying proficiency and qualifications as artists or teachers will be given to those finishing the entire course. Each student receives two hours' instruction per week and has the use of a piano for private practice one and one-half hours daily. The rudiments of music are taught and chorus singing practised in classes.

PIANOFORTE COURSE.

"*First Year.*—Richardson's Methods and pieces by Baumbach, Grove, etc.

"*Second Year.*—Studies by Duvernoy and Czerny, and pieces like 'Monastery Bells,' Wely; 'Carnival of Venice,' Bellak, etc.

"*Third Year.*—Czerny studies, Dr. Callcott's Musical Grammar, Zundel's Harmony, Overtures to Stradella and Der Freischutz.

"*Fourth Year.*—Cramer studies, Sonatas of Beethoven and Clementi, Marx Musical Composition."

Mr. Cawthorne remained in charge for another year when he was succeeded by Oscar Mayo, who came highly recommended from the Ohio Wesleyan Female College. With the advent of Mr. Mayo the following announcement was made: "The Music Department of the College offers extraordinary facilities to students of the Piano, Organ or Vocal Music. The Department is under the supervision of Professor O. A. Mayo, an educated and scientific musician, a thorough teacher and a brilliant performer of classic as well as modern Piano and Organ music." Mr. Mayo was to appoint his own assistants and the following courses were announced:

Organ Course.—Zundel and Rink.

Piano Course.—Rudiments, practice of easy exercises, Mason's Technics, Heller studies, Etudes of Chopin, Mendelssohn, etc.

As assistant, Professor Mayo had Count Laurent de Fosso, who also taught French, Spanish, and Italian. Piano, organ, melodeon and guitar were the branches taught, and from sixty to seventy students took music.

In 1871 the Northwestern Female College was merged into the Evanston College for Ladies, with Miss Frances Willard as President. Professor Mayo continued in charge of the Music Department, and there are evidences of an attempt to improve and enlarge the musical advantages. Only ten names appear as music students on the catalogue this year, but these obviously studied music to the exclusion of other studies, while previous student lists included those who had taken music as a supplementary study as well.

In 1873 the absorption of the Evanston College for Ladies by the Northwestern University was announced, together with plans for the formation of a Conservatory of Music on the European plan. This went into effect with the completion of the present Willard Hall, and the top story was devoted to the study of art and music. An attempt was evidently made to secure a good faculty, as arrangements were made with some of the best known musicians of that date in Chicago. Professor Mayo remained at the head. Mr. Silas G. Pratt, a pianist and composer of attainments, who had recently returned from his studies in Berlin, appears to have been head instructor of the piano. Mr. Pratt organized the present

Apollo Club in the city, and was later chiefly instrumental in promoting the movement which resulted in the Auditorium Building and the Orchestral Association. James Gill, who was for many years the most prominent baritone in Chicago, was engaged as instructor in voice culture, and Hans Balatka, the veteran chorus and orchestral conductor, had charge of chorus and quartette classes. The following year Mr. Pratt's name disappeared from the catalogue and later Mr. Balatka's, their places being filled by musicians of less celebrity. Eighty-eight students appeared on the list after the installation of the Conservatory of Music, but catalogues of the succeeding three years are missing. In 1876 Professor Mayo was succeeded by Oren E. Locke and the Conservatory of Music appears for the first time in the University Catalogue. Professor Locke had been a student in both the Leipzig and Boston Conservatories, and introduced the so-called "Conservatory System" into the school. The characteristic feature of this system was the teaching of piano, voice and orchestral instruments in classes instead of private individual instruction. The University catalogue gives but thirty-three students in the Conservatory at the end of Professor Locke's first year, and the attendance increased but slowly for the three succeeding years. In 1880-81 matters improved materially, one hundred and sixteen students being enrolled, and the number steadily increased until the maximum of two hundred and thirty-one was reached in 1886-87. James Gill was the only faculty member left over from the previous regime. From time to time Professor Locke had associated with him E. S. Metcalf, voice instructor; Joseph Singer, instructor of violin; Professor R. L. Cumnock, instructor of elocution; Professor A. S. Carhart, lecturer on the laws of sound; Warren Graves, instructor of piano and or-

gan, and C. M. Hutchins, instructor of band instruments. In 1880 and 1881 the present Dean of the School of Music was instructor of piano and organ, prior to his departure for Europe for a three years' course of study in Berlin, Vienna and Paris. In June, 1884, Professor Locke, in a printed report to the Board of Trustees, makes mention of nine thousand lessons having been given during the year, of fifteen pianos being in use, and calls attention to the growth and future possibilities of the school. Three students were graduated this year and the following courses were in operation:

Course 1.   Piano.
Course 2.   Voice.
Course 3.   Organ.
Course 4.   Orchestral Instruments.

In the year 1887-1888 the numerical prosperity of the school declined and continued to do so until 1890-91, when Professor Locke resigned, leaving the affairs of the school in a somewhat chaotic condition. There was a strong sentiment in favor of discontinuing the Conservatory of Music, but yielding to the wishes of Miss Nina Gray Lunt, an effort was made to continue the study of music in the University. At her suggestion Peter C. Lutkin, of Chicago, was put in charge, and gave a portion of his time to the reconstruction of the music department. A faculty was hastily organized, of which the principal members were: J. Harry Wheeler, a widely known vocal instructor, formerly a prominent member of the New England Conservatory of Music, Boston; Allen Hervey Spencer, a well-known concert pianist and teacher of Chicago; Joseph Vilim, violin instructor, and William Smedley, choir-master of St. James' Church, Chicago, as instructor of choral singing and sight-reading. A Glee Club was organized for the first time in the University, and also a Cecilian Choir for the young women. Eighty-nine students attended during the year, and a creditable concert was given at its close in the First Methodist Episcopal Church, in which the advanced piano and voice students, the Glee Club, and the Cecilian Choir took part. Three students were graduated.

This first year's work was looked upon as tentative and, at its completion, a formal proposition was made by the Director, which included a professorship in the College of Liberal Arts, and the severing of his city connections in order to devote his entire time and energies to the up-building of the music school. Largely upon the recommendation of Mr. James H. Raymond, the then chairman of the committee on the Conservatory of Music, the Executive Committee accepted the proposition of Professor Lutkin. The official appellation of the school was changed from "Conservatory of Music" to "Department of Music," and the courses were rearranged so as to mark a distinction between those studying as amateurs and those studying professionally. Diplomas were not issued at all and certificates only to those completing the Professional Course. One hundred and twenty-eight students attended this second year and the income of the school increased about seventy-five per cent.

The financial stringency of the year 1893-94 was felt to the extent that the attendance and income were practically at a standstill. Several changes were made in the faculty. Harold E. Knapp, who had recently returned from two years of study at the renowned Leipzig Conservatory of Music, succeeded Joseph Vilim as instructor of the violin. William H. Knapp, as instructor of voice and 'cello; William H. Cutler, as instructor of piano; and William Hubbard Harris, as instructor of piano and harmony, were added. A choral society, confined to students of the University, had been organ-

ized and gave two concerts at the Congregational Church. The works performed were Gaul's cantata of "Israel in the Wilderness" and Haydn's "Creation." In both cases the solo parts were nearly all taken by members of the University. An important event was the formation of a String Quartette, of which the personnel was as follows:

First Violin, Harold E. Knapp.
Second Violin, Joseph Bichl.
Viola, Caspar Grilnberger.
Violoncello, William H. Knapp.

This organization permitted us to give five recitals of Chamber Music, which added greatly to the interest of the school year. Sixteen recitals were given by the students and four were graduated from the Professional Course.

The year 1894-95 saw a large increase in the attendance and prosperity of the school. The number increased from one hundred and twenty-nine to two hundred and three, and the graduates from four to eight. Mrs. George A. Coe, who had recently returned from extended studies in Berlin under Heinrich Barth and Moritz Moskowsky, was added to the faculty as instructor of the piano, and instruction in wind instruments was provided for. Eighteen recitals were given by the students, and at the eight faculty recitals, many important works by Beethoven, Mendelssohn, Dvorak, Schubert, Chopin, Goldmark and Weber were given with the assistance of the University String Quartette. The Director gave a number of lectures analyzing the thematic structure of important works given by the Thomas Orchestra.

As the attempt to establish a good choral society within the University had not been altogether successful, owing to the constant shifting of membership, Professor Lutkin assumed the conductorship of the Evanston Musical Club, in the hope that the larger field would give more favorable results. In this he was not disappointed, and the history of that organization will be found elsewhere in these pages. Membership in the Club has always been open to students of the University, and the privilege has been taken advantage of, more particularly by the members of the Department of Music. The theoretical courses were greatly extended this year, and arranged on a four-year plan to conform to the courses in the College of Liberal Arts. The student recitals presented, in an excellent manner, a higher grade of compositions than had ever been given before, notably piano concertos by Beethoven, Mozart and Mendelssohn. A small pipe organ was added to the equipment of the school, which greatly increased the study of that instrument. The Department had now reached a point where its self-maintenance was fully assured, and it was sadly in need of larger and better quarters.

In the following year (1895-96) the official title of the school was changed from "Department of Music" to "School of Music," thus putting it upon the same basis as the other professional schools of the University. Mr. J. Harry Wheeler was succeeded by Karleton Hackett as Director of the Vocal Department. Mr. Hackett had recently come to Chicago after three years' study with Vincenso Vannini, the famous voice instructor of Florence. He had formerly studied singing with Cornelius Chenery of Boston, and theory under Professor Paine while a student at Harvard. Miss Carlotta M. Glazier was added as instructor of piano. The various courses were considerably strengthened, and the theoretical study of music was made the kernel of all graduating requirements. The theoretical studies embraced harmony, musical history, counterpoint, and musical form. The ground was taken that mere technical facility, even when allied to distinct musical

talent, was not sufficient to complete a course in a University school, but rather a comprehensive understanding of the nature and material of music, and the fundamental principles of good art. The scholarly aspects of music are thus emphasized, and the endeavor is to graduate well-equipped musicians rather than superficial and showy performers. The same theoretical studies are required of all candidates for graduation, be he pianist, organist, singer or violinist.

Professor Lutkin was appointed Dean of the reconstructed school, the other members of the faculty ranking as Instructors. As the Dean was also .Professor of Music in the College of Liberal Arts, the theoretical classes in the School of Music were open to the College students as electives in their various courses. Owing to the prevailing financial stringency there was but a slight increase in the attendance this year. The number of graduates remained the same. Fifteen student recitals, two student concerts with orchestra, eight chamber music recitals and four faculty concerts were given. A student orchestra of twenty-five had been organized, which gave very creditable performances. One of the chamber music recitals was devoted exclusively to serious works by various members of the faculty, including a String Quartette by Harold Knapp, part of a Trio for Piano, Violin and 'Cello, by P. C. Lutkin, and songs by Hubbard W. Harris. Among important works brought out were the Brahm's Quintette for Piano and Strings, Op. 67, in which Mrs. Coe assisted the University String Quartette, the Dvorak Quintette, Op. 81, and Quartettes by Schumann and Beethoven. Under Mr. Harold Knapp the violin department greatly increased in numbers, and furnished an excellent nucleus for the school orchestra.

In his annual report to the Board of

Trustees, President Rogers called attention to the urgent need of providing a suitable building for the School of Music, adding that after the Academy—which had been provided for—it was the next most desirable acquisition. The recommendations of President Rogers bore fruit more promptly than was expected. The lack of accommodations for the school in Woman's Hall, the poorly adapted rooms for instruction and practice, not to mention the unavoidable annoyance to college students by the incessant playing and singing, rendered it all but imperative that other quarters should be supplied. Although the finances of the University were in a somewhat crippled condition owing to the temporary loss of income from the Grand Pacific property, it was decided to erect a building for the special and exclusive use of the School of Music. A site was decided upon immediately to the north of Woman's Hall, and ground was broken during the summer of 1896. The building was completed during the following fall and winter, and taken possession of at the beginning of the spring term, in 1897. In Woman's Hall fourteen rooms had been in use by the school. Music Hall, as the new structure was named, provided us with nineteen rooms and a small recital hall, seating about three hundred. Seventeen of these rooms were at once put into service, and the year's records showed an increase from 207 to 218 students. The dedication of the new building was marked by two faculty concerts and a students' recital. At the first of them a chorus from the Evanston Musical Club and the School of Music Orchestra assisted in the following program, given on the evening of April 26, 1897:

Chorus, "The Heavens Are Telling"............Haydn
        Prayer by President Henry Wade Rogers.
Aria, "Rejoice Greatly"........................Handel
        Miss Helen Buckley.
        Address by Professor P. C. Lutkin.
Overture, "The Marriage of Figaro"............Mozart
        Orchestra.

Andante for Violin and Orchestra..........P. C. Lutkin
        Mr. Harold E. Knapp.
Songs, "The Broken Lyre," "Shepherd of
        Israel," "From the Bosom of Ocean
        I Seek Thee"..................Hubbard W. Harris
        Miss Buckley.
Quartette for Strings, C major.........Harold E. Knapp
        The University String Quartette.
Sanctus, from Messe Solonelle...................Gounod
        Mr. W. F. Hypes, Chorus and Orchestra.

After the concert a reception was held and the building was thrown open for inspection. On the following evening a Chamber Music Recital was given, in which Mrs. George A. Coe, pianist, Miss Mabel Goodwin, soprano, and the University String Quartette took part. The program was as follows:

Trio for Piano, Violin, and 'Cello, Op. 97....Beethoven
Songs, La Serenata ....Tosti
        Ecstasy ....Beach
        May Morning ....Denza
Quartette for Strings, G Minor..................Grieg

Nine students were graduated this year in the Normal Course, and one from the advanced, or Artist's Course. Twenty-four recitals and five concerts, with orchestra, were given by the students, and six chamber music recitals and four concerts by the faculty. The student orchestra assisted the Evanston Musical Club in their performances of Handel's Messiah and Haydn's Creation. In all directions the year showed substantial progress.

The first complete year in the new building (1897-98) found its capacity tested to the utmost. The attendance increased from 218 to 293. The theoretical courses were extended by the addition of classes in Analysis and Sight-reading. The recitations in Musical History under the charge of Mrs. Coe were doubled. The classes in Sight-reading were thrown open to students of the Garrett Biblical Institute, and the latter part of the year was devoted to hymn music with the object of demonstrating the fundamental principles of good church music. A good pipe-organ, with two manuals and pedals, and blown by a water-motor, was erected in the recital hall. Miss Carlotta M. Glazier was succeeded by Miss Una Howell, a graduate of the advanced course of the school, and Mr. Franz Wagner of the Thomas Orchestra, succeeded Mr. W. H. Knapp in the University String Quartette, and was added to the faculty as Instructor of Violoncello. Mr. Walter Keller was also added as Instructor of Piano. The usual student and faculty concerts were given and the commencement concerts presented a distinct advance on previous efforts, both in the selections and in the performance of the same. Twelve students were graduated from the Normal Course. Doubtless the added dignity and importance given to the school by being housed in its own building had much to do with the general prosperity.

The succeeding year was a repetition of the previous experience, that a very decided gain in one year was followed by a slight reaction in the following. The scholastic year 1898-99 showed a decrease of nine students, but a gain of ten per cent in the income. The discrepancy between the loss in attendance and the gain in income meant that a larger percentage of students remained through the year, and that there was a corresponding decrease in the unsatisfactory patronage, composed, for the most part, of triflers who enter and remain but a term or two.

The basement of Music Hall had been originally designed for a gymnasium for women, and the prospect of soon having a properly equipped plant was hailed with much delight and enthusiasm by those interested. It was a keen disappointment to many when it was decided to sub-divide the ground floor to make space for the imperative demands of the music school. The results of this change added ten practice rooms and a much-needed class room, seating seventy-five, to the equipment of the

school, and temporarily relieved the pressure for more space.

The student recitals averaged one per week and evidenced a very good standard of attainment. Nine students were graduated from the Normal Course, and three from the Advanced Course. The usual series of chamber music concerts was interrupted by the loss of the viola player in the University String Quartette, owing to his departure from the city.

The year 1899-1900 exhibited an increase of about five per cent in the attendance (the total number being 297) and of fifteen per cent in the income of the school. The largest class in the history of the school was graduated, ten in the Normal Course and three in the Advanced Course. The most important event of the year was the rearrangement of courses, requiring four years for graduation. The theoretical requirements consist of ten terms of harmony, four terms of musical history, four terms of sight-reading and musical dictation, eight terms of counterpoint, two terms of musical form, eight terms of analysis and four terms of ensemble playing. In addition the candidate is required to show distinct talent as a performer in the Practical School, or as a composer in the Theoretical School. In the former case, two programs are required of standard classical compositions. Students creditably finishing two years of this course are entitled to a certificate, but a diploma is given only for the longer course. These requirements are equaled by but few schools in the country.

Mr. Arne Oldberg, who had recently returned from extended studies in Europe, was added to the faculty as Instructor of Piano. Mr. Oldberg studied piano in Vienna with Leschetitzky and, later, composition in Munich with Rheinberger. His abilities, both as a pianist and composer, have attracted the favorable attention of the profession in Chicago. Mr. Day Williams, one of the most gifted of local 'cellists, succeeded Mr. Franz Wagner both in the String Quartette and as instructor of the violoncello. Mr. Walter George Logan succeeded Mr. Caspar Grilnberger as assistant in the violin department, and Mr. Frank Lee Robertshaw was put in charge of the sight-reading classes. The regular faculty of the school now consisted of fifteen members, of whom six taught piano, two violin, two voice culture, two organ, two theory, and one each, musical history, composition, violoncello, flute, clarionet, oboe, bassoon, cornet, French horn and trombone.

The first decade of the music school under its present head was completed with the year 1900-01, and the event was marked by several matters of interest in the development of the school. A decided increase in attendance crowded the capacity of the building to the utmost, and forced many students to make arrangements for their practice at private houses. The total number of students for the year was 348—a gain of fifty-one over the previous year. For the first time a fixed sum per term was charged for the regular courses, instead of a graduated scale depending upon the individual instructor. This charge was thirty-five dollars per term, and included private instruction from the principal instructors in instrumental or vocal music, and the privilege of attendance at the required classes. Considering the advantages offered and the quality of instruction given, the charge was put at a very reasonable figure. In fact, the results at the end of the year proved that the sum was hardly sufficient to cover the expenses of the course, and a recommendation to increase it to forty dollars per term was put into effect the following year.

The record for the ten years showed an increase in attendance from eighty-nine to 348, and, in income, of over 400 per cent. Six members of the faculty give their entire time to the school as against none in 1890-91. Extended and comprehensive courses have been developed and the reputation of the school is such as to bring a better class of students each year. Graduate students from the smaller music schools come to us and expect, as a matter of course, that much of their work is not up to our requirements. In fact, there are very few who are able to enter the second year's work.

The following changes took place in the faculty: Walter G. Logan was succeeded by Lewis Randolph Blackman, a young violinist of excellent reputation in Chicago. Mr. John Harlan Cozine, an experienced and well known voice specialist and choral conductor, and Mr. Anthony Stankowitch, an instructor of the Clavier method, were added to the list of instructors. During the year an interesting series of historical recitals was given by various members of the faculty, beginning with a lecture on Primitive Music, with illustrations, by Mrs. Coe. This was followed by Bach, Mozart, Beethoven, Schubert, Schumann and Chopin programs, in which various members of the faculty assisted. The University String Quartette had a number of outside engagements which brought forth a number of flattering press notices of their excellent ensemble work. This was notably the case at Cleveland, where Mr. Oldberg assisted in the performance of a new Trio of his own composition for piano, violin and 'cello. During the year the Dean of the school was honored with the degree of Doctor of Music by the Syracuse University.

Some five years ago a Preparatory Department was formed for giving thorough and systematic instruction to beginners in music. The instructors are drawn from the more talented graduates of the school, the present list including Mr. Louis Norton Dodge, Director; Mrs. Nina Shumway Knapp, Miss Elizabeth Raymond, Miss Mabel Dunn, Miss Edna Eversz, Miss Katherine Hebbard, Miss Laura Case Whitlock and Mr. Curtis A. Barry. This department has been very prosperous. It has its own solo classes and recitals which stimulate ambition and emulation, and it produces far better results than the usual private home-training of young children. It also prepares the more gifted ones for the regular courses and accustoms them to public appearances.

The year 1901-02 was signalized by advancing to professorships Mrs. Coe, Mr. Oldberg and Mr. Harold E. Knapp, in their respective specialties of piano and musical history, piano and composition, and violin and ensemble playing. In other regards the faculty remained the same, with the exception of Miss Una Howell, who resigned at the middle of the previous year, and was replaced by Miss Margaret Cameron, a pupil of Leschetitsky, who has won an enviable position as pianist and teacher in the city. The registrations numbered 366 for the year, and the income exceeded that of the previous year by about 20 per cent. Some ten students completed the Certificate Course, while three were graduated from the Diploma Course. Of the thirty-five or more student recitals, thirteen were individual recitals, giving many important musical compositions and, for the most part, the programs were memorized. Advanced students played the following concertos: For piano, the Beethoven C minor, Mendelssohn G minor, Rubinstein D minor, Grieg A minor and St. Saens G minor; for violin, the Beethoven D major (first movement), Mendelssohn E minor and Vieuxtemps A minor.

Advanced classes have done very creditable work in eight-part counterpoint, as well as in double and triple counterpoint, fig-ured chorals and fugue up to four parts. Many typical works by Bach and Beethoven have been analytically dissected and also concertos, chamber music and symphonies from full score. Capable students have assisted at the meetings of the musical section of the Woman's Club, the Thomas Orchestral Class, local concerts, and have given bimonthly Sunday afternoon entertainments at the University Settlement. Two important compositions of Professor Oldberg's have received their first performance at the faculty concerts, a Trio for piano, violin and 'cello, and a String Quartette. This latter work was repeated at a concert of the Chicago Manuscript Society, of which Professor Oldberg is President. Other numbers on the same occasion were the Finale from a String Quartette by Professor Knapp, and a sacred solo for contralto with violin obligato by Professor Lutkin.

A matter of congratulation has been the steady increase in the interest and appreciation of the Chamber Music Recitals by our faculty. Works of this character are the most difficult to comprehend in all musical literature, and many of the greatest composers have confided their loftiest inspirations to this most refined form of composition, calling, as it does, upon a company of individual artists for its proper representation. The patience, devotion and zeal necessary to produce a good ensemble of concerted instruments is something enormous, and the school and the community are very fortunate in having professional musicians of such high ideals and ambitions. For the sake of those interested, a list is appended of the works given during the past seven seasons, a number of which are but rarely performed:

Bach, Concerto for two Violins.
Bargiel, String Quartette No. 3, Op. 15.
    Trio for Piano, Violin, and 'Cello, Op. 6, No. 1
    Trio for Piano, Violin, and 'Cello, Op. 6, No. 3.

Beethoven, String Quartette, Op. 15, No. 1.
　　　　String Quartette, Op. 18, No. 2.
　　　　String Quartette, Op. 18, No. 6
　　　　String Quartette, Op. 59, No. 1.
　　　　String Quartette, Op. 59, No. 3.
　　　　String Quartette, Op. 18, No. 2.
　　　　String Quartette, Op. 18, No. 4.
　　　　String Quartette, Op. 95.
　　　　String Quartette, Op. 74.
　　　　String Trio, Op. 9, No. 3.
　　　　Trio for Piano, Violin, and 'Cello, Op. 97.
　　　　Serenade for Violin, Viola, and 'Cello, Op. 8.
　　　　Serenade for Flute, Violin, and Viola. Op. 25.
　　　　Septette for Clarionet, Bassoon, Horn, and
　　　　　　Strings, Op. 20.
　　　　　　(Four movements. The wind instruments
　　　　　　supplied upon the organ.)
　　　　Concerto for Violin, Op. 61.
　　　　　　(First movement with Leonard Cadenza.)
　　　　Sonata for Piano and Violin, Op. 17.
Borodine, Serenade Espagnole for Strings.
Brahms, Quintette for Piano, two Violins, Viola, and
　　　　'Cello, Op. 34.
　　　　Sextette for Strings, Op. 18.
Chopin, Polonaise for 'Cello and Piano, Op. 3.
Dvorak, String Quartette, Op. 51.
　　　　Quintette for Piano, two Violins, Viola, 'Cello,
　　　　　　Op. 81.
　　　　Bagatelles for two Violins, 'Cello, and Organ,
　　　　　　Op. 47.
　　　　Bagatelles for two Violins, 'Cello, and Organ,
　　　　　　Op. 85.
　　　　String Quartette, Op. 96.
Cesar Franck, Sonata for Piano and Violin.
Foote, Arthur, Quintette for Piano, two Violins, Viola
　　　　and 'Cello, Op. 38.
Gade, Trio for Piano, Violin, and 'Cello, Op. 42.
Godard, Trio for Piano, Violin, and 'Cello, Op. 72.
Goldmark, Quintette for Piano, two Violins, Viola, and
　　　　'Cello, Op. 30.
Golterman, Concertstueck for 'Cello, Op. 65.
Grieg, Sonata for Piano and Violin, Op. 45.
　　　　Sonata for Piano and Violin, Op. 13.
　　　　String Quartette, G. minor.
Hubbard W. Harris, Sonata for 'Cello and Piano.
　　　　　　(Second and third movements.)
Handel, Sonata for Piano and Violin, A. major.
Haydn, String Quartette, Op. 77, No. 1.
　　　　Variations from Kaiser Quartette.
Hoffmann, Sonata for Violin and Piano, Op. 67.
Harold E. Knapp, String Quartette in C major.
Liadow, Scherzo for Strings.
P. C. Lutkin, Trio for Piano, Violin, and 'Cello, Op. 1.
　　　　　　(Second movement.)
　　　　Andante for Violin and Orchestra. Op. 6.
　　　　　　(Orchestral part arranged for strings and organ.)
Mendelssohn, String Quartette, Op. 12, No. 1.
　　　　Trio for Piano, Violin, and 'Cello, Op. 66.
　　　　Sonata for 'Cello and Piano, Op. 45, No. 1.
Mozart, Quintette for Clarionette and Strings.
　　　　String Quartette No. 14.
Arne Oldberg, String Quartette, C minor.
　　　　Trio for Piano, Violin and 'Cello, E minor.
　　　　String Quartette, D major.

Rubinstein, Sonata for 'Cello and Piano, Op. 18.
　　　　　　(First movement.)
　　　　Sonata for Violin and Piano, Op. 13.
　　　　　　(First movement.)
　　　　String Quartette, Op. 17, No. 3.
Charles Schubert, Andante and Caprice for 'Cello.
Schubert, String Quartette, Op. 29.
　　　　　　(Two movements.)
　　　　String Quartette, D minor.
　　　　　　(Two movements.)
　　　　String Quintette.
　　　　Trio for Piano, Violin, and 'Cello, Op. 99.
　　　　Trio for Piano, Violin, and 'Cello, Op. 100.
　　　　　　(Two movements.)
　　　　Quintette for Piano, Violin, Viola, 'Cello, and
　　　　　　Bass, Op. 114.
Schumann, String Quartette, Op. 41, No. 2.
　　　　Quintette for Piano, two Violins, Viola, and
　　　　　　'Cello, Op. 44.
　　　　Quartette for Piano, Violin, Viola, and 'Cello,
　　　　　　Op. 45.
Saint Saens, Quintette for Piano and Strings, Op. 14.
Svendsen, Allegro Scherzando.
Tschaikowsky, String Quartette, Op. 11.
　　　　Trio, for Piano, Violin and 'Cello, Op. 50.
Wathall, A. G., Suite for Strings.
Weber, Concerto for Clarionet, Op. 74.
　　　　(Orchestral part arranged for Organ and Strings.)
Weber, Josef Miroslav, String Quartette in B minor.

It is with difficulty that the business of
the School is properly attended to in its
present inadequate quarters. Thirty rooms
with as many pianos, are in constant use for
instruction and practice. Ten more would
only relieve our immediate necessities. A
concert hall, with larger seating capacity,
and a good-sized organ are also much needed. That the conditions exist in Evanston
for the development of one of the largest
and most influential schools of music in the
country, there can be no doubt. Students
have been registered from China, East India,
South America, Mexico, France, England,
Newfoundland, Quebec, Ontario, Manitoba
and twenty-eight of the United States. Each
year brings us a more talented and desirable
class of students, as our reputation expands.
Very capable students have been graduated
and at least three prominent Chicago
churches have been supplied by us with
organists, where the duties are as exacting
as any churches in the West. A gifted
violin student, who has received his entire

training in the school, recently played for one of the most capable judges in the country, and his work was most highly commended and a brilliant future for him predicted. Alfred G. Wathall, one of our graduates in theory, has written the music to a light opera in conjunction with George Ade, and it has had an unprecedented run at the Studebaker in Chicago. Our piano graduates have appeared professionally with success and many have established good teaching connections and send capable students to us every year. Another has gone to Madison, Wis., where he is instructor in the University of Wisconsin, has the most important church position and conducts two choral societies, one of which he organized. These instances are cited to show some of the practical results of the School.

A crying need in the musical education of America is a more thorough training in the theory of composition in music. Without this we can never attain to artistic prominence in the world of art, as far as original work is concerned. The average American composer has a smattering of harmony and, possibly, a faint idea of strict counterpoint. With this limited equipment he rushes into print with the hope of meeting the popular taste and gaining notoriety and wealth. Of the exacting discipline that · would place the material of musical composition at his ready command, the close study of the masters, the comprehension of the subtle laws of esthetics, of proportion, balance and contrast, of even the mechanical outline of musical forms, he knows little and cares less.

A University School of Music should strive to supply this great lack and to establish not only a high standard of musical learning, but of general culture as well. It should guard against the one-sided tendencies of professional education and add to it such elements as will serve to broaden the

vision, enlarge the sympathies, and sharpen the intellect and understanding. Scholarliness and thoroughness should characterize its teachings and its faculty should stand for the highest ideals of art. Of equal, if not greater, importance should be its moral tone and influence. The sensitive and emotional nature associated with the artistic temperament should be safeguarded in every possible way. In large cities there is, unhappily, a tinge of the moral laxity prevalent in European capitals among professional men. It is by no means confined to musicians. It is a most dangerous and pernicious environment for the young in their formative years, and not infrequently ends most disastrously. Against these lamentable possibilities the wholesome surroundings of Evanston offer a marked contrast. Its churches and Christian associations, its freedom from saloons and questionable resorts, together with its educational facilities and attractive location, make it an ideal home for the pursuit of a musical education.

Evanston, with its beautiful homes and cultured residents, should take a peculiar pride in the cultivation of the fine arts, and should loyally support all educational efforts in that direction. The School of Music has grown steadily from small beginnings and its one advertisement has been its own work. It has drawn to itself an able faculty thoroughly in accord with University ideals. It has an unusual proportion of men actively engaged in composition of the better sort. It attracts talented students and holds them to such an extent, that, in several instances, the entire family have changed their mode of life in order to live in Evanston, so that the student could reap the full benefit of the advantages offered by continuous residence here. With its Preparatory Department it has given opportunity to a number of its capable graduates to make a start professionally. Its faculty and student recitals have been open to the public without charge, and they have formed, together with the concerts of the Evanston Musical Club, by far the larger and more important part of the musical attractions in Evanston. Concert programs that are arranged to please the average audience are rarely of real educational value. The school has consistently and persistently held to the highest standards, and the value of such a rigid policy is not always readily recognized, but the wisdom of it has been amply justified by the steady increase in attendance and appreciation. There is no surer gauge of real refinement and culture than the measure of esteem in which good music is held in a community.

But Evanston should not confine its ambition or interest to the welfare of a Conservatory of Music. Great possibilities exist here for the development of the art outside the scope of a good music school. Music Festivals, after the plan of Cincinnati or Worcester, are quite feasible here. They are managed successfully, both from an artistic and a financial point of view, at such small places as Ann Arbor, Mich., and Oberlin, Ohio, where they have but a fraction of our advantages or facilities. Still they contrive to have good choruses and orchestras and to engage really great artists. We are more fortunately situated here, in that we have better choral resources, and that an unsurpassed orchestra can be obtained without the great expense that is entailed by transportation and hotel accommodations in places remote from large cities. The only essential lack in Evanston is a suitable hall. The rest is merely a matter of enterprise and ambition.

The music festival presents peculiar conditions for the effective performance of music—conditions that are almost a necessity for a satisfactory rendition of certain great works. These works require an enthu-

siastic and responsive state of feeling as regards the audience, and this condition is difficult to arouse without the festival spirit. The stimulating atmosphere of excitement, the cumulative effect of successive performances, the concentration of artistic talent, the relaxation from the ordinary daily pursuits, all tend to put the hearer in a receptive and appreciative attitude. All these elements react upon the performers and, as a consequence, results are realized which would be quite impossible at isolated concerts.

The permanent establishment of annual or biennial festivals would give Evanston an artistic prominence obtainable in no other manner. With its great University and its superior moral surroundings, it already enjoys a most enviable reputation as an educational center. Add to this the attraction and distinction of notable musical festivals, and Evanston will be unique among the cities of the West as an artistic and literary community. And the larger portion of gain would not be to the residents of our favored town, but to the student hailing from the farm or the country village. What an education it would be to him if, in the course of his college life, he would have the opportunity to hear the great masterworks of music given under inspiring and uplifting conditions! Coming, as they do, from all quarters of the Union, many of them would return to their homes as so many musical missionaries, fired with an ambition to do what they could for good art. Hundreds would go forth from us every year with their esthetic sense stirred and enlarged, with a wholesome respect for the great names in music and an appreciative familiarity with the standard oratorios and orchestral works. The seeds of musical culture, thus sown, would bear fruit in scores of communities, and would play no small part in the higher development of our country.

Events of 1902-03.—The year 1902-1903 was made notable by an increase of an even hundred students in attendance and of over six thousand dollars in income. Courses in English language, English literature and modern languages were added to the graduating requirements with the result of bringing to the University a better class of students, as far as general education was concerned. A series of eight concerts, known as the "Artists' Series," was begun, given alternately by members of our own faculty and by visiting artists. The latter included Minnie Fish-Griffin in a song recital; Arthur Hochman, of Berlin, in a piano recital; Bruno Steindel in a 'cello recital, and Glenn Hall, of New York, and Allen Spencer, of Chicago, in a joint song and piano recital. These concerts attracted a large attendance, both on the part of the students and the town people.

Additional quarters for the kindergarten work of the Preparatory Department were acquired in the Y. M. C. A. building, and the school was unable to supply all the non-resident students with pianos for their practicing. The graduating concerts brought brilliant performances of the Schumann A minor, and the Rubinstein D minor piano concertos, and the Pagannini concerto for violin. Four diplomas and thirteen certificates were added to our list.

Enlarged Attendance of 1903-04.—The year 1903-1904, brought the attendance just over the five hundred mark and the income up to $35,000, with eight graduates in the diploma course and eighteen in the certificate course. The first concert in the Artists' Series was a decided novelty in the way of a programme of chamber music for piano and wood-wind instruments, participated in by Messrs. Starke, Meyer, Demare, and Kruse of the Thomas Orchestra and Professor Oldberg

of our faculty. Later there was a song recital by Gwylim Miles, a violin recital by Leopold Kramer, concert-meister of the Thomas Orchestra, and a piano recital by Augusta Cotlou. As usual, the University String Quartette, under Professor Knapp, gave four excellent concerts, while Miss Cameron, Miss Hull, Mr. Blackman, and Mr. Williams of the faculty all appeared on interesting programmes. Professor Stanley of the University of Michigan gave a most entertaining lecture on early Venetian opera, and Gustav Holmquist gave a most artistic recital of Scandinavian songs. A further matter of interest was the first performance of an elaborate quintette for piano and string, by Professor Oldberg, which proved to be a work of unusual scope and worth.

Five of the advanced students and graduates went to Europe at the end of the school year to continue their work in Leipzig, Berlin and Paris, and several of them at once won prominence by reason of their talents and the schooling they had received in Evanston. Over fifty student recitals were given during the year, and many hundred compositions for piano, organ, violin and voice were performed. A house opposite Music Hall was rented and filled with pianos for practicing purposes.

Conditions of 1904-05.—The year 1904-1905 again showed a recoil in attendance after successive gains of the previous years, the enrollment dropping to 466. The loss in income was not relatively so great, as a large proportion of students remained through the year. As usual, a number of inquiring students failed to appear upon learning that the official boarding places could not accommodate them; as they or their parents objected to boarding in town, principally upon the score of expense. The graduates were four in the graduate class and fifteen in the certificate class.

The Artists' Series of concerts was a notable one. With the co-operation of the Thomas Study class and the Evanston Musical Club, famous artists and organizations appeared. The first of these was the celebrated Kneisel Quartette of Boston, who gave us a fine program, remarkable for its charm of tone, refinement of shading, and artistic interpretation. This was followed by a song recital by Muriel Foster, the greatest contralto now upon the concert stage. On the evening previous to her recital, Miss Foster appeared with the Evanston Musical Club in Dvorak's "Stabat Mater" and upon the same occasion Professor Oldberg played for the first time his new symphonic concerto for piano and orchestra, a brilliant and most difficult work, in which he scored a great success both as composer and pianist.

In February the Pittsburg Symphony Orchestra, under the magnetic baton of Emil Paur, gave Beethoven's Overture to Egmont, the same composer's Emperor Concerto for piano and orchestra with Mr. Paur at the piano, Tscharkowsky's Pathetic Symphony and Wagner's Vorspiel to the Meistersaenger. The concert provoked the utmost enthusiasm, due to the energy and virility of Mr. Paur's conducting.

The last concert by visitors was an evening of old-time music by Arnold Dolmetsch's party, performed upon the instruments for which the music was originally written, such as the spinet, harpsichord, dulcimer and viola of various kinds. In the four concerts given by our own faculty a number of standard classical string quartettes were played, and a first performance of a Quintette by Cæsar Franck, in which Mrs. Coe supplemented the University Quartette at the piano. With the assistance of Mrs. Lida Scott

Brown as reader, Mrs. Coe gave a performance of her popular melodrama, "Hiawatha," before a large and appreciative audience. The musical themes for this work are largely drawn from Indian sources, and are judiciously and effectively applied as a back-ground to the recitation of this famous poem.

The Outlook of 1905-06.—The present year (1905-1906) bids fair to be the most prosperous of all in a material sense, and the school shows, in many ways, the benefits accruing from fifteen years of endeavor to establish an institution for musical instruction upon a worthy academic basis. A new department of Public School Methods was inaugurated in the fall, designed to fit candidates for the position of supervisor of music in the public schools. There is but one school in the West that specializes to any considerable extent in this branch of work, and it would seem that such a department, with the collateral advantages of a College of Liberal Arts and a well-equipped School of Music, would be very attractive. This department is in the very capable charge of Miss Leila M. Harlow, supervisor of music in the Evanston grade schools.

The Artists' Series brought the Kneisel Quartette for its second appearance here and a song recital by George Hamlin, and will include a chamber music recital of wood-wind instruments, at which a new Quintette for piano, oboe, clarinet, French horn and bassoon of Professor Oldberg's will receive its first production, and a piano recital by Emil Paur.

That there is a coterie of ardent and sincere music lovers in Evanston is evidenced by the increasing interest taken in chamber music. The concerts of the Kneisel Quartette have been patronized to an extent which puts Chicago to the blush, and the keen and discriminating appreciation for string quartette music is largely due to the unceasing efforts of Professor Harold Knapp in this direction. He has labored for the cause in season and out of season, with unflagging zeal and enthusiasm, despite discouragements and lukewarm interest, and it is pleasant to chronicle that his high ideals and abiding faith in the best in art have at last won recognition. His capable quartette has played repeatedly in the homes of our music lovers and chamber music in every sense of the term has come to its own. Professor Knapp's able colleagues are Messrs. Lewis R. Blackman, Charles Elander and Day Williams.

Changes in Teaching Force.—The well-known contralto, Mrs. Eleanor Kirkham, was added to the vocal force of the faculty and, upon her removal to New York, was succeeded by Mrs. Lillian French Read. Provision for the study of the harp was made by the appointment of Mrs. Clara Murray, who was succeeded by Walfried Singer of the Thomas orchestra. Mr. Walter Keller and Mr. Anthony Stankowitch resigned, the latter to accept charge of a large music department in a Southern school. Mr. Alfred G. Wathall, a graduate of the school who had been appointed instructor in harmony, and who played viola in the University String Quartette, resigned in order to pursue his studies in London. The Evanston Musical Club performed a very creditable cantata of Mr. Wathall's, entitled "Alice Brand," for chorus, soli, and full orchestra. His undoubted ability as a composer has enlisted the active interest of Sir Villiers Stanford and Sir Frederick Bridge, of the Royal College of Music, London.

John Skelton was succeeded by Charles S. Horn as instructor of band instruments, and also took charge of the University Band. Mrs. Elizabeth Raymond Woodward, Mrs. Nina Shumway Knapp, and Miss Bertha A. Beeman were advanced from the Preparatory Department to the regular faculty. Mr. Irving Hamlin was appointed Secretary of the school in 1902, and greatly improved the business relations of the school, which had formerly been in the hands of inexperienced students.

The following names appear on the faculty of the Preparatory Department since 1902: William E. Zench, Mrs. Carrie D. Barrows, Grace Ericson, Elizabeth L. Shotwell, Mrs. Hila Verbeck Knapp, Sarah Moore, Juliet Maude Marceau, Nellie B. Flodin and John M. Rosborough. The last five mentioned are still upon the faculty.

Necrology of the Year.—The sad duty remains of making record of the death of two who were intimately connected with the school — the one as teacher and the other as student. Mrs. Saidee Knowland Coe, Professor of Piano and Musical History, and wife of Professor George A. Coe, of the College of Liberal Arts, died at Alameda, Cal., August 24, 1905. Mrs. Coe was a member of the faculty of the School of Music for eleven years and performed her duties with great fidelity and success. As a pianist, teacher and lecture recitalist Mrs. Coe had an extended reputation, and she was particularly interested in bringing forward new or comparatively unknown works. The courses in the History of Music were greatly extended under her direction and compared favorably with those of our greatest schools and universities. Her lectures on the music of the American Indians and on the Wagner music-dramas were especially noteworthy. Mrs. Coe had resigned her position in the School of Music and had been appointed as a special lecturer on music in the College of Liberal Arts. Her plans for a year's vacation in Europe for recreation and study were rudely shattered by her sudden death. A large circle of friends and pupils mourn her loss and untimely end.

Earle Waterous, for ten years a violin student under Professor Knapp, died at his home in Evanston November 15, 1905. Evincing signs of unusual ability as a mere child, he was given a thorough schooling and before he was out of his 'teens had acquired a very unusual technical mastery of his instrument. Interested friends sent him to Europe and he immediately took a commanding position in the Leipszig Conservatory, eliciting the most flattering comments from the local press and winning predictions of high rank as a virtuoso from his teachers. With every promise of a brilliant career he was seized with a dread disease and barely reached his home ere he passed away.

CHAPTER XVI.

UNIVERSITY SCHOOL OF ORATORY

Professor Cumnock as Founder—Growth and Standing Due to his Labors—First Class Graduated in 1881—Its Aim and Branches Taught—Building Erected—Is Dedicated in 1895—Location and Description—Advantage over Private Institutions of Like Character—Training in English Composition and Rhetoric—Enrollment According to Last Catalogue—Promising Outlook for the Future.

The existence, growth and high standing of the School of Oratory of the Northwestern University (generally known as the Cumnock School of Oratory), is largely the outcome of the life and labors of Prof. R. L. Cumnock. Entering the service of the University in the fall of 1868, he labored for ten years, doing the work assigned him in the curriculum of the College of Liberal Arts. In the fall of 1878 an urgent demand for advanced work in vocal expression and interpretation resulted in the organization of a special department known as the School of Oratory. The first class was graduated in 1881. The special purpose involved in the organization of this new department was to furnish instruction and training in three subjects, viz: Elocution, English and Physical Culture.

The chief aim of the school was to prepare young men and women to teach these subjects in colleges, academies, high and normal schools. For many years the students in this department were accommodated in the College of Liberal Arts. From 1890 to 1894 the applications for admission to the school were so numerous that many could not be accepted by reason of the meager accommodations in University Hall. In the spring of 1894 Professor Cumnock secured from the Trustees a site on the University campus and assumed the entire responsibility of erecting a building for the special use of the School of Oratory. The building, with its equipment costing $30,000, was, at its dedication on May 16, 1895, handed over to the President of the University by Professor Cumnock, entirely free from debt.

The building was named the Annie May Swift Hall, in memory of one of Professor Cumnock's former pupils, whose father, Gustavus F. Swift, of Chicago, generously contributed to its erection. It stands just northeast of the Liberal Arts Building, near the lake shore. Many of the windows look directly upon the water, and from every point the view is beautiful. The building is of the Venetian style of architecture. The basement is of rock-faced Lemont limestone, and the upper stories are a buff-colored Roman brick and terra cotta. The roof is of red tile. There are three main entrances, the one on the south leading to the broad corridor that opens into the auditorium, and the other two on the east and west sides of the building.

The auditorium, though not large, is the handsomest room in any of the University buildings. No pillars obstruct the view, as the roof is supported by iron trusses stretching from the roof girders. The floor has a gentle incline to the stage from the sides and rear of the auditorium, so that from every seat an excellent view may be obtained. This building gives the department the best facilities of any school of oratory in America, and enables it to offer special advantages to all students pursuing its course of study.

The unique feature in the organization of the work of the school is the emphasis placed upon private training. Two private lessons in elocution are given, weekly, to each student during the entire course. Being free from rent and taxes, which other schools of like character are compelled to pay, the management can afford to provide this personal training which other schools of oratory cannot, or do not, offer.

In a large measure the same personal training is carried on in English composition and rhetoric. The number enrolled in the last catalogue of the school is 214, and the patronage is increasing slowly, but steadily. The graduates of the school are filling important positions in many of the leading colleges and schools of the Middle West, while a flourishing school of oratory, named after the Director and managed by one of the former teachers of this Department, is located at Los Angeles, California.

It is safe to say that the future of this Department is secure, and that students, as they come to learn the high grade and quality of the work done here, will enroll themselves, where the highest art in public speaking and writing are essential conditions for graduation.

CHAPTER XVII.

UNIVERSITY ATHLETICS
(By PROF. J. SCOTT CLARK, A. M., Lit. D.)

The noblest and the most interesting chapter in the history of athletics at Northwestern University grows out of the fact that its founders selected for the University a site near what had long been known to lake mariners as a dangerous point on the shore of Lake Michigan. As the determination of this site settled the site of Evanston, so the configuration of the shore at this point made it inevitable that, sooner or later, there should be established here a life-saving station. Long before the days of football teams, coaches, trainers, and the like—long before a gymnasium was even asked for, a volunteer band of Northwestern students made themselves immortal and won the praise of the nation by their heroic rescue of passengers from the ill-fated steamer, the "Lady Elgin." On the 8th day of September, 1860, a merry company of four hundred souls set out from Chicago for an excursion trip. The story of the rapid destruction of the steamer by fire and the death by drowning and otherwise of all but 98 of the passengers, is one of the tragic episodes in the history of Chicago. As the terrified victims came floating toward the shore line of the University campus, clinging to bits of the wreckage, only to be tossed cruelly back by the breakers, while horrified friends who lined the bluff shrieked in agony, several students, led by Edward W. Spencer, of the class of 1861, stepped out from the crowd, attached ropes to their waists, and plunged into the surf, to risk their lives in an effort to save drowning women and children. Again and again they made their way through the angry waves and deposited in safety some fainting victim of the disaster. It was only when their own strength gave out completely that they desisted. Spencer was carried to his room in a fainting condition. He is still living (1903) in California, and it is asserted on apparently good authority that his health, throughout his long life, has been seriously affected by his voluntary exposure in behalf of the victims of the "Lady Elgin" disaster.

The wide interest excited by the action of the Northwestern students in connection with the burning of the "Lady Elgin" resulted in the organization, in October, 1872,

177

of a volunteer crew of five men from the Senior class of the College of Liberal Arts. The members of this crew have since become well known in high circles in the Central West; they were L. C. Collins, George Lunt, E. J. Harrison, Eltinge Elmore, George Bragdon, F. Roys, and M. D. Kimball. Soon afterward Dr. E. O. Haven, then President of the University, received from Commodore Murray, then in charge of the United States life-saving service, a present of a fine life-boat, and Dr. Haven committed the boat to the care of the Senior class, from whose members the crew were selected. The boat was presented with the provision "that proper care will be taken of it and that it will be officered and manned by students, who will train themselves and do their best, if an emergency arises, to help any craft that may be in danger on the coast of the University." We find no record of any immediate provision for housing the boat; but, in 1873, the students petitioned that the life-boat be taken from the exclusive control of the Senior class and be placed in charge of a crew selected from all classes, according to their best physical and moral qualifications. No action seems to have been taken during 1874, but in 1875 the boat was placed in the hands of such a crew as was called for by the petition.

In December, 1876, it was announced that an agreement had been reached with the Federal Government, by the terms of which a life-saving station was to be immediately erected by the Government on the University campus, and that a crew of five was to be selected from the student body, irrespective of classes, which was to be captained by an experienced seaman paid by the Government.

In April, 1877, E. J. Bickell, '77, was appointed captain of the new crew, and sixty other students applied for the subordinate positions. They were to receive $40 per month during the season and $3 extra for every wreck trip. In the following June the college faculty nominated as members of the crew: Warrington, '79; Hobart, '79; King, '79; Piper, '80; Shannon, '81; and M. J. Hall of the Preparatory School, and these students were duly accepted by the Government. For a time the life-boat was housed in a temporary structure on the beach, but in 1876 the Government erected the eastern two-thirds of the present Life-Saving Station at a cost of about six thousand dollars. The site selected was on ground now covered by Fisk Hall. Prior to the erection of the latter building, in the summer of 1899, the station was removed to its present site on land then newly made near the water's edge.

Since the formal organization of the Evanston life-saving crew, in 1877, as a regular part of the government service, over four hundred lives have been saved by its agency. The following tabular statement is taken from the records somewhat at random, and is typical of the work of the crew since 1883. To such rescues as these must be added scores of cases where vessels have been relieved from awkward or dangerous situations, but where it was not found necessary to remove either passengers or crews. Besides the aggregate of over four hundred lives the local life-saving crew has saved property amounting to millions in value:

Date.	Name and Class of Vessel	No Brought Ashore in Surf-boat.
May 9, 1883.	Schooner, "Kate E. Howard."	8
Sept. 10, 1886.	Schooner, "Sodus,"	5
June 10, 1887.	Schooner, "Sunrise,"	7
Nov. 24, 1887.	Schooner, "Halstead,"	10
Oct. 22, 1889.	Schooner, "Ironton,"	8
Nov. 28, 1889.	Steamer, "Calumet,"	18
May 18, 1894.	Schooner, "Lincoln Ball,"	4
May 20, 1895.	Schooner, "J. Emory Owen,"	27
Nov. 26, 1895.	Steamer, "Michigan,"	9

Of these, the rescues from the vessels "Calumet," "Owen," and "Michigan," are the most noteworthy. By reference to the dates it will be seen that two rescues were made very late in November, nearly a month after the crews were off from regular summer and autumn duty. In both cases the rescues were made in the teeth of fierce gales and blinding snowstorms. Both involved tremendous and heroic exertion on the part of the crew, in order to get the surf-boat launched at the points opposite the wrecks. The "Calumet" was stranded at the very unusual distance of one thousand yards from the shore. The aggregate value of the three vessels, with their cargoes, was over $252,000. Not a life was lost in any of the rescues enumerated in the foregoing table. Mention should also be made of the large number of persons who have been rescued from capsized row-boats and of the rescued children who have fallen from the piers.

The present captain, Patrick Murray (1904), was appointed July 18, 1903, after having served as surfman seven years at the North Manitou Island station, two years at Muskegon station, and five years at Evanston.

Captain Lawrence O. Lawson, who made such a worthy record for twenty-three years at the head of our station, was born in Sweden in 1843, and began the life of a sailor at the age of eighteen. He came to America in 1861, and sailed on the Great Lakes during the following three years. He became a citizen of Evanston in 1864, engaged in fishing for a time, and was appointed Captain of the crew in 1880. In addition to his services in aiding to save nearly five hundred lives, Captain Lawson originated the system of righting the Beebee-McClellan surf-boat, which has since been adopted by the Government for use by all the crews of the service. In rescuing the "Calumet," as already described, Captain Lawson and his crew manifested such courage and endur-

ance that Congress awarded to each man a gold medal for "saving life from the perils of the sea." The medal consists of a gold bar from which hangs a broad ribbon supporting a golden eagle, sustaining in his beak a heavy disk of gold. The medal complete weighs about four ounces. In a circle on the face of the medal are the words "United States of America—Act of Congress, June 20th, 1874." In high relief is a representation of a crew in the act of saving a drowning person. On the obverse, in a circle, are the words: "In memory of heroic deeds in saving life from the perils of the sea." In relief is a tablet, surmounted by an eagle, with a woman's figure on the left, while on the right are an anchor and seals. Each medal is inscribed to its owner: "For heroic services at the wreck of the 'Calumet,' Nov. 28, 1889." In addition to Captain Lawson, the crew who thus honored Evanston in honoring themselves were: W. M. Ewing, F. M. Kindig, E. B. Fowler, W. L. Wilson, G. E. Crosby, and Jacob Loining, all University students at the time.

BASEBALL.

Little seems to have been done in the way of general college athletics during the first twenty-five years of Northwestern's existence. In fact, systematic athletics were as yet undeveloped in this country. Lawn tennis had not been imported, track athletics were in an incipient stage, and the modern game of football was unknown. The village of Evanston was small, and the college was smaller. There was plenty of wood to saw, and there was now and then a citizen's cow to be pulled out of the slough that existed in all its depth along the present line of our railways. In such diversions as these did the early sons of Northwestern engage for the development of their physical strength and, incidentally, the repletion of their thin purses. With the incoming of the 'seventies baseball began to be called "the national game," and our boys, like all normal youths, soon caught the fever.

As early as the spring of 1871, we read of inter-class games, and in June of that year a nine, of which Mr. James Raymond was a member, placed on record the first publicly recorded score, which stood Northwestern 35, "The Prairies" (a local Chicago nine) 7. On the 4th of July, 1871, occurred a memorable series of events, no small part of which were athletic in character. This was the day when ten thousand people gathered from all the surrounding country in the campus grove; when the Ellsworth Zouaves paraded under General John L. Beveridge as Grand Marshal; when $10,-000 was raised to set the young University on its feet, and when the corner-stone of the "Evanston College for Ladies" (now Willard Hall) was laid. This was an independent school until June, 1873. Of the $10,-000 raised on this memorable day, $2,500 was given by Governor Evans, whose name our city bears; several thousands were given by other friends of higher education, and no small sum was raised, as the college paper says, "by sales and exhibitions." These exhibitions seem to have consisted of what would now be called, in the parlance of track athletics, various "events," such as jumps, ball-throwing, tub-races, boat-races on the lake, etc., etc. So we may say with much of accuracy that Northwestern's formal athletics began with a field day. Some features of this first field day are worth chronicling in detail. Here they are:

"Baseball match between Ladies' College nine and Northwestern University; prize a silver ball; score, 57 to 4 in favor of Northwestern." (What an ominous beginning for co-education!)

"Regatta—Yachts, six-oared barges, and sculls; prize an ice-set and three flags."

"Exhibition drill by the Ellsworth Zouaves."

"Baseball match with the 'Atlantics' of Chicago."

During the spring and fall of 1871 the University nine played ten games with non-college nines, including the afterward famous White Stockings of Chicago, whom the college boys beat by a score of 18 to 12, and two with Racine College, in which each side scored but once. The highest recorded score of the season was 68—a fact that speaks volumes as to the crudeness of the game and the players of those early days. Of the twelve games, our team won ten.

During the next decade, and longer, the four colleges of what was then literally the Northwest were Northwestern University, Chicago University (the old institution, discontinued in 1885), Racine College, and, later, Lake Forest University. The great State Universities that have since so largely dominated Western college athletics, were then either unborn or still in their infancy, and the custom of making long trips for intercollegiate games had not become established. We find no records for 1872 and 1873, but during 1874 a team, which included John Hamline as short-stop and Charles Wheeler as center-fielder, played nine intercollegiate games. In the "final" for "the championship of the Northwest," Racine won by a few points. As compared with "our ancient enemy," Chicago, the total score for the season was Northwestern University 42, Chicago University, 34.

From 1875 to the present day the baseball records of Northwestern are chequered but not discreditable. In 1875 we won the silver ball and "the championship for the Northwest," with Charles Wheeler as left-fielder. W. G. Evans, '77, son of Governor Evans, and George Lunt, '72, were the leaders in the University athletics of the early seventies. In 1876, at Waukegan, was formed the first intercollegiate baseball association in this section, and the games of the season transferred the silver ball and the championship to Chicago. During this year batting records of the college nines began to be published. By the terms of the constitution of this intercollegiate association, each college was to play two games with each of the other three institutions. In 1877 Chicago again won the championship. During 1878 the colors white and brown were adopted by the Northwestern players, and a regular baseball diamond was laid out, "resodded, and rolled," on the site where the Orrington Lunt Library building now stands. It was during this year that the first efforts were made to check the already growing tendency toward professionalism. Before this year the custom seems to have been to use, as players on any college team, the best men obtainable, without much scrutiny as to their actual relation to the scholastic curriculum of the college. But in the constitution of the "Intercollegiate Baseball Association" that was in force during 1878, I find the following article:

"The captains of the respective nines must file with the secretary of the Association, before April 20th, the names of their respective nines and of the substitutes, together with a certificate from the secretary of the Faculty showing that the players have been in daily attendance at their respective institutions for twenty days previous to the first announced league game."

It will be seen that, while this action did not prevent a student from entering college for a course in baseball, it was the first step toward pure college athletics in the Central West.

During 1878 the silver ball went to Racine College.

In 1879 our team defeated Racine once and Chicago twice. In 1880 the games of the Association resulted in a tie between Racine and Northwestern; and, as Racine refused to play off the tie, thus retaining possession of the silver ball trophy, Northwestern withdrew from the association.

Because of the disruption of the old league there seems to have been no intercollegiate baseball here during 1881, but in December of that year delegates from Racine College, the University of Wisconsin, the University of Michigan, Chicago University and Northwestern met in Chicago and formed a new league. The limits of our space forbid a detailed account of the baseball games from 1881 to 1903. Over our defeats it is fair to draw the mantle of oblivion: over our victories we have a right to rejoice. In 1883, when the University of Michigan had withdrawn from the base ball league, and when Beloit College had been admitted instead, Northwestern won the championship of the league without losing a single game. The team for that year consisted of Plummer, Huxford, Rollins, Stewart, Bannister, Polley, Tillinghast, Dillman and Tomlinson.

Again in 1889 we won the championship of the Northwest and a pennant, with a team consisting of T. C. Moulding, J. A. Rogers, A. P. Haagenson, M. P. Noyes, F. C. Chapin, A. B. Fleager, C. C. Johnson, L. H. Stewart, and H. H. Jones; and in 1891 the championship was again awarded to Northwestern. In 1892 we won the championship in the smaller league (the old league), and secured the second place in a new league, including the great State universities of the Middle West. In 1894 our team defeated Chicago in three excellent games, one of 12 and one of 10 innings, the scores being, respectively, 3-2, 8-1, and 6-4 in our favor. During this season we also defeated Wisconsin 9 to 8, Oberlin 11 to 6, Wisconsin again 4 to 1, and Minnesota 6 to 2.

So the season of 1894 is the banner year of our baseball history; for, by winning nine games in succession, we were fairly entitled to the intercollegiate baseball championship of the Central West. The men who thus shed undying glory on Alma Mater were: John H. Kedzie (Captain), Frank Griffith, C. N. Jenks, J. K. Bass, C. D. McWilliams, Otis Maclay, W. D. Barnes, T. H. Lewis, W. A. Cooling, C. D. Reimers, A. E. Price and C. L. Leesley. The loss of several of these star players by graduation left the team of 1895 unable to win many victories, and the team of 1896 was not much more successful. In '97 the fates were kinder to us, and we defeated Nebraska, Beloit, Ohio State, and Wisconsin, by good scores; '98 was another off year in Northwestern baseball; in '99 we defeated Chicago once and Wisconsin once; in 1900 we defeated Chicago once and Oberlin once; in 1901 Illinois was our only victim among "the big nine"; in 1902 we defeated Chicago twice, Nebraska once, and Beloit once. The seasons of 1903 and 1904 have not been successful.

THE OLD GYMNASIUM.

The movement for the erection of a gymnasium was begun by under-graduates. In October, 1875, two young men, since prominent in Evanston and Denver, Messrs. Frank M. Elliot and W. G. Evans, issued a circular setting forth the project of building a gymnasium and soliciting aid from the friends and graduates of the institution. They soon perfected an organization, under the laws of the State, with F. M. Elliot, W. G. Evans, F. M. Bristol, F. M. Taylor, A. W. McPherson, and J. A. J. Whipple as commissioners. These under-graduates proceeded to issue $4,000 worth of stock in shares of $10 each, whose duration was for

ninety-nine years. It must be remembered that the University was then still in its early infancy and that the students were few in number and poor in purse. But their faith in themselves and in the future was sublime. Fourteen hundred dollars was soon raised by sales to one hundred and twenty-nine subscribers, nearly every one being an under-graduate. Work was begun in December, 1875, and by the 1st of February the building, 40x80, resting on a brick foundation, was erected, enclosed, and partially equipped, at a total cost of $1,900. It was not found possible, at that time, to complete the exterior of the building by casing the walls with brick, according to the original plan. A bowling alley was built in the basement by the Sigma Chi fraternity, and the "gym" was very popular with the under-graduates until 1878, when it began to lose its attractions. To quote one of the original commissioners: The new generation of students did not or could not raise money to veneer the building in order to protect it and to repair the worn-out apparatus. It was necessary to do something before all should be lost or ruined. It was finally decided to have the University take the property and maintain it as a "gymnasium." Through the indefatigable efforts of Mr. George Lunt, of the class of '72, a majority of the stock was finally secured, and was transferred to the Trustees, on condition that they should complete the building, furnish it with necessary apparatus, assume all liabilities of the association, and maintain the building and the apparatus in good repair for gymnasium purposes only. The transfer was completed in the spring of 1881, and one of the first acts of Dr. Joseph Cummings, then recently elected President of the University, was to induce the Trustees to veneer the building. The interior was cased with lumber by the students and members of the Faculty, including the venerable President, the trustees furnishing only the lumber and the nails. New apparatus was put in, and the rejuvenated "gym" was opened with a public entertainment on February 20, 1883.

The feelings of the under-graduates were expressed thus by Mr. M. M. Gridley, editor-in-chief of the college journal in 1882-83: "Once more the gymnasium is a topic of great interest. It is not now, as it was last year, a source of grumbling and discontent. Instead of a broken-down, weather-beaten old building, an eye-sore to the campus, it is a fine-looking brick structure, a thing of beauty and a joy forever. . . . . We now have one of the finest and most complete gymnasiums in the West." (*Sic.*) As an assurance of better things in the college athletics, the Trustees at this time engaged a regular instructor in physical culture, Mr. C. A. Duplessis, who held the position until October, 1883, when he was succeeded by Mr. Philip Greiner. Mr. Greiner continued to act as physical instructor until June, 1894, when he was succeeded by Mr. W. L. Bryan. At the opening of the college year 1898, the gymnasium and the physical work passed into the hands of Dr. C. M. Hollister, who held the place until December, 1902. The present physical director (1903) is Mr. Horace Butterworth, who has made an enviable reputation in such work at the University of Chicago.

THE TUG-OF-WAR TEAMS.

During the later 'eighties and the early 'nineties the athletes of Northwestern obtained wide fame in a test of muscle not ordinarily given much emphasis in college athletics. We refer to our memorable tug-of-war team, of which the instructor was the organizer and a prominent member. We find the first notice of the team in 1886. In 1887 they won a medal in a contest with a team from the Casino Gymnasium, then recently established in Chicago, and later in the same year they won "the championship" and a silver cup by defeating a team from the Illinois National Guards. This original tug-of-war team consisted of Philip Greiner, H. Caddock, C. T. Watrous, W. W. Wilkinson, and C. Greenman.

During 1888, when E. B. Fowler, H. R. Hayes, J. B. Loining, J. G. Hensel, A. H. Phelps, and J. T. Hottendorf had been added to the team, Messrs. Wilkinson and Greenman having dropped out, they defeated a Pullman team, the Casino Gymnasium team of Chicago, the Chicago Amateur Athletic Club team, and the Illinois National Guard team; and in April of that year, in a contest with three teams at the Casino Gymnasium, they proved themselves champions and won five gold medals. During 1889 they continued their victories over all local teams, winning various prizes and securing possession of the Meriden cup. It was this team that really began the practice of inter-department contests at Northwestern; for we read that, on University Day, in January, 1890, the tug-of-war team defeated teams from our Medical and Dental Schools, respectively. During the spring of 1890 they defeated several local teams, and won the championship of the West, securing permanent possession of the Hub cup. After several local victories early in 1891, the team made an Eastern trip, with the intention of meeting teams from the Massachusetts Institute of Technology, Harvard, Columbia, and other Eastern Universities. Only one of these proposed contests was ever held. After beating the Technology team in three trial contests, our team, in the final contest, lost the "drop" by five inches, and were defeated by two and one-half inches. But their display of skill and brawn was such that the teams from the other great institutions of the East found it wise to excuse themselves from pulling, on the ground of illness, etc. This was not the last time that an Eastern team has declined to match conclusions with one from the West.

THE MOVEMENT AGAINST PROFESSIONALISM.

We have spoken of the beginning of the movement against professionalism in Western college athletics. In this movement the representatives of Northwestern University have had a prominent and very creditable part. In 1883 the Western Baseball Association, then made up of Racine, Wisconsin, Chicago, Northwestern, and Beloit, enacted further rules forbidding a student player to play on a professional team during the college season or to take pay for playing anywhere during such a season, requiring a previous residence in college of at least two terms, and making ineligible any man "whose college expenses are in any way borne by men connected with baseball interests." The new association of 1891 advanced the good work by enacting that a candidate for a college team position must be carrying at least five hours of work in class per week, must not receive in any way compensation for playing on the college team or on any other team, must be registered at least two months before the first scheduled intercollegiate game, must not play on a college team for more than an aggregate of five years, must be prepared to make affidavit, on demand, as to his eligibility, and must present a certificate of eligibility signed by three members of his Faculty. In March, 1892, a local association was formed, in which the four branches of athletics now generally recognized as such—namely: baseball, football, track athletics, and tennis—were each represented on a joint committee consisting of two men representing each branch, two alumni, and a secretary, chosen by this joint committee.

This committee was to audit the accounts of the four branches, to have general oversight of the athletic grounds, to ratify the elections of all captains, and to have power to demand resignations and to order new elections in case of incompetency or malfeasance in office. The prime object of this arrangement seems to have been to eliminate from our athletics the sometimes harmful influence of fraternity preferences in selecting men and officers for the various teams.

At the beginning of the college year 1892-93, our Faculty appointed a committee on athletics consisting of Professors Coe (chairman), Hatfield, and Gray. No formal rules were at first laid down, but the *Annual* of that year informs the students that they must not hereafter play with professional teams; that members of all our local teams must be students in full and regular standing; that all schedules of games must be submitted to the committee for approval, and that, before joining a team, men will be subjected to a physical examination. During the year 1893-94 Professor Coe remained as chairman, supported by Professors Sheppard and Gray, and additional restrictions were announced, forbidding a student to play on any other team while a member of a university team and requiring the selection of players to be submitted to the committee for approval. In these days of comparatively pure college athletics, the restrictions already named seem mild indeed. But they were regarded by the under-graduates in 1892-94 as severe. That first faculty committee made a brave fight. Their greatest victory was in demonstrating to the student body that athletics was a subject legitimately within the control of the faculty. After undergoing a vast amount of abuse and obloquy, Professor Coe settled that question conclusively, and his efforts and sufferings in a good cause should not be forgotten.

With the beginning of the college year of 1894-95 the Trustees took athletics from the direct control of the Faculty and placed it in the hands of a "Committee for the Regulation of Athletic Sports," consisting of three professors, three alumni, and three under-graduates. At that time and ever since, the Faculty and alumni members of the committee have been appointed by the Trustees and the student members by the general student body. During 1894-95 the Faculty members were Professors Holgate (Chairman), Sheppard, and Gray. This committee continued the good work already begun, and dropped summarily from a team one of the worst offenders of the early days. Although hampered by a deadlock in the committee lasting nearly all the year, they stood for higher ideals in college sport.

The restrictions on the various teams during 1894-95 seem to have been substantially those in force during the previous year. But the call for more stringent measures was everywhere heard; and so, early in January, 1895, a meeting of the presidents of the universities then familiarly known as "the big seven" was held in Chicago. The fruit of this presidents' conference was "The Presidents' Rules," the first general enactment for the government of college athletics in the Central West. In brief, these rules required that a student, to be eligible for a team in any of the universities concerned, must be a *bona fide* student, must have been in residence in his college at least six months, must receive no pay for his athletic services, must not play under an assumed name, and must not be delinquent in his studies. It was further provided that a graduate student might play during the minimum number of years necessary to secure a degree in his graduate school (thus allowing a medical student, for example, to

play altogether seven years on a college team); that college games might be played only on grounds controlled by one or the other team participating; that the selection of managers and captains must be submitted for approval to the governing boards; that no college teams should play with professional teams; and that the respective registrars should certify to the proper selection of the various teams. These rules were published in our *Annual* of 1894-95, and were promptly put into effect here.

At the beginning of the college year 1895-96, the Trustees formed an entirely new committee, of which the Faculty members were Professors Clark (Chairman), Young, and White, while Messrs. Fred Raymond, Frank Dyche, and Charles Wheeler were the alumni members. With the exception of Mr. Wheeler, who resigned in 1898, this committee remained unchanged as to Faculty and alumni during the succeeding four years. It was during these years that the Conference Rules were gradually developed into substantially their present form. The chairmen of the boards of control in the "big seven" universities, who endeavored to enforce "The Presidents' Rules" soon found that they must be amended if the desired ends were to be attained. Consequently a conference of chairmen was called at Chicago early in the winter of 1896, and a mutual interpretation of the rules was agreed upon, while the term "professional" was more clearly defined.

At every one of the successive conferences the lines were drawn more sharply and the restrictions made more severe. In November, 1896, we lengthened the required probation of a player in residence from six months to one year; we reduced the possible time-limit for a graduate-student player from three or four to two years; we restricted all games to contests between "educational institutions"; and where a student had not been in residence over half of the year preceding his proposed admission to the under-graduate team, we required him to be on probation still six months longer. In the conference of 1897 we reduced the combined graduate and undergraduate limit to four years of playing on a 'varsity team; we enacted that, after September 1, 1898, all preparatory students should be barred from playing on a 'varsity team, and we ordered that, thereafter, there must be an exchange of lists of proposed players at least ten days before any intercollegiate game. In the conference of 1898 we defined professionalism still more closely, adopting the now famous clause requiring the candidate to make affidavit that he has "never used his athletic skill for gain." We also shut out from the teams all persons who were receiving from any of the universities concerned any remuneration for their services as teachers. A few minor changes in the conference rules have been made since 1898. By the gradual enactment and honest enforcement of these rules the universities of the Central West have secured a degree of purity in their athletics of which they may well be proud.

FOOTBALL.

During the autumn of 1878 the old-fashioned Rugby game of football began to be played on the campus in a general way, and the college colors were changed to purple and gold. In February, 1880, the first local football association was formed, the Rugby rules were published in the college paper, and regular team practice was begun.

Little seems to have been done in this game during 1881, but in November, 1882, we find that Northwestern defeated Lake Forest in what was later to become the most intense of college sports. During '83, '84, '85, and '86 the records hardly mention football. In November, 1887, a challenge for a Thanksgiving game with Michigan University was declined on the ground that our team was not in training. There was a team during 1889, but we find no mention of any intercollegiate games. The first recorded game with an institution of similar rank was in November, 1890, when Northwestern defeated Wisconsin by a score of 22 to 10. A little later we beat Beloit 22 to 6. In the autumn of 1891 a Football League was formed with Wisconsin, Beloit, and Lake Forest, and five intercollegiate games were played, our men winning two and tying one.

In 1892 Northwestern first took a prominent place in football, defeating Michigan by a score of 10 to 8, Beloit by a score of 36 to 0, Wisconsin by a score of 26 to 6, tying both Chicago and Illinois, and thus winning second place in the big Western League. This first great team was captained and trained by Paul Noyes, and included VanDoozer, Oates, Culver, Kennicott, Wilson, Pearce, McCluskey, Oberne, Griffith, and Williams. The games of 1893 and 1894 did not redound to our glory. In 1895 the team was strengthened by such men as Potter, Gloss, and Siberts, and defeated Beloit 34 to 6; Armour Institute 44 to 0; Chicago 22 to 6 (in the return game Chicago won, 6 to 0); Purdue, 24 to 6; and Illinois 43 to 8. The year 1896 was the banner year in football for Northwestern, up to the present. The team consisted of the famous veteran half-backs, Potter and VanDoozer, aided by such helpers as Hunter, Pearce, Levings, Perry, Sloane, Andrews, Thorne, Gloss, and Brown. These were the famous "cripples," so happily caricatured in the *Chicago Record*, who defeated Chicago on Marshall Field by the score of 46 to 6; who tied Chicago in the return game, with a score of 6 to 6; who went down to Champaign with a crowd of three hundred roaring student supporters in a special train, and gave to the Illini their first defeat in football on their home grounds to the tune of 6 to 4; and who, in that famous Thanksgiving game on our home grounds, before a crowd of four thousand people, played Wisconsin to a standstill. The score was 6 to 6; but the conditions and circumstances were such that unbiased observers generally counted it a victory for Northwestern. The team was managed during 1896 by Mr. Frank Haller, and much was done in the way of providing a training-table and a coach that had not been so thoroughly done before. After paying all expenses of the season, we were able to settle a bill of $1,000 which had been hanging over the local athletic association ever since the grand stand was built and partially paid for in 1891-92.

The season of 1897 was not a successful one, although the remarkable kick from the middle of our field by O'Dea of Wisconsin must be mentioned as one of the most sensational features in the history of Western football. During the season of 1898 particular effort was made in the way of hiring a high-priced coach from the East and a professional trainer, providing a large training table, etc. But our unwise plan of changing coaches and methods every year could have but one result, and that was defeat. With the coming of Dr. C. M. Hollister, in September, 1898, to act as general manager and coach for all branches of our college athletics except tennis, a great advance was made in every way. It now became possible to gain in momentum every year by continuing the same style of play and by taking advantage of the specific training given to particular men on the team of a preceding year. Although we were far from regaining the glories of 1896, we made some improvement during 1898, and in 1899 we defeated Minnesota 11 to 5, Indiana 11 to 6, and Purdue 29 to 0. In 1900 we defeated Chicago 5 to 0, Indiana 12 to 0, tied Beloit

6 to 6, tied Iowa 6 to 6, and secured third place in the "big nine" group of Western universities. The game with Iowa, which was played at Rock Island on Thanksgiving Day, was one of the great surprises of that year, for the Iowa giants had defeated nearly all comers so far during that season, and had widely advertised their intention to "do up" Northwestern. In 1901 our team defeated Illinois 17 to 11, Chicago 6 to 5, and Purdue 10 to 5. With the graduation of the class of 1902 we lost five great players: Johnson, the Dietz brothers, Elliott, and Hansen. The team of the following season was therefore composed largely of new, untrained material, and the results were what was to be expected under the circumstances.

An interesting social feature connected with football at Northwestern has been the football "banquets" that have been held for several years in the old chapel room of "Old College" during the week after the close of the season. To Dr. R. L. Sheppard, who has annually paid the bill for "feeding" the members of the team and the "scrubs" at these banquets, thankful recognition is here due.

THE ATHLETIC FIELD AND GRAND STAND.

It was not until 1892 that the field sports of Northwestern could be said to have a home. Prior to 1891 the teams had played, as before stated, where the Orrington Lunt Library now stands, and the spectators had been compelled to use the turf for grand stand and "bleachers." In September, 1891, the Trustees formally set apart the present field for athletic purposes, and at the same time Mr. George Muir, Evanston's long-time genial bookseller, whose Davis Street store, where Smith's studio is now, was for decades the downtown headquarters for students, started an energetic movement to raise money for a grand stand. In this effort Mr. Muir was ably assisted by Mr. Louis S. Rice, of the class of '83. These two men worked indefatigably and most unselfishly, soliciting aid from every alumnus whom they could reach, and within a few months they succeeded in raising about $1,500 from citizens, alumni, and undergraduates. Strong in faith in the loyalty of future students, these two gentlemen went ahead with the building, and completed the present structure at a cost of about $2,500. The grand stand was opened with appropriate ceremonies on the 15th of October, 1892. Meantime the Trustees had done some work in grading and partially draining the baseball field. But we were still without an enclosing fence, so that there were no certain means of collecting revenue by charging an admission to the games. But in the autumn of 1893 Dr. Sheppard—always the most generous local supporter of our athletics, and the man for whom the students later unanimously and very properly named the present grounds "Sheppard Field"—came forward with an offer to furnish lumber for a fence. His offer was promptly accepted, a boss carpenter was hired, also through Dr. Sheppard's generosity, and scores of under-graduates turned out with saw and hammer, with the result that the present enclosure was soon completed.

During the summer of 1896 the present quarter-mile cinder track was made entirely by student and Faculty enterprise, and was paid for largely from the football receipts of the previous year. In the autumn of 1896 the first of the now existing "bleachers" were built, the work being entirely done by students and professors under the direction of the Chairman of the Committee for the Regulation of Athletic Sports. The northern half of the west "bleachers" and all the east "bleachers" were built in the fall of 1898, and the work and material were paid for out of the treasury of the athletic association.

TRACK ATHLETICS AND TENNIS.

We have already spoken of the field sports connected with the great celebration held in the campus grove on the 4th of July, 1871. Some of the records made then are interesting by way of comparison with more recent records. We learn that T. C. Warrington kicked the football 147 feet 6 inches and threw the baseball 304 feet 10 inches; that Frank Andrews won the hurdle race (120 yards and five hurdles) in 18 seconds; and that George Lunt won the pole vault, making 6 feet 7 inches. The first formal University field day was held in 1879, and this observance has been a part of the college athletic life pretty regularly ever since. The most noteworthy records ever made on the home field by Northwestern students are as follows:

100 yard dash, 10 seconds	A. R. Jones, '99
200 yard dash, 22 1-5 seconds	A. R. Jones, '99
440 yard run, 52 seconds	R. S. Sturgeon, '00
800 yard run, 2 minutes 2 seconds	R. S. Sturgeon, '00
1 mile run, 4 minutes 55 seconds	H. Baker, '01
2 mile run, 10 minutes 21 1-5 seconds	F. E. Morris, '04
220 yard hurdles, 26 2-5 seconds	J. A. Brown
120 yard hurdle, 16 2-5 seconds	J. A. Brown
High jump, 5 feet 9 1-4 inches	Claude Smith
Broad jump, 22 feet 5 inches	O. Davis
Pole vault, 10 feet 6 inches	R. E. Wilson, '08
Hammer throw, 126 feet 1 inch	Arthur Baird
Shot-put, 39 feet 9 inches	Arthur Baird
Discus Throw, 121 feet 3 inches	Arthur Baird

The first three of the present seven College and Academy tennis courts were laid out and partially completed in the spring of 1895. In the following autumn, under a new administration, these were completed and paid for and a fourth was built, thus completing the courts of the University proper. The Academy courts were built in 1900. Our local courts have been the scene of many a well-fought battle between our own students and between the many professors and instructors who seek health in tennis, and they have witnessed several intercollegiate contests.

CHAPTER XVIII.

GARRETT BIBLICAL INSTITUTE
(By PRESIDENT CHARLES J. LITTLE)

Historical Sketch—Origin of the Institute Due to the Munificence of Mrs. Augustus Garrett—Building Erected in 1855 and Institute Opened in 1856—Additional Buildings Erected in 1867 and 1887—The Republican "Wigwam" of 1860 Becomes the Property of the Institute—Reverse Caused by Fire of 1871—Disaster Averted in 1897—Growth of the Institute—Personal History—Large Number of the Alumni in Missionary and Other Fields—Members of the Faculty and Board of Trustees.

In the winter of 1839 Mr. Augustus Garrett and his wife, Eliza Garrett, joined the Clark Street Methodist Episcopal Church of Chicago, of which the Rev. Peter R. Borein was then pastor. Mr. Borein was a man of unusual eloquence and piety, but of imperfect education. He often attributed this fact to the lack of a school in which men like himself might obtain a proper preparation for the ministry, and frequently said this in conversations with Mrs. Garrett.

In 1848 Mrs. Garrett was left a widow and in possession of what subsequently developed into a large property. In the year 1852 she authorized her legal adviser, Grant Goodrich, to ascertain the views of persons whom he might deem worthy of

special regard and consultation as to the field of greatest promise for her beneficence, and in October, 1853, her last will and testament was formally executed, in which she set apart the residue of her estate for the founding of Garrett Biblical Institute.

During the autumn in which her will was executed the Rev. Dr. John Dempster visited the West with the intention of planting an institution for the training of Methodist ministers. On passing through Chicago he learned of Mrs. Garrett's purpose, and, after an interview with her, a meeting of the Church in Chicago was called to determine what course should be pursued. Rev. John Clark presided. A committee consisting of John Clark, Philo Judson, Orrington Lunt, John Adams and Grant Goodrich, was empowered to adopt such measures as it was believed would result in the speedy erection of a building in which to open a school and to provide the means to sustain it until Mrs. Garrett's bequest should become available. They took upon themselves the responsibility of providing a building at Evanston and of furnishing an annual revenue of $1,600. Dr. Dempster undertook to provide whatever amount above that sum might be necessary to support the faculty. A building capable of accommodating forty students was completed in 1855, and the first term was opened in charge of Rev. John Dempster, D.D.; Rev. William Goodfellow, A.M., and Rev. William P. Wright, A. M. The institution was opened with interesting services, in which Mrs. Garrett participated. The first term began with four students and closed with sixteen. The second began with twelve and closed with nineteen. The greatest number in attendance at any one time was twenty-eight. Annual conferences passed encouraging resolutions and individuals and churches contributed to support the school. Mrs. Garrett was so anxious to disencumber her estate and make it available for her benevolent designs that for several years she would accept only $400 a year for her support, nearly half of which she devoted to pious purposes. This estimable and excellent woman died on the 23d of November, 1855, the last act of her life being to confirm to the now chartered institute the munificent bequest that she had made for its endowment.

An excellent portrait of Mrs. Garrett now hangs in the President's office in Memorial Hall. It is the picture of a sweet-faced, intelligent woman, and corresponds with all that has been said and written of her goodness and piety. Her death was sudden and unexpected, but she died in great peace—indeed, in great triumph. She was greatly beloved and greatly lamented.

The temporary organization was brought to a close in the spring of 1856, and in May of the same year the Trustees, under the charter of 1855, appealed to the General Conference of the Methodist Episcopal Church for recognition. This recognition was granted and the Bishops were requested to act as an advisory committee to counsel with the Trustees. A permanent organization was effected and the Institute opened on the 22d of September, 1856, about three years from the time that Mrs. Garrett determined upon its founding.

When the Institute was first opened at Evanston there was not, in the whole distance between Chicago and Waukegan, a single Protestant church. There was great need of evangelical effort in the villages that were springing up along the lake shore. The students of the Institute established and maintained regular appointments at which they preached, exhorted, taught Sunday schools, distributed tracts, and in connection with which they visited the people to converse with them concerning their religious welfare. Great interest was taken by the faculty in this evangelical activity. At the same time earnest efforts were made to connect with the Institute a department for missionary training. In an early catalogue the leading design of the Institute was stated in these words: "It is to make thinking, speaking, acting men." The founders of the Institute had a vivid forecast of the future of Chicago, and believed that a special Providence had directed its location; but they were compelled to face much prejudice and often deplored the lack of earnest co-operation, both of laymen and ministers.

The first building was a wooden structure accommodating forty students. In a few years a new building became necessary, and in 1867, through the efficient agency of Rev. J. S. Smart and the Women's Centennial Association, a building, now known as Heck Hall, was erected at a cost of $57,000. This served for lecture rooms, library and chapel, as well as a dormitory for students until 1887, when the present Memorial Hall was finished during the presidency of Rev. Dr. Henry B. Ridgaway. The older building, which has recently been completely renovated, is now devoted solely to the use of students.

The portion of Mrs. Garrett's estate which came into the hands of the Trustees consisted chiefly of the ground where in

1860 the "Wigwam" was erected in which Abraham Lincoln was nominated for President of the United States. In 1870 a block of brick stores was built upon this ground, but all these buildings were destroyed in the fire of 1871, and the estate was left with a debt of $92,000. The generous liberality of the church contributed a sum of $62,500 for the relief of the Institute in this critical time, and in 1872 a larger block of buildings was erected upon the same site. The debt incurred in this enterprise was removed by the active efforts of the Rev. W. C. Dandy, D.D., who was appointed financial agent. Among the numerous gifts obtained by him was one of $30,000 from Mrs. Cornelia Miller for the endowment of the Chair of Practical Theology. Under the wise management of the Trustees the property of the Institute gradually increased in value, but in 1897 another crisis occurred, the results of which were averted by the careful management of the present treasurer of the Institute, the Rev. Dr. R. D. Sheppard. The magnificent building now occupied by Reid, Murdock & Co. was erected under Dr. Sheppard's supervision after a lease had been negotiated which promises to afford a large revenue for immediate needs. The debt created in this connection the Trustees hope to extinguish by the sinking fund which they have started.

The Institute has deviated but little from its original ideal. It has met, from time to time, the demands of the period; thus, in the summer of 1892, it enlarged its facilities for the study of the English Bible, a systematic scheme for English Bible study being substituted in the diploma course for the study of Hebrew. In 1895 it took steps for instruction in Sociology. The Library has grown rapidly under the careful management of the Rev. Dr. Terry, and includes the splendid collection of Methodist books and original documents—the finest in the world—purchased for the Institute by Mr. William Deering. The records of the Seminary show that, since 1854, nearly 3,500 persons have enjoyed the privileges of the school. Of this number 700 have completed a three years' course, and of these 365 have received the degree of Bachelor of Divinity. The large majority of these graduates are pastors, many of whom are now filling conspicuous pulpits with ability. Among those now living may be mentioned: James S. Chadwick and George E. Strobridge, of the New York East Conference; Charles B. Wilcox, of Kansas City; Polemus H. Swift, W. E. Tilroe, John N. Hall, John D. Leek and John P. Brushingham, of Chicago; Edward S. Ninde, of Ann Arbor; Edwin A. Schell, of Greencastle, Ind.; Hugh D. Atchison, of Dubuque, Iowa; A. E. Craig, of Ottumwa, Iowa; E. G. Lewis, of Grand Rapids, Mich.; William A. Shanklin, of Reading, Pa.; James S. Montgomery, of Minneapolis; E. B. Patterson, of Baltimore; James H. Senseny, Des Moines, Iowa.

Forty of the Alumni have gone to the foreign field as missionaries. Among these are two Missionary Bishops, Joseph C. Hartzell and F. W. Warne; in China are Virgil C. Hart, William T. Hobart, Myron C. Wilcox, H. Olin Cady, Spencer Lewis, F. L. Guthrie, W. H. Lacey, W. C. Langdon and Quincy A. Meyers; in India are J. H. Gill, D. O. Fox, James S. Messmore, J. W. Waugh, J. C. Lawson, William H. Hollister, Harvey R. Calkins, D. C. Clancy and John W. Robinson; in Burmah, Julius Smith; in Southeast Africa, John M. Springer; in Singapore, John R. Denyes and Ernest S. Lyons; in Mexico, Ira C. Cartwright; in South America, M. J. Pusey and H. B. Shinn. Homer C. Stuntz, formerly of India, is now in the Philippine Islands.

Thirty-three are serving as Presidents

and professors in schools and colleges. Among these are: Nathan Burwash, President of Victoria College, Canada; William H. Crawford, President of Allegheny College, Pa.; Eli McClish, President of Pacific College, Cal.; Nels E. Simonson, Principal of the Norwegian-Danish School, Evanston; J. Riley Weaver, Professor in DePauw University; Robert D. Sheppard and Amos W. Patten, Professors in Northwestern University; Charles Horswell, Solon C. Bronson and Charles M. Stuart, Professors in Garrett Biblical Institute; Melvin P. Lackland, Professor in Illinois Wesleyan University; Orange H. Cessna, Professor in Iowa State Agricultural College; Thomas Nicholson, President Dakota Wesleyan University, South Dakota.

Among the earliest graduates in the class of 1861 was Bishop Charles H. Fowler. In the same class was Oliver A. Willard, the brilliant brother of the lamented Frances E. Willard.

The Norwegian-Danish Department was organized in 1886 under the principalship of Rev. Nels E. Simonson, D.D., an alumnus of the English Department. During the thirteen years of its operation, it has had in attendance more than one hundred students.

The Presidents of the faculty have been: John Dempster, Matthew Simpson, William X. Ninde, Henry B. Ridgaway and Charles J. Little.

The members of the faculty have been: John Dempster, William Goodfellow, William O. Wright, Daniel P. Kidder, Henry Bannister, Francis D. Hemenway, Miner Raymond, Robert L. Cumnock, William X. Ninde, Henry B. Ridgaway, Charles F. Bradley, Milton S. Terry, Charles W. Bennett, Charles Horswell, Charles J. Little, Solon C. Bronson, Charles M. Stuart, Doremus A. Hayes.

The Trustees have been: Grant Goodrich, Orrington Lunt, John Evans, Philo Judson, Stephen P. Keyes, Luke Hitchcock, Hooper Crews, Thomas M. Eddy, John V. Farwell, E. H. Gammon, Charles H. Fowler, A. E. Bishop, S. H. Adams, William Deering, Robert D. Sheppard, Oliver H. Horton, William C. Dandy, Frank M. Bristol, Frank P. Crandon, Amos W. Patton, Polemus H. Swift.

John Dempster, the first President, belonged to that vigorous Scotch-Irish stock which has been so potent in American history. His natural powers were very great, and though himself without a theological training, he may be said to be the founder of the theological schools in American Methodism. He exercised great influence, not only among his brethren, but in the general community, and was one of the committee that waited upon Mr. Lincoln in the crisis of the war to strengthen his hands and to assure him of the unfailing support of his fellow-citizens of Illinois.

Matthew Simpson, the eloquent Bishop, was the greatest preacher that recent Methodism has produced. His influence during the war surpassed that of any clergyman in the land, partly because of his great endowments and excellent character, and partly because he represented a church that "sent more men to the field and more prayers to heaven" than any other in the land.

Bishop Ninde, who succeeded him as President, drew all hearts to himself. His personal appearance was singularly attractive; his behavior was brotherly and his spirit so Christ-like that students revered him and the community trusted him implicitly.

Dr. Ridgaway came to Evanston from Cincinnati. He brought with him a great reputation as an eloquent preacher and a successful pastor. During his administration Memorial Hall was built. He, too, was greatly beloved.

Of the many distinguished members of the faculty the most conspicuous was Dr. Miner Raymond. No man in Methodism possessed a clearer mind. His words were weighty and his sentences, many of them, have become household words to his pupils. He lived to be more than four score years of age and continued his teaching until his eighty-second year.

Among the Trustees Orrington Lunt was, by reason of his personality and his many years of service, the most conspicuous and the most useful. He gave to the Institute unstinted service. He watched over its interests as he watched over his own, and prayed for it as he prayed for his family. Few institutions have enjoyed such devotion as Orrington Lunt gave to Garrett Biblical Institute, and his name will be connected with it so long as it shall last.

CHAPTER XIX.

EARLY DRAINAGE

First Steps in Organization of a Drainage System for Evanston—Natural Conditions—Early Legislation of 1855—The Late Harvey B. Hurd, Member and Secretary of First Board of Commissioners—Construction of Ditches Begun—Drainage Amendment of the Present Constitution Adopted in 1878—Extension of the System—Local Opposition—A Tax Collector's Experience—A Flood Converts the Opponents of the System.

The drainage of Evanston forms an important and interesting chapter in its history. There is plenty of evidence showing that all the territory now included in the towns of Evanston, Niles, Jefferson, Lake View and the southeastern portion of New Trier, were at some time covered by the waters of Lake Michigan. There are, in this territory, three distinct ridges made by the lake which mark several distinct recessions of its waters. The west one, sometimes called "Dutch Ridge," commences at Winnetka, at the south end of the clay bluff stretching along the west shore, and runs thence southwesterly, spreading and flattening out in fan-shape towards the north branch of the Chicago River and terminating at that stream near Niles Center. East of this, from a mile in width at the north end, to two or three miles at the south end, is Evanston's "West Ridge," which com-

mences where Ridge Avenue strikes the lake and runs almost directly south to Rosehill, where it turns sharply to the west, forming a J and flattening out considerably at Bowmanville, and also terminating at the north branch near that place, leaving between these two ridges a valley partly wooded and partly prairie. The east one of the three ridges commences at the lake shore in the University campus and runs southerly through Evanston, and bending slightly to the eastward through Lake View, ends at Lincoln Park.

Natural Conditions. — These several ridges, to a certain extent, cut off the drainage of the land between them, and this land was subject to occasional overflow, and was to some extent swampy during the entire year. Portions of it were impassable during most of the year. At quite an early day a small ditch was constructed midway between the east and west ridges, emptying into the lake through a ravine in the College campus and the site of the first Biblical Institute building erected in 1854, but afterward destroyed by fire. This ditch was called the Mulford Ditch, from the fact that Major E. H. Mulford was principally instrumental in its construction; Edward Murphy was associated with him in the making of it.

At the time of the location of Evanston this ditch had pretty much gone to decay

169

and the land between the two ridges was so swampy it was difficult to pass from one ridge to the other except in one or two places. Something in the way of drainage was accomplished by the throwing up of the streets when Evanston was laid out in 1853.

First Drainage Commission.—By an act approved February 15, 1855, "The Drainage Commission" was created for the purpose of draining the wet lands in Townships 41 and 42, in Range 13 and 14, and Sections 1, 2, 11 and 12, in Township 40 of Range 13. This Commission was given power "to lay out, locate, construct, complete and alter ditches, embankments, culverts, bridges and roads, and maintain and keep the same in repair." The Commissioners named in the act were Harvey B. Hurd, George M. Huntoon, James B. Colvin, John L. Beveridge and John H. Foster. As Dr. Foster resided in Chicago and did not wish to engage in the undertaking, A. G. Wilder was put in his place. Mr. Hurd was Secretary of the Commission, and to a considerable extent managed its operations.

At that time the only road on the prairie west of Evanston was one running north and south along the east edge of the Big Woods, leading from what was known as "Emerson's barn" to Chicago by way of Bowmanville. This road was passable only during a portion of the year—late in the summer and when the ground was frozen up.

Construction of Ditches Begun.—The first ditch constructed by the Commission was along the west side of this road; the excavation being thrown up in such a manner as to make a fairly passable road from "Emerson's barn" neighborhood to Bowmanville.

The next work of the Commission was the construction of what is known as the "Big Ditch," about half way between the Big Woods and West Ridge. It was so shaped that the north end of it from the north side of Center Street, on the town line between Evanston and New Trier, emptied into the lake, and from the south side of Center Street the water was carried south, emptying into the North Branch at a point about three-fourths of a mile northwest of Bowmanville.

Later several ditches were laid out and constructed across the prairie; these were so laid out and constructed as to create roads. One of them is the Rogers Road, commencing just west of what was then the home of Philip Rogers, after whom Rogers Park was named, running thence west to Niles Center. Another is the Mulford Road: another extended on Church Street west to the Big Woods, and another was the Emerson Road, now Emerson Street.

These roads have all become prominent thoroughfares; the last three have been extended west to Dutch Ridge, and Church Street has been extended to the Glenn View Golf Club grounds. The Commission enlarged the Mulford Ditch so that it furnished pretty fair drainage for the territory lying between the east and west ridges in the Village of Evanston until the sewerage system was put in. Later a ditch was constructed across the east ridge from a point just west of Tillman Mann's house, at the distance of about three blocks south of Rogers Park depot to the lake.

A. G. Wilder having died, Michael Gormley of Glencoe was put on the Commission in his place, and the Commission undertook to drain the Skokie, lying west of Winnetka, Glencoe and Highland Park. It first constructed a ditch emptying into the east fork of the North Branch, but it was found that in flood times the water set back in the North Branch and up this ditch, flooding the Skokie. Another outlet was therefore made through the Dutch Ridge, at a point about half way between Winnetka and the Gross Point settlement, carrying the water into the lake through what is now Kenilworth. The Skokie being about forty feet above the lake level, ample fall was found, and this last ditch redeemed a large amount of valuable lands at the south end of the Skokie, now covered by some of the best farms in that neighborhood.

The subsequent efforts of the Commission to enlarge the Skokie ditch and extend it further north, were opposed by some of the land-owners who were assessed for the expense of their improvement, and two cases were carried to the Supreme Court to test the constitutionality of the law. In the case of Hessler vs. The Drainage Commissioners (reported in 53 Ill. Reports, page 105), the court held the law to be unconstitutional. This decision was rendered in January, 1870, and put an end to the operations of "The Drainage Commissioners." This was one of several decisions of like import, for there were several other commissions in different parts of the State, acting under similar laws, where assessments for benefits had been held unconstitutional, but so much interest had been created in favor of drainage that a clause was put into the Constitution of 1870, designed to permit the General Assembly to pass laws for that purpose. This clause was amended by vote of the people in November, 1878, adopting an amendment of the Constitution, which is now the authority for the drainage laws found in the statutes generally known as the Farm Drainage Acts.

Extension of the System. — The north portion of the big ditch was later, under one of these acts, very considerably enlarged and extended south so as to draw the water lakeward from Church Street, but all those parts of the Big Ditch and Mulford Ditch within the corporate limits of Evanston have been supplanted by sewers constructed by the City of Evanston. The Rogers Park Ditch has been supplanted by a main sewer on Pratt Avenue, which carried all the drainage of Rogers Park west of the East Ridge into the lake. All the roads which were constructed by the Commission are not only maintained, but have been extended and improved and are now principal highways. The law under which they were constructed having been declared void, the owner of the land upon which they were laid out might have fenced them up, but they were of such evident utility and propriety that no one has shown any disposition to do so, and having now been in use over twenty years, they have become legal highways.

Local Opposition.—The opposition of the owners of the lands proposed to be benefitted was not confined to the validity of the law. When the first ditch was being laid out along the west side of the Big Woods Road, the Big Woods people came out with pitch-forks and clubs to drive off the engineer and his assistants, but fortunately the engineer was a good-natured man, but very firm, and did not allow himself to be driven off.

Later, when the Rogers Road ditch was projected, a very vigorous protest was made, the people insisting that they did not need any more drainage; that they would rather have their land as it was without further drainage, and I am of the opinion that had I not put on my pleasantest manner with them, I should have received rough treatment on one of my visits to the neighborhood in the collection of assessments. I had the satisfaction, however, later in the season, of turning the tables on them. It occurred in this way: Our ditchers, for the purpose of protecting their work from being flooded, threw up their excavation in such a way as to create a dam on each side of the ditch. In the midst of haying time, when a large quantity of hay was down, and considerable of it was in cocks, and when the ditch was about two-thirds across the prairie, there came a heavy rain which flooded the prairie. To save their hay, the people rallied in force, drove off the ditchers, cut the dams and let the water off, and thus saved much of their hay which would otherwise have been all spoiled. We had the ring-leaders arrested, brought over to Evanston and fined. Though they were not quite happy in the payment of their fines, they were much more reconciled to the payment of their assessments, acknowledging that after all the drainage was a pretty good thing.

All the work done by "The Drainage Commission" was by special assessment. Unfortunately, the Chicago fire in 1871 destroyed all our assessment rolls, or I should take pleasure in showing you how much more economically work was done by commissioners interested in the land as owners than is now done by municipal authorities who have no interest in common with those who have to foot the bills.

CHAPTER XX.

PUBLIC UTILITIES

(By ALEXANDER CLARK)

Area and Topography of the City of Evanston—The Drainage Problem—A Period of Evolution—Municipal Development—Electric Light System Installed—Street Improvements—Parks and Boulevards—The Transportation Problem—Steam and Interurban Railway Connections—Heating System—Telephone Service—Evanston as a Residence City.

The total area of the city of Evanston is about 4,000 acres. The lots generally have a frontage of fifty feet. As they average about five lots to the acre, this would make a total of 20,000 lots within the city limits. Estimating a population of five persons to each lot, would give the city a total population of about 100,000 when the territory is fully built up. The present population is about 20,000. It consists largely of residents who do business in the City of Chicago, while there is a large local population, residing permanently in the city, of whom a large proportion are in the employment of the other class.

Topographically the territory consists of an area intersected by two ridges running north and south, one known as the East, and the other as the West Ridge. The East, or Chicago Avenue Ridge, has an elevation of twenty to twenty-five feet above Lake Michigan, while Ridge Avenue (West Ridge) rises about forty-five feet above the lake level.

There is a large area to the west of Ridge Avenue which was at one time very low and swampy in its character. The opening of sewers through these two ridges to the lake has drained this area, and, although relatively low, it is actually about twenty feet above Lake Michigan, which is, on an average, about a mile and a half distant. The difference in elevation, therefore, affords a very good fall when the sewers are cut through.

Drainage.—The drainage of this area west of Ridge Avenue was a serious problem for early Evanston. The first drainage district ever organized in the State of Illinois was created for the purpose of accomplishing this purpose. In 1855, the Legislature, by special act, created a drainage corporation, consisting of the late Harvey B. Hurd and four other members, for the purpose of draining this territory.

Early in the 'sixties, this act was declared unconstitutional, and, in the meanwhile, the ditch leading from the prairie west of Evanston had been cut through to the lake at a point just north of the city limits, and also a connection had been made about the north line of Kenilworth, through the Gross Point Ridge to the Skokie. There two ditches carried away great volumes of surface water that flooded these areas at certain seasons of the year.

The first sewer in Evanston which tapped this west prairie country was the Emerson Street sewer, which was made of large capacity and was intended to drain this area included within the limits of the city of Evanston; as has already been stated, it has rendered the territory entirely habitable. There is a large area south of the portion included in the City of Evanston, part of which is in the Town of Evanston (now Ridgeville) and part within the Town of Niles, which as yet has no drainage, and must ultimately look for its drainage to a connection with the North Branch of the Chicago River, either through an open channel into which the Evanston drainage will be diverted, or by sewers constructed in the City of Chicago and connected with the Drainage Canal. A line of brickyards is gradually working its way along the east edge of this low ground, and, in time, will work out an open channel which will amount to an extension of the North Branch.

A Period of Evolution.—It is exceedingly interesting to trace the evolution of an open farm country into the complex development of a city. It is difficult for the early residents of such a district to contemplate the possibilities of paved streets, sewers, water mains, gas and electric supply, and to work with reference to the ultimate establishment of these improvements. Hence, such development goes on in a very tardy and expensive manner, the work being performed largely on experimental lines and with reference to the demands of the immediate present, and not with any comprehensive grasp of the needs of the future.

In the south end of the present City of Evanston, which constituted the village of South Evanston, the first attempt at drainage was by means of wooden box-drains

from the railroad leading down to the lake. One of these was constructed in Keeney Avenue, and a similar construction was placed on Main Street, but cut through Chicago Avenue Ridge, so as to drain the low-lying territory through the two ridges. It speaks well for the foresight of the men who performed this work, that, when they cut through Chicago Avenue Ridge, excavated to a depth sufficient to drain this outlying territory and constructed the drain of brick, when later it was found necessary to change it into a sewer, it was only necessary to reconstruct the portion between the ridges up to Chicago Avenue Ridge and then to excavate across Ridge Avenue to the city limits on the west.

Municipal Consolidation.—The present city of Evanston is made up of what was originally three municipal corporations: Evanston proper, South Evanston and North Evanston. The boundary of Evanston proper, or Evanston center, was originally on the south by Hamilton and Crain Streets, and on the north by Foster Street.

The first attempt at merging was in 1873. The Village of Evanston as it then existed was desirous of securing a water supply, but did not have the means to do so, and under the constitutional limitations as to indebtedness could not issue bonds in sufficient amount to accomplish this purpose. In order to increase its bonding capacity the plan was devised of uniting the Village of Evanston and North Evanston. The Village of South Evanston remained a distinct corporation until 1892, when, after some previous attempts, which proved unsuccessful, the question of annexation to the Village of Evanston was taken up and, after a hotly contested campaign, was carried through.

The Village of South Evanston owes its existence to the fact that no land was owned within its limits by the Northwestern University. In the early days this Uni-

versity owned a large portion of the property included the original City of Evanston, and as this property was largely unimproved and not subject to taxation, this exemption threw a very serious burden upon the portion of the village not owned by the University. To escape this taxation was the incentive for the organization of the new Village of South Evanston.

The framers of our present Constitution in their wisdom, saw fit to so hedge about the municipality that no margin for extravagant expenditure should be allowed, and by inserting the provision in the Constitution that no municipal corporation should become indebted, including present indebtedness, in excess of five per cent of its property, so hampered an increase of indebtedness that it is utterly impossible for any small municipality to have metropolitan facilities; so that, just as soon as these facilities are desired, it becomes necessary to consolidate in order to enlarge the bonding and taxing area.

The same principle that applies in business, and influencing the merging of several disconnected establishments in the same line of business into one, thereby securing greater economy in their management and operation, applies, up to a certain limit, with even greater force to municipalities.

The desperate struggles of some of these corporations to assume metropolitan airs, without the means, are very amusing. For instance, the Village of South Evanston desired a water supply, and, in order to secure it, first bored an artesian well about 2,600 feet deep, which spurted up like an oil gusher sixty feet above the surface; but the water was so hard that it could not be cut with an axe, and left a residuum of its organic elements upon the foliage that happened to be sprinkled with it.

The residents then began to clamor for lake water; but, in order to get a pure sup-

ply, it was necessary to go out some distance from the shore and construct a pumping station. A block of ground between Main Street and Kedzie Avenue was found which the lake was gradually eating up. It had been taken by foreclosure by Eastern parties, and they were in danger of losing their holdings by the erosion of the water. It was found, therefore, that the whole block could be purchased for about $1,600. A frontage of about 800 feet on Lake Michigan was thus secured at this nominal figure. The question then arose how to get the money to protect this land from the encroachments of the lake, grade it and secure a water supply. The first problem was solved by levying a special assessment on every lot between the Ridge and the lake—on those lots between the railroad and the lake $5.00 each, and on those between the Northwestern Railroad and Ridge Avenue $3.00 each. By this means $7,000 was raised, which was spent upon breakwaters, grading and setting out trees, and the present little park is the result of that investment. The extent of the ground has already been nearly doubled by accretion, and is capable of much greater enlargement at a trifling expenditure. About $20,000 was added to the bonded indebtedness and a pumping station and water-tower were built.

Electric Lighting.—The town then having started on the highway of progress, it was thought that it would be a good thing if an electric lighting system could be installed; bids were called for and it was ascertained that such a system could be established with a capacity for lighting the town at about $7,000. But the town was already bonded up to its full constitutional limit, and the improvement being a public one, it did not seem possible that any more money could be raised by special assessment. This device was then resorted to: a contract was made with an electric light company whereby it constructed a plant in the village and leased it to the municipality at a rental to be paid quarterly, with an agreement that, when a certain amount of rent was paid, the title to the plant should vest in the village. This plan was borrowed from the method pursued by impecunious females in purchasing sewing machines, pianos and furniture. To the credit of the people of the village and the lawyers residing in it, no effort was made to test the doubtful legality of this proceeding, and South Evanston soon had the satisfaction of being the only municipality electrically lighted between Waukegan and Chicago. The same boilers, the same engineers and fireman that operated the water plant also operated the lighting plant, and the success of the experiment is a very instructive lesson in the municipal management of public utilities.

But it was soon found that the sewerage which poured into the lake on Main Street, about 600 feet from the pumping station, was threatening contamination of the water supply, and it was necessary that the inlet be pushed far out into the lake. By none of the devices before discovered could any additional funds be secured, and ·it became a question with South Evanston of annexation or impure water; and this, more than any other fact, contributed to the merging of the two municipalities. Shortly after they were merged, the City of Evanston was organized, with seven wards and fourteen Aldermen.

Street Improvements. — The surface soil of most of the area upon which Evanston is built is sand, excepting the west prairie, where it consists of a light stratum of black soil over blue clay. On the sandy area the first method of street-making was confined to what is known as claying and graveling. Loads of blue clay from the west prairie were dumped along and spread

upon the street to a depth of four or five inches, this being covered by a layer of three or four inches of lake gravel. When the rains fell the gravel worked itself into the mud, and, for a lightly traveled street, it was not bad. The claying and graveling of a strip twenty feet wide in the center of a street cost about 50 cents per running foot, and the writer has a very distinct recollection of the clamor that was raised when the assessment was levied upon the abutting property for this improvement. The bearing of the burden of assessments is purely a matter of education. As the Irishman said about hanging: it is not so bad when you get used to it, provided you do not die in the meantime; and the same property owners that so bitterly contested the 50 cents per running foot assessment have since then borne with the greatest equanimity an assessment of three or four dollars per front foot for paving and curbing.

I have a very distinct recollection of the paving of Davis Street with clay and gravel. The abutting owners desired that there should be plenty of clay put on; so they stood around in the hot sun and bossed the job, and the contractor gave them all they wanted. Six or eight inches of it was put on and the gravel dumped on this, and, for the next year and a half, Davis Street was a hog-wallow during the greater part of the year. This ended the era of clay and gravel. The next pavement laid upon Davis Street was macadam. This was not found satisfactory and brick was laid upon the macadam. I think the history of the paving of Davis Street illustrates most forcibly the expensive evolution by which municipalities are educated up to the management of their affairs. "Vox populi" may be "vox Dei," but it is an exceedingly expensive voice when it comes to dealing with business matters. I think a careful investigation will establish the fact that generally what the people want in a business proposition is the thing they ought not to get. Such questions can not be settled by town meetings. I remember very distinctly when James Ayers attempted to pave Hinman Avenue. After an immense amount of oratory, discussions back and forth, theories and protests from people who wanted the street kept like a country village street and who dreaded city improvements, James finally gave the matter up and said in his opinion Hinman Avenue could never be paved—that there was "too much brains on the street."

With the advent of paved streets came the problem of providing for the cost of their maintenance, and the City of Evanston to-day, with its increased area and valuation, finds itself in almost as great financial straits as the old village of South Evanston in its early struggles.

The wooden block pavement craze struck quite hard in South Evanston, and the result is miles of streets to be repaved at the expense of the abutting owners. Perhaps the best and most durable pavement ever laid in Evanston is the piece on Chicago Avenue from Davis Street north. It is of brick, and has been down ten years and is practically as smooth and good to-day as when first laid. It was laid by experts. It consists of a layer of sand with a layer of brick laid flatwise, this being surmounted by another layer of sand and a layer of brick laid edgewise. The only possible objection to such a pavement is its noise.

Evanston has to-day some of the finest macadamized streets in the country. Associations have been formed on quite a number of streets for their care and maintenance, and it has been found that a street can be kept clean and in perfect condition for less than the cost of sprinkling on the individual plan. Property owners are gradually waking up to the proposition that the care of the street in front of abutting property is just as much a duty on the part of the owner as the care of his front yard and household surroundings.

Evanston is shut in on the south by Calvary Cemetery, which extends from the lake to Chicago Avenue. Chicago Avenue is an extension of Clark Street; Asbury Avenue an extension of Western Avenue, and Sheridan Road an extension in South Evanston of Ashland Avenue in the City of Chicago.

In the early '6os an effort was made by the township authorities to extend Evanston Avenue through Calvary Cemetery, and the attempt was resisted, *vi et armis*, by the then Archbishop. But along in 1887 an association, known as the North Shore Improvement Association, was organized by citizens along the North Shore for the principal purpose of constructing a driveway along the lake for the use of the shore towns from Lincoln Park north. So much enthusiasm and public spirit was generated in the matter that Archbishop Feehan generously donated a 100-foot strip through Calvary Cemetery, and public-spirited citizens in Evanston, headed by Mr. Volney W. Foster, raised about $3,000 to level down the sand-hills and clay and gravel the roadway. This opened up an outlet for driving purposes from Evanston to Chicago.

Parks and Boulevards. — The driveway thus opened up was known as the Sheridan Road. Except at a few points it constitutes a good highway all the way from Fort Sheridan to Chicago, with portions in Lake Forest and Waukegan. In 1893 the passage of an act of the Legislature was secured authorizing the formation of park districts along the shore of Lake Michigan, and vesting in such districts the title to the submerged land. An effort was made to organize such a district to include the City of Evanston, but times were hard and taxes were high, and the people could not see their way clear to establish a new taxing municipality. The portion of the West Side of Rogers Park, however, organized itself into a district under this law, and has constructed on Ridge Avenue a mile and three-quarters of the finest driveway in or around the city. This little district took this street as a sand-heap and has improved and beautified it in every particular with trees, sod and every requisite for residence purposes. Spurred to emulation, the East Side of Rogers Park, after a bitter contest, succeeded in organizing another district, and these people have taken hold of the Sheridan Road on the east side and are now duplicating the improvements made on Ridge Avenue.

Township Organization.—An effort is now being made by the City of Evanston to abolish the useless and expensive township organization system by which the territory is burdened. (As will be seen by the first chapter of this work, relating to the present territorial boundaries of the City of Evanston, the object just mentioned has been accomplished by the organization of the territory embraced within the City of Evanston into a single township under the name of "Ridgeville," with boundaries identical with those of the city.) The territory embraced within the City of Evanston previously included portions of three townships, and each of these townships placed a different valuation on property. The result was that a lot on one side of McDaniel Street, in North Evanston, bore 50 per cent more of all the burden of taxation than a lot on the opposite side of the street in the township of Niles, equally well situated. Moreover, the city was burdened with three sets of Highway Commissioners; three sets of Assessors; three sets of Collectors, and three sets of Town Clerks, necessitating an immense amount of bookkeeping. These Highway Commissioners were vested with taxing powers equal to about one-half of the taxing power of the municipality itself, with a provision that one-half of all the money raised in the area of the City of Evanston must be expended on the farm territory outside of the city limits. The whole method of township organization, as it existed in the City of Evanston, was one of the most outrageous illustrations of municipal mismanagement that could be well devised. The consolidation alluded to—which was accomplished under an act of the Legislature passed in 1903—has resulted in the abolition of the useless offices of Highway Commissioner, Town Clerk and Town Collector, and the consolidation of the township business with the city business, as well as the abolition of township elections on a separate day. As a result of this change greater economy will be secured and the City of Evanston will be enabled to organize itself into a park district under the law of 1893, and it will also be in position to take possession of the submerged land on the lake front, with a view of establishing, in the future, parks and drives along the whole shore. No man with an atom of prevision can fail to see the great possibilities of such a right to the city. Of course, to attempt to fill in the great areas of this submerged land under previous conditions would have meant bankruptcy to the city. The money heretofore spent under the complicated township organization, if spent in this direction, would have added immensely to the future prosperity and beauty of the city. Under the new arrangement rights and property can be secured at the cost of a few hundreds of dollars that, ten years hence, would have cost thousands. The best illustration of this is the history of the little park in South Evanston heretofore narrated. What was then secured for $1,600

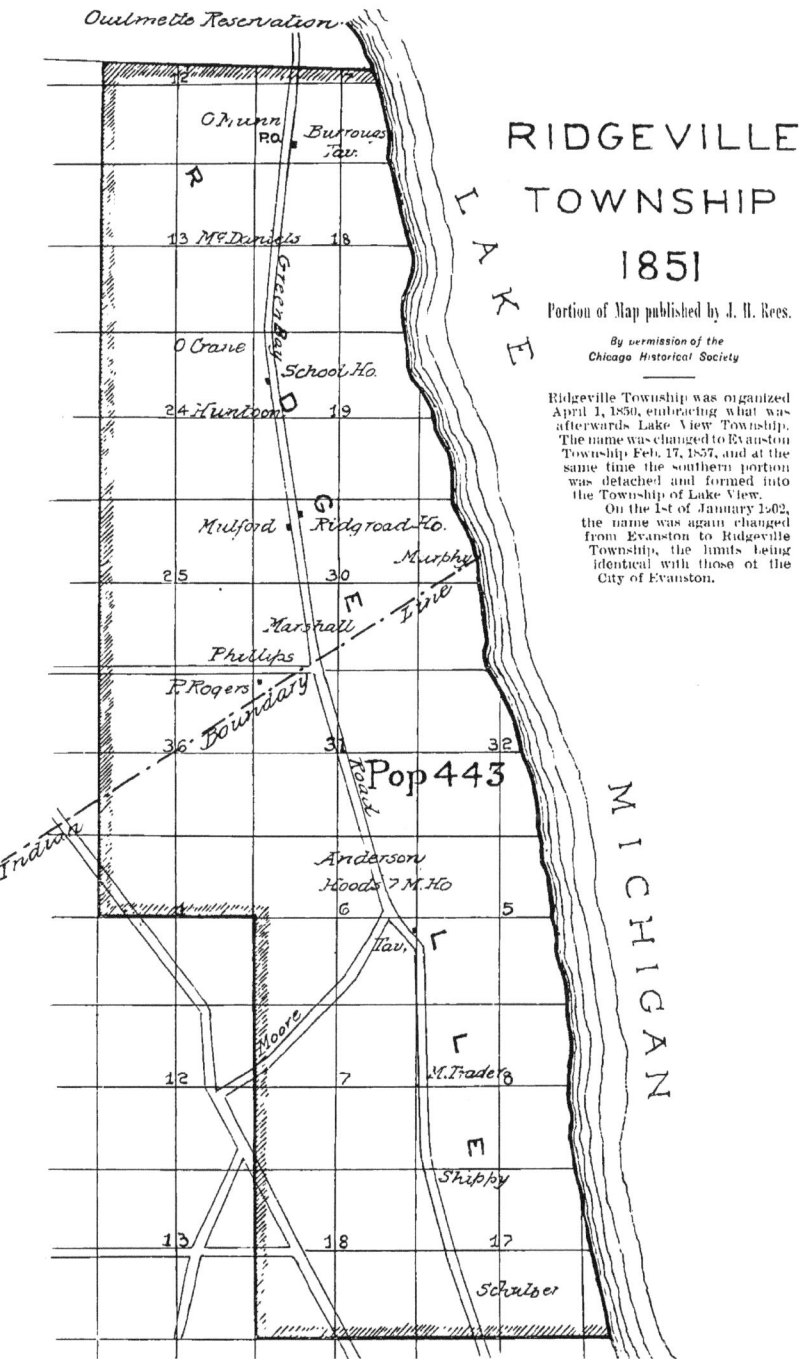

Ouilmette Reservation

RIDGEVILLE

TOWNSHIP

1851

Portion of Map published by J. H. Rees.

By permission of the
Chicago Historical Society

Ridgeville Township was organized
April 1, 1850, embracing what was
afterwards Lake View Township.
The name was changed to Evanston
Township Feb. 17, 1857, and at the
same time the southern portion
was detached and formed into
the Township of Lake View.

On the 1st of January 1902,
the name was again changed
from Evanston to Ridgeville
Township, the limits being
identical with those of the
City of Evanston.

O Munn
P.O.
Burrows
Tav.

R

13 McDaniels   18

O Crane
School Ho.

24 Huntoon   19

Mulford   Ridgroad Ho.
Murphy

25   30

Marshall   Line
Phillips
P. Rogers

36 Boundary   31   32

Indian   Pop 443

Anderson
Hoods 7 M. Ho
6   5

Tav.

12   7   M. Trade 8

Moore

Shippy

13   18   17

Schuler

LAKE

MICHIGAN

would probably now cost from twenty to thirty thousand dollars.

Transportation.—About the time of the incorporation of the Village of Evanston, along in 1856 or 1858, the Chicago & Northwestern Railroad was completed between Chicago and Milwaukee, and a suburban service was installed and carried on upon a single track until along about 1885, when the present double-track service was installed. In 1864 a corporation consisting of Orrington Lunt, John Evans and some other persons, was created under the title of the Chicago & Evanston Railroad Company. The object of the scheme was to construct a horse or steam road from the City of Evanston to the City of Chicago, the intention being to connect about Fullerton Avenue with the horse cars. The road got no farther than some rights along the river up to Fullerton Avenue, and it then slumbered under the blanket of an injunction until along in 1887, when it was revived and pushed to completion up to Calvary Cemetery, and a new corporation was then organized known as the Chicago, Evanston & Lake Superior Railroad Company, which obtained rights to construct the road through South Evanston and Evanston. The road soon after came under the control of the Chicago, Milwaukee & St. Paul Company, which was then looking for another entrance into the city, its lease over the Panhandle being about to expire. The property was bought for this purpose, but its use was not needed and it has been operated since as a local line, with very little profit to the company.

In 1892 the writer, D. H. Louderback, and John L. Cockran organized a company known as the Chicago & North Shore Street Railway Company to construct a street railway line from Evanston to Chicago. The installation of this service in Evanston was very bitterly contested by many of the residents, who claimed they had come out to Evanston to get away from this sort of thing; but it was pointed out to them that, with the growth of the City of Chicago, in order to get away from it, it would be necessary to get farther out than twelve miles from the center of the city. One resident was particularly solicitous about the effect of this innovation upon the Lord's day. He afterward agreed, however, that in consideration of $1,500 he would withdraw his opposition and leave the Lord to take care of his own day. The $1,500 was not paid. The road was finally installed and has proved a very fair success, and it is believed to be a benefit to the people of the city.

The City of Evanston is now anxious to get some benefit from the construction of the Northwestern Elevated. The present service is not satisfactory on account of its slowness and the necessity for transfers. When the road was completed it was expected that the St. Paul would make some traffic arrangement by which a connection could be secured with the elevated by an incline, and its cars could pass without transfer from Evanston down into the city over the express tracks of the elevated. Negotiations up to the present time have not resulted in the success of such a scheme; but it is so much to the interest of all parties concerned that it can be safely assured that this plan will finally be carried out, and that the St. Paul line will be equipped with electricity and operated in connection with the Northwestern Elevated to Evanston. If such an equipment were made, and stops made at frequent intervals through the city, with an express service from the city down over the elevated without any stop, say to Kinzie Street, and a frequent service given with a ten-cent fare, it is believed that the building boom that has set in at the terminus of the elevated would extend up along the shore and include the City of Evanston.

A line leaving this main line at Oakton Avenue and going west to Asbury, and along on Asbury, Florence and Ashland, and along the Northwestern up through to Gross Point, would bring a large area of the City of Evanston, which is now remote from depots, into close touch with the city by the very best kind of service, provided the cars were carried through without transfer over the elevated down into the city. A trolley line from Evanston to Waukegan has been installed, and a branch line leaving this line at Lake Bluff is now being built across to Libertyville, with the intention of being pushed into the Fox Lake region. When this line is completed it will certainly be the greatest pleasure riding and picnic line around Chicago, and the people of Evanston will be put in close connection with some of the most beautiful country around Chicago.

Gas and Electric Lighting.—At a very early day in the history of Evanston, Edwin Lee Brown, one of the city's public- spirited citizens, organized a company known as the Northwestern Gas Light and Coke Company, and started a gas plant. Pipes were laid to the principal buildings in the village. This plant has now been finally merged with the People's Gas Company of Chicago and gas rates run about the same as they do in the city, and the service has been extended practically over the whole city of Evanston.

Another corporation was organized by some of the citizens of Evanston eight or ten years ago for the purpose of furnishing electric light to the then village of Evanston, known as the Evanston Illuminating Company, and it has done for the City of Evanston what has not been done for any other city of its size in the United States, namely: put most of its wires underground. Its franchise for the use of the streets runs for about seventeen years, and it has a contract with the City of Evanston for public lighting running about ten years.

Heating System.—A couple of years ago a corporation was organized by Mr. Yaryan, of Toledo, Ohio, known as the Evanston Yaryan Company, and a franchise secured for furnishing heat by hot water carried through pipes connected with the houses. Recently a plant has been constructed and the service extended to about two hundred houses with the most gratifying results. Ashes, smoke and coal dust are eliminated from the home, and heat is furnished at a rate less than the actual cost of coal for private heating. It is very generally admitted that this single improvement adds fully twenty-five per cent to the value of property thereby benefited for residence. If any man is going to build a home he would be willing to pay that much more, provided he could secure this service; and the demand is spreading all over the city for the extension of the same.

Telephone Service.—The Chicago Telephone Company has extended its service into Evanston and erected a very beautiful building on Chicago Avenue, just south of Davis Street, for its offices. The local charge for residences is very reasonable, and the service has been found extremely satisfactory.

As has already been suggested, the territory embraced within the limits of the City of Evanston is capable of furnishing comfortable homes with plenty of air-space for about 100,000 people. There is no reason why this city should not be a model one. The problems of municipal government and management are live ones, and some of the best thought of the country is devoting itself to their solution. Perhaps nowhere could be found a more ideal spot or a better environment for the practical solution of many of these problems, and the residents of the City of Evanston are of a class to lend themselves readily to assisting along these lines.

CHAPTER XXI.

WATER SUPPLY—LIGHTING SYSTEM
(By THOMAS BATES)

Conditions Prior to 1874—First Move for an Adequate Water Supply—Charles J. Gilbert Leader in the Movement—Holly Engines Installed in 1874 and 1886—Annexation of South Evanston—The Consolidated City Incorporated in 1892—Increase in the Water Supply in 1897—Source of Supply—Revenue—Extent of System—Street Lighting by Gas Introduced in 1871—Introduction of Electric Lighting in 1890—Installation of the Evanston-Yaryan Light and Heating System.

Prior to 1874 the supply of water used by the citizens of Evanston was procured from their own private wells and cisterns. However, for two years before that time, the Village Board of the then Village of Evanston had been considering and discussing the possibility of a more satisfactory means of furnishing the people with water, but, as it involved the building of a water-works plant, putting down sewers and water-pipes and the purchase of an engine, it involved an expense which, to some of the learned fathers of that time, was appalling.

Leader in the Movement for an Improved Water Supply.—The man who was most active and persistent in his fight for the establishment of a water-plant was Charles J. Gilbert, who has, ever since that time, been known as the father of the Evan-ston Water-Works. He not only gave liberally of his time, but also contributed liberally of his private means in traveling about the country for the purpose of ascertaining the best system, the best engines and the best sort of plant for the village, and, in 1874, the first engine and pumping station were installed.

The engine was named the "C. J. Gilbert." It is a quadroduplex Holly engine, with a rated capacity of 2,000,000 gallons per day; but after it was installed and, in cases of emergency, it pumped in the neighborhood of 3,000,000 gallons per day. This engine is still running and in good condition, and it is a somewhat remarkable fact that Samuel B. Penney, who was installed as second engineer of the Evanston Water-Works in 1874, is still in charge of them, and has been in the continuous service of the village and city successively since the old "C. J. Gilbert" pumped the first gallon of water.

This engine was run for seventeen years, night and day, and during those seventeen years it ran on an average of 23.7 hours out of each 24 for the entire time.

The largest amount of water ever pumped in one day during the year 1875 was 656,-918 gallons, and for the entire month of May, 1876, there was pumped 6,636,448 gallons in the thirty-one days. As compared with this record, it may be said that, on August 8, 1900, the amount of water pumped in one day at the Evanston pumping station was 10,156,132 gallons, almost one-third more than was pumped for the entire month of May, 1876.

The Cost—Second Engine Installed in 1886.—The cost of the first Holly engine bought in Evanston, together with boiler, was $24,000. In the year 1886 it became apparent to the authorities of the then Village of Evanston, that the engine which had run night and day since 1875 was, in its capacity, inadequate for the wants of the people, and thereupon, after the usual investigation, consideration and discussion, a second Holly engine was purchased, of the Gaskill type, and, in the year 1888, it was installed with a rated capacity of 5,000,000 gallons a day, which, under pressure, could be increased to 5,500,000 per day.

It is a little remarkable that, upon the installation of this second engine, the then Village Board of Trustees were divided as to whether they should throw out the first engine or sell it for what they could get, upon the theory that this second engine, with a 5,000,000 gallons capacity, would be sufficient for the needs of the village for the next twenty years. It was, however, finally decided to retain the first engine for a time at least, and the wisdom of this decision was shown by the fact that, in less than three years, the second engine was found inadequate, and from that time until the year 1896, the water required at times taxed the full capacity of both engines.

Annexation of South Evanston.—A few years after the installation of the second engine, the Village of South Evanston was annexed to Evanston, and one month later (March, 1892), the consolidated village was incorporated as the City of Evanston. Prior to the annexation of the Village of South Evanston, it had received its water supply largely from an artesian well; but after the annexation, the water-mains were extended or connected with the mains of the City of Evanston, and it then became apparent that the capacity of the engines was insufficient to supply the needs of the people, and, therefore, in 1896 the City Council of Evanston took into consideration the question of the purchase of another engine to meet the increased demand.

Third Engine Installed in 1897.—Great diversity of opinion arose in the minds of the Aldermen composing the City Council as to what kind of an engine was best fitted for the purpose. The discussion at times was bitter and personal, but it resulted in the purchase, in 1897, and the installation of another Holly engine, of the Decrow type, with a pumping capacity of 12,000,000 to 14,000,000 gallons per day. This last mentioned engine, up to this time, has been found fully adequate to supply the needs of the city. The second engine, without any boilers or fittings, cost about $12,000, and the third engine, together with foundations and such fittings as were necessary, cost about $35,000.

The supply of water to these engines is procured through two in-take pipes, the first being 16 inches in diameter, which was laid on the bed of the lake in 1875, and which extends out 1,200 feet from the shore. In 1889, this in-take pipe being found insufficient, another in-take pipe 30 inches in diameter was laid on the bottom of the lake, extending out 2,600 feet to a submerged crib, and it is through this latter pipe that all of the water pumped for the City of Evanston is received, except in summer time, when much water is used for the sprinkling of lawns, and then both pipes are necessary to supply the demand.

Much inconvenience has been experienced in the coldest weather of the winter months, from what is known as anchor or slush ice, which sinks and accumulates about the openings of the submerged cribs and clogs

GROSS POINT LIGHTHOUSE
Sheridan Road and Central Street
Tower completed June 30, 1873.   Light exhibited Spring of 1874

the flow of water, and many expedients have been resorted to in order to overcome this difficulty, none of which, however, have been entirely successful. With a view to accomplishing this object, within the past year, connections have been made with the mains of Rogers Park and the City of Chicago, by which, in case of emergency, the valves may be opened and the supply of water, if cut off by anchor ice, may be obtained from the mains of the City of Chicago through Rogers Park. At the present time the question of a tunnel out under the surface of the lake is being agitated and seriously considered for the purpose of, at all times, securing an adequate supply.

At the present time the City of Evanston is also furnishing to the Village of Wilmette its supply of water.

The pressure upon the mains on an average is 40 pounds to the square inch, which can be raised to 80 pounds to the square inch in case of fire. The coal consumed in the year 1901 was 2,000 tons.

Income—Extent of System.—The revenue received from water-tax in 1901 was $65,000, which does not include the water permits; including the water permits, the total receipts of the Water Department for the year 1901 was about $70,000. It, perhaps, would not be advisable to state how much of this $70,000 is clear profit to the city, but it may be sufficient to add that, whilst the water-tax in the city is not higher than that of other cities—in fact, is considerably less than the water-tax of many cities—still the Evanston water-works plant, today, is proving an exceedingly profitable investment for the city.

The water, for which this $70,000 is paid, is distributed to the citizens of Evanston through sixty-one miles of water-mains. The supply is abundant. No restrictions are placed upon the citizens in regard to lawn sprinkling, and the beautiful trees and lawns of the city bear witness to the fact that the water-plant of Evanston, today, is a decided success.

Lighting.—Prior to 1871 a few smoky, flickering oil-lamps were the only guide which an Evanston citizen had at night to aid him in keeping out of the mud and the ditches of the unpaved and unsewered streets; but it was during this year that the Northwestern Gas-Light & Coke Company erected a small plant and furnished to a very limited number a substitute for the oil-lamps in the form of gas. It was nearly five years after this, however, before gas street-lamps came into anything like general use.

Evanston then, as now, was a city of homes. The people who settled there desired large lawns and plenty of room. A comparatively few people covered a large area, and to light effectively all the streets with gas involved an expenditure which was out of all proportion to the number of inhabitants who derived the benefit; and, therefore, it was not until about the year 1890 that an Evanston citizen could boast that his town was well lighted. Indeed, it was not until about the year 1895 that the lighting of the streets of the city could be said to be entirely satisfactory.

Evanston Electric Illuminating Company.—In the year 1890 the Evanston Electric Illuminating Company built its plant in Evanston, and, within one year after that plant was established, it entered into a contract with the City of Evanston to supply arc-lights of 2,000-candle power at the rate of $83.75 each per year, under what was known as the Philadelphia Moonlight Schedule.

In the month of July, 1895, the city entered into a contract with the Evanston Electric Illuminating Company by which it was agreed that the latter should furnish arc-lights of 2,000-candle power at a yearly cost of $65 per light, which contract provided that, at the end of five years, the illuminating company should have the right to raise the price to $67.50 per light.

The five-year contract expired in July, 1900, but in the spring of 1900 the Evanston-Yaryan Company applied to the City Council for an ordinance permitting them to establish an electric light and heating plant, and it was represented by the latter company that, by combining the two and furnishing both light and heat to the citizens, they would be able to furnish electric light at a greatly reduced price.

The ordinance for which the new company petitioned was granted by the Council, and the Evanston-Yaryan Company at once entered into competition with the Evanston Electric Illuminating Company for the street lighting contract, the result of which was that the City Council were enabled to make and close a contract with the Evanston Electric Illuminating Company, by which the latter agreed to furnish arc-lamps for lighting the streets of Evanston at $60 per light of 2,000-candle power, for a period of ten years, upon a schedule much more liberal than that known as the Philadelphia Moon-light Schedule. Under this contract the City of Evanston is now paying for 273 lights at an aggregate cost of $16,380.00 per year.

Yaryan Light and Heating System.—
The Evanston-Yaryan Company erected its light and heat plant in the year 1900. It experienced great difficulty in securing permits for the extension of its wires, the result being that it was able to furnish electric light only to a comparatively small number of consumers; but it immediately placed its mains in the central portion of the city for the furnishing of heat by means of hot water, which was pumped through those mains and into the houses from force pumps located in the central plant. In the summer

or fall of 1902 it consolidated its electric plant with the Evanston Electric Illuminating Company, and, at the present time, the electric lighting of Evanston is again controlled by one corporation.

The franchise granted by the City Council of Evanston to the Evanston-Yaryan Company fixed a limit upon the price that it might charge for furnishing heat to consumers, and in the summer of 1902 the company complained to the City Council that, under the limit thus fixed, it was unable to furnish heat upon a paying basis; and, in fact, it complained that it was running its plant at a loss. Thereupon, in September, 1902, further concessions were granted to the company by the City Council, under which it is now running its heating plant, and by reason of which it is enabled to secure a higher price for the heat furnished to consumers.

There can be no question that the heat thus furnished is ideal and very satisfactory to the consumers; but the question remains whether the Evanston-Yaryan Company will be enabled to furnish heat to its patrons at a price which they can afford to pay. In other words, the present prices charged are something in excess of what it would cost the consumer to heat his premises with a plant of his own. However, whilst this plant may be said to be now in an experimental state, there can be no question that the furnishing heat from a central plant is coming more largely into favor every year, and it is therefore predicted that the heating plant erected by the Evanston-Yaryan Company is now, and hereafter will be, a success.

It is claimed by this company that it can furnish heat to residents living a mile from its central plant, the hot water being forced out through pipes that are protected from the influence of the cold and returned by other pipes to the central heating plant, where the water is again heated to a high temperature and again forced out through the pipes to the consumers. But whilst the company claims that it can heat buildings a mile from its plant, still it is doubtful whether the heat can be profitably furnished to buildings situated three-quarters of a mile away.

It is estimated that the Evanston-Yaryan Company are, at this time, supplying heat to about 250 consumers, and, from the reports received, it is fair to assume that but few of those consumers would be willing to go back to the old system of heating, even though the expense of the hot-water heat from the Yaryan plant is somewhat greater than would be the cost of heating their buildings by the old process.

In conclusion, it may be said today that, in the matter of water supply and in city lighting, there are few, if any, cities more fortunate than the city of Evanston.

CHAPTER XXII.

EDUCATION

(By PROF. HENRY L. BOLTWOOD, late Principal Township High School)

The Public Schools of Evanston—Day of the Log School House—Early Schools and their Teachers—Sacrifice of School Land —Present School Buildings—Township High School—Preliminary History— —School Opened in September, 1883— Prof. Boltwood its First Principal— Present School Building—Manual Training—A Mimic Presidential Election— Drawing Department—List of Trustees.

The earliest records of Evanston public schools begin with May 9, 1846. This was about eleven years before the existing school laws of Illinois were framed. In those days the Township Trustees constituted the Board of Education, unless more than one district existed in the township. These trustees were appointed by the County Commissioners. The trustees of Township 41 North, Range 14 East, in 1846, were E. Bennett and O. Munn, Jr., with George M. Huntoon, Secretary and Treasurer.

Prior to the above date, a log school-house had been erected, probably by private subscription, on the northwest corner of Ridge Avenue and Greenleaf Street, on a lot which Henry Clark had deeded to the township for school and cemetery purposes. A private or subscription school had been maintained as early as 1844. The first teacher employed was a Mrs. Marshall, who taught at first in a cooper shop on the

Ridge road, nearly opposite the residence of the late Ozro Crain. The log school-house occupied in 1846 was probably built in 1845. One of its logs is now in the Central school at South Evanston. It seems to have needed repairs in 1846.

Before 1857, public schools in Illinois were not free schools. The public funds derived from the State and from the income of the school lands were not ample enough to maintain school except for a brief time. Teachers kept a schedule of attendance, and all the expenses for fuel, repairs and teachers' wages, were distributed among the parents of the several pupils in proportion to the number of days of attendance, regardless of property. The poorest man in the district might be called upon to pay the heaviest tax. This was the case in Connecticut as late as 1853. Parents were also required to board the teacher a certain number of days, according to the number of pupils sent from their family. This "boarding 'round" was the rule, and not the exception, in New England in those days, and is occasionally to be found even now. In case of a refusal to board the teacher, the teacher might, after due notice, select a boarding place, and the board-bill could be legally collected of the recusant family. The per diem rates do not appear in the school records, but from tuition bills in the possession of some of the old residents, they varied

187

from three-fourths of a cent to six cents, according to the number of pupils or the wages of the teacher.

The first teacher employed by the Trustees of the Evanston District was Miss Cornelia Wheadon, daughter of the well-known "Father Wheadon." Miss Wheadon now Mrs. C. A. Churcher, is still living (1903) at 2044 Sherman Avenue. She was engaged at a salary of $1.25 per week—very fair wages for the time. A motion was made at the board meeting to repair the schoolhouse and to purchase a water-pail and dipper. The repairs were voted down.

Pupils who lived along Chicago and Hinman Avenue, then known as the East Ridge, were sometimes unable to cross to the school-house except in boats or on rafts, on account of the deep water. Ozro Crain shot wild ducks, and occasionally a deer, about where Crain Street crosses Benson Avenue, just south of the present high school building. Before Miss Wheadon, Elmira Burroughs (Mrs. Palmer), and a Mr. T. H. Ballard taught. Miss Wheadon had also taught five weeks before her recorded engagement, and was allowed six shillings a week for her services.

Miss H. W. Barnes succeeded Miss Wheadon. She was married to Sylvester Hill, and continued to teach after marriage. Her wages were two dollars a week. In the winter of 1846 nine cords of wood were required to warm the little one-room school-house.

School Funds.—In the famous Ordinance of 1787, Congress declared that "schools and the means of education shall be forever encouraged," but did not specify how this should be done. But when, in 1818, Congress passed the act enabling the people of Illinois to form a State Constitution, it was provided that Section 16 in every township should be granted to the State for the use of the inhabitants of such

township for the support of schools. In case that Section 16 had already been disposed of, other lands equivalent thereto, and as contiguous as may be, were to be granted. The State Constitutional Convention accepted this provision.

But as Evanston is only a small fraction of the west side of a township whose legal designation is 41 North, Range 14 East, Section 16 is under the lake. To provide for such and similar cases, a law was passed in 1826, allowing townships so situated to select lands elsewhere. Accordingly Evanston, then known as Gross Point or Ridgeville, obtained as school land a tract lying in Section 12, Township 41 North, Range 13 East, a part of Niles Township, containing 153.48 acres. This land lay between Simpson Street on the south and Grant Street on the north, Dodge Avenue on the east and Hartrey Avenue on the west.

Most unwisely, as it now seems, the School Trustees sold this land at the minimum Government price of $1.25 per acre. One of the purchasers was Wendel Ellis, whose patent to the land was granted December 27, 1847, by Augustus C. French, Governor of Illinois, upon a return made by George Manierre, School Commissioner of Cook County. The money obtained by the sale of this land disappeared when School Treasurer Green defaulted in 1873.

To prevent such sales as the above, several of the younger States have laws that fix a minimum price for school lands, far in excess of the Government rate, and thus secure to the schools a permanent fund of great value. The school lands of Texas will ultimately give the schools of that State a permanent fund of not less than thirty millions. If Chicago had today all the original school lands of its several townships, the income would be almost enough to run its schools.

The early records are sadly defective.

Nothing is recorded for the year 1847. The Trustees in 1848 were O. A. Crain, E. Bennett and M. Dunlap. G. M. Huntoon was Treasurer. His bond was fixed at $400. The regular meetings were held at the Ridge House in Gross Point. A special meeting was called to be held "at early candle light." In that year it was voted that a sale of cemetery lots be held on the school premises, but no record of sale appears.

In March, 1848, it was voted to divide the township into two school districts, putting all of the township north of the south line of Section 19 into District One. Legal notice of a meeting to vote on the proposed change was ordered, but there is no record of any vote upon the question, and the probability is that the matter was dropped without a vote. It was not till February, 1852, that the division into districts was legally made. District 1 comprised the south part of the township, and District 2 extended "from the south line of Eli Gaffield's farm" to the north boundary of the township. So reads the record. But a subsequent vote makes the north District No. 1, and makes its south boundary the middle line east and west of Section 19.

In a list of by-laws adopted in April, 1860, trustees who were absent without excuse from a regular meeting were to pay a fine of fifty cents, but no record is made of any collection of a fine. Teachers were required to teach twenty-two days each month. They were also required to use exertions to have the children go to and from school in an orderly manner, and make it a rule that they should not play by the way, or bear tales of any of the transactions in school or during intermission. "Scholars shall be required to come with clean faces and hands under pain of being expelled from school."

When District 2 was organized, the school funds were divided upon a property basis, and District 1 received $25.49, and District 2, $13.50.

By vote of the township, February 14, 1856, District 2 was divided, and that part south of the Indian boundary was designated as District 3, but there is no record of its organization, though the organization of Districts 1, 2 and 4 are preserved. In 1870 District 3 was annexed again to District 2. The bond of the School Treasurer for 1856 was for $1,000.

The first regular school-tax was levied in 1856—fifty cents on each hundred dollars of taxable property. This amount was expected to provide for the running of the schools, and to pay up a deficiency.

District 4 was organized in April, 1857. It included "all that part of Evanston" north of the center of the south half of fractional Sections 7 and 12, in Townships 13 and 14. The first teacher of this school was M. E. Budlong.

The first recorded school census was in October, 1857. All white children under twenty-one were to be enumerated. C. Thomas took the census, and was allowed six dollars for his services, but no record of the result appears.

It seems that the Directors of District 2 bought a school-house lot of George M. Huntoon for $250, and received a deed from him, running to the Directors. Treasurer H. B. Hurd took the necessary legal action to restrain the Directors from paying the sum to Huntoon until the proper deed was made, vesting the title in the School Trustees. This result was not secured without a lawsuit.

In 1859 District 4 was re-annexed to District 1. This seems to have been because of the small number of children in the district. There are no records of the trustees between May, 1862, and October, 1868. Samuel Greene was elected Treasurer.

In April, 1870, "Section 12, and so much of Section 7 as lies west of the Ridge road and in the town of Evanston," was made a separate district, to be known as District 3. At a subsequent meeting, all of Section 7 was set back to District 1.

An appraisement of property was made in July following, to determine the allotment of school funds. The valuation of District 1 was $307,399, and of Section 12, $6,470.

Upon petition of residents of New Trier and of "lots No. 1 to 19, both inclusive, in George Smith's sub-division of the south part of the Archange Ouilmette Reservation," Union District No. 3,—the North Evanston district—was legally constituted, October 3, 1870.

District No. 4, the Rogers Park District, was also constituted in October, 1870. There was some difficulty about its boundaries, but it was finally settled that it should include all of the township lying south of the south boundary of Calvary Cemetery.

In April, 1875, Union School District No. 5 was organized. It included the northeast part of Evanston Township, and a part of New Trier Township, or the "Ouilmette Reserve."

Samuel Greene, Township Treasurer, defaulted in 1873. His bondsmen, apparently, paid the amount due from him in 1876, $5,397.10.

The first school-house built in District 1 was a one-story, one-room building, which was erected on the north side of Church Street, just east of Maple Avenue. Another story was added to it later. It was afterwards removed to 1618 Orrington Avenue, and is now occupied as a laundry. It was probably built in 1852, the year of the organization of the district. The upper story was used as a polling place for several years.

About 1860 the Benson Avenue school-house was erected, just south of Clark Street. It was twice enlarged; the last time in 1870. In this same year the lots on which the Hinman Avenue and the Noyes Street schools now stand were purchased, and school-houses were probably built soon after, but all the records of the district prior to 1870 are missing, and some records of later years are incomplete.

The original Noyes Street building is still standing on the north side of Gaffield Place, just west of the Milwaukee and St. Paul Railroad. The Hinman Avenue frame building was removed in 1881, to make room for a new brick edifice. It was taken to Benson Avenue, near Clark Street, and used as a church by the Second Baptist congregation till destroyed by fire in 1889.

In 1879 the three schools had outgrown their accommodations, and there was much discussion as to the proper means to provide more room. The Board of Education recommended a consolidation of all the schools on the block then known as the Lakeside property between Sherman and Chicago Avenue, north of Greenwood and south of Lake. The citizens, however, disapproved of this, and a new building was voted, to be placed on the Hinman Avenue lot, and a lot was purchased on Wesley Avenue, on which a large one-story brick building was erected. This was known as the Wesley Avenue School until 1900, when the name of David B. Dewey School was given it in honor of one of Evanston's most efficient citizens, who was for many years a member of the School Board. Both the Hinman Avenue and the Wesley Avenue buildings were constructed of one story only. The idea was, in this way, to avoid stair-climbing and to lessen danger in case of fire. The present high cost of land in Evanston will be in the way of any more buildings of this sort, but the Wesley Avenue building still has all its eight rooms on the ground floor.

The Benson Avenue building stood on leased ground, directly on the right of way of the Milwaukee & St. Paul Railroad. Its removal became necessary when that road was built in 1892. It was moved in three sections to the south side of Emerson Street, just west of Maple Avenue. The Haven school was then built on Church Street. It was very appropriately named after Dr. O. E. Haven, who was Superintendent of Schools from 1873 to 1882, and afterwards on the Board of Education till his untimely death in 1888.

In 1892 the Noyes Street School was provided with a new and enlarged building, which has been already outgrown, and a large addition was completed early in 1903. In 1894 the Larimer School was erected on Crain Street, on the very south boundary line of the district. It was named in honor of Joseph Larimer, a valued member of the School Board, and a man whose love for young men, and whose good influence upon them, well merited such a tribute to his memory. The Hinman Avenue School received a new building in 1898. This gives District 1 (or 76 in the present county enumeration) five large buildings, containing forty-nine rooms, with a seating capacity of about two thousand. Three additional rooms are also rented on Asbury Avenue, to accommodate the overflow of the D. B. Dewey School.

There appears to be no record of the earliest teachers of this district. The names of Echenbracht and Edwards are found among the earlier Principals. P. C. Hanford, who was murdered in Chicago, was also a Principal. Charles Raymond, who is still living here, was the first to grade the schools and to receive the title of Superintendent. He was succeeded in 1873 by Otis E. Haven, son of Bishop Haven of the University of Michigan. Mr. Haven was a born teacher of rare executive ability.

He not only brought the schools to a high degree of efficiency, but secured for himself a remarkable personal affection which still remains fresh in the minds of his numerous pupils.

He was the first to organize a high school. There was no small opposition to the idea of a high school at first; especially from those who thought that the academy of the Northwestern University, which was already in the field, was fully competent to do the work of such a school. However the school was established in 1876. It had no building, and was quartered in Lyons hall and elsewhere. From the very beginning it had an excellent name for scholarship, and sent its graduates to several of the best colleges. It had many tuition pupils from South Evanston, Rogers Park and elsewhere.

Among its early teachers was Dr. E. J. James, now President of the University of Illinois, from January, 1878, to May, 1889. His successor was J. Scott Clark, now Professor of English in Northwestern University.

George S. Baker, now a lawyer in Evanston, succeeded Mr. Haven in 1882, and was Superintendent for four years. Mr. Baker is a graduate of Michigan University and came to Evanston from McGregor, Iowa. He resigned his position to take up the study of law, as Mr. Haven did of medicine. During his administration the schools steadily grew and prospered.

Homer H. Kingsley, a graduate of Michigan University, succeeded Mr. Baker in 1886, and still continues in charge. Mr. Kingsley has been especially successful in thoroughly grading the schools, and in securing excellent buildings. The introduction of the kindergarten, of manual training and of domestic science is also due largely to his exertions, seconded and encouraged by the Woman's Club, and by many citizens. His work is widely known throughout the State, and the schools of Evanston attract many visitors from abroad and are most cordially supported by the tax-payers.

This district was one of the first to give women a place on the School Board, and Mrs. Louise P. Stanwood was the first woman to serve on the Board.

The value of the grounds and buildings now owned by the district is about $250,-000, and its bonded debt about $70,000. These bonds, at 4 and 4½ per cent, command a premium. The finances of the district have been very ably managed by our prominent business men. A. N. Young, Simeon Farwell, F. P. Crandon, and H. H. C. Miller may be mentioned as having done much in regard to the finances.

Evanston was among the first to incorporate the kindergarten in its school system. The first kindergarten was established in 1892. There are now four, and the experiment has proved very satisfactory.

Manual training was introduced in the form of shop-work as early as 1897, but a new impulse was given to it in 1901. Mrs. Alfred H. Gross and her brother, Irwin Rew, are the generous donors of funds to equip a Manual Training and a Domestic Science Department. Mrs. Gross offered an unlimited sum for the equipment of a Domestic Science school, only stipulating that it should be the finest in the country and the best that money could furnish. The Board furnished the building in which the two new departments are housed.

Mr. Rew offered $500 to equip the manual training room, and both Mrs. Gross and Mr. Rew offered $1,000 toward the salary of the requisite teachers, if the buildings were provided for by the Board.

The equipment of the Domestic Science department cost over $1,700. Mr. Rew's first gift to equip the Manual Training Department was $500. He subsequently gave a dozen lathes, of the latest and most improved pattern, at a cost of about $400. The building cost $8,000. Classes of twenty-four are taught at the same time. About two hundred boys and the same number of girls receive instruction weekly. The cost of the material used and all incidental expenses are paid by the regular appropriations of the Board.

The tenure of office among Evanston teachers is worthy of notice. Miss Nannie M. Hines and Miss Celia Sargent have completed their thirtieth year of service, and many others are nearing twenty years of continuous work.

District Two (South Evanston).—The modern history of District Two begins in 1871, in which year a four-room brick building was erected on the present site of the Central School, on Main Street. The cost was $18,000. This building was greatly enlarged in 1890, at a cost of $10,000.

In 1893, while the school was in session, fire broke out and entirely destroyed the building. By heroic efforts on the part of the teachers, no lives were lost, though several persons were injured. In 1901 a memorial fountain was erected to commemorate the names of the teachers who were most active in the rescue work.

A new building was at once erected on the same site, at a cost of $47,000. While this was under construction, the schools were accommodated in rented rooms. The eighth grade pupils occupied part of the high school building till the end of the school year.

In 1886 a four-room building was erected on the east side of the railroad, on Main Street near Forest Avenue. This was soon outgrown, and the present Lincoln schoolhouse was erected in 1895, at a cost of $47,-000.

In 1900 another building, known as the

Washington School, was built on the west side, on the northwest corner of Ashland Avenue and Main Street, at a cost of $35,-000.

It may safely be said that all these buildings are unsurpassed in their adaptation to school work and in the completeness of their equipment. The lighting, heating and ornamentation can hardly be improved. They attract many visitors who are seeking for models and suggestions.

Township High School.—In the winter of 1883, the attention of the citizens of Evanston village was called to the fact that additional school accommodations were needed for all the schools, and especially for the High School, which had been maintained for several years without any regular home. It had been moved about from hall to hall, and was greatly hindered in its work by its cramped and uncomfortable quarters, in rooms which were in no way suited to school uses. The rapid growth of the village had filled all the school buildings to overflowing. As the villages of Evanston and of South Evanston were in close proximity, and as all of the population of the township was distributed along the line of a single railroad, the idea of a Township High School was received with favor from its first mention. After considerable discussion in private circles and in the local papers, a public meeting was announced to be held in Lyons' hall, on the evening of February 11, 1882. The call for the meeting was headed by John L. Beveridge, L. C. Pitner and H. A. Pearsons.

The meeting was held according to announcement. Henry L. Boutelle presided. After free discussion, a committee was appointed consisting of John H. Kedzie, George O. Ide, William Blanchard, Oliver Adams and Harvey B. Hurd, who were instructed to prepare a report to be pre-

sented at an adjourned meeting to be held February 18th. This committee reported at the adjourned meeting, presenting the facts and figures which, in their judgment, favored the establishment of the proposed school. After considerable discussion, the following resolution was unanimously adopted:

"Resolved, That it is the sense of this meeting that a Township High School be established at an early date, and that a committee of seven be appointed by the chair, the duty of said committee being to interest the citizens of the town in the matter, and especially in those districts in which there has been thus far least interest in the matter."

These districts were, naturally, North Evanston and Rogers Park, which were farthest from the center of the township. South Evanston had been sending many pupils to the village high school from its first organization, upon payment of tuition.

The committee appointed in accordance with the foregoing resolution was composed of W. H. Crocker, Oliver Adams, Alexander H. Gunn, A. G. Bell, F. P. Crandon, Norton W. Boomer, and George O. Ide.

The report of the committee appointed on the 11th of February and the proceedings of the meeting held on the 18th of that month were published in the "Index" of the week following the 18th.

On the 9th of March, a petition, headed by Hugh A. White and H. B. Hurd, and signed by eighty-seven other legal voters, was filed with the Township Treasurer, Ambrose Foster, requesting that the question of the establishment of a Township High School be submitted to the legal voters of the township at the next election of School Trustees. This election resulted in a vote of 611 in favor of the school to 147 against it. William Blanchard was elected School Trustee. Thomas A. Cosgrove resigned from the Board of Trustees and Norton W. Boomer was elected in his place. Mr. Cosgrove's resignation was because both Mr. Blanchard and himself were residents of the same school district, contrary to law.

On the 10th of July, 1882, a notice was issued calling an election to be held on the 22d of the same month, to vote upon two propositions:

First. To authorize the Trustees of the township to purchase a site for building and to erect a suitable building upon it.

Second. To authorize them to borrow not exceeding $40,000, for the purchase of a site and the erection of a building, and to issue bonds for the amount actually borrowed.

The question of a site, of course, was of great interest, and several sites were proposed. Charles Raymond, once Principal of the schools in District 1, advocated the selection of the public park; but it was found that this property was not available except for park purposes. Others advocated the block then known as the Lakeside Block, between Chicago and Sherman Avenues, north of Greenwood Boulevard, then occupied by a building which had been used for a private school. The site proposed in the election call was the corner of Benson Avenue and Dempster Street, fronting west 250 feet on Benson Avenue, and measuring 200 feet on Dempster Street.

At the election held in accordance with the above call, 176 votes were cast in favor of this site, and two against it. Only one vote was cast against issuing the bonds.

The purchase price of the site selected was $4,000, or $16 per front foot. The ground was very low, and $2,200 was expended in filling. The building of sewers has since entirely changed the conditions. The bonds issued bore 5 per cent interest, payable semi-annually, and were all taken

by the Hide and Leather Bank of Chicago, at par. The plan selected for the building was furnished by W. W. Boynton, a Chicago architect. The contract price of the structure was $32,500. The furniture, library, and apparatus cost about $2,500. The mason work was done by Charles T. Bartlett of Evanston, and the woodwork by A. H. Avers of Chicago. McDougal Brothers, of Evanston, did the plumbing, and J. B. Hobbs, of Evanston, took the contract for painting. Ground was broken for the building October 18, 1882, but owing to the severity of the weather, little was done until the spring of the following year. The work was completed and the building formally dedicated August 31, 1883.

At the dedicatory exercises prayer was offered by Rev. F. S. Jewell. Addresses were made by Dr. O. E. Haven, former Superintendent of the village schools; by Albert G. Lane, County Superintendent of Schools; Rev. Dr. Cummings, President of the Northwestern University, and others. William Blanchard, President of the Township Trustees of Schools, presented the keys of the building to the Principal-elect, and Prof. R. H. Cunnock, of the School of Oratory, gave selected readings.

The Board of Trustees, at the date of the opening of the school, were William Blanchard, S. Goodenow and S. D. Childs. Mr. Childs was chosen at a special election called to fill a vacancy caused by the death of Norton W. Boomer, who did not live to see the completion of an enterprise in which he had taken great interest.

The school was opened September 3, 1883. The following teachers were employed:

Principal, Henry L. Boltwood, A. M. (Amherst.)

Science, Lyndon Evans. A. B. (Knox.)

Mathematics, Eva S. Edwards (Oswego Normal School.)

Latin and English, Mary L. Barrie.
German and History, Ellen L. White.
Music, O. H. Merwin.

Mr. Boltwood, who came to Illinois from Massachusetts in 1865, is widely known as the father of the Township High School in Illinois. In 1867 he organized in Princeton, Bureau County, the first school of this kind. Its success was an important factor in procuring the passage of the present State law pertaining to high schools. The Princeton school was organized under a special act. After teaching eleven years in Princeton, he organized another township high school at Ottawa, LaSalle County. Mr. Evans came from the High School in LaSalle. Miss Edwards and Miss White had been teaching for two years in the High School of Evanston. Miss Barrie came with Mr. Boltwood from Ottawa.

On the morning of December 20—the first very cold day of the winter—the building was found to be on fire. A register had been carelessly placed directly upon woodwork, only a few feet above a furnace. The school session was just commencing when the fire was discovered. The pupils behaved admirably. When it was apparent that the fire could not be controlled, they quietly removed their books, and assisted in carrying the library and apparatus to neighboring houses. Only one piece of apparatus, of trifling value, was injured. The fire department worked admirably, but it was very difficult to reach the fire. Aid was summoned from Chicago, and after three hours of hard work the flames were extinguished. The greater part of the building was uninjured except by water and smoke. The loss was about $4,000, fully covered by insurance. By extra hard work the building was reopened for school in a little more than two weeks, although with many unfavorable conditions. An even one hundred pupils were enrolled at the outset.

Among them were several who had graduated in former years, but who wished to carry their studies farther with improved conditions. The general course of study was lengthened from three years to four. In consequence there was no regular class to graduate at the end of the year. Five pupils graduated, however, of whom all but one had been in the school four years. The total enrollment for the year reached one hundred and forty-three.

Drawing had not been taught in the village high school, nor in the graded schools, but Miss Edwards was kind enough to take up this subject, and the high quality of the drawing work of the school from the first has been largely due to her energy and perseverance. O. H. Merwin had charge of the music, but the interest in this subject has never been very great, and it was retained in the course only three years. While it was retained, the pupils furnished the music for the graduating exercises.

Prize Speaking.—In the spring of 1884 a prize-speaking contest was held, open to pupils of the third year. An admission fee was charged and the prizes were paid out of the receipts. Any surplus was expended for the school, especially for the benefit of the Athletic Association. After a few years the prizes were given by two of our citizens, and the proceeds were applied to the class fund of the Junior Class. It soon became a custom for the Junior Class to give a reception to the Seniors on the occasion of graduation. This reception is generally held in the school building.

The enrollment of 1883-84 reached one hundred and fifty-five. The drawing work was increased. Typewriting was introduced as a voluntary study in connection with bookkeeping, and a class in shorthand was conducted outside of school hours. Forty different pupils took up typewriting, some of whom became reasonably expert.

Mr. Evans, having been elected Superintendent of the South Evanston schools, resigned at the end of the first year, and was succeeded by William Harkins, A.M., as teacher of Science and English.

Near the close of this year an industrial exhibit was given by the school, to which the pupils were requested to bring something of their own handiwork, not necessarily anything connected with school work. Most of them complied, and a very interesting display was made. Besides drawing, writing in English and German, typewriting, shorthand and map-drawing, which might be considered as school work, there were exhibited scroll sawing, wood carving, pieces of philosophical apparatus, bread, butter, confectionery, a great variety of needlework, and various collections of plants, insects and postage stamps. A large number of visitors inspected the exhibit. A class of twelve graduated this year.

One hundred and sixty pupils were enrolled in the fall of 1885, and the total enrollment of the year was one hundred and seventy-one. This necessitated more teaching force, and Miss Jane H. White was added to the corps. Mr. Harkins was succeeded as teacher of Science by Benjamin B. James, now (1903) Superintendent of Schools in West Superior, Wis.

The increased number of pupils required a remodeling of the assembly room, which had been arranged on the original plan for only one hundred and forty-four pupils. By doubling the number of desks in part of the room one hundred and eighty were accommodated.

In 1885 the school competed for the first time in the State Fair Exhibit, sending five sets of examination papers. Three of these took first prizes of $5 each. In 1886 ten sets of papers were sent, which took eight first prizes and two seconds, besides the two "sweep-stake" prizes for the best six and the best ten sets. For seven successive years the school carried off the highest honors, and received, in cash, $424, which was expended in pictures, casts and books for the library. At the end of this time the former system of awarding prizes was changed, and the school has not competed since.

The industrial exhibit of 1886 surpassed that of the former year, both in quantity and quality. The drawing and clay modeling attracted no little attention. A class of fourteen graduated this year.

Mr. James was succeeded at the close of the year by Lorenzo N. Johnson, A. B., of the Wesleyan University of Middletown, Conn. Mr. Johnson remained five years and did splendid work. He took great interest in school athletics, which, under his general charge, were very successful. He resigned in 1891 to accept a position as Instructor in Botany at Ann Arbor University, Mich., where he remained until his lamented death in 1897.

From the first, the school took special interest in athletics. For several years in succession Evanston won the pennant in the Cook County Baseball League. It has also won high honors in indoor baseball. In football it has not been able to compete very favorably with the larger schools. The loss of Crain field, near the schoolhouse, was a great drawback to good practice. The names of Frederick W. Poole, John H. Kedzie, Irving McDowell, Richard Carr, Arthur Sickels and Frederick Lanphear, not to mention many others, will long be remembered in the school.

Without following further in detail the history of the school it may briefly be said that the growth was very regular for several consecutive years, the increase averaging about thirty a year, and requiring an additional teacher each year. The annexing of Rogers Park to Chicago, in 1893, prevented the usual increase in that year.

While no effort has been made to secure pupils from abroad a considerable number have attended, chiefly from the towns on the north. New Trier Township—in which are located Wilmette, Winnetka, Kenilworth and Glencoe—was a regular contributor to the attendance until it established a Township High School of its own. In the first semester of 1900-01 all the High School pupils of that township, seventy-seven in number, attended the Evanston school, while their own building was in process of erection. Their tuition, amounting to $1,525, was paid by New Trier Township.

The total enrollment of the school in twenty years is almost exactly 2,900. Comparing this number with the number of graduates, 549, and not counting the 420 enrolled this year (1903), it will be seen that about 22 per cent of all that enter the school complete the course.

Nineteen classes have graduated, containing in all 549 pupils. Of these about forty per cent have gone to colleges, or higher institutions, besides many who have entered college without completing the High School course, or who have completed their preparation elsewhere.

Of these graduates 205—or about 37 per cent—were boys; a much larger proportion than is usually found among the graduates of high schools. In one class the boys outnumbered the girls, and in another they were equal in number.

Graduates or under-graduates have entered the following colleges and professional schools, though the list is undoubtedly incomplete: Amherst, Boston University, Bowdoin, Dartmouth, Harvard, Williams, Yale, Massachusetts School of Technology, Holyoke, Smith, Wellesley, Vassar, Bryn Mawr, Wells, Baltimore Female College, Cornell, Princeton, Syracuse, Annapolis, West Point, Lehigh University of Michigan, University of Wisconsin, University of Minnesota, Wesleyan University of Bloomington, Northwestern University, Lake Forest University, University of California, Berkeley, Colorado, Denver, Beloit, Rockford, Oberlin, Lewis Institute, Armour Institute, School of Mines at Golden, School of Mines at Rolla, School of Mines at Houghton, Art Institute at Chicago, Cumnock School of Oratory, besides several law and medical schools. Many have taken high honors, and several are professors or instructors in various colleges.

The original school building was planned to satisfy the needs of the Evanston of 1883 rather than with any view to the future. Evanston then had a population of about 8,000. Before four years had passed, the original assembly room was too small to accommodate the pupils, and a remodeling of the building was necessary. The growth continued, and in 1889 a large wing on the south side, containing ten recitation rooms, was added to the building at a cost of $22,000. This, in turn, proved too small, and in 1899 a new front and a north wing were added. This involved a virtual reconstruction of the whole building, and the problem of fitting the new to the old was much more difficult of solution than the building of an entirely new structure. Mr. Charles R. Ayers, however, proved equal to the occasion, and the present building is both attractive in appearance and convenient for work. The cost of the improvement was about $90,000.

The north wing contains the Biological, the Physical and the Chemical laboratories, and a lecture room which is used in common by the different teachers. The Manual Training Department occupies the north basement. On the second floor of this wing are the rooms assigned to the Drawing Department. There are three study-rooms, one for the Senior class, one occupied by the second and third year pupils, and one (the original assembly room) allotted to the entering class. The pupils generally study in these rooms when not in recitation.

The building contains thirty-six rooms above the basement, and is intended to accommodate at least six hundred pupils. The present enrollment (1903) is 420. One of the rooms is designated as the Infirmary, and is equipped as an emergency hospital. Two large recitation rooms, thrown together, are used as a sort of gymnasium. There is not room enough on the premises for a regular gymnasium. The proximity to two railroads is the greatest defect in the location. Twenty teachers are now employed besides an office clerk.

Manual Training.—In 1886 the Board purchased tools for woodwork, enough to equip a class of twelve, and Mr. T. E. Skinner, a carpenter and contractor, gave instruction outside of school hours to classes. Each pupil paid a fee of twenty-five cents a week for instruction. Twenty took instruction at first. They constructed their own benches and tool chests, and made easels enough to furnish the drawing department, but there was no regular course pursued. The hours after school were not favorable to work. In winter it became dark too early and in the milder weather it interfered with school athletics. Manual training was therefore dropped for some years.

When the enlarged and remodeled building was planned two large rooms in the basement were set aside for mechanical training. Improved benches and new tools were provided. A three horse-power dynamo was furnished, which takes the requisite current from the city electric plant. Four wood lathes were provided. Mr. Clarence M. Thorne took charge of the work. A regular course was laid out, in connection with

mechanical drawing. The work was done in school hours, and received credit like any other study requiring equal time.

Mr. Ward W. Pearson took charge of the work in 1901 and is still in charge of it. This year two lathes, a circular saw, a band-saw, a drill and a forge have been added to the plant, which altogether cost about $1,500. As a rule, the pupils have taken interest in their work. Conditions of room prevent any other than woodwork and a course longer than two years.

Citizenship.—On the day of the Presidential election the school has twice had a lesson in practical citizenship by going through the form of holding an election. Judges are appointed; voters are registered in regular poll-books by clerks; votes are challenged; regulation polling-booths are erected, and the specimen ballots sent out by the county officials are used instead of the official ones. Careful instruction is given in regard to the marking of the ballot. These elections have excited no little interest.

Drawing Department.—Twenty years ago—except in Massachusetts—few schools outside the larger cities included drawing, or any kind of manual training, in their regular courses of study. At the opening of the Evanston Township High School, the Principal said, "We must make a beginning, no matter how small it is," and the beginning was made.

The pupils enrolled in that first drawing-class, almost without exception, had never had any previous instruction in that study. However, their interest and faithfulness gave promise of success to the experiment, and the results justified it. From the first the aim was to be practical. The allotted time was forty-five minutes daily, on alternate days, for two years. The work was planned to open to the pupil as many avenues as possible, leaving him to choose and specialize later.

Form-drawing and design from given units were the basis of the first year's work; representation and construction followed as the pupils gained confidence and power. "Correlation" was an important feature; the drawing department supplemented the work in science and history. Under the superintendence' of the drawing teacher, charts and sketches in zoology and botany were prepared.

. Clay modeling was introduced in 1885. In those days the drawing and mathematics were taught in the same room, and the pupil who went to the board to demonstrate a problem in Algebra and Geometry threaded his way cautiously around and among easels, tables, drawing boards and all the other "needfuls" that were slowly but surely accumulating. Increasing numbers and lack of space made it necessary to omit the modeling until 1889, when it was again taken up under much more favorable conditions: not as before, as a supplement to drawing, but as an independent study, taken daily for a full year.

In 1887 Historic Art was introduced. The introduction of drawing in the public schools relieved our course of some of the elementary work which before had been necessary. No feature of the course has proved more satisfactory, and no other has brought, in after years, more emphatic testimonials as to "value received." The pupils receive lectures which they themselves illustrate with their own drawings, and also insert in their note books whatever comes to hand from magazine and other illustrations. The Egyptian, the Assyrian, the Greek, the Roman and the Gothic are all treated. This department has nearly a hundred books of its own, more than two hundred large charts of mounted magazine clippings and illustrations, several hundred mounted prints and photographs, besides the use of the pictures and charts belonging in other departments and about a hundred and fifty lantern slides.

In 1899 clay modeling, under the efficient supervision of Miss Maud I. Moore, a graduate of the school, and later of the Chicago Art Institute, assumed new life and interest. It is a third-year study, and is open to none who have not done excellent work in art.

In 1900 the introduction of Manual Training as a part of the school curriculum made it necessary to increase the work in mechanical drawing; consequently, in addition to the regular free-hand drawing, those who elect can have a two years' course in mechanical.

Twice the department has outgrown its quarters. It now has commodious rooms, well equipped with store-rooms and cases, in which to house its material. Modern and improved adjustable tables are provided for the mechanical and charcoal drawing; another room is devoted to historical art and design, and still another to the clay modeling.

The school has, from time to time, sent its work to competitive exhibits, and although compelled to compete with schools that carry drawing through a full four years' course, has won honors and received honorable mention.

A fair proportion of our pupils have gone to art schools, and are now professional teachers, illustrators, designers, architects, draftsmen and civil engineers, while others, in different professions, testify that their High School work in art has been of great service.

It is due to the people of Evanston to say that the drawing department has always had their hearty support. They may justly congratulate themselves that they were among the first, and not the last, to recognize its value and give it an honorable place.

It is simply an act of justice to say that Miss Eva S. Edwards, who has had full charge of the work from the beginning and developed it from feeble infancy to full maturity, is entitled to the highest credit for its present and past success. Few teachers have been privileged to witness such a happy growth, or have worked more patiently and unsparingly for its realization.

List of Trustees. — The following were the Trustees of the school under the school law of 1870:

William Blanchard, President (1882-1890); S. D. Childs, deceased (1882-1884); S. B. Goodenow (1882-1890); Henry J. Wallingford (vice Childs), (1884-1890).

By the law of 1889 the High School passed, in April, 1890, under control of a Board of Education, consisting of five members. The Board then chosen was as follows:

Chas. B. Congdon, President (1890-1897); John W. Bynam (1890-1891); Edward D. Coxe (Rogers Park), (1890-1893); Thomas Bates (1890-1900); Howard G. Grey (1890-1902).

Mr. Coxe resigned in 1893 in consequence of the annexation of Rogers Park to the City of Chicago.

The following have served since: L. H. Bushnell (1891-1900); David S. McMullen (1894-1901).

The present board consists of the following:

William S. Lord, President, appointed 1897; Conrad H. Poppenhusen, appointed 1900; Harold Dyrenforth, appointed 1901; Dorr A. Kimball, appointed 1901; George P. Merrick, appointed 1902. Winsor Chase is Secretary.

(Prof. Henry L. Boltwood, who prepared the preceding chapter, died January 23, 1906, terminating a career of over fifty years in connection with the cause of education, of which over forty years were spent in the State of Illinois and more than twenty-two years as Principal of the Evanston Township High School.)

CHAPTER XXIII.

EVANSTON AUTHORS

(By J. SEYMOUR CURREY, President Evanston Historical Society)

Establishment of Northwestern University Marks the Beginning of Evanston Literary Life — Effect of the Gathering of Professors, Instructors and Students — Growth of Literary Activity — Edward Eggleston and Frances E. Willard Begin their Careers Here — Miss Willard's "A Classic Town" — Miss Simpson's Catalogue of Evanston Authors in 1900 — Growth of Nine Years — Alphabetical List of Authors with Bibliography and Biographical Records.

The literary life of Evanston began with the establishment of the Northwestern University in 1855, and has flourished and kept pace with the intellectual development of the people. Naturally the location of an institution of learning attracted a large number of dwellers here who were in sympathy with the University and its work, or who were connected with it as professors, instructors or students. This created an atmosphere that was favorable to the growth of every form of literary activity, and the book publishers, as well as those of journals and periodicals, soon became familiar with the names of Evanston people as authors and contributors. Various weekly and monthly publications have been established here and have enjoyed prosperous careers.

It was in Evanston that Edward Eggleston lived when he began to write his re-markable series of books, beginning as a writer of fiction and afterwards becoming a historian of great reputation. It was here that Frances Willard began her literary work, and, possessing wonderful talents, attracted the attention of the world to her work in the Woman's Christian Temperance Union. There were others who were writers of wide reputation before coming here, but who continued their literary work in this favorable environment. Many societies of a literary character have enjoyed successful careers, and their records are a valuable possession of the community.

The first account of the literary history of Evanston is embodied in Frances Willard's history, entitled "A Classic Town," published in 1891, in which she says: "The amount of scholarly ink which has been put to paper by Evanston pens will compare favorably with that of any other community of its size and age in the world." "The literary atmosphere," she says, "is the highest charm of Evanston;" and adds, "literary people, be they great or small, hover by instinct around a center of books and thought and character."

At a meeting of the Young Woman's Missionary Society of the First M. E. Church, in 1900, one of the features was the sale of a "Catalogue of Evanston Authors" for the benefit of the society. The catalogue was in pamphlet form and was compiled by Miss Frances Simpson, who, with the help of the staff of the Evanston Public Library, prepared a list of 214 authors, with the titles of their books or contributions to the press in one form or another. In Miss Willard's book, published nine years before, she had given the names of sixty-four authors and journalists. Thus it would appear that there had been a large increase in the number at the time that Miss Simpson's list was prepared. This was predicted by Miss Willard who said in 1891, "It is safe to predict that the coming thirty-five years will show ten times as much work of this kind as the past thirty-five can show."

The authors whose names and works are given below are those who do now, or, at some period of their lives, have resided in Evanston, and who have published their works in book form. The list does not include journalists, contributors to periodicals, or writers of pamphlets. The attempt has been made to make the list fairly complete, but omissions are likely to be found. The reader's indulgence is asked for any shortcomings of this kind.

The people of Evanston take a just pride in the work of their writers, denoting, as it does, the intellectual status and culture of the community; and they will, no doubt, be surprised and gratified at the record here shown.

BIBLIOGRAPHY—PERSONAL SKETCHES.

Isaac Emens Adams.—Born at Mendham, N. J., October 29, 1857; graduated at Northwestern University; received degree of A. M. from same institution in 1882; on staff of "Chicago Times" for several years; and afterwards practiced law.

Author: "Life of Emory A. Storrs" (1886).

A. T. Andreas: "History of Cook County, Illinois, from the Earliest Period to the Present Time" (1884); "History of Chicago from the Earliest Period to the Present Time" (3 v., 1884-86).

Mrs. Rena Michaels Atchison: "Un-American Immigration: Its Present Effects and Future Perils: A Study from the Census of 1890" (1894).

Charles Beach Atwell.—Born at Theresa, N. Y., April 11, 1855; educated in Watertown (N. Y.) High School and Syracuse University; Professor of Botany in Northwestern University since 1894.

Author: "The Alumni Record of the Northwestern University" (1903).

M. Helen Beckwith: "In Mythland." (2 v., 1896); "Storyland with the Scissors" (1899).

Katharine Beebe: "First School Year for Primary Workers" (1895); "Home Occupations for Little Children" (1896); "School Room Plays" (1898); "Story of Longfellow" (1899); "Story of George Rogers Clark" (1900).

Charles Wesley Bennett.—Born at East Bethany, N. Y., July 18, 1828; educated at Wesleyan (Conn.) University; Professor of History at Syracuse (N. Y.) University, 1871-85; Professor of Historical Theology in Garrett Biblical Institute, 1885-91; died at Evanston, April 17, 1891.

Author: "Christian Archæology" (1888).

Henry Leonidas Boltwood.—Born at Amherst, Mass. Jan. 17, 1831; died at Evanston, Jan. 23, 1906; was graduated at Amherst College; in 1864 entered the service of the U. S. Sanitary Commission; was principal of the High School at Princeton, Ill., from 1867 to 1878; and occupied a similar position at Ottawa, Ill., for the succeeding five years; in 1883, came to Evanston where he became Principal of the High School and remained in this position up to the time of his death.

Author: "English Grammar and How to Teach It." (1871); "Topical Outlines of

General History" (1889); "Higher Speller" (1893).

Lewis Henry Boutell.—Born in Boston, Mass., July 21, 1826; died at Washington, D. C., January 16, 1899; was graduated from Brown University in 1844 and from Harvard Law School in 1847; on Jan. 1, 1848, was admitted to the bar in Boston; came West in 1863 and, in 1865, began the practice of law in Chicago. In 1893 he left the law practice for literary pursuits.

Author: "Alexander Hamilton, the Constructive Statesman" (1890); "Thomas Jefferson, the Man of Letters" (1891); "Life of Roger Sherman" (1896).

Frank Milton Bristol.—Methodist Episcopal clergyman, born in Orleans County, N. Y., January 4, 1851; graduated from Northwestern University, Ph. B., 1877, (A. M., D.D.); was pastor of leading churches in Chicago; now pastor Metropolitan Methodist Episcopal Church, Washington, D. C.

Author: "Providential Epochs"; "The Ministry of Art" (1897); "Shakespeare and America" (1898).

Solon Cary Bronson.—Born at West Union, Iowa, July 26, 1855; graduated at Upper Iowa University, Fayette, Iowa; became a professor in the Cornelia Miller department of Practical Theology, of the Garrett Biblical Institute, in 1896; has received the degree of Doctor of Divinity from two institutions, viz.: Garrett Biblical Institute, 1894, and Cornell College, Iowa, 1903.

Author: "Delusions: A Volume of Addresses" (1895).

Walter Lee Brown.—Born at Melrose, Mass., August 24, 1853, graduated at Northwestern University and Columbia College School of Mines; died at Evanston, April 6, 1904.

Author: "Manual of Assaying Gold, Silver, Copper and Lead Ores" (Ed. 6, 1896).

William Caldwell.—Born in Edinburgh, Scotland, November 10, 1863; educated in Edinburgh; graduated from Edinburgh University (M. A.) in 1884; post-graduate student in Germany, Paris, and Cambridge (England), 1887-91, inclusive; received degree of Doctor in Mental and Moral Science, Edinburgh; obtained high honors at Edinburgh; called to Sage School of Philosophy, Cornell University, N. Y., 1891; to University of Chicago, 1892; to Northwestern University, 1894, where he has been Professor of Moral and Social Philosophy.

Author: "Schopenhauer's System in its Philosophical Significance" (1893).

Henry Smith Carhart.—Born, Coeymans, N. Y., March 27, 1844; graduated from Wesleyan University, Middletown, Conn., in 1869; later studied at Yale, Harvard and Berlin; Professor of Physics and Chemistry at Northwestern University, 1872-86; President of Board of Judges, Department of Electricity, Columbian Exposition, 1893; member of Electrical Societies; Professor of Physics, University of Michigan since 1886.

Author: "Primary Batteries" (1891); "Elements of Physics" (with H. N. Chute) (1892); "University Physics" (1894-6) "Electrical Measurements" (1895).

George Chainey.—Unitarian minister, born in England in 1851; educated in Evanston and Boston; pastor Unitarian Church, Evansville, Indiana, 1877-80; engaged in work on Biblical Interpretation.

Author. "Foundation Stones," a Series of Unitarian Sermons (1879); "The New Version: Discourses on the Bible in Boston" (1882); "She: An Allegory of the Church" (1889); "Jeanne D'Arc, the Flower of France" (1888); "The Ten Commandments" (1900); "Book of Ruth: An Idyl of Friendship between the Heavens and the Earth" (1901); "Unsealed Bible"; v. 1, Genesis (1902).

J. Scott Clark.—Born in Copenhagen, N. Y., September 23, 1854; graduated from

Syracuse University in 1877; Principal of Evanston High School, 1879-82; Professor of Rhetoric and English Criticism, Syracuse University, 1882-92; Professor of English Language, Northwestern University, since 1892.

Author: "Practical Rhetoric" (1886); "Briefer Practical Rhetoric" (1892); "Study of English Prose Writers" (1898); "Study of English and American Poets" (1900).

Samuel Travers Clover.—Born in London, England, August 13, 1859; educated there; began newspaper career in 1880, making trip around the world; worked on newspapers in Dakota five years; staff correspondent of "Chicago Herald;" Managing editor of "Chicago Evening Post," from 1894 to 1901; "Los Angeles (Cal.) Evening News," 1905.

Author: "Paul Travers' Adventures" (1897); "Glimpses Across the Sea" (1900); "Rose Reef to Buluwayo" (1896); "Poets and Poetry of Dakota" (1898); "Zephyrs from Dakota" (1898).

George Albert Coe.—Born Monroe County, N. Y., March 26, 1862; graduated from University of Rochester; Ph. D., Boston University, 1891; John Evans Professor of Philosophy, Northwestern University since 1893.

Author: "The Spiritual Life: Studies in the Science of Religion" (1900); "The Religion of a Mature Mind" (1902).

Lyman Edgar Cooley.— Born Canandaigua, N. Y., December 5, 1850; graduated from Rensselaer Polytechnic Institute, C. E., 1874; Professor in Northwestern University, 1874-77; Associate Editor "Engineering News," 1876-78; Assistant Engineer of railroad bridge over the Missouri River, Glasgow, Missouri, 1878; Assistant United States Engineer on Mississippi and Missouri River improvements, 1878-84; Editor "American Engineer," 1884; Consulting

Engineer for Chicago Sanitary District (Drainage Canal). Member of the International Deep Waterways Committee, 1895-96.

Author: 'The Lakes and Gulf Waterway."

Edwin C. Crawford.— Born at Fostoria, Ohio, April 10, 1845; educated at High School, Ft. Wayne, Ind., and graduated at Dartmouth College in 1874.

Author: "Civil Government of Illinois and the United States"; Special Chapters on Chicago and Cook County (1890).

Henry Crew.—Born Richmond, Ohio, June 4, 1859; graduated from Princeton College, B. A., 1882; Fellow at Princeton, 1882-84; Fellow Johns Hopkins, 1884-87, Ph. D., 1887; Instructor in Physics, Harvard College, 1888-91; Astronomer Lick Observatory, 1891-92; Assistant Editor "Astrophysical Journal"; Professor of Physics, Northwestern University, since 1892.

Author: "Elements of Physics," for Use in High Schools (1899); "Laboratory Manual of Physics," for Use in High Schools (with R. R. Tatnall) (1902); Editor: "Wave Theory of Light"; "Memoirs of Huygens, Young and Fresnel" (1900).

Robert McLean Cumnock.—Born in Ayr, Scotland, May 31, 1844; came to America in the following year; graduated at Wesleyan University in 1868; and soon after became Professor of Elocution at Northwestern University, which position he has held to the present time.

Author: "Choice Readings"; "School Speaker."

Nathan Smith Davis, Sr., M. D., LL. D.— Born at Greene, N. Y., January 9, 1817; graduated from College of Physicians and Surgeons, Fairfield, N. Y., 1837; received honorary degree A. M. Northwestern University, and LL. D. from Illinois Wesleyan University; practiced medicine in Chicago from 1849; Professor in Rush Medical College, Chicago, 1849-59; one of the founders (1859) of Chicago Medical College, now Medical Department Northwestern University; Professor there for thirty years and Dean of Faculty until 1898, resigned; editor of various medical journals; President of the International Medical Congress, 1887; one of the founders of Mercy Hospital, and one of its physicians, for over forty years; a founder and Trustee of Northwestern University, Chicago Academy of Sciences, Chicago Historical Society, Illinois State Microscopical Society and Union College of Law; a member of various other Medical Associations in Chicago and New York; died June 16, 1904.

Author: "Principles and Practice of Medicine," and various pamphlets on medical subjects and on temperance.

Nathan Smith Davis, Jr., M. D.—Born in Chicago, September 5, 1858; graduated from Northwestern University, 1880, A. M. 1883; graduated from Chicago Medical College, 1883; has since practiced in Chicago; Associate Professor of Pathology, 1884-86; since then Professor of the Principles and Practice of Medicine and of Clinical Medicine, Chicago Medical College; Physician to Mercy Hospital since 1884; Member of the Ninth International Medical Congress, Pan-American Medical Congress, etc.

Author: "Consumption: How to Prevent It and How to Live With It"; "Diseases of the Lungs, Heart and Kidneys," etc.

Edward Eggleston.—Born Vevay, Indiana, December 10, 1837; died September 2, 1902; educated at country and village schools in Indiana; entered Methodist Episcopal ministry in 1857; editor of "Little Corporal," Chicago, 1866-67; chief Editor of the "National Sunday School Teacher" (1867-70) and other religious papers; President of the American Historical Association in 1900.

Author: "Hoosier Schoolmaster" (1871); "End of the World" (1872); "Mystery of Metropolisville" (1873); "Circuit Rider" (1874); "Hoosier School Boy" (1883); "History of the United States and Its People" (1888); "First Book in American History" (1889); "Beginners of a Nation" (1896); "Transit of Civilization from England to America" (1900); Editor, "Christ in Art" (1874); "Christ in Literature" (1875).

Finley Ellingwood. — Born Dearborn County, Ind., September 12, 1852; educated in Kankakee, Ill.; graduated from Bennett Medical College in 1878; Professor in same institution from 1885 to present time.

Author: "Manual of Medical Chemistry" (1889); "Annual of Eclectic Medicine" (1890, '91 and '92); "Systematic Treatise on Materia Medica" (1899); "Treatment of Disease" (1906).

Frank Macajah Elliot.— Born at Corinna, Me., March 27, 1853; graduated at Northwestern University; President Evanston Hospital Association since 1896.

Author: "History of Omega" (1885). George H. Ellis: "Analysis of White Paints" (1898).

Joseph Emerson: "Lectures and Sermons on Subjects connected with Christian Liberal Education" (1897).

Marshall Davis Ewell.—Born in Oxford, Michigan, August 18, 1844; educated in Michigan; LL. B. University of Michigan 1868; A. M. Northwestern University, 1879; Professor of Common Law, University College of Law, Chicago, from 1877 until the founding of Kent College of Law —also known as Microscopist; President of the American Microscopical Society, 1893.

Author: "Leading Cases on Disabilities"

(1876); "Treatise on Law of Fixtures" (1876); "Essentials of the Law" (1882); "Manual of Medical Jurisprudence" (1887).

Editor: "Blackwell on Tax Titles"; "Evans on Agencies"; "Lindley on Partnership," and other works.

Charles Samuel Farrar: "Art Topics: History of Sculpture, Painting and Architecture" (1885).

Randolph Sinks Foster.—Born Williamsburg, Ohio, February 22, 1820; educated at Augusta College, Kentucky; entered itinerant ministry of Methodist Episcopal Church 1837, in Kentucky Conference; later was transferred to Ohio and, in 1850, to New York, remaining until 1857; President of Northwestern University 1857-60; again in pastorate work in New York and Sing Sing, 1860-68; Professor of Systematic Theology, 1868-69; President of Drew Theological Seminary, Madison, N. J., 1869-72; died in 1903.

Author: "Objections to Calvinism" (1849); "Centenary Thoughts" (1884); "Beyond the Grave" (1878); "Studies in Theology" (1886); "Philosophy of Christian Experience"; "Christian Purity" (1851).

Francis Gellatly: "Necklace of Liberty" (1886); "Love Made to Order, and Temper Tempest."

Anna Adams Gordon.—Born in Boston, July 21, 1853; educated in Newton (Mass.) High School and at Mt. Holyoke College; for twenty-one years private secretary of Miss Frances E. Willard; Vice President at Large of National W. C. T. U.

Author: "Marching Songs"; "White Ribbon Hymnal"; "Beautiful Life of Frances E. Willard" (1898).

Ulysses Sherman Grant.—Born in Moline, Illinois, February 14, 1867; graduated from the University of Minnesota in 1888; Ph. D., Johns Hopkins, 1893; Assistant State Geologist, Minnesota, 1893-99; Instructor in Geology in the University of Minnesota, 1897-98; Assistant Geologist on the Geological and Natural History Survey of Wisconsin since 1899; Assistant Editor of the "American Geologist" since 1897; Professor of Geology and Curator of the Museum, Northwestern University, since 1899.

Author: " Preliminary Report on the Copperbearing Rocks of Douglas County, Wisconsin (1900); "Wisconsin Geological and Natural History Survey" (v. 6, 1900); "Final Report of the Geological and Natural History Survey of Minnesota" (with N. H. Winchell) (1899-1900).

John Henry Gray.—Born in Charleston, Illinois, March 11, 1859; graduated from Harvard in 1887; Ph. D., Halle, Germany, 1892; Studied also at Paris, Vienna and Berlin; Instructor in Political Economy at Harvard, 1887-89; Chairman of the World's Congress Auxiliary on Political Science in connection with the Columbian Exposition, Chicago, 1893; Chairman of the Municipal Committee of the Civic Federation of Chicago; 1894-96; First Vice President of the American Economic Association, 1897-98; appointed by Labor Commissioner, C. D. Wright, to investigate labor conditions in England, 1902; Professor of Political Economy and Social Science, Northwestern University, since 1892.

Author: "Die Stellung der Privaten Beleuchtnugsgesellschaften zu Stadt und Staat"; "Die Erfahrung in Wein, Paris und Massachusetts," Jena (1893).

Evarts Boutell Greene.—Born at Kobe, Japan, July 8, 1870; was educated in a private school at Yokohama, Japan, and in the public schools of Westborough, Mass., and Evanston; student at Northwestern University, 1885-88, and at Harvard, 1888-93; A. B., A. M., Ph. D.,—all from Harvard; at University of Berlin, Germany, 1893 to 1894; Professor of History, University of Illinois.

Author: "The Provincial Governors in the English Colonies of North America" (Harvard Historical Series, Vol. 7, 1898), "The Government of Illinois, Its History and Administration" (Macmillan, 1904); "Provincial America" (Harpers, 1905).

James Stanley Grimes: Geonomy: The Creation of Continents by Ocean Currents" (1857); "Human Nature and the Nerves" (1857); "Improved System of Geonomy" (1866); Mesmerism and Magic Eloquence" (1862); "Mysteries of the Head and Heart" (1870); "New System of Phrenology and Evolution of the Brain" (1869); "Philosophy of the Mind" (1870); "Phreno Geology, the Evolution of Animals and Man" (1850); "Phreno Physiology, Human Nature, the Evolution of Mind and its Instruments" (1901).

Mrs. Elizabeth Morrisson Boynton Harbert.—Born in Crawfordsville, Indiana, April 15, 1845; graduated from Terre Haute Female College 1862; for eight years editor Woman's Department, "Chicago Inter-Ocean."

Author: "Out of Her Sphere" (1871); "The Golden Fleece" (1867); "Amore"; Composer of the songs, words and music of "On Arlington Heights," "What Shall we Do With the Hours?" etc.

James Taft Hatfield.—Born in Brooklyn, N. Y., June 15, 1862; graduated from Northwestern University, 1883; A.M. 1886; Johns Hopkins University, Ph. D., 1890; traveled and studied in Japan, China, India and Egypt, 1883-84; Professor of Classical Languages in Rust University, Holly Springs, Mississippi, 1884-85; graduate student and Fellow at Johns Hopkins University, 1887-90; Professor of German Language and Literature at Northwestern University, 1890; studied at Berlin, Weimar and Oxford, 1896-97; served in Spanish-American War as Captain of a five-inch gun on the U. S. cruiser "Yale," June to August,

1898; Professor of German Literature at Northwestern University since 1890; Contributing editor "Americana Germanica"; Member of the American Oriental Society since 1884; Member of the Modern Language Association of America, etc.

Author: "Elements of Sanskrit Grammar" (1884); "Index to Gothic Forms in Kluge's Wœterbuch" (1889); "Freytag's Rittmeister von alt-Rosen" (1894).

Editor of German texts; Translator of German poems.

Erastus Otis Haven.—Born in Boston, November 1, 1820; died in Salem, Oregon, August 1881; graduated from Wesleyan University in 1842; in 1848 entered Methodist Episcopal ministry in New York Conference; in 1853 Professor of Latin in University of Michigan, which he exchanged the next year for the chair of English Language, Literature and History; given degree of D. D. in 1854 by Union College; resigned in 1856, and returned to Boston, where he was editor of "Zion's Herald" for seven years, during which period he served two years in State Senate, and a part of the time was an Overseer of Harvard University; President of University of Michigan, 1863-69; President of Northwestern University, 1869-72; in 1880 was ordained a Bishop of the Methodist Episcopal Church.

Author: "American Progress; The Young Man Advised" (1855); "Pillars of Truth" (1866); "Rhetoric" (1869).

Henry Bixby Hemenway. — Born at Montpelier, Vt., December 20, 1856; graduated at Northwestern University, 1879; practicing physician since 1880.

Author: "Healthful Womanhood and Childhood" (1894).

Newell Dwight Hillis.—Born in Magnolia, Iowa, September 2, 1858; educated at Iowa College, Lake Forest University and McCormick Theological Seminary

(M. A., and D. D., Northwestern University) ; entered Presbyterian ministry ; pastor at Peoria, Illinois, 1887-90 ; at Evanston, Illinois, 1890-94 ; succeeded late Prof. David Swing as pastor of Central Church, Chicago (an independent church), 1894 ; pastor of Plymouth Church, Brooklyn, since January, 1899.

Author: "The Investment of Influence" (1898) ; "A Man's Value to Society" (1896) ; "How the Inner Light Failed"; "Foretokens of Immortality" (1897) ; "Great Books as Life Teachers" (1899) ; "Influence of Christ in Modern Life" (1900).

Rosa Birch Hitt.—Born at Elkhart, Ind., April 25, 1863 ; educated at the High School, Marion, Ind., and at Northwestern University ; married Isaac R. Hitt, Jr., in 1889.

Author: "The Instrument Tuned" (1904).

Jane Currie Hoge.—Born in Philadelphia, Pa., July 31, 1811 ; educated at Miss Longstrength's school in Philadelphia ; engaged with the U. S. Sanitary Commission during the Civil War, visiting more than one hundred thousand men in hospitals ; died at Chicago, August 26, 1890.

Author: "The Boys in Blue" (1867).

Thomas Franklin Holgate.—Born in Hastings County, Ontario, April 8, 1859 ; graduated at Victoria College, Toronto, 1884 ; Professor at Northwestern University since 1893.

Author: "Elementary Geometry, Plane and Solid" (1901).

George Washington Hough.—Born in Montgomery County, New York, October 24, 1836 ; graduated from Union College in 1856 ; Astronomer and Director of Dudley Observatory, Albany, N. Y., 1860-74 ; Director of Dearborn Observatory and Professor of Astronomy in University of Chicago, 1879-87 ; discovered more than 600 new double stars and made systematic study of the planet Jupiter ; invented many instruments pertaining to astronomy, meteorology and physics ; Professor of Astronomy at Northwestern University and Director of Dearborn Observatory since 1887.

Author: "Annals of the Dudley Observatory" (2 v., 1866-1871) ; "Annual Reports of the Chicago Astronomical Society."

Mary Hess Hull.—Born at Miltonville, Ohio, April 22, 1845 (maiden name Mary Ann Hess) ; educated in schools of her native town ; married Morton Hull, December, 1863 ; died in Chicago September 13, 1905.

Author: "Columbus, and What He Found" (1892) ; "Browning's Christmas Eve," (1900).

Harvey Bostwick Hurd.—Born in Huntington, Connecticut, February 14, 1828 ; came to Chicago in 1846 ; admitted to the bar in 1848 ; LL. D. Northwestern University ; Professor in the Chicago Law School (now a department of Northwestern University), 1862-1900 ; first President of the Village of Evanston ; official reviser of General Statutes of Illinois ; edited State edition of the same, 1874 ; has since edited sixteen editions of General State Laws ; originator of the great Chicago Drainage Canal scheme ; died January 20, 1906.

Author: "Torrens Act of Illinois for Registration of Land Titles"; also of "Juvenile Court Act of Illinois," April 22, 1899.

Edmund Janes James.—Born in Jacksonville, Illinois, May 21, 1855 ; educated at Illinois State Normal School and Northwestern and Harvard Universities, A. M. ; Ph. D., University of Halle, Germany (1877) ; Principal of Evanston High School (1878-79) ; Principal of Model High School, Normal, Illinois (1879-82) ; Professor of Public Finance and Administration, Wharton School of Finance and Economy, University of Pennsylvania (1883-95) ; Professor of Political and Social Science, University of Pennsylvania (1884-95) ; Edited the publications of the University of Pennsylvania, Political Economy and Public Law Series (1886-95) ; Vice President of the American Economic Association ; President of the American Academy of Political and Social Science since 1889 ; Vice President of the Board of Trustees of the Illinois State Historical Library since 1895 ; Professor of Public Administration and Director of Extension Division in the University of Chicago (1896-1902) ; President of Northwestern University (1902-04) ; then became President University of Illinois at Urbana, Illinois.

Author : "Relation of the Modern Municipality to the Gas Supply" (1886) ; "The Legal Tender Decisions" (1887) ; "The Canal and the Railway" (1890) ; "Federal Constitution of Germany" (1890) ; "Federal Constitution of Switzerland" (1890) ; Education of Business Men in Europe" (1899) ; "Government of a Typical Prussian City" (Halle) (1900).

James Alton James.—Born in Hazelgreen, Wisconsin, September 17, 1864 ; graduated from University of Wisconsin in 1888 ; held scholarship and fellowship in History, Johns Hopkins University, 1891-93 ; Ph. D., 1893 ; Professor of History Cornell College, Iowa, four years ; Member of the American Historical Society ; Member of Council and Secretary of Northwestern Settlement ; President of the North Central History Teachers' Association ; Professor of History, Northwestern University since 1897.

Author : "Constitution and Admission of Iowa into the Union" (1900) ; "Government in State and Nation" (with A. H. Sanford) (1901).

William Patterson Jones.—Born about 1827 ; founder (1855) of the North-

western Female College, and for many years President of same ; in 1862 was sent as Consul to Macao, China ; later became President of Fremont (Neb.) Normal School, where he died about 1890.

Author : "Myth of Stone Idol, a Poem" (1876) ; "Inter-Ocean Curiosity Shop."

John Hume Kedzie.—Born in Stamford, N. Y., September 8, 1815 ; graduated from Oberlin College in 1841 ; admitted to the bar in 1847 ; member of Illinois Legislature, 1877 to 1879 ; died at Evanston, April 9, 1903.

Author : "Solar Heat, Gravitation and Sun Spots" (1886).

Daniel Parish Kidder.—Born at Darien, N. Y., October 18, 1815 ; graduated at Wesleyan University, Middletown, Conn., in 1836 ; from 1837 to 1840 was a missionary to Brazil ; and from 1844 to 1856 editor of the Sunday School publications of the Methodist Episcopal church ; compiled and edited more than eight hundred volumes for Sunday School libraries ; the list of which would fill many pages of this history ; in 1856 became Professor of Practical Theology in the Garrett Biblical Institute, where he remained until 1871, when he was called to a like chair in the Drew Theological Seminary ; died at Evanston, July 29, 1891.

Author : "Mormonism and the Mormons" (1844) ; "Residence and Travel in Brazil" (2 vols., 1845) ; in conjunction with Rev. J. C. Fletcher, "Brazil and the Brazilians" (1857) ; and "Treatise on Homiletics" (1868).

Homer H. Kingsley.—Born at Kalamazoo, Mich., June 9, 1859 ; graduated at Michigan University in 1881 ; Principal of Evanston Public Schools (Dist. No. 1) since 1886.

Author : "The New Era Word Book" (1901).

Nellie Fitch Kingsley.—Born at Peoria, Ill., October 4, 1862 ; educated at Kalamazoo (Mich.) High School; married to Homer H. Kingsley, August 18, 1886.

Author: "History of the Lewis and Clark Expedition" (1900); "Four American Explorers" (1902).

Marshall Monroe Kirkman.—Born in Illinois, July 10, 1842; entered railway service with Chicago & Northwestern Railroad in 1856; Second Vice President of Chicago & Northwestern Railway since 1889.

Author: "The Science of Railways" (12 v., 1894); "Classical Portfolio of Primitive Carriers" (1896); "Romance of Gilbert Holmes" (1900); "The Air Brake" (1901); "Building and Repairing Railways" (1901).

Samuel Ellsworth Kiser.—Born Shippensville, Pa., February 2, 1862; educated in Pennsylvania and Ohio; editorial writer "Chicago Record-Herald."

Author: "Budd Wilkins at the Show" (1898); "Georgie" (1890); "Love Sonnets of an Office Boy" (1902); "Ballads of the Busy Days" (1903); "Charles, the Chauffeur" (1905).

Loren Laertes Knox.—Born at Morrisville, N. Y., January 8, 1811; educated at Cazenovia (N. Y.) Seminary, and Wesleyan University (Middletown, Conn.); Professor of Greek in Lawrence University, Appleton, Wis.; died at Evanston, January 18, 1901.

Author: "Evangelical Rationalism" (1870).

John Harper Long.—Born in Ohio, December, 1856; educated at Tuebingen, Wuerzburg and Breslau, Germany; member of several scientific societies; Professor of Chemistry in Medical School, Northwestern University, since 1881.

Author: "Elements of General Chemistry" (1898); "A Text Book of Wine Analysis" (1900); "Laboratory Manual of Physiological Chemistry" (1894).

William C Levere: "Imperial America" (1899); "Twixt Greek and Barb" (1900).

Arthur Wilde Little.—Episcopal clergyman.

Author: "Reasons for Being a Churchman" (1886); "The Times and Teaching of John Wesley"; "The Intellectual Life of the Priest"; "The Character of Washington"; "The Maintenance of the Church Idea."

Charles Joseph Little.—Born in Philadelphia, Pa., September 21, 1840; graduated at University of Pennsylvania, 1861; Professor in Dickinson College, 1874-85; at Syracuse University, 1885-91; President Garrett Biblical Institute since 1891.

Author: Comprehensive History of America" (1896).

William Sinclair Lord.—Born in Sycamore, Illinois, August 24, 1863.

Author: "Verses" (1883); "Beads of Morning" (1888); "Blue and Gold" (1896); "Jingle and Jangle" (1899).

Mrs. Catherine Waugh McCulloch.— Born in Ransomville, Niagara County, N. Y., June 4, 1862; educated in Illinois; graduated from Union College of Law, Chicago, 1886; practiced law in Rockford, Illinois, 1886-90, since which time she has been engaged in the practice of law in Chicago.

Author: "Mr. Lex; or, the Legal Status of Mother and Child" (1902).

William Smythe Babcock Matthews.— Born in Loudon, N. H., May 8, 1837; educated in New Hampshire; studied music in Boston; practical teacher of music since 1853; since 1867 has been living in Chicago; in 1891 established and has since been editor of "Music" (a magazine).

Author: "How to Understand Music" (2 v., 1880 and 1888); "Primer of Musical Forms" (1890); "Music and its Ideals" (1897); "Popular History of Music" (1891); "The Great in Music"—first and second series (1900-1902); "Dictionary of Musical Terms" (1895); "The Masters and Their Music" (1898).

Samuel Merwin.—Born in Evanston, October 6, 1874; educated in Evanston, Detroit and Northwestern University.

Author: "The Short Line War" (with H. K. Webster) (1899); "Calumet K." (with same) (1901); "The Road to Frontenac" (1901).

Mrs. Emily Huntington Miller.—Born in Brooklyn, Conn., October 22, 1833; graduated from Oberlin College, 1857 (A. M.); Editor of "Little Corporal," afterwards combined with "St. Nicholas"; Dean of Woman's College, Northwestern University, 1891-98.

Author: "From Avalon" (poems) (1896); "The Royal Road to Fortune"; "The Kirkwood Series"; "Captain Fritz"; "Little Neighbors"; "What Tommy Did"; "The House that Jack Rented"; "Songs from the Nest" (poems) (1894); "For the Beloved" (poems).

Wilbur Dick Nesbit.—Born, Xenia, Ohio, September 16, 1871; educated in public schools, Cedarville, Ohio.

Author: "Trail to Boyland" (1904); "Little Henry's Slate" (1903); "An Alphabet of History" (1905).

Mary Louise Ninde: "We Two Alone in Europe" (1886); "William Xavier Ninde: a Biography" (1902).

Mrs. Minerva Brace Norton.—Author: "In and Around Berlin" (1889); "Service in the King's Guard" (1891).

Simon Nelson Patten.—Born in Illinois, May 1, 1852; educated in Illinois; took degrees of A. M. and Ph. D. at University of Halle, Germany; studied law in Law School Northwestern University; in 1888 elected Professor of Political Economy in the Wharton School of Finance and Economy, University of Pennsylvania.

Author: "Taxation in American States and Cities"; "Premises of Political Economy"; "The Stability of Prices"; "Consumption of Wealth"; "Theory of Prosperity" (1902).

Charles William Pearson.—Born in Leeds, England, August 7, 1846; graduated from the Northwestern University in 1871, and afterwards became professor of English literature in the same institution; he resigned this position in 1902, and became pastor of the Unitarian church at Quincy, Ill.; died in England, July 11, 1905.

Author: "Methodism: a Retrospect and Outlook: A Poem" (1891); "The Carpenter Prophet; a Life of Jesus Christ and a Discussion of His Ideals" (1902).

William Frederick Poole.—Born at Salem, Mass., December 24, 1821; died at Evanston, March 1, 1894; educated in Massachusetts; graduated from Yale College in 1849; in 1851 became Assistant Librarian of the Boston Athenæum and, in the following year was made Librarian of the Mercantile Library of that city—a flourishing institution subsequently merged into the Boston Public Library; in 1853 attended the first gathering of librarians ever held in the world, Edward Everett Hale and Dr. Henry Barnard, of Hartford, being among those present; in 1856 returned to Boston Athenæum, where he remained thirteen years; in 1873 was called to the Public Library of Chicago; in 1887 took charge of the Newberry Library, Chicago; contributed many papers to the reports published by the United States Bureaus of Education; in 1887 was President of the American Historical Association; in 1882 received the honorary degree of LL. D. from Northwestern University; died at Evanston, March 1, 1894.

Author: "Poole's Index to Periodical Literature" (with W. I. Fletcher) (4 v., 1882-1893); "Anti-slavery Opinions before the Year 1800" (1873); "Columbus and the Finding of the New World" (1892).

Miner Raymond.—Born in New York

City, August 29, 1811: graduated from Wesleyan Academy, Wilbraham, Mass., in 1831; instructor in same; LL. D. in 1884; Professor of Systematic Theology in Garrett Biblical Institute, 1864-97; died at Evanston November 25, 1897.

Author: "Systematic Theology" (3 v., 1877).

Henry Bascom Ridgaway.—Born in Talbot County Md., September 7, 1830; graduated from Dickinson College (Penn.) in 1849; Professor of Historical Theology in Garrett Biblical Institute in 1882; President of same in 1884; died March 30, 1895.

Author: "The Lord's Land." (1876); "Life of Alfred Cookman" (1871); "Life of Bishop Janes" (1882); "Life of Bishop Waugh" (1883); "Life of Bishop Simpson" (1885).

Charles Humphrey Roberts.—Author: "Down the O-hi-o" (1891).

Henry Wade Rogers.—Born Holland Patent, N. Y., October 10, 1853; graduated from University of Michigan, 1874; (A. M. and LL.D. Wesleyan University, Conn.); admitted to the bar in 1877; Professor of Law in the Law School of the University of Michigan, 1883; Dean of same, 1885-90; President of Northwestern University, 1890-1901; Chairman of Worlds' Congress on Jurisprudence and Law Reform, World's Columbian Exposition, Chicago, 1893; General Chairman of the Saratoga Conference on the Foreign Policy of the United States, 1898; Professor of Law in Yale University, since September, 1901.

Author: "Illinois Citations" (1881); "Law of Expert Testimony" (1883—2d ed., 1891).

Robert Dickinson Sheppard.—Born near Chicago, Ill., July, 23, 1847; graduated at Chicago University in 1869; at Garrett Biblical Institute 1870; Professor of History at Northwestern University, 1886 to 1903.

Author: "Abraham Lincoln" (1903).

Edwin Llewellyn Shuman.—Born in Manor Township, Pa., December 13, 1863; educated in Cook County Normal School and Englewood High School; editorial writer on "Chicago Journal," 1892-95; literary editor and editorial writer on "Chicago Tribune," 1895-1901; literary editor "Chicago Record-Herald," 1901 to date.

Author: "Steps into Journalism" (1894); "Practical Journalism" (1903).

Matthew Simpson.—Born at Cadiz, Ohio. June 20, 1811; attended Madison (Pa.) College; became tutor in same; in 1837 Professor of Natural Science in Alleghany College; President of Indiana Asbury University 1839-48; elected Bishop of Methodist Episcopal church in 1852; President of Garrett Biblical Institute in 1859; died in Philadelphia June 18. 1884.

Author: "Cyclopædia of Methodism" (1878); "One Hundred Years of Methodism" (1876); "Lectures on Preaching" (1879); "Sermons" (1885).

Alice Bunker Stockham.—Born in Ohio, in 1833, of Quaker parentage; graduated from the Eclectic Medical College, Cincinnati; practiced in Indiana and Chicago; established the Stockham Publishing Company, of which she is President, to publish her own works and other "advanced" books; was a leader in the introduction of "sloyd" in Chicago public schools; active worker for social purity, woman suffrage and social reform.

Author: "Tokology: a Book of Maternity" (1883); "Koradine" (1893); "Karezza" (1896); "Tolstoi: a Man of Peace" (1900).

Charles Macaulay Stuart. — Born in Glasgow, Scotland, August 20, 1853; graduated from Kalamazoo College in 1880; D. D., Garrett Biblical Institute; Associate editor of the "Michigan Christian Advocate" (1885-86); Assistant editor "Northwestern Christian Advocate" (1886-96); Professor of Sacred Rhetoric in Garrett Biblical Institute since 1896.

Author: "Text of Photogravures of the Holy Land" (1890); "Life and Selected Writings of Francis Dana Hemenway" (with C. F. Bradley and A. W. Patten) (1890); "Vision of Christ in the Poet" (1896); "Story of the Master Pieces" (1897).

Milton Spenser Terry.—Born Coeymans, N. Y., February 22, 1840; educated at Troy University and Yale Divinity School; A. M. Wesleyan University, 1871; D. D., same institution, 1880; LL. D., Northwestern University, 1895; Professor in Garrett Biblical Institute, Evanston, since 1885.

Author: "Commentary on the Old Testament" (1875); "Biblical Hermeneutics" (1883); "The Sibylline Oracles" (1890); "Rambles in the Old World" (1894); "Biblical Apocalyptics" (1898).

David Decamp Thompson.—Born April 20, 1852, at Cincinnati, Ohio; graduated at Ohio Wesleyan University; editor of "Northwestern Christian Advocate" since 1901.

Author: "Abraham Lincoln"; "John Wesley as a Social Reformer."

Edward Thomson. — Born at Portsea, England, October 12, 1810; came to America with his parents in 1818; graduated from the medical department of the University of Pennsylvania; in charge of Norwalk (Ohio) Seminary, 1838-43; elected Bishop of Methodist Episcopal Church in 1864; died March 22, 1870.

Author: "Evidences of Revealed Religion"; "Moral and Religious Essays" (3 vols.); "Oriental Missions" (2 vols.).

Charles Burton Thwing.—Born at Theresa, N. Y., March 4, 1860; graduated from Northwestern University, 1888; Ph. D., Bonn, Germany, 1894; Professor of Physics, Knox College, Galesburg, Ill., since 1896.

Author: "An Elementary Physics,"(1894).

Henry Kitchell Webster.—Born in Evanston, September 7, 1875; graduated from Hamilton College, N. Y., 1897, (Ph. M.); Instructor in Rhetoric Union College, Schenectady, N. Y. (1897-8).

Author: "The Short Line War" (with Samuel Merwin) (1899); "The Banker and the Bear" (1900); "Calumet K" (with Samuel Merwin) (1901); "Roger Drake" (1902).

David Hilton Wheeler.—Born at Ithaca, N. Y., November 19, 1829; attended Rock River Seminary; Professor of Greek in Cornell College; U. S. Consul at Genoa, Italy, 1861 to 1866; Professor of English Literature at Northwestern University, 1867 to 1875; for a part of this time (1867 to 1869) being acting president; editor of "The Methodist," 1875 to 1883; President of Allegheny College, 1883 to 1892; died at Meadville, Pa., June 18, 1902.

Author: "Brigandage in South Italy" (1864); "By-Ways of Literature" (1883); "Our Industrial Utopia."

Mrs. Irene Grosvenor Wheelock: "Nestlings of Forest and Marsh" (1902).

John Henry Wigmore.—Born in San Francisco, Cal.; graduated from Harvard University with degree of A. B., 1883, LL. B., 1887; Professor of Law at Northwestern University from 1893.

Author: "Materials for the Study of Private Law in Old Japan" (1892); "The Australian Ballot System" (1889); "Sixteenth Edition of Greenleaf on Evidence," Vol. I.(1899); "Treatise on Evidence" (4 vols., 1904-5).

Mrs. Caroline McCoy Willard.—Author: "Life in Alaska" (1884); "Kin-da-shon's Wife; an Alaskan Story" (1892).

Frances Elizabeth Willard.—Born September 28, 1839, at Churchville, near Rochester, N. Y.; graduated from Northwestern University and took degree of A. M. from Syracuse University; in 1862 was

Professor of Natural Science at the Northwestern Female College, Evanston, Illinois; in 1866-67 was Preceptress in the Wesleyan Seminary, Lima, N. Y.; in 1871 was President of the Women's College of Northwestern University, and Professor of Aesthetics in the University; in 1874 was appointed Corresponding Secretary of the National Women's Christian Temperance Union and, in 1879, was made President of that body—the largest society ever organized, conducted and controlled exclusively by women. She traveled extensively in the interest of the society and visited every State and Territory in the Union; in 1884 helped establish the Prohibition Party; originated a petition against the importation and manufacture of alcohol and opium, which was signed by seven million persons; was editor of the "Chicago Post," the "Union Signal," and other journals; died in New York, February 18, 1898.

Author: "Nineteen Beautiful Years" (1863); "Hints and Help in Temperance Work" (1875); "Women and Temperance" (1883); "How to Win" (1886); "Woman in the Pulpit" (1888); "Glimpses of Fifty Years"; "The Autobiography of an American Woman."

Josiah Flynt Willard.—Born in Appleton, Wisconsin, January 23, 1869; educated in Berlin University (1890-95).

Author: "Tramping with Tramps" (1899); "Powers that Prey" (with Francis Walton) (1900); "Notes of an Itinerant Policeman" (1900); "World of Graft" (1900).

S. R. Winchell.—Author: "Latin Prose Composition" (1875); "Lessons in Greek Syntax" (1886).

Erwin E. Wood.—Born at Plainfield, Ill., February 6, 1848; student at Northwestern University and Garrett Biblical Institute, 1864 to 1869; engaged in editorial work in Chicago and New York.

Author: "Epigraph Album" (1880).

Abram Van Eps Young.—Born in Sheboygan, Wisconsin, June 5, 1853; graduated from the University of Michigan in 1875; Fellow in Chemistry, Johns Hopkins University; Assistant in Chemistry, Harvard University; Professor in Chemistry at Northwestern University since 1885.

Author: "The Elementary Principles of Chemistry" (1901); "Suggestions to Teachers, Designed to accompany the Elementary Principles of Chemistry" (1901).

Jane Eggleston Zimmerman.—Author: "Gray Heads on Green Shoulders."

Charles Zueblin.—Born in Pendleton, Indiana, May 4, 1866; graduated from Northwestern University in 1887, and from Yale in 1889; founded Northwestern University Settlement, 1892; was the first Secretary of the Chicago Society for University Extension, 1892; Secretary of Class Study Division of the University Extension Department of the University of Chicago, 1892; member of various municipal, political and social science leagues; associate Professor of Sociology in the University of Chicago since 1896.

Author: "American Municipal Progress" (1902).

The general character of the works of the authors given above is shown in the following classification, arranged in the order given in "Dewey's Manual of Classification:"

Bibliography	4	(= 1.5 per cent)	
Political Economy and Law	26	(= 10.0	")
Philology	14	(= 5.4	")
Science	51	(= 19.5	")
Art and Music	9	(= 3.4	")
Fiction, Essays and Poetry	103	(= 39.5	")
Biography	25	(= 9.6	")
History	29	(= 11.1	")
Total	261	(= 100.0	"

Among the works thus fortuitously brought together as those of Evanston authors, we find a wide range of authorship, from the comics of Nesbit and Kiser to the profundity of Raymond's "Systematic

Theology" and Poole's "Index to Periodical Literature." As usual in a general line of literary productions, the Fiction, Essays and Poetry in the above table form about 40 per cent of the whole, corresponding in a general way with the proportion observed in the circulation of a public library. Science, Political Economy and Physiology, taken together, make up about 35 per cent; and when the 25 per cent of the remainder is shown as History, Biography and the Fine Arts, the solid and serious character given to the whole is sufficiently apparent. From this may be inferred a high general average of culture and learning among the writers. The works mentioned in the above list are not confined to the English language, for here we find the productions of Hatfield and Gray in German; and it is likely, if the search had been more thorough, there would have appeared others in tongues far remote from our beloved vernacular. Had it been a part of the plan of this chapter to enumerate the contributions to periodical literature and to the printed proceedings of learned societies, the intellectual activities of the writers who now make their dwelling place in Evanston or have done so at some time in the past, would have shown a much more extended range and increase in number.

Macaulay said that "one shelfful of European books was worth more than the whole native literature of India." Here is presented what may be the equivalent of a "shelfful" and even more, and it is a satisfaction to find this weighty characterization of Macaulay thus fairly applied to the productions emanating from one community among all the great numbers of centers of intelligence to be found in our country.

CHAPTER XXIV.

LIBRARIES—PUBLIC AND PRIVATE
(By MARY B. LINDSAY, Librarian)

Evanston's First Library—Major Mulford, the "Gentleman Pioneer of Evanston"— Some Specimens of His Library—First Sunday School Library—Private Libraries of Today—Unique Collection of Curios—History of Evanston Free Public Library — Edward Eggleston Prime Mover in Its Founding—First Step in Organization—Later History and Growth —Roll of Librarians and Other Officers —Cataloguing and Library Extension— Internal Management and Conditions— Site for a Library Building Secured in 1904.

The first collection of books brought together in Evanston was, without doubt, that of the private library of the late Major Edward H. Mulford, who came here in 1835 and settled on the Ridge road. The old Kirk mansion on Ridge Avenue, we are told, contains within itself a part of Major Mulford's old home, the first place occupied by him in what was at a later date called "Ridgeville." The later home of the family was the homestead which still stands on the corner of Ridge and Mulford Avenues. This place, with its background of wooded grove, its grounds fragrant with flowers, facing Ridge road, whose avenue of oaks extended to the Rogers Park line, was one of the most picturesque of the early homes of the place.

Major Mulford was called the "gentleman pioneer of Evanston," because it was rare in those early days to possess much education or to own a library. Of the size of this library we have no exact data. Mrs. Pliny Brown of Chicago, Major Mulford's granddaughter, says her earliest recollection is of three large book cases full of books.

Major Mulford died March 5, 1878, and the books, with the rest of the property, were divided among the members of the family. Many of these books are retained by Mrs. Pliny Brown, who kindly furnished a list of them. Of these some of the interesting early editions are:

"John Quincy Adams," by W. H. Seward. Derby, 1849.

Macaulay's "History of England." Harper, 1849. (1st Amer. ed.)

"Life and Writings of Dr. Chalmers." Harper, 1849-52.

"Washington's Agricultural Correspondence," by Franklin Knight, 1847.

"Louis the Fourteenth and the Court of France, in the Seventeenth Century," by Miss Pardoe, Harper, 1847.

"The Near and Heavenly Horizon; Remarks on Ecclesiastical History," by John Jastin. Holbourn, 1752.

A notable book of local interest is "Waubun; or, The Early Day in the Northwest," by Mrs. John H. Kinzie of Chicago, pub-

217

lished in 1856. Of this book the "London Athenæum" of that date said: "Written in perfectly simple, unpretending style, but with a keen perception of humor and a genuine love of adventure, which makes it very fascinating to read."

The old family Bible is dated 1813, the year of Major Mulford's marriage.

Among Major Mulford's books left in trust of later tenants of the old homestead, are a number of school-books, many of which bear interesting autographs and notes made by members of the family. We are indebted to Mr. Francis J. McAssey for many descriptive notes upon these books. In Lindley Murray's English Reader, Lexington, Ky., 1824, the poem by Wordsworth, the "Pet Lamb," is marked (apparently in Major Mulford's handwriting), to the effect that this poem was "learned by Ann at the age of seven years for her father, who was to pay her 25 cents." The names also occur of E. H. Mulford, George G. Mulford, James Johnson Mulford; Anna Mulford, Monticello Female Seminary; Mary Mulford, Kemper Hall, Kenosha, Wis.

The autograph of William S. Gibbs, Chicago High School, is found in Hilliard's First Reader, Boston, 1857.

Among other school books used in those early days was "Abercrombie's Intellectual Philosophy," Boston, 1841; "Porter's Analysis," Andover, 1828; "Newman's Rhetoric," Andover, 1839. "Comstock's Philosophy," New York, is inscribed as belonging to William Orr "Junor," "Covington Presbyterian Collegiate Institute."

An animated school-room correspondence had evidently been conducted upon the fly-leaves at intervals during the study of philosophy, between the owner and a rival in regard to their affections for one C. Lindley, who is described as "anjellick." It is interesting to speculate who "Bill"

Orr and his rival, "John Mc," were, and what finally became of their beautiful "Miss C. Lindley," all of whom "went to school to Mister Heir."

We note the contents of "Specimens of American Poetry," arranged by Samuel Kettell, Boston, 1829; Whittier, Richard Henry Dana and George Bancroft are each represented by one poem, Longfellow by three, Bryant by nine and John G. C. Brainard by ten. Whittier is spoken of in a biographical sketch as "one of the most youthful of our poets, and his verses show a more than common maturity of power . . . the editor of the 'American Manufacturer,' a newspaper of Boston."

"Hoyle's Games," New York, 1829, contains, among other games, "A Practical Treatise on the Game of Goff, or Golf," showing that golf was played "according to Hoyle" even in those early days.

The following quotation is found written on the last page of Chesterfield's "Men and Manners," New York, 1831: "To do justice, to love mercy, and to walk humbly with thy God," signed "E. H. Mulford"— this quotation, evidently, as the present owner of the book observes, "describing a Christian gentleman better, to the Major's mind, than the whole book he had finished reading."

"Thomas Jefferson's Manual of Parliamentary Rules," Philadelphia, 1853, is another book worthy of note. "The New York Book," New York, Geo. Dearborn, publisher, 1837, compiled from poetical writings of natives of New York State, contains "An Address to Black Hawk," evidently inspired by witnessing Black Hawk led captive through some eastern city. This book contains the autograph of Mrs. Bertha Gibbs.

Another contribution to the history of New York is "Rochester and Western New York," by Henry O'Reilly, Rochester, 1838, containing maps and illustrations of the city, also steel engravings of Colonel Rochester, after whom the city (Rochester) was named, and Vincent Matthews, the first lawyer admitted to the bar of Ontario County, then (1790) comprising all that part of the State west of Seneca Lake. This book also covers fully the development of the Erie Canal and early railroad projects. Henry O'Reilly, the author of this book, is said to have edited the first newspaper published west of New York City.

The "Musical Carcanet," New York, 1832, contains the words and music of "the most admired popular songs arranged for the voice, flute and violin." In a collection of poems, entitled "Elegant Extracts," is included a poem called "The Lighthouse," credited to Tom Moore, which is not to be found in any of the current editions of Moore's works.

Perhaps the most interesting book, in its bearing on local history, is "Laws of Illinois," published at Vandalia in 1833—that city being at that time the capital of the State. This book is now the property of the Evanston Historical Society. It is especially interesting from the fact that Major Mulford was a Justice of the Peace, and is said to have held the first court in Cook County—which would not be at all surprising when we consider that, in 1833, Chicago had only twenty-nine voters, comprising the entire adult male population in the election of that year. This book probably furnished Justice Mulford all the legal lore necessary to the settlement of all litigation arising from cattle breaking down fences, etc., in what is now the City of Evanston. Another book, now in possession of the Evanston Historical Society, is Dr. Isaac Mulford's "History of New Jersey," 1845. The author was a brother of Major Mulford, and the book bears the names of "Isaac Mulford" and "E. H. Mulford,

Ridgeville, Ill." "Scott's Lessons," a school book, published in 1823 and bearing the autograph of E. H. Mulford, was also presented to the Evanston Historical Society.

An example of the progress of science of that day is furnished in "Bigelow's Technology," published in 1815, and especially interesting from the fact that its author deemed it incomprehensible that the steam engine could ever be improved beyond its capacity at that time.

Among the works in the line of fiction current in the first few years of Major Mulford's residence in Evanston may be mentioned: Beaconsfield's "Young Duke," 1831, and "Vivian Grey," 1826: Cooper's "Homeward Bound," Philadelphia, 1838. One of the novels of a later date is "The Schoenberg-Cotta Family," by Mrs. Charles, 1863.

First Sunday School Library.—Closely allied with the history of this first Evanston library was the first Sunday School Library. This Sunday School, which was the seed from which sprang the present First Methodist Sunday School, was started at the old Mulford place and afterward moved to the log school-house which stood on the corner of Greenleaf Street and the Ridge. Mr. Abraham Wigelsworth was then the Superintendent. Mrs. Kate Hagarty, now of Ravenswood, then Mrs. Edward Mulford, who was at one time Superintendent, librarian and choir leader, brought with her from the East, about 1854, a collection of fifty books, which she presented to this Sunday School, thus founding the first Sunday School Library in Evanston.

Private Libraries of Today.—The library belonging to Dr. Daniel Bonbright, Dean of the College of Liberal Arts, Northwestern University, is without doubt the oldest of the existing private libraries of Evanston. Dr. Bonbright, who came to Evanston in 1855, is the oldest member of the

Faculty of Northwestern University; his library has grown up in connection with his chair of instruction in the Latin language and literature, and naturally its most important scope is in that direction.

Notable among the early libraries of Evanston may be mentioned that of the late Rev. Francis D. Hemenway, D.D., who came here in 1857 as Principal of the Preparatory Department of Garrett Biblical Institute and later became Professor in the Institute. He was Librarian of the Institute for many years and until his death in 1884. Dr. Hemenway was a member of the sub-committee to revise the Methodist Hymn Book in 1876, and during this work he gathered about 200 volumes on hymnology. This remarkable collection was presented to Garrett Biblical Institute in 1891 by his son, Henry B. Hemenway, M. D. About seventy-five volumes, once a part of this early library, are now in the possession of the Evanston Free Public Library, having been presented by Dr. H. B. Hemenway.

Besides possessing the remainder of his father's library, Dr. Henry B. Hemenway has a collection numbering about 600 volumes, more than one-half of which are medical works. This library contains the following quaint old volumes: "The Crucified Jesus; or, A Full Account of the Nature, Design and Benefits of the Lord's Supper," by Anthony Harneck, D.D., published by Lowndes in London, 1700; an extract from Mr. Law's "Serious Call to the Holy Life," by Rev. John Wesley, Philadelphia, 1803; "Rhetorical Reader, with Rhetorical Exercises," by Ebenezer Porter, D.D., New York, 1835—a very popular reader some sixty years ago and probably the first work published on oratory; a very early medical work, "Nine Commentaries Upon Fevers and Two Epistles Concerning the Smallpox," London, 1730; a rare old

book entitled, "Some of the Beauties of Free Masonry," by Joshua Bradley, 1816, has quite a history, having been left by an American soldier at the home of Mrs. Hemenway's grandmother, at Matamoras, Mexico. It bears its early owner's signature, John R. Bowdish, 1822.

Among other early Evanstonians, whose libraries were a source of inspiration to the youth of that day, may be mentioned the following:

Judge Harvey B. Hurd, who came to Evanston in 1855, and whose library was unfortunately destroyed by fire in recent years.

Rev. Henry Bannister, D.D., who lived and taught in Evanston twenty-seven years, coming here in 1856.

Dr. Oliver Marcy, who became Professor of Natural History in Northwestern University in 1862, and left at his death, in 1899, a well selected library.

Mr. L. H. Boutell, who came to Evanston in 1865 and was identified with the founding of the Public Library. His private library was a carefully selected, scholarly collection.

Edward Eggleston, who came here in 1866 as editor of the "Little Corporal," and whose private library had such an important part in the initial steps that led to the founding of the Free Public Library.

Probably the largest and most valuable private collection of books in Evanston is that belonging to Mrs. Charles J. Morse, whose library of about 10,200 volumes consists of three departments: (a) Professional Engineering; (b) General Literature; (c) Art, with especial reference to Oriental Art (Japan, China and India).

The Art Collection serves to trace the history of Oriental Art from India into China, from China into Japan, and its development in each country. The collection of books in English, French and German, relating to the History. Religions, Arts and Industries, etc., of Japan, China, India, Ceylon and other Buddhist countries, is more complete than any similar collection to be found in any of the large libraries of Chicago.

Supplementing the above library is a collection of (a) "The Art; or, Illustrated Books of Japan," and (b) "The Art, Literature and History of Art of China." The former is an attempt to form a complete collection of the art and illustrated books of Japan from the beginning of their publication, about 1608, to the present time, so far as they were of value to art. This collection of about 700 titles is representative and probably more complete than any in this country or in Europe, the similar department in the Bibliotheque Nationale of Paris containing, in 1900, only 581 titles.

The Chinese books consist of some 5,000 volumes, containing nearly the complete literature of the art of painting in China, as well as Encyclopedias, Histories, the Classics, Essays and Belles-Lettres. In this department is found the largest encyclopedia ever published in any country, consisting of 1,628 volumes, profusely illustrated.

One of the largest of the private collections in Evanston is that of Dr. Robert D. Sheppard, whose library, occupying a beautiful room on the east side of his home, facing the lake, contains about 5,000 volumes. Dr. Sheppard has made special collections of English and American history and economics.

Mr. Walter Lee Brown's library, of about 4,000 volumes, contains many sets of the earlier authors of England and America and few of the present. It consists largely of first editions of Cooper, Hawthorne, Irving and Poe, and contains special collections of the various editions of the "Meditations of Marcus Aurelius Antoninus" and White's "Natural History and Antiquities

of Selborne." Mr. Brown has also made a special collection of "Chap Books," most of which were published during the eighteenth century, one being dated as early as 1696.

Mr. Frank M. Elliott has a library of about 2,200 volumes, consisting of standard books in fiction and miscellaneous classes. Mr. Elliott also has made a valuable collection of works on Lincoln and Illinois, and Mrs. Elliott has a useful musical library.

The library of Mr. Charles Cleveland, of about 1,600 volumes, is one of the most valuable private collections in Evanston. Most of the volumes are large paper and de luxe editions, and represent not only the highest typographical excellence, but the most artistic examples of book-binding in existence, forming a collection which is probably not equaled in this respect by any in the West. Among these fine bindings are specimens of the art of Cobden-Sanderson, Riviere, Zaehnsdorf, Cockrell, Roger de Coverley, Tout, Prideaux, Chambolle-Durer, Mercier, Ritter, Michel, David, Joly and Lortic.

Of the more notable works may be mentioned : A majority of the Kelmscott Press publications ; a full set of Caxton Club publications ; full sets of Eugene Field's first editions and presentation copies ; Fiske's "History of the United States," extra illustrated ; Shakespeare's Works, sixteen volumes, extra illustrated ; de luxe editions of Hawthorne and Emerson and first edition of Ruskin's Works. Many of the volumes in this library have appeared in loan exhibitions, both in Chicago and in Evanston.

The late J. H. Kedzie's library consists of some 600 volumes of standard authors, with a special collection of scientific works, notably on astronomy, in which subject Mr. Kedzie had made special research.

The Orrington Lunt Library of Northwestern University and the Garrett Biblical Institute Library, both of which are so densely identified with the early history of Evanston, will be found described in the chapter devoted to the history of those institutions.

The Margaret C. Way Memorial Library was presented to the Woman's Educational Aid Association by Mrs. Kate V. McMullen in memory of her mother, Mrs. Margaret C. Way, who was for eighteen years a member of this Association. This library, which contains about 400 volumes, is for the special use and benefit of the students and teachers who reside at the College Cottage, now known as Pearsons Hall.

The Evanston Township High School has a good working library of some 1,600 volumes. The graded schools are also provided with reference libraries.

Collection of Curios.—A collection —not of books, but of equal value in point of historic interest—is that of Honorable George S. Knapp, who has gathered together what is probably one of the most remarkable collections of historic and scientific curios in the country. Mr. Knapp was the general manager of the Columbian Liberty Bell, which was one of the most interesting exhibits of the World's Columbian Exposition in Chicago of 1893, and to the making of which the pennies of 250,000 children were contributed, together with many historic pieces of metal, identified with various struggles for liberty. The most remarkable of these relics was that contributed by Mrs. Roger A. Pryor, of New York, which was formed of two bullets—one from the North and one from the South—which met in the air and so imbedded themselves into each other as to form a solid mass and assume the shape of the letter "U," typical of the Union of to-day.

Many things pertaining to the bell are still in Mr. Knapp's possession, the most interesting being the "International Rope," which was used by representatives of all nations in ringing the bell on "Chicago Day," 1893. The idea, which is a unique one, was conceived by Mr. Knapp. The rope, which is fifty-four feet long, is made of materials from all nations of the earth. The central strand, consisting of a piece of rawhide contributed by the United States, is covered by strands from the other nations, the whole being wrapped with the "red, white and blue." The first contribution to this rope was from Queen Victoria— a skein of linen thread spun by her own hand. The last was a piece of a meteor. Thus, as the owner says of it, "Heaven and earth helped to make it."

The Columbian Peace Plow was made from the relics, mostly swords and bayonets, which could not be used in making the Liberty Bell. On the beam of the plow are the words, "And they shall beat their swords into ploughshares, and their spears into pruning hooks. Nation shall not lift sword against nation, neither shall they learn war any more."

Another interesting reminder of the World's Fair is the beautiful American flag —the official flag of the Exposition—which was made of American silk, spun from cocoons by women of twenty-six States of the Union. This flag was dedicated to the women of America at the opening of the Woman's Building in 1893, and was presented to the Board of Lady Managers by Mr. G. S. Knapp and his son, G. M. Knapp, and was then presented back to them by that board. The staff is made of cherry and inlaid with pieces of wood furnished by the World's Fair Commissioners from each State and Territory in the Union, each piece being of great historical value.

Among the Revolutionary relics in this collection may be mentioned the following: Piece of Paul Jones' flag, the first to be saluted by a foreign power; sword used at Bunker Hill by Mr. Knapp's great-grandfather; lanterns used by Washington's body guard; blunderbuss taken from the boat from which the tea was thrown overboard in Boston harbor. This eighteenth century gun is a wicked looking piece, which bears on its large mouth the words, "Happy is he that escapes me."

Relics of a later historic period are: Cup of white china used by Lincoln; cigar-holder used by Grant; gavel composed of a picket from the late President McKinley's fence at Canton (given to the owner by Mr. McKinley himself) and a piece of the plank on which he stood at his inauguration; a Confederate flag found in a bale of cotton on board a ship which arrived in Liverpool, England, in 1864, after having run the blockade of New Orleans; an American flag carried by Mr. Knapp through the campaigns of Grant, Garfield, Blaine, Harrison and McKinley; a piece of an old fort at San Juan, in the capture of which some of our own Evanston troops assisted; a collection of swords and daggers used by the Filipinos in the late war, and on which the stains of blood still show, in spite of cleaning and polishing; a bow used by Black Hawk; a "Rob Roy" pistol from Sir Walter Scott's collection; a revolver carried by Robert E. Lee in the Civil War.

Among relics of a local interest may be mentioned: A carved staff made of wood from the old City Hall, which stood on the present site of the Rookery Building, Chicago; a frame made from the steps of the old Ogden House, which stood on the present site of the Newberry Library; the newel-post of the Ogden house. The first two were carved by Mr. Knapp, who has done several pieces of very intricate carving with a pen-knife, notable among which is a series of frames held together by links, emblematic of events in the history of the world—

the whole cut with a pen-knife from one solid piece of black walnut, the links being cut without disjoining. Not the least interesting in this unique collection is a piece of the first water-pipe laid in the City of Chicago, as well as samples of every kind of pipe used there since that time.

Evanston Free Public Library.—The Evanston Free Public Library had its origin in a plan to form "The Evanston Sabbath School Union Library" in February, 1870. For the inception of the idea of such a library, however, we must go back to 1867 or 1868, when Dr. Edward Eggleston, then Superintendent of the First Methodist Sunday School, formed a class of boys who met at his house, which stood until recent years at 1017 Davis Street. This class, which was not confined to boys of any one church, held a brief religious meeting, after which they were invited freely into Dr. Eggleston's library and allowed to choose books for their home reading. We quote from an article in "The Index" of December 18, 1897, by Dr. Henry B. Hemenway, who, describing this class, speaks of Dr. Eggleston as the "Father of the Public Library":

"My mental picture of Edward Eggleston generally shows him in the half hour after the meeting. He sits in a large, easy chair, his heavy brown hair pushed back, and his face lit up as he looks first to one, then to another of his hearers. A boy sits on each knee, another on each arm of the chair, one or two more hang on its back, while the rest get close to his feet on the floor, or on low stools. Then he told us stories—stories of his boyhood, or of the frontier. Some of them have since been printed. Before we parted he took us into the little library and helped us to select books for our week's reading. He did not object to books of adventure for spice, but I remember that he tried to instill into our minds a taste for books of more value, like Abbott's histories. The class grew until he had to move it into the Kindergarten building, which he had built for his sister in the yard east of the house. He added to his library, but it was too small. Then he began to appeal to some of our old citizens, L. L. Greenleaf among others, for the forming of a public library."

The impetus thus given resulted in the realization of Dr. Eggleston's cherished plan, and although his name is not found in the records of the library, he having moved to Brooklyn just about that time, yet there is no doubt that the beloved author of "Roxy" and the "Hoosier Schoolmaster" and many other books dear to young and old, was the inspiration of the present Public Library.

The first organization was formed at the residence of William T. Shepherd, 1738 Chicago Avenue, by the following named persons: L. L. Greenleaf, Rev. M. G. Clarke, Dr. E. O. Haven, A. L. Winne, William P. Kimball, William T. Shepherd. The next recorded meeting was held August 26, 1870, at the residence of William T. Shepherd. Those present at this meeting were: L. L. Greenleaf, A. L. Winne, Rev. E. N. Packard, H. C. Tillinghast and William T. Shepherd. At this meeting it was voted that the name of the Association be "The Evanston Library Association," the plan for a Union Sabbath School Library not being feasible. A committee which was appointed to draft by-laws and a constitution consisted of Rev. E. N. Packard, Dr. J. S. Jewell and William T. Shepherd. On October 18, 1870, this constitution was adopted at a meeting held in the Methodist Church, Dr. E. O. Haven, chairman, and E. S. Taylor, Secretary. This constitution provided that the name of the Association be "The Evanston Library Association"; that the object be "to establish and maintain a public library and reading room, and in connection with this, by all suitable means to awaken a desire for sound knowledge and a correct taste, and to provide for the gratification of the same among all classes of the community."

Two classes of membership were provided for, viz.: Ordinary and Life—the first being open to all residents of Evanston upon the payment of $5.00 per annum. The second was open to residents of Evanston upon the payment of $30.00 for gentlemen and $20.00 for ladies. Annual meetings of the Association and monthly meetings of its Board of Directors were provided.

The Nominating Committee who selected the first Board of Officers consisted of General (afterwards Governor) John L. Beveridge, Messrs. E. R. Paul, Merrill Ladd, Samuel Greene and Ambrose Foster. The following officers were elected: President, L. L. Greenleaf; Vice-President, H. G. Powers; Corresponding Secretary, Charles Randolph; Recording Secretary, Samuel Greene; Treasurer, Lyman J. Gage; Directors, Rev. E. O. Haven, D.D.; Ambrose Foster, Andrew Shuman, L. H. Boutell, J. S. Jewell, M. D., and J. H. Kedzie.

On October 25th at a meeting of the Board of Directors at the residence of H. G. Powers, the first Committees were appointed as follows: Books and Periodicals, L. H. Boutell, Andrew Shuman, Dr. E. O. Haven; Rooms and Furnishing, Samuel Greene, J. H. Kedzie, H. G. Powers and L. L. Greenleaf; Finance, H. G. Powers, Ambrose Foster, L. J. Gage and L. L. Greenleaf; Lectures, Dr. J. S. Jewell, Charles Randolph and L. H. Boutell.

Besides fees from members, many donations of money were made by friends of the enterprise, the largest of which was $575 from L. L. Greenleaf. Some revenue was also derived, later, from lectures and from rent of the Association rooms. Valuable donations of books were made by H. G. Powers, Andrew Shuman, J. S. Jewell, L. J. Gage and others.

On December 3, 1870, the Book Committee were authorized to purchase books to the amount of $1,000. Rooms were secured on the second floor of Dr. W. S. Scott's building, now numbered 613 Davis Street, and the Library was formally opened on February 9, 1871. The Association was organized as a body corporate under the laws of the State of Illinois on February 23, 1871. At this time a Constitution was adopted, which was practically the same as that adopted by the Association October 18, 1870. The first monthly report of the Library showed one hundred Life and Annual members, thirty-three weekly subscribers, ninety books in circulation.

On October 29, 1872 a Committee consisting of Messrs. L. L. Greenleaf, L. H. Boutell and J. S. Page were appointed to see what measures were needed to bring about the transfer of the Library to the town. Through the efforts of this Committee the matter was brought to a vote of the people at the Spring election, and in April, 1873, the citizens of the Village of Evanston, without dissent, voted for a two-mill tax for a free public library, under the provisions of the Illinois Library Law, which was passed in March, 1872. The Trustees of the Village of Evanston thereupon appointed as Directors of the Free Public Library, Messrs. L. H. Boutell, J. S. Jewell, O. E. Willard, J. H. Kedzie, Samuel Greene, E. S. Taylor, Andrew Shuman, L. L. Greenleaf and Thomas Freeman.

On May 22, 1873, the Evanston Library Association authorized the Trustees to transfer the books and other property of the Association to the Directors of the Free Public Library of the Village of Evanston, upon condition that the same be forever kept as a Free Public Library for the use of the inhabitants of the village, and upon the further condition that said Directors assume the indebtedness of the Association. In accordance with these instructions the 913 volumes, and other property belonging to the Association, were transferred by the Trustees on July 3, 1873. The first meeting of the Board of Directors of the Free Library of the Village of Evanston was held at the Library rooms on June 21, 1873. The ballot for officers resulted in the choice of J. H. Kedzie for President and Samuel Greene for Secretary. In April, 1889, the Library was moved to the lower floor of Anton Block's building, 522 and 524 Sherman Avenue. Upon the erection of the new City Hall in 1892, rooms on the second floor were assigned to the Public Library. These rooms were planned and adapted to the needs of the Library under the direction of N. C. Gridley, the President of the Board, and in April, 1893, the Library was removed to these rooms in the City Hall, its present quarters. Thus began a period of greater growth and expansion. The yearly accessions of books which, for the twenty-one years since its foundation, had averaged 465 volumes per year, now ranged from 1,142 volumes added in 1893, to 2,907 volumes added in 1897. This impulse toward a larger purchase of books was given through the generosity of John R. Lindgren, who, during the year 1891-92, turned over to the Library for a book fund, his salary as City Treasurer, amounting to $1,502.36.

Officers and Directors.—J. H. Kedzie, the first President of the Free Public Library Board, was succeeded by L. H. Boutell in April, 1877. Mr. Boutell, who, as we have recorded, was identified with the first Board of Directors of the Library Association, continued in faithful service as a member of the Board and of the Book Committee for twenty-nine years until his death, January 16, 1899. In May, 1882, N. C.

Gridley was elected to the office of President, which he held until his resignation, in June, 1895, after twenty years membership upon the Board, executing as President not only the duties of this office, but much of the work incident to the purchase of books, etc., usually devolving upon the librarian. To the many years of active service of these two gentlemen, is due, in large part, the successful growth of the library and the careful selection of books which formed the foundation of a collection well balanced in all departments.

Mr. J. W. Thompson, who was appointed a member of the Board in June, 1890, has been, since June, 1895, its faithful and efficient presiding officer. The first Secretary, Samuel Greene, served from October, 1870, to November, 1873. The successors to this office have been as follows: E. S. Taylor, H. M. Bannister, N. C. Gridley, H. G. Lunt, J. S. Currey and Wm. S. Lord, the last three named having served for eight years each, Mr. Lord still holding this office.

Charles A. Rogers is the oldest in service of the present Board of Directors, having served continuously since 1876. The remaining members of the present Board, not before mentioned are: J. Seymour Currey, Vice-President; Richard C. Lake, Charles G. Neely, Fred W. Nichols, George W. Paullin, Walter Lee Brown (resigned).

Librarians.—Mr. Thomas J. Kellam was the first librarian, serving from January to March, 1871. The compensation of the Librarian was fixed at $5 per week, this amount being understood to cover all expense incurred in the care of the room. Mr. Kellam was succeeded by Miss Mary E. Greene, who held the position until March, 1872, when Miss L. H. Newman was elected, and was retained by the Free Library Board, thus becoming the first Librarian of the Free Public Library.

Those succeeding to this position have been, as follows:

Miss Nellie A. Lathrop, October, 1875, to September, 1876.

Miss L. H. Bannister, September, 1876, to November, 1880.

Miss Lizzie R. Hunt, November, 1880, to September, 1882.

Miss Ada L. Fairfield, September, 1882, to September, 1883.

Miss Anna P. Lord, September, 1883, to November, 1888.

Miss Laura R. Richards, November, 1888, to May, 1891.

Miss Mary S. Morse, May, 1891, to October, 1891.

Miss May Van Benschoten, October, 1891, to June, 1894.

In December, 1893, it was resolved by the Board that the increasing work of the Library required the services of a trained librarian. In accordance with this resolution, the present Librarian, Miss Mary B. Lindsay, was appointed and entered upon her duties, June 1, 1894.

Classification and Cataloguing.—In 1896 the simple classification under which the books were arranged was found to be inadequate to the growth of the Library, and the work of reclassifying the Library under the Dewey Decimal system was begun in March of that year, under the direction of Dr. George E. Wire, late of the Newberry Library, and formerly identified with this Library as First Assistant Librarian. Miss Mary E. Gale was employed to make the card catalogue. This work was completed in December, 1896, having been accomplished without closing the library or materially interfering with its use. The first printed catalogue was published in December, 1873, and included a historical sketch of the Library for the three years since its organization. Later catalogues were published in 1877, 1887, 1889 and

1892. An "Annotated Finding List of Fiction, Books for Young People and Selected Lists" was published in 1897. The card catalogue, which is in dictionary form, under names of authors, titles and subjects, is kept up to date by a trained cataloguer, and thus takes the place of a printed catalogue, with continuous supplements. Bulletins of new books are published quarterly during the year and distributed free to readers.

Library Extension.—One of the chief means of promoting and extending the work of the Library on broader lines was inaugurated in March, 1896, when, in compliance with a request from F. W. Nichols, Superintendent of School District No. 2, about 100 books were loaned to the schools in that district to be circulated under the direction of the teachers. In the following year a system of separate school libraries was adopted. These school libraries of about one hundred books each were sent in turn to the schools farthest removed from the library, including all the school districts. One of these libraries was the gift of Mr. Richard C. Lake, of the Board of Directors. This circulation of books through the schools, besides giving the children the benefit of a careful selection of books, has been an effectual means of bringing into touch with the library the families of those children, who, residing in the remoter parts of the city, were otherwise not acquainted with the library and its privileges. A graded and annotated list of the 500 books in the school libraries, compiled by the Reference Librarian, has just been published. In October, 1897, the work for children was made a part of the work of the Reference Librarian and further co-operation of the library with the school was made possible by her visits to the schools and conference with the teachers.

A "Children's Corner" was established in the reading room of the library in October, 1898, and here, even in its crowded quarters, is seen something of what might be accomplished in this very important line of library work, in a building equipped with a separate children's room. A Children's Library League was organized January 26, 1899, with the object of promoting among the young people a better care of the books and other property of the library and the cultivation of a taste for the best books.

Reference Department.—The Reference Department of about 900 volumes is said to be better equipped than most libraries of its size. The usefulness of this Department was greatly enhanced in October, 1897, when the position of Assistant Librarian for Reference and Children's work was created. The placing of this department in charge of a trained assistant has made possible a much larger work by the preparation of reference lists on special subjects for clubs and for individuals, and by bringing to young people and adults a better knowledge of the various reference books and their use.

As a means of further extension of the library's usefulness and of increasing knowledge of its methods and work among the citizens, an annual "Library Day" was inaugurated on December 10, 1897. This annual event has taken the form of a reception or "open house," day at the library, during which books were not circulated, but the staff and Directors served as a reception committee and explained the various departments and methods of work. Special exhibits of books and curios, loaned by friends of the library, added to the interest of the occasion. The twenty-fifth anniversary of the opening of the Free Public Library was celebrated in this way on October 13, 1898. The crowded condition of the library rooms has made it necessary for the past two years to abandon, temporarily, this popular annual feature.

Hours.—The Library was open from 3 p. m. to 9 p. m., every day, except Sundays and holidays, until October, 1871, when the great Chicago fire made it necessary to curtail expenses. The hours were therefore limited at that time to Saturday afternoons and evenings, from 2 to 4 and from 7 to 9. In 1873 the hours were extended to three afternoons and evenings of the week. In April, 1893, the patronage of the library warranted its opening every day except Sunday from 2 to 9 o'clock p. m. In December, 1895, the hours for opening were made 1 p. m. to 9 p. m. daily and from 9 a. m. to 9 p. m. Saturdays. Beginning March 15, 1897, the present hours were inaugurated, viz: 9 a. m. to 9 p. m., daily, and in January, 1901, the plan of holiday and Sunday opening was inaugurated—the reading room being open on those days from 2 p. m. until 6 p. m.

Privileges, Etc.—Since the organization of the Free Public Library, membership has been free to all residents of Evanston upon the furnishing of written guaranty. The family card, good for three books and the individual card good for one book, were exchanged in August, 1896, for individual cards issued to each resident, without limit of age, allowing two books on each card. A fee of fifty cents per month, or $2.50 per year, gives the privileges of the library to non-residents. Non-resident students were at first allowed the use of the library for reference; in October, 1896, the privilege of drawing books from the library was granted to them. Since September, 1898, the public have been admitted to the shelves as far as practicable with the limited room.

Staff.—On August 29, 1895, the matter of employment of Librarian and staff of assistants was placed under the jurisdiction of the Civil Service Commission. The Staff at present (1905) consists of the following: Mary B. Lindsay, Librarian;

Elizabeth P. Clarke, Reference Librarian; Cora M. Hill, Superintendent Circulating Department; Gertrude L. Brown, Cataloguer; Bertha S. Bliss, Arthur H. Knox, Eddy S. Brandt, Assistants; Wm. E. Lee, Janitor.

From the 913 volumes which formed the nucleus of the Free Public Library in 1873, the number has grown to about 30,000 volumes—an average growth of about 1,000 volumes per year. From the small beginning represented by about 9,000 books circulated during its first year, the circulation has grown to 114,551 volumes, which went into the homes and the schools for the year ending June 1, 1901. The annual income of the library has risen from twelve hundred to about ten thousand dollars. The purchase of books, which in 1874 amounted to $260, has, for the last ten years, averaged about $2,000 per year, the book purchases for the year 1900-01 being 2,557 volumes, amounting to $2,459.49.

It has been the aim of the Public Library to keep in touch with the larger library interests of the country. To this end the Library has, in recent years, been represented at the meetings of the American Library Association and the Illinois State Library Association, President J. W. Thompson serving for a term as President of the latter Association. In February, 1898, an Inter-State Library Conference was held in Evanston, which was attended by some 170 delegates, eleven States being represented. A number of citizens generously aided the Public and University Libraries in the entertainment of this conference.

Library Building.—On May 31, 1884, the need for more room becoming apparent, Mr. Holmes Hoge was appointed "a committee of one to consult with Mr. Deering, about the erection of a library building suitable for the necessities of the people of the village." The annual report of the same date contained an appeal to the citizens of Evanston to provide a building for the Library. In April, 1887, Mr. William Deering offered $5,000 toward the erection of a library building, following which a circular letter was issued signed by the President of the Board, urging that a generous response be given to the Committee who would call upon the citizens for further subscriptions. After earnest efforts made to raise the required amount, the plan was abandoned in June, 1887, owing to the slight encouragement given by the citizens.

During the next ten years, though no action was taken, the question was often discussed by the Board, and endeavors made to create sentiment toward obtaining a building. In December, 1897, Mr. Charles F. Grey, of Evanston, offered $10,000 toward a $100,000 building. A committee from the Board was appointed to confer with Mr. Grey and to take up the matter of a new building. Though there were no offers toward the remaining $100,000, yet the Board felt confident that the required amount would be forthcoming, and efforts were continued toward securing a suitable site. In October, 1898, a committee was appointed to ascertain possible consent of property owners abutting on the City Park in case the City would grant permission to place the library building there. This committee canvassed the matter and reported almost unanimous refusal on the part of property owners to consent to having the park used as a site.

In June, 1899, resolutions were adopted by the Board asking the City Council to appropriate $35,000 for a site for the Library. These resolutions were referred by the Council to the Judiciary Committee in consultation with the Corporation Counsel. The appropriation was not granted. In January, 1900, Mr. C. F. Grey offered to give $100,000 for a library building, provided a site should be furnished, cleared of buildings, free of cost or incumbrance, and the premises after purchase removed from the tax list. A committee from the Board was appointed to raise funds for the purchase of a site. Anticipating the securing of the amount necessary for the building, the Board had previously made efforts to secure the property facing east on Chicago Avenue, extending north from the Baptist church to Grove Street, but efforts to obtain options on all of this property failed, and before the money could be secured that part of this property on the corner of Grove Street was sold to the Christian Science Church. Options were then obtained on the property facing west on Chicago Avenue, extending from the alley south to Grove Street.

In June, 1900, the Site Committee issued a circular letter to citizens of Evanston calling a meeting of citizens to consider ways and means of raising the needed funds to obtain a site. This meeting was held July 6, 1900, in the City Council chamber, and it was voted to attempt to raise the required amount on the voluntary assessment plan, and a committee of citizens was chosen to act with a committee from the Library Board in spreading and collecting the assessment. An equal per cent of each taxpayer was determined according to the tax lists and notices were sent them stating amount of share of each. Notices were also sent to non-tax-payers, asking for a percentage of their income. In response to this voluntary assessment, there was received $2,709.85 in cash from one hundred and twenty people. Pledges were received from forty-one people aggregating $2,116.80. The total amount necessary to purchase a suitable site in a central location was about $40,000. Realizing that this plan had failed, the money was returned to the donors and a final report made by the Treasurer of the fund, Rev. F. Clatworthy, in August, 1901.

In the meantime another attempt was made toward securing the City Park. This movement was started by Rev. J. H. Boyd, D. D., who interested a number of citizens in the matter and announced the subject for discussion at his "Conversazione," December 13, 1900, at the First Presbyterian church. This was made a public meeting, and the subject was fully discussed and resolutions were passed requesting the Library Board to ascertain whether the Park could be secured under the law, and to endeavor to secure consents of abutting property owners and the preferences of the legal voters of Evanston as to the site for the Library. A special committee was appointed from the Library Board, and made a careful canvass of the property owners abutting on the Park, but they were obliged to report in February, 1901, that they had been unable to obtain consent of all the owners. Though many who had formerly objected now consented, yet a few adhered to the opinion that their property would be largely damaged by the use of any part of the park for the purpose contemplated. January 31, 1901, Mr. J. C. Shaffer suggested the probability of securing a site on Chicago Avenue between Church and Davis Streets. A Committee was appointed to act with Mr. Shaffer towards securing this site.

On April 6, 1901, following upon the passage of a State law giving to cities the power to levy a tax for the purpose of purchasing sites for public library buildings, the Board of Directors passed resolutions determining to purchase a site, the estimated cost of which was $45,000, the collection of such cost to be spread over a period of fifteen years. A copy of these resolutions was sent to the City Council and

approved by them, but it was subsequently found that the City of Evanston was already indebted to its full legal limit; hence such action of the Council was found illegal and was rescinded.

In May, 1901, the Site Committee reported pledges received to the amount of $12,000. In June, 1901, Mr. Joseph M. Lyons was authorized to raise subscriptions to the site fund at a compensation of one per cent, conditional upon his raising a sum in addition to that already subscribed sufficient to pay for the site. Although pledges to the amount of $17,000 were secured, this enterprise also resulted in failure. After various other unsuccessful attempts, in June, 1904, the effort to secure a site was crowned with success, through the purchase of one by the city at the corner of Orrington Avenue and Church Street at a cost of $31,600.00.

A glance at the history of the library movement throughout the country shows the wonderful possibilities of the work of the public library in educating the masses, and thus making for a higher citizenship.

The Management of our Public Library is still confident that, in due time, some solution of our site problem will be reached, and Evanston's Public Library will not be long hampered by lack of room from attaining to that larger educational work toward which, during its twenty-nine years of history, it has steadily been advancing.

The movement for a new building for the Public Library culminated in the offer of Mr. Andrew Carnegie to provide $50,000 towards the cost of such a building. This was supplemented by a bond issue of the City of Evanston of $31,600, for the site at the north-east corner of Church Street and Orrington Ave., and $25,000 towards the cost of the building. This, with some other funds at the disposal of the Library Board, will enable the authorities to erect a building to cost approximately $100,000.

The corner-stone of this new building was laid on June 2, 1906. A box was inclosed in the corner-stone containing a written account of the efforts made to provide for the new building, reports, photographs of the various persons connected with the library and the city administration, newspapers of the day, and various mementoes. The general design of the building is pure classic, fronting on Orrington Avenue, constructed of steel framework with Bedford stone in the exterior walls, and with a portico supported by Grecian columns. The capacity of the space for books is double that needed for the present collection, thus making ample provision for future growth.

CHAPTER XXV.

UNIVERSITY LIBRARY
(By LODILLA AMBROSE, Ph. M., Assistant Librarian)

First Step in the Organization of a University Library—President Foster's Gift —Advance of Fifty Years—The Greenleaf Library—University Library is Made a Depository for Government Publications—Recent Notable Donations— Orrington Lunt Library Building is Dedicated in 1894—The Orrington Lunt Library Fund—Internal Administration —List of Those who have Served as Librarians—Libraries of Garrett Biblical Institute and Professional Schools.

The Northwestern University Library is an integral part of the institution whose name it bears. The beginnings of the Library were small and unheralded; its growth has been gradual, but constant and substantial. The earliest mention of a library in the University records occurs in the minutes of the annual meeting of the Board of Trustees, June, 1856, this being the first meeting after the University was opened to students. The report of the Faculty then submitted touched on the question of a library. This led to the appointment of a committee that made the following report: "The Committee on Library recommends that the Executive Committee be authorized to expend one thousand dollars in the purchase of books for the commencement of a library during the present year, and that the same amount be set apart from

year to year, for additions thereto, the catalogue to be selected under the direction of the Faculty."

A little later President Foster gave his first year's salary for the purchase of books; and in December, 1856, the Financial Agent was authorized to fit up a room in the University building to accommodate the Library. In June, 1857, the librarian reported 1,977 volumes and 37 pamphlets; these volumes, with a few exceptions, having been selected and purchased by President Foster. The annual meetings of 1857 and 1858 suspended the action taken in 1856 making an annual appropriation of one thousand dollars for books. In 1860, 675 volumes, chiefly philosophical and historical, were purchased from President Foster's library. In 1868, a printed catalogue of the library, prepared by Charles K. Bannister, '69, was published; a summary of the entries in this slight, green-covered pamphlet shows that the library then contained about 3,000 volumes. In June, 1870, the librarian reported 3,635 volumes; twenty years later there were 23,279 volumes, and April 30, 1903, there are 51,658 volumes and 35,000 pamphlets.

The first great addition to the library came through the gift of Mr. Luther L. Greenleaf. Negotiations, begun in 1869 in Berlin with the heirs of Johann Schulze, Ph. D., a member of the Prussian Ministry of Public Instruction, resulted in securing for the University the valuable library of this eminent German scholar and publicist. In recognition of Mr. Greenleaf's liberality the collection is known as the Greenleaf Library. It contains 11,246 volumes, and a very large number of unbound dissertations and other monographs, the publications of universities and learned societies. It includes a collection of the Greek and Latin classics, with the subsidiary literature, remarkable for its range and completeness. There are also choice selections of works in history, philosophy, and other leading subjects.

In 1874, the library of the late Prof. Henry S. Noyes, containing 1,500 well chosen volumes, was purchased by the University for the library. In 1878, Mr. William Deering and the Hon. Lyman J. Gage bought and presented a portion of the library of the late Oliver A. Willard, chiefly volumes of State and local history and political science.

In 1895, Mrs. R. W. Patterson gave nearly 500 volumes, largely biblical and philosophical, from the library of her husband, the late Rev. R. W. Patterson, D. D.

In 1896, the joint gifts of friends enabled the library to purchase a complete set of the Hansard Parliamentary Debates. In 1898, similar gifts secured complete sets of the Reports of the United States Supreme Court and of the Illinois Supreme Court, and also created a fund of $1,850 for the purchase of the later editions of the Greek and Latin classics, supplementing the Greenleaf collection of earlier date.

Another gift received in 1898 was the library of German authors (2,533 volumes) collected by Geheimer Regierungsrath Schneider, of Schleswig, Germany. It includes many first and second editions, and some early Reformation prints. Gifts from leading German citizens of Chicago, se-

cured by the late Assistant Professor Cohn, made possible the purchase of this collection.

In 1900, Dr. Herbert F. Fisk obtained for the Academy a supplementary library of over 500 volumes. In the same year Mr. Norman W. Harris gave $750 for the purchase of books on political economy; Mrs. Oliver Marcy gave selected volumes from the scientific library of her husband, the late Dr. Oliver Marcy, Professor of Geology; and Mrs. Henry Cohn presented valuable works from the linguistic library of her husband, the late Henry Cohn, Assistant Professor of German.

A generous donor to the library is the United States Government. The library was designated as a depository of government publications by Senator John A. Logan, May 26, 1876. In April, 1903, its collection of these documents numbers 6,740 volumes and 10,154 pamphlets. In addition to these, some 3,000 volumes of the official publications of States and cities have been collected.

In 1870, the Librarian's report gave the list of periodicals regularly received, comprising 39 titles; in 1890, this list contained 105 titles, and in 1903, 320 titles.

The hours of opening in 1870, according to the record, were four hours each weekday afternoon. These hours have been gradually extended in response to greater demands, until in 1903 the library is open thirteen hours each day for six days a week, during the college year. Early reports mention appreciative use of the library. Records of later years show a marked increase in its use along all lines —an increase that quite outstrips the growth of the library, as well as the advance in the number of students.

The library's first habitation was a room in the building now called Old College. In December, 1869, it was transferred to

ORRINGTON LUNT LIBRARY—NORTHWESTERN UNIVERSITY

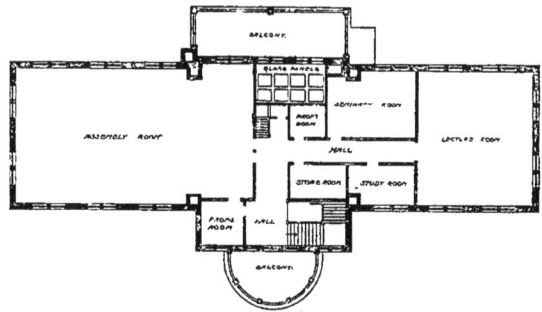

PLAN OF SECOND FLOOR

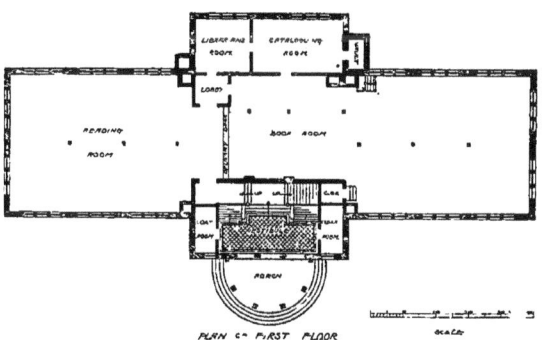

PLAN OF FIRST FLOOR

SCALE

rooms in the new University Hall. In August, 1894, came another migration, this time to the Orrington Lunt Library Building. As early as 1859 a prudent Trustee urged the necessity of a fireproof library building; in 1885 the need was emphasized in the report of the Committee on Library, and, in 1891, the subject was prominent in the President's report. July 22, 1891, Mr. Orrington Lunt, Vice-President of the Board of Trustees, signified his readiness to give $50,000 toward a library building. As an addition to this generous gift, $15,-000 was contributed in varying sums by other friends of the University. Among these contributions was a gift of $5,000 made by Mrs. Robert M. Hatfield as a memorial of her husband, the late Rev. Robert M. Hatfield, D.D., for years a Trustee of the University. The amount thus given through personal beneficence was raised to $100,000 by an appropriation from the funds of the University.

The building is situated on the University campus at Evanston, facing Sheridan Road, and covering an area of 73 by 162 feet. It is planned so that future additions may be made without sacrificing exterior effect or interior convenience. The outer walls are of buff Bedford limestone, the roof is red conosera tile. The building is constructed on the slow-burning, or practically fireproof, system, sometimes called mill-construction. The style of the building is an adaptation of the Italian Renaissance; its outlines are simple with little ornamentation, but the whole is harmonious and pleasing. The large semi-circular porch is supported by Ionic columns; on the frieze, in raised lettering, is the inscription, "Orrington Lunt Library."

On either side of the entrance are cloak rooms; a broad oak staircase leads to the second floor, which provides an assembly room seating 500 persons, art rooms and seminar rooms. The third story, extending only over the central portion of the building, is devoted to offices and recitation rooms. The basement, well lighted and thoroughly furnished, contains among others a large document room, seminar rooms, work rooms, and toilet rooms.

The first, or main, story is devoted entirely to library uses; in one wing is the reading room and in the center and in the other wing is the book room, the two being separated by the delivery desk and card catalogue cases. The windows are large and placed so that all light comes from above. All the wood-work and furnishings of this floor are of polished red oak. The reading room seats 120 persons. All the stories are connected with the book room by a book-lift and speaking tube. In a central extension of the building, as shown in the ground plan, are the Librarian's room and the cataloguing room. The heating is by steam from a detached station and the lighting is by gas and electricity. The architect is William A. Otis, of Chicago.

The Orrington Lunt Library was dedicated, September 26, 1894. In the afternoon in the assembly room of the building, the exercises of formal opening were held. The program was as follows: invocation by the Rev. Franklin W. Fisk, D.D., LL.D., President of Chicago Theological Seminary; address of presentation by Mr. Orrington Lunt; address of acceptance by President Henry Wade Rogers, LL.D.; dedication ode, by Mrs. Emily Huntington Miller; address by Charles Kendall Adams, LL.D., President of the University of Wisconsin. In the evening, in the First Methodist Episcopal Church, a public address on "The Development of the Library" was delivered by the late Justin Winsor, LL.D., Librarian of Harvard University.

Various gifts of books and money have already been noted. It remains to mention the Orrington Lunt endowment property,

In 1865 Mr. Lunt conveyed to the University 157 acres of land in North Evanston, thereby cancelling certain subscriptions previously made, and designating the generous remainder as a permanent endowment. Three years later this was set apart by the Board of Trustees as the foundation for a library, and named the Orrington Lunt Library fund. At an early date, a portion of the land was sold, expensive improvements have since been made on the property; its present valuation is $90,000. When the property becomes productive, it is expected to yield an increasing income for the purchase of books.

The details of the administration of the library are too technical for presentation here. The present system is the result of gradual growth and development along the lines shown to be important by the great library movement of the last twenty-five years. During the earlier years, some one of the professors was appointed librarian; among those who acted in this capacity were W. D. Godman, David H. Wheeler, Louis Kistler and Charles W. Pearson. In 1875-76 the Rev. W. H. Daniels served as librarian. For the following ten years the name of Horace G. Lunt appeared in the catalogue as Librarian. During the last two of these years, George E. Wire was Assistant Librarian. No one now bears the title of Librarian, but Miss Lodilla Ambrose, Ph. M., has been Assistant Librarian since January 1, 1888. Aside from student assistants, the present staff are: Miss Olinia M. Mattison, Ph. B., First Assistant since September, 1898; Miss Frances C. Pierce, Ph. B., Assistant in the reading room since September, 1901, and Miss Adaline M. Baker, B. L. S., cataloguer since September, 1902. A committee on the library, from their own number, reports annually to the Board of Trustees on the state of the library. The Library Committee of the faculty co-operates with the As-

sistant Librarian in the administration of the library. Of this important committee, the late Dr. Daniel Bonbright was, for many years, the Chairman, and the library owes much to his careful oversight.

The library of the Garrett Biblical Institute, numbering 16,260 volumes and 2,200 pamphlets, is also on the campus, and is open to all students.

The Dearborn Observatory has an astronomical library of about 1,000 volumes and 1,000 pamphlets.

The professional schools, located in Chicago, have special libraries as follows:

	Volumes	Pamphlets
Medical School	3,252	5,200*
Law School	6,789	No report
School of Pharmacy	810	No report
Dental School	2,452	2,000*

*Estimated.

The several collections of books belonging to the University make a total of 65,961 volumes and 43,200 pamphlets.

The Library of the Law School has made large gains in the current year, 1903. It has completed its sets of the Reports and compiled statutes of all of the States, and has added about 500 volumes of text-books and treatises. Two large gifts have been received but are not yet enumerated. The Hon. Elbert H. Gary, class of 1867 in the Law School, has presented a collection of the judicial decisions and leading law journals of eight European countries, namely: Germany, France, Austria, Switzerland, Holland, Belgium, Spain, Italy. This gift contains about 2,500 volumes. The late Charles C. Bonney gave to the University Library some 400 volumes from his own law library.

Thus has the library progressed from small beginnings to days of greater things. With a generous endowment property increasing in value, and with the fostering management of the great University, of which it is so vital a part, the rapid growth of the library is a thing assured.

CHAPTER XXVI.

EVANSTON NEWSPAPERS
(By WILLIAM C. LEVERE)

*The Newspaper as a Necessity—Introduc-
tion and Growth of Local Journals—The
"Suburban Idea," The "Evanston Index"
and Other Early Papers—Story of the
"Evanston Press"—Advent of the Daily—
The Chicago Printer's Strike of 1898—
Temperance Organ—College Journals—
A "Frat." and "Barb." Advertising Con-
test—Quarterly and Monthly Publica-
tions—High Standard of Evanston
Journalism.*

In an intellectual community the newspaper is a necessity rather than a luxury.
It is an index to the character of Evanston
that, despite its proximity to a great city,
it has been the home of several strong and
able periodicals, the beginnings of one of
these dating several decades back. In recent years, when the competition with metropolitan papers has become keener than
ever, with a large staff of local reporters
representing the great dailies of our neighboring city, the local papers have not only
survived, but have increased in usefulness
and prospered in material things.

It is the purpose of this chapter to deal
especially with the publications which have
made a marked impress on the civic, social,
educational and business life of Evanston.
To give a history of every publication
which has appeared in the city would require a volume rather than a chapter, for

there is scarcely one of the very numerous
literary organizations, social clubs, and religious societies, which has not, from time
to time, fathered a small magazine or journal, the existence of which was ephemeral
and yet which served its purpose for the
brief period it lived. Due attention will be
given to the more important of these in
this article. The newspaper which will forever possess the honor of being the pioneer
of Evanston journalistic enterprise was
"The Suburban Idea." It first appeared in
1864 and continued one year. Its editor
and publisher was Rev. Nathan Sheppard,
who, after his removal from Evanston some
years later, became famous as the author
of a number of well-known books, the
most widely circulated of which was, "How
To Speak in Public." Mr. Sheppard was a
man of superior literary attainments, and
the tone of "The Suburban Idea" was always high. It was published weekly, had
four pages and four columns. During its
short life it served a useful purpose to the
little village, and cultivated the desire for
a local newspaper of high grade which was
to be so amply met by its successor.

In any history of Evanston, the second
of June, 1872, ought to figure as one of the
most important dates, for it was on this
day the first number of "The Evanston Index" appeared. Seldom has a paper become part and parcel of a community, of

its homes, its official life, its every activity, as this paper has been in the thirty-two years it has been published. The credit for the founding of "The Index" belongs to Mr. Alfred L. Sewell. Mr. Sewell, together with Mr. John E. Miller, had been publishing "The Little Corporal," a paper for youth, which attained national circulation. Mrs. Emily Huntington Miller was the editor of "The Little Corporal." Mr. Sewell saw the possibilities of a village newspaper from a business standpoint, and that the commercial reasons which were his inspiration for the venture were satisfied, an inspection of the advertising columns of the little sheet will show. That it was a little sheet, the interesting files on exhibition at "The Index" are proof, for by actual measurement each of the four pages was but 15 by 20½ inches. When the first number of "The Index" appeared the Village of Evanston did not contain a printing establishment large enough to handle such a publication, despite its tiny dimensions. Each week Mr. Sewell would take the "copy" to Chicago, and there the paper was printed at first. Later in the year, after Mr. Sewell had disposed of his Chicago establishment, the paper was printed by the Chicago Newspaper Union. When "The Index" was a year old, Mr. Sewell opened a printing office in Evanston, and from that time "The Index" has known no home either for editorial room or publishing office, save that in the city it has served. In November, 1875, Mr. John A. Childs, who had been connected with the paper from the first, and Mr. David Cavan bought all of Mr. Sewell's interest in the paper and two years and two months later, in January, Mr. Childs became the sole proprietor by purchasing the interest held by Mr. Cavan.

It was just before the sale of "The Index" to Cavan & Childs that "The Evanston Herald" appeared; but in the spring of 1876 it was amalgamated with "The Index." For some time the latter paper was published in a building which stood on Davis Street, one door west of where the present Century building stands. A fire broke out one night and threatened to destroy the plant. When the good citizens realized that danger threatened their family paper, they rushed to the rescue, and dumping the type into buckets, they triumphantly carried it to safety. The humor of this incident will best be appreciated by those who are familiar with the printing business. The entire building at 526 Davis Street is now given up to the "Index" plant. The three floors are filled with the latest and finest make of presses, while several linotypes are kept busy on twenty-four hour runs, all the year round. It is not too much to say of "The Index," as it now appears, that it is the handsomest weekly newspaper in the United States. Since 1903 Mr. Albert H. Bowman has been associated with Mr. Childs in its publication, and is now Secretary and Treasurer of the corporation of which Mr. Childs is President.

The story of "The Evanston Press," its conception, evolution and present day popularity, is of exceeding interest. The modern novelists who are finding the background for their stories in business life, could write many interesting pages in recounting the incidents which surround the growth, struggles, and triumphs of "The Press" during its upward progress to its present career. The first number of "The Evanston Press" appeared January 5, 1889. Enterprising at the start, it was fortunate enough to secure the services of Miss Frances E. Willard, who contributed, weekly for a year, a chapter under the caption, "An Old Timer's Story of Evanston." This series of reminiscences attracted wide attention and, before the third issue of the paper appeared, it had over one thousand paid subscribers. The founders of "The Press" were two young men, both fresh from college, Mr. Robert O. Vandercook and Mr. Edwin L. Shuman. The latter withdrew after one year, but Mr. Vandercook has continued to manage and publish the paper, with the exception of one year, since its first appearance. In telling of the beginnings of "The Evanston Press" Mr. Vandercook goes back twenty-five years and gives a glimpse of an Evanston boyhood of rare interest, for it brings a picture to many of experiences along the same line. Mr. Vandercook, in telling of the little seed that was planted, says: "It came about like this. Big brother traded a boyish knick-knack for a little toy printing press. The younger brother was very envious of the toy and longed to possess it. Big brother said he would sell it for $1.50. The small boy said he would take it, but he didn't have any money, but would pay for it in a week. The $1.50 was paid from the earnings of the printing press within the time named. As fast as other money was earned it was added to the outfit. The little toy was soon discarded for a more practical machine. That in its turn was discarded for others, until at the time of leaving high school, about $500 had been invested in a printing plant. All was earned except one item of $40, which was a present toward a new press."

From this first start, so vividly depicted, came "The High School Budget," and though it lived but a year, Mr. Vandercook considers the experience gained but one more step toward the ultimate goal, "The Evanston Press." The corporation which first published "The Press" was known as The University Press Company. Mr. Vandercook tells the story of this publishing company in the following words, "It was at the end of the sophomore year when good old Dr. Cummings, the President of the University, called one of the founders of what was then known as The University Press, and gave him the kindliest words of fatherly advice. The good old Doctor said, 'I hear you have just formed a University Press Company and have spent considerable money for type and equipment. I want to warn you to go slow. You know nothing, or practically nothing, of the printing trade. What little experience you have had may have been all right along lines you were pursuing, but I am fearful that branching out will only result in failure to yourself and disappointment to your friends!' Some people called it obstinacy, some perseverance, that caused disregard of Dr. Cummings' advice, but in later years it seems to us it was as much obstinacy as perseverance. Much additional equipment was added to the little printing plant and the University Press Company, capital stock $1,000, was fully organized and incorporated under the laws of the State of Illinois, H. H. C. Miller, attorney. The University Trustees, in order to assist the new corporation, gave it office room, janitor's service, light and fuel free. The plant was set up in the basement of the gymnasium building. Here four or five students earned their way while in college by setting type on "The Northwestern," the college paper and the college catalogue, and a number of others also earned a large share of their college expenses. This was the 'quid pro quo' why the university furnished what it did."

It was not until "The Evanston Press" had been published two years that the name of the corporation was changed to the Evanston Press Company. For six years, "The Press" was published in the Simpson Market Building on the south-east corner of Fountain Square. The next five years it was located in the Park building, between the Davis Street depots. Since 1900 "The

Press" has occupied the three story brick building at 609 Davis Street, and there it has had the most successful period of its life. Mr. Robert O. Vandercook continues to retain the financial and editorial control, and the outlook is, that this publication will continue for years to come to give valuable service to the cause of honorable journalism and integrity in civic affairs.

An interesting incident in the history of "The Index" and "The Press" is that at one time they became dailies and were sold on the streets of Chicago as such. It was during the Spanish-American War. There was a strike in the mechanical department of the Chicago dailies, and all of them had suspended publication. The great sea fight at Santiago was fought and the people of Chicago were mad for news. For several days the cry of "Index!" "Press!" sounded on the city streets, instead of the familiar names the people were wont to hear. "The Press" became so enterprising that it published three editions a day. It secured a special correspondent at Washington and still preserves in its office the telegram it received announcing the destruction of Cervera's fleet.

Evanston for a brief period had a regular daily paper. It was called "The Evanston Daily News," and was published by Milton A. Smith, who came to Evanston from Anniston, Ala., to establish the paper. At Anniston Mr. Smith had been the successful publisher of "The Hot Blast," but the people of Evanston did not regard his scheme with favor and the life of the daily was short, the first number appearing in November, 1897, and the last in February, 1898. The paper had eight pages, half of which were devoted to news from throughout the country. As this was plate matter and was considerably later than the date when the same matter appeared in the Chi-

cago dailies, it was not an overwhelmingly popular feature.

Old-timers in Evanston remember two publications which flourished many years ago. Just after the Chicago fire of 1871, Mr. L. C. Pitner issued "The Real Estate News." It had no regular time of publication, but appeared at intervals for two years. It had four pages and these were filled with real estate advertisements and local news items. The other of the two was "The Lake Breeze." It was published monthly during 1875 by Harry W. Taylor. Miss Frances E. Willard wrote a serial story entitled "Miriam," which appeared in "The Lake Breeze."

William Duffell was editor and publisher of "The Evanston Citizen," a weekly newspaper, the first number of which was issued November 3, 1882. It was a strong advocate of the prohibition cause and it was a popular paper during its life. The last number appeared the last week in December, 1891.

Since December, 1903, Evanston has been the publication headquarters of "The Union Signal," the national organ of the Woman's Christian Temperance Union. This weekly publication with its large circulation, has brought new fame to Evanston as the home of important periodicals. Together with "The Union Signal" is fostered "The Crusader Monthly," a child's paper, published by the temperance workers.

Northwestern University has been the home of many publications, the best known of which has been and is "The Northwestern," which is now published tri-weekly. "The Northwestern" is the successor of two college papers, "The Tripod" and "The Vidette," which united in January, 1881, and adopted the now familiar name. "The Tripod" was a monthly and first appeared January, 1871. It was published by the literary societies of the university. It was a twelve-page, three-column magazine. "The Vidette" was a semi-monthly and its publishers were the entire student body. When "The Northwestern" first appeared it was published semi-monthly.

In 1890 a college war broke out between the fraternity and non-fraternity students of the university. "The Northwestern" was controlled by the fraternity students, and their rivals, wishing an organ of their own, established "The Northwestern World." The first number appeared October 17, 1890, and it was published weekly during the college year until June, 1892. Its demise was caused by its last elected editor becoming a fraternity member. An amusing phase of the struggle for advertising patronage between the two journals has been told in the college novel, " 'Twixt Greek and Barb," which is devoted to the story of college life at Northwestern. The contest was such a unique feature of journalistic adventure that we quote the story as it appears in the book. The genesis of the contest is first told as follows:

"The big Sophomore grinned blandly at his friends as he said, 'If you howling maniacs will be cool, calm and collected for a brief space of time, I'll tell you something interesting. Harburton has told you that I have been getting 'ads' for the new paper. Tedlon, the dry-goods man, does as much advertising as any merchant on Davis Street. I called on him today, and he declared that he would be able to advertise in only one of the two papers. I made a tremendous stagger to get his business, but the old man was foxy, and declared that he wanted to find out which paper would do him the most good. In the next issue of both papers, he will advertise a special sale for Saturday. In "The Northwestern" he will advertise underwear, and in "The New World," kid gloves. The advertisement

bringing in the greatest returns will win for its paper his advertising for the year. The sale will begin at eight o'clock in the morning, and will close at five in the afternoon. Now, fellows, here is a chance to let your patriotism wax warm. The fraternities know of the offer, and they intend to land that advertising contract for their sheet. Every mother's son and daughter of the Greeks will stock up with enough underwear to last them the rest of their lives. This will be the first clash, and we must draw first blood. Everyone of us ought to buy enough gloves to cover the fingers of an octopus. Each fellow must make himself a committee of one, and get all his friends to buy their season's supply of gloves next Saturday, and above all buy them at Tedlon's. These fraternity people must learn that we mean business. 'It's war to the knife, the knife to the hilt and the hilt to the heart.'

"Keg's speech aroused the enthusiasm of the crowd. The contest arranged by the shrewd merchant furnished the rival factions a tangible basis upon which to begin the struggle for supremacy. When the meeting adjourned, the crowd poured down the stairway with many suggestions of method and prophecies of victory."

The result of the fight between the factions in this queer journalistic war is told in another chapter as follows:

"The sole topic at the breakfast table was the contest to take place that day between the frats and the barbs for Tedlon's advertising. Excitement ran high in university circles, and both sides were as full of prophecies as politicians at election time. After finishing breakfast, Steve and Leslie started for Tedlon's, where the sale was to commence at eight o'clock. It was a few minutes before the hour when they arrived there, and they found a long line of students waiting for the doors to open. At eight o'clock, Mr. Tedlon appeared and throwing back the doors, welcomed them in with a gesture. The struggle had begun. The first man to buy a pair of gloves was the veteran captain of the Life Saving Crew, who said that, being a barb himself, he would have to stand by the cause. The fraternity men and women came in force, and, as each left with great packages of goods, the eyes of the proprietor glistened. At noon the contest seemed about even. There had been more barbs who had made purchases than Greeks, but the latter had purchased greater amounts, and Harney Dale, who was acting as one of the managers for the frats, declared that they were sure to win. Later in the afternoon as he stood on the edge of the walk before the store, he cried, 'Great Scotland, we are undone.' The sight that brought forth this exclamation was a long line of 'bibs,' who were approaching. It was known that the sympathies of the Heck Hallites had been enlisted by the Barbarians, but the fraternity men had hoped that the 'theologs' would simply lend their moral influence to the foe. Now that they saw them approaching, led by Jack Williams, who had rounded them up with the skill of a veteran politician, they were seized for the first time with the fear of defeat. There were more than a hundred 'bibs' in line, and, from the looks on their faces, it was evident they meant business.

"Harney stepped in front of Jack and demanded, 'Say, old man, are you going to ring in the whole Methodist conference on us?'

" 'Just watch my smoke,' said Jack, winking, as he steered the first of the crowd into the store.

" 'Oh, Lord! Rennick,' whispered Harney to his friend, 'what shall we do?'

" 'Bless me, if I know,' was Tom's reply, 'I'm afraid they've got us on the hip.'

" 'Can't we turn in a fire alarm,' asked Harney, 'and tell them that Heck Hall is burning to the ground?'

" 'Why not set it afire?' suggested Tom, 'What a sweet revenge that would be.'

" 'Stop fooling, and let's get our thinking caps on, or we are done for.'

" 'Well, then,' said Rennick, 'they've brought down Heck Hall; we might go up and bring down the fair flowers of Willard Hall.'

" 'Why, half of them have been here already,' said Harney, 'but I'll go up and see Laura Merrill, and have her try to persuade the rest of the girls to come to our rescue, while you go and hunt the fellows and tell them that they must come and buy again.'

" 'Buy again! Why half the fellows who have been playing this game, have gone broke now, but it's all for the cause, and I'll see what I can get them to do.'

"Harney and Tom gathered all the fraternity folk that they could find, and sent them to bring the needed aid. A strong rally was made, and the hopes of the Greeks began to rise once more. Five o'clock came at last.

" 'We've won,' cried Jack Williams.

" 'We've won,' cried Harney Hale.

" 'You both deserve to win,' cried Mr. Tedlon, rubbing his hands together with joy. It had been the greatest day for sales in the history of the store. No matter who else had won, Mr. Tedlon, was certainly a winner by a large majority.

"It was a brief matter for the sales of the day to be counted up, and the beaming face of Mr. Tedlon again appeared at the door. The street was blocked with students—Greeks, barbs, 'bibs,' 'preps' and 'co-eds,' all anxious to hear the announcement.

"Mr. Tedlon waved his hand to silence the cheers. 'Dear friends,' he said, 'I will not keep you in suspense. The contest has been won by the friends of the Northwestern World.' If the Barbarians, when they sacked Athens, had uttered such a cry as then went up to the heavens, it is no wonder the inhabitants were stricken with terror. The latter-day Greeks, at least, fled as precipitously, and left the field to the victorious enemy."

Numbered with other college publications are "The Northwestern University Record," a quarterly edited by a joint committee from the faculties; "The Euphronian," published by the Euphronian Literary Society; "The Academian," the organ of the students of Northwestern Academy, and "The Northwestern Magazine," a literary magazine which appeared for one college year, that of 1903-04.

Among the papers of general circulation which are now published in Evanston, are: "Correct English," a magazine dealing with the intricacies of the language, appearing monthly and published and edited by Mrs. Josephine Turck Baker; "The National

Stenographer," a monthly published and edited by C. H. Rush. Our colored citizens are represented by the "North Shore Colored American," the editor of which is Francis Stewart and the publisher W. H. Twiggs. This is not the first periodical which the colored citizens have had. During the year 1889, "The Afro-American Budget," a monthly magazine, attracted favorable attention.

"The Day," a weekly, appeared during 1904. It survived a short time. Its editors and publishers were Wesley Stanger and Charles Van Patten. "The Noon," a magazine of selected poetry, made its initial appearance in October, 1900, and continued for two years. William S. Lord was editor and publisher.

Looking back over this list of publications, representing the aspirations, interests and progress of the community, Evanston has reason to take pride to herself. The standard has always been high; the ideal, the best.

CHAPTER XXVII.

MEDICAL HISTORY
(REGULAR)
(By HENRY BIXBY HEMENWAY, M. D.)

Primitive Health Conditions — Freedom from Malarial Diseases — Some Old-Time Physicians—Sketch of Dr. John Evans—Drs. Ludlam, Weller and Blaney —Dr. N. S. Davis the Nestor of Medical Education — An Early Drug Store — Sketches of Later Day Physicians—Drs. Webster, Bannister, Burchmore, Brayton, Bond, Phillips, Haven, Hemenway, Kaufman, and others — Evanston Physicians' Club.

When Marc Anthony said:

"The evil that men do lives after them;
The good is oft interred with their bones."

he clearly was not speaking of physicians. If any of them ever made mistakes, those errors have been covered with the daisies of charity and hidden by the snow of oblivion, while their good deeds continue to grow and multiply as the years pass by.

Evanston is itself a memorial to the medical profession. It is called in honor of a distinguished member of a former faculty of Rush Medical college. Its principal business street was named after the Nestor of the American Medical Association. The old village depended upon the Northwestern University for its existence. The first subscription for starting the University bore obligations to the amount of $20,600, and of this amount $5,500 was subscribed

by Drs. John Evans, N. S. Davis and William Justice. Of the amount actually paid in on this subscription physicians gave over one-third. A regular practitioner of medicine has been the chief executive of the village; another was Postmaster, and doctors have borne their share of the work of education, and other public service.

Early Health Conditions.—Before 1855 there was no doctor residing in Ridgeville, as the place was then called. Then, as now, this was a particularly healthy section. Whereas, Chicago, and the ground south of the river, was only eight feet above the lake, here it was three times as high, and drainage was correspondingly better. B. F. Hill said to the writer that he never knew of a case of fever and ague occurring in those early days, along this north shore and east of the North Branch. The early settlers were familiar with the use of boneset for malarial fevers, rue for worms, lobelia for fevers, butterfly weed for pleurisy, tansy, camomile, saffron and other herbs. They knew how to use poultices and the wet pack, as well as other home remedies. Many of the better educated had such books as "Beach's American Practice." Seldom was a physician sent for to attend any one here. Alonzo Burroughs, who lived then in the campus at what is now the edge of the lake opposite Memorial hall, never had the assistance of a physician in his house until after the birth of his seventh child. I find that, for a time, a young doctor by the name of Smith lived with the Dennis family near the present Gage place on the shore in Wilmette. Dr. John Kennicott, who lived at Northfield, covered th' territory in his "drive." Dr. Hoffman in Niles practiced among our German citizens.

Dr. John Evans, from whom the place has its name, was born at Waynesville, O., March 9, 1814, of Quaker ancestry. His parents at one time lived in South Carolina, but they were obliged to emigrate on account of abolition . . . . . . In ohio his father continued . . . . anufacture of tools for which the family had been somewhat noted for three generations. John was graduated from Clermont Academy and, in 1836, having received his medical degree, he began the practice of medicine along the Illinois River. Later he settled in Attica, Ind. While there he began the agitation which resulted in the establishment of the first State Insane Asylum at Indianapolis, of which he was appointed the first Superintendent. In 1845 he moved to Chicago and took the chair of midwifery in Rush Medical College, which he held for ten years. He also edited the "Northwestern Medical Journal." He inherited a taste for business and gradually devoted more attention to secular affairs. He aided largely in building the Chicago and Fort Wayne Railroad. He secured for them their terminal facilities in Chicago. As was before stated, he took an active part in starting the Northwestern University, and he was the President of its Board of Trustees for forty-two years.

In 1855 he built and moved into his Evanston home. It was a Gothic cottage which has since been moved to 1317 Chicago Avenue. It still retains many of its older decorations, but it has lost some of the original Gothic beauty by the substitution of clapboards for battens. Originally it stood facing south on Clark Street in the middle of the block from Hinman to Judson Avenue. It was surrounded with a white picket fence, the east half of the block being a rolling lawn, while the Hinman Avenue side was given up to flowers and shrubs, among which gravel walks wound in geometric designs. Behind the house was the Gothic barn (now the residence of Sandy Trent, No. 1815 Benson Avenue), the hot-beds and vegetable garden, and further back the modest cottage of the doctor's man, Mike Cavenaugh. I have described this, my old playground, as a type of the better homes of the village.

In 1862 Dr. Evans became Governor of Colorado, and was never here much of the time afterward, though the family home was nominally here until 1867. From '63 to '65 the house was occupied by Luther L. Greenleaf. While in Evanston the Doctor practiced little, chiefly in consultation. Of his deeds in politics and railroad building we have nothing here to say further than that, to him more than to any other one man, does Colorado owe her present prosperity. As a student and practitioner of medicine he was literally in the front rank. In opposition to the prevailing opinion of the profession of that time, he affirmed, in the 'forties, the contagiousness of cholera, and yet, as late as 1862, his wife rode in a carriage with the casket containing a victim of scarlet fever, and on returning home took her little Margaret upon her knee. The result was another little grave in Rose Hill.

While teaching in Chicago he spent much time perfecting an extractor which he had invented. He was quite proud of his results and showed the instrument to his class. One of the students obtained a patent on it. Dr. Evans, instead of attempt- ing to have the patent set aside, so thor- oughly condemned the patenting of any professional article, and so perfectly showed forth every possible objection to the use of that particular instrument that, today, there are very few living who ever have heard of it. Dr. Evans died in Den- ver, Colo., July 3, 1897.

Dr. James W. Ludlam.—After Dr. Evans, Orrington Lunt and others had completed the purchase of the Evanston farm for the University, they stopped to water their horses at the tavern kept by Major Mulford. This tavern was a por- tion of the building since known as the James S. Kirk home, and is now used by the Sisters of St. Francis as a hospital. Vis- iting the Major at the time were Dr. and Mrs. Jacob Watson Ludlam. They had come West to see their sons Reuben and James, who had located in Chicago. After talking with the university folks, Dr. Lud- lam became impressed with the future of the town and purchased of the Major ten acres of land on the west side of Ridge Avenue. He built there his first Evanston house just south of Oakton Avenue. The locust trees that he planted show the loca- tion of the house which was burned some twenty years ago. When Dr. Ludlam found that the new town would not be near the old settlement, he first purchased the southeast corner of Hinman Avenue and Clark Street, opposite Dr. Evans, which he later exchanged for the present site of the Evanston Club. Here he erected the house since moved to 1206 Hinman Avenue, and now occupied by his children, Jacob Wat- son, Jr., and Miss "Mollie."

Dr. Ludlam was born at Camden, N. J., November 28, 1807. He graduated from the University of Pennsylvania, and prac- ticed at Deerfield, N. J., until he came to Evanston, March 31, 1855. He died here

July 11, 1859, and his body was the first interred in Rose Hill. With the exception of Dr. Blaney, Dr. Ludlam was probably the most thoroughly educated man in the profession among the early settlers. In those days it was not unusual for a man to begin practicing after from three to six months' study, but Dr. Ludlam took three years, and as long as he lived in the East it was his custom to frequently spend a month at one of the schools of medicine. Tall in stature and polished in manner, he was an ideal physician.

The Ludlam family were not an unim- portant part of the social life of the burgh. Of Reuben, the who later be- came President of the State Board of Health, the old Doctor said to one of the then old settlers: "I have a boy practicing in Chicago; I have this satisfaction about him, that he will never kill any one with his medicines." Reuben remained in Chi- cago, but James, or Major, as he has since been known, went with the Evanston boys —General Beveridge, Major Russell, Lieu- tenant Harry Pearsons and others—into the Eighth Illinois Cavalry. And 'Miss Mol- ly!' I remember hearing one of the young ladies remark one day after a wedding: "Now, Molly Ludham has been a brides- maid seven times, and that is a sign that she never will be married." She never has. For many years she taught in the old Ben- son Avenue School, and she did her work well.

Evanston's Second Physician.—The sec- ond physician to locate here was Fayette Montrose Weller, who came in the summer of 1855, and settled on Ridge Avenue op- posite the present site of the Academy of the Visitation. His ancestors were early settlers of New England from Bavaria, Holland, Scotland and England. He was born at Sardinia, N. Y., April 13, 1825. He first studied for the ministry, but changed his mind and graduated from the medical department of the University of Michigan in 1854. His first wife, Marie Antoinette Hypolite, died in Evanston in 1858. Three years later he married Philena M., the eldest daughter of George M. Huntoon, one of the earliest settlers of Ridgeville. Dr. Weller was for three or four years the village Postmaster, using the Max Hahn building, which stood at 619 Davis Street. Here he kept the second drug store opened in the village, though it could not have been as attractive as the colored lights and soda fountains are at present, for it did not impress itself upon the memories of the girls of the day. When Ed. Clifford became Postmaster, Dr. Weller sold to him the drugs which he moved into the little store, No. 1610 Chicago Avenue. Dr. Weller was a thick-set, dark-complexioned man, of medium height and a good practitioner. In 1865 Dr. Weller sold his practice to Dr. Ira B. Geier, but he returned to Evanston in the 'seventies for a short time. In 1878 he moved to Chicago, where he died at the age of 70.

Dr. Blaney.—James V. Z. Blaney was born at Newcastle, Delaware, May 1, 1820, into a family known for its refinement and education, with ample means to provide a thorough education. The son was graduated from Princeton College when eighteen and, as soon as he reached his majority, he received the degree of Doctor of Medicine from Jefferson Medical College. In 1842-43 he was on duty at Jefferson Barracks, St. Louis. A year later he located in Chicago, and became Professor of Chemistry at Rush. He also edited the "Northwestern Medical Journal." In 1857 he added to his other work the chair of Chemistry in the University and moved to Evanston. He built and occupied the house which recently gave place to Mayor Patten's new one on Ridge Avenue. As with Dr. Evans, Dr.

Blaney's Evanston practice was chiefly consulting. At the outbreak of the war Dr. Blaney was ordered East as Medical Inspector, and never returned to Evanston to reside. Later he was returned to Chicago as Medical Purveyor, and at the close of the war he was mustered out as a Lieutenant Colonel. He died in Chicago, December 11, 1874.

After the death of Dr. Ludlam, Dr. J. H. Hobbs, a recent graduate from Rush, made a short sojourn in our midst. About the same time a dapper little graduate from the University of Pennsylvania, in the class of '54, made his appearance. He wore eyeglasses—the only ones in town, perhaps. He was a perfect gentleman, and the admiration of all the young ladies. He started the first baseball club in the village. But William Varian was also a man of skill. He was the nephew of one of America's best surgeons—Washington Atlee—and at the beginning of the war he became a Brigade Surgeon. On one occasion, on reaching a new post, he was at once arrested as a spy, being mistaken for a Confederate General whom he strongly resembled. At the close of the war he settled in Titusville, Pennsylvania, where he is now an honored member of the profession.

I am told that in '61 there was a woman physician living in the house on the campus formerly occupied by Alonzo Burroughs, but she was probably not a graduate. At the same time there was a Dr. Barker living opposite the old Methodist church, corner of Orrington and Church Streets. He served in the army and after the war he settled in Wisconsin.

Ira B. Geier, a brother of Mrs. Mary F. Haskins, came in '65. He was a bachelor, and at the last lived in a cottage which he built on the northeast corner of Benson Avenue and Davis Street. He was a native of Central New York. He was a very well informed physician, but he never had a large practice. He lacked the decision, energy and backbone which are necessary for the work. A slight indisposition always caused him to fear his coming dissolution. On the other hand, he was an enthusiastic Mason, and was the real founder of Evans Lodge, for the first two years acting, and the next real, Worshipful Master of the lodge. He moved to Florida in 1872.

Dr. Leonidas P. Hamline, son of Bishop Hamline of the Methodist Church, was born at Zanesville, O., August 13, 1828. He graduated at Castleton Medical College, Vt. He moved to Evanston with his family in 1865, and built the residence now occupied by his daughter, Mrs. T. S. Creighton, at 1722 Judson Avenue. There he died January 22, 1897. During his early days in Evanston Dr. Hamline did most of the surgery performed here and saw an occasional sick patient, but he had practically retired from practice when he came here.

Later Physicians.—Dr. Washington S. Scott came to Evanston March 1, 1865. Born near Wellsburg, Brooke County, Vt., he went to college at Meadville, Pa. He received his medical education in Philadelphia, Cincinnati and New Orleans. Before coming to Evanston he practiced for some time in Iowa. He was not in active practice long here, but sold out to Dr. Poole in 1867. He threw all his energy into business. He started a drug store at 613 Davis street, almost on the same spot on which a man by the name of Donovan started the first store several years earlier; but, whereas Donovan soon went out of business, Dr. Scott's is still in existence, two doors west, now under the ownership of Hill & Leffingwell. Dr. Scott was a Democrat, but not offensively so. Naturally a Southern sympathizer, few ever heard him say it. He put forth his best thought in the interest of Evanston. He built the first brick business block in town, 611 and 613 Davis Street, and the first public hall. He built the first building intended for a postoffice, and the first Masonic temple. He died at the age of 70, in Springfield, Ill., June 25, 1901.

Dr. Isaac Poole was born in Halifax, Plymouth County, Mass., July 26, 1837. He was graduated in medicine from the Berkshire Medical College, Pittsfield Mass., in November, 1862. For two years he was interne at the Kings County, N. Y., Hospital. For two years he served as a Surgeon in the United States Navy. He came to Evanston in February, 1867, and has practiced here ever since. He is now the oldest physician in Evanston, and the oldest in the practice of medicine. He is of revolutionary and of Puritan descent. His grandfather, John Poole, was a minute man during the entire War of Independence. He is also descended from Dr. Samuel Fuller, the physician of the Mayflower.

James Stewart Jewell was born at Galena, Ill., September 8, 1837. He was graduated from the Chicago Medical College in 1860. He was Professor of Anatomy in the same institution from 1864 to 1869, and of Nervous Diseases during the later years of his life. In 1870 he received the honorary degree of A. M. from Northwestern University. He died in Chicago, April 18, 1887.

Dr. Jewell was naturally a brilliant man. He was a most entertaining lecturer and conversationalist. He was a linguist of more than ordinary ability. Soon after he came to Evanston, about 1868, he started a Bible class in the Methodist Sunday-school, then under the superintendence of Edward Eggleston. The class grew rapidly, and it was soon postponed until after the regular session of the school for two reasons: first, that they might have more room; and second, that members of other churches might attend. So popular was he that the old Methodist church, then the largest auditorium in the village, was filled every week. He illustrated his lectures with large charcoal sketches and maps of his own drawing. So interested did he become that he started to write a book on the Life and Travels of St. Paul, and with that in view, he took a party of Evanston young men to Palestine in 1870. In his party was Frederick Huse, later a doctor of medicine. The book was never finished. He became interested in psychology, and through that he began a closer study of the nervous system. This led to a study of the diseases of the nervous system, to which he limited his later practice. He started a "Journal of Nervous Diseases," and left a partially completed work upon this subject, but death overtook him in the midst of his labor. I have heard them tell how he first appeared in the medical school, a tall, awkward boy, wearing blue-jeans trousers. I have heard him narrate about his weary work in country practice before he came to Evanston, often sleeping as he rode upon his horse's back, awakening with a start as he unconsciously ducked his head to avoid an overhanging branch. He killed himself by overwork, and a disregard of the very rules which he so well taught us.

James Henry Etheridge, the son of a physician, was born in Johnsville, N. Y., March 20, 1845. After studying at Ann Arbor he graduated from Rush Medical College in 1868, and settled in Evanston. His sister was the wife of Lyman J. Gage, who then lived on Hinman Avenue. After practicing here for a year and a half, Dr. Etheridge married Harriet, the daughter of H. G. Powers, and, in 1870, went to Europe for further study. When he returned he settled in Chicago, where he died in 1891, having been a professor in his alma mater for thirty years.

It is not probable that any man has exerted a more powerful influence upon the medical profession of the United States than my old preceptor, Dr. Nathan Smith Davis. The Davis family lived opposite the First Methodist church from 1871 to 1881, and it had been the doctor's expectation to spend here the remainder of his life, but the untimely death of his son Frank changed his plans.

The Nestor of Medical Education.—N. S. Davis, the youngest of seven children, was born on a farm which his father had cleared at Greene, N. Y., Jan. 9, 1817. This son, after attending Cazenovia Seminary, began the study of medicine in 1831 with Dr. Daniel Clark, at Smithville Flats. According to custom the boy lived with his preceptor, taking care of his horses and doing other work. In 1837, before he was of age, he graduated with honor from the College of Physicians and Surgeons, at Fairfield, N. Y. His thesis was upon animal temperature. While in college he boarded himself much of the time. He settled first at Vienna, N. Y., and then at Binghamton, where, for a time, he had as an associate, Dr. A. B. Palmer, later the Dean of the Medical Department at Ann Arbor. In 1847 Dr. Davis became a professor in the College of Physicians and Surgeons in New York City. Two years later he came to Chicago as a Professor of Practice in Rush Medical College. Dr. Davis early began to advocate a more systematic course in the study of medicine, and in 1859, he started the Chicago Medical College, now owned by the Northwestern University. This was the first medical school in this country to insist upon a graded course of three years' study, Harvard being the second, more than a decade later. Chiefly at his own expense he started a hospital in the old Lake House, which later became Mercy Hospital. In honor of Dr. Davis the American Medical

Association, several years ago, had a medal struck, thus recognizing him as its founder. It was his pen that drew up the code of ethics which still governs that body.

Dr. Davis was a clear thinker and forcible speaker. He was tireless in his original investigations. He did his share of editorial work, the last being upon the "Journal of the American Medical Association." Dr. Davis always took a most active part in sanitary matters. In Chicago and in Evanston, by popular lectures and constant agitation, he did much toward the establishment of public water supply and sewerage systems. There was a time in Chicago when he was spoken of as "Pope Davis," because of his influence over the Irish people. This influence was noted in the dark days of the Civil War, when recruits were badly wanted but were slow to come. Then Dr. Davis, standing on the court house steps, so eloquently pleaded with them that large numbers came forward to enlist.

Dr. Davis was one of the first physicians to decry the use of alcohol as medicine, and later, through his efforts, the Washingtonian Home was started in Chicago for the care of inebriates.

Dr. Davis was always an active member of the Methodist Church, and while he lived in Evanston he seldom was absent from the morning or evening service, and as regular as the hour for Sunday-school, you might see him walk down the middle aisle to his Bible class. For two or three years he was President of the Board of Village Trustees. On one occasion a Trustee sent in a bill for hotel and livery entertainment of some visitors to the village. Dr. Davis cast it aside with the remark that such matters were private and should not be paid from village funds. "I think we should pay the bill," said one of the Trustees, indicating thereby a dissent from the decision of the chair. "All right," said Dr. Davis, putting

his hand into his pocket, "I'll give five dollars, what will you give?" "One," was the feeble reply.

Dr. Davis was always the poor man's friend. On one occasion a lady brought her daughter to the doctor, insisting that she wanted him to give her special attention, and she was willing to pay whatever he asked. The Doctor's head was bent over as he listened to her. Then he replied: "My fee is one dollar. I give my best care to every patient, the poor as well as the rich. I cannot do more in your case."

The son of Bishop Whitehouse once came to consult Dr. Davis. He was dressed in the height of fashion. The office girl gave him a number and requested him to take a seat; but, looking with scorn upon the long line of working people ahead of him, he rapped at the private door. He explained to the Doctor that he wished to consult him. "Take a seat," was the reply. "Probably you do not know who I am," said the young man. "I am the son of Bishop Whitehouse." "Take two seats," responded Dr. Davis, as he turned to hear the troubles of "next."

The Doctor's advice to his students as to treatment was, "First determine what is wrong. Then find the cause and remove it. Lastly determine what in your judgment is the best remedy to be used in the case and use it." I have often heard him tell with a twinkle in his eye how he once sent to an eclectic physician for some simple remedy for one case and of his neighbor's boastful pride over the fact. Dr. Davis received the honorary degrees of A. M., and LL. D. from Northwestern University. He died June 16, 1904.

An Early Drug Store.—In the early 'seventies Dr. T. S. Blackburn, a native of Canada and graduate from Ann Arbor, opened a drug store in the brick building east of the Central Street station of the

Northwestern Road. The North Evanston practice was divided between Drs. Blackburn and Jenks, both of whom are now dead.

In the late 'seventies there appeared in the village a fine looking gentleman, of middle age, who promised to cut a wide swath in the local profession. Whence he came or where he studied I have not found. His name was Trimble. In a short time he had upon his list the names of several prominent families, but an unfortunate series of fatal accidents discouraged him and he sought the balmy air of Florida, followed by a threat of shooting if ever he were seen in town again.

Latter Day Physicians.—Dr. Edward H. Webster was born of old Puritan stock at Wells River, Vt., in 1851. He traces his ancestry in this country to the middle of the seventeenth century. In 1867 the family moved to Evanston, where the father was known for his generosity to the poor. Edward attended the university and was a member of the Sigma Chi fraternity. He graduated from the Chicago Medical College in 1877, and has been located in Evanston since '79. In his later student days, and for two years following, he was in charge of the infirmary of the Chicago & Northwestern Railway in Chicago, and ever since he has been the District Surgeon of that company.

Henry Martyn Bannister, son of Professor Henry Bannister, D. D., of the old Institute faculty, was born at Cazenovia, N. Y., July 25, 1844. The family came to Evanston in 1856. Here the son received his degree of A. M. From 1864 to 1873 he was connected with the Smithsonian Institute, at Washington. He was badly frozen, separated from his companions and nearly lost his life, while on the exploring expedition sent out by the Government before we purchased Alaska. He was graduated from the medical department of Columbia University in 1871. For some years he was a physician at the Kankakee Asylum, but during much of his professional career he has been engaged in medical journalism. He is now on the staff of the "Journal of the American Medical Association."

Gustav A. Fischer, born in 1846, came here about 1875. He was graduated from the University of Prague, Austria, in 1871. He now resides in Chicago. John J. Scheuber came here from Switzerland about the same time. He had quite a practice among the Germans. He treated cancer with plasters, and had a diphtheria cure which still has some reputation. He married a sister of J. H. Stephen, the genial manager of Muno's bakery. Dr. Scheuber died in Joliet, in 1900, at the age of 64.

John H. Burchmore was born November 12, 1840, in Salem, Mass., where his family had resided since before the Revolution. He was graduated from the medical school of Harvard University in 1875, and, after serving as interne in the Massachusetts General Hospital and resident physician in the Boston Lying-in Hospital, in 1877 he located in what was then North Evanston. He married a daughter of John W. Stewart, one of the most prominent residents there.

Dr. Sarah H. Brayton was born in England in 1849. She was graduated in medicine by the New York Free Medical College for Women, in the spring of 1875. In 1883 she settled in Evanston.

Thomas Sheldon Bond, the son of a Congregational minister, was born at Lee, Mass., December 14, 1842. He graduated from Amherst College with the degree of A. M., in 1863, and taught at Lake Forest. In 1867 he graduated from the Chicago Medical College and the next year received a like degree from the College of Physicians and Surgeons of New York. From 1869 to 1874 he was demonstrator of anatomy and from 1874 to 1879, Professor of Anatomy in Chicago Medical College. He then retired to private life and, in 1882 moved to Evanston, where he died December 4. 1895. Dr. Bond was as fine an anatomist as there was in Chicago, and a most excellent teacher.

William A. Phillips, son of William B. Phillips, was born in Chicago, January 18, 1861. His genealogy in this country reaches back to George Phillips, who came to Salem, Mass., in 1632. In 1870 the family moved to Evanston. Here the son received the degree of Ph. B. He studied in the Northwestern Medical School, and in 1887 received the degree of M. D. from Harvard. After spending a year at Vienna he settled in Evanston. For a time he was lecturer on comparative anatomy in the University. He is an enthusiastic student of anthropology, and his valuable collection is one of the attractions of the University Museum.

Otis Erastus Haven, the eldest son of Bishop E. O. Haven, once President of the University, was born in New York City, July 2, 1849. He was graduated as an A. B. from Ann Arbor, in 1870, and went to Iowa to teach. In 1873 he received his master's degree, and came to Evanston as Superintendent of the Public Schools. Then he studied medicine while teaching, and was graduated from Rush in 1882. He spent some months in New York Hospital and then opened an office here. He was at once elected a member of the Board of Education and served until his death, February 3, 1888. His professional career had been short, but he was universally beloved as a man and physician.

Henry Bixby Hemenway was born at Montpelier, Vt., December 20, 1856. He traces his family in Salem, Mass., back as far as 1636. He came to Evanston in September, 1857, where his father became professor in the Theological School. He received the degrees of A. B. and A. M. from the University, and was licensed to practice in 1880 by State examination. He was graduated from Chicago Medical College in 1881 and located at Kalamazoo, Mich. While there he was City Health Officer, Secretary of Board of United States Examining Surgeons, Division Surgeon of the Michigan Central and of the Grand Rapids & Indiana Railways, and held offices in the local and State Medical Societies. In the fall of 1890 he returned to Evanston. He taught one year in Rush College and gave a course of lectures at the College of Physicians and Surgeons in 1900, during the illness of Professor Carter. He is the Surgeon of the Chicago, Milwaukee & St. Paul and the Chicago & Milwaukee electric roads.

Gustav W. Kaufman was born in Hanover, Germany, in 1860. He was educated in the German Gymnasium and School of Pharmacy. In 1881 he came to America and engaged in the drug business in St. Louis. He was graduated from the St. Louis College of Pharmacy in 1886, and four years later received the doctor's degree from the St. Louis College of Physicians and Surgeons. He settled in Evanston in 1890.

Lack of space prevents more than the mere mention of Dr. Gray, a copy of Jewell, who conducted a small private asylum here in the 'eighties; of Bentz, who at one time lived in North Evanston and moved to Wheeling; of O. T. Maxson, who graduated from Rush in 1849, and came to South Evanston in '84, taking great interest in that village; he died in '95, as did also Hawley, after a short residence here; or Leonard, also of the south wards; of Lyford, who came in the 'eighties, and returned to Port Byron; of Stewart, who was killed by the cars in '93; of Josiah

Jones, who gave up the Health Commissionership to dig gold in the Klondike; of Drs. O. Mueller, Bernard Miller, Frazier and Kimmet, returned to Chicago; of W. A. Palmer, removed to Minnesota, and Ivaats, returned to England; of Harriet Wolfe, who became a Goodrich and retired from practice; of Wilder, who married Marie Huse, and died in Iowa; of Harding, who married Mary Clifford, an old resident, and in '91 returned to Evanston from Goshen; of Dakin, an Evanston boy, who graduated from Physicians and Surgeons, New York, in '90, and came back two years later; of Bjorkman, who died in 1903; of Harder, Stockley, Baird, Balderston, Mars, East, the McEwens, Clyde, who came here since 1890, and the various specialists who have resided here: such as Ridlon, the leading orthopedic surgeon of the West; Dodd, the eye surgeon; Ballenger and Walters, the laryngologists; Pusey and Andrews, all of whom now reside in Evanston.

William R. Parks, our present Commissioner of Health, was born in Milwaukee in 1869. He received the degrees of Ph. B. and Ph. M. from Northwestern University, and in 1893 graduated from Rush Medical College. After two years in the Presbyterian Hospital he returned to Evanston to practice.

In 1883 a Medical Society was organized by some of the more recent settlers in the profession in Evanston. It was known as the Physicians' Club. Its meetings were held at the Avenue House. Its Officers were Dr. Hemenway, President; Kaufman, Vice-President; and Palmer, Secretary and Treasurer. At the close of the year the organization was a thing of the past.

In 1902 one of the first branches organized of the Chicago Medical Society was established in Evanston. Its membership is not limited to Evanston, but it includes resident physicians of the North Shore to the County line. In the effort to unify the profession, this society opens its doors to all reputable practitioners.

CHAPTER XXVIII.

MEDICAL HISTORY
(HOMŒOPATHIC.)
(By DR. N. C. BRAGDON)

First Case of Homœopathic Treatment in Evanston — Successful Results — Early Homœopathic Physicians—Dr. Hawkes First Local Practitioner—He is Followed by Dr. C. D. Fairbanks—Sketch of Dr. Oscar H. Mann—His Prominence in Local Educational, Official and Social Relations—Founding of the Evanston Hospital—Doctors Marcy, Clapp and Fuller —Roll of the Later Physicians and Surgeons.

About 1854 a child living in the neighborhood of the Mulford tavern was taken sick one night, and the family feared that she could not live till morning. There was no doctor nearer than Chicago, and it was not likely that one could be obtained before the next day, too late to save the patient. It was ascertained that the wife of one of the early settlers then stopping at the tavern had a case of homœopathic remedies. The gentleman did not believe in that mode of treatment, but his wife did. As she was ill, the husband took the case of pills in one hand and a manual of practice in the other, and went to the patient's relief. He knew little, if any, of the signs of disease, but he sat by the bed and studied the book. He said, in telling of the incident, that while he was not very hopeful of doing good, he felt sure that he would do no

harm. In the morning the patient was sufficiently recovered so that it was not considered necessary to send for a physician. So far as known, this was the first record of homœopathic treatment in Evanston.

Many of the early residents were accustomed to this method before they came to Evanston. It was not uncommon to find a copy of Small's "Manual of Homœopathic Practice" on the book shelf, or some other book for family use, and the more common remedies were kept on hand, even by those who were accustomed to employ the old school doctors. The simplicity of the system, the ease with which it could be used, and the freedom from harmful results, recommended it.

Homœopathy in Evanston has always had the support of many of the best educated people in the village, and among the earlier residents were many strong believers in the new school. Doctors Adam Miller, J. Nicholas Cooke, Reuben Ludlam, and other Chicago practitioners, made frequent professional trips to the village.

First Resident Practitioner.—At that early time there were few homœopathic schools. Most of the practitioners were graduates of the old school who had become dissatisfied with the heroic treatment then in vogue, and so had taken refuge in this more simple system. Many of them however did not adhere strictly to the law of similars. In 1856 one of this style came and settled in the village. His name was Hawkes. So far as the writer has been able to find, he was not related to Prof. W. J. Hawkes who came later, though they have often been confounded with each other. This man was in some way related by marriage to Dr. Moses Gunn, one of the foremost surgeons of half a century ago in Chicago, and to Mr. Gould, who long occupied the position of clerk at Rush Medical College. He was also a distant connection of the Judson family, and for his use Rev. Philo Judson had erected the commodious house which was removed to give place to the Young Men's Christian Association building in 1898. Dr. Hawkes remained only a year.

From that time until the middle 'sixties there was no resident homœopathic physician. Dr. C. D. Fairbanks lived in Evanston about 1865. Little is known of him. All who knew him spoke well of him, both as a man and as a physician. It is said that he moved from our midst to Englewood, but this is uncertain.

Dr. Oscar H. Mann.—In 1866 Oscar H. Mann took the place vacated in the community by Dr. Fairbanks. Dr. Mann was born at Providence, R. I., November 24, 1835. His great-grandfather was an officer in the American Revolution. The doctor received his earlier medical education in New York City, and began practicing. He received the degree of Doctor of Medicine from Hahnemann Medical College, Chicago, March, 1866. Afterward he came to Evanston where he was for many years a prominent factor in the life of the village, socially and politically. For about three years he lectured on Chemistry and Hygiene at the Northwestern Female College, which was familiarly called the Jones College from its founder and Principal. Dr.

Mann was one of the prime movers, and the first President of the Evanston Social Club, the first organization of the kind in our midst. Under its auspices were held theatricals, dances, and card parties. At this time it is hard to realize with what horror such an organization was then generally regarded. It occupied the rooms now devoted to the Odd Fellows, 604 Davis Street. Dr. Mann served as Township, and Village Trustee. He was the last President of the village, and the first Mayor of the city. Under his administration the old Village of South Evanston, which was organized because its residents did not wish to be taxed for a general water supply, was merged with Evanston, in order to get the benefit of our superior water system. The present City Hall was erected with rooms for the Police and Fire Departments, and for the Public Library. His home, once the scene of frequent parties, stood where the present Mann building now houses the Postoffice and Masonic Temple. In 1889 the house was removed to 811 University Place, where it now stands. He was one of the first officers of the Evanston Commandery Knights Templar, and served one year as President of the State Homœopathic Medical Society. He gradually retired from practice, and, on the completion of his service as Mayor, spent some years on his ranch at Okobojo, South Dakota, though still retaining his legal residence and interest in Evanston.

Dr. M. C. Bragdon.—In the summer of 1873 Dr. Mann took into partnership a young man from Evanston, then fresh from his studies in Vienna. Merritt Caldwell Bragdon was born at Auburn, N. Y., January 6, 1850. His father, Rev. Charles P. Bragdon, was sent to Evanston in 1858 as the pastor of the First Methodist Episcopal Church. The family moved into the house which had been built for Dr. Hawkes, on

Orrington Avenue. Here the father died, leaving his widow, three boys and two girls. Merritt, the second son, was graduated in 1870 from the Northwestern University, served as a clerk in the State Senate, studied in Chicago Medical College, and finally, in 1873, was graduated from the Hahnemann Medical College and Hospital of Philadelphia. After some months spent in foreign study, he entered upon his duties in Dr. Mann's office. He is a trustee of his father's church, and a member of the University Board of Trustees. He has devoted his attention to the practice of his profession. He is a member of the State and National Homœopathic Medical Societies. His chief public service in the community was the establishment of the Evanston Hospital, of which he is now one of the staff of physicians. Seeing the need for such an institution, he urged it upon one of his patrons, Mrs. Rebecca Butler, and his old neighbor, Mrs. Marie Huse Wilder—now Mrs. Daniel Kidder—and those ladies undertook its organization. Beginning in a small way, it has steadily grown until now it is one of the most modern, well equipped and best managed hospitals in America.

Dr. Anson L. Marcy.—After Dr. Bragdon left the office of Dr. Mann, Anson L. Marcy took his place. Dr. Marcy was a nephew of Prof. Oliver Marcy, of the University, and a classmate of Dr. Bragdon in the Hahnemann Medical College of Philadelphia, where he received his Doctor's degree in 1873. He came here originally as a student in the Academy and University, though he did not graduate. In his student days he was an expert taxidermist, and there are still many evidences of his skill to be found in the University Museum. After graduating in medicine he settled in Dakota, but having made a matrimonial alliance with the daughter of 'Squire Curry, he was drawn back to this village. He is now practicing in Richmond, Va.

Dr. Clapp.—Eben Pratt Clapp, the son of one of the oldest homœopathic practitioners in the State, Dr. Ela H. Clapp, was born at Rome, Ill., March 10, 1859. The family came to Evanston to educate the son, and he was graduated from the Northwestern University in 1881. He was graduated from the Hahnemann Medical College of Chicago in 1882, and after studying in Europe, settled in Evanston, where he has since practiced. For six years he served as an efficient Commissioner of Health for the City of Evanston. He is a member of the staff of physicians at the Evanston Hospital. He has now retired from active practice and spends his winters in California.

Dr. Ela H. Clapp was the second homœopathic physician to settle in Illinois He first studied in Cincinnati and began practice in Ohio, and later, after practicing for some years, he went to Cleveland for special study. After leaving Ohio he settled in Central Illinois. Having retired from active work he came to Evanston in 1874. His home overlooked the lake, and stood at the northwest corner of Church Street and Judson Avenue. Though not engaged in practice in Evanston, his position among the profession of the State entitles him to recognition here. He died April 12, 1888, of paralysis.

Later Homoeopathic Physicians.—Harry Parsons was the son of an Evanston merchant. The family lived in the northern part of the village. Harry was graduated from Hahnemann Medical College of Chicago in 1880. He practiced in Evanston after graduation, but later moved to Ravenswood, where he is now enjoying an active practice.

Prof. William J. Hawkes, a native of Pensylvania, came here in the 'eighties, but returned to Chicago, and later removed to Southern California. He was graduated from the Hahnemann Medical College of

Philadelphia, in 1867. During his residence here, Dr. Hawkes continued to occupy the chair of Materia Medica in Chicago Hahnemann College. He was a man of good address, genial, well posted in his profession, and successful in practice; yet for some reason he never took root in our soil.

Dr. Allen Benjamin Clayton came to Evanston in 1885, and was the only one of our homœopathic practitioners to die while practicing here. He was born January 26, 1849, at Aylmer, Ontario. His preliminary education was obtained in the schools of Aylmer and Saint Thomas. He received his medical training in the College of Physicians and Surgeons at Toronto, and in the Hahnemann Medical College of Chicago, being graduated from the latter school in 1869. He settled first in Chatham, Ontario, moving thence to Marinette, Wis. He came to Evanston in 1885. He was a gentleman of fine literary tastes, affable in manner, and at one time he had a lucrative practice. His father had wished him to enter the legal profession, but this was not to his liking. He died in Chicago, of rectal cancer, September 15, 1900.

Eugene E. Shutterly was born at Cannonsburg, Pa., January 2, 1862. He came to Evanston in 1877. He studied in the Academy, graduating in 1886. He then entered the Hahnemann Medical College of Chicago, from which he was graduated in 1888. He immediately began practice in Evanston. He has also served the city as its Commissioner of Health, conducting the office with satisfaction to all concerned. He is a member of the staff of physicians at the Evanston Hospital.

Mary F. McCrillis was the first woman homœopathic physician to settle among us. She was born in New Hampshire in 1856, of New England parentage. She was graduated from the Boston University School of Medicine in 1882. She came to Evanston in 1888, and has since that time been engaged here in general practice. She is a member of the staff of Physicians at the Evanston Hospital. Quiet and unobtrusive in manner, and well versed in her profession, she has proved a worthy member of the fraternity.

Frances B. Wilkins, a graduate of the Hahnemann Medical College of Chicago in 1876, has several times resided in Evanston. Her husband, John M. Wilkins, received his M. D. degree from the Chicago National Medical College in 1896.

Alice B. Stockham, born in Ohio in 1835, and graduated from the Chicago Homœopathic Medical College in 1882, came to Evanston about 1894. Here she did not enter general practice, but devoted herself to literary and commercial pursuits. She was the author of several books and pamphlets, the best known of which are "Tokology" and "The Koradine Letters."

Charles Gordon Fuller, born at Jamestown, N. Y., April 9, 1856, has resided in Evanston over fifteen years. Having received his early education in the schools of Jamestown and at Columbia College, he entered the Chicago Homœopathic Medical College, graduating in 1880. Later he took special studies at the College of Physicians and Surgeons, New York, at the New York Ophthalmic College and Hospital and the New York Ophthalmic and Aural Institute. He is ex-Major and Surgeon of the First Regiment Infantry of the Illinois National Guard, Ophthalmic and Aural Surgeon to several Chicago Hospitals and a member of the consulting staff of the Evanston Hospital. He is also a member of the American Institute of Homœopathy, the American Homœopathic Ophthalmological, Otological and Laryngological Society, ex-Assistant Surgeon to New York Ophthalmic Hospital, Fellow of the Royal Microscopical Society, England, member of the A. A. A. S. Association, Military Surgeons of the United States, and the American Microscopical Society. Dr. Fuller's office is in Chicago, where he has confined his attention to diseases of the eye and ear.

Burton Haseltine graduated from the Hahnemann Medical College of Chicago in 1896, and, after being associated with Dr. Shears of Chicago for two years, came to Evanston, limiting his practice to diseases of the eye, ear, nose and throat. He is the author of numerous monographs, Secretary of the State Homœopathic Medical Association, member of the National and Chicago Homœopathic Societies, Senior Professor of Nose and Throat in his alma mater, and attending Eye and Ear Surgeon to Cook County Hospital and Home of the Friendless. He has now removed to Chicago.

Samuel M. Moore, a native of Kentucky, and a graduate from the Chicago Homœopathic Medical College in 1895, and also serving as interne at Cook County Hospital, came to Evanston in 1897. For several years he enjoyed a prosperous hospital practice. He was a member of the staff of Physicians at the Evanston Hospital, but he retired in 1904 to engage in mercantile pursuits. He has now resumed his practice in Sheridan Park, Ill.

Guernsey P. Waring was graduated from Dunham Medical College in 1897, and is a Professor of Materia Medica in the Hahnemann Medical College of Chicago. He is a member of the State and National Medical Societies.

Dr. James T. Kent, who received his degrees from the Eclectic School in Cincinnati in 1871, and the Homœopathic College of St. Louis in 1884, is now Professor of Materia Medica at Hahnemann Medical College of Chicago, a member of the State and National Homœopathic Medical Societies, and the author of "Kent's Repertory," "Kent's Materia Medica," and "Kent's Philosophy."

Edwin H. Pratt was graduated from Hahnemann Medical College of Chicago in 1877. He is the author of a work on Orificial Surgery, is known as a successful operator and has for many years been one of the leading homœopathic surgeons. He has resided in Evanston since 1900.

Abbie J. Hinkle was born in Philadelphia in 1853. There she received her preliminary education. After several years spent in teaching in the public schools, she turned her attention to medicine, being graduated from the Hahnemann Medical College of Chicago in 1887. She first settled in Chicago. In January, 1895, she located in Evanston. During her student days she was an officer in the college clinical society, and more recently she has been a Vice-President of the Illinois Homœopathic Medical Association.

Thomas H. Winslow, a native of Norway, was graduated from the Herring College in Chicago in 1896. Since graduation he has practiced in Evanston. Having taken special work in the branches pertaining to diseases of the nose, throat, ear and eye, in February, 1904, he moved to Oakland, Cal., to practice that specialty.

Ransom M. Barrows, born in Michigan in 1849, is a brother of the late Rev. Dr. John H. Barrows, previous to his death President of Oberlin College, Ohio. Dr. Barrows received his education in his native State, being graduated from the Michigan University Medical School in 1877. In 1884 he took a degree from the Hahnemann Medical College of Chicago. After several years spent in Chicago he located in Evanston in 1901. He moved to Wilmette two years later.

George F. M. Tyson was born in Chicago, October 30, 1872. He has practiced in

Evanston since his graduation from the Chicago National Medical College in 1898.

Frank H. Edwards grew up in Evanston. He was born in Irving Park, Cook County, November 16, 1871. He was graduated from the Evanston High School, and began his professional studies under the direction of Dr. Clayton. In 1895 he was graduated from the Chicago Homœopathic Medical College, and began his career at Rockford, Ill. After three years he returned to Evanston. In 1902 he received a diploma from Rush Medical College. He then spent some time studying in Vienna, and later with his uncle, Dr. Ira Harris, in Tripoli, Syria. He is the author of several monographs. He has joined the Christian Scientists.

G. F. Barry was born in Chicago, January 12, 1875. He was graduated from the Chicago Manual Training School in 1894, and from the Hahnemann Medical College and Hospital of Philadelphia in 1902. He immediately settled in Evanston. He is a member of the Illinois Homœopathic Medical Association and a graduate of the Chicago Lying-in Hospital. He is a member of the staff of Evanston Hospital.

Dwight M. Clark, who took the practice of Dr. Moore, was born at Yellow Springs, Ohio, March 20, 1878. He studied at the Michigan University, was graduated from Chicago Homœopathic Medical College, in 1901, served as an interne at Cook County Hospital, received a diploma from Rush Medical in 1903, and came to Evanston in January, 1904. He is a member of staff of Evanston Hospital.

From the foregoing it may be seen that the homœopathic practitioners of the city have not been entirely occupied with private affairs. To members of this profession is largely due the praise for the present existence of two of our public buildings,—the City Hall, and the Hospital. Two of these doctors have served the city well as Commissioners of Health. Aside from these, others have done much toward the development of the city in a more quiet way, by the improvement of vacant property, erecting thereon residences and business blocks. Three for years showed an interest in the University by maintaining therein prizes for oratory, declamation, and scholarship. One is a director in one of our banks, and one is a Trustee in the University. But beyond all that has been said, in the quiet every day work of relief of distress and suffering the disciples of Hahnemann have done their full share.

CHAPTER XXIX.

EVANSTON HOSPITAL
(By WILLIAM HUDSON HARPER)

The Evanston Benevolent Society—First Steps in Founding a Hospital—Organization is Effected in 1891—First Board of officers—Medical Staff—Fund and Building Campaign—Enlargement of the Institution Projected — Munificent Gift of Mrs. Cable — Other Donations — The Endowment Reaches $50,000—Hospital of the Present and the Future—Internal Arrangement and Official Administration — List of Principal Donors — Present Officers.

When the exigencies of life in the growing Village of Evanston had made the care of its dependent and other sick more and more inadequate; when lives had been lost in the transportation of the afflicted to Chicago, and in insufficient ministration to those sought to be cured within the village, a movement arose in Evanston to bring on a better day. This movement was not based upon an abstract philanthropy. It was the offspring of the Evanston Benevolent Society, whose charitable service had, for several years, met an appealing emergency.

The Beginning.—The seed of the Evanston Hospital was planted at a meeting of citizens at the Avenue House, November 17, 1891. Strictly speaking, it was a meeting of the Evanston Benevolent Association, called to consider the report, on the establishment of a hospital in Evanston, of a special committee consisting of J. J. Parkhurst, Dr. D. R. Dyche, Mrs. Maria Huse Wilder and Mrs. Rebecca N. Butler. There were present William Blanchard, Dr. D. R. Dyche, H. B. Hurd, J. J. Parkhurst, J. M. Larimer, W. A. Hamilton, Frank M. Elliot, W. E. Stockton, Mrs. Jane Bishop, Henry A. Pearsons, Mrs. J. M. Larimer, Mrs. Davis, Mrs. Frank M. Elliott, Mrs. Butler, Mrs. Wilder, Mrs. Pearsons and Mrs. Bishop. It was agreed that Evanston should have an emergency hospital, and there were appointed as a committee on incorporation Mr. Hamilton, Mr. Larimer, Dr. D. R. Dyche, Mrs. Butler, and Mrs. Wilder. The meeting authorized overtures contemplating assistance by the Village Trustees and Board of Health; and from Mr. Parkhurst, on behalf of the executive committee of Northwestern University, assurance was received of the possibility that the University would lend financial help to the enterprise.

Organization — First Officers. — One week after, in the same place, a meeting of citizens affirmed the decision of the previous meeting that "an emergency hospital is a necessity for the village of Evanston." Incorporation followed December 2, and on December 4, 1891, there was organized the Evanston Emergency Hospital. The first administration of the institution, now in its successor almost unique in its perfections, was entrusted to the following citizens:

President—John R. Lindgren;

Vice-President—Julia M. Watson;

Secretary—Marie Huse Wilder;

Treasurer—Frank E. Lord;

Executive Committee—Wm. Blanchard, J. M. Larimer, John H. Kedzie, F. Stuyvesant Peabody, Frank M. Elliot, Maria A. Holabird, Rebecca N. Butler, Marie Huse Wilder, and Catherine I. Pearsons.

The hospital organization began its existence with sixty-three directors—public-spirited and influential, and with a truly liberal conception of the mission of the institution contemplated. The directors, soon afterwards reduced to thirty, were elected for service in three classes, severally for one, two, and, three years. The site chosen for the hospital, after resources and proposed service had been considered, was on No. 806 Emerson Street. Here was bought for $2,800 a lot, 45 by 170 feet, bearing an eight-room cottage which was duly made suitable for hospital purposes at a cost of about $1,500. It was not an imposing structure, but well enough adapted to the needs of the time, and it was a very healthy acorn. Then fifty feet of adjoining property, costing $1,050, was bought, and thus-wise Evanston seemed safeguarded for many years. To make this unpretentious start in the founding of an institution indispensable to Evanston, many active people had done much efficient work when, at the first annual meeting, November 1, 1892, the hospital was reported in possession of funds amounting to $7,-702—a total composed of subscriptions, dues from annual and life members, a donation of more than $3,000 from the proceeds of a summer kirmess conducted by the Woman's Club and others, and by a donation of $320 from the Apollo Club of Chicago,

which had sung the "Messiah" in public concert in Evanston.

First Medical Staff.—The hospital was opened for service, March 27, 1893, with Miss Emily E. Robinson, matron, and the following physicians as a medical staff: Isaac Poole, M. D.; E. H. Webster, M. D.; W. A. Phillips, M. D.; Sarah H. Brayton, M. D.; H. B. Hemenway, M. D.; A. B. Clayton, M. D.; M. C. Bragdon, M. D.; O. H. Mann, M. D.; E. P. Clapp, M. D.; Mary F. McCrillis, M. D.; I. V. Stevens, M. D.; and S. F. Verbeck, M. D. The hospital recognized all accepted schools of medicine and opened its doors to patients both paid and free. Month by month the management perfected equipment and system, the rate of charge for service in the wards being from $5.00 to $10.00, and for a private room from $15.00 to $25.00 a week. Directing an institution for public service, the hospital management in these early years looked with justifiable hopes toward the city authorities for assistance. By no means was it promptly vouchsafed; and when the executive committee was informed at its meeting in June, 1893, that it was impossible to get an appropriation from the Evanston Common Council, it was felt by more than one public-spirited member that the service of the new institution to the common weal was receiving but scant recognition. None too robust a child was the Emergency Hospital at this period. Funds were not too plenty, and citizens at large were not yet so trained in systematic benevolence as to make excessive provision for this municipal necessity. So, along with the manifold activities of committees and directors to keep and improve Evanston's first refuge for the afflicted, there arose discussion about the inauguration of the practice of Hospital Sunday. This happy and profitable way of contributing to hospital support in time took hold, and is

EVANSTON HOSPITAL

to-day, in Evanston, as in other cities, a reliable vehicle for large public benevolences.

Official Board.—At the first annual meeting of the hospital corporation, November 14, 1893, the following officers were elected:

President—Arthur Orr;

Vice-President—Mrs. Rebecca N. Butler;

Secretary—Marie Huse Wilder;

Treasurer—E. B. Quinlan.

Mr. Orr subsequently resigning, Hon. J. H. Kedzie was elected in his stead. Not long after, Mrs. Wilder resigning, Miss Mary Harris, February 5, 1894, was elected to the secretaryship, and began a period of service long, meritorious, and of a character that goes not a little unrewarded.

Raising Funds.—In 1894, reaching about for popular ways and means to let the public know that a hospital in Evanston was up and doing, and that it would welcome all possible support, the institution's friends conducted a so-called "magazine entertainment" in Bailey's Opera House. The entertainment proved a novel and sprightly potpourri of "stunts" by home talent, and brought into the hospital treasury $319. But the little hospital was truly an emergency institution, itself not infrequently its own chief emergency; and so to meet its needs, its industrious sponsors fell upon a venture of considerable magnitude and genuinely artistic attributes. This was an open-air performance of Gilbert and Sullivan's charming opera, the "Mikado." A stage was erected on the vacant lot at the northwest corner of Davis Street and Judson Avenue, and with clever principals, and equally clever auxiliaries from the young people of the village, the opera was sung on four successive evenings, in July, 1894, and before large and delighted audiences. The net proceeds of this very praiseworthy entertainment amounted to $2,000. Among the efficient managers of this enterprise were W. J. Fabian, Mrs. William Holabird, W. L. Wells, John M. Ewen, Mrs. F. A. Hardy, and Frank M. Elliot.

The Evanston Emergency Hospital was now a fact. It was at work. The public knew it was at work, and had gratefully profited by its ministrations. But it was not big enough, complete enough, modern enough—in short, it was inadequate. It simply would not do. So it was quite in order at the annual meeting of the association, November 6, 1894, that the following, presented by Henry A. Pearsons should have been, as it was, unanimously adopted: "Resolved, that it is the sense of this meeting that the board of directors be requested to appoint a committee to consider the question of procuring a more suitable site, and commencing the erection of a more suitable building for use of the hospital."

Plans for Extension.—The committee authorized to take up this proposition was Frank M. Elliot, William Blanchard, Dr. Sarah H. Brayton, and Henry A. Pearsons, this committee working under the administration of the following new board of officers:

President—Hon. J. H. Kedzie;

Vice-President—Mrs. William Holabird;

Secretary—Miss Mary Harris;

Treasurer—E. B. Quinlan.

The Committee on Building and Grounds was shortly re-enforced by one consisting of Wm. H. Bartlett, Dr. Charles G. Fuller, and Dr. Sarah H. Brayton, who, with broad outlook and knowledge of the relation of a hospital to the many-sided needs of a growing community, set out to determine the scope and functions of the proposed institution. On February 11, 1895, the corporation, desiring to disassociate from its name and work anything suggestive of an impromptu, transient, or tentative character, formally changed its name from Evanston Emergency Hospital to Evanston Hospital Association. Having enlarged its name, it was appropriate that the new association should enlarge its place of work, and so, on April 13, 1895, at a meeting of the Directors to consider the report of the committee on a proposed new building site, it was unanimously ordered that negotiations be opened for the purchase of a lot on Ridge Avenue, in the University sub-division, 280 feet on Ridge Avenue, and extending 600 feet to Girard Avenue, for $12,000, the terms being $6,500 and the transfer of the existing hospital property at a valuation of $5,500. A committee to raise the necessary money was appointed, consisting of Frank M. Elliot, John R. Lindgren, and E. H. Buehler. At a meeting on May 2d, purchase of the lot in question was authorized for the above price, a mortgage of $3,500 being ordered assumed, and a two years' lease of the Emerson Street property made. The building site was deemed an exceptionally desirable acquisition, and its subsequent improvement has been worthy its natural advantages. A month later plans for a hospital building were laid before the executive committee by George L. Harvey, architect.

A Fund and Building Campaign.—A building site and building plans meant large prospective drafts upon a none too plethoric treasury, and the association again tried the magic of an open-air opera as a benefit performance. Again, under professional guidance, social Evanston threw itself at the jolly task, and through the agency of the opera of "Powhattan," contributed $1,800 to the hospital's funds. Again Mr. Fabian and assistants received official thanks for their happy management of the agreeable enterprise. At a meeting of the Hospital Directors, July 8, 1895, it was resolved to raise $25,000 for the proposed administration building, in addition to

funds for purchase of site. The new association year 1895-1896 was inaugurated November 8th by the election of the following officers:

President—Frank M. Elliot;
Vice-President—Julia M. Watson;
Secretary—Miss Mary Harris;
Treasurer—E. B. Quinlan.

The new administration entered the campaign for hospital funds by making its entire Board of Directors a subscription committee. At a meeting of the directors, March 30, 1896, the services of Mr. Harvey, as an expert in hospital construction, were accepted, and the subscriptions to date were found to be $12,780; the cost of the proposed first or administration building was estimated at $22,000, and it was determined that, to open the new place free of debt, there would be needed $26,750. This was too expensive and the administration building was reduced in size to bring the cost within the limits of the fund that could then be realized.

The hospital year of 1896-1897, beginning with the election of officers November 10, 1896, was marked with but one change among the executive officers, Mr. Quinlan yielding to William G. Hoag as Treasurer. A rushing stream was to be crossed before the hospital should appear, and horses would better not be swapped. So Mr. Elliot continued President. At this stage in the financing of the new hospital project, an unusual opening developed to make an honest penny. Mr. Uriah Lott, an Evanston citizen, wishing to dispose of his household effects—and they were of more than ordinary elegance—offered to the hospital association a liberal percentage of the gross receipts of a public sale, should the association lend the sale its direction and patronage. The offer was accepted, and through the activity of Mr. Elliot, Miss Harris, and Mrs. Charles J. Connell, the hospital fund was increased $1,364. This, recruited by a contribution of $136 from the surplus of a citizens' Fourth of July fund, was welcome money in a year when much energy and organization were needed to raise the building funds to achieve the level of the plans proposed, and when indeed curtailment and modification were finally pursued. But energy and organization on the part of the association, and co-operation on the part of Evanstonians at large, determined this, the summer of 1897, to be the hospital's building summer the committee in charge being Frank M. Elliot, William H. Bartlett, Dr. Sarah H. Brayton, Howard Gray, and William B. Phillips. When October came, contracts for over $15,000 of an authorized expenditure of $16,000 had been let, an incumbrance of $3,500 had been paid, and the new and perfect hospital was a no distant fact. And, to rush the building fund, there came out of the hurly-burly of a football game in November, a sturdy little check for $210. The association, at the annual meeting, November 2, 1897, continued its retiring officers, and fixed the endowment of a bed in terms of an annual donation of $300 or a single donation of $5,000. Subsequently there was determined an important matter in executive policy, in a resolution that adjoining towns should not be allowed to endow beds in the new institution.

The new hospital building (the administration building) was opened for the reception of patients February 8, 1898. The association had a credit balance in bank of $2,707; and through its executive committee it unanimously thanked Dr. Sarah H. Brayton for efficient work in procuring the proper furnishing of the building without cost to the association.

New Enlargements Projected.—The annual meeting of the Evanston Hospital Association, assembling at the Avenue House, November 1, 1898, was a meeting of congratulation and a declaration of progress in a branch of public service that was doing honor to its workers and to all sympathetic citizens who had lent aid and comfort. The main building of the hospital, capable of sheltering as many as eighteen patients, was now a monumental fact. As complete as it was, its very usefulness emphasized its inadequacy, and its friends already looked forward to needed extensions: to wards for contagious, infectious and obstetrical cases, and to minor new accommodations. Noteworthy in the hospital's new equipment was an ambulance for service, a gift of Mrs. John M. Ewen, as a thank-offering for preservation in an hour of great danger; and, to bind it closer to the public, the hospital had now the temporary endowment of four free beds—one being supported by the Ladies' Aid Society of the Presbyterian Church, two by Northwestern University, and one by Mrs. Watson, Vice-President of the association. Further sustained on strong shoulders, the hospital felt itself to be, by the gratuitous service, two months each, of its entire medical staff. An abstract from the treasurer's report for one year made at this annual meeting will suggest the financial career of the hospital at this period; a period, be it remembered, marked between 1894 and 1898 by general strenuous effort in recovery from national panic and depression.

Subscriptions for building fund and site: 1895, $250; 1896, $4,615; 1897, $11,040; 1898, $9,513.

Amount allowed for old hospital, $5,500.

Expended on new site, $14,691.

Expended on new building, $17,140.

Receipts from entertainments, $1,802.

Receipts from memberships, $500.

Receipts from donations, $115.

Receipts from patients' board, $2,108.

Receipts from support of beds, $575.

Receipts from subscriptions for furnishing, $1,725.

Expenses for maintenance, $5,707.

The association continued for 1898-1899 the officers of the previous year. Early in 1899 the City of Evanston, without specified obligations upon the hospital, made to the institution an appropriation of $300. At the annual meeting of the association, November 7, 1899, the latter prepared for the aid and prestige which future donations might prove to the institution, by determining the privileges which should pertain to endowments of various amounts, and fixing classification for the same. With renewed persistency now appeared the need of a contagious ward, as well as of a wing to the hospital, and both interests were committed to a special committee. Another year the association continued its efficient executives in office, and strengthened its medical staff by the addition of a consulting staff in the persons of eminent Chicago specialists— Dr. Christian Fenger, Dr. John Ridlon, and Dr. Charles Adams. But the year 1900 brought to Evanston and its hospital a real loss in the death of Hugh R. Wilson. When the hospital association came to formally deplore the death of this stanch friend and good citizen, it did so, in part, in these feeling words: "Resolved, That, in the death of Mr. Wilson, the hospital loses one of its most active and interested supporters. In his readiness to assist the suffering; in his broad-minded and judicious charity; in his kindliness and gentleness of action, Mr. Wilson has, at all times during his connection with the association, been a helpful inspiration to those who have worked with him. His foresight and good judgment, together with his generosity of support, have served to advance our work in every practical way."

Munificent Gifts of 1900.—Institutions, like men, must be in the way of opportunity if they would have fortune knock at their door. A rather mysterious notice summoned to a special meeting the directors of the Evanston Hospital Association, March 19, 1900. When met, F. F. Peabody, Chairman of the Finance Committee, threw his associates into happy consternation by the following remarks:

"Mrs. Herman D. Cable wishes me to say that she will give $25,000 for the erection of a needed addition to the hospital to be known as the Herman D. Cable Memorial Building, and that, if this gift is accepted, she will give an additional $25,000 to endow a children's ward in the new building."

We may be sure this gift was accepted, and that the thanks, then formally voted Mrs. Cable, were deep and sincere; and it is also to be recorded that the Directors made it their duty to amplify the unexpected opportunity, to enlarge the existing building, and to raise, on their own part, an additional endowment fund of at least $25,000.

The hospital year of 1900-1901, inaugurated by continuance in office of the retiring executive officers, was also marked by resignation from the directorate of Hon. J. H. Kedzie, long identified with hospital interests, and the election of Mrs. Alice A. Cable, whose gift of a memorial building, with alterations in the main building, the Board now formally voted to realize. The year 1901 was one of expansion and construction in hospital interests. From a "rummage sale" in January the hospital received $1,813. In April Mr. Irwin Rew, a public-spirited citizen of Evanston, offered—and the offer was accepted—to equip the hospital with a heating and laundry plant at an estimated cost of $4,680. In October there was borne in upon the hospital management, both by the City Board of Health and by the hospital staff, the need of an extension in the way of an isolation ward. At the annual meeting, November 5th, the retiring officers were re-elected, and the very important additions to the institutions represented by the gifts of Mr. Rew and Mrs. Cable were formally acknowledged—the Cable Memorial Building being characterized as completely furnished and the children's ward endowed in memory of Anita Hutchins Cable.

Endowment Secured.—The association began its hospital year of 1901-1902 with its same efficient officers, and welcomed from another "rummage" sale a donation amounting to $1,440. In February the endowment fund had reached $46,000 of the contemplated $50,000; and in April the coveted goal was finally attained. As the good year closed divers talented amateur artists of Evanston contributed as the receipts of a performance of the "Rivals," at the Country Club, more than $500 to increase the usefulness of this popular refuge of rest and healing. In the history of amusements in Evanston this admirable presentation of the sterling old comedy will prove of long life in local reminiscence. So well in hand was the work of the association now coming, that the reduction of the floating debt of about $11,000 became an achievement to be undertaken until accomplished. Feeling its strength in the substantial work done, and in the officers whom it re-elected for the year 1902-1903, the association was also brought to know its weakness when, on April 10th, it was confronted with the death of Hon. John H. Kedzie, and on May 20th of Mr. Dorr A. Kimball. In terms of sorrow and appreciation Mr. Kedzie was formally lamented as "a friend who has met every emergency of the association's existence with generous words and generous deeds"; and, to Mr. Kimball's memory, the association offered no mean tribute when it declared him "an upright business man and honorable citizen of

Evanston, whose pure life and public spirit made him an example for all." When the association, at its eleventh annual meeting, November 10, 1903, elected its former officers, and checked off a reduction of nearly half the floating debt in pledges received, the feeling was general that the hospital was truly founded and that its beneficiaries, the public, would never permit it to decline.

Hospital of the Present and the Future. —When this volume— the story of a remarkable American community—shall have received more than one supplement, there will still be rising on the highest land in Evanston—the city itself but a borough in a mammoth municipality of 5,000,000 or 10,000,000 people—a group of buildings enveloped in the kindly shade of many trees, and looking to be, what it probably will be, a haven for the afflicted. What the hospital of that day will be to the city of that day none knows; but we do know that the Evanston Hospital of today is, to the Evanston of today, the most complete agency for practical philanthropy that any institution of its kind in the world, with the same equipment, fulfills. The Evanston Hospital, as it stands today—structure, equipment, and administration—is briefly this:

On the summit of Ridge Avenue, No. 2650, at right angles to the thoroughfare and several rods removed, rises the hospital's administration building. It is of stone and vitrified brick, the latter a structural material of the highest resistance and of good color tone. The building is of three stories, with high pitched and tile roof. Its architectural style has decorum, and suggests repose. An ample porch front, with balcony, looks eastward over a falling landscape toward the lake, a quarter of a mile distant. At right angles to this building connected therewith by a two-story and basement corridor, rises the second of the hospital buildings, the

memorial gift of Mrs. Alice A. Cable. This
is in architectural keeping with its dignified
fellow, and the forerunner of others yet to
rise in stately alignment westward and
northward to the boundary of the institution's property. The following taken
from the President's report for 1905 is
interesting:

"For several years reference has been
made in our annual reports to the necessity of providing a maternity hospital, and
last year particular emphasis was given to
this subject. In response to this appeal, Mr.
Lucian M. Williams, on behalf of himself,
his brother and sisters, made known their
desire to build this hospital, and requested
the Board of Directors to prepare plans and
obtain estimates for a most approved and
scientifically constructed building, to be
erected as a memorial to their mother,
Elizabeth Williams. Such plans and estimates were secured and presented, and the
sum of $25,000 was promised for this pur-
pose. It is expected this much needed hospital will be completed and ready for occupancy by June 1, 1906. The erection of this
building will be the consummation of a
hope long deferred. It will be located north
of the administration building, fronting on
Ridge Avenue, and will correspond in material and style of architecture with our
present buildings. There will be thirteen
beds for patients, an operating room with
dependencies, diet kitchens, children's nursery, etc. The rooms for private patients
will be on one floor and those for ward and
free patients on the other floor. The private
rooms will be arranged with adjoining bath
rooms and so planned as to give the utmost
privacy and comfort. This generous gift
will open the way for enlarging the charitable work of the Hospital. It is expected
the income will be augmented by the use
of the private rooms, and that it will be sufficient to meet the expenses of this addition-

al building after the first year. The need
of this new and thoroughly equipped Hospital has become more apparent with each
year. This magnificent gift is, therefore,
most timely, and will be a valuable addition
to our present admirably equipped hospital. This is another instance in which
generous friends, desiring to perpetuate the
memory of some beloved member of their
family, have made it possible to erect a
building as a memorial that will be constantly in use for the benefit of the sick and
afflicted."

This, then, is the main architectural mass
of the Evanston Hospital. When this system of buildings shall have its complete
setting of verdure, when its hundreds of
trees and shrubs, selected and planted with
design, shall have arisen to enfold it, the
tourist of the north shore will linger with
delight in its presence, and the household
word will become fixed, that the Evanston
Hospital is a place to behold as well as a
place to seek new life in. But a hospital
is what it is within.

In operating equipment the Evanston
Hospital is highly efficient. A visiting and
consulting staff of the first class, commanding the support of a community of intelligence and wealth, would naturally lead
this to be secured. Therefore this hospital
has a special room for the administration of
anæsthetics, whence the patient is wheeled,
an ample hydraulic elevator being used
when necessary, to any part of either building. The hospital also has a generous receiving room hard by a driveway approaching the connecting corridors from the rear;
and here, where water may be applied with
convenience and profusion, an emergency
case may be prepared for the operating
table. The operating room, with apparatus
for water and instrument sterilization adjoining, is placed in a swelling bay with
top and side lights and north exposure. Its

table, operating outfit, plumbing, and snowy enameled walls tell the story of an American warship—the cleanest place in the world, and the most effectual instrument for the purpose for which it is created. Supplementing these main factors for perfect operating service are medicine closets and lavatories for the professional staff.

The first and last impression of the domestic equipment of the Evanston Hospital is, that it is scientifically chosen and used; that such parts of it as should be dainty and feminine are superlatively dainty and feminine; and that, through all, spreads the genius of reason, cleanliness, and order. These various characteristics are generally expressed in the exquisite neatness and refinement of the institution's housekeeping: in the furnishing of the private rooms; in the simple, restful details of ward furnishings; in the ample dining-room for nurses, as well as in their ample and beautiful club room; in the home-like sleeping rooms of the nurses; in the practical machinery for bathing, cooking, storage; and in the clerical service of administration. So much for operating equipment, but the right people must use it; and so much for domestic furnishings, but not yet do walls, tools, and furnishings make a hospital. There must be a soul in the place, a god in the machine.

Arrangement and Internal Administration.—The administration of the Evanston Hospital is full worthy its physical outfit; and this is so because it stands in every way for the high technical and humanitarian standards of the institution's founders. With far more effort than the average citizen of Evanston appreciated, the sworn friends of the enterprise, now so firmly assured, shaped its early fortunes, besought donations of money and utilities, showed it worthy of confidence and large bequests, and finally with such capital built their grand work high upon a hill. So it is in the

nature of things, this hospital being a monument to sacrifice, that a strong, wise, and tender spirit should vitalize its administration. In Miss Annie L. Locke, who has been Superintendent eight years, is this spirit personified.

In this sketch of one of Evanston's most important institutions, ranking next to the municipal departments of police, fire, water, and public works, two types of inquiry about the place should find satisfaction. How good a place is it to get well in? What about it should interest the tourist and general visitor? To both of these inquiries answer has in the main been made; but there remain details of equipment and administration that should not go unnoted. The first floor of the administration is the greater part of the governing department of the hospital. Here is the reception parlor for visitors, office and apartments for the Superintendent, and rooms for surgical treatment. Beneath, in the basement, is the private dining-room of the Superintendent, the nurses' dining-room, and an extensive culinary equipment. On the second floor are private rooms and semi-private wards, occupants of the former enjoying an environment and retiracy surpassing that of a private home, and occupants of the latter being privileged to have a private, as well as a hospital, physician. On the third floor are rooms for domestic use. Two long sunny corridors—enticing haunts for convalescents—unite the administration with the Herman D. Cable Memorial Building. This latter, in structure, equipment and contented occupants, is, like its companion, something good to see. It is the house of the men's ward, the women's and children's wards, and the private rooms of the nurses. On the first floor, with outlook east and south, is the ward for men with seven beds, and the ward for women with ten beds. The building's southern end is one enormous bay, furnishing a sun-room annex to the women's ward on the first floor, and to the children's ward on the second. Capacious and comfortable are these sun-rooms—blissful half-way houses to health. The top floor shelters, in home-like chambers void of the institutional air, the members of the nursing staff, and has space for their large and inviting club and lecture room. Characteristic details of equipment in this building are the marble outfittings of the men's bath-room, the treadle action plumbing in the administration room, the ventilator system by steam exhaust fans, the diet kitchen, and the commodious elevator. On every floor of the combined buildings are reels of hose and extinguishers for emergency fire uses. A pumping service auxiliary to city pressure is also supplied.

An important and complete annex to the ward and administration buildings of the hospital, is an auxiliary building housing its steam-plant and laundry. The heating agent of the hospital is hot water circulated from boilers in this same building, where a reserve set of boilers promise capacity sufficient for future additions in the way of buildings, which the unoccupied area of the present hospital grounds can accommodate. The steam laundry, located on the second floor of the heat and power plant building, is admirably equipped for dispatch and perfection of work. Its centrifugal wringer and extensive drying compartments include apparatus nowhere excelled. The wood finishings of the hospital buildings are in oak, save where stained or white painted wood is used to supplement the more domestic furnishings of private apartments.

The grounds of the Evanston Hospital have ample space for departmental additions; and, it is the hope of its management, that there shall, in the near future, be added a pavilion for contagious, and a building for private patients—such addi-

tions taking systematic place along lines westward of the Herman D. Cable Memorial Building and parallel thereto. When the time is opportune the buildings will be provided.

To remind the management of the hospital's need of a maternity retreat, there came one season, to a friendly niche in the hospitable structure, a busy home-making robin which mothered two broods. This, explains the superintendent with a smile, is the Evanston Hospital's first maternity ward. The hospital in 1899 opened a training school for nurses. It has now graduated twenty students, all pupils of the selected practitioners of Evanston lecturing at the hospital, and nearly all, at one time and another, members of the hospital nursing staff. In the school at present are thirteen pupils.

Such has been the evolution of the Evanston Hospital, and such, in the main, is its characteristic equipment and administration. But for those who will read this record in years to come, as well as for the prospective beneficiaries and benefactors of today, still further information about this unique place of refuge and health should be supplied. And, first, no applicant whose condition will not imperil the institution is turned from its doors. The children's ward is specially endowed by Mrs. Cable for the free use of crippled and sick children, and there are also private rooms for children. In the women's and men's ward a patient may pay as much as $1.00 a day or nothing. In the semi-private wards the charge is $10.00 a week; in the private rooms, $15 to $30 per week. It is the income from the private rooms—and more such rooms are needed—that helps supply the deficiency in hospital revenue caused, in part, by increasing charity work in the general wards. The hospital work of 1905 may be expressed as equivalent to 7,561 service days given its free and pay patients. Of this over 34 per cent was service to free patients. The expense of hospital maintenance in 1905 was $24,182.41, to defray which receipts from hospital service contributed $14,854.11. The paid-in endowment fund is $50,500. The only indebtedness was incurred for buildings, and this has been reduced to $5,010. To operate the hospital with its present mechanical equipment and staff, consisting of Superintendent, its efficient Assistant Superintendent, Miss Edith A. Bird, and fifteen nurses, there is needed, from voluntary subscribers (aside from material donations, income from receipts and endowment income—the latter amounting to $2,259) the sum of $7,500. A free bed in a ward may be perpetually endowed for $5,000; a bed and a room for $10,000. The hospital has eighteen free beds and fifteen rooms. A gift of $100 or more to the endowment fund makes the donor an endowment member, or a like sum to the general fund, a life member. A gift of $10 secures a year's membership in the Hospital Association. The hospital stands—including the maternity hospital and 100 feet of land recently purchased for $4,250— as a total investment of about $130,000. Since organization the hospital has cared for 1,082 patients, and, in 1905, 491 people contributed to the institution's support. From its start, the hospital in every form of favorable publicity has been upheld by the "Evanston Press" and the "Evanston Index."

The administrative policy of the hospital is, of course, non-sectarian. Its receipts from the Protestant churches, on Hospital Sunday, February 14, 1905, were $4,394.13. The City of Evanston appropriates yearly to the hospital the sum of $300. Free beds are maintained by the Presbyterian and Congregational churches, and by Northwestern University. The medical and surgical attendance is the voluntary and unpaid daily attendance of two competent Evanston practitioners, rotating in service with associates, composing a total volunteer staff of twelve. For consultation the resident staff calls upon the most eminent physicians and surgeons of Chicago. The ambulance of the Evanston Hospital, is modern, up-to-date, with full equipment, and is under the direction of the superintendent.

Official Administration.—The affairs of the Evanston Hospital are guided by its executive officers and thirty Directors, operating in twelve committees. In all co-operative effort certain people voluntarily take—or, are besought to take, and do take—posts high and posts humble, but all of laborious duty. Hundreds of public-spirited citizens united to raise the Evanston Hospital, and hundreds continue to unite to make it the most attractive and useful place of its scope and equipment in the United States. Among these hundreds there must be some, even more than others, whom circumstances have elected to service peculiarly long, difficult and efficient. Of this smaller band common consent would approve the mention of Frank M. Elliot, President; Julia M. Watson, Vice-President; and Mary Harris, Secretary, the association's executive officers for eleven consecutive years; of F. F. Peabody, Charles R. Webster, David R. Forgan, John R. Lindgren, Rollin A. Keyes, Irwin Rew, William G. Hoag, for their service in finance and investment committee work; of William B. Phillips, for care of the variegated plant life that beautifies the grounds; of Mrs. Charles J. Connell, Mrs. Julia M. Watson, Mrs. Virginia Creighton, P. R. Shumway and William B. Phillips for faithful and sympathetic service on the Executive Committee; of Dr. Sarah H. Brayton, for work contributed to the furnishing of the hospital; of the Visiting Committee, Mrs. James A. Patten, and of E. H. Buehler on the Medical Supply Committee.

List of Donors.—Donors to the funds of the Evanston Hospital have been many, and at least two sources of income, not directly personal, are an interesting illustration of how an enterprise of this character may profit by public movements animated by belief in its merits and faith in its future. These two sources are the fixed annual institution of Hospital Sunday, and the benefit entertainment conducted by clubs or by society at large.

Benefactions have been generally measured by the competency of benefactors. While many small contributions have been, and continue to be, as the breath of life of this institution, certain large ones, at critical periods, have fixed the lines of its growth and the scope of its mission.

The Endowment Fund of $50,500 was contributed by the following Endowment Members: I. F. Blackstone, William Liston Brown, Mrs. Alice A. Cable, Frank E. Lord, James A. Patten, Mrs. Lilly Parker Stacey, Thomas I. Stacey, Mrs. Julia M. Watson, Mrs. Hugh R. Wilson, and unnamed friends in sums of $5,000, 1,500 and $2,500, respectively.

The following Life Members have each contributed $100 or more to the hospital: M. C. Armour, Mrs. M. C. Armour, C. A. Barry, William H. Bartlett, Dr. M. C. Bragdon, Mrs. W. L. Brown, Mrs. Edwin F. Brown, Mrs. Rebecca N. Butler, Daniel H. Burnham, William Blanchard, William H. Bartlett, William L. Brown, Rev. Charles F. Bradley, E. H. Buehler, Mrs. W. B. Bogert, Charles T. Boynton, E. J. Buffington, Mrs. W. H. Burnet, Mrs. Alice A. Cable, David S. Cook, Mrs. Louise Condict, Mrs. T. S. Creighton, C. P. Coffin, J. J. Charles, Ira B. Cook, Charles B. Congdon, Charles B. Cleveland, William Deering,

Frank M. Elliot, John M. Ewen, Mrs. John M. Ewen, C. W. Elphicke, Mary Fabian, W. J. Fabian, D. R. Forgan, Frank P. Frazier, J. H. Garaghty, Mrs. P. W. Gates, P. W. Gates, Charles F. Grey, Clara Griswold, A. H. Gross, Mrs. A. H. Gross, Mrs. Virginia Hamline, Mrs. A. J. Harding, F. A. Hardy, Mrs. C. H. Hall, E. A. Hill, Mrs. Janet W. Hubbard, William G. Hoag, Mrs. T. C. Hoag, W. H. Jones, Marshall M. Kirkman, N. C. Knight, E. S. Lacey, Richard C. Lake, John R. Lindgren, Thomas Lord, George S. Lord, Frank E. Lord, David R. Lewis, P. L. McKinney, M. D., Roger B. McMullen, Mrs. James A. Patten, F. F. Peabody, F. S. Peabody, H. A. Pearsons, William B. Phillips, Kate C. Quinlan, Irwin Rew, George B. Reynolds, Fleming H. Revell, W. T. Rickards, Mrs. C. H. Rowe, George Scott, R. L. Scott, R. S. Scott, J. E. Scott, Rev. H. P. Smyth, J. S. Shaffer, George M. Sargent, George Watson Smith, Robert D. Sheppard, William E. Stockton, Philip R. Shumway, Mrs. Lucy D. Shuman, Mrs. T. I. Stacey, H. C. Tillinghast, Leroy D. Thoman, H. J. Wallingford, C. A. Ward, Mrs. J. F. Ward, Mrs. Julia M. Watson, Margaret S. Watson, Milton H. Wilson, Mrs. H. R. Wilson, John E. Wilder, Charles E. Yerkes, A. N. Young.

The total cash receipts to the Evanston Hospital since its organization have been $308,719.00. This sum has been expended as follows:

Buildings and land.............$128,086
Endowment Fund............... 50,500
Maintenance for twelve years..... 130,133

On May 15, 1906, Mrs. Julia M. Watson died suddenly, depriving this association of one of its most devoted and valuable members. Mrs. Watson had been identified with the hospital from the beginning, and during these sixteen years had been an officer and active worker in its behalf. The hospital was peculiarly near to her heart and the object of her special devotion.

At a special meeting of the Executive Committee of the Hospital Association the following memorial paper was adopted:

"The sudden and, to mortal vision, untimely death of Mrs. Julia M. Watson, on the 15th inst., has not merely deprived the Evanston Hospital Association of its honored Vice-President, and this committee of one of its most active and valuable members, but has taken away one who has, from the very beginning of the institution to the present time, been so closely identified with its growth and development, so constant in her unselfish devotion to its interests and so generous in its support, that she had become an essential part of its very existence.

"Her wise counsel, her faithful attention to the duties of the various committees upon which she has continuously and most efficiently served and her strong and inspiring personality, no less than her generous gifts have contributed in a very large degree to the splendid results that have been accomplished.

"To express a proper appreciation of the value of such services as she has rendered, and of the loss this committee and the association have sustained is impossible. We can only record our profound sense of sorrow in her loss. Its more adequate appreciation will not be expressed, but will be preserved in the grateful and affectionate remembrance which we shall ever cherish in our hearts.

> "FRANK M. ELLIOT, Chairman,
> WM. G HOAG,
> WM. B. PHILLIPS,
> PHILIP R. SHUMWAY,
> ROLLIN A. KEYES,
> IRWIN REW,
> MRS. T. S. CREIGHTON,
> MRS. C. J. CONNELL,
> MRS. JAMES A. PATTEN,
> MARY HARRIS, Secretary."

Present Officers.—The complete governing body of the Hospital Association for the year 1906, is as follows:

General Officers—Frank M. Elliot, President; Julia M. Watson, Vice-President; William G. Hoag, Treasurer; Mary Harris, Secretary; Annie L. Locke, Superintendent; Edith A. Bird, Assistant Superindent.

Executive Committee—Frank M. Elliot, Chairman; Mr. William B. Phillips, Mr. Philip R. Shumway, Mr. Rollin A. Keyes, Mr. Irwin Rew, Mr. William A. Hoag, Mrs. Julia M. Watson, Mrs. T. S. Creigh-

ton, Mrs. C. J. Connell, Mrs. James A. Patten.

Finance Committee—Mr. Irwin Rew, Chairman; Mr. Frank H. Armstrong, Mr. Charles R. Webster.

Investment Committee—Mr. William G. Hoag, Chairman; Mr. J. R. Lindgren, Mr. Rollin A. Keyes.

Auditing Committee—Mr. Philip R. Shumway, Chairman; Mr. W. B. Phillips, Mr. Clyde M. Carr.

House and Grounds Committee—Mr. William B. Phillips, Chairman; Mr. M. C. Armour, Mr. Frank P. Frazier.

Admission Committee—Mrs. C. J. Connell, Chairman; Mrs. James A. Patten, Miss A. L. Locke.

Supplies Committee—Mrs. Julia M Watson, Chairman; Mrs. W. J. Fabian, Mrs. Caroline S. Poppenhusen.

Medical Supplies Committee—Mr. Edward H. Buehler, Mr. R. J. Bassett.

Printing Committee—Mr. Philip R. Shumway, Chairman; Miss Mary Harris, Mr. William G. Hoag.

Training School Committee—Mrs. Julia M. Watson, Chairman; Mrs. Alice A. Cable, Miss Mary Harris.

Hospital Saturday and Sunday Committee—Mrs. T. S. Creighton, Chairman; Mrs. Parke E. Simmons, Mr. C. F. Marlow.

Visiting and Delicacies Committee—Mrs. James A. Patten, Chairman; Mrs. W. S. Powers, Mrs. Irwin Rew, Mrs. A. R. Barnes, Mrs. E. J. Buffington, Mrs. M. A. Mead, Mrs. H. H. Hoyt, Mrs. John C. Spry, Mrs. T. M. Holgate, Mrs. J. H. Garaghty, Mrs. W. H. Warren, Mrs. James W. Howell, Mrs. Philip R. Shumway.

Directors.—Term Expires 1906—Mr. William B. Bogert, Prof. J. H. Gray, Mr. William B. Phillips, Mrs. W. L. Brown, Mr. Rollin A. Keyes, Mrs. William Holabird, Mrs. James A. Patten, Mr. Frank M. Elliot, Mr. E. H. Buehler, Mr. Clyde M. Carr.

Term Expires 1907—Mrs. H. D. Cable, Mr. Philip R. Shumway, Mrs. C. S. Poppenhusen, Mrs. John C. Spry, Mrs. T. S. Creighton, Mr. M. C. Armour, Mr. Irwin Rew, Mrs. E. J. Buffington, Mr. R. L. Scott, Mr. Charles F. Marlow.

Term Expires 1908—Mr. F. P. Frazier, Mr. F. F. Peabody, Mr. C. R. Webster, Mr. D. R. Forgan, Mr. Robert J. Bassett, Mrs. Julia M. Watson, Mrs. C. J. Connell, Mrs. Lucy J. Rowe, Mr. William G. Hoag, Mr. Frank H. Armstrong.

Medical Staff.—E. H. Webster, M. D.; W. A. Phillips, M. D.; William R. Parkes, M. D.; P. D. Harding, M. D.; Sarah H. Brayton, M. D.; Frank C. Dakin, M. D.; M. C. Bragdon, M. D.; E. E. Shutterly, M. D.; Mary F. McCrillis, M. D.; Dwight Clark, M D.; B. C. Stolp, M. D.

Consulting Staff.—Charles Adams, M. D.; C. S. Bigelow, D. D. S.; Frank Billings, M. D.; Arthur R. Edwards, M. D.; Charles G. Fuller, M. D.; D. W. Graham, M. D.; Fernand Henrotin, M. D.; Hugh T. Patrick, M. D.; John Ridlon, M. D.; Will Walter, M. D.; W. S. Alexander, Pathologist.

CHAPTER XXX.

LOCAL MUSICAL ORGANIZATIONS
(By PROFESSOR SAIDEE KNOWLAND COE)

Evanston as it Existed in 1856—Primeval Church Music—War Songs—A Commencement Concert—The Hutchinson Family—Jules Lumbard—O. H. Merwin Becomes A Choir Leader—Other Notable Musicians—Evanston's First Musical Club—Some Famous Teachers and Performers—Thomas Concert Class Organized—Mrs. Edward Wyman—Musical Department of Evanston Woman's Club —Women's Clubs as a Factor in Musical Training—Evanston Musical Club— Maennerchor Organized — Programs — Officers.

Evanston has become such an acknowledged musical as well as literary center, that the tracing of the steps leading up to its present high state of development affords unusual interest. Let us close our eyes and picture to ourselves the town in 1856. It consisted, as a reliable authority informs us, of a few houses: the University represented by the old Academy building, which then stood on the corner of Davis Street and Hinman Avenue; the Northwestern Women's College, further south on Chicago Avenue; the Methodist Church, a wooden building which everybody attended; and a general store and postoffice. At this stage it is natural that musical interest should have centered around the music in the church. This, at first, consisted of sing-

ing by the congregation of old familiar hymns. A little later a choir was formed of the young people of the church, led first by Mr. Hart P. Danks, who afterwards became well known as a composer of songs and church music. Mrs. Mary Willard was a member of this choir, which sang not only the hymns and old-fashioned anthems for the church service, but was always on hand for prayer meetings, lectures, sociables and even sleigh-rides and picnics. Mr. Danks was succeeded as choir-leader by Mr. John A. Pearsons. In the war meetings, held in the old University chapel, the choir thrilled its hearers with its rendering of patriotic songs.

The first brass band in the town was organized in 1857, and was led by Frank Steel, an Evanston boy, who afterwards achieved some reputation as bandmaster in a New York regiment during the war. About this time Mr. J. B. Merwin—a distant relative of Mr. O. H. Merwin, whose notable work for music in Evanston will be mentioned later on—succeeded in stirring up considerable musical enthusiasm among the young people. Under his direction they gave one or two sacred cantatas, which were greatly enjoyed. At commencement time a concert was always given in the Methodist Church by the music teacher and pupils of the Women's College. This was the most pretentious musical event of the year for the town. From time to time various musicians from outside gave concerts in Evanston. Among these are remembered the Hutchinson Family and Jules Lumbard, whose singing was very popular during the war.

In 1869 Mr. O. H. Merwin came to Evanston and was made director of the choir, a position he held for thirteen years, until 1882. The period of Mr. Merwin's activity in this work may be said to mark the musical transition between the Evanston of the past and the Evanston of the present. During his regime the choir, which was made up from the young people of the church and students of the University, numbered from forty to seventy members. Among the names we find many familiar ones. Miss Ella Prindle, now Mrs. Amos W. Patten, was leading soprano for eight or ten years; Mrs. Frank P. Crandon and Mrs. H. F. Fisk occupied front seats in the soprano row, while Professor James Taft Hatfield reinforced the tenors. Mr. and Mrs. John B. Kirk, Miss Lindgren (now Mrs. Nels Simonsen), Mr. and Mrs. Inglehart, Miss Nellie Hurd (now Mrs. Comstock), the Raymond brothers, Mr. Scott Matthews, Miss Pomeroy, and many others whose names are well known to old Evanstonians, mingled their voices in Mr. Merwin's choir. This organization gave frequent entertainments for the benefit of the church, on which occasion the choir was reinforced by all the singers in the town. In the spring of 1870 a concert was given in which Miss Annie Louise Cary took the leading part. The following year "The Messiah" was produced with Myron Whitney as basso. In 1882 Mr. Merwin was succeeded by Mr. Locke, director of the Music Department of the University.

The Evanston Amateur Musical Club.— The first important musical club in Evanston was the Evanston Amateur Musical Club,

a musical and social organization which flourished for five years—from 1882 to 1887. Its founder and presiding genius was Miss Nina G. Lunt, to whose perseverance and untiring energy the success of the enterprise was due. She started the club with fourteen young amateur musicians as a nucleus. The membership grew with such rapidity that it comprised large active, associate and honorary lists. The last included the names of many prominent Chicago musicians, notably Mrs. Regina Watson (who was always a great source of inspiration and help to the club), Miss Fannie Root, Miss Amy Fay, Mr. Carl Wolfsohn, Mr. Fred W. Root, Mr. Emil Liebling and others. For two years fortnightly afternoon musicals were given during the season at the homes of the members. The programs were furnished largely by the active members. Frequent evening recitals by well known artists added much to the interest of the association. It was finally deemed best to do away with the afternoon meetings and have the entertainments all given in the evening, the programs to be furnished by artists of established reputation. At the same time the term "amateur" was dropped, the name of the club appearing as the Evanston Musical Club. The list of artists who appeared in recitals before this club is a notable one. It includes Seeboeck, Amy Fay, Carl Wolfsohn, Emil Liebling, Frank Root, Mrs. Walter Wyman, Mme. Carreno, Sherwood, Annie Rommeiss, Mrs. May Phoenix Cameron, Mme. Hopekirk, Mme. Trebelli, Jacobsohn, Musin, Fannie Bloomfield Zeisler, The Mendelssohn Quintette Club of Boston, Rummel, Lilli Lehman and others. There were also Chamber Concerts given under the direction of Mr. William Lewis.

Church Music.—With the growth of Evanston, churches of various denominations have sprung up and their choirs have added no little to the musical development of the town. The Congregational Church choir has become noted as a training-ground for some of our best known concert singers. Among them are Mr. Francis Fisher Powers, Mrs. Minnie Fish Griffin and Mrs. Minnie D. Methot, who has recently gone into opera. The following excerpt is taken from an interesting article on "Church Music" by Mr. Frank M. Elliot, in which he sketches the musical history of the Evanston Congregational Church:

"One of the choirs long to be remembered was, in 1875 and 1876, known as the Powers Quartet, composed of Miss Emily Powers, Miss Lottie Powers (now Mrs. Ullman), Mr. Francis Fisher Powers and Mr. Fred Powers. They were all musical and their singing was always enjoyed.

"In 1881, 1882 and 1883 the music was under the direction of Mr. George H. Iott. This was the first of our paid choirs. Mr. Iott entered upon his duties with enthusiasm, and unquestionably did more to educate our people in good sacred music than anyone before or since. His selections were always of a high order of merit. His exactness with the musicians, his fine appreciation of music, together with the superb quality of his voice, gave a rendering that was always satisfactory and helpful to his listeners. The Te Deum became one of the most enjoyable of the selections given. It was his custom to give a Te Deum at every morning service, and this feature became so characteristic that his choir was known ever after as the 'Te Deum choir.'

"In 1890, 1891 and 1892, the choir composed of Miss Grace E. Jones, Miss Esther A. Pitkin, Mr. Henry Taylor, Jr., and Mr. J. P. McGrath, gave an excellent rendering of all their music. They were together so long that they became accustomed to each other's singing. Their ensemble work was, perhaps, as good as that of any choir we have had. By far the best choir we ever had was composed of Mrs. Minnie Fish Griffin, Miss Alice Hayes, Mr. Johnston and Mr. William Richards. Unfortunately this choir was together only three months. Their voices were evenly balanced, and all were experienced and artistic singers, so that every selection that they undertook was sure of proper interpretation.

"There have been other excellent choirs, but, as a rule, one or more of the voices were defective. The singers who have endeared themselves to our people—and who will always be regarded with the highest esteem, both for their musical ability and for their sincerity and devotion to their work while in the choir—are Miss Owens, Miss Carpenter, Mrs. Bartlett, Mrs. Goetz, Mrs. Brewer, Mrs. Lamphere, Mrs. Minnie D. Methot, Mrs. Stella Lawrence Naramore, Mrs. Grace Jones Taylor, Mrs. Esther Pitkin-Bartlett, Mrs. Jennie Sugg Carson, Mrs. Minnie Fish Griffin, Miss Hayes, Miss Sohlberg, Miss Kelley, Mr. George H. Iott, Mr. Homer F. Stone, Mr. James F. Bird, Mr. Charles A. Dew, Mr. Henry Taylor, Jr., Mr. J. P. McGrath, Mr. William Richards, Mr. James F. Johnston and Mr. L. F. Brown.

"The organists, who, by their association with this church, have become a part of its history, are J. W. Ludlam, Clarkson Reynolds Larabee, Arthur Cutler, Prof. W. S. B. Mathews, Prof. Oscar Mayo, Miss Mollie Ludlam, Miss Lydia S. Harris, R. H. L. Watson, L. P. Hoyt, H. D. Atchison, Hubert Oldham, W. W. Graves, A. F. McCarrell, John A. West, Edwin Barnes, Irving Proctor, John Mills Mayhew and Scott Wheeler."

In recent years the most marked feature of the music of the Congregational Church has been the artistic singing of Mrs. Sanger Steele.

St. Mark's (Episcopal) Church has a vested choir, which furnishes the music for the regular service throughout the year and in addition, usually performs the St. Cecilia Mass at Easter.

In June, 1897, a series of free organ recitals was inaugurated in the Presbyterian Church. These were continued through four seasons. The expenses were borne by private citizens who contributed each year in response to an appeal from the pastor, Dr. Boyd. The organists who furnished the programs were Miss Tina Mae Haines, organist of the church, to whom the credit of the enterprise is largely due, Scott Wheeler, Arthur Dunham, James Watson, A. F. McCarrell, Francis Moore, Ada Williams, Francis Hemington, William Zeuch and Clarence Dickinson. During the summer of 1899 the entire group of six recitals was given by Miss Haines, assisted by prominent vocalists. Among the soloists who assisted during the four seasons the most notable are George Hamlin, Charles W. Clark, Jennie Osborne, Helen Buckley and Holmes Cowper. One of the most notable concerts ever given in the church was the Farewell Concert given for Miss Haines before her departure for a year's study in Paris. The program was given by Miss Haines, Harrison Wild, Charles W. Clark, Leon Marx and Mrs. Edwin Lapham.

During the summer of 1904-5, the summer concerts were resumed and were so successful that a series will be given the coming summer, 1905-6. The programs are given by Miss Haines, with the assistance of prominent soloists. The most important concert ever given in the church was by the organist, Guilmant, in October, 1904. Miss Greta Masson assisted on this program, with soprano solos. In the summer

of 1901 a series of organ concerts was given in the First Methodist church by Professor P. C. Lutkin, Miss Mary Porter Pratt, Miss Tina Mae Haines, Mr. William E. Zeuch and Mr. A. F. McCarrell. After the installation of the new organ especially noteworthy recitals were given with the following programs:

Toccata and Fugue, D minor...................Bach
          Prof. P. C. Lutkin
Anthem—"Praise the Lord"..............A. Randegger
  (a) Chorus—"Sing unto God"..........G. F. Handel
  (b) "La Cygne" (The Swan)..........C. Saint-Saens
  (c) Nuptial March......................A. Guilmant
          Mr. Clarence Eddy
Quartette—"Thou Shalt Bring Them In"...A. S. Sullivan
          Quartette
Allegro Cantabile. From the fifth Organ Symphony
Toccata ....C. M. Widor
Lamentation, op. 45.....................A. Guilmant
          Mr. Eddy
Soprano Solo—"I will Extol Thee, O Lord".......Costa
          Miss Ridgeley
Barcarolle ....E. H. Lamare
March and Chorus from Tannhauser............Wagner
          Mr. Eddy

The following program was given by Mr. Frederick Archer on February 28, 1901:

Allegro Moderato from Organ Symphony....W. Faulkes
  (a) Pastorale ....Jorgan
  (a) Scherzo ....Gigout
Chorale in B minor.....................Caesar Franck
  (a) Chanson sans Paroles..............E. H. Lamare
  (b) Humoritisque ....J. Callaerts
Toccata in F..........................Claussman
Poeme Symphonique—"Rouet d' Omphale"....St. Saens
Theme and Variations.....................Schubert
Finale from Octette for strings...........Mendelssohn
Serenade ....Molique
Overture—"Love's Triumph"..............W. V. Wallace

During the summer of 1902 a series of organ recitals was given in the Presbyterian and First Methodist churches, alternately, by Mr. Clarence Dickinson, assisted by prominent vocalists. Among the noteworthy vocalists who have been members of the choir are Mr. Frank Hannah, Jenny Osborn Hannah, Mrs. Furbeck, Minnie Fish Griffin and Mr. Frank Webster. The present organist (1905) of the church, Miss Katherine Howard, has carried on with much success monthly musical vesper services during the winter and a series of organ concerts during the summer.

The Thomas Concert Class.—The Thomas Concert Class was started in October, 1896, and has had nine thoroughly success-'ful years. The membership is limited to subscribers to the Thomas Orchestra Concerts. Mrs. Edward T. Wyman and Miss Cora Cassard, now Mrs. Toogood, were the starters of the enterprise, going about among their musical friends to stir up an interest in the new venture. They soon enlisted the co-operation of Mrs. C. L. Woodyatt, Mrs. Curtis H. Remy and Mrs. Charles G. Fuller, and to the energy and devotion of these five ladies the Class owes its launching into a most successful career. The purpose has been, primarily, the study in advance of the numbers announced on the programs of the orchestral concerts. Since its organization, the Class has regularly held meetings on the day preceding each concert, when members have played and analyzed the program numbers of the following day. The value of this work to the members can hardly be over estimated. It has aroused and stimulated an interest in the greatest works of orchestral composition, while the study necessary for analyzing and playing these masterpieces has amounted to more than an ordinary course of music study. The devotion and perseverance shown by the ladies in preparing and presenting these programs, through nine consecutive seasons, are worthy of emulation.

In addition to the direct study of the Thomas programs, courses in Theory of Music have been given before the Class by Professor P. C. Lutkin and, through the season of 1900, a course in History of Music, outlined by Mrs. Coe, was finally carried out by the members. Theodore Thomas, during his life, always took a lively interest in the work of the Class, and Mrs. Thomas has addressed the members on several occasions. Artists' recitals, given under the auspices of the Class, have included the Brahms Piano Recital by Mr. Arthur Whiting and a program for the wood-wind instruments, besides a Histori-

cal Chamber Music Recital given by members of the Chicago Orchestra.

The Presidents of the Thomas Concert Class have been: Mrs. Curtis H. Remy, Mrs. Charles G. Fuller, Mrs. Frank M. Elliot, Mrs. John R. Lindgren, Mrs. H. D. Cable and Mrs. Newell C. Knight, each of whom has been responsible, in no small degree, for the uniform success which has attended the work of this organization. Mrs. C. L. Woodyatt has always been the presiding genius to whom, more than to any other individual, is due the harmony which has prevailed among the members and the spirit of helpfulness which has pervaded each meeting. The analytical work of Mrs. Woodyatt and Miss Tina M. Haines is especially worthy of mention, as well as the valuable work done in piano illustrations by Mrs. William Vance, Mrs. George Lord, Mrs. Knight, Mrs. Goldschmidt, Mrs. John H. Gray, Mrs. John R. Lindgren, Mrs. Underwood, Mrs. Hypes and Mrs. Seymour. The following resume, prepared by Mrs. Woodyatt at the close of the fifth year, gives a comprehensive idea of the work accomplished:

"The Thomas Concert Class, being an original venture without precedent or example, has felt its way along from its beginning in 1896, evolving year by year its own method of procedure. The musical numbers assigned by Mr. Thomas for our study do not afford much consecutive relation from week to week. For this reason it was recognized, at the outstart, that continuity and cohesion could only be secured by giving a portion of the time each morning to systematized theoretical study. With so large a membership, and one including so many grades of musical experience, this has been perhaps the most difficult question we have had to meet. Professional instruction can seldom be adapted to such mixed requirements, and, by the close of the fourth year, we had pretty well exhausted the possibilities along this line, without entering upon study of too technical a nature to be of value to the class as a whole. At the same time, it became evident that, with most of us, a mass of detached ideas and knowledge had been accumulating which would bear crystallizing into symmetrical form.

"With these facts in mind the list of topics was drawn up, which has formed the basis of the morning papers for the year just closing. This course, it was hoped, would form a clear outline of the history of the development of music. I am sure that I voice the opinion of the Class in saying, that this hope has been justified, and that the papers of this series have told— and told well—the story of music's growth from the primitive utterance of emotion in the savage, down through the centuries, until it has become the art we know to-day. The first paper was ably given by Mrs. Coe, to whose interest and experience we are indebted for the arrangement of the list of subjects. A few weeks later, in November, we had the pleasure of listening to a beautiful essay upon the period of the Troubadours, generously given to us by Miss Lunt. In January and in March important topics of the course were treated by Professor Lutkin, whose unfailing readiness to respond when occasions call for his assistance, has been of immeasurable value to us throughout our five years' experience. The second of these lectures—I refer to the one upon the 'Representative German Composers of the 19th Century,' in which he summarized and contrasted the influence of the great masters upon the development of the art—was the product of a comprehensive and keenly discriminating mind. The last paper of the course was given by Mrs. Theodore Thomas in the form of a resume of musical production in this country, particularly during Colonial and Revolutionary times. The remaining twelve papers were written and read by members of the Class. To the gifted women who have loyally and skillfully carried this course through without a single interruption, we cannot too warmly express our gratitude and appreciation, sentiments not unmixed with pride.

"Taking the courses collectively, they represent an immense amount of faithful research and study. The cream of all this reading has been placed before us from week to week, and has afforded those in regular attendance such an understanding of the general subject as could have been obtained only by the devotion of a large amount of time to the exclusive study of Musical History, while the variety afforded by the methods of the different essayists has added great interest and unfailing charm. To those who have been with the class from the first, a glance at what has been accomplished during the five years cannot fail to afford deep satisfaction. In 1896, when, through the enthusiasm and personal effort of Mrs. Edward Wyman, the little band was marshalled, in closing her remarks at the introductory meeting, I remember that she said, 'of course we have high hopes.' A group of women holding subscriptions to the concerts of one of the greatest orchestras the world has ever known, unite into a class with the purpose of becoming better fitted to appreciate this beautiful music. With this single aim they meet, each gladly giving to the others whatever she can perform, whether of artistic effort or of the silent inspiration of the listener. These are the simple conditions. But which of us can measure the growth in herself resulting from the interchange? —and, in the community in which we are a part, it is said that our influence is wide; that we occupy a position of responsibility.

May we continue to realize our supreme privilege of listening to the greatest music of the centuries under the leadership of the greatest of living conductors. May we continue to hold to the 'high hopes' with which we began, always mindful that such measure of success as has been ours, has been in exact ratio to our obedience to the divine law which orders all of Giving and Receiving."

During the past three years, in addition to the study of the Thomas programs, the subject of chamber music has been taken up under the direction of Professor Harold Knapp.

Music Department of the Evanston Woman's Club.—In 1897 it was decided to add a Music Department to the other thriving departments of the Evanston Woman's Club. Mrs. H. D. Cable was made chairman and Mrs. Coe was engaged, during the first season, to give a series of illustrated lectures on musical topics. The second season's work consisted of miscellaneous programs. In 1899 Mrs. Coe was made Musical Director of the department, a position which she held for three years. During that period she planned in detail all of the work of the department, personally superintending the presentation of each program. Through the season, 1899-1900, a unique course was carried out, devoted exclusively to the compositions of women. Several of the composers themselves took a lively interest in the work, and letters of encouragement and appreciation were received from Mrs. H. H. A. Beach and Cecile Chaminade.

The following programs were given:

JANUARY 9, 1900.

Lecture— "Women Composers"......Mrs. Crosby Adams
Vocal Illustrations....................Miss Una Howell
PROGRAM

Where Go The Boats?......}
The Swing. ....}...........Eleanor Smith
Christmas Song............}
Pleading.................}
Welcome.................}........Marguerite Melville
Hope.................}

Ghosts.............. ......}
Night...................... }..Margaret Ruthven Lang
Lydia...................... }
"Look out, O Love"............Clara Kathleen Rogers
The Spring Has Come.....}
To Mary..................}.....Maude Valerie White
The Throstle.............}

TUESDAY, FEBRUARY 13, 10 A. M.

Clara Schumann

Paper................................Mrs. W. M. Green
Piano—Scherzo................Miss Elizabeth Raymond
Two Songs........................ .....Mi. Whitehead
Piano—Andante and Allegro.......Miss Grace Erickson

Fanny Mendelssohn

Paper................................Mr. T. B. Dyche
Piano—Caprices...................Miss Edna Flesheim
Two Songs........................Miss Florence Stevens

MARCH 13, 1900.

Jessie L. Gaynor

Sketch of Work in Composition......... .Mrs. Gaynor
Selections from "Songs from the Child World"...Gaynor
L'Enfant.
If I Were a Bee
Hush-a-Bye, Baby Dear.
If I Knew.
The Wind Went Wooing the Rose.
Because She Kissed it.
A Valentine.
Discontented Duckling.
Slumber Boat.
Japanese Doll.
Fire Flies.
Jerushy.
Spring Song.
Accompanist, Mr. F. F. Beale.

APRIL 10, 1900.

Mrs. H. H. A. Beach

Paper............................Mrs. T. P. Stanwood
Anita.....................}..Miss Louise E. Whitehead
Ecstasy...................}
Piano, "Fireflies".................Miss Mabel Dunn
Dearie........................ ....}
Scottish Cradle Song..............} Miss Alta Miller
Oh, Were My Love You Lilac Fair.}
Personal Letter to the Club................Mrs. Beach
Read by Mrs. George A. Coe
Forgotten..................Miss Louise E. Whitehead
Piano—"Phantoms"..................Miss Grace Erickson
Wouldn't That be Queer?.}
The Year's at the Spring..}........Miss Alta Miller
Piano and Violin, Sonata, op. 34, Allegro Moderato
Miss Edna Eversz and Mr. W. G. Logan

MAY 22, 1900.

Cecile Chaminade

Short Sketches of Life and Work...Mrs. George A. Coe
Deus Pastorale...........}
Scarf Dance ....}........Mrs. Irene Stevens
C lierbe.................}
Vocal—Sombrero...................Mr. Alfred D. Shaw
The Flatterer..................Mrs. W. H. Knapp
Bourree, B. minor.........}
Pierrette.................}........Miss E na Eversz
Vocal—"Veins, Mon Bien Aime"...............
..................Miss Winifred Nightingale
Two Pianos "Le Soir"........Mrs. John R. Lindgren
"Le Matin"...Miss Harriet Engle Brown
Vocal—O's reverte.......... }... Mr. Alfred D. Shaw
( ) Villkomen...}
Concert Study "Autumn".......Miss Edna Flesheim
Vocal—"Ritournelle"...........Miss Winifred Nightingale
Courtstruck..................Miss Carrie Holbrook
Orchestral Accompaniment on Second Piano. Mrs.
George A. Coe.

Through the season of 1900-1901 the following programs were given, devoted to American composers:

JANUARY 8, 1901.

Paper......................Mrs. Chancellor Jenks, Jr.
William Mason
Piano—Amitie pour Amitie.) ......Miss Grace Erickson
  Improvisation.......)
John Knowles Paine
Vocal—The Matin Song....)
  I Wore Your Roses) ....Miss Alta Miller
Piano- Nocturne, op. 45......Miss Elizabeth Raymond
Dudley Buck
Vocal- Spring's Awakening...Miss Louise E. Whitehead
Piano— By the Brookside, op. 8, No. 2.Miss Mabel Dunn
Vocal— Sunset................................
  Where Did You Come From,
    Baby Dear................)
  When the Heart is Young.) ..Miss Alta Miller
Salve Regina.........................Miss Whitehead
George Whitfield Chadwick
Vocal—The Danza.................. (....Miss Miller
  Oh, Let Night Speak to Me. (
Piano—Irish Melody...............) ....Miss Dunn
  Scherzino, op. 7, No. 3...)
He Loves Me....................
Allah............................) ...Miss Whitehead
Sings the Nightingale to the Rose..)

FEBRUARY 12, 1902.

Suite Characteristique...................Arne Oldberg
Au Revoir.................)
White (aps............... |
Revery................... | ....Mr. Oldberg
Song to the Moon......... |
Le retour...............)
"The Child and His Music." An Illustrated Talk....
..............................Mr. W. H. Neidlinger

MARCH 12, 1901.

Illustrated lecture on 'The National Music of America."
  Mr. Louis C. Elson, Professor of Musical Theory and
  Lecturer on the Orchestra and on Musical History
  in the New England Conservatory of Music, Boston,
  Mass.

APRIL 9, 1901.

Arthur W. Foote
Paper.........................Mrs. William A. Dyche
Piano—Suite, D. minor.....)
  Prelude and Fugue. } ..Mrs. William L. Vance
  Romance..........)
  Capriccio...........)
Vocal—Through the Long Days)
  and Years.............) Miss Margaret Easter
  On the Way to Kew.....)
Piano—Selections from Poems (after Omar Khay-
  yam............ ....Mrs. George A. Coe
Vocal Memoirm..........)
I'm Wearing Awa........ (.............Miss Easter
Sweetheart. ....)
Piano and Violin—Sonata, G minor.
  Allegro Appassionata.
  Alla Siciliano.
  Adagio.
  Allegro Molto.
  Miss Elizabeth Raymond and Mr. Lewis Blackman

MAY 28, 1901.

Edward A. MacDowell
Short Talk on the Composer with selections from
  Sea Pieces ....Mrs. George A. Coe
Piano The Witches' Dance........Miss Mabel Dunn
The Eagle....................)
Improvisation.............. (,Mrs. William L. Vance
Poem.....................)
March Wind...............) .....Miss Grace Erickson
Songs to be selected........Miss Annie Louise Daniels
Czardas.........................Mrs. William L. Vance

In view of the activity along musical lines throughout the various organizations of women, it is a matter of especial interest to note the following opinion expressed in a private letter by the eminent American composer, Mr. Arthur Foote, of Boston:

"From circumstances, I am more acquainted with the work done by those clubs than most people right here, and I do not hesitate to give my belief that the most efficient factor for music in America now is just that done by those clubs, chiefly, naturally, in the Middle West, although there has been a surprising and healthful growth in the same direction about here; but, run as they are, generally by levelheaded and truly musical people, their effect, I firmly believe, will be more than either of us can imagine in the next twenty years."

During the season of 1901-1902 the Music Section of the Evanston Woman's Club, under the direction of Mrs. Coe, carried out the following Historical and Analytical Course:

JANUARY 14, 1902.

Lecture Recital—"Primitive Music"..................
..............................Mrs. George A. Coe
Vocal Illustrations..........Miss Louise Whitehead
The Development from Crude Beginnings among the
  Savages to the Attempts of the Early Christians.
Beginnings of Folk Music.
Development of the Scale.
The Music of the Chinese, Japanese, and Hindoos.
MUSICAL ILLUSTRATIONS.
Japanese and Hindoo Songs
Negro Folk Songs
The Lady Picking Mulberries..........Edgar S. Kelley
  (Written on Chinese scale.)
Suite for Piano—"Miniatures in Chinese Colors"....
..............................Lillian Statson Miller
Movement from Chinese Suite for Orchestra........
..............................Edgar S. Kelley

JANUARY 28, 1902.

Lecture Recital—"Music of the American Indians"....
..............................Mrs. George A. Coe
Vocal Illustrations........Miss Mary Florence Steve
Indian Legends, Superstitions and Sense of Musical
  Rhythm.
Scalping Songs, Prayers, Cradle Songs.
Songs of Joy and Sorrow.

FEBRUARY 11, 1902.

MUSIC OF THE GREEKS.
The Greek Drama.............Mrs. Doremus A. Hayes
The Greek Music System........Mrs. George A. Coe
Musical Illustrations................Mr. Arthur Burton

FEBRUARY 25, 1902.

Development of Church Music (from Ambrose and
  Gregory to beginning of the Netherland School).
Music in the Bible.
Musical Attempts of the Early Christians.

Paper.......................Mrs. C. D. B. Howell
Musical Analysis, including Development of Notation..
....Mrs. Coe
Vocal Illustrations of Ambrosian and Gregorian Chants
and Hebrew Hymns.............Mrs. H. W. Knapp

MARCH 11, 1902.

Lecture Recital—"History of Folk Music"..............
.........................Mrs. Joseph W. Hines
Folk Songs of Scandinavia.
Russian and Slavic Songs.

MARCH 25, 1902.

"EPOCH OF THE NETHERLANDERS"
Papers by Mrs. E. L. Harpham and Miss Elizabeth P.
Clarke.
Musical Illustrations by Vocal Quartette under the
direction of Miss Tina Mae Haines.

APRIL 8, 1902.

THE OPERA.
Italy—Peri to Verdi.
France—Beaujoyeux to Gounod.
Germany—Kaiser to Wagner.
England—Purcell to Handel.
Paper........................Mrs. Homer H. Kingsley
Vocal Illustrations.....Mr. A. D. Shaw and Mrs. Smith
Piano Numbers......Miss Grace Ericson, Miss Marion
Titus and Miss Hoff.

APRIL 22, 1902.

Analytical Lecture on Wagner's "Siegfried," with illustrations from the score.........Mrs. George A. Coe

MAY 13, 1902.

THE ORATORIO.
Papers.
Oratorio in Italy.................Mrs. W. A. Illsley
Oratorio in Germany.......Mrs. E. W. Goldschmidt
Oratorio in England.............Miss Mary B. Lindsay
Vocal Illustrations................Mr. Conrad Kimball
Piano Illustrations
........Mrs. Goldschmidt and Mrs. W. F. Hypes

MAY 27, 1902.

Lecture Recital—"Spanish Folk Music"..............
.................Senora Blanca de Freyre Tibbits

Work of Woman's Club.—The following resume of the three season's work was
prepared by Miss Tina Mae Haines:

"An inquiry into the cause of the steady
growth of general culture among an industrial busy people would reveal the presence of a multitude of important forces,
all working toward a broader and deeper
knowledge of the arts and sciences. One
of these important forces is the universal
spirit of investigation which continually
asks to know why things are as they are;
that spirit which insists upon dissecting
the component parts of everything—which
probes into the very mind and heart of
every one who has given a part of his best
self to the world—the spirit which seeks to
uncover the mysteries of creative power
itself.

"Music, the most elusive of all the arts,
has not escaped this microscopic examination. It is only within recent years, however, that the general public has shown any
perceptible desire to really understand the
science of music. It has been content to
have its ears tickled and its feet inspired,
to declare one's self fond of music meant
simply that one was fond of the 'tune.'
The number of such is steadily diminishing,
and moreover the time is rapidly passing,
when a musician, who knows nothing but
his music, can pass muster.

"The better class of conservatories, the
establishment of orchestras and organizations for the analytical study of orchestral
literature, the appearance on the scenes of
competent musical lecturers, and the exertions of our impressarios to appeal to the
cultivated musical palate, are all large factors in contributing to a more intelligent
comprehension of music as an art, and not
merely as a form of entertainment. Within the past few years these forces have received powerful impetus from the various women's clubs, many of which have incorporated in their courses of study departments of music.

"The Woman's Club of Evanston is a
notable example. It has just completed
the third year of a splendidly-conceived
and well carried out course of study. The
club showed excellent judgment in engaging Mrs. George Coe for the musical director, and the wisdom of the selection has long
since been proved by the steady growth of
the department and the increasing interest
in the examination of the course of study
shows the extensive scope of the work undertaken. During the season of 1899 and
1900 the general subject was, 'Woman in
Composition, and special features were an
illustrated lecture talk by Mrs. Jessie Gay-

nor of 'Methods of Work in Composition.' The subject of the study course, during the season of 1900 and 1901, was 'American Composers.' Among other interesting things, Mr. Louis C. Elson, of Boston, gave an illustrated lecture on 'The National Music of America,' and Mr. W. H. Neidlinger gave a talk on 'Children's Songs.'

"The series running through the season just closed has been devoted to the study of the development of music from its earliest beginnings. Many well-known soloists have furnished illustrations for the various programs. Some of the papers were prepared by members of the club, and Mrs. Coe herself, besides contributing a number of lectures and papers, has added to every program from her ample store of information.

"Mrs. Coe, in preparing her lectures, has added to her wide experience as a teacher and her thorough knowledge of the general history of music, a detailed study of the development of music among all nationalities, sparing no pains to secure rare and authentic material; and those who have heard these lectures, fully realize the careful selection of interesting matter, the absence of superfluous details and the artistic and logical arrangement of the information so carefully gleaned. Mrs. Coe should have the satisfaction of feeling that, in addition to interesting and entertaining her auditors, she is wielding an educational influence of immeasurable value and stimulating a desire for a more sincere study of the science of music."

During the season of 1902-1903, a series of lecture recitals was given before the club by Madam de Rooele Rice. During 1903-1904 a series of miscellaneous programs was given, including the first public performance of the "Melodrama of Hiawatha" for speaking voice and piano by Saidee Knowland Coe, given with the composer

at the piano and Miss Mae Neal, reader. A series of interesting and instructive lecture-recitals has been given the past season by Miss Tina Mae Haines, who is to furnish another course next winter.

The Evanston Musical Club.—One great cause of encouragement in the musical development of America is the broadening of general education to include some knowledge of the fine arts, notably music, and a corresponding enlargement of musical training to include culture along literary and scientific lines. It follows, therefore, that in towns where are situated colleges or universities of importance, one may, at the present time, as confidently expect to become acquainted with some at least of the masterpieces of music as with the great works of literature.

That the Evanston Musical Club has done real musical culture work no one can doubt who has watched its progress during the last few years and noted the number of new, as well as standard, works that have been brought to the attention of many persons who, perhaps otherwise, would never have heard them. One cause for congratulation in the work of the club is that the audiences are not made up solely of people sated with musical opportunities. The concerts prove a musical feast for many students and others whose opportunities for hearing great choral works have been very limited.

The following "Retrospective," published by officers of the club, gives a history of its start and first four seasons' work:

"In 1894 a Mænnerchor of twenty voices was organized in the Country Club, under the direction of Professor P. C. Lutkin, and gave its first concert at the club house on November 30th, with Max Bendix violinist, and Miss Fanchon Thompson, contralto, as soloist. The same program was repeated at the Congregational church and was the first public performance of the Evanston Musical Club. In the meantime, a ladies' auxiliary chorus was formed, which also gave a concert at the Country Club. On February 19, 1895, the two organizations united in a public performance at the Congregational church, with Francis Walker, baritone, and Frederick Archer, organist, as soloists. On May 7th an oratorio was attempted, and Sullivan's "Prodigal Son" was given with a quartette of home talent. The full chorus had grown to ninety voices and, largely through the efforts of the first President, Mr. John R. Lindgren, an associate member list of sixty-six was secured.

"The work of the Club had given so much pleasure and satisfaction that more pretentious plans were laid for the coming season. The concerts were all given at the Congregational church, beginning with the Mænnerchor on November 12, assisted by Bruno Steindel, 'cellist. On December 17th the first performance of the 'Messiah' was given and met with hearty approval. The solo quartette consisted of Miss Anita Muldoon, of Cincinnati, Mrs. Anna Rommeis Thacker, Mr. Walter Root and Mr. William Richards. A Part-song Concert was next given on February 7, 1896, with Mme. Lillian Blauvelt. The crowning feature of the year was the performance of 'Elijah,' on April 24, with Mrs. Janet Boyd Brown, Mrs. Foresman Bagg, Mr. William F. Hypes, and Mr. Plunkett Greene, as solo quartette. At both oratorios Mr. Clarence Dickinson presided at the organ. At the end of the season the active members numbered over one hundred, and the associate members eighty-nine.

"With its third season the Club adopted its present policy of giving three concerts annually—the 'Messiah' at Christmas tide, a Part-song Concert, with an eminent soloist, in February, and a great oratorio in April. The new season was inaugurated with the first appearance of an orchestra, and to provide the necessary stage-room, and also to accommodate the increasing attendance, the concerts of the Club were transferred to the First Methodist church, where they have since been held. The performance of the Messiah, with its proper orchestral setting, created much enthusiasm and received high praise from Chicago critics. The solo quartette included Miss Helen Buckley, Mrs. Anna Rommeis Thacker, William J. Brown, and Charles W. Clark. The following artists assisted at the Part-song Concert: Mlle. Alice Verlet, from the Paris Opera Comique, and Mr. Leo Stern, 'cellist, from London. The season closed with a successful performance of Haydn's 'Creation,' with orchestra, and Miss Helen Buckley, William F. Hypes and George Ellsworth Holmes as soloists. The chorus now numbered one hundred and twenty members, and there were about an equal number of associate members.

"The high standard the Club had set for its 'Messiah' performance was fully maintained at the opening concert of the fourth season. The assisting artists were Mrs. Genevieve Clark Wilson, Mrs. Sue Harrington Furbeck, Mr. George Hamlin and Mr. Lewis Campion. M. Henry Marteau, the eminent violinist, was the attraction at the Part-song Concert. In place of the usual oratorio at the last concert, an English Idyl, entitled 'St. John's Eve,' for solo, chorus and orchestra, was given with Mrs. Proctor Smith, Mrs. Christine Neilson Drier, George Hamlin and Sidney Biden in the solo parts. So great was the enjoyment in this beautiful work that a repetition was demanded. A second performance was given for a worthy charitable object, Miss Eolia Carpenter and Mr. William Hypes replacing Mrs. Drier and Mr. Hamlin. The chorus had increased to one hundred and thirty members and the associate members to nearly one hundred and fifty."

During the succeeding years the following programs have been presented:

FIFTH SEASON.

DECEMBER 13, 1898.

"THE MESSIAH."

Miss Jennie Osborn, Soprano; Mrs. Sue Harrington Furbeck, Contralto; Mr. Holmes Cowper, Tenor; Mr. Charles W. Clark, Bass; Mr. Curtis A. Barry, Organist.

FEBRUARY 23, 1899.

PART SONG CONCERT.

Soloists— Mr. Bruno Steindel, Violoncello; Mr. Holmes Cowper, Tenor.
Accompanists—Mrs. Bruno Steindel; Mr. Elias Arnold Bredin.

PROGRAM.

Cantata—"The Pilgrims"..............G. W. Chadwick
Evanston Musical Club.
Le Desir...Servais
Mr. Steindel.
Anthem for Tenor Solo and Chorus......P. C. Lutkin
Mr. Cowper and Evanston Musical Club.
The Elizabethan Madrigals........C. Williers Stanford
Evanston Musical Club.
Polonaise for Piano and 'Cello..................Chopin
Mr. and Mrs. Steindel.
Winter Days................................Caldcott
Evanston Musical Club.
Homewards................................ Rheinberger
Ladies' Chorus.
Hunting Songs.............................
Two Lovers................................Hecht
Evanston Musical Club.
Adagio....................................... Mozart
Tarantelle ....Popper
Mr. Steindel.
The Song of the Vikings...............Eaton Fanning
Evanston Musical Club.

APRIL 28, 1899.

MENDELSSOHN FESTIVAL.

Miss Jennie Osborn, Soprano; Miss Alton Littleton Smith, Soprano; Mr. George Hamlin, Tenor; Miss Una Howell, Pianist.

PROGRAM.

Concerto for Piano and Orchestra, op. 25..............
.................................Miss Una Howell
Motette ."Hear My Prayer".Miss Osborn and Evanston Musical Club.
A Hymn of Praise.

SIXTH SEASON.

DECEMBER 14, 1899.

"The Messiah"................................Handel
Soloists -Mrs. Sanger Steele, Soprano; Miss Mabelle Crawford, Alto; Mr. Glenn Hall, Tenor; Mr. Arthur Van Eweyk, Basso.

JANUARY 2, 1900.

Northwestern University Settlement, Chicago.
"The Messiah" ....Handel
Soloists- Mrs. Sanger Steele, Soprano; Miss Mabelle Crawford, Contralto; Mr. Glenn Hall, Tenor; Mr. Harry R. Parsons, Basso.

FEBRUARY 5, 1900.

PART SONG CONCERT.

Soloists- Leonora Jackson, Violinist.
(Mr. Ernest H Jackson, Accompanist.)
Incidental solos by Mrs. Alton Littleton Smith, Soprano; Harry R. Parsons, Basso; Russell Wilbur, Tenor; William A. Stacey, Baritone.
H. M. Tilroe, Reader.

PROGRAM.

1. Gallia, Motette for Soprano Solo and Chorus..Gounod
Solo -Mrs. Smith.
2. Chaconne, for Violin alone...................Bach
Miss Jackson
3. Two Part Songs for Ladies' Voices—
a In Spring...........................Bargeel
b Cradle Song.................Gilbert A. Alcock
4. Two Part Songs, for Mixed Voices—
a Madrigal-"The Miller's Daughter".............
..................................Horace Ellis
b Full Fathom Five.................Charles Wood
5. Violin Solos—
a Nocturne, D flat...............Chopin Sarasate
Humoresque.................... Tschaikowsky
c Dance.................. Brahms-Joachim
6. Six Ancient Folk Songs of the Netherlands—(A. D. 1626) arranged by.................E. Kremser
For Maennerchor, Baritone and Tenor Solos
7. Chorus, for Ladies' Voices and Soprano
The Sailors' Christmas.................Chaminade
Solo.................................Mrs. Smith
8. Ballad, for Baritone and Chorus—
Young Lochinvar...................Liza Lehmann
Solo.........................Mrs. Stacey
9. Violin Solo—Hungarian Themes with Variations....
.... Ernst
Miss Jackson
10. Two-Part Songs for Mixed Chorus—
a Evening and Morning Hymn........Rheinberger
b Gypsy Life........................Schumann

APRIL 27, 1900.

The Elijah...............................Mendelssohn
Soloists- Mrs. Genevieve Clark Wilson, Soprano; Mrs. Sue Harrington Furbeck, Alto; Mr. George Hamlin, Tenor; Mr. Charles W. Clark, Basso.
Wilson Reed, Soprano (The Youth).
Richard Uhlemann, Mezzo Soprano.
Armand Peycke, Alto.

SEVENTH SEASON.

DECEMBER 18, 1900.

The Messiah................................Handel
Soloists—Mrs. Jennie Fish Griffin, Soprano; Miss Mabelle Crawford, Alto; Mr. Frederick Carberry, Tenor; Mr. Charles W. Clark, Basso.

FEBRUARY 19, 1901.

PART SONG CONCERT.

Soloists—Madame Fannie Bloomfield Zeisler, Pianiste; Mr. Chauncey Earle Bryant, Tenor.

PROGRAM.

1. Credo........................}
Sanctus—From St. Cecilia Mass.} ....Gounod
2. Piano Solos—
a "Hark, hark, the lark"................Schubert
(Translated for Piano by Liszt).
b. Marche Militaire....................Schubert
(Duet arranged as a solo by Tausig).
Mme. Zeisler.
3. Part Song for Mixed Voices—
"When Spring Comes Laughing"....Eaton Fanning
4. The Twenty-third Psalm, for Ladies' Voices—
"The Lord is my Shepherd"............Schubert
5. Piano Solos—
Berceuse, op. 57.......
Etude, op. 10, No. 4.... | ....Chopin
Valse, op. 64, No. 1.... |
Valse, op. 64, No. 2.... |
Mme. Zeisler
6. Two Part Songs, for Mixed Voices—
Two Maidens.......................P. C. Lutkin
(Dedicated to the Apollo Musical Club.)
The Babbling Brook...................P. C. Lutkin
(Dedicated to the Evanston Musical Club.)
7. Two Part Songs, for Mixed Voices—
a Spring.............................Cowen
b Lover's Counsel....
Piano Solos—Liebestraum (Nocturne, No. 31)....Liszt
Caprice Espagnole, op. 37...............Moszkowski
Mme. Zeisler.
9. March and Chorus from Tannhauser.

APRIL 21, 1901.

CENTRAL MUSIC HALL, CHICAGO.

"The Elijah"............................Mendelssohn
By the combined Evanston and Ravenswood Clubs, under the direction of Professor P. C. Lutkin.
Soloists—Mrs. Genevieve Clark Wilson, Soprano; Miss Elaine De Sellem, Alto; Mr. George Hamlin, Tenor; Mr. Charles W. Clark, Basso.

MAY 7, 1901.

Stabat Mater................................ Rossini
Hiawatha's Wedding Feast.........S. Coleridge Taylor
Soloists—Miss Helen Buckley, Soprano; Miss Elaine De Sellem, Alto; Mr. Holmes Cowper, Tenor; Mr. F. B. Webster, Bass.

EIGHTH SEASON.

NOVEMBER 21, 1901.

Hiawatha's Wedding Feast. }
Hiawatha's Departure...... } ....S. Coleridge Taylor
Soloists—Mrs. Maria Hoag-Haughley, Soprano; Mrs. Ella Pierson Kirkham, Alto; Mr. L. E. Rollo, Tenor; Mr. Joseph Baernstein, Basso.

FEBRUARY 27, 1902.

PART SONG CONCERT.

Soloists—Mme. Corinne Moore Lawson, Soprano; Mr. Gustav Holmquist, Basso.

PROGRAM.
PART I.

1. "Hear My Prayer"....................Mendelssohn
   Motette for Soprano Solo and Chorus.
   Mrs. Lawson and Chorus.
2. The King's Prayer from Lohengrin..........Wagner
   Bass Solo, Quintette and Chorus.
   Mr. Holmquist.
   Miss Anna L. Beebe, Soprano; Miss Louise Whitehead, Alto; Mr. A. D. Shaw, Tenor; Mr. C. N. Stevens, Baritone.
3. Te Deum, opus 103......................Dvorak
   Soprano and Bass Solo and Chorus.
   Mrs. Lawson, Mr. Holmquist and Chorus.
PART II.
1. The Dance, opus 27, No. 1...........Edward Elgar
   From the "Bavarian Highlands.".
   Evanston Musical Club.
2. a Norwegian Shepherd Song.Old Melody 10th Cent.
   b Bid Me Discourse.. }
   c Love Has Eyes..... } ....Old English
3. Lullaby, opus 27, No. 3.......; {
   Aspiration, Opus 27, No. 4. } .....Edward Elgar
   Evanston Musical Club.
4. a The First Love Song..........Carl Grammann
   b The Sand Carrier.............August Bungert
   c Serenata........................... Moszkowski
   Mrs. Lawson.
5. The Marksmen, Opus 27, No. 6........Edward Elgar
   Evanston Musical Club.

APRIL 22, 1902.

VERDI'S.

Manzoni Requiem.

Soloists—Mrs. Genevieve Clark Wilson, Soprano; Miss Jessie Lynde Hopkins, Mezzo Soprano; Mr. John B. Miller, Tenor; Mr. Joseph Baernstein, Basso.

Other especially important works presented by the Club are "Caractacus" and "King Olaf" by Elgar, and Dvorak's "Stabat Mater." Interest in the club was greatly augmented by the winning of the second prize of $3,500 in the choral contest at the Louisiana Purchase Exposition at Saint Louis, in 1904, under the direction of Professor Lutkin. In the concert of January 30, 1905, a concerto for piano and orchestra by Arne Oldberg had its first performance, and the celebrated English contralto, Muriel Foster, was the most notable soloist.

The Presidents of the Evanston Musical Club have been Mr. John R. Lindgren, Mr. W. F. Hypes, Mr. Frank W. Smith, Mr. Chancellor Jenks and Mr. C. N. Stevens.

Let us hope that the great development along musical lines, which has taken place in Evanston during the last few years, may lead some public spirited citizen to erect a large hall suitable for concert purposes. Mendelssohn has said, "I know of no aim more noble than that of giving music to one's native language and to one's native country." What more noble monument could an Evanstonian erect than a building in his own town, which would make possible an annual musical festival whose strains would mingle with the majestic organ point of our beautiful Lake Michigan, in fulfilling the musicians' calling which, according to Schumann, is "to send light into the deep recesses of the human heart."

CHAPTER XXXI.

EVANSTON BANKS
(By WILLIAM G. HOAG)

Banking in Evanston, however intimate this city's relations with near-by Chicago, has been prosperous and permanent when conducted with discretion, and ephemeral and disastrous when otherwise undertaken. The story of banking in Evanston is largely that of the older of its two institutions, and a story by no means without interest to all who profit by and have pride in the successes of conservative finance.

Effect of the Chicago Fire.—With the influx of population after the Chicago fire of 1871, the growing business of Evanston invited the creation of banking facilities furnished by Evanston capital and operated by Evanston citizens. Into this field, in the early 'seventies, came Merrill Ladd, who founded the private bank of Merrill Ladd & Company. Speculation worked this venture ill; and the panic of 1873, that shook the financial strongholds of New York, Boston, Philadelphia and Chicago, left the enterprise of Evanston's first money-lender a memory only. In 1874 a new bank started in Evanston, and became a corner-stone for the village's wealth and growth.

Bank of Hoag & Co. Established.— In 1874, on the southeast corner of Davis Street and Chicago Avenue, Thomas C. Hoag & Company started a private bank. Mr. Hoag, of the Chicago grocery firm of Goss & Hoag, one of the largest in the city, and situated on North Clark Street near the bridge, had suffered the destruction of his property in the great fire, and was free to find a new opening wherever he might. Living as he had in Evanston since 1857, and having done a grocery business by railway express with North Shore villages, he now began a local grocery business in Evanston, and soon thereafter went into banking on the aforesaid site. Mr. Hoag already was the Treasurer and Business Agent of the Northwestern University, and with this and other advantageous connections, he conducted with increasing success the Evanston bank that had come to stay. The business grew, justifying a building next door exclusively for banking purposes, and further establishing itself as an indispensable institution in the development of the commercial life of Evanston. In 1891 the banking firm of Thomas C. Hoag & Company moved to the southwest corner of Davis Street and Chicago Avenue, there installing the first modern safety deposit vaults offered to the Evanston public.

State Bank Incorporated.—On May 10, 1892, was incorporated the State Bank of Evanston, to which Mr. Hoag sold his interest, his banking firm then retiring from business. The incorporators of the new institution—its charter being of the date of March 10, 1892, and conferring powers to conduct a general commercial and savings bank business—were Robert D. Sheppard, Charles F. Grey, and John R. Lindgren. The first board of directors of the State Bank of Evanston were the following well-known citizens:

William Blanchard, Frank M. Elliot, William G. Hoag, H. H. C. Miller, Robert D. Sheppard, H. B. Cragin, Charles F. Grey, John R. Lindgren, Henry A. Pearsons, William E. Stockton, and Charles T. Bartlett.

The first officers of the new bank were John R. Lindgren, President; William Blanchard, Vice-President; William G. Hoag, Cashier. Mr. Lindgren was already prominently identified with Chicago banking as Cashier of the State Bank of Chicago. Mr. Blanchard was a retired lumberman and capitalist, and Mr. Hoag brought experience from his associations with his father in the firm of Thomas C. Hoag & Company. The Evanston State Bank began business with a capital, all paid in, of $100,000 and deposits from Thomas C. Hoag & Company of $306,000. Among the stockholders, together with the officers and directors, were J. H. Kedzie, Henry R. Hatfield, D. S. Cook, M. S. Terry, George H. Foster, William Deering, T. C. Hoag, C. H. Quinlan, Lucy D. Shuman, Daniel

Bonbright, William L. Brown, Frank P. Crandon, Charles T. Boynton, Thomas Lord, Fleming H. Revell.

At the close of 1892, the year of organization, the bank's deposits amounted to $369,590.60. On January 13, 1894, Robert D. Sheppard succeeded John R. Lindgren as President, and continued in direction of the bank until succeeded in February, 1903, by Henry J. Wallingford. From organization to the present time, William G. Hoag has been the bank's Cashier. In March, 1900, E. F. Pierce was chosen Assistant Cashier and continues in this office. Prominent citizens who have served in the bank's directory from 1892 to 1905, other than those composing the original board are: D. S. Cook, Thomas Lord, Dr. M. C. Bragdon, E. B. Quinlan, Henry J. Wallingford, Frank W. Gerould, William A. Dyche. In 1897 Thomas Lord was elected Vice-President. At present writing, in 1906, the officers of the State Bank of Evanston are:

President—Henry J. Wallingford.

Vice-President—H. H. C. Miller.

Cashier—William G. Hoag.

Assistant Cashier—Edwin F. Pierce.

The following tables statistically tell the story of the growth of the State Bank of Evanston in its general banking and savings departments, but do not especially declare the policy which has built up this popular banking house. The policy is that which makes for slow growth but for sure—the policy of prudence and conservatism.

GROWTH OF DEPOSITS IN STATE BANK OF EVANSTON FROM 1892 TO 1906.

1892	$ 324,029.18
1893	390,381.44
1894	532,265.86
1895	557,103.15
1896	539,673.67
1897	715,112.57
1898	733,844.59
1899	967,774.80
1900	1,128,518.67
1901	1,171,016.54
1902	1,133,123.75
1903	1,160,244.29
1904	1,122,029.17
1905	1,315,098.62
1906	1,460,000.00

This bank, since the first year after incorporation, has paid dividends at the uniform rate of six per cent. Its excess of earnings, carried over to the surplus, now makes this guarantee of security over $100,000. The last reported quotation of this bank's stock was 240.

The Test of 1893.—The policy that has shaped the development of business, recorded in the foregoing tables, is characteristic of all the financiers, capitalists, and business men who have contributed to the growth of this conservative institution. One of its banking principles is never to sacrifice security to interest. Beginning its corporate existence a year before the great panic of 1893, it was put to the earthquake test while still quite young. In that memorable year, when there were 15,508 business failures; when 154 National and 184 State banks suspended; when 598 banking institutions of all classes, with estimated assets of $184,281,014 and liabilities of $170,295,581, suspended—in that disastrous time, no savings bank in Cook County was less severely jarred than the State Bank of Evanston. Indeed, it may be said that, in that fateful year, this bank, safe if not colossal, never felt serious pressure from its depositors; and it is well remembered by its officers that, if at any period of unusual popular timidity, money has flowed out from one window, a compensating stream has flowed in by another. The following from the "Evanston Press," of May 20, 1893, suggests the stamina of this bank in a time that surely tried men's souls:

"Thursday morning a slight run was made on the State Bank, but it was soon over, only a very few dollars having been drawn out. The State Bank is perfectly sound, and has made arrangements to stand a heavy run. Cashier Hoag said, Thursday, that every cent now on deposit can be drawn out, and that the bank has in its vaults the cold cash to meet all of its indebtedness. By order of President Lindgren the bank was kept open for an hour after the usual closing hour on Thursday, but this was not necessary, as the 'run,' if such it could be called, was over long before the usual hour for closing."

This bank's history has been one almost without losses from injudicious banking. It has had almost no litigation. On real estate investments it has never lost a dollar; and, for twenty years, during the life of the antecedent company and of its own corporate life, its total losses have not exceeded $2,000 or $3,000. So discreet, yet so mutually just, is it in the management of credits, that in a certain statement its cashier reported deposits of $1,300,000 with over drafts amounting to just one cent. Needless to say, that the Evanston State Bank eschews speculation.

Influence on Local Business.—The business of Evanston has grown because of its own local banking facilities. Its banks have drawn, held, and made wealth here. Here Evanston merchants have received their accommodations, and to this prosperous sub-station of Chicago banking come people of neighboring towns and thrifty farmers from tributary country. Evanston banks hold all the public funds of the city of Evanston, and some of the funds of neighboring towns and villages; and the Evanston State Bank and its predecessor for thirty years have been the depository of Northwestern University. One source of the strength of this bank is the support given it by its large number of children depositors, whose many pennies in many little toy banks make many large dollars.

Of course, the nature of the business of the State Bank of Evanston, and the character of its clientele, demand that it shall have the status of a Chicago bank as regards the conveniences and privileges of the associated banks of a money center. This bank is a secondary member of the Chicago Clearing-house, whereby it reports to that institution as if it were a Chicago bank, and its checks are accepted throughout the country as if drawn on a Chicago bank. It deals, of course, in foreign exchange and sells drafts and letters of credit good in all parts of the world.

The tendency of the times is toward individuality in bank architecture. A bank is becoming more than a floor in a business block. It is becoming a monument ennobling an entire city. The State Bank of Evanston proposes to erect a bank building for its own use, approved in style and equipment, and steps have been taken to this end by the securing of a long term lease on certain property on the northwest corner of Davis Street and Orrington Avenue.

A National Bank Venture.—The first National bank started in Evanston was born in a strenuous time, and in it passed away. On June 29, 1892, was organized the Evanston National Bank. On July 5, 1892, it began business. Its capital was $100,000. Its officers were Henry Wells, President; J. C. Austin, Vice-President; J. C. Terhune, Cashier. Its directors were Benjamin F. Hill, L. A. Goddard, E. T. Paul, N. A. Hill, T. J. Whitehead, O. G. Gibbs, Henry Wells, J. C. Austin, J. C. Terhune. On March 6, 1893, a published statement showed deposits to be $100,000. But in 1893 only the strong stood the tempest. A shrinkage of its assets set in. On May 16th and 17th a heavy run on this bank resulted from the failure of the Cairo Lumber Company, of which Henry Wells, the President of this bank, was treasurer. On May 18 there was posted on the doors of the Evanston National Bank the following notice:

"Owing to heavy drains made on our deposits, and the stringency of the money market, this bank suspends payments. Depositors will be paid in full.

"Henry Wells, President.
"Nat. A. Hill, Vice-President."

On June 8, 1893, Charles Winslow took charge as receiver under appointment by the Comptroller of the Currency. At the present writing the approved claims of creditors amount to $80,971, upon which 73.7 per cent has been paid.

In 1892 J. C. Terhune started a private bank in Evanston, which continues business at the present writing.

A More Successful Venture.—As Evanston grew in wealth and population, capitalists and men of affairs began to see that, were the city removed from the suburban touch with a metropolis, its business would support a half-dozen banks rather than one, and that, even as it was, a second bank would not be a precarious undertaking. So representative citizens, resolved to found a national bank that should become a strong tower to this community. On February 14, 1900, Marshall M. Kirkman, James A. Patten, David R. Forgan and Thomas Bates signed articles of association for the incorporation of a national bank. With these incorporators was associated Joseph E. Paden, attorney. On April 10th of the same year there was issued a charter creating the City National Bank of Evanston, and the first directing board of this institution was made up of the aforesaid incorporators, together with Rollin A. Keyes, Henry A. Pearsons, and Joseph F. Ward. The bank began business in its present quarters, the Century Building, southwest corner of Davis Street and Sherman Avenue, June 21, 1900, with Joseph F. Ward, President; Thomas Bates, Vice-President; and Charles N. Stevens, Cashier. The deposits of the first day amounted to $16,220, and the first depositor was William S. Lord.

the dry-goods merchant, who thereby recorded the testimony of Evanston business men, that this city was big enough and wealthy enough to sustain two strong banks in healthful rivalry.

The City National Bank of Evanston started in with a paid-up capital of $100,000, and the price of the stock before business opened on the first day was $105 per share. In stanch and stable communities the banking class is the conservative class. Behind the City National Bank of Evanston among its first stockholders were Hugh R. Wilson, Joseph E. Paden, A. N. Young, M. H. Wilson, P. R. Shumway, C. D. Cleveland, L. D. Thoman, A. M. Foster, George W. Wall, W. B. Bogert, George A. Foster, William S. Lord, George Taylor, N. P. Williams, Charles N. Stevens, J. L. Hebblethwaite, W. O. Dean, John E. Wilder, Robert S. Clark, C. H. Poppenhusen, Daniel McCann, W. H. Jones, Newell C. Knight, James Wigginton, John H. Boyd, A. S. Van Deusen, J. R. Woodbridge, James B. Huse, F. E. Griswold, George A. Coe.

In its first year the bank earned six per cent on its capitalization, but turning this and the earnings of the next year into surplus account, it refrained from declaring a dividend until 1903, when it began its present six per cent payments. This bank deals in such securities as are customary with National banks, receives savings as well as checking deposits, and conducts a general banking business. It clears, of course, through the Chicago Clearing House. With the State Bank of Evanston it shares in the custody of the municipal funds of Evanston, and also has been distributing agent in the matter of the construction of the postoffice.

This bank's growth is noteworthy. Beginning business June 21, 1900, with deposits amounting to $16,220.00, it reported deposits June 21, 1902, of $345,152.24. On June 21, 1903, deposits had risen to $703,640.53; and a year later they were $842,074.73. On June 14, 1905, they had reached $1,197,053.35. The stock of the bank at this writing, judging from a private bid refused, is 175. This bank carries 5,000 accounts. A statement of the condition of this new and promising institution, at the close of business, April 6, 1906, is as follows:

RESOURCES.

Loans and Discounts	$1,069,565.60
Overdrafts	2,167.46
United States Bonds	100,000.00
Premium on U. S. Bonds	3,000.00
Other Stocks and Bonds	89,864.47
Furniture and Fixtures	7,754.84
Cash on Hand and in Banks	208,000.02
Due from U. S. Treasury	5,000.00
	$1,485,352.39

LIABILITIES.

Capital Stock	$ 100,000.00
Surplus and Undivided Profits,	53,190.13
Circulation	100,000.00
Deposits	1,232,162.26
	$1,485,352.39 $1,485,352.39

Officers.—The present officers of the City National Bank of Evanston (1906) are:

President—Joseph F. Ward.

Vice-President—William S. Mason.

Cashier—Charles N. Stevens.

Directors.—Henry A. Pearsons, Thomas Bates, Rollin A. Keyes, Joseph A. Paden, David R. Forgan, William S. Mason, James A. Patten, Joseph F. Ward.

A considerable improvement lately added to the City National Bank is a safety deposit vault, commodious and of extraordinary strength of construction. Its auxiliary conveniences for patrons are complete and elegant.

CHAPTER XXXII.

EVANSTON REAL ESTATE
(By FRANK M ELLIOT)

Primary Geological Conditions—Early Roads—The Indian Trail—A Period of Growth—"The Path the Calf Made"— Influence of the University — Evanston Over-boomed—Effect of the Chicago Fire —Local Real Estate Rivalries—Notable Residences—The Transportation Problem —The Park System—Taxation—Evanston Homes—Real Estate Values.

We are told that Evanston, at one time, was entirely submerged by Lake Michigan, but that gradually, through unknown ages, the waters receded. The battle-field of the two contending forces—land and water— is distinctly marked by the alignment of land fortification or ridges. This great struggle had continued year in and year out, with the land forces conquering and adding much territory to their possession. These lines of fortification are visible to-day. The highest and most prominent of all, runs along the Gross Point Road, three miles distant from the Lake; another on Ridge Avenue, a mile distant; one on Hinman Avenue, a quarter of a mile distant, and still another along the lake shore, where the battle of land and water is still raging. This contest between the land and water is one of great importance to the real estate of Evanston. Practically the last stand has been reached, for the force of the waters of Lake Michigan is so great, that it

is no longer possible to extend the land, with any degree of safety. Covering this territory conquered from the lake, there has grown a beautiful forest of oak, maple, elm and linden, a portion of which has withstood the violence of the elements and the ruthless depredations of man.

Early Roads.—There were two roads running from Chicago to Green Bay which passed through Evanston — one on the Gross Point highland, and the other, known as the Green Bay Road, running along Ridge Avenue. East of the latter was an old Indian trail, the route of which can still be traced by a number of trees with large branches bent to the ground. The best example of these is a tree at the State line just east of the Electric Road. The large oak at the entrance of the College Campus, and the one at the northeast corner of Forest Avenue and Lake Street, mark the direction of the trail. There was only one cross road located in Rogers Park along the Indian Boundary Line. The low land between the ridges was filled with water and marsh, resembling in effect the present condition of the Skokie. These roads were, for the most part, built of corduroy and were maintained at private expense. A toll was exacted for the use of them and one of the oldest toll stations, and the last to exist, was in Rogers Park at the intersection of Chicago Avenue and the Indian Boundary Line. The toll house was discontinued about 1875.

A Period of Growth.—The development from a "forest primeval" to a city lot is interesting, for into this development enters the human element, which is a never ending source of interest. The low and marshy places, the hills and the ridges, the obstruction of trees and tangled wood—all of these must be brought under the control of man. Streets must be made, sewers built, and much digging, cutting and burning, before a city lot is defined. This, in brief, is what has taken place in Evanston.

There have been periods of immigration that have added to the material growth of Evanston. The western march of civilization brought farmers into this country. These acquired title to their farms from the Government. They planted fruit trees, and especially a large number of the peach variety. These prospered and brought rich harvests until the time when the forests, which extended to the North Branch of the Chicago River, were destroyed. The climatic changes which ensued after this destruction made it impossible for peaches to grow on this side of Lake Michigan.

In 1853 the Northwestern University was established here. From a few homes and a store on Ridge Avenue—a settlement called Ridgeville—grew a new town, named Evanston in honor of the late Governor Evans, of Colorado, one of the founders of the University. There was the infusion of a new element into the community; professors and their families, scholars and trades people. The coming of these represented the second immigration.

"The Path the Calf Made."—The growth of a town can sometimes be traced from its foot-paths. First comes the trail of the Indian, or frontiersman, who marks his way with a broken branch, or a blaze on the trees. The settler, with his flock and herds, then follows nature's own survey for a future city's thoroughfare in "the path the calf made," of which the poet, Sam Walter Foss, thus graphically sings:

"One day, through the primeval wood,
A calf walked home, as good calves should;
But made a trail all bent askew,
A crooked trail as all calves do.

Since then two hundred years have fled,
And, I infer, the calf is dead.
But still he left behind his trail,
And thereby hangs my moral tale.

The trail was taken up next day
By a lone dog that passed that way;
And then a wise bell-wether sheep
Pursued the trail o'er vale and steep,
And drew the flock behind him, too,
As good bell-wethers always do.

And from that day, o'er hill and glade,
Through these old woods a path was made;
And many men wound in and out,
And dodged, and turned, and bent about,
And uttered words of righteous wrath
Because 'twas such a crooked path.
But still they followed—do not laugh—
The first migrations of that calf,
And through this winding woodway stalked,
Because he wabbled when he walked.

This forest path became a lane,
That bent and turned, and turned again;
This crooked lane became a road,
Where many a poor horse with his load
Toiled on beneath the burning sun,
And traveled some three miles in one.
And thus, a century and a half,
They trod in the footsteps of that calf.

The years passed on in swiftness fleet,
The road became a village street;
And this, before men were aware,
A city's crowded thoroughfare;
And soon the central street was this,
Of a renowned metropolis.
And men two centuries and a half,
Trod in the footsteps of that calf."

In the early settlement, for foot passengers there were first walks of clay and gravel extending from the Lake Shore in Davis Street to the business portion; afterward the single plank, laid lengthwise; then the double-barreled walk of two planks, with a space between, the invention of Obadiah Huse, President of the Village Board; next the board walk, three or four feet in width, the wider board or dirt walk, and then the flag stone, brick or cement walk of the present day—each serving its day or purpose until superseded by something better. All these walks mark with distinctness, the growth and evolution that has taken place in our community.

Influence of the University.—The influence of the University brought, as early inhabitants, a class of people who have been of great benefit to Evanston. They were people of refinement who desired quiet with the delights of intellectual and congenial society. They established homes here and many of their friends, attracted by their example, came to live in this quiet and scholastic atmosphere.

The University purchased large tracts of land amounting to 343 acres. In July, 1854, the Plat of Evanston was made by Andrew J. Brown, Philo Judson and the Northwestern University. As an illustration of the rapid advance of land values, take for example the southwest quarter of Section 18, Township 41, Range 14, being 160 acres, lying between Church and Dempster Streets, and Asbury and Chicago Avenues. In 1840, James Carney bought this land from the Government for $1.25 per acre, a total of $200. In 1854, Carney sold this land to Andrew James Brown for $13,000. After the subdivision was made the best lots sold for $350 each. The lot on southwest corner of Davis Street and Maple Avenue, 70 by 215 feet, sold, in 1855, for $350. In 1865, it sold for $600. In 1870 the same lot, only 115 feet deep, sold for $2,000, and in 1889 for $7,000. It is worth to-day, without improvements, $17,500. Let us take another example on the East Side. In 1865, the Northwestern University bought the "Snyder farm," 60½ acres, for $24,227. This farm ran from Hamilton to Greenleaf Streets, and from Chicago Avenue to Lake Michigan. As platted to-day, there are about 6,660 feet frontage and a conservative value would be $100 per front foot, or $666,000. Other examples might be cited to show the increase in value of real estate in Evanston; but it would be about the same story, and would only repeat what is well known of the substantial and fixed value of real estate throughout the entire city.

Expansion of 1872.—During the Civil War, when the unsettled condition of the country was making its influence felt—even at this distance from the field of action—while Evanston was sending the best of her manhood to the front, she still made advances, and had enough surplus energy to contribute generally toward the building up of the town. The greatest expansion took place in 1872. In common with the rest of the State, and, indeed, with many parts of the country, Evanston was over-boomed. It needed the bursting of the bubble in 1873 to bring values to their legitimate level. During the subsequent decade, real estate values and the movement of property wore slowly down to a more rational pace.

Effect of the Chicago Fire.—Up to the time of the Chicago fire in 1871, the University was the dominant influence which brought people to Evanston. The loss and ruination brought about by that fire enforced the sale of much property, and this caused a depreciation of prices. Rigid fire ordinances followed that great catastrophe, and the enforcement of stringent regulations drove beyond the Chicago city limits those people, who, desiring to build houses for themselves, had not means for the erection of structures of brick or other fire-proof materials. These circumstances acted decidedly in favor of suburban localities, to which professional men, clerks, and others of moderate income were attracted. A feature of the real estate business since then has been the suburban trade. Evanston receiving a large influx of people at the time of the Chicago fire. They were attracted by its accessibility, its delightful surroundings, and the high character of the people who already resided in the village. The restriction of the liquor traffic, making it illegal to sell or manufacture alcoholic beverages, has had a beneficial effect, not only in giving the community a high standard, but in maintaining and enhancing the value of property within its limits. The preference of the people for homes outside of Chicago created an unusual demand for houses and lots in Evanston. Prices advanced rapidly, and the building of houses and the selling of them became a profitable business. Keen and wide-awake business men were quick to grasp the situation, and soon there were new sub-divisions of land into lots. These were disposed of rapidly and other sub-divisions made, and sold out. There was a boom in real estate. The buying of acres and subdividing them was so extensive that, to this day, the growth of our city has been inadequate to bring them into the market for residence purposes. As we view some of these outlying sub-divisions, now occupied, fallowed or returned to nature, we wonder at the credulity, the misguided judgment and the almost criminality of the men who made them. It does not seem possible that any one could have been so misguided as to expect these sub-divisions to become the homes of other beings than the musk-rat or the gopher. The time of disillusion came in the panic of 1873. Prices took a tumble from which, after thirty years, they have scarcely recovered. Evanston was tainted by the same wild speculation as Chicago. Many people suffered the bitter experience of losing their property by foreclosure and many were burdened with property they could not afford to keep. Values were brought to the lowest level, and, after several years of adjustment, a healthful progress began which has continued up to the present time.

During the last twenty-five years there have been many interesting changes in the character and property of certain localities, and a shifting more or less of popular favor as to residence sections and business localities. While prices in some parts of the city have not yet come back to the speculaton values of years ago, the present value of most of our Evanston real estate has never before been reached. In the business center of the city there is some property that has never decreased in value. The property along Davis Street has held its own, notwithstanding the establishment of business centers at Main, Dempster and Central Streets.

Local Rivalries.—There has always been more or less of a good natured rivalry between the East and West Side property owners, the railroads passing through the middle of the city being the dividing line. The East-Siders have the Library University, banks, several clubs and the leading stores and parks, together with the lake, as their chief attractive features; while the West-Siders claim the rise of land along the Ridge, the High School, the Country Club, the unobstructed view of the sunsets, and protection from the harsh winds which sometimes sweep over the lake. The point of excellence in fine residences is about equally divided between the two sides. It has been my observation, however, during an experience of twenty-five years in the real estate business, and as a resident of Evanston, that the difference between the East and West sides is a species of fancy rather than of fact; that it is largely a question of neighbors and friends. Upon whichever side a person first makes his home there he will soon form acquaintances and friendships that will bring contentment and happiness. This is the truth of the whole matter in a nut-shell. Values are about equally divided on both sides. Property held at the highest price is found on each side, and from this to the lowest priced lots there is about an equal division. This, however, was not true in the early days. The finest residences were on the West Side, and the value of Ridge Avenue lots was considered twice as great as that of lots in the Lake district. The change of value has been greater in this district because of its recent improvements and its new buildings.

Evanston Residences.—The residences of Evanston, for the most part, are of frame structure. There have been some typical houses which represent the time in which they were built. The oldest of these is the residence of D. H. Burnham, which is unique in having the walls of cement or grout. It was built by Mr. Geo. H. Bliss about 1859, and was then considered one of the finest in the town. The house of Mr. James Rood, on Davis Street, which was built by L. L. Greenleaf in the early 'seventies, was typical of many houses of a similar structure. Other old-timers may be mentioned. Mr. O. F. Gibbs built the Mulford home on Ridge Avenue, which was sold to James S. Kirk, and is now owned by the Saint Francis Hospital. Then there are T. C. Hoag's residence, corner of Davis and Hinman, built in 1856; Judge Harvey B. Hurd's home on Ridge Avenue; the Purington home, a part of which is now included in the residence of Mr. Frank C. Letts on Greenwood Boulevard; the brick residence on Ridge and Greenwood, built by Mr. Geo. F. Foster in 1863 and sold to the late Charles Comstock; Mrs. Watson's house on Ridge Avenue, and the Somer's homestead on Chicago Avenue and University Place. Among the finest residences built within the last twenty years may be mentioned those owned by W. H. Bartlett, Milton H. Wilson, R. D. Sheppard, Arthur Orr, Mrs. C. H. Rowe, J. C. Shaffer, Mrs. Virginia M. Hamline, James A. Patten, Mrs. H. R. Wilson, John B. Kirk, R. C. Lake and C. A. Ward.

During the past five years there has been an evolution in building, and the first flat and apartment buildings have made their appearance in our midst. This is in line with the progressing movement of real estate, as they bring a far greater income than can be obtained by other improvements. Property that is losing attractiveness for residence purposes, and which cannot, by the nature of the case, become business property, can thus be utilized for profitable investment. Sadly deficient are our hotel accommodations. What is needed is a first-class, fire-proof hotel, with modern appointments, a new library building and an auditorium. The churches are now used extensively for all public meetings. Evanston has passed the lyceum era, and is now ripe for the buildings which modern up-to-date cities possess. Every public improvement adds to the comfort of the people and, consequently, enhances the value of real estate.

During the time prior to the Chicago fire, Evanston had among its population many men who, a few years later, were to make it famous through their achievements. The foundations of many of the best homes were laid, and definite plans for future development were made. They were, of course, crude and incomplete; but the men of Evanston had a fair conception of the possibilities here for a city of homes. The men who were actively engaged in real estate at this time were L. L. Greenleaf, Rev. Obadiah Huse, Charles E. Brown, D. P. Kidder, J. H. Kedzie, J. H. Keeney, Merrill Ladd, C. L. Jenks, O. A. Crain, J. W. Stewart, L. C. Pitner, I. R. Hitt, Andrew J. Brown, George M. Huntoon, Gen. White, Eli Gaffield, O. F. Gibbs, Charles J. Gilbert and Joseph M. Lyons.

There have been other eras when the immigration to Evanston has induced somewhat more than the natural growth. In 1892, during the World's Fair, when Evanston prospered with Chicago, there were many new residences built, some of them costing from $50,000 to $75,000 each.

The Transportation Problem.—One of the striking features of the real estate situation just now is the effect of rapid transportation upon it. Electric and steam railroads have had marked influence on the value of residence property. There is no question that this influence is felt on real estate values all along the lines of railroad extension. Outlying properties in communities more remote have been brought into competition with those which heretofore have had the advantage of accessibility. Fast train facilities make it possible for a man to have a home thirty miles distant from Chicago where land is cheap. Competition is thus extended. Other and better inducements for real estate within the nearer districts of Chicago, must be made to meet this outside competition. That inducement is best solved by the reduction of price, and this is what has happened in many suburban towns, including Evanston.

Evanston has two railroads and two electric street car lines. When these were started the increase of population in our city was noticeable. These roads have created a market for property, and values have been stimulated thereby. It is reasonable to expect a great increase in the growth of our city. With better equipment for transportation service, and when passengers can be landed in the heart of Chicago, many people will come here to live. The importance of Evanston is, in a large measure, determined by its relationship with Chicago. It is dominated, with all other cities in the Northwest, by that great metropolis.

The Park System.—The parks of Evanston have been limited to the lake shore south of the University campus, and the block bounded by Chicago, Hinman, Lake and Grove Streets. These parks were given by the Northwestern University, when the original plat of Evanston was made. During the last ten years considerable attention has been given to the development of our park system, especially along the Lake Shore, where the city has filled and graded and planted trees and shrubs. The trees which were planted by the early settlers along the park way of the streets, have become strong and vigorous, and in many streets their tops have spread out until they meet, forming beautiful archways. Our elms are noted for their beauty and hardiness. They line the streets everywhere and are so manifestly symmetrical and vigorous, that the city seems to be nestling in the forest. Nowhere, except in the old New England towns, are they so attractive. There are few fences dividing the ownership of lots and, with its well groomed lawns, the whole city is, in a certain sense, a great park. Flowers, shrubs and trees adorn most of the grounds.

In the early days the streets were simply as nature made them. The cedar-block pavement was cheap and, perhaps, the best that could be had at that time, but it had to be replaced by modern pavements, divided between macadam, brick and asphalt. With few exceptions, all the streets are now paved with these substantial and durable pavements.

Taxation.—When the subject of taxes is mentioned, there always arises the question of the non-payment of taxes on the property owned by the Northwestern

University. Before the University had sold much of its property this was a serious matter: for under its charter the University was exempt from paying all general taxes. However, in street improvements, such as sewers, water mains and side-walks, the University has always paid its full share. The policy of the University has been liberal in the selling of its property. In 1874, a restriction was imposed by Gov. Evans, who had given a large sum of money ($100,000), as reported), with the understanding that one-quarter of every block remaining unsold should be held by the University for leasing purposes only. The leasing of property for business purposes was on the basis of six per cent on a conservative valuation for a period of fifty or ninety-nine years, with the added condition of a revaluation every ten years. On residence property the rate of interest was four per cent. Considering the fact that there was no general tax to be paid except on the improvements, and none on the land, many of these leases were made. As long as high rates of interest continued, these leases were considered desirable, but since money rates have become reduced, they are no longer in demand. The restriction imposed by Gov. Evans has since been rescinded, and the University can sell any of its property. The policy, however, has not been to sell where leases have been made. The tax rate is about one per cent on the actual value of the property. If the real estate is valued at $10,000, the tax will be about $100. The Assessor, however, in making his valuations, places it at one-fifth the real value. The tax covers the amount needed for public schools, which are of the highest order of excellence, and consequently expensive to maintain. It also covers the amount

used for the Public Library, State, County and City.

The University, as a landlord, has been conservative, and the sale of its property is made only at current valuation. It has made only limited improvements on its property, when it might have made others which would have been helpful in developing districts where it owned large tracts of land. It is not difficult to conceive that the policy of building homes on its residence lots would have contributed to the benefit of the University, as well as to the interests of the city at large.

Evanston Homes.—One great charm of Evanston lies in its homes. Lake Michigan is the prime element in its landscape. The meandering shore, with its borders of sand, is a source of unfailing delight. To the west is a commanding view of the setting sun, with its glory of color. Mr. D. H. Burnham, the Director of Works of the World's Fair, in a recent address pays this tribute to our city: "Evanston," he says, "is the most beautiful city in the world. There are cities that surpass Evanston in natural scenery and in other single points many are superior; but take the city as a whole, as a place of residence, there is none to equal it. Evanston has the most beautiful streets to be found anywhere, and their bordering trees make of the town a veritable park. Many of its residences also are incomparable as examples of high class architecture.

"Besides these points of beauty, there are the lake shore and the bordering fields. Perhaps the greatest charm about the city is its atmosphere of refinement and culture that is reflected in every one's daily life. It has resulted from the gathering here of a higher class of people than is usually found in a city, and this condition is constantly drawing to it more people of the same class."

It is seen, therefore, that the market for real estate in Evanston has been made, first, by the influence of the Northwestern University; second, by the immigration following the Chicago fire; third, its transportation facilities; and fourth, by the character of its citizens, its substantial improvements, and its attractive surroundings.

Real Estate Values.—The value of property in Evanston for business purposes is from $100 to $500 per front foot; for residence lots of the better localities, from $50 to $300 per front foot. In the outlying districts lots are valued from $10 to $40 per foot. The fact that Evanston is not exclusive or made up of one class of people, with high priced building restrictions, but is cosmopolitan, including all classes, with every kind of artisan, workman and professional business man,

makes it an ideal place for residence. During each decade it has won new and added interest. Its school and home circles have been "stamped with a propriety seal;" its churches, representing every denomination and creed, are tolerant and full of enthusiasm; its civic government, made up of the best representation of its people; its healthfulness, the absence of the degrading influence of vice—these, and much more, make Evanston a place where men, women and children may live in security, in the enjoyment of many privileges and much happiness.

On returning from excursions into regions far and near, one is eager to reaffirm these beauties and the restful welcome of Evanston. This is why real estate in this city has a value so completely entrenched and so strongly fortified that it can never be effaced.

CHAPTER XXXIII.

EVANSTON ARCHITECTURE
(By EDGAR O. BLAKE, Architect)

Historic Progress—Influence of the Architect on the City's Growth—The "Georgian" Style follows the Log and Grout Houses—Churches and Private Residences—Advent of the Victorian Gothic Style—University Hall and Union Park Congregational Church—Architect G. P. Randall the Designer—Asa Lyons Evanston's First Resident Architect—Others who followed him—Description of Some Notable Buildings and their Designers—Public Library—Enumeration of Principal Private and Public Buildings.

The credit for historical progress should be given not only to the soldiers, politicians, preachers and financiers, but the men who create our environment should be remembered for the permanent objects of influence they leave behind them. Too often the architect, who designs the monument, is forgotten and the man who paid for it remembered.

It is the first purpose of this article to serve as a reminder of some of the men who have influenced Evanston, not by giving their wealth but by giving their ideas; by putting themselves into the buildings which they designed. It will also be attempted to give a list of the most interesting buildings, not for size or cost but for architecture. It is difficult, however, in a short sketch, to cover every work of architectural art in a city like Evanston, which has been served by at least fifty men as designers of its many buildings.

Historical.—In the later eighteenth and the early nineteenth century, a style of architecture, called the "Georgian," was in quite general use in this country. Books of designs in this style were published and used quite freely by builders in the scarcity of professional designers. It is evident that some of these old books found their way to Evanston in the early days; for, after the log houses and "grout" houses, many of the old buildings show quite plainly the ear-marks of these publications.

Under this head come the Bull-head Tavern, still standing on east side of Ridge Avenue north of Noyes Street; the old Kline house in same neighborhood; the Hoag homestead, on the southwest corner of Hinman Avenue and Davis Street; the Crain house, now standing on University Place, just west of Sherman Avenue, and another old house on the east side of Ridge Avenue south of Simpson Street. Most of these buildings were erected prior to 1860. Dempster Hall, built on the Campus in 1854, was probably the first important building erected. It was destroyed by fire thirty years ago, but pictures show it to have had no more style than the old Preparatory Building, which was erected in 1855.

The first church built by the Methodists, in 1856, was a well proportioned example of the Georgian style; also the Northwestern Female College, which was erected in 1857 on grounds west side of Chicago Avenue, between Lake Street and Greenwood Street, and the old Benson Avenue School, with its queer belfry, built in 1860.

One of the oldest residences at present standing was erected in 1862, by General Julius White, on the northwest corner of Davis Street and Chicago Avenue. It was moved in 1872 to its present location at 1028 Judson Avenue.

Most of the work between 1860 and 1870 had very little interest. The original church buildings erected by the Baptists (in 1865), the Presbyterians (in 1866) and the Congregationalists (in 1868), were of no special style, and all disappeared twenty years ago to make way for modern buildings, the present Presbyterian church being the third erected on the same site.

The so-called Victorian Gothic style was now making its appearance, and examples may be seen in Heck Hall, built on the campus in 1867, and Willard Hall, built in 1871, with their mansard roofs and other characteristic details. The present building of the First Methodist church was built in 1870, and is interesting because it has so long been the principal auditorium in the city.

In 1873 was completed Evanston's first real work of architecture—University Hall—and it still has no superior among Evanston buildings. It was designed as an American adaptation of the English Collegiate Gothic by Architect G. P. Randall, who was one of Chicago's leading architects at that time. He was a Ver-

monter by birth, a self-educated man, an author of several books on architecture, and designed a large number of churches, schools and other public buildings. He died in 1885 and, for a number of years previous, lectured on scientific subjects. One of the best of his buildings in Chicago was the Union Park Congregational church. He claimed to be the first architect using the dished floor and semi-circular arrangement of seats in churches. Mr. Randall showed his originality and genius in selecting the style he did for University Hall, so totally different from the conventional buildings being built here at the same period. Its fitness is attested by the fact that Chicago University, after long consideration, has selected a very similar general style. Is it too much to claim that the constant proximity of this work of art has affected, not only the architecture, but the general life of Evanston since that time?

Evanston's first resident architect was Asa Lyons, and he deserves credit for establishing himself in such a small town. It is also a credit to Evanston that it was willing to support an architect at that early day. Architect Lyons came in 1872 and designed a great number of the houses being put up by Warren and Keeney in the south end of town. Later he erected the second building of the Presbyterian church. He was "the" architect for ten years. A pretty good example of his style is the house at 1043 Hinman Avenue. Among his last works in Evanston were the Simpson market on corner of Davis Street and Sherman Avenue, built in 1882 and famous at that time for its tile floor and fountain; and the original township high school building erected in 1883, and since incorporated in the present edifice.

Two good examples of the work done between 1870 and 1880 are the C. J. Gilbert house, on Ashury Avenue, near Emerson Street, now owned by Mr. T. L. Fansler, and the Haskins house on the northeast corner of Hinman Avenue and Davis Street. At this time there were several places especially admired for their landscape architecture—the Kirk homestead, at the south end of Ridge Avenue, the Edwin Lee Brown place, at the foot of Hamilton Street, and the Old Soldier's Home grounds, at the foot of Main Street. The Kirk homestead is the only one remaining in nearly its former beauty.

The next architects to leave their impress on Evanston architecture were Isaacson & Bourgeois, and when it is told that they designed the Congregational church in 1886, that is sufficient to keep them in long remembrance.

During the ten years from 1880 to 1890, the firm of Edbrooke & Burnham put up quite a number of houses in Evanston. It was the period of the "Queen Anne" in architecture. Probably the residence of Dr. M. C. Bragdon, 1709 Chicago Avenue, is as typical of this period as any other.

Now began building on a large scale by many architects of all degrees of ability. About the time that Architect Lyons sought other fields for his genius, Mr. S. A. Jennings began the practice of architecture here on a small scale, but Evanston was growing fast and, through the force of circumstances, he became the busy architect from 1885 to 1895. During that time he designed several hundred buildings for all purposes and of all sizes and varying cost, but all in one style. A critic who has seen two or three of his houses can recognize his hand in all the others, and there is hardly a block in the entire city where he has not left his mark. There is no doubt he designed more Evanston buildings than any other one man before

or since. The substantial homes of J. W. Low, 1560 Oak Avenue, and Timothy Dwight, 730 Hinman Avenue, are typical "Jennings" houses. Perhaps the most expensive of his houses was the W. H. Jones house, 1232 Ridge Avenue, now owned by W. H. Redington.

During the period of building activity between 1890 and 1895, a number of other architects especially identified themselves with Evanston—another Jennings with initials J. T. W., Mr. J. T. Lane, Charles R. Ayars, P. C. Stewart and, last of all, the author of this article. The work of these later men will be mentioned in the descriptive portion of this article.

Foregoing are all the architects who have been especially identified with Evanston architecture, although many whose principal practice was elsewhere have lived here and have, possibly, added more to the beauty of its buildings than the local men.

Descriptive.—The first appearance of Evanston is not prepossessing to the architectural critic. Davis Street is not especially a poem in brick and stone. In fact, some of it is still wood. This, however, is a general characteristic of American cities and on overlooking this, a number of good designs appear. Those most worthy of mention are the City Hall, a work of Holabird and Roche; the Century Building in renaissance style, by C. R. Ayars; the Rood Building, by J. T. W. Jennings; and the new Simpson Building, No. 616, by John D. Atchison.

On Grove Street, just west of the Police Station, the building of the Evanston Heating Company is worthy of notice as a reasonable expression of purpose in design. It is the work of Myron Hunt. Another important building in this vicinity is the Y. M. C. A. Building by Holabird and Roche.

At the east end of Davis Street one enters the residence district. On the southwest corner of Forest Avenue is a good house in French domestic Gothic style by Burnham & Root. At 1616 Forest Avenue, north of Davis Street, is the house of C. A. Ward, in Southern Colonial style, by G. L. Harvey. The house of F. S. Martin, corner of Forest Avenue and Church Street, is a good sample of the modern plastered building.

The University buildings are, of course, the most studied by strangers. Nearest to the lake is the very conveniently arranged Academy building by D. H. Burnham & Co. The only criticism ever made on it was by some wag, who pitied the poor little bear up on the top trying to hide behind a stone shield. At the end of Hinman Avenue is Science Hall, by Holabird & Roche, north of this University Hall, which has already been mentioned. The School of Oratory, in Venetian Gothic style, is the work of C. R. Ayars. Heck Hall is one of the older buildings mentioned in the historical sketch. Memorial Hall was designed by W. W. Boyington, and is supposed to be Romanesque in style. This architect also designed the Observatory. One of the finest of the University buildings is Orrington Lunt Library, in pure classic style, by W. A. Otis.

On the west side of Sheridan Road, facing the Campus, are a number of artistic houses. The comparatively small residence at No. 1902 is considered by many one of the best proportioned houses in Evanston. North of this are several of the S. A. Jennings houses. No. 2016 is the home of Dr. C. J. Little, designed by W. A. Otis. No. 2110 is Dr. Bonbright's house by C. R. Ayars. No. 2114 is the residence of J. Scott Clark, designed by

himself with the advice and assistance of D. H. Perkins, architect.

This neighborhood is favored by men who are their own architects. On the south side of Noyes Street are two houses, designed by Vernon J. Hall for himself, and at 620 Hamlin Street is Professor Crew's own design. On the northwest corner of Sheridan Road and Milburn Street is the house of E. F. Brown, by Handy & Cady. At 2645 Sheridan Road is the house of C. W. Deering. The light house is a very good specimen of the latest principles in construction of that class of buildings. North of the light-house is a pretty group of houses called Ingleside. One of the best of S. A. Jennings' smaller designs is next to Sheridan Road on the north side of the park. Beginning at the north end of Orrington Avenue are a number of good examples of modern plaster architecture, mostly belonging to professors in the University. Numbers 2340 2110, 2042, 2038, 2030, 2026, and 1925 are all of this material in varying styles. Three good apartment buildings, designed by Myron Hunt, come farther south; the Boyleston, 614 Clark Street; the Cambridge, Clark and Orrington, and the Hereford, corner of Chicago Avenue and Church Street—this last being an especially good example of the English country style.

The block on the west side of Orrington Avenue contains, besides the old Willard Hall, the School of Music, a modern brick design by W. A. Otis, and Chapin Hall, a Colonial design by C. R. Ayars.

The new Public Library, a classic building by C. A. Phillips, will stand on the the northeast corner of Orrington Avenue and Church Street. On the southeast corner of the same streets is the Fowler studio, an artistic design, both exterior and interior, the work of P. C. Stewart. One block west the new Post Office is being erected from designs by the government architect.

On Ridge Avenue, near the north city limits, is the Evanston Hospital, an excellent brick building in the style of the Georgian period by G. L. Harvey. A little farther south, after passing the old Kline house and the Bull-Head Tavern, comes the Academy of Visitation. Only the south wing has been built. The design is drawn from Royal Hollaway College, at Egham, England. H. J. Schlacks is the architect.

Over in the vicinity of Church Street and Wesley Avenue is a group of interesting houses designed by Myron Hunt —Nos. 1613, 1617, and 1606 Wesley Avenue are among them.

The United Presbyterian church, in the same vicinity, is a good piece of brick architecture in Italian Romanesque style. No. 1456 Ridge Avenue, the residence of John B. Kirk, is a good example of modern English country architecture.

The finest private residence in Evanston is that of James A. Patten, on the southwest corner of Ridge Avenue and Lake Street. The house, stable, grounds, fences, decorations and furniture were all designed by George W. Maher, and it is a very good example of what is known as the "Art Nouveau."

Across the street is St. Mark's Episcopal church, in Norman style, by Holabird & Roche, who also designed the Country Club, a large Colonial building a little way east on Lake Street. The interior of St. Mark's is very rich and elaborate.

St. Mary's Catholic church, on the corner of Lake and Oak, was designed by S. A. Jennings. Next door east is St. Mary's Hall, probably the best public

auditorium in Evanston at the present time. It is the work of Murphy & Camp.

The residence of W. J. Fabian, No. 1509 Ridge Avenue, is an elaborate design in timber work, a very beautiful work.

A description of interesting houses on Ridge Avenue would mean a list of nearly all and, in a sketch like this, only the most prominent can be mentioned. The Catherine White house, on the northeast corner of Ridge Avenue and Dempster Street, is a good example of Myron Hunt's work.

On the west side of Ridge Avenue, between Crain and Greenleaf Streets, are three houses in New England Colonial style by W. C. Zimmerman, who also designed a group of very artistic shingled houses on Oak Avenue just east of the above. The residence at 1123 Ridge Avenue is one of Handy & Cady's designs. The W. H. Jones house, 1232, has been mentioned before.

A little west of Ridge Avenue, on corner of Asbury and Lee, is a very handsome little Colonial church designed by D. H. Perkins.

St. Nicholas Catholic church, on Ridge Avenue, south of Main Street, is the work of Hermann Gaul.

Over at the west end of Main Street is the Washington School, designed on general Renaissance lines by Patton and Miller. It is most unique in arrangement of floor plan.

On the corner of Main and Benson is the Central School, by Thomas & Rapp. The Episcopal chapel, corner of Main and Sherman, was built by J. T. Lane.

On the northwest corner of Main Street and Chicago Avenue is the Sheridan building in Italian Renaissance style by J. E. O. Pridmore—a very successful piece of remodeling and adding to an old building.

Across the street south are the Park

Apartments, in English half-timbered style —very successful in appearance in connection with the park in front—designed by the author of this article.

A little north of Main Street on Chicago Avenue is the Hemenway Methodist church by J. T. Long. The house Mr. Long designed for himself on Sheridan Road just north of Main Street, is interesting, as it contains a mantel removed from the old Governor's house in Kaskaskia.

The Lincoln School, corner of Main Street and Judson, is a very good Romanesque design by J. T. W. Jennings.

The gateway to Calvary Cemetery, at the extreme south end of town, is a graceful Gothic design by J. J. Egan, the well known church architect.

Villa Celeste, the home of P. L. McKinnie, at 721 Sheridan Road is by P. C. Stewart.

Hinman Avenue is another street lined with fine residences. Beginning at the south end, No. 730 is the home of Timothy Dwight mentioned previously. The Colonial house, No. 740, is the home of L. L. Smith. The Second Presbyterian church is on the northeast corner of Main and Hinman. The houses at 918 and 1014 are interesting examples of remodeling old houses. The work was done by architects, but more than usually following suggestions by the owner, Dr. A. W. Herbert.

The Evanston Apartments and Enslee Apartments, on opposite corners of Lee Street, are by John D. Atchison. The house at 1043 was previously mentioned as Asa Lyons' work. No. 1211 is a neat Swiss villa by C. R. Ayars. Numbers 1115, 1118, 1119, 1126, and 1209 are all worth repeating. The Hinman Avenue school on the corner of Dempster Street is a perfect colonial design by D. H. Burnham & Co. On the southwest corner of

Hinman and Lake is one of Irving K. Pond's artistic designs.

Around the park at this corner are grouped the unique Congregational church; the Presbyterian church, a Byzantine design by D. H. Burnham & Co.; the Evanston Club by Holabird & Roche, and the graceful Baptist church built in 1875.

Further north is the Methodist church, before mentioned. The houses at 1707 and on the corner of Clark Street were designed by W. A. Otis, the first in English country style and the second in French Gothic.

Forest Avenue has a number of notable houses. No. 1324 is by W. G. Barfield. Dr. Fuller's house, No. 1305, is an interesting shingled house, especially as it is said that D. H. Burnham, who stands at the head of his profession in this country, not only originated the design but made most of the drawings with his own hands.

No. 1314 is a design by Handy and Cady. Farther south at the corner of Greenleaf Street are the Wilson houses, a group in stone, designed by Beers, Clay & Dutton. At the east end of Greenleaf Street is the Boat Club.

Sheridan Road and Judson Avenue are both worth seeing in this vicinity.

At the foot of Hamilton Street the old Edwin Lee Brown place has been subdivided, and built up with a number of beautiful homes, with the slightly discordant proximity of the Melwood Apartment building. One of the largest is a combination design by Wilson & Marble at 1225 Sheridan Road.

Greenwood Boulevard is worth a tour. At the east end are the residences of Arthur Orr at 202 by Holabird & Roche, Dr. Sheppard's residence at 225 by F. Edwards Ficken of New York, and the home of W. H. Bartlett on the corner of Forest Avenue.

On the northwest corner of Judson Avenue is a block of houses by Myron Hunt. At 1424 Judson, is one of W. A. Otis' designs.

Dr. Webster's house, on the corner of Chicago Avenue, is one of the best designs in Evanston. The Unitarian Church, on Chicago Avenue, near by, is the work of a woman architect, Marion Mahoney.

West of the railroad a little south is the High School, a Renaissance design by C. R. Ayars. On the corner of Greenwood and Oak is the Emanuel church, one of the last designs of John W. Root in association with D. H. Burnham. His death occurred soon after it was started.

Greenwood between Maple Avenue and the Ridge contains a number of well designed houses.

Up in the woods, at what was formerly North Evanston, are a large number of moderate priced artistic homes, in particular a group at corner of Lincoln Street, and Evanston Avenue, by P. C. Stewart. D. H. Perkins, architect for the Chicago Board of Education, has built himself a summer home at 2319 Lincoln Street. The interior decorations are by Lucy Fitch Perkins.

The Methodist church, on the corner of Central Street and Prairie Avenue, is a neat piece of wood architecture, by C. H. Whittlesey.

The new buildings now in progress on Davis Street will add greatly to Evanston's architectural beauty. The one on the northwest corner of Chicago Avenue is designed by George W. Maher. The one being erected on the site of old Lyons' Hall, at 621 and 623 Davis Street, is the work of H. W. J. Edbrooke, and the new State Bank Building has for its designer C. A. Phillips.

CHAPTER XXXIV.

STREET NOMENCLATURE
(By J. SEYMOUR CURREY, President Evanston Historical Society)

Origin of Street and Avenue Names in Evanston — Village Platted in 1853 and Named for Dr. John Evans — Postoffice Previously Known as Ridgeville, and Still Earlier as Gross Point — Evanston Office Established in 1855—Street Names Derived from Prominent Methodists, Early Residents or Noted Statesmen — History and Biography thus Incorporated in Street Nomenclature — System of Street and Avenue Numbering — List of Principal Streets and Persons for Whom Named.

The village of Evanston was laid out and platted in the winter of 1853-4 under the superintendence of Rev. Philo Judson, who was at that time business agent of the Northwestern University. The name of Evanston was adopted at this time by the Trustees of the University in honor of Dr. John Evans, one of the incorporators of the University and a liberal contributor to its endowment. Before that time there was no village on the site of Evanston, but a postoffice was in existence known as Ridgeville. In an earlier time the post-office had been known as Gross Point. The latter was established December 28, 1846. This was changed to Ridgeville, April 26, 1850; and again changed to Evanston, August 27, 1855. After laying out the village the form of government still re-

mained vested in the Board of Township Trustees as it had been before. On the 29th of December, 1863, the village was regularly incorporated. This form of government continued until April 19, 1892, when Evanston was incorporated as a city.

Owing to the preponderating influence on the new community of the Northwestern University, which had been established here under Methodist auspices, the names bestowed on the streets were largely those of distinguished Methodists. When, however, later additions were made to the village, the names were given by the new proprietors and the field of selection was much widened. Many of these names are in honor of old residents or of statesmen, or those known to the promoters of the new additions, or were selected arbitrarily because of their fitness to the natural surroundings, or even dictated by fancy.

Thus, in the names of the streets of Evanston there is embalmed much of history and biography. In the main these names are of especial interest to Evanston people, being intimately associated with its character and development. There are a few such names as Main Street, Central Street, and the like, which are common to very many towns, and which convey little or no meaning. But in general the usual poverty of street nomenclature, so painfully apparent in most towns of its size, is in conspicuous contrast with the body of names found here, which in so great a degree reflect the character and sympathies of the founders and builders of Evanston, and are so rich in historical associations.

The plan of this chapter of street names is to give the name of the street followed by the name of the person after whom it was called, with a few brief particulars, or descriptions. Full particulars are available in a great variety of records. The names of some streets have been omitted because it was not possible to learn the origin of them. Some again are sufficiently obvious and require no mention, as for example Washington Street, Madison Street, Chicago Avenue and the like.

It will be observed that the spelling of a street name does not always follow that of the person for whom it was named. This is the case with Hamlin Street, as now spelled, though named after Bishop Hamline who used a final e in the last syllable of his name. So, also, with Forest Avenue, the usual spelling at the present time, though named after a man who spelled his name Forrest. A number of streets are called after the first names of the persons honored. For example, we have Orrington Avenue, Lee Street, Chancellor Street, Florence Avenue and the like, a reference to which will show that these are the Christian names of the persons for whom they were named.

The streets of Evanston are called "Avenues," "Courts," "Streets" and "Places," according to the following rule: Avenues and Courts are such as run north and south; Streets and Places such as run east and west. Exceptions to this rule occur in two instances. The "Sheridan Road" is called "Road" to conform to the general usage of the cities and towns north

and, south of the City of Evanston. The "Indian Boundary Line" is so called because it is a street coinciding with the "Line" established by treaty with the Indians, as described below. The house numbers on the Avenues and Courts begin at the southern limits of the city and run about 800 to the mile, an even hundred beginning at each street intersection; and those on the streets and places begin at the lake and run about 1200 to the mile, an even hundred beginning at each street intersection.

Following will be found the names of the more noted and historic streets, avenues, etc., with a concise reference in each case to the person, locality or circumstance from which the name is derived:

Arnold Street: Named for Isaac N. Arnold, a prominent citizen of Chicago, born 1815, died 1884; was member of Congress 1861-65; and owned land in the vicinity of where this street is located.

Asbury Avenue: For Francis Asbury, first Bishop of the Methodist Episcopal Church in America, 1745-1816.

Ayars Place: For James Ayars, a citizen of Evanston, once President of Board of Village Trustees.

Bennett Avenue: For Mrs. C. C. Bennett, a sister of John Culver, now and for many years past a teacher in the Chicago Public Schools.

Benson Avenue: For Francis H. Benson, a resident of Evanston in an early day.

Boomer Place: For Norton W. Boomer, for many years Principal of a public school in Chicago.

Botsford Street: For J. K. Botsford of Chicago, who was one of the Trustees of the Northwestern University.

Browne Avenue: For Charles E. Browne, one of the original proprietors of North Evanston.

Chancellor Street: For Chancellor L. Jenks, Jr., a son of Chancellor L. Jenks, a citizen of Evanston.

Chicago Avenue: This name was given when the northern limits of Chicago were at North Avenue, and a long stretch of open country lay between Evanston and Chicago. The road connecting the two places was an extension of Chicago Avenue in Evanston southward, which joined North Clark Street at the Chicago city limits. The road was sandy and its condition so bad that a corporation was formed in 1859 to grade it, and it was then called the gravel road. On this road were two toll-gates, one at the intersection of the Indian Boundary Line and the other at Graceland.

Clark Street: For John Clark, a member of Rock River Conference, and the minister in charge of Clark Street church, Chicago, at the time that Mrs. Garrett made her gift to Garrett Biblical Institute.

Clinton Place: Name adopted by city ordinance, February 11, 1902.

Colfax Street: For Schuyler Colfax, Vice-President of the United States, 1869-73.

College Street: Original name of that portion of Davis Street west of Sherman Avenue. Name was changed to Davis Street in 1871.

Crain Street: For the Crain family, who were among the earliest settlers of Evanston.

Darrow Avenue: Named by Morton Culver in laying out a subdivision after a man of that name who was prominent among colored Masons of Chicago.

Davis Street: For Dr. Nathan S. Davis, one of the Trustees of the Northwestern University; born in 1817 and died in 1904.

Dempster Street: For Dr. John Dempster, born in 1794, died in 1863; Professor at Garrett Biblical Institute 1854 to 1863.

Dewey Avenue: For two sisters, Electa E. Dewey and Mary J. Dewey. Name given by Morton Culver in laying out a subdivision; the Misses Dewey were teachers in the Jones School, Chicago.

Dodge Avenue: For Miss Kate Dodge, a teacher in the Jones School, Chicago.

Emerson Street: For Benjamin Emerson, a pioneer resident of Evanston.

Ewing Avenue: For Adlai T. Ewing, who had control for several years of Ewing's addition to Evanston.

Florence Avenue: For Miss Florence Tullis, a teacher in the Jones School, Chicago.

Forest Avenue: For Thomas L. Forrest, born 1819, died 1904; was a banker of Chicago and owned some property in Evanston; for thirty years was cashier of the Hide and Leather Bank. Residents have preferred a spelling different from the name of Mr. Forrest.

Foster Street: For Randolph S. Foster, born 1820, died 1903; was the second President of the Northwestern University, 1856-59.

Gaffield Place: For Eli Gaffield, a pioneer resident of Evanston.

Grant Street: Named in honor of General U. S. Grant.

Greenleaf Street: For Luther L. Greenleaf, born February 7, 1821, died November 23, 1886; lived in Evanston from 1860 to 1875.

Grey Avenue: For Charles F. Grey, a resident of Evanston since 1866.

Hamilton Street: For James G. Hamilton, for many years a resident of Evanston; was the secretary of the Board of Trustees of the Northwestern University.

Hamlin Street: For Leonidas L. Hamline, born May 10, 1797; elected Bishop of the Methodist Episcopal Church 1844; died March 23, 1865.

Hartzell Street: For Joseph C. Hartzell, Methodist Bishop of Africa. While a student at the Garrett Biblical Institute, was the hero of a rescue of four men from the wreck of the schooner "Storm" in May, 1864.

Haven Street: For Erastus O. Haven; born 1820, died in 1881; was President of the Northwestern University 1869 to 1872; in 1880 was elected a Bishop of the Methodist Episcopal Church.

Hinman Avenue: For Clark T. Hinman, first President of the Northwestern University, 1853-55; was born in Kortright, N. Y., August 3, 1817; graduated from Wesleyan University in 1840; died at Troy, N. Y., 1854.

Indian Boundary Line: This street follows the line of the boundary established by a treaty with Ottawas, Chippewas and Pottawatomies, August 24, 1816. The line begins at the lake shore (in the language of the treaty) at "a point ten miles northward of the mouth of Chicago Creek," and runs southwest, crossing the Sheridan Road about one block from the starting point. A half block farther it crosses the southern city limits. It is known as Rogers Avenue after it crosses the limits into Chicago.

Isabella Street: Named by Charles E. Browne after one of his daughters.

Jackson Avenue: For A. B. Jackson, long a resident of Rogers Park.

Jenks Street: For Chancellor L. Jenks, born January 29, 1828; practiced law in Chicago 1851-67; died January 10, 1903.

Judson Avenue: For Philo Judson, born in Otsego County, N. Y., March

1, 1807; was business agent of the Northwestern University, 1854-76; died March 23, 1876.

Kedzie Street: For John H. Kedzie, born September 8, 1815; died at Evanston, April 9, 1903; was a resident of Evanston forty-two years.

Keeney Street: For James F. Keeney, for some years a resident of Evanston.

Kirk Street: For James S. Kirk, born in 1818; lived in Evanston from 1859 to the time of his death; died June 15, 1886.

Lee Street: Named by L. C. Pitner for his son, Lee J. Pitner; name given in 1871 when "Union Addition" was laid out.

Leon Street: Named for Louis Leonhardt, a portion of his name being taken for the purpose.

Library Street: That part of Hamlin Street extending from Orrington Avenue to Sherman Avenue, changed to this name because of its proximity to the Lunt Library, by city ordinance, June 21, 1904.

Livingston Street: Named for Livingston Jenks, a son of Chancellor L. Jenks.

Lyons Street: For Joseph M. Lyons, a resident of Evanston since the '60's.

McDaniel Avenue: For Alexander McDaniel, born in 1816; came to Evanston in 1836; Postmaster at Wilmette 1870-89; died October, 1898.

Mulford Street: For Edward H. Mulford, born 1792; commissioned paymaster (with rank of Major) of a New York regiment in 1825; came to Evanston in 1840; died March 4, 1878.

Nate Street: Former name of Clinton Place; originally named for Rev. John Nate, a minister of the Methodist Church, long a resident of Evanston.

Noyes Street: For Henry S. Noyes; Professor of Mathematics, Northwestern

University, 1855-60; acting President of same 1860-69; died May 24, 1872.

Orrington Avenue: Named for Orrington Lunt; born December 24, 1815; one of the founders of Northwestern University; died April 5, 1897.

Payne Street: For Henry M. Payne, a resident of Chicago.

Pitner Avenue: For Levi C. Pitner, long a resident of Evanston.

Pratt Court: For the Pratt family, of whom two brothers, George and Paul, came to Evanston in 1837.

Reba Place: Named for Miss Reba Poor, a daughter of John E. Poor.

Reese Avenue: For Theodore Reese, surveyor, long a resident of Evanston.

Ridge Avenue: There are two well defined ridges running north and south through Evanston, the west ridge being the more prominent of the two. The general course of Ridge Avenue is along the summit of the West ridge. In an early day this neighborood was often described as "the Ridge." This is the oldest street in Evanston and follows the route of the old Green Bay Road. This route was established as a military road by the United States Government in 1832. It was also the route of the Frink & Walker stage line established in 1836, and which continued in operation until the railroad was opened in 1855.

Rinn Street: For Jacob Rinn, long a resident of Evanston.

Sheridan Road: Named in honor of General Philip H. Sheridan. This great pleasure driveway along the shore of Lake Michigan was planned by Volney W. Foster in 1887, and he is therefore known as the "father of the Sheridan Road." An act of the State Legislature was passed March 27, 1889, authorizing "Pleasure driveways in incorporated towns," under which the Sheridan Road Association was organized. The Evanston City Council passed an ordinance, July 25, 1892, establishing and naming that portion of Sheridan Road which passes through Evanston. Alexander Clark was associated with Mr. Foster in this great enterprise. Mr. Foster died August 15, 1904. Mr. Clark died September 26, 1903. The Sheridan Road is now complete from Lincoln Park in Chicago to Waukegan, and eventually will extend to Milwaukee. Gen. P. H. Sheridan was born March 6, 1831, and died August 5, 1888.

Sherman Avenue: For Alson Smith Sherman, born April 21, 1811; came to Chicago in 1836; Mayor of Chicago, 1844; one of the incorporators of the Northwestern University, 1851; removed to Waukegan in 1856; and died there September 22, 1903.

Shuman Street: For Andrew Shuman, for many years editor of the "Chicago Evening Journal;" Lieutenant-Governor of Illinois 1877-81; born 1830; died 1890.

Simpson Street: For Matthew Simpson, born 1811, elected Bishop Methodist Episcopal Church 1852; President of Garrett Biblical Institute 1861-65; died June 18, 1884.

Stanley Avenue: For B. F. Stanley; name given by C. L. Jenks.

Stewart Avenue: For John W. Stewart, one of the original owners of North Evanston.

Stockham Place: For Mrs. Alice B. Stockham, long a resident of Evanston.

Thayer Street: Named by John Culver for his wife, whose maiden name was Thayer.

Warren Street: For Henry A. Warren, formerly a resident of Evanston.

Wesley Avenue: Named in honor of John Wesley, the founder of Methodism.

Wilder Street: For Aldin G. Wilder, a lumber dealer in Evanston in 1866, who also subdivided lands in the western part of the city.

Willard Place: For Frances E. Willard, born September 28, 1839; President of Woman's College, Evanston, 1870; President of Woman's Christian Temperance Union, 1879; President of World's Christian Temperance Union, 1888; died February 17, 1898.

A notable deficiency in the street nomenclature of Evanston is the absence of Indian names. No street perpetuates the name of tribe or chief, and but one—the "Indian Boundary Line"—has reference to a locality connected with the Indian occupation. The Pottawatomie Indians, who inhabited this region, possessed too ungainly and barbarous a name to make use of, and there were no leaders of distinction among them who might be thus honored. This absence of picturesque Indian names is unfortunate, but is made good in the distinction and character of the names that have been chosen.

The origin of street names is usually neglected until the occasion of them begins to grow dim in the vistas of the past. Then laborious research is necessary to learn the origin and significance of these names which have become household words. The effort to trace accurately the names given to streets, even within a compass of fifty years, is fraught with difficulty, and, as it is seen in older communities, the time comes soon when it is often a matter of conjecture.

The aspect of the streets of Evanston, as we see them today, is in strong contrast with the face of the land as looked upon by the founders of the town. Then was spread before them woodland and fields where farmers and woodmen had, in twenty years of ceaseless toil, changed the face of the country from its primeval condition to one of diversified forest and farm lands. Dwellings and locations of streets began to appear in accordance with the plans of the founders. Extensive lines of shade trees were planted which today, after many years' growth, have developed into stately avenues of lofty elms and maples. Parks beside roadways, well paved streets and walks, spacious and well cultivated lawns, the glimpses here and there of the blue waters of Lake Michigan, and the comfortable and often palatial homes of its residents, have combined to form a "city beautiful," and to earn for itself the well deserved title of a "city of homes."

CHAPTER XXXV

THE FOUR-MILE LIMIT
(By WILLIAM A. DYCHE)

Act Incorporating Northwestern University Amended—Prohibition District Established—Sale of Spirituous Liquors Within Four Miles of the University Prohibited—Local Sentiment in Favor of the Law—Violations and Anti-Saloon Litigation—Citizens' League Organized—Supreme Court Decisions.

On January 18, 1855, Senator Norman B. Judd, of Cook County, offered in the State Senate an amendment to the charter of Northwestern University, entitled: "An Act to amend an act to incorporate Northwestern University," approved January 28, 1851. The proposed amendment consisted of five sections, the second, as finally passed, being as follows:

"Section 2. No spirituous, vinous, or fermented liquors shall be sold, under license or otherwise, within four miles of the location of said University, except for medicinal, mechanical, and sacramental purposes, under a penalty of twenty-five dollars for each offense, to be recovered before any Justice of the Peace of said County of Cook: *Provided*, that so much of this act as relates to the sale of intoxicating drinks within four miles, may be repealed by the General Assembly whenever they may think proper."

Senator John M. Palmer, of Sangamon County, moved to strike out this section. The vote was: yeas 6, nays 14.

Senator Joseph Gillespie offered, as an amendment, that part of the second section which reserves for the General Assembly the right of appeal. The other four sections of the amendment, like the charter, constitute a perpetual contract between the State of Illinois and Northwestern University.

The amendment of Senator Gillespie was agreed to and, on vote, the act was passed, 18 yeas to 2 nays.—(Senate Journal, 1855, pages 126-127.)

The measure was reported to the House February 2, 1855, and read for the first time on February 7th; it was referred to the Committee on Miscellaneous Affairs. On the 9th it was reported by the Committee and ordered to third reading. It was passed February 13th, yeas 51, nays 0.—(House Journal, 1855, pages 205, 295, 378 and 538.)

This amendment was formally accepted by the Trustees of the University June 13, 1855.

Local Sentiment.—There has always been, on the part of citizens of Evanston, a strong sentiment in favor of the strict enforcement of the provisions of this act. It is safe to assert that, from its enactment to the present, Evanston has been freer from the illegal sale of liquor than almost any other community located near the borders of a great city like Chicago. Our local government has always had among its ordinances stringent measures based on this amendment, and usually has made earnest efforts to enforce them. Numerous violations, of course, frequently occur, but there has never been a place within the limits of the corporation where these ordinances were openly violated. Outside of the city, but within four miles, the violations have been more frequent, but at the present time there are very few open saloons within four miles of the University, except to the south, where the prohibition district extends far into the city of Chicago. Here saloons are numerous and flourishing, though they exist contrary to law.

Litigation.—Three cases in which fines have been levied for the illegal sale of liquor within the four-mile limit, have been appealed to the Supreme Court of the State, two of which involved the constitutionality of the amendment to the charter of the University, and the third raised the question of the competency of testimony of detectives pa'd by the city. The first case was decided at the April term of the Court, 1862, being entitled, John O'Leary, Appellant, vs. The County of Cook, Appellee. The constitutionality of the amendment was questioned. The attorneys for the appellant argued that it was in contravention of the 23d Section of Article III. of the Constitution, in that it embraces two separate and independent subjects- -the one of a private character, viz.: the amendment to the corporate powers of the University; the other of a public nature, viz.: the prohibition of the sale of liquor within a given locality under penalty—two subjects not germane to one another and having no natural or necessary connection with each other, while

only one subject is expressed in the title of the act.

This was successfully refuted by Messrs. Hurd, Booth & Potter, attorneys for the appellee, and the constitutionality of the act was upheld in a decision rendered by Chief Justice Caton. The following quotation from the opinion from the Chief Justice is interesting:

"The object of the charter was to create an institution for the education of young men, and it was competent for the Legislature to embrace within it everything which was designed to facilitate that object. Every provision which was intended to promote the well being of the institution, or its students, was within the proper subject matter of that law. We cannot doubt that such was the single design of this law. Although this provision m ght incidentally tend to protect others residing in the vicinity from the corrupting and demoralizing influences of the grog-shop, yet that was not the primary object of the law, but its sole purpose was to protect the students and faculty from such influence."

It is of interest to note that the appellant, John O'Leary, and his descendants have been involved in more or less litigation with Evanston for nearly half a century; it is also worthy of notice that the illegal sale referred to in this case was made to Mortimer Russell, Russell being a name well known in the early annals of the village. The greatest item of interest in this case, aside from the favorable decision is, that the cause of law and order was ably advocated by Hon. Harvey B. Hurd, who, for more than half a century, had been one of Evanston's foremost citizens. Though more than forty years have come and gone since this decision, until his death in January, 1906,

Mr. Hurd still remained to lend his vigorous aid in seeing that the law was enforced.

From 1882 to 1893 the Citizens' League of Evanston was active in prosecuting violators of this law. Among those frequently prosecuted were Trausch Brothers, and other saloon-keepers on the West Ridge, just north of Rose Hill. With the hope of protecting themselves from further prosecutions, these saloon-keepers and their friends, on November 28, 1890, incorporated the village of West Ridge, out of territory heretofore not included within any city or village. Said village, by ordinance, regulated the sale of intoxicating liquors within its limits by licensing the sale thereof. Henry Trausch was granted a license; shortly thereafter the Citizens' League obtained evidence that he made two separate and distinct sales of liquor. Action was brought against Trausch and a fine levied on him. He appealed the case and it finally reached the Supreme Court.

Supreme Court Decision.—Chief Justice Shope, in rendering the opinion of the Court, makes it clear that any license granted by any city, village or town for the sale of liquor within the four-mile district is null and void. The following is a quotation from his opinion:

"While the power is given to license, regulate and prohibit the selling and giving away of intoxicating liquors, such power is not to be so construed as to affect the provisions of the charter of Northwestern University, it being a literary institution, the charter of which was granted before the General Incorporation Act."

The chief contention of the attorney for the appellant was, that the amendment had been repealed by the general act, approved May 4, 1887. This was overruled. It is made clear in this decision that any license issued for the sale of liquor within the four-mile district, even though it be issued by a city, town or village within said district, is null and void. It is worthy of note in connection with this case that Hon. Harvey B. Hurd again appeared as attorney for the appellee, associating with him the law firm of Beach & Beach.

During the past twenty-five years several different organizations have been formed to assist in the enforcement of this act. On August 24, 1882, the Citizens' League of the Township of Evanston was incorporated, with Frank P. Crandon and David R. Dyche, Millard R. Powers and H. W. Chester as charter members. Mr. Dyche served as its President till his death in August, 1893. He devoted much time, energy and no insignificant contributions from his own purse to forward the objects of the League. The next President was Mr. Crandon. He, also, made large donations of time and money to this important work.

Four-Mile League.—In 1894 it seemed wise to form a new organization as a successor to the Citizens' League, and through the efforts of Henry Wade Rogers, who was then President of Northwestern University and greatly devoted to the cause of temperance, the Four-Mile League was organized, with Charles B. Congdon, Henry Wade Rogers, Hugh R. Wilson, Charles H. Aldrich, William A. Dyche, William H. Bartlett, Frank P. Crandon, George M. Sargent and Charles J. Little, as charter members. The charter was dated September 11, 1894. Mr. Crandon was its first President; he was succeeded by Mr. J. C. Shaffer. Mr. Shaffer conducted a vigorous warfare against illegal sale of liquor and met with marked success. Mr. Newell C. Knight was the third and last President of the League. His administration was equally vigorous.

In 1902 the Municipal Association was incorporated. This organization, though having wider aims than the Four-Mile League, which it succeeded, is especially interested in the same good cause and is doing excellent work. Mr. Charles R. Webster has been President since its incorporation.

On January 3, 1893, William H. Lyman, a Chicago member of the House of Representatives, introduced House Bill 282, which sought to repeal a portion of the City and Village Act of 1872. This act, among other things, gives cities and villages power to issue licenses for the sale of liquor under certain conditions. It provides, however, "that nothing in the act shall be construed to affect the provisions of the charter of any literary institution heretofore granted." The introduction of this bill created much excitement and great indignation. Large delegations at once went to Springfield and exerted such influence that the bill never reached a second reading.

Mayor's Report.—The citizens of Evanston have been greatly annoyed by the existence of saloons outside of, but near to, the limits of the corporation. The following quotation from the Mayor's report for the year 1895 gives an instance of this:

"For some years the western portion of our city has been greatly annoyed by the existence of several saloons on the prairie west of us. Some of these saloons were resorts of the lowest character, and to their other evils gambling and prostitution were often added. For some years they were licensed illegally by the Cook County Commissioners; but this summer, in response to your request and the urgent effort of Commissioner Munn, these illegal licenses were not reissued. The Four-Mile League provided funds to carry on a vigorous warfare against them. Our Chief of Police, Wheeler Bartram, greatly aided the League with his advice and work, as did also our City Attorney. The result was that, after a brief but energetic fight, these saloons were practically closed. Some of them are still running, but very quietly. A renewed and continuous effort by the League, aided by our city authorities, will undoubtedly close them. The only way to successfully fight this enemy is to make it too expensive for him to stay in business."

During the latter part of 1896, and for some time thereafter, the city was greatly hindered in its attempts to prosecute violators of its prohibitory law by adverse decisions of the courts located in Chicago. The following, from the Mayor's report for 1896, is to the point:

"One W. H. Meyers was arrested in July, 1896, on several charges of violating our liquor ordinances. He was fined in sums from $10 to $100. From these judgments the said Meyers appealed to the Criminal Court, where the cases were dismissed on the grounds that the evidence had been obtained by witnesses who were in the employ of the city for the purpose of bringing action against the said Meyers. The city took an appeal from this decision to the Appellate Court, where it again met defeat, the Appellate Court sustaining the decision of the Criminal Court.

"While it is comparatively easy for our policemen to discover the resorts where liquor is sold illegally, it is very difficult for them to obtain evidence of this, for the reason that they are well known, hence it is necessary to use detectives, but both the testimony of our policemen, as well as that of the detectives, was rendered useless by the decisions above referred to, and the difficulty of successfully prosecuting the keepers of these resorts was greatly increased. The case just referred to was carried to the Supreme Court of the State, by the direction of the Council, and the judgments of the Criminal and Appellate Courts were reversed. The entire case was in charge of City Attorney George S. Baker, and to him belongs unstinted praise for the obtaining from the Supreme Court of so far-reaching benefit, not to Evanston alone, but also to numerous other communities. The difficulty of prosecuting these cases and obtaining satisfactory results is far greater than most people imagine."

Difficulties Owing to Nearness to Chicago.—One who, for the first time, is called upon to assist in enforcing the ordinances of Evanston, based on the amendment to the charter of the University, has no idea of the difficulties of the task, and it too frequently happens that both officers of the city and of the voluntary associations above referred to not only receive too little support from the community, but are most unjustly criticised for failure to obtain their complete enforcement. Occasionally they have deserved severe condemnation for their indifference, but, as a rule, they have been earnest and active, meeting with decided success. Though at times our citizens seem indifferent to appeals for aid as in this work, they are in reality greatly interested and in emergencies respond most generously. The

greatest danger in my mind to our law is the City of Chicago. The "four-mile limit" extends about two and one-half miles into the City of Chicago, and, in this prohibition territory in Chicago, numerous saloons exist. I do not know if Chicago at present licenses these saloons. When I last investigated this in 1896, I found that Chicago did not issue them any license, but that the saloon-keepers at the end of each quarter paid the City Collector a sum equivalent to a quarter's license. Whether licensed or not, they exist illegally, and ought to be closed. If they are allowed by Chicago to flourish on Devon Avenue, some day she will permit them on the very north line of her corporate limits— a stone's throw from Calvary Cemetery. Unless Evanston puts up a vigorous fight, this will happen. Of all the blessings Northwestern University has brought Evanston, this amendment is first. It gives us a unique place in the ranks of American cities, and helps to make it possible for us to maintain a local government of unusually high standard. Let us give every aid and encouragement to our officials and especially to those men who, from time to time, we ask to act as our leaders in the great work of enforcing the provisions of this amendment and the ordinances based thereon.

CHAPTER XXXVI.

HOMES AND HOME-MAKERS—1846-1870
(By ELIZABETH M. BOYNTON HARBERT, Ph. D.)

Some of the Early Homes of Evanston— Men and Women Who have Left Their Impress on the City's History—What Evanston Owes to Its Early Home Builders—Historic Names on the City Map— Abraham Lincoln and other Distinguished Visitors—The Willard and Eggleston Families—Notable Workers in the Field of Religion, Education, Literature and the Arts.

"The language of a ruder age gave to the common law the maxim that every man's house is his castle: the progress of Truth will eventually make every home a shrine."

"I think that the heroism, which, at this day, would make on us the impression of Epaminondas and Phocion, must be that of a domestic conqueror."

Thus wrote our poet-philosopher Emerson, concerning the value and importance of wise home-making, while our poet-scientist, Henry Drummond, has left for us the following statement:

"So long as the first concern of a country is for its homes, it matters little what it seeks second or third.

"The one point, indeed, where all prophets meet, where all sciences, from biology to ethics, are enthusiastically at one, is in their faith in the imperishable potentialities of this yet most simple institution. In a far truer sense than Raphael produced his "Holy Family," nature has provided a Holy Family. Not for centuries, but for millenniums, the family has arrived. Time has not tarnished it; no later art has improved upon it; no genius discovered anything more lovely, nor religion anything more divine."

Of one important branch of home-making, that great "Apostle of the Beautiful," John Ruskin, has written:

"Cookery means the knowledge of Circe, Medea, and of Calypso and Helen, and of Rebekah and of all the Queens of Sheba. It means the knowledge of all fruits and balms; of all that is sweet in fields and groves. It means the economy of your great grandmothers and the science of thoroughness, French art and Arabian hospitality." And, if Mr. Ruskin had lived on this side of the Atlantic, might he not have added, "American Adaptability?"

Mr. Frank Grover, in a valuable historical sketch (printed elsewhere in this volume) refers to one of the first typical Evanston homes as follows:

"The father, Antoine Ouilmette, was of French descent; the mother, Archange, was of true American (Indian) parentage. In this family were four daughters: Elizabeth, Archange, Josette and Sophia, and four sons: Joseph, Louis, Francis and Mitchell."

Surely all lovers of symbolism or all philosophers, thinkers, who recognize the law that, in order to secure harmony, we must combine differences, will promptly recognize in the variety and balance of this pioneer home, prophecies of the resultant harmony and equilibrium which has caused so many discriminating tourists to repeat the trite question, "Is this Heavenston?" Thus, in its very infancy, the presiding Fates seem to have decreed that the honor of having founded our beloved Evanston belonged equally to its sons and daughters, while our subsequent cosmopolitanism may be traced to that French father and American mother.

For a number of years William and James Carney represented the entire police force, and so firmly, kindly and humanely did they preserve law and order, that the village was exempt from depredations, and the very name "Carney" became a synonym for law and order; as instance, the incident of an Evanston child exclaiming at sight of a Chicago policeman, "There goes another good Carney."

In preparing this fragmentary sketch, we have been interested in the typical character of the early settlers who, by their tastes and pursuits, foreshadowed the æsthetic development of after years.

Mr. and Mrs. Alonzo Burroughs were among the earliest agriculturists. Mr. and Mrs. Samuel Reed seem to have made Beauty and Service the patron saints of their home. We are told that Mr. Reed was the original path-finder or roadmaster of the village, and that a certain apple-tree planted by Mrs. Reed was, for forty years, because of the fragrance of its bloom and the rare flavor of its fruit, a joy to succeeding generations of children.

These pioneer path-finders and homemakers doubtless would have been cheered and encouraged in many toilsome wanderings, could they have foreseen the tree-fringed avenues, streets and courts, whose names enshrine the memories of many subsequent path-makers, and honored citizens; e. g., "Judson," "Hinman," "Irvington," "Benson," and "Kedzie" Avenues; "Dempster," "Davis," "Noyes," "Mulford," "Crain," "McDaniels," and "Lyons" Streets; "Ayars Court" and "Willard Place," etc.

"Joy," that notable but too frequently neglected "Fruit of the Spirit," hospitality, industry and faith (faith in God and faith in humanity) seem to have been characteristic of many of these pioneer homes. The altruistic cheerfulness, so notable in his philanthropic daughter, Mrs. Helen Judson Beveridge, as well as in other members of that merry household, was early interspersed in the village life by the genial father. Rev. Philo Judson. We are told that Mr. Judson's optimism and constant cheerfulness "enabled him to make perpetual holiday of the hard work and privations incident to the life of a circuit-rider through the wilds of Illinois," while his wife, Mrs. Huddleston Judson, was in all respects a notable helpmeet, bravely bearing the added responsibilities resultant from his numerous absences.

Truly, if "all the world loves a lover," the residents of small frontier villages, where life is often too strenuous to permit of much pleasure-seeking, must always delight in a wedding. We are confident that, if the villagers could have foreseen in the groom a future General and Governor, and in the bride a notable philanthropist, even greater interest, if possible, would have centered in the marriage, in 1848, of Miss Helen Judson and Mr. John L. Beveridge.

Who can estimate the amount of good

influences that have emanated from the family circle of children and grand-children, whose father, mother and grandparents commenced their home-making in a small cottage near where the Congregational Church now stands? We refer to Mr. and Mrs. John A. Pearsons. Mr. Pearsons, aside from his business interests and industry, was ever a promoter of harmony in the village, as he was, for a number of years, the first and only chorister; while Mrs. Pearsons has, for more than half a century, been a constant benediction to home and friends and church.

Another group of contributors to the peace, health and harmony of the early village life was the family of Dr. and Mrs. Jacob W. Ludlam. The early annals of Evanston contain frequent references to this tree-embowered home as a social and musical center of most gracious influences. The Evanston Club House now occupies the beautiful grounds of this one-time influential home-center.

The home of Major and Mrs. Mulford, "The Oakton" of 1840, is also remembered with loving appreciation by all who comprehend the influence and power of a bountiful hospitality, which is at the same time brave enough to exclude temptation in any form from both young and old. We are told that, in those early days, from their most abundant table, wine was excluded, even on New Year's day.

Theirs was, indeed, the home of Justice and hospitality and temperance. Major Mulford was one of the early and honorable Justices of the Peace.

About this time arrived the families of Mr. and Mrs. George M. Huntoon, General and Mrs. Julius White, Major and Mrs. Edward Russell, Mr. and Mrs. Leander Clifford, Mr. and Mrs. George F. Foster, Mr. and Mrs.

Andrew J. Brown, Mrs. Mary Foster, Mr. and Mrs. Simon J. Kline, Professor and Mrs. William Jones, Mr. and Mrs. E. R. Paul, Mr. and Mrs. Benjamin F. Hill, Mr. and Mrs. O. A. Grain.

If still with us, the lamented editor of this volume might enter his editorial protest; yet we would still insist upon the privilege of emphasizing in this record, the debt of gratitude which, not only Evanston, but the entire State and Nation, owe to some of these pioneers. In 1855, Hon. and Mrs. H. B. Hurd commenced their home-making in Evanston; and every one in any way affected by the laws, the ethics or spiritual development of our loved "Prairie State," was thereby directly benefited. For half a century Judge Hurd, by his legal acumen, his patriotic citizenship, his true fellowship in neighborhood, club and church, his loving fatherliness and grandfatherliness, proved a benediction to his generation and, at his passing onward on January 20, 1906, no citizen was ever more sincerely mourned. Many citizens who cherish loving memories of "the good old times," refer with kindliest interest to the home of Judge and Mrs. Hurd, while children and grandchildren pronounce them "blessed."

As early as 1858, in the happy, wisely orderd home of Mr. and Mrs. J. F. Willard, a young girl was rapidly developing into the gifted philanthropist who, more than any other citizen, has made Evanston a house-hold word throughout the world, and "Rest Cottage" a veritable "Mecca" to thousands. The motherhood of Mrs. Mary Thompson Willard has become historic, but as we wish to refer to it in another connection, we omit further comment here.

In 1885 Mr. and Mrs. Allen Vane commenced their home-building here, laying the foundations, as was notably the case of so many of Evanston's early residents, of outside philanthropies, as well as fireside pleasures. Other notable arrivals about this time were Rev. and Mrs. Obadiah Huse—the charming personality of Mrs. Huse, the dignified bearing of Mr. Huse and the intellectual alertness of their children rendering their home a most attractive place.

Citizens whose memories are enriched by pictures of the childhood and youth of Evanston, refer with loving appreciation to the home of Mr. and Mrs. L. L. Greenleaf, whose most generous hospitality included almost every human interest and object—educational, philanthropic and reformatory. Mr. Greenleaf was one of the first of our citizens to make a valuable gift to the library of the University. He organized the Temperance Alliance, and Mrs. Elizabeth M. Greenleaf, his coadjutor in every good word and work, accepted service as President of the first Board of Trustees of "The Woman's Educational Association."

Two notable friends of education arrived when Mr. and Mrs. C. G. Haskin brought their "Lares and Penates" to the village, and afterwards built the attractive house on the northeast corner of Hinman Avenue and Davis Street, which has successively served as the home for such representative citizens as Mr. and Mrs. Simeon Farwell and Mrs. Mary Raymond Shumway.

An all-inclusive altruism is always characteristic of the true parental heart, which cannot rest content until comfort, opportunity and education are secured for "all the other children," as well as for one's very own; hence, we are not surprised to find it recorded that, "early in 1868, Mrs. Mary Haskin started forth alone, from her well ordered home on a most important mission. Her object was

to submit to such well known Christian philanthropists as Mrs. Melinda Hamline and Dr. Henry Bannister, her plans for a "Woman's Educational Association." The marked success which attended her effort belongs to the Educational Chapter. We deem it our province, however, to refer to the practical interest in this plan—and doubtless personal sacrifice— to give the first financial aid, which developed in the home of Rev. Obadiah and Mrs. Huse, one of the interesting and influential home centers already referred to. Studying the results enjoyed in the Evanston of to-day, we realize what patient, faithful, self-sacrificing seed-sowing was done by these faithful pioneer home-makers in order to insure such a "Harvest Home" as the citizens of our bountiful and beautiful village enjoy to-day. As we think of the tradition of one notable "City Father," planting miles of trees, we rejoice in the day when Mr. and Mrs. Eli Gage and their household inscribed their names upon the now rapidly enlarging directory.

One participant in "those good old times" informs us that, at one time, the social interests of the village seemed to converge in the cheerful home of Mr. and Mrs. Richard Somers, where, amid all good influences, a happy group of children were growing into manhood and womanhood.

Another friend cherishes, as an almost sacred picture, that Madonna-faced young mother tenderly ministering to her own little "coming woman:" the sweet voiced mother being Mrs. Lucy Stone; the baby daughter, the gifted Alice Stone Blackwell. Meanwhile, in imagination, we see that noble father (the justice-loving patriot to whom every American woman owes a debt of gratitude), Mr. Henry Blackwell, at his daughter's cradle, highly resolving to do all in his power to secure freedom of opportunity, not only for his own, but for every other child without distinction of race, color, creed or sex.

Of the home life of Rev. and Mrs. George C. Noyes, we find the following interesting silhouette in "A Classic Town:" "Few have the intersphering nature that would lead them to lend a hand in enterprises so varied as those that shared the beneficent activities of Dr. Noyes. Indeed, there was no movement for the good of Evanston into which he did not throw the momentum of his well-poised mind and the warming influence of his opulent heart."

"Beside this valiant servant of Christ, there stood, during the first twelve years of his Evanston pastorate, a wife strong and capable as she was winsome and tender. I shall never forget, nor will any one who shared their blessed help, their faces so full of inspiration, their voices so vibrant with sympathy, their hands so frequently outstretched in deeds of love."

Mrs. Noyes was another illustration of the fact that the true mother-heart is inclusive, for while surrounded by her own group of six children, she found time to aid in the temperance work, and to meet the various demands made upon the wife of a pastor of a large church.

"For a term of years, Miss Emily Noyes rendered most faithful service in her brother's home until the only daughter of Rev. and Mrs. Noyes, now Mrs. Ellen Noyes Orr, began to preside, as a little mother-queen, among her group of brothers."

Of the beloved Professor Francis D. Hemenway, it is said that not even the "Hemenway Memorial Church" is his true monument, but the "Hymnal" of the Methodist Church. Dr. and Mrs. Hemenway came to Evanston in 1857, and for

almost a quarter of a century lived, loved and served among us. A most beloved instructor in the University, the record of his refined, helpful and harmonious life belongs there: his wife has claimed, as her richest inheritance, the fact that "she had been the privileged home-maker for one of the purest, truest and best of men, who fully appreciated the meaning of that sacred word "Home."

The historian in search of facts in regard to the substantial growth of Evanston between the years 1850 and 1860, is aided by the following paragraph from an interesting letter written by Mrs. Sara Bailey Mann, one of the pioneer daughters. Mrs. Mann writes: "You ask when my parents moved to Evanston? They came here in 1859. The location of the Northwestern University was just then decided upon, and father moved here because of the educational advantages Evanston then promised." Some of these children for whom these loving parents, Mr. William S. and Mrs. Sarah Bailey, were thus planning, were soon called to the severe educational experiences of our Civil War, as three of their sons responded to the call of their country, the daughters subsequently (as was so often the case) bravely bearing added responsibilities.

In preparing this little sketch, the writer is often tempted to pause, as before sacred shrines in recognition of the really heroic sacrifices and endeavor manifest in these homes. Words written by a friend concerning Mr. and Mrs. Bailey are so true of them and of many other parents, that we reproduce them here: "What a history two simple names suggest. What sunshine, shadow, struggle, heroic sacrifice, noble living and final victory."

As no well regulated village is without

its universal "aunt" or "uncle," so, in 1863, there came to Evanston one who was soon familiarly known as Uncle Mark De Coudres. At ninety years of age, he with his own hands shingled his home in order to contribute $100 for African Missions.

In a copy of *The Index*, of 1864, we find the following record of the closing of one of the early homes—that of Dr. and Mrs. James T. Jewell: "Mrs. Jewell, the devoted and beloved wife of Dr. James Jewell, died at her home on Greenwood Street last Tuesday." Those who can read between the lines will comprehend the pathos of such a record as the following, which was so often true of the self-sacrificing mothers of those early days: "She received an education, during her girlhood, far above that which it was possible, at that time, for many to attain. From early life she entertained strong desires to enter upon a life of study and into literary work. After her marriage she saw no immediate way to carry out her desires and plans without neglecting her duties in her home. She considered the matter carefully and deliberately elected as her life work, the making of a home for her husband and children." While some students of motherhood and home-making sometimes conclude that, if the mother can serve the literary feast in addition to the more material ones, it is better for home and children, yet all who knew of the absolute devotion of Mrs. Jewell to her husband and home, will gratefully remember her faithful administrations therein.

Another notable home-maker who seems to have yielded herself as a loving sacrifice in her home, was the wife of Bishop Randolph Foster. Bishop and Mrs. Foster, with their group of eight most interesting children, lived in a home among the magnificent group of oak trees which formerly adorned the lot upon which the hospitable home of Mr. and Mrs. Hugh Wilson now stands.

This spot seems to have ever been one noted for its generous hospitality. Mrs. Foster was, as Elder Boring once said, "a wholly selfless woman. She was a Miss Sarah Wiley, one of the best, truest, purest, most unselfish women that ever lived, devoted to her husband, lost and swallowed up in him; she lived for him, planned for him, took care of him, and kept a home that was always open to his friends with the most generous hospitality."

We build monuments—the world is filled with them—to the fathers who yield life for others on the world's great battlefields; let us enshrine the memories of the self-sacrificing mothers and fathers, who, amid the imperious cares of home or the overwhelming duties and responsibilities of business, yield their lives for their children. As those who have entered into their labors, let us endeavor to secure wiser household and business conditions by replacing intense competition with Christian co-operation.

We have with hesitation referred to these facts in the hope that, with hundreds of similar ones that have come to each of us, they may incite us to throw the weight of whatever influence we may possess in favor of simpler manners, wiser laws, which will inevitably "Ring out the false, ring in the true."

The more spiritual and intuitional the wife and mother, the more is she needed by husband and children, and the greater the loss to the highest good of all, if she yields to the wifely and motherly temptation to effect her own effacement and utter self-sacrifice for her loved ones.

These same years seem to have been

auspicious ones for Evanston in many ways. In addition to the several names mentioned, we find recorded the arrival of Mr. and Mrs. Francis Bradley and Mr. and Mrs. Simeon Farwell.

In 1862 a young couple arrived in the village who were destined to make valuable additions to its life in many ways; and most interesting is the story of the service rendered by Dr. Oliver and Mrs. E. E. Marcey, to science, literature, philanthropy and religion. The pleasant homestead on the northeast corner of Chicago Avenue and Church Street has been, for forty years, a favorite rallying point for students and friends. Of Dr. Marcey's valuable services as an educator, mention will be made elsewhere, while, for adequate record of Mrs. Marcey's faithful ministrations as wife, mother, missionary-worker and philanthropist, a volume would be required. The parental pride centered in the beautiful and gifted daughter, Mrs. Anna Marcey Davis, whose memory is still sacredly cherished by many friends.

About this time we find our illustrious patriot, Mrs. Jane C. Hoge, not only wisely guiding and guarding and ministering to her own, but also including, in her true mother-heart, thousands of semi-motherless boys, who, during those crucial years of war, watched for her coming, or for the result of her loving care, as for an angel. Reproducing a statement made some years since at the historic "Foremother's Day in Evanston," we repeat: Because our lake-bordered, tree-fringed village was once her home, we place lovingly on our scroll of honor, the name of Mrs. Jane C. Hoge, while just underneath, we trace that of Mrs. Arza Brown, the first woman in the United States of America to receive the badge of the Christian Commission.

Any thoughts of the philanthropic mother include memories of the beautiful and hospitable home on Chicago Avenue, where the interests of the whole world were studied, and so far as possible, aided by Mr. and Mrs. Isaac R. Hitt. This home is one of the treasured land-marks of Evanston. Mrs Arza Brown, the patriotic mother of Mrs. Hitt, included in her active interest "A Christian Commission of the United States of America;" Mrs. Mary Brown Hitt, the daughter, included in her plans missionary service to the whole world.

When we assert of Mr. Isaac R. Hitt, Mr. Andrew J. Brown and other of our prominent and influential men, that they supplemented and aided their wives in public philanthropic work, we record their true heroism and self-sacrifice, since it required true courage for a loving husband to hear and read the oft-time bitter criticisms of those days, upon any work performed by woman outside of the home, even though such service was rendered for the Church or the State.

During the years from 1864 to 1867, inclusive, many strong links were forged in the chain of helpful influences which was to encircle Evanston for generations, since many of the children of these rapidly developing home-shrines are numbered amongst the most useful and honored citizens of the present time. Art, literature, science, health, education, philanthropy, religion, happiness, beauty and joy have been the rich fruitage yielded from the homes of Mr. and Mrs. Charles F. Grey; Dr. and Mrs. Oliver Marcy; Dr. and Mrs. Miner Raymond; Dr. and Mrs. O. H. Mann; Rev. and Mrs. Lucius H. Bugbee; Mr. and Mrs. L. H. Boutelle; Mr. and Mrs. Andrew J. Brown; Mr. and Mrs. Nicholas G. Iglehart; Mr. and Mrs. Towner K. Webster; Mr. and Mrs. Francis Bradley; Mr. and Mrs. Simeon

Farwell; Mr. and Mrs. H. C. Tillinghast; Mr. and Mrs. Charles E. Browne; Mr. and Mrs. H. F. Olmstead; Hon. and Mrs. Andrew Shuman and Mr. and Mrs. Frank L. Winnie.

Among the earliest patrons of art were Mr. and Mrs. Charles F. Grey, and the carefully selected canvases, which have adorned their beautiful and home-like family residence on Forest Avenue, have rendered this home center a most attractive spot to all art-lovers, while in the church and in the beautiful courts of philanthropy, they have rendered constant, cheerful and most generous services. Music and religion were indigenous to the spiritual atmosphere of the home of Mr. and Mrs. Nicholas G. Iglehart. The records of the Baptist Church are replete with the facts of Mrs. Iglehart's abundant helpfulness.

Abounding cheerfulness, and that true hospitality which includes every homesick, lonely stranger, were conspicuously characteristic of the home of Mr. Charles E. and Mrs. Martha Evarts Browne. No literary, musical or artistic prophet, philanthropist or reformer was without honor in Evanston, during the years when Mr. and Mrs. Browne lived and served amongst us. At one time during the year 1869, sixty-nine authors, musicians and literateurs were numbered among the guests at this home.

Another home where, for many years, one met with a rare hospitality and with most beautiful object lessons in high-thinking and simple living, was that of Mr. and Mrs. H. F. Olmstead. In addition to the wise and careful mothering of her four sons, Mrs. Olmstead was one of the most discriminating and appreciative students of philosophy and literature amongst our Evanston women, while Mr.

Olmstead was noted for his business integrity.

If ever a man caused his neighbors and friends to walk a flower-strewn path, it was Mr. H. C. Tillinghast. His sermons in flowers, silently exhaling from the pulpit of more than one church, constantly reminded us that "Beauty is the smile of God." Mr. and Mrs. Tillinghast have been blessed in their home life, and in turn blessed the village and the church, while children and grandchildren refer to them as their richest inheritance.

How many care lines have faded from the faces of anxious young mothers upon the appearance of Dr. O. H. Mann. He was successful and progressive in his medical practice, which included the then novel hints and suggestions in regard to the prevention of disease by hygienic nursing and cheerful surroundings. The home of Dr. and Mrs. Mann was the scene of generous hospitality both to friends and to ideas.

In the pleasant home of Mr. and Mrs. Francis E. Bradley the Congregational Church was organized. From it many other religious and philanthropic influences emanated, and ever the purest atmosphere of culture, refinement and true religion permeated this home of beautiful daughters and obedient sons. For many years, this home, together with those of Mr. and Mrs. J. L. Williams, Mr. and Mrs. L. H. Boutelle and Mr. and Mrs. J. H. Kedzie, seemed to be the "social annex" to the Congregational Church.

During these years the University, the Methodist Church and the Social Circle of the village, gladly welcomed Dr. Miner Raymond and his gracious and estimable wife, Mrs. Elizabeth Henderson Raymond. To the historian of the University belongs the rich and interesting record of the good Doctor's many useful years. The memories of the early and faithful ministrations of the loving mother belong to us all, and are cherished as a rich legacy by her children and grandchildren, as are the more scholarly labors and Christian philanthropies of the noble father.

About this time Mr. E. W. Larned came to build the second brick house in Evanston, to be the future home of Mr. and Mrs. I. P. DeCoudres. In the following year Mr. and Mrs. Larned located permanently in Evanston.

To all appreciating the value of the kindergarten and the importance of the early years of childhood, a most important and far-reaching event occurred, when, in the spring of 1866, Rev. and Mrs. Edward Eggleston commenced their home-making in our village. Mr. Eggleston was among the first of our American fathers to comprehend and appreciate the methods and aim of the great Froebel. Finding it impossible to obtain a good translation of Froebel's songs, he studied German for that purpose; translated the songs, built a cottage for the kindergarten and taught the kindergartners, and, meanwhile, superintended the Methodist Episcopal Sunday School, while carrying on his literary work.

Another inmate of this "Children's Home" was a gifted young sister, Miss Jane Eggleston, who subsequently became the wife of Rev. Charles Zimmerman. Mrs. Zimmerman, although possessed of unusual intellectual gifts (as all who have read her "Gray Heads on Young Shoulders" recognize), has been far more than a quarter of a century a most faithful mother and home-maker, as Rev. Mr. Zimmerman is one of our enthusiastic reformers.

In this same year, 1866, much interest centered in the arrival of many other most interesting families and in the erection of some beautiful homes in our suburb, notably the residence of Mr. and Mrs. W. N. Brainard, on Hinman Avenue. The homes of those days, although not equaling, in many respects, some of the more massive structures of modern times, possessed all the essentials of ideal homes, namely: large grounds, grassy parks shadowed by beautiful trees, flowers, books, music, happy children, and genuine altruism. In the home of Mr. and Mrs. Brainard, for a quarter of a century, a most charming hospitality was dispensed. While fulfilling every duty incident to motherhood and home, Mrs. Brainard found time for helpful service in the church and in social circles, and also for extensive and discriminating reading along philosophic and spiritual lines, which has caused her opinions to be highly valued by all who love the good, the beautiful and the true. Mr. William N. Brainard served as a member of the State Board of Railroad and Warehouse Commissioners, and was a most public-spirited citizen.

In this same historic year, still other names, destined to be loved and honored in Evanston, first became known in church, in journalistic and social life. We refer to those of Hon. and Mrs. Andrew Shuman. As editor of the "Evening Journal," of Chicago, and subsequently as Lieutenant-Governor of the State, Mr. Shuman reflected honor upon the home of his adoption, while his wife soon became an accepted authority in the most refined and intellectual circles. The family homestead, embowered in stately evergreens and majestic elms and oaks, was a radiating center of many helpful influences.

In 1867 came such helpful citizens as Mr. and Mrs. T. K. Webster, Col. and

Mrs. E. S. Weeden, Mr. and Mrs. Alfred Sewell, Mr. and Mrs. Charles H. Gilbert —each and all referred to elsewhere.

Many pleasant memories and much loving interest center in the home of Professor and Mrs. H. S. Noyes. From 1860 to 1869 Professor Noyes was the Acting President of the Northwestern University, and was ably seconded in his manifold duties as parent, educator and citizen, by his gifted and accomplished wife. What the most ideal home of any college President has been to any village have been the homes of the Northwestern's Presidents to Evanston. In the list, which includes such honored names as Bishop and Mrs. Foster. Dr. and Mrs. Hinman. Professor and Mrs. Noyes, Bishop and Mrs. E. O. Haven, Bishop and Mrs. Charles Fowler, Dr. and Mrs. Oliver Marcy, Dr. and Mrs. Cummings, Dr. and Mrs. Henry Wade Rogers, and Dr. and Mrs. Edmund James, we recognize a succession of influences which have greatly enriched and ennobled the life and civilization of this great Northwest.

Among the names of influential citizens which will appear and re-appear in the reports of clubs (Philosophical, Educational and Social), business enterprises, church organizations and village interests, are those of,

Mr. and Mrs. George Reynolds,
Mr. and Mrs. Heman G. Powers,
Mr. and Mrs. A. P. Wightman,
Mr. and Mrs. George M. Huntoon (1841),
Mr. and Mrs. E. R. Paul,
Mr. and Mrs. A. J. Brown,
Mr. and Mrs. D. B. Dewey.
Mr. and Mrs. Addison de Coudres,
Major and Mrs. Edward Russell (1855),
Mr. and Mrs. John A. Childs,
Prof. and Mrs. Julius F. Kellogg,

Mr. and Mrs. William Wycoff,
"Deacon" and Mrs. Hill,
Mr. and Mrs. Alexander Gunn,
Mr. and Mrs. Eugene Chapman,
Mr. and Mrs. A. G. Wilder,
Mr. and Mrs. John A. Lighthall,
Mr. and Mrs. D. I. Crocker,
Mr. and Mrs. John Lyman,
Mr. and Mrs. F. M. Weller,
Mr. and Mrs. P. G. Siller,
Mr. and Mrs. H. C. Cone,
Mr. and Mrs. I. H. Haywood,
Mr. and Mrs. William C. Comstock,
Mr. and Mrs. Charles Comstock,
Mrs. Sarah Roland Childs,
Mr. and Mrs. Edward S. Taylor,
Mr. and Mrs. Charles Wightman,
Mr. and Mrs. S. A. Kean,
Mr. and Mrs. John H. Hamline,
Mr. and Mrs. Thomas Cosgrove,
Mr. and Mrs. R. S. King,
Mr. and Mrs. L. C. Pitner,
Mr. and Mrs. C. S. Burch,
Mrs. Caroline Murray,
Mr. and Mrs. Alfred L. Sewell,
Mr. and Mrs. J. J. Parkhurst,
Mr. and Mrs. David R. Dyche,
Lewis M. Angle.

Those who would most deplore any loss of tenderness or refinement in women, or any diminution in love of, or loyalty to, home or children, as a result of more inclusive and public interests, are referred to page 236 of " A Classic Town," and are requested to study the faces of four of Evanston's most illustrious mothers, housekeepers and home-makers: i. e., Mrs. Mary Thompson Willard, Mrs. Lucy Bannister, Mrs. Henriette S. Kidder and Mrs. Melinda Hamline. Before referring to these noble mothers of illustrious children, we would be glad if Miss Frances Willard had given us, on the opposite page of her volume the equally interesting faces of the fathers in these not-

able homes: Mr. J. G. Willard; Rev.
Henry Bannister. D. D.; Rev. Daniel
Kidder, D. D., and Bishop Hamline—for
in each case, at a glance, one would have
discovered that in these ideal homes there
was always found the poet's dream of
"Two heads in council." The face of
Mrs. Mary Thompson Willard is the first
of the notable group of home-makers to
arrest our thought. The story of the life of
the beloved and honored Willard family in
our midst is so familiar that its re-telling
here is unnecessary, and we content ourselves with reproducing a single scene.

On January 3, 1885, one of the most
notable gatherings ever held in the West
convened at "Rest Cottage," in recognition of the eightieth birthday of "Madame
Willard." The father, Mr. J. G. Willard,
the daughter "Mary" (whose "nineteen
beautiful years" have been so beautifully
photographed by her illustrious sister),
and the brilliant son, Mr. Oliver Willard,
had all passed to the Spirit Realm; but
the mother, calm, poised, genial and radiant with the pure joy resultant from re-
warded self-sacrifice and great enthusiasms, was still spared to us. Never did
she seem more truly great than in the dignified simplicity with which she received
the homage paid to her, as the noble
mother of the great daughter.

Writing of this event at the time, we
said the very cards of invitation seem
pregnant with suggestions, although they
merely hint of the inclusive home-making
of this great mother. They, however, remind those who have the *entrée* to this
veritable "Rest Cottage," of a pleasant
fact, namely: that here, under one roof,
divided by an open doorway, are the
homes of Madame Willard and her
daughter Frances, and of the beloved
daughter-in-law, Mary Bannister Willard, with her group of children.

The words written for this occasion by
Mrs. Mary A. Livermore are so obviously true of many fathers and mothers in
Evanston, that we presume to produce
them here:

"My Dear Mrs. Willard:

"I have come to know you through
your children. A mother is indeed honored, whose children rise up and call her
'blessed.' I also call you blessed; not
alone because of your children, but because you have learned so well the lessons and mastered so nobly the tasks assigned us here in the first school of the
soul.   Yours truly,
                    "Mary A. Livermore."

Equally appropriate are the lines written for this occasion by the dearly loved
adopted daughter of this home, Miss
Anna Gordon:

"We join tonight to honor one,
    Whose crown of eighty years
Reflects a faith that's born of love,
    A hope that conquers fears.

"A life enriched by blessed deeds,
    All through its blessed days;
A soul that, e'en in darkest hours,
    Still sings its song of praise."

Many parents, themselves deprived of
early advantages, congratulating their
children or grandchildren who enjoy the
glorious opportunities of the "present,"
re-echo the words of this grateful mother: "Your opportunity is my pleasure;
your duty is my delight."

Isabel Somerset (Lady Henry) in the
"Rest Islander," has preserved for us this
picture:

"In October, 1891, I stood for the first
time on the platform of the railway station in the "Classic Town of Evanston."
It was a sunny, autumn day. The rare

tints of ruby and gold that gleam as summer's funeral torches in the glad, new world, were flaming in brilliant beauty along the shady park-ways of that lovely spot on the shores of Lake Michigan.

"A few minutes later, I was in 'Rest Cottage,' as it was then in its completeness, for since that day, the sun has set on that great life that was the center of the home circle. Mrs. Willard stood there then in the doorway to meet me, erect and queenly still, in spite of her eighty-six years. She greeted me with that gentle kindness that showed at once her innate, refined and quiet dignity, and, as we sat around the supper-table that night, amid the dainty brightness, yet simple surroundings of that charming home, and later gathered round the open hearth in Miss Willard's den, or walked next day in the yard with its trees and flowers, grape arbor and rustic dove-cote, I felt that, in all my wanderings up and down the world, I had never found a more harmonious home; a spot in which seemed combined the breezy atmosphere of the great wide world, with the fragrant family life which remained unruffled in its holy calm."

The second picture is that of Mrs. Melinda Hamline. During a Sabbath afternoon in the 'sixties, strangers were sometimes surprised to see numbers of people leaving the attractive lakeside home of one who was always known as "Mrs. (Bishop) Hamline." Curiosity was speedily assuaged, however, by the statement, that these were members of the "Bible Class" taught by this gentle, little blue-eyed woman, who combined with the tenderness of the violet the poise and strength of the eternal hills.

We are told that "the first home that the stranger student was invited to enter in Evanston between the years of 1856 and

1870 was likely to be that of Rev. Dr. and Mrs. Daniel Kidder." Miss Willard writes in her historical sketch, "That roomy mansion among the trees, so long known as the 'Hitt Homestead,' was one of the first, if not the foremost, social center of old-time Evanston. Its way was undisputed; its associations were delightful. True Christian hospitality has rarely had a more adequate exponent; for here were comfort, cordiality and culture without luxury, fashion or display. The timid girl, working her passage through college, salutes the distinguished head of the University, and the youth who sawed wood or milked cows to earn his board, met the rich Chicago business man without feeling any gulf between them."

We are glad to call attention to the fact that this recognition of the true dignity of industry was not confined to those earlier years. During the notable feast of oratory incident to the fiftieth birth-day of the Northwestern University, no sentiment received greater applause than the following voiced by the youngest representative on the programme: "Evanston is not ashamed of her college stokers."

Rev. George E. Strowbridge, another of Evanston's representative children, the son of Mr. and Mrs. M. M. Conwell, writing of this home, after referring to the most generous hospitality of Dr. and Mrs. Kidder, says: "It was of incalculable benefit to those whose opinions were then forming, that this 'home,' with its large library lined with well chosen books, its roomy parlors and its broad piazza on which we delighted to promenade when summer nights were fair and sweet, brought to our young hearts the conception of Christ and Christians as a social force."

The fourth face upon this interesting page is that of Mrs. Lucy K. Bannister, another mother of notable children and grandchildren, philanthropists, literateurs, musicians, authors. In this home we find the father ever a most potent factor, since, whenever Dr. Henry Bannister presided, there was a recognized "McGregor at the head of the table." Friends, pupils, citizens, attest to the good influences constantly emanating from this home. Our Common Schools, "Free Library," The "Philosophical Association" and the "Temperance Alliance," each found in Dr. Bannister a most helpful friend; while he, in time, sought and found his inspiration and help in the beautiful and spiritual woman who, for half a century, was the light of his home.

We have previously referred to the pleasant home of Rev. and Mrs. C. P. Bragdon (the latter a sister of Dr. Bannister), where were developing into helpful manhood and womanhood another group of children, who were to render this name historic in the annals of Evanston.

Having written and quoted the foregoing in regard to these notable homemakers, our attention is arrested by a page containing another group of names almost equally notable as mothers, literateurs, poets and philanthropists. This is the page on which appear the portraits of Mrs. Mary B. Willard, Mrs. I. R. Hitt, Mrs. E. E. Marcey and Mrs. Emily Huntington Miller. As one thinks of that slight figure of Mrs. Miller, in those earlier days, so beautifully administering her home; then, of her contributions to the "Little Corporal," still later of acceptable lectures at Chautauqua, one wonders at her strength. Then, as we revert in thought to the herculean work and petite stature of Frances Willard, of the work of Mary B. Willard, Mrs. Marcey and others, all small of stature, we are reminded of one of Mrs. Mary Livermore's stories, which she prefaced with the statement, "Oh, the power of these little women!" She stated that when she called a meeting of women in Chicago, to counsel with them in regard to the name of a journal she was thinking of publishing, some large woman who appeared to be physically able to overturn a State, would rise, and, in the softest, gentlest tones would say: "Madame Chairman, I move that the paper be called the 'Morning Light' or the 'Dawn of Day.'" Then, some little woman would arise and in clear, unmistakeable tones would say, "O do not vote for 'The Dawn of Day,' or 'Morning Light,' but for the 'Revolution' or the 'Agitator.'"

Just at this point we would ask permission to explain that, if in this record of home-making, the work of the fathers does not always receive equal emphasis with that of the mothers, it is because the fathers are to appear in other records.

In almost every one of the homes mentioned there were, from the beginning, imperious duties and interests requiring the joint action of both parents. It would be a labor of love to allow this chapter to enlarge into a volume, and to chronicle the name, not only of every pioneer, but the name and fame of all the beloved "later arrivals," but that pleasure must be enjoyed by some future historian.

The necessary limits of this fragmentary sketch prevent other than the briefest reference, especially to such names as will appear in specific records of churchly, educational, industrial and philanthropic interests. However, in gleaning from the facts of road-making, house, church and school building, the manifold altruistic and philanthropic plans devised by these fathers and mothers (surrounded by their groups of little children); one is reminded of the story of Bernini, the celebrated Italian Master. Upon one occasion, this versatile genius gave a public opera in Rome, for which, as Vasari tells us, "he built the theater, painted the scenery, invented the engines, composed the music and wrote the poem."

We greet the children and grandchildren of these pioneers in every honorable occupation to-day; in business, literature, science, music, the drama, art, philosophy and religion, and as we greet them thus, we re-affirm the thought that nothing pays so well as wise, loving, true and faithful parenthood.

Surely the notable and useful children and grandchildren who have emerged from these homes, were developed in an atmosphere of plain living and high thinking, since, in 1853, the taxable property of Evanston was assessed at six hundred dollars, and we find on the tax-list of that year, the names of George Huntoon, Eli Gaffield, William Foster, Paul Pratt, Mrs. Pratt, O. A. Crain and Charles Crain.

Mrs. Beveridge reports a church service in 1854, at which all but three of the women appeared in the old time sun-bonnets, and the clerical dress of the pastor consisted of blue cotton "overalls."

Judging from the helpful lives of the children of these simpler homes, we are convinced that the foundations of our beautiful Evanston were laid by those who had learned "the true secret of culture," thus beautifully defined by the "Concord Sage:"

" The secret of culture is to learn that a few great points steadily re-appear, alike in the poverty of the obscurest farm and in the miscellany of metropolitan life, and that these few are alone to be regarded, namely: the escape from all false ties; courage to be what we are and to love what is simple and beautiful; independent and cheerful relations. These are the essentials; these, and the wish to serve, to add somewhat to the well-being of man."

A charming story could be written concerning the distinguished guests who have been welcomed to these homes. A list including such names as those of Abraham Lincoln, who was entertained by General and Mrs. Julius White; Lady Henry Somerset, of England; Susan B. Anthony, A. Bronson Alcott, Presidents, Bishops, literateurs, Judges, poets, philosophers, scientists, statesmen and philanthropists, ad infinitum.

We also delight to record that our somewhat too puritanic Evanston of the "airly days," was at times capable of great enthusiasms, and we gladly reproduce the picture of a most unusual scene preserved for us by Miss Willard, in connection with a charming biographical sketch of Bishop Simpson and his wife, and of their three years' residence here. She writes:

"While he lived in Evanston, 1860 to 1863, the Bishop's official duties called him to California, and half the town formed in procession going with him to the train, an honor never before or since accorded to mortal, that I know of, by our staid and thoroughly equipoised Evanstonians. When he returned, coming all the awful distance overland by stage, and in peril of the Indians a large part of the way, we all turned out again, and carrying the Bragdon melodeon and led by the Ludlam voices, we young folks serenaded our revered chief with,

'Home again, home again,
From a foreign shore!' "

Difficult, as it doubtless is, for their descendants to realize the manifold self-sacrifices, the anxieties and discouragements of pioneer life, yet do not those who have lived to enjoy the luxuries of "apartments," "steam-heat" or "Yaryan"; of butlers' pantries," and modern "receptions." often revert to the good old-fashioned open fires, the old-fashioned family singing or the neighborhood singing school, and the blessed old-fashioned tea-parties, when there was leisure for high-thinking and opportunity to express one's thoughts; when the patriotism of the home and the public spirit of the fathers and mothers were manifested in the children and over-flowed into the groves, at least once a year, on the Fourth of July?

If, added to those conscious pleasures, some seer or prophet could have appeared and voiced some such words as the following, would not the ever-recurring daily duties have been performed with added joy? "Congratulations, good friends!" must have been the exclamations, as upon the "screens prophetic" were thrown, in rapid succession, scenes from the future lives of some of these growing, questioning children. Suppose we could have foreseen Frances E. Willard presiding in England's capitol over a World's Temperance Convention; General and Mrs. Beveridge "receiving" at the executive mansion at Springfield; Hon. Lyman J. Gage serving as a member of the United States Cabinet at Washington; Mrs. Emily Huntington Miller reading her poems, or serving as a Trustee of the Northwestern University; Mary Bannister Willard as a beloved teacher in Germany's capital; Kathryn Kidder receiving plaudits incident to her success upon the histrionic stage; and Harry Boutell serving in State and National legislative halls.

Imagine the joy of the aged parents of our notable architect, Mr. D. H. Burnham, could they have foreseen him, crowned with the knowledge of having aided in creating that diapason of architecture, the Court of Honor, at the Columbian Exposition! Or, how the hearts of Mr. and Mrs. Andrew J. Brown—who, for almost half a century, have lived and served so faithfully in the home and the church—would have been thrilled, could they have foreseen their beautiful and gifted daughter, Mrs. Jessie Brown Hilton, voicing, with womanly earnestness, her helpful thoughts and suggestions to listening mothers throughout the State! It could but have pleased Dr. and Mrs. N. S. Davis, could they have glimpsed the interesting scene in connection with the inauguration of Dr. James as President of "Northwestern University," when, in manly bearing and clearness of thought, their son should stand almost peerless among many of the leading educators of the world.

Would that Elder and Mrs. Boring could have foreseen the varied activities of their children in church, philanthropy and in the home; and that Mr. and Mrs. William G. White could have imaged to their loving, parental eyes the manifold and helpful influences their children were to set afloat in our schools and homes; that Mrs. Way could have foreseen the ever-increasing usefulness of the College Cottage for which she did so much, or Mr. Charles Way, the fond father and co-operating home-maker, could have seen his daughter, Mrs. Catherine Way Mc-Mullen, presiding over the Illinois Congress of Mothers, ably assisted in every good word and work by her husband, Mr. Roger McMullen. Could these things have been foreseen, every cloud of discontent would have melted before the sunshine of gratitude.

With the exodus to Evanston, which occurred as a result of the great fire of 1871, a new life dawned upon our heretofore almost idyllically peaceful village. New interests were developed, new methods introduced, new social circles formed and the village began to assume some of the desirable, as well as some of the undesirable, aspects of a city. To those who saw with regret the magnificent oak trees dying, the optimists pointed out the more regular parks, fringed with rapidly growing elms and the glowing maples; to those who saw, with regret, the beautiful grounds surrounding the homes of Mr. and Mrs. A. J. Brown, Mr. Purington, General and Mrs. Ducat, being divided into small city lots, the same cheerful friends replied: "Ah! but think of the beautiful homes that are being builded, and the charming people who are coming to reside in them." To those who would lament the loss of the "big woods," where the violets and hepaticas grew in such abundance, the reply would be made — "Rejoice in the beautiful sward that forms such a perfect setting to hundreds of homes."

The fame of Evanston, as a city of beautiful homes, became so wide-spread that fathers and mothers who desired to secure for their children educational advantages and the environment of a moral and temperate community, came in such numbers that some future historian must devote volumes to the record of their manifold services.

Recognizing, as we do, "the beautiful times we are in," and the value of the rich inheritance enjoyed by the children of the present generation, let us highly resolve, here, in our truly beautiful, lake-bordered, tree-fringed, flower-crowned Evanston, to build such a monument to these pioneer home-makers as has never yet been attempted, namely, *a city in which there cannot be found a neglected or friendless child.* If, in those early days, there was money enough, wisdom enough, time enough, Christianity enough and love enough to build the libraries, the schools, the colleges, the railroads and the churches, there is now money enough, wisdom enough, time enough, Christianity enough and love enough to make life for every child within our borders full of blessedness, opportunity and joy.

From the beginning of its history, Evanston has offered almost ideal conditions for true home-making. The great University has offered rare educational facilities for every lad and lassie. The wise legislation which has resulted in rendering the village peculiarly free from the temptations incident to the liquor traffic; its proximity to a great city, and the spiritual and educational influences which have predominated, have made it "beautiful for situation" and greatly to be desired.

While in every village and locality one finds a certain coterie of influential people and home makers, in Evanston this coterie has been so unusually large that the present historian is limited to the merest catalogue of names of those who, with their descendants, have made the name of our village known throughout the world.

Those early days were enriched by the most helpful co-operation of friends and neighbors, "in sickness and in health," in feasting and fasting, in poverty and in wealth. We have referred to the cheerful services of Mr. John A. Pearsons as the first choir master; the future historian will record the years of cheerful service, subsequently given by Mr. O. H. Merwin. Mr. Merwin and Mrs. Bannister Merwin were one of the young couples who arrived just in time to be entered upon the Pioneer Roll of Honor, together with our gifted Prof. Robert Cumnock and his wife.

Notwithstanding the manifold and imperious home duties of these useful homebuilders, the true club spirit was manifested as early as 1864, when, in the spacious and hospitable home of Mr. and Mrs. Charles Comstock, the "Eclectic Club" was organized. In a more truly inclusive spirit than the name indicates, every alternate week witnessed a hospitality which included a genuine flow of soul as well as a reasonable feast. This interesting story, however, belongs to the record of Club Life.

While the village life was remarkably free from "cliques," or divisions, and while, upon all important occasions the entire community seemed to be of one household, yet about this time, owing to geographical reasons and the limitations of the home-parlor, the social and literary life seemed to be forming around two centers. One such center was the University and the rapidly enlarging Methodist Church; another seemed to have as a nucleus the Episcopal Church and the "Eclectic Club."

Thus, while one group of friends enthusiastically recall the good old times enjoyed in the pleasant homes of Mr. and Mrs. Charles Comstock, Hon. and Mrs. H. B. Hurd, Mr. and Mrs. William Page, Mr. and Mrs. L. C. Pitner, Mr. and Mrs. George Watson, Mr. and Mrs. George Purington, Mr. and Mrs. Thomas Cosgrove, Mr. and Mrs. S. H. Burch, Mr. and Mrs. George Bliss, Mr. and Mrs. R. H. King, Mr. and Mrs. J. J. Parkhurst, Gen. and Mrs. Julius White and Mr. and Mrs. William Blanchard, another will claim that never were there such gatherings of charming people as those enjoyed in the homes of Dr. and Mrs. Judson, Rev. and Mrs. Bragdon, Dr. and Mrs. Ludlam, Mr.

and Mrs. T. C. Hoag, Dr. and Mrs. Bannister, Mr. and Mrs. Isaac R. Hitt, Mr. and Mrs. J. M. Williams, Mr. and Mrs. Francis Bradley, Mr. and Mrs. W. N. Brainard, and Mr. and Mrs. Andrew Shuman. While some homes have surpassed others in richness of tapestries, draperies, marbles and pictures, yet in almost every one are to be found well selected libraries, flowers, good music, high thinking and altruistic service.

This limited record is submitted to the citizens and home-makers of our beautiful Evanston, with the hope that even the fragmentary glimpses herein revealed may cause many to rejoice in the vast amount of good, helpful and inspiring influence that may emanate from a single home.

With grateful memories for each and all of these pioneers may we conclude by uniting in a "Lang Syne" recognition and consecration.

Then here's to Love, and Joy, and Truth
  And Beauty everywhere;
The cornerstones on which we build
  Our Temple rich and rare.

For bairnies of all time, my dears,
  For bairnies of all time—
We'll keep a cup o' kindness here
  For bairnies of all time.

These crystal walls of living light
  Reflect, from base to dome,
How faithfully we're building here
  Love's Temple of the Home.

For bairnies of all time, my dears,
  For bairnies of all time—
Then keep a cup o' kindness here
  For bairnies of all time.

CHAPTER XXXVII.

EVANSTON CHURCH HISTORY

(The matter in the following chapter devoted to general church history, is arranged in chronological order as related to individual church organizations, but under independent heads.)

METHODIST CHURCHES
(By F. D. RAYMOND)

First Methodist Episcopal Church.— The earliest preaching of Methodist cir-cuit-riders in the territory called "Grosse Point," of which I have knowledge, was in the home of George W. Huntoon, on Ridge Avenue, near Main Street, during the period from 1838 to 1843. These services were occasional and were usually held on Tuesday evenings. In the summer of 1846, Rev. Edward D. Wheadon and Rev. Solomon F. Denning were assigned to an extensive circuit which included Grosse Point, and in turn they preached at the Grosse Point School House—a log structure standing in the the burial ground at the corner of Ridge Avenue and Greenleaf Street. Other preachers from Fort Dearborn sometimes supplied the pulpit.

In 1850 the town of Ridgeville was organized and thereafter that log school house was in the town of Ridgeville. The land in the town of Ridgeville, purchased by the Northwestern University, was platted as "Evanston" in the winter of 1853-54. The school house was outside the plat. The spring of 1854 saw the arrival of several Methodist families, among them the families of John A. Pearsons, Rev. Philo Judson (the University agent), John L. Beveridge, James B. Colvin and A. Danks. Soon after his arrival Mr. Judson organized a Methodist class, the nucleus of a Methodist church, of which George W. Huntoon was appointed leader; and on July 13, 1854, the first quarterly conference for Evanston charge was held by Presiding Elder John Sinclair, "at the log school house in the town of Ridgeville." Some time prior to that date a Sunday school had been organized at the school house, of which Abram Wigglesworth was Superintendent, and at that time Rev. John G. Johnson was preaching there by appointment of the Presiding Elder. Philo Judson and J. G. Johnson, preachers, and George W. Huntoon, class leader, were the members of that first quarterly conference. The Sunday school was reported as having thirteen officers and teachers and eighty-four scholars. John L. Beveridge, A. Danks and J. B. Colvin were elected stewards and Abram Wigglesworth was elected Superintendent of the Sunday school. Mr. Johnson was recommended to the Annual Conference for admission to the itinerary connection; evidently he was a local preacher. He remained at Evanston only about six months after the organization of the church. Mr. Beveridge soon succeeded Mr. Wigglesworth as Superintendent of the Sunday school, but during the next year three schools seem to have been maintained by this church—one in the village plat under Mr. Beveridge, one in the aforementioned log school house on the South Ridge, in the "Huntoon" district under Mr. Danks, and still another conducted by Mr. Wigglesworth, in the other log school house on the North Ridge, or "Stebbins" district. During subsequent years Sunday schools at Winnetka, Glencoe, Rockland (Lake Bluff), Deerfield, and Bowmanville were tributary to this church.

January 1, 1855, the first building of Garrett Biblical Institute—later called Dempster Hall—was completed, and the preaching services were transferred from the school house to the Institute Chapel, the Sunday school remaining in the old location. Professor P. W. Wright, of the Institute, was appointed preacher in charge. About May 1, 1855, the preaching services and the Sunday school were transferred to the upper story of a building erected and owned by Mr. Judson, at the corner of Davis Street and Orrington Avenue. In November of that year (1855), the University building was opened at the corner of Davis Street and Hinman Avenue, and all services were transferred from the Judson Building to the University Chapel. In September of the same year, Rev. John Sinclair, the former Presiding Elder, was appointed preacher in charge. In the summer of 1856, the first church building was erected at a cost of $2,800, at the northeast corner of Church Street and Orrington Avenue and dedicated July 27th, by Rev. John Dempster, D. D., assisted by W. D. Godman and Rev. John Sinclair. A. L. Cooper succeeded John Sinclair as pastor in October, 1859. In the quarterly conference records of that year, the committee appointed to estimate the table expenses of the pastor reported that he should be allowed $400 for such purpose, which, with his disciplinary allowance of $200, made $600, the society furnishing him a house in addition. G. M. Huntoon was appointed a committee to collect unpaid subscriptions, and was instructed to present those who, in his judgment, could but would not pay the same, to the preacher in charge by way of complaint for trial. In the autumn of 1858, Rev. Charles P. Bragdon was appointed pastor, and after filling his full term of two years' service died in Evanston on January 8, 1861.

The records of the Official Board during these pastorates furnish us some interesting glimpses of old fashioned Methodism. Cases of delinquency in attendance upon class-meeting were reported

OLD FIRST METHODIST CHURCH

and discussed, and committees were appointed to labor with the delinquents and report at the next meeting. Committees were appointed to investigate, adjust if possible and report upon cases of disagreement between members of the church, also to investigate and report upon cases of questionable financial dealings on the part of certain members, all of which reports were set out in full in the records. The committee appointed to investigate the affairs of Brother B., in connection with the failure of the banking firm of which he was a member, reported that there appeared no just cause of complaint against him. Brother and Sister S. were tried and expelled from the church for breach of rules in not attending class meeting. Dr. W. was tried and sentenced to be admonished by the pastor for buying, through a third party, a judgment against himself, thereby depriving his creditor of part of his just due. Sister T. and Brother W., two of the younger members of the church, were deemed disorderly in having engaged in dancing at a picnic "on or about" the 4th of July, and were called upon to acknowledge their fault and do so no more. Probationers were dropped in blocks, for neglecting class-meeting, some of them being reinstated again and again.

The Board resolved that they would sustain the preacher in charge in strictly enforcing the disciplinary requirement, that members should attend class, and instructed the secretary to read the resolutions in the public congregation on the following Sabbath.

The class leaders of those days were: L. Clifford, J. W. Clough, A. C. Stewart, A. Vane, William Triggs, F. H. Benson, John Fussey, G. W. Reynolds, I Smith, P. Judson, S. Springer, and H. S. Noyes.

In 1860 Rev. R. K. Bibbins was appointed pastor and remained one year, being succeeded by Rev. J. R. Goodrich. In 1862, Rev. O. H. Tiffany, D. D., came to the pastorate, widely known as one of the finest orators that the Methodist Episcopal Church has known. During his pastorate the church building was enlarged, so that it assumed the form of a Greek cross.

In the autumn of 1864, Rev. Miner Raymond, D. D., Professor of Systematic Theology in the Garrett Biblical Institute, was appointed pastor. He served the church ably for three years and was succeeded by Rev. W. C. Dandy, D. D., in October, 1867. Plans were discussed for a new church, and committees appointed for that purpose. Much discussion and difference of opinion were encountered in determining the location of the new edifice. It was not until October, 1869, that they settled on the corner of Hinman Avenue and Church Street, a site donated by the Northwestern University, adjoining the lot on which the parsonage had been built four years before. Dr. Dandy was made Presiding Elder in 1869, and Rev. James Baume was appointed pastor of the church. The corner-stone of the new edifice was laid with appropriate ceremonies, July 4, 1870. The lecture room was dedicated September 24, 1871, when a subscription of $20,597 was raised to cover the cost of the building in excess of previous subscriptions up to that point. The value of these subscriptions was much affected by the Chicago fire, in October of that year, which postponed the day of liquidation. In October, 1872, Rev. M. C. Briggs, D. D., was transferred to Evanston from Cincinnati. During his pastorate the church was finished and dedicated at a cost of $63,837.73, and a large organ provided at a cost of $4,500.

In December, 1875, Rev. J. B. Wentworth, D. D., was transferred from New York and stationed at the First Church, Evanston. He is described as an intellectual giant and a great theologian who often preached over the heads of his congregation. During his pastorate the ladies of the church, under the leadership of Mrs. E. E. Marcey and Mrs. Jane Peek, began a systematic collection of funds, which resulted in reducing the debt fully $8,000.

Rev. R. M. Hatfield, D. D., was appointed pastor in 1877, and served the full time allowed by the laws of the church. In October, 1880, Rev. Amos W. Patten succeeded to the pastorate, remaining three years. During his administration, and largely by his efforts, the last of the building debt was provided for by subscription, on September 23, 1882, when at a banquet in the church parlors arranged by the trustees, $14,200 was subscribed for the payment of the funded debt. By subsequent solicitation this was increased to $18,000, and, on September 6, 1884, the final payment of the funded debt was made, and the mortgage on the church property released. The period of the building of the new church and the payment of the building debt was one of great activity on the part of the trustees. Those who served as trustees and bore the grievous burdens of the office during those days were:

Elected in 1868—L. P. Hamline, W. H. Lunt, D. P. Kidder, E. Haskin, L. J. Gage, A. J. Brown, O. Huse, E. Russell; 1869—E. A. Gage, W. T. Woodson, J. S. Kirk, J. L. Beveridge, O. Marcy; 1870—E. O. Haven, S. A. Matteson; 1873—W. B. Phillips, I. R. Hitt, N. S. Davis, A. B. Jackson; 1876—W. C. Wilson, H. V. Smith, M. C. Bragdon, J. D. Easter; 1878—Chas. Munson, Wm. Deering; 1882—T. H. Traver, E. S. Taylor.

Trustees elected since 1884 have been: 1886—O. E. Haven, G. M. Sargent, W. H. Jones, D. Bonbright, H. R. Wilson, C. B. Congdon; 1888—H. H. Gage; 1892—P. R. Shumway;

1900—W. H. Whitehead; 1901—W. G. Hoag, I. G. Hatcher; 1903—E. P. Clapp.

Rev. Lewis Curts succeeded Dr. Patten in October, 1883. One year later, South Evanston was put on a circuit system with the First Church, and Dr. Ridgaway and Dr. Terry were associated with him in the pastorate. In October, 1885, Dr. Ridgaway was appointed acting pastor and, assisted by Dr. Bennett, served until the following March, when Rev. S. F. Jones, D. D., was appointed pastor, being succeeded in October, 1890, by Rev. W. S. Studley, D. D. Dr. Studley died at Evanston, February 27, 1893. During his pastorate the conference collections reached the highest point to which they have attained in the history of the Church. After the death of Dr. Studley and until the annual conference in October following, Dr. Chas. J. Little, President of Garrett Biblical Institute, was acting pastor. During that summer the parsonage was reconstructed at a cost of about $4,500, and fifteen hundred dollars was spent in refurnishing. In October, 1893, Rev. Frank M. Bristol, D. D., was appointed pastor, and remained nearly five years until the spring of 1898, when on his departure for Washington, D. C., Dr. Little again assumed the duties of acting pastor. During that summer the church was redecorated and refurnished and the parsonage partly refurnished, at a cost of $6,000. In September, 1898, Rev. William Macafee, D. D., came to the pastorate and remained five years. In January, 1901, the organ built by the Austin Organ Company at a cost of $12,500, was completed and in October of that year the Annual Conference met a second time in Evanston, the first time being in Dr. Jones' pastorate. In closing his pastorate in October, 1903, Dr. Macafee reported to the Annual Conference benevolent contributions amounting to over $19,000, which, with the expenses of the church, made a total of over $31,000 for the year. In October, 1903, Rev. Dr. T. P. Frost was appointed pastor, which pastorate continues at this writing to the great satisfaction of his people.

The following is a complete list of the Sunday School Superintendents of the First Church since 1855:

Elected	Superintendent	Assistant Supt.
1855	J. L. Beveridge	————
1859	F. H. Benson	T. C. Hoag
1859	P. Judson	G. M. Huntoon
1860	H. S. Noyes	G. M. Huntoon
1860	B. T. Vincent	G. M. Huntoon
	B. T. Vincent	J. L. Beveridge
1860	F. D. Hemenway	J. L. Beveridge
1861	J. L. Beveridge	H. L. Stewart
1861	W. Taplin	G. M. Huntoon
	W. Taplin	W. A. Spencer
	W. Taplin	A. C. Lynn
1862	E. S. Taylor	G. E. Strowbridge
1863	H. B. Hurd	G. E. Strowbridge
1864	E. S. Taylor	A. L. Sewell
1865	W. A. Spencer	W. E. Clifford
1866	L. J. Gage	P. B. Shumway
1866	E. S. Taylor	P. B. Shumway
1867	Edward Eggleston	L. H. Bugbee
	Edward Eggleston	L. J. Gage
	Edward Eggleston	W. T. Shepherd
1870	W. T. Shepherd	L. G. Gage
	W. T. Shepherd	W. M. Wyckoff
	W. T. Shepherd	Mrs. Gillespie
1872	J. E. Miller	W. T. Shepherd
	J. E. Miller	W. M. Wyckoff
	J. E. Miller	J. J. Crist
1877	H. F. Fisk	Wm. Deering
	H. F. Fisk	F. D Raymond
1880	F. P. Crandon	F. D. Raymond
	F. P. Crandon	T. H. Traver
	F. P. Crandon	H. H. C. Miller
1882	C. B. Congdon	C. B. Atwell
1892	C. M. Stuart	G. A. Coe
	C. M. Stuart	C. B. Congdon
1894	W. H. Dunham	————
1896	B. D. Caldwell	————
1896	R. H. Johnston	————
1897	W. E. O'Kane	J. A. Burhans
1899	L. G. Westgate	C. M. Stuart
1900	T. F. Holgate	L. S. Grant
1902	W. H. Dunham	————
1904	A. L. Lindsey	W. H. Dunham

The following is a complete list of persons who have served the First Church as Stewards—the date given being that of first election:

1854—A. Danks, J. B. Colvin, J. L. Beveridge; 1855—H. S. Noyes; 1856—G. W. Reynolds, G. M. Huntoon; 1858—J. W. Ludlam, T. C. Hoag, Geo. F. Foster, Hiram Clark (Northfield circuit); 1859—W. T. Woodson, G. H. Bliss, W. P. Jones, Jr.; 1860—John

Evans, William Gamble, E. Haskin; 1862—J. A. Pearsons, J. F. Willard, A. C. Langworthy; 1863—H. B. Hurd, A. Vane, O. Marcy; 1867—A. J. Brown, L. J. Gage, W. H. Lunt, A. J. Hanchette, A. L. Sewell; 1868—L. P. Hamline; 1870—O. Huse; 1871—E. Newman; 1872—A. B. Jackson, I. R. Hitt, S. P. Lunt, W. M. Wyckoff, H. A. Pearsons; 1873—E. A. Clifford; 1874—R. Baird; 1875—Wm. Deering, J. E. Miller; 1876—J. J. Parkhurst, L. C. Pitner, J. H. Raymond; 1877—S. Farwell, H. S. Carhart, C. E. Wiswall; 1878—F. D. Raymond, H. H. C. Miller; 1880—D. R. Dyche; 1881—O. E. Haven; 1883—F. P. Crandon; 1884—W. H. Whitehead, N. W. Harris, L. C Tallmadge, E. S. Weeden; 1885—R. B. McMullen; 1886—M. H. Bass, F. A. Fletcher; 1887—G. G. Calkins; 1888—G. A. Foster; 1890—J. F. Ward; 1892—A. L. Butler, I. Bailey; 1893—W. A. Dyche; 1894—R. R. McCabe, B. D. Caldwell; 1895—T. M. Hubbard, W. M. Scott, J. R. Fitch; 1896—J. C. Shaffer; 1899—B. F. Crawford; 1900—C. N. Stevens, A. F. Townsend; 1901—W. J. Morphy; 1903—R. E. Barrett, H. B. Prentice.

Central Street M. E. Church.—At the quarterly conference of the First Methodist Episcopal Church, held August 9, 1870, a resolution was adopted approving of the setting off of North Evanston as a separate charge. Pursuant to this action Mr. and Mrs. D. W. Warren and Mr. John Culver took their letters of membership from the First Church, and, with Rev. E. G. W. Hall, a local preacher, set about the organization of the second Methodist Episcopal society in Evanston. Others joined them, and the society was organized on the sixth day of September of that year. The first official members were: John Culver, A. C. Fulton, D. W. Warren, A. F. Kleise, John Picket and Joseph McCallum. John Culver was Sunday School Superintendent and classleader. Soon after the organization steps were taken to secure a site for the erection of a building in which to hold service. Mr. Culver donated a lot on West Railroad Avenue near Lincoln Street. Rev. D. P. Kidder encouraged the enterprise by a very liberal contribution. Further pledges being secured of sufficient amount to warrant the commencement of building operations, the rear part of the church building was finished and occupied for some months. The completed edifice was dedicated August 11, 1872, the property being then valued at $2,500. The society worshiped in this building until 1891, when the property was sold for $1,100, and the lot at the corner of Central Street and Prairie Avenue was purchased for $1,600. Upon this lot a new building was erected at a cost of nearly $5,000, and dedicated December 13, 1891. The improvements added since have increased the value of the property to about $8,000.

The following is a list of the pastors of this church:

E. G. W. Hall .... Sept., 1870
Wm. Craven .... Mar., 1871
Samuel Paine .... Sept., 1873
J. J. Tobias .... Oct., 1875
Wm. Daws   ⎫
T. Van Scoy   ⎮   Oct., 1876
R. J. Hobbs   ⎬ ....   to
C. E. Lambert   ⎮   Nov., 1879
V. F. Brown   ⎭
A. H. Kistler .... Nov., 1879
W. F. Stewart .... Oct., 1880
C. H. Zimmerman .... Oct., 1882
J. H. Alling .... Oct., 1883
J. E. Farmer .... Sept., 1884
E. H. Brumbaugh .... Oct., 1886
C. S. Dudley .... April, 1889
H. W. Waltz .... Mar., 1892
A. S. Haskins .... June, 1893
G. P. Sturges .... Oct., 1898
R. H. Pate .... Oct., 1900
E. G. Schultz .... Oct., 1902

Norwegian-Danish M. E. Church.— Organized Christian work among the Scandinavians in Evanston began in the year 1870, when Karl Schou, a native of Denmark and a student in the University, gathered around him a group of friends

for Bible study, meeting on Sunday afternoons in the Benson Avenue school house. From the membership of this Bible class a Methodist class was organized, which formed the nucleus of a church. The number of class members increased, and preachers from Chicago visited them. At the Annual Conference held in Milwaukee, October 9, 1871, Bishop Simpson appointed Brother Schou pastor of this church. He was also the first appointed teacher of a class of young men preparing for the ministry, and leader of one of the two classes into which the church was divided, Oliver Hansen being leader of the other. The membership of the church at this time numbered thirty-three.

In the year 1872 the frame building vacated by the First M. E. Church was purchased and moved to the lot on the south side of Church Street between Orrington and Sherman Avenues, the lot being leased from the University. The building was repaired, and a parsonage added; the whole at a cost of $7,800, part of which remained as a debt. In February, 1873, Brother Schou left Evanston to take up the work assigned to him as Superintendent of the Mission in Denmark. Rev. C. Willerup, the former Superintendent of the Mission in Denmark, succeeded Brother Schou as pastor of this church until the next conference, when B. Johannessen was appointed pastor. In October, 1874, the Swedish members of the society, desiring services in their own language, withdrew and organized a society of their own.

In October, 1876, M. Nilsen was appointed to supply this church; but his work was of brief duration. Before the close of the conference year he withdrew from the work, and sometime afterward connected himself with the Lutheran church, with whose doctrines he was more in accord. Otto Sanaker, a student, acted as pastor during the remainder of the conference year. At the next conference C. F. Eltzholtz was appointed to the Second church in Chicago and Evanston. In 1878, Chr. Treider was appointed editor of *Den Christelige Talsmand* and pastor of the church in Evanston. At this time the membership of the church numbered thirty-nine in full connection and three on probation.

In October, 1879, Mr. Willerup was appointed pastor and remained one year. From October, 1880, until September, 1884, A. Haagensen was pastor of the church, and also at the same time editor of the church paper before named. B. Smith was pastor in 1884 and 1885.

In November, 1885, N. E. Simonsen, being transferred from the Norway Conference, took up the work as pastor in connection with his work as President of the Norwegian-Danish Theological Seminary; but the Annual Conference, recognizing that his work as teacher demanded his entire attention, appointed M. Rye, a student, as pastor in 1886. Bro. Rye did faithful work for about a year and a half, when failing health compelled him to retire. He died in Utah in 1888.

E. M. Stangland, a student in Garrett Biblical Institute, took up the work during the conference year 1888-1889. His report to the annual conference showed fifty-seven persons in full connection and four on probation. G. Anderson received his appointment as pastor in September, 1889; the following February he was transferred to San Francisco, Cal. Chr. Arndt, a student in the Norwegian-Danish Theological School, then became pastor for sixteen months, when he was succeeded by H. P. Berg, assistant teacher in the theological school, who served two

years. During Bro. Berg's pastorate the church lot on Clark Street was bought. A. Anderson, a student in the Norwegian-Danish Theological School, followed Bro. Berg, and was pastor two years.

In 1895 Paul Haugan was appointed pastor. At this time the membership numbered eighty-eight in full connection and eleven on probation. Of seventeen pastors up to this time four were teachers in the theological school, two were editors of *Den Christelige Talsmand*, and six were students in the educational institutions in Evanston. Such combinations of duties were necessary in view of the fact that there are not many Norwegians and Danes in Evanston, and the congregation has never been large. During Bro. Haugan's pastorate the present church building on Clark Street was erected. He both made the plans for the building and superintended the erection.

In 1897 Gustav Mathesen became pastor and served until 1901, when he was succeeded by Charles J. Johnson, the present pastor.

Swedish M. E. Church.—The society organized in the year 1872, of which Karl Schou, a Dane, was appointed the first pastor—now the Norwegian-Danish M. E. Church—was styled the Scandinavian Methodist Episcopal Church in Evanston. Although the Swedes were in the majority, the new society was soon connected with the Norwegian-Danish work; and the request of the Swedish members to have occasional meetings conducted in their language being denied them, they withdrew and formed a separate society. Meetings were first held in Ladd's Hall, where quite a revival followed. Later the society worshiped in Union Hall, where, on October 17, 1874, the church was formally organized. J. B. Anderson acting as chairman and Charles J. Wigren as secretary of the meeting. The five Trustees elected were: Charles J. Wigren, L. O. Lawson, A. B. Johnson, John A. Oberg, and Otto Johnson. The first quarterly conference was held the same evening, presided over by Rev. A. J. Anderson, of Chicago, and J. B. Anderson, a theological student, was appointed the first pastor. The following year O. J. Stead, also a theological student, was appointed pastor. During his time the church building on the corner of Grove Street and Sherman Avenue was erected, and dedicated on the 11th of June, 1876. The cost of the building was $5,000. Later a parsonage was built and the entire property of the church freed from debt.

The following is the complete list of pastors: J. B. Anderson, 1874-75; O. J. Stead, 1875-76; Wm. Henchen, 1876-77; Fr. Ahgren, 1877-78; James T. Wigren, 1878-79; S. B. Newman, 1879-82; John Lundgren, 1882-83; Albert Ericson, 1883-86; N. O. Westergreen, 1886-90; Alfred Anderson, 1890-91; Richard Cederberg, 1891-94; O. F. Lindstrum, 1894; Jas. T. Wigren, September, 1899; John W. Swenson, September, 1903.

The present trustees are: Frida Hanson, Hanna Barck, Carl Anderson, Leonard Gustafson, J. A. Holmgren, Tina Carlson and Mary Nelson. J. A. Holmgren is Superintendent of the Sunday school and Ernest Johnson is President of the Epworth League.

Hemenway M. E. Church.—The Methodist church in South Evanston had its inception in the spring of 1872. Lots for a site of a church building were secured at the northwest corner of Lincoln Avenue (now Main Street) and Benson Avenue. Regular services were held several months in a small school house on Ridge Avenue just south of Lincoln. The permanent organization of the church was effected Thursday evening, July 17, 1873, and ground was broken for the first church building Tuesday, July 22nd. The corner-stone was laid Monday, August 11th, the religious ceremonies having taken place the previous Sunday. The church was dedicated Sunday, November 9, 1873, only the basement being finished. About ten years later, on Wednesday, May 9, 1883, this building was completely demolished by a cyclone. The society rallied at once, began rebuilding, worshiping in the meantime in Ducat's hall. The second church edifice was dedicated Sunday, November 11, 1883. This structure was destroyed by fire early on the morning of Saturday, January 23, 1886. Worship was resumed in Ducat's hall. A new location on the east side of Chicago Avenue a little north of Lincoln (now Main Street) was decided upon, March 20, 1886. A lot one hundred and fifty feet front, and containing a house suitable for a parsonage, was purchased. Ground was broken for the new church edifice Saturday, August 28, 1886. The corner-stone was laid October 9th, the formal ceremonies occurring Sunday, October 10th. About this time it was decided to call the church "Hemenway M. E. Church," in honor or Rev. Francis Dana Hemenway, D. D., Professor in Garrett Biblical Institute, and a former pastor of the church. The new church edifice, a substantial building of red pressed brick with white stone foundations and trimmings, was dedicated Sunday, December 25, 1887, Rev. T. P. Marsh being the pastor. The program of dedication week, beginning on the previous Sunday, is interesting as showing the names of the men active in the Methodist churches about Chicago and Evanston at that time. On the first Sunday there was preaching in the morning by Rev. R. M. Hatfield, D. D., and in the afternoon by Rev. Frank M. Bristol, with a platform meeting in the evening presided over by Charles B. Congdon, Esq., and addressed by Judge O. H. Horton, J. B. Hobbs, F. P. Crandon, and H. S. Towle. There was preaching on subsequent evenings of the week by C. E. Mandeville, H. W. Bolton, H. G. Jackson, and S. F. Jones, with another platform meeting on Friday evening presided over by Rev. L. Curts and addressed by Rev. William Smith, pastor of the Presbyterian church, Rev. D. S. Smith, rector of the Episcopal church and former pastors Burns and Zimmerman. On Sunday, "the great day of the feast," Doctor Ridgaway preached in the morning, Rev. B. I. Ives in the afternoon and Miss Frances E. Willard delivered an address in the evening. Others taking part in the exercises of the week were Drs. Stowe, Boring, Edwards, Jutkins and Rev. C. M. Stuart. At the time of dedication the Trustees were: Thomas Purnell, President; John W. Byam, Wesley L. Knox, W. H. Blake, M. D. Ewell, W. G. Miller, Edwin Benjamin. The stewards were Thomas Purnell, E. Benjamin, J. F. Hathaway, James H. Thomas, Thomas Blackler, J. Milhenning, F. W. Brown, James Wigginton. Charles O. Boring was Sunday School Superintendent.

The following is the complete list of pastors who have served this church:

A. G. Button	Jan. ——Sept. 1873
W. H. Burns	Sept. 1873— Oct. 1874
W. X. Ninde (supply)	Oct. 1874— Oct. 1876
J. C. R. Layton (supply)	Oct. 1876— Apr. 1877
C. H. Zimmerman (supply)	June ——Sept. 1877
F. D. Hemenway (supply)	Oct. 1878— Oct. 1881
S. H. Adams	Oct. 1881— Oct. 1882
I. Linebarger	Oct. 1882— Oct. 1884
H. B. Ridgaway ⎰	
L. Curts ⎱ (supply)	Oct. 1884— Oct. 1885
M. S. Terry	
T. P. Marsh	Oct. 1885— Oct. 1888
W. H. Holmes	Oct. 1888— Oct. 1893
W. E. Wilkinson	Oct. 1893— Oct. 1897
O. F. Mattison	Oct. 1897— Oct. 1903
R. B. Kester	Oct. 1903—

Wheadon M. E. Church.—In February, 1887, Rev. Edward D. Wheadon formed a class which, for a time, met in the homes of the members in the neighborhood of Wesley Avenue, and north of Emerson Street. Later a tent was pitched on Foster Street, and preaching services held in it. In 1888 a hall was secured on (West) Foster Street; a church was organized by Rev. Dr. Luke Hitchcock, Presiding Elder of the Chicago District, and "Father" Wheadon was appointed the first pastor. The first Trustees were: E. D. Wheadon, Adam Tait, John Owens and John Culver. In 1889, Rev. E. G. Lewis was appointed pastor; and a lot 120 feet by 192 feet was' secured on the corner of Ridge Avenue and Leon Street. It is recorded that the enterprise was kindly encouraged by Rev. S. F. Jones, pastor of the First Church, and by William Deering, Frank P. Crandon, John B. Kirk, and James H. Raymond. Under the pastorate of Rev. F. G. Boylan, a chapel was built on the property costing $1,750, which was dedicated in February, 1890. Rev. H. D. Kimball, Dr. Hitchcock, Dr. Jones and Dr. Ridgaway taking part in the dedication. The chapel was built on the rear part of the lot facing north on Leon Street. In 1903 it was turned around to face Ridge Avenue, and much improved at a cost of about $3,500. Up to 1902 over 500 persons had united with the church by letter or on probation, the average resident membership being 100, the average congregation about 130, and the average membership of the Sunday school about 150.

The following is a complete list of pastors, with dates of entrance upon their pastorates: E. D. Wheadon, April, 1888; E. G. Lewis, May, 1889; F. G. Boylan, October, 1889; J. B. Lucas, October, 1890; R. H. Wilkinson, October 1891;

John Lee. October, 1894; R. H. Wilkinson, October, 1896; J. R. Smith, October, 1898; W. T. Euster, October 1900; W. C. Reuter, July 1901; M. L. Norris, October, 1903.

The present officials of the church are: Trustees—William Campbell, R. H. Baldwin, J. W. Travis, F. Flood, A. B. Crosby, C. J. Tisdel, W. A. Dyche; Stewards —Charles Beck, A. C. Pearson, Charles Rose, George Fellingham, G. F. Starkweather, Joseph Justice, J. P. Sloan, Miss Cora Marsh, Mrs. F. M. Crosby, Mrs. H. L. Lincoln; Sunday School Superintendent—G. F. Starkweather; President Epworth League—Stanley Ward; President Junior Epworth League—Miss Myrtle English.

Emmanuel M. E. Church.—March 10, 1889, a Sabbath School was organized in the High School building, west of the railroad track. Charles O. Boring was Superintendent, S. A. Kean, Assistant Superintendent, and Charles G. Haskins was secretary and treasurer. This school was under the control of the First Church. At the quarterly conference of the First M. E. Church, held November 25, 1889, Rev. Dr. S. F. Jones being pastor, the following resolution was offered by C. O. Boring and unanimously adopted:

"Whereas, it is the sense of this quarterly conference that the time has come to arrange for the purchase of a lot, looking toward the ultimate erection of a church on the west side of Evanston; and,

"Whereas, a committee was recently appointed, at a meeting of gentlemen living on the west side, for the purpose:

"Be It Resolved, that this quarterly conference appoint a committee to cooperate with said committee in the selection of a lot south of Davis Street, and that the lot so selected may then be purchased

with the full consent of this quarterly conference."

The chairman, Dr. Jones, appointed as such committee, C. O. Boring, William Deering, D. R. Dyche, C. B. Congdon and R. B. McMullen.

At the quarterly conference, held September 22, 1890, the committee reported that a lot had been purchased at the corner of Greenwood Boulevard and Oak Avenue, and the report was accepted. A communication was received from the Secretary of the Board of Trustees of Emmanuel M. E. Church, stating the facts of the organization of that church, as follows: On the evening of June 9, 1890, a meeting was held at the residence of Mr. and Mrs. Charles G. Haskin, 203 Maple Avenue. There were present: Hon. Harvey B. Hurd, Dr. S. F. Jones (pastor of the First Church), Mr. William H. Jones, Mr. Charles O. Boring, Mr. David B. Dewey, Mr. David R. Dyche, Mr. Frank P. Crandon, Mr. Henry H. Gage and Mr. and Mrs. Charles G. Haskin.

Dr. Jones, the pastor, stated that he had nominated, and Presiding Elder Truesdell had approved, the following gentlemen for Trustees of the new church: H. B. Hurd, W. H. Jones, D. B. Dewey, J. B. Kirk, J. J. Shutterly, H. H. Gage, F. P. Crandon, D. R. Dyche and C. G. Haskin.

The meeting was organized by the election of H. B. Hurd, Chairman, and C. G. Haskin, Secretary; the name of the church was declared to be Emmanuel Methodist Episcopal Church of Evanston the persons above named were elected the first Board of Trustees; and the secretary was directed to file a certificate of organization in the Recorder's office of Cook County. At a regular meeting of the trustees, held June 13th, the following officers were elected: H. B. Hurd, President; C. G. Haskin, Secretary, and D. B. Dewey, Treasurer. The secretary's communication further stated that the site selected for the erection of the church building, at the northeast corner of Greenwood Boulevard and Oak Avenue, has a frontage of seventy feet on Greenwood Boulevard and 214 feet on Oak Avenue; that it was bought in two parcels, the total purchase price being $11,500, all of which had been paid, and the title placed in Emmanuel M. E. Church; that it was proposed to erect a church edifice to cost, when finished and furnished, about $35,-000, which, with the cost of the lot — less the sale of old buildings to be credited— would make an investment of about $45,-000; the seating capacity of this church to be about 600, with a Sunday school room ample for all needs for several years to come.

The first Stewards of Emmanuel Church were: H. B. Hurd, W. H. Jones, R. B. McMullen, S. A. Kean, J. J. Shutterly, C. O. Boring, George S. Baker, John Freeman and George A. Bass. C. O. Boring was the first Sunday School Superintendent. Of the first Board of Trustees Messrs. Gage, Crandon, and Dyche were members of the First M. E. Church.

In October, 1890, Rev. Sylvester F. Jones was appointed the first pastor of Emmanuel Church. During the construction of the church edifice the society worshiped in the building on (West) Davis Street, formerly occupied by St. Mark's Episcopal Church.

The church building was finished and dedicated in August, 1892. The total cost of the property was $80,000. Doctor Jones served as pastor three years and was succeeded, October, 1893, by Rev. C. A. Van Anda, who remained one year.

From October, 1894, to October, 1895, the pulpit was supplied by Rev. S. J. Herben and Rev. M. S. Terry, D. D. October, 1895, Rev. N. M. Waters was appointed pastor and remained four years. Rev. W. O. Shepherd was pastor from October, 1899, to October, 1901; Rev. W. E. McLennan, from October, 1901, to October, 1903, when he was succeeded by Rev. F. S. Rockwell, the present pastor.

The present officers of the church (1905) are:

Trustees.—H. B. Hurd (now deceased); W. H. Jones, W. O. Dean, Dr. W. R. Parkes, M. L. Record, L. M. Sawyer, C. S. Graves, S. J. Llewellyn, J. L. Whitlock; Stewards—J. M. Barnes, C. O. Boring, W. L. Boettcher, G. J. Dart, G. W. Eddy, G. N. Friend, J. P. Grier, J. C. Turner, S. R. Winchell, J. L. Whitlock, E. R. Prickett, J. S. Crosby; Sunday School Superintendent—W. A. Burch; President Epworth League—H. H. Young.

FIRST BAPTIST CHURCH
(By REV. B. A. GREENE, D. D.)

Those interested in forming a Baptist church in Evanston met in the chapel of the Northwestern University April 24, 1858. Mr. E. H. Mulford was elected moderator and Moses Danby clerk. "Articles of Faith and Practice" were adopted, and it was voted to call the church "The Evanston Baptist Church." The six constituent members were: E. H. Mulford, Rebecca Mulford, Francis M. Iglehart, Judith W. Burroughs, Rebecca Westerfield and Moses Danby.

For two years previous to this time Mrs. Francis Iglehart had been the leader in Sunday school work in the vicinity of Oakton. Her leadership, at this early stage, and her hearty, generous, continued helpfulness afterward, made her the mother of the Baptist interest in the city. A marble tablet may be seen in the present church edifice commemorating her conspicuous fidelity.

A council for the recognition of the church was held April 29th in the Methodist church. Five churches in Chicago and the church in Waukegan were represented by delegates. Dr. W. G. Howard, pastor of the First Baptist Church, Chicago, was elected moderator. E. H. Mulford stated that a lot worth $600, on the northeast corner of Hinman Avenue and Church Street, had been given to them by the Northwestern University, and the Trustees had further given the use of their chapel until a new house of worship should be built. This surely was very generous help from Methodist friends. Those who participated in the recognition were: Rev. Dr. Foster, President of Northwestern University, who read the scripture: Prof. Goodman offered the prayer; Dr. Howard preached the sermon; Rev. A. J. Joslyn, of Union Park Church, gave the charge to the church; Rev. A. Kenyon, of the Berean Church, offered the closing prayer and pronounced the benediction.

At a business meeting, on May 6, 1858, the following were elected Trustees of the church: N. P. Iglehart, President; E. H. Mulford, James Sudlam, Moses Danby and Mr. Trumbull. A month later, at a church meeting, the following were received for baptism, and the next day, June 6th, were baptized in the lake: Isaac Burroughs, Betsy Burroughs, Almina Burroughs and Hannah Newell. This month, also, the church was admitted to the Fox River Baptist Association, held at Plainfield, having sent as delegates F. M. Iglehart and E. H. Mulford.

The church, although small, seemed to be well started and entering upon a career of organic and spiritual life. But it was very soon found that they must pass through a stage of struggle and disappointment. The preaching service was irregular. Supplies for the pulpit came sometimes from neighboring churches and sometimes from the University. The next year, 1859, when four of their most active members were temporarily absent, the church became discouraged, and voted in July "to suspend further efforts toward erecting a building for the church, and also to give up public worship for the present." However, social gatherings and prayer meetings continued to be held, and so they were kept together in sorrowing hope until the next spring. They had given up the use of the chapel, and the Congregational people occupied it. In the meantime Mr. Iglehart had erected a building, twenty by thirty feet, on their home lot at Oakton, near what is now Ridge Avenue and Oakton Street. This building was put up for a billiard room, but was christened instead as "Oakton Chapel," and here public services were resumed.

Rev. Ira E. Kenney began his pastorate March 11, 1860. In August of that year, as the Congregationalists had given up their service in the University chapel, it was voted to hold a four o'clock service there and have an evening prayer meeting at Oakton. In their letter to the Fox River Association, this year, they report fourteen members, $460 raised for expenses and benevolence, a sewing society and sociable every other Friday afternoon and evening, a sewing society for little misses every Saturday afternoon, and that scholars in the Bible school learn ten verses each, every Sabbath. In 1861 they left Oakton Chapel and worshipped in the schoolhouse near by; and, for a while, they had preaching only once a month. Mr. Kenney closed his pastorate March 9, 1862, having accepted a call from Niles, Mich.

Rev. J. S. Mahan was then called to the pastorate from Waukegan, May 4, 1862. The compensation was not flattering—"$2.50 to $3.00 every two weeks." He preached his farewell sermon October 19th of that year. Preaching service was again suspended. Prayer meetings were kept up for a while, but the records say that, as Mrs. Iglehart and family removed temporarily to Chicago in the winter of 1863-64, all preaching and prayer-meetings were suspended until the family should return. The Civil War had its depressing effect, not only on business life, but upon social and religious life as well.

The next spring there was a concerted movement on the part of the members and of friends in the city to get the church into such condition as to receive those who had moved out from Chicago. Thomas Goodman, of the Union Park Church, and afterward editor of *The Standard*, the Baptist denominational paper of the Northwest, was a leader in the advisory work. A meeting was held in June. Minor matters in the "Articles of Faith" were corrected. A proper record was made of the former election of E. H. Mulford as deacon. Then, ten persons were received into membership. S. E. Jackson, who had served as clerk since 1860, resigned, and A. W. Ford took his place. The latter soon moved to Freeport and, October 20th, J. N. Whidden became clerk. Thomas Goodman and J. N. Whidden were elected deacons. "The Evanston Baptist Society" was constituted, and the following trustees elected: B. F. Johnson, Richard Somers, James Maclay, Riley M. Graves, John Clough and I. P. Iglehart. Their report to the

Association, in June, 1865, begins with this sentence: "Our long night of anxiety has passed, and the full light of a new and, we trust, a better day has dawned." They received twenty-six by letter and had dedicated their new house of worship, costing $6,500, free of debt. Many friends from Chicago came February 16, 1865, and Dr. Everts, pastor of the First Baptist Church, of that city, preached the sermon. The next Sunday, February 19th, after Dr. Tiffany preached in the afternoon, the entire indebtedness was provided for. Rev. N. Sheppard was engaged to preach once on the Sabbath until further arrangement could be made, and his pay was to be $10 per Sabbath.

June 28, 1865, William J. Leonard was called to be pastor, at a salary of $1,000. He was young and unmarried. He was ordained in the church September 7th. Dr. E. J. Goodspeed preached the sermon, Dr. J. C. Burroughs offered the ordaining prayer, Dr. Raymond, of the Methodist Church, gave the charge to the candidate, and Rev. N. Sheppard the charge to the church. Previous to the coming of the pastor, on July 17th, Theodore Reese was elected treasurer, L. L. Greenleaf having resigned. Riley M. Graves, John Clough and John Goebel were elected deacons. During this pastorate quite a number were received by letter, bringing the membership up to seventy-three. There is a story still in circulation, which used to be told with much gusto, as throwing light upon customs and comments behind the scenes, especially touching up long-winded parsons. One day a visiting clergyman, stopping with the pastor, was asked to "say grace" at the table. The pastor's little nephew was very hungry, and, after he had waited and waited for the words of blessing to cease, when the "amen" was pronounced, he burst forth,

"Hocus-pokus, what a long prayer!" A parsonage was built. Messrs. Greenleaf, Graves and Clough advanced the required capital; but, as the church became financially involved, the "so-called parsonage" was sold in the same year, 1867. A baptistry was built in November of this year. Mr. Leonard's pastorate closed in November, 1868, amid considerable disturbance of feeling. He was a man of intellectual ability, generous instincts and fine taste, but was lacking in some of those tactful qualities so essential in a struggling church.

It is to be noted here that, on Thursday evening, August 18, 1868, Theodore Reese was elected clerk, and, for the next seven years, served faithfully. He had been immediately preceded in short terms by J. R. Hearsey and J. W. P. Hovey.

In January, 1869, Dr. M. G. Clark, a retired minister living in Chicago, began preaching. His services proved so acceptable, tending to restore harmony in the church, that he was given a unanimous call, at a salary of $1,500. He was a strong man and received into the church, in the next two years, about eighty persons. The Trustees at this time were: John Clough, Andrew Shuman, H. C. Tillinghast, R. S. King, R. M. Graves, C. F. Grey, J. W. P. Hovey and E. R. Paul. The Treasurer was Towner K. Webster. During this pastorate "The New Hampshire Articles of Faith" were adopted by the church, in place of those which had given trouble in earlier days. The trouble was verbal and of minor character, rather than theological. There was feeling on the part of some that the pews should be free; but they voted, January 10, 1870, to rent them as before, and Mr. C. F. Grey was made chairman of the committee to solicit the renting of them. In February of that year it was

voted to have a covenant meeting both afternoon and evening. In May, 1870, they reported a membership of 105—twenty-three having recently been baptized; $3,200 for home expenses and benevolence, and the Bible school was supporting two native Garo preachers in Burmah, and members were working in four mission schools.

Dr. Clark befriended the janitor of the church, a colored man, because he was shamefully abused, and, on that account, came near being mobbed by the "hoodlum element." His friends shielded him, and his enemies were afterward ashamed of their folly. Dr. Clark's wife was editor of "The Mother's Journal." He resigned in March, 1871, to become district secretary of the Home Mission Society in the State of New York.

On Sunday, May 28, 1871, a unanimous call was extended to Rev. F. S. Chapell, of Middletown, Ohio, at a salary of $2,500. This double fact of unanimity and of large increase in salary shows advance. And, within a week, they entertained the Fox River Association for three days.

Mr. Chapell began work July 2d. The church now entered upon longer pastorates and larger activity. They decided upon quarterly business meetings, appointed a committee on music and selected a new hymn-book. Within a year they decided to secure a more central location and fixed upon the lot now occupied, the northwest corner of Chicago Avenue and Lake Street. The price of the lot was $6,000. C. F. Grey, C. E. Brown, H. C. Tillinghast, W. C. Clark, A. S. Shuman were appointed a committee to have charge of building the new house. The last service on Hinman Avenue was held August 18, 1872. The next four Sundays they occupied "Lyons' Hall." At the end of that time the little wooden church had been moved and located on the rear of the new lot. There the congregation worshiped until the present brick church was finished, in November, 1872.

Sunday evening, November 3, 1872, a crowd of people had come to hear one of a series of sermons for the young and to witness a baptism. Just as the pastor began preaching "nearly half of the floor gave way and precipitated the congregation into the basement, about nine feet below." None were seriously injured. Nathan Branch, a highly esteemed colored brother of the church, was sitting in a pew that was fastened to the side of the building. When he felt the floor giving way, and glanced at the confusion below, he leaped to a window-sill from his lofty perch and plunged through the window, breaking sash and glass. He came around to the treasurer the next morning and offered to pay the damage.

Sunday, April 27, 1873, the fifteenth anniversary of the church was celebrated. The pastor preached a historical sermon in the morning and Rev. Dr. W. W. Everts preached in the evening. During the day the sum of $19,400 was subscribed for the new church.

In June, 1874, Riley M. Graves and four others were dismissed, to help form a new Baptist church at Winnetka. The church was organized, but it did not continue long, as the leaders in the work soon left the village.

In December of this year the church adopted revised and elaborated "Rules of Order" for the church, and also a "Constitution of the Bible School." A financial report for the year 1874 shows $3,714.32 received and $3,305.35 expended, with $178 for benevolence. The following officers were elected for the year 1875: Deacons: E. H. Mulford, James B. Van

Buren, John Goebel, H. C. Tillinghast. F. S. Belden, C. H. Rudd and S. Harbert. Trustees: C. F. Grey, C. F. Brown, D. F. Keeney, R. S. King, John Goebel, Andrew Shuman and E. R. Paul; Clerk, Theodore Reese; Treasurer, George D. Mosely. Finance Committee: D. B. Dewey, George D. Mosely, C. F. Grey, Francis B. Belden and H. C. Tillinghast.

February 17, 1875, the church was reincorporated "under and by virtue of Section 44 of an Act concerning corporations, approved April 18, 1872," and the corporate name adopted was "First Baptist Church of Evanston." In March of this year fourteen names were dropped from the roll of membership. In June it was voted to establish three mission schools, the financial obligation of the church not to exceed $150 per annum. John Goebel was elected superintendent of the South Mission, F. S. Belden of the North Mission, and C. H. Rudd of the West Mission. The latter was the more successful, and brought a number of members to the church afterward. In July letters were granted to J. G. Westerfield and three others, to help form a new church in Wilmette; but this movement, like the one in Winnetka, was short-lived. It will thus be seen that the church was feeling the vigor of growing life. They had business enterprise. They could clear the decks for effective action, and they had the missionary zeal to reach out into the surrounding regions. In November, 1875, N. L. Stow was elected clerk of the church, and has served with conscientious, painstaking fidelity up to the present time, a period of twenty-seven years.

The building of the new church progressed rather slowly, on account of the hard times. A loan of $10,000 was secured in June, 1875, to pay off the floating debt and for completing the church. N. L. Stow, in his address at the fortieth anniversary, has this to say of the condition of things: "The foundation for the new building was laid in the autumn of 1873. The panic of these years caused the work to drag slowly, and two years went by before we saw the completion. The building committee had so attended to the main work, the ladies to the furnishing and the pastor to the bell, that the house was very complete; the spire being finished, the entire floor carpeted and the seats cushioned. It was a beautiful day — this Sabbath, the 21st of November, 1875. A large congregation assembled, morning, afternoon and evening. Dr. Everts preached in the morning. The afternoon service was a children's service, H. C. Tillinghast, the superintendent, having charge. Other schools of the village were represented. Rev. Mr. Packard, of the Congregationalist Church; Rev. Dr. Noyes, of the Presbyterian, and Prof. Hemenway, of the Methodist, gave addresses. Col. Fairman, the artist, made the closing speech. Dr. Northrop, President of the Chicago Baptist Theological Seminary, preached in the evening. The subscriptions this day amounted to $14,000. The bell was made especially for the church. The motto cast in the metal was selected by the pastor, and is as follows: "Gather the people together, men and women and children, and thy stranger that is within thy gates, that they may hear and that they may learn and fear the Lord your God." Many subscriptions were made by citizens outside the church, that Evanston might have at least one church bell centrally located. The building cost $31,000, which, added to the cost of lot, bell and furnishing, made a total of $40,000. Mrs. Rebecca J. Mulford, wife of Major E. H. Mulford, re-membered the church generously in her will; and her name, in memory of her devout character, was placed in one of the windows beside the appropriate emblem of a sheaf of ripe wheat.

It was a large undertaking to keep up the running expenses and meet the maturing obligations involved in the new construction. Heavy lifting there was on the part of many; but in March of the following year, 1876, the auditing committee insert this statement in their report with regard to H. C. Tillinghast:

"We find that, in addition to the usual cares incident to the position as Treasurer and Chairman of the Building Committee, rather than see the work stop, he has loaned his own individual credit, giving his notes, endorsing subscription notes to make them negotiable, advancing money when the funds of the church were low, and at the present time, the church is indebted to him over $1,400. We owe Brother Tillinghast a lasting debt of gratitude and that some acknowledgment of these services be placed on record."

Record is made July 4, 1876, that the new bell was consecrated to patriotic service by being rung thirty minutes at sunrise, noon and sunset. Ivy was also planted at the south of the spire. The church contributed to the new Moody movement in Chicago. Thursday, November 9th, of this year, a large social gathering met at the pastor's house, to celebrate his fortieth birthday by giving him a set of "Johnson's Encyclopedia."

In December, 1877, Pastor Chapell tendered his resignation to take effect the following July. He felt it was impossible for the church to keep up his salary; that the pastorate was, already as long as the average, and a change might be beneficial to the health of his family. He had wrought a noble work, and there was the best of feeling in the separation. Resolutions were spread upon the records, affirming that it was through the pastor's pulpit ability, his zeal and consecration, that .the church had come to its present state of growth. He was devout and at the same time practical. He believed in attending to details and statistics and discipline. He was untiring in labors and, during the last year, acted as Superintendent of the Bible school. During the seven years of his pastorate he preached 684 sermons, conducted 535 devotional meetings, married 34 couples, attended 66 funerals, baptized 83, received into the church 204, and there has been raised in money $53,250. He went to Janesville, Wisconsin.

It is very evident from the report of the Trustees, the December following, that the church was passing through financial straits, owing to the loss of several valuable members and the general business depression. When overtures were made to Rev. Mr. Custis, of Chicago, to become pastor, he felt that he could not come for less than $2,000. That salary they could not then pay. March 31, 1879, a unanimous call was extended to Rev. George R. Pierce of Oneida, N. Y., at a salary of $100 per month. He accepted April 8th, and immediately entered upon his work. Nothing unusual marked the early part of his pastorate. July 27th the records state: "Service this morning was made more than usually interesting, because of the first introduction of a quartette choir." The pew question came up for consideration, and the evening preaching service was repeatedly discussed and voted upon, while the church, exercising the usual Baptist prerogative, instructed the Trustees not to order any "further collection to be taken, unless the matter be first submitted to the church." At the opening

of the second year the pastor's salary was raised to $1,300 per annum, and, a little later, he was granted a vacation of five weeks. During the year 1880, the Eddy mortgage of $10,000 became due. It was arranged to pay $1,000 by November 1st and let the remaining $9,000 run until May, 1885, at 7 per cent interest—it being understood that the church could, at any time, pay any portion of the principal. On November 28th of that year Mr. Kimball, of Chicago, spent the day trying to raise the entire debt. In the morning $6,000 were subscribed and in the evening $1,000. In order to raise 25 per cent more, a committee of ladies was appointed to solicit help from every individual. These ladies were: Mrs. Goebel, Mrs. Craine, Mrs. Somers and Miss Sarah Webster. But not until March, 1883, was there recorded any special reduction of the debt. Then, by the aid of R. S. King's bequest of $5,000, the bonded debt was reduced to $3,000, and the interest to the rate of 6 per cent per annum. An amended and revised constitution for the Bible school was reported by J. W. Thompson, and this was adopted April 18, 1881. November 15, 1882, Nathan Branch and nine other persons were dismissed to become constituent members of the First Colored Baptist Church to be organized in Evanston.

March 19, 1883, Pastor Pierce resigned, stating as his reason that "general dissatisfaction has sprung up in the minds of the members of the church." A week from that time the resignation was accepted by a vote of 29 to 16, the resignation to take effect September 30th.

Sunday, April 22d, they began celebrating the twenty-fifth anniversary. Dr. William M. Lawrence, of the Second Church of Chicago, preached in the morning, and Dr. Anderson, of the Chicago University, in the evening. In the afternoon the pastor gave a history of the church and read letters from Rev. W. J. Leonard and Rev. F. Chapell, former pastors. Two constituent members were present, Mrs. Iglehart and Mrs. Burroughs. On the following Tuesday evening, in response to an invitation, many friends from Chicago and Evanston rallied, and, after listening to the pastor in a brief recital of church history and short addresses from Rev. Mr. Burhoe, Rev. Mr. McGregor and Dr. Hatfield, they repaired to the vestry where bountiful tables awaited them.

At the quarterly meeting, June 25; 1883, the motion accepting the pastor's resignation was rescinded and he was asked to remain. The pastor wished time for consideration, but finally decided that he must go. There was considerable feeling stirred, and D. B. Dewey with some others withdrew from the church. This pastorate ended December 30, 1883. Although 65 had been added to the church in the four years, losses had made the net gain only three, and the number reported to the Association the next year showed a net loss of three.

Rev. Fred Clatworthy, of Norwalk. Ohio, was given a unanimous call, January 9, 1884. This call, coming as it did after so much commotion, and with an offer of $2,000 salary ($500 of it to be made up by private subscription), when much financial strength had been lost to the parish, spoke highly of the church's regard for the man. This esteem was well placed, for, beginning March 1st, he did a rare work in settling disturbed conditions and rallying forces for the beginning of even a larger prosperity than ever. The work began with revising the church rules of order and a new election of officers. For Deacons they elected C. H. Rudd, A. O. Bassett and E. S. Turner;

for Trustees, H. C. Tillinghast, John Goebel, C. F. Grey, J. W. Thompson, L. K. Gillson; for Clerk, N. L. Stow; for Treasurer, H. G. Grey; for Superintendent of Bible School, J. W. Thompson.

In March, T. K. Webster reported from the Trustees that they had decided to secure the income for the church from voluntary offerings, and, in April of the next year, they reported a floating debt of $500 wiped out, the additional $500 for salary met, the chapel painted and decorated, a good choir kept up, all bills (aside from mortgage) paid, and a small balance in the treasury. The amount expended this year was $4,305.44. There was a net increase in membership of 37 making a total of 198, and the church was thoroughly united. P. N. Fox followed H. G. Grey as Treasurer, while James E. Low took the place of J. W. Thompson as Superintendent of the Bible School.

May 6, 1885, the church sent delegates to help form a city Mission Society in Chicago. A tablet in memory of the wife of Rufus King was placed on the east wall of the church, carrying out the condition on which he bequeathed to the church the $5,000, before referred to.

During December, 1887, a new organ, made by Steere and Turner, was placed in the church, and on the thirty-first of the month a concert was given by Mr. Clarence Eddy of Chicago.

May 5, 1889, Mr. Clatworthy resigned to go to the church in Adrian, Michigan. It was with regret that the resignation was accepted, for "exceedingly pleasant relations characterized the pastorate." He preached his farewell sermon June 30th.

During his pastorate 197 were added to the church roll by baptism and by letter and, the total membership was increased from 169 to 284.

Before the pastor left the field, a committee, of which J. W. Thompson was chairman, reported in favor of calling Rev. H. A. Delano, of South Norwalk. Conn. It was with the hearty endorsement of the retiring pastor that this was done. Such a call was extended June 13, the vote standing 54 to 19, and the salary to be $2,000. Mr. Delano accepted July 1st, and began his labors September 1, 1889.

The work started in a prosperous way. At the following Easter enough money was raised to close up the old year and begin the new year "in the best possible condition." Treasurer James E. Low, April 7, 1890, reported they had expended for the year just closed $3,727, and there was on hand $271. There was an increasing demand for pews and it was decided to go back to pew rentals. The church building was equipped for electric lighting, and they began agitating the question of a new chapel, as the old one was in bad condition and not at all in keeping with the new structure in front.

In September of the following year, 1891, Mr. C. F. Grey very generously offered "to donate towards a new chapel, all the mason and carpenter work, with material for all the building, except the roof, plumbing, painting and finishing—provided the church would complete the building without incurring debt in so doing." With a vote of hearty thanks to the donor, the Trustees were authorized to secure plans and provide for the additional money needed. Plans were reported and adopted March 6, 1892, and on March 27, at the close of the sermon, the amount required ($6,500) was very nearly pledged and the work on the new chapel began.

The last service in the old chapel was on Sunday evening, June 12, 1892. The new chapel was first occupied Sunday, June 11, 1893. The Bible school session was first, as they had before changed the hour of the school from 12 m. to 9:30 a. m. The service was, in part, an installation of the new officers and in part a dedication. The morning preaching service was also held here. The chapel was solidly built, conveniently arranged and beautiful, giving completeness to the church property. Its cost reached about $22,000.

For a while, previous to this, the mid-week prayer-meeting was held in "Union Hall." The Presbyterian church very kindly offered the use of their vestry. And this courtesy was reciprocated when, in 1894, the Presbyterian church building was burned. They were invited to use the Baptist auditorium, and did so for a while.

Dr. Delano's salary was raised twice, $500 at a time. His ministry was an able one. He was interested in public affairs and social reforms, and was everywhere acceptable as a platform speaker. His hearty, companionable way won him hosts of friends in the community. When his resignation came, March 23, 1896, to take effect May 1st, it was with great reluctance his friends consented to have him go. He accepted a call to the Belden Avenue Baptist church, Chicago. In the seven years of his pastorate the church had received 295 additions; but removals had been so frequent, the net gain was only about 60, leaving a membership of 354.

During the following year the pulpit was supplied, for the most part, by Prof. Albion W. Small, of Chicago University. He preached only in the morning. The evening preaching service, which had been a perplexing problem even in the hands of the popular pastor, Dr. Delano, was suspended. November 18, 1896, a

unanimous call was extended to Rev. D.
B. Cheeney, of Racine, but he did not feel
justified in leaving his field.

January 20, 1897, a unanimous call was
extended to B. A. Greene, D. D., of Lynn,
Massachusetts, at a salary of $3,000. The
church had not heard him preach, neither
had he known the church; but the call
was given on the strength of reports
gained from many sources as to his fitness for the place. J. W. Thompson and
J. S. Dickerson were selected to confer
with the man of their choice. Dr. Greene
accepted and began work March 2, 1897.
The last nine years have been prosperous
and harmonious. There have been 290
additions. The finances have been generously cared for. In addition to pew
rentals, and to provide beforehand against
deficiency, it is a custom to secure pledges
at some selected morning service. Annual
expenses amount to about $7,000; be-
nevolences, about $3,000.

The church has adopted as its own the
Delano Mission, corner of Maple Avenue
and Foster Street.

The following is a list of officers at the
present time (1906):

Pastor—B. A. Greene, D. D.; Deacons
—James E. Low, J. S. Dickerson, Peter
Lemoi, L. K. Gillson, W. G. Sherer, A. M.
Zimmerman, A. E. Wright, Rev. M. Bar-
ker; Trustees—J. E. Scott, J. W. Low, H.
G. Grey, Dr. D. J. Harris, J. H. Mac-
Gregor, L. R. Wing, J. F. Piersen; Treas-
urer—E. R. Gilmore; Clerk—N. L. Stow;
Bible School Officers—L. A. Trowbridge,
Superintendent; Wm. Hanchett, Associate
Superintendent; Fred Richards, Secretary;
J. Q. Adams, Treasurer; Women's Socie-
ties—Mrs H. W. Tate, President of Wo-
man's Aid and Home Mission Department;
Mrs. W. P. Parker, President of Foreign
Mission Department; Mrs L. K. Gillson,
President of Home Missions; Young Peo-

ple's Society (B. Y. P. U.)—Mr. S. S.
Crippen, President; Harold Hanchett, Vice-
President; Miss Mabel Piersen, Secretary;
Miss Helen Talbot, Treasurer.

PRESBYTERIANISM IN EVANSTON
(BY REV. JOHN H. BOYD, D. D.)

The City of Evanston is the offspring
of a Methodist University, and very naturally, the first church organized was the
noble First Methodist Church, who is the
mother of us all. In the days of small
population and primitive simplicity the
religious life of the village was nurtured
solely by her; but as the community
grew, the uniformity which marks the
early stages of every infant society passed,
and little groups of kindred faith and spirit
drew off, one by one, to organize separate
churches; the Baptists in 1858 and the
Episcopalians in 1864.

First Presbyterian Church.—In July,
1866, the Rev. James B. Duncan, of the
Presbyterian Church of Canada, came to
Evanston upon invitation, with a view to
establishing a Presbyterian Church, but
after a canvass of the field a union church
alone was deemed possible of success.
Accordingly, on the first of August a small
company of Congregationalists and Presbyterians united in forming an independent church. The ministry of Mr.
Duncan continued over a period of about
two years. The Northwestern University,
continuing the generosity shown to all
previously organized societies, presented
this new church with a lot situated on the
northwest corner of Hinman Avenue and
Greenwood Boulevard, where the Greenwood Inn now stands. This lot was
afterwards exchanged for one at the corner of Lake "Avenue" and Chicago Avenue, and the church thereafter was known
as the "Lake Avenue Church." Upon this

site was erected a simple wooden structure, without lecture or Sunday School room, with about 250 sittings. At the end of two years, after a most harmonious and profitable association, each of the elements constituting this society felt strong enough to separate and organize churches of their own order. The Presbyterians purchased the interest of the Congregationalists, and remained on the original site. By appointment of the Presbytery of Chicago the Rev. Robert W. Patterson, D. D., and the Rev. James T. Matthews organized "The First Presbyterian Church of Evanston, July 27, 1868," with thirty-eight members, all except three of whom had been members of the "Lake Avenue Church." Three of these original members live today: Mrs. Frances Winne, Mrs. Priscilla Poole, of Evanston, and John McLean of Chicago. At its organization, Brainerd Kent, George E. Purington, Lewis M. Angle and A. L. Winne were chosen and ordained ruling elders. But one member of this original session is living today—Mr. George E. Purington of Chicago.

In October following the Rev. George Clement Noyes, of LaPorte, Ind., was called to the pastorate. He began his ministry November 22, 1868. The rapid growth of the congregation made it necessary to enlarge the building the year after his coming. One hundred sittings were added to the auditorium and a pleasant lecture room annexed. On May 2, 1875, the building, with its entire contents, was destroyed by fire. The loss was a most serious one for the little congregation. Many men of business had been financially embarrassed by the great Chicago fire, and a long period of depression in business ensued, but the spirit of the people was undaunted ,and their liberality and enterprise are manifest in the fact that,

at the following Christmas season, services were held in the completed lecture room. The entire building was ready for dedication July 23, 1876. The cost of this edifice with furnishings was about twenty-two thousand dollars.

The ministry of Dr. Noyes was one of remarkable fruitfulness, evidenced in a net growth of the Church from a membership of thirty-eight to four hundred and sixty-four—nine hundred and sixty-three persons having been received into the Church during his pastorate of twenty years. The benevolences for the last five years of his ministry amounted to more than twenty-three thousand dollars, but the power of his ministry cannot be measured in concrete facts, however large and significant. Dr. Noyes, through his massive and sweetly spiritual personality, begat a spirit and created an atmosphere in which this congregation still lives. He possessed and represented the highest style of Presbyterian Christianity. Profoundly serious, earnest, broad and tolerant, believing God too great and too good to be exhausted by human definitions, and the ways of love and grace too many and too mysterious to be traced and numbered by formulas and creeds, he tolerated, he welcomed, he embraced all who loyally and lovingly clung to the Divine Master.

During his long pastorate of more than twenty-one years, he represented—it would be more true to say that he embodied—in his own personality the Presbyterianism of Evanston, making it conspicuous and noble before the eyes of the Church and the world. For many years he was an editorial writer and weekly correspondent of the *New York Evangelist*. The words of "Clement" were read throughout the land as messages of wisdom. In the great controversy between the Reverend David Swing and the

Reverend Frank L. Patten, Mr. Swing chose Dr. Noyes as his counsel, and he was so appointed by the Presbytery of Chicago. He conducted the defense with distinguished ability. For a long term of years he was Chairman of the Committee of Home Missions of the Chicago Presbytery, the aggressiveness and efficiency of that body being in a large measure due to his splendid leadership. The ministry of Dr. Noyes was closed by his death January 14, 1889. Miss Frances E. Willard, who knew Evanston so long and intimately, writes thus of the places which this noble Presbyterian had in the life and affection of the community: "I think," says she, "no other death, unless it be that of Dr. Otis Haven, in all the years I have been an Evanstonian, ever drew forth so many expressions of sorrow, or from quarters so various, including the wide gamut that separated our municipal council from the freshman class of our University."

The Church, thus so sadly vacated, remained pastorless until a worthy successor to Dr. Noyes was found in the Rev. Newell Dwight Hillis, then pastor of the First Presbyterian Church of Peoria. The congregation invited Dr. Hillis to become pastor on February 6, 1890. He accepted and entered upon his labor April 6th.

The work prospered under the younger prophet as it had under the elder. He had the joy of seeing the work and Kingdom of God ever enlarging under his hand, and the congregation was happy in watching the unfolding of that power and eloquence which have placed him in a position where he addresses, through tongue and pen, an audience which may well be the admiration of any man who desires to reach his fellows with the message of God as he understands it.

The years of Dr. Hillis' ministry were very fruitful. The membership of the Church grew from four hundred and sixty-four to seven hundred and twelve. Benevolent gifts increased to unprecedented largeness, while every branch of the work showed thorough organization and won ever enlarging successes. The traditions of the Church were all preserved and the spirit of the great soul who had preceded him and had molded the congregation was that of his own soul.

In the fourth year of this pastorate the Church went through its second fire bath. On a quiet Sabbath morning, February 24, 1894, the assembling congregation, instead of entering the Sanctuary to worship, stood by and saw it consumed by the flames. They were not, however, difficult to comfort. The loss of the building was not a serious disaster. It was rather an unlooked-for solution of a difficult problem. The growth of the audience had made is necessary to consider the question of either enlarging the old building or erecting a new one. The charred timbers and ashes of the old answered the question. The congregation moved with such characteristic energy that, on the 7th day of the following October, the corner-stone of the present structure was laid with appropriate ceremonies, and, less than a year from that date, the building stood completed and furnished, being opened for worship September 1, 1895, the pastor-elect preaching the sermon.

This new building is a splendid, massive structure, built of Lemont limestone, with interior finishings of red oak, the roof beams of Georgia pine. It cost, complete with decorations and furnishings, $63,500, the organ costing $6,600 additional. The main auditorium, of 75x90 feet, with a gallery in the rear, has a seating capacity of about fourteen hundred. It is lighted by two great memorial windows—that on the north commemorating the Rev. Robert W. Patterson, D. D., who was a noble father of Chicago Presbyterianism, from the beginning the friend of this Church, and afterwards coming with his family to be, for many years, a member of the congregation; that on the south dedicated to the memory of the Rev. George Clement Noyes, D. D. It is most fitting that the worship and the work and fellowship of the congregation of the First Presbyterian Church should exist between windows sacred to the memory of these two men; for, as the fair auditorium is lighted by the rays of the sun which fall through the rich glasses, so the life of the congregation has been, and will in the future continue to be, illuminated by the rays of the Sun of Righteousness which shine through their holy characters.

During the erection of this edifice Dr. Hillis retired from the pastorate, presenting his resignation in December, 1894, having accepted an invitation to minister to the Central Church (Independent) of Chicago. On the 10th of July following, a call was extended to the Rev. John H. Boyd, D. D., then pastor of the Second Presbyterian Church of Charlotte, N. C. The call was accepted and the new pastorate opened on the 6th day of October, 1895. Dr. Boyd still remains in the field, and under his charge the prosperity which has always characterized the organization continues. The roll of church membership, after careful expurgation, showed at the beginning of his pastorate six hundred and fifty-nine names. This has been increased to eight hundred and sixty-three. During the seven years past $14,716 have been contributed to the cause of Home Missions, and $10,618 to Foreign Missions. Other Boards and benevolences have received $25,813, while in the payment of debts and self-support the con-

gregation has expended $109,602, making a grand total of $160,749, or almost $23,-000 per year. During the past seven years 219 persons have been received on profession of faith, and 449 by letter—making a total of 668 additions to the membership.

A notable event in the recent life of the congregation was the payment of a large debt which existed after the new church was completed. This amounted to $21,-500. After three years this amount was reduced by $4,000, leaving $17,500 indebtedness. On Sunday morning, April 23, 1899, after a discourse by the pastor, the congregation with enthusiastic liberality swept the whole debt away, in forty minutes time contributing more than sufficient to pay the whole.

The Church, as now organized, is a splendid piece of religious machinery, embracing sixteen different organizations, which engage the active co-operation of more than six hundred workers. The present session consists of twelve elders: Homer C. Hunt, who has served for more than twenty-two years; Thomas Lord, with a record of twenty years of service; Andress B. Hull, nineteen years of service; Thomas H. Linsley, Adam E. Dunn, Edward B. Quinlan, Otis R. Larsen, Frank S. Shaw, Cornelius D. B. Howell, Harry B. Wheelock, Charles C. Cox and Frank Marimon.

The Board of Trustees consists of nine members: Henry J. Wallingford, Jerome A. Smith, Philip P. Lee, Andrew Patterson, Adam E. Dunn, Frank W. Gerould, J. H. Nitchie, David B. Forgan, M. Cochrane Armour. This roll of esteemed and earnest men fully represents that greater list of officers who have served the church during the thirty-two years of its existence. The splendid personnel of the governing body and their positions of leadership is the explanation of the years of unarrested prosperity and continued peace which have marked this Church. The Sunday School, with a membership of five hundred, is under the leadership of Elder H. B. Wheelock, who, with his diligent officers and teachers, has brought the work to a high state of efficiency. The school is excellently graded. Miss Laura E. Cragin is in charge of the Kindergarten, Mrs. George H. Ludlow, the Primary, and T. K. Webster, the Intermediate. The Superintendent conducts the main department, and Mr. Fleming H. Revell and Mr. Newell C. Knight are leaders of Bible classes. The other minor organizations, devotional and benevolent, operate along the whole front of religious opportunity and are accomplishing large results.

The enlargement of Presbyterianism in Evanston is represented in two movements; one resulting in the organization of the Second Church in what was then the village of South Evanston, and the second and more recent one the building of a chapel whose future is full of promise. For nine years a prayer-meeting and Sunday School were sustained in a store house at 1315 Emerson Street. This was known as the Emerson Street Chapel. In the winter of 1902 the Church felt justified in placing this work upon a more substantial footing. A lot was bought at the corner of Emerson Street and Dewey Avenue. A neat little Chapel, well equipped for a neighborhood church, seating about 250, was erected. It was first occupied May 4th and was dedicated, amid the rejoicings of Children's Day, on June 8, 1902.

The Second Presbyterian Church grew out the interest of the Rev. Dr. Noyes of the First Church, in the people of the village of South Evanston. Having moved with his family to the corner of Greenleaf Street and Judson Avenue, he began to hold cottage prayer-meetings in the neighborhood. These gatherings quickened the desire of the people in that locality to have a church of their own. The growth of the movement and career of the church is here given from the pen of Mr. George W. Hotchkiss, who was from the beginning active in advancing the cause and who remains, today, to enjoy the large measure of success which has come to the effort of the earnest men and women of that congregation:

Second Presbyterian Church. — The Second Presbyterian Church of Evanston, located on the northeast corner of Hinman Avenue and Main Street, originated in February, 1884, from the gathering together of a few citizens of the then Village of South Evanston (now comprising the Third and Fourth Wards of the City of Evanston), to consider the spiritual needs of the village, which, with about 1,500 inhabitants, had but one church organization, that of the Methodist Episcopal denomination. The preliminary and several successive conferences were attended by Messrs. Charles Randolph, Gen. Julius White, A. H. Gunn, J. M. Brown, T. Winter, S. E. Norton, A. L. Winne, J. B. Lamkin, E. A. Downs, Wm. M. R. Vose and George W. Hotchkiss, and a general call was promulgated addressed to—

"All persons who believe that the time has arrived when an earnest effort should be made to organize either a Presbyterian or Congregational Church in South Evanston, and those feeling any interest in the subject are requested to assemble in Ducat's Hall on the afternoon of Sunday, February 24, 1884, at four o'clock, to consider the question and to inaugurate such action as will lead to the accomplishment of such an organization."

At this meeting eighty-five persons were assembled, and by a practically unanimous vote, it was decided to canvass the village and thus ascertain if financial and religious support could be relied upon. This resulted in a report to a meeting, held March 9th, that the movement could rely upon the approval and support of two hundred and three adults, while one hundred and two children and youth had been found who would gladly attend the Sabbath School, and the Committee recommended that immediate steps be taken toward permanent organization and the securing of subscriptions for a building fund. At a meeting held April 13th subscriptions to the amount of over $6,000 were reported as having been pledged, and it was formally decided to go forward as rapidly as possible with the work of organization and the erection of a house of worship. At this meeting articles of association were adopted for the formation of a religious society and received the signatures of one hundred and twenty-five persons. On Saturday evening, April 19th, a formal organization was effected by the adoption of by-laws, and a two-thirds majority of those present being in favor of a Presbyterian form of government, the new organization was designated as the Presbyterian Church of South Evanston, and, as such, was certified by the Secretary, George W. Hotchkiss, to the County Clerk of Cook County in accordance with the laws of the State of Illinois. At this meeting A. H. Gunn, John M. Brown and O. F. Gibbs were elected Trustees to serve one year, and Thaddeus Winter, Charles Randolph and H. C. McClary to serve for two years. The first meeting of the Board of Trustees was held April 23d, at which time it was voted to purchase a lot of 114 feet frontage on Hinman Avenue, northeast corner

of Lincoln Avenue (afterwards named Main Street), for the price of $3,500. April 25th a building committee was appointed to act in conjunction with the Board of Trustees. June 7th Messrs. Holabird and Roach were selected as the architects, and their plans of a building to cost about $8,000 were approved. These plans were subsequently remodeled and the final structure, as it now stands, represents an outlay of about $20,000. The edifice has seating capacity for about four hundred and fifty persons. So much for the origin and completion of the temporalities of the Church which, upon the incorporation of the two villages of South Evanston and Evanston, became known as "The South Presbyterian Church of Evanston." In June, 1901, the corporate name was again changed to conform to existing conditions, and it is now known as "The Second Presbyterian Church of Evanston."

During the progress of events from the initiation of the movement looking to the formation of the Society and during the interim of building, neighborhood prayer-meetings were held, ladies' societies formed and every preparation made for the final organization as a religious body. By June, 1885, the church building had so far progressed that, on Sabbath Day, June 28th, a committee from the Presbytery of Chicago consisting of Rev. George C. Noyes (pastor of the First Presbyterian Church of Evanston) and Rev. R. W. Patterson, D. D., met and examined the letters of forty-four members of other churches who had decided to join the new organization, and who, together with six persons who presented themselves upon confession of their faith, were declared to form the thus constituted church. At this, the first religious service held in the church, Rev. R. W. Patterson, D. D., administered the ordinance of baptism to three adults, after which he preached a sermon from Luke 13:18-21. Dr. Patterson was assisted in this service by Rev. Clatworthy, pastor of the Baptist Church of Evanston, and the Rev. Lewis Curts, of the Methodist Episcopal Church of Evanston, while the service of dedicating the building to the worship of Almighty God was conducted by Rev. George C. Noyes, D. D., the dedicatory prayer being offered by Rev. A. J. Scott, pastor of the Congregational Church of Evanston. From this time regular church service was held in the lecture room, a Sabbath School organized and a Wednesday evening prayer-meeting established. On July 15th, at the close of the prayer service, it was decided to elect but two elders at that time and William H. Spencer and William M. R. Vose were elected to that office. During the remainder of that year the Rev. R. W. Patterson, although of advanced age and infirmity, assisted the young Church as pulpit supply, until November 11, 1885, when a call was extended to Rev. William Smith, of Hudson, N. Y., who, accepting, came at once to his new pastorate and continued to the great edification of the Church until his death, February 23, 1892. In June, 1892, the Rev. John N. Mills, of Beatrice, Neb., was called to the pastorate which he filled acceptably until May 8, 1895, when failing health compelled him to present his resignation, much to the regret of the membership, and his farewell sermon was preached on the 26th of the same month. From that time until March, 1896, Prof. M. Bross Thomas acted as pulpit supply with great acceptability and, on March 4, 1896, a call was extended to Rev. A .W. Ringland, D. D., late of Toledo, Ohio, which, being accepted, Dr. Ringland entered upon his pastorate April 5, 1896. He continued a most successful and harmonious pastorate until February 25, 1898, when failing health compelled his resignation, taking effect April 1st of that year. Loath to accept the resignation of so faithful a pastor, a resolution prevailed granting to Dr. Ringland a year's vacation in the hope that, with restored health, his pastorate might continue; but, in February, 1899, he deemed it judicious to make his resignation absolute, and it was accepted. During the interregnum the pulpit was again supplied, to the great edification of the Church, by Prof. M. Bross Thomas, of the Lake Forest University, until February 26, 1899, when a call was extended to Rev. John W. Francis, of Richland Center, Wis., who was installed as pastor on June 4, 1899, and still occupies that position, at this writing (April, 1902), the Church under his charge having greatly prospered. The present membership is 220.

During all the years since the organization of the Church a Sabbath School, which now has a regular attendance of about 185, has been maintained. A society of Christian Endeavor has engaged the attention and interest of the young women of the Church, while various societies in different branches of church work have done effective service. Of these, the Ladies' Home and Foreign Missionary Societies, the Ladies' Aid Society and the Forward Circle of the younger ladies have been prominent in effective work. The weekly prayer-meeting has been well sustained from the beginning, and the Second Presbyterian Church of Evanston justly holds a position of prominence among the many churches of the city.

EPISCOPAL CHURCHES
(By REV. ARTHUR W. LITTLE, D. D., L. H. D.)

In the year 1864 there were in Evanston only three or four families who really belonged to the Episcopal Church. There were, however, several leading citizens who loved the Prayer Book, and were ready to aid in starting a parish church. There were also certain other public-spirited men who, from considerations of civic pride, desired to see an Anglican church in the village. Thus the way was opened for the founding of St. Mark's Church.

In the spring of 1864 the Rev. John Wilkinson, a priest, and chaplain to the Rt. Rev. Dr. Whitehouse, Bishop of Illinois, was permitted by the courtesy of the Methodists to give notice in the chapel of the University that a parish would be organized according to the canons of the Diocese of Illinois, and that the organization would take place on April 20th. At this meeting a canonical organization was effected under the title of St. Mark's Parish, and Mr. Charles Cumstock and Mr. D. J. Crocker were chosen church wardens. St. Mark's, therefore, started as a parish, and was never a mission.

The first service was held on the third Sunday of May, 1864, in the building then known as the First Methodist church. After that the services were held in the chapel of the University, the Rev. Theodore I. Holcombe being priest in charge. There are many interesting reminiscences of his ministry here as a temporary supply for about a year, although it was indeed the day of small things.

Early in the spring of 1865 the Rev. Mr. Holcombe was transferred to the Diocese of Wisconsin, and for several weeks there seem to have been no public services of the Church. Meantime, however, the Trustees of the University kindly gave the parish a lot of land on the north side of Davis Street, between Ridge and Oak Avenues, sixty feet front by 150 feet deep, upon which a small wooden church was built. On September 15th of the year 1865 the church, being free of debt, was consecrated by Bishop Whitehouse, the solemn function being attended by the clerical and lay members of the Diocesan Convention, which was in session that week in Chicago. At the same time the Rev. John W. Buckmaster, a priest of the Diocese of New York, was made rector of the parish. From that day to this there has been no interruption in the parochial work of this church. The eucharistic sacrifice has been offered, and all the sacraments have been duly celebrated, while divine worship and preaching of the gospel have been maintained, with much charity and good work for the bodies as well as for the souls of men. When there has been a vacancy in the rectorship, there have always been temporary supplies.

The first class of candidates for confirmation was presented by the rector, Mr. Buckmaster, on March 26, 1866. It consisted of ten persons who were confirmed by the Rt. Rev. J. C. Talbot, D. D., Bishop co-adjutor of Indiana, acting for the Bishop of Illinois. That was a great event in Evanston. It was like the day when St. Peter and St. John came down from Jerusalem to Samaria, and laid their hands in apostolic benediction upon the first converts who had been baptized by St. Philip. This was the only class presented by the first rector; ten confirmations in two years—an average of five a year. This rectorship lasted from September, 1865 to April, 1867.

During much of the history of St. Mark's, the parish undoubtedly suffered from the shortness of the rectorships—a thing which seriously interrupts parochial work and the pastoral relation. The first ten years show four rectorships, besides two years of supplies. The next thirteen years show three rectorships, with about two years of supplies; in short, up to the year 1888, the average rectorship was less than three years. This seems like the Methodist system grafted upon the Old Church. It is wholly contrary to the Church idea, and was the cause as well as the result of evil.

The second rector of St. Mark's was the Rev. Thomas Lisle of Philadelphia, who was the parish priest here from the 20th of May, 1867, to the 7th of June, 1869. Great progress was made during this rectorship. The fact is, the people of the village began to realize that St. Mark's Church was here, that it stood for something, and that it had come to stay. Moreover, the village was growing quite rapidly at that time. It is recorded that the number of families and communicants in the parish doubled in those two years. The church building was also greatly enlarged by being lengthened, and a small wooden tower was built, containing a bell made by the Meneely Bell Company of Troy. So that, from that day St. Mark's has never been without "the sound of the church-going bell," to tell of God and to summon to the House of God, except during the time after the new church was built and until the beautiful chimes of St. Mark's were installed.

Bishop Whitehouse made his first episcopal visitation for confirmation on April 19, 1868, confirming a class of four persons; and again, on April 25th of the year 1869, when he confirmed ten, making fourteen who received the sacrament of confirmation during this rectorship—an average of seven a year.

From January, 1869, until April, 1872, there was one short rectorship with several priests in charge as temporary supplies. Not much work was done. There were no confirmations. The rectorship was that of Rev. A. J. Barrows, from November, 1869, to September, 1870—less than a year.

In April, 1872, the Rev. C. S. Abbott became rector, and remained until in 1875. He was a kindly and faithful priest and pastor. He presented three classes for confirmation, containing, respectively, one, five and twelve souls, making eighteen confirmations—an average of four and one-half a year.

During this rectorship, as early as in the year 1873, plans for building a new church began to be formed. The scheme, however, was rejected by the vestry on what were probably wise and prudent considerations. There had been what is familiarly known as a great "boom" in Evanston. After the Chicago fire, many Chicago people were left homeless and came out to this suburb to live. Among them were many Church folk. Thus the parish received a great accession of numbers and strength. But the vestry knew that many of these would go back to Chicago, and that the boom was an artificial one and could not be depended on. Consequently they were not willing to undertake either the building or enlargement of the church. But, as often happens in such cases, the women of the parish were roused to action, as appears from the following extract from the minutes of the vestry of St. Mark's under date of July 11, 1875:

"A proposition of the women of the parish to enlarge the church-building at their own cost, by widening it about twelve feet on the east side and making some other minor improvements incidental thereto, was laid before the vestry. After a discussion of the plan proposed, it was unanimously resolved" (note the unanimity with which it was resolved), "that the ladies of the parish be allowed to enlarge the church building at their own expense, provided that the contract be so made as in no way to make the vestry liable or to incumber the church building for any part of the cost of the contemplated improvement."

The good women were not abashed; they took hold and built what, in ecclesiastical language, is known as the south aisle of the church. The example of the women produced an effect which was that, subsequently, the Men's Guild of the parish built and added to the old church the north aisle.

I have thus very briefly sketched the first ten years of the parochial life of St. Mark's. God alone knows the unrecorded works; the faith and charity that went on all through that decade; the earnest, devoted and faithful struggles of the laymen to maintain the church; the faithful pastoral work, and the preaching by the three rectors and the various temporary supplies. These things are written in the Lamb's Book of Life.

Toward the close of the period of ten years, hard times came upon the parish and the town. Many of the refugees from the Chicago fire had moved back to their own rebuilded homes. There had been a great panic in the financial world, and men felt the pressure of straightened resources. The congregation fell off. It is recorded that the Sunday morning congregation that used to fill the church had now dwindled down to thirty-five or forty persons, hardly more than the present choir.

The first ten years of parochial administration of St. Mark's were years when the parish work was done on what may be called protestant lines. The general teaching and tone of the church, aside

from the irresistible influence of the Prayer Book, were hardly above the average Puritan level. One may see something of this, for example, in the fact that, during those ten years there were but fifty confirmations—an average of five a year. There was, comparatively speaking, little brightness in the service; there seemed to be a fear of making the worship of God beautiful; and the senseless cry of "no popery" was raised by some, over things that are a part of the Anglo-Catholic heritage. The building itself was unchurchly and unattractive. The altar was a wooden box only four feet long, without cross, vases, altar lights, altar vestings, or even a full set of altar linens. There was no credence or prothesis. In celebrating the Holy Eucharist, instead of the unleavened bread which our Lord used, common bread was employed. The mixed chalice was not used. Eucharistic vestments were unknown; the celebrant wore a long white surplice and black stole. The ablutions were not performed. There were no early communions, and the Saints' days and many of the Church's holy feasts and fasts were not generally observed.

With the coming in of the new rector, the Rev. J. Stewart Smith, which coincided with the advent of the new Bishop of the diocese, a new system was inaugurated; and, from that time St. Mark's has known prosperity and progress undreamed of before. For thirty years, then, after the first ten, the parish has been administered on what may properly be called Anglo-Catholic lines. In the History of Evanston by our late brilliant fellow-townswoman, Miss Willard, are these words, describing the rectorship of the Rev. J. Stewart Smith:

"This was the beginning of a new order of things, wherein was a striking contrast to the old; the change was a marked difference in Catholic teaching and practice, and the work then earnestly begun has been faithfully increased and widened by Mr. Smith's successors. The trend of this movement has steadily been in harmony with the Catholic revival in the Anglican Church, and St. Mark's has been highly favored in the men who have filled her pulpit since then."

It is impossible to overestimate the work of the Rev. J. Stewart Smith, the fifth rector of St. Mark's. He was the curate of the Rev. William E. McLaren, D. D., rector of Trinity Church, Cleveland, when Dr. McLaren was made Bishop of this diocese. Mr. Smith was then in deacon's orders, but the Bishop, knowing the worth of his young curate, nominated him to the rectorship of St. Mark's. He was elected by the vestry on the 30th day of January, 1876, with the understanding that he should become rector as soon as he was advanced to priest's orders, for a deacon cannot be rector of a parish. He was advanced to the sacred order of the priesthood on the 30th day of January of that year, and on the 14th day of February—known as St. Valentine's Day—Mr. Smith became the rector of this church. He remained as rector for about four years; that is, until January, 1880.

He found the parish very sadly run down. The services, as has been said, were protestant in tone and unattractive. That, however, was characteristic of the church services in general throughout this part of the land. But the clergy and a few of the parishes were beginning to feel the uplifting tide of Catholic reform which was then spreading over England and the East.

Immediately upon the coming of J. Stewart Smith, an improvement was seen all along the line, and no one would wish to go back to the condition of things that prevailed before he accomplished his great work. But his work was not accomplished without heroism, perseverance and indomitable courage. Almost every improvement that he made in the character of the services was opposed or criticised by some section of the parish. But he was a man whom nothing could discourage, whom nothing could daunt. The fact is, the whole subject of the Church's ritual on which so much has been said of late years, after all is simply this: Whether we shall have reverent behavior in the House of God and a decent adornment of the House of God, or whether we shall treat God and His House worse than we treat ourselves and our own domestic dwellings.

A bare summary of the chief restorations and improvements introduced by Mr. Smith must suffice: He secured a good cabinet organ in place of the old melodeon. The church was repaired and decorated in as churchly a style as the limitations of the old building would permit. A large altar was placed in the Sanctuary, with cross and vases and proper vestings for the various seasons of the Christian year. A credence was procured. Proper vestments were worn. All Holy Days were duly observed. Requiem masses were celebrated. Services and instructions were greatly multiplied and the pastoral care of souls greatly increased.

The opposition against him was such as is always met with when a sleepy and protestant parish is brought under the leadership of a truly Catholic priest. But his loving kindness, his tact, and his perseverance conquered; and when finally he left, the parish found itself transformed, and has never been willing to sink back into the condition in which it had previously been. Father Smith is still living and active, the rector of St. Mary's, Kansas City. All subsequent rectors have simply built upon the foundations that he laid. If any honor is due to any rector of this parish, it is above all to the Rev. J. Stewart Smith.

Aside from purely local and parochial work, Mr. Smith also launched forth into missionary work and Church-extension. He began the services of the Church in the neighboring villages of Winnetka, Wilmette, North Evanston and Rogers Park, where, today, four flourishing churches, which may be called daughters of St. Mark's, remain as monuments of Mr. Smith's zeal and devotion. The time had not yet come for starting a mission in South Evanston. That was done a few years later.

Every year of his rectorship Mr. Smith presented good classes for confirmation, numbering, respectively, sixteen, eighteen, nine and seven per year—an average of twelve a year instead of four, which had been the previous average. After his departure, there was a vacancy for about a year, during which time four persons were confirmed.

The sixth rector of St. Mark's was the Rev. Dr. Frederick S. Jewell, 6th May, 1880, to August, 1885. Dr. Jewell had been a Presbyterian minister, but had been converted to the older Church, had been confirmed, ordained a deacon and then advanced to the priesthood. He was a Catholic Churchman and a strong and brilliant preacher. His work here for about five years was fruitful. One interesting feature of this rectorship was that, in the year 1882 there was organized what was called the "Men's Guild." During the five years of its existence the guild raised nearly $4,000. It was

the Men's Guild that paid for building the north aisle of the church; for the enlargement of the choir, and in large part for the purchase of the new pipe organ, which was considered a fine instrument for those days. One of the great objects of the guild was to promote fellowship in the parish, visit the newcomers, get acquainted with strangers, and support the rector in every one of his works. The result was that everything in the parish was strengthened, directly or indirectly, by the Men's Guild. It was during this rectorship that the mission in "South Evanston" (now the flourishing parish of St. Luke's, Evanston) was started, not without the help of Dr. Jewell and the Men's Guild of St. Mark's.

Dr. Jewell was the first to complete the adornment of the altar by placing upon it altar lights. During his rectorship Dr. Jewell presented classes for confirmation every year, numbering respectively, nine, four, fifteen, nine and ten candidates—being an average of nine and one-half per year.

Dr. Jewell, during the latter part of his rectorship, also introduced some choral services which are now so dear and uplifting to the people of the parish and of the community. Yet, strange to say, this induced opposition which spread throughout the parish. After faithfully upholding the standard of the Cross here for more than five years, the good doctor resigned.

The seventh rector of St. Mark's was the Rev. Richard Hayward, who held the rectorship from February, 1886, to May, 1888. He had previously been a chaplain in the United States Navy. He was a sound Churchman and a good preacher. Two notable events marked his brief rectorship of less than three years. The first was the successful introduction of the vested choir, which took place on Whitsunday in 1887, and has been the greatest blessing to the public worship of the Church ever since. The faithful and beloved choirmaster, Mr. Robert Holmes, has been the choirmaster nearly all the time since then.

The second notable event in the rectorship of Mr. Hayward was the revival of the scheme of building a new church and a rectory. Ten thousand dollars (or nearly that) were pledged, payable as soon as the church should be begun. During his rectorship Mr. Hayward presented three classes for confirmation, numbering respectively, four, thirteen and ten—an average of nine a year. When Mr. Hayward left in May, 1888, for about six months the parish was vacant, but was chiefly in charge of a faithful priest, the Rev. Walter H. Moore, afterwards dean of Quincy.

The eighth rector of St. Mark's was a young priest from the diocese of Maine, the Rev. Arthur W. Little. Mr. Little had been for seven years rector of St. Paul's, Portland. He was a member of the Cathedral Chapter and of the Standing Committee of the Diocese; had represented Maine in the General Convention of 1886, and was well known as the author of a popular work entitled "Reasons for Being a Churchman." His rectorship began on All Saints' Day, November 1, 1888. He was formally instituted by the Bishop on the 18th of November, being the twenty-fifth Sunday after Trinity, and is still the rector of the parish. In 1895 he received a doctor's degree from Hobart College. He has been for many years Examining Chaplain to the Bishop, a member of the Board of Missions and of the Standing Committee of the Diocese, and Lecturer on Ecclesiastical History in the Western Theological Seminary. Still

later he was a delegate to the General Convention in 1904.

Mr. Little at once began to push forward the building of the new church. A desirable lot on the corner of Ridge Avenue and Grove Street was bought and paid for. A beautiful stone church of early English type, designed by the distinguished architects, Holabird & Roche, was built. The corner-stone was laid by the Bishop on the Sunday after Ascension, May 18, 1900. The first services were held on Easter Day, March 29, 1901. On the following Wednesday, at a high celebration of the Holy Eucharist, at which most of the clergy of the diocese were present, an office of Benediction was said by the Bishop, the Rt. Rev. William E. McLaren, D. D., D. C. L., who also preached the sermon. At evensong the Rt. Rev. George F. Seymour, D. D., LL. D., Bishop of Springfield, preached. On St. Mark's Day, April 25, 1895, the church, including the chapel of St. Mary, in the north choir aisle, being entirely free from debt, was solemnly consecrated by the Bishop in a splendid and memorable service.

This was the last public service at which the venerable Charles Comstock, for thirty years the Senior Warden and constant benefactor of the parish, was present. He died on the 5th of the following September, in the eighty-second year of his age.

In 1899 a commodious rectory or parsonage was bought on Ridge Avenue, near the church. A beautiful Rood Serene, of carved oak, separating the choir from the nave, was placed in the church in 1899, as a memorial to the late Franklin G. Beach. The church contains some beautiful windows of the best English stained glass, made by Ward & Hughes of London. The great east window over the high altar, representing *The Institution of the Holy Eucharist*, is considered the finest example of stained glass in the West. It is a memorial to the late Franklin G. Beach and Elizabeth, his wife. The windows in the north aisle depict scenes from the Old Testament, and those in the south aisle from the New.

In the fall of 1891 a superb chime of nine bells was placed in the tower of the church, along with an automatic attachment for playing the beautiful "Westminster changes" at the quarter hours. The following Latin inscription was cast on the great bell:

A. M. D. G.
AEDI PAROCHIAEQUE SANCTI MARCI ME, OCTO CUM ALIIS CAMPANIS, GRATO CORDE DEDIT AMICUS MENSE SEPTEMBRE, MDCCCCI.
RDO. ARTURO W. LITTLE, L. H. D., PAROCHO.
LAUDE SONO DOMINI: POPULUM VOCO AD OSTIA CAELI.

(To the greater glory of God. To the church and parish of St. Mark's, a friend, out of a grateful heart, gave me, along with eight other bells, in the month of September, 1901, during the rectorship of the Rev. Arthur W. Little, L. H. D. I resound with the praise of the Lord: I summon the people to the gates of heaven.)

The parish during 1903 erected a large and beautiful Guild Hall or Parish House, adjoining the church, for the use of the Sunday School, and the various guilds and other charitable and social organizations of the parish.

During the rectorship of Dr. Little the church has enjoyed a steady and healthy growth in numbers and influence and in all departments of worship and of work,

especially in the cause of missions and charities. In the seventeen years of his rectorship Dr. Little has presented five hundred and ten candidates for confirmation, being an average of thirty a year. In the previous twenty-three years, one hundred and sixty were confirmed—making six hundred and seventy confirmations in the forty years of parish life.

In the summer of 1904 a superb marble altar and reredos were presented to St. Mark's by the children of the late Senior Warden, Charles Comstock, as a memorial to him and his beloved wife, and to their daughter-in-law, Eleanora K. Comstock.

In 1905 the interior of the choir and sanctuary was rebuilt of massive carved stone, the walls of the clear-story being covered with gold. The effect is very fine. This was the gift of Mr. William C. Comstock, and is a memorial to his beloved wife, Eleanora K. Comstock.

The year 1905 also witnessed the organization of the Men's Club of St. Mark's, a society for literary and social as well as for ecclesiastical purposes. It has had one prosperous year under the presidency of Mr. William B. Bogert. The President for 1906-7 is Mr. William S. Powers. Any citizen of Evanston is eligible to membership in this club.

St. Mark's is a strong and united parish. It numbers among its adherents some of the best citizens of Evanston, and has the respect and esteem of the community.

A few items from the last Parochial Report — May, 1906 — must close this sketch:

St. Mark's.
Rector, Dr. Arthur W. Little.
Church Wardens, Messrs. Henry S. Slaymaker and Edward H. Buehler.
Members, about 1,500.
Communicants, 775.
Value of property, about $125,000.

St. Matthew's Mission.[1]—The first service in connection with the starting of "St. Matthew's" Mission was held in the public school-house and was conducted by the Rev. J. Stewart Smith, Rector of "St. Mark's," Evanston, on Sunday, May 14, 1876. Services were maintained every third Sunday until 1878, when these were discontinued. The Sunday School was organized September 8, 1878, soon finding a home in the house of Mr. T. A. Turner. March 7, 1878, a Sunday evening service was begun in the same place. This continued until January, 1880.

After Mr. Smith's departure from St. Mark's, lay-readers conducted the service. In 1862, May 21st, a lot was donated by Mr. Jenks, and by July 1, 1883, the church building was ready for occupancy. It was in May of this year that the Mission was duly organized, being put in charge of the Rev. Dr. Jewell, rector of St. Mark's.

The Rev. George B. Whitney was appointed priest in charge June 24, 1883, having also in his care Christ Church, Winnetka. Mr. Whitney remained in charge until November 1, 1885. Through the kindness of friends in St. Mark's and elsewhere, the indebtedness on the building was cancelled, and the church consecrated by the Rt. Rev. William E. McLaren, D. D., Bishop of Chicago, October 30, 1884.

The years following the departure of the Rev. Mr. Whitney were marked by various and ofttimes trying experiences, but the life was maintained by the faithful women of the Mission and the assistance of students from the Western Theological Seminary, the Rev. John C. Sage, now of St. John's, Dubuque, serving in this capacity for a year. He left in September, 1870, and on November 2, of the same year, the Rev. H. R. Neely took charge, remaining until May, 1897. In

the fall of 1897 the Rev. H. C. Granger, at that time assistant at St. Peter's, Chicago, was given charge of "St. Matthew's;" he is still the incumbent.

Several fitting memorials have recently been placed in the church, such as a pair of three-branch candlesticks for the altar, in memory of the late Mr. C. O. Ferris, and a beautiful oak lecturn.

While credit is due to many kind friends for their undiminished interest in St. Matthew's during all these years—especially to the rectors of St. Mark's, Evanston—it is not too much to say that among the names deserving of very particular mention are those of Mr. and Mrs. T. A. Turner, by whose unceasing and loving care the lamp, once lighted, was never suffered to go out.

From the Parochial Report of St. Matthew's Mission, May, 1906:

Priest in charge, the Rev. Henry C. Granger.

Members, 200.

Communicants, 70.

Estimated value of property, $3,000.

St. Luke's Parish.[2]—St. Luke's Church was organized as a mission early in July, 1885, and the first service was held in Ducat's Hall. In August a store was rented on Chicago Avenue and fitted up for use of the mission. In June, 1886, the Rev. Marcus Lane, who had been priest in charge for this first year, resigned, and was succeeded, August 1, by the Rev. Daniel F. Smith, who continued in charge until August 1, 1904.

In October, 1886, ground was broken for the erection of a church on the northeast corner of Lincoln Avenue (now Main Street) and Sherman Avenue. In May, 1887, this was so far completed as to be

[1] This sketch of St. Matthew's Mission was furnished by Rev. Henry C. Granger.

[2] The sketch of St. Luke's, up to 1904, was furnished by the Rev. D. F. Smith, D. D.

available for the services, though still quite in the rough. Improvements have been made almost continually, and twice the church has been enlarged. It was solemnly consecrated November 10, 1889, being free from debt.

On January 1, 1891, the mission was re-organized as a parish, which, on May 26 of that year, was admitted into union with the Convention of the Diocese of Chicago, with the following officers: David L. Thorp, Josiah C. Lane, Wardens.

In twenty-one years since the organization of St. Luke's the number of communicants has increased from twenty-seven to four hundred and sixty-two. The parish is now numbered among the stronger and more active in the diocese, is united and prosperous and abounds in good works.

In 1904 the Rev. Daniel F. Smith, D. D., resigned, and was elected *rector emeritus*, carrying with him the love and esteem of the people to whom he had ministered so faithfully and so long. He was succeeded by the Rev. George Craig Stewart who became rector of St. Luke's, August 1, 1904.

Mr. Stewart is an able and energetic priest. Among the notable events in the history of Evanston during the last two years has been the great progress of St. Luke's. Strong preaching on Catholic lines, improvement in the ritual and ceremonial of public worship, large confirmation classes, the organization of the Men's Club of St. Luke's, and great parochial activity are signs of his progress. A large lot has been bought on the corner of Hinman Avenue and Lee Street, and plans had been adopted for a large and beautiful stone church, to cost, when completed, $125,000. The building will be begun in June, 1906, and the work will be pushed forward with the energy which characterizes the rector and the people of St. Luke's.

From the Parochial Report of St. Luke's Parish, May, 1906:

Rector Emeritus, the Rev. Daniel F. Smith, D. D.

Rector, the Rev. Geo. Craig Stewart.

Church Wardens, Messrs. C. H. Cowper and C. E. Dudley.

Members, 1,000.

Communicants, 462.

CATHOLIC CHURCHES
(By FR. H. P. SMYTH)

Among the earliest settlers of Evanston were a few Catholic families. They worshipped either at St. Joseph's Church, Gross Point, or at St. Henry's, High Ridge, according to their convenience.

However, in 1864 a concerted effort was made to establish a church in Evanston. Accordingly, on July 20th of that year, the property upon which St. Mary's Church now stands, corner of Lake Street and Oak Avenue, was purchased; the deed being made to "the Catholic Bishop of Chicago."

The few families that then constituted the Catholic population of Evanston, found that the purchase of property had exhausted their resources, leaving them little hope of erecting a church in the near future. Yet, so confident were those pioneers of the ultimate success of their enterprise, that, as it were, burning the bridges behind them, they had inserted in the deed a clause making the property revertable to the original owner, in the event of its being used for other than Catholic Church purposes. This limitation of title, though prudent at the time, afterwards gave trouble; and has been removed at considerable expense within the last few years. The few people continued as formerly to attend mass, either at Gross Point or Rose Hill.

In 1866 the foundation of a church was laid, but it was found impossible, through lack of funds, to construct the edifice according to plans. A smaller structure forty feet by twenty, which still stands on the rear of an adjoining lot, was erected. In this church the small congregation worshipped for three years. In 1869 the little building was moved south on the property, and work was begun on another structure according to the original plan. This second church was finished towards the close of the year.

Still there was no resident pastor in Evanston. Father Heskemann, of Gross Point, had superintended the construction of the first church, and, for two years after its completion, came every alternate Sunday to Evanston.

Early in 1868, the priest in residence at Rose Hill, Father Heamers, succeeded Father Heskemann, in charge of the small congregation and church. He, too, however came only on Sundays. He continued to minister to St. Mary's, Evanston, as long as he remained at Rose Hill. In 1869 or 1870 he was succeeded in both charges, first by Father Marshall and later by Father Michels, who like their predecessor attended Evanston as a mission from Rose Hill.

During Father Heamer's pastorate a school was established, and two nuns of German birth taught and resided in Evanston for one year. Lay teachers were employed subsequently.

In the fall of 1872, Rev. M. Donohue came from Waukegan to St. Mary's, Evanston, as its first resident pastor. When he came he found the church which continued to be used for the succeeding twenty years, and also the parochial residence, which is occupied today, awaiting him.

In 1874 the Dominican Sisters of Sinsin-awa Mound, Wis., were invited to take charge of the school which was now established. They have continued to work uninterruptedly to the present.

Father Donohue had, at some time in the 'seventies, been created Rural Dean by Bishop Foley, and, in 1887, was made permanent rector by Archbishop Feehan. The former title is honorary and, in the Chicago archdiocese, brings with it no responsibility. The latter is more substantial and was conferred upon Father Donohue purely as a personal compliment; the parish, as it then was, not being of sufficient importance to warrant the honor.

In the same year, 1887, Catholics of German birth and blood, became sufficiently numerous to support a church; and Archbishop Feehan sent Rev. Otto Greenebaum to organize a new congregation. Father Greenebaum came in July, 1887, and, in November of the same year, a two-story building, intended as a school and temporary church, was opened.

Father Donohue's declining health compelled him to ask for an assistant, and, in the fall of 1883, Rev. W. J. McNamee, who had recently come from Ireland, was sent to help him. Father McNamee, however, was soon transferred to a more important parish in Chicago, and his place was filled by a priest from the Servite Church, Chicago, who came occasionally as required. This condition obtained until 1888, when Rev. M. Foley, present pastor of St. Patrick's church, Dixon, came to Evanston as assistant to Father Donohue. In the summer of 1889, he was succeeded by Rev. P. C. Conway, who remained four years.

The new St. Mary's church was begun in 1891 and was opened to worship in May, 1892.

On March 12, 1893, Father Donohue died. The formalities governing the succession to an irremovable rectorship, delayed for some weeks the appointment of a new rector. Toward the end of April the present pastor, Rev. H. P. Smyth, was selected by the Archbishop, and on May 6, 1893, took possession of the parish.

Father Conway, who had been acting pastor, was transferred to St. Mary's Church, Chicago. On November 1, 1893, Rev. Thos. M. Burke came as an assistant, and an out-mission at Rogers Park was immediately opened. During the following summer the present St. Jerome's church was built and dedicated. The mission continued to be attended from St. Mary's, Evanston, until it became important enough to need the attention of a resident pastor.

In July, 1897, Father Greenebaum died; and in August of the same year the present pastor of St. Nicholas' Church, Rev. P. L. Biermann, came to Evanston. On February 3d, following, the structure which had for ten years served as church and school was burned to the ground. The fire occurred during school hours, but the children and teachers escaped in safety. St. Nicholas' congregation then again worshipped in St. Mary's Church for some months during the erection of the present church and school, which were opened in the spring of that year. A handsome parochial residence was also built simultaneously.

In the fall of 1897 a Community of Visitation Nuns, twenty-five in number came to Evanston to establish an Academy for young ladies. They rented a large residence on the northeast corner of Davis Street and Wesley Avenue, where they resided for four years. In 1899 they purchased the tract of land known as the Freeman Place on Ridge Avenue, and in 1901 erected the south wing of an im-

posing structure designed for them by Architect Schlaachs. They took possession of the building on the eve of Thanksgiving Day, 1901.

In the autumn of 1900, Fathers Smyth and Biermann, acting for the Franciscan Sisters, purchased the Kirk Mansion and grounds on Ridge Avenue in South Evanston, and on December 1st of the same year, the nuns took possession of it. The mansion was, in 1901, fitted up as a hospital and patients were received. In December of the same year the Catholics of both parishes came together to establish "The St. Francis' Hospital Auxiliary Association"

The growing needs of St. Mary's Church necessitated the purchase of a lot adjoining the church property in January, 1897. In June, 1900, Rev. Thomas Egan came to fill the place of the pastor who was setting out on an extended tour through Europe and the Orient. On the return of Father Burke, who is now traveling, as we write, it is the purpose to have three priests at St. Mary's.

The Catholic Church of Evanston has not grown as rapidly as the church in Chicago and its other suburbs, yet there has been considerable growth. A census, taken in the interest of church work in the summer of 1900 gave the Catholic population about 3,400. It would seem that was somewhat of an exaggeration. The question put by the canvassers bore upon preference rather than affiliation. It has been ascertained that some expressed a preference for St. Mary's who have no affiliation with it. But, today, as we write, February, 1902, we are safe in saying that the Catholics of Evanston number at least 3,400. These are of various nationalities. Those of Irish and German blood predominate. Besides these, there are English, French, Scandinavian, Italian, Greek and

Dutch. Nearly all European nationalities are represented. These attend two churches and support two schools, with six hundred pupils. There are five priests and four communities of nuns.

The Dominicans, eleven in number, teach St. Mary's Parochial School; six Sisters of St. Agnes have charge of St. Nicholas' School; seven Franciscan nuns take care of the new Hospital, and, in the Visitation Convent and Academy, there is a community of about thirty nuns.

Recent Changes.—In bringing the story of Catholic work in Evanston down to date (May, 1906), we have a few important changes to note: Rev. Thomas M. Burke was intrusted by the Archbishop of Chicago with the formation of a new parish in Chicago, and Rev. P. J. Hennessy came to succeed him at St. Mary's June, 1903. Rev. L. J. Maiworm came to assist at St. Nicholas' church in 1902. In the spring of 1904, ground was broken for the new St. Mary's School, which was ready for occupancy in the following September. Later the new parochial residence was commenced. On its completion in the spring of the present year (1906) the old presbytery, which had done service for thirty-five years, was removed. The splendid new Gothic church of St. Nicholas' Parish, begun over a year ago, is approaching completion as we write.

FIRST CONGREGATIONAL CHURCH

(By REV. JEAN FREDERIC LOBA)

The very first Congregational Church in Evanston was organized on December 8, 1859. A preliminary meeting had been held to consider the possibility of such a step on November 13, 1859, and another preparatory to organization the week following; but the final step was taken on the first date above mentioned, when, by a council called for that purpose, meeting in the Chapel of the Northwestern University, the Church was organized, consisting of five members. Of this council the Rev. W. W. Patton, pastor of the First Church of Chicago, was Moderator, and E. W. Blatchford, Esq., was scribe. A. T. Sherman was clerk, and S. S. Whitney and Isaac D. Guyer were deacons of the Church. During the six months of the following year (1860), the membership was increased to eleven members, and it is interesting to note that of these only seven were originally Congregationalists, the others coming from different denominations.

This first Congregational Church attained to no strength nor did it long continue to exist. In the records of that Church, kept by Mr. Sherman, we find a note to the effect that, on June 15, 1860, at a meeting of the Church, it was resolved: "That as so many of the members contemplated removing from the place, the services could not be sustained, and that the clerk be authorized to grant letters to any who might desire them." A final note informs us that letters were granted by the clerk to all except himself, he keeping up the organization by paying the annual assessment to the Association until the year 1865, at which time the organization was suspended, as he saw no hope of reviving the church. This is the pathetic little story of an early effort to organize a Congregational Church in the weak, scattered and unsettled conditions of the early days of Evanston.

There was, however, a growing sense of the need of such a church, for in that same year, as we learn from the late L. H. Boutell, "One Sunday afternoon in the summer of 1865, as I was sitting in the library of Dr. Bannister, that large hearted man suggested the propriety and feasibility of forming a Congregational Church in Evanston. That suggestion bore fruit in the autumn of that year when, on the 6th of November, a few families met at the house of Francis Bradley and organized a weekly prayer meeting, out of which grew the Lake Avenue Church, an independent organization composed of Congregationalists and Presbyterians."

In 1868 this Lake Avenue Church organized the First Presbyterian Church of Evanston from which, in 1869, the Congregationalist members withdrew with perfect good feeling on both sides; so that this Lake Avenue Church, it seems, did not long continue its existence, but, in turn, became the mother of at least two of the present churches of Evanston—the First Congregational and the First Presbyterian. A little later on Mr. Boutell narrates: "The twenty-two persons who, on the first day of August, 1866, gathered in the Baptist Church, which then stood on the corner of Church street and Hinman Avenue, to form the Lake Avenue Church, little thought that, in so short a time, two strong churches would be the outcome of an enterprise so insignificant."

It is a very singular fact that, so soon after the disbanding of the First Congregational Church under what seemed to be hopeless conditions, a new organization, covering practically the same ground and on the same basis, should spring up under such auspicious circumstances. The pathetic final note of the clerk of that first church affords us a loop-hole through which we may see the very uncertain and changeable conditions of the population of Evanston at that time.

When in August, 1869, the Congregationalists withdrew from the Lake Avenue Church, they left the property in the hands of the majority who were Presbyterians. The winter of 1869-1870, or three months thereof, was spent chiefly in organizing a Congregational group, the formal organization taking place upon the 8th of September, 1869, and recognition by Council on January 13, 1870.

During these early and formative years, it is interesting to note the spirit of harmony, fellowship and co-operation among the different denominational representatives in Evanston which has subsisted to the present time. The first suggestion of a Congregational Church seems to have originated with the earnest Methodist, Dr. Bannister. The first meetings of the Congregationalists were held in the Chapel of the Northwestern University, which then was the only building of that institution. These services were conducted by different pastors and teachers, prominent among whom were such men as Dr. Bannister, Dr. Hemenway, E. O. Haven, President of the University, and others.

Mr. Luther D. Bradley, who, as a youth, was present at these early meetings of the Congregational Church, thus writes of them: "The prayer-meeting in our little front room I remember very well, but the one at the Baptist Church but dimly; but there was one season of services which is very fresh in my mind— that during which Dr. Hemenway preached for us. These services were held in the old chapel of Northwestern University. The sole building of those days was the old frame structure, now standing on the campus north of the Preparatory—or, as I believe they call it, the 'Old College' —building. The structure was then standing on the northwest corner of Davis Street and Hinman Avenue, fronting south. The east room on the ground floor was the chapel, a plain old room

with fixed pews of pine, painted a drab
color, with blackboards around the walls.
Here the meetings were held on Sunday
afternoons, and here, I think, Mr. Duncan,
the first pastor of the church, began his
work. I think some mention must be
made of Mr. Duncan, both on account
of his importance as the first settled minister of the church, and also because of his
very picturesque personality. He was a
Scotch-Canadian, a very agreeable preacher and good man, but not exactly like any
of his people and not precisely at home in
the community.

"I remember that some of the most
telling sermons that were preached in the
old chapel at this time were by Dr. S. C.
Bartlett, later President of Dartmouth
College, who filled the pulpit for a few
Sundays, though this was before Mr.
Duncan's arrival."

However uncertain, interrupted and in-
adequately recorded were these early
steps toward organization, they all crys-
tallized on the 13th of January, 1870, into
the First Congregational Church of Evanston. Very few of the early members now
survive. But the roll of the church of that
time contained some noble names such as
those of Francis Bradley, L. H. Boutell,
Rev. D. Crosby Green (now and for many
years a missionary in Japan), Heman
Powers, J. M. Williams, Orvis French,
besides many others who won for
themselves enviable reputations as men
and women of character, of more than
usual intelligence, of capacity, energy and
a wide-reaching influence.

Immediately upon the organization of
the First Church, it called, and on the 13th
day of January, 1870, installed its first
regular pastor, the Rev. Edward N. Packard, D. D., now of Syracuse, N. Y. The
University again granted the new church a
lot on which to erect a suitable structure

for worship. Mr. Dorr A. Kimball gives us
an interesting sketch of the method by
which the lot on which the present church
edifice stands, became Congregational property. He says: "At that time the lot on
which this church edifice is located, was
a little park originally given to the Village
of Evanston by the Northwestern University, to be used for Park purposes only.
Immediately after the meeting held at Mr.
Green's residence for the organization of
a Congregational Society, our trustees
had made a very satisfactory arrangement,
which was this: On payment of the sum
of $600 to the Village Trustees, they va-
cated the park and, the title reverting to
the University, they persuaded the University Trustees to deed the property to
the First Congregational Society without
further compensation." Upon this lot,
then the trustees having secured $6,000 as
a building fund, "General Julius White
moved that they proceed to build a church
edifice costing not less than $10,000."
From Mr. Kimball's sketch, it would appear that they "succeeded in getting the
lecture room completed in July, 1869 ,and
the main auditorium was wholly completed in the month of January, 1870."
This ten thousand dollar church, however, was to cost the little society not
far from $25,000, leaving them with a
debt of $7,000, with interest at nine and
ten per cent.

The maintenance of a church during
these days of poverty and struggle was
not all smooth sailing, for in 1871 came
the Chicago fire which impoverished
many of its members, and immediately
thereafter one of the greatest financial
panics that this nation has ever experienced swept over the country bringing
financial ruin and distress upon many
households. With self-sacrifice and stern
resolution the society and the church

held on, although it required the wisest management to meet current expenses and keep up interest on the bonded debt. In March, 1879, Dr. Packard resigned to accept a call to a church in Boston. He was succeeded, September 10th, of the same year, by Rev. A. J. Scott. In 1883 the church edifice was enlarged, repaired and in part refurnished at a cost of $5,000, greatly increasing the seating capacity. On the night of November 23, 1884, after the first service in the renovated church, the entire edifice was destroyed by fire. The next morning, as the friends gathered about the smoking ruins, sums of money were at once pledged toward rebuilding. These sums, together with the insurance of $25,000, enabled the trustees to proceed at once to the erection of a new edifice. Before the fire was extinguished, invitations had been received from the trustees of the First Methodist, Presbyterian and Baptist Churches to use their buildings on Sabbath afternoons and for social meetings as they might desire. Similar invitations were also received from the Woman's Christian Temperance Union, to occupy Union Hall free of charge, and the Northwestern University again generously offered Heck Hall on the same terms. The new structure was completed and dedicated upon the 11th of April, 1886, and has continued in use ever since.

From the very earliest days the church has been marked by a spirit of harmony and benevolence. When it numbered less than fifty members it erected and furnished its own church building at a cost of about $25,000. Before the burden of this debt was fully removed, it enlarged and improved this building at a cost of $8,000. In 1884, it erected and furnished the present edifice at a cost of over $50,-000. During this time its current expenses increased from $3,000 to $10,000 a year.

During the first twenty-five years its benevolences to Home and Foreign Missions aggregated $103,854, making an average of $4,154 a year. One of its first members has been himself a missionary to Japan for forty years. One of the most earnest and devoted Japanese Christians was baptized in this church and returned as a preacher to his own people in Japan.

In 1886, on the resignation of Rev. A. J. Scott, the Rev. Nathan H. Whittlesey, D. D., was called to the pastorate, which continued harmonious and unbroken until May 1, 1892. In October of the latter year, Rev. Jean Frederic Loba, D. D., was called and installed November 17, 1892.

During more than thirty years the church has been characterized, first of all, by a spirit of harmony. No serious dissensions have ever existed among its members, and, whenever any misunderstandings have arisen, they have quickly been adjusted and smoothed away. It has stood for a perfectly simple evangelical faith, its present articles of faith being the ones which were adopted by the Lake Avenue Church in which Dr. Francis Bradley characteristically substituted the word "privilege" for "duty." It has ever shown interest in every form of philanthropic benevolence. It was among the first supporters and benefactors of the city settlement movement. Its interest in education has been shown by its hearty sympathy and co-operation with the Northwestern University. Its benevolences have been unstinted and generous. During the year 1901 these exceeded its home expenses by $1,500, and during the year 1905 they aggregated over $13,000. It has been foremost in its love of all that was tasteful and artistic in its form of worship, having been generous in its expenditure for the best church music. A chapter might well be written upon the history of its devotion to sacred music. Many of its singers and organists were artists of the highest rank. For the first ten years of its existence the expense for music was from $331 to $1,912 a year, making an annual average of about $1,295. From 1890 to 1895 the average was $2,390 a year, and the total cost of music from 1880 to 1895 was $24,759.

The church has been interested in city missions and has been a liberal supporter of the Chicago City Missionary Society. For two years it supported an independent mission on Halsted Street. In 1894 it purchased a lot on the west side of Evanston on which it erected a substantial and neat house of worship. For this, on one Sabbath, $4,800 were subscribed and a thousand dollars more secured for lot and structure. Here it co-operated with a small congregation in the support of a pastor, so that it may be truly said that the church, while interested in foreign missions, has never neglected home culture and home benevolences. In 1903 it was thought best to discontinue this work or place it in other hands, and the property was sold to the Christian Church by which a flourishing church organization is now conducted. The proceeds of this sale were donated to the Chicago City Missionary Society for its endowment fund.

During 1905 and 1906 the Church has contributed about $2,500 per year through the Chicago City Missionary Society, for the support of Bethesda Mission in Chicago, besides furnishing some eighteen or twenty teachers and officers in the various branches of this work. It has also an active interest in a promising mission at Rose Hill, in Chicago.

Charity has begun at home, but it has not stopped there. The church has always maintained a most cordial relation with the sister churches in Evanston and, with them, has always been ready to co-operate in every religious, social and civic effort for the improvement of the higher life of our city. Its six hundred members are now thoroughly organized for work in and out of its own organization. Its Sabbath School of about 350 scholars has long been one of the most prosperous and thoroughly equipped in the city, being carefully graded into primary, intermediate and senior schools, each with a competent head of department.

The benevolences of the Church are fostered and directed by the Home, Foreign and Young Ladies' Missionary Societies; to which should also be added the missionary departments of the Young People's Society of Christian Endeavor and the Light-Bearers.

Grateful for its history and successes, the Church goes forward full of faith and hope, assured that its Master, who has instituted and prospered it thus far, will lead it to yet larger successes.

LUTHERAN CHURCHES
(By REV. J. D. MATTHIUS)

German Evangelical Lutheran Bethlehem Church.—It was in the year 1872, when a small number of Germans, living in Evanston and professing faith in the religion of Martin Luther, first assembled for regular Evangelical Lutheran services. They did not possess a house of worship, so they met in those little cabins down on Clark Street, near the locality of the present Electric Light plant. Several of the first Lutheran pioneers had settled in that neighborhood. A pastor they found in Rev. A. H. Reinke, of Chicago. He agreed to come to quiet little Evanston on Sunday evenings and preach God's message to the attentive little group which was seated on up-turned wash-tubs, laundry-benches, and whatever could be used as stool or pew. The majority of this small congregation had emigrated from the "Old Country." Having become tired of the hardships which they had to endure under landlordism in Mecklenburg-Schwerin, they had come to America in the hope of enjoying the freedom of this country. But poor they were, indeed—the most of them—and the plain, simple mode of their living bore ample proof of it. Some of them experienced many sad and gloomy hours on their "arrival at this village in the woods," far away from their native home, without their church so dear to them, without a German school, without a pastor to teach and console them. Their delight was great when, at last, they had their own religious services in the dwellings of their fellow-people.

Twenty-five years later the Rev. A. H. Reinke wrote as follows concerning the first Lutherans of Evanston: "When I first began to preach at Evanston and organized a congregation, there were, according to my knowledge, the following people among the members and hearers: H. Voigts, H. Witt, Joh. Witt, Joachim Witt, P. Claussen, Martin Becker, A. P. Handke, F. Lass, Joh. Vorbeck, F. Strokey and others."

The names of the above are also found in the records of the church attached to a constitution which was adopted August 8, 1875, for the "German Evangelical Lutheran Bethlehem Church of Evanston, Cook County, Illinois."

We find that Rev. A. H. Reinke baptized children here, from June 16, 1872, until May 18, 1873. After that time a number of baptisms were performed by Rev. G. S. Lober, of Niles, Illinois. For some unknown reason it appears the little flock of Lutherans were without services for a while after June, 1873. Again, however, Rev. Reinke, missionary as he was, turned his attention to his small mission post at Evanston, and, though overburdened with work, took up the care of the Evanston Lutherans with a zeal and devoutness not often to be found. Rev. H. Wunder, of Chicago, too, found his way here and preached to the people occasionally.

The year 1875 was an epoch in the annals of the Bethlehem Church. Glencoe, about seven miles north of Evanston, had had a Lutheran congregation since 1847, but had always been attended to by the Lutheran ministers of Chicago, especially by Rev. Prof. C. A. T. Selle, Rev. H. Wunder and Rev. J. Grosse. In 1874 they rejoiced to have the young Rev. Ed. Doring take up his residence at Glencoe as their ordained minister. In the following year, January, 1875, we find the first records of holy communion celebrated in Evanston by the Rev. Ed. Doring. He it was then who conducted the services of the congregation until 1881, when he accepted a call to a mission post at Portland, Oregon. In the meanwhile the Lutherans had come into possession of a little church property on Florence Avenue, near Lake Street, and built a small frame church on it. Later this little church was sold to the Swedish Lutherans and was moved to Lake Street near Sherman Avenue. Now it is the church of the Danish-Norwegian Lutherans, and is to be found on Greenwood Boulevard, near Sherman Avenue, west of the Northwestern Railroad.

Until the departure of Rev. Doring the congregation had not taken very great strides to prosperity; still it had among its members several young, enterprising and good Lutherans, one of which was the late Wm. E. Suhr. They were not without a minister very long. In the fall of 1881 a young energetic pastor, Rev. A. Detzer, a graduate of Concordia Seminary, St. Louis, Mo., was installed in his calling as pastor of the German Lutheran Church (at Evanston), with his residence at Evanston. In future there were services every Sunday. The new pastor also took charge of the parish at Glencoe and preached there every two weeks.

As soon as Rev. Detzer had become acquainted with his people, he had them found a parochial school. He undertook the task of teaching the children himself. The school was opened with twelve pupils in attendance. The schoolroom was in the attic of a small dwelling house in the "prairie." The venture, however difficult for pastor and people, who gladly paid their taxes for public schools, and besides upheld their private school, proved so successful that they soon saw themselves compelled to build a school-house of their own. They erected a house for this purpose at a cost of $1,450, where now the parsonage is to be seen at 1410 Greenwood Boulevard.

In 1885 we find a school of fifty-three pupils learning the rudiments of the Evangelical Lutheran denomination, and all elementary branches necessary for a good secular education. The congregation understood how great a burden their pastor had taken upon his shoulders and relieved him of it by appointing Mr. H. Feuchter as provisory teacher, and by calling Mr. M. E. Bittner, in 1886, as their ordained school-teacher. Mr. Bittner still holds this position, having held it sixteen years. He now teaches the upper class only.

As the number of pupils increased, so also did the number of members of the church. The congregation, therefore, soon found its first church too small, and without delay built a handsome new church edifice at the corner of Greenwood Boulevard and Wesley Avenue, which was dedicated November 21, 1886. It was a great day for the German Lutherans. After a period of fourteen years since their first services, they now were in possession of their second church, which, though not as large as some of our present churches, was far larger than their first one and far more artistic and inviting. After having stood sixteen years, it still deserves to be mentioned as one of Evanston's notable buildings.

When the year 1899 came, the class of pupils had outgrown the school. There was not room enough for a new scholar, so the enterprising congregation, numbering about sixty male voting members by this time, did not hesitate to purchase a new building site at the corner of Lake Street and Ashland Avenue. Here they erected a two-story brick-veneered schoolhouse containing two spacious classrooms, with all modern improvements. The "Evanston Press," of March 8, 1890, devoted its entire second page to the description of the dedication of this school. It said: "Our German patrons are to be congratulated on the enterprise and devotion to the cause of education which has prompted them to this progressive move."

Soon after the new school had been pressed into service, Rev. Detzer received a call from St. Paul, Minn., where he was wanted to build up an English Lutheran mission. Though he had been serving a German congregation in Evanston, he was an able English scholar and therefore regarded this call as one which his conscience urged him to accept. It was a painful parting when he left.

Again the founder of the congregation,

Rev. A. H. Reinke, of Chicago, then pastor of the largest German Lutheran congregation in America, was asked to take care of his forsaken flock in Evanston. He gladly did so. He preached and performed all other pastoral duties, attended their meetings and assisted them in every manner to get a new pastor. They extended calls to a number of ministers, but in vain. Several months passed by, and Evanston was still looking for a minister. In August, 1890, a call was sent to the undersigned, Rev. J. D. Matthius, of Chicago, son-in-law of Rev. A. H. Reinke. He accepted and was installed September 3, 1890. He was a native of Staten Island, New York, the son of a prosperous business man. When thirteen years old he entered Concordia College, Fort Wayne, Ind., took an academic course of six years, graduated there in 1885, and in 1888 from Concordia Seminary, St. Louis, Mo. From that time until his charge in Evanston he was assistant of Rev. A. H. Reinke in Chicago.

From 1890 up to the present day (February, 1902) the congregation has enjoyed constant prosperity. It still clings to the infallible divine inspiration of the Bible and to Faith in Christ Jesus as the only way to salvation. The congregation now consists of over 200 German Lutheran families and many single persons. It has 130 male voting members, 135 pupils in its school and, besides Mr. M. E. Bittner, has Mr. R. Mangelsdorf as teacher of the second class. In 1893 a handsome parsonage was erected in the rear of the church.

The congregation belongs to the "Evangelical Lutheran Synod of Missouri, Ohio and other states."

Besides the German Lutheran, Evanston has also a Norwegian-Danish Lutheran, a Swedish Lutheran, and, of late, also a small English Lutheran congregation. The latter conducts its services in the church of the Danish-Norwegian Lutherans, and is attended to by Rev. J. K. Reed of Chicago, a member of the General Synod.

Norwegian-Danish Lutheran Church.— The following notes have been kindly compiled by the pastor, Rev. D. Larsen:

The Evanston Norwegian-Danish Lutheran Church was organized July 29, 1891, under the supervision of Rev. N. J. Ellestad and Rev. J. N. Kildal of the Bethlehem Norwegian Lutheran Church in Chicago, and, until the new congregation could secure a pastor, Rev. Kildal temporarily served it in connection with the Chicago church.

Admission into the United Norwegian Lutheran Church of America was applied for and granted in June, 1892. In March of the same year Rev. T. Aarrestad began to serve the congregation as its ordained pastor, and remained in that capacity until October, 1893.

John Hetland, the next pastor, served from February, 1894, till June, 1900.

In January, 1894, the Young People's Society, "Nordlyset," was organized.

The congregation had, as yet, owned no place of worship, but services were held in rented quarters. In 1899, however, a lot was bought on Greenwood Boulevard between Sherman and Benson Avenues, and the chapel, owned first by the German and then by the Swedish Lutheran congregation, was bought and moved to the above-mentioned location. This chapel will serve as a temporary house of worship until the congregation becomes able to build a church. The present pastor, Ditman Larsen, was installed July 21, 1901.

Swedish Evangelical Lutheran (Immanuel) Church.—This congregation was organized in 1888, by Rev. S. A. Sandahl of Lake View, with thirty-four communicant members. The first installed pastor was Rev. J. Edgren, who served the congregation a number of years. The next pastor was Rev. C. Solmonson. During his ministry in Evanston the Swedes built their present handsome new church and parsonage at Sherman Avenue and Lake Street. Their present minister is Rev. G. K. Stark.

Our information concerning the Swedish Lutherans is very scant.

We should have gladly inserted a chapter from the pen of the present pastor, but our efforts to obtain such an article were in vain.

Supplemental.

Since the above chapter was written work among the Lutherans of Evanston has kept on. The English Lutherans now have a handsome little edifice of their own at Benson Avenue and Greenleaf Street.

In Bethlehem German Lutheran congregation the parochial school has experienced some changes. Mr. R. E. Mangelsdorf, on account of failing health, was obliged to accept a position as teacher of a parochial school at Black Jack, Mo. Likewise, Mr. M. E. Bittner, after having been at the head of the school for almost nineteen years, accepted a call to Kankakee, Ill., in 1905, where he now is Principal of a parochial school. The respective vacancies have been filled by Mr. F. Toenies, for many years teacher at Strassburg, Ill., and by Mr. L. O. Schaefer, one of the graduates of the Addison Lutheran Teachers' Seminary in this State, in 1905.

EVANSTON CHRISTIAN CHURCH
(By ULYSSES GRANT BUCK)

The Evanston Christian Church has had humble beginnings, but gives promise of becoming a strong power for good in this city of churches, and has found a place and a work that would indicate that no mistake has been made in bringing it into being.

The Reformation Movement, which this organization represents, had its inception in Western Pennsylvania about one hundred years ago, and has been one of rapid growth on lines parallel to the lines of immigration, with the result that the northern and southern parts of our country have few, if any, more prosperous churches. However, there have gone into all parts of the country, as happens with our shifting population, a few representative active members, and these have been gathered together to form a working nucleus, and thus have grown up large congregations where once there was no work done. This is the history of the Evanston Church.

The Christian Missionary Society of Chicago had its attention called to the possibilities of a work being started in Evanston in the year 1895. Accordingly on the 24th day of November, 1895, City Evangelist E. W. Darst, accompanied by W. B. Taylor, pastor of the North Side Christian Church; E. S. Ames, of the Disciples' Divinity House of the University of Chicago, met with the few disciples to be found in this community, among whom were Mr. and Mrs. E. E. Starkey, of Wilmette; Dr. and Mrs. R. C. Knox, of Rogers Park, at the home of Mr. and Mrs. Milton O. Naramore, at 925 Main Street, to discuss the idea of attempting to organize a Christian Church at some point in Evanston. The urgent need of a church organization was conceded, and it was unanimously decided to take steps to hold a meeting, and in the meantime to hold preliminary cottage meetings in order to enlist the co-operation of all persons who might be found to be members of the Church.

Meetings were held at the same place on each of the Lord's Days in December, making six preliminary and preparatory meetings, during which the whole situation was thoroughly canvassed and all arrangements were made to hold a series of meetings at Union Hall, 807 Davis Street, beginning on Sunday, January 5, 1896. At 3 o'clock on that day a large audience assembled at the above place, among whom were many representatives from the city churches, and, as an inaugural service, Rev. W. F. Black, of the Central Church, Chicago, preached a learned and able discourse.

On the evening following, Evangelist E. W. Darst, assisted by local members, began a series of meetings which lasted for the next eleven weeks, without interruption, every week day evening except Saturday and twice on Sunday. At the end of this series of meetings there were forty-two persons who had made confession and thirty-four who had been received by letter, making a total of seventy-six, who thus became the nucleus of the Evanston Christian Church.

Upon the completion of this series of meetings the church proceeded to the organization of all the departments common to Evangelical churches, and soon it had an active Sunday School, a live Christian Endeavor Society, a Ladies' Aid Society and a Woman's Missionary Society.

On the 17th day of May, 1896, the church called Edward Scribner Ames, of the Disciples' Divinity House, as its first pastor. He continued with the church for about one year, when he was followed by Rev. A. L. Chapman.

On the 1st day of May, 1897, the church was moved from 807 Davis Street to Odd-Fellows' Hall, 604½ Davis Street, where it continued to meet until it was removed to the Y. M. C. A. Building.

Mr. Chapman remained as pastor until the autumn of 1898. On the 30th of October of that year E. W. Darst was called as pastor, and continued until September, 1899, when Wallace C. Payne, of New York, became his successor. Mr. Payne's work continued until March 24, 1901, when he was succeeded, after a short interval, by Dr. E. V. Zollars, President of Hiram College, Hiram, Ohio. Dr. Zollars is one of the ablest men in the Christian Church, and gave the church in Evanston a standing second to none. He was succeeded on October 27, 1901, by Mr. W. D. Ward, a graduate of Hiram College under Dr. Zollars, and formerly of Mantua, Ohio. Under his guidance and preaching the church has prospered and grown, and his relations with the church have been so pleasant that he is liable to remain yet many years.

In 1900 the church, under careful and wise financial management, began to accumulate a building fund, and after about three years' saving, was able to purchase a lot at the corner of Oak and Church Streets, where it was proposed to build a church home, and which it still owns; but the unexpected, which often happens, came when the opportunity was presented of securing a commodious property at the corner of Lee Street and Asbury Avenue, known as the Plymouth Congregational Church.

This came near the end of 1903, and the generous offer of the First Congregational Society of Evanston was soon accepted, and, for the first time in its history, the Evanston Christian Church became an established fact in the community.

In June, 1905, the church celebrated, in befitting manner, the clearing off of all indebtedness; and with all its equipment and with the simple gospel plea which it presents, is bound to continue to prosper and grow, and lead men and women and children to a knowledge of better things and to lives of better deeds, until the time when it shall be known as one of the most potent influences for good in this splendid city of splendid people.

FIRST CHURCH OF CHRIST (SCIENTIST)
(By HOLMES HOGE)

The First Church of Christ (Scientist), of Evanston, was organized under a charter granted by the State of Illinois, January 23, 1895, with a membership of twenty-six. It is a branch church of the First Church of Christ (Scientist), Boston, Mass., which was founded in 1879. Since that time six hundred and sixty-three churches and societies of this denomination have been organized in this country and foreign lands. The branch churches have the power to govern local affairs and elect their First and Second Readers, Boards of Trustees and Directors, and other officers, annually.

The Evanston church has had a steady growth and has received one hundred and fifty-two persons into membership. The meetings were first held in a private house, but that was soon found too small to accommodate the increasing congregation, and larger quarters have been sought from time to time, until now the church owns the handsome property on the southwest corner of Chicago Avenue and Grove Street.

The present form of Sunday service observed in all of the churches of the denomination was inaugurated in 1895. The sermons consist of selections taken from the Bible and the Christian Science Text Book, "Science and Health," with Key to the Scriptures, by Rev. Mary Baker G. Eddy, the discoverer and leader of Christian Science. The lesson sermons of all the churches are arranged by a committee appointed by the First Church of Christ (Scientist), of Boston, and are read by the First and Second Readers, reading from the Bible and from "Science and Health," respectively.

Following the Sunday morning service the Sunday School assembles. Since its organization progress has been the keynote with these little workers, who are bringing out in their daily lives beautiful proofs of the power of good in overcoming evil, as this religion teaches.

On each Wednesday evening in this church, as well as all other churches of this denomination, a meeting is held for the purpose of giving testimonies of the benefits received physically, morally and spiritually from the study and practice of Christian Science.

In accordance with a by-law of the First Church of Christ (Scientist), of Boston, a reading room has been established and is open daily, affording an opportunity to those who are seeking knowledge on the subject of Christian Science to read and procure literature.

The theology of Christian Science includes healing the sick, as well as reforming the sinner, by the prayer of faith with a spiritual understanding of the Scriptures, basing its authority upon the teachings and works of Christ Jesus and the Apostles, as recorded in the Bible.

The following item from one of the

Chicago newspapers of a year ago—the exact date is not known—furnishes an interesting fact in connection with the history of the First Church of Christ (Scientist), of Evanston:

"When the temple building of the First Church of Christ (Scientist), of Evanston, was destroyed by fire two and a half years ago, the one hundred persons who comprised the membership of the church erected a new building at a cost of $25,-000, and then set out to wipe out the debt within three years. Last evening, at the regular prayer service, Holmes Hoge, treasurer of the church and assistant cashier of the First National Bank of Chicago, announced that the last payment on the mortgage was made yesterday."

CHAPTER XXXVIII.

YOUNG MEN'S CHRISTIAN ASSOCIATION
(By ARTHUR B. DALE, General Secretary)

Evanston Young Men's Christian Association — Organization Effected in 1885 — First Board of Officers — General History — Association Building Erected and Dedicated in 1898 — Gymnasium and Natatorium Constructed — List of Former and Present Officers.

The Young Men's Christian Association of Evanston, as elsewhere, arose in response to a public need for the care of the young men of the community, and since its organization has steadily grown, both in size and efficiency, until now it occupies a place of unquestioned utility in the city and has become one of the most effective arms of the church for its work among young men. Differing from the usual social or athletic club in breadth of purpose, it has steadily aimed to reach the young man in his entirety and to benefit him morally, intellectually, physically and socially. It firmly stands for the symmetrical growth of all of these sides of his life, believing that only thus does a man approach the plan designed for him by his Maker.

The local organization was called into being as the result of a meeting of pastors and lay members of the various churches of the city, held June 26, 1885, at which were present Rev. Messrs. Scott, Curts and Noyes for the pastors, and Messrs. H. G. Grey, D. S. McMullen, Martin, Miller, Adams, Gillson and Benjamin for the laity. This meeting had under discussion the question whether an organization for young men was needed, on which point they were unanimous; and whether such organization should be the Young Men's Christian Association. On the latter point, some difference of opinion arising, the matter was referred to a committee of five, who afterward reported to a mass meeting in favor of the Association, which was finally launched on November 17, 1885, with the following Board of Managers: M. P. Aiken, Jos. M. Larimer, W. E. Stockton, Capt. L. O. Lawson, J. H. Nitchie, W. H. Spenser, O. E. Haven, S. A. Kean, C. B. Congdon, H. G. Grey, L. K. Gillson and P. O. Magnuson. This Board organized with the following officers: President—M. P. Aiken; Vice-President—J. M. Larimer; Recording Secretary — J. H. Nitchie; Treasurer — Howard G. Grey.

Under this Board of Directors the Association was duly incorporated as "The Young Men's Christian Association of Evanston," on November 17, 1885, and has continued under these articles to the present time. Rooms were secured in the Rink Building, at the corner of Davis Street and Chicago Avenue, and on March 16, 1886, Mr. W. S. Mather was engaged as General Secretary, to take charge of the work.

From this date the Association pursued the usual course of such organizations, meeting with difficulties and achieving successes from time to time, but persistently holding to its one purpose of reaching and benefiting the young men of the community. After a period in the Rink Building, the rooms were moved to the Block Building, on Sherman Avenue, south of Davis Street, where the work continued to prosper. Among the successful enterprises conducted by the Association during this period were the religious meetings addressed by Rev. C. H. Yatman, of Newark, N. J., in the fall of 1887. These meetings were held in conjunction with the city churches and resulted in 218 professed conversions, of which 115 were young men, and a general quickening of the religious life of the city.

During the General Secretaryship of Mr. F. D. Fagg, agitation for a building began, and the following resolution was adopted at a meeting of the Board of Directors on June 3, 1892: "Resolved, That it is the sense of this Board that the Association proceed, at the earliest possible date, to secure a site and take the necessary steps to erect a building commensurate with the public need." Pursuant to this resolution, a committee of five was appointed to select a site and solicit funds for its purchase. This agitation finally resulted in the purchase of the present Association lots, in March, 1893, at a cost of $27,-000.

Just when matters were growing bright for the accomplishment of the long-desired purpose of beginning work for a building, the Association met with a great loss in the death of Mr. J. M. Larimer, who was, at the time, its President. Mr. Larimer had been for a number of years a most active friend and supporter of the work, giving both of his time and money with unusual generosity, and to his efforts was largely due the progress that had been made up to that time.

Shortly after the death of Mr. Larimer, Mr. John R. Lindgren was elected President, and Mr. William Boyd having just entered upon the duties of General Secretary, the work of canvassing for funds for the new building was taken up and pushed to a successful issue. A great stimulus was given the project by the State Convention of the Association, which was held in Evanston in 1895, and gave the people of the city an enlarged view of the extent and importance of the work at large, of which the local organization was a part. After much hard work and patient continuance in the solicitation of funds, the present building was finally completed, and on October 6, 1898, was dedicated to the interests of young men in Evanston in a public reception, at which a very large number of the citizens were present.

With the completion of the front building, the interest in the Association took on a renewed vigor, and work was immediately begun for the building of the gymnasium, without which the work planned would have been most incomplete. This was carried on in a most systematic and successful manner, and on November 28, 1899, the Gymnasium Building was formally opened, complete in every detail with the exception of the Natatorium that had been contemplated in the original plan. For this latter feature the Association waited until July 1, 1903, when two of Evanston's most liberal citizens contributed $5,000 each, for this purpose, and one of the finest swimming pools in

the country, of tile and marble construction, was installed as part of the physical equipment.

The completion of the Gymnasium and Natatorium gave the Evanston Association not only one of the most complete equipments in the country, but also one most admirably adapted to the work to be performed. The greatest wisdom has been shown by those having the matter in hand in providing not only for the present membership, but also for the probable increase of future years. Since its completion, the International officers of the Association have frequently referred others to the Evanston building as a model to be followed, and calls for inspection by visiting officers or architects are of common occurrence.

Together with the completeness of its equipment, however, the Association has never lost sight of the real purpose of its organization, viz., the extension of the kingdom of Christ among the young men of the city. Aided by the active co-operation of the churches, it has conducted its physical, educational and social work, as well as its more specifically religious work, with this object in view, and by this policy has won a place for itself among the permanent factors going to make up the better citizenship and life of the city.

Presidents and General Secretaries of the Association since its organization, with their terms of service, have been as follows:

Presidents:
M. P. Aiken, 1885-1886.
C. B. Congdon, 1886-1891.
J. M. Larimer, 1891-1894.
J. R. Lindgren, 1894-1903.
John E. Wilder, 1903-.....
General Secretaries:
W. S. Mather, 1886.
Jesse Lockwood, 1886-1887.
W. A. Hill, 1887-1888.
E. A. Barrett, 1888-1889.
John M. Dick, 1889-1890.
F. D. Fagg, 1890-1893.
Wm. Boyd, 1893-1901.
A. B. Dale, 1901-.....

The present Board of Directors is composed of the following gentlemen: John E. Wilder, President; Richard C. Hall, Vice-President; Wm. Hudson Harper, Recording Secretary; Wm. A. Dyche, Treasurer; Frank H. Armstrong, Thos. L. Fansler, Livingstone P. Moore, John H. Hardin, John R. Lindgren, James F. Oates, Thos. I. Stacey, Wm. G. Sherer, Alfred L. Lindsey, Milton H. Wilson.

The present executive force is as follows: Arthur B. Dale, General Secretary; J. Graham Stewart, Assistant Secretary; Lewis O. Gillesby, Physical Director.

Frances E. Willard

CHAPTER XXXIX.

WOMAN'S CHRISTIAN TEMPERANCE UNIONS
(By SUSANNA M. D. FRY, A. M., Ph. D.)

Women's Temperance Alliance—Evanston Woman's Christian Temperance Union Organized in 1875—Working Departments — Enforcement of Four-Mile Limit Law — Industrial School — Children's Organization — Loyal Temperance Legion and Gospel Temperance Meetings — Miss Frances E. Willard and Other Noted Leaders — Manual Training School—The Evanston W. C. T. U.—Reiley and South Evanston Unions—Young Woman's Organization.

The forerunner of the Woman's Christian Temperance Union in Evanston was the Women's Temperance Alliance. This was formed March 17, 1874, and was a part of the general awakening which followed the Woman's Crusade of the winter of 1873-74. The name, "Woman's Christian Temperance Union," was as yet practically unknown, and that the organization took the name it did was probably due to the fact that Mr. L. L. Greenleaf had, several years earlier, formed an Alliance which met at his own and other homes in Evanston. The chief object of the Women's Temperance Alliance was the prosecution of violators of the University charter law, which forbade saloons within four miles of the college campus. As soon as the village of Evans-

ton was incorporated a local ordinance had been passed in harmony with the University charter. Other objects of the Alliance were the circulation of the pledge and the visiting of places within the four-mile limit, where liquor was believed to be sold, or where gambling was carried on. Mrs. A. J. Brown was elected the first President, but declined to serve, and Mrs. Dr. O. Marcy was elected. Mrs. Prof. H. F. Fisk was the first Secretary. Among those who were particularly interested were Mrs. Dr. David Noyes, Mrs. Edward Russell, Mrs. A. P. Wightman, Mrs. Francis Bradley, Mrs. Arza Brown, Mrs. Charles E. Brown, Mrs. Emily Huntington Miller, Mrs. John E. Kedzie, Mrs. T. C. Hoag, Mrs. Helen E. Hesler, Mrs. J. F. Willard, Mrs. Mary B. Willard, Mrs. Rev. F. L. Chappell, Mrs. Caroline F. Corbin, Mrs. M. C. Van Benschoten. The records of the Alliance include the names of about seven hundred citizens of Evanston who signed the total abstinence pledge at that time. The men and women signers were about equal in number, and the last fifty-four names are noted as coming from the University and the College Cottage, and were handed in by Miss Jessie Brown, afterward Mrs. Hilton, who became National W. C. T. U. Superintendent of Mothers' Meetings.

THE EVANSTON W. C. T. U.

May 1, 1875, the Alliance changed its name to the Evanston Woman's Christian Temperance Union, and September 18, 1878, became auxiliary to the State and National W. C. T. U. The following have served as Presidents of this Union from 1874 until 1906: Mrs. Dr. O. Marcy, Mrs. Mary Thompson Willard, Mrs. W. E. Clifford, Mrs. Francis Bradley, Mrs. A. J. Brown, Mrs. M. M. Conwell, Mrs. Mary Bannister Willard, Mrs. Jane Eggleston Zimmerman, Mrs. Mary H. Hull, Mrs. William Bradley, Mrs. Gertrude M. Singleton, Mrs. Lucy Prescott Vane, Mrs. John B. Finch, Mrs. A. De-Coudres, Mrs. Robert M. Hatfield, Mrs. Harriet Kidder, and Mrs. George R. Brown, who became President in 1899.

For many years the W. C. T. U. and the Ladies' Union Prayer Meeting met as one body. The Evanston Union has, at different times, carried on the following lines of work: Law Enforcement, Gospel Temperance Meetings, Kindergarten Work, Night School, Industrial School, Reading Room, Band of Hope, Loyal Temperance Legion, Hospital and Rescue Work, Distribution of Literature, Scientific Temperance Instruction, Work Among Colored People, Temperance Teaching in the Sunday School, Parliamentary Usage, Medal Contest, Work Among Railroad Employes, Mothers' Meeting, Pledge Signing, and other departments of the National W. C. T. U. work, some of which will be taken up somewhat in detail in this sketch. This Union is still doing good work under the leadership of Mrs. George R. Brown, President, and Mrs. G. W. Price, its faithful, long-time Recording Secretary. It has a paid-up membership of sixty.

Law Enforcement.—In the early days

Mrs. Arza Brown, mother of Mrs. Mary H. B. Hitt, who was for many years President of the Northwestern Branch of the Woman's Foreign Missionary Society of the M. E. Church, used to take Mrs. Dr. Marcy with her in her buggy to Gross Point, a German settlement north of Evanston, where they visited saloons and did regular temperance missionary work among the people. The women prosecuted those found selling liquor within the four-mile limit and generally gained their case, but too often an appeal was taken and the case was finally lost. The members of the Union did not hesitate to go into the court and testify. Mrs. Arza Brown, when nearly eighty years old, went fearlessly into the most forbidding places and searched most diligently into the statutes concerning liquor-selling, and, withal, was most fervent in prayer, not only in the Union, but among the offenders whom she visited.

The following appeared in the "Evanston Index" while the Union was still called the Alliance:

"The Women's Temperance Alliance of Evanston, appreciating the embarrassment systematically thrown in the way of all who attempt to prosecute the secret and open venders of intoxicants, at its last meeting created a committee of vigilance, consisting of many influential ladies and gentlemen, whose duty it will be to attend the courts to prevent, as far as possible the intimidation of witnesses and to do whatever else may be necessary to insure a prompt and vigorous prosecution of all violators of the University charter law, and the laws of this State and village, within reach of the influence of the Alliance."

The same paper reported at another time a liquor case before Justice Huntoon, which was attended by Mesdames

Arza Brown, Charles E. Brown, A. J. Brown, Marcy, Bradley, Fisk, Willard, Boutell, Goebel, Woodson, Ninde, Newman, Moore, Stout, Butler, Curtis, Lane, Van Benschoten, Hoag, Pitner, Pitt, Clifford and Miss Jackson.

In 1883 a Law and Order League was organized among the men of Evanston, at the suggestion of Rev. Dr. Bannister, of which Dr. D. R. Dyche was for many years President, but the Union never lost its interest in this phase of temperance work and no single feature has been of more general interest to the citizens of Evanston. The minutes of the Evanston Union show, from time to time, that the "saloon on wheels" was still rolling up and down the streets, and that the Union was called upon for greater activity in law enforcement.

October 16, 1880, the Y. W. C. T. U., which had been organized the year before, moved that the society communicate, through its Secretary, with the Trustees of the Northwestern University, respectfully calling their attention to the fact that, in direct opposition to published laws, beer was sold on the streets, and that there were seven saloons in operation within less than four miles of the University; also that the society would furnish witnesses who would testify to the facts as above stated.

The National W. C. T. U. has a department of Legislation and Law Enforcement, and even in Evanston, which has never had a legalized saloon, constant vigilance is needed on the part of officials and other citizens to minimize illicit selling of intoxicating drinks. Hence the continued activity of the Unions in this direction.

Industrial School.—One of the earliest efforts among poor children was made by Mrs. Dr. O. Marcy. Those most needing instruction along the lines of temperance, industry, cleanliness, et cetera, were gathered together in a school, which some persisted in calling the ragged school, but which the leader always dignified with the title of "Industrial." The children were taught in a very simple and practical way. Texts were often selected which had something to say about "clean hands." To illustrate the Scripture, "Make a chain, for the land is full of bloody crimes and the city is full of violence," the children were taught to make a chain of their pledge cards. These had all been decorated with hand-painted flowers, and upon them were the names of those who signed the following pledge: "We all, whose names are on this pledge, promise not to drink anything that will intoxicate." The children were taught that "crimes" and "violence" were to be lessened by their sobriety and industry. The chain of pledge cards is still in existence. The school met in uncomfortable places until taken to Union Hall. They were trained to recite pieces and sing, together with sewing for the girls and some simple manual work for the boys. Mrs. Cornelia A. Churcher and others of the long-time residents of Evanston were greatly interested in this school.

The Star Band of Hope.—February 23, 1875, Mrs. S. M. I. Henry, afterward a National W. C. T. U. evangelist, organized the Star Band of Hope among the children, which soon numbered seventy. Mrs. A. J. Brown was the presiding genius, and Dr. Eben Clapp was her most faithful co-laborer. The meetings were held in Mrs. Brown's house at first, then in the old Evanston Hotel on Davis Street, and afterward in Union Hall. Dr. George C. Noyes, then pastor of the First Presbyterian Church, helped to corral the unruly boys, and assisted in many ways, as did Mr. George Wire, Dr. William B. Phillips and others. Many of the boys were wild and reckless, and a system of military drill was instituted among them by Captain Julian R. Fitch. Evanston ladies met and made caps and belts for the boys. A band of musicians was trained among them, and they marched through the streets with their wooden guns, the band playing such military airs as were supposed to indicate that they were "soldiers fighting for good habits." Mrs. Marcy wrote some songs for them, notably, "I Heard a Little Bird One Morning Sing, Sip, Sip No Wine."

Mrs. Edward Russell had charge of the Girls' Brigade, which was a part of the Band of Hope. The children of many prominent families belonged to the organization, and the testimony is that never was better temperance work done among the children than during the five years' existence of the Band of Hope.

The Loyal Temperance Legion.—The National W. C. T. U. adopted the name, Loyal Temperance Legion, for its temperance society among the children in 1886, and these Legions succeeded the Bands of Hope. The same year Miss Anna A. Gordon, now Vice-President-at-large of the National W. C. T. U., and Edward Murphy formed a Legion in Evanston, which met in the First M. E. Church. It was formally adopted by the Evanston Union at a meeting on December 6, 1886, with Miss Gordon as Superintendent. The Legion numbered 200 members, with an average attendance of about 100. Mrs. Mary Owens Denyes, now President of the Straits Settlement W. C. T. U., and residing at Singapore, was a member of the Legion, as were others whose names are now widely known.

After the completion of Miss Gordon's first book of "Marching Songs" for the L. T. L., her legioners gave a demonstration in the church. The banners with mottoes, the marching and singing and declaiming, were new to the audience and were wonderfully impressive. Later, Mrs. Culla J. Vayhinger, then a student in the University and now President of the Indiana W. C. T. U., was Superintendent of the Legion. The children had courses of instruction which have come, through repeated revisions and improvements, to be exceedingly fine manuals of study, adapted to Junior, Senior and Normal grades. Several L. T. L.'s have succeeded each other, but Evanston has never been long without such an organization. The L. T. L. is a branch of the National W. C. T. U., and in its entirety numbers about 200,000.

Gospel Temperance Meetings.—Sunday afternoon, September, 1879, a Gospel temperance meeting was started under the leadership of Mrs. M. M. Conwell, in the waiting-room of the old Northwestern depot. These meetings continued until 1895 or 1896. After leaving the depot they were held in a rented room on the corner of Davis and Maple Streets, and, later still, were regularly maintained in Union Hall. Mrs. Jane Eggleston Zimmerman was leader of these meetings for about eight years, beginning in 1881. Among the devoted workers were Mrs. R. H. Trumbull, Mrs. Mary Bannister Willard, Mrs. T. C. Reiley, Mrs. R. Somers and scores of others.

When Lady Henry Somerset, now President of the World's W. C. T. U., made her first visit to this country, 1891-92, she and Miss Willard spoke at the Gospel temperance meeting on Sunday, March 13, 1892. The hall was packed and the interest intense. A farewell meeting for Lady Henry Somerset had been given in Central Music Hall, Chicago, the evening before, and both she and Miss Willard were extremely weary, but they did not find it in their hearts to refuse to speak on the occasion named.

Miss Julia Ames, Miss Helen L. Hood, Miss Ruby I. Gilbert and Mary Allen West, editor of "The Union Signal," all closely identified with the National W. C. T. U., and domiciled in the northern half of Rest Cottage, were frequently at these meetings. Mrs. Elizabeth Boynton Harbert, Mrs. M. L. Welles, afterward National W. C. T. U. lecturer, and many others belonging to the Union, spoke at these meetings, as well as the pastors of the various churches. Temperance papers from all over the world were received by Miss Willard at Rest Cottage, and these were carried over to Union Hall every Sunday and distributed.

The following, which appeared in the "Evanston Index" at the time, shows the inspiring cause of the meetings:

"Father Wheadon was roused from sleep one night by a young man living near him, who came to him saying: 'I have signed the pledge, but I must have God's help to keep it.' From the spirit aroused by the recital of this incident came the combination of effort on the part of Mrs. Conwell, Mrs. Clifford, Miss Willard and others, which resulted in the Gospel meetings."

An incident will illustrate the character of the work:

When Miss Willard was to speak, Union Hall, with all side rooms opened up, was always crowded. On one such occasion a man was observed to be eagerly seeking admittance. To Mrs. T. C. Reiley, who sought to make room for him, he said he must see Miss Willard. He was informed that he could not see her then, as she was about to speak, but

might do so at the close of the meeting. Observation of the man suggested the wisdom of an after meeting, and a note to Miss Willard prompted its announcement. When the man had an opportunity he asked if the Union took care of men's wives. He said he had gone to ethical culture lectures and many others, and no one could tell him how to reform, and now it was time to drop all such efforts. A word of prayer was proposed, and when the meeting closed the man said that if God was what they represented Him to be, and would keep him from falling through the week, he would come again next Sunday. He was given a Bible, a white ribbon was pinned on his coat, and he was sent to his Chicago home. Before going he said he had come to Evanston with the intention of killing himself, had walked past Rest Cottage six times without the courage to enter, and then went to the meeting with his revolver in his pocket. After reading the Bible many times, he said to his wife: "If this God will take me past the saloons, I'll take Him." Influence was brought to bear to secure employment for the man, he joined the church, and at last accounts was still doing well.

The attention of the Union, however, came to be turned more and more to prevention by work among children, as the experiences of this and thousands of other unions showed that a large percentage of reformed men eventually went back to their cups. The Salvation Army came in with the same kind of Gospel work, and in time this particular field in Evanston was largely left to them.

Kindergarten Work.—In the winter of 1885 a kindergarten was started which continued until April, 1896, when the work was introduced into the Haven public school. Mrs. Mary Bannister Willard was chiefly instrumental in raising the necessary funds at the beginning, through what was termed $15 scholarships, and in honor of her work the school was later named the Mary Bannister Willard Kindergarten. Mrs. Hester E. Walker had the school in charge and was most successful in winning both children and parents. The ladies of the First M. E. Church earned the first $200 for the kindergarten. The Y. W. C. T. U. and other young people lent a helping hand, chiefly through the sale of home-made candies, which was a source of considerable revenue to the Union for many years. Miss Mary McDowell, now at the head of the Northwestern University Settlement in Chicago, did much to aid the kindergarten work. Miss Kate Jackson, Mrs. John A. Childs, Mrs. Dr. O. H. Mann, Mrs. R. M. Hatfield and Mrs. Henderson were also moving spirits. The need for the school did not exist after the work became a part of the public school system. During the more than eleven years of its existence it cost the Union, for hall rent, salary to the Superintendent, supplies, et cetera, about $1,000 per year, which was cheerfully contributed by the citizens. It is related that some of the little folks won their fathers from drink by the instructions which they had received in the kindergarten and carried to their homes.

Manual Training School.—This school was started about 1883 and suspended in January, 1887. Mrs. H. H. C. Miller was Secretary of the Union during a part of that period, and she was especially active in raising funds for the school and in carrying on the work. Other able women assisted her. Miss Lu Bushnell was a devoted teacher and Mr. William Lindley taught the boys carpentry. The meet-

ings were held in Union Hall and the practical work was done in another building. The especial aim was to gather in the neglected children, or those who for reasons had the greatest need, and to teach them temperance, industry and other virtues.

Other Undertakings.—The Evanston Union inaugurated many other lines of work beside those already named. At one time a night school was opened for youths who were obliged to work and could not attend the day schools. This numbered about eighty, and was sustained through the generosity of Mr. William Deering, Rev. Henry Delano, Mr. Charles Congdon and others, until the Public School Board was induced to open a night school. A reading room was carried on from 1881 to 1886, and cottage prayer meetings were held frequently. At one time open air meetings were held on the University campus and on the corner of Ayars Court and Ridge Avenue. In 1886 the Good Times Club of girls, organized to illustrate that the best of good times consist in doing good to somebody else, became a part of the Union.

Much attention was given to mothers' meetings. Mrs. Jessie Brown Hilton was, for a number of years, the inspiring and instructive leader. She served as National W. C. T. U. Superintendent of Mothers' Meetings several successive years, and gave many special lectures in Evanston by invitation of the Union. A sewing school for girls was maintained for some time.

Social purity also had its place. Mrs. Isabel Wing Lake, for many years National Superintendent of Rescue Work, Mrs. Major Singleton, Mrs. R. H. Trumbull and others went regularly to the Cook County Hospital, interested themselves in the welfare of the girls in that institution, and in many cases did practical rescue work.

Thousands of pages of temperance literature were distributed every year. Active interest has always been taken in the teaching of scientific temperance truths from proper text-books in the public schools. As is well known, this plan originated with the W. C. T. U., and the Evanston Union did its part in securing the State law and the amendments which have been made from time to time, and in helping to make the law effective locally.

The Union was instrumental in organizing a union among the colored people of Evanston at one time, and it has regularly supervised a number of other departments of the National W. C. T. U., such as Non-Alcoholic Medication, Anti-Narcotics, Flower Mission, whereby thousands of bouquets, with Scripture texts, have been given to the sick and unfortunate, but first, last and all the time, it has striven to promulgate the two basic principles of total abstinence and prohibition. The Union assisted the Delano Mission and has always been active in home charities, besides sending many boxes and barrels of clothing to needy Western territory.

As indicative of the practical work of the Union, the following, taken at random from its minutes, may be noted:

"December 23, 1878, the anniversary of the Temperance Crusade was observed in the M. E. Church, which was decorated for the occasion, the President, Mrs. M. M. Conwell, presiding. Miss Willard delivered, in her own peculiarly charming manner, her lecture on "Home Protection," at the close of which 150 signatures to the petition to the Illinois Legislature were secured. (Some 600 in all were taken.)

"January 10, 1879, temperance day in the week of prayer, was observed, Mrs. Converse presiding. Mrs. Arza Brown spoke with energy against the use of tobacco.

"March 19, 1879, the Union petitioned a certain railroad to remove intoxicating liquors from its dining-cars and a committee reported having visited all of the churches of Evanston urging the use of unfermented wine at the sacrament.

"May 7, 1881, Mary B. Willard, President, a committee was appointed to protest to druggists against unnecessary Sabbath trade, and to the town authorities against a gambling den known to exist."

For several years lately the W. C. T. U. has had representation on the Board of Associated Charities of Evanston, Mrs. G M. Price having been the representative so far.

Many lecturers have been brought to Evanston by the Union to address public audiences or union meetings. Among these may be named John B. Gough, Joe Hess (the reformed pugilist), Francis Murphy, Col. George Bain, John B. Finch, and of our own, Mary T. Lathrap, Mary H. Hunt, Narcissa White Kinney, Caroline B. Buell, Esther Pugh, Helen M. Barker, Mary A. Woodbridge, Katharine Lent Stevenson, Mary Allen West and Mrs. Robinson, an evangelist, who held meetings for two months, sometimes five a day. Those heard most frequently were, of course, our own citizens: Mesdames Emily Huntington Miller, Elizabeth Boynton Harbert, S. M. I. Henry, Jessie Brown Hilton, Dr. Kate Bushnell and Frances E. Willard.

The Sunday Gospel temperance meetings were addressed by people from

Japan, Persia, India, Mexico, and from many of our own States, besides many pastors and others citizens of Evanston. Frequent mass meetings and receptions were held during the early years.

It is related that when Miss Willard made her first public address in Evanston, in the old M. E. Church which stood on the site now selected for the new Public Library on Church Street, she did not remove her bonnet. Before the meeting opened, a friend suggested that she take it off, saying the lines were not just suited to Miss Willard's face. "O no, dear," she replied: "I mustn't do it. Some of the sisters might not just like it," which is illustrative of her thoughtful care of the feelings of others.

When Mr. Murphy was lecturing in Evanston, Miss Willard used to occupy fifteen or twenty minutes before he began. One night a $5 gold piece was put in the collection-box by a gentleman who, upon inquiry as to whether a mistake had been made, said that this piece had come to him in a very peculiar manner and was to be used for his own personal pleasure; that he came to hear Mr. Murphy and heard Miss Willard, and knew the time had come to use the $5 gold piece. He said he regarded her perorations as worth many times the value of the coin.

Not a few members of the Evanston Union have been prime movers in National W. C. T. U. matters, as, for instance, Mrs. Dr. O. Marcy was one of the committee which founded the first National paper, called "Our Union." Plans for it were discussed in Evanston and investigations were made in Chicago as to the printing of the paper, which was finally published in Philadelphia, and if Miss Willard's work were to be taken account of, it would mean an enumeration of much

of that which is of greatest value in the National W. C. T. U.

Suffrage was a dangerous question in the early days. Mrs. Harbert relates that at a meeting of the Union she was nominated as Secretary. She rose and said: "Ladies, I think I ought to tell you, before you go any further, that I hold in my hand an invitation to become the President of the State Suffrage Association"; whereupon the presiding officer quickly said, "Do sit right down, Mrs. Harbert, or you will turn this meeting into a suffrage discussion." Mrs. Harbert sat down, contenting herself mostly thereafter, she says, by offering to furnish scalloped oysters and angel food on occasions, believing these would create no discussion.

The anniversary meeting for Miss Willard, on her fiftieth birthday, was the first public recognition of the department of equal suffrage, which the National had adopted years before. Mrs. Elizabeth Wheeler Andrew, afterward round the world W. C. T. U. missionary, presented Miss Willard with a basket of beautiful flowers decorated with white and yellow ribbons, and explained that the white stood for temperance and the yellow for equal suffrage. The Unions, State and Local, had long since learned that they were free to accept or reject departments according to their likings and beliefs, which had allayed the fears of some who could not accept all of the departments proposed by the National W. C. T. U.

The Reiley Union.—For many years there was but the one Union in Evanston, except those among the young women called the "Ys." In later years, it was thought a union west of the railroad tracks would appeal more particularly to residents in that locality, and January 21, 1896, the Reiley Union was organized. The Presidents have been Mrs. Caroline Franklin, Mrs. Ella DeCoudres and Mrs. T. C. Reiley, who had served many years as Treasurer of the Evanston Union, and who was President of the Fourth District for nine years, beginning in 1893. The Fourth District then included Chicago and Evanston, and in fact, all of the north shore. The work and the departments of the Reiley Union have been similar to those of the Evanston Union during the same years, and a number of its members were previously identified with the older union and had a share in what has been related of it. It may be noted, however, that the Reiley Union has sent quantities of literature to needy places and to other States; has worked the department of Soldiers and Sailors, supplying the soldiers with many comfortbags during the Spanish and Philippine wars. It has been an ardent supporter of the one time affiliated interests of the National W. C. T. U., and it secured the organization of the present Y. W. C. T. U. It has many devoted workers in its membership of thirty.

The **South Evanston Union.**—This Union was organized by Mrs. Reiley in 1894 and continued the work for seven years. Its presidents were Mrs. D. D. Thompson, Mrs. K. R. Whitman and Mrs. George Hoover. It numbered twenty-five or thirty members, distributed a large amount of literature, held most excellent mothers' meetings and had a fine Loyal Temperance Legion.

The **Ys of Evanston.**—The Young Woman's Christian Temperance Union is a branch of the W. C. T. U., and these Unions among the young people have come to be known as "the Ys." Tradition says that Evanston has had three different organizations of the Ys, but written records supply information of two only. The first of these was organized January 2, 1879, with a speedy enrollment of thirty-seven members. It was organized at Rest Cottage, the home of Miss Willard, she and Miss Gordon both being present and assisting in the organization. Miss Belle Webb was elected President and Miss Justina A. Pingree, Recording Secretary. Miss Webb declined to serve and Miss Fannie Wiswall was elected. The Union took up temperance teaching in the Sabbath schools, securing subscriptions to "Our Union," the official organ of the National W. C. T. U., and supplying the papers with temperance items and reports of the work of the Y. The society was pledged to total abstinence and also to use its influence against the use of tobacco. Many signers of the Home Protection Petition and the total abstinence pledge were obtained. As has already been stated, this Union lent its aid to the efforts for law enforcement and to the other undertakings of the mother Union, the Evanston W. C. T. U. It secured lectures by Prof. George E. Foster, Mrs. Harbert, Mrs. Hannah Whitall Smith, Miss Lucia Kimball, Miss Willard and others. Miss Martha Button was the President in 1880. A temperance school was conducted by the Ys, and they aided the Gospel temperance meetings and edited and read at their monthly meetings a little paper fitly called, "The Waterspout." Prof. Haven of the public schools, Dr. Garnsey and Miss Brace conducted experiments in the temperance school. The membership came up to forty and the meetings were moved from private houses to Room 4 of Union Hall, and later to a building on the corner of Davis and Maple Streets. In 1880, leaflets were distributed to the number of 10,000, and 132 total abstinence pledges were secured, exclusive of children. The temperance school was held every Saturday except for two summer months. It numbered sixty. Julia Colman's Juvenile Temperance Manual, picture tracts and reward cards were used. The society subscribed for fifty copies of "Illustrated Temperance Tales" and Miss Willard donated fifty copies of "The Youth's Temperance Banner." A number of public entertainments were given. Miss Mary Ninde was the President for 1881, but on March 12, 1881, after two years and a quarter of separate activity, the Y voted to become a part of the Evanston W. C. T. U.

The next Y, of which there are records, is the present Evanston Y. W. C. T. U. It was organized November 8, 1902, by Mrs. Minnie B. Horning, Corresponding Secretary of the Illinois W. C. T. U., and Miss Kathryn Sawyer, State Y Secretary. It began with eight active members, and numbers, at the present time, twenty-four young women and eighteen young men, the latter being honorary members. Its Presidents have been as follows: Miss Sibyl Horning, Miss Mildred Auten and Miss Erma Hoag. Their work has been mainly connected with the Flower Mission, Press, Hospital and Literature. A necessary requirement for membership in all Ys, as well as Ws, is the signing of the pledge against the use of intoxicating drinks, and this one has also declared against the use of tobacco, though this is not made a requirement of membership They have contributed to the White Ribbon Missionary Fund, which, at present, helps to sustain Miss Kara Smart as a resident W. C. T. U. missionary in Japan, and to the Frances E. Willard Memorial Fund, which is used to enlarge and perpetuate the work at home, and also to the state work. Considerable attention has been given to parliamentary usage, that the meetings may be conducted properly.

At this writing it is proposed to supply teachers from their membership for a new Junior Loyal Temperance Legion being organized among the children.

At one time, in order to increase the interest in the meetings, a continued story was a part of the program, each chapter being written by a different member. This Union is made up of University and High School young people, and bids fair to be a worthy member of the trio of Unions now working in Evanston, viz.: the Evanston W. C. T. U., the Reiley W. C. T. U. and the Y. W. C. T. U.

Brother Helpers.—The ministers and other good men of Evanston have lent their aid during the more than thirty years of active service by the Unions. Chief among the early helpers may be mentioned Dr. Martin C. Briggs, of the Methodist Episcopal Church; Rev. Edward N. Packard, of the Congregational Church; Rev. F. L. Chappell, of the Baptist Church, and Dr. Geo. C. Noyes, of the First Presbyterian Church; and, in later years, Dr. Robert M. Hatfield, Dr. Frank Bristol, Dr. Frederick Clatworthy, and Dr. Henry Delano, who often spoke for the W. C. T. U. and whose church was always open for its meetings. Dr. N. S. Davis was ready to help at the public meetings with valuable contributions from his professional knowledge.

Among the other notable Brother Helpers were Mr. William Deering, Dr. O. H. Mann, Dr. Eben Clapp, Mr. C. B. Congdon, Major W. F. Singleton, Mr. F. P. Crandon, Mr. John B. Finch, Dr. Milton Terry, and other University professors, including Prof. H. F. Fisk and President Joseph Cummings.

All the Unions have been greatly indebted from time to time to the Brother Helpers who have aided in many ways.

CHAPTER XL.

CHARITABLE ASSOCIATIONS
(By MRS. LOUISE BROCKWAY STANWOOD)

Benevolent Society Organized — Hospital Projected — New Society Takes the Name "Associated Charities" — Auxiliary Organizations — Mothers' Sewing School — St. Vincent de Paul Society— Needle Work Guild — Mothers' Club — Visiting Nurse Association —, King's Daughters — Camp Good Will — Its Service in Behalf of Poor Mothers and Children — Receipts and Expenditures.

The distribution of charity in Evanston, up to the year 1883, had been a matter of individual effort or church discrimination; but the winter of 1883 opened very bitter and stormy and, on one particularly cold day, Mrs. William Blanchard was distressed at the thought of the suffering there must be amongst the poor of the town. Calling her coachman, she inquired if he would think it inhuman to take his horses out and drive her about to look after cases of suffering. The children coming home from school reported that, in one family, a baby had been frozen to death the night before. When Mrs. Blanchard reached this home, she found the family in a desperate condition; several children partially frozen and the whole family in need of every comfort—clothes, food, and heat. After relieving their immediate necessities, she went home to think over the situation, and the idea of a

benevolent society for the relief of the poor and suffering in Evanston took shape in her mind. Mrs. Blanchard inserted a notice in the village paper, calling on all ladies who might be interested in the formation of such a society to meet at her house on a given day, to talk the matter over and to organize. Many ladies responded to the call and the Benevolent Society of Evanston was duly organized.

Benevolent Society Organized.—It was decided to hold meetings for sewing at the different homes, to have a relief and investigating committee and a committee to solicit funds. The response to the request for funds was hearty and generous, as Mrs. Blanchard herself says, only one person who was approached for money refusing to give. The names of the first workers in the Benevolent Society included those of Mrs. Edward Taylor, Mrs. George Watson, Mrs. L. C. Tallmadge, Mrs. N. A. Coble, Mrs. N. C. Gridley, Mrs. Tillinghast, Mrs. William Deering, Miss Josephine Patterson, Mrs. A. L. Butler, Mrs. Frank M. Elliot, Miss Alice Blanchard and Mrs. Blanchard, Miss Katherine Lord and Mrs. Frank Wilder.

The sewing meetings were continued all the winter of 1883-84 and Mrs. Blanchard's house was used as the depot for the storing and distributing of clothing. Mrs. Blanchard also made such arrangements with the Cook County hospital that, on her request and recommendation, any case of sickness could be taken to the hospital to be taken care of. This Society, while it provided for the needs of many of the poor, did not prevent frequent cases of duplication in individual charity nor the special efforts of churches in relieving their own people. That was a development that was to come later.

The first records of the Association show the list of officers elected in the winter of 1887-88, when Mrs. Edward Taylor was made President, Mrs. L. C. Tallmadge, Vice-President-at-large, with a Vice-President from each of the following churches: Congregational, Presbyterian, Episcopal, Methodist and Baptist; Miss Josephine Patterson, Secretary; and Mrs. J. E. Burke, Treasurer.

A sewing school, to teach young girls belonging to needy families to sew, had been organized in 1883-84 and in this year (1887) Mrs. Edward Belknap was appointed the chairman of the sewing-school. During this same winter—which is memorable for organization—the Kitchen Garden Association was formed, for the purpose of giving some instruction in cleaning, setting tables, making beds and other housework, that would make it easier for girls to secure positions where they could earn something to help themselves and their families. This Kitchen Garden was first taught by Miss Gardner of Chicago, who trained several of the younger Evanston ladies to be teachers and to continue the school. In the year 1887, Mrs. L. C. Tallmadge and Miss Kate Lord were appointed to have charge of the Kitchen Garden. Mrs. Blanchard, Mrs. Watson, and Mrs. Balding formed the committee to raise funds. The amount of money received was in no sense insignificant, for from the first of November, 1887, to the first of November, 1888, the Treasurer's books show receipts of over $800.

Another form of benevolence had been maintained by the Flower Mission, an organization of young women in the village whose chief duty it was to gather and send to Chicago, for distribution, both garden and greenhouse flowers. This society also had done some relief work, but in October, 1887, the Benevolent Society and the Flower Mission were consolidated, a constitution was adopted, and one more step was taken in the thorough organization of charity work in the village.

The work done by this Society at this time consisted chiefly in clothing the poor, and it had also helped with actual money in the payment of rents, but as the village grew, the needy increased in numbers and, in the very last of 1887, it was decided that society could not afford to pay out money for rents, nor could it provide coffee, sugar, and butter, except in cases of illness. Throughout the records of the Benevolent Society the reports of the Sewing School and the Kitchen Garden furnish interesting reading; and the generosity of various merchants of Evanston and of the doctors in rendering professional services free are many times gratefully acknowledged. In October, 1888, it was decided to confine the work of relief strictly within the villages of North Evanston, Evanston and South Evanston. Tickets were also distributed amongst householders in these three villages, which were to be given to all applicants for relief, directing these latter to the proper authorities.

In October, 1889, the Society decided to hold an open business meeting at the beginning of each sewing meeting, and to ask for reports from each department connected with the work. This had a tendency to increase the attendance at the meetings and to further the interests of the Society. Up to this time the money had been solicited either by representatives from the churches or by a general finance committee; but in this year (1889) a solicitor was appointed for each side of the village — these being Mrs. Bishop and Mrs. Gridley for the east side and Mrs. George Judd for the west. The minutes of October 29, 1889, are interesting to read, because the problem of furnishing fuel to the poor was so well met by the offer of Mr. Hugh Wilson to give ten tons of coal, and the enumeration of garments (old and new) blankets, shoes, etc., indicates that the work afterwards performed by the Needle Work Guild was so well done at this time by the general Society. Another point noticed in these minutes is the suggestion of Miss Lord's growing out of her experience as the head of the Kitchen Garden, that steps should be taken to found a cooking school in Evanston. The teachers of the Kitchen Garden drilled their girls for a public entertainment which was given very successfully and the money received was afterwards applied to that purpose.

Hospital Projected.—In the minutes of February 11, 1890, occur these words: "The hospital question was agitated, and it was decided to call a meeting on Tuesday, February 15th, at Mrs. Tallmadge's, of a committee of six ladies, one from each church, to discuss the propriety of establishing a hospital in Evanston." The names of this committee were as follows: Baptist Church, Mrs. Charles F. Grey; Presbyterian Church, Mrs. H. E. Daniels; Methodist Church, Mrs. Tallmadge and Mrs. A. L. Butler; Congregational Church, Mrs. Joseph Larimer; Episcopal Church, Mrs. H. W. Hinsdale; and from the village at large, Mrs. William Blanchard. In this year, also, it was decided to organize an auxiliary society in North Evanston, and the names of Mrs. Comstock, Mrs. Carson and Mrs. Boomer are associated with the reports of work done by this society.

The cooking school proposed by Miss Lord was established in the basement of the Congregational Church in the winter of 1889 and 1890, under the care of Miss Lord and Miss Mary Bradley. The young girls were very well instructed as cooks, waitresses and house maids.

In 1890 other names appear amongst the list of officers, Mrs. P. S. Shumway being made President, Mrs. Hugh R. Wilson Vice-President from the Methodist Church, Mrs. W. E. Stockton from the Presbyterian, Mrs. Fred Washburn from the Congregational, Mrs. Morse from the Baptist, Mrs. David Cooke from the Episcopal, Mrs. Charles Haskins from the Immanuel, Miss Lindgren from the Swedish Methodist, Mrs. Magill from the Catholic; Secretary, Miss Maud Wycoff, and Treasurer, Mrs. Whitely; and Miss Boutell the chairman of the Flower Mission. On December 1, 1890, the Treasurer reports the treasury empty and in debt, but a little later in the month she reports $72 in the treasury and Mrs. Stockton for the Presbyterian Church reports a collection of $105, so the response to the solicitors was always to be depended upon. Mrs. Wilder, the visitor, reported at this same meeting that she had provided nineteen families with Thanksgiving dinners. This, of course, was in addition to many such dinners provided by individuals and churches. By the last day of the year 1890 the Treasurer reported $527 on hand, a part of which was given by the Business Men's Association of the town and part by the collection taken at the union services on Thanksgiving day. About this time the Society begins to recognize the work of the King's Daughters, who are reported as making garments for the Benevolent Society and acting as visitors to some poor families.

Another reference to the need of an Evanston hospital is found in the minutes of April 6, 1891, when Mrs. Butler reports upon a plan of founding a small hospital. At the meeting of October 14, 1891, Mrs. Wilder suggested that, as the amount in the treasury ($367) was unusually large, a part of it be appropriated for hospital purposes; and in accordance with this suggestion, $300 was set aside for that purpose. By this time the attempt to divide the sewing hitherto done at the afternoon meetings among the churches was tried, although the cutting was still done by the cutters appointed by the general society.

The annual meeting for the year 1891 shows total receipts of $734 and disbursements $666. The Flower Mission reported that year having sent 70 crates of flowers to the Chicago hospitals. The Kitchen Garden seems to have served its purpose and, for a time, it was thought wise to abandon it. The work for the Relief Committee had increased so much by 1891 that it was found necessary to hire a cab for its use, although the number of cases visited is not enumerated.

At Christmas time of 1892, Mrs. Butler reported that she had provided twelve families with Christmas baskets, and it is interesting to see that the names of the same families appear, year after year, amongst the poor and needy, although sickness and drunkenness in the head of the family seem to be the prevailing causes of this poverty.

At the annual meeting of 1892, Mrs. Walworth was made President, with Vice-Presidents Mrs. P. B. Shumway, from the Methodist, Mrs. H. L. Boltwood from the Congregational, Mrs. W. B. Top-

liff from the Presbyterian, Mrs. L. K. Gilson from the Baptist, Mrs. H. W. Hinsdale from St. Marks, Mrs. Wm. Cowper from St. Lukes, Mrs. Herman Poppenhusen from the Presbyterian South, Mrs. J. O. Foster from the Methodist South, Mrs. F. M. Forrey from Wheadon, Mrs. M. J. Boomer from the Central, Mrs. H. W. Brough from the Unitarian and Mrs. Robert Magill from the Catholic Church. Buying Committee, Mrs. Wilder; Visiting Committee, Mrs. A. D. Sanders.

It was at this meeting that it was decided to change the name of the Society to the Associated Charities of Evanston, and an amendment was added to the constitution to this effect, the number of vice-presidents increased, as is to be seen by the foregoing list of officers, and all charities in the three parts of the city were represented on the board. The following quotation from the report of the Relief Committee of this year shows how the work of the Benevolent Society had increased from the time of the informal meeting in Mrs. Blanchard's parlors to October 3, 1892:

"During the past year we have cared for one or more members of thirty-two different families. These have been furnished food, medicine, fuel, clothing, nurses, hospital services, and in a few cases, funeral expenses. We have had surgical cases, partial blindness, consumption, diphtheria, typhoid fever, scarlet fever, inflammatory rheumatism, erysipelas, deformities, confinement cases. We have furnished work of all varieties for both sexes. We have provided all sorts of things, from a nursing bottle to a load of hay, the last being given in order that the father of eight children—one of whom, together with the mother, had been sick eight weeks with typhoid fever—should not be obliged to sell his cow which provided the greater part of food for the sick and little ones. One of the greatest difficulties met with has been that of procuring nurses willing to go into the homes of these families. But the completion of the hospital now near at hand, will, we trust, obviate the necessity."

This report of Mrs. Butler's pointed forward not only to the necessity for a hospital in Evanston, but to the need of a visiting nurse. This need was soon met as will be see further on in this chapter.

The Flower Mission reported that fall a distribution of 49½ crates of flowers, three baskets of bouquets and 5½ crates mostly of hot-house roses, the gift of Mr. Weiland. The Kitchen Garden reported a class of twenty-four, the Sewing School reported an attendance of ninety scholars and eleven teachers. The receipts for that year were over $800.

Change of Name.—The change from Benevolent Society to Associated Charities made it desirable, and even necessary, to seek a permanent place of meeting, and Mrs. Whitely and Mrs. Tallmadge volunteered to see the Mayor and ascertain if a small room in the new City Hall could be secured. The report of the next meeting shows that the Mayor readily acceded to the request. At this time the Society had been meeting in the different church parlors instead of in the individual homes as at first. The room in the City Hall was not yet finished in November of 1892 and it continued to be necessary to meet in different churches. At one of these meetings the minutes relate that a large clothes basket was heaped with new garments made during the day. By Dec. 19, 1892, the room in the City Hall was furnished and was made the depot for garments old and new, and it was announced in the city press that the room was open to all comers.

The relief committee of this year volunteered to distribute Christmas dinners to those needing them, which were promised by Sunday schools and private parties. It was reported at this meeting that Mr. McMahon had received $100 from an Evanston gentleman to invest in chickens and turkeys, and that they would be distributed from one of the markets on Christmas eve.

At the annual meeting of 1893, it was reported, among other benevolences, that an Evanston gentleman had offered to furnish new shoes to any one recommended by a committee from the Associated Charities. The annual report of this year (1893) speaks of the difficulty a stranger experiences in believing that there can be want and destitution in so beautiful a place as Evanston. The report says the poor are usually in that condition because of shiftless habits, lack of training as to the use of money, spending freely when not earning, not laying by for winter, but adds: "It is hard to refuse coal and food, even to the shiftless, when they are found suffering." Another large gift of coal from Mr. Wilson and help from the grocers in the matter of discount is gratefully acknowledged. It is reported that 265 new garments were made and given out from the City Hall in this year. The reports of the Society show a constant improvement in organization, investigation and discrimination, and new names are constantly being added to the lists of officers and visitors. This increased care in the distribution of charity was gradually reducing the relief formerly given from door to door and the claim that the charity of the kindly disposed was abused by the unworthy poor was being surely undermined. It was in 1893 that the ladies decided to interview the ministers of the town and seek to have the entire collection of the union Thanksgiving service given to the Associated Charities. By this time the Society recognizes the gifts of the Needle Work Guild, an organization

whose work will be referred to later. The
generosity of the merchants of Evanston
is constantly noted, and the distributing
station was made available for the distribution of the donations from the grocery
stores and bakeries as well as for clothing.

Auxiliary Organization.—In 1894, when
Mrs. J. E. Scott was President of the Associated Charities, a Mothers' Sewing
School was organized as an additional
means of helping mothers to clothe their
children. A careful record was kept in
1894 and 1895, not only of the officers,
visitors and committees, but also of the
pastors of all churches and the representatives from each church on the Executive Board of the Associated Charities.
The boundaries of the wards are given
and the visitors are named according to
their wards. October 1, 1894, Mrs. H. L.
Boltwood was elected President; Mrs. J.
E. Scott, Vice-President; Mrs. C. J.
Whitely, Treasurer; Mrs. L. G. Wescott,
Secretary; Mrs. A. D. Sanders, Chairman
of the Visiting Committee, and Mrs. J. E.
Scott, Superintendent of the Sewing
School. Out of the sewing class for mothers had come a sewing class for children,
and Mrs. Strawbridge, a teacher of sewing, came out from the city on Saturday
afternoons to teach them. A regular systematic course of instruction was given,
which secured the interest of the children
and uniformity in the work. The children were required to come with clean
hands, faces and aprons. The receipts for
the year 1894 are reported at $1,630 and
the work of visiting the poor was much
more efficiently carried on because of the
division of labor. No help was given until
the homes had been visited and great
pains taken to ascertain the exact state of
the family.

The work of the different wards is interesting as showing where the greatest

needs were. In the First Ward 20 families were helped; in the Second, 6; in the
Third, 11; in the Fourth, 24; in the Fifth,
45; in the Sixth, 32; in the Seventh, 67;
and in North Evanston, 47.

At the meeting of November 21st, in
order to have some uniformity in the distribution of groceries, the following rule
was adopted: "The following articles can
be ordered by the visitor: beans, potatoes
by the peck or half peck only, cheap coffee or tea in small quantities, sugar in
small quantities, corn-meal or oat-meal,
rice, salt, flour, laundry soap by the bar;
no meat, except in the case of sickness."

In 1895 occurs the last mention of the
Kitchen Garden, when it was decided to
donate the material used in the instruction
to the Northwestern University Settlement of Chicago. At the annual meeting
it was reported that there had been received $831 and that $795 had been disbursed. The President reported over 1,500
garments, the value of which is not included in the money receipts. Of these,
the new garments were contributed by the
Needlework Guild. At this meeting Mrs.
Brewer was elected President, Mrs. Boltwood, Vice-President, Mrs. Sanders, Secretary, and Mrs. Whitely, Treasurer, with
representatives from each of the churches.

In 1896 the German Catholic Church reported that it would care for all its poor
and needy, and any Catholics applying to
the Associated Charities were almost sure
to be unworthy. This lessened the field
for the society. At the annual meeting of
1896 Mrs. J. E. Scott was made President
and Mrs. Cragin, Secretary, with Vice-
Presidents representing the different
churches as usual. The winter of 1896
opened early and the women began casting about for means to employ the men
and women who applied for aid that they
might earn the relief that was granted

them. October 28th, at a meeting in the Congregational Church, Rev. Mr. Southgate was asked to be present and he spoke of the possibility of arranging such work for both men and women. A wood yard was proposed for the men where they could saw and split wood and a work room for women, where, under a superintendent, they could be instructed in repairing and making garments, receiving either clothing or provisions as compensation. After this talk a committee was appointed to see the city officials, and to ask them to help in establishing a wood yard. The report of this committee was given at the next meeting and was very favorable. The Mayor offered to furnish work and a superintendent to supervise it, the wood being obtained by cutting off the piles of the old Davis Street pier. A great deal of cleaning was secured in the public schools during this winter for the women, an arrangement which worked well in both directions—making the recipients of the city's charity feel that they had earned it, and making the schools much more sanitary and wholesome for children. Twenty-eight men were employed on the streets of Evanston. The new plan instituted this year, of requiring work from all the able-bodied who had been assisted, proved very successful, the records showing that only three persons refused to work, and that many had expressed their satisfaction at being allowed to do so. This year it is recorded that over 1,200 visits were made by the visitors of the Society.

At the annual meeting of 1897, Mrs. William M. Green was made President; Mrs. J. L. Whitlock, Vice-President; Mrs. S. G. White, Secretary; and Mrs. Joseph Lyons, Treasurer. It was decided to give no assistance to the able-bodied this year without its equivalent of work, and two

rooms in the City Hall were given to ladies for their use as a distributing center.

From this time on the work of the Associated Charities runs in regular grooves, well organized, systematized, and admirably accomplished. The next year Mrs. Whitlock was made President and has served in that capacity up to the present writing. The records show the increasing use of the plan of no aid without services rendered, and the number of unworthy applicants has been reduced to almost nothing. With the aid of the visiting nurse, the sick poor have been cared for; the homeless old people have been put into proper institutions or sent to their own people in more or less distant places; children have been clothed and fed and kept in school; and any one who wishes to give to the relief work in the city can do so with every assurance that his contribution will be wisely and carefully administered. The work of the Associated Charities has shown an increasing co-operation with the other forces of the town that make for the comfort of the needy and for righteousness. The Supervisor, the Chief of Police, the Officer of the Humane Society, the Probation Officer, the Associated Charities, the Hospital, the Visiting Nurse, and the Needle Work Guild, have so interwoven their advice, their special knowledge of needs and their means of relief, that the best results have been obtained. The work of soliciting funds is still done by the representatives of different churches on the Board, and the successful efforts of the officers of the Society to secure work supplement these actual money donations. At the annual meeting of the twentieth anniversary of the founding of the Society (1903), the Secretary reported that the work of the Society began early on account of the prevalence of smallpox in the city. Nearly all the afflicted families were those of laborers who were necessarily kept from their work and, in some cases, the fathers were the only nurses for wives and children. The Society furnished an abundance of clothing suitable for the sick, and when this was destroyed upon the recovery of the patients, furnished still other outfits. But this is the only epidemic which the Society has had to contend with. Seventeen hundred and sixty garments, old and new, were distributed this year. The report closed with these words: "If success is measured by activity and conscientious effort, this year deserves to be placed in line with those preceding it."

St. Vincent De Paul Society.—In 1887 the Evanston branch of the St. Vincent de Paul Society was organized and became auxiliary to the great Catholic Society of the same name three or four years later. This society is composed of men in the Catholic Church who are devoted to the relief of distress, the care of the sick and the burying of the dead. It is unique in Evanston in being a society composed of men, aided, when necessary, by an auxiliary society of ladies. It is non-sectarian in its work, aiding any cases of distress, although later, after time for investigation, if found to be non-Catholic, the case is turned over to the proper church or institution.

It co-operates with the Visiting Nurse and the Associated Charities and the ladies of the auxiliary are members of the Needle Work Guild, their contribution to the Association being returned to them for distribution by this Society. It has raised in money about $4,700 in the last seventeen years, although one of its fundamental principles is never to give money directly, preferring to furnish provisions and, if possible, to aid the recipi-

ent in earning the assistance. In many cases the women so aided have been glad of the opportunity to pay for it by scrubbing and cleaning in the parochial school and the church. This is a society which seldom makes public reports but prefers to do its work without the sound of trumpets. The society has been served by the same officers since its founding: Mr. Daniel McCann, President; Mr. Cullen, Secretary.

The Woman's Club.—Although the Woman's Club was founded in 1889 for social and literary purposes, the organization was very early interested in philanthropic work, since so many of its members were interested in particular charitable enterprises and sought the opportunity to lay them before the Club and seek its support. In 1891 before the Club was divided into departments (as it was later), there was a meeting well remembered by the old members, when Mrs. A. L. Butler spoke on behalf of the need of a hospital in this community. Her plea for the sick amongst the poor and helpless and the strangers in our midst was so touching, that it was immediately determined by the Club to endeavor to raise money to help found a hospital. A committee was appointed with Mrs. Joseph Hubbart Chairman, and it was determined to give a kirmess, the plans for which were minute and, at the same time, elaborate and kept the ladies of the town busy the entire summer preparing for it. A most successful kirmess was held, continuing for five afternoons and evenings and netting a sum of $3,500, which was handed over to the Hospital Board, which had already acquired a small property, for hospital purposes.

Later Mrs. H. W. Rogers made a plea in behalf of the Kindergarten of the

Northwestern University Settlement, and $100 was appropriated from the club funds to apply on the rental of better rooms for the children. When, after eight years of service as President of the Club, Mrs. Harbert refused a renomination, it was decided by the Executive Board to recognize her long and faithful service to the Club by making some gift in her name which should be a source of comfort and blessing to humanity. A drinking fountain, properly inscribed, was erected on Grand Avenue, near the corner of Union Street, in a neighborhood where no such convenience existed and where thousands pass every day. While this token of appreciation was not erected in Evanston itself, it is none the less one of the expressions of brotherly love that Evanston feels for the great neighboring city.

About this time the records show the formation of a separate department in the Woman's Club to be called the Philanthropic Department, the purpose of which was to give the members special opportunities for the study of philanthropy and sociology and to enable them to work more directly in the interests of any charitable project that they chose. The very first record of this department showed an appropriation of $150 for the benefit of the Kindergarten of the Northwestern University Settlement, the Vacation Schools, Probation Officer, and Visiting Nurse. These appropriations vary in amount, but invariably they result in an empty treasury which was refilled by entertainments, lecture courses, readings, and various such methods of raising money, besides individual pledges and dues of the members. Many noted speakers and workers in charitable and philanthropic fields appeared before the department, and its members were thus educated in the idea of scientific, organized charity, and were made acquainted with the needs of all kinds of endeavor.

One of the most interesting of the purposes for which this department has worked is that of the Probation Officer maintained by funds raised in Evanston through the efforts of members of this department, from September 1, 1900, to May 1, 1903, under the chairmanship of Mrs. W. O. Dean. The records of January 31, 1902, refer to a meeting held at the house of Mr. H. B. Hurd, where Mr. Hurd and Miss Clark, a probation officer in Chicago, related the history of the Juvenile Court Bill, told of the work of the court and of the probation officers. This bill was drawn by Mr. Hurd and went into operation July 1, 1899. In three years previous to the opening of the Juvenile Court, there were 1,705 children (that is, boys) under sixteen years of age in the county jail, while in the three years following the opening of the court, there were but forty-eight. Fourteen hundred and seven of the cases of delinquent children, out of 2,854 heard in the year 1902, were placed in charge of a probation officer, and these are the very pivot of the success of the law. The formation of the law itself removes children from the police stations and from jail; but it is the faithful, patient work of the probation officer which makes this removal of real value to the child. These facts appealed to the members of the department so strongly, that, after supporting an officer of the Children's Aid Society for a time, as a probation officer of this court, they finally took entire charge directly of one probation officer (Miss Clark) and paid her salary until it was necessary for her to resign her work. Up to the present time, the minutes of the Philanthropic Department show a constant interest in this work, and it is noted in one place that during that year seven children from Evanston had been taken before the Juvenile Court. This care of neglected children is not only a charitable work but one of real economy.

The visiting nurse has been aided directly and indirectly in the discharge of her labors. The management of her work lies in the hands of a committee chosen from this department, and monthly statements of her work, with detailed information about the individual cases, are regularly given. Any special need which the nurse finds for medicine, clothes, or delicacies for the sick are always met on appeal to this department.

The Needle Work Guild.—The Needle Work Guild of Evanston was organized in 1892 as a branch of the Needle Work Guild of America. Mrs. Charles Hamill, of Chicago, came to Evanston upon the invitation of Miss Nina Lunt, to meet the ladies of Evanston at the house of Mrs. Arthur Orr, and by her enthusiastic presentation of the work of this society, persuaded the ladies present to organize. Miss Lunt was made Honorary President, Mrs. Frank Wilder President, and Mrs. C. F. Bradley Secretary, but no records were kept of the work of the first two years. The purpose of the Needle Work Guild is to collect and distribute new, plain, suitable garments to meet the great need of hospitals, homes, and other charities, and permits each branch to elect its own beneficiaries. At the annual meeting of the Guild in November, 1896, the following officers were elected: Honorary President, Miss Lunt; President, Mrs. J. E. Scott; Treasurer, Miss Sarah W. Gillett; Secretary, Miss Ethel Grey. Sectional Presidents to the number of twenty-one were appointed, as follows: Mrs. Connell, Mrs. Chapin, Mrs. Shum-

way, Mrs. Clark, Mrs. Brooks, Mrs. Stevens, Mrs. Whitely, Mrs. Fabian, Mrs. W. J. Littlejohn, Mrs. Gallop, Miss Hoge, Miss Harrows, Mrs. Hanford, Mrs. Ward, Mrs. Isbester, Mrs. Magill, Mrs. Murphy, Mrs. O'Connell, Mrs. Howard Gray, Mrs. J. C. Connor, and Mrs. J. E. Scott. The number of garments gathered at this meeting is not stated in the records.

At the meeting of 1897 the officers of the last year were re-elected. The garments were distributed as follows: To St. Vincent de Paul Society, 152; Evanston Hospital, 187; Girls' Industrial School, 150; special cases, 266; Associated Charities, 1,053—Total, 1,810.

At the annual meeting in 1898, the garments were distributed as follows: To the visiting nurse, 398; Girls' Industrial School, 217; The Evanston Hospital, 141; Old Ladies' Home, 67; Associated Charities, 944; special cases, 43; St. Vincent de Paul Society, 163—Total, 1,973.

At the annual meeting in 1899 the garments were distributed to the same beneficiaries as the year before, with the addition of the King's Daughters' Fresh Air Home, which, by that time, had been established in Evanston. At this time there were 1,560 garments completed. At the annual meeting in 1900, the same list of beneficiaries were maintained, and a total of 1,574 garments were distributed. In 1901, with the same board of officers, 1,684 garments were distributed. At the election of officers in 1902, Miss Hempsted was elected Secretary and Mrs. C. T. Connell was made Honorary Presirent. This year the total number of garments collected was 1,256. At the annual meeting of 1903, Mrs. T. P. Stanwood was elected President, the other officers remaining the same. The number of garments collected this year was 1600.

The total money receipts during these

years was $198, and it has been the annual custom, after deducting the dues for membership in the National Society for the Needle Work Guild, to contribute nearly the balance to the Visiting Nurse fund.

Mother's Club of Noyes Street.—In 1896 a group of mothers and teachers gathered in the rooms of the Noyes Street School House, to talk over the needs of the neighborhood. It was found that there were many children attending that school who were poorly clothed and whose mothers, from illness or poverty, were not able to provide as they would for their children. An informal sort of a neighborhood society grew up, which, at first, devoted itself to supplying those needs of the people which were evident to the eyes of the teachers, and all mothers of the neighborhood were invited to join. The club met by permission of the School Board in the school building and made over and renovated all garments that were contributed. There developed a feeling of friendliness and neighborliness which carried the work of helpfulness into the homes, and at the occasional evening meetings which were held in the school house, entertainment in the form of music, readings, and lectures was freely given and enjoyed by the fathers, mothers, and young children of the neighborhood. Christmas trees were contributed and decorated, and from year to year it was so managed that the gifts on the tree were largely the manufacture of the children for each other and for their fathers and mothers.

From the first the desire to help others has been a conspicuous characteristic of this neighborhood club, and for seven years it has been the custom of the women to invite from 300 to 350 women and children from the city, from the least favored quarters, to an all-day's picnic on the lake shore in Evanston. These mothers and children have been brought out, entertained, fed and returned to their homes in entire safety and at the expense of the treasury of the Mother's Club.

A knitting machine owned by the Woman's Club of Evanston has been for several years in the home of one of the members of this Mothers' Club. On it she has knit the legs of nearly 500 pairs of stockings which have been footed by the mothers who knew how to knit, at the regular meetings of the club. In one year this Club has distributed 1,000 garments, including these stockings.

Visiting Nurse Association.—In the year 1897 a mother, who had been recently bereaved, felt that she would like to do something in the name of her daughter for other mothers who were trying to care for sick children. She called a few women who were experienced in the charity work of the city into consultation, and asked their advice as to the need of a visiting nurse among the sick poor of Evanston. The women were unanimous in believing that there was much suffering and sickness which could be relieved by the visits that such a nurse could give, and upon their advice Mrs. McMullen offered a sum of money sufficient to keep a nurse at work for four months, as a memorial to her daughter. Miss Faltz, a trained nurse, was chosen to inaugurate the work and, going about the town from north to south and far out on the prairie, she found plenty of work to keep her busy.

So impressed were the women who had been consulted in the matter with the success of the experiment, that they decided that this beautiful work must not be allowed to stop, and there was organized the Visiting Nurse Association of Evanston. Mrs. C. H. Chandler was made President and served in this position until her death in 1903. Mrs. P. C. Lutkin was made Secretary and Treasurer, and is still serving in that capacity. Mrs. C. F. Grey, Mrs. R. B. McMullen, Mrs. R. H. Wyman, Mrs. J. C. Bundy, Mrs. T. P. Stanwood, Mrs. O. F. Carpenter, Mrs. T. K. Webster are among those who have served on this Association, but the devoted, intelligent, increasing attention paid by Mrs. Chandler and Mrs. Lutkin have been the real backbone of these years of its work. It would be a beautiful thing if the Visiting Nurse could be endowed in memory of Mrs. Chandler.

Only one nurse has been employed and she has been maintained by friendly gifts of money. She visits among the sick poor, carrying out the orders of the physician, if one is employed, bathing and caring for mother and babe in maternity cases, dressing wounds, cuts, burns and bruises, making poultices for pneumonia, and giving instructions in cleanliness and sanitation. Where a case proves too severe for care at home, she recommends it to the hospital where the response has been most generous.

Besides this care of the actual sick, the services of this nurse are invaluable in the prevention of the spread of infectious diseases. Many families, feeling unable to call a physician, will ask for the services of the Visiting Nurse, and she is often able to decide that a case, which seems simple to an ignorant father and mother, is really a danger to the community. Several cases of scarlet fever, in different years, have been so discovered and isolated and the possibility or probability of the spread of these diseases through the schools, where other children of the same family were in attendance, has been avoided.

Besides rendering assistance as a trained nurse, the endeavor is made to treat each individual case as its peculiar necessities seem to demand, giving help in time of greatest need and saving the small wage-earner, so far as possible, from the worry of debt and discouragement consequent upon severe illness. It is just at this point that co-operation between the Associated Charities and the Visiting Nurse Association has been most valuable. This sympathetic aid is looked upon as the larger part of the nurse's work. The nurse goes everywhere within the limits of Evanston free of charge, except where patients prefer to pay a small fee. At first the nurse was able to go about on her bicycle during the large part of the year, but it was found that this mode of conveyance exhausted her strength and unfitted her for much of the arduous labor that she is called upon to perform. The necessity for providing a carriage of some sort has increased the cost of maintaining this charity somewhat. The Visiting Nurse Association is made up chiefly of members of the philanthropic department of the Woman's Club, and monthly reports of its work are given this department, but the department is not able to maintain the charity, and aids it only so far as its funds make it possible.

Miss Faltz was the Visiting Nurse in Evanston from November 1, 1898, to November 1, 1902. In the year 1898 she made 2,105 calls, and the expense for the year was $661.62. In 1899 she made 1,710 calls at an expense of $915.23. In 1900 she made 2,035 calls and the expense was $1,293.90. On November 1, 1901, Miss Brown took Miss Faltz's place and continued the work until December 1, 1902. In 1901 there were 2,361 calls, costing $1,274.80. December 1, 1902, Miss

Warren took up the work and, in that year, made 2.505 calls, and the expense was $1,341.85. In 1903 the Nurse made 2,554 calls and the expense was $1,312.50. In 1904 the Nurse made 2,608 calls and the expense was $1,350.75.

In cases of protracted illness, which for any reason cannot be carried to the hospital, the Association sends a special nurse to take charge of the case. The money is solicited by means of a little circular, which is issued each year and sent by post to the people of Evanston. Kindly disposed friends have many times given special entertainments for the benefit of this fund, and some particularly fine dramatic entertainments have been given by the dramatic department of the Country Club. The little circular bears on its face the significant words: "I was sick and ye visited me." "Inasmuch as ye have done it unto one of the least of these, my brethren, ye have done it unto me."

King's Daughters. — The Evanston King's Daughters Society was founded by Mrs. Daniel B. Gardner in 1893, the first membership consisting of ten young women of Evanston who wished to devote some time to charity work. Mrs. Lucian Harding was the first President, and the first work undertaken was the support of a bed in the Burling Street Half Orphan Asylum, which is still maintained by the King's Daughters. A few years later it was decided to open a fresh-air home in North Evanston for the poor working girls of Chicago, and this has continued to be the chief work of the Circle up to the present day.

The King's Daughters own their home at 2339 Hartzell Street, North Evanston, for which they paid $3,000. This money was raised chiefly by the management of a golf club during several years, and

also by donations from generous friends. About one hundred girls from Chicago are given a two weeks' outing every summer, the home being open generally fourteen weeks at an annual expense of about $500. The money to carry on the summer's work in the home is raised each winter by the King's Daughters in various ways. The receipts for the last year show a candy sale and musicale as sources of income, as well as the membership fees from active and associate members.

The society is now incorporated and the active membership is limited to fifty. There is an associate membership of 123 well known citizens of Evanston, who pay one dollar annually for the support of the home. The annual report just published at this writing shows the election of the following board of officers: President, Miss Mary Manson; Vice-President, Mrs. George Peaks; Corresponding Secretary, Miss Alma McDonald; Recording Secretary, Mrs. Elmer M. Scott; Treasurer, Miss Hoge; with Mrs. Fred P. Vose and Miss Daisy Fansler, Directors. The receipts for the year have been $757 and the disbursements $505, which leaves the society in a good financial condition.

Camp Good Will. — A meeting was held in the rooms of the Young Men's Christian Association on Monday evening, March 12, 1900, to listen to Mr. Charles F. Weller, Superintendent of the West Side District of the Bureau of Associated Charities of Chicago, who called attention to the great benefit of giving to the poor mothers and children, living in the unsanitary and crowded parts of the city, some relief during the hot summer months. Mr. Weller explained the purpose and method of the Camp Good Will at Oak Park, which has been in successful operation for three years. Three members of the executive committee of that Camp were present and gave interesting details.

The meeting manifested hearty interest in the work, and it was thought that, if this humane enterprise were fully brought to the attention of the people of Evanston, it would be supported and carried through to complete success. Accordingly it was voted to issue a call for another meeting, to be held at the rooms of the Young Men's Christian Association on Monday evening, March 26th, at 8 o'clock. Mr. Weller was present with stereopticon views of life in the congested wards of Chicago, and contrasting views of the Summer Camp at Oak Park. Mr. A. H. Standish, Secretary and Treasurer of the Camp, was present and furnished information.

All the Churches, the Clubs and the Associated Charities of Evanston were invited to attend, with a view to definite action and organization, if, upon consultation, the work was approved and undertaken. The call for this meeting was signed by the following: J. F. Loba, D. D., B. A. Greene, D. D., J. L. Whitlock, Julia M. E. Hintermeister, Committee; with W. L. Cobb, Chairman and C. B. Foote, Secretary.

The different aspects of country and city life for the poor were brought vividly before an audience by Mr. Chas. F. Weller in 1900. After some informal discussion, on motion of A. W. Kimball, it was voted that "this meeting is cordial in its support of this movement, and enthusiastically recommends it."

It was voted to begin the organization of a summer camp by appointing a General Council to consist of two from each of the churches there present, and further that each of the Evanston Churches be asked to send two representatives to a meeting to be held on Monday evening,

April 2d, to complete this organization. Mr. A. W. Kimball and Mr. F. H. McCulloch were appointed members of the Executive Committee from the First Congregational Church; Mr. D. D. Thompson and Mr. C. O. Boring from the Emmanuel M. E. Church; Mr. C. K. Pittman and Mr. J. R. Guilliams from the Church of all Souls. The First Baptist Church was represented by two members who promised delegates to this committee for the next meeting, and communications were reported from the pastors of the First Presbyterian and South Presbyterian Churches, expressing sympathy with the work and a desire to help. Votes of thanks were given Mr. Weller and Mr. Standish, and also to Prof. Nichols of South Evanston, who furnished and operated the stereopticon.

Those who were interested in the project of establishing Camp Good Will in Evanston were glad to learn that its success was assured. At a meeting held Monday evening a permanent organization was effected, with A. W. Kimball as Chairman; F. D. Raymond, Treasurer; and C. B. Foote, Secretary. The following committees were also appointed: Grounds—A. W. Kimball, F. P. Crandon, J. R. Guilliams; Plans—J. R. Guilliams, Dr. B. A. Greene, Dr. J. F. Loba, Rev. J. W. Francis, Louis S. Rice; Finance— C. K. Pittman, J. L. Whitlock, F. D. Raymond, F. E. French, C. Poppenhusen. The following announcement was made:

"The camp will be opened in July and will continue for several weeks. It is hoped that, in that time, as many as 500 tired mothers with their children will have enjoyed a week of fresh air and sunshine, coming in sections of 100 at a time.

"The Bureau of Associated Charities of Chicago, through its friendly visitors, selects needy and deserving people, and experience has shown that their visit brings as much blessing as it gives. This was proved at Oak Park by the fact that the work was continued for three years and is still going on. It is an enterprise that will enlist the sympathy of the people of Evanston and all will have an opportunity to co-operate."

A meeting of the General Council was held at the rooms of the Young Men's Christian Association, Tuesday evening, May 8th, with Mr. A. W. Kimball in the chair. Nine members were present. Mr. C. Poppenhusen was appointed Secretary, pro tem., and minutes of the previous meeting were read and approved. Mr. J. Guilliams, Chairman of Committee on Selection of Grounds, reported they had in view a tract of ground which seemed to his Committee very desirable for the use of the Camp. The property belongs to the Northwestern University, and the chairman thought it would probably be available. A meeting of the Trustees of the University was to be held May 21st, at which time this matter was to be considered. This selection was approved.

The Finance Committee through Mr. C. K. Pittman, its chairman, advised having a union meeting of the churches on Sunday evening, May 27, if practicable, at the First Methodist Church, to be addressed by Franklin MacVeagh, President of the Chicago Bureau of Charities, and Mr. Charles F. Weller, Superintendent of the West Division of the Chicago Association. The plan was approved and Mr. Kimball was appointed to arrange for a public meeting as outlined.

The following plan of organization for the summer camp was presented by Mr. Guilliams: "We recommend the following additional committees, to have special executive duties, but under the instruc-

tion of and reporting to the Executive Committee: Commissary Committee; Entertainment Committee; Committee on Grounds and Tents (sanitary, etc.); these committees to be appointed from among the members of the General Council.

"There shall be an auditor of accounts appointed by the General Council, and that auditor shall not be a member of the Council.

"A resident superintendent, man or woman, satisfactory to the executive committee, shall be appointed, who shall have general supervision of all affairs of the camp, such as the cooking, laundry work, all needful sanitary rules and rules of behavior, etc., etc. And this superintendent shall be paid and shall engage the other paid servants, such as the cook, laundry workers, and any others found necessary; and the superintendent engaging these servants shall also discharge them, if need be, for any reason. But the superintendent shall report any such matters to the executive committee, if requested to do so. The superintendent also shall be under the authority of any committee having special executive functions, such as Committee on Tents and Grounds, Commissary Committee, etc. But these committees shall deal with the superintendent, and not with the servants and employes direct.

"The several churches shall each assume charge of the special needs of the camp, under the superintendent, or under any special committees that may be appointed—such needs as waiting on the table, pleasant social service and association and entertainment for the pleasure of the guests; and this responsibility shall be apportioned among the several churches according to their ability and willingness, so that one church may assume the special duty for one week, another for three days, and another for two days, etc.; and the manner in which each church shall discharge this responsibility, by committees, or in whatever way, shall be left to the arrangement of the church itself. It shall be the duty and power of the General Council to apportion and appoint the service and time of duty for each church, and the special time for each church shall be arranged and appointed in the beginning.

"All donations of food must be sent to the Commissary Committee, and not to the guests direct. This is a point that shall be exclusively under the daily control of the Superintendent acting under the Commissary Committee.

"The Executive Committee shall determine what, if any, shall be the order of the day in the Camp on Sunday, and what, if any, shall be the meetings held for religious purposes; but no one of the guests shall be obliged, or even urged beyond a kind invitation, to take part in any meeting or take part in any religious form, or assembly, or service.

"The General Council to have supreme power, except as to any limitations provided herein, and except that it must not take away or abridge the responsibility of any individual church once assumed and appointed, at the beginning or thereafter, without the consent of the church being first secured."

Promoters of Camp Good Will, which was to be established on the lake shore north of Sheppard field this summer, were more than pleased with the result of the appeal for funds made at a union mass meeting of all local churches, held in the First Presbyterian Church. More than $1,400 was raised by subscriptions. This amount was made more conspicuous to the camp enthusiasts by the fact that the

Oak Park outing camp, which has been so successful the last three years, started out with only $23 to back it.

The church was well filled when Dr. J. F. Loba, of the First Congregational Church, introduced C. F. Weller, Superintendent of the West Division office of the Chicago Bureau of Associated Charities, who gave an interesting talk about the slum districts on the West Side of Chicago. Stereopticon views of the wretched dwellings called home, the foul-smelling play-grounds of the children about garbage boxes in the ill-kept streets and alleys, and also of the transformation which takes place when the children are given fresh air and freedom in the Camp Good Will at Oak Park, were thrown upon the screen. He told of the methods which the different churches employed in caring for their charges when they assumed control. Each church would have charge of the camp for a week. The women of the church would wait on the Chicago mothers and children and do all the necessary work. The Evanston camp planned to follow the same plan, and hoped to do much more with such a bank account and the ideal location of the lake front. Dr. William Macafee and Rev. J. H. Boyd made short addresses, saying that the opportunity of showing practical Christianity had been offered to Evanston people in their joining in and pushing forward this new charitable movement.

A blackboard, with a number of small squares, each representing a subscription ranging from $5 to $50, was placed upon the platform. Dr. Loba auctioned these squares off until $1,000 was raised. Then slips were passed through the congregation and $400 more was promised. The committees and officers held meetings during the week and organized a plan of procedure. The camp was to open in July.

Camp Good Will is Open.—(July 11, 1900.)—"Evanston Camp Good Will opened this afternoon when the two chartered cars of the Chicago Street Railway company unloaded the 100 women and children, selected from the poor districts by the Bureau of Associated Charities. Those who will take part in this week's outing at the Camp gathered from the different poor districts at Madison and Halsted Streets, and were taken directly to Evanston.

"Camp Good Will is situated just north of the University grounds, and is on the lake shore, with the woods stretching to the north open for the children to romp in. One of the Evanston local Committeemen will have charge of the camp and will be assisted by members of the committees from the Evanston churches, who are the founders of the camp. The camp will last for five weeks, and each week 100 more women and children will be taken out to take the place of those who have had their week. Tents have been provided for the use of the campers. Each tent is supplied with two double-decked beds, making each tent capable of holding eight persons."

Report.—"Babies hold Sway. With the 120 guests who arrived yesterday afternoon at 5 o'clock at Camp Good Will, came sixteen children in arms. Baby carriages and high chairs are now in great demand. There is no time in the day when the babies' presence is not made well known, and these very young campers constitute the main attraction to the church women. Exclamations as (too · cute for anything), (how cunning!) and (the little dear) were heard on all sides.

"That's a pretty good speech." This was the opinion of a ten-year-old camper advanced to Superintendent Riddle, when the latter had tried to impress some salient point of good conduct upon the little fellow. The culprit is inclined to be tough, it is said.

"It was announced in the local churches Sunday, that more blankets were necessary for the comfort of the Camp Good Will visitors. The result of the appeal has not been so favorable as wished. The hospital loaned many coverings, but came after them today. This leaves the "Good Willers" subject to the cold breezes from the lake on stormy and chilly nights.

"The First Methodist Church assumed control of the camp this week. The Congregationalists are ready to receive congratulations on their efficient and painstaking management of the initial week's camp. Dr. William Macafee will lead the song service in the assembly tent tonight. The usual program of kindergarten and mothers' meeting in the morning, and the carriage riding and bathing in the lake in the afternoon, was carried out today.

"Charles F. Weller, Superintendent of the West Side Division of the Chicago Bureau of Associated Charities, had a narrow escape from an infuriated mob of Italians yesterday. Mr. Weller selects the most deserving families to be given an outing in the summer camp and, in the course of his rounds, takes down the number of members in each family. In the Italian district he had chosen enough families to aggregate twenty-five persons according to their own count, but when they made their appearance for transportation the surprised Superintendent counted forty expectant persons. He asked an explanation and soon found that the mothers had failed to name all their children for fear they would not be selected. Some of the families had to be sent home again, and the fathers became angry. They threatened all kinds of vengeance, and it looked as though a mad rush would be made for Mr. Weller, but the latter succeeded in quieting the foreigners and a possible riot was averted.

Report of the Treasurer.

```
Promotion: prospectus, expense of union meeting.$  52 15
General Expense: stationery, printing, postage...   11 85
Preparing Camp: sewerage, plumbing, tent floors 289.47
Hire of tents, cots and bedding..................  321.50
Equipment, utensils, towels, bathing suits.......   64.68
Transportation: car fares........................   74.95
Superintendence and Labor: wages of Superinten-
   dent, cook and help; Superintendent's travel-
   ing expenses .. ............................ .  148.75
Entertainments, stereopticon, etc................   16.00
Incidental expenses, lighting supplies, etc........   42 45
Provisions: tea, coffee, sugar, butter, eggs, po-
   tatoes, soap, ice, bread, milk................  309.95
                                               _____
   Total expenses, paid from general fund......$1,320.75
Subscriptions, paid ...................$1,165.80
Subscriptions, unpaid ................    25 00
Discounts on bills ..................    40 15
Plumbing returned .................:....    34.00
Lumber sold ......................    50.00
Deficit ..........................     5.80
                               _____
                                           $1,320.75
                              F. D. RAYMOND,
                                          Treasurer.
```

"Camp Good Will, which was such a feature for good in Evanston last summer. is to be continued. During July and August last year, five hundred and eighty-five mothers and children enjoyed a weeks' vacation—a bright spot in many a weary life—in Camp Good Will.

"The eminent success of last year's work, the ease with which it was done, the liberality and interest of many citizens, and the unbounded joy of both guests and hosts make it a pleasure again to undertake this noble work. Much property has been left over which will materially reduce the cost of inauguration, and, with the same generous support and effort, it is certain that this year will be a far greater success than the first attempt."

"Moved by a deep conviction that this work is building where needed, and that its report is not alone to be found in benefit to the present, but also to future generations, those people who carried it forward last summer are to engage in it again this summer, and through the gen-

erosity of the Trustees of the Northwestern University, the use of the grounds had last year is to be had again for the camp this year.

"On next Sunday, June 16, at 7:45 o'clock in the evening, a general mass meeting will be held in the interest of this work in the First Presbyterian Church in Evanston. The Rev. Professor Graham Taylor, of the Chicago Theological Seminary, and who is head resident of the Chicago Commons, will address the meeting."

"An illustrated lecture will be given by Mr. James Minnick. Superintendent of the West Side Division of the Chicago Bureau of Associated Charities, during which views depicting the home life and the surroundings of the poor of Chicago will be shown.

"It is hoped that all of Evanston's citizens who did not join in the work of last year will do so this year, and through the undersigned, the organization having the matter in hand extends an invitation to all to attend the meeting."

The appeal is signed by J. R. Guilliams. First Vice-President: Charles B. Foote, Secretary: Joseph F. Ward, Treasurer.

The result of this appeal was so encouraging that, on June 18th, an announcement was sent to each church stating that the camp would open on Wednesday noon, July 10th, and continue for five weeks. Permission to use the same beautiful grounds was granted by the Trustees of Northwestern University, and the Superintendent of the preceding years, Mr. J. R. Riddle, who had proved most wise and efficient, agreed to act again in the same capacity. The experience of former years was repeated in giving rest and joy to groups of many women and children and the money collected through the churches was entirely adequate for all purposes. The cost of maintenance was practically the same as that of the preceding year—i. e., $1,320. The camp has now become a regular feature of the summer life of Evanston, and those who participate in its service feel that those residents who are in the habit of spending their summers elsewhere lose a privilege and satisfaction that they can hardly estimate. The past three summers have seen the work conducted in the same systematic and hearty way as at first, although since every church now contributes service, the period that each church serves is shorter than it was during the first year. In 1903, Mr. Crosby was the Superintendent, but in 1904, Mr. J. B. Riddle resumed the task for which he is so admirably fitted.

In 1903, at the request of Miss Addams of Hull House, the camp was kept open one week longer and boys' clubs of Hull House and Northwestern University Settlement were entertained. This increased the cost of that year to $2,124. The same plan was carried out during the summer of 1904, and everyone interested in the work of the camp rejoiced in helping to extend its services for this additional week. It is easy to maintain discipline where the privilege of living in the camp is so highly esteemed, and the experience of a few unruly boys in being sent home has been sufficient to hold any temptation to waywardness in check. The Evanstonians who have waited on their guests of Camp Good Will at table, entertained them in the evening, talked to the mothers in the informal Mothers' meetings, led the children in kindergarten games, songs and occupations, or given personal service in any way, have received far more of blessing than they have given. We cannot all go to Chicago to work in the neglected and forlorn places for the downtrodden and hopeless, but Camp Good Will brings them to us, and the cordial response that has been given to appeals for money and service to maintain this summer outing proves that Evanston welcomes the opportunity. "Thou shalt be served thyself by every sense of service that thou renderest."

CHAPTER XLI.

SOCIAL LIFE IN A UNIVERSITY TOWN
(By EMILY HUNTINGTON MILLER)

Transitions of a Half Century—Social Life as It Existed in Early Days—The Building up of a Great Christian Institution as Its Dominant Motive—Reminiscences of Some of Its Early Factors—Influence of Hospitality on Student Life and Character—Some of Those Who Were Influential in Establishing Evanston's Reputation as a Hospitable Center.

It would be a difficult, if not an impossible thing, to present from individual impressions the spirit of social life in the University to-day. Society is no longer a unit, but broken up into a multitude of groups; and its aspect, as in any community, will differ with the point of view held by the observer, or the special development noted.

But looking back to the early days of the University, one finds, among the witnesses who shared and helped to create its social life, a practical unanimity of sentiment. To some extent most of them agree in the opinion expressed by one of their number—

"I am reminded of the sentence with which the writer of an encyclopædic article on 'Owls in Ireland' introduced his disquisition: *'There be no Owls in Ireland.'* "

Social life as an end certainly did not exist in those first strenuous days, when the University was Evanston, and the noble ambition which dominated every other purpose, and united all her citizens in a bond of brotherhood, was the hope of building up a great Christian institution that should be an opportunity, an invitation, and an incentive to a multitude of young men whom the older universities could never reach.

Naturally, in the days of its small beginnings, when faith and courage and energy were taxed to the utmost, many things seemed of more vital consequence than any special provision for the social instincts. But the greatest charm of that early fellowship was its purely instinctive character; the shining out of a spirit of friendliness that took little thought for any formal expression.

Making reasonable allowance for the mellowing effect of distance, and for the happy illusion through which memory shows "the days that are no more," there is still sufficient testimony to the idyllic character of that early life to justify the declaration of one who shared it:

"No doubt there were hardships and deprivations and necessary crudities, but, as I look back upon it, it seems to me like Eden, in its peace, and simplicity, and good-fellowship; people of every denomination worshiping together in one church, and living like one family; old and young meeting in friendly intercourse by hearth and fireside, and counselling together for that

425

which most concerned us all, the welfare of the students and the prosperity of the University."

There seems no more effective way of presenting the salient features of a society that was only impressive because of its spirit, than by employing the old class-meeting methods of that day, and calling up individual testimonies.

The University owes to its comparative youth the happy possibility of summoning a few such witnesses, even for its very earliest times, though year by year the calling of the roll brings fewer responses, and much that might have illuminated this record has passed beyond our reach.

The writer is especially indebted for valuable material to Mrs. Harriette S. Kidder, whose clear and comprehensive recollection of the time is fortunately supplemented by her diary, and who, to-day in her eighty-fourth year, is a beautiful example of spiritual and mental vigor.

"Of course I knew largely what was passing in Evanston in its earliest days, and was deeply interested in all that concerned it. It seemed to me there never was a better opportunity offered to build up 'a model community. As the families that settled there came from different localities, and were strangers to each other, they were ready to respond to any movement that would bring them into closer social relations. I was deeply impressed with the idea that, in this rural place, we need not take for our standard all the customs that were perhaps best suited to city life and a more mixed society. Since we were generally intelligent Christian people, we might be really fraternal in our social relations. So, for myself, I made it a rule to call upon every new family that came to Evanston, and to invite them, as opportu-

nity offered, to a place at my table and a share in our social intercourse.

"Many of us who were connected with the University went to Evanston because of our deep interest in the training of the young people who were to be drawn there by these schools, founded for their benefit, and we felt that, away from their own home influences, congregated in clubs or scattered through the village, they needed to be brought under the influence of our homes and such home-association as we could give them. As their number was for several years comparatively small, we could invite them in a social way, providing rational entertainment, and thus a strong bond of union between students and citizens was formed that was valuable to both parties.

"The instructors of the young men who were to mingle among the people as ministers of the gospel, felt it specially important that they should share the social life of the community, as a necessary part of the training for their work. So there were gatherings in the homes of the professors, bringing together, in a social way, students, teachers, trustees and citizens. At these gatherings, after a substantial supper was served, there was singing, sometimes short talks, and always prayer before separating. In all the social gatherings of that day we met early, and generally left before eleven o'clock. I doubt if any community ever enjoyed a more delightful social life. The six or eight families of the professors often took dinner together in each other's homes, and, as each of us had frequent visitors whom we wished others to enjoy, they were introduced into our social circle in this neighborly way. This simple form of social life was a striking feature of our community for several years, and people outside of our church, who had only known more formal society and more elaborate entertainments, seemed greatly to enjoy this friendly sort of home visiting."

Dr. Daniel Bonbright, whose memories cover the whole existence of the University, adds some vivid touches to the picture of its early days.

"In those first years, when the University counted in its catalogue scarcely fifty students, collective social life could hardly be said to have existed. There were, to be sure, two literary societies, and Greek letter fraternities in germ. These, in their way, must have been centers of association, but I doubt if they counted for much in the life of the student body as a bond or spur.

"There were no athletic games; public entertainments of any sort were rare and unimpressive. I recall the Cantata of Queen Esther. It was gotten up by the Sunday School as an event of pomp and circumstance. One can judge, from this example of the extraordinary, what must have been the average quality of the social satisfaction of the epoch.

"The families of the faculty were thoughtful of the students, as were also a good number of families in the village. One may hear from the older graduates grateful reference to hospitalities and cheer which they enjoyed from those sources during their student life. But housed as the students were at hap-hazard, in a community itself scattered and struggling, there could have been among them but feeble collective consciousness, and sense of a mutual life. I suspect there was little escape from lonely isolation, save in the self-forgetfulness of hard work, a recourse more in honor in that primitive age than in these piping times of merry-go-round, cigarette and song.

"As for social life in the faculty itself, including that of the Biblical Institute, there was nothing characteristic which would not

be implied by its constituent elements. The families were nearly all from New England, and brought with them the qualities of their birthright. They were people of education, intelligence and Christian sobriety. As your letter reminds me, cards and social dances were not yet; neither were Browning Clubs nor other idolatry. I remember only one coterie: I forgot what it called itself. (See Chapter XLII., on "Social and Literary Clubs," in this volume.) It was composed of gentlemen from the faculties of the University and Institute. They met, perhaps, once a fortnight, for the discussion of questions in religious philosophy. But they took their separate convictions too seriously for controversy. In the interest of good-will and harmony it was found safest to disband. The immediate occasion of the disruption, I believe, was the introduction of some explosive speculation by Dr. Dempster on the subject of the 'Eternal Now.'

"But the peaceful unity that prevailed, both in the schools and in the community around them, is illustrated by the fact that the entire Protestant population worshipped together, Sunday after Sunday, in the same church. Methodists, Baptists, Episcopalians, and the rest, they all listened to the Gospel proclaimed from the same pulpit; each, as in Apostolic times, hearing the word, as it were in his own tongue, wherein he had been born."

Probably no individual is more closely associated with memories of the University days in the thought of a great majority of its graduates, than Dr. Oliver Marcy. One can scarcely recall the older or the newer Evanston, the shaded streets, the classroom, or the campus, without seeing his fine patrician face, and his dignified figure with its impressive bearing of genial courtesy. The Marcy home was generously opened for the hospitalities of the University, and many of the early classes could testify to the readiness with which their attempts at class entertainment were helped out by placing its resources at their service.

Mrs. Marcy has furnished some recollections, beginning with the time of their coming to Evanston in 1862, a date at which it must have required a vivid imagination to speak gravely of the existing school as a University.

"When we came to Evanston things were in a very primitive condition, though about seven years before there had been a 'boom' in the settlement of the town. Dr. Kidder had built a commodious house, near what was then the center of the town, and his family had occupied it five or six years. They were leaders in hospitality, and no one came to town who was not soon made the recipient of their cordiality. Garrett Biblical Institute was well established, but though Dr. Dempster was its official head, there was no doubt Dr. Kidder's open doors were the magnet that drew the student body, as well as others who came to town, for Evanston itself is indebted in no small degree to the University for its early social life.

"I think it had been the habit of Mrs. Kidder to entertain, and she continued the practice so that, sooner or later, every member of the schools then in operation had been included. Some of the young men who underwent this initiation into society were, of course, not exactly up to date in matters of etiquette, and while appreciating the courtesy, sometimes dreaded the ordeal; but the hearty good-will with which they were received by old and young soon removed any sense of discomfort.

"The 'Female College' was then in the hey-day of its popularity, under the management of Professor Jones, who did his part to make it conspicuous in social happenings, making the most of his anniversaries, and inviting the '400' with a very liberal inclusiveness.

"Bishop Simpson lived here at that time, the greatest of our living preachers, a most genial and lovable man in his prime. Governor Evans was with us the first years, but soon left for Colorado. They were quite distinctive features of Evanston society in those early days. Mrs. Evans was a woman of superb presence, and the daughter, Josephine, a favorite among young people. Her wedding, which took place on the lawn between the house and the lake, was a notable event of the time.

"On the Ridge were Mr. Hurd, Mr. Kedzie and other families of position and character, who gave entertainments as they had probably been accustomed to do, and helped to maintain the cordial spirit of friendly interest and co-operation between the town and the University, although in that day no such distinction was ever thought of: we were all 'University people.'

"Mrs. Bragdon, at that time struggling with the effort to 'college her boys,' did not forget that her calling and election had been the care of the churches as a minister's wife, and interested herself in a sisterly way in every social scheme or kindly project.

"The history of our social life would be incomplete without reference to Professor Bonbright, who from the beginning watched over these interests in a most tactful manner, and without whose presence in those days no social function would have seemed complete. He not only made himself agreeable, but, in some sense, responsible, that the University influence should be brought to bear even in its social affairs, and nothing overlooked that might contribute to tone and popularity. I remember the brotherly way in which he used to discuss with me matters great and small, making the most valuable suggestions in his courteous deferential manner that always carried conviction with it.

"A score of worthy names arise in my memory of those whom the University might well delight to honor, because of their early ministry to its social well-being, but they had their reward in 'having served their day and generation,' and most of them have 'fallen on sleep.' "

Mr. Andrew J. Brown, the Secretary of the University's first Board of Trustees, and now the only surviving member of that board, brought his family at an early date to the little community and took an active interest in its development. Mrs. Brown adds to the history of the time some reminiscences:

"I should like to begin with my first impression of the village, that in 1866 formed the nucleus of the University, and was scarcely in thought separated from it. We were sitting upon the piazza at Dr. Bannister's, just at twilight, and the sweet sound of a hymn came to us. It was the hour of family prayer, and the melody was soon mingled with that from another home, until from the whole circle of firesides went up the voice of praise and prayer, the spirit of social fellowship giving a new power to individual worship. These two characteristics, Christian devotion and Christian fellowship, were the strong and impressive features of University life at that day.

"Though the number of students was comparatively small, we soon found that there were many lonely young men in town, and it was our practice, for many years, to invite to our tea-table on Sunday as many as chose to join us. There were many families where the students were most hospitably received, besides their own class

gatherings and receptions, and our ingenuity was sometimes taxed to the utmost to provide amusement for young people who might not indulge in card-playing or dancing. But, however strong may be the protest against church rules to-day, I do not think there ever was a happier time than when we were all held to their strict observance.

"We had at that time a most delightful society. Governor and Mrs. Evans had a beautiful home on the Lake Shore, always open to the young people. Dr. and Mrs. Bannister, Professor and Mrs. Godman, Professor Bonbright, Professor Blaney and his charming family, Colonel and Mrs. Eaton on the Ridge, the Pearsons with their unfailing interest in the students, Bishop Foster and his family so genial and gracious in their hospitality, Mr. and Mrs. Greenleaf, and Dr. and Mrs. Marcy—it seems invidious to mention names where the spirit of hospitality was universal. We were one great family whose highest aspiration was to build up this school, which was to rival Harvard in its literary standard, but set above all other learning, that knowledge of God which is the beginning of wisdom."

It would be interesting, as well as enlightening, if one could set beside these testimonials from what might perhaps be considered the governmental side of social life, the unbiased confessions of the party of the second part, now happily removed from the pressure of fear or favor, and learn exactly how things looked from the student point of view. It would, perhaps, be instructive to know whether the young man of that day felt the deep necessity of recreation, and yearned, though in a half conscious, unenlightened way, for foot-ball and track athletics.[1] One would like to discover what relief they themselves contrived for the social instincts, and what were the delights of class-socials and kindred dissipations. Such things there must have been even in the days when the simplest entertainments gave pleasure, and the young people were not burdened with bills for flowers, music and carriage-hire at their social parties.

One would like for the benefit of coming generations, to know how it was done, and how it was found practicable to maintain a rational balance between the pleasures of life and the serious duties of University work. But a mist seems to have gathered over the memories of those who might testify, and nothing definite is available. One of them indeed declares:

"In the days which I remember, it seems to me few persons had any respect for social functions as a part of any earnest life. I remember that President Foster had receptions, and Professor Noyes, Dr. Kidder, and others had 'evenings'—especially for married 'Bibs'—and that all the town seemed to swing about the students. But, so far as I know, the students themselves did nothing but grind and haunt the Female College."

Co-education, with its far-reaching complications, had not yet presented itself to trouble the placid counsels of trustees and faculty. Possibly some wise women already saw its Star in the East, but they dreamed only of a related college after the pattern that Radcliffe has since so successfully adopted. But the feminine nearness, even in purely unsympathetic institutions, is too intimately related to Dr. Dempster's "*Eternal Now*" to be lightly ignored.

The friendly homes that welcomed the students held daughters to whose presence they owed their attractions and humanizing influence, quite as much as to the

hospitable tea-table and the courtesies of more formal receptions. And the home society was amply supplemented by the Northwestern Female College, from whose incongruous title the Woman's College inherited its designation of "Fem. Sem." The students were ready to avail themselves of its friendly overtures for all established ceremonials, and, it may be surmised, found further opportunity in its halls and laurel groves, for which human nature was the only authority consulted.

The University, from the very outset, took its students as a trust, and made itself responsible for them in a measure far beyond the mere furnishing of opportunity for learning. In the days of its poverty nothing made this possible but the bond of sympathy and mutual interest between the University and the community outside of it. It is not easy to say how far the influence of an individual or an institution may have been effective in the shaping of community life, so many obscure and apparently unrelated forces go to determine its character. But looking back to those earliest days it seems reasonable to claim that Evanston owes much to the direction given its development when the University, laying its own foundations, laid those of the village also. Social fraternity, civic responsibility,

_____

[1] An interesting reminiscence of this period of the history of the University is that of Melville C. Spaulding, of the class of 1860, who relates the origin of athletics in the college:

"When we had about sixty students in the old building ('Old College') I solicited 10 cents each from the students—on the co-operative plan—and with the $6.00 in hand, created an out-door gymnasium (the first), the uprights, parallel bars, etc., being placed in the northwest corner of the college lot, and much use was made of the simple apparatus. This diminutive beginning or 'Commencement'—outlay, $6.00—sounds strange when contrasted with the proposed $50,000 gymnasium."—(Letter to the editor, May 9, 1904.)

and that broad religious sympathy which is far nobler than toleration, were fruits of the spirit springing naturally from seed sown in that day of small things.

The deep religious spirit that was so marked in its beginnings when one church sufficed for the whole community, found its natural outgrowth in later years, when the denominations had gathered each one into its own fold in practical Christian unity. Its spirit of brotherhood still survives in a disregard of social distinctions; its teaching of civic responsibility long held citizens of all persuasions to alliance for the public good irrespective of party politics, and the unwritten law which made brain and culture the stamp of its aristocracy rather than money and birth, has never been revoked.

It was inevitable that, with the expansion of the little rural village into the suburban city, its residents should become absorbed in diverse interests, and the prosperity of the University cease to be the ever present motive and ambition. The growth of the University itself from feebleness to strength tended to this change of sentiment, since the personal interest one might feel for a small body of students and instructors, with whom individual acquaintance was possible, could not exist when, in place of a little coterie of friends, one had to consider that vague impersonal thing—an institution.

But while it would be impossible to restore the simplicity and unity of early social life, it is most desirable for both town and University that the bond of sympathy between them should, in every way, be guarded and strengthened.

And in closing this chapter it may not be out of place to say, that to accomplish this end and re-establish this active interest in promoting University interests with a generation to which the earlier history is only an uncertain tradition, was the purpose for which the University Guild was organized, and which it seems, in some encouraging measure, to be attaining.

(The foregoing chapter is copied by permission of the publishers from the "Northwestern University. A History, 1855-1905," edited by Arthur Herbert Wilde, Ph. D., Assistant Professor of History in The College of Liberal Arts, Northwestern University.)

CHAPTER XLII.

SOCIAL AND LITERARY CLUBS
(By PROF. HOMER H. KINGSLEY)

A Reminiscence of Noah's Ark — Social Instincts of Evanstonians — Philosophical Association — Its Founders and Their Favorite Topics — The "O. R. Circle" Blossoms Out as the "Legensia" — Bryant Circle — Pierian Club — Woman's Clubs — The Fortnightly Succeeds the "Woman's Reading. Circle" — Its Service in the Field of Charity and Philanthropy — The Coterie — Twentieth Century and Present Day Clubs.

It is said that the coat of arms of the Montmorency family contains the picture of a servant with a box under his arm running after Noah's Ark, while a legend issues from his mouth expressing these words: "Make room for the archives of the Montmorency family!" Evanston is yet so young that the organization of all of her clubs is a matter of history. They are not like Melchizedec, "without father or mother, or table of descent." Fortunately in all of them we have official records of origin, purpose and, in many, of their final dissolution. This history can touch only the more pretentious clubs. An attempt to define the scope and to give the history of all the various church societies, neighborhood circles, social and card clubs, would use up the limits of this paper largely in their simple enumeration.

The social instincts of Evanstonians are much like those of any community. As soon as any neighborhood discovered that it contained a band of congenial spirits, it generally desired to form a club in order to give these instincts play and development. In the early days, when Evanston was smaller and when outside interests attracted less of the attention of business men and professional men; when the people on the Ridge knew the people on Forest Avenue; before the Evanston Club, the Boat Club, the Country Club, or any of the various whist clubs were organized; in the days when people took time to read and think and discuss, and not simply prophesy smooth things; back in the early '60s, in the days when the names of Bannister, Willard, and Kidder were household words in Evanston, a club of young women was organized known as the Iota Omega Club. The symbolic letters were believed to signify Independent Order; at least, the motto of the club—"No others need apply"—would seem to make it capable of that interpretation. This club was organized in 1860, and during its various vicissitudes and ramifications, it developed into, or was absorbed by, the Eclectic Society, the Social Club, and finally by the well known club of the present day, the Evanston Club. As this club is to have a separate chapter in this History, it is not necessary

423

to go more into detail in this account. Intellectual improvement and social enjoyment were the fundamental features of all of these clubs.

Perhaps the most pretentious club in Evanston's early days was the

Philosophical Association.—This club had enough importance to be incorporated, and received a charter from the Secretary of State, bearing date, February 28, 1867. Dr. Bannister was the father of the society, and a study of the list of subjects discussed shows that they were of no trifling nature, and were handled in no inferior manner. The records show that papers were discussed bearing such formidable titles as the following: "The Relation of the Unconditioned, the Absolute, and the Infinite to Human Faith and Knowledge"; "Is a Science of History Possible?" "Science, Religion and Theology"; "The Nature and Province of Instinct"; "Religious Controversy between Deism and Christianity." The foregoing are not specially selected subjects, but are taken at random from the records, and illustrate the fact that, in those early days, the men who discussed subjects did much original work, and did not rely upon the encyclopædia to inform them as to what some one else had said or done upon the subject in hand. Economics, Sociology, Political Economy, Electricity, Astronomy, Physics, Chemistry and pure Mathematics came in for a fair share of the discussion; in fact, it is not impossible to find men today who think the society might be still living if it had not been for its sensitiveness about having the tariff discussed. If this is a matter of history, it serves to show that the tariff is not entirely an unmixed good; for there ought to be a place in Evanston for a club which would discuss the more serious things of

life. It is, however, hardly to be expected that another club like this will ever exist in Evanston. The changes in theological thought and discussion in the last twenty-five years, perhaps a certain lack of seriousness in the present day life, the demands that are made on professional and business men, make it quite impossible to get together a set of men who could give time and energy to such subjects as the old Philosophical Association used to consider. The society had an existence of sixteen years, and finally disbanded after its meeting of February 13, 1882. During its period of prosperity, the society kept up, for a time, a course of free public lectures, and the public were frequently invited to hear papers of the members when such papers promised to be of more than ordinary interest or merit. The successive Presidents of the society were: Henry Bannister, Oliver Marcy, Francis Bradley, L. H. Boutell, F. D. Hemenway, Andrew Shuman, D. H. Wheeler, N. S. Davis, Miner Raymond, N. C. Gridley, J. G. Forest, H. S. Carhart, C. W. Pearson, H. F. Fisk.

Legensia Club.—Perhaps the next most important club in Evanston was "Legensia." The original name of this club was the O. R. Circle. This was the abbreviated way of writing "Our Reading Circle." It had its origin January 30, 1880. On that date a few congenial friends met at the home of Mr. and Mrs. H. B Cragin and formed a club whose object, as stated in its call, should be "the forming of a club for literary exercises, having in view both the profit and pleasure of its members." In a short time the name of the club was changed to "Legensia"—a name which was compounded by Professor J. Scott Clark from the last three syllables of Collegensia and the syllable leg from the Latin word *lego*, to read.

The development of this club was much like that of a child. It passed through its years of infancy, youth, maturity and decline. A study of its successive programs shows clearly the working out of those lines of work and thought which characterize childhood, youth and maturity. Its first notion was to meet and read something serious, then something light and humorous, and to have each program interspersed with some descriptions of people or places by members who might be qualified to speak along these lines. The club soon gave up this desultory work, and took up a line of work which had continuity and serious purpose in it. The Life and Works of Daniel Webster formed the theme of reading for the first year, and the Life and Letters of Ticknor the second year. At the beginning of the third year, Legensia began to show precocity by writing its own compositions. The biographical spirit was still rampant and strongly impressed the society, and accordingly all of the essays were biographical. No system obtained in the selection of authors, and there was a frisky skipping from Holmes to John Adams. Then Legensia took a run down to the sixteenth century, to Martin Luther, and then back to the nineteenth century to Elizabeth Barrett Browning, with an alacrity of disconnectedness which would have been the envy of the promoters of the International Sunday School Lessons. The novelist, poet, statesman, historian, essayist, philosopher, and philanthropist were made, in succession, the subjects of Legensia's praise and criticism. During this year a famous debate arose as to the relative merits of Webster and Sumner as statesmen. The debate was as hot and as protracted as any in which those famous statesmen ever engaged in the halls of congress. Curiously enough, all of the women of the club sided with Sumner, while all of the men yielded their allegiance to Webster. Finally one member was won over to the side of the Webster camp, and the question was settled in this way, and never disturbed the dreams of the club thereafter. In 1883, Legensia thought it was old enough to forego writing essays upon persons whose lives had been carefully and thoughtfully written beforehand by competent historians, and it took up the matter of writing about things. American History became the theme of this year's work. The following year was spent in a study of the English poets from Chaucer to Wordsworth. By 1886, the society thought it could wrestle with the deep problems of life, and so took up the discussion of the mysteries of the protective tariff, with the usual result, that after a year of discussion, everyone understood it perfectly, but no two persons had the same understanding about it. In 1887-88, the Victorian Reign, and the next year French History from Julius Cæsar to that date, were considered. In 1889, nothing in the old lines was quite satisfactory to the society. Several programs were suggested, but were all thrown out, and the club spent a year on the study of "Socialism." This proved to be one of the most interesting years in the history of the society. After 1890 the club had an existence of four years during which it discussed art, architecture, Alaska, Australia, Africa, Aldrich, Agassiz, and numerous problems of government, ethics, schools, and also the practical problems of life. In fact, the latter subject was frequently a matter of discussion in the club, and the manner in which it took hold of the subject was an ample testimony to the witticism of the bright Evanston woman who said she was sick and tired of hearing about her soul, but wanted to know how to keep her kitchen drain clean. The last year of Legensia was devoted to a consideration of Bryce's American Commonwealth. Whether or not this proved too severe a task, or whether other attractions abbreviated the membership, the club never got beyond December, 1894. This club never attempted the solution of the deep things of life, as did the old Philosophical Association. It never had soarings after the infinite nor divings after the unfathomable, nor did it ever attempt Browning.

The annual banquets of Legensia were meetings of great enjoyment. The first one was a complete surprise upon the gentlemen of the club, having been secretly prepared in advance by the ladies. It consisted of a fine collation of chicken salad, celery, cheese - sticks, cream, candy, and numerous other attractive articles of diet, and when the business of this evening was over, the gentlemen were ushered into the presence of the feast. As a literary feature of the evening, each man was asked to give his favorite author and a quotation from his works, and also to name his native State. As this was entirely impromptu, it led to some embarrassment, and men who had never quailed before the cannon's mouth were suddenly struck dumb at the audacity of the ladies, and their natural eloquence was abated. One of the most eloquent members of the club could only repeat the first verse of Genesis, while one of the most learned members of the faculty of Northwestern University could only describe his favorite state — into which he shortly afterward entered. Fourteen banquets in all were held, and it would be impossible to recount all of the bright things that were said and done on these occasions. One of the most unique was where each member was required to bring in an original poem, or at least alleged poetry; and these poems varied in length from four lines to one which took two rolls of wall paper to contain it. From the latter episode Mr. Dorr A. Kimball earned the title of poet laureate of the club. It would be impossible to speak in detail of the personnel of the club. There were in all about three hundred members during its fourteen years of history, including every class of society except the crank; all degrees of wealth, one Governor, three members of the Legislature, one Attorney-General of the State, business men, bankers, professional men, college Presidents and Professors unnumbered. One of the early members of the club made it a point, at every meeting, to have on hand the autograph or some former personal belonging of the person under discussion, and succeeded in every case except in the case of Julius Cæsar. When Martin Luther was under consideration this member is said to have had with him ink-stained samples of ingrain wall-paper, which he declared were taken from the room where Luther threw the ink bottle at the Devil. The higher criticism was not rampant in those days, but in spite of that fact, some members were so incredulous as to doubt the identity of this particular paper.

The papers of Legensia were always of a dignified nature. The flippant never entered into its discussions, and even the discussion of the protective tariff never precipitated any lifelong animosities, and the club will ever remain in the memories of older Evanstonians as a pleasant recollection of fourteen years of earnest, profitable, wholesome and most enjoyable work, coupled with a spirit of hospitality, generosity and friendship, which have become a permanent part of many lives made sweeter by the privileges of this association.

The following persons have acted as Presidents of Legensia: C. A. Flanders, F. P. Crandon (two terms), H. B. Cragin, W. S. Harbert, II. H. C. Miller, O. E. Haven, C. W. Pearson, Dorr A. Kimball, H. H. Kingsley, C. B, Atwell, L. K. Gillson, R. B. McMullen, J. Scott Clark and Fleming H. Revell.

Bryant Circle.—The Bryant Circle can claim the distinction of having had thus far the longest life of any literary society in Evanston, it now being in the twenty-first year of its existence. It was organized in 1885 as a "Chautauqua Literary and Scientific Circle." In the winter of 1883-84 several ladies of Evanston were pursuing independently the studies as laid down by the Chautauqua Association. Realizing, however, the benefit that would come from united action, the regular meeting together of those interested in the same line of study, both from the information each would impart to the other and from the stimulus that would be aroused by such union, they resolved to call a meeting of the ladies of the village interested in forming an after-noon circle for the following winter. Accordingly, there appeared in the "Evanston Index" of September 19, 1885, a notice calling such a meeting, the result of which was seen in the coming together of ten ladies, meeting with Mrs. Carsewell at the Avenue House Cottage. The charter members of the society which was organized were Mrs. Carsewell, Mrs. H. H. Gage, Mrs. George Bancroft, Mrs. H. J. Edwards, Mrs. W. H. Crocker, Mrs. G. H. Thompson, Mrs. W. H. Lewis, Mrs. Baskin and Mrs. Balding. New members were constantly added and in-

terest continued unabated. The name "Bryant" may possibly be something of a misnomer to those not familiar with the beginnings of the society. When a name for the circle was under discussion at one of the early meetings the name Bryant seemed especially fitting, that day being the birthday of the poet, and also one of the memorial days in the Chautauqua calendar; hence it was chosen. As no study of that poet has ever been pursued by the circle, it has been thought by many, during late years, that it is misleading, and there has been an attempt made to change the name, but, possibly from the sentiment of long association, the vote of the circle decided to retain its original name. The Chautauqua outline of work was strictly followed for four years, at which time (1889) the course was completed. The Circle then departed somewhat from the prescribed line, and for three years followed the outline pertaining to History and Literature, leaving out the sciences. At the end of that time it discontinued the Chautauqua study and a program committee from the club has, each year, presented a program which met the expressed desires of the Circle—the preference being generally given to literary and art studies. During the winter following the World's Fair papers were prepared on the various exhibits, more especially pertaining to the arts, crafts and industries, each paper being the result of personal observations. Various countries have been studied, and altogether the Circle's work, during its long career, has touched upon many branches of culture —intellectual, aesthetic, moral and religious. The fact that every member has contributed her share of the written papers, and taken part in the discussions, has been a distinctive and pleasing feature of the society. The active membership of the Circle is limited to thirty. There is an associate list, limited to ten, containing the names of those who, having been active members, are for good reasons unable to be constant attendants at regular meetings; these, however, are expected to participate, as far as possible, in the programs of the Circle. There is usually a number of names on the waiting list ready for election into the Circle whenever a vacancy occurs, thus showing the sustained interest and popularity of the society. These names must be presented by some member of the society. The election is by ballot, and a unanimous vote is required to gain admission. The Circle holds its meetings on alternate Monday afternoons at the homes of its members, and not the least delightful feature of the exercises is the social one—the cup of tea and the friendly chat which follow the more formal program. During the last few years it has been the custom, each winter, to hold one evening meeting to which the husbands and friends of the members have been invited, and an address has been given by an invited speaker on some topic kindred to the line of study of the year. A number of clergymen of Evanston and University professors have favored the Circle; also delightful musical numbers have been given by Evanston artists.

The following persons have acted as Presidents of the Circle: Mrs. G. W. Candee, Mrs. W. H. Whitehead, Mrs. A. F. Townsend, Mrs. L. D. Norton, Mrs. H. R. Wilson, Miss Mary Harris, Mrs. E. A. Dawson, Mrs. H. H. Kingsley, Mrs. Thomas Balmer, Mrs. W. A. Smith, Mrs. C. S. Raddin, Mrs. F. M. Bristol, Miss Alice Houston, Mrs. Howard Field, Mrs. P. L. McKinnie, Mrs. J. C. Turner.

Pierian Circle.—The Pierian Circle was organized February 27, 1891. It was the outgrowth of a porch reading circle, which had been enjoyed by a few ladies in the same neighborhood during the preceding summer. As they wished to continue the pleasant custom, and also to widen the scope of this little circle, they decided to make it a regular organization, under as informal a rule as possible. For this purpose, a meeting was called at the above date at the home of Mrs. P. L. McKinnie, 108 Davis Street. Twelve ladies were present, and after freely discussing the matter, a study club was formed, the object of which should be to stimulate, in an enjoyable way, the intellectual development of its members, and combine the advantage of literary and social culture. The name "Pierian" was chosen for the Circle with much hesitation as being rather ambitious for a circle of learners, the suggestion coming from Pope's Essay on Criticism: "Drink deep, or taste not the Pierian Spring." This objection was counteracted somewhat by the motto selected for the Circle: "Let Knowledge grow from more to more." The number of members was limited to thirty, to be elected by vote of the club after having been considered by a membership committee, the meetings to be held twice a month at the homes of its members. The subject selected for the first season's study was American History, and current events were given at roll call. The President elected at the initial meeting was Mrs. C. E. Thayer, one of the original porch circle.

While early in its history some philanthropic work was done by the club, its main object has been of a literary nature. The regular afternoon meetings have been occasionally varied by evening meetings, with invited guests and lectures by those outside of its own membership.

The interest in the Pierian Club has been steadily increasing and warmly maintained. Its list of membership has always been full, with several on the waiting list. The subjects which have been studied during the years succeeding the first one already mentioned are as follows: Ruskin for three seasons; Magazine Reviews; The Victorian Reign: London; France; The English Colonies; The Industrial Arts.

The office of President has been held by the following named persons: Mrs. P. R. Woodford, Mrs. R. P. Hollett, Miss Mary Harris, Mrs. J. A. Battle, Mrs. Nelson De Golyer, Mrs. J. M. Bond.

The Fortnightly.—Preparatory to the ascension of the great White City on the shores of Lake Michigan, a thousand fantasies possessed the imaginations of the people, anticipating the marvelous phantasmagoria soon to be practically realized. It is not surprising that the highly favored inhabitants of Evanston should have shared in the general enthusiasm to the extent of seeing visions by night and dreaming dreams by day. Hence it so happened that the genesis of the "Fortnightly" was the product of a revelation communicated to a few friends with mutual sympathies and common aims, who entered into an informal partnership for higher education, diversified by friendly chat and the consequent attrition of many minds. On this purely unconventional basis, the Fortnightly Club commenced business nearly fourteen years ago. This chrysalis of inexperience was destined to mature beyond the stage of the ephemeral fledgling, and while building better than it knew, to earn an enviable reputation for stability and intelligence second to none

of its kindred societies. The first women to extend a helping hand to this union were, in order, as follows: Mrs. Lucretia Morgan, Mrs. Henrietta Day, Mrs. Alexander Clark, Mrs. Sereno Norton, Mrs. Thomas L. Fansler and Mrs. George Graley. These few founders stand for charter members of an unincorporated club which has never formed any alliance with State or National Federations. It was originally christened as the "Woman's Reading Circle," and made its initial bow to the public with the assistance of a single official, Mrs. Alexander Clark acting as Director, and filling the position most acceptably and efficiently. With the lapse of years this infant industry grew in stature and in grace. Having an increased membership, it naturally drifted with the tide into broader thought expressed in more conventional channels, and became, like all well-regulated associations of the time, governed by parliamentary rules, selecting regular presiding officers, and finally adopting the more dignified title of the Fortnightly Club of Evanston. As any trustworthy narrative must include a definite list of topics for study, the various subjects are appended herewith: History of Spain; Arts and Industries; Countries of the World; Celebrated Historians; Parliamentary Law and Socialism; Miscellaneous Program in 1896-7—History of Chicago; Cuba and the Philippine Islands; Russia, Customs and Manners; Holland and Her Dykes; Fiction and Philosophy.

These topics were interspersed with current events of interest, discussions on higher education, the amenities of home and fireside, with the practical solution of vexed problems and the burning issues of the hour.

The life of the Fortnightly has not,

however, been one of serious contemplation. It has frequently had brought to mind the old adage, that "All work and no play makes life dull every day"; so, metaphorically speaking, the club has taken up the "fiddle and the bow," while resting from the exertions of the "shovel and the hoe." As comparisons are odious, it may not be well to chronicle any of the gay larks indulged in by this clique of sober and serious matrons. Let it suffice that the Fortnightly has held dignified receptions, listened to lectures and addresses, played hilarious games galore; has been feted and feasted at the hospitable homes of its members, and last, but not least, has disported gaily in honor of Saint Valentine, where, if not wined in this prohibition town, the club has certainly dined to its heart's content. As this is a many-sided club, it has never turned a deaf ear to appeals for philanthropic and charitable enterprises. During the winter many a fire has been kept burning, and the wolf diverted from the doors of the sick and needy. Money has been contributed for the collection of books, a room furnished in a public institution, and last year all moneys were turned into the general fund of the Associated Charities.

At the commencement of the fourteenth year of the history of the Club, it has a full roster of thirty members. Good fellowship has always been its aim. On the solid rock of the sacredness of home and family ties, the Club stands as a unit. Births and deaths and burials have been fitly commemorated alike in kind words and loving deeds, and the fragrant ministry of flowers—the pink carnation being the floral emblem of the Club. In the flight of time but one member has been gathered by the unrelenting scythe of death. Many changes have occurred

in the roll call, but vacancies are speedily filled, while some of the original members and a little of the old leaven still remain intact.

Thirty daughters under one roof-tree have inevitably held different opinions, yet uniformly agreeing to disagree in a spirit of tolerance, the general weal being the paramount consideration. Collectively the Fortnightly Club is composed of wide-awake, intelligent, progressive women living up to the spirit of the motto of the Club, "Whatever the subject, it deserves our pains."

The Club has a very promising future, and it is enthusiastically hoped that it may attain to that spirit of high idealism expressed by one of its members: "That the coming years may bring to all its members a still larger charity and greater loving kindness, forming an indissoluble union of heart and hand, a loyal copartnership that shall abide 'for better or worse, for richer or poorer, in sickness and in health, till death do us part.'"

The Coterie.—In 1893 an invitation was sent to the ladies living on Michigan Avenue between Kedzie and Keeney Avenues, to come together for the afternoon, and bring their sewing and children, if necessary, while one lady would read to them from some recently published book. "The Prince of India," by General Lew Wallace, was chosen; and each week a few chapters of the book were read, after which a social hour was passed and light refreshments were served.

The afternoon was much enjoyed, and the ladies decided to meet every week at their various homes. There were present at each meeting ladies of musical talent who pledged themselves to furnish either piano or vocal music. Several books were read during 1893-4.

October 5, 1894, it was decided to organize a society with the understanding that
the closing hour for conversation and
social pleasure be not infringed upon.
Accordingly, a constitution was presented and unanimously adopted. Mrs.
E. L. Waddell was elected President,
and she has retained the office up to the
present time, 1902. With no desire to
be called a literary club, it was decided
to call the Club "The Coterie." The social requirements form a large part of
the afternoon entertainment. As the
members are, for the most part, too busy
to prepare papers, the literary features
of the afternoon have consisted largely in
reading from books, magazines and various other sources.

The later history of The Coterie embraces a study of foreign countries, and
an annual program is followed every
year, in which pleasure, entertainment
and culture, as well as social enjoyment,
are the leading characteristics. The literary features of the afternoon have
never been a burden to the Club, and
once a year there is an annual dinner and
a children's party, which are not the least
pleasing features of this very delightful
and enthusiastic club.

The Coming Century Club.—The Coming Century Club of Evanston was first
suggested February 18, 1894. It originated in a meeting of eight men: W. E.
Wilkinson, H. L. Tolman, D. D. Thompson, F. W. Nichols, C. O. Scudder, W.
H. Webster, E. O. Blake and A. E. A.
Shinner. It was proposed to form a society of gentlemen to discuss the live
topics of the day.

A meeting was called by this gathering, and over a supper at the home of
H. L. Tolman, the Club was organized.
The name, "Coming Century Club," was
suggested by Mr. J. J. Flinn, and the

following is Mr. Scudder's record of the
meeting:

"Coming Century Club.—On Monday evening, February 25th, Messrs. Adair, Blake, Flinn, Graham, Hibhen,
Knox, Milhening, Nichols, Rowe, Scudder, Thompson,
Tolman, Webster, and Wilkinson, met at the home of
Mr. Henry L. Tolman and organized the above named
club for the free discussion of current questions, on the
following basis:

Negations.

No Accounts	nor	Axes,
No By-Laws	nor	Bores nor Business,
No Club House	nor	Constitution,
No Debts, Dress Coats	nor	Dudes nor Dues,
No Fines	nor	Formality,
No Long Speeches	nor	Late Sittings,
No Officers	nor	Organizations,
No Preaching	nor	Profanity.

"Messrs. Nichols, Scudder, Tolman, Thompson, and
Wilkinson were made an Executive Committee with power
to do all business, with Mr. Tolman as Chairman and
Mr. Scudder as Secretary.

"The Club meets on the second and fourth Monday
evenings of each month; on the second Monday evening at
eight o'clock sharp, at the house of some member; on the
fourth Monday at six-thirty P. M., for dinner, discussion
afterward, at some place hereafter designated, the same
to cost not to exceed seventy-five cents.

"The Club adjourns at ten o'clock. The introductory
speakers are allowed twenty minutes each, with five
minutes additional to close. Other speakers are limited
to five minutes. The next meeting will be held at the
residence of Mr. Nichols, 932 Hinman Avenue, Monday
evening, March 11.

"Question: Should the United States adopt the bi-
metallic standard?
"Affirmative—Mr. Adair.
"Negative—Mr. Tolman.
                                    "C. O. SCUDDER, Sec."

The membership was at first limited
to thirty-five, and meetings have always
been held at the homes of members. The
early popularity of the Club came from
its unique constitution, all business being transacted by the Executive Committee without coming before the Club
to distract from its social and literary
character. Its continued vitality has also
been due to the freedom given to all members to take part in the discussions,
which have frequently been wise as well
as witty.

Meetings have been held twice each
month during the winter months of each
year ever since the organization. Banquets have been held two or three times
each year, generally served by church ladies.

In 1897 the membership was doubled
by the admission of ladies, and has several times been enlarged to accommodate
the demand for admission of new mem-

bers. The present membership is one hundred and the homes are often taxed to accommodate the meetings.

At the opening of the year 1898 it was thought best by the committee to adopt a constitution, which embodied mainly the past practices of the Club. The first printed annual programs were used in 1896 and have been printed each year since.

Of late years there have been a few meetings each year, when outside talent has been called in to entertain the Club. Perfect harmony has prevailed in the meetings and the discussions have settled nearly all the questions of the day—political, religious, literary and scientific.

With the opening of the season of 1901-2 the name of the Club became "The Twentieth Century Club" and will probably remain so during the present century.

Present Day Club.—The Present Day Club, while one of the youngest clubs in Evanston, is thoroughly an up-to-date club. It was organized about 1899 by six women living in the vicinity of Sheridan Road and Lee Street, for the purpose of discussing the best news of the day, and keeping in touch with the literary world. The Club, which is limited to fifteen members, meets every two weeks in the homes of its members. The annual fee is used for a book fund. The leading works of the present day are purchased, read and discussed, and distributed, pro rata, to the members at the close of each club year. Among the works of fiction discussed during the first year

were "Janice Meredith," "When Knighthood Was in Flower" and "Richard Carvel." In connection with the reading of the last-named book, which was valuable for its wholesomeness as well as for its historical worth, a scholarly lecture on the Revolutionary Period was given by one of its members. All the points of interest were traced on the map, and comparisons were drawn with the characters and events depicted in the book. "Eben Holden" served as a pleasant dessert to the year's literary menu. Tolstoy's life, country and works were studied during the second year, his last work of fiction being considered a strong work for people of mature years who are studying the sociological questions of the day. The work of fiction which found greatest favor among the members of the Club was "The Crisis," and it was especially noticeable that the literary criticisms of the Club were frequently at wide variance with those of the professional reviewers. The program for the present year includes current events, lives of editors, magazine articles and late works of fiction. After reading such books as "Lazarre" and admiring Gilbert Parker's strong literary strokes in his "Right of Way," rest and refreshment are to be found in turning to Van Dyke's "Little Rivers," or reading his "To Be Glad of Life, because it gives you the chance to love and to work, and to play and to look up at the stars; to be satisfied with your possessions, but not contented with yourself until you have made the best of them."

CHAPTER XLIII.

THE EVANSTON WOMAN'S CLUB
(By MRS. RICHARD H. WYMAN)

Origin of Evanston Woman's Club — Julia Ward Howe's Advice — Organization and First Officers — Club Programs — Auxiliary Organizations — Work of the Traveling Library Committee — Field Day at Lake Geneva — Object of the Club Defined in Its Constitution — Club Motto.

All great and successful organizations have their origin in consecration of thought and purpose. The seed-thought of the Evanston's Woman's Club flickered into existence deep in the heart of a woman whose desire was for the activity of all women striving for the good of all women. The thought was cherished and confided to a few kindred spirits. Nourished by their sympathy, strengthened by their zeal, it grew into an impulse to reach out for co-operation.

Early in 1889 Mrs. Elizabeth Boynton Harbert invited to her home a little group of earnest women, to take counsel together as to how they might unite in promoting a Woman's Club. For inspiration they read with interest and profit Julia Ward Howe's address on the "Organization of Women." That great and wise leader, desiring to help others, says:

"Deliberation in common, mutual instruction, achievement for the whole, should be the spirit of associations: work faithfully, fervently and in sincerity with the motto, 'The good of all, the aim of each.' Question: What are the most pressing needs of society? What can we, as a body corporate, do to meet and answer them? Learn to act in the light of experience. Work with the conviction that the possibilities of Women's Clubs are as broad as the land, as diverse as are the requirements of mankind."

Pondering these sentiments and encouraged by the enthusiasm of their hostess, who proved herself in every sense a leader, these women continued to meet informally until in March, 1889, when they associated themselves together to form "The Woman's Club of Evanston."

Mrs. Harbert was made President and Mrs. Thaddeus P. Stanwood Secretary. Early in 1890 the membership had grown to a dignity requiring a constitution and regular officers. This form of organization continued until March, 1898, when the club was duly incorporated in accordance with the laws of the State of Illinois.

Mrs. Harbert was the Mother of the Club in the deepest and broadest sense of the relation expressed by the word. It has been well said that what Alice Cary accomplished in Sorosis, Mrs. Harbert accomplished and amplified in Evanston.

443

To her personal inspiration and wise direction the Club owes its early activities and its healthful development. She was its President for eight years, when, at her own instance, the honor was transferred to another. Mrs T. P. Stanwood was then elected to the office. Being a woman of exceptional ability, keen perception and rare graciousness, she was well qualified to guide the Club through a critical period and to thoroughly establish its prosperity.

At the end of two years she was succeeded by Mrs. Richard H. Wyman, who, after two years' service, was followed by Mrs. H. H. Kingsley, a charter member and loyal worker. With charming tact and grace she conducted the affairs through a very successful year, when, positively declining re-election, she was succeeded, in April, 1902, by Mrs. C. A. Goodnow. These Presidents have always been splendidly supported by fellow-officers and a Board of Managers showing ability and devoted zeal. Every department and branch of the club work have received the special attention of women who have devoted heart and hand to the attainment of highest standards.

The program of the earlier years, though not thoroughly systematized, was profitable and enjoyable. It consisted usually of a special topic with prepared essay, which was followed by two short speeches on the subject, supplemented by informal discussion. This method furthered one of the primary objects of the Club—to train women to become easy speakers; to help them to acquire the habit of thinking and speaking readily and connectedly on their feet before an audience.

An indication of one of the early-time interests and activities, which has since grown to importance, is given in the fact that a large reception was tendered the teachers of Evanston at Mrs. Harbert's home, where an address was made by the late Colonel Parker on the Relation of the Home to the School.

During the time from 1891 to 1894 the Club sustained a World's Fair Department, for the purpose of study and investigation in the various lines of interest connected with the World's Columbian Exposition. This was under the leadership of Miss Mary Harris, and proved a marked success.

A Household Economic Department was organized at about this time, at whose meetings, held twice each month, papers on Domestic Science, previously read at the World's Fair Congresses, were presented. This department merged into the Department of Philanthropy, which has led the Club into the line of broader work and great achievements.

From this time the work of the Club developed into departments, serving as channels for each member to pursue investigation and to derive pleasure, according to her taste and desire—all uniting in one general club meeting each month; all serving loyally any cause for the general good.

The Art and Literature Department was formed in September, 1894, and the Child and Home Department in 1897. The Press Department was organized a little later. A French Study Class, under Professor Oudshorn, was formed in 1897; a class in German, under Miss White, in 1899, and a class in Civics, under Miss Childs, in 1902. Also a class in singing, under Professor Niedlinger, was carried on during the winter of 1902.

The first, and one of the greatest efforts of the Club in outside work, was the impetus which it was the means of giving to the Evanston Emergency Hospital. At a meeting held in November, 1891, the words of Mrs. A. L. Butler stirred the members to form a Hospital Committee with Mrs. Joseph Hubbart as Chairman. It was resolved to give a festival and kirmess. The enterprise met with the cordial and generous support and efficient co-operation of citizens, both in and out of the Club, and was a brilliant success, netting $3,600 for the hospital fund.

A course of lectures was given during the winter of 1895, by Professor Charles G. Moulton, which afforded means to assist the Convalescent Home at Lake Geneva and to support a teacher for a sewing school. As a mark of appreciation of the hospitality of the Evanston Boat Club in offering the use of its rooms, a complimentary lecture by Professor Moulton, followed by a reception, was given.

Among other good deeds, the Woman's Club has extended substantial aid to the Northwestern University Settlement; it has placed a beautiful drinking fountain in the vicinity of the Chicago Commons; it has contributed to the Forward Movement and the Vacation Schools of Chicago; the local charities have received generous co-operation; a Day Nursery was established and sustained for a time, and several successful Mothers' Clubs have been conducted at the homes of members and at school houses.

Sewing classes and housework classes for young girls were, during one season, conducted by members at their own homes. At Thanksgiving and Christmastide the overflowing spirit of giving and doing has been directed in proper channels by a Club Committee, who thoroughly canvassed the town and knew just where the bounty was most needed and would be best appreciated. The purpose was that there should not be a child within reach who should not know the blessings of the season. Over two hundred families have thus been reached, while over one thousand public school children have been carefully examined to ascertain and assist those suffering from defective sight or hearing. The teeth of the children have also received attention.

A successful entertainment, in the form of a children's operetta, "The House That Jack Built," was given under the auspices of the Child and Home Department, which netted a substantial sum for the benefit of the Domestic Science Department of the Evanston Public Schools. As a memorial to a beautiful young daughter, one of the prominent mothers of the Club installed a Visiting Nurse to minister to those needing, but not able to pay for, such service. This noble work has been sustained through the Philanthropic Department. The bright face, untiring devotion and ready skill of the Club's representative, Miss Galtz, in this beautiful charity, has been appreciatively welcomed by scores of sufferers.

In response to an earnest talk from the President, much of personal service was undertaken and accomplished during Mrs. Stanwood's administration. It was interesting to note the varied character of the responses. Some offered the use of their carriages to those who might especially need them; others, a view of their pictures; still others, their time to read, to tell stories, to mend, to make over clothing, to teach some common or unusual branch of home accomplishments. One of the tangible results of this movement was the purchase by the Club of a knitting-machine for the use of the different Mothers' Clubs, where the call for stockings was constant and imperative.

A letter, sent through Mrs. Grey, appealed to Marshall Field & Company for a guarantee of garments manufactured under sanitary conditions. Thus was a beginning made towards one of the great objects aimed at later by the Consumers' League. One of the members skilled in bird lore gave a series of interesting talks upon her favorite subject. Another member led a course in parliamentary law, which was very profitable and enjoyable. A Legislative Committee has watched and reported bills and legislative matters of importance and interest to the women, and the proper influence has been used to further them. A course of lectures and demonstrations in cooking and housekeeping, by Mrs. Hiller, was managed by the Child and Home Department. These were attended by over a hundred women, both mistresses and maids, who gave their enthusiastic approval.

In May, 1900, the Club invited the Illinois Congress of Mothers to meet under its auspices in Evanston. An exceedingly interesting series of meetings was held, lasting over three days. These meetings were addressed by eminent men and women, and were attended by delegates from all parts of the State. The conference closed with a beautiful reception given by Dr. and Mrs. McKinney, at their palatial home on the lake shore. Baroness Schimmermann, the German philanthropist, gave an interesting talk during her stay in Chicago concerning herself and her work among sailors. Committees are maintained to promote the work of the Juvenile Court and

support a probation officer; also to assist the Vacation Schools and to guard and enforce the ordinances of the city of Evanston.

The Traveling Library Committee sent out its first library in 1900. This was the first library in the world to be taken in charge by the Rural Delivery. Since that time ten libraries of fifty books each, packed in a complete case, have been sent on their way to cheer the barren places where books are unattainable. Magazines and periodicals are constantly being sent in packages to various institutions and hospitals, for both adults and children.

For several seasons the privileges of the Club have been extended to all the teachers of Evanston, and during the past season the husbands of members and gentlemen "connected by marriage" have been invited to attend the meetings. Those who have been able to avail themselves of the opportunity have expressed their approbation and enjoyment, as they have lingered to chat over the cup of tea or coffee which is always served at the close of the meetings.

The Club is affiliated with the Illinois Federation of Woman's Clubs, the Illinois Congress of Mothers, the Illinois Society for Child-Study, the Chicago Art Association and the Cook County League, and in the Club rooms is a tempting supply of books and current magazines.

A word as to the local habitation of this organization. It was born in the home of Mrs. Elizabeth Boynton Harbert, and there it was carefully watched through its young and tender years. As it grew the members realized that this charming home had its limitations in space, though never in hospitality. The mention of this hospitality brings to the minds of the early members the vivid memory of the devotion of Arthur Harbert, who so cordially assisted in providing for the comfort and entertainment of his mother's friends. With the greatest reluctance to leaving the environment around which so many associations clustered, the Club gratefully accepted the generous offer of the Evanston Boat Club, in December, 1894, and for two seasons occupied its attractive assembly hall. The membership at this time was about two hundred.

During the two following seasons the Club enjoyed the hospitality of the Country Club, but in the autumn of 1898 the members entered upon the occupation of a suite of rooms of their own in the new Young Men's Christian Association Building. These rooms, furnished completely and in excellent taste, have been the Club headquarters for five years. With the truest instinct of women and the best spirit of a club, the members look forward with longings and hope to the vague future, which may hold for them a home of their own. Surely, with entire possession and complete control of the premises, this ideal club would make an ideal home.

The first and only "Field-Day" of the Club was celebrated at the charming home of Mr. and Mrs. Harbert, at Lake Geneva, in July, 1894. Fifty members made up the happy party, and they will ever cherish the memory of the occasion with keen pleasure and a consciousness of fresh inspiration.

The programs of the twelve years of the Club's history contain many names illustrious in art, literature, education, music, philanthropy and science. The very best to be obtained in professional and practical lines has been brought before the members, both in the departments and in the general meetings.

The membership numbers over three hundred and fifty, and includes many prominent women, among whom are the President of the Illinois Federation of Clubs, the President of the Illinois Congress of Mothers, the President of the Illinois Suffrage Association, the Dean of Woman's Hall, the Musical Director of the Northwestern University, and Presidents of several smaller clubs. There are a lawyer, a doctor, a librarian, teachers, wives of judges, editors, professors, clergymen, and—honor be to them— scores of women who are devoted to that most exalted sphere of woman—the Home.

Twenty members have passed beyond the activities of this life to the higher life Beyond. Their memories are a benediction to those who knew them here.

"There is no death
To the living soul, nor loss, nor harm."

In 1898 a Club pledge, color and pin were adopted. The pin is in form of a shield, with emblems of heart, distaff and torch, above a scroll bearing the words, "Unity, Charity, Liberty." The colors are green and gold. The Pledge voices unfailing loyalty and active devotion to the Club and its interests.

There is no better way to epitomize the cause of the existence and the course of the vitality of the Evanston Woman's Club than to quote, in closing, its own words, taken from its Constitution:

"The objects are mutual helpfulness in all affairs of life, and united efforts toward the higher development of humanity."

Surely there could be no higher standard than that expressed in its motto:

"In essentials, unity;
"In non-essentials, liberty;
"In all things, charity."

CHAPTER XLIV.

THE EVANSTON CLUB
(By N. C. GRIDLEY)

On the 24th day of November, 1888, at the request of Marshall M. Kirkman, the following-named citizens of Evans- ton met in the Committee Room of the Hotel Richelieu, in the city of Chicago, for the purpose of organizing a Club in Evanston, namely: Curtis H. Remy, Daniel H. Burnham, Marshall M. Kirk- man, Nelson C. Gridley, Francis A. Hardy, James K. Armsby, Frederick W. Clarke, Milton W. Kirk, Edward P. Wil- son, David B. Dewey, John B. Kirk, Wil- liam E. Stockton, Josiah J. Parkhurst, George E. Gooch and Frank M. Elliot.

Mr. Kirkman stated the object of the meeting, and, on his motion, Mr. C. H. Remy was elected Chairman; and, on motion of Mr. D. B. Dewey, Mr. C. G. Phillips was elected Secretary. There- upon it was—

"Resolved, That measures be at once taken to incorporate the Club under the laws of the State of Illinois," and on the 26th of November, 1888, a certificate of incorporation of "The Greenwood Club" was duly issued by the Secretary of State of Illinois.

Subsequently, at a meeting held in the Grand Pacific Hotel, Chicago, November 28, 1888, the following-named gentlemen were duly elected as the officers and Di- rectors of "The Greenwood Club:" President, Marshall M. Kirkman; First Vice-President, Daniel H. Burnham; Sec- ond Vice-President, Milton W. Kirk; Treasurer, David B. Dewey; Directors— Hugh R. Wilson, Charles W. Deering, Nelson C. Gridley, Curtis H. Remy, Wil- liam E. Stockton, James K. Armsby and Charles F. Dwight.

Thereupon the officers and Directors adopted By-Laws and House Rules for the government of the Club, and elected Frank M. Elliot as Secretary.

The By-Laws provided that "The ob- ject for which this Club is formed is the promotion of social, athletic and aesthetic culture; its immediate purpose the recre- ation and amusement of its members and their families; that the membership should be limited to one hundred mem- bers of the age of twenty-one years; that the initiation fee shall be $300 and the annual dues $50; that junior members, between the ages of sixteen and twenty- one years, and the sons of or related to members, may be admitted to all the privileges of the Club except voting; that the ladies of every member's family, and the males between the age of sixteen and twenty-one years, shall be entitled to the privileges of the club; and that no liquors shall be allowed in the Club House or upon the premises, nor any gambling or betting—the purposes of the Club being to afford its members and their families a place where they may go to seek the recreation and amusement that are commonly to be found at clubs."

The following named gentlemen, residents of Evanston, were duly elected members of the club, each of whom paid the initiation fee of $300, and to each of whom was subsequently issued a certificate of membership:

James K. Armsby	William E. Stockton
Daniel H. Burnham	Frederick W. Clarke
Hugh R. Wilson	Charles W. Deering
Curtis H. Remy	David B. Dewey
George E. Gooch	Charles F. Dwight
Milton W. Kirk	Edward P. Wilson
Francis A. Hardy	Morris R. Eddy
Arthur Orr	John B. Kirk
William Holabird	Nicholas G. Iglehart
William D. Hitchcock	Arthur S. Kirk
Frederic T. Peabody	Thomas A. Balding
Nelson C. Gridley	Henry M. Kidder
Josiah J. Parkhurst	Richard L. Dakin
Augustus A. Buell	Frank M. Elliot
Aaron N. Young	Hugh A. White
James H. Deering	William D. Porter
Marshall M. Kirkman	Charles G. Fuller
William Blanchard	Volney W. Foster
Simeon Farwell	Harry S. Farwell
Nelson De Golyer	Charles P. Mitchell
George A. Foster	David S. Cook
William B. Phillips	Harold Smith
George M. Sargent	Martin M. Gridley
Henry R. Pearsons	Birney J. Moore
William T. Rickards	H. H. C. Miller
Edward H. Webster	Richard W. Lynch

At the meeting of November 28, 1888,

a committee, consisting of Messrs. Dewey, Burnham and M. W. Kirk, were appointed to investigate as to the most desirable location for the Club, which committee, on the 17th day of December, 1888, reported the selection of the "Ludlam" lots (on which the Club House now stands) situated on the northwest corner of Chicago Avenue and Grove Street, 132 by 210 feet, and which could be purchased at $11,000; and thereupon the Executive Committee were authorized to make the purchase of said lots. The money for the purchase of said lots was obtained by the issue of the bonds of the club, of $500 each, secured by mortgage, all of which bonds were purchased by members of the club. There was situated upon said lots a frame dwelling house, which had been occupied by Mrs. Ludlam and family for many years, and which was removed by her as a condition of the purchase of said lots.

At a meeting of the members of "The Greenwood Club," held at the Avenue House, Evanston, January 14, 1889, it was unanimously

"Resolved, That the name of this corporation, 'The Greenwood Club,' be, and the same is hereby changed to 'The Evanston Club.'"

And, thereupon due proceedings were taken for the change of same in compliance with the laws of the State of Illinois.

On the 15th of March, 1889, the Board of Directors adopted plans and specifications for the building of a Club House, which had been prepared by Holabird & Roche, architects, under the supervision of a committee consisting of F. W. Clarke, D. H. Burnham and William Holabird, and thereupon a building committee, consisting of D. H. Burnham, D. B. Dewey and N. C. Gridley was duly appointed, and instructed to proceed with the erection of a Club House.

"The Evanston Club" Club House was practically completed, and a meeting of the Board of Directors was first held in the Club House on September 24, 1889.

In consequence of the cost of the building and its appurtenances exceeding the estimates therefor, it became necessary to raise funds for the furnishing of the Club House, whereupon twenty-three members of the Club voluntarily subscribed $100 each, for that purpose, which money was subsequently repaid by the Club.

A committee consisting of Mr. and Mrs. Charles F. Dwight, Mr. and Mrs. William Holabird, and Mr. and Mrs. Frederick W. Clarke, was appointed to select and purchase furniture and fixtures for the Club House. The opening party of the Club was given on the evening of Tuesday, October 1, 1889. The guests, consisting of members and their wives, sons and daughters of members over the age of sixteen, and invited guests, in all about 600, were received by a Reception Committee consisting of Mr. and Mrs. Marshall M. Kirkman, Mr. and Mrs. Daniel H. Burnham, Mr. and Mrs. Milton W. Kirk, Mr. and Mrs. Frank M. Elliot, Mr. and Mrs. Hugh R. Wilson, Mr. and Mrs. Charles Deering, Mr. and Mrs. James K. Armsby and Mr. and Mrs. Charles F. Dwight.

On August 28, 1890, the By-Laws were so amended that "The membership of this Club shall be limited to one hundred and sixty (160), and shall consist of sixty (60) charter members, or those having paid $300 membership fee and holding certificates of membership, and one hundred (100) Associate Members without any ownership in the property of the Club." Subsequently, on November 2, 1891, the By-Laws were again amended so as to increase the membership to 200,

to consist of sixty (60) charter and one hundred and forty (140) Associate Members.

In July, 1896, the distinctions theretofore existing in the membership of the Club were abolished, and all members were granted equal rights in the government and property of the Club. This was accomplished by the charter members surrendering their certificates of membership and releasing all interest in the property of the Club, in consideration of new certificates of membership providing that the dues of each holder of a certificate shall not exceed $25 per annum.

During the fall and winter months in each year from the opening party in October, 1889, to and including 1894-5 — the Club took the lead in the social amusements of Evanston in providing for its members, their wives and children, concerts, vocal and instrumental; musicales and theatricals by members; sociables, with music, dancing and cards; children's entertainments, card parties, dancing parties, lectures, readings, song and violin recitals, and, in many of the entertainments, the Club hired artists of national and international reputation.

In consequence of the organization of other social clubs in Evanston, as "The Country Club" and "The Boat Club," the general features of social entertainment by "the Evanston Club" were curtailed, and have been limited, since the fall and winter of 1895-6, to bowling, billiards and cards, with bi-monthly card parties or "Ladies' Nights," for the special entertainments of the wives and daughters of members of the Club.

The property of "The Evanston Club," consisting of real estate and the Club House with its furnishings and fixtures, is of the value of about $50,000, with a bonded indebtedness of only $12,000, and having a balance in the hands of the Treasurer, on January 1, 1902, of about $1,000.

OFFICERS AND DIRECTORS OF THE EVANSTON CLUB FROM ITS INCEPTION

Year	President and Director	First Vice-President and Director	Second Vice-President and Director	Secretary	Treasurer and Director	Director
1888	M. M. Kirkman	D. H. Burnham	M. W. Kirk	F. M. Elliot	D. B. Dewey	C. W. Deering
1889	M. M. Kirkman	D. H. Burnham	M. W. Kirk	F. M. Elliot	D. B. Dewey	C. W. Deering
1890	M. M. Kirkman	D. H. Burnham	M. W. Kirk	F. M. Elliot	D. B. Dewey	C. W. Deering
1891	M. M. Kirkman	M. W. Kirk	N. C. Gridley	F. M. Elliot	W. T. Rickards	F. A. Hardy
1892	M. M. Kirkman	M. W. Kirk	N. C. Gridley	F. M. Elliot	W. J. Fabian	F. A. Hardy
1893	M. M. Kirkman	W. H. Bartlett	J. B. Kirk	F. M. Elliot	W. J. Fabian	F. A. Hardy
1894	M. M. Kirkman	W. H. Bartlett	J. B. Kirk	N. G. Iglehart	W. J. Fabian	F. A. Hardy
1895	M. M. Kirkman	W. H. Bartlett	N. C. Gridley	G. M. Sargent	G. R. Jenkins	F. A. Hardy
1896	M. M. Kirkman	N. C. Gridley	W. Holabird	W. T. Rickards	G. R. Jenkins	F. A. Hardy
1896	N. C. Gridley	W. Holabird	F. A. Hardy	W. T. Rickards	G. R. Jenkins	M. M. Kirkman
1897	N. C. Gridley	W. Holabird	F. A. Hardy	W. T. Rickards	G. R. Jenkins	M. M. Kirkman
1898	N. C. Gridley	W. Holabird	F. A. Hardy	W. T. Rickards	G. R. Jenkins	M. M. Kirkman
1899	N. C. Gridley	W. Holabird	F. A. Hardy	W. T. Rickards	G. R. Jenkins	C. H. M'Farland
1900	A. N. Young	G. R. Jenkins	W. T. Rickards	A. Millard	C. H. Harbert	C. H. M'Farland
1901	G. R. Jenkins	B. F. Adams	G. S. Marsh	N. G. Iglehart	N. G. Iglehart	C. H. M'Farland

Year	Director	Director	Director	Director	Director	Director
1888	J. K. Armsby	H. R. Wilson	W. E. Stockton	N. C. Gridley	C. F. Dwight	C. H. Remy
1889	J. K. Armsby	H. R. Wilson	W. E. Stockton	N. C. Gridley	C. F. Dwight	C. H. Remy
1890	J. K. Armsby	H. R. Wilson	W. E. Stockton	N. C. Gridley	C. F. Dwight	C. H. Remy
1891	N. G. Iglehart	H. R. Wilson	W. E. Stockton	W. Holabird	A. C. Buell	A. N. Young
1892	N. G. Iglehart	H. R. Wilson	W. H. Bartlett	W. Holabird	A. C. Buell	W. D. Hitchcock
1893	N. G. Iglehart	N. C. Gridley	H. A. Pearsons	W. Holabird	A. C. Buell	W. D. Hitchcock
1894	N. G. Iglehart	N. C. Gridley	H. A. Pearsons	W. Holabird	D. A. Mudge	C. H. Remy
1895	N. G. Iglehart	W. J. Fabian	C. J. Connell	W. Holabird	G. M. Sargent	C. H. Remy
1896	N. G. Iglehart	W. J. Fabian	C. J. Connell	W. H. Bartlett	G. M. Sargent	C. H. Remy
1896	N. G. Iglehart	W. J. Fabian	C. J. Connell	W. H. Bartlett	G. M. Sargent	C. H. Remy
1897	N. G. Iglehart	E. S. Lacey	C. T. Boynton	W. H. Bartlett	G. M. Sargent	H. S. Stevens
1898	N. G. Iglehart	E. S. Lacey	C. T. Boynton	W. H. Bartlett	G. M. Sargent	H. S. Stevens
1899	N. G. Iglehart	E. S. Lacey	R. C. Lake	D. A. Kimball	W. T. Rickards	H. S. Stevens
1900	N. G. Iglehart	F. W. Gerould	J. A. Patten	D. A. Kimball	N. C. Gridley	H. S. Stevens
1901	A. N. Young	F. W. Gerould	J. A. Lawrence	D. A. Kimball	N. C. Gridley	H. S. Stevens

CHAPTER XLV.

EVANSTON COUNTRY CLUB

To the minds of the older individual members of Evanston's representative society, that class which typifies the best achievement and highest aspiration of the city's social life, any reference to the "Country Club" has been suggestive, in other days, of a larger volume of pleasurable thoughts, remembrances and anticipations than were called forth by the mention of any other feature of that community. This responsive sentiment, moreover, was not confined to those who made their home in the beautiful city with which the Country Club is identified, but extended to urban residents of the vicin-

age, where dwelt congenial souls, who, as guests, were wont to partake of the enjoyment signalizing memorable gatherings within the hospitable portals of the Club's "Home." And thus, although its existence is measured by less than a score of years, its name long since became a synonym in Evanston for all that is worthiest and best in an association of kindred spirits, with the common purpose of fostering inspiriting diversions and wholesome sports, commingled with exercises of the mental faculties, and uplifting endeavors in the domain of music and art. The first conception of the projectors of the club was, doubtless, little else than as a medium for indulgence, on a more comprehensive scale, in the popular sports of the day, such as basket ball, tennis, billiards, pool, and other games devoid of strenuous exertion, and as an opportunity for unconventional gatherings, in a "home" common to the membership, of those who sought to cultivate a wider and better acquaintance than occasional neighborhood visiting afforded. Almost in its infancy, however, the organization began to develop into a broader scope, and continued enlarging its sphere of activities until it became the most conspicuous feature in Evanston's social life.

Previous to the inception of "The Country Club," many well-known gentlemen of

Evanston, largely of the younger element, were wont to indulge their social inclinations for fellowship, by fraternizing in coteries of limited membership, under various designations and for various specified purposes. This manner of dividing into small groups led to a habit of invidious criticism, and the members of one set were not infrequently the objects of depreciatory allusions by those of another, the basis of organization being narrow and the methods arbitrary. In none of these was the gentler sex eligible to membership, and public social functions of a comprehensive nature were unknown. In 1880 but two clubs of any pretentions were known in Evanston, viz.: the "Evanston Social Club," which was shortly afterwards disrupted, and the "Evanston Boat Club," devoted to a single purpose, and having an enrollment of two score of the stylish young men of the town. Somewhat later, another organization of young men was formed under the title of the "Idlewild Club," for the promotion of athletic sports, chiefly indoor ball and tennis. The Idlewild Club was subsequently merged with the Evanston Boat Club. The "Evanston Club," of present high repute, had not then been ushered into existence.

The ladies of Evanston, to a certain extent, were associated in those days in small, companionable bodies of their own sex, each comprising from a dozen to a score of members, designated by odd and enigmatic titles in the form of initial letters, such as the M. As; the N. Gs; the X. Ys; and the J. Js. These feminine groups were quite out of social touch with each other, making no effort towards harmonious relations, and, as between clubs of the sterner sex, unseemly rivalry engendered petty jealousies and harsh aspersions, at times approaching animosity.

Under the conditions which then prevailed in Evanston society, it was thus reserved for a new blending of social factors, the necessity for which had long been tacitly recognized in various quarters, to mold into cordial harmony, upon a broad and enduring basis, all kindred spirits of both sexes, composing that element which was conceded to be truly representative of the better and more highly aspiring social life of the city, in which all felt a fond pride.

The project of the Country Club of Evanston was first made a subject of discussion at a select social gathering at the residence of Frederick W. Clarke, on Hinman Avenue, in April, 1888. The suggestion of such an idea touched a common chord of responsive sentiment in all the guests, prominent among whom were A. T. Cutler, George T. Judd, Frederick Arnd, George Lunt, E. A. Chapman and William L. Brown. One of the ladies present was Mrs. Thomas S. Creighton (then Virginia Hamline), who was emphatic in urging an immediate movement toward organization. The gentlemen present withdrew into seclusion for a brief conference in regard to the practical features of the scheme, and their consultation resulted in a decision to induce, if possible, one of Evanston's most prominent and popular citizens to take the initiative in formative effort. The particular patron on whom the minds of all in attendance centered, was Marshall M. Kirkman, then, as now, a recognized leader in all worthy enterprises in Evanston. To Misses Hamline and Barlow, in conjunction with Thomas S. Creighton, was intrusted the mission of soliciting Mr. Kirkman's co-operation as the principal organizer of the new club. This committee and its proposition met with a cordial reception from that gentleman, who became a ready sponsor of the movement, and at his residence, on the evening of May 14, 1888, two committees were appointed, one to formulate a constitution, and the other to nominate officers, for the forthcoming organization. Their duties were accomplished on the spot. The nucleus of the present elaborate constitution was submitted to the assemblage and promptly ratified, and the officials designated by the committee on nominations were confirmed by vote, as follows: President, Marshall M. Kirkman; First Vice-President, Frederick W. Clarke; Second Vice-President, Milton W. Kirk; Treasurer and Recording Secretary, Thomas S. Creighton; and Corresponding Secretary, Catherine Aishton. The original enrollment included a membership of 150, composed of persons representing the most reputable element in Evanston society, associated for the purpose of promoting a higher degree and wider range of sociability, and encouraging physical exercise in the practice of athletic games. The aim of the club was, as declared by one of its projectors, the "making of life in Evanston even more pleasant than it is at present," and in the by-laws adopted at the outset, the object was formally stated to be "the promotion of social, athletic and esthetic culture, and its immediate purpose, the recreation and amusement of its members."

Formative details having been disposed of, the next step in the progress of the Country Club was, naturally, the establishment of suitable quarters for its occupancy. Its first "home" was built on Hinman Avenue, within an environment of most pleasant grounds. It was known by the quaint name of "The Old Shelter," and although of limited dimensions and unpretentious aspect, well served its purpose during the inceptive period of the club's existence. A snug retreat, of rustic design with a generous fireplace and cozy veranda, it was uniquely decorated within and without, and, altogether, was keenly suggestive of ease and comfort. Delightful indeed are the recollections that cluster about "The Old Shelter," and the thoughts of early members of the club who frequented it often revert to its homelike attractiveness, with feelings of pleasure not unmingled with a tinge of sadness. Many of them, then in the fervid flush of youth, but now staid matrons or sedate sires, both smile and sigh as they recall the gayeties of old-time summer gatherings there, under moonlit foliage, or the mirthful hours of cider symposiums on long winter evenings. Of the familiar faces of yore that reflected cheer on the festivities of "The Old Shelter," not all remain. Some of them are now known in connection with new scenes of activity, while the earthly abodes of others will miss them evermore. The memory of the early members who have vanished from this world's habitations, notably, George T. Judd, George Lunt and E. A. Chapman, is sacredly cherished by their surviving contemporaries among the founders of the club.

At a business meeting of the members held March 22, 1889, a committee was appointed to secure the incorporation of The Country Club under the laws of Illinois, and a petition for that purpose was drafted and forwarded to the State capital, to which twenty-eight names were appended. The gentlemen having charge of this matter were Martin M. Gridley, Harry P. Pearsons, J. Stanley Grepe, Thomas S. Creighton, Edwin F. Brown, Arthur Orr, Nicholas G. Iglehart, George Lunt, Harry S. Farwell and Frederick W. Clarke. A charter was issued, and the club was thus ushered into existence with the sanction of law. The first Board of Directors under the act of incorporation was composed of William Holabird, William L. Brown, John H. Kedzie, Jr., Charles H. Matthews and John W. Scott. Applications for membership were numerous from this period, and the strength of the organization rapidly increased. At the outset its influence was chiefly manifest in widening the circle of pleasant acquaintance of worthy men and women, who had hitherto been kept apart by barriers of formality. While the rules regulating admission were carefully administered, arbitrary restrictions were ignored, and the stiffness of mere conventionalism, in the better element of Evanston society, was soon materially relaxed under the genial sentiment dominating the club. The principal entertainment features under its auspices were in the form of select dancing parties, and the popular sports on its program were those then mostly in vogue—tennis and indoor ball.

Early in its fifth year, the numerical strength of the organization had grown to such a degree, and the social and athletic activities projected had so far exceeded the original plans, as to disclose the need of more ample accommodations as to space and convenience of arrangement, than "The Old Shelter" afforded. Measures were thereupon taken to provide new quarters. Plans were drawn under the supervision of the management, and the task of construction was commenced in the early summer of 1902. In the autumn of that year the present commodious and inviting structure, at the intersection of Lake Street and Oak Avenue, was completed. On the evening of October 18, the new edifice was suitably dedicated. The cost of the house and grounds was about $40,000, which in-

volved an issue of bonds to the amount of $33,500. The occupation of the present "home" signalized the inauguration of a more attractive series of social festivities, and a course of highly-interesting athletic competitions, which occasionally involved the participation of noted clubs from other localities. The Country Club "germans" date from that period, as does also the Lady Directors' custom of New Year's Day receptions, which have since constituted the most elaborate and enjoyable society "affairs" known in Evanston. From the time of the club's inception, one day has been set apart in summer, and one in winter, as "Children's Day," devoted to childish merry-making. On these occasions, the little folk monopolize the club house and its environs for a time of blithesome frolic. Music, refreshments and youthful sports abound, and the periodical recurrence of "Children's Day" is awaited by the juvenile element in Evanston with eager anticipation.

During the period intervening between 1892 and 1895, the Country Club played the part of host in many entertainments on an elaborate scale, in which its guests were well-known pleasure clubs, athletic organizations, and civic and military bodies. Among the prominent Lady Directors of that time whose conspicuous charms and accomplishments lent peculiar dignity and grace to these brilliant functions, were Mrs. Thomas S. Creighton, Mrs. Frederick Arnd, Mrs. George R. Jenkins, Mrs. Charles G. Fuller, Mrs. David A. Mudge, Mrs. William A. Hammond, Mrs. John B. Kirk, Mrs. Christopher L. Williams, Mrs. Milton W. Kirk, Mrs. Andrew Hazelhurst, Mrs. Frank M. Elliot, Miss Cornelia G. Lunt, Mrs. William J. Fabian, Mrs. Milton M. Kirkman, Mrs. Benjamin F. Adams, Mrs. Nicholas G.

Iglehart, Mrs. Edwin F. Brown, Mrs. Stewart Clark, Mrs. A. C. Buell, Mrs. Harry P. Pearsons, Mrs. Charles J. Connell, Mrs. George Lunt, Mrs. Curtis H. Remy, Mrs. Henry R. Post, Mrs. William Holabird, Mrs. William H. Harper, Mrs. Daniel H. Burnham, Mrs. B. J. Moore, Mrs. Francis A. Hardy, and Mrs. Herman D. Cable.

About the year 1890, was put into practical operation the policy of promoting branch associations for the purpose of fostering the talent and skill of the club's membership in particular lines of accomplishment. Between that year and 1895, seven flourishing subordinate branches were formed under the fostering care of the parent body, and whatever were the predilections of individual members as to esthetic culture, or their aptitude in the line of popular sports, each found in one of these different associations a satisfactory medium for the gratification of a peculiar taste, or the cultivation of a special talent. This policy of the club proved signally successful, and has done more to bring into prominent notice and stimulate to a high degree of development, the home talent of Evanston in musical and histrionic rendition, than all other local agencies combined. As early as 1895 the concerts given and the operas and dramas rendered by the members, and under the auspices of The Country Club, were hardly inferior to professional presentations, and the new club house had become the musical and artistic center of Evanston.

In the winter of 1893-94 was formed the Dramatic Association of the club. Prominent among the organizers were Louis F. Brown, William J. Fabian, Archer Gifford, Henry Raeder and William L. Wells. In addition to these gentlemen, and the wives of the last four, the following were original members of the associa-

tion, namely: Mr. and Mrs. Frederick Arnd, Mr. and Mrs. William H. Harper, Mr. and Mrs. Harry Cobb Kennedy, Mr. and Mrs. William A. Hammond, Mr. and Mrs. Charles P. Spining, Mr. and Mrs. Harley C. Winchell, Messrs. Gardner Read, Charles H. Dalgleish, Edward Hurd Smith, Hugh Talbot, George Stanford, Frederick H. Tackaberry, Frank M. Gould, John W. Scott, Ernest H. Eversz, Louis A. Ferguson, Frank M. Savage, Hanson McDowell, William C. Evans, and Misses Bessie Fletcher, Lida Scott, Anna Ives Hotchkiss, A. Louise Redfield, Maria Reynolds, Flora Gardner, Louise Rice, Sarah Ward, Mae Talbot, Mary T. Wilson, Virginia Boteler, Alice Spaulding, Mae Dingee, Anna Jane Wilcox, Lily M. Parker, Mrs. Elizabeth Boynton Harbert, Rosella Ward, Jessie E. Eversz, Ruth Farwell, Catherine Aishton and Louise Hoge. The officers were as follows: William J. Fabian, Manager; Miss Jean McN. Matteson, Secretary; and Mrs. Charles P. Spining, Miss Mary W. Lord, Archer Gifford, Henry Raeder and Harvey Cobb Kennedy, Directors. The new "Shelter" was remodeled in 1895, in order to admit of an enlargement of the stage to meet the necessary requirements of the Dramatic Association, and after this was made suitable, and the requisite mechanical appointments were provided, the plays thereupon produced, with roles filled by association's members, were presented in a manner as complete, entertaining and artistic as many witnessed in the theaters of Chicago.

The Cycling Association of the Country Club, for the purpose of which the smooth and shady streets of Evanston and its environs afforded peculiar facilities, was formed in 1894. A special feature in its program of recreation was the club rides on Saturday afternoons, when the members sallied forth from the club house, and wended their way to some appointed destination in the surrounding country. There they partook of refreshments and whiled away the waning day with pleasant converse in scattered groups, returning homeward in the dusk of evening, in jovial procession. The tasteful and variegated attire of the lady cyclists on these occasions presented a gay spectacle, the animated discourse of all, as they glided along in the twilight, giving evidence to throngs of interested observers, of the enjoyable hours they had passed. A large proportion of the early members of the club were enrolled in this association. It was managed by a Board of Directors, the regular excursions being under the conduct of Dr. Frank Dakin or Edwin C. Belknap. The association also included a body of cyclists composed exclusively of ladies organized for daily rides, under the guidance of Mrs. Frederick Arnd and Miss Bessie Chapin.

The Country Club "Musical Association" was formed in 1894, its nucleus being a singing society previously organized by a few of the members. Through the efforts of President Kirkman, who was ever on the alert to devise measures for broadening the scope and enhancing the usefulness and prestige of the club, this association received its first impetus. Mr. Kirkman was aided by the earnest co-operation of Walter M. Anthony, who had been prominent in the musical circles of Worcester, Mass., before establishing his home in Evanston. At the instance of these two gentlemen, a meeting of all the members interested in the project was convened on February 20, of the last mentioned year. In that gathering The Country Club Musical Association was launched into being, with the following board of Directors, namely: Mrs. George

R. Jenkins, Miss Cornelia G. Lunt, Miss Annie W. Lord, John W. Scott, Prof. A. F. McCarrell, Ernest H. Eversz, and Walter M. Anthony. Mr. Anthony was afterwards elected President, and Mr. Eversz, Secretary and Treasurer. The association was subsequently divided into two separate bodies—a woman's musical organization, at first styled the "Friday Morning Musical Club," and a society of male vocalists, called the Country Club Maennerchor. The practice of the latter was under the direction of Prof. McCarrell, and later, under that of Prof. P. C. Lutkin. In conjunction with Messrs. McCarrell and Lutkin as founders of the Maennerchor, were William Richards, Charles Dickinson and John R. Lindgren. Mr. Lindgren, who had been an orchestra leader in Chicago, succeeded Mr. Anthony as its President. Associated with him as officers were Charles S. Burch, Vice-President; Albert D. Shaw, Secretary; Thomas Beard, Treasurer; and Robert Holmes, Librarian. The Maennerchor, whose first efforts were limited to college songs and old-time melodies, gradually attained proficiency in a higher degree of musical art, and became one of the leading organizations of its kind in the West.

The Woman's Musical Association of The Country Club, at first known as the "Friday Morning Club," was composed of about thirty active members, and constituted the Ladies' Choir of The Country Club. Together with the Maennerchor, it formed the well-known "Evanston Music Club of that period. The original officers of the Woman's Musical Association were as follows: Mrs. William Holabird, President; Mrs. Arthur W. Underwood, Vice-President; and Mrs. Marshall M. Kirkman, Mrs. Daniel A. Mudge, Mrs. William L. Vance, Mrs. Charles P. Spining, Mrs. Charles R. Webster and Miss

Helen M. Ide, Directors. The membership represented a superior order of musical talent, and acquired, by reason of diligent practice, an excellent artistic culture. It was recognized as the bright esthetic feature of Evanston society.

A large number of members of The Country Club gathered in its reception rooms on May 28, 1894, and perfected the organization of the Equestrian Association, in which riders of both sexes were represented. Francis A. Hardy was elected Director, with William C. Hoag as Secretary and Treasurer; and Francis O. Frazier, William B. Bogert and Hamilton E. Grepe were chosen as a board of managers. The event at once stimulated a new interest in horsemanship throughout the town. Many superb riding horses were purchased and brought to Evanston from Kentucky and Missouri, States noted for their fine grade of saddle horses, and scores of mettlesome steeds were soon seen prancing in the knightly sport which the association was formed to promote. Its members, mounted on chargers caparisoned in saddle-blankets of blue broadcloth with yellow bindings and showing, brightly embroidered in their corners, the four-leaf clover emblematic of the club, presented a gay and imposing sight to the beholder. The riding parties were wont to meet for country-road excursions on Saturday afternoons, and to the practice of graceful horsemanship acquired in many spirited jaunts, is attributable much of the skill for which Evanston society people have been noted in connection with this robust and exhilarating diversion. At the period of its inception, thirty-one gentlemen, all prominent members of The Country Club, joined in the regular riding parties of the Equestrian Association. Among the accomplished equestriennes who graced these occasions were Mrs.

Louis F. Brown, Mrs. Charles Buckley, Mrs. Thomas S. Creighton, Mrs. Frederick E. French, Mrs. Francis A. Hardy, Mrs. Marshall M. Kirkman, Mrs. George W. Whitfield and Misses Katherine Buehler, Cora Cassard, Elizabeth Fletcher, Minnie Kirkman, Maude Parker, Kate C. Quinlan and Mary T. Wilson. In the summer of 1895, as an off-shoot of the Equestrian Association, a number of its members organized themselves for competition in the game of pony polo. This body acting in concert with the former, afterwards inaugurated what was observed as "The Country Club Field Day," on which polo matches, hurdle races, pony races and premium "turnout" exhibits constituted the attractions. Marshall M. Kirkman was the projector of The Country Club Polo Association, and its organization was effected at his residence on the evening of April 12, 1895. Besides the host of the occasion, those in attendance were Albert Tracy Kirkman, Marshall Jay Kirkman, W. Bruce Kirkman, George H. Sargent, John H. Kedzie, Jr., Gabriel F. Slaughter, Henry W. Dakin, John M. Allen, Frederick S. Chapin and George K. Armsby. George S. Chapin was elected Captain of the Association, and Frederick S. Chapin was made Secretary and Treasurer. Grounds were leased and suitably prepared at the corner of Grant Street and Asbury Avenue, and an experimental game of polo was there played one month from the date of organization.

A feature of instrumental music was supplied by the club in October, 1894, in the formation of a Banjo and Mandolin Association, each instrument being at first represented by a distinct organization, the former having fifteen members, and the latter, eleven. These were under the direction, respectively, of Ralph H. Smith and Signor Salvatore Tomaso. The two societies were subsequently united under one leadership. Prominent among the original members were the Misses Mae Rice, Grace Hess, Lily Rice, Susanna Rowe, Lucy Pinney, Blanche Eversz, Elizabeth Boynton Harbert, Frances Rickards, Teresa Metcalf, Louise Rice, Emily D. Rowe, Mrs. Lucian E. Harding, and Messrs. Charles George Lewis, Thomas H. Lewis, William C. Gilbert, John W. Scott, Dwight Willing, Frank Savage, Winter D. Hess, Will Gilbert, William McCormick, Charles H. Matthews, Marshall Jay Kirkman and Benjamin Miller. Some of these "branch associations" were discontinued in after years. Among the most notable "functions" of the parent club which have been maintained ever since its inception, are the New Year's receptions and the Children's Day festivals, which are still characterized by undiminished vivacity and eclat.

From the organization of the Country Club, on May 14, 1888, until and including the annual election of officers in 1898, its subordinate executive officials were as follows: First Vice-Presidents—Frederick W. Clarke, Arthur Orr, William E. Stockton (who served two terms), and Frederick Arnd (who served seven terms); Second Vice-Presidents—Milton W. Kirk, Frederick Arnd (who served two terms), Frank M. Elliot, and Benjamin F. Adams (who served seven terms); Treasurers—Thomas S. Creighton and Nicholas G. Iglehart, of whom the latter served ten terms; Secretaries—Catherine Aishton, Edwin F. Brown (who served seven terms), William B. Bogert, and John H. Kedzie, Jr., (who served two terms). In the course of time above mentioned, the following gentlemen were Directors of the club: Marshall M. Kirkman, Nicholas G. Iglehart, Edwin C. Belknap, Benjamin F. Adams, Thomas S. Creighton, Arthur

Orr, Frederick Arnd, George Lunt, Roscoe L. Wickes, Edwin F. Brown, Martin M. Gridley, William E. Stockton, William Holabird, Frank M. Elliot, Harry S. Stevens, Francis O. Frazier, Francis A. Hardy, E. A. Chapman, Milton W. Kirk, Hugh R. Wilson, John Scott, Hanson McDowell, Charles H. Matthews, William B. Bogert and Charles T. Boynton.

Marshall M. Kirkman served continuously as President of the club from the time of its organization until the official term covering 1898. William Holabird succeeded Mr. Kirkman as President and Francis A. Hardy became First Vice-President; Francis O. Frazier, Second Vice-President; Rufus C. Davis, Treasurer; and Lucien E. Harding, Secretary. The directors then elected were: for three years—Frederick Arnd, John H. Kedzie, Jr., John W. Scott and William W. Gates; for two years—Hugh R. Wilson and Walter W. Ross; for one year—Marshall M. Kirkman, Rollin A. Keyes and Edwin A. Sherman. In April, 1901, Judge Leroy D. Thoman succeeded Mr. Holabird as President, serving in that capacity four years.

The present President of the Club, Franklin C. Letts, was elected May 1, 1905, when the following officials were also elected, namely: First Vice-President, Charles E. Yerkes; Second Vice-President, Charles G. Davis; Secretary and Treasurer, Charles N. Stevens; Directors—Murray B. Augur, Charles H. Barry, Marshall Clarke, David R. Forgan, George T. Kelly, William Holabird, Marshall M. Kirkman, C. F. Marlow, F. F. Peabody and William H. Warren.

The present membership of The Country Club numbers 800. Its sole honorary member is Nicholas G. Iglehart. The list of life members, a relation involving a fee of $400 for gentlemen and $85 for ladies, is as follows: William Blanchard, Charles

T. Boynton, William L. Brown, John M. Ewen, William J. Fabian, Francis P. Frazier, Francis A. Hardy, William Holabird, John H. Kedzie, Jr., John B. Kirk, Walter W. Kirk, Marshall M. Kirkman, Richard C. Lake, Charles G. Lewis, Dr. Thomas H. Lewis, Benjamin W. Lord, Uriah Lott, Arthur Orr, Henry P. Pearsons, Henry Raeder, George M. Sargent, Roscoe L. Wickes, Hugh R. Wilson, Mrs. Charles T. Boynton, Mrs. William L. Brown, Mrs. John M. Ewen, Mrs. William J. Fabian, Mrs. Francis P. Frazier, Mrs. Francis A. Hardy, Mrs. William Holabird, Mrs. J. W. Howell, Miss Margaret Kedzie, Miss Emma Kirk, Mrs. John B. Kirk, Mrs. Walter W. Kirk, Mrs. Marshall M. Kirkman, Miss Ella Gates Kirkman, Miss Mary Lewis, Mrs. Uriah Lott, Mrs. Henry Raeder, Mrs. Martha C. Stockton, Miss Julia K. Watson, Mrs. Hugh R. Wilson and Miss Mary T. Wilson.

CHAPTER XLVI.

BIOGRAPHICAL

ORRINGTON LUNT.

"A man he seems of cheerful yesterdays,
And confident tomorrows."

Orrington Lunt, one of Chicago's pioneers and one of the founders of Evanston, attained to the very ideal of the public-spirited, patriotic citizen, without a blemish upon his record as a merchant, a gentleman and a Christian. He was born in Bowdoinham, Maine, December 24, 1815. He came of old New England stock. His first American ancestor, Henry Lunt, who emigrated to this country from England in 1635, was a grantee in the original allotment of land in Newburyport, Mass., and, in 1636, was made a freeman of the colony. His grandmother was a daughter of General Joseph Vose of Revolutionary fame, one of the founders of the Society of the Cincinnati and a direct descendant of a family noted for courage and prowess. His father, William Lunt, represented his county in the Maine Legislature and was everywhere recognized as a thrifty and enterprising man of affairs. He was a merchant in the little town of Bowdoinham and during a long life-time enjoyed the esteem and confidence of the community in which he lived. His mother, Anne Matilda Sumner, was of the same lineage as Governor Sumner of Massachusetts, and the distinguished Senator of that name. She was a woman of rare cleverness and beauty, and from her apparently her oldest child derived many of his principal traits. And the gifts bestowed upon him at his cradle were among the best at God's command; physical strength and manly beauty, a sweet and sunny temper, a quick strong mind, a rich quaint humor, a fearless spirit and a tender heart. Besides all these, a glad delight in natural beauty and a joy in human fellowship.

When the lad was nine years old he sat one wintry afternoon watching his mother's face by the light of the fire. Her beloved features changed to such unutterable sadness that he burst into tears. Roused from her reverie she put her arms about him and tried to comfort him. But the solemn sweetness with which she urged him to be a good boy and a good man, never to forget her, never to forget her counsels, revealed the truth, and ere many months he stood beside her grave. After that, it was said, the neighbors seldom saw him smile. But he learned rapidly and eagerly all that the village schools could teach him. The vigorous and ambitious boy was everywhere known as a hard worker and an apt scholar. Apparently a bright future opened before him as a student, but at the call of duty he went forth to prepare for the great battle of commercial life, being then in his fourteenth year.

On leaving school he entered his father's store, taking hold of his assigned tasks with the same hearty good will and high purpose that so distinctly marked his whole after career. He showed from the first the steady light of sterling integrity, of persistent effort, and of unweariedness in well doing. He remained in the store, a growing favorite with all who dealt there, until the attainment of his majority when he was taken into partnership. The character of Mr. Lunt was well established. He had attracted the confidence of his neighbors and was honored by them publicly. In his twenty-second year he was elected Clerk and Treasurer of the town, and was also appointed Justice of the Peace. These positions he held until he left the State.

But Bowdoinham was too small and too slow a place for his active and enterprising nature. He had married on the 16th of January, 1842, Miss Cornelia A. Gray, the oldest daughter of the Hon. Samuel Gray, a leading attorney in the village, who served as Representative, Senator, and member of the Governor's Council of the State; and as trade grew dull he and his young wife determined to try their fortune in the then distant and unknown West.

He sold out his interests in Maine at a heavy sacrifice, realizing little more than enough to pay off his mercantile indebtedness. They started west on the first of November, 1842, and arrived in Chicago on the eleventh of that same month, it taking ten days of constant travel to make the journey. Chicago then, according to the census of 1840, had a population of less than five thousand, and it was then at its lowest ebb, real estate selling for less than at any time since the

crisis of 1837. The condition of trade was at a standstill and it was impossible to embark in business during the winter, as navigation was closed. At that time there were no railroads in the Western State. To add to their discouragement, in the spring Mrs. Lunt became alarmingly ill, and during her partial convalescence they decided to return to Maine. He was now thoroughly disheartened, but the spirit of the pioneer was not to be denied. He had looked upon the prairies and the Lakes, and the narrower horizon of New England robbed him of that new sense of liberty he had learned to value. He felt, with the intuition of a faith he never lost, that in the West was the seat of opportunity, and that Chicago, then a village of five or six thousand inhabitants, was to be the metropolis of that West. So about the last of July they again turned their faces westward, his entire capital consisting of letters of recommendation from Eastern firms, mercantile houses in Boston and New York.

Mr. Lunt began his business career in Chicago as a commission merchant by purchasing a set of books on credit, and at once started the shipments of such produce as he could obtain. His first transaction of any considerable magnitude was the buying of several hundred barrels of cranberries in lots, as they were offered at fifty cents per bushel, for a Boston house. He was soon busily at work purchasing almost anything that offered. He succeeded so well that, by the summer of 1844, he was fairly started in the grain trade, which he began by receiving from Buffalo a small cargo of oats to sell for this market. After the ensuing harvest he began to purchase wheat from teams. At that time this product had to be hauled by the farmers in their wagons to Chicago, sometimes coming from the distant fields in Indiana and from the prairies of Central Illinois. At Chicago it was transferred to boats and thence transported eastward by way of the Lakes. The business steadily increased, his operations became more extensive, his careful energetic management attracted confidence and esteem. In 1845 he leased a lot on the river front and erected thereon a warehouse having a storage capacity of 100,000 bushels—no mean capacity in that "day of small things." Wheat came in quite freely after the harvest, and with a brisk trade, on a continually advancing market, he had his house full by the close of navigation. He made one sale of fifty thousand bushels, which was a very large transaction in those days.

In business Mr. Lunt was an honest man in the strictest sense of the word—not only honest in his personal dealings, but he never tolerated dishonesty in subordinates or employes. In those days, when grain was drawn to Chicago, sold to buyers on the street and weighed in at South Water street warehouses, the farmers who sent their boys to the young city repeatedly told the inexperienced youths to "wait for Orrington Lunt or one of his buyers," and it became known on the street that instructions were given that, even if he offered lower prices than any other buyers, "not to leave him, for his honest weights would more than make the difference." He was strong, self-reliant and enterprising, and soon prosperity made him over-sanguine. He bought boldly and lost in a single season all that he had made. He took the lesson to heart. He never speculated again, and was ever afterward noted for his cautious and conservative sagacity. Frontier life is a severe test of character. Many a man has forgotten, in the hurry and excitement of a rapidly growing town, his

moral training and his religious experience. But Orrington Lunt never neglected his vows to God during the years of strenuous commercial activity, in which he laid the foundations of his success. His probity became proverbial.

With the entry of railroads into Chicago, the conditions of trade materially changed, and, in the year 1853, Mr. Lunt leased his warehouse for a term of years and retired temporarily from the handling of grain, but in 1859 he again took charge and continued until 1862 handling as much as three and a half million bushels of grain annually. He always kept himself familiar with all the transactions of the Board of Trade, which had seen its first struggles into existence in 1848. He had joined with those who were taking the initiatory steps for its formation, and was at the first meeting called to pass resolutions and adopt a constitution. He was a charter member, at one time a Director on the Board, and was one of the noted pioneers in that period of its history. In 1851, at its third annual meeting, the official reports presented an extremely discouraging aspect of affairs. Not only had the membership fallen off, but those in good standing who had paid their dues numbered only thirty-eight, and during the following year business transactions "on change" became so insignificant that attendance dropped at times to nothing. It is noteworthy that on the record for July 12th there was present one man. It was Orrington Lunt. And during nine days only five members had sufficient interest to put in an appearance at the place appointed for daily sessions. From that Board of Trade, to which he belonged from its organization, he never resigned his membership.

Mr. Lunt was pre-eminently a builder whose conservatism was only matched by his steady, persistent push in everything he undertook. He exercised a potent influence in the city of his adoption. Every enterprise calculated to further its prosperity deeply interested him. His zeal, conservatism, and strenuous endeavor made him an important factor during the formation period of the civic, railroad, educational, church and business life of Chicago and all the country tributary to it during that period. His geniality was as proverbial as his sterling honesty. His generosity was without narrowness. His hand and his home were open to all good men and all good causes, and the wisdom of his counsel was eagerly welcomed in all the varied interests connected with the growth of the Northwest. He early held many honorable positions. Rarely does it fall to the lot of one man to be equally wise in the Council Chamber and strong in executive action. Places upon boards of directors always came to him. He did not have to seek them nor did he shun them. He responded to every call upon his conscience and his judgment, and was ever ready to share in doing anything that would develop Chicago and the country about it. His love for his adopted city grew with its growth, and lasted all his life long; and the name of Orrington Lunt commanded respect, confidence and affection in all Chicago. Men loved him for his gentleness, yet he knew how to achieve his purpose. His plans were pushed with tranquil energy, and none could swerve him where his conscience was involved.

In 1853 Mr. Lunt was appointed a member of the Committee of the Board of Trade to visit Washington and urge upon Congress the improvement of Chicago harbor. In 1855 he was elected a Water Commissioner for the South Division of Chicago, and con-

tinued in that position for six years. At the end of his first term in office, he was re-elected for three more years, and during the last three, the City Department having been consolidated in the Board of Public Works, he held the position of Treasurer and President of the Board. He was often solicited by his friends to allow his name to be used as a candidate for Mayor and various high city offices, but his ambition never ran in that direction. He was one of the most modest men that ever blessed the human family. He shrank from ostentation and from public applause. Like most men of that early period he made investments in real estate. He became interested in Fire and Life Insurance, and was a Director in the Chicago Fireman's and the Chicago Mutual Life Insurance Companies. He devoted much attention to railroad enterprises, particularly to the Galena & Chicago Union, of which he was a director from 1855 until it became a part of the Chicago & Northwestern Railway Company's System. He was also one of the Auditors of the Board of Directors and devoted close attention to the duties of the office for several years. During the last two years of his connection with the road, up to the time of its absorption by the Northwestern, he was its Vice-President.

During all its years, until his resignation a few months before his death, he was a member of the Board of Trustees of the Young Men's Christian Association; he was President of the Chicago Bible Society and one of its life-members, and worked earnestly and with decided success to establish the Chicago Orphan Asylum, of which he was one of the builders and early benefactors. In connection with one other member of the Building Committee, in the summer of 1854, he raised nearly twenty thousand dollars to complete the edifice. In 1854 he also became a Trustee of Dearborn Seminary, which, after a trying struggle, succeeded in erecting its building in 1857. He was one of the original Trustees of Clark Seminary at Aurora, which was built by a private corporation but subsequently turned over to the church, the first holders transferring their interest without compensation. He was one of the Board of Directors of the first Homœopathic Hospital established in 1854, and a Trustee of the Hahnemann College, whose charter was drafted in the office of Abraham Lincoln who personally exerted himself to secure its passage. Quinn Chapel was organized in 1847 to shelter a little congregation of colored people. With a quiet courage that never failed him, Mr. Lunt helped these unfortunates when they were the objects of much persecution. He had sold to them a lot at a minimum price, receiving a very small first payment. The passage and the approval of the Fugitive Slave Act in 1850 had caused great consternation among the colored population of Chicago, and resolutions intensely antagonistic to the bill were passed and even a Vigilance Committee appointed. In one of the journals of that period it is related that many of the little congregation fled to Canada to prevent the provisions of the bill being enforced upon them. A local historian describes their pastor as "having very strong lungs, and being well versed in the prophecies and Revelations, but with a weak heart and doing nothing for the church." He refused to sign any papers, nor would he do anything toward collections, or aid in any payments on Queen Chapel lot. A committee, therefore, waited upon Mr. Lunt to explain their indigence and inability, to whom he replied, "Give yourselves no uneasiness; you shall not lose the prop-

erty," and immediately donated three hundred of the five hundred dollars due him. He purchased lots for the Swedes, Germans and other church societies, and his name became a household word in all of them. A liberal man at the beginning of his Christian life when only twenty years of age and when his means were slender, his benefactions increased in variety and magnitude with his enlarging fortune.

When Mr. Lunt first came to Chicago he and his wife immediately connected themselves with the First Methodist Episcopal Church, in which he became one of the Trustees and for a long time was the Secretary of the Board. In the counsels of the church his words were not many, but always wise and brave. For Orrington Lunt united shrewdness with sentiment. He planned for others as well as for himself. He gave thought and toil as well as speech and song. It has been said of him that there is not a Methodist institution, general or local, in the city of Chicago, which is not, in one way or another, a beneficiary of his enthusiastic and invincible love for the Church and Kingdom. The State Street Methodist Episcopal Church originated with Orrington Lunt. In 1847, realizing the necessity of a church edifice further south, he bought a lot which he offered to the Clark Street at the purchase price less his own contribution, and held this offer open for five years. The Wabash Avenue M. E. Church was the result of his foresight and generosity. To the church of his early love he gave unstinted energy and a thrifty and far-seeing wisdom. His piety was fraught with rare intelligence, and to him more than to any other man the Methodists in Chicago owe many of the plans that made their growth so rapid. In spiritual as well as financial affairs he was active. In the social meetings he was a conspicuous and beloved figure. When he sang in the prayer meetings he captured all hearts. Not unfrequently in those early days he sang alone. His voice was rich and resonant, strong, with a supporting, inspiring quality that made the heart glad. "I believe," he wrote in his old age, "that if one sings so as to help the meeting he must have the spirit to sing." And he sang, as he gave, with the spirit and desire to help. He had the keenest sense of righteousness without a tinge of bitterness toward anybody. Religious faith wrought in him not so much to transform as to refine, to preserve, to illuminate and to perfect him. And the vital thing about Orrington Lunt was the divine atmosphere in which he moved for over sixty years. It clothed him with an invisible armor. It urged him on to secret prayer and open goodness. It strengthened and perfected the virtues he inherited. It guided him into large and generous enterprise. It made his home luminous and glorified his old age. His character, to many who thought they understood him, seemed quite simple. But it was, in reality, a harmony of many qualities too seldom found together. There was nothing astonishing about him, and yet no human being in all Chicago taught more perfectly the dignity of manhood and the sweet magic of loving kindness. Other men have had more fame; no man was ever dearer to the hearts that knew him. Other men have made more money; he made enough to accomplish far more for the public good than most of them. True to every trust, eager to urge and swift to aid in every work of mercy, the association of his name with a new project became almost a guarantee of its success.

When the Civil War broke out Mr. Lunt consented to serve upon the Committee of Safety and Finance, appointed at the Bryan Hall Meeting, held April 13, 1861. That was a day long to be remembered in Chicago, a beautiful, cloudless spring day, such as seldom visits the West so early—and in the fresh April air, from spire and balcony, church and dwelling, floated the flag which had been lowered at Fort Sumter. To raise it once more—to preserve its honor as a priceless heritage—was the all-absorbing passion and purpose. He was a figure in the war meetings crowded with excited and patriotic citizens, and he spent the first Sabbath after the fall of Fort Sumter in raising supplies and starting the first regiment to the front from Chicago. And this was but the beginning of his efforts to aid the Union cause. His work was continuous, faithful and nobly generous. He threw himself into the arduous work of the committee with the zeal of an enthusiast whose patriotism knew no more doubt than his religious faith. While the war lasted his devotion never flagged. And whatever Orrington Lunt did was not only sure to be well done, but it was done in a spirit of gentleness and cheerfulness that was a constant wonder and joy to his fellow-workers in those days of National trial. And four years after the commencement of the bitter struggle, he had the delight of seeing the old flag again flung to the breeze from the battlements of Sumter, and later, in company with distinguished generals and civilians, he visited Charleston and Richmond. His was also the proud privilege of witnessing, at our National Capital, the never to be forgotten Grand Review of our victorious armies at Washington on May 24, 1865.

Travel had always been to Mr. Lunt a source of keen enjoyment, and he lost no opportunity to familiarize himself with large regions of his own country. In 1865 he started with his family on a journey to the Old World. He visited the noted cities and countries of Europe and the East and traveled extensively for over two years. He loved nature and he loved art, and to the last moment of his stay abroad he showed for both a tireless interest. No one of his children, alert and active as they were, could keep pace with him. What he liked he remembered vividly and tenaciously, what he disliked he forgot. He had the rare quality of seeing quickly and passing by easily the trivial and unpleasant, and he had a childlike happiness in the beautiful, the curious and the wonderful. Returning to Chicago he devoted himself to the care of his estate and to the enterprises that had become the central interests of his life. In 1877 he was elected President of the Trustees of the Care Fund for the lot owners of Rose Hill Cemetery, and was their Treasurer to within a short period of his death, rendering, as was his wont, entirely gratuitous service. Under the skillful and faithful management of the Trustees $100,000 was collected and invested in city and Cook County bonds. Simply to mention the religious, philanthropic, and educational enterprises which were and are indebted to his munificence and foresight, is to make no inconsiderable catalogue. He displayed an enviable largeness of spirit, and a monumental lavishness in gifts.

But the crowning activity of Mr. Lunt's public life was that in connection with the Northwestern University and the Garrett Biblical Institute, to which he gave more affection and gratuitous service than any other man who has been connected with them. It is a blessing rare and seldom paralleled that a man of large private interests should render, through so long a period and without pecuniary compensation, such painstaking, judicious and

devoted service. And though responsible for many and extensive interests, which in the vicissitudes of business were often imperiled; and though in constant demand by important civic, philanthropic and religious enterprises for service which was always ungrudgingly rendered, Mr. Lunt still gave to those institutions the richest treasure of his sagacity, his patience, and his tireless devotion. As early as 1851 Mr. Lunt, with two others, purchased the quarter of a block at the northeast corner of La Salle and Jackson Streets, Chicago, with a view to the possible location there of a preparatory school for the projected University. But, after the University had been founded at Evanston, this property, of which they still held possession, as they had given their personal obligations for its full payment, was leased to provide an income for the University which still owns it. It is the valuable land on which they have reared, as a permanent investment, that noble building occupied by the Illinois Trust and Savings Bank. Mr. Lunt's connection with the Board of Trustees of the University was continuous from the granting of the charter in 1851, in which he was named one of the incorporators, until his death in 1897. For a time he was Treasurer of the Board, and he served for several years as a member of the Auditing Committee. In 1875 he became First Vice-President and Acting President of the Board of Trustees, and continued as such until 1895, when he accepted the Presidency which had been repeatedly urged upon him. The University had frequently been the object of his generosity. It was characteristic of him that, at the time when he was planning for the special pleasure and profit of his family, he should also plan for the advancement of the institution he was wont to watch over almost as if it had been one of his children. Just before his departure for Europe he deeded to the University one hundred and fifty-seven acres of land, fifty-four of which yet remain unsold and constitute an endowment fund for the Library. In 1855 he was one of the charter members of the Garrett Biblical Institute, and was its Secretary and Treasurer and the Manager of its financial and business matters until his death. His policy was to sacredly keep intact the landed property willed by Mrs. Garrett, believing it to be the most permanent endowment. His was the steadfast, practical wisdom that no booming prosperity or speculative enterprise could swerve from the principles of true conservatism, and that no financial disasters could waver or discourage. His unwearied and unremitting services, rendered with such judgment and power of prevision, gave him a unique place among the benefactors of the schools. Only those intimately associated with him in the development of that work could appreciate the laborious exactive management of infinite detail which he voluntarily assumed. Not only their material interests, but the selection of fit men for the Boards of Instruction, the framing of educational policy, and the fostering of the spirit of earnest evangelism were subjects of his constant care; and his sagacious counselling and liberal devising were resorted to as unfailing sources of light and inspiration.

And his chief success was here at Evanston. A history of Evanston would have Mr. Lunt's name inscribed on its very first page, for to him more than to any other man is due the location of this city. He was the actual discoverer of the Evanston site and, therefore, the cause of the purchase of the magnificent location now owned and occupied by the University. He helped to plant the Institute and University in the Grove that enchanted him. He helped obtain the charters that safeguard their endowments, and safeguard also the children of this city from the dread destroyer worse than death. He lavished upon these Institutions an unceasing industry. He poured out for them his money and his time. The noblest building on the campus is a visible monument of his generosity, but no architect that lives could frame a structure beautiful enough to symbolize the loving fidelity, the almost passionate affection, with which Orrington Lunt fathered the progress of these schools. They had grown fast to his heart.

When the great fire of 1871 laid Chicago in ashes, and reduced multitudes to want, Mr. Lunt's home on Michigan Avenue went with the rest, and with it went all the buildings from which he derived an income. But there was that about this quiet man, with the smiling kindly eyes, that neither flood, war, fire nor famine could daunt. He began amid the smoking ruins to lay the foundations for the restoration of his own fortune, as well as for the salvation of Garrett Biblical Institute and the rebuilding of the Methodist churches. With the wisdom that always requires most of the busiest men, Mr. Lunt was chosen a member of the Relief and Aid Society which had charge of the distribution of the World's contributions for the relief of Chicago's destitute. The $150,000 collected from generous Methodists in all parts of the country passed through his hands and was disbursed to the satisfaction of all parties.

In 1874 Mr. Lunt with his family removed to Evanston. He had first looked with the eye of a Seer on the beautiful grove. He had watched with pride the growth of the charming suburb. His home in Chicago had melted under a fiery hand. His memory, crowded with past scenes, with happy visions of cherished plans accomplished and noble enterprises started for centuries to come, made it natural for him to choose Evanston as the home of his old age. Yet, in one sense Orrington Lunt had no old age. His four-score years were not "labor and sorrow." His strength, his good cheer, his vivacity, his sagacity remained with him, so that his life at Evanston was an ideal existence for him and his beloved. The home was the center of his heart's affection. He never forgot that a perfect human home is the joy and the triumph of human endeavor. A lover after half a century of wedded life; a father who was at the same time as elder brother to his children; he never did, and never could, live his life in any sense apart from those dearest to him. Whatever interested him he took to them. Whatever interested them was to him like something of his own. The sunny smile, the hearty hospitable word, the cordial hand-grasp, the heart warmth that always found leisure to make a welcome for the guest, the quick sense of humor and ready laugh that answered every jest, the lowering of the voice that showed his sympathy with every trouble, the swift responsive interest in human life and work left in every heart the sense of a perennial and perpetual youth. Happy in the wife of his youth and his children, his hearthstone was the center of perpetual gladness, and there gathered rapidly a cluster of far reaching activities and friendships in Evanston that made their home upon the Lake Shore as beautiful, for its moral outlook, as it was for its enchanting views of Lake Michigan.

On the evening of January 16, 1892, that home of Mr. and Mrs. Lunt was thronged with friends who came to celebrate their Golden Wedding. Fifty years since the newly wedded pair had turned their hopeful eyes toward Chicago; fifty years since, with youthful courage, they had made their venture to the unknown West. What wonders they had seen! Of what marvelous achievements they had themselves been a part! It was, indeed, a notable company that assembled to greet this pioneer citizen—to bring to the much beloved benefactor and equally beloved wife the congratulations of the community and the gratitude of thousands. All day long letters and telegrams had been pouring in from far and near; friends of his youth and friends of his later years, from bishops of the church, civic rulers, merchants, bankers, lawyers, physicians, officers and professors of the colleges, neighbors and relatives—all vied with each other to honor him and the wife who had furthered all his plans, who had delighted alike in his prosperity and his generosity, and who, with quiet skill, had ruled the household and trained the children. Costly presents and elaborate addresses were laid at their feet. He looked and listened with gracious satisfaction. Benignity and contentment beamed from his features. He had completed half a century of faithful, happy and honorable domestic and parental life. This unstinted appreciation, these expressions of love and admiration and reverence were the fitting coronation of a life so rich in helpfulness, so radiant with intelligent benevolence, so thoroughly alive with kindly energy. He had shown himself friendly, and now he had friends. He was recognized everywhere as an example the largeness and wisdom of whose life had come to its golden fruition of victory and peace.

During that culmination of International Expositions, the World's Columbian Exposition of 1893. Mr. Lunt displayed remarkable vigor and vivacity. He visited the White City almost daily. It was to him the grandest enterprise ever carried through. He exulted in it all as a great educational work and it was to him the demonstration of how great Chicago could be. Those palaces and temples of the whole world's science and art and industry and zeal were studied with keenest enthusiasm and appreciation. Not counting the fatigue or exertion, he attended most of the celebrations held amid those surroundings. He spoke of it always with a challenging pride, he talked much of its far-reaching and beneficial results, and he astonished his whole circle by his intimate acquaintance with its wonders. The advancement of our Nation in art, science and invention filled him with a personal joy. On Chicago Day— that greatest pacific gathering the world had ever seen—he was one of the happiest in the happy throng. In that Fair his smiling eyes beheld all the promises of Chicago fulfilled fourfold; for as one has ably put it, "creation had been brought together in harmony and in brotherhood."

As the Orrington Lunt Library rose above its foundations he watched its progress with ardent delight, and surprised his friends by his alertness and activity. But, as it approached completion, his strength began to fail. When in the fall of 1894 the building was dedicated, Mr. Lunt, to the joy of his friends, was strong enough to be there and to read his address of presentation. No one who saw it can ever forget the scene; some could hardly take in his words—so pathetically beautiful was the sight. The touch of death was upon him, and they knew they would hear his voice in public no more. His words

told them that he knew it also when he said:—"And, if I may now speak a few words to the young men and women who are to gather here that they may gain strength and enthusiasm for lofty purpose and noble endeavor, I would earnestly say to them—remember that, whatever you are, your chief effectiveness in life will be due to the high ground you take; that your weight in advancing any cause will be measured in the end by your standard of character. That which is personal, small and intolerant soon dies, and only what is rational and noble, in the hard struggle for truth, survives to wield eventually its just power unfettered and free. The treasures of the past, the possessions of the present, and the promise of the future seem to one of my age, looking back upon many deprivations and an entire lack of these splendid chances, to be all yours for the seeking, all within your reach . . . I seem to see the light which touches even as the sunrise touches the hill tops, the heads of the young and ardent workers of today. We, whose feet are rapidly nearing the Shadowy Valley, have hope of the better things to come. Well do we know that all things which are true and honest, just and pure, come from Him who is the perfect beauty and perfect truth. And so believing, we look patiently for that revelation which is to turn darkness into light, falsehood into truth, hatred into love, and the whole earth from evil unto good. . . . Here is the Library. It is yours with its class rooms, its lecture rooms, its books, its periodicals, its newspapers. Yours with its inspirations and possessions, given to this University in cheerful love, and in full confidence that it will be consecrated by patient industry and fruitful research, and that the gift will be multiplied by centuries of use; that it will enlighten all who come into its studious and quiet atmosphere, and more firmly establish that which you—living men of progress and lovers of learning —are aiming to teach and embody. I pray, in hope and faith, that it may become a great, active and potential force for good. I shall never speak to you all again. Standing before you where I have so seldom stood in my life before, all unused as I am to the platform and wholly a novice at public speaking; reminded, as one of my age must constantly be reminded, of those who have passed beyond our human vision, whither all feet are surely tending—reminiscence has had, perhaps, too large a share in my thought and speech. This you will pardon to my years. And in closing— not mournfully but rejoicingly—I quote, and may even dare to appropriate, a sentence of Carlyle's, spoken of his father, whom he loved and whose death left him conscious of irreparable loss, yet kindled his faith into exalted expression, "I, too,"—as that father did—"feel my feet upon the Everlasting Rock, and through time, with its death can to some degree see into Eternity with its life." He was indeed seeing into Eternal Life.

One of the distinguished journalists of Chicago records the city's estimate in an editorial, under the distinctive heading, "End of a Beautiful Life":

"Full of years, crowned with good works, beloved (as few men are) by all, with not an enemy in the wide world, Orrington Lunt, the founder of Evanston and one of the Fathers of Northwestern University, died at his residence in our northern suburb yesterday morning. Mr. Lunt was in his eighty-second year, and for fifty-five years of his life he had been a sweet and wholesome influence in the stirring scenes marking the development of Chicago from the hamlet to a metropolis. He was one of our pioneers, and he brought to this city a disposition so singularly limpid, gentle

and pure; a nature so full of love for his fellow men; a character so free from the fierce energy of action that is usually associated with the founding of cities, that his career was another illustration of the truth that

"The bravest are the tenderest,
The loving are the daring."

"In the early history of Chicago the name of Orrington Lunt figures in almost every enterprise that went toward centering here the trade of this vast continent. And as Chicago grew to be a city of mark in the land, the same name was found enrolled wherever action was being taken to yoke the refining elements of education and culture with its material activity and growth. It is impossible to fully estimate or appreciate the priceless value of such a life to such a stirring community as that with which Orrington Lunt united his fortunes. It imparted a leaven to the grosser lump which has never ceased to work for the purification and elevation of this city.

"Of recent years it has been a joy to look upon the beautiful face of this pioneer. Crowned with an aureole of silver hair, as pure white as his own spotless nature, he has walked among us a being beneficent. He has gone, but his public benefactions, his private virtues, and the memory of his gentle, successful life remain to bless the community in which he lived.

"Yes, Orrington Lunt was indeed a rare being, a very radiant human energy, a just man, very beautiful with love. He died on the morning of April 5, 1897. He was buried on the following Thursday. On the day of the funeral the schools were closed, business was practically suspended, and the National colors were half-masted in Evanston. The entire city mourned as if he represented every interest there. A vast multitude gathered in the First Methodist

Church of Evanston to honor his memory and to listen to the beautiful ceremonies of his funeral. In place of the ordinary depressing and oppressive black, the prevailing color of the funeral drapery was purple. That color accorded better with the sunny life, earnest spirit, and ministering works that had adorned his personal history. The many tributes to his memory were marked by an unusual tenderness and reverence. All who knew him sorrowed and were grateful. The overflowing buoyancy of his nature had made sunshine wherever he was, and left inevitably an unlifting shadow on every life out of which his smile had gone. Tears and thanksgiving mingled in every mention of his death, for by his manly and beneficent life he had brought men nearer to the heavenly world. No wonder, therefore, that his departure touched them like a benediction. The words spoken over his bier sounded like words of triumph.

"All that we loved him for is now immortal, and the shadow of him will linger with us while we remain and remember. It is not simply his name that is woven forever into the history of this community and its institutions, but his character has penetrated them and us and made us nobler than we were. Like some subtle mystery of climate that gives rare beauty and rare vigor to the happy children of the soil, so his influence will work its quiet marvels as the days go by, and brighten the lives of many with transfiguring touch. The building that bears his name to posterity may crumble to its foundation; but so long as yonder Lake that charmed him hither murmurs to human listeners, the power of his faith and his example, carried from generation to generation, will break in praises of human blessing at the feet of God."

HARVEY B. HURD.

Hon. Harvey B. Hurd was born in Huntington, Fairfield County, Connecticut, February 14, 1828, and died at his home in Evanston, Ill., January 20, 1906. On his father's side he was of English descent, and of Dutch and Irish lineage on the side of his mother. His youth was spent on his father's farm, during the summers at work and in the winters at school, until he was fifteen years of age, when, on May 1, 1842, he made his start in life, breaking the home ties and journeying on foot with his little pack to Bridgeport, Conn., to become an apprentice in the office of the "Bridgeport Standard," a Whig newspaper. After two years and more of work as a printer, with a company of young men he turned his face westward to seek his fortune. He landed in Peoria County, Illinois, and for more than a year attended school at Jubilee College, founded by Bishop Philander Chase. His funds having been exhausted, he sought employment in Peoria as a printer, but failing to find it, took passage on a baggage stage for the growing city of Chicago. There he obtained work as a printer in the office of the "Evening Journal," which was then published by Wilson and Geer. A little later he was employed for a time on the "Prairie Farmer." In the fall of 1847 he began studying law in the office of Calvin De Wolf, and was admitted to the bar in 1848, forming a partnership with Carlos Haven, and soon after with Henry Snapp. From 1850 to 1854 he was in partnership with Andrew J. Brown, with whom he was interested in the purchase and platting of a large tract of land on the West Side of Evanston, which has since become one of the most attractive parts of that suburb. In the summer of 1854, he built his home in Evanston, where he lived continuously till the day of his death, an exemplary, industrious and public spirited life, taking a vital interest in all the concerns of his home town, of the city in which he worked, the State and the Nation. No interests were too small or too large to enlist his attention and active labor. He became the first President of the Evanston Village Board and retained his active interest in all its steps of progress throughout his life.

Mr. Hurd was an anti-slavery man of the abolitionist type, and took an active part in the stirring events which took place in Chicago, both before and after the repeal of the Missouri Compromise. He was a member of the convention which met at Buffalo, N. Y., at which a national committee was formed to aid, arm and protect the Northern settlers in Kansas, and was appointed Secretary of its Executive Committee by this convention, with headquarters at Chicago. When the Kansas crop proved a failure in 1856, adding to the strife of factions, the committee in New York instructed the Executive Committee at Chicago to purchase the necessary seed for the crop of 1857, at the same time appropriating $5,000 to aid John Brown to organize and equip the Free Soil settlers for the purpose of protection. There were not funds enough in the treasurer's hands to meet both requirements, so he decided that the first requisite was seed, which was forwarded. When John Brown called for the appropriation the treasury was empty. Serious complaint was made by Gerritt Smith and other martial friends of John Brown, but the joy with which the seedgrain was hailed on its arrival at Lawrence, Kans., vindicated the action of Mr. Hurd, and made it possible for the settlers to hold their ground, without which their cause would have been lost. When John Brown left Kansas with a price upon his head, he found an asylum in the house of John Jones, later the colored County Com-

missioner of Cook County, who had escaped from slavery. Brown's clothing was in tatters, but it was unsafe for him to venture out to the tailors to be fitted with a new suit. Mr. Hurd became his proxy and was measured for the suit, which in due time reached Brown. Mr. Hurd used often to refer to the incident and the humor of it, and remarked that he was glad he was not in it when John Brown was hung.

The firm of Booth & Hurd was formed in 1862. The Hon. Henry Booth was deeply interested in legal education, and his partner likewise accepted a position as lecturer in the Law School of the old University of Chicago. In 1868, the law firm of Booth & Hurd was dissolved and Mr. Hurd retired from private practice, accepting in 1869 the appointment from Governor Palmer of a place on the Board of Commissioners to revise and rewrite the General Statutes of the State of Illinois. His colleagues soon withdrew from the work and he carried it on alone, completing it with the adjournment of the Twenty-eighth General Assembly in April, 1874, and he was appointed by that body to edit and supervise the publication of a volume of revised statutes made necessary by the adoption of the Constitution of 1870. This task he accomplished so satisfactorily that it stands as a monument to his industry and skill. Seventeen editions have since been edited by him following successive sessions of the Legislature, and "Hurd's Statutes" has become a household word among the legal profession of the State.

When the Law School of the Chicago University became the Union College of Law in 1876, under the joint supervision of Northwestern University and the University of Chicago, Mr. Hurd continued as a Professor in the School and remained for many years after it became exclusively a department of Northwestern University.

until he felt that he could no longer carry the burden in addition to affairs which taxed his declining strength. The deep regret of his associates and students that was manifested at his leave-taking made very apparent the large place that he held in their esteem. His logical mind and large acquaintance with affairs, his geniality and democratic spirit made him an ideal teacher. His interest in young men and in legal education kept him fresh and young, and imparted an element of enthusiasm to his work that made it a joy to himself and his pupils. The importance of the public question of drainage, as it pertained to the city of Chicago and the communities adjacent, early appealed to him as to others to such an extent that he has been credited by many with being the father of the system. However that may be, he was certainly the author of the plan creating, for the benefit of the municipal district of Chicago, "The Chicago Sanitary District," which was adopted. He was the author of the first bill introduced in the Legislature on the subject in 1886. When a legislative committee was appointed to further investigate the subject and present a bill, such a bill fashioned upon the Hurd Bill was presented by them and passed in 1877.

For a number of years Mr. Hurd was at the head of the Committee of Law Reform of the Illinois State Bar Association, and gave the subject the same public spirited and conscientious care which he was accustomed to bestow on all matters of public interest. Many able reports on this subject emanated from his pen, among them one on the subject of the transfer of land titles, which resulted in the appointment of a commission by the State to consider the subject. Mr. Hurd was made Chairman of the Commission which recommended, in December, 1892, a system of registering land titles based upon the Australian or Torrens system. In 1897 the recommendations of this commission culminated in the act for the registration of land titles which is now in our statutes, and which has been imitated in many other States of the Union. Another of his activities was in connection with the Children's Aid Society of Chicago, which grew out of his earnest endeavor to protect the young who were victims of crime and poverty, and evil association in their tender years. He was constantly calling attention to the necessity of this work in the interest of the State, and was the sponsor of the Juvenile Court Bill, which, under the administration of such Judges as Tuthill and Mack, is working so beneficently in the interest of the youth of Chicago and Cook County in the prevention of crime and the saving of the children.

Not alone did he lend his natural powers, his wide observation and his consummate skill to the formulation of legislative acts for the numerous causes that enlisted his sympathy, but was constantly importuned for aid by various causes seeking changes in the interest of justice and progress or the public good, and only those who were intimately associated with him can realize the amount of valuable time and consideration he gave to these matters of public service without expectation of material reward. In all matters pertaining to township, village, city, State and national affairs, he was an interested public spirited citizen. His home reflected his culture and his domestic virtues. He was thrice married to lovely and cultured women, who made the Hurd home in Evanston a synonym for refinement and taste and hospitality. Two daughters survive him: Mrs. George S. Lord, of Evanston, and Mrs. John A. Comstock. His funeral was held in the Evanston home and memorial services were likewise held in the Emmanuel

Methodist Church, to the building of which he had generously contributed. Judges Horton, Kohlsaat and Tuthill each spoke feelingly and appreciatively of Mr. Hurd's well spent life in the interest of the community, and Dr. R. D. Sheppard spoke of his relations in the home town where he was best known. It was the universal testimony that a noble, useful and many-sided career had closed with the death of Mr. Hurd, that the life of the State and Nation had been enriched by his living, and to him should be accorded the tribute, "Well done, good and faithful servant."

ROBERT DICKINSON SHEPPARD.

Robert Dickinson Sheppard, A. M., D. D., former Professor and present Trustee of Northwestern University, was born in the city of Chicago July 23, 1846, the son of Robert and Samantha (Dickinson) Sheppard. The father was a native of Dundee, Scotland, who came to America in 1830, locating first at Buffalo, N. Y., whence five years later he came to Chicago, where he became a building contractor and later engaged in the lumber business. Robert Sheppard, Sr., was an early Methodist and erected the first brick building occupied by the First M. E. Church on the site of the present Clark Street church. His wife, Samantha (Dickinson) Sheppard, mother of the subject of this sketch, was born in Granby, Hampshire County, Massachusetts, the daughter of Zenas Dickinson, who came to Chicago in 1835, where the daughter was a pioneer teacher.

The son, Robert D., was educated in the Foster School, the Chicago High School, the Northwestern University and the old University of Chicago, graduating from the latter in 1869. At an early period he formed the purpose to qualify himself for the ministry, and accordingly devoted much of the time during his college vacations to the study of theology. As a consequence it was necessary for him to spend only one year at the Garrett Biblical Institute to complete his theological course, receiving his certificate of graduation from the Institute in 1870, when he was immediately admitted to membership in the Rock River Conference of the Methodist Episcopal Church. His first charge after entering the ministry was as pastor of the Michigan Avenue Church, Chicago, with which he was connected for a period of three years, which was the full limit at that time. His second charge was in connection with the Third Street Church at Rockford, Ill., after which he spent three years (1874-77) as pastor of the Western Avenue M. E. Church, Chicago. In the fall of 1877 he went abroad and spent the following year in travel, visiting Italy, Greece, Palestine, Asia Minor and Egypt, with a view to extending his acquaintance with countries and peoples connected with Biblical history, besides devoting six months to study in Germany. On his return to Chicago in 1878 he was appointed pastor of the Grace Methodist Episcopal Church, Chicago, where he remained three years, when he became pastor of the First Church at Aurora, Ill., remaining there a like period when he returned to Grace Church. Three years after graduating at the University of Chicago, he received from that institution the degree of A. M., in course, and in 1875 an honorary degree of the same rank from the Northwestern University. Mr. Sheppard's official connection with the latter institution began in 1878, when he became one of its Trustees, in 1884 accepting a similar relation with the Garrett Biblical Institute, which he has retained up to the present time. In 1884 he was elected by unanimous vote of the Board of Trustees of the Northwestern University to the chair of History and Political Economy in that institution, and was immediately granted one year's leave of absence, which he utilized for travel and study abroad. Returning at the end of the year, he entered upon his studies, which he continued to discharge in full until the burden of care in the business office of the University made it necessary for him to share some of his professional work with his colleagues. In 1892 he was elected Treasurer and Business Manager of the University, resigning this position in 1904, with the intention of resuming his work in history after a vacation granted him by the Trustees. Excepting the President, no one has occupied a more prominent and responsible position in connection with the material growth of Northwestern University than Dr. Sheppard, and his fitness has been demonstrated by his long connection therewith and the confidence manifested in him by the Trustees and friends of the institution. After an active professional experience of over thirty-five years, of which more than twenty years has been spent in connection with the Northwestern University, Dr. Sheppard is still in the midst of a successful career with apparently many years of usefulness before him.

Dr. Sheppard was married on June 13, 1872, to Miss Virginia Loring, a daughter of Nahum Loring, who settled at Naperville, Ill., at an early day, and there established a mercantile business at a time when that place was considered, in a certain sense, a rival of Chicago. Four children have been the result of this union, namely: Robert Loring, Margarethe, Virginia and Dorothea, all of whom are living.

FRANCES E. WILLARD.

(By MRS. L. M. N. STEVENS, President National W. C. T. U.)

Frances E. Willard was born of New England ancestry in Churchville, N. Y., September 28, 1839, reared in Wisconsin and educated at the Northwestern University, Evanston, which was the family home for well-nigh forty years. Here, beginning as a teacher in the public schools, Miss Willard, by what she liked to call "honest hard work," achieved the position of Dean of the Woman's Department of the University, and Professor of Rhetoric in a faculty otherwise composed of men, nearly all of whom had been graduated from European universities. She studied abroad two years or more (from 1868 to 1870), French, German, Italian, history and the fine arts being the subjects to which her attention was devoted. It was her ambition to be a literary woman in connection with her work as a college professor. She was perhaps more celebrated for her method of school government than for any other one thing at this time. She organized what amounted to a senate and a house of representatives of the young women in the college, and practically placed their government in their own hands. This method worked so well for the good order of the institution and for the development of a high standard of honor among the young women students, that it has since been introduced into many colleges and public schools.

In 1862 Miss Willard wrote her first book, "Nineteen Beautiful Years," which was published by the Harper Brothers, with an introduction by the poet Whittier, and since has been translated into several languages. She also wrote "How to Win," a book for girls; "Woman and Temperance," a history of the Woman's Christian Temperance Union; "A Classic Town," a history of the beautiful university town of Evanston; "A Young Woman Journalist," intended to inspire young women to take up a profession in which Miss Willard herself had been engaged for many years. "Glimpses of Fifty Years," her autobiography, of which 50,000 copies have been sold, was written in 1889 by request of the National Woman's Christian Temperance Union. "A Great Mother" is, perhaps, her best book, containing as it does the theory and practice of bringing up children according to her mother's plan; and Madam Willard was, in the estimation of everyone who knew her, a truly "Great Mother." Miss Willard's hand-book for the world's white ribboners, entitled "Do Everything," is packed full of hints and helps for local workers. She also wrote "Woman in the Pulpit" and "How I Learned to Ride the Bicycle."

In 1883 Miss Willard and Miss Anna Gordon made a temperance organization trip, visiting each of the States and Territories of the United States, traveling 30,000 miles or more, from Puget Sound to the Gulf of Mexico. Such a trip had never before been made by man or woman in any cause, so far as we know. In the same year Miss Willard founded the World's Woman's Christian Temperance Union, of which she became President, and which has made the White Ribbon Society known in every English speaking country of the globe.

In 1892 Miss Willard and Miss Gordon went to England by invitation of Lady Henry Somerset, their devoted friend, who then led the movement in Great Britain. There they helped to develop white ribbon methods and to edit the English white ribbon paper. Editions of several of Miss Willard's books were brought out about this time, thus making her known to the reading public in the mother country. A great reception was tendered her in Exeter

Hall, which was participated in by fifty philanthropic societies of London, with such speakers as Canon Wilberforce, Lady Henry Somerset, Mrs. Ormiston Chant, William T. Stead, Rev. Hugh Price Hughes, Rev. Mark Guy Pearce and several members of Parliament.

They returned to America from this visit in the summer of 1894, Lady Henry Somerset coming with them. In March, 1895, they again went to England. Miss Willard and Miss Gordon returned to the United States in time for the National W. C. T. U. Convention, held that year in Baltimore. In April, 1896, Miss Willard made her last voyage to England, accompanied by Miss Gordon, and it was in the autumn of this year that she and Lady Henry did their notable work for the Armenian refugees at Marseilles, her interest in their welfare never waning. She reached her native land in October, 1896, spent the following winter in Castile, N. Y., and the last summer of her life was spent in New England. In October, 1897, Miss Willard presided over the World's W. C. T. U. Convention, held in Toronto, Canada. Her address as President of that convention was pronounced to be one of the finest, most powerful and eloquent that she had ever delivered. A few days later she presided over the National Convention at Buffalo, N. Y.

Miss Willard originated the "Polyglot" Petition addressed to all the Governments of the world, praying for the prohibition of the liquor traffic and the opium trade, which, with seven million names and attestations of great societies, was presented to the President of the United States in February, 1895, and in London before an audience of ten thousand people in June, 1895. In April, 1898, the petition was presented to the Dominion of Canada at a great meeting in Ottawa, arranged by the Canadian W. C. T. U., when it was received on behalf of the Canadian Government by the Premier, Sir Wilfred Laurier. Miss Willard's active interest on behalf of social purity, labor reform and woman suffrage was in consistent accord with her belief in the "do everything" policy of dealing with the great problem of the day.

In 1894 the honorary degree of LL. D. was conferred upon Miss Willard by the Ohio Wesleyan University.

How Miss Willard Came Into the Work of the W. C. T. U.

Miss Willard has repeatedly said that, when the Crusade came, in 1873, she as well as her mother, became absorbingly interested in it. Miss Willard resigned the presidency of the Woman's College and her professorship in the University in June, 1874. Attractive positions at the head of educational institutions were offered her, but she felt more and more drawn to the women of the "Crusade." She was not in Chautauqua when the preliminary committee for organized work was formed, but was at that time in Maine, consulting with Neal Dow, and in Boston, consulting with Dr. Dio Lewis. Meantime she wrote to Bishop Simpson, who had been an honored friend of her family for years; also to Mrs. Mary A. Livermore, whom she and her mother greatly admired, and to other leaders, as well as to her own family, friends and relatives, not one of whom sent her a favorable reply except Mrs. Livermore, who encouraged her, telling her by all means to follow her leadings. Miss Willard's resolution to join the crusade movement was taken independently. One morning in August, 1874, there came to her a letter from Mrs. Louise S. Rounds, who had led the crusade movement in Chicago during the winter, asking her if she would come to Chicago and act as President of the local W. C. T. U. They were a weak band of

middle-aged women without financial resources, and Mrs. Rounds wrote Miss Willard that they could offer her no salary. On the same day that this letter reached her at Cambridge, Mass., Miss Willard received a definite offer from the principal of a ladies' school in New York City, near Central Park, offering her $2,500 a year if she would act as preceptress, teaching as little or as much as she pleased, but exercising a helpful influence over the young ladies and among the patrons. She was entirely without income, and had not laid up a penny, as those who knew her do not need to be told. Her mother was advancing in years, and Miss Willard was her only support. The crusade movement had passed away and there seemed to be a lull in the work. Yet so profound was the impression that God called her to the work of the Woman's Christian Temperance Union, that she at once wrote to New York declining Dr. Van Norman's offer, and to Mrs. Rounds, accepting the position of President of the W. C. T. U. of Chicago, entering upon its duties a few weeks later.

At the organizing convention of The National Woman's Christian Temperance Union, held in Cleveland, Ohio, November, 1874, Miss Willard was elected Corresponding Secretary of the organization, which position she held until she was elected President at the Indianapolis Convention in 1879. She was re-elected as President each year, holding that position at the time she passed away. Miss Willard was the founder of the World's Woman's Christian Temperance Union, which was organized in 1883, and was its first and only President during her lifetime. Lady Henry Somerset, who was Vice-President, succeeded Miss Willard in the Presidency and still holds that office, having been re-elected at the sixth biennial convention held at Geneva, Switzerland, in

1902. This society is composed of National Unions organized in over fifty nations. The other officers are: Mrs. Lillian M. M. Stevens, Vice-President, who is also President of the National W. C. T. U. of the United States; Miss Anna A. Gordon, one of the Secretaries and also Vice-President-at-large of the W. C. T. U. of the United States; Miss Agnes Slack of England the other Secretary; and Mrs. Sanderson, of Canada, Treasurer.

Many memorials have been erected in many places in honor of Miss Willard. The National Woman's Christian Temperance Union decided that its most fitting memorial would be to extend and perpetuate the work to which she gave her life. For this purpose, contributions to the Frances E. Willard Memorial Organization Fund are made each year, and the society is constantly gaining in membership and influence.

Miss Willard's home State of Illinois, through the action of its Legislature, has placed a statue of Miss Willard in the Hall of Fame in the United States Capitol Building at Washington, D. C. Miss Willard is the first woman to be thus honored. On occasion of the acceptance of this statue by the United States Congress, on February 17, 1905, memorable addresses were made by Senators Cullom and Hopkins of Illinois, Beveridge of Indiana and Dolliver of Iowa. In the House, Representatives Foss, Graff and Rainey, of Illinois; Littlefield, of Maine, and Brooks, of Colorado, also delivered notable addresses.

These addresses were fitting eulogies of the great good woman who had the heart and mind of Christ in her yearning love for humanity. At the hour of unveiling the statue, thousands of little people paid the tribute of childhood, as each one placed a flower at the foot of the statue.

"Stand, radiant soul,
Here in the center of our nation's heart,
Forever of its best life thou'rt a part;
Here thou shalt draw thy land to what thou art.
 Stand, radiant soul."

A commemorative meeting was held in the evening, at which forty-three States were represented by speeches, messages or telegrams. Miss Willard will live on and on in the hearts of multitudes of grateful men and women, who, with desires like her own, are working to redeem our country from the curse of impurity and intemperance.

The following tribute to Miss Willard, as the type of "The American Woman," was delivered in the United States Senate by Senator Albert J. Beveridge, of Indiana, on the occasion of the unveiling of the Willard statue in Washington, above referred to:

Mr. President: From the beginning woman has personified the world's ideals. When history began its record it found her already the chosen bride of Art. The things that minister to mankind's good have, from the very first, by the general judgment, been made feminine—the ships that bear us through storm to port; the seasons that bring variety, surcease of toil and life's renewal; the earth itself, which, through all time and in all speech, has been the universal mother. The Graces were women, and the Muses, too. Always her influence has glorified the world, until her beatitude becomes divine in Mary, Mother of God.

Mark how the noblest conceptions of the human mind have always been presented in form of woman. Take Liberty; take Justice; take all the holy aspirations, all the sacred realities. Each glorious ideal has, to the common thought, been feminine. The sculptors of the olden time made every immortal idea a daughter of the gods. Even Wisdom was a woman in the early concept of the race, and the unknown genius of the youthful world wrought Triumph itself into woman's form in that masterpiece of all the ages—The Winged Victory. Over the lives and destinies of men the ancients placed Clotho, Lachesis, and Atrophos, forever spinning, twisting, severing the strands of human fate.

In literature of all time woman has been Mercy's messenger, handmaid of tenderness, creator and preserver of human happiness. Name Shakespeare—Miranda and Imogen, Rosalind, Perdita and Cordelia appear; name Burns—the prayer "To Mary in Heaven" gives to the general heart that touch of nature which makes the whole

world kin; name the Book of Books—Rachel and
the women of the Bible, in beauty, walk before
us, and, in the words of Ruth, we hear the ultimate formula of woman's eternal fidelity and
faith.

So we see that, through all time, woman has
typified the true, the beautiful, and the good on
earth. And now Illinois, near the very heart of
the world's great Republic and at the dawn of
the twentieth century, chooses woman herself as
the ideal of that Commonwealth and of this
period; for the character of Frances E. Willard
is womanhood's apotheosis.

And she was American. She was the child of
our American prairies, daughter of an American
home. And so she had strength and gentleness,
simplicity and vision. Not from the complex
lives that wealth and luxury force upon their
unfortunate children; not from the sharpening
and hardening process of the city's social and
business grind; not from any of civilization's
artificialities, come those whom God appoints to
lead mankind toward the light.

Moses dwelt alone on the summit of mystery
and human solitude. The Master abode in the
wilderness, and there the power descended on
Him with which He put aside the tempter. In
the forests the Father of our Country learned
Liberty's lessons from Nature, Liberty's mother,
and from the valleys and the heights, the fields
and pouring streams, got understanding of the
possibilities of this land, a knowledge of its uses,
a perception of its people's destiny. We cannot
imagine Abraham Lincoln coming to us from a
palace. No! We can understand him only as
he really was—man of the people and the soil,
thinking with the people's mind the grand and
simple truths, feeling with the people's heart an
infinite compassion for and fellowship with all
the race.

So, Mr. President, all the saints and heroes of
this world have come, fresh and strong from the
source of things, by abuses unspoiled and un-
weakened by false refinements. And so came
Frances E. Willard, the American woman. The
wide, free fields were the playgrounds of her
childhood. The great primeval woods impressed
her unfolding soul with their vast and vital calm-
ness. Association with her neighbors was scant
and difficult, and home meant to her all that the
poets have sung of it, and more. It was a refuge
and a shrine, a dwelling and a place of joy, a
spot where peace and love and safety and all
unselfishness reigned with a sovereignty un-
challenged. And so this child of our forests and
our plains, this daughter of that finest of civilization's advance guard—the American pioneers—
early received into her very soul that conception
of the home to which, as the apostle of universal
womanhood, her whole life was dedicated.

To make the homes of the millions pure, to
render sweet and strong those human relations
which constitute the family—this was her mission and her work. And there cannot be a
wiser method of mankind's upliftment than this—
no better way to make a nation noble and enduring; for the hearthstone is the foundation
whereon the state is built. The family is the

social and natural unit. Spencer wrote learnedly
of "the individual and the state;" but he wrote
words merely. The individual is not the important factor in nature or the nation. Nature
destroys the individual. Nature cares only for
the pair; knows in some form nothing but the
family. And so, by the deep reasoning of nature
itself, Frances Willard's work was justified.

But hers was no philosopher's creed. She got
her inspiration from a higher source than human
thinking. In her life's work we see restored to
earth that faith which, whenever man has let it
work its miracle has wrought victory here and
immortality hereafter. Such was the faith of
Joan, the inspired maid of France; such that of
Columbus, sailing westward through the dark;
such the exalted belief of those good missionaries
who first invaded our American wilderness to
light, with their own lives on civilization's altar,
the sacred fire that never dies. The story of
Frances Willard's faith in the conquest of evil
by the good seems incredible to us who demand
a map of all our future before we take a step.

For Frances E. Willard knew no questioning.
The Master's message was at once her guaranty and her command. The Bible was to her,
in very truth, divine. What immeasurable and
increasing influence that one book has wielded
over the minds of men and the destiny of the
world! If it be the word of God, as we
profoundly believe, surely it comes to human
ears with all the dignity and peace and power
that His word should command. If it be the
word of man, then even the doubter must admit
that the ancient Hebrews had miraculous skill
to cast a spell across millenniums which,
strengthening with the years, spreads wider
today than ever and embraces the future as far
as even the eye of imagination can behold. Not
all invention, or all statesmanship, or all of literature have so touched and bettered human life as
this one book. And it was the Bible that gave
Frances E. Willard her mission, her strength,
her hope, her argument and her inspiration.

Thus prepared and thus equipped she went
out into the world and to her work. No method
can measure what she did. The half million of
women whom she brought into organized co-operation in the Women's Christian Temperance
Union, is but a suggestion of the real results of
her activities. Indeed, the highest benefits her
life bestowed were as intangible as air and as full
of life. She made purer the moral atmosphere
of a continent—almost of a world. She rendered
the life of a nation cleaner, the mind of a people
saner. Millions of homes today are happier for
her; millions of wives and mothers bless her;
and countless children have grown into strong,
upright and beautiful maturity, who, but for the
work of Frances E. Willard, might have been
forever soiled and weakened.

Mother of all mothers, sister of all wives, to
every child the lover, Frances E. Willard sacrificed her own life to the happiness of her sisters.
For after all, she knew that, with all her gifts
and all the halo of her God-sent mission, nevertheless the humblest mother was yet greater far
than she. But it was needful that she should so

consecrate her strength and length of years. For how shall the service of utter unselfishness be achieved save in the utter sacrifice of self? So Frances E. Willard gave up her life and all the rights and glories of it, that all of her sisters might lead fuller, richer, happier, sweeter lives themselves.

So, Mr. President, by placing her statue in the hall of our national immortals, a great commonwealth today forever commemorates the services of this American woman to all humanity. And the representatives of the American people—the greatest people in this world—in Congress formally assembled, today are paying tribute to the little frontier American maid who heard and heeded the voices that came to her from the unseen world, and, obeying their counsels, became the first woman of her generation, the most beloved character of her time, and, under God, a benefactress of her race.

WILLIAM DEERING.

William Deering, merchant and manufacturer, was born at Paris, Oxford County, Maine, April 24, 1826. His parents were James and Eliza (Moore) Deering. His ancestors emigrated from England in 1634, and, in all of the histories of New England from that time, the name of Deering finds most honorable mention. William Deering's boyhood was much the same as that of other boys reared by earnest Christian parents. His scholastic education consisted of the full and regular course of studies in vogue at that time in the common and graded schools, and was finished in the high school at Redfield, Maine, in 1843. While yet in his early manhood he occupied the position of manager of a woolen mill in Maine, discharging every trust reposed in him to the eminent satisfaction of his employers. After the termination of his labors there he engaged in various business enterprises, to which is largely due his marked genius for handling large manufacturing details. His greatest achievement has been the building up of the works of William Deering & Company, for the manufacture of harvesters and agricultural machinery. The firm was founded in 1870,

the name being changed in 1894 to the Deering Harvester Company, but is now the "National Harvester Company," in which Mr. Deering holds the controlling interest. The works are now located in Fullerton Avenue, along the line of the Chicago & Northwestern Railroad, with docks on the North Branch of the Chicago River. At the present time eighty-five acres are occupied by the plant, which is compactly arranged. The works comprise large woodworking shops, knife and section shops, machine and blacksmith shops, bolt and rivet works, a foundry, a large malleable iron plant, and an extensive twine plant. The works consume annually 45,000 tons of steel and a like quantity of pig iron, comprising both Northern and Southern coke-iron. Some 72,000 tons of coal and coke are annually consumed, 4,817,750 gallons of oil and 31,000,000 feet of lumber.

The force employed in the shops is usually 7,000 hands, and many of the departments work with regular night shifts, the establishment operating its own electric light plant, which gives it facilities for producing a larger number of machines of all kinds than any other harvester company in the world. It receives a part of its raw material from many foreign countries, including the Philippines, and distributes its products all over the globe. The sales department embraces fifty-eight branch houses and general agencies, and the sales extend over Europe, Australia, New Zealand and South America. Mr. Deering, the founder of this immense plant, continues actively identified with its operations, ably assisted by his two sons, Charles and James.

Mr. Deering has been twice married. His first wife was Miss Abby Barbour, of Maine, daughter of Charles and Joanna (Cobb) Barbour, to whom he was married October 31, 1849. Of this union there was one child, Charles, born in 1852, now Secretary of the Deering Harvester Company. The second marriage, on December 15, 1857, was to Miss Clara Hamilton, of Maine, daughter of Charles and Mary (Barbour) Hamilton. The issue was two children, James and Abby Marion, born in Maine—the former in 1859, and the latter 1867. James Deering is the present Treasurer of the Deering Harvester Company. William Deering removed with his family to Evanston, Ill., in 1873, where he now resides in his beautiful home. He is liberal, public-spirited and benevolent, and his business career has been noteworthy from the absence of controversies with his employes. He has been, for a number of years, one of the Trustees of the Northwestern University at Evanston. He is also a Director and stockholder in several financial institutions. One of his latest acts of beneficence was the giving of Fisk Hall to the Northwestern University.

CHARLES COMSTOCK.

Charles Comstock (deceased), for over thirty years a prominent citizen of Evanston, Ill., and during his business career, a leading member of the Chicago Board of Trade, was born in Camden, N. Y., May 7, 1814, and spent his early life in the central portion of his native State. In 1861 he came to Chicago as the Western Agent of the Onondaga Salt Company, of which he was a stockholder, and at once located at Evanston, which continued to be his residence for the remainder of his life, covering a period of thirty-four years. Soon after coming to Chicago he became a member of the Chicago Board of Trade and, at the time of his death in September, 1895, was, with one single exception, the oldest in continuous membership connected with that organization.

As a business man Mr. Comstock was noted through his life for his energy and aggressive character, occupied with rare business judgment and a public spirit that tended to promote the interest of the city and any enterprise with which he might be connected. Always possessed of ample means, he contributed liberally to the support of religious and benevolent enterprises, and was a leading factor in the founding of St. Mark's Episcopal Church in Evanston in 1865, of which he was a generous supporter and which he served as Senior Warden continuously for thirty-one years. For five years he acted as President of the Traders' Insurance Company, in which he retained a large interest, besides being interested in several leading banks of Chicago. On account of age and failing health he was practically retired from active business during the latter years of his life, but always maintained a deep interest in business affairs and in operations on the Board of Trade. The late Judge George F. Comstock, of the New York Court of Appeals, was his brother, and together they were largely interested in the Onondaga Salt Company, of which Mr. Charles Comstock was the representative after coming West in 1861.

Mr. Comstock was twice married, his first marriage being with Mary Griswold of the State of Massachusetts and a niece of Bishop Griswold, an early American Bishop of the Episcopal Church. One son by this marriage—who is a namesake of Bishop Griswold—is now living. Mr. Comstock's second marriage was with Miss Julia J. Sprague of New York State, who survived him five years. Of this marriage five children are living—two sons and three daughters. The golden wedding anniversary of this marriage was celebrated in September, 1892, three years before Mr. Comstock's death. That event occurred at his home at 1326 Ridge Avenue, Evanston, September 5, 1895, at the age of over eighty-one years, as the result of a lingering illness from which he had suffered for many years. Both the local and the Chicago press paid a generous tribute to his memory as an upright citizen and a public-spirited and enterprising business man. The following testimonial to his integrity of character by one who had been brought in close association with Mr. Comstock and knew him intimately—Mr. George F. Stone, Secretary of the Chicago Board of Trade—is worthy of reproduction here: "He always enjoyed a reputation for being conscientiously honest and punctilious in all his affairs, and commanded the respect of every one who knew him. He was an extremely upright man in business and charmingly affable and courteous in a social way."

HUGH ALEXANDER WHITE.

Hugh Alexander White (deceased) was one of the solid men of Chicago, the scene of his business life, and of Evanston, the place of his residence for upwards of thirty years, and where he resided at the time of his death, after a short illness, March 25, 1894. He was a believer in work, and one of his most prominent characteristics, even from childhood, was his unremitting industry. It was not a hardship for him to work—it was a pleasure. He did not believe in royal roads to success in life, or in short cuts. There was, consequently, no time in his life when he was not successful to the measure of his undertakings. He was one of those who, if he thought he could go a mile, could go two. He did not lack ambition, but it was not for display—not to shine for a time—it was to go steadily on in the discharge of the duties belonging to the trusts reposed in him, reaping the rewards he knew were sure to follow. Such was his dislike to intruding himself upon public attention that he would never consent to being "written up," and so seldom talked of himself that the writer of this sketch, though intimate with him for nearly thirty-five years, knew little of his early life except what was gained from others; and, whatever his success in business, he seldom talked of them by way of self-gratulation. He was a public-spirited man, and took an active part in bringing about better conditions, the enactment of better laws and greater fidelity in their enforcement. By the thoroughness of his investigations into the subjects committed to him, and the practical nature of his suggestions for reform, he rendered most valuable service. He was clear-headed, outspoken and sturdy, and left no one in doubt where he stood.

Mr. White was born near Quincy, Ill., in 1830. Both parents having died before he was nine months old, he was left to the care of his maternal grandparents. He was brought up on a farm in the neighborhood of Quincy by an uncle by marriage, Moses Gutherie, and was educated in the Illinois College at Jacksonville. From there he went to Quincy and entered the law office of Williams, Grimshaw & Lawrence as a student, where he remained until he came to Chicago in 1856 and opened the law office of Williams & White. His partner was Archibald Williams, the senior member of the firm with which he had studied, and who was about that time United States District Attorney, one of the great lawyers in Illinois.

Mr. White continued in the active practice of the law, trying cases in court until about 1874, when, in consequence of an affection of the throat and a large increase in his office business, he discontinued his court practice and confined himself to the more profitable and congenial business of

managing the several large estates that had
been entrusted to his care, examination of
abstracts and other office business. Among
the estates which he managed were the
Allen C. Lewis estate, which grew in his
hands to its present magnificent proportions; the Bigelow estate, the De Haven
estate, and the Francis C. Sherman estate.
To the management of these estates he
brought that same conscientious, painstaking care, executive ability and strict integrity that marked his whole business life.
He wanted no unfair advantage of others,
and he did not allow others to take unfair
advantage of him. The upright found it
very agreeable to do business with him, but
the quibbling and dishonest were sometimes
made to regret that they had shown these
undesirable traits to him.

Mr. White was married to Catherine Mc-
Intosh Sands, of New York, in 1860, who
died a few years after her husband, a public benefactress, mourned by many friends,
by those who had sustained to her the relation of neighbor and by the general public
of Evanston. They had no children. Soon
after their marriage they moved to Evanston, and not long after that erected the
beautiful home where they lived to the time
of his death. Mr. White was a great lover
of flowers, among which many of his early
morning and evening hours were spent in
their culture. His grounds, half a block
on Ridge Avenue, one of the most beautiful streets in the town, have been the pride
and delight of the people of Evanston. He
was a connoisseur of pictures, and a great
lover of books. His house was well filled
with the best paintings of the masters, and
his library was well stocked with rare and
most valuable books. There were few men
better posted upon almost every topic, or
who could talk more entertainingly, than
Mr. White. He cared little for general
society, and did not aspire to office. His

pleasure was in his home, which he provided with every luxury, where, in company of his devoted wife, whom he delighted to honor and to whom he left his
fortune, he spent the hours of leisure among
his flowers, his books and gems of art.

During his active business life Mr. White
was unostentatious in his private benevolence, often extending his charities to
worthy persons and objects, on the principle that "the left hand knoweth not what
the right hand doeth." After his demise
many instances came to light of persons
whom he had befriended, saying, "What
shall I do, now that my best friend is
gone?" His widow, by her will, left a
generous bequest to the Chicago Art Institute, thus carrying out the purposes which
Mr. White had entertained during his life.
.Through the same source his library of
miscellaneous and law books has become
the property of the University of Chicago.

CHANCELLOR LIVINGSTON JENKS.

Few names upon the roll of honor of
Evanston's loyal and successful citizens are
better known than that of Chancellor L.
Jenks. During the greater part of his active
life he was either a resident of, or largely
interested in, Evanston. His energetic nature, guided as it was by sound business
acumen and sterling honor, made him a
most conspicuous and influential figure in
the civic and industrial life of the city and
of Chicago. He was born in the town of
Warren, Bradford County, Pa., January 29,
1828, and was one of a large family of
children born to Livingston and Sarah
(Buffington) Jenks. His father was a native of Rhode Island, the cradle of the family in America, and came of a sturdy line of
ancestors whose lives form part of the glorious history of New England patriotism.

Three in the direct line of his ancestry—all bearing the name of Joseph Jenks—had much to do in molding the destinies of the Colonies. All were called upon to serve as members of the General Assembly, and one was four times elected Governor of Rhode Island. Livingston Jenks, the father of Chancellor L. Jenks, settled in La Salle County, Ill., in 1836, where he combined the several vocations of farmer, merchant and lawyer, until his death in 1863 closed a life of usefulness and honor.

Chancellor L. Jenks spent his boyhood in La Salle County, receiving his education at the country school house and at Granville Academy. From 1849 to 1850 he taught school in Ottawa; but his ambition had always been to engage in the legal profession. In 1851 he came to Chicago and began the study of law under Calvin De-Wolf. Nine months later he was admitted to the bar. Success came at once. His tremendous activity of mind, his fertility of resource, his power of grasping instantly the important points of a case, his fearlessness and his great physical strength, aided by a reputation for "good luck," attracted a large clientage. He was an indomitable worker and a firm believer in the policy of "keeping everlastingly at it."

He was married to Pamella M. Hoisington, May 6, 1855, at the First Methodist Church in Chicago. She was the daughter of Jasper A. Hoisington, whom many residents of Evanston and Chicago will recall with pleasure, and who lived to the ripe age of ninety-four years. Mrs. Jenks died in San Diego, Cal., April 5, 1890, while visiting her son Chancellor, then a resident of California.

Mr. Jenks became early convinced of the great future of Chicago and vicinity and believed that careful investments in real estate would prove remunerative. From time to time, as his means allowed, he made purchases in different parts of Chicago and its suburbs. In 1868, in connection with Charles E. Brown and others, he acquired a large tract of land in what is now the Sixth Ward of Evanston, and laid out the sub-division known as North Evanston. He was also one of the founders of Glencoe and, in addition to his holdings in Chicago, invested largely in Englewood, Hyde Park and elsewhere. Mr. Jenks' real estate interests having become so extensive as to demand his entire attention, he was compelled, with great reluctance, to give up the practice of the law not long before the great Chicago fire. That catastrophe violently checked his career of prosperity. In the second great fire of 1874, he again suffered a heavy loss. But like thousands of his energetic fellow-citizens, he managed to rise above his misfortunes and, in a few years, realized that these great financial disasters had merely cleared the ground for the foundations of a more enduring and genuine success.

During his long residence in Evanston Mr. Jenks served several terms as a member of the Board of Trustees and the School Board, and was a strong influence in the development of the municipality. In politics he was always a stanch Republican, and, in ante-bellum days, he and his father were active champions of abolitionism, and maintained upon the farm in La Salle County a station of the so-called "Underground Railway," established to aid runaway slaves in escaping to Canada.

An interesting incident in connection with Mr. Jenks' efforts in behalf of the negro has been often related. One day he saw a runaway slave girl struggling in the grasp of her master, Stephen F. Knuckles, and Jack Newsom, a commissioner under the Fugitive Slave Law. Mr. Jenks promptly rushed to the assistance of the negress with the result that the entire party were soon rolling over each other in the gutter. Police officers arriving on the scene, they were all taken into custody. The slave alone was imprisoned; the others being well known and responsible, were released on their own recognizance. Mr. Jenks immediately swore out a warrant charging the slave with disorderly conduct, Justice Calvin De Wolf issuing the writ at 10 o'clock at night. George Anderson, Deputy Sheriff (who with Justice De Wolf was in the "conspiracy") served the warrant at once, and took the girl from the police station with the apparent purpose of producing her before the magistrate. On the street he was surrounded by a howling mob of several hundred persons, and, when the crowd was dispersed, the prisoner was not to be found. The Federal Grand Jury, which was then in session, promptly indicted Mr. Jenks, Calvin De Wolf and George Anderson on the charge of violating the Fugitive Slave Law. The affair coming to the knowledge of President Buchanan, he made the somewhat natural mistake of supposing "Chancellor" Jenks to be a judge of one of the State courts on the chancery side. Indignant at this instance of open violation of a cherished United States statute, he telegraphed the United States Attorney at Chicago as follows: "Prosecute Chancellor Jenks to the full extent of the law. For a private citizen to be engaged in such nefarious practices as he is charged with is bad enough; but a high officer of the court, who is concerned in them, should be severely dealt with. James Buchanan, President." Shortly after Abraham Lincoln was elected President, the War of the Rebellion broke out, the political complexion of the Federal officers at Chicago changed, and the indictment was nolle prossed.

Mr. Jenks was a member of the First Baptist Church of Chicago for more than forty years. He closed his eventful, successful and honored life January 10, 1903, at San Francisco, Cal., while on a visit to his son, Livingston Jenks. The children born to Mr. Jenks and wife were eight in number, of whom but two survive their parents—Chancellor L. Jenks, Jr., who resides at 1217 Ridge Avenue, Evanston, and who is a practicing attorney, and Livingston Jenks, whose residence is in San Francisco, and who also is a member of the legal profession.

JOHN HUME KEDZIE.

John H. Kedzie (deceased), for over forty years a leading resident of Evanston, Ill., was born in Stamford, Delaware County, N. Y., September 8, 1815, and, after reaching the school age, until his seventeenth year attended the district school in winter while working on his father's farm in the summer. At eighteen years of age he began teaching in a district school, but being ambitious to acquire a liberal education, he began a course of preparation for college at Oneida Institute, and later entered Oberlin College, Ohio, from which he graduated in 1841. Having studied law and been admitted to the bar in his native State, in 1847 he removed to Chicago and there established himself in practice. At the time of the California gold excitement, in common with many others, he was seized with the desire to visit the El Dorado of the Pacific Coast, but was prevented by the accumulation of business on his hands. He was compelled to content himself with making financial advances to others. Of four or five whom he aided in this way, not one ever made any return to him as promised.

In 1850 Mr. Kedzie was married to Mary Elizabeth Austin, who died four years later, leaving an infant daughter named for her mother, but who died during the following year. On June 17, 1857, he was married to a second Mary Elizabeth, whose maiden name was Kent, and who still survives in Evanston. Of five children born to Mr. Kedzie's second marriage, two—Margaret Frances and John Hume, Jr.—are still living. The oldest daughter, Kate Isabel, who became Mrs. George Watson Smith, died over twenty years ago, and two daughters—Laura Louise and Julia Hume—died in childhood.

A steadfast Republican in his political views, in the fall of 1876 Mr. Kedzie was elected a member of the lower branch of the Thirtieth General Assembly from Cook County, and in the contest for United States Senator which followed, gave his earnest support to Gen. John A. Logan for that position. It becoming apparent that Gen. Logan could not be elected, Mr. Kedzie finally gave his support to Judge David Davis, who was elected as an "Independent." His prominence in connection with the business affairs of both Evanston and Chicago is indicated by the fact that public highways have been named in his honor in both cities —that in the former being Kedzie Street and in the latter Kedzie Avenue. An office building at 120-122 Randolph Street also bore his name. The names of both the Kedzie and the Hume families, from both of whom he was descended, are traced to Scottish origin, each being prominent about the time of Oliver Cromwell and earlier.

In 1861 Mr. Kedzie took up his residence in Evanston, and from that time bore a prominent part in the affairs of that place. He first purchased and occupied a house erected by Francis H. Benson, which was subsequently destroyed by fire. Another house built on the same site met a like fate on New Year's Day of 1880, and during the same year he erected the residence on the southwest corner of Ridge Avenue and Grove Street, which he occupied during the remainder of his life.

Mr. Kedzie gave evidence of his originality and his fondness for philosophical investigation in the preparation of a volume entitled "Solar Heat, Gravitation and Sun Spots," which was published in 1886, and which has attracted the attention of many interested in the unsolved problems of nature. He took a prominent part in the establishment of the Evanston Free Public Library, and from the date of its organization in 1873, for the first four years of its existence, serving as President of the Library Board. He also served for many years as a member of the Board of Education, was one of the original members of the Philosophical Society organized in 1866, and took a prominent part in connection with church affairs, being one of the organizers of the St. Mark's Episcopal Church in 1864, and in the latter part of his life a member of the First Congregational Church, which he served for many years on its Board of Trustees. Mr. Kedzie's death occurred April 9, 1903, in the eighty-eighth year of his age.

JOSEPH CUMMINGS, D. D., LL. D.

Rev. Joseph Cummings (deceased), one of the most eminent clergymen and educators in the United States, and widely known as the honored President of Northwestern University from 1881 until 1890, was born at Falmouth, near Portland, Me., March 3, 1817. His parental ancestors were of Scotch nativity. His father was a zealous and faithful minister of the Methodist Episcopal Church, whose labors covered a large portion of the State of Maine and extended into the Canadas.

His worthy wife, the steadfast and devoted helpmate in his pastoral labors, was
a member of a family of local note in the
field of Methodism, and especially active
in the work of the church. Thus the subject of this sketch was a Methodist by
birth, domestic training and institutional
instruction.

In early youth Dr. Cummings enjoyed
the advantages of the public schools in
the vicinity of his home. He underwent
his preparation for college in Maine Wesleyan Seminary at Kent's Hill, and afterwards entered Wesleyan University at
Middletown, Conn., through which he
worked his way by teaching school at intervals. From this institution he was
graduated with the Class of 1840, and
shortly afterwards became a Professor
in, and subsequently Principal of, Amenia
Seminary, at Amenia, New York. While
engaged in teaching he pursued a course
in theology, and in 1846 was ordained
by the Methodist Episcopal Conference
a minister of the Methodist Episcopal
Church. He rapidly gained prominence
in his calling, being recognized as an
impressive and convincing speaker, a profound logician and a forceable expounder
of doctrinal points.

In 1853, Dr. Cummings was called to
the chair of Theology in the Methodist
Biblical Institute at Concord, N. H., and
thence went to Lima, N. Y., where he
assumed the presidency of Genessee Wesleyan College, of which he was the head
from 1854 to 1857. In the latter year,
the success he had achieved in this capacity resulted in his election to the presidency of his alma mater, Wesleyan University. Here was first revealed, in a
remarkable degree, his possession of that
superior constructive faculty, capacity for
organization and high quality of leadership, which made him famous among the

educators of the United States. For
eighteen years he conducted the affairs
of this institution, and these were years
of marvelous growth and development in
its history. The grand results which he
achieved in this connection were fittingly
recognized in a memorial address delivered, shortly after the death of Dr.
Cummings, by Rev. James Marcus King,
D. D., of New York, in which he said:
"It was the proud boast of a Roman Emperor that he found the 'Eternal City'
brick and left it marble. Of Dr. Cummings it may justly be said, that he found
the college buildings at Middletown
meager, inadequate and unattractive—
formerly the dingy quarters of an abandoned military academy—and he crowded
that classic hill on High Street with massive structures as noble and inspiring as
can be found on this continent. In these
eighteen years he reared a triple monument in buildings of imperishable old red-
sandstone, that will stand as imposing
reminders of the splendidly successful administration of Joseph Cummings as long
as the river they overlook shall flow to
the sea."

During the presidency of Dr. Cummings, the alumni of Wesleyan University contributed about $30,000 towards a
library fund for the institution, and Isaac
Rich and Daniel Drew pledged $200,000
to the endowment fund. The old boarding hall was remodeled and transformed
into an observatory hall, being surmounted by a tower containing a telescope of
extraordinary power. The memory of
"Wesleyan's" heroic dead, fallen in the
War for the Union, was perpetuated
by the erection of a memorial chapel. A
model gymnasium was provided; large
additions were made to the scientific collections; the faculty was increased in
numbers, and the course of study extend-

ed; the halls of the University, with their opportunities, were for the first time opened to women; and finally the work of this administration was crowned by the erection, through the beneficence of Orange Judd, of a structure—one of the most complete and elegant in the land—as a temple of natural science. Mr. Judd also originated and prepared at great labor and expense, a work of incalculable value to his alma mater, in the shape of an alumni record, which is the only approximately perfect catalogue of this kind known to American colleges. In 1875, Dr. Cummings resigned the office which he had held for nearly a score of years, his administration having spanned the pre-eminently constructive period in the history of the University.

After his resignation Dr. Cummings continued for three years to occupy the chair of Mental and Moral Philosophy and Political Economy in the institution, and then resumed his ministerial labors, feeling that his career as an educator was at an end. It was not so to be, however, as the fame of his ability, not only as a builder of institutions of learning, but as a developer of character and men, was widespread. His services were needed in an enlarged field of activity and a broader sphere of usefulness. In 1881 he was called from a successful ministry in New England to the presidency of Northwestern University. To this position he brought ripe experience, rare wisdom, mature judgment, and that spirit of progressiveness which had been one of the distinguishing characteristics of his career. In addition to these, he brought to the scene of his last endeavor the prestige of a great name. Here he speedily won the confidence of the official board and of wealthy and kindly disposed friends of the University. Financial claims against

it were met, new buildings were erected, its income was increased, and the period of its highest prosperity began. He governed wisely, planned judiciously for the future, and directed the affairs of the institution, which is now the pride of Western Methodism, almost to the end of his life. At his death it was truly said, "Methodism has lost its greatest College President." In terms of endearment, and almost of adulation, those who came under his care and guidance at the Wesleyan and Northwestern Universities, speak of this great educator—stern and exacting as he was at times—as one who seemed to grapple his pupils to himself with hooks of steel. Possessed of rare moral and physical courage, a chevalier in defense of the right, and a knight-errant in boldly and vigorously assailing the wrong, "he seemed," says one of his students, later associated with him as an instructor at Wesleyan University, "to sum up and embody all that can vaguely be conceived of tenacity of will, fearlessness, superb power of achievement—in short of the heroic." Dr. Cummings had a hatred of feebleness and indolence of nature, vacillation, dallying with wrong and weak-kneed sentimentality. "He taught us," said another of his pupils, "that the first duty of a man is to be strong; yet this man, so stern—at times so harsh—had a heart as tender, a hand as soft, and a voice as gentle as a woman's, wherever there was pain to soothe or sorrow to console." Another, who was an elder and lifelong friend, said: "For the student, he had a personal and tender interest. He encouraged the despondent, assisted the sick, prayed with the penitent, and pleaded and labored with the erring. He imparted his spiritual life to thousands who have thereby been quickened into noble living. He lived on towards three-score years and ten, genial, optimistic, planning, until the last, greater things for our educational institutions. Withal, he was so modest and unassuming, and did his work with so little of the spirit of display, that we have but faintly realized how great was the place he filled."

Busy as was the life of Dr. Cummings in the fields of education and ministerial work, he still found time to give considerable attention to social, economic and governmental problems. He was a member, and at one time Vice-President, of the National Reform Association, and also a member of the American Association for the Advancement of Science. His was a powerful influence in promoting the cause of temperance, and throughout his long career he missed no opportunity to aid in the suppression of the liquor traffic. A great preacher, as well as a great educator, he stood high in the councils of the Methodist Church. He participated as a delegate in many of the General Conferences of the Church, and, in 1864, was a member of the committee appointed by the Conference to formulate resolutions conveying to President Lincoln an expression of the loyal sentiment and co-operation of the church. He prepared and presented to Mr. Lincoln the address which drew from the great Emancipator the following historic answer:

"Gentlemen: In response to your address allow me to attest the accuracy of its historic statements, endorse the statements it expresses, and thank you in the nation's name for the sure promise it gives. Nobly sustained, as the Government has been, by all the churches, I would utter nothing which might, in the least, appear invidious against any. Yet without this it may fairly be said that the Methodist Episcopal Church, not less devoted than the best, is, by its greater numbers, the most important of all. It is no fault in others that the Methodist Church sends more soldiers to the field, more nurses to the hospitals and more prayers to Heaven, than any. God bless the Methodist Church! Bless all the churches and blessed be God, who, in this, our greatest trial, giveth us the churches!"

During the war Dr. Cummings was among the most active supporters of the Union cause in New England, bringing all his powerful influence to bear to strengthen the armies, care for the sick and wounded, and provide for those dependent upon the soldiers in the field.

In recognition of his distinguished services as educator and minister of the gospel, both Harvard and Wesleyan Universities conferred upon Dr. Cummings the degree of D. D., and he received the degree of LL. D. from Northwestern University.

The domestic life of the subject of this sketch, like his professional and public career, was ideal in its character. In 1843 he was united in marriage with Deborah S. Haskell, a member of one of the most prominent and worthy families of Augusta, Maine, represented by ministers and lawyers of local distinction. Mrs. Cummings was a broad-minded, capable woman, and her assistance in furthering the plans and endeavors of her husband cannot be overestimated. She was endowed with fine social gifts, and her home was delightfully hospitable. She survived her husband and, after his decease, served as one of the Trustees of Northwestern University. Her death occurred in 1901. Mrs. Bonbright, wife of Dr. David Bonbright, Professor of the Latin language and Literature in Northwestern University, is the only child left by this noble couple.

Dr. Cummings departed this life on May 7, 1890. In that event a great career was ended and a great soul entered the communion of saints. His strong individuality is indelibly impressed upon the city which was his last home, and upon the famous educational institution of which he was the head; and his memory lingers, like a benediction, with those who knew him as guide, philosopher and friend during the years when his labors were drawing to a close. His field of activity was wide and his fame national; but his name is indissolubly linked with Evanston, with Northwestern University, and with Western Methodism.

GEORGE MYRICK SARGENT.

George Myrick Sargent, manufacturer, Chicago and Evanston, Ill., was born in Sedgwick, Me., March 29, 1830, the son of Benjamin Choate and Susannah (Cole) Sargent, being the youngest of a family of eleven children, of whom six (January, 1904), are still living. The family name has had more than thirty different forms of spelling at different periods and in different countries, beginning, as it is believed, in Normandy in the latter part of the twelfth century, with the name "Serniens," and after undergoing various transformations in the intervening centuries, has taken on its present form. The founder of the family in America was William Sargent, who was born in Northampton, England, in 1602, and came to Charleston, Mass., in 1638, from whom Mr. George M. Sargent is sixth in line of descent. Heads of various other branches of the family on the maternal side came to Plymouth Colony in the days of Pil-

grim immigration, some of them coming on the "Mayflower" in 1620, and their descendants took part in most of the colonial wars, including King Philip's War, and later in the War of the Revolution, the War of 1812 and the Mexican War. The children of Benjamin C. and Susannah Sargent were: Benjamin Cleaves, born June 12, 1808, died in infancy; Wyer Groves, born June 24, 1810; John Oliver, born December 18, 1812; Sarah Jane, born February 2, 1815; William Haskell, born February 4, 1818; Lucius Bolles, born January 18, 1820; Thomas Cole, born November 6, 1821; Albion Keith Parris, born October 24, 1823; Mary Merrill, born June 4, 1826; Jasper Newton, born January 6, 1828; and George Myrick. The five last named, with William Haskell, are still surviving.

The subject of this sketch was reared on his father's farm, meanwhile attending the common schools in his native State until eighteen years of age, when he entered into the employ of his brother, Wyer G., as clerk in his store at Sedgwick (now Sargentville), Maine. Here he remained four or five years, during part of the time serving as the first Postmaster of that place; later removed to Boston, Mass., where for the next four years he was employed as clerk by J. N. Dennison & Co. Then returning to Sedgwick, Maine, he entered into partnership with his brother under the firm name of W. G. Sargent & Brother, continuing four years. Retiring from this partnership, he next engaged in the ship-chandlery business in Boston with his brother-in-law, Joseph J. Durham, the firm taking the name of Durham & Sargent. In 1861 Mr. Sargent went to New York, where he formed a partnership in the same line of business with Robert H. Thayer (firm name Thayer & Sargent), remaining until about 1870. On account of the sturdy political position of the members of this firm during the Civil War period, their place of business became known as "The Black Republican Store."

Coming west in 1870, Mr. Sargent purchased an interest in the malleable iron works at Moline, Ill., with which he remained three years, the concern first being known by the firm name of Hill, Heald & Sargent, but later being incorporated as the Moline Malleable Iron Works. Having severed his connection with the iron works enterprise at Moline in 1873, he removed to Des Moines, Iowa, where for three years he was connected with the Des Moines Scale Company in the manufacture of farmers' scales. Then, in 1876, coming to the city of Chicago, he established there the first manufactory in the United States for the exclusive manufacture of the brake-shoe for railway cars, under the firm name of George M. Sargent & Co. In 1877 the concern was reorganized as a stock company, known as the Congdon Brake-Shoe Company. The business grew rapidly and, in 1893, a new corporation was formed under the name of the Sargent Company, with a capital stock of $250,000, Mr. Sargent being its President. Later the stock was increased to $500,000, the plant being located at Fifty-ninth and Wallace Streets, Chicago, and covering an area of about five acres. Furnaces for the manufacture of steel castings were erected, the output consisting chiefly of brake-shoes and railroad couplers. The business grew so rapidly that it was found necessary to increase the facilities for the production of cast-iron brake-shoes, and a new plant was erected at Chicago Heights, covering an area of ten acres, the plant at Fifty-ninth Street being thereafter devoted to the manufacture of coup-

lers and knuckles almost exclusively for railroads. In 1901 the plant at Chicago Heights was sold to the American Brake-shoe & Foundry Company, and the steel plant at Fifty-ninth Street to the American Steel Foundries, the former representing a capital stock of $4,500,000. Mr. Sargent is still a director in the first named company, but not in active business. His son, William Durham Sargent, who promoted its organization, was its first President, remaining until January, 1904, when he resigned, and is now Second Vice-President of the American Steel Foundries (representing a capital of $40,000,000), in charge of the operating department.

Mr. George M. Sargent is a director of the Railway Appliance Company of which his son, George H., is the Vice-President. Other business enterprises with which he has been connected include the "Live Poultry Transportation Company," of which he was President for some years, and the Vessel-Owners' Association, of which he was a director while in New York. It was through the efforts of a committee of the latter association, of which Mr. Sargent was a member, that the builders of the East River Bridge were induced to increase the elevation of that structure from 120 feet, as originally projected, to 135 feet. His prominence as a business man is indicated by the fact that, in 1901, he was elected Vice-President for Illinois of the National Association of Manufacturers of the United States, and, at the present time, is a member of the Committee on Commerce of the National Business League.

Mr. Sargent was married at Winterford, Maine, September 15, 1858, to Helen Marie Durham, who was born in Freedom, Maine, February 15, 1834, the daughter of William and Emily Durham, and they have had four children: Emily Helen, born October 3, 1860, died aged eleven months; William Durham, born in Lynn, Mass., June 16, 1863; George Hamlin, born in Brooklyn, N. Y., October 5, 1865, and Annie Cushing, born in Marlboro, N. H., November 27, 1870. William Durham Sargent married, February 14, 1899, May Alene Partridge, daughter of C. W. Partridge; Annie C. married, September 19, 1895, Henry K. Gilbert of Chicago; and George Hamlin married, January 12, 1904, Elizabeth H. Pittman, of Detroit, Mich.

In religious belief Mr. George M. Sargent is a Methodist and in politics a Republican. For two terms he served as a member of the Evanston Board of Trustees, and is a member of various fraternal and social organizations, including the Royal Arcanum and Blue Lodge A. F. & A. M., Evanston Chapter and Commandery K. T., Evanston; the Mystic Shrine, Medinah Temple; Union League Club, Chicago; Country Club and Evanston Club, Evanston; besides the Evanston, Glenview and St. Augustine Golf Clubs. For several years he was President of the Society of the Sons of Maine, Chicago, and is present Vice-President of the New England Society. After a long and conspicuously successful business career, Mr. Sargent, with his faithful and devoted wife, is spending the evening of his days in their delightful home in Evanston, practically retired from active business, though still retaining his official connection with the manufacturing enterprises in which he has been financially interested and an important factor for more than a quarter of a century.

ALEXANDER CLARK.

The death, on September 26, 1903, of Alexander Clark, at Antioch, Ill., where he was bringing to successful completion one of -the many enterprises which his genius for large and useful undertakings had conceived, and which his indomitable energy and splendid organizing ability had made possible, removed a man who had given generously of his talents and time to the furtherance of Evanston's civic welfare. Almost from his settlement in Evanston to his latest hours on earth, he had taken a deep and active interest in everything that concerned the community. Although he never sought or accepted office, he commanded, by reason at once of his high personal character and his unselfish devotion to public interests, a measure of respect in the ranks of influential citizenship, which made his opinion an important political factor, and which never failed to give weight to his voice, whenever he felt called upon to raise it, in support or condemnation of the policy of those entrusted with the conduct of municipal affairs. It was mainly through his instrumentality that the villages which now constitute the City of Evanston were consolidated under one government, and it is a peculiar, yet a characteristic, coincident that only a few months subsequent to his death, his fellow citizens ratified at the polls a measure upon which he had been quietly working for years, and one which rendered this consolidation more secure—the practical combination of the city and township governments.

While South Evanston was still a village and Mr. Clark was among the newest of its residents, he was foremost in the movement for securing a water supply, and when the artesian well, then installed, proved inadequate to meet growing needs, he assisted materially in creating the means whereby the village was enabled. by the erection of waterworks, to draw its supply from Lake Michigan. and to establish in connection therewith an electric light plant. He was a strenuous advocate of good streets and sidewalks, and it was largely through his efforts, and in consequence of his unceasing agitation for improvement in this direction, that South Evanston became the best paved of the North Shore suburbs and was the first among them to introduce the cement sidewalk. He was the first to see the necessity for the creation of a local park system; it was he who secured the strip of lake frontage between Main and Kedzie Streets. He was one of the founders of the movement for the creation of Sheridan Road, and was Secretary of the Sheridan Road Association from its organization to his death.

The advice of Mr. Clark was sought and followed in the establishment of the city government; he gave wise counsel to its first officials, and prepared, or assisted in the preparation of, many of the ordinances under which the municipality is now operating. Although engrossed in an extensive law practice in Chicago, he was always ready to give liberally of his thought and time to the public affairs of the community in which he made his home and for which he always entertained and expressed the greatest affection. To him is Evanston indebted for the conception and construction of electric railway communication with Chicago, an enterprise in which he enlisted capital, and for which he secured the necessary frontage consents and right of way through its entire length. The ability which he displayed in this undertaking won for him a hearing later, when he proposed the construction of the Union Loop in Chicago—a conception which was entirely his own, and which was carried into execution, so far as its legal phases were concerned, in accordance with plans which he had formulated long before capitalists were asked to consider it as an investment. In his lifetime, so unmindful was he of any form of personal praise, he was never heard to claim credit for what many knew him to be entitled to—the origination of the scheme which has made possible the success of the present elevated railway systems of Chicago.

At the time of his death Mr. Clark was engaged in promoting the electric line between Waukegan and Kenosha, since completed, one of his principal associates being Volney W. Foster, another distinguished and beloved citizen of Evanston, who was one of his pall-bearers and who, only a few months later, was also borne to his last resting place.

Alexander Clark came of Scotch-Irish stock; his father, Alexander Clark, and his mother, Eliza McCullom, having been born in the North of Ireland, the former on June 7, 1819, the latter on July 1, 1821. His parents emigrating to America, Alexander was born in Paterson, N. J., on June 15, 1851. The family came West when he was 12 years of age, settled on a farm in Knox County, Ill., later moving to a larger place in Ford County. He was educated in Wabash College, Crawfordsville, Ind., from which he was graduated in 1877. After reading law in the office of Judge Woods, Chicago, he was, in 1878, admitted to the bar. On March 10, 1881, he married Miss Emma Osgood of Oneida, Knox County, Ill., and the same month the young couple settled in Evanston. Mrs. Clark and two children—John Alexander and Helen Osgood—still survive.

Following the death of Mr. Clark, the City Council of Evanston adopted resolutions setting forth the great loss which the community had suffered in his demise, recounting the useful services which he had rendered the community, and naming the lake front park, which he had secured for the City, Clark Square, as a lasting testimonial to his honored memory.

DR. JARED BASSETT.

Dr. Jared Bassett (deceased) was born in East Montpelier, Vt., January 26, 1814, the son of Joel and Ruby (Metcalf) Bassett, and grandson of Jared Bassett, who emigrated from Connecticut and became one of the early settlers of the "Green Mountain State." While the genealogy of the family is not now accessible, it is believed to have been of Huguenot origin, the first American ancestor of the name having crossed the ocean in 1621, the year after the landing of the "Mayflower" at Plymouth Rock. Dr. Bassett's mother was a devout member of the Society of Friends, while the father, who was a farmer by occupation and held many offices of honor and trust in the community, shared the faith and mode of life of his wife. Although not strictly a Quaker in religious faith and practice, the son inherited many of the traits of his ancestors, including the strength of character, simplicity of manner and quiet self-control which were marked characteristics of the followers of that faith. After having spent his boyhood and youth on the farm engaged in farm work and in attendance at the district school, at the age of twenty-two years, having decided to adopt the medical profession, he entered the office of Dr. James Spaulding, of Montpelier, as a student in that line. In

1836 he attended medical lectures at Woodstock, Vt., later took a course in the medical department of Dartmouth College, New Hampshire, and in 1839 received the degree of M. D. from the Medical College at Albany, N. Y. Then having settled at Plainfield, Washington County, Vt., he engaged in practice, but later removed to Northfield in the same State, where he remained seven years, winning the experience of the old-school practitioners of that period.

On May 29, 1844, Dr. Bassett was married to Miss Harriet Sherman, a daughter of Col. Nathaniel and Deborah (Webster) Sherman, of Barre, Vt., and sister of the late Alson S. and Oren Sherman, who were prominent business men of Chicago at an early day. Two years later his attention having been attracted to the advantages offered in the West to those entering upon a business career, Dr. Bassett, accompanied by his wife, started for Chicago, making the journey by stage to Lake Champlain, across the lake to Whitehall by steamer, thence to Rochester by canal-boat, and from there to Buffalo by a newly built section of what is now the New York Central Railroad. At Buffalo they took a lake steamer for Chicago, arriving at their destination on September 10, 1846, after a lake journey of ten days. Chicago, a primitive city of some ten thousand inhabitants, was then just entering upon the development which, in the growth of the next sixty years, made it the second city in the United States with a population of two million souls.

In Chicago Dr. Bassett found a temporary boarding place on West Washington Street, and opened an office in the second story of a frame building on Lake Street, where he displayed a sign indicating his profession. A year later he bought a small house and lot on Clark Street, near Monroe, then a pleasant neighborhood of frame cottages in the outskirts of the town, paying for the land about fifteen dollars per front foot. After a few years residence here he converted his home into business property and removed to the West Side, taking up his residence at the corner of West Adams and Morgan streets, where he purchased a small brick cottage (the first of its kind erected west of the river, with about an acre of ground. In 1857 he removed to Waukegan, where he resided until 1868, when he returned to Chicago, in the meantime giving attention to his landed interests in Chicago, making daily trips between his suburban home and the city by the Chicago & Northwestern Railroad, the pioneer suburban line for the accommodation of dwellers along the North Shore. After his return to Chicago he erected a more commodious dwelling on the site of his West Side home. After practicing his profession in Chicago for about twelve years, Dr. Bassett turned his attention to the improvement of his real estate, keeping pace with the growth of the city. In common with the mass of property holders of the city of Chicago, he was a heavy loser by the great fire of 1871, the retrievement of which cost him many years of labor and anxiety. In politics he was a zealous Republican, before the days of the Civil War maintaining the anti-slavery views of his ancestors. He was one of the founders of the People's Church, which grew out of the exclusion of Dr. H. W. Thomas from the Methodist denomination. In 1894 he removed to Evanston, where he continued to reside until his death. Mr. and Mrs. Bassett had one son, Robert J., a lawyer, who continued to reside with his parents during their latter years. Dr. Bassett died May 10, 1905, his wife having preceded him, dying August 14, 1900.

HENRY BASCOM RIDGAWAY.

Henry Bascom Ridgaway, D.D., LL. D. (deceased), for thirty years a most able and efficient minister and pastor of the Methodist Episcopal Church, and for ten years President of Garrett Biblical Institute, Evanston, Ill., was born in Talbot County, Md., September 7, 1830. His father, James Ridgaway, one of the most extensive and prosperous farmers in Talbot County, was a man of strong mental and moral characteristics, a devout Christian, and a much valued official of the church. Mary (Jump) Ridgaway, mother of the subject of this sketch, was a daughter of Alumbey Jump, a veteran of the Revolutionary War, who served the State of Maryland in official positions, and was Representative in the Legislature from his county shortly after the successful termination of the Revolution. Henry B. Ridgaway's parents moved to Baltimore when their son was quite young, and there he attended the public school. He subsequently graduated from the high school, the principal of which left a lasting impress upon the after life of his pupil. In 1847 he entered Dickinson College, at Carlisle, Pa., and was graduated from that institution in June, 1849. While pursuing his course there he preached the gospel at frequent intervals, and after his graduation taught a common school for one year. In 1851 he joined the Baltimore Conference, was ordained a Deacon in 1853, and an Elder, in 1855, by Bishop Beverly Waugh. For four years he was engaged as an itinerant upon circuits in Maryland and Virginia, and in 1856 was assigned to the Harford Avenue Church in the City of Baltimore, which, with two other churches there, formed a city circuit. He afterwards served High Street Church, Baltimore, then in its most flourishing condition, and after that, Grace Church, which had one of the finest edifices and largest congregations in Baltimore. In 1858 he was placed in charge of the Chestnut Street Methodist Church in Portland, Maine, which had just completed an ornate and imposing place of worship. Its new pastor attained the climax of his pulpit and parochial effectiveness while ministering to this flock, by which he was held in the highest esteem and affection. The country was just passing into the throes of the Civil War, and a Southern man in a Northern pastorate confronted a severe ordeal, from which he emerged without the slightest distrust of his patriotism.

From Portland Dr. Ridgaway was called to St. Paul's Church, in New York City, then the most conspicuous church in the Methodist denomination. The Washington Square Church was his next pastorate, and the size of the parish made his three years of service there an intense strain upon his powers of endurance. During 1867, however, he enjoyed a most pleasant ministerial experience at Sing Sing, on the Hudson River. From 1868 to 1870 he was again in charge of St. Paul's Church, New York City. Following this, he spent three serviceable years at St. James Church, in Harlem, and then, after a long tour abroad was pastor, for one year of St. James Church, Kingston, New York. His foreign journey was devoted to visiting Egypt, crossing the desert, traveling through Palestine, and going to Constantinople and Greece. He had, on a former occasion, traveled through Great Britain and the Continent. Having been transferred to the Cincinnati Conference, he was three years in charge of St. Paul's Church, Cincinnati, and three years at Walnut Hills, then a suburb of that city. In both parishes his labors were highly effective. In 1882 Dr. Ridgaway was elected Professor of Historical Theology in Garrett Biblical Institute, Evanston, Ill., and in 1885, became President of this institute and Professor of Practical Theology. In 1892 he availed himself of an extended vacation to make a tour of the world, journeying through Europe; visiting the Riviera, Florence, and Rome, Italy; passing through the Suez Canal, stopping at Bombay and making extended journeys in India, spending a month in China, traveling through Japan and returning by way of the Pacific Ocean and the Canadian Pacific Railroad.

Dr. Ridgaway was one of the editors of the "Methodist" during the entire period of its publication, and was the author of several interesting and popular works. He was also a most entertaining lecturer on various topics. As a preacher he was earnest, forceful and convincing; as an educator, erudite, yet simple and lucid. The enforced limits of this sketch forbid a detailed mention of his manifold efforts of pen and tongue, or of the numerous honors bestowed upon him by different religious bodies. In 1868 he received the degree of D.D. from Dickinson College, and that of LL.D. in 1889.

Dr. Ridgaway was married, February 22, 1855, to Rosamond U., daughter of Professor Caldwell, of Dickinson College. Mrs. Ridgaway still survives her husband, having shared all his experiences of joy and sorrow during forty years of wifely companionship. His widely lamented death occurred March 30, 1895.

ELLIOTT ANTHONY, LL. D.

Among the names that are justly entitled to be enrolled among the makers of the great commonwealth of Illinois and of the City of Chicago, is that of Judge Elliott Anthony, whose more than forty years residence has left its impress upon the State and the Nation. Although born in Central New York, he early saw the great possibilities which the West afforded, and, as a consequence, left his home and native State within one month after being admitted to the bar at Oswego on May 7, 1851, and took up his abode, first at Sterling, the county seat of Whiteside County, Ill., where an elder brother was at that time living. The next autumn he removed to Chicago, where he spent his life in connection with his profession, officially or otherwise, though a resident during later years of the city or Evanston. He came at that fortunate period when everything was in the formative state, when there were not more than fifty lawyers all told. His rise was rapid, and in less than three years he was known as one of the most promising lawyers at the bar. Judge Anthony's forefathers were Quakers, who, early in the seventeenth century, came to the land to which Roger Williams was exiled, and with which the family history has been closely identified for generations. His father, Isaac Anthony, was born on the island of Rhode Island, eight miles from Newport. His grandmother on his father's side was a Chase, who was connected with the well known Chase family of which the late Chief Justice Chase was a member, and his mother a Phelps, belonging to the Phelps family of Vermont, who at an early period were residents of Connecticut and Massachusetts. The grandfather and his family were residents of Rhode

Island when the Hessians held it during the Revolutionary War, and for some alleged infraction of martial law, the grandfather and a younger brother were taken prisoners and compelled to perform various menial duties, which greatly embittered them against the British. Mr. Anthony's father was an able historian, thoroughly familiar with the facts concerning all the Indian wars and the uprising of the colonies against their mother country, having obtained them from his own father and grandfather, and thus the son acquired familiar acquaintance with those stirring events in our history which has had a most lasting effect on all of the descendants of the family.

Removing from New England about the same time, Mr. Anthony's grandfathers on both sides settled in Washington County, N. Y., and purchased lands in the town of Cambridge, some twenty miles from Albany. Here the father of Judge Anthony first met Parmelia Phelps, to whom he was married, and one daughter and three sons were born of this union, when the father removed to Spafford, the southwestern town of Onondaga County, and commenced the life of a typical pioneer. There, on June 10, 1827, the son Elliott was born. This region was then an almost unbroken wilderness, and here his early years were spent in cutting down and clearing the forests and assisting in work on the farm. Three sisters were born while the family resided in this locality, so that there were in all four brothers and four sisters who grew to manhood and womanhood. The children attended the country schools, and attained a considerable proficiency in the common branches, later each in turn taking a course at Cortland Academy, located at Homer. At the age of eighteen Elliott, who was the fourth son, left the farm to take a preparatory course before entering college. Cortland Academy was at that time under the charge of Samuel B. Woolworth, who subsequently became one of the regents of the State University at Albany. Here he remained two years studying Greek and Latin and some of the higher branches of mathematics, and in the fall of 1847 entered the sophomore class at Hamilton College, Clinton, N. Y., graduating there with high honors in 1850. Prof. Theodore W. Dwight, afterwards so distinguished, was at that time Professor of Law and Political Economy, and commenced private lessons to a few students who chose to avail themselves of his services. A class having been formed for the year 1850-51, Mr. Anthony returned to Clinton for a year's course, and was admitted to the bar at Oswego, May 7, 1851. It was during this period that he and a classmate by the name of Joseph D. Hubbard had charge of the academy located in the village of Clinton, and he had as one of his pupils Grover Cleveland, afterwards President of the United States. Soon after his admission to the bar he came west and stopped for a short time at Sterling, Whiteside County, Ill., where he commenced the practice of law and where he tried his first case in a court of record. Returning east the following year he was on the 14th of July, 1852, married to Mary Dwight, the sister of his law preceptor, and a granddaughter of President Dwight, so well known in connection with Yale College. In the fall of the same year he came to Chicago, and from that time until elected to the bench in 1880, he pursued his profession with a zeal and success rarely equaled. During his first year's residence in Chicago, with the aid of his devoted wife, he compiled "A Digest of the Illinois Reports," which was soon after published and received with favor

by the profession throughout the State. In 1858 he was elected City Attorney for Chicago, and distinguished his administration of that responsible office by the energy and ability with which he conducted the legal business of the city. Later he was for several years specially retained by the city to conduct many important cases in the local courts and in the Supreme Court of the State and the United States. While acting for the city he established several new and interesting law points, among which was that the collection of special assessments could not be enjoined by a court of chancery; next, that the city of Chicago could not be garnisheed to collect the salary or wages of any of its officers or employes; and, lastly, that no execution could issue against the city to collect a judgment; and at a later period, that the city could not tie up its legislative powers by making contracts with the gas companies for the supply of gas so as to interfere with its legislative prerogatives. In 1863 he was appointed the general attorney and solicitor of the Galena & Chicago Union Railroad, which during the next year was consolidated with the Chicago & Northwestern Railway. A contest arose over this consolidation, and he was shortly after retained by a number of bondholders and non-consenting stockholders to test the validity of the consolidation, and in connection with the case prepared and printed a most remarkable argument upon the law of the case, which grew into a treatise which he entitled "The Law Pertaining to the Consolidation of Railroads." The late Samuel J. Tilden was directly interested in the questions involved, as well as many of the leading capitalists and railway magnates in New York, and the array of legal talent was formidable, the late Judge Beckwith leading on behalf of the consolidationists, and Judge Anthony leading on behalf of the minority bond-holders and minority stockholders. It was tried as a chancery case before Judge David Davis of the United States Supreme Court, then on the circuit, who associated with him the late Samuel H. Treat, United States District Judge for the Southern District of Illinois, and the positions maintained by Mr. Anthony were upheld and affirmed in almost every particular. Soon after the parties met and settled their differences to the satisfaction of all, as the consolidationists found that it would be disastrous to them if the litigation should be continued. At this time Mr. Anthony received numerous letters from some of the most prominent lawyers and Judges in this country, complimenting him upon his masterly exposition of the law. Among them were the late Josiah Quincy and Sidney Bartlett of Boston, Mr. Justice Swayne of the United States Supreme Court, the late Thomas A. Ewing, of Ohio and many others. His brief, which was in the shape of a bound volume of several hundred pages, was in great demand in this country and in Europe, and was most kindly reviewed by several of the leading journals in Great Britain.   •

It fell to the lot of Judge Anthony to serve as a member of two of the conventions called to frame constitutions for the State of Illinois—the first held in 1862, which framed a constitution that was rejected by the people, and the second held in 1870, and which framed the present constitution. In both of these conventions Judge Anthony took a prominent part, and was regarded in many respects as a leading expert in that body upon constitutional questions and methods of procedure. He was made Chairman of the Executive Committee and

reported the article as it now appears in the constitution relating to the Executive Department. He also served upon the Judiciary Committee, and the committee upon railroads, and many of the provisions in the judiciary articles, and most of those in regard to railroads, are the work of his hands. He was instrumental in providing for the organization of Appellate Courts and for additional Judges of the Circuit and Superior Courts of Cook County, as the population should increase and public business might require. At an earlier period he took part in the formation of the Republican party in this State, and was a delegate to the first Republican convention ever held in Cook County, and was for years most active in everything relating to the welfare and success of that party. In 1880 when the third term question came up, he took a most conspicuous part in that movement, was elected Chairman of the Cook County convention, at which a portion of the delegates withdrew, was elected a delegate to the State Convention, and was then selected as a contesting delegate to the National Convention at Chicago; was, after one of the stormiest debates on record, admitted as a delegate and participated in the proceedings which resulted in the nomination of General Garfield for President. In the fall of that year he was nominated and elected to the office of Judge of the Superior Court of the city of Chicago, and six years later was re-elected to the same position. Among the marked traits in Judge Anthony's character were his indomitable industry, and his devotion to business which, coupled with executive ability, enabled him to try and dispose of cases with great promptness and celerity. Judge Anthony was a voluminous writer, and his contributions to various legal magazines and periodicals would, if collected, fill volumes. He was also the author of several books of a historical character, among which may be enumerated "The Constitutional History of Illinois," "The Story of the Empire State," and one of local interest upon "Sanitation and Navigation," which has special reference to the disposition of sewage of the city of Chicago and the construction of a ship canal to unite the waters of Lake Michigan with those of the Mississippi River. While acting as Corporation Counsel of the city of Chicago in 1876, he wrote an interesting work upon taxation and the rules which had been established regarding the levy and collection of taxes. This work involved great labor and research, and has proved a useful and timely contribution to the general subject, and is very frequently referred to. In 1887, while holding the Criminal Court of Cook County, which includes the city of Chicago, he wrote a most interesting work on the "Law of Self-Defense, Trial by Jury in Criminal Cases and New Trials in Criminal Cases," which attracted a great deal of attention in this country, and is the first bold stand ever taken by any jurist of distinction against the wanton abuses which have arisen by invoking the doctrines of self-defense. One of his latest and most valuable contributions is an extended chapter entitled "Reminiscences of the Bench and Bar of Chicago," published in a two volume edition of the "Bench and Bar of Illinois" under the editorship of the late ex-Gov. John M. Palmer. Other contributions from his pen include a sketch of all of the courts of England; a treatise upon the "Law of Arrests in Civil Cases," and a series of articles upon "Old Virginia," published in the "Western Magazine of History." By special invitation of the State Bar Association, he delivered a memorable address at

their annual meeting in January, 1891, upon "The Constitutional History of Illinois," and another in the following year, entitled, "Remember the Pioneers," which is replete with the most interesting reminiscences.

Judge Anthony was one of the incorporators of the Chicago Law Institute, having drawn up its charter and, at his own expense, visited Springfield twice in one winter, while the Legislature was in session, to urge its passage, and for several terms served as its President. He was also one of the founders of the Chicago Public Library, and one of its first Board of Directors with which he was connected for a number of years.

From his youth Judge Anthony was a omniverous reader, and had at the time of the Chicago Fire, one of the largest private libraries in the city. He made several trips to Europe, during the last of which he visited Denmark, Sweden, Russia, Turkey, Greece, Italy, Spain and all the regions along the Mediterranean and Southern France. Many of his letters relating to these countries were published and read with great interest. In 1889 Judge Anthony was honored by his alma mater with the degree of Doctor of Laws. His death occurred at his home at Evanston, February 24, 1898.

VOLNEY W. FOSTER.

Volney W. Foster (deceased) was born near Jefferson, Wis., February 27, 1848. He attended the public schools and the Academy in Portage City, Wis., to which place his father moved when Volney was an infant. When he was thirteen years of age his father moved back to Jefferson. Wis., on a farm where Volney attended the district school. Afterwards he attended Milton College at Milton, Wis., one year. His mother, who was a gifted woman, helped him to acquire a fairly good classical education. At Jefferson he taught school several terms, holding the position of Principal of the Public Schools of that city. Afterwards he was engaged in business for himself as a partner in the firm of Platt, Gray & Foster, general merchants, at Manitowoc, Wis. He sold his interest in this firm and came to Chicago. There he was employed first by the Northwestern Railway. Later he became agent for a Wisconsin Lumber Company and, still later, was employed as cashier and the representative of Schulenburg & Boeckler's interests in the lumber firm of James McDonnel & Co., Chicago. Afterwards he was employed by Thompson & Barber, Wholesale Grocers on South Water Street, Chicago, as a traveling salesman.

In 1874 Mr. Foster went to Chatham, Ontario, and there purchased a half interest in the lumber business of A. R. Schulenburg. In the following year he purchased the entire business of the Georgian Bay Lumber Company. In 1879 he sold his lumber business at Chatham, and joined William D. Hitchcock in the purchase, sale and manufacture of lumber, shingles, railway ties, telegraph poles, etc., the business being carried on under the firm name of Hitchcock & Foster. In 1883, in connection with Mr. Hitchcock, Amos H. Perkins and W. H. Watson, he organized the Western Paving & Supply Company. In 1898 this company entered extensively into the asphalt-paving business, establishing offices in Indianapolis, Ind., Milwaukee, Wis., Evansville, Ind., and in Chicago. In 1892 the firm name of Hitchcock & Foster was dissolved, Mr. Hitchcock continuing the lumber business

and Mr. Foster taking over the paving business. In 1898 he sold out his interest in the paving business, and, in 1901, at Mexico City, in association with Mr. Enrique C. Creel, now Governor of the State of Chihuahua, Mexico, he organized the Almacenes Generales de Deposito de Mexico y Vera Cruz, S. A., which is a bonded warehouse organization, with warehouses at Mexico City and Vera Cruz. Of this company Mr. Foster was Vice-President. He was also President of the United States Repair & Guaranty Company, the United States Silica Company, the Chicago, Waukegan & North Shore Railway and the Chicago, Kenosha & Milwaukee Electric Railway Company, and he was largely interested in the North Shore Gas Company of Waukegan, Ill., in the North Coast Development Company, of San Francisco, Cal., and the Foster Contracting Company of Illinois. None of the companies or corporations in which he was interested ever failed in business.

Mr. Foster was the possessor of one of the finest private libraries in Evanston, and was a diligent and discriminating reader, being especially fond of history and philosophy. There were few departments of literature with which he was not well acquainted, and he had a remarkable memory and an unusual gift of language, so that he was able to appear to advantage in any company of cultivated gentlemen of which he was a member. In 1901 he was appointed by President McKinley a delegate to the Pan-American Conference, held in Mexico City in the Winter of 1901-02. He there had charge of formulating projects on International Sanitation, the re-organization of the Bureau of American Republics, the Exchange of Diplomas, and he originated and presented to the Conference the project for the establishment of an International Archæological and Ethnological Association, with its headquarters at Washington. All of these projects were unanimously adopted by the Republics represented at the Conference. In 1903 he was appointed by the President one of the American Commissioners to the Convention held at Washington, December 21, 1903, for the organization of the International Archæological and Ethnological Association. In 1904 he was appointed by the Peruvian Government as representative of Peru in this Association.

In 1900 he was appointed and served as Assistant Treasurer in the National Republican campaign. In 1887 he organized at his home, with the assistance of a few friends, the Sheridan Road Association, its purpose being to promote the construction of a free pleasure driveway on and near the Shore of Lake Michigan between Chicago and Milwaukee. Of this Association he was President up to the time of his death, and gave to it largely of his time and money. This Association secured State legislation for the establishment of park districts and pleasure driveways, and also the passage of the bill authorizing the reclamation of submerged lands on Lake Michigan by municipalities for parks. In 1891 he organized the Back-Lot Studies Society, and devoted to it premises near his home in Evanston and erected thereon a building for its use. These were known as the Back-Lot and the Shelter. The object of this was the instruction of boys selected by the Principal of the High School and the Principal of the Preparatory Department of the University. The attendance for several years averaged sixty-five. Weekly meetings were held in the Shelter and the boys were addressed by practical and successful business men on the different kinds of human activity called business. In the summer of 1903 he maintained on these premises a nature study class, in charge of an able director, where eighty-five young people were taught.

In 1876 Mr. Foster was married at Brockport, N. Y., to Eva Adele Hill, the daughter of Ezra N. Hill, of that city. Of this marriage were born two children, Albert Volney Foster, born in 1877, and Eva Cornelia Foster, born in 1879. Albert graduated from Harvard University and Eva at Smith College, Northampton. Eva married Mr. Walter Leisenring Righter, and now resides at Plainfield, N. J. Mrs. Foster died in 1887.

Mr. Foster was a member of the Glen View Golf Club, a charter member of the Evanston Club and a member of the Union League Club of Chicago, of which he was President in 1901. He organized the Evanston Ethical Club, which held its meetings at his home for several years and afterwards at his rooms at his hotel. He was also a charter member of the Evanston Country Club and an honorary member of the University Club of Evanston, a member of the Society of Colonial Wars, and of the Society of Mayflower Descendants. He was also a member of the International Peace Society, and author of the bill introduced in both Houses of Congress, in 1893, for the establishment of the National Arbitration Tribunal. This bill attracted very general attention and it is believed that, of he had lived, its essential features would have been incorporated into a national law. He regarded this as the most important work of his life. Mr. Foster's death occurred August 15, 1904.

JOHN B. KIRK.

John B. Kirk (deceased), former manufacturer, Chicago, with residence in Evanston, was born in Utica, N. Y., November 8, 1842, the second son of the late James S. Kirk, who was a native of Glasgow, Scotland, and was brought in his infancy by his father to Montreal, Canada. Here James S. Kirk grew to manhood, married Nancy Ann Dunning, of Ottawa, Canada, in 1839, and the same year located at Utica, N. Y., where he entered into mercantile business with his father. In 1859 the firm removed to Chicago where they founded the house of James S. Kirk & Company, which at the time of James S. Kirk's death, in 1886, was one of the most extensive manufacturers of soap, perfumery, etc., in this country. John B. received his early school training in the public schools of his native place, where he remained until seventeen years of age, in the meantime receiving a sound English education. At first he had a strong predilection for a professional career, but yielding to the wishes of his father, entered upon a business career, finally succeeding the latter in a branch of manufacturing industry which has grown to large proportions. Under his father's eye he was initiated into the mysteries of chemistry connected with the manufacture of the various products turned out by the firm of James S. Kirk & Company, meanwhile being trained in bookkeeping and business methods. After serving a regular apprenticeship under such thorough tutorship, having demonstrated his qualifications while still a young man, he was admitted as a partner of the concern, sharing with his father the responsibility of its management. In this way he was able to render his father most valuable assistance during the period of depression immediately following the great fire of 1871, in which the firm suffered a loss of nearly a quarter of a million dollars. In the work of reorganization he bore a prominent part, and the business was soon placed on a substantial basis. It is worthy of note here that the site of the plant now occupied by the Kirk Manufacturing Company, on North Water Street, is that of the first home occupied by permanent white settlers in Chicago, known as the historic "Kinzie Mansion."

Besides the manufacturing interests in which he held the position of President, Mr. Kirk had been connected with a number of financial enterprises, including the late American Exchange National Bank (merged a few years ago in the Corn Exchange Bank), of which he was President from 1890 to 1894. He was also deeply interested in the prosperity of the Northwestern University, which he served for several years as Trustee, and in connection with which he founded the $100 prize for oratory, which was of deep interest to the students of the Senior Class.

Mr. Kirk was married October 4, 1866, to Miss Susie MacVean, the daughter of Mr. D. McVean, of Chicago, and of this union four children were born: James M., Frederick I., Josephine and Susie. For many years his home was in Evanston, where he enjoyed the confidence and respect of a large circle of friends. On November 1, 1904, Mr. Kirk's notable career as a business man and public-spirited citizen was terminated by his sudden death, in New York City, while on a business visit to that place.

SIMEON FARWELL.

Simeon Farwell, merchant and head of one of the most widely known mercantile houses in the West, has been a resident of Evanston since 1876. He was born at Campbelltown, Steuben County, N. Y., March 22, 1831, the son of Henry and Nancy (Jackson) Farwell, and a descendant in the seventh generation of Henry Farwell, who was one of the founders of the colony of Concord, Mass., incorporated in 1635. Back of its advent in this country, the history of the Farwell family is traced to the thirteenth century, and to Richard Farwell of Yorkshire, who gained distinction in the reign of King Edward I. The American branch of the family has had many prominent representatives in various walks of life in New England, and in later years in many States of the Union. The father of Simeon Farwell, who removed from Massachusetts to New York State, was a farmer by occupation in the last named State, and later became one of the pioneer agriculturists in Ogle County, Ill. He removed with his family to this State in 1838, and the son, Simeon, passed the next few years of his life on the farm near Oregon, aiding as a boy to bring under cultivation the prairie lands which his father had acquired. He was educated at Mt. Morris Seminary, Mt. Morris, Ill., fitting himself for a commercial career. In July of 1849 he came to Chicago, and had his earliest experience in this city as Deputy Clerk of the Circuit Court, of which the pioneer Chicagoan, L. D. Hoard, was then Clerk. After filling this position about two years, Mr. Farwell entered, as a clerk, the noted old-time banking house of George Smith, in its day the most famous financial institution in the West. A year later he resigned this position to become a clerk in the dry-goods house of Cooley, Wadsworth & Co., accepting a lower salary than he had been receiving in order that he might learn the business to which he had decided to devote his after life. When he entered the employ of this firm, he took charge of its books and accounts, bringing to the discharge of his duties untiring energy, a thorough knowledge of his business and strict integrity, which constituted an excellent basis for success. He continued to act as bookkeeper of the firm until 1860, and in 1870 was admitted to a partnership. In the meantime, in 1860, the firm had become Cooley, Farwell & Co., Mr. Farwell's elder brother, John V. Farwell, since widely known as a merchant, being the junior partner. John V. Farwell had preceded the younger brother to Chicago, as had also another brother, Charles B. Farwell, later merchant, banker and United States Senator. In 1865 the firm became John V. Farwell & Co., a name which it has since retained, with slight change, although the co-partnership was succeeded in 1890 by the J. V. Farwell Company, incorporated. This pioneer dry-goods house, known now and for many years past throughout the United States, and which annually has a trade aggregating many millions of dollars, has graduated from its salesrooms some of the most famous merchants in the world; among them, Marshall Field, Levi Z. Leiter, H. N. Higinbotham, and others. The connection of Simeon Farwell with this house and its predecessors has covered a period of fifty-five years, and for twenty-five years he has taken a leading part in its conduct and management. He became Vice-President of the J. V. Farwell Company at the time of its incorporation in 1890, and since 1900 has been its President. To the building up of this great commercial institution his activities have been mainly given, although for some years he was a Director of the Metropolitan National Bank. The measure of its success evidences the measure of his ability as a merchant, and the breadth and scope of his genius in the field of commerce. In the early years of his business career in Chicago his home was in this city, but as previously stated, he became a resident of Evanston in 1876. Since then he has been a leading citizen of this classic suburb of Chicago, and a leader in advancing the interests of the little city and its institutions.

Mr. Farwell is a Methodist in religious belief, and a communicant of the First Methodist Church of Evanston. In 1857 he married, at Sardinia, Erie County, N. Y., Miss Ebenette M. Smith, daughter of Rev. Isaac B. Smith, a Methodist clergyman of the Empire State. Their living children are Henry S. Farwell, now connected with the great mercantile house which his father helped to build up, and Mrs. Ruth (Farwell) Gridley, of Evanston. Their eldest daughter, Anna Pearl Farwell, died in 1893.

WILLIAM HUGH JONES.

William Hugh Jones, Evanston, Ill., President of the Plano Manufacturing Company, one of the substantial industries of the city of Chicago, was born in Wales in 1845, one of eight children—six sons and two daughters—of Hugh and Jennett Jones. His father, who was a farmer in comfortable circumstances, came to America in 1812, locating near Utica, N. Y., where his first wife died. He later returned to Wales, where he married his second wife, the mother of the subject of this sketch. In 1857 he

again came with his family to America, first locating in Wisconsin, whence he removed in 1873 to Iowa, dying in Howard County in that State in 1876, aged eighty-two years. His widow, who survived her husband about four years, was a daughter of Richard Jones, an extensive farmer of Wales, who reached the age of ninety-two years.

William H. Jones remained in his native land until twelve years of age, when he came with his parents to Wisconsin, and there spent his youth in farm work with his father until he reached his majority. In 1866 he became agent for the Dodge Reapers and Champion Mowers at Berlin, Wis., remaining in this business until 1868, when he entered into the employment of L. J. Bush & Co., of Milwaukee, as traveling salesman. Two years later (1870) he formed a connection with E. H. Gammon for the sale of the Marsh Harvester and Dodge Reapers. This concern afterwards became the firm of Gammon & Deering, which was dissolved in 1879 by the retirement of Mr. Gammon. Mr. Jones remained with Mr. Deering until 1880 and in 1881 organized at Plano, Ill., The Plano Manufacturing Company, assuming the office of President, which position he has retained to the present time. In 1893 this concern erected a new factory, covering an area of twenty acres in West Pullman (now One Hundred an Twentieth Street, Chicago), which was furnished with improved machinery and facilities, which has resulted in a largely extended trade, both home and foreign. Mr. Jones' early experience as a farmer fitted him to judge the needs of the farming class, while his later connection with practical manufacturing enterprises has enabled him to apply this knowledge in a way greatly to benefit the farmers and extend the trade. In 1877 he opened a wholesale implement house at Minneapolis, which carried on a large business, and with which he continued to be connected until 1889.

Mr. Jones was married in 1867 to Miss Elizabeth Owens, and three sons were born of this union—Hugh W., William O. and Garfield R. The parents are members of the Methodist Episcopal Church, in which Mr. Jones holds the position of Trustee. In political views he is an adherent of the Republican party, but votes independently on local questions, and has never been a seeker for office in his own behalf. Since 1872 he has been a resident of Evanston, with the exception of a short time spent at Minneapolis and at Plano, Ill., and is held in high estimation as a public-spirited and enterprising citizen. Mr. Jones is now a Vice-President, and Director of the International Harvester Company.

CHARLES GATES DAWES.

Charles G. Dawes, President of Central Trust Company of Illinois, and former Comptroller of the Currency, was born at Marietta, Ohio, August 27, 1865, the son of Gen. Rufus R. Dawes, who served as Colonel of the Sixth Wisconsin Volunteer Infantry (which constituted a part of the "Iron Brigade" under command of Gen. Edward S. Bragg) during the Civil War, and at the close of the war was brevetted as Brigadier-General for gallant service. Mr. Dawes' mother, Mary (Gates) Dawes, was a member of one of the oldest families of Southern Ohio, her father being Beman Gates, a prominent business man and banker of his time, and his great-grandfather the celebrated Manasseh Cutler, who was a prominent representative of the Ohio Land

Company just after the close of the Revolutionary War, and is credited with having been the author of the anti-slavery clause of the Ordinance of 1787, protecting the territory northwest of the Ohio River from the admission of slavery.

Charles G. Dawes was educated in the common schools and at Marietta College, graduating from the latter in 1884. Two years later he graduated from the Cincinnati Law School, during his vacation working as a civil engineer on the Toledo & Ohio Central Railroad, of which he later became Chief Engineer. In 1887 he went to Lincoln, Neb., where for the next seven years he was engaged in the practice of his profession. Having in the meantime made a special study of the question of railroad freight rates, he was retained by a number of Nebraska shippers in the prosecution of suits against railroad companies for violation of the Inter-State Commerce Law, in which he displayed marked ability.

In 1894, having acquired an interest in a gas company, Mr. Dawes removed to Evanston, Ill., which has since been his home except when in the Government service. While a resident of Nebraska he had gained much prominence as a champion of the principles of the Republican party, and, on coming to Illinois, at once became an important factor in the movement to secure the nomination of William McKinley for President. Largely through his influence and active efforts the Republican State Convention at Springfield, in 1896, adopted resolutions instructing the delegates to the National Convention there appointed to cast their votes for McKinley, and Mr. Dawes was appointed a member of the Executive Committee of the Republican National Committee and bore an important part in the following campaign. In January,

1898, he was appointed by President McKinley Comptroller of the Currency as successor to James H. Eckels, retaining this position until October, 1901, when he tendered his resignation with a view to becoming a candidate for the United States Senate. In May, 1902, having withdrawn from the candidacy for the Senate, he was, a few days later, elected President of the Central Trust Company of Illinois, with headquarters in Chicago, a position which he has retained continuously to the present time. Having made banking and finance a study for many years, he is regarded as an authority on these questions, and is the author of a volume on "The Banking System of the United States."

Mr. Dawes was married on January 24, 1889, to Miss Caro Dana Blymyer, of Cincinnati, Ohio.

MERRITT C. BRAGDON, M. D.

Dr. Merritt C. Bragdon, one of the most prominent and successful physicians and surgeons of Cook County, Ill., whose career as a skillful practitioner in Evanston, the city of his home, extended over a period of more than thirty years, was born in Auburn, N. Y., January 6, 1850, the son of Rev. Charles P. and Sarah (Cushman) Bragdon, natives of the State of Maine, born in the towns of Acton and East Poland, respectively. Rev. Charles P. Bragdon was reared to manhood in his native State, and there, in early youth, made diligent use of the opportunities for mental training afforded by the public schools. At a later period he became a pupil in Cazenovia Seminary, N. Y., where he pursued a course of study, which fitted him for his subsequent long and eminently useful career in the ministry, covering a wide field of activity. He entered the ministry of the Methodist Episcopal Church in Maine, and was afterwards stationed at Auburn, N. Y., until he was called to the agency of the Methodist Book Depository at Springfield, Mass., where he remained until 1854. · In that year he made his home in Illinois, becoming a member of the Rock River Conference. His first pastoral charge was at Waukegan, where he remained for two years. His next appointment was at Aurora, from whence he was transferred to Evanston, where, in 1858, he became one of the early pastors of the First Methodist Church. He was greatly beloved by the pioneer residents of Evanston who founded and built up the "First Church," which is now one of the leading churches of the Northwest, conspicuous in Christian work, abounding in material prosperity, and noted for the moral and intellectual culture of its members. On the termination of a useful pastorate of two years in this connection, the health of Mr. Bragdon having become seriously impaired, he was compelled to relinquish his ministerial labors and withdraw from active labor. He departed this life in Evanston on January 8, 1861. His estimable wife survived her husband for more than forty years, during which period she continued to reside in Evanston. She passed away on January 29, 1902, at the age of eighty-three years.

At the time when the Bragdon family established their home in Evanston, the subject of this sketch was eight years of age. He received his primary mental training in the local schools, and after pursuing a course of preparatory study, matriculated in Northwestern University, from which he was graduated in the class of 1870. Immediately after graduation, he began reading medicine under the preceptorship of Dr. Nathan Smith Davis, whose extended and distinguished career as a physician and educator placed him at the head of his profession, and whose fame as author and founder of the American Medical Association spread throughout the scientific world. Dr. Bragdon attended his first course of lectures at the Chicago Medical College, and subsequently became a student in the Hahnemann Medical College at Philadelphia, from which he was graduated in the class of 1873. After receiving the degree of M. D. from this institution, he went abroad and continued his studies at Vienna, devoting particular attention to obstetrics and surgery. On completing his postgraduate researches he returned to Evanston, and entered into a professional partnership with Dr. O. H. Mann, who then had a large practice, but is now retired. This connection lasted three years, and since the end of that peirod, Dr. Bragdon has continued in practice alone. His growth in popular favor has been rapid and continuous, and he long ago became one of the leading practitioners of his section of the State. The devotion which he has manifested to professional duty has been of an intense and useful nature, and nothing has been permitted by him to interfere with the attention due to those who required his treatment or sought his friendly counsel. He was chosen to a professorship in the Hahnemann Medical College of Chicago, but declined the honor, lest an acceptance should prove detrimental to his success as a practicing physician in Evanston—the college being located at so great a distance from his field of labor. He is, however, a member of the American Institute of Homœopathy, and the Illinois State Homœopathic Association.

Dr. Bragdon has taken an active interest in public affairs, and has been a steadfast advocate and supporter of all that is wholesome and desirable in connection with the material and educational interests of Evanston. He was one of the founders and an original stockholder of the State Bank of Evanston, and has for a number of years been a member of the directorate of that admirably managed financial institution. Of the welfare of the Northwestern University he has always been a helpful promoter, and has contributed to its prosperity through individual effort, and as a member of its Board of Trustees. As a churchman he has used his best endeavors to advance the interests of the First Methodist Church of Evanston, with the official board of which he is identified.

On June 6, 1876, Dr. Bragdon was united in marriage with Elizabeth Wayne Byerly, a lady of many virtues and graces, and a daughter of David Byerly, who was a representative of one of the old Quaker families of Philadelphia. The children resulting from this union are as follows: Elizabeth, Wayne, Charles Ridgaway, Sara Frances, and Merritt Caldwell, Jr.

In politics, the subject of this sketch is an adherent of the Republican party, to which he lends an unselfish support. As boy and man, he has been a witness of the progress of Evanston and its institutions from an early period, and has borne his full share in their development. Throughout the community he is held in high esteem.

LEVI CARROLL PITNER.

Rev. Levi Carroll Pitner, retired, Evanston, was born in Wilson County, Tenn., January 24, 1824, the son of Michael and Catherine (Rouble) Pitner. Michael Pitner was born in Rockingham County, Va., the son of John Pitner, a native of the same State. John Pitner was a soldier in the Revolutionary War for the entire period of seven years, and Michael Pitner was a soldier in the War of 1812, serving with General Jackson at New Orleans. At the age of eighteen, Michael Pitner removed to East Tennessee, near Knoxville, and here his marriage took place. In the year 1799, this heroic couple crossed the Cumberland Mountains and went to Wilson County, West Tennessee. where they purchased a farm, which, for thirty-two years, continued to be their home. On this homestead twelve children were born—seven sons and five daughters,—eleven of whom grew to maturity. Four of these sons preceded the family to Illinois, and so glowing were the accounts sent back, that the remainder soon followed, arriving at the home of Montgomery Pitner, a relative, on the second day of September, 1837, and locating soon afterward on a farm in North Prairie, nine miles northwest of Jacksonville. Before a permanent home could be provided, the head of the family was stricken with disease, which proved fatal, and ended his life at the age of sixty-two.

Levi Carroll Pitner, the subject of this sketch, was then sixteen. He was greatly distressed at the death of his parent, and, as a result of that father's example and death-bed solicitude, the son gave his heart to God and united with the M. E. Church. From the day of his conversion the conviction grew upon him that his life-work was to be preaching the Gospel. At length he was appointed class-leader; next he received a license to exhort, and later a license to preach from the Quarterly Conference of the Jacksonville Circuit. He was next recommended for admission to the Illinois Conference, which he joined September 4, 1845. In those

days the conferences maintained a strict course of study, which Mr. Pitner successfully completed. His first work was on the Jerseyville Circuit as junior colleague of the Rev. James Leaton, and there had a happy and prosperous year. He later had charge at Quincy, Carlinville, Beardstown, Bloomington, Jacksonville and Decatur. One of the twenty-three years of Mr. Pitner's connection with the Illinois Conference was spent as agent to raise $40,000 with which to build the Quincy College, now known as Chaddock College. In 1866 he was appointed Conference agent for the purpose of raising $100,000 to aid the conference institutions of learning, including Garrett Biblical Institute. This large amount, by the aid of the ministry and the laymen, was raised during that year. Mr. Pitner served three years as Presiding Elder of the Danville district, and was an active force in many large camp-meetings so popular during that period of church history. The arduous labors in which he had so long indulged were a severe strain on his physical strength, and at the advice of his many friends he at length asked for location, Bishop Janes signing his release from service.

On August 30, 1848, Mr. Pitner was married to Miss Arminda F. Cartwright, daughter of Rev. Peter Cartwright, D. D., famous among the pioneer preachers of Western Methodism. Their only child is Lee J. Pitner of Evanston.

After his retirement from the itinerary service, deciding to locate in Evanston, Ill., Mr. Pitner was confronted with the serious problem of making a living. He finally went into the real estate business, and as his venture began just at the time when Chicago was having "a boom" and when buyers were plentiful, he made a success, clearing about $200,000 in three or four years. The panic of 1873, however, swept away all but his home. In the early 'eighties the tide of fortune again turned in his favor. He was happy in making investments in Hammond, Ind., and also in Seattle, Wash., and has since that date lived in the enjoyment of a comfortable competency. In his political views, Mr. Pitner, after having voted twice for Lincoln, because of his temperance principles went over to the Prohibition Party in 1884. In 1888 he was Chairman of the State Central Committee for his party, and led the campaign for Fiske and Brooks. At that election the party cast a larger number of votes in Illinois than has been cast at any Presidential election since, with the exception of that of 1904. Notwithstanding the fact that he was Southern born he was an ardent Unionist during the Civil War, supporting the cause with all the means and influence at his command. It is equally noteworthy that he was a strong anti-slavery man before the war, voting for General John C. Fremont in 1856. When the war had settled the slavery question, his strong convictions on the subject of prohibiting the liquor traffic carried him in 1884 into the Prohibition party, and he has been a consistent and forceful champion of the principles of that party ever since. He is now a local elder in Emmanuel M. E. Church, Evanston, and a member of the official board.

REV. MINER RAYMOND, D. D., LL. D.

January 2nd, A. D. 1636, the town of Salem, Mass., granted a half acre of land at Winter Harbor, to Richard Raymond, "for fishing trade and to build upon." Richard was a mariner who later engaged in coastwise trade and died at Saybrook,

Conn., in 1692, "ae. abt. 90." Richard's son, John, and John's son, Thomas, lived at Norwalk, Conn., and Thomas' son, Comfort, and Comfort's son, Comfort, Jr., lived at New Canaan, Conn. Here was born Nobles Benedict, a son of Comfort, Jr., September 29, 1788. Nobles Benedict, who was by trade a shoemaker, was married in 1808, in the City of New York, to Hannah Wood, a daughter of a Revolutionary soldier. Of their union Miner Raymond was born in New York City, August 29, 1811.

Two years later the family removed to Rensselaerville, Albany County, where Miner helped in the home and the shop and attended the village school until he was twelve years old. By that time he had mastered all that the village school could teach him and he began to yearn for something larger and better. His father was not able to send him away to school, nor could he allow him to be idle: so, to use his own language, "he set me on a shoe-bench drawing the cords of affliction on the stool of repentance for six years, and I wanting to go to school all the time."

In 1830, when he was nineteen years old, the way opened for him to go to the Wesleyan Academy at Wilbraham, Mass. He succeeded in paying his way, in part, by means of his skill as a shoemaker. Three years later he became a teacher in the Academy and continued for seven years in that relation, first in charge of the English department and later as instructor in mathematics. His remarkable aptness as a teacher, as well as the power of his commanding personality, is witnessed by a lawyer of New York who was a student under him, and declared long afterwards that "Miner Raymond was the greatest mathematical teacher on God's earth." He evinced from the first that he was one of those born teachers who are gifted beyond ordinary men to make things clear. In 1840 the Wesleyan University honored him with the degree of Master of Arts and in 1854 with that of Doctor of Divinity. Thirty years later the Northwestern University conferred on him the degree of Doctor of Laws.

Meanwhile his ability as a preacher began to attract wide attention, and in 1841 he left the Academy and became a pastor in the New England Conference of the Methodist Episcopal Church, preaching successively in Worcester, Boston and Westfield, Mass. Of him, as a preacher, the historian of Wesleyan Academy writes, that "his first attempts at preaching evinced the careful thinker. But while the principles and main proposition were laid down carefully as well as clearly, the preacher was sure to kindle as he advanced and to break into a tornado in the peroration. Though gifted with large capacity for astute and accurate thought, he was heard gladly by the people, because his logic usually came to white heat." After his coming to Evanston he was for three years the pastor of the First Methodist Episcopal Church of this place, and the older inhabitants often speak of his great power as a preacher, and of the overwhelming effect some of his sermons had upon the large assembly. He was six times a member of the (quadrennial) General Conference of the Methodist Church, and was chairman of the Committee on Slavery in the General Conference at Indianapolis in 1848.

But it was not as a pastor and preacher that he was destined to work out the great ministry of his life. In 1848, when he was thirty-seven years old, exigencies at the Academy at Wilbraham led the Trustees to turn to Miner Raymond as the man above all others to take charge of the institution. It was with great reluctance that he at last consented to leave the pastorate and become the Principal of Wilbraham. But he obeyed the call which seemed divine, and the sixteen years that followed were probably the most brilliant period of his entire career. The same historian of the Wesleyan Academy says that his election as Principal "marked a new era in the history of that honored institution. Of all the Principals, his term was at once the longest and most fruitful in important results. Under the touch of his genius and the control of his unconquerable will, old things disappeared and almost everything about the institution became new. Difficulties, which to weaker men would have proven altogether insuperable, vanished in the presence of one so able to influence men and to command resources. To this wise master-builder the friends of the institution owe an immense debt of gratitude."

But if those sixteen years were the most brilliant in his career, the next period of over thirty years made him more conspicuous in the eyes of both the Church and the world. In the summer of 1864 Dr. Raymond was called to succeed Dr. John Dempster, as Professor of Systematic Theology in Garrett Biblical Institute, and the rest of his life work was performed in connection with that institution. "When I came here," he once remarked, "and walked up and down along the lakeside, and considered the field and its opportunities, I felt that I had come to my kingdom : and though it was unexpected and unsought, the place and the work came to me as that which, above all others in the gift of the Church, was the one for which I had been providentially prepared."

Dr. Raymond died November 25, 1897, and at his funeral services his colleague,

Dr. M. S. Terry, said: "For the last thirty years his life has been a part of the history of Evanston. His name is to the people of this community a household word; his memory as ointment poured forth! How magnificently that whole record of a life of eighty-six years opens up to our thought! Almost three generations have come and gone since he was born, and his life was nearly co-extensive with the nineteenth century. He has built a character and work that cannot perish from the annals of the Church of God. Dr. Raymond was the last survivor of a great faculty—that older faculty of the Institute in its heroic days. Successor of Dempster, the founder of theological schools in the Methodist Episcopal Church, he was the fitting colleague of Kidder and Bannister and Hemenway. They passed on before him into God's higher school many semesters ago. But Dr. Raymond lived on to see almost another generation pass. A Bennett and a Ridgaway have come and gone, and seem already like the transfigured forms of a beautiful vision that vanished long ago. But this saintly man lived on and taught, and prayed, and smiled, and wept, and pronounced many a loving benediction on the younger folk."

Of Doctor Raymond President Little wrote: "He was one of the last and one of the greatest of a marvelous group of Methodist preachers—a group illustrious with the names of Olin, and Fisk, and Bascom; of Simpson, and McClintock, and Durbin, and Stevens. And even in the class-room he could not cease to preach. For the truths that he expounded were to him the substance of eternal life. Other teachers might be more erudite and more subtle; none could be more luminous or more reasonable; and few, indeed, could so challenge the student to admira-

tion, or so encourage him to strenuous effort and to independent thought. Hence, the unbounded affection of the men that sat at his feet. Many of them have reached the highest station of influence and authority in the Church; some of them are preaching the gospel in distant lands; others are working quietly and faithfully at home. But to all of them the echoes of his deep, sonorous voice are an imperishable treasure, for the words he spoke to them were spirit and life."

During the first years of Doctor Raymond's residence in Evanston he was not only professor in the Institute and pastor of the Methodist Church, but he was also President of the Village Board of Education; and it was during his administration that the Hinman Avenue School was organized and the first building erected for that school.

When the University purchased the Snyder farm in 1867 the Trustees voted "that the street on the north line be called Dempster Street, and that the street nearest the lake shore be called Raymond Avenue." Raymond Avenue has been swallowed up in Sheridan Road, but the City Council recently voted that the public park between Chicago and Hinman Avenues, and between Grove and Lake Streets, be named Raymond Park; so that Dr. Raymond's name is still perpetuated on the city plat.

Doctor Raymond married, at Webster, Mass., August 20, 1837, Elizabeth Henderson, who died at Evanston, September 19, 1877. She was the mother of his children: Charles Wesley and Francis Asbury, who died in infancy; Mary, widow of Philip B. Shumway, who died at Evanston, December 22, 1903; William M., who died in Chicago, February 5, 1896; Samuel B., now living in Chicago;

and James H. and Frederick D., who are living in Evanston.

On July 28, 1879, Doctor Raymond married, as his second wife, at New Haven, Conn., Mrs. Isabella (Hill) Binney, who died at Evanston February 6, 1897.

FREDERICK D. RAYMOND.

Frederick D. Raymond, who has been a resident of Evanston for more than forty years, was born in Wilbraham, Mass., September 16, 1852. His father, Rev. Miner Raymond, D. D., LL. D., was born in New York City, August 29, 1811; and his mother, Elizabeth (Henderson) Raymond, was a native of Ireland, born in Mt. Hall, County Tyrone, August 12, 1814. The former was a minister of the Methodist Episcopal Church, and an eminent teacher. (See sketch of Rev. Miner Raymond in this volume.)

Frederick D. received his primary education in the public schools of his native State, and came to Evanston with his parents in August, 1864, and there, for one year, attended the "Grove School," with Miss Frances E. Willard as his preceptress. He then became a pupil in the Preparatory Department of Northwestern University where he continued three years. Subsequently he finished the university course, requiring four more years of study, and graduated with the class of 1872. During his undergraduate period, he was a member of the Hinman Literary Society and the Sigma Chi fraternity, and later was elected a member of the honorary Phi Beta Kappa Society. On completing his education, Mr. Raymond spent a year in connection with the adjustment of the affairs of a Chicago fire insurance company, which was rendered insolvent by the great fire of 1871. He then taught

in the Preparatory Department of Northwestern University during the first year of the principalship of Rev. Dr. Fisk—1873 to 1874.

Since 1874, Mr. Raymond has devoted his attention to the construction and operation of railroads. The first three years of this period were spent at Streator, Ill., engaged in construction work and in the freight department of the Chicago & Paducah and the Chicago, Pekin & Southwestern Railroads, now, respectively, the Chicago division of the Wabash System and the Atchison, Topeka & Santa Fe Railway. He was subsequently engaged in the construction of the "Monon" line, from Chicago to Indianapolis, and served as general freight agent of the Chicago & Great Southern Railway (now the coal line), in Indiana, of the Chicago & Eastern Illinois Railroad. Since its organization in 1887, he has been a director, and Secretary and Treasurer of the Elgin, Joliet & Eastern Railway Company; and since 1899 has acted in the same capacities in connection with the Chicago, Lake Shore & Eastern Railway Company, both of which companies are controlled by the United States Steel Corporation. In the construction of all these roads, except that last mentioned, Mr. Raymond was associated with his brother-in-law, the late Philip B. Shumway.

On October 24, 1877, Mr. Raymond was united in marriage at Evanston, Ill., with Carrie M. Wyckoff, of that city. Mrs. Raymond is a daughter of William M. and Mary A. Wyckoff residents, successively, of New York City, Bellefontaine and Cincinnati, Ohio, Chicago and Evanston. Mr. and Mrs. Raymond are the parents of the following named children: Ruth, born October 6, 1878; Mary, born October 18, 1880; Philip W., born

October 28, 1886; Margaret, born August 9, 1891; and Frederick D., Jr., born July 6, 1896.

Politically, Mr. Raymond is a supporter of the Republican party. His religious connection is with the First Methodist Episcopal Church, of Evanston, of which he has been a member of the official board since 1878. In fraternal circles he is identified with the Royal Arcanum, and is a member of the University Club, of Evanston. He is now acting in the capacity of Treasurer of the Municipal Association of Evanston.

CAPT. JOSHUA P. BOUTELLE.

The first American ancestor of Captain Joshua P. Boutelle, of Evanston, Ill., was James Boutelle, who came from England to America early in the seventeenth century, the original family seat being in Massachusetts. From Massachusetts Captain Boutelle's branch of the family emigrated to Maine, and at Edgecomb and at other places in the latter State Dr. John Boutelle, the father of the subject of this sketch, practiced medicine for many years. Dr. Boutelle was a zealous anti-slavery champion and for many years was actively interested in colonization movements in the interest of ex-slaves and other negroes in the United States. Captain Boutelle's grandfather, William Boutelle, was a soldier in the Revolutionary War, and received for his services a land warrant from the Government, which he located on land in Maine.

Captain Joshua P. Boutelle was born at Edgecomb, Maine, September 20, 1822, where he was reared on a small farm, receiving a common school education during his boyhood. Later he attended an academy at Newcastle, Maine,

where he gave special attention to navigation, and at seventeen years of age adopted the life of a sailor, making his first trip to Cuba on board the brig "Damascus," under the command of Captain Chase. In 1848 he became master of the ship "St. John," upon which he won for himself the title of the "yellow fever captain," in consequence of having taken this vessel to Vera Cruz to remove a number of American soldiers to the States, after the close of the Mexican War. In the performance of this duty he took the place of the regular commander of the "St. John," who feared to expose himself to contracting the yellow fever. In 1849 Captain Boutelle sailed the ship "Archelaus," which foundered off the coast of Wales, after which, in 1850, he took the ship "State of Maine" around Cape Horn to California, and thence sailed across the Pacific and Indian Oceans, making the circuit of the globe and finally reaching London by way of the Cape of Good Hope. In 1852 he assumed command of the "Arabia," which, for four years, sailed between New York, Mobile, New Orleans and Liverpool, after which a company, of which he was a member, built the "Niagara," which in 1859 was engaged in trade between the United States and Liverpool. The last vessel on which he sailed was the "Saginaw," which, in company with others, he built in 1863, and which made its first voyage to Panama the same year. During the Civil War this vessel narrowly escaped capture by the Confederate cruiser "Alabama," but was burned in 1866 off the Island of Madeira while bound from Cardiff, Wales, to Panama.

This closed Captain Boutelle's sea-faring life, and in 1867 he engaged in coal-mining in Nova Scotia, having charge, as superintendent for one year, of mines which he had opened there. He then came to Chicago, but in 1869 returned to New York, where he embarked in the wholesale sewing machine trade for one year, when, in 1870, he came to Evanston, Ill., which continued to be his home for the remainder of his life. Here he invested in real estate and engaged in building and other improvements; in 1871 erected the Boutelle & Wesley Block, and later improved considerable residence property. From 1875 to 1881 he was engaged in the hardware trade in Evanston, since then being retired from business life.

Captain Boutelle was married first to Frances A. Robbins, of Maine, who died in 1850, and in 1868, he married as his second wife Margaret A. Patten, of Brunswick, Maine, who died in 1872. His third marriage was with Miss Augusta A. Reed, of Chicago, in 1880. Mrs. Boutelle is a native of New York, but came to Sterling, Illinois, in girlhood, still later spent some years in the South and East, finally returning to the West. An intimate friend of Mrs. Boutelle for many years was the widow of the late Judge David Davis, of Bloomington, Ill., now Mrs. Greene of North Carolina. Captain Boutelle's only child is now Mrs. Ada (Boutelle) Briggs of Evanston. The Hon. Charles A. Boutelle, late Congressman from Maine (now deceased), was a nephew of Captain Boutelle.

Captain Boutelle was a member of the Odd Fellows' fraternity, in politics was a Republican, and served for eight years as Justice of the Peace and one year as Collector for the city of Evanston. He lived an active and strenuous life, and at the age of eighty-two years was in possession of his mental faculties, and retained a vivid memory of past adventures and events which made him a most

charming companion. Death came to him at his home in Evanston, June 21, 1905. His daughter and her husband, Mr. John A. Briggs, accompanied the remains to Union, Maine, where they were interred in accordance with his wish, by the side of his first wife.

WALLACE REYNOLDS CONDICT.

Wallace Reynolds Condict (deceased), a well known and highly respected resident of Evanston from May 1, 1875, until August 30, 1899, was born in Newark, New Jersey, June 1, 1824. His parents were Sidney and Charlotte (Reynolds) Condict. Sidney Condict was a prominent and prosperous dry-goods merchant in the East. In New York and New Jersey the Condicts are an old and influential family, and the Reynolds family is of Mayflower stock. The circumstances of Wallace R. Condict's parents enabled them to give him an excellent high school education, and his business training was received in the dry-goods line under his father's supervision. When about twenty years of age the son came West, to Racine, Wis., and was connected with an elevator concern until he was about twenty-five years old, when he went to Michigan City, Ind., and engaged in the dry-goods business on his own account. There he remained until near the termination of the Civil War, when he sold out and came to Chicago, but did not enter upon any active business enterprise on his own responsibility after his arrival there. On May 1, 1875, he established his residence in Evanston, where he lived during the remainder of his days. Politically, Mr. Condict supported the Republican party. He attended the Congregational Church, to the maintenance of which he was a regular contributor.

Mr. Condict was married in Chicago,

January 31, 1874, to Louise Albridge, a daughter of Isaac and Armina Albridge, of Plattsburgh, New York. The issue of their union was Wallace Reynolds and Jessie Haskell, both of whom are married and living in Evanston.

The subject of this sketch was honorable, conservative and level-headed in his business transactions, and one whom all could trust. He was a home-loving, quiet man who devoted himself to his business and family, and cared nothing for club life or political honors.

OLIVER M. CARSON.

Oliver M. Carson (deceased) was born in Sweden, March 31, 1853, and in early childhood came to America with his parents who settled in Galesburg, Ill. His education was received in the public schools near his home and at Knox College, Galesburg. While pursuing his course in that institution he supported himself and secured his diploma by his own unaided efforts. He then entered the well-known dry-goods house of Charles Gossage, where he remained until his health became so impaired as to necessitate a change, when he went to Minnesota and tried agricultural pursuits for a brief period. An improvement in his health enabled him to return to mercantile pursuits, which first took him to Farmington, Minn., later becoming connected with the dry goods firm of Carhart & Co. of St. Paul, with which house he remained for a period of eleven years. Returning to Chicago, Mr. Carson, after a brief experience in trade, began operating in real estate, located in the main along the North Shore, and also in Oak Park. Always enthusiastic over the development of North Shore realty, his confidence was unbounded, and the improvements made under his management were many and of an important character. The subject of "riparian rights" was ever uppermost in his mind, and he acquired much property in this connection. In his business undertakings he was intensely active, such being the nature of the man, but of all enterprises none was dearer to his heart than the improvements along the North Shore. He promoted a number of sub-divisions between Chicago and the suburban cities to the north, as well as 48 acres of land in Oak Park.

On October 18, 1882, Mr. Carson was united in marriage to Miss Clara, daughter of G. L. Wetterland, of Chicago, and of this union one daughter (Miss Mildred) was born. In his political affiliations Mr. Carson was a Republican. He was a member of the Presbyterian Church. Until 1892 his residence was in Chicago, but at that time he removed to Evanston, Ill., his home being at No. 222 Stockham Place, one of the most charming locations in the classic town. Active, genial, enterprising, Mr. Carson's interest in all pertaining to the improvement of North Shore property continued to the close of his successful career. His decease occurred on September 11, 1902. Mrs. Carson, who survives her husband, resides at Hotel Monnett, Evanston. Mr. Carson was domestic in his habits, delighting in the society of his family and of his intimate friends. He was cordial, approachable, and his home was a center where one met this most affable and engaging of men, whose death was lamented by many.

WILLIAM J. CANFIELD.

William J. Canfield (deceased), formerly a leading merchant of Evanston, Ill., was born in Salisbury, Conn., November 14, 1832. His parents were Lee and Ruth (Butler) Canfield. The Canfield family was originally of English extraction, and the subject of this sketch was a descendant of Thomas Canfield, one of the early colonists who settled at Milford, near New Haven, Conn., and was one of the original proprietors of the place. Lieut. Col. Buel, of Revolutionary fame, was one of the ancestors of Mr. Canfield, as was also Governor Wells, one of the early Colonial Governors. Lee Canfield was an iron manufacturer by occupation, and worked the noted Salisbury mines from which iron was taken for vessels in the Revolutionary period. These mines were once operated by Ethan Allen, and were among the first worked in America.

In his boyhood Mr. Canfield attended the public schools of Salisbury, and was afterward a pupil in Amenia Academy, at Amenia, N. Y. He grew up at Salisbury, and was trained to the iron business. In early manhood he was associated with his father in the manufacture of iron at Salisbury, which he continued until 1881, when he came with his family to Evanston. Here he established himself in the grocery business and was one of the principal merchants of the city until his death, which occurred December 19, 1896.

Mr. Canfield was married, March 3, 1856, to Frances C. Caul, who survives her husband. Her parents were William and Dorcas (Crowell) Caul, of Salisbury, N. Y., and on the maternal side, she is a descendant of John Alden, of the Mayflower, and also of Richard Warren, who was one of the same company of Pilgrims. Her ancestors were represented in the Revolutionary army.

The children of Mr. and Mrs. Canfield are: Mrs. Carrie (Canfield) Dean, and Mrs. Nellie (Canfield) Lee, both born in Salisbury. The former is the wife of Marvin A. Dean, of Evanston, and the latter married Rev. Frank T. Lee, of Maywood,

Ill. In politics Mr. Canfield was an adherent of the Republican party.

ADAM FRIES TOWNSEND.

Adam Fries Townsend (deceased), for twenty-one years special agent of the Northern Assurance Company of London, England, and a most highly esteemed citizen of Evanston, Ill., was born in Philadelphia, on May 9, 1834. Reared as a boy in that city and educated at Pennington Seminary in New Jersey and Dickinson College in Pennsylvania, the educational bent of his nature led to his choice of the teacher's profession, and he entered life's active service as Superintendent of Schools at Dubuque, Iowa, where he organized that city's system of graded schools. Later, he undertook and accomplished a similar work at Galena, Ill. While success had crowned his work as an educator, and while his chosen profession proved fully congenial to his intelligent spirit, it soon appeared that the sedentary conditions of his vocation were detrimental to his physical well-being. He reluctantly changed the direction of his life energies from a professional sphere to the business arena, entering the employ of the Western Manufacturers' Mutual Fire Insurance Company. At this time he came to Evanston and soon after was appointed special agent of the Northern Assurance Company of London, serving the interests of this company with unflagging faithfulness for the long period of twenty-one years and up to the very day of his death. While in East St. Louis, Ill., in the faithful discharge of his business obligations, he fell and fractured the bone of his thigh, an injury which resulted in his death on February 13, 1904, in Henrietta Hospital, East St. Louis.

While in charge of the Galena schools,

Mr. Townsend was married by Bishop Vincent, of the Methodist Church, to Miss Sarah P. Burr, daughter of Hudson Burr, well-known merchant of Dubuque, Iowa.

The subject of this sketch united with the Methodist Episcopal Church, in Salem, New Jersey, at the early age of fourteen. Committed by holy vows to the fellowship of the church, he was ever devoted to her interests. For many years and in many places he was an office bearer in the church, attending with conscientious fidelity to whatever was committed to his hand. Of him it should be said that he was regular and punctual at the place of worship, devout in his ways, pure and blameless in Christian life, uniform and steadfast in his religious confession, and always ready to do his part in every good work—a living epistle, a steady light, that grew not dim, but brightened with the years.

HUMPHRYS H. C. MILLER.

Humphrys H. C. Miller, lawyer, Evanston, Ill., with office at 1415 Marquette Building, Chicago, was born in New York City, October 17, 1845, the son of George and Isabella (Clark) Miller, the former born at Ballybay, County Monoghan, Ireland, April 14, 1796, and the latter in New York City in 1820. After coming to America the father was engaged in the book publishing business, also keeping a book store, until 1855, when he removed to the vicinity of Hanover, Jo Daviess County, Ill., and engaged in farming, later removing to Carroll County, Ill., where he continued in the same business. Still later the father lived in Jackson County, Mo., and died at Greenwood in that State in 1876, the mother dying there the same year.

Until about nine years of age, the subject of this sketch lived in New York City, but coming with his parents to Illinois in 1855, worked on his father's farm in Jo Daviess County, and then in Carroll County except while attending school. He taught school one winter in a small log schoolhouse in Carroll County, at a place called Zion's Grove, receiving a salary of $25 per month. While in Carroll County he prepared for college in Mt. Carroll Seminary, and entering Union College, at Schenectady, N. Y., in the fall of 1864, remained there two years, when he was admitted to the Junior Class at the University of Michigan, graduating from that institution with the degree of A. B. in 1868. From 1868 to 1870 he was Principal of the high school at Channahon, Will County, Ill., when he went to Morris, Grundy County, serving as School Superintendent there for five years, after which he occupied the same position at Pittsfield, Ill., for one year. Always fond of reading, his mind naturally turned toward the law; and, in 1875, he was admitted to the bar, during the following year coming to Chicago, where he entered into partnership with Charles W. Needham, which was continued five years, when the partnership was terminated by Mr. Needham's removal to Washington, D. C. While maintaining his office in Chicago, Mr. Miller has continuously made his residence in Evanston.

The official positions held by Mr. Miller include those of Corporation Counsel for the Village of Evanston (1886-87), and Village President from 1888 to 1890, being elected to both of these positions without opposition and by unanimous vote. At the close of his term he was complimented by a public reception given in his honor by the citizens of Evanston. He has also been President of the Evanston Board of Education since 1880, and has held a like position in connection with the Civil Service Commission since 1895. From 1900 to

1904 he served on the staff of Gov. Richard Yates, with the rank of Colonel. The public positions held by Mr. Miller indicate the estimation in which he is held as a lawyer and as a citizen.

JOHN MARSHALL WILLIAMS.

Mr. John M. Williams was born in the village of Morrisville, Madison County, N. Y., on the 6th day of December, 1821. His parents were Amariah and Olive (Read) Williams, both of whom were natives of Connecticut. There were four sons and two daughters in the family, of whom he was the third son. He was sent to the district school and, later, to an academy at Morrisville. At eighteen years of age the course of his studies was interrupted by ill-health, which led to his taking a sea-voyage in the hope of improvement. Five months spent in cruising upon the banks of Newfoundland, with the active life and plain wholesome fare of a cod fisherman, so restored his strength that he resumed his course of education, going to The Oneida Conference Seminary at Cazenovia, N. Y. Here he pursued his studies for eighteen months, having in view preparation for college, to which his taste and ambition led him. At this time his eyesight having become impaired, he was obliged to leave school and abandon the idea of obtaining a liberal education, but desired a wider and more active field than was offered by the life of a farmer among the secluded valleys of Madison County. An advertisement of Mr. S. Augustus Mitchell, a noted publisher of maps in Philadelphia at that time, met his eye, and thinking it offered a favorable opportunity for commencing business and seeing something of the country, he opened a correspondence which led to his undertaking the sale of maps. With one hundred dollars advanced by his father—the only pecuniary aid which he ever received during the lifetime of his parents—he procured a supply of outline maps, suitable for use in schoolrooms, and commenced a tour through the villages of New York and Pennsylvania. His success was such that Mr. Mitchell, though he knew his customer only by correspondence, offered him an agency for the State of Ohio for the sale of a wall-map of the United States, which he had just published. With a supply of these maps he set out in the spring of 1843 for Ohio, by way of the Erie Canal and by steamboat on Lake Erie, and commenced work in Cleveland. The maps sold readily, and after canvassing a large part of the Western Reserve he later took the agency for New Orleans, meeting there with fairly profitable success, and in early spring embarked on a sailing vessel for New York, visiting Cuba on the way. His sales so far had yielded him a net capital of $800 for the year. In the following year he pursued his map business in New York and the South, but soon after had an earnest desire to go West.

An older brother, Mr. Read A. Williams, had already located in Chicago, and was there engaged in the lumber business. At the solicitation of his brother, and impressed with the advantages which the young city offered for business, Mr. Williams came to Chicago in the spring of 1848, accompanied by his cousin, William W. Farwell, a lawyer, who afterwards was a Judge of the Superior Court of Cook County for many years. He soon formed a partnership with Mr. Walter Lull and opened a yard for the sale of lumber. Having occasion to visit Michigan for the purchase of lumber during the summer, he was there attacked by a severe and dangerous fever. While upon the sick-bed the tidings of the discovery of gold among the alluvial sands of California reached the East, and stimulated a wild emigration to that distant, and then almost inaccessible, region. Mr. Williams disposed of his lumber business and determined to join the ranks of the gold-hunters. At St. Joseph, Mo., the fitting-out place for overland emigrants, he joined a party of them, in company with his cousin, Mr. Farwell.

The story of the journey across the plains and over the mountains by the emigrants of 1849 has often been told, and Mr. Williams' experience was not unlike that of others. He drove oxen, toiled along dusty trails, crossed deserts, starved and suffered thirst through the long stretches of sagecovered plains, guarded the camp by night, repulsing attacks from stealthy savage marauders, climbed the ascent of the Rocky Mountains, and wandered among the precipices of the Sierra Nevadas. At the sink of the Humboldt River, having tired of the slow and toilsome progress of the ox-train, he procured a horse and pushed on with his cousin for the remainder of the journey, arriving at Sacramento on the first of September, 1849, after a three months' journey. He lost no time in seeking the placer grounds, which he entered upon at Goodyear's Bar on the Yuba River. With a shovel and rude rocker he began working the gravel of the bar, and in twenty-two days had taken out $900. Supplies of food, at this place and time, cost $3.50 per pound. The work was hard and the society rough. With the winter floods approaching, he left the diggings and returned to Sacramento. Going down to San Francisco he invested his little capital in such goods as sperm candles, bacon, etc., and for two or three months carried on a lively little trade in the small towns along the river. He had accumulated $1,000 by his labor and enterprise, when, in January, 1850, in consequence of the news of his father's death, he started for his former home in New York, by way of the Isthmus of Panama.

Among his fellow-voyagers were General John C. Fremont and his wife, the renowned Jessie (Benton) Fremont. After walking across the Isthmus, where he saw new and strange forms of tropical vegetation and a novel type of human life, he again embarked on the Atlantic, and reached Morrisville, his former home, in the early summer.

On July 17, 1850, he was there married to Miss Elizabeth C. Smith, a daughter of Nathan and Roxana Smith, of Nelson, Madison County, N. Y. She accompanied her husband on his return to Chicago and, for forty-five years, shared his home at Chicago and at Evanston, to which they removed in 1868. Uniting with the First Congregational Church in its infancy in Chicago, Mr. and Mrs. Williams both bore a prominent part in the work of that denomination as charter members of the First Congregational Church of Evanston. In the latter part of the summer of 1850, Mr. Williams went to Elgin, which was then the temporary terminus of the Galena & Chicago Union Railroad, and there opened a lumber yard. The next spring he formed a partnership, in Chicago, with Messrs Ryerson & Norris, of which firm Mr. Martin Ryerson was a member. The firm of Williams, Ryerson & Company opened a lumber yard on the corner of Fulton Street and the River, adjoining that of Leonard & Williams, and carried on the business for five years. He continued in the lumber business until 1860, when he established a wholesale grocery business, but retired from that a few months later. In 1861, in connection with W. D. Houghteling, he engaged in the grain-buying and commission trade, continuing it for several years. In 1869 he went into a wholesale hardware business, and was so engaged when the Chicago fire of 1871 swept it away and all the improvements upon his business lots. Being largely insured in English companies, his loss was not as great as that of many others, and he was one of the first to rebuild his business block on the corner of Fifth Avenue and Monroe Street, it being ready for occupancy early in the following spring. After being destroyed by fire again in 1898, a modern fire-proof building was erected in its place.

Mr. Williams was a purchaser of lots in the west part of the city at the sales held by the Canal Trustees, and dealt in other realty with profitable results. He had confidence in Chicago and did not hesitate to stake his fortune on her growth and prosperity. In business matters he seems to have been gifted with an accurate judgment. He was cautious and prdluent, and invested freely when the times seemed propitious. Fortune seems to have favored him, for, from the time he started out from his early home to engage in a humble trading venture up to the time of his death, his fortune had grown without any serious set-backs, until he was numbered among the many wealthy men of the city. He was one of the original stockholders of The First National Bank, of Chicago, and always continued his ownership in its stock. He was also one of the organizers of that wonderfully prosperous corporation, The Elgin Watch Company, in which he retained a large financial interest. His early knowledge of the lumber trade caused him, during the period of 1880 to 1885, to invest largely in pine timber-lands adjacent to the north shore of Lake Superior, Minn., on what is now termed the Mesaba Range of iron and pine lands. These lands embrace the famous Biwabik Iron Mine, one of the richest and most extensive iron mines on the range.

While Mr. Williams' business career has been chiefly sketched thus far, it should not be overlooked that he was prominently identified with the moral and religious movements of the period of his active life. His early home in New York was in the neighborhood of one of the early apostles of emancipation, the gifted Gerrit Smith, and he brought to the West such a lively sense of the abomination of slavery, that he classed himself with the then execrated, but now honored, abolitionists, and identified himself with all the agitations which preceded the war of the rebellion and the culmination in the adoption of the policy of emancipation. He was ever afterward a steadfast friend of the colored man, and exemplified his friendship by his numerous benefactions for their education and the moral elevation of the race. He was also a liberal supporter of the religious and city mission work in Chicago, prosecuted by the Congregational churches. The Chicago Theological Seminary, long struggling with embarrassments, which repressed its growth, but now happily placed in an independent position, owes much to his liberal contributions, and the Chicago Commons also received much aid from him, and after his death his children manifested the same spirit by giving the family residence at the Commons as a memorial to his honor, while the new Maternity Building of the Evanston Hospital is a memorial to their mother.

Mr. and Mrs. Williams had a family of eight children, three boys and five girls. Lucian Marshall married Lucile Seaton, and they reside in Chicago. Walter Smith married Elia Gilbert, daughter of Mr. C. J. Gilbert, of Evanston, but died in 1891, leaving two children—John Marshall Williams and Margaret Williams. Another son, Nathan Wilbur, married Elizabeth Cook, and they reside in Evanston. Isabella married Charles L. Blaney, a son of Doctor J. V. Z. Blaney, formerly of Chicago, and they live at San Jose, Cal., and Anna married another son of Dr. Blaney, but both are deceased. Helen G. married Joseph J. Husser, and they reside in Chicago. Edith married Robert C. Kirkwood, and they reside in Mountain View, Cal. Jessie B. married Parke E. Simmons, and they reside on the old homestead, in Evanston, at the corner of Hinman Avenue and Clark Street.

Mr. Williams was at one time President of the Village Board of Evanston, and identified himself with various interests of the city. During the last four years of his life he made his home in Mountain View, Cal., where he died on March 9, 1901, leaving a widow, Mrs. Annie (Dearborn) Williams, and a son Alan.

ALDIN J. GROVER.

Aldin J. Grover (deceased), pioneer settler of Chicago and early resident of Evanston, was born at Holland, Erie County, N. Y., near Buffalo, August 24, 1822, the son of Chester J. and Susan (Davis) Grover, both of whom were natives of Bradford, Vt. His parents moved to Western New York while that region was still a wilderness, and settled upon the famous "Holland Purchase." Here the father died when the subject of this sketch was about three years old. Thus left fatherless at an early age, the son was compelled to face the problem of life about the time when most children are entering school. Having learned the carpenter's trade by the time he was twenty-two years of age he had accumulated sufficient means to enable him to come to the city of Chicago, which he did in September, 1844. There being no railroad connection from Chicago with the East at that time, the journey was made from Buffalo by the steamer "Empire State" around the lakes. He soon found employment with the American Car Works, which later came into the hands of the Illinois Central Railroad Company. For many years thereafter he resided in Lyons Township, Cook County, owning several farms in the vicinity of Riverside and La Grange. In 1866 he removed to Evanston for the purpose of securing better educational advantages for his children. In Evanston he engaged in business as a contractor and builder, and was quite an extensive dealer in real estate, in the meantime building for himself and others many of the older dwellings and business blocks in that city. His residence in Evanston, Ill., from 1866 to 1895 was at the corner of Grove Street and Sherman Avenue, on the present site of the "Grover Block," recently built by his executors.

In the early days Mr. Grover held several Evanston township offices, and was a member of the Grand Jury that returned the indictments against the Chicago Anarchists after the Haymarket riot of 1886.

Mr. Grover was married twice, first to Eliza D. Reed, of Erie County, N. Y., and, as his second wife, to Mrs. Mary E. Skinner of Waukegan, who survives him. Six children—two sons and four daughters—were born of the first marriage, all still living, viz.: Frank R., Chester A., Etta (wife of Dr. Charles H. Thayer), Katherine S., Caroline G. (wife of Dr. Warren R. Smith of Lewis Institute), and Louise M. A stepson, Mortimer B. Skinner, also survives.

Some ten years before his death Mr. Grover retired from business, and seven years later removed to Wilmette, where he spent the last three years of his life. His death occurred in his home at Wilmette on Sunday, April 6, 1902.

Mr. Grover is remembered as a man of great physical and mental energy and industry, his business activity extending until he was advanced in life. He left a name for sterling integrity and as a Christian gentleman of which his family may justly be proud, and which is recognized by a large circle of friends and fellow-citizens.

FRANK REED GROVER.

Frank Reed Grover, lawyer, Chicago, with residence in Evanston, Ill., was born on a farm in Lyons Township, Cook County, Ill., September 17, 1858, the son of Aldin J. and Eliza D. (Reed) Grover. In 1866 he came with his father's family to Evanston, and there received his education in the public schools, being a member of the second graduating class of the Evanston High School in 1877. Later he attended the Union College of Law of the Northwestern University for one year, and thereafter, until 1881, was engaged in business as a traveling salesman. During the year last named he entered the law office of Ela & Parker, Chicago, where he continued his law studies and was admitted to the bar in 1883. Upon the dissolution of this firm in 1885, he entered into partnership with one of its members and his former employer, John W. Ela, late President of the Chicago Civil Service Commission, under the firm name of Ela & Grover, and later under the name of Ela, Grover & Graves, which was continued until Mr. Ela's death in 1902. Since that date the business has been carried on by Mr. Grover and his surviving partners, without change of the firm name.

The official positions held by Mr. Grover include that of member of the Board of Trustees of the former Village of Evanston, in which, although the youngest member ever elected to the Board, he held the chairmanship of many important committees. Having declined a re-election he was subsequently appointed Village Attorney, and while occupying this position, carried through all the legal work incident to consolidation of the village of Evanston and South Evanston, laying the foundation for the present city government for the consolidated corporation. He was then elected as the first City Attorney and Corporation

Counsel, and bore a prominent part in organization of the new city government in its various departments, which was accomplished in 1892. For the service thus rendered he received high commendation from the City Council in resolutions adopted by that body on his retirement from office.

Mr. Grover is a member of the Chicago Bar Association and has conducted a successful practice of his profession for the past twenty years. For several years he was Chairman of a Committee appointed by citizens of Evanston in connection with the proposed constitutional amendment pending in the Legislature, providing for a new charter for the City of Chicago. The duties of this committee were to protect the City of Evanston from any scheme looking to the annexation of Evanston to the city, and in this they were entirely successful, as shown in the character of the amendment as finally adopted. Mr. Grover is a charter member of the Evanston Historical Society, was elected its first Vice-President and has served in that capacity ever since. During this period he has been an important factor in promoting the success of the Society, not only in the way of organization and subsequent work in its behalf, but by his contributions on historical topics, especially with reference to matters connected with Indian history of this locality. An example of this is furnished in a chapter in this work relating to Indian history connected with the North Shore. (See Chapter II., "Our Indian Predecessors.")

Mr. Grover's father, Aldin J. Grover, was one of the pioneers of Cook County, who came to Chicago from Erie County, N. Y., in 1844, and his mother, Eliza D. (Reed) Grover, who came from the same locality, was a member of the same family as Charles H. Reed, a former State's Attorney of Cook County. (See sketch, Aldin J. Grover, in this volume.)

Mr. Frank R. Grover was married in 1884 to Ella F. Smith, of Olmsted County, Minn., and one son has been born to them, namely: Mortimer C. Grover.

WILLIAM EICHBAUN STOCKTON.

William Eichbaun Stockton was born in Pittsburg, Pa., December 18, 1840, the son of Robert Clark and Martha Celeste (Little) Stockton, the father born near Meadville, Pa., and the mother in Pittsburg. The father was a member of the firm of Johnston & Stockton—afterward R. C. Stockton—who were engaged in the printing, publishing, bookselling and paper manufacturing business in Pittsburg. Among the publications issued by Johnston & Stockton was the "Western Calculator," an arithmetic which was popular and used for many years in Western schools. The author was Joseph Stockton, A. M., the father of Robert C. Stockton, and grandfather of the subject of this sketch, who had studied theology with the noted John McMillan and, in 1801, became pastor of a church at Meadville, Pa., whence he removed to Pittsburg to become Principal of the Academy at that place, now the Western University of Pennsylvania. In 1819 he gathered together a little group of worshippers in Allegheny City, and established the first church in that city. He published a series of school books, which proved a valuable aid to popular education of that period. Besides his interest in education he was skilled in medicine, and his services as a missionary and pastor of local churches were given, largely without compensation or reward, throughout all that region from Allegheny City to the United States Arsenal, and from Sharpsburg to Pine Creek, the churches at the two points last named being built under his care. This was before the days of railroad transportation, and travel was solely by means of horses or on foot. His father, Robert, was one of the first elders of the Presbyterian Church at Washington, Pa., and his grandfather (Thomas Stockton) was an elder of the church of Dr. Craighead, at Rocky Springs, Pa., when that patriot pastor left his pulpit to lead the male members of his church into the ranks of the Continental Army.

William E. Stockton was first employed in the railroad business at Pittsburg, Pa., but is now engaged in the iron and steel trade with office at 536 Rookery Building, Chicago, and, with the exception of one year, has been a resident of Evanston since 1872. On April 25, 1861, he enlisted under the first call for troops issued by President Lincoln in defense of the Union, was mustered into Company I, Twelfth Regiment Pennsylvania Volunteer Infantry, and after serving the three-months' period of his enlistment, was discharged at Pittsburg, Pa., August 5th following. On the last day of the same month (August 31, 1861), he re-enlisted as a member of Company A, First Regiment Illinois Volunteer Artillery, but was discharged under surgeon's certificate, for disability, at Memphis, Tenn., February 15, 1863. A year later (February 15, 1864) he enlisted a third time as a member of Company A, Fourteenth Pennsylvania Cavalry, was promoted to be Sergeant-Major of his regiment in the field September 20, 1864, and was discharged at Pittsburg, Pa., January 16, 1865, on account of a gunshot wound received at Fisher's Hill, Va.

The civil offices held by Mr. Stockton include those of Trustee of the Village of Evanston and Director of the Evanston Public Library. He is a pronounced Republican in political principles, but has not been a seeker for public office. His religious affiliations are as a member of the First Presbyterian Church of Evanston, in which he has held the position of Elder. He is a member of the John A. Logan Post, No. 540, Grand Army of the Republic, and of Evans Lodge A. F. & A. M., Evanston.

Mr. Stockton was married at Shields, Pa., May 7, 1872, to Eliza Leet Cook, a great-granddaughter of Major Daniel Leet of Virginia and Pennsylvania, who was an officer of the Continental Army during the War of the Revolution and a personal friend of Gen. George Washington. Two children have been born of this union: Martha Cook Stockton and John Wilson Stockton. The latter is a resident of Evanston and is associated in business with his father in the city of Chicago.

CHARLES CRAIN.

Charles Crain, who was one of the earliest settlers on the site of the present city of Evanston, and whose family still reside at the old homestead, thereby linking the earliest history of the city with the present, was born in Stockton, Chautauqua County, N. Y., July 16, 1822. He came of an old New England family, which is now widely represented throughout the United States, the names Crain and Crane being traceable to the same origin, and their genealogy to the same parent place in New York State, and here Mr. Crain gained his early education in the schools of Stockton. In 1833, his father's family removed to Ohio and settled in the town of Leroy, where they lived during the next three years. From there they came west as far as Hamilton, now in Steuben County, Ind., where Charles Crain received his last schooling and was fitted, by thorough industrial training for an active business life. He made his first visit to Illinois in 1840, coming to Chicago, which then had a population of about four thousand souls. The same year

he traversed the North Shore region, which was later to become his home, and saw much of the then unbroken and totally unimproved land about Chicago. His cousin, John Miller, had settled at what was then called Dutchman's Point, now Glenview, and Mr. Crain was in his employ during part of the following year. Then returning to Indiana in 1841, he remained there until after the death of his mother in 1842. In company with his brother, O. A. Crain, he then came again to Illinois, determined to make here his permanent home. The settlement, which a little later became known as Ridgeville, and still later developed into the Town of Evanston, was then called Gross Point, and here the brothers cast their lot with the few pioneers then to be found in this region. In 1844, they settled on the farm by which they were afterward so closely identified with Evanston, and which is now part and parcel of the city. From 1845 to 1850 the brothers were engaged in the cooperage business there and were pioneer craftsmen in that line.

The gold discoveries in California, in 1849, stirred the spirit of adventure within them, however, and, early in 1850, they were members of a company that outfitted a wagon train for the long and, in those days, perilous trip across the plains and over the Rocky Mountains to the Pacific Coast. There were thirty men in the company, in all, which, besides Charles Crain, included three of his brothers and a cousin of the same name. On April 8, 1850, the company left what was known as the Buckeye Inn, an old-time Evanston tavern, and reached Georgetown, Cal., in August following, having been a little more than four months on the way. This was considered a very quick trip in those days, and by reason of the fact that this wagon train passed pretty near everything on the road, it was called the "Lightning Express." After mining for something less than a year, with varying degrees of success, the company returned to Illinois in 1851, bringing with them the recollection of many thrilling and interesting experiences. Safely they had crossed the arid plains of Kansas, the tortuous steeps and chasms of the Rocky Mountains, and the desert wastes beyond. They had traversed, unharmed, a region infested with wild animals and wilder men. They had seen herds of buffalo so vast that they seemed like moving plains; and they came back, if not rich in purse, rich in knowledge and stories of adventure with which to regale their children and grandchildren, neighbors and friends, in later years. Upon their return, Mr. Crain and his brother, O. A. Crain, turned their attention to farming and gardening, and carried on a profitable business in this line for many years, and until the growth of the city created a demand for the subdivision of the lands and the building up thereon of city homes. Mr. Charles Crain bought a 44-acre tract of land on which he originally settled in 1846, upon which he resided during the remainder of his life, dying at his home on this farm, June 2, 1891. In all respects he was a typical pioneer. Honest, upright, generous and kindly, he was much esteemed by the pioneers who were his earliest neighbors and friends, and equally esteemed by the later generation who grew up around him. He was one of the pioneer members of the Masonic Order in Evanston, and very soon after its organization he affiliated with the Evans Lodge, and died a member of this Lodge, which buried him with the honors due a steadfast and faithful brother.

Mr. Crain was married, in 1846, to Miss Sarah Burroughs, who was born in Ashtabula County, Ohio, and came with her sister, Mrs. Captain Beckwith, and her broth-

er, Alonzo Burroughs, to Gross Point in 1842. There was a bit of history kindred to romance connected with the coming thither of the pioneer Beckwith. He sailed a vessel on the lakes for fourteen years prior to 1841 without accident, but in the fall of that year his boat went ashore at what is known as Hubbards Hill. The captain was not aboard himself at the time of the wreck, but soon reached the disabled boat, and while making his way to Chicago by wagon, fell in love with the country along the lake shore and determined to settle here, where his wife, sister-in-law, and brother-in-law joined him the following spring. Mrs. Crain's father, David Burroughs, who was a soldier in the War of 1812, came from Ashtabula County, Ohio, to what is now Evanston, with the rest of his family in 1843. He rented, for a time, the farm which Charles Crain purchased two years later, and this place has now been Mrs. Crain's home continuously for more than sixty years. The old homestead is still a cherished possession of Mrs. Crain, and here, where she passed her later girlhood and young womanhood, she is growing old gracefully, a veritable encyclopedia of information concerning the pioneers and pioneer life of Evanston and its environments. From time to time she has contributed to the local press and to the Evanston Historical Society much interesting data of this character. The history of her family, as well as that of her husband's family, is closely interwoven with the earliest history of Evanston, and representatives of both families bore an honorable part in laying the foundation of "the Classic City."

Crain Avenue was so named in honor of the Crain family. Besides Mrs. Crain, the members of this pioneer family living in 1905 were Mrs. Malvina (Crain) Angle, Mrs. Alice (Crain) McDougal, Miss Lucy J. Crain of Evanston. William

E. Crain, living in Wayne County, Ill.; Charles E. Crain of Pittsburg, Pa.; Mrs. Francis (Crain) Blake of non City, of Colo.; George H. Crain, real estate operator of Evanston, and Harvey E. Crain of Park Ridge, Ill.

ROBERT McLEAN CUMNOCK.

Robert McLean Cumnock, A. M., L. H. D., Director of the School of Oratory, Northwestern University, at Evanston, Ill., has been a resident of Evanston for thirty-eight years. Professor Cumnock is of Scotch nativity, having been born in the town of Ayr, Scotland, on May 31, 1844. At a very early period of his life he was brought to America by his father, who settled in New England, and the years of his boyhood were spent in Massachusetts and New Hampshire. His preparation for a collegiate course was obtained at Wilbraham Academy, Wilbraham, Mass., and, in the fall of 1864, he entered Wesleyan University at Middletown, Conn., from which he was graduated with the class of 1868. Three years later his Alma Mater conferred upon him the degree of A. M., and in 1903, he received from Dickinson College the degree of L. H. D.

Professor Cumnock was married, in 1877, to Annie E. Webster, of Evanston. The children resulting from this union are Wallace Webster Cumnock, who was born April 28, 1880, and Claude B. Cumnock, born July 31, 1884. Professor Cumnock has been connected with the Northwestern University since 1868, and to his assiduous care, in the special department of instruction over which he presided, has been entrusted the mental molding of many pupils who have achieved useful and notable careers.

JOSIAH SEYMOUR CURREY.

The Currey family traces its ancestry to Richard Currey, who came from Scotland when a young man and settled in Westchester County, N. Y., about the year 1700. The county records and Bolton's History of that county mention the names of Richard Currey and his descendants frequently during the period from 1707 to the present time. Richard Currey had a son of the same name, born in 1709, who died in 1806, having attained the extreme age of ninety-seven years. His son Stephen, one of nine children, was born in 1742 and died in 1830. Stephen married Frances, a daughter of Thomas Moore of New York City, and they reared a family of seven children. Stephen served in a New York regiment for a time during the Revolutionary War. The family lived near Peekskill, in Westchester County, almost from the beginning of the settlement of that region, and many of the descendants, now very numerous, are still living there. One of the sons of Stephen was Thomas, who was born in 1773 and died in 1862. He married Rebecca Ward and their children were nine in number. The youngest was James, the father of the subject of this sketch, who was born in 1814 and died in 1891. He married Eliza Ferris of Peekskill and had a family of six children.

Josiah Seymour Currey, the eldest son of James and Eliza (Ferris) Currey, was born on a farm near Peekskill, N. Y., October 2, 1844. In his childhood he attended the schools of the neighborhood, and when thirteen years of age, removed with his parents to Illinois, the family making its home at Channahon, in Will County, where his father carried on the farming business. In 1862 the family removed to Chicago, and in 1867 to Evanston. His father was engaged for some years in the lumber business at

Evanston, frequently receiving cargoes from lake vessels at the old Davis Street pier, now in ruins.

In 1862, Seymour Currey, as he is usually known, enlisted in the Sixty-seventh Regiment Illinois Volunteer Infantry (a 3-months' regiment). After serving the period of his enlistment on guard duty at Chicago and Springfield, he was discharged October 6th, following. Later in the war he enlisted again in one of the "hundred-day" regiments—the One Hundred and Thirty-fourth Illinois. During and after the war Mr. Currey became engaged in various employments, one year as teacher in a country district school near Aurora, Ill., for some years serving as an assistant in the oldtime drug-store of Bliss & Sharp at 144 Lake Street, Chicago, and later spending a year in attendance at the Northwestern University in Evanston. His first appearance in the place where he has since made his home was in the spring of 1867, and in the following fall he regularly entered the University as a member of the class of 1871. His course was not finished, but the next year other activities were entered upon, and since that time he has been engaged in various mercantile employments, most of the time as an accountant, in which capacity he attained considerable proficiency. In 1895 he became connected with the New England Mutual Life Insurance Company of Boston, which has been continued to the present time.

Mr. Currey was married November 24, 1875, to Miss Mary Ella Corell, by Rev. E. N. Packard of the Congregational Church of Evanston. Miss Corell was born at Portland, Chautauqua County, N. Y., September 11, 1852, the daughter of Joseph Corell of that place. The Corell family had lived in Chautauqua County since the days of the "Holland Purchase" early in the nineteenth century. Mr. and Mrs. Currey

have had seven children, six of whom are living. The oldest, Helen Marguerite, was born May 27, 1877, graduated from Vassar College in 1901 ; the second, Harold Young, born June 10, 1879, graduated from the Massachusetts Institute of Technology in 1902; the third, Frances Moore, born March 21, 1882, married Ralph M. Ashby, November 2, 1905; the fourth, Rachel, born October 25, 1883, graduated from Wellesley College in 1905 ; the fifth, Frederick Seymour, born August 5, 1885, died December 21, 1888; the sixth, Richard Channing, born September 20, 1891; the seventh, Ruth Seymour, born July 28, 1896. All were born in Evanston, and the two last named are attending the schools in Evanston.

Among the ancestors of, and those immediately related to, the Curreys are the names of many well known families and men who have attained eminence. Frances Moore, previously mentioned, was the daughter of Thomas Moore of New York and Elizabeth Channing, who was the daughter of William Channing, the agent of the British navy in New York. Frances was one of a family of eleven children, born in 1750 and died in 1824. A brother of Frances, John Moore, was the agent of the British government in New York from 1765 to 1783, and was naturally unfriendly to the American cause. He was denounced in a report made to the Provincial Congress in 1776. The sympathies of the family were divided, however, as another brother, Stephen Moore, was Colonel of an American regiment, and was owner of the land on which the buildings of the West Point Academy are now situated, which he sold to the American Government after the war for $10,000. Ann Moore, a sister of Frances, became the wife of Jedediah Huntington, a Major-General in the American army, and Frances herself was the wife of

Stephen Currey, a private in the same army. Another brother of Frances was Richard Channing Moore, who was the Protestant Episcopal Bishop of Virginia from 1814 to 1841, and rector of the Monumental Church of Richmond.

Going back a generation we find that John Moore, the father of Thomas Moore, held appointments from the British government in colonial times, was a member of "His Majesty's Council" in New York, and Colonel of a city regiment. He married Frances Lambert, a member of a Huguenot family, and they were the parents of eighteen children, one of whom, Thomas Moore, above mentioned, is in the line of ancestry we are here tracing. The line of descent is as follows: John Moore, 1687 to 1749; Thomas Moore, 1722 to 1784; Frances Moore, 1750 to 1824, who married Stephen Currey, previously mentioned. In Trinity churchyard, New York, within a few yards of the passing throng in Broadway, may be seen the family vault of the Moore family. In this vault lie the remains of John Moore and Frances Lambert, his wife; Thomas Moore and Elizabeth Channing, his wife; and a number of the children of both families.

The Ward family were residents of Peekskill in colonial times, and at the time of the Revolutionary War, Benjamin Ward became Captain of a company of loyalists, or "Tories," and entered the British service. He was present at the storming of Ft. Montgomery in 1777, being one of the first to scale the walls. After the war he became reconciled to the new order of things and lived in Peekskill the remainder of his life. John Paulding, one of the captors of Major Andre, married a sister of Benjamin Ward, and one of the children, Hiram Paulding, became a Rear-Admiral in the United States Navy about the time of the Civil War. Benjamin Ward's daughter, Rebecca, was born in 1776 and died in 1864. She married Thomas Currey in 1796 and they had a large family of children, one of whom was James Currey, the father of the present subject.

Of the Ferris family the first mention is made of Jeffrey Ferris, who came from England about 1635, and was a resident of Stamford, Conn., where he died in 1666. His son John was born about 1650 and died in 1715. The next in order of descent was Peter, who became a resident of Westchester, N. Y., where in 1721 his name is mentioned in a deed in the county records. His son Jonathan was born in 1732 and died in 1798. Jonathan was a soldier in the Revolutionary War, and member of a company raised in Peekskill. It is a singular fact that Jonathan Ferris and Stephen Currey, previously mentioned, were members of the same company, namely; Capt. Ebenezer Boyd's company of Col. Drake's regiment of New York troops; and that their descendants—a great-granddaughter of the former and a grandson of the latter—should have become man and wife. And thus the present subject of this account, J. Seymour Currey, is able to trace his Revolutionary ancestry, on both the maternal and paternal sides to men who were fellow soldiers in the same company. Jonathan raised a family of fourteen children, the eldest of whom was Joseph, who was born in 1757 and died in 1841. He married Lydia Seymour in 1786, and they had a family of ten children. The eldest was Josiah Seymour, for whom the subject of this account was named. He was born in 1788 and died in 1882. He was married to Elizabeth Royce of Peekskill in 1814 and they had nine children. He was for many years a custom house officer in New York, where the family lived a great part of their lives. One of the daughters of the family was Eliza, who was born April 7, 1825, married James

Currey, October 22, 1843, and she is still living in good health at the age of eighty-one. The eldest child of this union is the subject of this sketch.

Of the uncles of Mr. Currey on his father's side one was Daniel Curry who spelled his name at variance with the usage of his ancestors. In 1827 he graduated from the Wesleyan University, Middletown, Conn., and entered the ministry of the Methodist Church. He received the degree of Doctor of Divinity, and in 1854 became President of Indiana Asbury University (now De Pauw). In 1857 he became editor of the New York "Christian Advocate," and was the author of numerous works. A biographical account of him is given in the American Cyclopedia, and in the New York papers at the time of his death in 1887. Another uncle, a twin brother of James Currey, was John Currey, still living in California at the advanced age of ninety-two years. John Currey was graduated at Wesleyan University and afterwards entered upon the practice of law in Peekskill. In 1849 he went to California and has resided there ever since. He was an occupant of the Palace Hotel, where he had lived some thirty years, at the time of its destruction by earthquake and fire, April 18, 1906, but escaped in safety, though suffering a severe property loss. In 1859 he was a candidate for Governor of the State of California, and though defeated, he conducted one of the liveliest campaigns in the political history of the State. In 1864 he was elected Chief Justice of the Supreme Court of the State, which office he held for eight years. In 1870 the degree of LL. D was conferred upon him by Williams College of Massachusetts. His decisions as Judge occupy a large space in the California reports, and are highly esteemed by lawyers. Edward Currey, a brother of Josiah Seymour, was at one time Secretary of State of the State of Arkansas, and was a prominent banker in the West at the time of his untimely death in 1904. Another brother, Arthur L. Currey, is a practicing lawyer of Chicago widely known in the community.

As will be observed, the family of Mr. Currey has been closely identified with the history of the country at all periods since colonial times. In the Revolutionary War some of its members were found in the ranks and some among the officers on both sides. They are found in the legal and ministerial professions, and some have risen to eminence. Large families and a remarkable average of longevity have been characteristics of the different branches above described. One of the family, who in 1883 was engaged in writing a family history (which, however, was not completed), estimated that there were (or had been) 600 descendants of Stephen Currey and Frances Moore.

Since his residence in Evanston, Mr. Currey has been honored by the citizens by being elected a Director of the Evanston Public Library, for a succession of terms. In the spring election of 1886, when Evanston was under a village form of government, he was elected for a term of three years, and re-elected twice thereafter. The village having been succeeded by a city form of government in 1892, the office of Library Director became thereafter an appointive one, and Mr. Currey has received the appointment each time his term has expired up to the present time, making a continuous service in this line of over twenty years. He is now Vice-President of the Board, and Chairman of the Building Committee having in charge the new Public Library building now in course of construction. In 1898 he was the principal mover in the formation of the Evanston Historical Society of which the late Harvey B. Hurd was President up to the time of his death in January, 1906, when Mr. Currey was elected his successor and is now President of the Society. Mr. Currey is a member of the Caxton Club of Chicago, the American Historical Association, the Illinois State Historical Society, the Illinois State Library Association, Grand Army of the Republic, the Sons of the American Revolution and the Society of the Colonial Wars.

CONRAD HERMAN POPPENHUSEN.

Conrad H. Poppenhusen, lawyer, Evanston and Chicago, was born on Long Island, New York, July 21, 1871, and is the son of Herman C. Poppenhusen, a former manager of the Long Island Railroad, and his wife, Caroline C. Funke. The family name is one of social and financial prominence and will, for a great measure of time, be perpetuated in the educational history of Long Island, because of the beneficence of Conrad Poppenhusen, the paternal grandfather of the subject of this narrative, who was a man of affairs, being then the controlling owner of the Long Island Railroad. Commemorative of his fiftieth anniversary, he presented to the village of College Point, Long Island, a suitable plat of ground, along with an endowment of one hundred thousand dollars, in which deed is written the initial chapter of Poppenhusen Institute.

The early education of Mr. Poppenhusen was obtained in private schools, and at the age of eleven years he was sent to Europe where he remained until his eighteenth year, attending the best schools during that entire period. Returning to America, he located in Evanston and entered the Evanston High School, from which he was graduated after six months' attendance. In the same year (1890) he matriculated in the Union

College of Law, now the School of Law of the Northwestern University, and received his degree in 1892. In the year 1893 he was admitted to the Chicago bar and then began the practice of his profession. Several years afterward he entered the law partnership of Gregory, Poppenhusen & McNab, which firm occupies a position of high rank in the Cook County Bar.

Following the precepts of his father and paternal grandfather, Conrad Herman Poppenhusen takes a leading interest in educational matters. From 1898 down to the date of this sketch he has been continuously a member of the Evanston High School Board of Education, serving with distinction during the term 1902-03 as President of that body. In his political affiliations, he is identified with the Republican party, and has been honored, at the solicitation of his party, with office. In 1895 he was Secretary and Chief Examiner of the Evanston Civil Service Commission, and from 1895 to 1897 served as Alderman in the Evanston City Council. He is a member of the Republican Club of Evanston.

The social status of Mr. Poppenhusen is exemplified by his membership in the following social and other organizations: Evanston Club, Evanston Golf Club; Onwentsia Club, Lake Forest; Union League, Chicago; Chicago Athletic Club; City Club, Chicago; Lawyers' Club, New York; Chicago Bar Association; Illinois Bar Association; Municipal Association, Evanston, and the Civic Federation of Evanston, and is also a member of all Masonic bodies. He is a believer in the Presbyterian faith and a member of the First Presbyterian Church of Evanston.

At Evanston, June 25, 1895, Mr. Poppenhusen was united in marriage to Miss Harriet Mae Gunn, born May 9, 1872, the daughter of Alexander H. Gunn, Esq., a graduate of Yale College, class of 1854, and of Yale Law School. Her mother, Emily (Dyer) Gunn, is a daughter of Charles Dyer, M. D., of Burlington, Wis., and a sister of Judge Charles E. Dyer, of Milwaukee, Wis.

SIMON VEDER KLINE.

Simon Veder Kline (deceased), whose residence in Evanston dates from 1850, before the advent of railroads at this point, was formerly a substantial and prosperous merchant of the place. He was born in Fonda, N. Y., June 12, 1821, and his ancestors were of German extraction. He was reared in the village of Fonda, where he attended the common schools, and in his youth learned blacksmithing. After living for a time in Syracuse, N. Y., he came to Chicago, where he engaged in the manufacture of threshing machines and farming implements under the firm name of Wemple, Kline & Company. In 1866, they disposed of the business, and Mr. Kline entered upon the manufacture of lumber at Glencoe, Ill., and also had a contract for supplying the Northwestern Railroad with wood for engines at that point. After the disposal of these interests along in the 'seventies, he did not engage again in mercantile pursuits, but operated a farm which he owned north of Evanston until 1880. At that time he went into the grain business in Evanston, and also conducted a grocery store. This he continued until 1891, when he withdrew from active business and lived in retirement until his death, December 18, 1893.

Mr. Kline served as Assessor of the Township of Evanston for several years; he was also Township Collector for a number of years, and subsequently served as Village Trustee.

The subject of this sketch was twice married. His first wife was Mary Foster, whom he wedded in 1851. She bore him one child, James D., born February 28, 1852, who married Anna Gedney; he died in 1880. For his second wife Mr. Kline married Laura Northrup Ostrander, of Watervale, N. Y., November 16, 1853. The issue of this union was George Romyne, Mary Virginia, Carrie Anna, Frank J., and Charles Gaffield. George Romyne was born November 15, 1854, and died October 20, 1901. Mary Virginia, who is deceased, married Fred. R. Merrill, of Evanston, and they had four children, three of whom are living. Frank J. married Anna C. Franz, of Evanston, and they have four children. Charles Gaffield, born January 6, 1863, married Harriet E. Franz, and they have six children. In politics, the subject of this sketch was a Republican, and in religious belief, a Universalist. Socially he was a member of the I. O. O. F. His widow is still living.

GEORGE ROMYNE KLINE.

George R. Kline (deceased), formerly a prosperous merchant of Evanston, Ill., where he lived forty-five years, was born in Chicago, November 15, 1854. His father, Simon Veder Kline, one of the pioneer residents of the place, who was a merchant and farmer, was born in Fonda, N. Y., June 12, 1821, and his ancestors were of German origin. His mother, formerly Laura Northrup Ostrander, was born in Watervale, N. Y., and was married to Simon V. Kline, November 16, 1853. George R. Kline came with his parents to Evanston when he was two years old, and there attended the public school, which stood a little north of the lighthouse and was very primitive in those days. Dwellings were few and the wolves could be heard howling around the home at night.

George was an apt pupil, and took pride in recalling the time when he won a picture of George Washington in the old school house, for being the best speller. He grew up in the midst of pioneers trained to farming, and was accustomed to till the soil where fine houses and grounds now mark the landscape and excite the beholder's admiration. About the year 1882, when the city of Evanston began to build up more rapidly, Mr. Kline abandoned the farming and dairying business which he had carried on in company with his father, and in company with the latter went into the flour and feed business, conducting also a grocery store. Shortly before the death of his father he sold his interest in the grocery, but continued in the flour and feed trade. In 1899, he disposed of his store and purchased a large farm near Lake Forest, to which he gave a large share of his attention thereafter until his death, which occurred at his country home October 20, 1901. He had led a very active life and died at a comparatively early age. Besides his farm he was owner of valuable real estate in Evanston, and had been for some time part owner and operator of an elevator at Rockwell, Iowa.

The subject of this sketch was married in Chicago, in 1875, to Mary Jones, a daughter of James W. and Margaret (Snyder) Jones, who still survives him. Mrs. Kline's parents came to Evanston from Peekskill, N. Y., in 1857. They first settled at what is now Wilmette, when Mrs. Kline was four years of age, but two years afterwards established their home on the site of the present corner of Church Street and Chicago Avenue, in Evanston. The children of Mr. and Mrs. Kline are Rolland R., Mrs. Laura (Kline) Thomas, of Evanston, and Mrs. Jennie (Kline) Payne, also of Evanston. Here Mrs. Kline spent her girlhood, removing subsequently with her father's family to Chicago, where she was married.

In political views, Mr. Kline supported the Republican party, and participated with lively interest in its campaign work. He served as Tax Collector in Evanston during the years 1898, 1899 and 1900. He was an estimable man, honest and upright in all his transactions and left a name free from reproach.

CHARLES GAFFIELD KLINE.

Charles G. Kline, President of the Kline Bros. Coal and Grain Company and former manager of the Evanston branch of the Peabody Coal Company, in which he is a stockholder, was born in Evanston, Illinois, January 6, 1863. His parents, Simon V. and Laura (Ostrander) Kline, were pioneer residents of Evanston. His father who was a merchant and farmer, was born in Fonda, N. Y., June 12, 1821, his ancestors being of German origin. He married Laura Ostrander, November 16, 1853.

Charles G. Kline was reared in Evanston, and enjoyed the advantages of the public schools. In 1884 he became associated with his father and brother in the flour and feed business, to which he had been trained in his father's store. Until 1890 he was junior partner of the firm of S. V. Kline & Sons. Then his brother, George R., took the feed business in which, in 1892, Charles G. became a partner with him. The same year they engaged in the coal trade, taking over the business of the Evanston Elevator and Coal Company. This connection continued until 1899, when George R. Kline retired from the firm. Charles G. Kline conducted the business until December 31, 1904, when the concern was absorbed by the Peabody Coal Company, whose coal interests in Evanston Mr. Kline superintends, having gained an extensive patronage. Mr. Kline has had this trade under his personal direction since 1892, and has developed it into large proportions. He has charge of all the interests of the Kline estate, acting also as administrator of the estate of his brother George, since the death of the latter in 1901.

Mr. Kline was married in Evanston, in 1885, to Harriet E. Franz, a daughter of Jacob Franz, of Evanston. Mrs. Kline's parents were early settlers in Chicago, and in later years made their home in Evanston. The children of Mr. and Mrs. Kline are: Carrie M., Merritt C., Elida F. Helen, Walter E. and Harriet E. Politically, the subject of this sketch is a Republican, and fraternally, he is a member of the Modern Woodmen of America.

TUNIS ISBESTER.

Tunis Isbester (deceased) was born in Kinderhook, N. Y., on May 10, 1849, and was engaged in business in Rochester, N. Y., until about 1887, when he removed to Evanston, Ill., which continued to be his residence until his death, which occurred January 15, 1902. During the latter years of his life and at the time of his decease, Mr. Isbester was the Western Manager of the Westinghouse Air-Brake Company, and was widely known in business circles throughout the United States. His parents were of Scotch descent, but resided in Kinderhook, N. Y., for many years, finally removing to Niagara Falls. Mrs. Isbester was born in Nashville, Tenn., in 1849, the daughter of John H. and Christene (Cullen) Campion, and comes of Scotch ancestry. Her family removed from Nashville, Tenn., to New York City about 1854, a few years after her birth, and she was married at Buffalo, N. Y., to Mr. Isbester December 29, 1873.

JOHN J. FOSTER.

John J. Foster (deceased) was born in Syracuse, N. Y., April 16, 1832, the son of William and Mary Foster, the former born in Ireland and the latter in New York State, who came West with their family in the fall of 1839, making their home for six months in Chicago. In the spring of 1840 they removed to Gross Point, purchased a farm and remained there for six years. Sometime in 1846 they came to the newly-laid-out town of Evanston, locating on what was known as the "Old Ridge Road," now Ridge Avenue and Grant Street. Mr. Foster received his education in the public schools, and in his seventeenth year (1849) left home with his father for an overland trip to California. Of the experience pertaining to this journey much might be said. It was at length accomplished in safety, and the young man spent three fairly successful years in the West. Upon his returning to Illinois, Mr. Foster located at Evanston, where he was engaged at different times, in the coal and lumber trades. While dealing in coal, he built what was known as the "Foster Pier," where much merchandise of various sorts was handled during a long period. This pier, which, during the last quarter of a century, was so important a feature of the lake trade at Evanston, as well as the landing place of passengers from lake vessels, was a place of much historic interest. Here schooners and other vessels were accustomed to discharge their cargoes of coal and other fuel for consumption in the city of Evanston and surrounding country, while numerous lake steamers used it as a landing place for parties of excursionists from Chicago and other points, who had come to visit and admire the college suburb. Through all its history was associated with it the name of Mr. Foster, its originator and builder.

On June 12, 1852, Mr. Foster was united in marriage to Miss Marietta, daughter of Oliver Jellerson, a native of Bangor, Maine, who came to Illinois in 1839, first settling in Chicago, but removing to Evanston in 1846, purchased land on what is now Ridge Avenue and Leonard Street. The old homestead where Mrs. Foster spent her girlhood days is yet standing. Mr. Jellerson accompanied Mr. Foster and his son, John J., on their overland California trip in 1849, and there the former died. Mr. and Mrs. Foster were the parents of six children, three of whom are living: Edward, John H., and Mrs. Olive M. Corlett, all residents of Evanston.

In his political views Mr. Foster was a Republican, and he and his wife were members of the Baptist Church. Mr. Foster had all of the pioneer resident's pride in the town in which he had always felt so loyal and deep an interest, and in the development of which he was so important a factor. The growth and prosperity of Evanston meant much to one who, like him, had never for a moment doubted the supremacy of the college town. His death, which occurred February 12, 1898, was sudden, being the direct result of an accident, in which he received an injury while unloading a coal vessel at Foster's Pier. His widow survives, residing at No. 2236 Ridge Avenue, Evanston.

ANDREW SCHWALL.

Andrew Schwall (deceased), former citizen of Evanston, Ill., was born near Berlin, Germany, October 11, 1846, the oldest son of Jacob and Katherine (Rieden) Schwall, both of whom were natives of the vicinity of their son's birthplace, where the father was a farmer by occupation. The parents came to America in 1847, when the son was one year old, and buying sixty acres of land at Gross Point, five miles northwest of Evanston, the father there resumed his vocation as a farmer. The opportunities then afforded for acquiring an education in that locality were extremely meager, and his mother having died when he was seven years old, the son Andrew assisted his father in supporting the family until he was fourteen years of age, when he came to Evanston, and there engaged in working wherever he could find employment. In this he was so successful that he soon after purchased an express wagon, and still later a carriage, which he used for some time for the accommodation of passengers arriving or departing by the Chicago & Northwestern trains. On January 1, 1873, he entered into partnership with Earl S. Powers in the livery business, the concern becoming the well-known firm of Powers & Schwall. Mr. Powers having died in August 1891, Mr. Schwall purchased his deceased partner's interest, thus becoming sole proprietor of the establishment, which he conducted successfully for the remainder of his life.

On November 23, 1881, Mr. Schwall was married at No. 1505 Ashland Avenue, in Evanston, to Lydia J. Kinder, who was born May 31, 1856, near the village of Des Plaines in the Town of Maine, Cook County, the youngest daughter of Edwin and Mary Kinder, who came from Yorkshire, England, in 1842. Mrs. Schwall's mother died October 3, 1903, at the age of eighty-four years, while the father is still living about the same age. Mr. and Mrs. Schwall had three children: Myrtle Lavinia, born December 15, 1882; Martha Marion, born August 11, 1885, and Rowland Rieden, born January 10, 1891. The older daughter, Myrtle, was married September 7, 1904, to John G. Seyfried, of Oak Park, Ill. The two other children still reside with their mother at 1423 Benson Avenue, Evanston.

Mr. Schwall was admitted to the Masonic fraternity as a member of the Evanston Lodge, May 9, 1870, in which he took the third degree, March 26, 1871, and on June 4, 1878, became a member of Apollo Commandery, Knights Templar. While not a member of any church, he was a lover of the highest order of personal integrity, adopting as his motto, "Let not thy left hand know what thy right hand doeth." His political affiliations were with the Republican party. As the result of a stroke of paralysis which he had suffered on May 28, 1901, his decease occurred at his home in Evanston, December 19, 1901, and he was buried in Rose Hill Cemetery on the 23rd of that month. He was a kind and loving husband and father, and his taking away was deeply lamented by a large circle of appreciative friends, especially by the poor of his locality who had been indebted to him for many favors.

JOSEPH McGEE LYONS.

Joseph McGee Lyons, retired banker, and a resident of Evanston, Ill., for more than forty-two years, was born in Coleraine, Franklin County, Mass., August 6, 1835, and is a son of Lucius and Jane Ross (McGee) Lyons. His father, who was by occupation a cabinet-maker, was born in 1803. The Lyons' family is of French extraction, and the ancestors of Joseph M. Lyons went to England with William of Normandy in the year 1000. In 1640 his more immediate ancestors came to America and settled at Roxbury, Mass. Mr. Lyons' grandfather, Jesse Lyons, was born in Roxbury, May 18, 1767, and moved to Coleraine while still a young man. The great-grandfather, was one of the famous Boston "Tea Party."

The house built by Jesse Lyons still stands, and is among the oldest houses in Coleraine.

Joseph McGee Lyons received his early mental training in the common schools, in Coleraine, and the academy at Shelburne Falls, Mass. When nineteen years of age, he went West and obtained employment in a bank in Cincinnati, Ohio. There he remained five years, serving the last as cashier of the bank. During that year his father died, and he returned home to settle up the estate. After remaining at home for two years, he came to Chicago in 1861 and established a banking and brokerage business, which he conducted for ten years. In 1864 he moved to Evanston, where he has since resided. After retiring from the banking business Mr. Lyons established a brick manufacturing plant in Evanston, which he operated until 1873, when he disposed of it.

When Mr. Lyons came to Evanston in 1864 he purchased a tract of twenty acres of land just west of Ridge Avenue. In 1870, in connection with Gilbert & Woodford, who owned the twenty acres adjoining he platted, improved and sold this ground, which became known as the Lyons, Gilbert & Woodford Addition to Evanston. In 1865, Mr. Lyons bought twenty acres more lying west of his former purchase, which he used for the manufacture of brick. This he sold in 1873 to Merrill Ladd, who subsequently platted it as an addition to the City of Evanston. One of the streets of Evanston is named for Mr. Lyons, and a building erected by him bears his name —"Lyons' Hall."

Mr. Lyons was married at Groton, Mass., on November 24, 1859, to Mary Helen Farmer, and three children were the issue of this union, all of whom died in infancy. Politically, Mr. Lyons is a Republican. He cast his first vote for John C. Fremont, and has voted for every Republican candidate for the presidency since that day. During the four years from 1876 to 1880, he was engaged in the office of the County Treasurer of Cook County. Prior to 1880 he served one year as Town Assessor, and with the exception of a year's interval, has filled this office continuously up to the present time. He was formerly a member of the Board of Village Trustees.

Mr. Lyons is the "Nestor" of Evans Lodge No. 524, A. F. & A. M. In 1857 he joined Woodward Lodge, No. 149, I. O. O. F., in Cincinnati, and was affiliated with that order for some time after coming to Evanston, but relinquished his membership on account of the pressure of other duties. He is a member of St. Mark's Episcopal Church.

HENRY LEONIDAS BOLTWOOD.

Henry L. Boltwood (deceased educator) was born at Amherst, Mass., January 17, 1831, the son of William and Electa (Stetson) Boltwood, both of whom were natives of Massachusetts, the former born at Amherst, July 3, 1802, and the latter at Abingdon, same State, April 7, 1808. His ancestors had been New England farmers for eight generations, which was the vocation of the father, and in which the son gave assistance during his boyhood and youth. Several of the family were killed during the Indian wars in New England, and Mr. Boltwood's great grandfather was an officer in the Provincial wars. His maternal grandfather moved from Abingdon, Mass., his mother's birthplace, in 1812. The father was a man of reserved temperament, well-informed and suffered from lameness most of his life. The mother died at Ottawa, Kan., a few years ago, aged nearly ninety-two years. Of their eleven children, of

whom Henry L. was the third, nine grew to maturity and six were living in 1905, previous to the death of the subject of this sketch. Lucius Boltwood, an uncle of Henry L., was the first candidate for Governor of Massachusetts on the old Abolition ticket in 1840, and a brother, Captain Edmund Boltwood, of Ottawa, Kan., served as a soldier for four and a half years in the Civil War, and was a Captain of the Twentieth Kansas Volunteers in the Philippines during the Spanish-American War, while still another brother (now deceased) was an engineer in the Government service during the Civil War.

Brought up on a farm in his early boyhood, Mr. Boltwood had the opportunity of only three months' attendance each year at the district schools, but between the ages of nine and fifteen, residing within a mile of Amherst Academy and College, he was naturally inspired with a desire for a higher education, although the family means did not permit its gratification. Through the influence of the Principal of the Academy which he first attended, his father was induced to grant him his time, except such help as he could give on the farm during vacation, or out of school hours. He obtained his board, washing and fuel at home during this period, but no other compensation for his labor. He thus worked his way through the Academy for three years, and for four years in college, graduating from the latter in 1853. This he was able to do without losing his rank in his class. A voracious reader and having access to the college library through the favor of student friends, he took a high rank in college, though often compelled to be absent to earn money by teaching or otherwise to pay expenses. During this period he taught every winter, at first receiving only four dollars per week while boarding 'round. His tastes were for the languages and literature, and he also became quite an expert in botany and chemistry.

After graduation in 1853, Mr. Boltwood took charge of an academy at Limerick, Maine, but six months later accepted the principalship of a high school at Palmer, Mass., where he remained one year, when he assumed charge of the Blanchard Academy at Pembroke, N. H., remaining there two years. In 1857 he went to Derry, N. H., and there had charge of the Pinkerton Academy for four and a half years, when he succeeded to the principalship of the high school at Lawrence, Mass., a little more than a year later accepting a business position as photographic chemist in New York City. Starting out with the intention of entering the ministry, he had by this time become deeply interested in educational work, although in the meanwhile doing much missionary and pastoral work in feeble and destitute churches, but without having taken a course in theology. For one year (1859) he also served as School Commissioner of Rockingham County, N. H.

On April 1, 1864, he entered into the service of the United States Sanitary Commission in the Department of the Gulf, remaining until June, 1865, and being present at the capture of Fort Blakeley near Mobile, which was the last battle of the war, occurring on the day of Lee's surrender at Appomattox. During this period he served for a time as Chaplain of the Sixty-seventh United States Colored Infantry, but was never formally mustered in.

After returning from the army, Mr. Boltwood came to Illinois and was soon after appointed School Superintendent

and Principal of the High School at Griggsville, Pike County, remaining there two years (1865-67). During the latter year he removed to Princeton, Bureau County, and there organized the first Township High School in the State, which proved a success, and in connection with which he remained eleven years, when (1878) he went to Ottawa, La Salle County, and organized a similar school there. Five years later (1883) he came to Evanston, there organized his third Township High School, of which he continued to be Principal for the remainder of his life—a period of over twenty-two years. He has been widely recognized as the father of the township high school system, with which he was continuously connected for nearly forty years, and for a longer period than any other teacher in the State. In all, his experience as a teacher, both East and West, covered a period of nearly fifty-three years. Incidentally, during his teaching service, Prof. Boltwood did much outside work as a teacher and lecturer in Teachers' Institutes in New Hampshire, Massachusetts, Iowa and Illinois. In 1876 he was appointed a member of the Illinois State Board of Education, serving eight years, and was elected President of the State Teachers' Association for the year 1891. He was never a candidate for political office, though once proposed for the nomination for State Superintendent of Public Instruction.

While in college, Professor Boltwood was a member of the Alpha Delta Phi fraternity, and became a charter member of the Phi Beta Kappa Society at Amherst; was also identified with most of the great religious organizations of the Congregational Church, of which he became a member in his college days, in his religious faith following in the footsteps of his parents. He was also connected with the Tariff Reform and Anti-Cigarette Leagues of Evanston, and various benevolent, literary and historical societies. Educated as a Whig and a protectionist, he was active at an early day in his support of the principles of the Republican party. The opportunity of seeing the condition of the factory operatives during his residence in Lawrence, Mass., led to a change in his views on the subject of protection, and he became a strong advocate of tariff reform and an "independent" in politics, as well as an earnest opponent of all classes of monopolies.

Beginning with his college days, Prof. Boltwood manifested a strong fondness for athletics, and was one of the best long-distance runners in college, often walking a distance of twenty miles or more. He kept up his practice in baseball and football until forty-five years of age, and was fond of hunting, fishing and forest life. His favorite sciences were chemistry and botany, and he was also an enthusiastic student of the languages, besides his vernacular and the classics, having gained a fairly intimate acquaintance with German, French, Italian, Spanish and Portuguese, besides some knowledge of Bohemian. He was also the author of an English Grammar, several readers, two spellers, a "Topical Outline of General History," besides many articles on educational topics. He was deeply interested in labor issues and, in 1889, delivered an address on Tariff Reform which attracted much attention and was widely quoted.

On June 17, 1904, after completing fifty years of actual school work, Professor Boltwood was tendered a public reception by the Evanston Township High School Board, which was attended by several hundred of his friends and former pupils. Near the close of the exercises

he was presented by President George P. Merrick with a purse containing fifty ten-dollar gold pieces, and still later the alumni of the school presented him with a beautiful silver loving-cup. In the fifty-odd years of his school experience he had never lost a day on account of illness until within the last three or four years of his life. While connected with public school work, he received several invitations to accept positions in connection with colleges, but, being devoted to the work in which he was already engaged, invariably declined. Of some 6,000 pupils who came under his instruction, nearly one thousand have entered over forty different colleges, professional or technical schools, scattered over the world. These have included foreign missionaries, regular officers, professors, doctors, lawyers, financiers, railroad officials, eminent teachers and a host of prominent business men and refined and useful women.

Professor Boltwood was married at Charlemont, Mass., July 31, 1855, to Helen Eugenia Field, born in that city, June 18, 1830, the daughter of Eugene and Abigail (Hawkes) Field, and granddaughter of Joseph Field, who was a pastor of the Congregational Church at Charlemont for many years, later becoming a Unitarian, and who lived to be ninety-four years of age. An uncle, Dr. Joseph Field, was with Fanning's command which were the victims of a brutal massacre at the hands of the Mexicans, at Goliad, Texas, during the war for Texan independence, but was spared by the victors to care for their wounded, finally escaping after a season of great peril and hardship. Professor and Mrs. Boltwood had one son, who was born at Pembroke, N. H., April 28, 1856, graduated from Amherst College in 1881, and died of diphtheria at Peoria, Ill., unmarried, December 23, 1884. Professor Boltwood died at his home in the city of Evanston, January 23, 1906, deeply lamented by a large circle of appreciative and admiring friends. His widow, Mrs. Helen E. Boltwood, still survives.

WILLIAM LISTON BROWN.

William Liston Brown, a longtime resident of Chicago and Evanston, Cook County, Ill., the record of whose career, as herein contained, speaks with no uncertain sound, was born in St. Joseph, Mich., August 23, 1842. He is a son of Hiram and Jane Reese (Liston) Brown, the former born in Locke, N. Y., June 15, 1804; and the latter, born in Columbia, Pa., June 15, 1810, and a member of a Quaker family who settled in Michigan in 1830. The paternal grandfather, Liberty Brown, recruited a company of troops in Western New York during the War of 1812, which he led to Fort Niagara. Hiram Brown first embarked in business in Rochester, N. Y., whence, in 1834, he removed to Michigan, locating in St. Joseph. There he remained until 1848, when he removed to Chicago, and for several years operated a line of boats on the Illinois and Michigan Canal, returning to St. Joseph in 1861. He died August 17, 1883, his wife passing away July 7, 1854.

Mr. Brown passed his early youth in Chicago in the manner customary for most boys in a large and growing village, such as Chicago was at that time. He was thoroughly familiar with all the streets and points of interest, and was ever on the alert for new and notable features. An intent observer, his watchful eyes left no occurrence unnoticed in the successive stage of development which the future metropolis of the West was undergoing. His education was mainly obtained in public and private schools in Chicago, and he completed his educational training in what was known as the Garden City Academy. After finishing the course of study there, he was employed as a clerk, and afterwards as bookkeeper, in a grain commission house, continuing in this position from 1857 until 1862. In July of the latter year, Mr. Brown enlisted as a private in the Chicago Mercantile Battery, Light Artillery, and actively praticipated in all of its field activities, serving with it in Tennessee, at the sieges of Vicksburg and Jackson, Miss., and later in the campaigns in Louisiana, Mississippi, Arkansas and Texas. During the entire period of his enlistment he was continually in active service. He was mustered out as Quartermaster's Sergeant in July, 1865. On returning home he became connected with the iron business in the capacity of a clerk, and, in 1870, was admitted to the enterprise as partner. In 1883 he reorganized the concern as Pickands, Brown & Co., which is its present designation. He also organized the Chicago Ship Building Company in 1890. He devotes his attention largely to the manufacture of pig-iron, iron ore mining, and ship-building, and has developed these industries in Chicago and the Northwest to extensive proportions.

In addition to his duties as President and member of the Board of Directors of Pickands, Brown & Co., Mr. Brown sustains numerous other important commercial and financial relations, as follows: as member, and chairman of the Board of Directors of the American Ship Building Company.; Director of the Bay City Ship Building Company: President and Director of the Calumet Transit Company; President and Director of the Chicago Ship Building Company; Director of the Dental Protective Supply Company of the United States; Director of the Detroit Ship Building Company; President and Director of the Federal Furnace Company; Vice-President and Director of the Federal Steamship Company; Director of the First National Bank of Chicago; Director of the First Trust and Saving Bank of Chicago; Director of the Interlake Company; Director of the International Steamship Company; Vice-President and Director of the Manitou Steamship Company; Director of the Milwaukee Dry Dock Company; Director of the National Safe Deposit Company; Director of the Sea & Lake Insurance Company; President and Director of the South Chicago Furnace Company; Director of the Superior Ship Building Company; and Director of the Zenith Furnace Company. Mr. Brown is also a member of the Board of Trustees of Northwestern University, and a member and Trustee of the Chicago (Thomas) Orchestral Association.

On September 27, 1871, Mr. Brown was united in marriage with Catherine Seymour, of Smithville, N. Y., a daughter of Dr. Stephen and Harriet (Weeks) Seymour, natives of New York and Vermont. Dr. Seymour was one of the founders of the Hahnemann Medical College, of Chicago, and was a physician of high standing during his life in that city. The attractive and hospitable residence of Mr. and Mrs. Brown is situated at No. 217 Dempster Street, Evanston. While the tastes and inclinations of Mr. Brown are strongly domestic, he is fond of outdoor recreation, and takes pleasure in occasional travel, having visited almost every point of interest in his own country, and made several tours in foreign lands. Socially he is a member of the Chicago, Mid-Day, Commercial, Glen View, Onwentsia, and Evanston Country clubs; the Ketchi-Gammi, of Duluth, Minn.; the Union & Tavern Clubs of Cleveland, O.; the Casta-

lia Fishing Club; the Point Moullie Shooting Club; and the Tolleston Club.

In politics Mr. Brown has always been a pronounced and unswerving Republican, although never an aspirant for political preferment. His religious connection is with the Chicago Society of the New Jerusalem (Swedenborgian) Church. Fraternally he is identified with the Grand Army of the Republic, and with the Ancient Order of Free and Accepted Masons, in which he is a Blue-Lodge member, although not at present actively affiliated with any lodge. Mr. Brown is one of the most prominent characters in the industrial, commercial and financial circles of the West.

ARTHUR W. LITTLE, D. D., L. H. D.

Arthur W. Little, D. D., L. H. D., Episcopal clergyman, Evanston, Ill., was born in Brooklyn, N. Y., October 6, 1856, the son of William H. and Caroline F. (Cobb) Little. The father was a native of Castine, Maine, born in 1806, and a merchant, manufacturer and banker by occupation, while the mother was born in Gouldsborough, Maine, in 1823. Both parents were people of education, refinement and personal piety. The son acquired his education in Dr. Pingry's school at Elizabeth, N. J.; Knox College, Galesburg, Ill., and the General Theological Seminary, New York. In 1881 he was ordained to the priesthood, and, during the same year, became rector of St. Paul's Church at Portland, Maine, where he remained until 1888, when he removed to Evanston, Ill., becoming rector of St. Mark's Episcopal Church of that city, where he has remained ever since, at the present time being the longest settled pastor connected with any church in Evanston.

The most notable work accomplished by Dr. Little since coming to Evanston has been the erection of a beautiful church edifice and parish-house and the building up of a prosperous parish, which has been attended by good work for the souls and bodies of his parishioners and others who have come under his influence. He has been a member of Standing Committees of the Dioceses of both Maine and Chicago, has represented both in the General Convention of the Episcopal Church, and has been a lecturer on Ecclesiastical History in the Western Theological Seminary of the Episcopal Church in Chicago. He has also been, for many years, Examining Chaplain to the Bishop of Chicago Diocese. His fraternal relations are with the Phi Delta Theta Society, Sons of the Revolution, Masonic Fraternity, and the University Club of Chicago. In politics he is a Republican.

In 1889 Dr. Little was married, in the city of New York, to Caroline Ferris, who was a native of Portland, Maine. In his religious and professional relations he is recognized as a hard-working parish-priest and eloquent preacher, a man of wide culture and scholarship and a successful writer. His principal publications are: "Reasons for Being a Churchman," which has passed through several editions and is recognized as a standard authority for the Anglican Church; "The Times and Teaching of John Wesley;" "The Intellectual Life of the Priest;" "The Character of Washington;" "The Maintenance and the Propagation of the Church Idea;" etc. Socially he is genial and witty, and much in demand as an after-dinner speaker.

MILTON S. TERRY, A. M., D. D., LL. D.

Milton Spenser Terry, A. M., D. D., LL. D., who has held a professorship in the Garrett Biblical Institute, at Evanston, Ill., for more than twenty years, and is a widely known minister of the Methodist Episcopal Church, was born in Coeymans, Albany County, N. Y., on February 22, 1840, the youngest son of John and Elizabeth (McLoen) Terry, of whom the former was born at Swansea, R. I., March 13, 1786, and the latter in New York City, on April 15, 1796. The occupation of John Terry was that of a farmer, in which he met with reasonable success. In 1794, he moved from Swansea, R. I., to Coeymans, N. Y., together with his father, Philip Terry, and his grandfather, George Terry. The family is of English origin, and some of Dr. Terry's ancestors settled at an early period in the New England colonies.

Milton S. Terry spent his early youth on the paternal farm, and, as a boy, was inclined to be studious and to make diligent use of his opportunities for mental instruction. He obtained the rudiments of an education in the public schools of his native place, and afterwards pursued a course of study at Charlotteville Seminary, in New York, and a theological course in the Divinity School of Yale College. After graduating from the latter institution, he entered the ministry of the Methodist Episcopal Church, having pastoral charges at Hancock, N. Y., and at Hamden, Delhi, Peekskill, Poughkeepsie, Kingston and New York City, in succession. From 1879 to 1883, he was the Presiding Elder of the New York District of the New York Conference, and since 1884 he has occupied the position of Professor in the Garrett Biblical Institute at Evanston.

On May 15, 1864, Dr. Terry was united in marriage at Delhi, N. Y., with Frances Orline Atchinson, who was born at Hamden, N. Y., on October 1, 1841. Her ancestors were of New England origin, and made their home in Schoharie County, N. Y., at an early day. Of this union there are two children, namely: Minnie Ruth, born in 1870, and Arthur Guy, born in 1878.

Politically Dr. Terry has been a supporter of the Republican party since 1864, when he voted for Abraham Lincoln, whose election to the Presidency he advocated in public speeches. Dr. Terry is a clear, forceful and convincing preacher, a highly efficient instructor, and a biblical scholar of profound research. His attainments as a theologian are recognized throughout his denomination and in other evangelical fields, and he is the author of a number of widely read books. Among these are volumes entitled, "Biblical Hermeneutics," "Biblical Apocalyptics," "Biblical Dogmatics," "The New Apologetic," "Moses and the Prophets," "The New and Living Way," "The Mediation of Jesus Christ," "The Prophecies of Daniel Expounded," "The Sibylline Oracles," "Commentary on Genesis and Exodus," "Commentary on Judges, Ruth, First and Second Samuel," "Commentary on Kings, Chronicles, Ezra, Nehemiah and Esther," and "Rambles in the Old World." Dr. Terry has been a most observant traveler in foreign lands, and has made good use, in his ministerial and institutional work, of the experience thus gained.

STEPHEN JOSEPH HERBEN.

Rev. Stephen Joseph Herben, Litt. D., D. D., of Evanston, Ill., editor of the "Epworth Herald," was born in London, England, May 11, 1861. In boyhood he underwent his primary mental training in the public schools. After completing a course of study in the Preparatory School of Northwestern University, in 1885 he entered the College of Liberal Arts of that Institution, from which he was graduated in 1889, with the degree of A. B. He then became a student in the Garrett Biblical Institute, graduating therefrom in 1891, with the degree of B. D. During his preparatory course, he was a member of the Philomathia Society, and in college, a member of the Hinman Literary Society and the Phi Kappa Psi Fraternity, and was President of the Twentieth Century Club. He is a member of the Phi Beta Kappa Fraternity. He was a successful contestant for the Marcy Botany Prize, the Hinman Essay Prize, and the Sheppard Political Economy Prize. He competed in the Kirk Oratorical Contest, and was on the editorial staff of the "Syllabus."

The subject of this sketch joined the Rock River Conference of the Methodist Episcopal Church in 1889. From 1890 to 1895, he was assistant editor of "The Epworth Herald," and from 1895 until 1904, was associate editor of "The New York Christian Advocate." In May, 1904, at the General Conference in Los Angeles, Cal., he was elected editor of "The Epworth Herald." Dr. Herben was a delegate to the Third Methodist Ecumenical Conference at London, England, in 1901. He received the honorary degree of Litt. D. from Syracuse University in 1897, and that of D. D. from Garrett Biblical Institute in 1904.

On May 27, 1891, Dr. Herben was united in marriage at Park Ridge, Ill., with Grace Ida Foster, and two children have been born to them, namely: George Foster, born March 17, 1893; and Stephen Joseph, born March 14, 1897.

Mrs. Herben was born at Lanark, Ill.,

September 19, 1864. In girlhood, she received her primary education in the public schools, completed a course in the Northwestern University Preparatory School in 1885, and in 1889 was graduated from the University, with the degree of B. L., and received the degree of M. A. from Allegheny College in 1890. During the undergraduate period, she was a member of the Eugensia Society; the Alpha Phi Sorority; the Ossoli Literary Society; and the Twentieth Century Club. From 1889 until 1891, she held the position of Preceptress in Allegheny College. In October, 1895, she was appointed Secretary of the Woman's Foreign Missionary Society in New York Conference, and in October, 1905, was elected Home Secretary of Northwestern Branch, W. F. M. S.

GEORGE PECK MERRICK.

George P. Merrick, attorney-at-law, Chicago, with residence in Evanston, Ill., was born at Manteno, Kankakee County, Ill., October 4, 1862, the son of Dr. George Clinton and Mary Elizabeth (Peck) Merrick, the former born in Franklin, N. Y., December 11, 1824, and the latter in Troy, same State. The father graduated at Rush Medical College, Chicago, after coming to Illinois, and practiced his profession at Manteno forty-four years. Dr. George C. Merrick removed with his parents from their home in New York to Fremont, Ohio, when he was about nine years of age, and later to Palmyra, Wis., where he married Mary E. Peck who was the daughter of Joel M. and Amanda Peck, the latter being a daughter of Judge Purdy of Steuben County, N. Y. Joel M. Peck removed about 1840 to Wisconsin and settled at

West Troy, Walworth County, later removing to Palmyra, where he spent the remainder of his life.

The parents of Dr. George C. Merrick —and paternal grandparents of the subject of this sketch—were Sylvester M. and Mercy (Loveland) Merrick, both of old Colonial families of Massachusetts. Thomas Merrick, the first of the name in America, came from Wales and settled in Springfield, Mass., in 1630. His descendants in direct line were: Joseph, James, Perez, Sylvester, George C. and George P.—making the latter of the seventh generation in America. James Merrick, the grandson of Thomas, was a soldier and served as a Lieutenant in the Continental army.

George P. Merrick received his elementary education under private tutors, after which he entered Northwestern University, graduating in the class of 1884. He then began the study of law in the office of Judge Elbridge Hanecy, and two years later (June, 1886) was admitted to the bar. In 1889 he entered into partnership with his preceptor, but since the promotion of Judge Hanecy to the Circuit Court bench in 1893, has practiced alone.

Mr. Merrick was married at Galesburg, Ill., January 21, 1885, to Miss Grace Thompson, daughter of James S. and Nancy (Willitts) Thompson. Mrs. Merrick was born in New Boston, Mercer County, Ill., and she and her husband are the parents of three children, namely: George Clinton, born January 18, 1886; Grace Willitts, born October 1, 1896; and Thompson, born March 29, 1900. George C., who is a student in Yale University, at the close of his freshman year (1906), was chosen a member of the editorial board of the "Yale Daily News" for the year 1906-07. Mr. George P. Merrick attends the Methodist Church of which his wife is a member, and for several years has been one of the Trustees of Northwestern University. The professional, fraternal and social organizations with which he is identified include: the American, the Illinois State and the Chicago Bar Associations; the Chicago Law Institute; the University and Evanston Clubs; the Glen View Golf Club; the Law Club; the Knights Templar and subordinate Masonic orders.

ANSON MARK.

Anson Mark, manufacturer, formerly of Chicago, but now a resident of Evanston, Ill., was born at Annville Mills, Dauphin County, Pa., April 21, 1867, the son of Cyrus and Rebecca (Strohm) Mark. His parents were both natives of Lebanon County, Pa., the father born August 8, 1836, and the mother March 11, 1840, the former being engaged in mercantile business. The subject of this sketch came to Chicago in boyhood, and was there educated in the public schools, after which he was engaged in the dry-goods trade as an employe of James H. Walker & Company, wholesale dealers, remaining with this firm from September 4, 1886, to July 1, 1890. On the latter date he became connected with the Mark Manufacturing Company, which had been established by his father and a brother in, 1889, and with which he is still identified. At the time Mr. Mark entered into the business, the company employed six men. It now maintains two manufacturing plants, one at Evanston and another at Zanesville, Ohio, employing twelve to fourteen hundred men. It is engaged in the manufacture of drive-well points, artesian and tubular well cylinders, pump fixtures, plumbers' and steamfitters' tools,

wrought iron pipe and other products in this line. The general offices of the company, formerly in the First National Bank Building, Chicago, are now located in the city of Evanston.

Mr. Mark removed from Chicago to Evanston in May, 1902, which continues to be his home. On September 5, 1893, he was married at Van Buren, Ark., to Allie Willis Ribling, who was born in that place January 27, 1867, and they have two children: Geraldine Rebecca Mark, born in Chicago, September 28, 1896, and Anson Mark, Jr., born in Evanston, September 9, 1902. Mr. Mark's success as a business man is demonstrated by the phenomenal growth of the manufacturing enterprise with which he has been connected during the past fifteen years of its existence.

AARON NELSON YOUNG.

Aaron Nelson Young, a grain merchant of the Chicago Board of Trade of long standing, who has been a resident of Evanston, Ill., for the past thirty-five years, was born in Morrison, Ill., in 1838, and married at Sterling, Ill., to Anna M. Correll. He received a common school education at Morrison and early embarked in the grain and lumber business. About the time of the great Chicago fire he moved to Chicago and became a partner in the firm of S. H. McCrea & Co.; later, in 1883, established the firm of Young & Nichols, in which he was actively interested until 1903, when he retired from business. He has always been deeply interested in the Evanston public schools, and served in the capacity of President of the Evanston Board of Education for many years, during a period when they required very able and careful financial management. He was Trustee of the Northwestern University for several years, and has been a Director in many business enterprises.

HOMER HITCHCOCK KINGSLEY.

Prof. Homer H. Kingsley, educator, Evanston, Ill., was born at Kalamazoo, Mich., June 9, 1859, the son of Moses and Clarissa (Beckley) Kingsley, the father born in Boston, Mass., March 5, 1810, and the mother in Chautauqua County, N. Y., in 1818. The occupation of his father was that of a farmer and, after reaching the school age, the subject of this sketch attended the district school five miles west of Kalamazoo until twelve years of age, when he spent six years in the graded schools of Kalamazoo, going from his home each day a distance of five miles and graduating from the Kalamazoo High School in 1877. Then entering the University of Michigan, he graduated therefrom in 1881, when at once he began teaching as instructor in mathematics in the high school at East Saginaw, Mich. This relation continued three years, when Mr. Kingsley went to Alexandria, the county seat of Douglas County, Minn., where he had charge of the city schools for one year. He was then recalled to the University of Michigan as Instructor in Mathematics, in place of one of the professors who was disabled by reason of sickness. After remaining in connection with the University two years, in 1886 he accepted the superintendency of the schools at Evanston, Ill., which he has retained continuously to the present time, a period of twenty years. From boyhood Professor Kingsley had a strong predilection for teaching as a profession, and his success in that line, during an experience of twenty-five years, has demonstrated the accuracy of his judgment. Undoubtedly one reason for that success is to be found in his enjoyment of his profession and the enthusiasm which he has thereby been able to impart to others. The estimation in which his abilities in his chosen profession are held is indicated by the fact that, during the summer of 1898, by special invitation he delivered a course of lectures on "School Supervision" at the University of Chicago.

Professor Kingsley was married at Hopkinton, Mass., August 18, 1886, to Nellie Appleton Fitch, who was born at Peoria, Ill., October 4, 1862, and three daughters have been born of this union, namely: Margaret Appleton, born July 3, 1887; Katharine Winslow, born June 18, 1892, and Helen Dewey, born December 3 1895. In politics, although in general accord with the principles of the Republican party on national issues, Mr. Kingsley is inclined to vote independently and for "the best man" on questions of a local character. In this he seeks to secure the best interests of the people.

Aside from his profession as a teacher, both Professor Kingsley and his wife have devoted some attention to literary work, as shown by the issue by the former in 1901 of a volume entitled "The New Era Word Book," and by the publication in 1900, from the pen of the latter, of a "History of the Lewis and Clark Expedition," and in 1902 of the story of "Four American Explorers."

NEWELL CLARK KNIGHT.

Newell C. Knight, manager of the Bond Department of the Royal Trust Company of Chicago, was born in St. Louis, Mo., April 25 1862, the son of Augustus and Fanny (French) Knight. He received his preparatory education in the Saint Louis public schools and the academic department of Washington University, and graduated from Yale University in 1884. After graduation, intending to engage in business as a shoe-manufacturer, and in order first to learn it, he entered the factory of the Hamilton-Brown Shoe Company, working at the block and handling machines. Two years' experience of ten hours a day physical labor somewhat impaired his health; he therefore accepted a position as Secretary of an investment company at Wichita, Kan., but soon after retired to engage with his brother, Harry F., in the same line of business, under the name of The Knight Investment Company, dealing in mortgages and commercial paper. This business was discontinued in 1893, when Mr. Knight came to Chicago, and in connection with Reuben H. Donnelley, organized the firm of Knight, Donnelley & Company. From a small beginning this firm became one of the very large stock, bond and grain houses in Chicago, being members of all the leading exchanges. Its failure in June, 1905, resulted in its dissolution, and Mr. Knight soon after became the Manager of the Bond Department of the Royal Trust Company.

A Cleveland Democrat politically, Mr. Knight, during the campaigns of 1896 and 1900, was an active supporter of McKinley and of Roosevelt in 1904. In 1899 he was elected President of the Evanston "Four-mile League" and later served as Chief of Police of the City of Evanston without pay, devoting his attention to the strict enforcement of all the city ordinances, especially the law prohibiting the establishment of saloons within four miles of Northwestern University. He kept the town clean. Mr. Knight was mar-

ried in 1886 to Annie Louise, daughter of James L. Sloss of Saint Louis. Five children have been born to them: Augustus, Francis McMaster, Katharine, Newell Sloss and Nancy Louise. His office is with the Royal Trust Company, 169 Jackson Boulevard, Chicago, and his residence is at 1326 Asbury Avenue, Evanston.

ALBERT R. JONES.

Albert R. Jones, oil operator, residing in Independence, Kan., and engaged in the production of crude oil, was born at Pekin, Ill., September 14, 1874. In boyhood he attended public school, and was a pupil in the Virginia (Ill.) High School in 1891-92. In the latter year, he entered the Northwestern Academy, from which he was graduated in the fall of 1895. He then matriculated in Northwestern University, graduating therefrom with the class of 1899, and receiving the degree of B. S. From 1899 to 1902, he applied himself to the study of law in the Law School of Illinois Wesleyan University, at Bloomington, Ill., from which he graduated with the degree of B. L.

Mr. Jones is a member of the Sigma Alpha Epsilon Fraternity. He was a member of the "Deru" Society, the Rogers Debating Club, Young Men's Christian Association, and was Captain of the University track team during the seasons of 1898 and 1899. On June 29, 1904, at Springfield, Ill., Mr. Jones was united in marriage with Mabel Neer, of that city.

NELSON LLOYD STOW.

Nelson Lloyd Stow, whose residence in Evanston, Cook County, Ill., covers the period of a generation, during which he has maintained a record free from reproach, was born in New Haven, Conn., January 8, 1833, a son of Henry and Lydia (Goodrich) Stow, both natives of Connecticut, where the former was born in Milford, December 15, 1804, and the latter in Berlin, September 9, 1805. The occupation of Henry Stow was that of a manufacturer of wheels and wheel material for vehicles, in New Haven, and he was the first manufacturer in the United States to make these by machinery. He was a devoted member of the Baptist Church in New Haven, in which he served as deacon for more than sixty years, and he died in that city at the age of ninety-one years.

The Stow family is descended in a direct line from Lord Thomas Stow, of England, and certain of the ancestors of the subject of this sketch came to this country previous to the Revolutionary War, and held superior rank in the Continental Army during that conflict. A fine monument in honor of one of them stands in the cemetery at Milford, Conn., erected by the State.

Nelson Lloyd Stow received his early mental instruction in the public and high schools of his native State. He finished his school studies at the age of sixteen years, and then spent five years in learning the trade of carriage manufacturing. On September 17, 1854, when twenty-one years old, he located in Chicago and engaged in selling carriage materials. He was the first dealer in such goods in Chicago and in the West, none being manufactured at that time west of New York. In this business Mr. Stow continued until 1880, when he was engaged as manager of the most extensive iron concern in the city, and acted in that capacity for twenty-five years. He became a resident

of Evanston in 1873, and has made his home there ever since.

In 1863, Mr. Stow was united in marriage, at Milford, Conn., with Sarah Maria Merwin, who was born May 21, 1844. She is descended from Puritan stock, belonging to one of the oldest families of Connecticut, and a monument to one of her ancestors, in the cemetery at Milford, marks the oldest grave in that oldest of Connecticut cemeteries. The union of Mr. and Mrs. Stow resulted in six children, namely: Ada Merwin, born September 17, 1864; Harry Jared, born December 8, 1866; Helen Webster, born July 8, 1870; Charles Goodrich, born October 2, 1871; Nelson Lloyd, born December 12, 1872; and Mary Goodrich, born October 5, 1875. Charles died in infancy and Nelson died at the age of twenty-two years.

In politics Mr. Stow has long been an unswerving adherent of the Republican party, and a prominent and influential factor in the local councils of that organization. In 1887 he was elected a member of the Evanston Board of Education for District No. 76, and served in this capacity eleven years, acting for six years as President of the board. He was elected Alderman from the Fourth Ward in Evanston in 1895, and twice re-elected, and filled the position of acting Mayor of Evanston one year. He drafted many of the statutes which conserve the welfare of the city, among them being the Curfew Law. The erection of street signs was accomplished through the personal efforts of Mr. Stow, and under his personal supervision as President of the School Board, the Lincoln and Central schools were erected. By individual exertion he also raised over $600, with which to put up the fountain on the Central School grounds, which commemorates the heroism of teachers who saved the lives of their youthful pupils, on the occasion of the destruction by fire of the old school building. The name of Mr. Stow is cut in panels on both of the school buildings above mentioned.

Since making his residence in Evanston, Mr. Stow has been identified almost continuously with the public affairs of the city. He was a member of the Cook County Federation, and served on the Drainage Canal Committee, acting with the late Judge Harvey B. Hurd, in tracing the route for the canal through West Evanston. He was also chairman of the Evanston Army and Navy League, organized in 1898. While a member of the City Council, Mr. Stow drafted the statute for the protection of animals and birds, the law to preserve street signs from damage, and that prohibiting the sale of cigarettes to minors, besides other statutory provisions. During the Civil War Mr. Stow was a member of the Sanitary Commission.

The subject of this sketch has long been a zealous adherent of the faith of the Baptist denomination. He united with the First Baptist Church of Evanston in 1873, being transferred from the Second Baptist Church of Chicago, and has maintained his membership in the former ever since. In 1875 he was elected clerk of that church, and has held that office continuously until the present time. He has conducted Sunday services at the Industrial School for Girls, in Evanston, since 1874, and served twelve years as a member of the Board of Directors of that Institution, acting as President of the board for three years. His influence has always been exerted in behalf of the best interests of the community.

LEONIDAS P. HAMLINE, M. D.

Dr. Leonidas P. Hamline, who became a resident of Evanston at a comparatively early date, and whose family has since been closely identified with the social and religious life of the city, was born in Zanesville, Ohio, August 13, 1828, the son of Bishop Leonidas L. Hamline, a distinguished member of the Episcopacy of the Methodist Episcopal Church, and a pulpit orator of rare force and eloquence. In the youth of the son Bishop Hamline was actively engaged in ministerial work, and under the itinerary system then prevailing in the Methodist Church, the family changed its residence at frequent intervals. Thus it happened that the younger Hamline was educated in the schools of Tarrytown, N. Y.; Yellow Springs, Ohio, and Greencastle, Ind., finally finishing his academic studies at Lebanon, Ill. He then began the study of medicine, and received his doctor's degree from Castleton Medical College, Castleton, Vt. For a time thereafter he practiced medicine at Hydeville, Vt., and was physician and surgeon to the corporation operating large marble quarries at that place. He came west from Vermont and first established his home at Mt. Pleasant, Iowa, where he gained professional distinction and was in active practice during nine years following. While the Civil War was in progress he took an active part in caring for the sick and wounded Union soldiers, acting as surgeon in the hospitals at Dubuque, Iowa. He retired from practice at the close of the war and removed to Evanston in 1865. He was among the pioneer men of means who established homes in Evanston, and one of the first to make building and other improvements which have since made the city noted for its beauty. His father,

Bishop Hamline, had been an early and fortunate investor in Chicago real estate, and the care and management of these interests occupied a large share of Dr. Hamline's attention in later years. After the death of Bishop Hamline at Mt. Pleasant, Iowa, in 1864, his widow removed to Evanston, and that city continued to be her home until her death, which occurred in 1881. It was in the infancy of Northwestern University and in the village days of Evanston that Dr. Hamline came to Evanston to live, and for more than thirty years thereafter he was an esteemed citizen of the place. He and Mrs. Hamline were members of the First Methodist Church established here, and attended services in the primitive church edifice in the days when the Methodists shared it with other denominations not able to have places of worship of their own. During the later years of his life, Dr. Hamline and Mrs. Hamline traveled extensively both in this country and abroad, and much of their time was spent away from Evanston. Dr. Hamline was married in 1850 to Miss Virginia Moore, daughter of John Moore of Peoria, Ill., and died in Evanston in 1897. Mrs. Hamline, who still survives, residing in Evanston, was born in Ripley, Ohio. The other surviving members of this pioneer family are: Leonidas N. Hamline, of Chicago, and Mrs. Virginia (Hamline) Creighton, of Evanston. Another son, John H. Hamline, a distinguished member of the Chicago Bar, died February 14, 1904.

JOHN H. HAMLINE.

John H. Hamline, lawyer (deceased), Evanston and Chicago, was born in Rotterdam, near Schenectady, N. Y., March 23, 1856, the son of Dr. Leonidas P.

Hamline, who was the son of a Bishop of the Methodist Episcopal Church. In 1865 his father, Dr. L. P. Hamline, removed with his family to Evanston, Ill., where the son spent his youth attending the public schools and Northwestern University, and graduating from the latter with the degree of A. B. in 1875. After two years of study in the Columbia Law School, New York, he graduated from that institution in 1877, taking his examination and was admitted to the bar September 14, 1877, and immediately entered upon the practice of his profession in the city of Chicago, which continued to be his professional headquarters during his business career. At this time his home was still in Evanston, where he served as Corporation Counsel from 1880 to 1884. While occupying this office he framed a complete municipal code for Evanston, which was published in 1882.

About 1885 he removed to 1621 Prairie Avenue, Chicago, where he continued to reside for the remainder of his life. In October, 1886, he entered into partnership with his life-long friend, Frank H. Scott, under the firm name of Hamline & Scott, which later, by the admission of Frank E. Lord, became Hamline, Scott & Lord, Redmond D. Stephens being admitted to the firm in 1902. In 1887 he was elected a member of the Chicago City Council, serving one term, during which time he won a great deal of prominence by advocating for the first time in that body the principle of compensation for municipal franchises. Though never afterwards a candidate for political office, he continued to take an active part in public affairs, and his opinions were often sought after in connection with municipal issues. Besides being associated with many local clubs and fraternal societies, he was a member of the American Bar Association, the Chicago Bar Association (of which he was elected President in 1891), and the Illinois State Bar Association, serving as President of the latter for the year 1896-97. In 1895 he was chosen President of the Union League Club, and also served one term as President of the Chicago Law Club.

One of the most conspicuous services rendered by Mr. Hamline was as member of a board consisting of three members appointed by Mayor George B. Swift, in 1894, for the purpose of devising a merit system in connection with the Police Department of the City of Chicago. In conjunction with his colleagues he gave a vigorous support to this measure, which resulted in the passage by the Legislature of the Civil Service Act of 1895. Later he was a zealous supporter of a similar measure for the whole State, and, although it failed at the time, the final enactment of the State Civil Service Law, approved May 11, 1905, authorizing the Governor to appoint a Civil Service Commission with power to prescribe rules for the examination and appointment of persons for service in connection with the State institutions, was undoubtedly the outcome of these early efforts.

Mr. Hamline was married May 19, 1880, to Miss Josephine Mead, daughter of Henry Mead of Norwich, N. Y., and two children were born to them—Josephine and John H., Jr. Mr. Hamline died at his home in the city of Chicago February 14, 1904, and the event was deeply deplored by a large circle of personal friends and members of the bar, who had learned to admire his profound modesty, his high integrity and unselfish devotion to public interests, and his talents as a citizen and a lawyer. His former partner, Frank H. Scott, Esq., in an "In Memoriam" pamphlet, paid the following tribute to his memory: "Taking into account not merely disposition toward public affairs, nor ability nor energy, but all of these combined, it may safely be asserted that, in the past twenty years, Chicago has had no better citizen. For himself he claimed nothing, giving credit to others for the fruits of his own efforts. He was concerned only in effecting results, and not at all as to where credit should be bestowed."

CURTIS H. REMY.

Curtis H. Remy, a well-known attorney-at-law, who has been a resident of Evanston, Cook County, Ill., for many years, is a native of the State of Indiana, where he was born in the town of Hope, Bartholomew County, April 29, 1852. He is a son of Allison Clark and Sophia R. Remy. The father was a farmer by occupation, and was successful in that sphere of industry. The subject of this sketch spent his early youth on the farm, utilizing the opportunities afforded by the district schools in the vicinity of his home. His education was acquired in part at Nazareth Hall, in Pennsylvania, and was completed at Transylvania College, Lexington, Ky.

Mr. Remy was married in Boone County, Ind., on October 28, 1875, and is the father of two sons and one daughter. In politics Mr. Remy is a supporter of the Republican party, and has served the public in several local offices, and often been suggested for others. Fraternally he is affiliated with the Masonic order, in which he has passed all the degrees, and he is also a member of several clubs. His religious belief is in accordance with the creed of the Methodist Church. He has made his home in Evanston since November, 1876.

CLAUDIUS BUCHANAN SPENCER.

Claudius B. Spencer, A. B., A. M., D. D., Litt. D., LL. D., Kansas City, Mo., was born at Fowlerville, Mich., October 20, 1856, prepared for college at Howell, Mich., matriculated in Northwestern University, Evanston, Ill., in 1877, and four years later (1881) graduated from the College of Liberal Arts with the degree of A. B., still later, in due course, receiving the degree of A. M. During his undergraduate career he was a member of Hinman Literary Society, his fraternity was the Phi Kappa Sigma. He is a Phi Beta Kappa. He was editor of "The Tripod" (the College paper), and succeeded I. E. Adams on the "Evanston Index." He edited the college "Musical Register." Immediately after graduation he joined the Detroit Conference of the M. E.'Church, and preached for two years on Lake Superior; four years in Detroit; three years in Owosso, Mich., and two years again in Detroit. In 1892, he was transferred to Christ Church, Denver, Colorado Conference. He was elected by the General Conference Commission editor of the "Rocky Mountain Christian Advocate." In 1895 he was assigned to Asbury Church, Denver. In 1896 he was again elected editor of the "Rocky Mountain Christian Advocate," by the General Conference Commission; and resigned the pastorship to devote his attention to editorial work. In 1900 he was elected, by the General Conference, held that year in Chicago, editor of the "Central Christian Advocate," at Kansas City, Mo., and four years later was re-elected at Los Angeles, Cal., to the same position, which he still retains. He was Secretary of the Conference of Young People's Societies, held in Cleveland, Ohio, in May, 1889, which organized the Epworth League. He is a member of the Board of Managers of the Freedmen's Aid and Southern Education Society. On October 20, 1886, Mr. Spencer was united in marriage with Miss Mary L. Mitchell, of Brockport, N. Y., and three children have been born to them, namely: Helen Mitchell, Marjorie Elizabeth, and Mildred Isabel.

THOMAS C. HOAG.

Thomas C. Hoag (deceased), former prominent citizen and banker, Evanston, Ill., was born in Concord, N. H., September 7, 1825. His father, who was a book-publisher in New Hampshire, came West with his family in the fall of 1840, and spent the following winter in Chicago, after which he removed to a farm near Plainfield, Will County. In 1845, Thomas C. Hoag came to Chicago and engaged in the wholesale and retail grocery business in partnership with Oliver L. Goss, under the firm name of Goss & Hoag. This business was continued until the great Chicago fire of 1871, when their stock having been destroyed with the mass of Chicago business houses, Mr. Hoag removed to Evanston and there established himself in the grocery business in a building still occupied by his successors in the same line. There being no banking facilities in Evanston in those days, in 1874 Mr. Hoag established a private bank in the rear of his store, which was conducted under the name of T. C. Hoag & Company. In 1894 it was removed to the building now occupied by the State Bank of Evanston, which was incorporated under that name in 1892, Mr. Hoag having, at that time, sold out his interest and retired from the banking business. In addition to his other business interests, Mr. Hoag was, for a time commencing in 1870, President of the Lumbermen's Fire Insurance Company of Chicago.

Mr. Hoag was married May 1, 1851, to Marie L. Bryant, who was born in Canterbury, N. H., in 1827. In 1857, while still engaged in business in Chicago, he became a resident of Evanston, purchasing the homestead at the southwest corner of Davis Street and Hinman Avenue, then directly across the street from the original building of the Northwestern University, of which he was a Trustee for thirty years, and for over twenty years business manager. Of four children born to Mr. and Mrs. Hoag, three are still living, namely: Dr. Junius C. Hoag, of Chicago; William G. Hoag, Cashier of the State Bank of Evanston, and Dr. Ernest B. Hoag, of Pasadena, Cal. A daughter, Rebecca B. Hoag, was one of the first two women to become students in Northwestern University, which she did in 1870, pursuing a classical course until her death in her junior year. On May 1, 1901, Mr. and Mrs. Hoag celebrated the fiftieth anniversary of their wedding, the occasion being memorable on account of the presence of a large number of their early friends in Chicago and Evanston.

Soon after retiring from the banking business in Evanston, Mr. Hoag removed to Pasadena, Cal., where he purchased a home, there spending the remaining years of his life in practical retirement, though still maintaining his interest in public enterprises. While a resident of Pasadena he served as a member of the Board of Trustees of that city, and on the Board of Trustees of the Throop Polytechnic Institute founded by Mr. A. G. Throop, a former resident of Chicago.

Mr. Hoag's demise occurred at his home in Pasadena, April 16, 1906, and his remains were brought to Chicago and interred in Rose Hill Cemetery, where impressive ceremonies were held in the chapel on the cemetery grounds on Sunday afternoon, April 22. He is survived by his widow and three sons mentioned in the preceding sketch.

WILLIAM GALE HOAG.

William Gale Hoag, Cashier of the Evanston State Bank, was born in Evanston, Ill., November 19, 1860, the son of Thomas C. and Maria L. (Bryant) Hoag, who were natives of New Hampshire, the former born at Concord in 1825, and the latter at Canterbury in 1827. The Hoag family was of New England Quaker stock, and the father of William G. was prominent in Chicago and Evanston business circles for more than fifty years. (See sketch of Thomas C. Hoag in this volume.) William G. Hoag received his education in the local schools and Northwestern University Academy, enjoying the rare advantages of books and friends from his youth in a university town.

After leaving school Mr. Hoag at once entered upon a business career in connection with his father in the private bank conducted by the latter—now the State Bank of Evanston—with which he has been continuously associated ever since, and of which he has been Cashier for twenty years. His whole life has been spent in the place of his birth without change of occupation or business relations. The official positions held by Mr. Hoag have been wholly in connection with local benevolences, having served as Treasurer and Director, and member of the Executive Committee of the Evanston Hospital for many years.

The literary, social and business organizations with which Mr. Hoag is associated include: The University Club, The Evanston Club, Evanston Country Club, the Evanston Golf Club, and the Bankers' Club of Chicago. His religious associations are with the First Methodist Episcopal Church of Evanston, and politically he supports the policies of the Republican party. Indulging the quiet tastes of a bachelor, he feels a deep interest in the social life and happiness of those around him, and takes pleasure in contributing his share to the comfort and welfare of others.

JEAN FREDERIC LOBA, A. M. D.D.

Jean Frederic Loba, pastor of the First Congregational Church, Evanston, Ill., was born in Lausanne, Switzerland, October 17, 1846, the son of Frederic and Julie (Sider) Loba. Both parents were natives of Switzerland, as their ancestors had been for an indefinite period—the father born in Berne Canton, December 25, 1809, and the mother at Echallens. The father was a chemist and lived in Canton de Vaud; came to the United States in 1853 and died in Illinois March 14, 1864. Mr. Loba was educated at Olivet College, Mich., at Basle in his native country, Yale College and Chicago Theological Seminary. Hampered by limited means, his youth was spent in toil and wandering from place to place in search of employment, but being a lover of books, he was a voracious reader of everything that came into his hands, thus acquiring a literary bent of mind. After leaving college he spent two years (1873-75) as teacher of Greek in Knox College, Galesburg, Ill., later was a student at Basle

University, Switzerland, 1875-76; a student in Yale Divinity School, 1876-77; pastor at Kankakee, Ill., 1877-78, and at Kewanee, Ill., 1878-82; Professor of Modern Languages at Olivet College, Mich., 1882-88; pastor at Kalamazoo, Mich., 1888-91; in Paris, France, 1891-92, and from 1892 to 1906 in his present position as pastor of the Congregational Church at Evanston. He has been a member of the Congregational Church since June, 1866.

On September 22, 1864, he enlisted as a soldier of the Civil War in Company I, Thirteenth Missouri Veteran Volunteer Cavalry, and after serving nearly two years, was mustered out May 17, 1866. He is a member of the Evanston Grand Army Post, and was Commander of the Post in Olivet, Mich. He is also a member of the Phi Alpha Pi Literary Fraternity. In politics he is a Republican, but on local questions is inclined to act independently, and on one occasion voted the Prohibition ticket.

On September 4, 1877, Mr. Loba was united in marriage at Penacook, near Concord, N. H., to Lucene M. Bradley, born at Adams, N. Y., January 10, 1851, and of this union five children have been born: Lucene S. (now Mrs. McConnell), born December 25, 1879; Julie B. (Mrs. Collins), born September 17, 1882; Winifred, born September 2, 1885, died April 25, 1905; Marguerite, born December 25, 1891, and Jean F., Jr., born September 10, 1894. The Bradley family, to which Mrs. Loba belongs, is of Revolutionary stock, and many still reside in Concord, N. H. Possessing no advantages until he had reached his nineteenth year, by a life of self-denial and sturdy effort, aided by a vivacious and enthusiastic temperament, Rev. Mr. Loba has developed a strong character which has placed him in the front rank of Evanston clergymen. A lover of nature, he is also a lover of men and of books, and enjoys life as pastor of his flock while contributing to the enjoyment of others and promoting their aspirations to a higher life. In 1876 he received the degree of M. A. from his Alma Mater and in 1891 the degree of D. D. from the same institution.

WILLIAM S. HARBERT.

William Soesbe Harbert, lawyer, born September 17, 1842, at Terre Haute, Ind., is the son of Solomon and Amadine (Watson) Harbert—the former a descendant of a Virginian family of English extraction, and the latter a native of Bardstown, Ky. At an early age the subject of this sketch attended the public schools of Terre Haute, preparatory to a course in Franklin College, at Franklin, Ind. From that institution he went to Wabash College, Crawfordsville, Ind., and from there to the University of Michigan, where he remained till he completed his sophomore year. In 1862 he enlisted as a volunteer in the Union Army, and on his return from the field, matriculated in the Law Department of the University of Indiana at Bloomington, Ind., remaining there one year, when he entered the Law Department of the University of Michigan, at Ann Arbor, where he received his degree in 1867. The same year he located at Des Moines, Iowa; was admitted to the bar, remaining there seven years, within that time serving as Assistant United States District Attorney, and being also a member of the law firm of Harbert & Clark. Success attended his stay in Des Moines, but the desire to operate in a field affording greater opportunities led to his removal to Chicago in 1874, where he resumed practice as the senior member of the firm of Harbert & Daly. This partnership was succeeded by that of Harbert, Curran & Harbert, the junior partner being the only son of the subject of this narrative. Upon the death of his son, Arthur Boynton Harbert, in 1900, the firm was dissolved, since which time Mr. Harbert has practiced alone.

The year following the outbreak of the Civil War and while a student, then twenty years of age, William Soesbe Harbert enlisted as a private in Company C Eighty-fifth Indiana Volunteers and was in active service until 1865. During the period of his military career, he served on the staff of Gen. John Colburn, Gen. Benjamin Harrison, and Major-General W. T. Ward. He was engaged in the campaigns against Atlanta and Savannah and was with General Sherman on his famous march to the sea. At the first battle of Franklin (Tenn.) he was taken prisoner and spent two months in Libby Prison. He was brevetted as Captain "for distinguished meritorious services." Mr. Harbert is prominent in philanthropic work and, for seven years, was President of the Board of Managers of the "Forward Movement," a social settlement organization having beautiful assembly grounds, which Mr. Harbert spent much time in procuring for the organization. He holds membership in and is active in furthering the enterprises of a number of philanthropic organizations.

In his religious and political affiliations, Mr. Harbert is independent. He believes in municipal control of public utilities, assisted in the establishment of the Juvenile Court, the adoption of the indeterminate sentence law and advocates the placing of a limitation on the power to grant, by will, large sums to single individuals.

Mr. Harbert, on October 18, 1870, was united in marriage to Miss Elizabeth Morrison Boynton, a woman of high literary attainments and social rank, a sketch of whom also appears herein. Three children, Arthur Boynton (deceased), Corinne Boynton, and Boynton Elizabeth, wife of Ashley D. Rowe, of Pasadena, California, were born to them. Continuously since 1874 the Harberts have been residents of Evanston, and their spacious home is not the least of its attractions. For twenty years they have dispensed a generous hospitality at their pleasant summer home at Lake Geneva, Wis.

ELIZABETH BOYNTON HARBERT.

Mrs. Elizabeth Boynton Harbert, author, lecturer, reformer and philanthropist, was born in Crawfordsville, Ind. She is the eldest child of William H. Boynton, of Nashua, N. H., and Abigail Sweetser Boynton, a native of Boston, Mass. Her maiden name was Elizabeth Morrison Boynton. Her journalistic signature was Lizzie M. Boynton. She was educated in the Female Seminary at Oxford, Ohio, and in the Terre Haute Female College, graduating from the latter with honors. Growing up in Crawfordsville, under the shadow of a college into which girls were not permitted to enter, she early learned the value of educational privileges and claimed them for her sister women.

After vain attempts to slip the bolts of prejudice and precedent that barred out the daughters of the State from the halls of learning, she strove to rouse, with pen and voice, those whose stronger hands could open wide the doors. The faculty of Wabash College had allowed, as an especial privilege, four young women— Emma Hough Fairchild, Mary Krout, Mary Cumberland Jennison and Elizabeth Boynton Harbert—to attend lectures

on Physics by Prof. John L. Campbell, who was later the Secretary of the Philadelphia Centennial Exposition. Although these lectures were substantially repetitions of those required in the college curriculum, the young men were excluded. Dr. White, the first President of Wabash College, shortly before his death, promised Mrs. Harbert a diploma upon the completion of her course. Not long after the same four young women, in company with nineteen others, petitioned the faculty for permission to enter the college and receive the benefit of its teachings. The letter written in reply to the petition of the young ladies was to the effect that the faculty expressed its extreme regret that the facilities of the preparatory department were such that the department was inadequate for its needs, and hence the college would not be able to admit the young women. Each one of these young women had progressed far beyond the "preparatory" department. It is difficult for Mrs. Harbert to speak of this letter without manifesting, in some manner, a slight touch of the profound impression it produced, although, when measured by its after effect upon her career, it should be considered of inestimable value. The first ten dollars she received as the result of her own work, was from the "New York Independent" for an account of this attempt to obtain a college education.

This group of twenty-three girls, under the leadership of the four, had purchased the town flag, the church organ and the first fire engine. In their indignation and disappointment, they determined to secure for their own use, and the town, a public library. With this object in view, they advertised the presentation of a comedy, entitled "The Coming Woman," in which they burlesqued themselves and their unsuccessful efforts. In a relentless manner, the male students issued burlesque handbills and posters. In one day not less than five varieties were issued. The ladies were styled "the Twenty-three Sorry Sisses," in an attempt to pun upon the word "Sorosis," which latter organization was attracting considerable attention in the East. It is needless to say that the adverse criticism attracted an unusually large audience, and a considerable sum was netted with which was purchased the nucleus for a circulating library. At that time Miss Boynton was but twenty years old.

Oberlin was then the only college which admitted men and women on an equality. At the suggestion of friends, Miss Boynton prepared an address which she entitled, "Before Suffrage, What?" which was a plea for the education of women as an essential preparation for their enfranchisement. This was delivered first in Crawfordsville, after a most flattering introduction by Gen. Lew Wallace. The following week the same address was given at La Fayette, and the next week at Cleveland before an immense audience. Following this was another success at Cincinnati in the opera house. Mrs. Mary A. Livermore, who was at this time a most helpful and encouraging friend of Miss Boynton, wrote to one of the Woman's journals, as follows: "The speech of the day and evening (referring to a convention in Ohio), was made by Lizzie Boynton, although among the speakers were Susan B. Anthony, Mrs. Stanton and myself. She held the audience on the platform, as well as that in the hall, spellbound for an hour." A journalistic sketch of Miss Boynton said, "by one stroke she had placed herself beside Fanny Fern and Gail Hamilton."

During the Civil War Miss Boynton energetically devoted her time to the care of the soldiers and the duties of the hour. Her sympathies were keenly allied to the cause of the Union, although she was always too inclusive in her love of humanity to indulge in any bitterness of feeling. Her first book, "The Golden Fleece," was published in 1867. In 1870 she was married to Capt. William S. Harbert, a brave soldier and successful lawyer. After their marriage Mr. and Mrs. Harbert lived in Des Moines, Iowa, and there Mrs. Harbert published her second book, "Out of Her Sphere," and her first song, "Arlington Heights."

While living in Des Moines, Mrs. Harbert took an active part in the Woman's Suffrage Movement, being elected President of the State Association. She succeeded in inducing the Republicans of Iowa to put into their State platform a purely woman's plank, "winning the members of the committee appointed to prepare a platform for the State Convention, by her earnest and dignified presentation of the claims of women." Thus was earned the distinction of being the first woman to design a woman's plank and secure its adoption by a great political party of a state.

In the winter of 1874, Mr. and Mrs. Harbert moved to Illinois, and from that time have made their home in Evanston. The family now consists of two daughters, Corinne and Boynton. In 1900 their only son, Arthur Boynton Harbert, heroically surrendered his earthly life, meanwhile bequeathing to parents, sisters and friends the memory of a beautiful, self-sacrificing, loving life, he being then in his twenty-eighth year.

Mrs. Harbert was for two years the President of the Social Science Association of Illinois. She was Vice-President of the Woman's Suffrage Association of

Indiana, President of the Woman's Suffrage Association of Iowa, and for twelve years President of the Illinois Woman's Suffrage Association. She was a member of the Board of Managers of the Girls' Industrial School of South Evanston, and Vice-President of the Association for the advancement of women, known as the Woman's Congress.

As editor for seven years of the "Woman' Kingdom," a regular weekly department of the *Chicago Inter Ocean*, she has exerted a widespread influence over many homes. As editor of the *New Era*, in which she was free to utter her deepest convictions, she devoted a year's service. In 1891 the Ohio Wesleyan College conferred upon her the honorary degree of Doctor of Philosophy.

During the year of the World's Columbian Exposition, and the World's Congress, auxiliary thereto, popularly known as the World's Parliament of Religions, Mrs. Harbert served on several committees, among which was the Committee on Organization of the World's Congress of Representative Women, otherwise known as the "Department of Woman's Progress of the World's Congress Auxiliary of the World's Columbian Exposition of 1893." Of that committee, Mrs. May Wright Sewell, of Indianapolis, Ind., was Chairman; Mrs. Rachel Foster Avery, of Somerton, Pa., Secretary, and Mrs. Sarah Hacket Stevenson, M. D., Mrs. Julia Holmes Smith, M. D., Mrs. Coonley Ward, Miss Frances E. Willard and Mrs. William Thayer Brown, members. These congresses resulted in a number of organizations of both national and international scope. Mrs. Harbert was also a member of the Committee of the Woman's Branch of the World's Congress Auxiliary on Government Reform Congresses, and subsequently became Associate Chairman of the Government Reform Congress of the World's Congresses.

The list of charter members of the Illinois Woman's Press Association contains the name of Mrs. Harbert. She was also a member of the Illinois Press Association. She was President and Director of the National Household Economic Association, and Vice-President for Illinois of the National Woman Suffrage Association.

The Woman's Club of Evanston was organized and presided over by Mrs. Harbert, and after seven years' service as such —during which time the meetings of the Club were held at the Harbert homestead —she was elected Honorary President of the Club, which honor she declined.

The immediate outcome of the World's Congresses was the formation of two organizations, namely: The Religious Parliament Extension, of which the late Hon. Charles C. Bonney was President and Dr. Paul Carus, Secretary; and The World's Unity League, of which Hon. Charles Carroll Bonney (until the time of his decease) and Mrs. Harbert were Associate Chairmen. At present Mrs. Harbert is the acting chairman, no one having yet been appointed to succeed Mr. Bonney. Mrs. Ella A. W. Hoswell and Miss Ida C. Heffron are its secretaries.

From the official report of Mr. Bonney, made to the representative participants in the "Congress Auxiliary," we quote the following:

The **Woman's Committee on Religious Parliament Extension**.—Mrs. Elizabeth Boynton Harbert, Chairman, and Mrs. Frederick Hawkins, Secretary thereof, have determined to circulate for signatures, in all parts of the world, the pledge of the World's Religious Unity, with which the Religious Extension Movement was inaugurated. This pledge, of which Mrs. Harbert is the author, was the bond of union presented and signed at the first Extension meeting and is in the following words:

· Mrs. Harbert is associated with many organizations which have for their object the recognition of the divinity of humanity, one of her favorite statements being, "There are no common people, since we all belong to the divine familyhood of the Creator and the created."

Notwithstanding all the work implied in filling so many important offices, Mrs. Harbert finds her greatest pleasure in her hospitable home and with her family. However, the basic principle of all her work has ever been found in the home, and the recognition of the fact that the civilization of tomorrow inheres in the children of today.

Mrs. Harbert is versatile to a remarkable degree. She has won the unstinted affection of her townsmen and women, which has manifested itself in the gift of a fountain, works of art, etc., from these. In all her endeavors she has been nobly sustained by her husband, whose clear judgment and generous sympathies have made his aid invaluable.

As a writer she is poetic, pointed, witty, vigorous, convincing. On two occasions she has addressed the Judiciary Committee of the Senate of the United States, making a plea for an amendment to the Federal Constitution prohibiting the disfranchisement of United States citizens on account of sex. She also addressed the New York General Assembly at a joint session of the Assembly and Senate of that State, upon the same subject. With Mrs. Catherine Waugh McCulloch, of Evanston, and Mrs. Helen M. Gougar, of La Fayette, Ind., Mrs. Harbert went to Springfield, Ill., where they addressed

the House and Senate in favor of the bill allowing the women of Illinois to vote upon school questions, and secured the passage of the bill.

She has made addresses before the Legislative Assemblies of Wisconsin, Iowa and Illinois. She was one of the two women appointed by the National Woman's Suffrage Committee, as delegates from the United States at large to the National Republican Convention that nominated R. B. Hayes, at which she made an address before the platform committee.

Among the most important of Mrs. Harbert's essays and lectures are the following: "Before Suffrage, What?" "Homes of Representative Women"; "The Domestic Problem"; "Men's Rights"; "Conversation and Conversers"; "The Ideal Home"; "George Eliot"; "Lucretia Mott"; "Statesmanship of Women"; "Aims, Ideals and Methods of Women's Clubs"; "A Woman's Dream of Co-operation"; "The Message of the Madonna"; "Lyric Poets of Russia"; "An Hour with the Strong Minded." Her publications are: "The Golden Fleece"; "Out of Her Sphere"; "Amore;" "The Illinois Chapter in the History of Woman Suffrage." Songs: "Arlington Heights"; "What Have You Done with the Hours?" "The New America" (words); "The Promised Land" (words). Poems: "The Little Earth Angel"; Lines to My Anonymous Friend," and others.

The narrative in the foregoing sketch, with but slight and immaterial changes, from the pen of Mrs. Harbert's, who passed from this life in 1890, was found among his papers after his death.

To Mrs. Harbert is due the full credit of the chapter in this volume under the title of "Homes and Home-Makers of Evanston."

FRANK M. ELLIOT.

Frank M. Elliot, who for nineteen years has resided at No. 225, Lake Street, Evanston, Ill., and is engaged in the real estate and loan business in Chicago, was born at Corinna, Maine, March 27, 1853, the son of Jacob Smith and Sarah (Moore) Elliot, both natives of New England. Jacob Smith Elliot, who was a physician by profession, continued to live in Maine until 1855, when the family moved to Minneapolis, Minn. He preempted 80 acres of land on which he established his western home and which is now within the limits of that city. Dr. Elliot was one of the leading practitioners of medicine in his locality for twenty-five years. Subsequently, he went to California, where he died, aged eighty-three years.

The subject of this sketch spent his boyhood on the paternal farm, and received his early mental training in the public schools of Minneapolis. He afterwards pursued a course of study in Northwestern University, at Evanston, from which he was graduated with the class of 1877. After his graduation he studied law, and then held a position in the Recorder's Office of Cook County, for two years. At the end of this period, he entered into the real estate and loan business in Chicago, in which he has since been successfully engaged. He attends to the management of estates and conducts a general business in real estate. He has been a director in the State Bank of Evanston, since the organization.

On November 13, 1878, Mr. Elliot was united in marriage, at Evanston, Ill., with Anna Shuman, whose father, Andrew Shuman, was for many years, the editor of the "Chicago Evening Journal" and who filled the position of Lieutenant Governor of Illinois. In politics Mr. Elliot has always been an earnest supporter of the Republican party. In 1887 he held the office of Village Trustee of Evanston. He has been an officer of the Evanston Hospital Association since its organization in 1891, acting for fifteen years on the Executive Committee and has been the President for eleven years. In 1884-85 he was President of the Alumni Association of Northwestern University. Socially, Mr. Elliot belongs to the Sigma Chi Fraternity, in which he was Grand Annotator from 1884 to 1886; and to the Evanston Club, the Glen View Golf Club, and the University Club of Chicago. His religious connection is with the First Congregational Church of Evanston. He is regarded as a public-spirited and useful member of the community.

BENJAMIN ALLEN GREENE, D. D.

Rev. Benjamin A. Greene, an eminent minister of the Baptist church, residing in Evanston, Ill., was born in Harrisville, R. I., November 6, 1845, the son of Alvin and Maria (Arnold) Greene, of whom the former was born in Killingly, Conn., in December, 1820, while the latter was a native of Rhode Island, where she was born in February, 1820. The occupation of Alvin Greene was that of superintendent of a cotton mill. The genealogical line of the family is traceable back to John Greene, who lived in Warwick, R. I., in 1639.

In early youth the subject of this sketch attended the common schools of his native place. After reaching the age of twelve years, he worked half of the time in the cotton mills and spent the other half at school. He recalls the fact that he began to read the "New York Tribune" editorials of Horace Greeley, at the beginning of the Civil War. For two years he lived in Yarmouth, Maine, but most of his later boy-

hood was spent at White Rock, R. I. He
spent 1866-68 in preparation for college, in
the Connecticut Literary Institute, at Suf-
field, and entering Brown University, graduated there in 1872, and from Newton Theological Institution in 1875. In 1893 he
received the degree of D. D. from the former institution. From July, 1875, to April,
1882, Dr. Greene followed his ministerial
calling in Massachusetts, during that period
serving as pastor of the First Baptist
Church at Westboro, and later as pastor of
the Washington Street Baptist Church, at
Lynn, Mass., from April, 1882, to March,
1897. Then coming West he assumed his
present charge in Evanston. Dr. Greene
has officiated as President of the Massachusetts Conference of Baptist Ministers, and
as lecturer on homiletics at Newton Theological Institution, Crozer Theological
School, Rochester Theological Seminary,
and Chicago University Divinity School.

On June 25, 1875, Dr. Greene was united
in marriage, at Providence, R. I., with Ella
Fairbrother, who was born in Pawtucket,
R. I., in 1849. Two children have been
born of this union, namely: Ruth M. (Mrs.
J. F. Pierson), born February 27, 1877; and
Marian F., born January 4, 1886. On May
12, 1891, the mother of this family having
died, Dr. Greene was married again, his
second wife being Nancy W. Maine, who
was born January 19, 1856. In his political views, Dr. Greene is a supporter of the
principles of the Republican party.

HENRY B. HEMENWAY, M. D.

Dr. Henry Bixby Hemenway, who
is successfully engaged in the practice of
medicine in Evanston, Ill., was born in
Montpelier, Vt., December 20, 1856, the son
of Francis Dana and Sarah Louise (Bixby)
Hemenway, natives of Chelsea, Vt., where

the former was born November 10, 1830,
and the latter, March 2, 1828. The paternal grandparents, Jonathan Wilder and
Sally (Hibbard—or Hebard) Hemenway,
were born in Barre, Mass., and Brookfield,
Vt., respectively. On the maternal side the
grandparents were Ichabod Bixby, born at
Belchertown, Mass., March 19, 1784, and
Susanna (Lewis) Bixby, in Walpole, N.
H., August 31, 1789. The maiden name
of the great-grandmother, on the paternal
side, was Sarah Davidson. The great-
grandparents on the maternal side were
Ichabod and Lydia (Orcutt) Bixby, James
and Grace (Paddock) Lewis—the first mentioned (Ichabod Bixby), born January 9,
1757. The great-great-grandfather of
Mrs. Hemenway, Solomon Bixby, was
born in 1732, and died January 27, 1813.
His father, Nathan Bixby, was born in November, 1694, the father of Nathan was
Benjamin and his father was Joseph Bixby,
who died in 1706. The father of Joseph
Bixby was Nathaniel Bixby, who came
from Boxford, Suffolk County, England
and settled in Salem, Mass., in 1636. Dr.
Hemenway's father, Francis Dana Hemenway, was a clergyman who, at the time of
the doctor's birth was pastor of a church
in Montpelier, Vt., and Chaplain of the
State Senate. He first located in Evanston
in 1857. During periods in 1861 to 1862
and 1863 to 1865, he had a pastoral charge
at Kalamazoo, Mich., and for a time in
1862-63, served as pastor of the First Methodist Episcopal Church in Chicago. On locating in Evanston he was elected to a professorship in the Garrett Biblical Institute
but from the fall of 1861 until the spring
of 1866, availed himself of leave of absence
from the institution. In 1876 he was a reviser of the Methodist Episcopal Hymnal.

Henry Bixby Hemenway received his
mental training in the Preparatory School
and College of Liberal Arts of Northwest-

ern University, receiving his degree of A. B. in 1879, A. M., in 1882, and that of M. D., from the medical department of the University in 1881. While taking his course in the College of Liberal Arts he taught a district school at Deerfield, Ill., in 1878-79. In 1881 he entered upon the practice of his profession in Kalamazoo, Mich., continued therein until 1890, when he moved to Evanston, where he has since practiced with successful results. He served in the capacity of Health Officer of Kalamazoo in 1884-85, was secretary of the Kalamazoo Board of the U. S. Examining Surgeons, from January 1887 to September 1890; was also Treasurer of the Michigan State Medical Society from 1886 to 1890 and was Secretary and Librarian of the Kalamazoo Academy of Medicine. He was a member of the Finance Committee of the Ninth International Medical Congress; is now a member of the American Medical Association, the American Academy of Medicine, the Chicago Medical Society, the Illinois State Medical Society, etc.

Dr. Hemenway has been twice married, first in Evanston, on May 2, 1882, to Lilla Maggie Bradley, who was born at Cottage Hill, Ill., August 25, 1856, and died March 29, 1883. She was descended from an old New England family, Benjamin Bradley, a London Apothecary, being the ancestor of the family. His son, Daniel, born in 1615, came to Massachusetts in 1635 and was killed by Indians August 13, 1689. The doctor's second wife was Victoria Stevenson Taylor, to whom he was united in marriage at Kalamazoo, Mich., October 13, 1885. She was born in Kalamazoo, February 16, 1861, a daughter of Andrew and Victoria (Bangs) Taylor, her father being a native of Kelso, Scotland. Her maternal grandparents were Samuel and Susan (Payne) Bangs, the birthplace of the latter

being in Virginia. Samuel Bangs received a grant of eleven leagues of land from the Mexican Government, for services rendered previous to 1840. Dr. Hemenway became the father of three children, namely: Ruth L., born March 23, 1883; Hazel, who was born March 24, 1887, and died March 28, of the same year; and Margaret, born December 14, 1888.

In politics, the subject of this sketch is a supporter of the Republican party, but is averse to mingling national with local issues. His religious connection is with St. Mark's Episcopal Church. In fraternal circles, the doctor is identified with the A. F. & A. M., belonging to the R. A. M., and Knights Templar organizations. He is also affiliated with the Knights of Pythias, the U. O. F.; the I. O. O. F.; and the Columbian Knights.

ANDREW J. BROWN.

Andrew J. Brown (deceased), one of the oldest and most favorably known citizens of Evanston, Ill., and a lawyer of distinction, was a native of the State of New York, born at Cooperstown, in that State, in 1820. Mr. Brown received his early education in the common schools of his native place, and subsequently studied law with Robert Campbell, of Cooperstown. In the autumn of 1840, he removed to Illinois and settled in De Kalb County, where, on his twenty-first birthday, he was elected Probate Judge of that county.

After remaining four years in De Kalb County, Judge Brown located in Chicago, where he rapidly built up a remunerative practice. In 1850, he entered into a law partnership with the late Harvey B. Hurd, of Evanston, which was continued until 1854. Soon after entering into this partnership he became interested in North Shore realty, and about the year 1863, became the owner of a tract of land containing 248 acres, which mainly constitutes the site of the present city of Evanston. In 1850 Mr. Brown, in conjunction with Grant Goodrich, Dr. John Evans, Orrington Lunt, and others, took part in a conference held in the city of Chicago, to consider the founding of "a university in the Northwest under the patronage of the Methodist Episcopal Church." Mr. Brown served as Secretary of this conference, was appointed a member of the committee to propose a form of charter which was adopted at a subsequent meeting, and still later, in an act passed by the Legislature in January, 1851, authorizing the establishment of such an institution, was named as a member of the First Board of Trustees. As one of the incorporators he assisted in the formal incorporation of the new institution, meanwhile serving as Secretary of the Board. Two years later (1853) he took a prominent part in the search for a permanent site for the University, which, on or about the Fourth of July of that year, resulted in the selection of the present location, and the founding of the village of Evanston named in honor of Dr. John Evans, at that time President of the Board of Trustees and a potent factor in the founding of the institution. It is claimed that, as early as 1852, Mr. Brown had selected this as the proper site of the coming university, thus anticipating the views of his colleagues on the Board of Trustees, of which he was the only member then living in Evanston. After the establishment of the University, Judge Brown, who had acquired considerable financial resources, was one of its most steadfast supporters, and became security for many of the loans negotiated to tide it over the emergencies in its early history. The land in that vicinity which he purchased early in the 'sixties in anticipation of the future development of his educational project, was disposed of by him in such a manner as to promote the best interests of the city of Evanston, and to him is largely attributable the reputation which Evanston now enjoys as a center of material elegance, intellectual culture, and sound moral sentiment.

Mr. Brown was married to Abigail Mc-Tagg, who survives her husband, as do also their son and daughter, Robert P. Brown, and Mrs. W. A. S. Graham. His death, as the result of an attack of grip, occurred at his home in Evanston early in the year 1906.

PETER CHRISTIAN LUTKIN.

Peter Christian Lutkin, whose career in technical music during the twenty-five years which have passed since his first connection with Northwestern University, has given him a high reputation throughout the West as a master of that art, is a native of Wisconsin, born at Thompsonville, in the vicinity of Racine, that State, March 27, 1858. His father and mother, who were of Danish nativity, came to the United States in 1844. In 1859, they moved from the small village where their son Peter was born to Racine, and thence, in 1863, to Chicago, where they spent the remainder of their lives. Both died in 1872.

Before the death of his parents, the subject of this sketch had made diligent use of the opportunities for mental training afforded by the Chicago public schools, and had been for one year a pupil in a select school in that city. On being left an orphan when just entering upon his 'teens, further attendance at school became impossible. He had gained some experience, however, at an earlier age, as boy-alto in the choir of the Cathedral of SS. Peter and Paul, in Chicago. He was the first boy to sustain that part in the church choirs of the city, as he was also the first one of his age in this section of the country to render solos in oratorio music. He was then nine years old, and three years later, without previous tuition, he presided at the cathedral organ during the regular daily services. At the age of thirteen years, in conjunction with W. F. Whitehouse, a son of Bishop Whitehouse, he played that instrument in the cathedral on occasions of Sunday worship. He was then appointed organist of the cathedral when fourteen years old, and acted in that capacity for nine years. During this period he had studied with Clarence Eddy, Regina Watson and Frederick Grant Gleason in organ, piano, and the theory of music, respectively.

On going to Europe in 1881, Mr. Lutkin became a pupil of August Haupt, Oscar Raif and Waldemar Bargiel, in Berlin, in the respective branches of organ, piano and composition. In 1882 he took a course in the Hochschule, in that city, and was one of the sixteen students (he being the only foreigner) accepted for the study of theory and composition in the Royal Academy of Arts, Berlin. Later he went to Vienna, where he attended the piano classes of Theodor Leschetitzky; and subsequently visited Paris, there becoming a pupil of Moszkowsky, in piano and composition. Mr. Lutkin then returned home and received the appointment of organist and choirmaster of St. Clement's Church, in Chicago. From 1890 to 1896, he acted in the capacity of organist of St. James' Episcopal Church, in the same city, which established the standard for ecclesiastical music in this section of the country.

Before entering upon his studies in Europe, Professor Lutkin had been a teacher of piano in the Conservatory of Music in Evanston, and after his return to this country, he was for a considerable period the principal theory teacher in the American Conservatory of Music in Chicago. In 1891, while temporarily retaining his connection with the latter institution, he was placed in charge of the Conservatory, to which he devoted a portion of his time, reorganizing the school and soon uplifting it from a state of deterioration to a condition of high efficiency and prosperity. In 1892 Professor Lutkin resigned his position in the American Conservatory, and was formally appointed Director of the Department of Music of Northwestern University and Professor of Music in the College of Liberal Arts. Five years later the progress of the Department warranted its reorganization as a separate School of the University, with Professor Lutkin as Dean of the new faculty. He was one of the organizers of the University Club, and received the degree of Mus. D. from Syracuse University in 1901.

The Evanston Musical Club was organized by Professor Lutkin during the 'nineties, and he has acted as its director since 1895. He was director as well of the Ravenswood Musical Club from 1897 to 1905, and that society made signal progress under his leadership. These two organizations were awarded $4,500 in prizes, during competitions held at the Louisiana Purchase Exposition at St. Louis in 1904. Professor Lutkin is the composer of music to a considerable extent for use in the worship of the Episcopal Church, to which denomination he belongs, and some of his compositions are used in the services of the Established Church of England. Although an Episcopalian, he was chosen as one of the two musical editors engaged on the revision of the hymnal of the Methodist Episcopal Church, a fact which notably attests the rank generally conceded to him in the musical profession.

CHESTER P. WALCOTT.

Chester P. Walcott (deceased), for a number of years one of the most worthy, useful and highly esteemed citizens of Evanston, Ill., was born in Providence, R. I., November 24, 1859, the son of Erastus L. and Harriet (Pratt) Walcott. Mr. Walcott was reared in his native place, where, in early youth, he made diligent use of the opportunities afforded by the public schools. In 1876, he located in Chicago, and sometime afterwards became connected with the business of dealing in plumbers' supplies. For many years, in partnership with Mr. Hurlbut, he carried on a large business under the firm style of Walcott, Hurlbut & Co., being identified with the trade in this line until the time of his death, which occurred April 25, 1899. He had established his residence in Evanston in the spring of 1891, and there passed away at his home, No. 1114, Judson Avenue. Although a quiet, undemonstrative man, Mr. Walcott was energetic in the conduct of his affairs, in which he manifested superior business capability and won merited success.

October 27, 1881, Mr. Walcott was united in marriage, at the Fourth Presbyterian Church in Chicago, with Martha C. Howe, a daughter of Samuel Howe, one of the pioneer grain merchants of that city. The children born of this union are: Chester H. Walcott, who graduated from Princeton University with the class of 1905 ; and Russell S. Walcott, who is a high school student in Evanston. Mr. Walcott was reared an Episcopalian, but after his marriage united with the Presbyterian Church, to which denomination his wife belonged and with which she is still connected. On settling in Evanston he became a member of the First Presbyterian Church, and took a prominent part in promoting its welfare. He was a member of the Board of Trustees and of its building committee. He was also a member of the committee which extended the call to the Rev. Dr. Boyd to become pastor of the church, in which relation that gentleman still officiates.

Socially, Mr. Walcott was identified with the Evanston Club. He had a wide acquaintance, and his genial nature, kindly deportment and helpful disposition, attracted to him hosts of friends. By those who were brought into intimate contact with him in the daily walks of life, he was regarded with warm affection, and his unswerving probity and sterling traits of character commanded the sincere respect of all with whom he had business transactions.

COL. NATHAN H. WALWORTH.

Col. Nathan H. Walworth (deceased), formerly one of the most prominent, popular and widely known citizens of Evanston, Ill., was born in Western (now Rome), Oneida County, N. Y., February 14, 1832, the son of Elisha and Sarah (Halbert) Walworth, natives of New York State. Elisha Walworth was a farmer and manufacturer by occupation. The Walworth family was one of the oldest and most noted in the Empire State, and among its most distinguished representatives was the eminent jurist, Chancellor Walworth.

The boyhood of Nathan H. Walworth was passed on the paternal farm in the Mohawk Valley, and he received his primary training in the public schools in the vicinity of his home. His education was completed at Rome Academy and in Cazenovia Seminary. He remained on the farm during his youth and, when about twenty-two years of age, after finishing his studies, he came west to Fulton County, Ill., where he operated a large farm in 1855 and 1856. At a later period he went to Oneida, Knox County, where he engaged in mercantile pursuits. In Oneida he was prominent both as a merchant and as a citizen, serving as Supervisor of his town, and filling other positions of trust and responsibility. While in New York, Col. Wadsworth had some experience as Captain of Artillery, in the National Guard of that State, and in the early summer of 1861, organized a company of infantry for service in the Union Army. This company became a part of the Forty-second Regiment, Illinois Volunteer Infantry, in which he was commissioned as Captain July 22, 1861. In December of that year he was promoted as Major, and in October, 1862, became Lieutenant Colonel. On February 15, 1863, he was promoted to the Colonelcy and was constantly in command of his regiment from the time he became Major until May 15, 1864, when he resigned. At the battles of Chickamauga and Mission Ridge he commanded a brigade. His services in the field began under Fremont and Hunter in Missouri. In February, 1862, he was sent to reinforce Grant at Fort Donelson, and was then ordered down the Mississippi River to Island No. 10. There he conceived the idea of surprising the Confederate water battery, located above the bend of the river. His suggestion was carried out by Col. Roberts in the famous exploit of April 1, 1862, in which the guns of the battery were spiked, and our gunboats ran the gauntlet at the island, cutting off the retreat of the Confederates and compelling them to surrender. The regiment was later engaged in the siege of Nashville, and became part of the Army of the Cumberland. Col. Walworth was a close personal friend of Gen. Sheridan, who relied much on his military judgment.

After leaving the army, Col. Walworth returned to Oneida, Ill., where he became a stock breeder in that vicinity, and operated a lumber yard in the town, which he con-

ducted until 1868. In that year he located in Chicago with C. H. Conger, and was largely interested in the firm of Conger, Walworth & Co., lumber dealers. About the same time the firm purchased the business of Roberts, Calkins & Hull, and Col. Walworth having bought the Conger interest, the firm became Bushnell, Walworth & Reed in 1871. In 1875 the company engaged in the manufacture of lumber at Cedar Springs, Mich., and also established lumber yards, drying kilns, etc., at that place, where it conducted business until 1880. The Chicago yard was sold in 1876, and Mr. Bushnell withdrew from the firm. Mr. Reed became President and the concern carried on a retail lumber business at a dozen or more points in Nebraska, having a trade in the aggregate of 30,-000,000 feet of lumber per year. The firm abandoned the lumber business in 1889, but Col. Walworth and Mr. Reed continued together in the real estate line until the death of the former, at his home in Evanston, October 29, 1892. They were also the owners of large live-stock interests, operating an extensive ranch at Holdredge, Neb., as the Holdredge Live Stock Company. Besides these interests, they owned mills at Muskegon, Mich., which the firm had bought in 1871 and continued to operate until 1885, when they moved to Minneapolis. In 1880 the firm sold a half-interest in the Cedar Springs plant, and moved the business to Montague, Mich., and in 1884, the Walworth & Reed Lumber Company was incorporated, with Col. Walworth as President.

In 1855, at Delta, N. Y., Col. Walworth was united in marriage with Adelia E. Cornish, who was a native of New York and a daughter of Hosea Cornish of that town. Mrs. Walworth is the only surviving member of the family, although she and her husband cared for and educated several children. Politically, Col. Wadworth was an earnest supporter of the principles of the Republican party. Socially, he was a prominent member of the Loyal Legion; the Union League and Evanston Clubs; and the George H. Thomas Post, G. A. R. His religious connection was with the Congregational Church. Throughout his active career, the strain of his varied and extensive business responsibilities was incessant and severe, and he found it necessary, in 1888-89, to indulge in a vacation for the benefit of his health, spending the period in European travel.

It was the nature of Col. Walworth to be kindly and helpful, and his friends loved him as few men are loved. He was ever charitable and took special interest in assisting young men. He was steadfast in friendship and devoted to his old comrades in arms. His home life was ideal, and his intercourse with his wide acquaintance was befitting the character of a brave soldier and chivalrous gentleman.

RICHARD CONOVER LAKE.

Richard C. Lake, retired, Evanston, Ill., was born in Montour County, Pa., July 20, 1846, the son of James and Hannah (Dey) Lake, natives of the State of Pennsylvania. Mr. Lake is most fortunate in his ancestry. On the paternal side, he is a descendant of John Lake, one of the Lady Deborah Moody party who constituted the first English settlement on Long Island in 1643; the line of descent being from John through Daniel, John, Richard, Benjamin and James to Richard C. On the maternal side, the Dey family are Holland Dutch, and were among the first emigrants to land in New Amsterdam, now New York City. Dey Street is named for this family. Thus it will be seen that through

descent, both maternal and paternal, as well as by collateral lines, the subject of this sketch is related to many of the most prominent and distinguished families known to American history, among them being the Randolphs, Harrisons, Berkleys, etc.

James Lake, the father of Richard C., was a well-known agriculturist, who at the time of his decease was an associate Judge in the County of Columbia, State of Pennsylvania. Richard C. received a common school education, which has been supplemented by study in later years. Until he was twelve years of age, his youth was spent upon a farm. He then went to Espy, Columbia County, Pa., where he was employed by a mercantile house until his seventeenth year, when, in company with some older brothers, he removed to Central City, Colo. There he went to work for a mercantile firm, later becoming a partner in the concern. In 1877 he disposed of his interest and embarked once more on the mercantile sea in Deadwood, S. D. A little later he engaged in the banking business in that city, and in 1879 was elected President of the First National Bank. For twenty years thereafter he continued in this business, becoming President of the First National Bank of Rapid City, S. D., in 1884, and later President of a bank in Hot Springs, S. D., and another at Chadron, Neb.

On September 14, 1871, Mr. Lake was married to Mary, daughter of John R. Randolph of Providence, R. I., whose father was a cousin of the celebrated John Randolph of Roanoake. Mr. and Mrs. Lake were the parents of six children: Jessie, Amy (now Mrs. Walter G. Pietsch), Richard Randolph, Margaret, George Ernest (now a midshipman in the U. S. Navy), and Gertrude. In 1893, the family removed to Evanston, Ill., where Mrs. Lake died September 14, 1894. Shortly after coming to Illinois, Mr. Lake disposed of his banking interests in the West, but was made Vice-President of the Union National Bank of Chicago, which relation he continued to occupy for nearly two years, when, having been elected President of the Masonic Fraternity Temple Association, and being a large stockholder therein, he resigned the vice-presidency of the bank and took personal charge of the Masonic Temple Building. For two years thereafter—or until the building was placed on a dividend-paying basis—he held this position. He then resigned, and since that time has devoted his attention exclusively to his private business affairs, most important among which may be mentioned the Range Cattle Industry in South Dakota and Texas, a business in which, for the past twenty years, he has been interested to a greater or less extent.

On February 9, 1899, Mr. Lake was united to Helen M. Kitchell, daughter of Mrs. E. E. Willis, of Evanston, Ill., but there is no living issue from this marriage. In his political affiliations, Mr. Lake is a Republican. He is a thirty-second degree Mason, and has filled nearly every position in the order. He is a member of the Union League Club of Chicago, the Glenview Golf Club, the Evanston Club, and the Country Club of Evanston. He is likewise a Director of the Evanston Free Public Library, and a member of the School Board of that city. He and his family are members of the Episcopal Church.

EDWARD W. LEARNED.

Edward W. Learned, a prominent resident of Evanston, Ill., since 1865, was born in the town of Homer, Cortland County, N. Y., April 30, 1823. His parents were Edward W. and Polly (Briggs) Learned.

Edward W. Learned, Sr., was a farmer by occupation and the son was reared in the neighborhood made famous in the story of David Harum. Here he enjoyed the educational advantages of the common schools of Homer and Solon, and after a course in the Cortland Academy at Homer, in his early manhood engaged in teaching. He came west in 1845, locating at Racine, Wis., on June 5, of that year. His elder brother had come to this section the year before, and he took a tramp beyond Rock River to visit some old New York friends. There he hired out to a farmer who lived near what was then Southport, but is now Kenosha. He worked there at $12.50 per month, taught school the following winter and, when the term was over, went to Port Washington, where he and his brother entered government land, receiving a deed therefor from President James K. Polk. Mr. Learned still owns this farm.

Except for a period of six years spent in California, Mr. Learned remained in Wisconsin, engaged in building and farming, for twenty-one years. He went to California in 1851, sailing from New York and rounding Cape Horn. The voyage from New York to San Francisco consumed 155 days, and during this period thirteen burials at sea and ten cases of yellow-fever came under his observation. He was engaged in the building line in San Francisco and Sacramento five years, was connected with the Vigilantes, and made money rapidly. In 1857 he returned from California, via the Isthmus of Panama, and returned to Port Washington where he resumed building and continued in this line until 1866, when he came to Evanston. Here he was actively engaged in building operations until he retired from business. Prior to his removal to Evanston (in 1865) he built the second brick residence in Evanston. He put up several buildings for himself, and made judicious investments in real estate. He also conducted a grocery in Evanston for a time, and, by diligent effort, secured a competency for old age.

In 1857, Mr. Learned was married in Homer, N. Y., to Carrie M. Shuler, a daughter of Jacob Shuler, of that place. Their only child was Ella Elizabeth (Learned) Betts, who died in 1884, leaving an infant son, who died seven weeks later. Politically, Mr. Learned is a Republican. He served one term of four years as Justice of the Peace, and was also a member of the city auditing board. His religious connection is with the First Methodist Church.

JOHN R. VAN ARSDALE.

John R. Van Arsdale (deceased), for eighteen years one of the most favorably known citizens of Evanston, Ill., was born in New Brunswick, N. J., March 10, 1824, and was reared in his native place, where he received his early training in the public schools, and where he also gained his first business experience. In 1869 he moved west to Illinois, and locating in Chicago, was first engaged in the manufacture of wall paper, as a member of the firm of M. A. Howell & Company. From 1870 to 1872, he was a grain commission merchant and an operator on the Chicago Board of Trade. In 1873, he became connected with the Mutual Benefit Life Insurance Company of Chicago, of which, in 1876, he was appointed cashier. This position he filled until the time of his death, which occurred February 15, 1890. He passed away at his residence on Ridge Avenue, Evanston, where he had established his home in 1872. During the seventeen years of his connection with the above-mentioned company, he was largely instrumental in advancing its interests to a high degree of prosperity.

In 1857, Mr. Van Arsdale was united in marriage with Mary E. Tannehill, of Brooklyn, N. Y., and their union resulted in the following named children: Robert T., a resident of New Brunswick, N. J.; William T., who is engaged in business in Chicago, and maintains his residence in Evanston; John R., Jr., who is also a business man of Chicago and lives in Evanston; Isabella (Mrs. Sutphen) of Brooklyn, N. Y., and Mary, whose home is in Evanston. In his religious associations Mr. Van Arsdale was an attendant upon the services of the Presbyterian Church. He was a man of excellent traits of character, superior business capacity and scrupulous integrity, and enjoyed the sincere respect and unreserved confidence of all who made his acquaintance.

LUCIUS A. TROWBRIDGE.

Lucius A. Trowbridge, a well-known banker of Chicago, and prominent resident of Evanston, Ill., was born in Danbury, Fairfield County, Conn., April 10, 1847, the son of Matthew Thomas and Agnes K. (Sherman) Trowbridge, who moved from Connecticut to Illinois in 1861, settling in Rockford, where the former passed the remainder of his life, dying in 1903. Both the Trowbridge and Sherman families are of old New England stock. Lucius A. received his early education in the public and high schools of Rockford, Ill., and, after finishing his studies, was employed for two years as a clerk in the "County Book Store," in that city. In 1863, he became bookkeeper in the private bank of Spafford & Penfield, and during the same year this bank became the Third National Bank of Rockford. Mr. Trowbridge remained with it in various capacities for twenty-seven years. He was successively book-keeper, teller, assistant cashier and cashier, and for several years, was also a director, and one of the principal stockholders. In 1891, he resigned his position as cashier, in order to engage in private banking in Chicago, and, in 1893, founded the private banking house of Lucius A. Trowbridge. This was succeeded by the corporation of Trowbridge & Co., in 1895, with Mr. Trow-bridge as Président and D. R. Niver as Secretary. In 1900 the corporate name was changed to that of The Trowbridge & Niver Co., and the house has been, and still is, largely engaged in the purchase and sale of high-grade municipal and corporation bonds. From the outset its main offices have been located in the First National Bank Building, in Chicago, while a branch office is maintained in Boston. In late years, the bonds owned and offered to the public by The Trowbridge & Niver Company have aggregated millions of dollars annual-ly. Mr. Trowbridge is also largely inter-ested in the Twin City Telephone Company, of Minneapolis and St. Paul, Minn., on be-half of his firm. He is a man of keen per-ception and excellent business judgment.

On June 9, 1881, Mr. Trowbridge was united in marriage with Carolyn Frances Cobb, a daughter of George Cobb, whose early home was at Sauquoit, N. Y. Mr. and Mrs. Trowbridge have three daughters, namely: Alice, Jessie and Carolyn. Relig-iously, Mr. Trowbridge has been for many years a prominent and active member of the Baptist Church. He is widely known throughout the State of Illinois as a Sun-day School worker and, in 1883, was Presi-dent of the Illinois State Sunday School Association. He is also active in the work of the Y. M. C. A., and was chairman of the Illinois State Executive Committee of

that organization from 1891 to 1895. He is still a member of the advisory committee of the association. Mr. Trowbridge estab-lished his home in Evanston in 1902, and is there held in high esteem.

DORR AUGUSTINE KIMBALL.

Dorr A. Kimball (deceased), who was for many years one of the most prominent and widely known business men of Chicago, was born in Dexter, Jefferson County, N. Y., June 4, 1849, the son of John B. and Louisa (Ryder) Kimball. His father was a shoe manufacturer and a Jus-tice of the Peace in New York State, and in political sentiment a zealous Free-Soiler, deeply interested in the abolition movement and the operations of the "Underground Railroad," and while living near Sackett's Harbor, frequently aided fugitive slaves to secure their freedom by escaping to Cana-da. Later he was a supporter of the Gov-ernment in the war for the preservation of the Union, assisting in the organization of troops for the suppression of the rebellion. On the maternal side, the Ryders were an old family of New York State, engaged in agriculture.

The subject of this sketch received his education in the public schools, and when about fifteen years of age obtained a clerk-ship in a store at Watertown, N. Y., where he remained a year when, in 1865, he came to Chicago and found employment as office boy with Fox & Howard, dredgers and con-tractors, continuing in this business until 1874. He then accepted a position as cash-ier with Marshall Field & Co., which he soon exchanged for a position at the head of the general credit department of the same firm, retaining the latter position for the rest of his life, covering a period of nearly thirty years. His long connection with the most important department in this extensive concern indicates the estimation in which he was held as a business man. Gifted with a retentive memory which enabled him promptly to recall faces and events, his judgment and integrity were implicitly trusted, and seldom, if ever, at fault.

Soon after coming to Chicago, Mr. Kimball became a member of the New England Congregational Church, but after moving to Evanston in 1876, transferred his membership to the First Congregational Church of that city, with which he remained identified up to the date of his decease. Although not a member of any secret society, he was identified with several social organizations, including the Evanston Club, the Evanston Country Club, besides various literary organizations, being Vice-President of the first named during the last year of his life. He was also one of the founders and most active supporters of the Home for Incurables, in connection with which he served as a Director from its establishment, was a member of the Evanston High School Board, a Director of the Evanston Hospital and, for several terms, a Trustee of the First Congregational Church. He was especially interested in the welfare and happiness of the children—the boys and girls—of his home city, and on his holidays was accustomed to lead a bicycle club of little girls about the city and adjoining country, ending the trip with an entertainment at a soda-fountain or an ice-cream parlor. The affection in which he was held by the younger class was one of the highest tributes that could be paid to his character, and affords his friends a pleasant memory of his many admirable qualities of mind and heart. In politics he was a Republican.

Mr. Kimball was united in marriage in the city of Chicago, April 24, 1871, to Miss Susie Woodford, daughter of Orin F. and Mary A. (Merrill) Woodford — both branches of Mrs. Kimball's family being descended from old prominent New England families. To Mr. and Mrs. Kimball were born three sons and three daughters, of whom two sons—Harlow M. and Dorr Edwin—and one daughter—Ruth Merrill —are now living. Of the other three children, two died in infancy, and the oldest born, Leonice Woodford, in 1900, at the age of twenty-six years.

Mr. Kimball's death occurred suddenly on May 20, 1903, at the Sanitarium at Lake Geneva, Wis., whither he had gone for treatment for a nervous affection, and was deeply deplored by a large circle of friends both in Evanston and Chicago who had learned to appreciate his high business integrity and his many admirable traits of character. His decease called forth many tributes to his memory.

It may be said of him that his fidelity and his honesty were never questioned. He was one of the most faithful and trustworthy of citizens in every relation of life. His deportment in all the relations of life was of the highest, and he was interested in everything that would tend to the betterment of the community — spending freely of his means, his time and his labor for the upbuilding of his home city and the promotion of the public good.

LEWIS CASS TALLMADGE.

Lewis Cass Tallmadge, for many years one of the most prominent and favorably known citizens of Evanston, Ill., was born in Springfield, Mass., January 23, 1842, son of Marcus M. and Abigail (Andrews) Tallmadge. Marcus M. Tallmadge was a man of independent fortune. In politics, he was a prominent Democrat and an intimate friend of Andrew Jackson. In religion he was a leading Episcopal churchman. Gen.

Benjamin Tallmadge, the grandfather, was a member of Washington's staff. Marcus A. Tallmadge moved with his family, at an early period, from Springfield, Mass., to East Granby, Conn., where he made his home for many years. He had a son and daughter, who were respectively named after Andrew and Rachael Jackson. The old family homestead was destroyed by fire in October, 1905, and with it were consumed many Revolutionary and other historical relics and family treasures. Among these were miniature portraits, on ivory, of General and Rachael Jackson, presented to their namesakes.

The Tallmadge family in New England was descended from James Tallmadge, who, with his son Robert, came from Holland to Boston in 1630. They moved to Connecticut in 1639, and were original grantees of lots in the town of New Haven. Many of the Tallmadge family participated in the Revolutionary War, and some of its representatives have, in later times, become distinguished in professional careers, among them, Rev. T. DeWitt Tallmadge, the noted pulpit orator.

Lewis Cass Tallmadge received his early education in the public schools of New Haven, Conn., relinquishing his studies at the age of seventeen years in order to enlist in the Union Army, where he served in a Connecticut regiment. After the war was over, he went to Washington, D. C., where he obtained a position in the War Department, and at the same time studied law. At a later period, he engaged in the business of adjusting naval claims, which he followed to a considerable extent during a residence of twenty years in Washington and thereafter. He was also interested in real estate operations, the building of telephone lines and various other enterprises. In 1881, Mr. Tallmadge located in Chicago, soon afterwards removing to Evanston, where he resided until the time of his death, which occurred in Chicago, October 16, 1902.

In 1874, the subject of this sketch was united in marriage, in the city of New York, with Mary Eliza Eddy, a daughter of Rev. Dr. Thomas M. Eddy, then Secretary of the Board of Missions of the Methodist Episcopal Church, and widely known in that connection. Dr. Eddy had previously held the position of editor of the "Northwestern Christian Advocate," in Chicago, and from Chicago went to Baltimore, where he became pastor of the old Charles Street Church, and afterwards built the beautiful Mt. Vernon Place church, and served as its pastor. Still later, he was pastor of the Metropolitan Methodist Episcopal Church in Washington, D. C., from which he went to New York, and died there while serving as Secretary of the Board of Missions of his denomination. He was one of the most eminent ministers of the Methodist Church, noted alike for eloquence in the pulpit and rare executive ability in the conduct of church affairs. Mr. and Mrs. Tallmadge became the parents of two children, namely: Thomas Eddy Tallmadge, of Chicago, and Abbie Louise Tallmadge, of Evanston.

Politically Mr. Tallmadge was a supporter of the Republican party. He enjoyed a wide acquaintance with public men, and personally knew every President of the United States, from Grant to McKinley, inclusive. In religion, he was reared an Episcopalian, but became a Methodist while in Washington, and was a communicant of the First Methodist Episcopal Church, of Evanston. Socially, he was a member of the Evanston and Country Clubs; the John A. Logan Post, G. A. R.; and the Sons of the American Revolution.

GEORGE ALBERT COE, A. M., PH. D.

George Albert Coe, John Evans Professor of Moral and Intellectual Philosophy, Northwestern University, Evanston, Ill., was born March 26, 1862, at Mendon, N. Y., son of the late Rev. George W. Coe, for about forty years a minister of the Methodist Episcopal Church. The Coe ancestry is English. The first member of this family to emigrate to America came to Boston in the ship Francis in 1654. The ancestry on the side of the mother (Harriet Van Voorhis) was Dutch, the first Van Voorhis ancestor in this country, coming from Holland to the Hudson River region in the year 1670.

Mr. Coe graduated with degree of A. B., from the University of Rochester, N. Y., in 1884, subsequently receiving the degree of A. M. from the same university. In 1887, after three years' study at Boston University, he received from that institution the degree of S. T. B., thereafter remaining at the University for another year of graduate study. On September 3, 1888, he was united in marriage to Sadie E. Knowland, daughter of Mr. and Mrs. Joseph Knowland, of Alameda, Cal., and during the next two years (1888-90) was a professor in the University of Southern California at Los Angeles. Then, having been appointed Jacob Sleeper Traveling Fellow of Boston University, he spent one year (1890-91)studying at the University of Berlin. In 1891 he received the degree of Ph. D. from Boston University, and the same year was appointed Acting Professor of Philosophy at Northwestern University, two years later being appointed the John Evans Professor of Moral and Intellectual Philosophy in that institution, which he still retains. Professor Coe has published numerous articles in psychological and theological journals, and is a member of the American Psychological Association, the American Philosophical Association, and the American Association for the Advancement of Science. He is the author of the following works: "The Spiritual Life" (N. Y., 1900) ; "The Religion of a Mature Mind" (Chicago, 1902) ; "Education in Religion and Morals" (Chicago, 1904). He has also delivered numerous popular lectures on educational topics. In 1900 he was Lecturer on the Psychology of Religion at Boston University School of Theology, and in 1902, and again in 1903, gave courses of lectures at the summer sessions of the Harvard Divinity School on The Psychology of Religion and Religious Education, respectively. Professor Coe is a member of the First Methodist Church of Evanston.

SADIE KNOWLAND COE.

Sadie Knowland Coe, late Professor of Piano and History of Music, Northwestern University School of Music, Evanston, Ill., was born in San Francisco, Cal. in 1864, the daughter of Mr. and Mrs. Joseph Knowland, was educated in the public schools and the high school of Alameda, Cal., and studied piano with Ernst Hartmann of San Francisco, and still later with Carl Baermann and J. W. Tufts, of Boston. On September 3, 1888, she was married to George Albert Coe, a Professor in the University of Southern California at Los Angeles. During the academic year 1889-90, she was in charge of the piano department of the University of Southern California, and for the next three years studied music in Germany—taking instruction in piano music with Heinrich Barth and Moritz Moskowski, Theory and Composition with Reinhold Succo, and Ensemble Playing with Waldemar Bargiel.

Mrs. Coe came to Evanston in 1893 and

started a class for private instruction of pupils in piano music, but was invited into the faculty of the University School of Music as Instructor of Piano, with which she was connected eleven years. Besides teaching piano, she developed a popular department of the History of Music, gave numerous recitals, and appeared often with the string quartette, repeatedly bringing out new compositions, or those heard here for the first time. In 1901 she was advanced in rank to Professor, which she resigned in 1905 in order to establish a private school. She was under appointment as Lecturer on Musical Aesthetics in the College of Liberal Arts at the time of her death, which resulted from cancer, at San Francisco, Cal., August 24, 1905.

Mrs. Coe was exceedingly active in promoting music as a means of popular culture. For some four years she took the lead in the music work of the Evanston Woman's Club, conducting or organizing each year a course of educational programs and recitals. In the meantime she gave numerous lecture recitals in Evanston and elsewhere. Her leading topics were historical, such as Primitive Music, Music of the American Indians, and the several music-dramas of Richard Wagner.

A few days before her death there appeared from the press of the Clayton F. Summy Company, her "Melodrama of Hiawatha" for speaking voice and piano, the text being from Longfellow's poem, and the music being based upon genuine Indian themes. This composition has been given repeatedly in Evanston, and a number of times in other cities. It has proved itself possessed of great beauty and emotional power. Besides being a brilliant player and an able teacher and lecturer, Mrs. Coe was possessed of rare executive ability, intellectuality and social power. Adhering to the same faith as her husband, Prof. George

A. Coe, she was a member of the First Methodist Church of Evanston.

ALANSON SWEET.

Alanson Sweet (deceased), pioneer merchant and legislator of the Middle West, and former well-known citizen of Evanston, Ill., was born in Owasco, Cayuga County, N. Y., March 12, 1804, the son of Wilbur and Anna (Leach) Sweet. Wilbur Sweet was a skilled stoneworker by occupation, and was also engaged in agricultural pursuits. His son, Alanson, was reared on the paternal farm and trained to farming, besides learning the stone-mason's trade. On the maternal side he was descended from Lawrence Leach, of English ancestry, who settled in Salem, Mass., eleven years after the landing of the Pilgrims, and was in the Colonial service under Governor Winthrop.

Left a half-orphan by the death of his mother in his early childhood, Alanson Sweet was thrown upon his own resources at the age of fourteen years. He had had few advantages of early schooling, but being naturally studious, as a result of self-training he became a man of broad general information. As a youth he had a varied experience, an incident of which was his service as driver of a canal boat on the Erie Canal. When but nineteen years of age he was a contractor for stone work, and in this connection, held Government contracts. In 1831 he journeyed to Chicago, and was at Fort Dearborn at the beginning of the Blackhawk War. He was First Lieutenant of a company of volunteers raised in Chicago at that time, to aid in checking the ravages of the Indians, and in this connection rendered considerable active service. While in Fort Dearborn he saw, for the first time, Emily Shaw, who had just arrived in Chicago from New York State, and who, on account of the threatened danger, had taken refuge in the fort. It was a case of love at first sight, and, in 1833, they were united in wedlock at St. Joseph, Mich. Soon after his marriage, Mr. Sweet engaged in building and other enterprises in Chicago, and was one of the earliest real estate owners there. He built the first two-story frame house in Chicago, and had the first inclosed grounds, comprising a quarter of an acre of land at the corner of Clark and Kinzie Streets.

In 1835, believing that on account of its fine harbor and other advantages, Milwaukee was destined to become the chief city of the lakes, he moved to that place, where he acquired large landed interests and became a leading man of affairs. For thirty-five years thereafter, he was one of the foremost citizens of Milwaukee, possessed of ample means, conducting extensive enterprises and manifesting great activity in every field of effort. It was his design to build up a new city and commercial emporium. Mr. Sweet held many positions of honor and trust in Milwaukee, and was one of the organizers of the Wisconsin Territorial and State Governments. He served as one of the five members of the first Territorial Legislature, and was chiefly instrumental in locating the capital of Wisconsin, afterwards named Madison, at "Four Lakes." He improved part of the harbor of Milwaukee, and constructed a number of lighthouses on Lake Michigan and Lake Superior. Mr. Sweet was a close personal friend of Governor Doty, the first Governor of the State, and co-operated with him and other noted pioneers in laying the foundations of a great commonwealth. For many years he was the leading grain merchant of Milwaukee, owning large elevators and handling vast quantities of grain annually.

In the early days, Mr. Sweet was an ardent champion of water as against railroad transportation, and was among the pioneers who were unfriendly to railroad enterprises. He lived, however, long enough to realize how largely the latter have contributed toward the development of the country. Having met with reverses, Mr. Sweet went to Kansas in 1870, beginning the life of a farmer again at Arkansas City. After remaining there about six years, he relinquished active efforts and settled in Evanston, where he passed nearly all his later life, dying in Chicago in 1891. His last days were spent near the scenes of his earliest labors in Illinois. On the spot which he had beheld in all its original barrenness, with hardly a human habitation outside of Fort Dearborn, he saw a city of more than a million people spring into existence almost within a generation.

The faithful, life-long companion of Mr. Sweet passed away in Evanston in 1892, and the only surviving members of this noted pioneer family are a son and a daughter—George O. Sweet, of Chicago, and Mrs. Mary (Sweet) Taggart, of Evanston.

OSCAR H. MANN.

Oscar H. Mann, M. D., who has been one of the prime factors in the development of Evanston, Ill., from a straggling, though pretty suburb of Chicago, to a handsome city and a seat of wealth and culture, was born in Providence, R. I., November 24, 1834. His parents, Timothy M. and Eliza (Tupper) Mann, were descended from families conspicuous for high mental and moral qualities. Dr. Mann's father was a cousin of Horace Mann, the famous educator and author, and Martin Tupper, the poet, was a member of the family from which the mother of the subject of this sketch was derived.

When Mr. Mann was but a child, his father moved to Albany, New York, and for several years was engaged in the transportation business on the Hudson River and the Erie Canal. The son at this period attended Whitesboro College, Whitesboro, N. Y., and then pursued a course of study in the Medical College of the University of the City of New York, where he received his diploma. Similar degrees were also conferred upon him by Hahnemann Medical College in Chicago, and the Chicago Homœopathic College.

In 1860 Dr. Mann came West and commenced practicing medicine at Shabbona Grove, Ill. From 1863 until 1866 he practiced in Ottawa, Ill., and then settled in Evanston, where he soon attained a professional status which ranked him among the leading physicians of the State for more than thirty years. He has been President of the Illinois State Homœopathic Association, and has filled other positions of honor and trust. Early in his career he became interested in promoting public enterprises and was an earnest advocate of honesty and economy in municipal government. He bought real estate and improved it substantially, erecting some years ago what is still one of the principal business blocks in the city. He served as a member of the Village Board and was the last President of that body before the incorporation of Evanston as a city. He was one of the chief organizers of the waterworks system, and under his administration the City Hall was commenced and completed. The annexation of South Evanston to Evanston was, to a considerable extent, the result of his active efforts, in conjunction with those of other public-spirited men whose sagacity and energy made the city

what it now is. He became the first Mayor of the city, and was re-elected to that office, serving, in all, three years, and organizing the city government in all its departments. To him was largely due the satisfactory settlement of the tax controversy between the city and the Northwestern University, the bringing to the city of the electric railroad, and the planning and beautifying of Fountain Square.

Shortly after his second term as Mayor expired, in 1895, Dr. Mann relinquished his medical practice, and moved to a large stock and grain ranch, which he owned near Pierre, South Dakota, where he remained eight years, returning to Evanston in 1903. Beyond the age of threescore and ten years, he is now living in retirement, enjoying well earned repose and the esteem of all his fellow citizens.

FRANK HERBERT ANDERSON.

Frank H. Anderson, a well known citizen of Evanston, Ill., where he is now serving as City Treasurer, was born in Forest, Ontario, Canada, October 11, 1866. He is a son of Andrew Sparahock and Helen (Jones) Anderson, both of whom were natives of the Province of Ontario; the former born at Prescott, and the latter at Kingston. The occupation of Andrew S. Anderson was that of a builder and stockman. The subject of this sketch received his early mental training in the public schools in the vicinity of his birthplace, and remained at home until his schooling was completed. He then pursued a course of professional study in the Ontario Veterinary College, from which he was graduated in 1889, beginning the practice of veterinary surgery at Evanston in the following year.

On November 29, 1893, Mr. Anderson

was united in marriage, at Evanston, with Anna Margaret Hartray, who was born in that city, December 2, 1870. She was a daughter of James Hartray, who is one of the earlier settlers of Evanston. Of this marriage there were two children, namely: Raymond Francis, born September 11, 1894, and Ruth Helen, born January 18, 1898. The mother of these children died March 21, 1899.

In politics Mr. Anderson is an earnest supporter of the Republican party, and is active and influential in its local councils. He was elected City Treasurer of Evanston in 1905, and is still the efficient incumbent in that office. He has served in the capacity of Assistant State Veterinarian of Illinois, since 1900. In fraternal circles, the subject of this personal record is identified with the A. F. & A. M. Religiously, he is an adherent of the Episcopal faith. He is an intelligent, energetic and popular man, and a public-spirited citizen.

JAMES MILTON BARNES.

James Milton Barnes, who is one of the most prominent and favorably known citizens of Evanston, Ill., was born at Hope, Warren County, N. J., December 29, 1858, the son of Samuel and Sarah Ann (Moore) Barnes, who moved from the East, in 1860, to Rochester, Mich. The subject of this sketch received his early mental training in the public schools of Rochester, Mich., and there his childhood years were spent. He then became a pupil in the Pontiac (Mich.) High School, and after graduating from that institution, pursued a two years' course of study in the University of Michigan, at Ann Arbor. Before completing his education, Mr. Barnes applied himself to teaching, in which occupation he continued four years.

In 1883 he entered the government service, securing a position in the Appraiser's office in Chicago, where he remained five years. After leaving the government service, he went into the employ of Marshall Field & Co., in Chicago. While thus engaged he studied law and was admitted to the bar. Subsequently, he was made attorney for Marshall Field & Co., and at a later period became head of the credit and legal departments in that establishment, which position he now holds.

On December 25, 1885, Mr. Barnes was united in marriage, at Rochester, Mich., with May Curtis, who was born near that place, October 13, 1860. Two children have been born of this union, namely: Myrtie Adella, born April 22, 1887; and Alice May, born February 10, 1889. In politics, Mr. Barnes is a supporter of the Republican party, and in religion he adheres to the faith of the Methodist Episcopal Church. His business reputation is of the best, and he is regarded in Evanston as a high-minded and public-spirited citizen.

SARAH H. BRAYTON, M. D.

Dr. Sarah H. Brayton, a well known and highly respected practitioner of medicine in Evanston, Ill., is a native of Carlisle, County of Cumberland, England, where she received her elementary education in the grammar schools. Her parents came to the United States during her early girlhood and settled in the State of New York, where the daughter grew to maturity. As she approached womanhood, she conceived the idea of becoming a physician, and intent upon the belief that the avenue of her usefulness in life lay in this direction, she diligently applied herself to a course of medical study, which she continued four years. In 1875 she received the degree of M. D., and during the same year began the practice of her profession in the City of New York. In 1876 she was appointed Professor of Materia Medica and Therapeutics in the Medical College for Women in that city, in which she soon attained a high reputation. She was also signally successful in her practice, which rapidly increased. Work in that city, however, proving detrimental to her health, she was obliged to relinquish it. While on a visit of recreation to the West during a vacation period, some of her friends in Evanston urged her to resign her position in New York, which she consented to do, and after arranging her affairs in the East, settled in Evanston, and has ever since been professionally and socially popular in her adopted city, where her practice has continued to meet with exceptionally good results.

Dr. Brayton has been prominent in many important and meritorious public enterprises, especially in securing the erection of the hospital building in Evanston, which is now one of the most creditable features of the town. She is a member of the Illinois State Medical Society; the Chicago Medical Society; the American Association for the Advancement of Science; the American Public Health Association; The Fortnightly of Chicago, and the London Lyceum Club. In 1891 she was appointed a delegate by the Auxiliary Congress of the World's Columbian Exposition, to the Seventh International Congress of Hygiene and Demography, held in London, England. In 1893 she was elected Chairman of the Woman's Committee of the International Congress of Public Health, which convened with the annual session of the American Public Health Association, in Chicago, during that year. In later years in addition to her large practice, Dr. Brayton has devoted much time to the establishment of a convalescent home for women and children in Evanston. She is a member and Secretary of the Evanston Hospital Staff.

CHARLES LYMAN WAY.

Charles Lyman Way (deceased), a noted expert in iron and steel work, whose residence in Evanston, Ill., began at the time of the great Chicago fire of 1871, in which he was one of the numerous sufferers, was born in New Haven, Conn., November 7, 1818, the son of William and Betsy Way, who were natives of New England. William Way, the father, was an iron-worker by occupation, and was the first man in that line of work to conceive and carry into effect the idea of manufacturing carriage hardware for the general trade, thereby obviating the necessity of making each part as needed. Since that time this branch of manufacture has grown into vast proportions. William Way was a man of rare skill as an artisan, and was possessed of remarkable energy and strong traits of character. In religious belief he was a Methodist, and belonged to the First Methodist Church of New Haven, Conn., for more than seventy years, being a class-leader for about sixty years of that period.

The early mental training of the subject of this sketch was obtained in the public schools of his native place, and after his schooling was over, he was employed with his father in the iron works, until he acquired an intimate knowledge of that art. From 1845 to 1855, he was superintendent of Peter Cooper's rolling mills at Trenton, N. J., and in the latter year, moving to Michigan, acted in the same capacity in connection with E. B. Ward's rolling mills at Wyandotte in that State. In 1863, he located in Chicago, where he assumed the position of superintendent of the North Chicago Rolling Mills, on Clybourn Avenue. Subsequently for more than twenty years, he served in the capacity of steel expert for the Chicago & Northwestern Railway Company. He was also connected with the Pennsylvania, and other railroad companies, as steel expert.

On September 21, 1851, at Trenton, N. J., Mr. Way was united in marriage with Margaret C. Raum, who was born in that city, July 23, 1829. One child was born of this union, namely, Kate Virginia, who was born April 27, 1858, and became the wife of Roger Barrett McMullen, on June 15, 1882. In politics Mr. Way was a supporter of the Republican party. Religiously, he was reared, in the place of his birth, in accordance with the creed of the Methodist Episcopal Church, but after his marriage became connected with the Baptist denomination.

Immediately after the fire of 1871, Mr. Way, abandoning the flaming ruins of Chicago, established his home in Evanston, on October 9, 1871, and from the time of his removal until his death was regarded as one of the worthiest and most useful members of the community in which he had cast his lot under circumstances so peculiar. He was a man of exceptional purity of character and scrupulous sense of justice. It was his habit never to pass an adverse opinion on others, and if nothing good was to be said, he said nothing.

JOSEPH M. LORIMER.

Joseph M. Lorimer (deceased), who was for about ten years a well known, exceptionally useful and highly respected citizen of Evanston, Ill., was born in Pittsburg, Pa., September 6, 1891, the son of William F. and Rachael (McMasters) Lorimer, who were natives of Pennsylvania. When Joseph was five years of age, the family went to Nebraska, and after remaining there a short time, settled in Leavenworth, Kans., where William F. Lorimer was engaged in freighting to Denver. He afterwards moved to a farm in the vicinity of Leavenworth, where his home was situated during the Civil war. The father of the family and four sons served in the Union army.

When Joseph M. Lorimer was eighteen years of age he located in Chicago and, as messenger, entered the employ of Jones & Laughlin, the Pittsburg iron manufacturers, who had established a branch in Chicago some years previously. Mr. Lorimer was advanced from one grade to another, until some years before his death, when he became manager of the western department of the business. At the time of his death, which occurred August 24, 1894, he had been in the employ of Jones & Laughlin nearly twenty-five years, and had established a very high reputation as a business man. He had charge of most important interests in this connection, and was the inventor of the Lorimer column, used in structural iron work.

Mr. Lorimer established his home in Evanston in 1884, and at once became a potent factor in promoting the best interests of the city. Seldom has any man, in a residence so comparatively brief in duration, impressed his individual worth upon the hearts of his fellow citizens as strongly as did Mr. Lorimer upon the people of Evanston.

In 1876, Mr. Lorimer was united in marriage, at Waukegan, Ill., with Fannie L. Sherman, a daughter of the Hon. Alanson S. and Aurora Sherman. Mrs. Lorimer's father was the fifth Mayor of Chicago, and, at a later period, was one of the founders of Northwestern University. Mr. and Mrs. Lorimer became the parents of the following named children: Helen (Mrs. Miller), of Pittsburg, Pa.; Robert Sherman; and Joseph McMasters Lorimer.

On settling in Evanston, Mr. Lorimer took an active part in church and educational work. He was a most active and useful member of the First Congregational Church, a liberal contributor to its needs, and earnest and zealous in all branches of its work. He was a member of the official board of the church, and his Sunday school efforts were highly effective. He was one of the organizers of the Evanston Y. M. C. A. and the prime mover in infusing life and energy into its operations. A leading spirit in starting the movement to erect its building, he aided the construction with his own means, and made loans to others for the same purpose. For several years Mr. Lorimer was a member of the Evanston School Board, and as chairman of the building committee, had charge of the erection of the Lorimer School, thus named in his honor after his decease. In politics, Mr. Lorimer was a strong Republican and took a spirited part in the campaigns of his party. He was a member of the Union League Club of Chicago and a director of the State Bank of Chicago. His death was deeply deplored as an irreparable loss to the community, and his memory is warmly cherished by all who closely knew him and felt the wholesome beneficence of his life.

ALANSON FILER.

Alanson Filer, a venerable and highly esteemed citizen of Evanston, Ill., and one of the few survivors among the original settlers of the Middle West, was born in Herkimer County, N. Y., March 10, 1812, the son of Alanson and Patty (Dodge) Filer, the former born September 12, 1774, and the latter October 25, 1784. The father was a farmer by occupation. In early youth the subject of this sketch attended the public schools of his native place for a limited period only, as, being the oldest son, his services were needed to assist his father in work on the farm. After having remained at home until he was fourteen years of age, he was apprenticed to a cabinet-maker, with whom he remained four years. His mother furnished his clothing during the period of this apprenticeship, and besides his board, he received from his employer, in return for four years' service, ten cents in wages or as a present. At the end of this connection he went to Utica, Oneida County, N. Y., to serve another apprenticeship lasting until he reached his majority, when he journeyed westward to Chicago, reaching that village July 6, 1833.

On November 22, 1835, Mr. Filer moved from Chicago to Root River (now Racine), Wis., where he made his home until April, 1891, when he moved to Evanston, Ill., where he has since resided. When Mr. Filer located at Root River, Wis., that State formed a part of Michigan Territory, and he was one of the pioneers in that region. He is now probably the oldest survivor of the original settlers of Southeastern Wisconsin.

On November 16, 1834, Mr. Filer was united in marriage, at Chicago, with

Maria Pilkington Green, who was born November 28, 1809, and died in 1889. Eight children born of this union were as follows: One daughter, born in October, 1835, and who died in infancy unnamed; Mary A., born February 22, 1837; Agnes Julia, born August 9, 1840; Charles A., born March 15, 1842; Roxanna M., born March 29, 1846; Martha, born April 14, 1849; Samuel H. (date of birth unknown); and Kittie M., born September 26, 1853. The survivors of this family are Agnes Julia and Martha, whose home is at Manistee, Mich. Charles A. was killed in the first battle of Bull Run, and "Charles Filer" Post, G. A. R., at Racine, Wis., is named in his honor. On January 28, 1893, Mr. Filer was married a second time, wedding Elizabeth Crews, who was born and reared at Fairfield, Ill.

In politics, Mr. Filer was originally a Whig, but became a Republican in 1856, maintaining his association with that party until 1884, when he joined the Prohibition party. He was a member of the lower house of the Wisconsin Legislature in 1855, and served as Sergeant-at-arms of the Senate of that State in 1857. Fraternally, he belonged to the order of Good Templars in the 'fifties, and held the office of Grand Worthy Chief Templar until the disruption of the order, about the time of the Civil War. Religiously, Mr. Filer is a member of the Methodist Episcopal Church, with which he united in 1828. He was President of the Board of Trustees of the First M. E. Church in Racine, Wis., from the time its place of worship was built until his removal to Evanston, in 1891. He has lived an exceptionally long, upright and useful life, and is held in the highest esteem and veneration by all who know him.

MYRON H. BASS.

Myron H. Bass (deceased), formerly one of the most worthy and highly esteemed citizens of Evanston, Ill., was born in Williamstown, Vt., December 24, 1836, the son of Joel and Catherine Wright Bass, natives of New England, where they were derived from Colonial ancestry, Myron H. Bass being a descendant in the seventh generation from Samuel Bass, who settled in Roxbury, Mass., in 1630, and was for many years a deacon of the first church established there. Mr. Bass remained in his native place until he was 18 years of age, obtaining his early education in the public schools. His primary studies were supplemented by an academic course at Meriden, N. H. In 1855, Mr. Bass removed to Illinois, to which State two of his brothers had preceded him—Perkins Bass, who located in Chicago, and another brother, Walter B. Bass, who was engaged in farming in Will County. Mr. Bass owned and operated a farm in Kankakee County until 1870, when he moved to Chicago and engaged in the real estate business, representing many large holdings. He continued to be prominently identified with the business interests of Chicago, although he removed to Evanston in 1884, which was his home during the remainder of his life.

In 1863, he was united in marriage, in Will County, Ill., with Ann Elizabeth Kelly, a daughter of James Ward and Nancy J. Kelly. In 1834 James W. Kelly moved from Greenbrier County, Va., to Illinois, and settled in Will County. At that period, the Indians were numerous in that section of Illinois, and Mrs. Bass, who was a native of that region, has vivid recollections of many thrilling experiences of pioneer life. The surviving members of the family born to Mr. and Mrs. Bass are: George A., of Philadelphia, Pa.; Perkins B., of Evanston; Stella (Mrs. J. E. Tilt), of Chicago; and James K., of New York City.

In religious belief, Mr. Bass was a Methodist, at an early period having become a member of the Grant Place Methodist Church, of Chicago. From the time when he became a resident of Evanston until his death, on June 3, 1890, he was a communicant of the First Methodist Episcopal Church of that city, in which he officiated as one of the stewards. He was possessed of most excellent traits of character, and was a genial, kindly man, the virtues of whose daily life gained for him the affectionate esteem and confidence of all who intimately knew him.

WILLIAM MORSE GRISWOLD.

Dr. William M. Griswold, who is engaged in the practice of dentistry at No. 23, Glockengiesserwall, Hamburg, Germany, was born in St. Charles, Minn., September 26, 1871. His primary mental training was obtained in the public schools and after completing his preparatory studies in Hamline University, he took a professional course in Northwestern University Dental School, Chicago, Ill., from which he was graduated, in 1897, with the degree of D. D. S. He received the class honor of an appointment as demonstrator in this institution.

Dr. Griswold is a member of the American Dental Society of Europe, and is serving on its Executive Committee for the term extending from 1903 to 1907. That body held its Easter session of 1904 in Hamburg, through an invitation extended in 1903 by Dr. Griswold, at Mad-

rid, where he was in attendance at the meeting of the International Medical Congress. The subject of this sketch is a member of the New York Institute of Stomatology, the Congris Dentaire Internation de Paris, and was elected first honorary member of the W. D. Miller Dental Club of Berlin.

SIDNEY BACHRACH MEYER.

Sidney B. Meyer, attorney-at-law, residing at No. 1627 Grace Street, Chicago, Ill., was born in Quincy, Ill., April 13, 1879. His primary mental training was obtained in the public schools and he pursued a preparatory course of study in the North Division High School, in Chicago. In September, 1898, he matriculated in Northwestern University Law School, from which he was graduated in June, 1901, with the degree of LL. B. In 1899, 1900 and 1901, he was pitcher in the Northwestern University baseball team. Mr. Meyer is a member of the Phi Alpha Delta Fraternity, and belongs to the Hampden, Washington and Lexington Clubs. In 1900, he was President of the First Voters' Club, in Chicago, and in 1902-1903, held a like position in the 24th Ward Republican Club in that city. His law offices are at Rooms 937-945 American Trust Building, Clark and Monroe Streets, Chicago.

WILLIAM MONTELLE CARPENTER.

William M. Carpenter, First Vice-President Walworth and Neville Manufacturing Company, with residence at 2010 Sheridan Road, Evanston, was born in Wooster, Ohio, October 15, 1866, the son of Charles and Mary (Blanchard) Carpenter, both born in the State of New York, the former in 1833 and the latter in 1836. The first of the Carpenter family to come to America was William, an Englishman, who crossed the ocean on the ship "Bevis" in 1638 and settled at Rehoboth, Mass. Genealogists have traced the name as far back as John Carpenter, who was Town Clerk of the City of London, died wealthy and founded a great school in that city at the corner of the Thames Embankment and John Carpenter Street,—"The City of London Schools." Another ancestor on the paternal side was Lieutenant John Hollister, who came from England to Connecticut in 1642, and married a daughter of Hon. Richard Treat, Sr., who was one of those to whom the original Connecticut charter was issued. The first of the Blanchards was Samuel, who came early in the seventeenth century from England to Charleston, now a part of Boston, and whose descendants intermarried with many of the families of Billerica, Mass. The last of the Blanchards was Mr. Carpenter's grandfather, Capt. Walter Blanchard, who was killed at Ringgold Gap, during the Rebellion, while leading his regiment, the Thirteenth Illinois. The wife of one of the Blanchards was a Tolford, whose claim to descent from "the nobility" is at least stoutly maintained. The Daniels, another maternal family, was of North-of-Ireland-Scotch stock and settled in Vermont. Of the different branches of these ancestral families many took part in the Colonial Wars, the Revolutionary War, the War of 1812 and the War of the Rebellion.

Mr. Carpenter's father's family removed from Southern New York to the central part of the State, and his mother's family to the same locality from Massachusetts. In the 'thirties of the last century his mother came to Du Page County,

Ill., and his father some years later, and there they were married during the Civil War, while the father was at home on furlough. The father of William M. Carpenter was a school teacher and court reporter for many years, and a respected citizen of Downers Grove, where he served on various boards and as Postmaster. He made a modest success in business, and lived a clean, honorable and useful life; he was, at the same time, of strong character and kindly temperament. The mother died in 1893; in the language of Mr. Carpenter himself, she "was of all mothers the best: a strong, forceful, noble character."

The subject of this sketch spent his boyhood and early youth in a village near Chicago, where he graduated from a high school, later taking a one year's classical course in college, and in the meantime acquiring the habit of reading, with taste for an active out-door life. He then became an errand boy in a law office in Chicago at a very modest salary, utilizing his spare time in the study of shorthand. In August, 1883, he went to New York as a stenographer in the office of the Western Electric Company, a year later returning West to enter school for a year. He then entered the employment of the Western Union Telegraph Company for a year, but returned to the Western Electric Company, with which company he continued for upwards of twelve years, making steady progress. During 1906 he connected himself with the lumber company above referred to.

For some years during the 'nineties he was a member of the Downers Grove Board of Education. Besides being a member of the Sons of Veterans, he belongs to the following social organizations and fraternities: Union League and Caxton Clubs, Chicago; Bibliophile Society, Boston; Evanston Municipal Association and Evanston Club, Evanston Historical Society, Sons of American Revolution and Sons of Colonial Wars, Masonic Fraternity, Modern Woodmen of America, National Union, American Civic Association, National Geographic Society and National Credit Men's Association. He has at times been President of The Electrical Trades Association of Chicago and of the National organization.

Mr. Carpenter's business has made it necessary for him to make frequent and extensive trips over the country, and he has visited every large city from Boston to San Francisco and from New Orleans to Duluth; has also, for several years, made annual trips to Europe, one to the Hawaiian Islands and one each to Cuba and the City of Mexico and beyond, besides frequent visits to Canada. He has thus been a visitor in practically every State of the Union, and in most of the large cities of the country has a more or less extensive acquaintance. Originally a Prohibitionist in his callow days, he later came to the conclusion that real regeneration never came through law, and is now willing to be classed as a "Mugwump" with pronounced Republican proclivities.

In July, 1888, Mr. Carpenter was married, at Downers Grove, Ill., to Florrie M. Schofield, who was born in St. Louis, Mo., in 1867, and of this union two children were born, namely: Hubert Montelle, born June 12, 1889, and Mary Blanchard, born December 19, 1890. On July 27, 1898, he was married in London, England, to Lucile Russell, of Hudson, Mich., and they have one son—Russell— born June 12, 1903.

Fond of good books and fine bindings, Mr. Carpenter has gathered a library containing some choice books. For years he has had an especial liking for the writings of Eugene Field, Rudyard Kipling and Thackeray, and of neither one does he ever tire. With a taste for art, he has collected some good pictures, and has studied potteries and picked up many samples in his travels. He has been especially interested in American art pottery specimens, including Rockwood, Van Briggle, Grueby, etc. He also made many original photographs of scenery and of ancient and modern buildings and other structures met with during his travels; and has in his collection some rare specimens of old Mexican zerapes, Indian rugs and potteries, Hawaiian calabashes and the like. Mr. Carpenter regards the people of the Middle West as the "salt of the earth," and would rather live in Evanston than in any other city he has ever seen.

WILBUR WALLACE McCLEARY.

Dr. Wilbur Wallace McCleary, physician and surgeon, whose office is located at No. 257 West Forty-seventh Street, Chicago, Ill., was born in Rock Island, Ill., in 1867. In boyhood, he availed himself of the advantages afforded by the public schools of his native town, and in 1881 began a course of study in St. Mary's College, Kan., from which institution he was graduated in 1886. In that year, he matriculated in the Medical Department of Northwestern University, graduating therefrom in 1889.

The subject of this sketch is at present acting in the capacity of physician to the Provident Hospital, in Chicago. He is a member of the American Medical Association, the Illinois State Medical Society and the Chicago Medical Society. On June 30, 1895, Dr. McCleary was united in marriage with Fannie Cleage, of Chattanooga, Tenn., and one child, Josephine, has been born of this union.

JOHN H. HUNGATE.

John H. Hungate, lawyer and banker of La Harpe, Hancock County, Ill., was born in that county June 2, 1838. His early education was obtained in the public schools of his native place, and he afterwards pursued a preparatory course in Knox College and Burlington University. Subsequently he qualified himself for the legal profession by taking a course in the Law Department of Northwestern University, from which he received the degree of LL. B. He then entered upon the practice of law in St. Louis, Mo., and was thus engaged for five years. From 1864 to 1868, he held the office of Circuit Court Clerk of McDonough County, Ill., and is the author of the law requiring an index of court records.

In 1876, Mr. Hungate was the candidate of his party for Congress, but met with defeat. He assisted in organizing the Title and Trust Company of Peoria, Ill., which was afterwards consolidated with the Dime Savings Bank of that city. In 1874, he organized the bank of Hungate, Ward & Company, of which he is now sole proprietor. He is President of the Board of Trustees of Gittings Seminary at La Harpe, Ill., and President of the Board of La Harpe High School.

On May 8, 1878, Mr. Hungate was united in marriage with Florence E. Matthews, of Monmouth, Ill., and they have four children: Ward, Edith, John and Harold. In fraternal circles, Mr. Hungate is identified with the A. F. & A. M. and the I. O. O. F. He is a man of broad information and has traveled extensively in the United States and in Europe.

MASON B. LOOMIS.

Judge Mason B. Loomis (deceased), formerly a prominent citizen of Evanston, Ill., and a lawyer and jurist of distinction, was born in Harrisville, Medina County, Ohio, April 14, 1837, the son of Milo and Lucy (Greenly) Loomis, who had moved to Ohio from New York. Milo Loomis was a merchant by occupation. The first known ancestor of Judge Loomis was a Spanish gentleman, who came to this country at an early period and settled in Connecticut. Both of Judge Loomis' parents died when he was fifteen years old, and he grew to manhood under the care of a guardian. After receiving his primary education in the public schools at Lodi, Ohio, he took a supplementary course in Oberlin College. He then spent several years in Illinois, returning to Ohio in 1859 and beginning the study of law there with Bliss & McSweeney. Both of his legal preceptors passed their professional examination at the Ohio Bar, and in later years, Mr. McSweeney, who was noted as a criminal lawyer, became widely known throughout that State as the "old man eloquent." Mr. Loomis was admitted to the bar in the spring of 1861, and thereupon moved to Kankakee, Ill., where he remained nine years, meeting with signal success in his profession. In 1868, he was elected State's Attorney for the circuit comprising the counties of Livingston, Iroquois and Kankakee, for a term of four years. At the end of two years, he resigned this office and located in Chicago, where he became a member of the firm of Runyan, Avery, Loomis & Comstock. Four years later he withdrew from this firm, and formed a partnership with Judge Charles H. Wood, under the firm name of Wood

& Loomis. This connection continued until 1877, when Mr. Loomis was elected County Judge of Cook County, for a term of four years. In this office he served, however, five years, an amendment to the State Constitution having, in the meantime, extended the term one year. At the expiration of this period, he resumed the practice of law under the firm name of Needham & Loomis. At a later period this partnership was dissolved, and he became associated with his son under the firm name of M. B. and F. S. Loomis, which existed until the death of the father, when the son succeeded to the practice. Judge Loomis established his home in Evanston in 1892. and died there at his residence on Washington Street, October 2, 1902, after an attack of sickness lasting four days. In addition to the offices of Judge and State's Attorney, he served as a member of the City Council of Evanston, and in this position did much towards the advancement of the interests of the city.

In 1859, at Harrisville, Ohio, Judge Loomis was united in marriage with Nellie Ainsworth, who was a schoolmate of her husband in their youth, and who still survives him, a resident of Evanston. In politics, Mr. Loomis was an earnest advocate of the principles of the Republican party, and participated in many campaigns. Religiously, he was a member of the Second Presbyterian Church of Evanston during his residence there, having previously been connected with the Third Presbyterian Church of Chicago. Socially, he was identified with the Illinois Club (of which he was an officer), the Irving Club, of Chicago,—an old literary organization,—and the Twentieth Century Club, of Evanston. These societies, as well as the Evanston City Council, adopted appropriate memorial resolutions on the occasion of his death.

Judge Loomis was a rare wit and an incisive, forceful and convincing public speaker. He was an exceptionally able trial lawyer, and a jurist of eminent ability, making an exemplary record on the bench. The "Chicago Evening Post" reflected public opinion in regard to him by saying: "In citizenship he won high esteem. He was a thorough Chicagoan, zealous for Chicago's supremacy, and always sought to enhance its repute, municipally and commercially. Honest local government commanded his continuous interest. He was identified with many movements leading towards the city's upbuilding, and education, charity and church all found in him an ardent advocate." The Twentieth Century Club paid him this tribute: "He was not only profoundly versed in the law, but he was abreast of the best literature of the day, and conversant with the best authors of the past. His convictions were deep, and he had the courage to maintain them. His wit was of the character that provoked only mirth; it had no sting. He used this dangerous faculty so skillfully that he never inflicted a wound. Judge Loomis was a Christian gentleman. He was an active participant in the religious work of the church to which he belonged. He was genuine, upright, pure and noble, and the loss to this community of such a man is immeasurable."

WALTER L. GALLUP.

Walter L. Gallup (deceased), formerly a very energetic, prosperous and reputable citizen of Evanston, Ill., was born at Poquonock Bridge, Conn., April 2, 1852, the son of Franklin and Sarah (Burroughs) Gallup, both members of old New England families. Franklin Gallup was engaged in the fish-oil business. The early education of Walter L. Gallup was obtained in the schools of Norwich, Conn., where his childhood was passed. When he reached the age of fourteen years he entered the Bank of Norwich, in which he received his youthful business training, becoming an expert accountant. A severe attack of sickness, however, caused him to relinquish this position, and to join his father in the oil business on the coast of Maine. At a later period, he was connected with a mercantile firm in New York City. Early in the 'seventies Mr. Gallup located in Indianapolis, Ind., where he became a member of the saw-manufacturing firm of E. C. Atkins & Co., and was prominently identified with the manufacturing interests of Indianapolis until 1889, when he established himself in business in Chicago, where he was engaged in advertising enterprises until the time of his death, which occurred in Evanston, in 1894. After starting in Chicago five years previously, he had, through diligent application and superior capacity, built up an exceedingly prosperous business.

In 1874 Mr. Gallup was united in marriage at Port Jervis, N. Y., with Ella H. Hunt, a daughter of Dr. Isaac S. and Sarah (Fleming) Hunt. Mrs. Gallup's father practiced medicine successfully for many years at Port Jervis, and there his death occurred. One child resulted from the union of Mr. and Mrs. Gallup, namely, Stella (Mrs. Pickerell), of Evanston.

Mr. Gallup belonged to the First Baptist Church of Evanston, in which he was a member of the Board of Trustees, having charge of the choir, and sustaining other official responsibilities. In fraternal circles, he was identified with the Royal Arcanum. He was a man of excellent traits of character and strict probity in his business relations, and was regarded as one of the worthiest and most useful members of the community.

JOHN H. VOJE.

Dr. John H. Voje, who is engaged in the practice of medicine in Oconomowoc, Wis., and is also proprietor of Sanatorium Waldheim in that city, was born in Germany, on March 12, 1853. In 1874, he entered the Chicago Medical College, now the Medical Department of Northwestern University, from which he was graduated in 1876, with the degree of M. D., and in 1884 received another degree from the University of Leipzig, Germany. Dr. Voje founded the Sanatorium Waldheim, in Oconomowoc, August 1, 1888. He is a member of the American Medical Association, the Wisconsin State Medical Society, and the Waukesha County Medical Society.

On June 19, 1879, Dr. Voje was married to Hannah Ulrich, who has borne him two children: Hertha, born July 24, 1880, and Henry, born December 14, 1885.

CHARLES W. BARLOW, D. D. S.

Charles William Barlow, dentist, Providence, R. I., was born in St. John, N. B., Canada, May 13, 1863. His boyhood and youth were spent in the place of his nativity, where his early mental training was obtained in the public schools. He pursued a course of dental surgery in Northwestern University Dental School, Chicago, Ill., from which he graduated with the class of 1894, receiving the degree of D. D. S. He is a member of the Northwestern University Dental School Alumni

Association. The marriage of Dr. Barlow occurred August 4, 1896, at which time he was wedded to Florence A. Angell, of Providence, R. I.

_____

WINFIELD SCOTT HALL.

Winfield S. Hall, Professor of Physiology in the Northwestern University Medical School since 1895, and a resident of Berwyn, Cook County, Ill., was born in Batavia, Ill., January 5, 1861. He began his preparatory studies under private tutors in Hastings, Neb., and entered the College of Liberal Arts of Northwestern University in 1881, continuing until the fall of 1883.. From 1884 until the fall of 1886, he pursued a professional course in Northwestern University Medical School, and in 1886-87, continued his literary and scientific studies in the University. In 1887-88, he was a student in the Medical School, and he also took a course in medicine in the University of Leipzig, Germany in 1893-94, and a course in philosophy in 1894-95. He received the degree of B. S. from Northwestern University in 1887, that of M. D. in 1888, and of M. S. in 1889, from the same source. The University of Leipzig conferred upon him the degree of Dr. Med. in 1894, and those of A. M. and Ph. D. (Magna cum laude) in 1895.

While in the College of Liberal Arts in Evanston, Ill., Prof. Hall was a member of the Hinman Literary Society and the Phi Kappa Psi Fraternity. He was awarded the Marcy Botany Prize in June, 1883, and received General Scholarship Honors in 1887. He belonged to the Honorary Fraternities—Phi Beta Kappa, Sigma Xi, and Alpha Omega Alpha. During his medical course, Prof. Hall was Class President of the class of '88. He was a successful contestant for the Fowler $100-Prize in Optics, and the Ingalls $100-Prize in "Scholarship: Literary, Scientific and Professional." In 1888-89 he held an interneship in Mercy Hospital, Chicago, after a competitive examination. From 1889 to 1893, Prof. Hall was Professor of Biology in Haverford College, Pennsylvania. From 1901 to the present time he has served in the capacity of Junior Dean of the Medical Faculty of Northwestern University Medical School.

From 1902 to 1906, Prof. Hall was President of the American Medical Association for the Study of Narcotics; in 1903-04, Secretary of the Association of American Medical Colleges; in 1904-05, Chairman of the Section of Pathology and Physiology of the American Medical Association; Primarius of the Alpha Omega Alpha, Honorary Fraternity, 1903 to date; and President of the American Academy of Medicine, 1905. He is now a Fellow of the American Academy of Science, a member of the American Association for the Advancement of Science, a Fellow of the Chicago Academy of Sciences, a member of the American Medical Association, the American Physiological Society, the Chicago Medical Society, etc., etc. He is also the author of several important contributions to medical literature in the form of volumes familiar to the profession.

On October 11, 1888, the subject of this sketch was united in marriage at Juniata, Neb., with Jeannette Winter, of Princeton, Ill., and they became the parents of the following named children: Ethel, born October 22, 1893; Albert Winter, born January 8, 1895; Reymond Ludwig, born January 20, 1897; and Muriel, born August 11, 1902.

ASAHEL O. BASSETT.

Asahel O. Bassett (deceased), formerly one of the most substantial and prominent citizens of Evanston, Ill., was born in Delhi, Delaware County, N. Y., January 2, 1837, the son of Hon. Cornelius Bassett, who was an extensive farmer, and owner of a fine country residence, and at one time a member of the New York Legislature. The Bassett family was of English extraction, and settled at an early period in Martha's Vineyard.

Asahel O. Bassett received his early training partly in the public schools of New York State and partly in Illinois. He grew up on his father's farm until he was about ten years of age, when his mother having died, he accompanied his uncle, Reuben Coffin, to Illinois, the family locating at Buffalo Grove, Ogle County. After remaining there two years, the family came to Chicago, and, on the trip, Mr. Bassett had a good opportunity of observing pioneer life in that section of the State from which the farmers were accustomed to haul their grain to Chicago by team. In 1849, Mr. Bassett went to New York City, where he remained five years, and was there trained to the grocery business. Thence he went to Tarrytown, N. Y., where he was first engaged in that line of trade on his own responsibility. At a later period he embarked in the manufacturing business, but shortly after his marriage, took charge of the large estate of his wife's father, who was an extensive land-owner at Tarrytown.

After living about ten years at Tarrytown, Mr. Bassett moved to Chicago, where he engaged in the plumbing and gas-fitting business. He suffered heavy loss by the fire of 1871, but at once resumed operations, and afterwards conducted a large business on the Methodist Church Block. Subsequently withdrawing from the plumbing trade, he embarked in the manufacture of picture mouldings and frames on a large scale, employing about 100 men, and shipping his product throughout the United States. In this connection he suffered further losses by fire, when he turned his attention to the lumber trade, in which he was engaged until his retirement from active business, a few years before his death. Mr. Bassett was always a very active and energetic business man, and maintained a wide acquaintance.

In 1859, Mr. Bassett was united in marriage, at Tarrytown, N. Y., with Nancy B. Decker. Her father, William J. Decker, was in early life a shipbuilder in New York City, but subsequently became an extensive landowner in Westchester County, N. Y. The Deckers were an old Knickerbocker family, and were also akin to the Bayles and Storm families, ancestors of Mrs. Bassett on the maternal side. Mrs. Bassett was born in New York City, but spent her youth in the Tarrytown home, which is located amid historic surroundings. It is within four miles of White Plains, a famous battlefield of the Revolutionary War. At Tarrytown, the noted British spy, Major Andre, was captured, a member of the family of Mrs. Bassett's mother having taken part in the capture. Within a mile of the Tarrytown home stood the headquarters occupied by Washington during a portion of the struggle for Independence. Of the Decker estate Mrs. Bassett is still part owner. In the vicinity are the summer homes of John D. Rockefeller, Edwin Gould, Helen Gould and other noted people. Mrs. Bassett's mother, who died at the old home in 1902, was born in the same vicinity on the Holland estate, afterwards the property of Cyrus W. Field.

Mr. and Mrs. Bassett became the parents of the following named children: William D., of Loveland, Colo.; George, who is connected with the First National Bank of Chicago; Etta (Mrs. Dr. Freeman), of Evanston; Harriet, wife of Harry H. Mallory, of Evanston; and Emma, who married Vernon S. Watson, of Oak Park, Ill.

In 1882, Mr. Bassett established his home in Evanston, purchasing a residence at No. 1124 Asbury Avenue. His home, which then stood almost alone, is now in a compactly built portion of the city. It was there that he departed this life on February 4, 1902.

In religious belief, Mr. Bassett was a Baptist, and for 18 years officiated as deacon of the First Baptist Church of Evanston. In fraternal circles, he was identified with the Royal Arcanum. He was devotedly attached to the home circle, and his domestic life was exceedingly pleasant. Although quiet and unassuming in demeanor, he was a man of genial, amiable nature and winsome disposition, and won many friends. In life he was cordially esteemed, and his death was deeply lamented.

THOMAS H. WATSON.

Thomas H. Watson (deceased), long and favorably known in connection with the wholesale grocery interests of Chicago for a period of thirty-five years and a prominent and highly esteemed citizen of Evanston, Ill., was born in a Quaker settlement called "The Union," fourteen miles from Plattsburg, N. Y., April 7, 1843. He was a son of Judge Thomas B. and Harriet E. (Powers) Watson, natives of New York.

Judge Watson was of English extraction and was reared in the Quaker faith. He was a lawyer of high reputation, and served on the judicial bench of New York for a number of years.

Thomas H. Watson passed his early youth in Plattsburg, N. Y., where he made diligent use of the opportunities afforded by the public schools. When seventeen years of age he located in Chicago, where his uncle, Heman G. Powers, was then established in business, as junior member of the firm of Durand & Powers. The head of the firm, Henry Durand, was a pioneer merchant of Chicago. Mr. Watson entered the employ of this firm as a clerk, and continued in that capacity until 1862, when he entered the Union Army as a member of the famous Board of Trade Battery, of Chicago, in which he served until near the close of the war. On his discharge from the service he returned to Chicago, and resumed his connection with Durand & Powers, remaining with this firm and its successors until 1879, when he became associated with the extensive wholesale grocery house of Franklin Mac-Veagh & Company. At different times he traveled extensively in the interest of this firm, and became widely known as a salesman. He was a close student of everything pertaining to the grocery trade, and gained a reputation throughout the West as one of the best informed men in the country, in that line of business.

Mr. Watson was especially prominent as a sugar expert, and for many years had entire charge of the sugar purchases of Franklin MacVeagh & Co., amounting to hundreds of thousands of dollars a year. He was also a leading member of the National Association of Wholesale Grocers, and served as the Committeeman of that organization charged with special attention to the sugar trade, until within ten months of his death. He was very active in business, bearing heavy responsibilities, and conducting large transactions.

In 1862, at Kankakee, Ill., Mr. Watson was united in marriage with Mary P. Hickox, a daughter of John R. Hickox, a well known member of the Bar of Illinois. Mrs. Watson was born at Dansville, Livingston County, N. Y., and spent the years of her girlhood in Syracuse, that State. In 1860 she moved from New York to Illinois, the journey westward being deeply impressed upon her memory by the fact that it was made in company with the New York delegates to the Republican National Convention held in Chicago, which nominated Abraham Lincoln for the Presidency. Mr. and Mrs. Watson became the parents of four children, as follows: Emma (Mrs. Knight), of Chicago; Thomas W., of Decatur, Ill.; Alice (Mrs. Jackson), and Ednah (Mrs. Russell), of Evanston.

Mr. Watson established his home in Evanston in 1869, and during the early years of his residence there was a member of the Board of Trustees of South Evanston and also a member of the School Board. He was an attendant at the services of the Congregational Church. His death occurred at Evanston, July 28, 1904.

He was regarded as one of the most worthy and useful members of the community, and his estimable widow is held in the highest regard by a wide circle of friends.

ISAAC R. HITT, Jr.

Isaac Reynolds Hitt, Jr., residing in Washington D. C., was born in Chicago, Ill., September 7, 1864. Mr. Hitt's childhood was spent in the city of his birth.

In 1871 his parents moved to Evanston, Ill., and there the subject of this sketch lived until 1898. Since February 1, of that year, he has been a resident of Washington, D. C., where his home is at No. 1334 Columbia Road. The primary mental training of Mr. Hitt was received in the public schools of Evanston, Ill., and he afterwards became a pupil in the Preparatory School of Northwestern University, graduating therefrom in 1883. He was graduated from Northwestern University with the class of 1888, receiving the degree of B. S., that of M. S., being conferred upon him by his alma mater in 1894, the year of his graduation from the Kent Law School, now Lake Forest University Law School.

During his preparatory course, Mr. Hitt belonged to the Euphonia Literary Society, and was Captain of the Football Eleven. In the University he was President of the Hinman Literary Society, and Captain of the University Football Eleven. While in that institution, he was one of the reorganizers of the Illinois Alpha Chapter of the Phi Delta Theta Fraternity, later Province President, and in 1891-93 was in the General Council of that fraternity. He participated in the "Hinman Essay Contest," acted in the capacity of business manager of "The Northwestern" (Magazine); served on the board of business managers of the "Syllabus;" and was one of the four organizers of the "University Press." Since making his home in Washington, D. C., Mr. Hitt has been, since its organization and is still, a member of the Council of the University Club, President of the Northwestern Alumni Club, and re-organizer of the Phi Delta Theta Alumni Club.

From 1898 to 1902 Mr. Hitt held the position of Law Clerk in the Law Division of the Internal Revenue Bureau in the Treasury Department, and became Chief of the Miscellaneous Division of that Department in the latter year. He is President of the Illinois Republican Association of the District of Columbia, and is President of the Board of Trustees of the Calvary Methodist Episcopal Church of Washington, D. C. He compiled the Internal Revenue Laws in 1900, and the Legal Tax Laws and Decisions. He is a member of the Bar of the United States Supreme Court, the Court of Claims, and Supreme Court and Court of Appeals of the District of Columbia.

On November 13, 1889, at Logansport, Ind., Mr. Hitt was united in marriage with Rosa May Birch (N. W. U. Ex. '87). Four children are the offspring of this union, namely: Ruth Emma, born October 8, 1890; Leila Birch, born July 29, 1892; William Birch, born July 17, 1895; and Isaac Reynolds, III., born June 7, 1901.

CARL ELLSWORTH BLACK, A. M., M. D.

Dr. Carl E. Black, physician and surgeon who is engaged in the practice of his profession in Jacksonville, Ill., was born in Winchester, Ill., July 4, 1862, the son of Green V. and Jane (Cohenour) Black, of whom the former is Dean of the Dental Department of Northwestern University. In boyhood the subject of this sketch received his primary mental training in the public schools of his native place, and graduated from the High School in 1881. He then entered Illinois College, from which he received the degree of B. S. in 1883. In 1887, he graduated from Northwestern University Medical School with the degree of M. D., afterwards pursuing post-graduate courses of medical study in New York City and Vienna. In 1903, the degree of A. M. was conferred upon him by Illinois College. He was awarded the prize for the best essay on the "Principle and Practice of Operative Surgery," and the Stephen Smith prize, inscribed by Dr. N. S. Davis, for the best Inaugural Thesis submitted to the faculty of the Chicago Medical College of Northwestern University, by the graduate class of 1887.

Since his graduation, Dr. Black has been engaged in practice in Jacksonville, and for a number of years his attention has been devoted almost exclusively to surgery. Dr. Black is a member of the American Medical Association; The Illinois State Medical Society, of which he was Chairman of the Legislative Committee from 1900 to 1903; Counsellor for the Sixth District, President in 1903-4, and Chairman of the Council in 1906-7, of the Mississippi Valley Medical Society; the Western Illinois Medical and Surgical Society, the Morgan County Medical Society, and the Jacksonville Medical Club. From 1896 to 1902, he was editor of the Morgan County "Medical Journal;" and, in 1903-06, was Chairman of the Committee managing the "Illinois Medical Journal," is also associate editor of the "Medical Fortnightly." He is a member of the Jacksonville Literary Union, President of the Morgan County Historical Society, a Trustee of Illinois College, a director of the Jacksonville Public Library and Vice-President and acting President of the Illinois State Library Association, 1905-06.

On June 12, 1899, the subject of this sketch was united in marriage, at Jacksonville, Ill., with Bessie McLaughlin, and four children have been born of this union: Kirby Vaughn, Carl Ellsworth, Dorothy Lawrence, and Marjorie Vauderman.

PROF. OSCAR OLDBERG.

Prof. Oscar Oldberg, a prominent pharmacist of Chicago, was born in Alfta, Helsingland, Sweden, January 22, 1846, the son of Andrew and Fredrika (Ohrstromer) Oldberg, both of whom were also natives of that country, the former born in 1804, and the latter, in 1808. Andrew Oldberg was a man of superior intellect and fine attainments. He was an author of note, and had a high reputation as an educator. In religious belief, he was an adherent of the Lutheran Church. He received his education in the University of Upsala, and for many years was the head of Prince Oscar's School, a connection which was terminated in 1845. In that year he was appointed rector of the Parish of Alfta. There, in 1866, he departed this life. His wife passed away in 1882.

Oscar Oldberg was the seventh of nine children. In early youth he made diligent use of the opportunities for mental training afforded by the public schools in the vicinity of his home, and afterwards pursued a course of study in the Gymnasium of Gefle, Sweden. His education was obtained to a considerable extent, however, through instruction received from private tutors. He was reared at Alfta on the Woxna River, where his childhood was passed among the mountains. During the period when he was approaching manhood he devoted considerable attention to music, having experienced throughout his juvenile years a strong inclination for that art. In 1861 he secured a position in the drug store of Sir. F. W. Helleday, at Falun, Sweden, and continued in the employ of that gentleman until 1865. At that period he became a licensed pharmacist, and during the same year left his native country and made his home in the United States,

locating in New York, where he spent two years engaged in his chosen profession. In 1882 he moved to Chicago.

Prof. Oldberg is a member of the American Pharmaceutical Association; the A. A. A. S.; the A. Chemical Society; the American Metrological Society; the National Geographic Society; and the Chemical Society, of Germany.

On May 17, 1873, at Youngstown, Ohio, the subject of this sketch was united in marriage with Emma Paritt, who was born at Atwater, in that State, and underwent her early mental culture in the Ohio schools. Three children resulted from this union, namely: Arne, a composer of music, born July 12, 1874; Olga, born April 16, 1876; and Virgil, a mechanical engineer, born December 17, 1877.

In political sentiment, Prof. Oldberg is an Independent Republican, and in religious belief, accepts the faith of the New Jerusalem (Swedenborgian) Church.

WILLIAM NEWELL BRAINARD.

Capt. William N. Brainard (deceased), for many years one of the most prominent citizens of Evanston, Cook County, Ill., was born in De Ruyter, Madison County, N. Y., January 7, 1823. He came of an old New England family, the earliest known representative of which was Daniel Brainard, who was brought to America when eight years of age, sometime after the landing of the Pilgrims. He became one of the proprietors of Haddam, Conn., where he settled in 1662, having previously lived in the Colony at Hartford. The maiden name of Captain Brainard's mother was Sally Gage, who was born in Dutchess County, N. Y., and the Captain's grandmother, on the maternal side, when a child, witnessed the tragic massacre at Wyoming, Pennsylvania, in which two of her brothers were killed. Another brother, who reached the age of one hundred years, was a soldier of the Revolutionary War. The father of Captain Brainard was Jonathan Brainard, who moved from New York to Painesville, Ohio, in 1831, but returned to New York a year later, where he was engaged in farming until his death.

Captain Brainard spent his boyhood on his father's farm, obtaining his education in the public schools and at the De Ruyter Institute. He began teaching when eighteen years of age, read law for a time and afterwards went to Rome, N. Y., where he was engaged in the forwarding and shipping business for five years. In 1850 he sailed from New York on the Pacific mailship, Georgia, from which he landed at Chagres, on the way to California, in company with nine others going to Gorgona on the Chagres River, by canoe, rowed by five naked natives, and thence to Panama, the baggage being carried on pack mules. From there he went by vessel to San Francisco, which he reached in the following December. After mining for a time on the North Fork of the American River, he went into the express and produce business at Sacramento, in which he continued until 1857. While living in Sacramento, he was elected city treasurer, and held that office during the formative period of the town.

In 1853, Captain Brainard returned east as far as Illinois, and became interested with others in fitting out a wagon train, which convoyed a herd of cattle across the plains to California. Then continuing his journey eastward to Syracuse, N. Y., on May 4, 1853, he was married to Malinda B. Coley, at her home in Syracuse, when they sailed together for California, and Mrs. Brainard shared with her husband the thrilling experiences of pioneer life there until 1857. During his residence in California, Mr. Brainard served as Captain of a company of Vigilants, and thereby gained the title which clung to him through life.

In 1857, Captain Brainard returned to his native State, and, after spending a year in Syracuse, moved to Chicago, where he became a member of the Board of Trade, engaging in the produce business, in which he continued until his death. In 1863, he made a trip to Pike's Peak. He served one term as President of the Chicago Board of Trade, and was acting President of that organization in 1872. He also filled a number of important official positions at different times. These included membership on the Board of Commissioners of the Illinois and Michigan Canal, by appointment of Gov. Beveridge, from 1873 to 1877, and as a member of the Railroad and Warehouse Commission, by appointment of Gov. Hamilton, from 1883 to 1885. From 1885 until 1893 he served on the Board of Trade committee for the inspection of grain.

In 1866, Captain Brainard established his home in Evanston, where he was a leading citizen during the remainder of his life. He served as a member of the Village Board and as Town Collector. In politics, he was a supporter of the Republican party, and fraternally, was a member of the I. O. O. F. and the California Pioneers' Association. His death occurred May 19, 1894.

Mrs. Brainard, who survives her husband, is a daughter of Col. George and Hulda (Norton) Coley, of Chenango County, N. Y., and her grandfather was a quartermaster during the Revolutionary War, under Washington. Besides Mrs. Brainard, the only member of this family living in 1905, was her daughter, Mrs. Frances Marian Belknap. A son, William Valejo Brainard, died in 1887, and a daughter, Hattie Belle, died in childhood.

JOHN R. WOODBRIDGE.

John R. Woodbridge (deceased), well-known in business circles of Chicago and throughout the West as merchant and manufacturer, and for some years before his death a resident of Evanston, Ill., was born at Fort Recovery, Ind., August 16, 1851, the son of Ebenezer and Eliza (Ripley) Woodbridge, and a descendant of Rev. John Woodbridge, who came from England and settled at Newberry, Mass., in 1683. Through its English ancestry, the lineage of the family is traced to King Henry I. of France.

When he was four years of age, and when Illinois was still regarded as a part of the "Far West," Mr. Woodbridge's parents removed to Lee Center in this State, and the son passed the years of his boyhood at that place, receiving the mental training in the public schools and at Lee Center Academy, which fitted him for a successful business career. Leaving home when he was seventeen years of age, he came to Chicago and obtained his first employment in the Methodist Book Concern—then, as now, one of the great church publishing houses in the West and a powerful agency in advancing church interests. In this institution he was well trained morally, religiously and industrially, and developed early into a capable man of affairs. After serving the Book Concern for several years, winning the approbation and gaining the high regard of those with whom in this connection he was brought into contact, severing his connection with the publishing concern, he engaged in business on his own account, becoming junior member of the firm of Eldredge & Woodbridge, pioneers in the manufacture of men's furnishing goods in the West. A few years after they began business Mr. Eldredge died, and thereafter

Mr. Woodbridge conducted the enterprise which they had founded under the firm name of Woodbridge & Co., building up a commercial house of high character and constantly expanding trade. In later years he conducted in connection with his factory a large laundry, located on the "West Side" in Chicago, and also operated salesrooms at 100 Madison Street. In the trade with which he was identified he became widely known throughout the West, and no business house in the city had a higher standing among its patrons. Those who knew him as a man of affairs esteemed him alike for his sterling integrity, his correct business methods and his uniform courtesy and fairness in all of his dealings. He had broad capacity for the conduct of business, was intensely active and energetic, and, all in all, was a fine type of the self-made western business man. In 1892 he came to Evanston to live and soon became a favorite in social and club circles by reason of his geniality, his kindliness and many lovable traits of character. A man of charming personality, he drew about him a large circle of devoted friends, to whom his death, on the 21st day of March, 1901, brought a deep sense of personal bereavement. He was a Methodist in religious belief and a leading member of the Emmanuel Church of Evanston, taking a deep interest in the upbuilding of the church and the advancement of its interests. When his business cares were laid aside, he found his favorite recreation from time to time in hunting and other out-door sports; was an active and leading spirit in the Evanston Gun Club and the Masonic Order, and also a member of the Evanston Club.

Mr. Woodbridge was first married, in 1872, to Mary H. Grannis, daughter of Amos Grannis of Chicago. She died in 1884, leaving two daughters, Anna May and Mary Grannis Woodbridge. In 1887 he married Miss Georgia E. Tanner, daughter of Charles Tanner of Chicago, who survives her husband, residing at the family homestead on Asbury Avenue. Their children are Helen Louise and John R. Woodbridge, Jr.

MARY BOYD LINDSAY.

Mary B. Lindsay, Librarian Evanston Public Library, was born in Peoria, Ill., the daughter of James Columbus and Sarah M. (Dinwiddie) Lindsay—the former born at McConnellsburg, Pa., June 20, 1829, and the latter at Gettysburg, Pa., November 3, 1834. The families of both parents became early settlers in Peoria, Ill. but in 1903 removed to Evanston.

Hugh Dinwiddie, the great-great-grand-father of Miss Lindsay on the maternal side, served as Captain in the York (Pa.) "Associators" during the Indian War, and was also a soldier of the Revolution, serving first as Major, and later as Lieutenant-Colonel, and dying in the service. Another ancestor on the same side, Henry Black, served in the American Revolution as Captain of a company of "Rangers."

Miss Lindsay was educated in the Peoria High School and in the New York State Library School, at Albany, in that State, and later taught one year in the Peoria public schools and a year in the Pettingill Seminary of that city. She also was connected with the Peoria Public Library for a time until 1894, when she came to Evanston to accept the position of Librarian of the Free Public Library of that city, which she has continued to occupy to the present time. In July, 1905, she was chosen Secretary of the Evanston Public Library, which position she still retains. She was President of the State Library Association for the year 1905-06. Her religious affiliations are with the First Presbyterian Church of Evanston. Miss Lindsay's long identification with library work, and her continuous reten-. tion of the position which she has occupied for the past twelve years, as well as the growth of the Evanston Library under her administration, attest the value of the service she has rendered in her chosen field of labor to the city of Evanston.

EDGAR OVET BLAKE.

Edgar Ovet Blake, whose reputation as a skillful architect has been thoroughly established during the successful pursuit of that profession in Evanston, Ill., was born in Evanston, July 22, 1866. The place of his birth is near the property now known as Number 1632, Chicago Avenue, Evanston. Mr. Blake is a son of Wallace Hoyt and Lucena Mariette (Herrick) Blake, the former born in Williston, Vt., and the latter a native of Watertown. N. Y. For many years the occupation of Wallace Hoyt was that of a wholesale grocery salesman, but he is at present living in retirement in Colorado. The mother of the subject of this sketch passed away in 1885. In 1870, the family moved to South Evanston, and were among the earliest settlers in the vicinity where they located. Mr. Blake's ancestry on the paternal side is traceable in America to the year 1700, when this branch of the family settled in Wrentham, Mass., where from that period its successive generations have continued to own and occupy land. On the maternal side, Mr. Blake is descended in a direct line from Edward Winslow, who landed from the Mayflower at Plymouth Rock. in 1620.

In early youth. Mr. Blake made diligent

use of the opportunities for mental training afforded by the South Evanston public school, and supplemented his elementary studies by attending the Evanston High School.

In 1881, he entered the employ of John M. Van Osdel, of Chicago, who was then one of the most prominent and successful architects of the West. This period marked the inception of Chicago's modern architecture, and in the year last mentioned, the Board of Trade Building and the John V. Farwell warehouse in that city, were erected. On the plans for the latter building, Mr. Blake assisted as office boy. When he left Mr. Van Osdel's employ, Mr. Blake became a pupil in the Art Institute of Chicago, where he remained until he went to Europe, finishing his architectual studies in Paris. With the exception of the period thus spent abroad, Mr. Blake has spent his entire life in Evanston and its vicinity. On returning from Europe, he was employed in the architect's office of the World's Columbian Exposition in Chicago, and worked on the plans of the famous buildings included in that memorable enterprise. During the six months of its continuance he had abundant leisure to attend the "World's Fair Congresses" on religious and economic questions, and there began the course of investigation which resulted in his present attitude in public affairs. Together with many others, he was affected by the financial depression which followed the termination of the great Exposition in 1893. In 1896, he applied himself to his chosen work in Evanston, and has since confined himself closely to the practice of architecture, making it a special point to attend personally (as a craftsman) to his work, as far as possible.

He has furnished plans for a number of business buildings and several fine apartment buildings in Evanston, beside a few churches in the neigboring towns. His specialty, however, has been along the line of moderate-priced residences, of which he has designed about 200, mainly in Evanston. Of these, quite a number were built for members of the Northwestern University staff of professors.

On November 13, 1890, Mr. Blake was united in marriage at Evanston with Annie Elizabeth Bradley, who was born in Nottingham, England, April 15, 1866. Two children have been born to Mr. and Mrs. Blake, namely: Marion Lucena, born October 18, 1891, and Eleanor Elizabeth, born June 16, 1896.

In religious association the subject of this sketch is identified with the Methodist Episcopal Church, and formerly was quite active in church work, and in the work of the Epworth League. During the past ten years, however, his attention has been almost entirely devoted to his professional and domestic duties. Politically, Mr. Blake was formerly a Republican, casting his first vote for Benjamin Harrison in 1888. In 1896, he became a Socialist, as the ultimate result of his study of sociological and economic problems, at the World's Fair Congress of 1893. Aside from his chosen occupation, he has always taken an interest in music, but never made a special study of that art. In 1890, during his absence in Europe, already mentioned, he visited the important points of interest in England, France and Italy. His professional reputation rests securely on the work that he has wrought, which amply attests his ability and skill as an architect.

JOHN JAY SHUTTERLY.

John Jay Shutterly (deceased), who established his home in Evanston in 1880, was one of its most active and progressive citizens. He was born in Philadelphia, Pa., July 14, 1826, and reared in the village of Carmichael, near Pittsburg, Pa. He received his education at Greene Academy and Jefferson College, Canonsburg, Pa. From the latter institution (now Washington and Jefferson College), he was graduated in 1857.

Mr. Shutterly began business in Pittsburg as a wholesale grocer, and subsequently engaged in real estate operations. For years he managed large realty interests for Dr. Hostetter, of "Hostetter Bitters" fame. In 1877 he came to Chicago, where he continued in the real estate business on an extensive scale for a long period. In 1881 he built fifty houses west of Deering, and later, thirty-six flat buildings on the "South Side." He also did some building in Evanston. In 1901 he retired to a small fruit farm in the vicinity of St. Joseph, Mich., where he died October 25, 1904.

Mr. Shutterly was a member of the Charleston Democratic National Convention of 1860.

During the Civil War, he recruited and assisted in equipping a company for the Fourteenth Regiment Pennsylvania Volunteer Cavalry, of which he was commissioned as captain. He participated in many of the principal battles of the war, including that of Gettysburg, and was for many years afterwards a member of John A. Logan Post, G. A. R., of Evanston. He married Ella Gillis of Canonsburg, Pa., and they had two sons, Eugene E. and John J., Jr., and two daughters, Mary and Lillie H.

Mr. Shutterly was a consistent Christian and was very active in church work. He was one of the founders of Emmanuel Methodist Episcopal Church of Evanston, in which he served on the building committee, as a member of the official board, leader of the Bible class, etc. As a biblical scholar

he acquired considerable reputation, and was a famous Chautauquan, having graduated with the highest number of points ever credited to a graduate up to that period. Twenty seals were awarded to him, each representing a special course of study. He was a man of uncommon mental vigor and untiring energy.

EUGENE E. SHUTTERLY.

Eugene E. Shutterly, M. D., a well-known physician of Evanston, son of John Jay Shutterly, subject of the foregoing sketch, was born in Canonsburg, Pennsylvania, January 2, 1861. He received his early mental training in the schools of Pittsburg and completed his education at Northwestern Academy. In 1888, he was graduated from the Hahnemann Medical College, Chicago, began practice of medicine in 1889, and has since gained an enviable standing in the profession. He has been a member of the staff of Evanston Hospital since the institution was founded, and has served as Health Commissioner of the city.

Dr. Shutterly was married in 1888 to Nettie Rugg, of New Lenox, Ill., who died in 1890. In 1897 he married Elizabeth Miller, of Louisville, as his second wife. He is a member of the First Presbyterian Church of Evanston.

JAMES HENRY RAYMOND.

James H. Raymond, patent lawyer, whose office is located at No. 1515 Monadnock Building, Chicago, Ill., and who resides at No. 2148 Sherman Avenue, Evanston, Ill., was born in Wilbraham, Mass., June 6, 1850. He is a son of Rev. Miner Raymond, D. D., LL. D., and Elizabeth (Henderson) Raymond. After finishing his primary studies in the public schools of his native place, Mr. Raymond became a pupil in Wesleyan Academy, at Wilbraham, Mass., and in September, 1864, entered Northwestern University at Evanston. He graduated from the College of Liberal Arts in 1871, and from the Law School of the University (then the Union College of Law) in 1875. In 1871 he received the degree of A. B., in 1873, that of A. M., and in 1875, that of LL. B. During his undergraduate period, he was a member of the Hinman Literary Society and the Phi Gamma Delta Fraternity, and won every prize contest which was open to him, with two exceptions. These were the contest for the Hinman Essay prize, from which he was debarred by sickness; and the Blanchard (now Kirk) oratorical contest, on which occasion for certain reasons the prize was divided between Mr. Raymond and E. R. Schrader of the Class of '71, by a divided vote of the faculty.

Mr. Raymond was admitted to the bar in 1875 and now devotes his attention, chiefly, to the specialties of patents, copyrights, trade-marks and corporations. From April 15, 1874, to November 21, 1884, under the title of "Secretary and Treasurer," he served in the capacity of actuary of the Western Railroad Association, a bureau of 103 railroad companies, organized for the purpose of investigating and adjusting all claims for the infringement of patents in use by them, and defending all patent suits brought against members of the association. Mr. Raymond was formerly a member of the firm of Raymond & Veeder, and subsequently, of that of Raymond & Omohundro; the present firm style is Raymond & Barnett.

Mr. Raymond is a member of the American Bar Association, having been for one term President of its section on patents, trade-marks and copyrights; of the Illinois State Bar Association; the Chicago Bar Association; the Chicago Law Institute; and the Chicago Patent Law Association, of which he was the founder and second President. In non-professional relations, he is an associate member of the American Society of Mechanical Engineers; a member of the Master Car Builders' Association and of the Railway Master Mechanics' Association.

In civic connection, he is a member of the Municipal Association of Evanston, and socially, he belongs to the Union League Club of Chicago and to the Evanston Club. For twelve years he has been a Trustee of the Northwestern University, and a member of the Board's Executive Committee; is also a director in many private corporations.

On October 13, 1874, Mr. Raymond was united in marriage, in Springfield, Ill., with Mary S. Edwards, a daughter of Hon. Benjamin Stephenson Edwards and wife of that city. Mr. and Mrs. Raymond have had four children born to them, namely: Edwards F., of Evanston; Elizabeth (Mrs. Frederick C. Woodward), of Evanston; Helena Van Wycke (Mrs. A. R. Carman), of Argyle, Ill., and Miner, a student in Northwestern University College of Liberal Arts, of the Class of 1907.

Politically, Mr. Raymond is a Sound-Money Democrat. In 1871-73, he was Secretary of the first Railroad and Warehouse Commission of Illinois. Religiously, he is a Methodist, and has been a member of the First Methodist Church of Evanston since 1865. In fraternal circles, he is identified with the A. F. & A. M., in which order he is a Knight Templar.

NATHAN SMITH DAVIS, JR., M. D.

Dr. Nathan Smith Davis, Jr., physician of Chicago, Ill., was born in that city, September 5, 1858, the son of Dr. Nathan S. and Anna M. (Parker) Davis, and a grandson of Dow Davis. His father was, for many years, one of the most conspicuous figures in the medical profession. Dr. Nathan Smith Davis, Jr., obtained his primary education in the schools of Chicago, and then pursued a literary course in Northwestern University, from which he was graduated in 1880, with the degree of A. B., receiving that of A. M. from the same source three years later. While an undergraduate, he was a member of the Hinman Literary Society and the Sigma Chi and Phi Beta Kappa Fraternities. On leaving the university, he began the study of medicine with his father, in Chicago, and took three successive courses of medical lectures in Chicago Medical College, which now constitutes the Medical School of Northwestern University. From this institution he was graduated in 1883. In that year he entered upon the practice of his profession in Chicago, where he has lived ever since. Dr. Davis took post-graduate courses in Heidelberg, Germany, and Vienna, Austria, in 1885.

In 1884, Dr. Davis became Associate Professor of Pathology in Northwestern University Medical College, and in 1886, was made Professor of the Principles and Practice of Medicine, and of Clinical Medicine. At a later period he became Secretary, and subsequently Dean, of that institution. In 1884 he was chosen physician to Mercy Hospital in Chicago. Dr. Davis was a member of the general business committee and more recently of the council and judicial council of the American Medical Association, having previously been Secretary of the Section of Practice and Chairman of the Section of Therapeutics in that body. He was a member of the Council of the Section of Pathology in the Ninth International Medical Congress, and of the Council of the Section of Practice in the Pan-American Medical Congress. In 1893, he was Chairman of the Section of Practice in the Illinois State Medical Society. Besides the American Medical Association and the Illinois State Medical Society, Dr. Davis is a member of the American Academy of Medicine, the American Climatological Association, the American Therapeutical Association, the American Tuberculosis, the Chicago Pathological Society, the Chicago Neurological Society, the Chicago Medical Society, the Chicago Medico-Legal Society and the Illinois State Microscopical Society. Of non-professional official relations, the doctor is a Trustee of Northwestern University, and formerly a member of the General Board of Management of the Y. M. C. A. of Chicago. He is also a member of the Chicago Academy of Sciences and the Chicago Literary Club, Chicago Art Institute and Chicago Historical Society. The subject of this sketch is the author of several medical works of high repute, among which are volumes entitled, "Consumption: How to Prevent it and How to Live with it"; "Diseases of the Lungs, Heart and Kidneys"; and "Diet in Health and Disease."

On April 16, 1884, Dr. Davis was united in marriage, at Madison, Wis., with Jessie B. Hopkins, a daughter of the late Judge Hopkins, of that city. Four children have resulted from this union, three of whom are living, namely: Nathan Smith Davis III.; Ruth Davis, and William Deering Davis.

REV. HUGH P. SMYTH.

Rev. Hugh P. Smyth, pastor St. Mary's Roman Catholic Church, Evanston, Ill., was born a little over fifty years ago in County Cavan, Ireland, attended college at All Hallows, Dublin and was ordained to the priesthood in 1881. He then came to America and, soon after arriving in New York, came to Chicago, and became assistant pastor of the Church of the Nativity, at Union Avenue and Thirty-seventh Street, retaining this position nine years. His first charge was as pastor of St. Patrick's Church at Lemont, where he remained two years, when he was called to the rectorship of St. Mary's Church in Evanston, being appointed to this position by Archbishop Feehan, and taking charge of the parish on May 6, 1893, which position he has retained continuously to the present time. (See "Catholic Churches," Evanston, in chapter on churches in the historic portion of this volume.)

In the thirteen years of Father Smyth's connection with St. Mary's Church it has greatly increased in the number of its communicants, the church property has been greatly improved, and he has acquired a wide popularity among all classes of citizens. The parochial school erected during this period at a cost of $70,000 is capable of accommodating a large body of pupils and the church membership has nearly doubled. Democratic and liberal in his tastes, Father Smyth is in much demand as a speaker on popular occasions, and has been frequently called upon to lecture before the students of the Northwestern University. He takes a deep interest in live questions and has proven himself a zealous champion of social, moral and business reforms. In an address made before a credit men's association, a few months before the

publication of this volume, referring to questions occupying much popular attention, he said: "I believe in pure food, pure water, clean streets, air free from grime and soot, and stand for the simple, sweet and peaceable life that brings out the best in man and woman."

The twenty-fifth anniversary of Fr. Smyth's ordination was celebrated in St. Mary's Church, Evanston, with impressive religious services on Sunday, June 24, 1906, followed by a banquet in the parochial school hall, which was participated in by some forty visiting priests. Much interest was manifested in the event by many outside of the popular priest's own denomination, and he was made the recipient of numerous generous gifts, not only from his immediate parishioners but also from non-Catholic friends, amounting in all to $4,500.

ELIZABETH EUNICE MARCY.

Elizabeth Eunice Marcy, wife of the late Professor Oliver Marcy, LL. D., of Northwestern University, was born at East Hampton, Conn., December 22, 1821. She is of Mayflower stock on both sides of her family, tracing her lineage in direct descent from Elder William Brewster and Stephen Hopkins of Mayflower fame. Mrs. Marcy's life, up to the time of her young womanhood, was spent in her home in East Hampton in the atmosphere of a thrifty New England family. Nathaniel Clark Smith, her father, was a man highly respected in the community. It may be said of him that he practically received every office in the gift of his fellow citizens. He was Justice of the Peace, Selectman, Notary Public and represented his town in the Legislature for several sessions. His family is directly traceable to the famous Eastham Colony, the first exodus from Plymouth about 1644. Her mother, Charlotte (Strong) Smith, is said to have been a woman of remarkable efficiency, being a lineal descendant, in the seventh generation, from Elder John Strong of England, who came to America in 1630.

Elizabeth was given the usual opportunities for education in the public schools, afterwards in private schools and still later in the Wesleyan Academy of Wilbraham, Mass., all contributing to her training, after which she had further development in the experience of teaching. She is of artistic temperament and has done creditable work in this line, as an amateur beginning at a very early age to copy simple designs. All these avocations have filled a long and busy life of one whose simple vocation was a housekeeper. Professor Oliver Marcy married Elizabeth Eunice Smith July 2, 1847, at which time he was a teacher in the Wilbraham, Mass., Academy. Professor Marcy was a member of a very old and distinguished family, being descended from John Marcy, son of the High Sheriff of Limerick, Ireland, who was born about the year 1662 and came to America in 1685. From him the direct line continues through successive generations down to Thomas, the father of Oliver. Oliver was born February 13, 1820, graduated at Middletown, Conn., in 1846, and received the degree of LL. D. from the Chicago University in 1873. In 1862 Professor and Mrs. Marcy came to Evanston, Ill., he having accepted a professorship in Northwestern University, with which institution he was identified until his death on March 19, 1899. His service to the University and the science of Geology gave him distinguished rank among American educators. To Mr. and Mrs. Marcy were born four

children: Annie Smith, born November 30, 1851, married Dr. Frank Davis April 21, 1875, and died February 22, 1900; Edwin Grosvenor, born January 23, 1854, died July 22, 1855; Frederic Malcolm, born November 2, 1856, died September 25, 1857; and Maude Elizabeth Olivia, born June 20, 1862, died February 1, 1875.

During a long and busy life, Mrs. Marcy has found time for public service of noble and enduring sort. Her passion for helpfulness found expression in her alliance with the Woman's Foreign and Woman's Home Missionary societies of the Methodist Episcopal Church, in both of which she was a charter member. The early history of these movements is a curious record of opposition and discouragement from other official agencies, and everlasting credit is due to the noble and intrepid band of women who declined to be overawed or discouraged, and among these Mrs. Marcy, by pen and voice, was a recognized leader. As a sort of corollary to her work with the Woman's Home Missionary Society, Mrs. Marcy undertook to found what is known as the Elizabeth E. Marcy Home in one of the destitute sections of Chicago. The home is conducted as a sort of religious settlement and is now a center of acknowledged help and usefulness, a source of beauty and strength to those who receive its benefits. Mrs. Marcy was also one of the founders of the Woman's Christian Temperance Union, to whose crusade she has ever been one of the most valuable auxiliaries. She is a member of the Daughters of the American Revolution, being entitled to this order by the service of her paternal grandfather, Sparrow Smith, who joined the Continental Army in his seventeenth year. She is also eligible to membership in the Colonial Dames, having for her progenitor on her mother's side

Josiah Cook, who rendered soldier service in King Philip's War in 1675. On her father's side she is a descendant of the Rev. John Norton, who in the French and Indian War was made Chaplain of a line of forts in Western Massachusetts. During the service he was carried to Canada, where he remained captive for a year. Afterward he settled in East Hampton, Conn., where he was pastor of the church during the remainder of his life of thirty years. She is also by lineal descent from the signers of the original Compact of the Pilgrim Fathers, a member of the Society of the Women of the Mayflower of the State of Illinois.

Mrs. Marcy's contributions to the press have been numerous. In prose they have been chiefly in the direction of her philanthropic work, some of them being of such importance as to warrant their distribution by tens of thousands in pamphlet form. In verse Mrs. Marcy has been less prolific but not less successful. She excels as a writer of occasional hymns and songs. One of her hymns, originally contributed to the Hymnal of the Methodist Episcopal Church, has been taken up by other hymnals and has been sung with great acceptance by congregations all over the world. In person, Mrs. Marcy is most approachable and companionable. The wide variety of her interests, her intellectual keenness, the breadth and geniality of her sympathies, the high quality of her culture and her deep spirituality invest her with exceptional charms. She has lived a long, diligent and useful life, and if, by reason of years, her range of activity is now restricted, she is none the less an inspiring and beloved figure in a wide circle of friends upon whom the blessing and the balm of a pure spirit have passed.

CHARLES C. BRAGDON.

Charles C. Bragdon, A. M., a teacher by profession, who is Principal of the Lasell Seminary for Young Women, at Auburndale, Mass., was born in Auburn, N. Y., September 6, 1847. In boyhood he attended public school, and in early manhood pursued courses of study in Northwestern Female College, and in the Preparatory Department of Northwestern University, where he graduated in 1865, and received the degree of A. M. in regular course in 1868. At a later period, the degree of LL. D. was conferred upon him by Northwestern University. From 1872 to 1874, Mr. Bragdon continued his studies in Germany. He is a charter member of the Alpha Phi Kappa Psi Fraternity, and during his collegiate course, belonged to the Adelphic Literary Society.

From 1865 to 1867, Mr. Bragdon taught in the Williamsport Seminary, in Pennsylvania, and from 1868 to 1872, in the Wesleyan Female College, at Cincinnati, Ohio. On June 30, 1869, he was united in marriage with Kate R. Ransom, of Williamsport, Pa., and they became the parents of two children, namely: Katherine Belle and John Ransom.

FRANKLIN SEXTON CATLIN.

Franklin S. Catlin, a worthy and promising representative of the younger element of attorneys-at-law in Chicago, Ill., was born in that city September 16, 1876, the only son of Charles and Mary Edith (Woods) Catlin, both of whom were natives of Chicago. On the maternal side he is descended from Michael Humphrey, who settled in Connecticut in 1647. Mr. Charles Catlin is Cashier of the Money Order Department of the Chicago Post Office.

The youthful mental training of Mr. Catlin was obtained in the "Lincoln" Public Grammar School, of Chicago, after which he became a pupil in the old Chicago Manual Training School, from which he was graduated in 1894. He then entered the Northwestern University Law School, graduating therefrom in 1896, and receiving the degree of LL. B. In that year he was a contributor to the "Northwestern University Law Review." As he was too young for admission to the bar, being but nineteen years old, he took a post-graduate course in the Chicago College of Law (the law department of Lake Forest University), which also conferred upon him the degree of LL. B. In November, 1897, Mr. Catlin was admitted to the bar, and became connected with the law firm of Loesch Brothers & Howell, with whom he remained three years. Since 1900 he has continued in practice alone.

In politics, Mr. Catlin is an earnest adherent of the Republican party, and takes an active part in the work of its local organization, having acted as secretary of his precinct and clerk of election for six years. His religious connection is with Unity Church (long under the ministry of Rev. Robert Collyer), of which he is secretary. In fraternal circles he is identified with the A. F. & A. M., being a member of Oriental Lodge No. 33, of Chicago, of which his father has been Secretary for the past twenty-seven years. He is also a member of the Board of Directors of the North Side Club, a social organization. Mr. Catlin is somewhat of an expert in aquatic sports. In 1896 he won the Junior Single Shell championship, and was one of the winners of the Junior Pair-oared Shell championship, in the regatta of the Mississippi Valley Amateur Rowing Association,

at Black Lake, Michigan. He is secretary of the Catlin Boat Club, which was organized in 1882, and a member of the American Canoe Association.

GEORGE W. WHITEFIELD, M. D., D. D. S.

George W. Whitefield, physician, D. D. S., was born near Boston, Mass., September 30, 1855, the son of Rev. John and Martha (Kemp) Whitefield, and a grand nephew of Rev. George Whitefield, the celebrated English evangelist of the eighteenth century. In boyhood, he was brought by his parents to Aurora, Ill., where he was educated in the public school and high school, his first employment after leaving school being as a bookkeeper. While still in his 'teens he opened an art store in Aurora, and, after reaching manhood, spent some time on the plains. In 1879 he began study and laboratory work preparatory to opening a dental office during the following year, in the meantime, while engaged in practice, pursuing medical and dental college courses, taking the D. D. S. degree at the Chicago Dental College in 1885, and that of M. D. from Rush Medical College in 1886. The official positions which he has held in connection with his profession include the chair of Dental Pathology in the American Dental College and that of Electrical Therapeutics in the Dental Department of the Northwestern University; also for some time was Aural Surgeon in connection with the Protestant Orphan Asylum, and Assistant Surgeon under the celebrated Dr. Gunn preceding the death of the latter in 1887. He is a member of the Chicago Dental Society, the Odontographic Society and the Electric Club, and served as delegate to the Ninth International Medical Congress; is also the inventor of several valuable instruments now in general use in connection with electro-therapy.

On January 31, 1895, Dr. Whitefield was married to Fannie Comstock, daughter of Charles Comstock, and they have one daughter, Julia Sprague. For five years he was a member of Company D, Third Regiment I. N. G., and served with his regiment in suppressing the riots at Braidwood, Ill., in 1877. Owing to failing health he entered commercial life, serving for a time as Vice-President of a company whose business interests led to his making a trip to the tropics. In a short time, having regained his health, he returned home in 1903 and resumed the practice of his profession, which he has followed continuously since. He was Vice-President of the American Fruit and Transportation Company and a Director of the Rio Bonito Company. His residence and office are at No. 1518 Hinman Avenue, Evanston.

FRANK LYNN BORTON.

Frank Lynn Borton was born near Philadelphia, Pa., in 1863, of Quaker parentage. Mr. Borton has been in the service of the Pennsylvania Railroad System for twenty years and is Assistant to the Manager of the Star Union Line, the through freight department of the Pennsylvania Lines. He has been a resident of Evanston for eleven years, is a member of the Official Board of Emmanuel Methodist Church, and has always taken an active interest in municipal affairs. Mr. Borton's home is at 740 Forest Avenue.

DAVID R. DYCHE, M. D.

Dr. David R. Dyche (deceased) was born near Red Lion, Warren County, Ohio, March 11, 1827, the son of William Dyche, who was a farmer by occupation. The son was brought up on a farm, meanwhile receiving his education in the public schools, at Lebanon Academy and under private tutorship, after which he began the study of medicine with Dr. Joshua Stearns of Lebanon, still later taking a course in the Medical College at Cincinnati, from which he graduated in 1854. He then began practice in the town of Monroe, Butler County, Ohio, where he remained nine years. In 1865, coming to Chicago, at the end of the year he engaged in the drug business, first at the corner of Randolph and Dearborn Streets. The fire of 1871 having destroyed his place of business, he soon afterward erected the Dyche building at the corner of Randolph and State Streets, in which he continued business until his death August 4, 1893.

Up to 1874, Dr. Dyche's residence was in the city of Chicago. He then removed to Evanston, where he continued to reside during the remainder of his life, taking an active part in the building up of that city. He was one of the active members of the Citizens' League, which did much to keep saloons from obtaining a foothold in the city in violation of the "Four-Mile Limit Law." He was an active factor in the founding of the Woman's Medical College, afterwards identified with the Northwestern University, and in the promotion of the medical department of the University; and was also one of the founders of the School of Pharmacy connected with that institution. He became a member of the Methodist Church in early life, and took a deep interest in church affairs and in the upbuilding of the Northwestern University, with which he was closely identified as a member of the Board of Trustees soon after coming to Evanston, and continuously thereafter until his death.

Dr. Dyche was married in Monroe, Ohio, in 1856, to Mary S. Boyd, a daughter of Andrew Boyd of that place, and they had two sons, both of whom survive, namely: William A., former Mayor of the City of Evanston, and present Business Manager of the Northwestern University, and Dr. George B. Dyche, who is a physician in the city of Chicago.

Liberal, public-spirited and enterprising, Dr. David R. Dyche was one of the most influential factors in promoting the benevolent, educational and moral interests of the city with which he was so closely identified for twenty years.

JOHN CARNEY.

John Carney (deceased), who spent his entire life of nearly fifty-four years in Evanston, Ill., and served twenty-three years, in all, as head of its police force, died September 21, 1899, within three blocks of the spot where he was born January 7, 1846. His parents were John and Mary (Lindsay) Carney, natives of County Mayo, Ireland. His father, born in Castlebar, County Mayo, was reared to farming, and on coming to the United States in 1835, sought what was then the Far West, and settled on the prairie twelve miles north of the village of Chicago, and on the site of the present city of Evanston. The tract of land on which he located is now bounded on the north by Church Street, south by Greenleaf Street, east by Railroad Avenue, and west

by the western limits of Evanston. Here he applied himself to farming, being one of the first of the pioneers to bring land under cultivation in this region. His old homestead is now No. 1314 Ridge Avenue, and he continued to reside there until the Northwestern University was established, and the ground on which it stood was purchased for the use of that institution. He then moved to a place near the present Rose Hill Cemetery, where he was occupied in farming for two years.

In the meantime, Evanston having been laid out, he established his home in the new village, where he became the owner of the block of ground on Asbury Avenue between Grove and Lake Streets. There he built the residence in which he lived during the remainder of his days, dying there April 3, 1874, at the age of ninety-seven years. His widow, who reached the age of ninety-two years, passed away August 12, 1896. Both of these worthy pioneers were typical early settlers, and throughout their long lives, enjoyed the high esteem of their contemporaries in early settlement, and that of the later generation that grew up around them.

John Carney, the subject of this sketch, was born at the early homestead on Ridge Avenue. He attended school in the primitive log school house in the village, then called Ridgeville, and was subsequently a pupil in the historic Catholic school in Chicago, known as St. Mary's of the Lake. He learned the butcher's trade as a boy, and he and his brother William were, for some time during his early manhood, engaged in the meat business in Evanston. Afterwards, he worked at the painter's trade until 1872, when he became a member of the pioneer police force of the Village of Evanston. Among the Village Trustees of that period were Lyman J.

Gage, Oliver Willard, J. J. Parkhurst and others who gained distinction in later life. Mr. Carney was the first Chief of Police of the incorporated City of Evanston, and became widely known for his ability as a police officer and detective. He had more than any other man to do with shaping the character of the force and making it what it is to-day. After 1895 he gave up all active pursuits and lived in pleasant retirement at his home on Asbury Avenue. Throughout his official life he was chiefly interested in preserving the best possible order in the community, and took a leading part in establishing the "four-mile limit," within which saloons are not allowed in Evanston.

Mr. Carney was married in St. Mary's Church, Evanston, June 12, 1870, to Ida Maria Guinan, a native of Burr, Kings County, Ireland. Mrs. Carney came to the United States with her parents, John and Anna Guinan, when she was five years of age. Her family settled at Dayton, Ohio, where she passed the early years of her life. The only child of Mr. and Mrs. Carney is Mrs. John M. James, the infant daughter of whom, Irene, represents the fourth generation of the family in Evanston, and the third generation born there.

Like his father before him, Mr. Carney was a Catholic Churchman. His widow, who survives him, and her daughter adhere to the same faith and are communicants of St. Mary's Church in Evanston.

JOHN BRENTON CALLIGAN.

John Brenton Calligan (deceased), formerly a well-known citizen of Evanston, Ill., was born in Machias, Maine, August 19, 1848, and there received his mental

training in the high school. His parents, Warren and Catherine (Hartley) Calligan, died when he was very young, and he was adopted into the family of William Lorimer, of Machias, where he was reared. At an early age he entered the employ of the Pope Brothers, who operated a large merchandising and lumbering concern in Machias, and for many years occupied a responsible position with this firm. About 1880, he went to Boston and became connected with the mercantile house of R. H. White. There he remained until 1887, when he resigned this position, and coming to Chicago, entered the wholesale hardware trade as a representative of the Colby Wringer Company, with which he continued until 1896. Retiring from this business, he then purchased a fruit ranch near Boise City, Idaho, to which he devoted his attention mainly during the remainder of his life. In 1887 he established his home in Evanston, where he lived until his death, which occurred October 6, 1904.

Mr. Calligan was twice married. His first wife, to whom he was wedded in 1873, was Frances Brown, a daughter of Capt. David Brown, of Machias, Maine, who was a prominent resident of that place. She died in June, 1882. Two children resulted from this union, of whom one died in 1882 and the other in 1883.

In June, 1884, Mr. Calligan was united in marriage to Annie F. Harlow, a daughter of Deacon Alden and Temperance (Bourne) Harlow, of Needham, Mass. On the paternal side, Mrs. Calligan, who survives her husband, is a lineal descendant of John Alden, the Puritan, and comes of a noted New England family. One of her ancestors in the paternal line was Col. Anthony Thomas, of Revolutionary fame. Another was Col. Briggs Alden, who was a close personal friend of Gen. Washington. On the maternal side, Mrs. Calligan has an equally distinguished ancestry. One of her ancestors was John Bourne, who walked a distance of forty miles to Boston in order to enlist in the Revolutionary Army. He was with Washington at Valley Forge, and the record of his military career constitutes a narrative of thrilling interest. He lived to be six months more than a hundred years old. Mrs. Calligan's grandfather, Eleazer Harlow, owned and lived on a farm adjoining that of Daniel Webster, at Marshfield, Mass. The two men were warm personal friends, and Mr. Harlow was one of the pall-bearers at the funeral of the great New England statesman.

The only child of Mr. and Mrs. Calligan is Mrs. Grace Brenton Williams, who is a Daughter of the Revolution, and preserves among her cherished possessions the cartridge box and bayonet of her ancestor, John Bourne, and other relics of the Revolution.

Politically, Mr. Calligan was a Republican of pronounced views. Fraternally, he was made a member of the Masonic Order in Norfold Lodge, at Needham, Mass., in 1883. His religious associations were with the Second Presbyterian Church of Evanston.

ROBERT DODDS.

Dr. Robert Dodds, physician and surgeon, who is located at No. 144 Oakwood Boulevard, Chicago, Ill., was born at Kirkmaiden, Scotland, February 12, 1856. In boyhood he was a pupil in the grammar schools of Scotland, and subsequently pursued a course of study in Ayr Academy, in that country. He graduated from the Medical Department of the North-

western University in 1890, with the degree of M. D. Dr. Dodds is Attending Surgeon to the Chicago Baptist Hospital and the Charity Hospital, Gynecologist of the Post-Graduate School and Hospital, and Lecturer in the Methodist Training School for Home and Foreign Missions. He is a member of the American Medical Association, the Illinois State Medical Society, the Chicago Medical Society, the Chicago Medico-Legal Society, and the Chicago Gynecological Society. Dr. Dodds was united in marriage with Jessie B. Brown in April, 1890, and one child has been the offspring of this union, namely: Mary West Dodds.

CASSIUS M. C. BUNTAIN.

Cassius M. Clay Buntain, lawyer, of Kankakee, Kankakee County, Ill., was born in Momence, in that county, October 15, 1876, the son of Thomas Jefferson and Anna (Vankirk) Buntain. His early youth was spent in his native town, where he obtained his primary mental training in the public school. On September 7, 1891, he entered the Momence High School, from which he graduated as class orator and valedictorian May 23, 1894. On September 12, 1894, he entered the Northwestern University Academy at Evanston, Ill., from which he graduated June 8, 1896. On September 21, 1899, he became a student in the law school of Northwestern University, from which he graduated June 19, 1902, with the degree of LL. B. He had previously (June 15, 1899) received the degree of A. B. from Northwestern University, and that of A. M. was conferred upon him by the College of Liberal Arts in Evanston June 19, 1902. In 1894-95, he was President of the Momence High School Alumni Association, and Chairman of its Executive Committee in 1895-96. The prizes which were awarded Mr. Buntain in connection with his studies in Momence, Ill., were as follows: a silver medal, October 15, 1890, at the Inter-State Hay Palace in that place, for the "best scholarship in arithmetic"; a $3 prize for the best map of the United States drawn from memory; a $3 prize for the best solution for a problem in mathematics; a prize for the best note-book kept during the year; first prize (a silver medal) in the Demorest declamation contest at Momence, Ill., April 3, 1891; first prize (a gold medal) in the Demorest declamation contest at Watseka, Ill., August 20, 1891; first prize (a gold medal) in a declamation contest at Chicago Heights, Ill., January 6, 1894; and first prize (grand gold medal) in the Demorest declamation contest at Urbana, Ill., September 7, 1894. In Northwestern University Academy, Evanston, Ill., Mr. Buntain won second place in the Columbian Oratorical Contest, May 25, 1895.

In the course of his academic and college connections Mr. Buntain received, in 1895-96, a State scholarship for four years. During the same period, he was chosen Trig Cremation orator. In 1896-97, he was a member of the Rogers Debating Club and was nominated by the class committee as editor of the "Syllabus." In 1897-98, he was Chairman of the Pan-Hellenic Association; leader of the Junior Promenade, February 18, 1898; member of the Junior Play Committee and cast, elected a member of the Rogers Debating Club team for 1898-99; and Delegate to the province convention of the "Phi Delta Theta" Fraternity at Lincoln, Nebraska, May 19, 1898. He also represented the same fraternity at its semi-centennial convention at Columbus,

Ohio, November 21-25, 1898. On September 29, 1904, at St. Louis, Mo., he was elected Vice-President of the General Council of the "Phi Delta Phi" Fraternity. He joined the "Phi Delta Theta" Fraternity December 7, 1895, and became a member of the "Theta Nu Epsilon" Fraternity May 13, 1898. He was initiated into the "Deru" (Senior Fraternity) on May 27, 1898. On May 11, 1900, he was initiated into the legal fraternity of "Phi Delta Phi." On May 24, 1901, he was elected President of the class of 1902, for the senior year (1901-02). During the summer of 1898, Mr. Buntain served as clerk in the Adjutant General's Office (War Department), Washington, D. C. On October 28th of the same year he was a member of the winning team in the first semi-final debate of the Inter Society Debating League. On January 13, 1899, he was a Cleveland declamation contestant and a Lyman J. Gage debate contestant April 14, 1899. On February 21, 1899, he was elected to membership in the Society of American Wars.

On October 7-8, 1902, Mr. Buntain passed the State Bar Examination at Springfield, Ill., and on October 17th, following, was admitted to practice. From February 2, to May 6, 1903, he was clerk in the law firm of Dupee, Judah, Willard & Wolf, of Chicago, and from May 14th to October 29th of that year he acted as assistant attorney for Farson, Leach & Co. of that city. On April 4, 1904, he opened up a law office at 25 Arcade Building, Kankakee, Ill., where he has since been successfully engaged in practice. In fraternal circles, the subject of this sketch is identified with the Royal Arcanum, Grove City Council No. 832; also Kankakee (Ill.) Lodge No. 389 of Ancient Free and Accepted Masons; Kankakee (Ill.)

Chapter No. 78 Royal Arch-Masons; and Ivanhoe Commandery No. 33 Knights Templar, Kankakee, Ill.

PETER THOMAS BURNS, M. D.

Dr. Peter Thomas Burns, physician, who is located at No. 531 South Leavitt Street, Chicago, Ill., was born in Osman, Wis., October 5, 1864. In early youth he attended the common and high schools of his native place, and in 1888 matriculated in the Medical Department of Northwestern University, from which he was graduated with the degree of M. D. in 1891. From the time of his graduation, Dr. Burns has been a teacher in the Department of Anatomy of the University Medical School, in which, since 1892, he has acted in the capacity of Assistant Professor of Anatomy. Dr. Burns is a member of the American Medical Association, the Illinois State Medical Society, and the Chicago Medical Society. The marriage of the subject of this sketch took place on June 21, 1892, when he was wedded to Mary Adelaide Davis of Meeme, Wis.

SOLOMON W. ZIPPERMAN, D. D. S.

Dr. Solomon William Zipperman, who is engaged in the practice of dentistry at No. 538 South Halsted Street, Chicago, Ill., is a native of the Russian Empire, where he was born in Chotin, Bessarabia, June 15, 1875. His boyhood and youth were spent in the place of his birth, and his earlier mental training was obtained in the public schools of Chotin, Russia, and in the high school there, of which he is a graduate.

Shortly after coming to the United States, Mr. Zipperman matriculated (in 1896) in the Northwestern University Dental School, from which he was graduated with the class of 1899, receiving the degree of D. D. S. He immediately entered upon the practice of his profession, in which he has met with successful results, and has secured a remunerative patronage.

Dr. Zipperman is a member of the Alumni Association of the Northwestern University Dental School, the Illinois State Dental Society, and the Chicago Odontographic Society; and is also fraternally affiliated with Apollo Lodge No. 642, A. F. & A. M., and Commercial Lodge No. 165, I. O. O. F.

ROSCOE TOWNLEY NICHOLS, M. D.

Roscoe Townley Nichols, physician and surgeon, who is engaged in the practice of his profession at Liberal, Seward County, Kan., was born at Allerton, Wayne County, Ia., on February 20, 1881. In early youth he attended public school in his native place, and, from 1895 to 1899, pursued a course of scientific study in the Kansas State Agricultural College, from which he was graduated in the year last named, with the degree of B. S. He then, in 1899-1901, studied medicine at St. Louis, Mo., in Barnes Medical College In September, 1901, he entered the Northwestern University Medical School, graduating therefrom with the degree of M. D. in June, 1902. In 1899 he was President of the Webster Literary Society of the Kansas State Agricultural College, and was on the editorial staff of the "Students' Herald," of that institution, in 1898-99.

Dr. Nichols is a member of the Southwest Counties Medical Society of Kansas, the Kansas State Medical Society, the American Medical Association, and the American Academy of Medicine. Fraternally, he is identified with the A. F. & A. M., having been made a Mason by Fargo Lodge No. 300 in May, 1903. On May 3, 1903, he was united in marriage with Osa Roscoe Clark, and two children have been born of this union: Harry Dale Nichols, born March 15, 1904, and Alice C. Nichols, born August 22, 1905.

CHARLES L. RICHARDS.

Charles L. Richards, lawyer, of Hebron, Neb., was born in Woodstock, Ill., March 21, 1856, and there, in boyhood, received his primary mental training in the public schools. At a later period he entered the University of Illinois, at Champaign, from which he was graduated with the class of 1878. He pursued his legal studies in the Union College of Law in Chicago, graduating therefrom in 1884 with the degree of LL. B. From 1886 to 1890, Mr. Richards held the office of Prosecuting Attorney of Thayer County, Neb., and in 1895 served in the capacity of member and Speaker of the Nebraska House of Representatives.

In fraternal circles, the subject of this sketch is affiliated with the A. F. & A. M. Religiously, he adheres to the faith of the Presbyterian Church. Mr. Richards is the father of four children, namely: Carl G., John Lowrie, Webb and Bessie.

WILLIAM J. CAMDEN.

William J. Camden, pharmacist, of Walhalla, North Dakota, was born in the Province of Quebec, Canada, on December 10, 1872, received his early mental training in the public schools of St. Paul, Minn., and in September, 1890, matriculated in the Northwestern University School of Pharmacy in Chicago, Ill., graduating in 1893 with the degree of Graduate in Pharmacy. In 1897, he engaged in business at his present location. In 1902-03, he served in the capacity of Vice-President of the North Dakota Pharmaceutical Association, of which body he was elected President in 1904. In fraternal circles, the subject of this sketch is identified with the K. of P., the A. F. & A. M., and the D. O. K. K. Mr. Camden was united in marriage with Mary Frances Horgan, of Walhalla, N. D., on February 7, 1906.

CHARLES H. MAYO, M. D.

Charles Horace Mayo, who is engaged in the practice of surgery at Rochester, Minn., was born in that city July 19, 1865. In youth he attended a private school, and was also a pupil in the public and high schools of his native place. In 1885 he matriculated in the Medical Department of Northwestern University, in Chicago, Ill., from which he was graduated in 1888 with the degree of M. D. He received the honorary degree of A. M. in 1904. Dr. Mayo is a member of the firm of Mayo, Stinchfield & Graham of Rochester, Minn., and is surgeon in St. Mary's Hospital in that city. He is also a member of the Minnesota State Board of Health, and is connected with various medical and surgical societies as follows: The American Surgical Association; the Southern Surgical Association; the Western Surgical Association, of which he was elected President in 1904; the American Medical Association; the Minnesota State Medical Society, of which he was President in 1905-06; the District Medical

Society for the Southern Counties of the Mississippi Valley; and the Olmsted County (Minn.) Medical Society. On April 5, 1893, Dr. Mayo was united in marriage with Edith Graham, who has borne him five children, namely: Dorothy, Charles, Edith, Joseph and Louise.

RAYNOR ELMORE HOLMES, M. D.

Dr. Raynor E. Holmes, physician and surgeon, Canon City, Colo., was born at New Lenox, Ill., November 2, 1871. In boyhood he attended the public school in his native place, and his later youth was devoted to special studies. In 1893 he entered the College of Liberal Arts of Northwestern University, at Evanston, Ill., and completed his course in 1895. In 1896 he matriculated in the Northwestern University Medical School, graduating therefrom in 1901, with the degree of M. D. Dr. Holmes acted in the capacity of interne in the Minnequa Hospital, in Pueblo, Colo., from June, 1901, to October, 1902. From October, 1902, until the present writing he has occupied the position of surgeon at Canon City and Brookside, Colo., for the Colorado Fuel & Iron Company.

The subject of this sketch is a member of the Colorado State Medical Society; the Fremont County (Colo.) Medical Society; and the American Medical Association.

THOMAS BATES.

Thomas Bates, a prominent attorney residing in Evanston, Ill., was born in Griggsville, Pike County, Ill., March 4, 1844. His parents, Thomas and Ann (Cleveland) Bates, were natives of Windsor, Vt., where they were born in 1815 and 1818, respectively. In the earlier period of his life, Thomas Bates, Sr., was engaged in farming, but later became a merchant and grain buyer. The son, Thomas, received his early mental training in the common schools, and spent one year in Illinois College, at Jacksonville. After leaving college he worked one year in his father's store, and then went west as assistant wagon-master in Sully & Sibley's expedition against the Sioux Indians. This occupied his time for about a year, when he returned home and in May, 1862, enlisted in Company B, Sixty-eighth Regiment Illinois Infantry, which was attached to the Army of the Potomac under Gen. McClellan. The regiment first enlisted as State Militia, but at the request of its members was mustered into the Federal service, and was engaged in guarding forts, etc., for a period of about four months, when it was mustered out at Springfield. Thomas Bates returned home when discharged, and taught school at Towanda and Gilman, Ill., for about nine years. In 1876, he came to Chicago and entered the law office of Leonard Swett, having previously read law under Mr. Swett's direction. In the autumn of 1876 he was admitted to the bar and formed a partnership with his legal preceptor, under the firm name of Swett & Bates. Subsequently Judge Van H. Higgins was admitted, and the firm name became Higgins, Swett & Bates. On Mr. Higgins' withdrawal Pliny N. Haskell was admitted, the style of the firm then becoming Swett, Bates & Haskell. This continued until 1884, when Mr. Bates retired from the partnership and practiced alone for three or four years, when Richard W. Barger, of Des Moines, Iowa, was admitted as a partner. Later the firm became Bates & Harding, and is now Bates, Harding & Atkins.

Mr. Bates has confined his practice chiefly to fire insurance cases, and is attorney for a large number of fire insurance companies doing business in the West. Among the famous suits which he has conducted may be mentioned those in Arkansas and in Kansas, known as the "Anti-Trust Suits," brought for the purpose of ousting all companies which were in combination and had fixed rates, etc. Mr. Bates was the attorney for the insurance companies and won the suits. He has defended the suits in both the above-mentioned States and in Missouri, and is attending to similar suits now pending in Illinois.

Mr. Bates was married at Turner, Maine, in December, 1872, to Sarah B. Ricker, whose mother was a sister of Leonard Swett and they have two children living, namely: Rose Cleveland, born in 1878; and Alfred Ricker, born in 1882. Politically, Mr. Bates was a Democrat until the Bryan campaign, when he became, and still continues, a Republican. He was one of the Trustees of the Village of Evanston for two terms, before its incorporation as a city. In 1899 he was elected Mayor of Evanston, serving one term; and was nominated for a second term but declined a re-election. Mr. Bates is a member of the Country Club, of Evanston, and of the Evanston Golf Club. He is an attendant of the Presbyterian Church.

EDWARD HEMPSTEAD.

Edward Hempstead (deceased), for twenty years a highly respected citizen of Evanston, is descended from a long line of Puritan ancestors who were among the first settlers of New London, Conn. His grandfather, Stephen Hempstead, born there in 1754, was a patriot and soldier in the American Revolution, who fought for his country from the first call for troops at Lexington until the close of the war. In 1811 he removed with his large family to St. Louis, Mo., where his son Edward Hempstead, a young and distinguished lawyer, had already preceded him, and who was the first Delegate in Congress from the region west of the Mississippi River. His father, Charles S. Hempstead, also a lawyer of marked ability, was intimately connected with the early development of St. Louis, and later of Galena, Ill., where for many years he had a large law practice extending over what was then a wide western territory, including Chicago in its early days. Edward Hempstead was born in St. Louis in 1820. His mother, Rachel Wilt, of old Pennsylvania Dutch lineage, died when he was a child, and his youth was passed with his father's relatives in that circle of early pioneers of St. Louis, where true New England hospitality, blended with the grace and polish of the French settlers, created such a charming society, among whose number were the most eminent people of those days. He was educated at Belleville, Ill., Seminary, and began his business career as a commission merchant in Galena. In 1854 he came to Chicago, and for nearly twenty years was engaged in business as a member of the firm of Hempstead & Horton, wholesale grocers. With many others he lost home and property in the great fire of 1871 and became, for a short time a refugee in Evanston. Soon after that disaster, retiring from business, he became a permanent resident in Evanston where he died in 1895.

A true Republican in sentiment, he took the deepest interest in the political welfare of his country, numbering among his acquaintances Abraham Lincoln, Gen. U. S. Grant, Hon. E. B. Washburne, and many other public men of Illinois of his time. He was a liberal promoter and contributor toward all the early enterprises of Chicago, one of the first members of its Board of Trade, the Historical Society and Art Institute, and always greatly interested in the growth and prosperity of that city. Mr. Hempstead was a man of the highest integrity, of excellent judgment and cultured taste, always loyal to his friends, of a most social and kindly disposition and highly esteemed by all who knew him. He was married in 1846 to Miss Mary Corwith, of Bridgehampton, Long Island. Six of their eight children are living.

CHARLES NEVILLE KIRKBRIDE.

Charles N. Kirkbride, attorney-at-law, who resides in San Mateo, San Mateo County, Cal., was born in Pueblo, Colo., November 15, 1868. In early youth he attended the public schools and in 1884, entered the University of the Pacific, at San Jose, Cal., where he graduated in 1887, with the degree of Ph. B. He matriculated in Northwestern University Law School at Chicago, Ill., in 1891, graduating therefrom in 1893, with the degree of LL. B.

In 1889-90, Mr. Kirkbride was the editor of the "San Mateo (Cal.) Leader," and in 1890-91, of the "Times-G- -ette," at Redwood City, in the same Sta :. He was admitted to the California bar in October, 1893, and was elected City Attorney of San Mateo, Cal., in 1895, and still holds that office. He is Secretary of the San Mateo Public Library, and has filled the position of Trustee of the San Mateo Union High School since 1902. He is also a Director of the San Mateo Athletic Club, and attorney for the San Mateo

Bank, and the local Building and Loan Association.

GEORGE WILLIAM DIXON.

George W. Dixon, lawyer, Secretary and Treasurer of the Arthur Dixon Transfer Company of Chicago, Ill., residing at No. 2706, Michigan Avenue, that city, is a native of Chicago. After finishing his primary studies in the public schools, and completing his preparatory course in the West Division High School in Chicago, he matriculated in Northwestern University, from which he was graduated in 1889 with the degree of A. B. He then entered Northwestern University Law School, graduating therefrom in 1892, with the degree of LL. B. During his under graduate course, he was a contestant for the Kirk Oratorical Prize, and was a member of the Phi Beta Kappa, Phi Kappa Psi and Phi Delta Phi fraternities.

From 1902 to 1906, Mr. Dixon represented the First Senatorial District of Illinois in the State Senate. He also served as a member of the staff of Governor Yates, with the rank of Colonel. In 1901-02, he was President of the Chicago Methodist Social Union. He is a member of the Union League, Hamilton and University Clubs of Chicago and of the Chicago Athletic Club, a thirty-second degree Mason, a Knight Templar and Mystic Shriner.

On March 2, 1903, the subject of this sketch was united in marriage with Marian E. Martin. They have one daughter, Marian.

JUDSON WILKES HOOVER.

Judson Wilkes Hoover, who is engaged in the drug business at 251 Main Street, Galesburg, Ill., was born in Avoca, Iowa,

March 2, 1876. His primary mental training was obtained in the public schools of his native town. After taking a preparatory course in the Iowa Wesleyan University, at Mount Pleasant, Iowa, on September 1, 1898, he matriculated in the Northwestern University College of Pharmacy, from which he was graduated with the degree of Ph. G., in June, 1899.

Mr. Hoover is a member of the M. W. A.; of the Northwestern University Alumni Association of Pharmacy, in which he holds the office of Secretary; a member of the Soangetaka Club, the Galesburg Cmmercial Club and Fraternal Tribunes of Galesburg, Ill. On April 15, 1894, he was united in marriage with Miss Kathryn Daugherty, of Mt. Pleasant, Iowa, and one child has been born to them, namely: Murlin Hoover, born June 30, 1895.

JAMES A. GARLAND, M. D.

James Asa Garland, physician and surgeon of Buchanan, Mich., was born in Peoria, Ill., January 15, 1871. In early youth he attended the Chicago public schools, and is a graduate of one of the high schools in that city. He entered Northwestern University in 1891, graduating from the medical department of that institution in 1895, with the degree of M. D. From 1898 to 1901, inclusive, he served as Health Officer of the city of Buchanan, Mich., and of the township.

Dr. Garland is a member of the American Medical Association, the Berrien County (Mich.) Medical Society, and the Red Cross Society, Berrien County Humane Society. In fraternal circles, he is identified with the A. F. & A. M. and the M. W. A. On November 27, 1901, Dr. Garland was united in marriage with Gertrude Friesleben, of Chicago.

AMOS A. L. SMITH.

Amos A. L. Smith, attorney at law, who is located at No. 2316, Grand Avenue, Milwaukee, Wis., was born at Appleton, Wis., September 8, 1849. His primary mental training was obtained in the public schools of his native place and he pursued his preparatory course of study in Lawrence University, at Appleton. He then entered Northwestern University in the Sophomore year, and was graduated therefrom with the class of 1872. He was a member of the Adelphic Literary Society and the Phi Beta Kappa Fraternity. In the English Literature contest, his essay on "Darwinism" won the "President's prize." He also won the one hundred dollar prize for oratory, by his oration on "Cavour." During the undergraduate period, he held the position of editor of the "Tripod." Mr. Smith has been a member of the Board of Trustees of the Milwaukee Woman's College, a Director of the Wisconsin National Bank, and of the Wisconsin Trust and Security Company. Socially he is a member of the Milwaukee Club, the Bankers' Club, the Milwaukee Athletic Club, and the Blue Mound Country Club.

Mr. Smith was wedded in 1874 to Frances L. Brown, who died in 1891. In 1893 he was united in marriage with Mary Niel Anderson. He became the father of four children, namely: Philip R., Edwin L., Laura L., and Walton K.

RICHARD R. JOHNSON, D.D.S.

Richard Roy Johnson, D.D.S., who was engaged in the practice of dentistry at Great Falls, Mont., was born in Whitehall, Mich., September 25, 1874. In early youth he attended the public schools of his native town, and prepared for college in the High School at Lisbon, N. D., whence he went to the University of Minnesota Dental Department, in which he completed the first year of the course in 1897. During the same year he matriculated in Northwestern University Dental College, from which he was graduated with the class of 1899, receiving the degree of D.D.S. He is a member of the Delta Sigma Delta Fraternity. Shortly after his graduation, he opened an office at Lisbon, N. D., but sold his practice in June, 1903, and moved to his present location, where his efforts have been attended with good results. He is at present lecturing on dentistry and hygiene at the Columbus and Deaconess Hospitals in that city. He is a member of the Montana State Dental Society.

During 1902, and until his removal to Montana, in June, 1903, Dr. Johnson held the office of City Treasurer of Lisbon, N. D., and in that city he was married on September 26, 1900, to Florence May Severance. Two children have resulted from their union, namely: Maude Lucille, born in Lisbon, N. D., June 25, 1902; and Winnifred May, born in Great Falls, May 30, 1904. Fraternally, Dr. Johnson is identified with the A. F. & A. M., and is Past Master of the Lisbon Lodge of that order. He is also a member of the R. A. Chapter and Commandery of Knights Templar.

C. PRUYN STRINGFIELD, M. D.

Dr. C. Pruyn Stringfield, physician and surgeon, whose office is located in the Western Union Telegraph Building, in Chicago, Ill., was born in Washington, D. C., December 12, 1866. In youth he made diligent use of the facilities for instruction afforded by the public schools of Topeka, Kan., and entered the Medical Department of Northwestern University in 1886, graduating therefrom in 1889. From that year until 1894, he assisted Prof. Ralph S. Isham in clinical surgery. He was President of the Chicago Medical Examiners' Association in 1902 and 1903. In 1895, 1896 and 1897, he was connected with the Health Department of the City of Chicago.

Dr. Stringfield was consulting physician of the Chicago Baptist Hospital; attending surgeon to the Cook County Hospital; is physician to the Actors' Fund of America; was Medical Director of the Marquette Life Insurance Company, and is now Medical Examiner for the Phœnix Mutual Life Company of Hartford; resident physician of the Grand Pacific Hotel, in Chicago; and ex-contract surgeon of the United States Marine Corp. He is a member of the American Medical Association; the Illinois State Medical Society; the Chicago Medical Society; the American Association of Life Examining Surgeons; Chicago Medical Examiners' Association and the Association of Military Surgeons of the United States. From 1901 to 1905, Dr. Stringfield served on the staff of Governor Yates, of Illinois, with the rank of Colonel.

Fraternally, the subject of this sketch is a Mason, a life-member of the B. P. O. Elks, and is Past Chancellor of the Knights of Pythias. He belongs to the Chicago Athletic Club; South Shore Country Club; the Chicago Yacht Club; the Hamilton, the Forty and the Chicago Automobile Clubs.

The marriage of Dr. Stringfield took place on August 14, 1889, when Miss Josephine Milgie, a most estimable and accomplished lady, became his wife. He is widely and favorably known in Chicago and the State, where he is held in high esteem, individually, professionally and as a citizen.

ALEXANDER F. BANKS.

Alexander F. Banks, a prominent railway official, whose residence is at No. 1908 Sheridan Road, Evanston, Ill., and who is widely and favorably known throughout the railway circles of Illinois, was born in Crawford County, Ind., on January 31, 1861. He is a son of Henry Bartlett and Julia C. (French) Banks, natives of Kentucky, his father born in Washington County, that State, in 1809, and his mother, in Maysville, in 1822. Henry Bartlett Banks, who was a farmer by occupation, moved with his family from Kentucky to Crawford County, Ind., in 1844, and there engaged in agricultural pursuits. His son, Alexander, attended the common schools of Indiana during the winter months, until he was thirteen years of age, and in the intervals between the school terms, assisted his father in the work on the farm. At that period he started out to work for himself.

In 1877, when sixteen years old, Mr. Banks entered upon his career in the railway service as a clerk at Evansville, Ind., and, in 1879, was appointed contracting freight agent of the St. Louis & Southwestern Railway. In 1880, he became connected with the Continental Fast Freight Line, and served in the capacity of Agent and General Agent of that company until 1888. In that year he entered the service of the Iowa Central Railway Company, at Peoria, Ill., as General Agent, afterwards serving successively as General Freight Agent, General Freight and Passenger Agent, and as Traffic Manager. In 1893 Mr. Banks left the services of the Iowa Central Railway Company, in order to become General Freight Agent of the Elgin, Joliet & Eastern Railway Company. He was appointed Traffic Manager of that company, and also of the Lake Shore & Eastern Railway Company, in 1894. In 1900 he was elected President of both of these corporations and still serves in that capacity.

In November, 1883, Mr. Banks was united in marriage with Blanche Nicholson, at Evansville, Ind., and of this union three children have been born, namely: Duke Nicholson, Blanche, and Charles Ackert. Mr. Banks has risen, step by step, from a lowly grade of railway service, through superior innate ability, to his present high and responsible position, and is regarded as one of the most thorough and capable railroad officials in this section of the country.

AUGUST AHLBERG.

August Ahlberg, Evanston, Ill., was born in Sweden, August 5, 1845, the son of Johan Gustave and Margaret Christina (Olson) Ahlberg, his ancestors on both sides having been natives of Sweden for generations. After receiving his education in his native country, he learned the cabinet-making trade and, in 1871, came to America, arriving in Chicago in July of that year. In 1878, he removed to Evanston, where he has followed the cabinet business continuously ever since. Mr. Ahlberg was married in 1872 to Margaret C. Oslund, who is also a native of Sweden, and they have three children: Theresa, Axel Renaldo and Gertrude. In religious faith he is a Baptist and a member of the Swedish Baptist Church, and in political opinions is a Republican, but is not identified with any secret fraternal organizations. His residence is at 2122 Harrison Street, Evanston.

DR. STEPHEN V. BALDERSTON.

Stephen Victor Balderston, a very favorably known and successful physician, of Evanston, Ill., was born in Prince Edward Island, Canada, November 5, 1868, a son of Hon. John and Sarah (Weeks) Balderston, both natives of Prince Edward Island. His father was born October 31, 1831, and his mother, May 3, 1841. The occupation of the former was that of a farmer and miller and, in his civic career, he attained prominence and distinction as a statesman. Hon. John Balderston first came into public notice at the age of twenty-eight years, in connection with the movement, in Prince Edward Island, for the abolition of landlordism in that colony. When thirty-two years old, he was elected to the Legislative Council, in which he served twenty-four years, during ten years of this period acting as President of that body. When Prince Edward Island became a Province of the Dominion of Canada, in 1870, the title of Honorable was bestowed upon Mr. Balderston, as a mark of favor, by Queen Victoria.

The paternal grandfather of Dr. Balderston was a native of Cornwall, England, and a descendant of an old border family which lived in the land of the Douglases. Grandmother Balderston's people were Protestant Irish, born in Wexford. One brother was condemned to be burned by Irish insurrectionists in a holocaust of some hundreds in a large barn, but was rescued at the last moment by a priest, who was a personal friend. The Weeks family were also Irish Protestants, and one member of it was a Captain of foot soldiers during the Irish Rebellion.

Stephen Victor Balderston spent his childhood on his father's farm, and was a sprightly lad of a somewhat studious disposition. In early youth he utilized the advantages afforded by the common schools in the vicinity of his home, and then pursued a course of study in Prince of Wales College, at Charlottetown, Prince Edward Island. After leaving college, he applied himself to teaching school for a time. His professional education was subsequently obtained in the University of Pennsylvania Medical Department, at Philadelphia, from which he was graduated in 1895. In the same year he took the position of interne in the hospital of the National Soldiers' Home, in Virginia, where he was promoted to be First Assistant Surgeon in 1897. This position he resigned in December, 1899, to take up private practice in Evanston. During the period spent in the hospital at Hampton, Va., he served through an epidemic of yellow fever. While there he became a citizen of the commonwealth of Virginia.

On January 5, 1903, Dr. Balderston was united in marriage, in the National Soldiers' Home, in Virginia, with Jessie Elizabeth Thompson, who was born August 17, 1873, in the National Military Home at Dayton, Ohio. Her father was a veteran of the Civil War, having served in the Third Regiment Kentucky Volunteer Infantry and lost an arm on the battlefield. He was a member of the staff at the National Military Home at Dayton, Ohio, and Governor of the National Soldiers' Home in Virginia. Mrs. Balderston is a graduate of the Woman's College of Baltimore, Md., and a member of the Alpha Phi Sorority.

Dr. Balderston is a member of the John Ashhurst, Jr., Surgical Society of the University of Pennsylvania, the Chicago Pediatric Society, the Chicago Medical Society, and the Illinois State Medical Society. In politics, he is inclined to favor the general policies of the Republican party, but is not in accord with high-tariff legislation. He voted for McKinley and Roosevelt. In religion, the doctor adheres to the faith of the Methodist Church.

Next to his love of good books and his partiality for microscopic investigation, the subject of this sketch is fond of out-door sports, especially golf. Most of all, in a practical sense, he likes to be regarded as a family doctor who tries to make peo-ple physically better and mentally hap-pier. He takes an earnest and intelligent interest in public affairs, and supports all measures tending to promote the welfare of the city of his adoption.

HENRY W. HINSDALE.

Henry W. Hinsdale, an old and widely known resident of Evanston, now living in honored retirement, was born in Benning-ton, Vt., August 19, 1825, being descended from an old New England family. His father, Hiram W. Hinsdale, was a farmer by occupation. The son attended the public schools of Bennington, and later, went to school at Grand Rapids, Mich., to which place his parents moved at an early date. Grand Rapids was then an Indian trading post. Henry stayed on the farm until he was seventeen years old, and then set out alone for Chicago, where he arrived with but two dollars in his pocket and having no acquaintance to advise him. He looked about for something to do, and finally se-cured employment with J. H. Dunham, then the leading wholesale grocer. His wages at first were two dollars per week. He was employed as a clerk in this store for ten years, his salary for the last five years of this period amounting to $2,500 per year. He was afterwards a partner in the concern for three years, and then bought

Mr. Dunham's interest and became the head of the firm of Hinsdale & Babcock. Later he built a block at the corner of South Wa-ter and River Streets, which he occupied as head of the firm of Hinsdale, Sibley & Babcock. He carried on this business until the spring of 1867, when he temporarily retired. He was the most extensive whole-sale grocer of his day in Chicago.

Just before the great fire of 1871, Mr. Hinsdale went to Grand Rapids, where he built a beautiful home, intending to live there. The fire destroyed property belong-ing to him, worth more than $500,000, and evidence of his high standing as a merchant is found in the fact that two of his New York correspondents telegraphed him au-thority to draw on them for $50,000 each.

Mr. Hinsdale has known Chicago since it was a small city, and can remember hunt-ing deer where the Board of Trade Build-ing stands. His business career began in Chicago during the 'forties, and continued for a period of more than fifty years. His first residence was on Wabash Avenue, where he built the first house north of Twelfth Street. Later he had a house on Prairie Avenue. He removed to Evanston in the 'sixties, where he lived for three or four years before going to Grand Rapids. He continued to reside at the latter place until 1879, engaged in loaning money for Eastern capitalists and in rebuilding Chi-cago property. During the years of his experience as a pioneer merchant, he had formed a wide acquaintance with Western business men, who had great confidence in his sagacity and foresight.

In 1879 Mr. Hinsdale moved from Grand Rapids to Evanston, and went into the brokerage business, in which he was en-gaged for fourteen years. At the end of this period he became manager of the Chamber of Commerce safety vaults. This position he held until July, 1904, when he abandoned an active business life. While in the brokerage business he represented three of the leading sugar refineries of the United States. After the capture of New Orleans in the Civil War, he sent north the first cargo of sugar, loading three vessels.

Mr. Hinsdale was one of the early members of the Chicago Board of Trade, and one of the first stockholders of the Elgin Watch company. The Merchants Loan & Trust Company was organized in the office of J. H. Dunham & Co., with which Mr. Hinsdale was connected. He was a passenger on the first train that ran west of Chicago on the Chicago & Galena Union Railroad. In 1866 he made an overland journey to California, returning by way of the Isthmus of Panama. The beautiful town of Hinsdale, on the Chicago, Burlington & Quincy Railway, was named after Mr. Hinsdale by its founders, who were his friends.

The subject of this sketch was married in Chicago, at the home of Mrs. Hinsdale, on State Street, opposite Marshall Field's present store, wedding Eliza Chatfield, a daughter of Judge John Chatfield, of Batavia, N. Y. The children born of this union are: Henry K. Hinsdale, now of New York; Mrs. Charlotte Hinsdale Mosely, and Benjamin Hinsdale, of Evanston.

Religiously Mr. Hinsdale is an Episcopalian, and served as Warden of Grace Episcopal Church in Chicago, for many years. He is now a communicant of St. Mary's Episcopal Church of Evanston.

THOMAS H. BEEBE.

Thomas H. Beebe, a venerable and greatly esteemed citizen of Evanston, Ill., who is passing his declining years in well-earned repose, was born in St. Louis, Mo., March 31, 1819, the son of Elijah and Sarah (Hempstead) Beebe, natives of Connecticut. The Beebe family came to America with Gov. Winthrop's colony. John Beebe started from Northamptonshire, England, with his wife and five sons, in 1650, but died on shipboard. The remainder of the family settled at New London, Conn. From its head, all the Beebes are descended. At a convention of citizens of Columbia County, N. Y., held June 24, 1776, Martin Beebe was made a member of a committee which was instructed to draft resolutions declaring for Independence. The Hempstead family is also of ancient and honorable origin.

Elijah Beebe journeyed from New England to St. Louis in 1813, making the trip to Pittsburg, Pa., overland. There he purchased a keel-boat and took a cargo of flour down the river. At Louisville, Ky., he took aboard John and Benjamin O'Fallon, men who afterwards became noted citizens of St. Louis. By trade Elijah Beebe was a saddler and harness maker, and established himself in that line in St. Louis. Subsequently, he took a contract to supply beef to the Government forts. On one of his excursions in this connection, Indians robbed him of a whole herd of cattle, for which loss he was reimbursed by Congress through the efforts of Col. Thomas H. Benton.

Thomas H. Beebe received his early education in the public schools of St. Louis and in the country schools of Belleville, Ill., and afterwards went to work in the dry goods store of his uncle, William Hempstead, in St. Louis. He was later employed by Hempstead and Beebe. This firm was in the river trade, and was interested in steamboats. Mr. Beebe afterwards became a clerk at different times on several of these boats, and followed the river for about four years. He then went to the Rocky Mountains with a wagon train, and on this trading expedition had an interesting experience among the Indians.

In 1841 Mr. Beebe went to Galena, Ill., where his uncle, William Hempstead, was in business, and was employed by him for two years, becoming his uncle's partner, at a later period, in smelting and dealing in lead. This connection lasted until 1853, when he came to Chicago and opened a branch house under the name of T. H. Beebe & Co., in the forwarding and commission line. Isaac L. Lyon and E. G. Merrick became members of the firm during its first year, and the business was transacted under the firm name of Beebe, Lyon & Co. Mr. Beebe bought his uncle's half-interest, and the firm purchased a half-interest in the lumber firm of Capt. Jesse H. Leavenworth, who owned mills and timber land at Peshtigo, Wis. The firm of Beebe, Lyon & Co. was dissolved in 1855, Mr. Beebe retaining his lumber interest with Capt. Leavenworth.

William B. Ogden, the first Mayor of Chicago, became a partner of Beebe, in 1856, and the Peshtigo Lumber Company was formed that year. Mr. Beebe afterwards became President of this company, and filled that office until 1873, when he resigned and disposed of his interest in the business.

In 1873, Mr. Beebe went to California as general superintendent of a large lumber concern. After a short time he returned to Chicago, and was subsequently connected with the First National Bank, of that city, and the Consolidated Paper Company. He was a sufferer from the great fire of 1871, after which he moved to Highland Park, where he lived six years and served as Mayor in 1874. He afterwards returned to Chicago, whence, in 1891, he moved to Evanston, where he has since resided. He was an early member of the Chicago Board of Trade, of which he was Vice-President for two years.

Thomas H. Beebe was married in 1844 to Catherine Eddowes, a daughter of John and Lydia Eddowes, of Galena, Ill. Mrs. Beebe was born in Newcastle County, Delaware. She died June 3, 1902, after fifty-eight years of wifely companionship. The children of this union who are living are as follows: Edward H., who lives in California; William H., Dr. John E., Christopher K., of Chicago; Archibald A., and Catherine E.; Mrs. Lydia (Beebe) Van Dusen and Mrs. Mary K. Valentine, of Evanston.

Politically, Mr. Beebe was a Whig in his early life, but later acted in co-operation with the Democratic Party until 1896, and since that time has been an Independent Republican. Religiously, he is classed as a Presbyterian.

JOHN G. BYRNE, M. D.

John G. Byrne, physician and surgeon, who is engaged in the practice of his profession at Spokane, Wash., was born in Chicago, Ill., January 22, 1871. He attended the Chicago public schools, and was a student in Dennison University, in 1887-89, and in Lake Forest Academy in 1890. In 1891 he matriculated in Northwestern University Medical School, from which he was graduated in 1894 with the degree of M. D. From April, 1894, to May, 1895, he acted in the capacity of interne in Wesley Hospital, Chicago. He is a member of the Phi Rho Sigma Fraternity.

On March 2, 1887, the subject of this sketch enlisted as a private in the Second Regiment, Illinois National Guard, and became Corporal of Company E, May 17, 1890; Sergeant, December 15, 1890; First Sergeant and Hospital Steward in 1896; Assistant Surgeon, December 22, 1897; First Lieutenant and Assistant Surgeon Illinois Volunteer Infantry, May 16, 1898, and resigned September 28, 1898. He was appointed Acting Assistant Surgeon U. S. Army, November 9, 1899, and served as such until March 20, 1903, spending one year in the Philippines, where he was wounded, June 26, 1900. He was Post Surgeon at Fort Wright from December 6, 1900 to March 20, 1903.

Dr. Byrne is a member of the Snohomish County (Wash.) Medical Society, and a life member of Northwestern University Alumni Medical Association. Socially, he is a member of the Spokane Club, and the M. W. A., the Royal Highlanders, and Surgeon to Spanish War Veterans.

On October 14, 1897, Dr. Byrne was united in marriage with Annie S. Hewitt, who has held the position of Superintendent of Wesley Hospital in Chicago, and of the West Side Hospital, in the same city. Dr. and Mrs. Byrne have one child—Katherine Anna, born November 7, 1903.

JOHN J. FLINN.

John J. Flinn became a resident of the village of South Evanston in the summer of 1880, when he purchased from General Julius White the house which he and his family have since occupied at 814 Michigan Avenue. The street was then called Congress Street, but later the name was changed to Wheeler Avenue. It became Michigan Avenue by adopting the name of the extension north of Main Street, which was then called Lincoln Avenue. With the exception of three years, Mr. Flinn has been continuously a resident of Evanston

from the time of his first removal here. He has thus witnessed practically all the changes that have occurred here for the last twenty-five years, and has taken an active part in connection with some of the most important of them.

Mr. Flinn was born in Clonmel, Ireland, December 5, 1851, his parents being James and Margaret (Cunningham) Flinn. Coming to America with his widowed mother in 1863, after receiving only an elementary education in his native country, he began life on this side as a cash boy in Boston. Thanks to the fact that the Boston Public Library was open to him, his education was uninterrupted. He read everything that he could lay his hands on, and kept this up when his family moved to Missouri. At eighteen years of age he began to contribute matter to the local newspapers, at twenty-one became a reporter in St. Joseph, Mo., and one year later secured a position under Joseph B. McCullagh (inventor of the "Interview"), on the "St. Louis Globe," now the "Globe-Democrat." At twenty-two he was made night editor of that journal, later was entrusted with the Legislative correspondence, and in 1873 reported the proceedings of the Missouri State Constitutional Convention. His days in St. Louis were contemporaneous with those of Eugene Field, Stanley Huntly, Stanley Waterloo, William Lightfoot Visscher, and others who have won celebrity in literature.

In 1875 Mr. Flinn became associated with Melville E. Stone in the editorship of the "Chicago Daily News," and was connected with that newspaper during the first seven years of its existence. In 1883 he was appointed Consul to Chemnitz, Saxony. Returning he became associated with Frank Hatton, who was Postmaster-General under President Arthur, and Clinton A. Snowden, in the publication of the "Chicago Mail," and later was managing editor of the "Chicago Times." Since 1897 he has been an editorial writer on the "Chicago Inter Ocean."

In addition to his newspaper work, Mr. Flinn has written numerous essays, lectures, poems, a novel, etc. In connection with John E. Wilkie, now chief of the United States Secret Service, he compiled a "History of the Chicago Police." He is the compiler, also, of the "Standard Guide to Chicago," and was appointed compiler of all the authorized Guide Books of the World's Columbian Exposition. He is a charter member of the Chicago Press Club, and was elected to its Presidency in 1906. He is one of the founders of the Twentieth Century Club of Evanston, and has been its President. He is serving his third term as a member of the Evanston City Council.

FRANK MYER FORREY.

Frank Myer Forrey, credit man State Bank of Chicago, was born in Cambridge City, Ind., November 1, 1859, the son of William Sharpless and Lydia (Myer) Forrey, the former a native of Milton, Ind., and the latter of Dublin, Ind. The father was engaged in the hotel business for many years, for ten years was in charge of the Hotel Phœnix at Shreveport, La.; one year with the Commercial Hotel at Muscatine, Iowa; five years with the Occidental Hotel at Wichita, Kan., and five years with the Glen House at Harper, Kan. He died in April, 1904.

Frank M. Forrey came to Chicago in 1864, acquired his education there and, in 1875, entered into the employment of the Central National Bank, remaining one year, when he became a clerk and later Exchange Clerk, in the Clearing House for two years. He was then offered the position of Assistant Cashier of the firm of A. T. Stewart & Co., where three years later he assumed the entire responsibility as Cashier without an assistant. In 1881 he became connected with the wholesale dry goods firm of James H. Walker & Co., as Cashier, remaining until the failure of the firm in 1893, when he became an employe of the State Bank of Chicago, in which, at the present time, he holds the position of credit man.

On November 1, 1881, Mr. Forrey was married in the city of Chicago, to Alida Churcher, who was born in Chicago in 1862 and is a granddaughter of Rev. Edward D. Wheadon, who was a prominent Methodist preacher and one of the early settlers of Evanston. Mrs. Forrey's mother was a teacher in the vicinity of Evanston a half century ago. Mr. and Mrs. Forrey have lived at the same location in Evanston, No. 2040 Sherman Avenue, since 1882, a period of nearly twenty-five years. They have two children: La Jeune C., born in Evanston, November 1, 1885, and Richard Lindgren, born in the same place, December 5, 1891. The daughter, La Jeune, won the oratorical contest of Literary Societies as a student in Northwestern University in 1904, being the first female student to gain that distinction in ten years.

Mr. Forrey served as Alderman of his ward two years (1897-98), is a member of the Republican party and in religious faith and association a Methodist. He is fraternally associated with the Royal Arcanum, the Royal League, of which he has been an officer since 1883; the Order of Columbian Knights, and formerly a member of the Boat Club, but later of the Evanston Club. He is also identified with the Evanston Musical Club, which includes in its membership a large proportion of the musical talent of the University city.

MITCHELL DAVIS FOLLANSBEE.

Mitchell Davis Follansbee, who is engaged in the practice of the law in Chicago, with offices in the Home Insurance Building, and in New York, with offices in the Trinity Building, is the son of George A. Follansbee, and was born in Chicago January 23, 1870. He obtained his education in the public schools, the South Division High School, Harvard School, and Harvard University, from which he was graduated in 1892, with the degree of A. B. He then entered the Northwestern University Law School, being graduated therefrom in 1894, with the degree of LL. B. He was on the first Board of the Northwestern Law Review, and a member of the Phi Delta Phi Legal Fraternity. He now holds the position of lecturer on Legal Ethics in the Northwestern University Law School and is Professor of Illinois Practice in that institution. He is a member of the University, Midday, Onwentsia, Forty, Saddle & Cycle, and Harvard clubs of Chicago, and belongs to the Legal Club, Law Club, the Chicago Bar Association, the Illinois State Bar Association, the Harvard Club and the Lawyers' Club of New York, and the Harvard Union of Cambridge, Mass. He is President of the District Council of the Lower North District of the Bureau of Charities, and is President of the Northwestern University Law Publishing Association, publishers of the new Illinois Law Review.

On April 14, 1903, Mr. Follansbee was married at Seabreeze, Fla., to Miss Julia Rogers McConnell. They have two children: Eleanor, born January 27, 1904, and Mitchell Davis Follansbee, Jr., born March 6, 1906. Their home is at 52 Bellevue Place, Chicago.

ROLLIN CURTIS WINSLOW, M. D.

Dr. Rollin Curtis Winslow, physician and surgeon, who is engaged in the practice of his profession at Sault Ste. Marie, Mich., was born at Laporte, Mich., August 11, 1873. He received his primary mental training in the public school, and afterward became a pupil in the Laporte (Mich.) High School. He then studied languages in a private school, for two years. His first course of medical study was pursued in the Saginaw Valley Medical College, from which he was graduated in 1899, with the degree of M. D. He matriculated in Northwestern University Medical School in the summer of 1901, and graduated therefrom with the class of 1902.

Previous to taking the university course, Dr. Winslow was engaged in the practice of medicine at West Branch, Mich., from June, 1899, to September, 1901. On graduating from the medical department of the university he entered upon practice in his present location.

He is a member of the American Medical Association; the Michigan State Medical Society; the Upper Peninsula (Mich.) Medical Society; and the Chippewa County (Mich.) Medical Society, of which he was elected Secretary in 1905.

On September 21, 1898, at Saginaw, Mich., Dr. Winslow was united in marriage with Edith May McAlpine. This union has resulted in one child, Madeline Eloise, born January 22, 1905.

WILLIAM HUDSON DAMSEL.

William H. Damsel, a well known and highly respected citizen of Evanston, Ill., was born in Westchester, Chester County, Pa., February 7, 1844, the son of Uriah and Catherine (Phipps) Damsel, natives of

Pennsylvania, the former born in Lancaster County and the latter in Chester County. The occupation of Uriah Damsel was that of a manufacturer. In early youth William H. Damsel obtained his education in the schools of his native town, and after his studies were completed, secured a position in the employ of the Central Ohio Railroad Company. April 17, 1861, he enlisted as a private in the Third Regular Ohio Volunteer Infantry, for a service of three months, being mustered out August 19, 1861, at the expiration of his term of enlistment. On May 1, 1864, he entered the service of the Adams Express Company, with which he has ever since been connected.

On September 15, 1870, Mr. Damsel was united in marriage, at Columbus, Ohio, with Susan R. Nace, who was born at Morristown, in that State, March 7, 1845. Five children were born of this union, namely: William Wynkoop, born December 27, 1871; Edna Murray, born January 14, 1873; Jessamine Phipps, born April 1, 1877; Ethel Birch, born June 20, 1879; and Percy, born June 10, 1882.

In politics Mr. Damsel is a supporter of the Republican party, and fraternally is identified with the Royal Arcanum and the Knights of Honor.

GEORGE OSMAN IDE.

George Osman Ide (deceased), formerly a well known attorney of Evanston, Ill., and a highly respected citizen, was born at Passumpsic, Vt., November 25, 1831. His father, Rev. George Barton Ide, a clergyman of the Baptist Church, was born in Coventry, Vt., February 17, 1804, and his mother, Harriet (Walker) Ide, was born December 21, 1807. The ancestry of the

Ide family dates back to an early period in New England history. John Ide, the great-grandfather of George O., born in 1742, and deceased in 1815, was a soldier in the Revolutionary army. Timothy Ide, another ancestor, whose life covered the period between 1660 and 1735, was an early settler of Bristol County, Massachusetts. He took an active part in the wars against the Indians, and was an ensign to the General Court of Massachusetts. Still another ancestor, Nicholas Ide, came from England to Massachusetts in 1643. He was one of the original settlers of Bristol County, and one of the first landowners there. He was active in the early settlements; was one of a committee appointed to settle disputes with King Philip, the Indian Chief, in 1689, and was the first of his name in America.

Rev. George B. Ide, father of George O., was pastor of the First Baptist Church of Philadelphia, Pa., from 1838 to 1852, and of the first Baptist Church of Springfield, Mass., from 1852 to 1872. He died in the city last named, April 16, 1872.

George O. Ide attended the public schools of Philadelphia, to which place the family had moved, and completed his education at Hamilton College, N. Y., where he graduated. He studied law under Rufus Choate, in Springfield, Mass., where he was admitted to the bar. Soon afterwards he came to Illinois and, about 1855, settled in Princeton, where he began the practice of law. In this he continued successfully until 1871, when he came to Chicago and formed a partnership with George L. Paddock, formerly of Princeton, under the firm name of Paddock & Ide, during the same year taking up his residence in Evanston, where he lived during the remainder of his life. About three years before his death the firm of Paddock & Ide was dissolved, and Mr. Ide thereafter practiced alone. He was Village Attorney of Evanston from

1874 to 1880, and attained a prominent position at the Chicago bar.   .

Mr. Ide was married at Princeton, Ill., January 29, 1862, to Helen M. Ide, a daughter of Cassander Ide, of that place. Mrs. Ide was born at Essex, Vt., and belonged to the same general lineage as her husband. The children born of this union who are still living are: William K. Ide, of the First National Bank, Chicago; Charles B. Ide, of the Corn Exchange National Bank, Chicago; Arthur C. Ide, an attorney of Chicago; and Mrs. Henry W. Dakin, of Detroit, Mich. The eldest of the sons of Mr. and Mrs. Ide, died in Evanston, August 6, 1894.

In politics, George O. Ide was a Democrat, and fraternally, was a member of the Masonic order, and in religious belief, a Baptist. His death occurred at his home in Evanston, February 7, 1885. The home at No. 1425 Maple Avenue, where the family have resided since 1881, is still occupied by his widow and three surviving sons.

ORRIN T. MAXSON, M. D.

Orrin T. Maxson, M. D. (deceased), formerly a prominent physician in Evanston, Ill., was born in the State of New York in 1825, being descended from an old New England family. In his early childhood he went to Wisconsin with his parents, who were among the earliest settlers in the northwestern part of that State. There he attended the public schools and received his early mental training. His professional education was obtained in Rush Medical College, Chicago. Dr. Maxson began the practice of medicine in Prescott, Wis., where he remained several years, when he removed to Chicago, and where he continued in practice. He subsequently lived and practiced for a time in Waukegan, Ill.

In the early 'eighties he moved to Evanston, Ill., where he devoted himself to his profession until his death, which occurred at Pasadena, Cal., in 1895. Dr. Maxson recruited Company A, Twelfth Regiment Wisconsin Volunteer Infantry for service in the Civil War, and served as its Captain during the entire war.

Dr. Maxson was married to Eunice McCray, of New York State. Those of their children who are living are: Dr. O. P. Maxson, of Waukegan; and Amelia (Maxson) Knox, who resides in Evanston. In 1882 the daughter, Amelia, became the wife of Laverne L. Knox, of Waukegan, who was engaged in business in Chicago, and died in Evanston in 1889.

Dr. Maxson was a physician of high standing in his profession and of superior accomplishments, and was a valued member of the leading medical societies. Politically he was an active Republican and took a good citizen's interest in public affairs. While living in Wisconsin he served as a member of the Legislature of that State. Fraternally, he was a Knight Templar, and in religious belief a Congregationalist.

FRANK WHEELOCK GEROULD.

Among the most prominent men in the social, political and religious circles of Evanston, Ill., whose business interests are in Chicago, is the gentleman whose name heads this brief personal record. Mr. Gerould was born in Smithfield, Pa., January 13, 1854, the son of Marcus B. and Mary E. (Bingham) Gerould, of whom the former was born in Smithfield, Pa., October 28, 1818, and the latter, in Towanda County, in the same State, January 2, 1827. Marcus B. Gerould was a merchant by occupation. In 1857 he moved from Pennsylvania to Rockford, Ill., where, with the exception of a few years spent in Byron, Ill., the family made their permanent home.

In youth the subject of this sketch diligently utilized the opportunities afforded by the public schools of Rockford, and, after completing his studies, secured employment as clerk in a shoe store in that city. In 1878 he located in Chicago and entered the employ of A. G. Spaulding & Bros., extensive dealers in athletic goods, in which connection he has remained until the present time. Mr. Gerould now occupies the position of managing director of the western department of that widely known establishment. He maintains a high reputation for executive ability in the commercial circles of Chicago, and is very popular among the employes and patrons of the concern with which he has been so long identified.

On September 1, 1881, Mr. Gerould was united in marriage, in the city of Chicago, with Mary S. Avery, who was born in Belvidere, Ill., on February 9, 1860. Three children have been born to them: Helen Louise, born January 9, 1890; Frank Avery, born August 15, 1893, and Walter Blakesley, born August 18, 1898. The mother of this family passed away in Evanston, March 11, 1901.

Mr. Gerould is connected with the First Presbyterian Church, of Evanston, and is a member of its Board of Trustees. In politics he is a supporter of the Republican party, and has represented his ward in Evanston, as Alderman, for the last eight years. Socially he is a member of the Evanston Club, of which he is President and director; a member of the Chicago Athletic Club, and of the Glen View Golf Club. He is one of the Directors of the State Bank of Evanston. In earlier life he belonged to the Illinois National Guard for six years. He is highly regarded throughout the community.

WILLIAM BECKLEY PARKES.

William B. Parkes (deceased), formerly a prominent citizen of Evanston, Ill., and a man of lovable and great force of character, was born in Saugerties, N. Y., March 19, 1838. He was a son of Joseph and Mary (Dunn) Parkes, who came from Dudley, England, five or six years before his birth, and a brother of the noted surgeon, Dr. Charles T. Parkes, of Chicago. Joseph Parkes was an iron master, with interests in Wheeling, W. Va., and St. Louis, Mo. He prepared his son, William, for a commercial career, the latter having graduated from a business college in Wheeling at the age of thirteen years. From that period he worked in his father's foundry and made himself independent, paying his own board and other expenses.

In the panic of 1857, the failure of his father's works at St. Louis, with which he was connected, together with his marriage at the same time, made it necessary for him to seek other employment. He accordingly went from St. Louis to Southern Illinois, and worked on farms in order to secure means to engage in business on his own account. In 1864, he bought a farm in Will County, Ill., which he operated for three years, and then, coming to Chicago, secured employment in connection with the North Chicago Rolling Mill Company.

In 1868, Capt. E. B. Ward, of Detroit, founded the Milwaukee Iron Works, and among other skilled workmen who were taken there from Chicago, was Mr. Parkes. He was soon promoted to the superintendency of a department in the plant, and subsequently, when the North Chicago Rolling Mill Company acquired possession of the works, he was made General Superintendent. This position he held for ten years or more, having an average of 2,000 men under his direction. He was especially happy in his method of dealing with his employes, and was successful in building up an industrious and prosperous community. In this connection he became widely known as a practical iron-master of ripe experience and broad general knowledge of all phases of the business. Besides his rolling mill connection, he was interested in iron mines and transportation companies to a considerable extent.

At this period ill health compelled Mr. Parkes to retire from active business, and he severed his connection with the concern in 1890. Disposing of his Milwaukee interests he purchased a home in Evanston, where he lived in retirement until 1899. He died August 4, 1899, in Milwaukee, where he had gone to visit his daughter.

Mr. Parkes was married at St. Louis, in 1857, to Mary Jane McNickle, a daughter of George and Jane (McCoy) McNickle, of that city. Mrs. Parkes, who is still living, was born in Pennsylvania and reared in Virginia. The children of this union are as follows: Ida Virginia Parkes, Mrs. Mary (Parkes) Llewellyn, Mrs. Jennie (Parkes) Grier, Mrs. Annie (Parkes) Phillips, and Dr. William Ross Parkes, all of Evanston, and Mrs. Sarah (Parkes) Treat, of Appleton, Wis.

Mr. Parkes became a member of the Methodist Episcopal Church when he was fourteen years of age, and when he removed to his farm in Will County, he helped to found a church at Monee. He was afterwards one of the founders of the Dixon Street M. E. Church in Chicago, and of Trinity M. E. Church in Milwaukee, where he served as Sunday-school Superintendent for twenty years. After coming to Evanston he was one of the builders of Emmanuel M. E. Church. For several years he was a member of the Board of Trustees and of the official board of the last named church. "Though dead he yet speaketh," and "his works do follow him."

JOSEPH WATERS WORK.

Joseph W. Work, who is successfully engaged in the real estate business in Evanston, Ill., was born in Dewitt, Carroll County, Mo., September 18, 1871. His father, Andrew Jackson Work, was a native of Charlestown, Ind., where he was born October 17, 1819, and his mother, Elizabeth (Waters) Work, was born in Lincoln County, Ky., October 15, 1835. Andrew Jackson Work was a farmer by occupation and his whole active life was devoted to agricultural pursuits.

The early education of Joseph W. was obtained in the public schools and the high school at North Salem, Ind., and Bunker Hill, Ill., and, after completing his studies, he became a traveling salesman. This occupation he followed for nine years previous to making his home in Evanston, where he located in 1894. In that year he established himself in the real estate business in partnership with his father-in-law, Lewis M. Perry, succeeding to the latter's interest in the firm, in 1897 and establishing at that time the firm known as The J. W. Work Agency.

On December 27, 1893, Mr. Work was united in marriage at Evanston, with Flora Perry, who was born in Murdock, Ill., December 10, 1871.

In politics, Mr. Work pursues an independent course, ignoring party lines. His religious connection is with the Evanston Christian Church, of which he is a charter member. Socially he is identified with the Evanston Club.

SUSAN LEONHARDT.

Mrs. Susan Leonhardt, one of the oldest living natives of Cook County, Ill., was born at Grosse Point, September 18, 1840, and enjoys the distinction of being the first white child born within the present city of

Evanston. She is a daughter of Paul and Caroline (Adams) Pratt, who were natives of Massachusetts; her mother Caroline Adams, being a daughter of Rev. Ephraim Adams, who was a member of the same family which furnished two Presidents of the United States—John Adams and John Quincy Adams. Her father was born in Weston, Middlesex County, Mass., September 11, 1807, and her mother, in Oxford, Worcester County, March 10, 1816. Paul Pratt was the owner of considerable landed property, for those times, and was engaged in agricultural pursuits. His father, also Paul Pratt, was one of the historical "Minute Men" of Massachusetts Colony, who sprang to arms from every village and farm in Middlesex County, when Paul Revere sounded the summons on his celebrated ride in 1775. Paul Pratt, Jr., the father of Mrs. Leonhardt, moved to Illinois at an early period, locating on the site of the present city of Evanston. On his land in that locality, he hewed timber and rafted it to the mouth of the Chicago River, to be used in building the first Government pier at Chicago in 1839. He had two sons who took part in the Civil War, Charles E. and Willard I. The former served three years in the Eighth Regiment Illinois Volunteer Cavalry; the latter was a member of Company C, Eighty-ninth Regiment Illinois Volunteer Infantry, and was taken prisoner at Dallas, Ga., and incarcerated in Andersonville prison, where he languished for seven months. He died at home in 1865. From their log cabin on Leon Avenue, the family moved in 1848, to a frame house, built that year, and which was one of the first frame dwellings constructed in Evanston.

Mrs. Leonhardt spent her childhood years in the way customary for farmers' daughters in a new settlement. Her early mental training was obtained in the country school at Ridgeville, now a part of Evanston, and she grew to maturity on the paternal farm. On September 30, 1857, she was united in marriage at Evanston, with Louis Leonhardt, and twelve children were born of this union: Charles E., born April 29, 1859; Arthur D., born November 3, 1861; Frank W., born November 29, 1863; Carrie E. (Mrs. Stiles) born February 4, 1865; Ella, who was born August 29, 1866, and died in 1867; George P., born March 7, 1868; Louis, born November 25, 1870, and died in 1880; Eva May, born January 21, 1873, and died in 1880; Paul, born February 10, 1875, and died in 1880; Fred. L., born July 30, 1877, and died in 1880; Richard J., born November 17, 1880; and Willard I., born January 7, 1882. Seven of this family still survive.

In religious faith, Mrs. Leonhardt is a Baptist, and a zealous member of the Missionary Society of the First Baptist Church of Evanston. She is an object of affectionate interest to her children, and of cordial esteem by a large circle of friends.

LEWIS TABOR BRISTOL.

Lewis Tabor Bristol, who is engaged in the practice of dentistry in Nogales, Ariz., was born in Cairo, Ill., September 1, 1872, the son of Walter L. and Louisa S. Bristol, natives of Illinois. In early boyhood, Dr. Bristol received his primary mental training in the public schools of his native town, where he spent the remainder of his youthful years. He entered the Dental School of Northwestern University in 1894, graduating therefrom in 1897, with the degree of D. D. S. He is a member of the Delta Sigma Delta Fraternity. Shortly after his graduation he entered upon the practice of his profession, in which he has continued successfully ever since. In politics, Dr. Bristol is an earnest supporter of the Republican party. In 1905, he served as a Representative of Santa Cruz County in the Legislature of Arizona.

VERNELLE FREELAND BROWNE.

Vernelle F. Browne, attorney-at-law, Farmer City, Ill., was born at De Witt, De Witt County, Ill., January 8, 1873. He acquired his primary education in the local high school and by home study, took a law course in the Northwestern University Law School at Evanston, Ill., with one semester in the Law Department of the University of Michigan at Ann Arbor in that State. While in the University he was much interested in athletics, and a member of the Masonic Club at the University of Michigan. He worked his way through the University, was admitted to the bar in October, 1899, and, starting in debt, since entering upon his profession has been very successful, having accumulated, in less than seven years' practice, an estate valued at $15,000. The official positions held by Mr. Browne since locating at Farmer City, Ill., include those of City Clerk for two years (May 1, 1901, to May 1, 1903); City Attorney since May 1, 1903, in which he is now serving his second term, which will expire May 1, 1907. He has been solicited at different times to become the candidate of the Republican party for County Judge, State's Attorney and Representative in the State Legislature, but believing that his best interests would be subserved by adhering to his profession, has declined. He is a member of the Knights of Pythias, Modern Woodmen, Red Men, a Thirty-second Degree Mason, the Order of the Eastern Star, the Rathbon Sisters and the Benevolent and Protective Order of Elks.

On December 6, 1899, Mr. Browne was married to Miss Daisy Gertrude Reeser, of Farmer City, Ill., and they have one daughter, Theresa Gertrude Browne, born February 5, 1903.

WALTER LAURANCE HERDIEN.

Walter Laurance Herdien, who is a successful representative of the younger element of rising lawyers who are becoming favorably known at the bar of Chicago, was born in Galva, Ill. August 8, 1874. He is a son of Peter and Martha (Johnson) Herdien, natives of Sweden In early youth he made diligent use of the opportunities for an education afforded by the public schools of his native place, and in September, 1894, matriculated in the Liberal Arts Department of Northwestern University, from which he was graduated in June, 1898, with the degree of A. B. He entered Northwestern University Law School in September, 1898, graduating therefrom in June, 1900, with the degree of LL. B. During his collegiate course, he was a member of the Beta Theta Pi Fraternity and the Deru Society. Shortly after graduating he was admitted to the bar, and at once entered upon the practice of his profession, in which he has since continued. In social circles, he is affiliated with the B. P. O. E.

On October 25, 1903, Mr. Herdien was united in marriage with Mabel Geneva Sharp, of Kewanee, Ill. Politically, he is a Republican.

ELMER FORREST HERDIEN, M. D.

Elmer Forrest Herdien, physician, Chicago, Ill., was born in Galva, Ill., May 22, 1876, the son of Peter and Martha (Johnson) Herdien, both natives of Sweden and a brother of Walter L. Herdien, a lawyer of Chicago. Elmer F. spent most of his early life in Chicago, was a graduate from the Lake View High School and from the Northwestern University, later taking a course in the Medical Department of the University, from which he was graduated in 1901. After graduation he served for a time as interne in hospital work, after which he was engaged in practice at Baker City, Oregon. On June 6, 1906, Dr. Herdien was married at Kewanee, Ill., to Miss Nelle Johnson, of that city, the event exciting much interest among society people, and being celebrated with much eclat in the presence of a large circle of friends of the bride and groom. Dr. Herdien's address is at 1317 Foster Avenue (Edgewater), Chicago.

HENRY BUTLER.

Henry Butler, a well-known and highly-esteemed citizen of Evanston, Cook County, Ill., where he has lived for nearly twenty-six years—during a considerable portion of this period being extensively and successfully engaged in the livery and teaming business—was born in Kenosha, Wis., April 7, 1860, the son of Cornelius and Barbara (Blanknheim) Butler, of whom the former was born in Richmond Va., in July, 1822, and the latter in Prue, a small town in The Netherlands, on February 17, 1831. Cornelius Butler was a carpenter by occupation, and followed that trade in Kenosha, Wis., of which place he became a resident in 1840. Early in the Civil War he enlisted in the Thirty-ninth Regiment Wisconsin Volunteer Infantry, with which he served until the end of the conflict, when he returned to Kenosha and resumed his customary work. Shortly afterward he moved to Evanston, where

he spent the remainder of his life. The mother of the subject of this sketch came to the United States when she was about sixteen years of age. Her marriage to Mr. Butler took place at Kenosha on March 13, 1851, and their union resulted in eleven children.   .

The early mental training of Henry Butler was obtained in the district schools in the vicinity of Kenosha, and in the public schools of that city. When not engaged in study, he applied himself to farm work. He was about seventeen years old when he came to Evanston, where he was employed for several years in various kinds of labor by prominent citizens of the place. In 1893 he started out on his own responsibility, establishing himself in the livery and teaming business, in which he has ever since been very successful. He now conducts two extensive livery barns, has about seventy teams in use, and employs forty men, besides an office force of four girls. He also operates large blacksmith and repair shops. His entire time is occupied in superintending this business, and his energy, diligence, close application and honorable methods have made the enterprise a pronounced and signal success. With the exception of a tour of inspection which he made through the Western States, he has not been absent from home to any extent since coming to Evanston.

On January 5, 1883, Mr. Butler was united in marriage, at Evanston, Ill., with Mary Hager, who was born July 4, 1864, at Florence, Ala., where, in girlhood, she enjoyed the advantages of the public schools. Mrs. Butler is a daughter of William Hager, a native of Pennsylvania, and a soldier in the Civil War, near the close of which he lost his life. Her mother is also deceased.

In religious faith Mr. Butler is a Baptist, being a consistent member of the Second Baptist Church, of Evanston. Politically he has always been a firm Republican, but never an aspirant for public office. To all charitable and benevolent enterprises in Evanston, he has always been a liberal contributor. He has led a life of exceptional personal purity, having never made use of tobacco or intoxicants, nor indulged in profane language. His strict observance of correct rules of living have enabled him to endure the strain of long and strenuous exertion in building up his extensive business, with no impairment of mental or physical faculties, and his upright and honorable dealings have gained for him, in an especial degree, the confidence and esteem of his fellow citizens. Mr. Butler is regarded as one of the most useful and exemplary members of the community.

JOHN T. BARKER.

John T. Barker, lawyer and Mayor of Evanston, was born in Derbyshire, England, October 27, 1860, the son of John and Mary (Shimwell) Barker. John Barker, Sr., was a blacksmith by trade, and his death occurred in England. This bereavement necessitated his son's finding a position at the age of eleven in a rolling mill, in order to help support his mother. When the lad was thirteen years old, with his surviving parent he took passage for America, locating in the city of Chicago. The boy enjoyed less than two years' schooling before he went to work in earnest for the North Chicago Rolling Mills. A little later he secured a position with the Chicago Steel Works, where, for fifteen years, he found steady employment; first as a common laborer, at fifty cents per day, spending his earnings at a

night school, being gradually promoted through the positions of stenographer, bookkeeper, cashier, etc., until he received the sum of $1,500 per annum. Here he paused long enough to take a course of lessons at the Chicago Athenæum. In 1890 he launched out in the real estate business, his evenings again being occupied with the study of law in the night schools of the great city. In 1893, his studiousness was rewarded by his admittance to the bar.

On December 14, 1881, Mr. Barker was united in marriage to Anna Laura Blanchard, and of this union two children have been born: John Lawrence, born August 27, 1884, and Marion Ethel, born July 22, 1888. In 1897, Mr. Barker removed with his family to the city of Evanston Ill., with the history of whose growth the present Mayor has been and is still intimately connected. In the year 1900, Mr. Barker was elected Alderman for the Third Ward, thus becoming an active member of the City Council. In 1901 he took an extended vacation, making a tour through England, Scotland, France and Belgium, and other European countries. Upon his return to Evanston in 1902, he was re-elected Alderman, which position he resigned in the spring of 1903, when he was made Mayor of the city as successor of James A. Patten. During his official connection with the city, Mayor Barker has been greatly interested in much legislation of an important nature, such as the annexing of the North Shore territory to the Drainage District, the consolidation of the towns included in the present city of Evanston, the amendment of the Library Act, and other measures pertaining to public improvement. In the year 1905, he was re-elected Mayor of the city whose interests he has served so disinterestedly and well. In his political affiliations, Mayor Barker is a Republican. He was one of the originators of the organization of the first Park District of the city of Evanston, an improvement recognized by all. He is a member of the A. F. & A. M., the National Union, and Royal League Fraternities, and also of the local Evanston Club, Hamilton and Golf Clubs. He belongs to the Episcopalian Church.

GEORGE E. GOOCH.

George E. Gooch, a well-known resident of Evanston, Ill., who has been prominent in the business circles of Chicago for many years, was born in Norwich, Norfolk, England, September 24, 1847, the son of George C. and Margaret (Brewer) Gooch. The son received his early education in the common schools of his native land, and came to Chicago in 1867. He became connected with the commission firm of Sherman, Hall & Pope, and soon afterwards engaged in the same line of business on South Water Street, under the firm name of Richards & Gooch. Subsequently, he identified himself with Charles Counselman & Co., and still remains in that connection. Since 1869 he has been a member of the Chicago Board of Trade. Mr. Gooch established his residence in Evanston in 1877, and is considered one of its intelligent and substantial citizens.

Mr. Gooch was married in November, 1874, to Miss Rhoda England, a daughter of William England, and they have seven children, all of whom were born in Evanston, and all are still living.

In his political views, Mr. Gooch is independent, and his action is untrammeled by party ties. He has served as Alderman of the Second Ward in the City Council. Socially, he belongs to the A.

F. & A. M. Royal Arcanum, of which he is Regent; Royal League, of which he is Orator; Modern Woodmen of America, and Sons of St. George. He is a charter member of the Evanston Club and the Evanston Boat Club. Mr. Gooch is a communicant in St. Mark's Episcopal Church, in which he officiates as vestryman.

JOHN W. GIBSON.

John W. Gibson (deceased), formerly a well-known resident of Evanston, Ill., was born in Batesville, Noble County, Ohio, October 20, 1853. His parents were William and Christine (Stattler) Gibson, the former being a merchant by occupation. The early childhood of Mr. Gibson was passed in Batesville, and his education was received in the schools of Newark, Ohio. He was trained to merchandising by his father, and on the death of the latter, succeeded to the business and conducted it for two or three years. About 1881 he came West and became identified with the nursery business, establishing his home in Davenport, Iowa. In this connection he traveled extensively, his transactions covering the States of Iowa, Illinois and Wisconsin. He continued to reside at Davenport until 1890, when he moved to Evanston, where he remained until his death, which occurred September 13, 1904.

Mr. Gibson was married at Monroe Center, Ill., December 26, 1882, to Ella Tyler, a daughter of Mrs. H. C. Tyler, of that place. Mrs. Gibson, who survives her husband, was born there and grew up in Illinois. The only child of Mr. and Mrs. Gibson is Harry W. Gibson, who has succeeded to the conduct and management of his father's business interests. Mr. Gibson was an attendant upon the services at the Baptist Church.

JOHN C. MURPHY.

John C. Murphy (deceased), who served as Justice of the Peace in Evanston, Ill., for nearly twenty-three years, was born in Evanston July 31, 1841, the first white child born in that place. His parents were Edward and Ann (Mack) Murphy, natives of Ireland, the father born at Kenmore, County Kerry, in 1805, and the mother at Castletown Bearhaven, County Cork. Edward Murphy was a teacher and mathematician by profession. Through the influence of the Marquis of Lansdowne, while still a young man, he was appointed to the position of Government teacher at London, Upper Canada, where he first located on his arrival in America. In the spring of 1837 he settled in Chicago, where he taught in the public schools, and was otherwise interested in educational affairs. In 1839 he was appointed Deputy Sheriff, under Sheriff Isaac R. Gavenfirst, was elected Coroner of Cook County in 1840, and re-elected in 1842. He was the first Supervisor for Evanston, having been elected to that office in 1850, the year of the adoption of township organization, and served in this capacity until 1856. His death occurred January 25, 1875. Eugene Mack a brother of Mrs. Edward Murphy, served in the United States Navy for forty years, and was an officer on board the Frigate "Cumberland" when that vessel was sunk. Six of Edward Murphy's children survived him—two sons and four daughters, namely: John C., the subject of this sketch; Edward, Mary A. (Mrs. Sampson), Anna E., Louisa D., and Elizabeth C.

John C. Murphy received his early education in the public schools of Chicago, where he subsequently pursued a course of study in a business college. His father owned a farm in the vicinity of Evanston, and upon this John C. lived until 1875. From that year until 1881, he was in the employ of Cook County. He always made his home in Evanston, and in his reminiscences of early times often recalls the rush of gold seekers, with their prairie schooners to California in 1849-50.

On July 19, 1877, Mr. Murphy was united in marriage, in Chicago, with Elizabeth M. Carroll, who was born at Ogdensburg, N. Y., August 4, 1857. Four children were born of this union, namely: Edward J., born April 30, 1879; J. Francis, born November 13, 1881; Joseph N., born January 7, 1891 and Nannie A., born August 23, 1886.

In politics, Mr. Murphy was an unswerving adherent of the Republican party. He was elected Justice of the Peace for Evanston Township in April, 1881, and held that office without intermission until the time of his death. In fraternal circles, he was identified with the K. of P. and the Catholic Order of Foresters. He belonged to the Historical Society of Evanston. In religion, he was a devout member of the Catholic Church, and as a citizen, was ever on the alert in his efforts to promote the best interests of the community. He was a member of the Evanston Historical Society.

Mr. Murphy departed this life on February 21, 1904, and his death was deeply lamented by all who knew him. He was a man of invariable good nature and, as a public official, was easily accessible. On account of the numerous wedding ceremonies which he performed, he was sometimes called "Bishop" Murphy. The dwelling in which he was born is still standing, in a slightly altered condition, on the northwest corner of Clark Street and Rogers Avenue.

EDWARD J. MURPHY.

Edward J. Murphy, Justice of the Peace, Evanston, Ill., is a native of Evanston, where he was born April 30, 1879, the son of John C. and Elizabeth M. (Carroll) Murphy, the father born in Evanston, Ill., July 31, 1841, and the mother in Ogdensburg, N. Y., August 4, 1857. John C. Murphy was the first white male child born in Evanston, and died in that city February 21, 1904. The grandparents, Edward and Ann (Mack) Murphy, were natives of Ireland (see sketch of John C. Murphy). Grandfather Edward Murphy was a teacher and mathematician, who came to Chicago from London, Canada, in the spring of 1837, and taught in the public schools. He was the owner of a farm situated where the City of Evanston now stands, and served as Deputy Sheriff and Coroner of Cook County, and as the first Supervisor of Evanston, to which office he was elected in 1850.

The gentleman to whom this record refers received his rudimentary mental training in the public schools of Evanston, and subsequently graduated from the De La Salle Institute, in Chicago. He then pursued courses of study in Canisius College, at Buffalo, N. Y., and Northwestern University, Evanston, graduating from the Law School of the latter in 1903.

In politics Edward J. Murphy is an earnest supporter of the Republican party. In 1904 he was elected to succeed his father as Justice of the Peace, and enjoys the distinction of being the youngest incumbent of that office ever elected in Cook County. Socially, he is identified with the Phi Delta Theta Fraternity, the Alpha Chi Law Fraternity, the Modern Woodmen of America, and the Knights of Columbus. He is regarded as one of the most promising young men in the community, and seems fully assured of a bright and useful future.

GEORGE HENRY MOORE.

George Henry Moore, Manager Insurance Company, Chicago, with residence in Evanston, was born in North Hartland, Vermont, January 20, 1848, the son of Reuben and Ann Maria (Hunt) Moore, the former born in Salem, Mass., November 18, 1808, and the latter in Concord Mass., December 6, 1812. The father's occupation was that of a railroad contractor and builder. On the maternal side Mr. Moore is the eighth in descent from Captain Thomas Brooks, seventh from Captain Timothy Wheeler and Captain John Prescott, and sixth from Ensign Humphrey Barrett, Captain James Minott, Captain Jonathan Prescott, Hon. Peter Bulkley, Simon Lynde and Francis Willoughby—all of whom were soldiers of the Colonial and Revolutionary Wars, and direct descendants of the famous Hunt family, whose progenitors settled in New England in 1635.

George Henry Moore commenced business for himself at Plattsburgh, New York, as clerk in a general merchandise store in 1864, in which he remained two years, when (in 1866) he engaged in the forwarding and shipping business and lumber trade at Detroit, Michigan. Twelve years later (1878) he entered into the fire insurance business, which he has followed continuously ever since. Having received an appointment as one of the managers of the Liverpool, London & Globe Insurance Company for the West, on January 1, 1893, he moved to Evanston. He still retains this position with office in the Home Insurance Building at 205 La Salle Street, Chicago. He was elected President for 1896-7 of the Fire Insurance Association of the Northwest, which is the largest insurance organization in the world.

December 16, 1870, Mr. Moore was married at Detroit, Mich., to Emma E.

Smith, and they have had six children: Carlton Ward, Ella Florine, George Albert, Louise Hurd and Irene Hunt (twins), and William Warren.

In his political sentiments Mr. Moore has always been a sturdy Republican, is an attendant upon religious services at the First Presbyterian Church of Evanston, and is identified with the following clubs and social organizations: Union League Club, Chicago; Sons of the Revolution, Colonial War Society, Evanston Club, Evanston, and Glen View Golf Club.

CHARLES CLARENCE POOLE.

Charles Clarence Poole, patent lawyer, Evanston, Ill., was born at Benicia, Cal., November 27, 1856, the son of Charles Henry and Mary A. (Daniels) Poole, was educated in the public schools at Washington, D. C., and fitted for practice in civil engineering by private instruction. During 1874-75 he served as Assistant Engineer in connection with surveys carried on by the Engineering Department of the United States Army. In 1882 he graduated from the Law Department of the Columbian University, Washington,, with the prize for an essay on Trademarks. During the same year he came to Chicago and, in partnership with Taylor E. Brown, engaged in practice as a lawyer, confining his attention chiefly to patents, copyright and trade mark laws, which he still continues, with offices in the Marquette Building. He is also a member of the bar of the United States Supreme Court, the Chicago Bar Association, and the Patent Law Association. In 1884 Mr. Poole was married in the city of Chicago to Miss Anna Poole, daughter of the late Dr. William Frederick Poole, at that time Librarian of the Chicago Public Library, but later occupying a similar position in connection with the Newberry Library. Mr. and Mrs. Poole have four children: Frances, Charles H., Clarence F. and Dorothy, their residence being at 939 Forest Avenue, Evanston. Mr. Poole's fraternal associations are with the Illinois Athletic and the Chicago Literary Clubs.

CHARLES S. RADDIN.

Charles S. Raddin, a prominent citizen of Evanston, Ill., where he has resided for twenty-five years, was born in Lynn, Mass., January 29, 1864, the son of Charles E. and Harriet Augusta (Rhodes) Raddin, natives of New England. Charles E. Raddin, who carried on the business of shoe manufacturing in Lynn, Mass., moved with his family from that city to Chicago in 1879, and thence to Evanston in 1881. The subject of this sketch obtained his early education in Chauncy Hall, Boston, Mass., and when the family located in Evanston, pursued a course of study in Northwestern University, from which he received the degrees of B. S. and M. S. During his undergraduate period he identified himself with the Phi Kappa Sigma Fraternity. Mr. Raddin's business interests are in Chicago, where he acts in the capacity of manager of the American Bank Equipment Company.

On June 28, 1892, Mr. Raddin was united in marriage, at Evanston, Ill., with Belle Elmira Alling, a native of that city, and the daughter of a well known Methodist clergyman. This union resulted in one child, Louise, born January 4, 1898. Politically Mr. Raddin is a supporter of the Republican party. Religiously he adheres to the faith of the Methodist Church. In fraternal circles he is affiliated with the National Union. He is a member and Vice-President of the Board of Trustees of the Chicago Academy of Sciences, Secretary of the Natural History Survey of Chicago, and a member of the Board of Directors of the Evanston Historical Society. He is the author of publications entitled, "Flora of Evanston and Vicinity," and "Flora of Chicago and Vicinity," issued as bulletins of the Chicago Academy of Sciences. Aside from his business relations, he is a man of studious habits and wide information, and is a useful and highly esteemed member of the community.

WALTER LEE BROWN.

Walter Lee Brown (deceased), formerly a chemist of high repute and for some time President of the Northwestern Gas Company, of Evanston, Ill., was born in Melrose, Mass., August 24, 1853. He was a son of Edwin Lee and Mary (Babcock) Brown. His father was a man of high attainments whose reputation extended beyond the limits of his State. The family came to Chicago about 1861. As a boy, Walter Brown attended the old Ogden School in Chicago. When seventeen years of age he returned to the East and entered the Pennsylvania Military Academy, at Chester, Pa., which he attended for three years. He completed his academic studies at Northwestern University, giving special attention to chemistry while there. From that institution he received the degree of Bachelor of Science. After completing his studies in Evanston, he entered the Columbia College School of Mines, from which he was also graduated at the end of a course of study in which he devoted much time to metallurgy. For two or three years thereafter he was a

lecturer at Columbia College, and acted as assistant to Dr. Charles F. Chandler, then, as now, at the head of the scientific department of that institution. About 1879, Mr. Brown returned to Chicago, where he purchased the pioneer laboratory, the oldest in the city—established at an early date by the late Dr. James G. Blaney. He conducted this laboratory five years, and became widely known as a chemist, assayer and metallurgist. In 1885 he disposed of the laboratory in order to organize a "test department" for the Chicago, Burlington & Quincy Railway Company, which then set on foot a plan to test all materials used in its railroad construction, equipment, etc. From 1885 to 1888, while conducting these experiments, he resided at Aurora, Ill. Business interests then compelled him to remove to Evanston, where he succeeded his father as President of the Northwestern Gas Company.

With the duties imposed on him by this relation he was occupied for the next five years. He disposed of his interest in this company in 1893, and virtually retired from business, devoting his attention to his books and the arts and sciences during the remainder of his life, which ended April 6, 1904. He bestowed much time on the collection of rare books and literary relics, and gathered together numerous first editions of American authors. Among his intimate associates in this occupation was James Fennimore Cooper, a grandson of the famous novelist. In the science of metallurgy he was eminent, and was the author of "A Manual of Assaying," which reached its eleventh edition, and has been adopted as a text-book by Harvard University and other higher institutions of learning in America and abroad. He traveled extensively throughout the mining regions of the United

States in connection with his work as metallurgist and mineralogist. He was a charter member of the National Society of Chemists, and was long an official of that organization. From June, 1894, to August, 1901, he was a member of the Board of Directors of the Evanston Free Public Library.

Mr. Brown was married October 16, 1884, at Boone, Iowa, to Ida B. Cosgrove, a daughter of Thomas A. Cosgrove, of Evanston. Mr. Cosgrove was an early resident of Evanston, having moved there from Champaign, Ill., in 1868. He was one of the prime movers in securing the location of the Illinois State University at Urbana. The children of Mr. and Mrs. Brown are: Lathrop Lee, who pursued a course of study at the Manner School in Stamford, Conn.; Lois Virginia, and Delight. Mrs. Brown is still living in Evanston.

The subject of this sketch was a man of undeviating rectitude of character. In religious views he was broadly liberal.

EDWARD H. WEBSTER.

Edward H. Webster, a prominent citizen of Evanston, Cook County, Ill., was born at Wells River, Vt., November 17, 1851. He is a son of Caleb Williams and Persis T. Webster. The father, Caleb William Webster, was a merchant by occupation.

The subject of this brief personal record received his early mental training in the public schools of his native State, and graduated from Northwestern University. Mr. Webster was united in marriage with Emily Roneyn Winne, and one child, Helen Christine, is the result of this union.

GEORGE P. K. VOLZ.

George P. K. Volz, of Arlington Heights, Cook County, Ill., Manager of the firm of Peter & Volz, manufacturers of sewing machines, opera chairs, and school desks, was born in Arlington Heights, April 7, 1878. From 1884 until 1891 he attended the public school in his native place, and from 1891 until 1895 was a pupil in the Jefferson High School in Chicago. In the last mentioned year he matriculated in Northwestern University, from which he was graduated in 1899, with the degree of A. B. He was a teacher in the Chicago public schools from 1899 until 1903, when he assumed the management of the Peter & Volz manufactory.

Mr. Volz is a member of the Arlington Athletic and Social Club, of which he was secretary 1901-1906. In 1902 he was appointed assistant chief of the Arlington Heights Volunteer Fire Department, and was appointed Chief in 1905. In fraternal circles, he is affiliated with the M. W. A., and was clerk of the Arlington Camp of that order, 1900-1906. He is also identified with the A. F. & A. M., being a member of Palatine Lodge No. 314, and of Lincoln Park Chapter, R. A. M., No. 177.

On June 29, 1904, at Aurora, Ill., the subject of this sketch was united in marriage with Miss Sallie Anderson, of Chicago, and they have one daughter, Donna Marie, born July 8 1905.

EZRA MARCH BORING, D. D.

The Boring family name was first known in America in Maryland. The progenitor of the American branch of this family was a sailor, who was separated from his family at Liverpool, England, when a lad. Together with companions, he was enticed upon a ship which sailed and carried them to sea. Because the boys were unable to pay their fare they were sold into servitude. Young Boring, on account of his vivacity, became a favorite of the captain and was made cabin boy. From this position he rose to that of mate and finally to be captain of a privateer. While commanding this vessel, he lost a limb in an engagement in the Mediterranean Sea, and after this incident determined to retire from the sea service. He returned to England and, unable to find his family, sailed for America and settled in Baltimore, Maryland. His business was that of a shoemaker. He was one of the early converts to Methodism, and the Boring family, which spread over the South and West, has been generally prominently identified with that denomination.

Some of the immediate ancestors of the family of a later period removed from Maryland to Kentucky, and early in the last century to Claremont, Ohio, where Ezra Marsh Boring was born near the village of Felicity, June 12, 1813. General U. S. Grant was also born in this village and was a boyhood friend. Temperance Boring, the mother of Ezra Marsh Boring, was a strong character, an ardent Methodist, and her home was one of the best known of the fraternity in Southern Ohio.

In 1832 Mr. Boring was soundly converted, and this change of heart turned his life into a new channel and he became an earnest student. Previous to this time he had learned the saddler's trade, and this fact, together with the assistance of his warm friend, William I. Fee, made it possible for him to attend the Methodist

school in Augusta, Kentucky. He graduated from this college in 1842, and, while the college curriculum was limited, he became reasonably proficient in Latin, Greek and Hebrew, which languages he continued to study and use until his closing years.

At the close of his school life, Mr. Boring married Rebecca Ann Barnes, and became Principal of Franklin Seminary in Washington County, Kentucky. This was a well known Southern Seminary of the M. E. Church, situated in the heart of the slave district. Ezra Marsh Boring received a liberal salary for his services for that day, and enjoyed great popularity among the planters, because of his great ability as an orator and his genial and happy nature. He was an ardent champion of the "Divine Right of Slavery" until he was suddenly converted to Abolitionism, which made it necessary for him to cross the Ohio River and separate himself from his friends. From that day he was an ardent friend of the black man, and his home was one of the stations of the "underground railroad." In 1843, he joined the Southern Ohio M. E. Conference and was stationed at Gallipolis. This was an old French town with marked infidel tendencies among its citizens. Here Mr. Boring's fearlessness, joined with his tact, made him many warm friends, so that the meager salary, customary in that day, was generously supplemented by fees and presents. He afterwards preached at Marietta, Newark and Lancaster, Ohio, and was made a Presiding Elder, at which time he resided at Athens, the seat of the Ohio State University. He was then a very young man for so responsible a position. In 1857 he was transferred to the Rock River Conference in Illinois, being stationed at Galena, where he remained for two years and made many warm friends. He also here renewed his acquaintance with U. S. Grant, his boyhood friend, which friendship continued through life. After a brief pastorate in Waukegan, he removed to Chicago and became Presiding Elder of the Chicago District, serving, in all, two terms in this position. He was pastor at Grant Place (now Wesley), Dixon Street and State Street, Chicago; also at Arlington Heights, Park Ridge, Crystal Lake, Woodstock and Wheaton, Illinois.

For many years he was Secretary of the Home for the Friendless in Chicago, giving to this Institution the best service of his life, and, as the result of his labors, leaving it well endowed for the future. The closing years of this long life in public service was spent as Corresponding Secretary of The Superannuates' Relief Association of the Rock River Conference, and here he also succeeded to a remarkable extent. The degree of Doctor of Divinity was conferred upon him by the Theological Institute of Greensburg, Ind. · Dr. Boring will be especially remembered by many as the founder of the Desplaines Camp Meeting, established in 1860, which he conducted or attended for twenty-eight consecutive years.

As a preacher, Elder Boring (as he was often called) spoke extemporaneously, and often with great power. He was an earnest but wise evangelist, an educator of great ability, and managed business affairs with remarkable sagacity. He was greatly beloved by many of all demoninations for his broad and tolerant spirit, and no man in Chicago was probably better known by those of every rank of life. He passed away November 21, 1892, having survived his wife about two years.

ERNEST HAMMOND EVERSZ.

Ernest H. Eversz, senior member of the firm of Eversz & Company, bankers, located at No. 220 La Salle Street, Chicago, was born August 3, 1872. His primary education was obtained in the Milwaukee public school, where he graduated in 1888. He subsequently pursued a course of study in Evanston Township High School, Cook County, Ill., graduating therefrom in 1891. In that year he matriculated in Northwestern University, from which institution he was graduated in 1895 with the degree of A. B. While taking the university course, he was identified with the Beta Theta Pi and Theta Nu Epsilon fraternities, and from 1891 to 1894, was a member of the Northwestern University Glee and Banjo Clubs. In 1895 he took the Harris Prize in the political economy contest.

From 1895 until 1901, Mr. Eversz was in the employ of N. W. Harris & Company, bankers, in Chicago. From 1901 to 1904 he was manager of the Chicago office of Redmond, Kerr & Company, bankers, and since 1904 has been engaged in his present connection. Mr. Eversz is a member of the Union League and Washington Park Clubs, of Chicago; the Chicago Yacht Club, and the Illinois Athletic Club.

On November 5, 1902, Mr. Eversz was united in marriage with Ruth Swift, a daughter of the late Gustavus F. Swift. One child, Barbara, has resulted from this union, born October 9, 1904. Mr. Eversz, resides at No. 3323 Michigan Avenue, Chicago.

WILBUR J. ANDREWS.

Wilbur J. Andrews, of Berwyn, Cook County, Ill., engaged in the real estate business, was born in Rockford, Ill.,

March 24, 1859. In boyhood he received his rudimentary education in the public schools of his native place, and otherwise pursued his preparatory studies until he entered Northwestern University, from which institution he received the degree of A. B. in 1887, and that of A. M., in 1890. While in the university, he was a member of the Hinman Literary Society and the Phi Kappa Psi fraternity. The subject of this sketch was united in marriage with Ada C. Redfield, of Evanston, Ill., in 1881 and they became the parents of three children, namely: Elliot Redfield, Jerome Edson and Kathryn Louise.

CHARLES EDWARD PIPER.

Charles Edward Piper, lawyer and real estate operator, Berwyn, Ill., was born in Chicago, Ill., June 12, 1858, the son of Otis and Margaret Piper—the former born at Sackett's Harbor, N. Y., in October, 1830, and the latter at Prescott, Canada, in 1837. Mr. Piper's father was a merchant, and one branch of his family was descended from old Massachusetts stock extending back to New Salem, Mass., in 1632.

Mr. Piper was educated in the Chicago public schools, the High School and Northwestern University, and after completing his literary course, served as Postmaster at the Union Stock Yards, Chicago, while pursuing the study of law in the Law Department of the Northwestern University. After his graduation from the Law School in 1887, he turned his attention to the real estate business and general practice of his profession. During 1894-95 he served as President of the Town Board of Cicero Township, and has also been a member of the School Board. Some years since he started the movement for the establishment of Sanatoria in different States for the benefit of tuberculous members of various fraternal organizations participating in the same, the first institution being located at Black Mountain, N. C.

In political views, Mr. Piper was born and bred a Republican, and in religious belief is identified with the Methodist Episcopal Church. He was one of the organizers of the Epworth League, serving as the first President for the Chicago District, and later as President of the State organization, and for eight years as Treasurer of the National organization. He has also been Supreme Secretary and General Manager of the Royal League, a member of the Phi Kappa Psi and Phi Delta Phi Fraternities, of the Royal Arcanum, Knights of Pythias, various Masonic bodies, Ancient Order of United Workman, Independent Order of Odd Fellows, Independent Order of Foresters, North American Union, and various other secret and benevolent orders.

At Indianola, Iowa, on August 15, 1882, Mr. Piper was married to Carrie Gregory, who was a native of Nauvoo, Ill., and whose great-grandfather was associated with Robert Morris in the manufacture of gunpowder for use of the American soldiers during the Revolutionary War period. Mr. and Mrs. Piper's children are: Carolyn E., born January 17, 1884, and now a member of the Senior Class in Northwestern University; Lulu Lane, born May 29, 1887, a sophomore in Macalester College, St. Paul, Minn; Robert G., born December 7, 1889, a graduate of Clyde High School, now entered Freshman in Northwestern; Margaret, born February 27, 1892, died September 16, 1894; and Charles E., Jr., born March 6, 1898. Mr. Piper's office as Supreme Scribe of the Royal League is located in Room 1601, Masonic Temple Building, Chicago.

CHARLES LYFORD LOGAN.

Charles Lyford Logan, clergyman, who is a minister of the Methodist Episcopal Church at Elizabeth, Ill., was born in Atkinson, Maine, June 10, 1850. When he was four years old his parents removed to Illinois and two years later to Minnesota. Here he received his primary education in the public schools and, after preparing for college at home, in the fall of 1873 entered the Freshman Class of Northwestern University, graduating therefrom in 1877. In that year he became Principal of Public Schools in Caledonia, Houston County, Minn., for one term. He joined the Wisconsin M. E. Conference in 1878, and in 1880, entered Garrett Biblical Institute, at Evanston, Ill., from which he was graduated in 1882. He received the degree of A. B. in 1877; that of A. M., in 1880; and that of B. D., in 1882. During his college course, he was a member of the Adelphic Literary Society and of the Owl Club. In the Junior year, he was one of those who took part in the "Junior Ex.," and was a contestant in debate between the Adelphic and a Chicago literary society. He was editor of the "Tripod," representing the Adelphic Literary Society, and was one of the orators in the commencement exercises, at the time of his graduation. In 1883 he transferred to the Rock River Conference. From 1886 to 1889, and from 1892 to 1895, a period of seven years, inclusive, he was principal of Inyo Academy, at Bishop, Inyo County, Cal.

On May 8, 1884, Mr. Logan was united in marriage with Grace Boehm Wood, and they have become the parents of the following children, namely: Mary Lois, born in 1885; Grace Sarah, born in 1887; Laura Louise, born in 1889; Helen Irene, born in 1891; Edith Evangeline, born in 1893; Frances Willard, born in 1896; Charles Lyford, Jr., born in 1898; and Ruth, born in 1904.

In fraternal circles, the subject of this sketch is identified with the I. O. O. F. and the A. O. U. A. M.

JEROME J. CERMAK.

Jerome J. Cermak, attorney-at-law, Chicago, was born in the city where he now resides, September 30, 1880. In boyhood he made diligent use of the opportunities afforded by the Chicago public schools, graduating from the Joseph Medill High School in June, 1898. In September, 1899, he matriculated in Northwestern University Law School, from which he was graduated in June, 1902, with the degree of LL. B. From 1902 to 1906 he has been Secretary of the Law Alumni Association of that institution. He was a member of the University Baseball Club in the spring of 1901, and of the Law School baseball team in 1901 and 1902. He belongs to the Phi Alpha Delta Law fraternity, and socially, is identified with the Royal League and the "Ceska Beseda." He is also a member of the Y. M. C. A.

GEORGE THOMAS FOX, D. D. S.

Dr. George Thomas Fox, who is engaged in the practice of dentistry at No. 5101 South Halsted Street, Chicago, Ill., was born in Chicago February 19, 1881, and received his rudimentary education in the Chicago public schools. He afterwards pursued a course of study in Wheaton College at Wheaton, Ill., and, in the fall of 1900, entered Northwestern University Dental College, from which he was graduated in 1903, with the degree of

D. D. S. In November, 1903, he commenced the practice of dentistry at the location above mentioned, where he has since continued with good results.

PHILIP E. ELTING.

Philip E. Elting, attorney-at-law, Macomb, McDonough County, Ill., was born in the vicinity of that city and spent his boyhood and early youth in his native place, where he enjoyed the advantages of the public schools. After completing his primary education, he pursued a course of study in the Law Department of Northwestern University at Evanston, Ill., from which he was graduated with the Class of 1892, receiving the degree of LL. B. He was immediately admitted to the bar (June 14, 1892), and at once entered upon the practice of his profession at Macomb, in which he has since continued with successful results. Although he has not sought political preferment, he has been endorsed by his county as a candidate for Circuit Judge in the Ninth Judicial Circuit of Illinois.

In fraternal circles, Mr. Elting is identified with the A. F. & A. M., in which he is a Knight Templar; and is also affiliated with Military Tract Lodge, No. 145, Independent Order of Odd Fellows, and with the Knights of Pythias.

SIDNEY G. McCALLIN, D. D. S.

Sidney Gilmore McCallin, who is engaged in the practice of dentistry at No. 830 West Sixty-Third Street, Chicago, Ill., was born in Rochester, Minn., September 7, 1878. In boyhood he made diligent use of the opportunities afforded by the public schools, and afterwards entered the Waukesha (Wis.) High School, from

which he was graduated in 1896. On October, 5, 1898, he matriculated in Northwestern University Dental School, graduating therefrom in May, 1900, with the degree of D. D. S. During his dental course he was a member of the Psi Omega Fraternity, and was on the Dental School football team in 1898-1899.

Dr. McCallin began the practice of his profession at No. 1124 West Sixty-third Street, Chicago, on July 7, 1901, and on June 7, 1904, moved to his present location. In 1904, he became a member of the Englewood Dental Society, of which he was elected President in 1905. He is also a member of the Englewood Men's Club and of the Jackson Park Yacht Club.

LOUIS GRANT HOTCH.

Louis Grant Hotch, dentist, who is located at No. 334 East Division Street, Chicago, Ill., was born in Carthage, Ill., March 15 1868. In early youth he attended the public schools of his native place, and afterwards graduated from the High School, subsequently taking a course in a Kansas City (Mo.) business college. In 1901, he graduated form Northwestern University Dental School. Dr. Hotch worked his way through school by industrious application to other pursuits, during his vacations and other periods of leisure. On June 30, 1900, he was united in marriage with Miss Tillie Nelson, and one child Marion Sophia, has been the result of this union.

SAMUEL CRAIG PLUMMER.

Samuel Craig Plummer, surgeon, who is located at No. 156 East Forty-second Place, Chicago, Ill., was born in Rock Island, Ill., April 22, 1865. In early youth he utilized the advantages of the public schools and, after finishing his primary studies, pursued a course in Augustana College, at Rock Island, from which he was graduated in June, 1883, with the degree of A. B. In the same year he matriculated in the Chicago Medical College, of Northwestern University, graduating therefrom March 23, 1886, with the degree of M. D. He is a member of the Phi Rho Sigma fraternity. In 1886-87, Dr. Plummer occupied the position of interne in the Cook County Hospital, Chicago. In 1891 he was appointed Assistant Demonstrator of Anatomy in the Northwestern University Medical School; in 1892 became Lecturer on Anatomy; in 1893, Professor of Anatomy, and in 1894, Demonstrator of Operative Surgery. Since 1899 he has been Professor of Operative Surgery in that institution, and from 1900 until the present time, has served in the capacity of Surgeon to Wesley Hospital, Chicago, and since 1902 has held the position of Chief Surgeon of the Chicago, Rock Island & Pacific Railway system. He has also been secretary of the Northwestern University Medical School since 1904.

Dr. Plummer is a member of the American Medical Association; the American Association of Railway Surgeons; the Illinois State Medical Society, the Chicago Medical Society, of which he was Secretary in 1900-1901; the Chicago Surgical Society; and the Chicago Pathological Society. Socially Dr. Plummer is a member of the Kenwood and Washington Park Clubs of Chicago, and fraternally of the Military Order of the Loyal Legion. He was united in marriage with Mary Louise Middleton, on March 18, 1902, and one child, Susan Middleton Plummer, has been born of this union.

ALBERT D. PERSONS, D. D. S., M.D.S.

Dr. Albert Dodge Persons, dentist, of Des Plaines, Cook County, Ill., was born in Chicago, Ill., July 20, 1879. His early mental training was obtained in the Chicago public schools and, in October, 1897, he entered the Northwestern College of Dental Surgery and matriculated in Northwestern University Dental School in October, 1898, graduating therefrom April 30, 1900, with the degree of D. D. S. He has also received the degree of M. D. S. Dr. Persons was a member of Northwestern University Dental School football team in 1898-1899.

The subject of this sketch is Professor of Oral Surgery in the American Post-Graduate School; Professor of Oral Surgery in the National Medical University; was formerly Professor of Orthodontia in the Illinois Medical School Dental Department, and is now Assistant Professor of Orthodontia in the Northwestern University Dental School.

Dr. Persons was united in marriage with Grace Bennett, of Des Plaines, Ill., on August 16, 1904.

WALTER B. HELM, M. D.

Walter B. Helm, physician and surgeon, of Rockford, Ill., was born at Butlerville, Iowa, October 12, 1859, and his primary education was received in the public schools of his native place. Subsequently he became a pupil in the Beaver Dam (Wis.) High School, finishing his studies there in 1876. He then matriculated in Northwestern University, and, after completing the literary course, in 1881 entered the Medical Department of that institution, from which he was graduated with the degree of M. D., in 1884.

He had previously received the degree of B. S. In 1884-85, he attended the clinics of Cook County Hospital, Chicago, and in 1895, took a course in the New York Post Graduate School of Medicine. During his undergraduate period, he was a member of the Hinman Literary Society, and from 1879 to 1883, was connected with the United States Life-Saving Service.

Dr. Helm acted as Attending Physician and Surgeon in connection with the Rockford City Hospital from 1886 to 1904, and, since the last named year, has occupied the position of Consulting Surgeon in that institution. He was local surgeon of the Illinois Central Railroad Company at Racine, Wis., in 1897. Dr. Helm is a member of the American Medical Association; the Illinois State Medical Society; the Central Wisconsin Medical Society; and the Winnebago (Ill.) Medical Society. Socially he is connected with the Rockford Country Club, and, in fraternal circles, is identified with the B. P. O. E.

Dr. Helm was married on October 26, 1887, to Mary C. Gibson, and two children are the offspring of this union, namely: Allan G., born November 8, 1888, and Elizabeth, born January 27, 1902.

GEORGE W. NESBITT.

George W. Nesbitt, physician and surgeon, of Sycamore, Ill., was born in that town March 13, 1869. His early education was obtained in the public schools of his native place, and from 1887 to 1889, he was a student in the Illinois State University at Urbana. In the fall of the latter year he matriculated in the Chicago Medical College of Northwestern University, from which he was graduated April 22, 1892, with the degree of M. D.

Dr. Nesbitt is a member of the American Medical Association; the Illinois State Medical Society; the DeKalb County (Ill.) Medical Society; and the Mississippi Valley Medical Society. He was united in marriage with Cora Whittemore, of Sycamore, Ill., on August 16, 1894.

PAUL SYNNESTVEDT.

Paul Synnestvedt, who is engaged in the practice of law, in Pittsburgh, Pa., where his office is located at No. 518 Frick Building, was born in Chicago, Ill., April 14, 1870. In his youth he enjoyed the advantages afforded by the public schools of Chicago, and, after finishing his literary studies, entered the Law School of Northwestern University at Chicago, from which he was graduated in 1897, with the degree of LL. B. The marriage of Mr. Synnestvedt took place in 1893, when he was wedded to Anna E. Lechner of Pittsburgh, Pa., their union resulting in eight children, namely: Arthur, Hubert, Elsa, George, Evan, Raymond, Kenneth and Virginia.

WILLIAM LEON STEVENS, D. D. S.

Dr. William Leon Stevens, who is engaged in the practice of dentistry at No. 1012 West Lake Street, Chicago, Ill., and resides at Clyde, Cook County, Ill., was born at Eaton Rapids, Mich., December 11, 1867. In early youth he utilized the opportunities afforded by the public schools, and on September 25, 1887, matriculated in the American College of Dental Surgery, from which he was graduated with the degree of D. D. S., March 25, 1889. In fraternal circles, Dr. Stevens is identified with the A. F. & A. M., having joined Lodge No. 610, August 14, 1893.

On June 17, 1897, Dr. Stevens was united in marriage with Anna Maude Stevens, and they have become the parents of two children, namely: Morton Leon, born October 27, 1898, and Ethel Grace, born May 17, 1891.

OLE HANSEN TUTTLE.

Ole Hansen Tuttle, dentist, Chicago, Ill., was born at Eaton, Ohio, April 17, 1867. In early youth he utilized the opportunities afforded by the public schools of his native town and graduated there in 1886. In 1891 he entered Northwestern University Dental College, and was graduated therefrom in 1894, with the degree of D. D. S. He was class treasurer in that institution during the last mentioned year, and special clinic in operative dentistry there in 1895-96. From 1893 to 1900, he served as secretary and treasurer of the Miami Club. Fraternally he is identified with the A. F. & A. M., being a thirty-second degree Mason, and a member of the Mystic Shrine.

On November 24, 1902, Dr. Tuttle was united in marriage with Grace M. Goss, a daughter of the inventor of the Goss Printing Press. One child, Genevieve Harriet, has been the offspring of their union. Dr. Tuttle is located at No. 1046 Jackson Boulevard, Chicago.

BENJAMIN WALDBERG.

Benjamin Waldberg, who is engaged in the practice of dentistry at No. 66 North State Street, Chicago, Ill., was born in Lemberg, Austria, December 25, 1851. In boyhood he received his primary mental training in the public schools of his native country, and graduated from the Classic Gymnasium in the city of his birth. He matriculated in Northwestern University Dental School for the term of 1897-8, and was graduated in 1901, with the degree of D. D. S. Dr. Waldberg was appointed Demonstrator in Prosthetic Technics, October 1, 1899, and in May, 1901, received the appointment of Demonstrator and Superintendent of Prosthetic Laboratories, a position which he still holds. He is a member of the Odontographic Society; the Psi Omega Dental Fraternity, and the A. F. & A. M.

Dr. Waldberg was married in 1869, but has been a widower since 1886. He has two sons, Bernard and Joseph.

AMOS R. SOLENBERGER, M. D.

Amos Rufus Solenberger, physician, and a resident of Colorado Springs, Colo., was born in 1853, at Canton, Ohio. After finishing his primary studies in the public schools of his native State, his parents removed to Illinois, where he pursued preparatory courses in Rock River Seminary and Northwestern University Academy, and in 1879 matriculated in the College of Liberal Arts of Northwestern University, Evanston, graduating therefrom in 1883, with the degree of Ph. B. In 1883 he entered the Northwestern University Medical School, from which he was graduated in 1885, with the degree of M. D. During his undergraduate course, he was a member of the Euphronean and Adelphic societies, and of the Phi Kappa Psi Fraternity, and was contestant for the Adelphic and Hinman prizes in oratory. He acted in the capacity of Field Marshal on Field Day in 1883.

Dr. Solenberger took special courses in Medicine, Laryngology, Rhinology and

Otology, in Berlin, Paris and London, and is the author of "Lectures on Hygiene of the Vocal Organs," and on the "Principles and Practice of Diseases of the Upper Respiratory Tract." From 1896 to 1899 he was Instructor in Laryngology and Rhinology in the Northwestern University Medical School. He is a member of the American Medical Association; the Chicago Academy of Medicine; the American Laryngological, Otological and Rhinological Societies, and of the Colorado State Medical Association.

He was united in marriage with Priscilla H. Stauffer, at Denver, Colo., on April 8, 1885.

JOHN RAYMOND HOFFMAN, M. D.

Dr. John Raymond Hoffman, who is engaged in the practice of medicine at No. 206 East Washington Street, Chicago, Ill., and resides in Ottawa, Ill., was born in the latter city, June 18, 1865. In boyhood he attended public school in Ottawa, and graduated from the High School there in 1885. He matriculated in Chicago Medical College of Northwestern University in 1888, and was graduated therefrom in 1891 with the degree of M. D. Dr. Hoffman entered upon the general practice of his profession in Ottawa, during the year of his graduation from the University, and continued therein until 1895, when he devoted his attention mainly to affections of the eye, ear, nose and throat. In 1897, he began this special line of practice in Chicago, on the establishment of the Eye, Ear, Nose and Throat College, of which he is secretary. In this institution, Dr. Hoffman has also filled the chair of Professor of Ophthalmology since the year of its establishment. From 1896 to 1898, Dr. Hoffman was Assistant Surgeon of the Illinois National Guard, and from 1897 to 1903 was Assistant Surgeon of the Illinois Charitable Eye and Ear Infirmary. He is a member of the Chicago Medical Society, the Chicago Ophthalmological and Otological Society, and the American Academy of Ophthalmology, Otology and Rhinology.

On June 2, 1891, the subject of this sketch was united in marriage with Mary T. Hapeman, of Ottawa, Ill., and their union has resulted in three children namely: Douglas T., Phœbe Ella, and Frances.